trotman

Brian Heap

39th edition

Degree Course Offers

2009 entry

**Winning your place
at university – the
essential guide**

Mander Portman Woodward

Degree Course Offers 2009

In order to ensure that *Degree Course Offers* retains its reputation as the definitive guide for students wishing to study at UK universities, thousands of questionnaires are distributed, months of research and analysis are undertaken, and painstaking data checking and proofing are carried out.

Every effort has been made to maintain absolute accuracy in providing course information and to ensure that the entire book is as up-to-date as possible. However, changes are constantly taking place in higher education so it is improtant for readers to check carefully with prospectuses and websites before submitting their applications. The author, compilers and publishers cannot be held responsible for any inaccuracies in information supplied to them by third parties or contained in resources and websites listed in the book.

We hope you find this 39th edition useful, and would welcome your feedback as to how we can ensure the 40th edition is even better.

Author Brian Heap
Compilation and Data Processing Dianah Ellis, Henry Ellis
Advertising Sales Sarah Talbot, Advertising Sales Director; Kerry Lyon, Senior Account Manager
(contact team on 020 8334 1617 or e-mail advertising@trotman.co.uk)

This 39th edition published in 2008 by Trotman Publishing an imprint of Crimson Publishing Ltd
Westminster House, Kew Road,
Richmond, Surrey, TW9 2ND
www.trotman.co.uk

© Brian Heap 2008

A CIP record for this book is available from the British Library

ISBN 978 1 84455 158 3

Typeset by RefineCatch Limited, Bungay, Suffolk
Printed and bound in the UK at the University Press, Cambridge

Founded in 1973, **Mander Portman Woodward (MPW)** is one of the UK's best known groups of independent sixth-form colleges with centres in London, Birmingham and Cambridge. It offers over 40 subjects at AS and A2 with no restrictions on subject combinations and a maximum class size of eight.

MPW has one of the highest numbers of university placements each year of any independent school in the country. It has developed considerable expertise over the years in the field of applications strategy and is frequently consulted by students facing some of the more daunting challenges that may arise in areas such as getting into Oxbridge, Medicine or Law. This expertise is available to a wider audience in the form of **MPW Guides** on higher education and the seminars that are run for sixth-formers at its London centre. We are grateful to Trotman for publishing the Guides and hope that this latest edition of **Degree Course Offers** will prove as popular and useful as ever.

If you would like to know more about MPW or MPW Guides, please telephone us on 020 7835 1355 or visit our website, www.mpw.co.uk.

Choosing Your University And Degree Course...And Completing Your UCAS Form?

Why not contact Brian Heap, the author of *Degree Course Offers*, *Choosing Your Degree Course and University* and *University Scholarships and Awards*, for a personal interview or a telephone consultation for advice on such issues as:

- Choosing A-level subjects (which are the best subjects and for which courses!)
- Degrees and Diploma courses (making the right choice from a list of thousands!)
- Completing your UCAS form (will the admissions tutor remember your personal statement?)
- Choosing the right university or college (the best ones for you and your courses)

For details of services and consultation fees contact: The Higher Education Advice and Planning Service

tel: 01386 859355 email: heaps@dsl.pipex.com

SO
employable.

Here at Southampton Solent University, we pride ourselves on education for the real world. The proof? Well, our most recent graduate survey showed that 80% of Southampton Business School graduates are in employment within six months of graduating*.

Our courses include:

Accountancy
Business
Marketing
Law
Human Resource Management
Sport Studies
Health and Fitness
Football Studies
Tourism

For further information about the Southampton Business School and its extensive range of undergraduate courses, please telephone **0845 676 7000** or email **sbs@solent.ac.uk**

*Figures from the most recent Destinations of Leavers from Higher Education Survey

solent.ac.uk

QUOTES

'The guru of university choice'
The Times, 2007

'For those of you going through Clearing, an absolute must is the Degree Course Offers *book. This guide operates subject by subject and gives you each university's requirements, standard offers and, most importantly, "course variations"'*
The Independent, August 2007

'Brian Heap, the guru of university admissions'
The Independent, September 2007

'Degree Course Offers *is probably the UK's longest running and best known reference work on the subject'*
www.universityadvice.co.uk, 2005

'This guide contains useful, practical information for all university applicants and those advising them. I heartily recommend it'
Dr John Dunford, General Secretary, Association of School and College Leaders, 2005

'An invaluable guide to helping students and their advisers find their way through the maze of degree courses currently on offer'
Kath Wright, President, Association for Careers Education and Guidance, 2005

'No one is better informed or more experienced than Brian Heap in mediating this range of information to university and college applicants'
Careers Education and Guidance, October 2005

'The course-listings bible'
The Guardian, June 2005

'After consulting this you won't be able to say "I didn't know!" For every school library'
The Teacher, Nov 2003

'A must buy . . . one of the best single reference sources to degree course offers available'
Career Guidance Today, July 2003

'The most comprehensive guide is Degree Course Offers *by Brian Heap'*
John Clare in The Daily Telegraph, April 2003

'Degree Course Offers *is an excellent resource and contains the type of information that prospective students and their parents need to know when making decisions about degree courses'*
Mandy Telford, NUS National President, April 2003

'This guide gives a valuable and objective insight into the country's universities'
Will Straw, President, Oxford University Student Union, April 2003

'The Bible for university applicants provides detailed information on pretty much every course in the land'
The Northern Echo, April 2003

'Going to university is one of the biggest investment decisions you will ever make in your own future. In order to make the right choices, you need to be armed with fair and accurate information of the wide variety of institutions and courses open to you. Brian Heap's Degree Course Offers *is an excellent source of information'*
Rt Hon Charles Clarke MP, Secretary of State for Education and Skills, March 2003

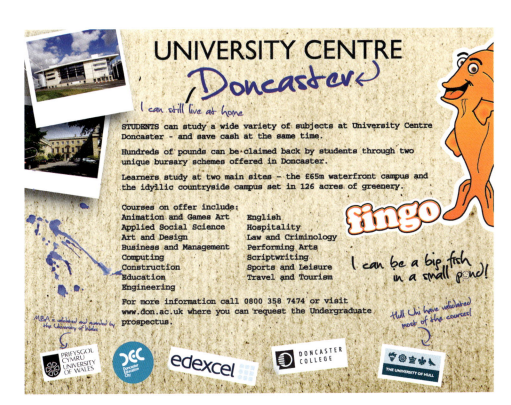

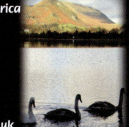

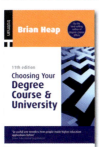

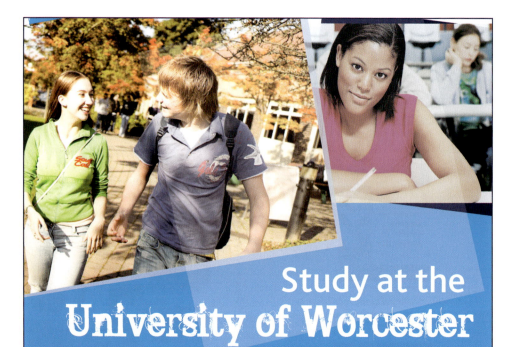

Study at the
University of Worcester

- Wide range of subjects on offer at postgraduate and undergraduate level
- Excellent facilities including Digital Arts Centre and Sports Complex
- Lively modern campus with a good range of accommodation available
- Nationally recognised professional courses in management, teaching and nursing
- Full and part-time study options
- Friendly and supportive atmosphere

Open Days 2008

See for yourself what the University of Worcester has to offer!

Sunday 22 June 10am-3pm
Sunday 21 September 10am-3pm
Wednesday 29 October 1-5pm
Thursday 30 October 1-5pm
Wednesday 12 November 1-5pm

To find out more:
Tel: 01905 855141
email: study@worc.ac.uk
www.worcester.ac.uk

IT'S YOUR WORLD.
WHAT WILL YOU CHANGE?

Middlesex University

[ART AND DESIGN

MIDDLESEX UNIVERSITY]

- BA Honours Design and Technology
- BA Honours Design, Interior and Applied Arts
- BA Honours Fashion
- BA Honours Fashion Design, Styling and Promotion
- BA Honours Fashion Textiles
- BA Honours Fine Art
- BA Honours Fine Art and Critical Theory
- BA Honours Graphic Design
- BA Honours Interior Architecture: Design and Practice
- BA Honours Jewellery
- BA Honours Fashion Jewellery and Accessories
- BA Honours Illustration
- BA Honours Interior Architecture and Design
- BA Honours Photography
- BA Honours Product Design
- BA Honours Sonic Arts
- BSc Honours Engineering Product Design

020 8411 5555
www.mdx.ac.uk

MIDDLESEX UNIVERSITY IN LONDON

degrees with added 'wow' factor

Enjoy great career prospects with our new 'world of work' skills programme

Liverpool John Moores University
Open Days 2008

Wednesday 2 July, Tuesday 7 or Wednesday 8 October 2008
at Liverpool Anglican Cathedral

to pre-register or enquire call: **0151 231 5090**
email: **recruitment@ljmu.ac.uk**   web: **www.ljmu.ac.uk**

CONTENTS

Northern School of Contemporary Dance

A unique dance training institution offering a select group of students the opportunity to develop and excel as dance artists in a conservatoire environment.

The School if a Higher Education College providing a Foundation Course in Contemporary Dance, a BPA (Hons) Degree in Contemporary Dance and an innovative Graduate Diploma Programme which now includes two distinct pathways:

• A highly successful graduate apprenticeship scheme which offers placements with some of the UK's leading dance companies.

• Verve, an exciting graduate dance company offering intensive performance experience and professional skills development.

For course and audition information contact:

T: +44 (0) 113 219 3000
E: info@nscd.ac.uk
www.nscd.ac.uk

The Northern School of Contemporary Dance is affiliated to the Conservatoire for Dance and Drama. HE provision is validated by the University of Kent.

the **arts institute** at bournemouth

WANT A CREATIVE CAREER?

Steve
Picture Editor
House & Garden
Magazine

Esther
Skilled Costumier
Royal Shakespeare
Company

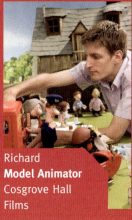

Richard
Model Animator
Cosgrove Hall
Films

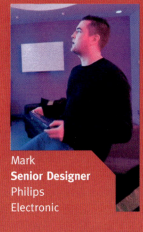

Mark
Senior Designer
Philips
Electronic

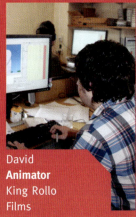

David
Animator
King Rollo
Films

Ed
Modelmaker
Richard Rogers
Partnership

START WITH A CREATIVE DEGREE

For further information visit www.aib.ac.uk

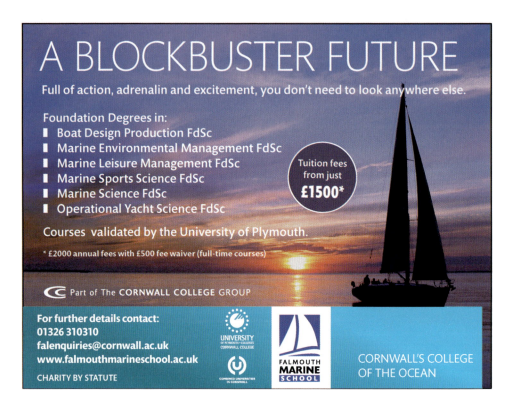

Choosing Your University And Degree Course...And Completing Your UCAS Form?

Why not contact Brian Heap, the author of *Degree Course Offers*, *Choosing Your Degree Course and University* and *University Scholarships and Awards*, for a personal interview or a telephone consultation for advice on such issues as:

- Choosing A-level subjects (which are the best subjects and for which courses!)
- Degrees and Diploma courses (making the right choice from a list of thousands!)
- Completing your UCAS form (will the admissions tutor remember your personal statement?)
- Choosing the right university or college (the best ones for you and your courses)

For details of services and consultation fees contact:
The Higher Education Advice and Planning Service

tel: 01386 859355 email: heaps@dsl.pipex.com

AUTHOR'S ACKNOWLEDGEMENTS

This year I must record my gratitude for the invaluable and extended support received from my daughter Jane Heap, who has provided additional research and advice in the compilation of this edition.

I acknowledge gratefully the efforts of the many university and college registrars, schools liaison staff, faculty and departmental heads and admissions tutors in providing detailed information about their courses.

In particular, I should also like to thank the staff at UCAS for their help, the Engineering Council UK, Sarah Hannaford of the University of Cambridge Admissions Office, Clare Woodcock of the University of Oxford Public Relations Office, Lee Hennessy, Head of Admissions at the University of Bath, and Dr Roger Ash, Head of Admissions at the University of Bradford, for providing me with up-to-date information on admissions procedures. In addition, my thanks are due to Professor Ian Johnson of Nottingham University Medical School for details of the UKCAT scheme, Dr Kevin Stannard of Cambridge International Examinations for information on the Cambridge Pre-U Diploma, and also to the Higher Education Funding Council (England, Scotland and Wales) for permission to publish information relating to research ratings and teaching quality assessments, and also to *Oxford Applications* for interview questions. In addition, I should like to express special thanks to the Higher Education Statistics Agency (HESA) for the use of data in *Destinations of Leavers from Higher Education 2005/6* and to the Quality Assurance Agency for information on subject assessment reports. I should also like to thank Susan McGrath of the Manchester Metropolitan University Careers Service for her assistance in providing data for the career information appearing under Graduate Destinations in the subject tables and finally those admissions tutors, teachers and their pupils who have sent me interview reports and other information which has provided useful supplementary data for the book. In particular, the following staff have provided information on their sandwich courses: Aston University (Biology), Prof Peter Lambert; (Business Studies) Nicola Bullivant; (Engineering) Louise Thomas and Graham Perry; (Mechanical Engineering) Dr P Upton. Bath University (Chemistry) Dr Simon Bedford; (Mechanical/Electronic/Electrical Engineering) Angela Harrington; (Mechanical Engineering) Robert Greenwood; (Mathematics) Jackie Wallen; (Physics) Dr Steve Andrews. Brunel University (All subjects) Michelle Kavan. Cardiff (UWIC) (Youth Work) Jan Huyton; (Education) Alan White and Natalie Hughes. Kingston University (Business and Law) Mari Zadeh; (Science) Diane Gillick. Loughborough University (Civil Engineering and Building) Dr Matthew Frost; (Product Design) Sid Pace.

Every effort has been made to maintain absolute accuracy in providing course information and to ensure that the entire book is as up-to-date as possible. However, changes are constantly taking place in higher education so it is important for readers to check carefully with prospectuses and websites before submitting their applications.

I also wish to thank Dianah Ellis for her continuing editorial advice and work, and the many readers who have written to me about the problems they have encountered in choosing courses and places to study. Such information adds to a valuable store of knowledge which can be passed on, thereby creating a better understanding of mutual difficulties.

Finally, my thanks to my wife Rita for her administrative help (and patience!) through 39 years of publication.

Brian Heap
January 2008

ABOUT THIS BOOK

Choosing a career or course of study is not easy. There is much that applicants need to know in order to make decisions that are right for them as individuals, and each year they will spend a great deal of time exploring various options. One option is higher education, although entry to degree and diploma courses can be highly competitive, and applicants need good advice on how to choose courses. Comprehensive and comparative information about selection policies and the range of courses available, therefore, is an essential part of this process. To assist applicants, *Degree Course Offers* (now in its 39th year) aims to provide a **first stop** reference for applicants choosing courses of higher education by providing information from official sources.

The purpose of this book is to provide essential information for all students preparing to go to university or college in 2009. It covers information about all stages of choosing degree course subjects, universities and colleges including:

* How to select the degree subject that is right for you
* The courses offered, what they involve and how they are taught
* How difficult or easy it will be to secure an offer of a place at your chosen institution(s)
* How to prepare your personal statement for the UCAS application
* How to cope in August if your grades don't match your offer
* Information about UK universities for international students, and the acceptability of international qualifications.

The subject tables in **Chapter 9** provide a brief overview of each subject area with useful websites and lists:

* Subject requirements/preferences
* Target offers for Honours degree courses in A-level grades and/or UCAS tariff points, including a selection of IB offers
* Alternative offers
* Examples of Foundation degrees
* Course variations
* Universities and colleges teaching quality
* Top universities and colleges (Research)
* Sandwich degree courses
* The number of applicants per place
* Advice to applicants and planning the UCAS personal statement
* Some misconceptions students have about courses
* Selection interviews
* Interview advice and questions
* Applicants' impressions of open days and interviews
* Reasons for rejection
* Offers to applicants repeating A-levels

* Graduate destinations and employment
* Career note
* Other degree subjects for consideration.

NEW FOR THIS EDITION

* Up-to-date information on bursaries and living costs;
* Advice on graduate careers in the subject tables;
* **Sandwich Courses and Professional Placements:** a new chapter with information from university staff, employers and students on, eg student pay, finding placements, employer requirements and career advantages;
* Expanded list of International Baccalaureate (IB) offers.

Degree Course Offers is updated each year from information supplied by admissions staff in universities and colleges and other sources. It is collated between October and March of each academic year for publication in the spring, so providing up-to-date advice on admissions policies and details of new courses for the next application cycle starting in the following September.

In **Chapter 9** the offers, made in terms of grades and/or UCAS tariff points, are often wide-ranging in order to suit the needs both of individual applicants and of universities and subject departments. The offers listed are the targets at which applicants should aim. However, offers can vary and are subject to change, so it is essential for applicants always to refer to websites for the very latest information.

Used in conjunction with *Choosing Your Degree Course and University* (the companion title to this book), *Degree Course Offers* takes the student through the entire guidance process for higher education. Once again, therefore, it provides in a single volume a comprehensive survey of selection information and guidance for applicants to higher education at a time when they need it most.

Note Every effort is made to ensure accuracy throughout this book. It is important, however, that readers always check websites and prospectuses carefully for any late changes in offers, admissions policies or courses, and, if they have any queries, contact admissions staff of their chosen institutions.

Brian Heap
January 2008

1 | YOUR FIRST DECISIONS

HIGHER EDUCATION OR NOT?

Why do you want to go on to higher education? If you are taking GCE Advanced (AL) and Advanced Subsidiary (AS) qualifications, this is an important question to ask. Last year (2007) there were 531,898 applicants, with 411,991 acceptances, for full-time first degree and diploma courses in the United Kingdom. Law, Psychology, Pre-clinical Medicine, Management Studies and Design Studies were the five most popular subjects. However, higher education is just one of two options you have. The other is employment, and perhaps it is important to note that higher education is not necessarily the best option for everyone. It is one which is appropriate for many and, therefore, should not be rejected lightly. Higher education is likely to open many doors and give you opportunities for work and leisure that otherwise you might not have. Also, very often and quite accidentally, it can lead into careers that you might NOT have considered before.

Choosing your AS/A-levels will normally be done on the basis of your best and most interesting subjects. However, leading universities (and, in particular, those with popular and competitive courses) will seek a grouping of subjects with 'academic weight'. Cambridge University has been specific in providing advice on the choice of A-levels.

They advise:

'To be a realistic applicant, students will normally need to be offering two traditional academic subjects, ie two AS/AL subjects **not** on the following list:

Accounting, art and design, business studies, communication studies, dance, design and technology, drama/theatre studies, film studies, health and social care, home economics, information and communication, leisure studies, media studies, music technology, performance studies, performing arts, photography, physical education, sports studies, technology, travel and tourism

For example, AS/AL history, mathematics and business studies would be acceptable but history, business studies and media studies would **not** normally be acceptable.

For IB students not more than **one** of the following subjects should be taken at Higher Level to count as part of the Diploma: business and management, design and technology, information technology in a global society, theatre arts, visual arts.'

Most courses in higher education lead to a degree or a diploma and for either you will have to make a subject choice. This can be difficult because the universities alone offer over 1200 degree subjects and over 50,000 courses within the UCAS scheme. You have two main options:

A   Choosing a course that is either similar to, or the same as, one (or more) of your examination subjects, or related to an interest outside the school curriculum, such as Anthropology, American Studies, Archaeology. See **Section A** below.

B   Choosing a course in preparation for a future career, for example Medicine, Architecture, Engineering. See **Section B** below and also **Appendix 2**.

SECTION A

Choosing your course by examination subjects

Deciding your degree or diploma course on the basis of your A-level (or equivalent) subjects is a reasonably safe option. Already you are familiar with the subjects and what they involve, and you may well look forward to studying at least one to a much greater depth over the next few years. If the long-term career prospects concern you, don't worry – a degree course isn't necessarily a training for a job. If you are taking science subjects, they can lead naturally on to a range of scientific careers, although many scientists follow non-science careers such as law and accountancy. If you are taking arts or social science subjects, remember that training for most non-scientific careers can start once you have your degree.

When choosing your degree course it is important to consider what A-level subjects you are taking as universities may 'require' or 'prefer' certain subjects for entry to some courses. To make sure you have the right subjects, check the course subject requirements in university/college prospectuses or on their websites. When choosing AS-level subjects, students sometimes prefer to select those with a similar subject base, for example four science subjects, or four arts, or four humanities subjects. However, some institutions welcome one, or even two, contrasting subjects (for example, Bradford, Brunel, Imperial London, the London medical schools), provided the required A-level subjects are also offered. Subjects and policies are likely to vary, depending on the subject requirements for specific degree courses, but subjects do not stand on their own, in isolation. Each subject you are taking is one of a much larger family. Each has many similarities to subjects studied in degree and diploma courses that you might never have considered, so before you decide finally on taking a subject to degree level read through the lists of A-level subjects below, each followed by examples of degree courses in the same subject field. Here you will find some examples of degree courses with similarities to the A-level subjects you might be taking. (These lists are also useful if you have to consider alternative courses after the examination results are published!)

Accountancy See Section B.

Ancient history Archaeology, Biblical Studies, Classics and Classical Civilisation, Classical Greek, Latin, Middle and Near Eastern Studies.

Applied ICT See Section B (Computing).

Archaeology See Section B.

Art and design; Applied art and design Art, Furniture Design, Photography, Graphic Design, Textile Design, Theatre Design, Three Dimensional Design, Typography and Graphic Communication. See also Section B.

Biology; Applied science See Section B.

Business; Applied business See Section B.

Chemistry; Applied science See Section B.

Classics and Classical civilisation Ancient History, Archaeology, Classical Greek, Classics, Latin.

Communication studies See Section B.

Computing; Applied ICT See Section B.

Dance; Performing arts/Performing studies See Section B.

Design technology; Applied art and design; Engineering Engineering, Industrial Design, Product Design. See also Section B.

Drama and theatre studies; Performing arts See Section B.

Economics; Applied business Accountancy, Banking, Business Administration, Business Economics, Business Studies, Development Studies, Estate Management, Financial Services, Management Science, Politics, Quantity Surveying, Social Studies, Statistics.

Electronics; Engineering Computing, Engineering (Aeronautical, Aerospace, Communication, Computer, Software, Systems), Mechatronics, Multimedia Technology, Medical Electronics, Technology. See also Section B.

English language and literature Drama, Information and Library Studies/Management, Journalism, Theatre Studies.

Environmental sciences; Applied science Biological Sciences, Biology, Earth Sciences, Ecology, Environmental Hazards, Forestry, Geography, Geology, Land Management, Marine Biology, Oceanography, Plant Sciences, Wildlife Conservation, Zoology.

Film studies See Section B.

French International Business Studies, International Hospitality Management, Law with French Law.

Geography Development Studies, Earth Sciences, Environmental Science, Estate Management, Forestry, Geographical Information Science, Geology, Land Economy, Meteorology, Oceanography, Surveying, Town and Country Planning, Urban Studies, Water Science.

Geology See Section B.

German International Business Studies, International Hospitality Management, Law with German Law.

Government/Politics Development Studies, Economics, Government, Industrial Relations, International Politics, Law, Politics, Public Administration, Social Policy, Sociology, Strategic Studies.

Health and social care See Section B.

History American Studies, International Relations, Law, Religious Studies.

Home economics Food Science, Hospitality Management, Nutrition.

Information and communication technology See Section B.

Languages Apart from French and German – and Spanish for some universities – it is not usually necessary to have completed an A-level language course before studying the many languages (over 60) offered at degree level, for example, Chinese, Japanese, Scandinavian Studies.

Law See Section B.

Mathematics Accountancy, Actuarial Mathematics, Aeronautical Engineering, Astrophysics, Building Science and Technology, Business Management, Chemical Engineering, Civil Engineering, Computational Science, Computer Systems Engineering, Control Systems Engineering, Cybernetics, Economics, Electrical/Electronic Technology, Engineering Science, Ergonomics, Geophysics, Management Science, Materials Science and Technology, Mechanical Engineering, Metallurgy, Meteorology, Naval Architecture, Physics, Quantity Surveying, Statistics, Systems Analysis, Telecommunications.

Media studies; Media communication and production See Section B.

Music Music Technology. See also Section B.

Philosophy Divinity, History of Science, Psychology, Religious Studies.

Physical education and sport Chiropractic, Coaching Science, Dance Studies, Exercise and Health, Exercise

Science, Golf Studies, Health Care/Education/Psychology/Science, Human Life Science, Nursing, Occupational Health and Safety, Occupational Therapy, Osteopathy, Outdoor Pursuits, Physical Education, Physiotherapy, Sport and Exercise Science, Sport and Health, Sport Coaching, Sport Equipment Design, Sport Management, Teaching (Primary) (Secondary).

Physics; Applied science Aeronautical Engineering, Architecture, Astronomy, Astrophysics, Automotive Engineering, Biomedical Engineering, Biophysics, Chemical Physics, Civil Engineering, Communications Engineering, Computer Science, Cybernetics, Education, Electrical/Electronic Engineering, Engineering Science, Ergonomics, Geophysics, Materials Science and Technology, Mechanical Engineering, Medical Physics, Meteorology, Nanotechnology, Naval Architecture, Oceanography, Optometry, Photonics, Planetary Science, Quantum Informatics, Renewable Energy, Telecommunications Engineering.

Psychology See Section B.

Religious studies Archaeology, Anthropology, Biblical Studies, Divinity, Philosophy, Psychology, Theology.

Social policy; Sociology; Health and social care Economics, Human Geography, Psychology, Social Work, Sociology. See also Section B.

Statistics Business Studies, Informatics. See also Mathematics (above) and Section B (Mathematics-related careers).

Travel and tourism; Leisure studies See Section B.

SECTION B
Choosing your course by career interests
An alternative strategy for deciding on the subject of your degree or diploma course is to relate it to your career interests. However, even though you may have set your mind on a particular career, it is important to remember that sometimes there are others which are very similar to your planned career. The following lists give examples of career areas, each followed by examples of some relevant degree subjects.

Accountancy Actuarial Science, Banking, Business Studies, Economics, Financial Services, Management Science.

Actuarial work Accountancy, Banking, Insurance.

Agricultural careers Agriculture and Countryside Management, Agricultural Engineering, Agricultural Surveying, Animal Sciences, Biological Sciences, Ecology, Environmental Science, Estate Management, Forestry, Horticulture, Plant Sciences, Surveying.

Animal careers Agricultural Sciences, Biological Sciences, Equine Science/Studies/Management, Veterinary Science, Zoology.

Archaeology Ancient History, Anthropology, Classical Civilisation and Classics, History of Art and Architecture.

Architecture Building, Civil Engineering, Construction Engineering and Management, Structural Engineering.

Art and Design careers Advertising, Architecture, Education (Art), Industrial Design, Landscape Architecture, Photography, Three Dimensional Design.

Astronomy Astrophysics, Mathematics, Physics.

Audiology Education of the Deaf, Nursing, Speech and Language Therapy.

Banking/Insurance Accountancy, Business Studies, Economics, Financial Services.

see you there

To make the right choice of university, you need the right information.

We could give you a whole host of compelling reasons to choose Coventry - an innovative University in a thriving city.

We could talk about our courses - designed together with some of the biggest names in industry, giving you the best chance of success. We could tell you about how much we're investing to ensure you receive only the very best teaching and leading edge facilities.

Or we could talk about the city - like the University – built on a spirit of reinvention and enterprise – and the surrounding area is surprisingly good too.

But if you'd like to see for yourself, log on to **www.coventry.ac.uk** for further information.

Or call our admissions team on **024 7615 2222.**

Coventry
University

Biology-related careers Agricultural Sciences, Biochemistry, Ecology, Education, Environmental Health, Environmental Science, Genetics, Immunology, Medicine, Microbiology, Pharmacy, Plant Science, Physiology.

Book Publishing Advertising, Business Studies, Communications, Creative Writing, Journalism, Media Communication, Photography, Printing, Publishing, Science Communication, Web and Multimedia.

Brewing Biochemistry, Chemistry, Food Science.

Broadcasting Film and TV Studies, Journalism, Media Studies, Media and Communications Studies.

Building Architecture, Building Services Engineering, Building Surveying, Civil Engineering, Estate Management, General Practice Surveying, Land Surveying, Quantity Surveying.

Business Accountancy, Advertising, Banking, E-Commerce, Economics, Estate Management, Hospitality Management, Human Resource Management, Housing Management, Industrial Relations, Insurance, Logistics, Marketing, Public Relations, Supply Chain Management, Transport Management, Tourism.

Cartography Geographical Information Science, Geography, Land Surveying.

Catering Consumer Studies, Dietetics, Food Science, Hospitality Management, Nutrition.

Chemistry-related careers Agricultural Science, Biochemistry, Botany, Ceramics, Chemical Engineering, Colour Chemistry, Education, Geochemistry, Materials Science and Technology, Pharmacology, Pharmacy, Physiology, Technologies (for example Food, Plastics).

Computing Artificial Intelligence, Business Studies, Electronic Engineering, Information and Communication Technology, Mathematics, Microelectronics, Physics, Telecommunications.

Construction Architecture, Building, Building Services Engineering, Civil Engineering, Landscape Architecture, Quantity Surveying, Surveying, Town and Country Planning.

Dance Drama, Movement Studies, Performance/Performing Arts, Physical Education, Theatre Studies.

Dentistry Biochemistry, Dental Materials, Dental Technician, Equine Dentistry, Medicine, Nursing, Pharmacy.

Drama Dance, Education, Movement Studies, Teaching, Theatre Management.

Education British Sign Language, Conductive Education, Psychology, Social Work, Speech and Language Therapy, Youth Studies.

Engineering Engineering (including Chemical, Civil, Computing, Control, Electrical, Energy, Environmental, Food Process, Manufacturing, Mechanical, Microelectronics, Nuclear, Product Design, Software, Telecommunications), Geology and Geotechnics, Mathematics, Physics.

Estate Management Architecture, Building, Civil Engineering, Economics, Forestry, Housing Studies, Landscape Architecture, Property Development, Town and Country Planning.

Food and Accommodation Culinary Arts, Dietetics, Home Economics, Housing Management, Nutrition.

Food Science and Technology Biochemistry, Brewing, Chemistry, Culinary Arts, Dietetics, Food and Nutrition, Food Safety Management, Food Technology, Home Economics, Nutrition.

Forestry Arboriculture, Biological Sciences, Countryside Management, Ecology, Environmental Science, Plant Sciences, Rural Resource Management, Tropical Forestry, Urban Forestry.

Furniture Design Furniture Production, History of Art and Design, Three Dimensional Design, Timber Technology.

Geology-related careers Chemistry, Earth Sciences, Engineering (Civil, Minerals), Environmental Sciences, Geochemistry, Geography, Land Surveying, Soil Science.

Graphic Design Advertising, Photography, Printing.

Health and Safety careers Biomedical Sciences, Community and Health Studies, Environmental Health, Exercise and Health Science, Fire Science Engineering, Health Promotion, Health Sciences, Nursery Nursing, Occupational Safety and Health, Paramedic Science, Public Health, Public Services Management. (See also **Medical careers**.)

Horticulture Agriculture, Botany, Landscape Architecture, Plant Science.

Hospitality Management Business and Management, Events and Facilities Management, Food Science, Food Technology, Heritage Management, Hospitality Business Management, Human Resource Management, International Hospitality Management, Leisure Services Management, Travel and Tourism Management.

Housing Architecture, Estate Management, General Practice Surveying, Social Administration, Town and Country Planning.

Law Business Studies, Commercial Law, Consumer Law, Criminal Justice, European Law, Government and Politics, International History, Land Management, Legal Studies, Sociology.

Leisure and Recreation Countryside Management, Dance, Drama, Fitness Science, Hospitality Management, International Tourism Management, Movement Studies, Music, Physical Education, Sport Development, Sport and Leisure Management, Sports Management, Theatre Studies, Travel and Tourism.

Library and Information Management Administration, Business Information Systems, Information and Communication Studies, Information and Library Studies, Information Management, Information Sciences and Technology, Museum and Galleries Studies, Publishing.

Marketing Advertising, Business Studies, Consumer Science, E-Marketing, International Business, Printing and Packaging, Psychology, Public Relations, Travel and Tourism.

Materials Science/Metallurgy Automotive Materials, Chemistry, Engineering, Glass Science and Technology, Materials Technology, Mineral Surveying, Physics, Polymer Science, Sports Materials, Textile Science.

Mathematics-related careers Accountancy, Actuarial Science, Banking, Business Decision Mathematics, Business Studies, Computer Studies, Economics, Education, Engineering, Financial Mathematics, Mathematical Physics/Sciences, Physics, Quantity Surveying, Statistics.

Media careers Advertising, Communications, Computer Graphics, Creative Writing, Film/Video Production, Journalism, Photography, Public Relations.

Medical careers Anatomy, Biochemistry, Biological Sciences, Chiropractic, Dentistry, Genetics, Human Physiology, Medical Sciences/Medicine, Nursing, Occupational Therapy, Orthoptics, Osteopathy, Pharmacology, Pharmacy, Physiotherapy, Radiography, Social Sciences, Speech and Language Therapy, Sports Biomedicine.

Microelectronics Computer Studies, Electrical/Electronic Engineering.

Music Drama, Performance/Performing Arts, Theatre Studies.

Nautical careers Marine Engineering, Naval Architecture, Nautical Studies, Oceanography, Offshore Engineering.

Naval Architecture Marine Engineering, Maritime Studies, Offshore Engineering.

Nursing Anatomy, Applied Biology, Biochemistry, Biological Sciences, Biology, Dentistry, Education, Environmental Health and Community Studies, Health Studies, Human Biology, Medicine, Midwifery, Occupational Therapy, Orthoptics, Physiotherapy, Psychology, Podiatry, Radiography, Social Administration, Speech and Language Therapy. (See also **Medical careers**.)

Nutrition Dietetics, Food Science and Technology, Nursing.

Occupational Therapy Art, Nursing, Orthoptics, Physiotherapy, Psychology, Speech and Language Therapy.

Optometry (Ophthalmic Optics) Applied Physics, Orthoptics, Physics.

Photography/Film/TV Animation, Communication Studies (some courses), Digital Video Design, Documentary Communications, Film and Media, Graphic Art, Media Studies, Moving Image, Multimedia, Photography.

Physical Education Exercise Sciences, Fitness Science, Leisure and Recreation Management, Sport and Recreational Studies, Sports Science.

Physiotherapy Chiropractic, Exercise Science, Nursing, Orthoptics, Osteopathy, Physical Education.

Physics-related careers Applied Physics, Astronomy, Astrophysics, Education, Engineering (Civil, Electrical, Mechanical), Medical Instrumentation, Optometry (Ophthalmic Optics).

Production Technology Engineering (Mechanical, Manufacturing), Materials Science.

Property and Valuation Management Architecture, Estate Management, Quantity Surveying, Urban Land Economics.

Psychology Applied Social Studies, Cognitive Science, Occupational Therapy, Psychology (Clinical, Developmental, Educational, Experimental, Occupational, Social), Social Work.

Public Administration Applied Social Studies, Business Studies, Social Administration, Social Policy, Youth Studies.

Quantity Surveying Accountancy, Architecture, Building, Civil Engineering, Surveying (Building, Land and Valuation).

Radiography Anatomy, Audiology, Biological Sciences, Medical Photography, Nursing, Orthoptics, Photography, Physiology, Physiotherapy.

Silversmithing/Jewellery Three Dimensional Design.

Social Work Anthropology, Health and Social Care, Journalism, Politics and Government, Public Administration, Religious Studies, Social Administration, Sociology, Town and Country Planning, Youth Studies.

Speech and Language Therapy Audiology, Education (Special Education), Nursing, Occupational Therapy, Psychology, Radiography.

Statistics Business Studies, Economics, Informatics, Mathematics, Operational Research, Population Sciences.

Technology Applied Chemistry, Chemistry, Dental Technology, Food Science and Technology, Paper Science, Polymer Science, Timber Technology.

Textile Design Art, Clothing Studies, Fashion Design, Interior Design, Textile Management.

Theatre Design Drama, Interior Design, Leisure and Recreational Studies, Theatre Management, Theatre Studies.

Three Dimensional Design Architecture, Industrial Design, Interior Design, Theatre Design.

Town and Country Planning Architecture, Environmental Science, Estate Management, Geography, Leisure and Recreational Management, Planning Studies, Population Sciences, Statistics, Transport Management.

Transport Business Studies, Town and Country Planning.

Typography and Graphic Communication Graphic Design, Packaging Design, Printing, Publishing.

Veterinary careers Agricultural Sciences, Agriculture, Animal Sciences, Equine Dentistry, Equine Science, Medicine, Pharmacology, Pharmacy, Veterinary Medicine, Veterinary Nursing, Zoology.

COURSE TYPES AND DIFFERENCES

When choosing an Honours (or Ordinary) degree course, the first factors to consider are the course and subject requirements or preferences. Courses in the same subject at different universities and colleges can have different subject requirements so it is important to check the acceptability of your GCE A/AS and GCSE subjects (or equivalent) for your preferred courses. Specific GCE A/AS-levels, and in some cases, GCSE subjects, may be stipulated. (See also the **Table of Equivalent Offers** in **Chapter 8** for information on the International, European and French Baccalaureates, Scottish Highers, the Welsh Baccalaureate and the Irish Leaving Certificate, and **Appendix 1** for international qualifications.)

You will then need to decide on the type of course you want to follow. The way in which Honours degree courses are arranged differs between institutions (see **Chapter 3**). For example, a subject might be offered as a single subject course (a single Honours degree), or as a two-subject course (a joint Honours degree), or as one of two, three or four subjects (a combined degree) or a major-minor degree (75 and 25% of each subject respectively). One variation on single Honours courses is that of the sandwich course, in which students will spend part of their degree course on work placements. These can be extremely advantageous, not only from the point of view of earnings but in many cases as a stepping stone to full-time employment on graduation. See **Chapter 4** for more about sandwich courses and professional placements.

Courses can also differ considerably in their content and how they are organised. Many universities and colleges of higher education have modularised their courses which means you can choose modules of different subjects, and 'build' your course within specified 'pathways' with the help and approval of your course tutor. It also means that you are likely to be assessed after completing each module, rather than in your last year for all your previous years' learning. In almost every course the options and modules offered include some which reflect the research interests of individual members of staff. In some courses subsidiary subjects are available as minor courses alongside a single Honours course. In an increasing number of courses these additional subjects include a European language, and the importance of this cannot be over-emphasised with the United Kingdom's membership of the European Union. Such links are also reinforced by way of the Erasmus programme which enables university students to apply for courses in Europe for periods of up to a year, some of the courses being taught in English.

Many institutions have introduced credit accumulation and transfer arrangements, especially in Scotland. This means that students are awarded credits for modules or units of study they have successfully completed which are accumulated towards a certificate, diploma or first degree.

When choosing your course it is important to remember that one course is not better than another – it is just different. The best course for you is the one which best suits **you**. To give some indication of the differences between courses, see **Course variations** in the tables of **Chapter 9**, and more fully in *Choosing Your Degree Course and University* (see **Appendix 3**). After provisionally choosing your courses, read the prospectuses again carefully to be sure that you understand what is included in the three, four

or more years of study. Each institution differs in its course content even though the course titles may be the same and courses differ in other ways, for example, in their:

* methods of assessment (eg unseen examinations, continuous assessment, project work, dissertations)
* contact time with tutors
* how they are taught (for example, frequency and size of lectures, seminars)
* practicals; field work requirements
* library, laboratory and studio facilities
* amount of free study time available.

These are useful points of comparison between courses in different institutions when you are making final course choices. Other important factors to consider when comparing courses include the availability of opportunities for studying and working abroad during your course, and professional body accreditation of courses leading to certain professional careers (see **Appendix 2**).

Once you have chosen your course subject(s) the next step is to find out about the universities and colleges offering courses in your subject area. The next chapter, **Choosing Your University or College** provides information to help you do this.

2 | CHOOSING YOUR UNIVERSITY OR COLLEGE

LOCATION, REPUTATION AND OPEN DAYS

For the majority of applicants the choice of university or college is probably the main priority, with location being a key factor. However, many students have little or no knowledge of regional geography and have no concept of where universities are located: one student thought that Bangor University (situated in North Wales) was located at Bognor on England's south coast!

Some institutions – probably those nearest home or those farthest away – will be rejected quickly. In addition to the region, location and immediate surroundings of a university or college, each applicant has his or her own priorities – perhaps a hectic city life or, alternatively, a quiet life in the country! But university isn't all about studying, so it's not a bad idea to link your spare time interests with what the university or college can offer or with the opportunities available in the locality. Many applicants have theatrical, musical or artistic interests while others have sporting interests and achievements ranging from rowing, horse riding, sailing and mountaineering, to even fishing for England!

Some other decisions about your choice of university or college, however, could be made for the wrong reasons. Many students, for example, talk about 'reputation' or base their decisions on league tables. Reputations are fairly clear-cut in the case of some institutions. Oxford and Cambridge are both top world-class universities in which all courses have been established for many years and are supported by first class facilities. In other universities certain subjects are predominant, such as the social sciences at the London School of Economics, and the sciences and technologies at Imperial London.

Many other leading universities in the UK are also very strong in certain subjects *but not necessarily in all subjects*. This is why it is wrong to conclude that a 'university has a good reputation' – most universities are not necessarily good at everything! In seeking advice, you should also be a little wary of school staff who will usually always claim that their own university or college has a 'good reputation'. Teachers obviously can provide good advice on the courses and the general atmosphere of their own institution, but they are not in a good position to make comparisons with other universities.

League tables are a popular source of information, particularly those that list 'teaching' scores, although these should not necessarily be taken at face value. Firstly, these 'inspections', or 'surveys', were done from 1998 to 2000 and are now more than eight years out-of-date and will not be updated. Secondly, these inspections were not like school inspections in which every member of staff was checked on presentation skills and the syllabus. University staff may well be extremely learned with high academic qualifications, but their ability to present their subject may fall short of your standards!

The best way to find out about universities and colleges and the courses that interest you is to visit your preferred institutions. Open days provide the opportunity to talk to staff and students although, with thousands of students wandering round campuses, it may be difficult to meet and talk to the right people. Also, many institutions hold Open days during vacations when many students are away which means that you may only hear talks from the staff, and not have any opportunity to meet students. However, it is often possible to visit a university or college in your own time and simply 'walk in'. Alternatively, a letter to the head of department requesting a visit could enable you to get a closer look at the subject facilities. But failing this, you will be invited automatically to visit when you receive an offer and then you can meet the students in the department.

ACTION POINTS

Before deciding on your preferred universities and courses it is important to check out the following points:

Teaching staff

How do the students react to their tutors? Do staff have a flair and enthusiasm for their subject? Are they approachable? Do they mark your work regularly and is the feedback helpful, or are you left to get on with your own work with very little direction? What are the research interests of the staff?

Teaching styles

How will you be taught, for example, lectures, seminars, tutorials? Are lectures popular? If not, why not? Are computer-aided packages used? How much time will you be expected to work on your own? If there are field courses, how often are they arranged and are they compulsory? How much will they cost?

Facilities

Are the facilities of a high standard and easily available? Is the laboratory equipment 'state of the art' or just adequate? Are the libraries well-stocked? What are the IT facilities? Is there plenty of space to study or do rooms and workspaces become overcrowded? Do students have to pay for any materials?

New students

Are there induction courses for new students? What student services and facilities are available? Is it possible to buy second-hand copies of set books?

Work placements

Are work placements an optional or compulsory part of the course? Who arranges them? Are the placements popular? Do they count towards your degree? Are work placements paid?

Transferable skills

Transferable skills are now regarded as important by all future employers. Does the department provide training in communication skills, teamwork, time management and information technology as part of the degree course?

Accommodation

How easy is it to find accommodation? Where are the halls of residence? Are they conveniently located for libraries and lecture theatres? Are they self-catering? Alternatively, what is the cost of meals in the university refectory? Which types of student accommodation are the most popular? What is the annual cost of accommodation? If there is more than one campus, is a shuttle-bus service provided?

Finance

Find out the costs of materials, accommodation and travel in addition to your own personal needs (and see **Chapter 5** for details of the average living costs for each university). What opportunities are there for earning money, on or off campus? Does the department or faculty have any rules about part-time employment?

It is important to note that, whilst financial help is available to all disadvantaged students at all universities, many universities also offer additional scholarships, bursaries and other awards covering a wide range of subject areas, often on the basis of academic excellence. See **Chapter 5**, and also *University Scholarships, Awards and Bursaries* (see **Appendix 3**) for full details of these awards for UK, EU and overseas students.

INFORMATION SOURCES

Prospectuses, websites and Open days are key sources of the information you need to decide where to study. Other sources include the books and websites listed in **Appendix 3**, the professional associations listed in **Appendix 2**, and the websites provided in the subject tables in **Chapter 9**. It is important to take time to find out as much as you can about your preferred universities, colleges and courses, and to explore their similarities and differences.

The following chapter **University Course Profiles** gives you information about the types of courses they offer and how they are organised. This is important information that you need to know when choosing your university or college because those factors affect, for example, the amount of choice you have in what you study, and the opportunities you have for sandwich placements (see **Chapter 4**). You therefore need to read **Chapters 2** and **3** in conjunction so that you can find the university or college that is right for you.

DIRECTORY OF INSTITUTIONS

SECTION 1: UNIVERSITIES

Listed below are universities in the United Kingdom that offer degree and diploma courses at higher education level. Applications to these institutions are submitted through UCAS except for part-time courses, private universities and colleges, and further education courses. For current information refer to the websites shown and also to the UCAS *Big Guide* for a comprehensive list of degree and diploma courses (see **Appendix 3**).

Aberdeen A city-centre university on Scotland's east coast. *(University of Aberdeen, University Office, King's College, Aberdeen, Grampian, Scotland AB24 3FX. Tel 01224 272000; Student Recruitment and Admissions Service 01224 272090/1; www.abdn.ac.uk)*

Abertay Dundee A modern city-centre campus. *(University of Abertay Dundee, 40 Bell Street, Dundee, Scotland DD1 1HG. Tel 01382 308000; www.abertay.ac.uk)*

Aberystwyth A coastal university with a striking campus. *(University of Wales, Aberystwyth, Old College, King Street, Aberystwyth, Ceredigion, Wales SY23 2AX. Tel 01970 623111; www.aber.ac.uk)*

American InterContinental Situated in central London, AIU London is a private university charging termly tuition fees from £4000. It is accredited in the UK by the Open University and is in the membership of the Quality Assurance Agency. *(American InterContinental University – London, 110 Marylebone High Street, London W1U 4RY. Tel 020 7467 5600; www.aiulondon.ac.uk)*

Anglia Ruskin Two main campuses in Cambridge and Chelmsford and over 20 partner colleges throughout East Anglia and north-east London. *(Anglia Ruskin University, Bishop Hall Lane, Chelmsford, Essex CM1 1SQ. Tel 0845 271 3333; www.anglia.ac.uk)*

Arts London The University consists of four Colleges of Art and Design (Camberwell, Chelsea, Central Saint Martins (including Byam Shaw School of Art) and Wimbledon), the London College of Communication and the London College of Fashion. *(University of the Arts London, 65 Davies Street, London W1K 5DA. Tel 020 7514 6130; www.arts.ac.uk)*

Aston A green campus university in the centre of Birmingham with academic, sporting and social activities on site. *(Aston University, Aston Triangle, Birmingham B4 7ET. Tel 0121 204 3000; www.aston.ac.uk)*

Bangor A central site in Bangor on the Menai Straits with partner institutions throughout North Wales. *(University of Wales, Bangor, Gwynedd, Wales LL57 2DG. Tel 01248 351151; Undergraduate Admissions 01248 382017; www.bangor.ac.uk)*

Bath A rural campus outside Bath and a campus in Swindon, with college-based programmes available in Bath itself and throughout Wiltshire. *(University of Bath, Claverton Campus, Bath, Somerset BA2 7AY. Tel 01225 388388; Admissions Office 01225 386959; www.bath.ac.uk)*

Bath Spa A new university (2005) located on two campuses near Bath. *(Bath Spa University, Newton Park, Newton St Loe, Bath, Somerset BA2 9BN. Tel 01225 875875; www.bathspa.ac.uk)*

Bedfordshire This is a new university (formed in August 2006 from the merger of Luton University and the Bedford campus of De Montfort University). The main campus (one of three) is in the centre of Luton. *(University of Bedfordshire, Park Square, Luton, Bedfordshire LU1 3JU. Tel 01234 400400; www.beds.ac.uk)*

Birmingham A 'red-brick' university on the Edgbaston site to the south of the city, with a second campus at Selly Oak. *(University of Birmingham, Edgbaston, Birmingham B15 2TT. Tel 0121 414 3344; Admissions 0121 415 8900; www.bham.ac.uk)*

Birmingham City (until recently the University of Central England in Birmingham) Eight teaching sites located around the city, each focusing on one subject. Four franchised colleges in Birmingham and Warwickshire also offer courses. *(Birmingham City University, Perry Bar, Birmingham B42 2SU. Tel 0121 331 5000; Course Enquiries: 0121 331 5595; www.bcu.ac.uk)*

Bolton A new (2005) university, situated on two campuses close to the town centre. *(University of Bolton, Deane Road, Bolton, Lancashire BL3 5AB. Tel 01204 900600; www.bolton.ac.uk)*

Bournemouth A compact university site in a large coastal resort, with seven partner colleges in the region also offering courses. *(Bournemouth University, Talbot Campus, Fern Barrow, Poole, Dorset BH12 5BB. Tel 01202 524111; www.bournemouth.ac.uk)*

Bradford The University's main campus is close to the city centre, with the management centre two miles away. *(University of Bradford, Richmond Road, Bradford, West Yorkshire BD7 1DP. Tel 01274 232323; www.brad.ac.uk)*

Brighton Situated on the south coast, the University has campuses in Brighton, Eastbourne and Hastings. University-validated courses are offered at several partner colleges. *(University of*

Brighton, Mithras House, Lewes Road, Brighton, East Sussex BN2 4AT. Tel 01273 600900; www.brighton.ac.uk)*

Brighton and Sussex Medical School *(BSMS Teaching Building, University of Sussex, Brighton, East Sussex BN1 9PX; Tel 01273 877864; Admissions 01275 644644; www.bsms.ac.uk)*

Bristol A city university with halls of residence in Stoke Bishop and Clifton. *(University of Bristol, Senate House, Tyndall Avenue, Bristol BS8 1TH. Tel 0117 928 9000; www.bris.ac.uk)*

Bristol UWE Four campuses in Bristol with additional campuses in Bath, Gloucester and Swindon. Links with the Bristol Old Vic Theatre School and the Royal West of England Academy. *(University of the West of England, Coldharbour Lane, Bristol BS16 1QY. Tel 0117 965 6261; www.uwe.ac.uk)*

Brunel A compact campus to the west of London at Uxbridge. Brunel also validates courses at the London School of Theology. *(Brunel University, Uxbridge, Middlesex UB8 3PH. Tel 01895 274000; Admissions 01895 265265; www.brunel.ac.uk)*

Buckingham A small independent university on a town campus some 40 miles north of London offering two-year (eight-term) degrees. *(University of Buckingham, Hunter Street, Buckingham MK18 1EG. Tel 01280 814080; www.buckingham.ac.uk)*

Bucks New A new university (2007) with two campuses in High Wycombe and one at Chalfont St Giles. *(Buckinghamshire New University, Queen Alexandra Road, High Wycombe HP11 2JZ. Tel 01494 522141; free phone 0800 0565 660; www.bucks.ac.uk)*

Cambridge Thirty-one colleges located throughout the city. **Colleges** Lucy Cavendish, New Hall and Newnham (women only); the following admit both men and women undergraduates: Christ's, Churchill, Clare, Corpus Christi, Darwin, Downing, Emmanuel, Fitzwilliam, Girton, Gonville and Caius, Homerton, Hughes, Jesus, King's, Magdalene, Pembroke, Peterhouse, Queens', Robinson, St Catharine's, St John's,

Be unique

Bath Spa University could help you change your future.
We offer teaching of the highest quality across a wide range of
courses, from Foundation Degrees to Master's programmes.
We provide an inspiring and supportive environment -
our campuses are stunning. And, of course, Bath is a superb city.

To find out more about a unique University where each
student is valued as an individual, contact us now.
We have Open Days in May and October.

Tel: 01225 875 875
email: enquiries@bathspa.ac.uk
www.bathspa.ac.uk

let's change our future

Selwyn, Sidney Sussex, Trinity, Trinity Hall, Wolfson. Clare and Darwin admit only graduates. *(Enquiries should be addressed to the Tutor for Admissions, . . College, Cambridge or to the Cambridge Admissions Office, Fitzwilliam House, 32 Trumpington Street, Cambridge CB2 1QY. Tel 01223 333308; www.cam.ac.uk)*

Canterbury Christ Church A new university (2005) located near the city centre with campuses at Canterbury, Folkestone, Medway and Tunbridge Wells. *(Canterbury Christ Church University, North Holmes Road, Canterbury, Kent CT1 1QU. Tel: 01227 767700; www.canterbury.ac.uk)*

Cardiff The Cathays Park campus of the University is located in the city centre, with the Heath Park campus a mile to the south. *(Cardiff University, Cardiff, Wales CF10 3XQ. Tel 029 208 74000; www.cardiff.ac.uk)*

Central Lancashire The University is located on a small campus in the city centre. It also has 23 partner colleges. *(University of Central Lancashire, Preston PR1 2HE. Tel 01772 201201; www.uclan.ac.uk)*

Chester A new university (2005) located on a campus in Chester, with a second campus in Warrington. *(Chester University, Parkgate Road, Chester CH1 4BJ. Tel 01244 511000; www.chester.ac.uk)*

Chichester A small new university (2005) with the main campus at Chichester and a second near Pulborough on the South Downs. *(University of Chichester, Westgate Fields, Chichester, West Sussex PO19 1SBE. Tel 01243 786321; www.chi.ac.uk)*

City The University is situated in central London; Foundation courses are offered at a local college of further education. *(City University, Northampton Square, London EC1V 0HB. Tel 020 7040 5060; www.city.ac.uk)*

Coventry The University has a number of teaching centres throughout the city with courses offered in six partner colleges. *(Coventry University, Priory Street, Coventry CV1 5FB. Tel 024 7688 7688; www.coventry.ac.uk)*

Cumbria A new university (August 2007) created by the merger of St Martin's College and Cumbria Institute of the Arts. *(University of Cumbria, Fusehill Street, Carlisle, Cumbria CA1 2HH. Tel 01228 616234; Enquiries 0845 606 1144; www.cumbria.ac.uk)*

De Montfort The University has two sites in Leicester and 12 associate colleges. *(De Montfort University, The Gateway, Leicester LE1 9BH. Tel 0116 255 1551; Enquiries 08459 454647; www.dmu.ac.uk)*

Derby The University has two campuses: one close to Derby city centre and the second at Buxton. It also has a wide network of partner colleges. *(University of Derby, Kedleston Road, Derby DE22 1GB. Tel 01332 590500; Course Enquiries 08701 202330; www.derby.ac.uk)*

Dundee A city-centre campus, with the Medical School and School of Nursing located at Ninewells Hospital to the west of the city. *(University of Dundee, Nethergate, Dundee, Scotland DD1 4HN. Tel 01382 383000; Admissions and Student Recruitment 01382 381160; www.dundee.ac.uk)*

Durham Two sites, the main one in Durham city; the second, at Stockton, has two colleges on the Queen's Campus. *(University of Durham, University Office, Old Elvet, Durham DH1 3HP. Tel 0191 334 2000; Admissions: 0191 334 6123; www.dur.ac.uk)*

East Anglia A parkland campus outside Norwich. *(University of East Anglia, Norwich NR4 7TJ. Tel 01603 456161; www.uea.ac.uk)*

East London Three campuses in London at Stratford, Docklands and Barking. Foundation degrees are offered at Barking, Newham and Redbridge Colleges. *(University of East London, Docklands Campus, 4–6 University Way, London E16 2RD. Tel 020 8223 3000; Admissions 020 8223 3333; www.uel.ac.uk)*

Edge Hill A new university (2005) with its main campus on the outskirts of Ormskirk near Liverpool. *(Edge Hill University, Ormskirk Campus, St Helens Road, Ormskirk, Lancashire L39 4QP. Tel 01695 575171; www.edgehill.ac.uk)*

Edinburgh A city university consisting of the University Central Area in the city centre and the University King's Buildings on a site a mile to the south. *(University of Edinburgh, Student Recruitment and Admissions, 57 George Square, Edinburgh, Scotland EH8 9JU. Tel 0131 650 4360; www.ed.ac.uk)*

Essex A parkland campus two miles from Colchester. The University and the South East Essex College Partnership also provide degree schemes at the new Southend campus. The University validates degrees offered by Writtle College. *(University of Essex, Wivenhoe Park, Colchester, Essex CO4 3SQ. Tel 01206 873333; Undergraduate Enquiries 01206 872002; www.essex.ac.uk)*

Exeter Two sites in Exeter: the Streatham campus is the largest, and the St Luke's campus is a mile away. A third campus is situated a short distance from Falmouth in Cornwall. *(University of Exeter, Northcote House, The Queen's Drive, Exeter, Devon EX4 4QJ. Tel 01392 661000; www.exeter.ac.uk)*

Glamorgan A single campus university and partnership arrangements with associate and partner colleges in England and Wales. *(University of Glamorgan, Treforest, Pontypridd, Mid-Glamorgan, Wales CF37 1DL. Tel 0800 716925; www.glamorgan.ac.uk)*

Glasgow Three main campuses, two on the outskirts of Glasgow and one on the Crichton campus at Dumfries. Glasgow School of Art and the Scottish Agricultural College in Ayr are associated institutions. *(University of Glasgow, Glasgow, Strathclyde, Scotland G12 8QQ. Tel 0141 330 2000; www.glasgow.ac.uk)*

Glasgow Caledonian A city-centre campus; courses are also offered through four associated institutions. *(Glasgow Caledonian University, Cowcaddens Road, Glasgow, Strathclyde, Scotland G4 0BA. Tel 0141 331 3000; www.caledonian.ac.uk)*

Gloucestershire Three campuses in Cheltenham and one in Gloucester. *(University of Gloucestershire, The Park, Cheltenham, Gloucestershire GL50 2RH. Tel 08707 210210; www.glos.ac.uk)*

Greenwich The main campus is the Maritime Greenwich campus, a second at Avery Hill Park, Eltham in south London and a third at Medway at Chatham Maritime. There are also eight partner colleges in east London and Kent. *(University of Greenwich, Maritime Greenwich Campus, Old Royal Naval College, Park Row, Greenwich, London SE10 9LS. Tel 020 8331 8000; Course Enquiries 0800 005006; www.gre.ac.uk)*

Heriot-Watt A large parkland campus seven miles west of Edinburgh, a second campus in the Scottish Borders at Galashiels 35 miles to the south and a third in Dubai. *(Heriot-Watt University, Edinburgh, Riccarton, Edinburgh, Lothian, Scotland EH14 4AS. Tel 0131 449 5111; www.hw.ac.uk)*

Hertfordshire Two campuses in Hatfield; courses also offered through a consortium of four Hertfordshire colleges. *(University of Hertfordshire, College Lane, Hatfield, Hertfordshire AL10 9AB. Tel 01707 284000; Admissions 01707 284800; www.herts.ac.uk)*

Huddersfield A town-centre university with links to over 30 colleges of further education throughout the north of England. *(University of Huddersfield, Queensgate, Huddersfield HD1 3DH. Tel 01484 422288; Admissions 01484 473969; www.hud.ac.uk)*

Hull The main campus is located in Hull, some two miles from the city centre, with a smaller campus in Scarborough. *(The University of Hull, Admissions Office, Cottingham Road, Hull, East Yorkshire HU6 7RX. Tel 01482 346311; www.hull.ac.uk)*

Hull York Medical School *(Admissions Section, University of York, Heslington, York YO10 5DD. Tel 08701 202323)*

Imperial London The College became an independent university, separate from the University of London, in 2007. The central site is in South Kensington. Medicine is based mainly at St Mary's Hospital, Paddington, Charing Cross Hospital and Hammersmith Hospital. *(Imperial College London, South Kensington, London SW7 2AZ. Tel 020 7589 5111; www.imperial.ac.uk)*

Keele A small university on a green campus five miles from Stoke-on-Trent. *(The University of Keele, Keele, Staffordshire ST5 5BG. Tel 01782 621111; Admissions 01782 584005; www.keele.ac.uk)*

Kent A spacious campus near Canterbury, and also campuses at Medway, Chatham, Brussels, Tonbridge, Wye and Transmanche, France. There are also three associated institutions – Mid Kent, South Kent and Canterbury Colleges. *(University of Kent, Recruitment and Admissions, Canterbury, Kent CT2 7NZ. Tel 01227 827272; www.kent.ac.uk)*

Kingston Four campuses in and around the town with easy access to London. *(Kingston University, Student Information and Advice Centre, 40–46 Surbiton Road, Kingston upon Thames, Surrey KT1 2HX. Tel 020 8457 2000; Admissions 020 8547 7053; www.kingston.ac.uk)*

Lampeter A small university in a rural town in west Wales. *(University of Wales, Lampeter, Ceredigion, Wales SA48 7ED. Tel 01570 422351; www.lamp.ac.uk)*

Lancaster Parkland site three miles south of the city centre. *(University, Bailrigg, Lancaster LA1 4YW. Tel 01524 65201; Admissions 01524 592028; www.lancs.ac.uk)*

Leeds The University is sited on a campus in the centre of the city. *(University of Leeds, Leeds LS2 9JT. Tel 0113 243 1751; Course Enquiries 0113 243 2336; www.leeds.ac.uk)*

Leeds Metropolitan Two main campuses, one in the city and a second in Headingley on the outskirts of Leeds. There are two smaller campuses in Harrogate and Ripon and a network of 14 partner colleges. *(Leeds Metropolitan University, Civic Quarter, Leeds LS1 3HE. Tel 0113 812 0000; Course Enquiries 0113 812 3113; www.leedsmet.ac.uk)*

Leicester The compact campus is located on the edge of the city. *(University of Leicester, University Road, Leicester LE1 7RH. Tel 0116 252 2522; www.le.ac.uk)*

Lincoln The Brayford and Cathedral campuses are in the city, with the Riseholme Park campus

some five miles away; there is also a campus in Hull. *(University of Lincoln, Brayford Pool, Lincoln LN6 7TS. Tel 01522 882000; www.lincoln.ac.uk)*

Liverpool A large city-centre campus. *(University of Liverpool, Liverpool L69 3BX. Tel 0151 794 2000; www.liv.ac.uk)*

Liverpool Hope A new university (2005) outside Liverpool. *(Liverpool Hope University, Hope Park, Liverpool L16 9JD. Tel 0151 291 3000; Admissions 0151 291 3295; www.hope.ac.uk)*

Liverpool John Moores Three campuses in and around the city. *(Liverpool John Moores University, Roscoe Court, 4 Rodney Street, Liverpool L1 2TZ. Tel 0151 2312 2121; Student Recruitment 0151 231 5090; www.ljmu.ac.uk)*

London – Birkbeck (Birk) The College is situated in Bloomsbury in the London University precinct. *(Birkbeck, University of London, Malet Street, Bloomsbury, London WC1E 7HX. Tel 020 7631 6000; Course Enquiries 0845 601 0174; www.bbk.ac.uk)*

London – Central School of Speech and Drama Main campus at the Embassy Theatre. *(Central School of Speech and Drama, Embassy Theatre, 64 Eton Avenue, London NW3 3HY. Tel 020 7722 8183; www.cssd.ac.uk)*

London – Courtauld (Court) The Institute is located, together with its gallery, in Somerset House on the Strand in central London. *(The Courtauld Institute of Art, Somerset House, Strand, London WC2R 0RN. Tel 020 7872 0220; Admissions 020 7848 2645; www.courtauld.ac.uk)*

London – Goldsmiths (Gold) The College is located in south-east London. *(Goldsmiths, University of London, Lewisham Way, New Cross, London SE14 6NW. Tel 020 7919 7171; www.goldsmiths.ac.uk)*

London – Heythrop College (Hey) The College is located on a site in central London. *(Heythrop College, University of London, Kensington Square, London W8 5HQ. Tel 020 7795 6600; www.heythrop.ac.uk)*

London – Institute in Paris The Institute's

Department of French Studies and Centre of Professional English operates in partnership with Queen Mary and Royal Holloway Colleges. *(University of London Institute in Paris, 9–11 rue de Constantine, 75340 Paris Cedex 07. Tel 00 33 1 44 11 73 83 76; www.ulip.lon.ac.uk)*

London – King's College (King's) Five campuses in central and south London including the School of Medicine, the Dental Institute and the School of Biomedical and Health Sciences. *(King's College London, Hodgkin Building, Guy's Campus, London SE1 1UL. Tel 020 7848 6501/6502; Strand campus (a) School of Humanities: Tel 020 7848 2374; (b) School of Law: Tel 020 7848 2503; (c) School of Physical Sciences and Engineering: Tel 020 7873 2271; Florence Nightingale School of Nursing and Midwifery, James Clerk Maxwell Building, 57 Waterloo Road, London SE1 8WA. Tel 020 7848 4698; King's College London, Strand, London WC2R 2LS. Tel 020 7836 5454; www.kcl.ac.uk)*

London – Queen Mary (QM) A city campus in the East End of London. *(Barts and the London Queen Mary's School of Medicine and Dentistry, Turner Street, London E1 2AD. Tel 020 7882 2240/2243); (Queen Mary, University of London, Mile End Road, London E1 4NS. Tel 020 7882 5555; www.qmul.ac.uk)*

London – Royal Holloway (RH) A large campus with halls of residence located at Egham, some 19 miles from central London and three miles from Windsor. *(Royal Holloway, University of London, Egham Hill, Egham, Surrey TW20 0EX. Tel 01784 434455; www.rhul.ac.uk)*

London – Royal Veterinary College (RVC) The College is located in north London. *(Royal Veterinary College, University of London, Royal College Street, London NW1 0TU. Tel 020 7468 5000; Admissions 020 7468 5149; www.rvc.ac.uk)*

London – St George's Located on a compact site in south-west London, St George's has extensive links with many hospitals and practices, and with Kingston University and Royal Holloway London. *(St George's, University of London, Cranmer Terrace, Tooting, London SW17 0RE. Tel 020 8672 9944; www.sgul.ac.uk)*

London – London School of Economics and Political Science (LSE) A central London site near the Aldwych. LSE entrance examination may be required: see **Chapter 7**. *(London School of Economics and Political Science, University of London, Houghton Street, London WC2A 2AE. Tel 020 7405 7686; Student Recruitment Office, W700, Tower 3, London School of Economics and Political Science, Clement's Inn Passage, London WC2A 2AE. Tel 020 7955 6613; www.lse.ac.uk)*

London – School of Oriental and African Studies (SOAS) The School is located in Bloomsbury and Islington. *(School of Oriental and African Studies, University of London, Thornhaugh Street, Russell Square, London WC1H 0XG. Tel 020 7637 2388; www.soas.ac.uk)*

London – School of Pharmacy The School has a central London site near to the London University precinct. *(School of Pharmacy, University of London, 29–39 Brunswick Square, London WC1N 1AX. Tel 020 7753 5800; www.pharmacy.ac.uk)*

London – University College London (UCL) The College is located in Bloomsbury in the London University precinct. *(University College London, Gower Street, London WC1E 6BT. Tel 020 7679 2000; www.ucl.ac.uk)*

London Metropolitan Two campuses, one in north London (with the largest (new) science laboratory in Europe) and one in the City, and six partner colleges. *(London Metropolitan University, 166–220 Holloway Road, London N7 8DB. Tel 020 7423 0000; Admissions 020 7133 4200; www.londonmet.ac.uk)*

London South Bank Campuses at Southwark, Whipps Cross Hospital in east London and at the Harold Wood Hospital in Essex. *(London South Bank University, 103 Borough Road, London SE1 0AA. Tel 020 7815 7815; course enquiries, 90 London Road, London SE1 6LN. Tel 020 7815 7815; www.lsbu.ac.uk)*

Loughborough A large rural single-site campus one mile from the town centre. *(Loughborough University, Loughborough, Leicestershire LE11 3TU. Tel 01509 263171; www.lboro.ac.uk)*

Manchester A large university precinct one mile south of the city centre. *(University of Manchester, Oxford Road, Manchester M13 9PL. Tel 0161 306 6000; Admissions 0161 275 2077; www.man.ac.uk)*

Manchester Metropolitan Five sites in Manchester and two in Cheshire, at Alsager and Crewe. *(The Manchester Metropolitan University, All Saints Building, All Saints, Manchester M15 6BH. Tel 0161 247 2000; Course Enquiries 0161 247 1039/1980; www.mmu.ac.uk)*

Middlesex Five campuses are located in the north of London, each focusing on a different subject area. *(Middlesex University, Admissions Enquiries, North London Business Park, Oakleigh Road, London N11 1QS. Tel 020 8411 5000; Admissions 020 8411 5555; www.mdx.ac.uk)*

Napier Four main campuses located in the centre and to the south-west of Edinburgh. *(Napier University, Edinburgh, Craiglockart Campus, Edinburgh, Scotland EH14 1DJ. Tel 0131 444 2266; admissions 08452 606040; www.napier.ac.uk)*

Newcastle A university campus in the city centre. *(Newcastle University, 6 Kensington Terrace, Newcastle upon Tyne NE1 7RU. Tel 0191 222 6000; www.ncl.ac.uk)*

Newport The University has two campuses, in Newport and Caerleon. *(University of Wales, Newport, Caerleon Campus, PO Box 101, Newport, South Wales NP18 3YH. Tel 01633 430088; Course Enquiries 01633 432432; www.newport.ac.uk)*

Northampton This new university (2005) is located on two campuses close to the town centre. *(University of Northampton, Park Campus, Boughton Green Road, Northampton NN2 7AL. Tel 01604 735500; Course Enquiries 0800 358 2232; www.northampton.ac.uk)*

Northumbria Three campuses in and around Newcastle and one in Carlisle. *(Northumbria University, Admissions, Trinity Building, Northumberland Road, Newcastle upon Tyne NE1 8ST. Tel 0191 243 7420; www.northumbria.ac.uk)*

Nottingham A large campus university to the west of the city. *(The University of Nottingham, University Park, Nottingham NG7 2RD. Tel 0115 951 5151; Course Enquiries 0115 951 5559; www.nottingham.ac.uk)*

Nottingham Trent The Clifton campus is four miles from the city and caters for Education, Humanities and Science whilst Brackenhurst, near Southwell, focuses on land-based subjects. *(The Nottingham Trent University, Burton Street, Nottingham NG1 4BU. Tel 0115 941 8418; Admissions 0115 848 2814; www.ntu.ac.uk)*

Open University The UK's largest university for part-time higher education, providing supported distance learning for undergraduate (and postgraduate) students who must be over 18. Application and registration is made direct to the OU, and not through UCAS (at present). *(The Open University, Student Registration and Enquiry Service, PO Box 197, Milton Keynes MK7 6BJ. Tel 0845 300 6090; www.open.ac.uk)*

Oxford Thirty colleges and seven private halls admitting undergraduates throughout the city. **Colleges** Balliol, Brasenose, Christ Church, Corpus Christi, Exeter, Harris Manchester (mature students only), Hertford, Jesus, Keble, Lady Margaret Hall, Lincoln, Magdalen, Mansfield, Merton, New, Oriel, Pembroke, St Anne's, St Catherine's, St Edmund Hall, St Hilda's (women only, but has voted to admit men), St Hugh's, St John's, St Peter's, Somerville, The Queen's, Trinity, University, Wadham, Worcester. **Permanent Private Halls** Blackfriars, Campion Hall (men only), Greyfriars, Regent's Park College, St Benet's Hall, St Stephen's House, Wycliffe. *(Enquiries should be addressed to The Tutor for Admissions . . . . College, Oxford, or to The Oxford Colleges Admissions Office, Wellington Square, Oxford OX1 2JD. Tel 01865 288000; www.ox.ac.uk)*

Oxford Brookes A campus university to the east of the city with 10 partner institutions and 10 overseas institutions. *(Oxford Brookes University, Headington Campus, Gipsy Lane, Oxford OX3 0BP. Tel 01865 741111; Course Enquiries 01865 484848; www.brookes.ac.uk)*

Choose your perfect degree!

Myerscough College
PRESTON • LANCASHIRE

With a great range of degree courses, a superb location, excellent teaching and amazing facilities, you'll find exactly what you're looking for at Myerscough College. Foundation Degrees and Honours Degrees are available in the following subjects:

- Agriculture
- Animal Welfare & Veterinary Nursing
- Arboriculture: Tree Care
- Ecology & Conservation
- Equine Studies
- Floral Design
- Football Coaching

- Golf, Sport & Leisure
- Horticulture
- Garden Design
- Landscape Management
- Mechanisation
- Motorsports
- Sportsturf
- Watersports

OPEN MORNINGS EVERY MONTH Check website for dates

uclan
University of Central Lancashire

Myerscough College is a partner institution of the University of Central Lancashire.

For more information, and to receive a prospectus, call Course Enquiries on **01995 642211** or visit **www.myerscough.ac.uk**

Peninsula College of Medicine and Dentistry
Campuses at Exeter and Plymouth Universities. *(Peninsula Medical School, The John Bull Building, Tamar Science Park, Research Way, Plymouth, Devon PL6 8BU. Tel 01752 437444; www.pms.ac.uk)*

Plymouth Two main campuses from 2008, one in Plymouth and the other, the Peninsula Allied Health Centre, four miles north of the main campus. Courses are also offered at 16 partner colleges. *(University of Plymouth, Drake Circus, Plymouth PL4 8AA. Tel 01752 600600; www.plym.ac.uk)*

Portsmouth The main campus is close to the town centre; courses are also taught at four colleges in Hampshire and Surrey. *(University of Portsmouth, University House, Winston Churchill Avenue, Portsmouth, Hampshire PO1 2UP. Tel 023 9284 8484; www.port.ac.uk)*

Queen Margaret (New university 2007) Located on a new campus on the Firth of Forth with student accommodation on site. *(Queen Margaret University, Queen Margaret University Drive, Musselburgh, East Lothian EH21 6UU. Tel 0131 474 0000; www.qmu.ac.uk)*

Queen's Belfast A large campus situated in the south of the city. *(Queen's University of Belfast, University Road, Belfast, Northern Ireland BT7 1NN. Tel 028 9024 5133; Admissions 028 9024 5133; www.qub.ac.uk)*

Reading A large rural campus on the edge of the city. *(University of Reading, Whiteknights, PO Box 217, Reading, Berkshire RG6 6AH. Tel 0118 987 5123; Course Enquiries 0118 378 8168/9; www.rdg.ac.uk)*

Richmond, The American International University in London A private university with degrees validated by the Open University and accredited to the Middle States Association of Colleges and Schools in the USA. There are four entry points to courses in each academic year. *(Richmond, The American International University in London, Queens Road, Richmond upon Thames, Surrey TW10 6JP. Tel 020 8332 8200; Admissions 020 8332 9000; www.richmond.ac.uk)*

Robert Gordon Two campuses in and near the city centre. *(The Robert Gordon University, Schoolhill, Aberdeen, Grampian, Scotland AB10 1FR. Tel 01224 262000; Admissions 01224 262728; www.rgu.ac.uk)*

Roehampton The University, located in southwest London, close to Richmond Park, consists of four Colleges: Southlands, Digby Stuart, Froebel and Whitelands. *(Roehampton University, Erasmus House, Roehampton Lane, London SW15 5PU. Tel 020 8392 3000; Admissions 020 8392 3232; www.roehampton.ac.uk)*

St Andrews A town-centre university situated on the east coast of Scotland. *(University of St Andrews, College Gate, St Andrews, Fife, Scotland KY16 9AJ. Tel 01334 476161; Admissions 01334 462150; www.st-andrews.ac.uk)*

Salford A city-centre campus university for all courses, except for Midwifery at Bury and Nursing at Eccles. *(The University of Salford, The Crescent, Salford, Greater Manchester M5 4WT. Tel 0161 295 5000; Course Enquiries 0161 295 4545; www.salford.ac.uk)*

Sheffield A campus university close to the city centre. *(University of Sheffield, Western Bank, Sheffield, South Yorkshire S10 2TN. Tel 0114 222 2000, Medical School 0114 271 2142; www.sheffield.ac.uk)*

Sheffield Hallam Three campuses are in the city centre, with two some two miles away. *(Sheffield Hallam University, City Campus, Howard Street, Sheffield, South Yorkshire S1 1WB. Tel 0114 225 5555; www.shu.ac.uk)*

Southampton The University has six main campuses in Southampton and Winchester. *(University of Southampton, University Road, Southampton SO17 1BJ. Tel 023 8059 5000; www.soton.ac.uk)*

Southampton Solent A new university (2005) close to the city centre. *(Southampton Solent University, East Park Terrace, Southampton, Hampshire SO14 0YN. Tel 023 8031 9000; www.solent.ac.uk)*

ACTING • MUSICAL THEATRE
CLASSICAL ACTING • SCREEN &
RADIO PERFORMANCE • THEATRE
DIRECTING • TECHNICAL THEATRE
ACTING • MUSICAL THEATRE •
CLASSICAL ACTING • MUSICAL
THEATRE • CLASSICAL ACTING
RADIO PERFORMANCE
THEATRE DIRECTING
TECHNICAL THEATRE

MOUNTVIEW
ACADEMY OF THEATRE ARTS

www.mountview.ac.uk
Tel: 020 8881 2201

Mountview is committed to equal opportunities

Staffordshire Sites at Stafford, Stoke and Lichfield. *(Staffordshire University, College Road, Stoke on Trent, Staffordshire ST4 2DE. Tel 01782 294000; www.staffs.ac.uk)*

Stirling A rural campus of 310 acres. *(University of Stirling, Stirling, Central Scotland FK9 4LA. Tel 01786 473171; Admissions 01786 467044; www.stir.ac.uk)*

Strathclyde Main campus in Glasgow city centre, with the Jordanhill campus to the west of the city. *(The University of Strathclyde, 16 Richmond Street, Glasgow, Scotland G1 1XQ. Tel 0141 552 4400; www.strath.ac.uk)*

Sunderland Main campus in the city centre, with the Sir Tom Cowie campus across the river accommodating the Business School and Informatics Centre. *(University of Sunderland, City Campus, Chester Road, Sunderland SR1 3SD. Tel 0191 515 3000; Course Enquiries 0191 515 3000; www.sunderland.ac.uk)*

Surrey A modern campus a mile from the city centre. Some foundation year teaching in local colleges. *(University of Surrey, Guildford, Surrey GU2 7XH. Tel 01483 300800; 01483 689305; www.surrey.ac.uk)*

Sussex A single site campus four miles from Brighton. *(University of Sussex, Sussex House, Falmer, Brighton, Sussex BN1 9RH. Tel 01273 606755; Admissions 01273 678416; www.sussex.ac.uk)*

Swansea A parkland site outside the city. *(Swansea University, Singleton Park, Swansea, Wales SA2 8PP. Tel 01792 205678; Admissions 01792 295111; www.swan.ac.uk)*

Swansea Metropolitan A new (2008) university and formerly Swansea Institute, situated in the centre of Swansea. *(Swansea Metropolitan University, Mount Pleasant, Swansea, Wales SA1 6ED. Tel 01792 481000; Course Enquiries 01792 481010; www.smu.ac.uk)*

Teesside A city-centre campus in Middlesbrough. Links with colleges in Teesside, Bishop Auckland and Derwentside. *(University of Teesside, Borough Road, Middlesbrough, Tees Valley TS1 3BA. Tel 01642 218121; Course Enquiries 01642 384277; www.tees.ac.uk)*

Thames Valley Based on four sites in west London and five associated colleges. *(Thames Valley University, St Mary's Road, Ealing, London W5 5RF. Tel 020 8579 5000; Admissions 0800 036 8888; www.tvu.ac.uk)*

Ulster Four campuses – at Coleraine, Jordanstown, Belfast, and Magee in Londonderry. *(University of Ulster, Cromore Road, Coleraine, County Londonderry, Northern Ireland BT52 1SA. Tel 08700 400 700; www.ulster.ac.uk)*

Warwick A single site campus three miles southwest of Coventry. *(University of Warwick, Coventry, Warwickshire CV4 7AL. Tel 024 7652 3523; Admissions 024 7652 3723; www.warwick.ac.uk)*

West Scotland A new university (2007) formed from the merger of the University of Paisley and Bell College. Four campuses, in Paisley, Ayr, Hamilton and Dumfries. *(University of the West of Scotland, High Street, Paisley, Strathclyde, Scotland PA1 2BE. Tel 0141 848 3000; www.uws.ac.uk)*

Westminster Four campuses (Cavendish, Marylebone and Regent in central London and Harrow) and eight associated colleges including the Trinity College of Music. *(University of Westminster, Headquarters Building, 309 Regent Street, London W1B 2UW. Tel 020 7911 5000; Course Enquiries 020 7915 5511; www.wmin.ac.uk)*

Winchester A new university (2005) situated close to the centre of the city with a part-time study centre in Basingstoke. *(Winchester University, West Hill, Winchester, Hampshire SO22 4NR. Tel 01962 841515; Course Enquiries 01962 841515; www.winchester.ac.uk)*

Wolverhampton Two campuses in Wolverhampton and others in Walsall and Telford. *(University of Wolverhampton, Wulfruna Street, Wolverhampton, West Midlands WV1 1SB. Tel 01902 321000; Course Enquiries 01902 322222; www.wlv.ac.uk)*

Worcester A small new university (2005) located on a campus a short distance from the city centre. *(Worcester University, Henwick Grove, Worcester WR2 6AJ. Tel 01905 855000; www.worc.ac.uk)*

York A parkland campus situated on the outskirts of the city and a second campus in the city centre. *(University of York, Heslington, York YO10 5DD. Tel 01904 430000; www.york.ac.uk)*

York St John This new university (2006) is located on an eight-acre site facing York Minster, five minutes' walk from York city centre. *(York St John University, Lord Mayor's Walk, York YO31 7EX. Tel 01904 624624; www.yorksj.ac.uk)*

SECTION 2: UNIVERSITY COLLEGES AND COLLEGES AND INSTITUTES OF HIGHER EDUCATION

Changes are taking place fast in this higher education sector, with several colleges becoming universities in the last year. Changes are also taking place in the further education sector (see Section 6) to give more degree course opportunities. All this means that you can study for a degree or diploma in a wide range of colleges, and it is important that you read prospectuses and check websites carefully and go to Open days to find out as much as you can about them and about their courses which interest you.

Applications for full-time courses at the institutions listed below are through UCAS. Refer to the *Big Guide* for details (see **Appendix 3**).

Bell College (Merged in 2007 with University of Paisley to form the University of the West of Scotland: see Section 1)

Birmingham University College (formerly Birmingham College of Food, Tourism and Creative Studies) Summer Row, Birmingham, West Midlands B3 1JB. Tel 0121 693 5959; www.ucb.ac.uk

Bishop Grosseteste University College Lincoln Newport, Lincoln LN1 3DY. Tel 01522 527347; www.bishopg.ac.uk

Bradford College Great Horton Road, Bradford, West Yorkshire BD7 1AY. Tel 01274 433333; www.bradfordcollege.ac.uk

Buckinghamshire Chilterns University College (now **Bucks New University**: see Section 1)

Colchester Institute Sheepen Road, Colchester, Essex CO3 3LL. Tel 01206 518000; *Course Enquiries* 01206 518777; www.colchester.ac.uk

Creative Arts University College The University College for the Creative Arts at Canterbury, Epsom, Farnham, Maidstone and Rochester, Falkner Road, Farnham, Surrey GU9 7DS. Tel 01372 728811; Admissions: Canterbury 01227 817312; Epsom and Farnham 01252 892696; Maidstone 01622 620150; Rochester 01634 888717; www.ucreative.ac.uk

East Lancashire Institute of Higher Education (at Blackburn College), Duke Street, Blackburn BB2 1LH. Tel 01254 292594; www.blackburn.ac.uk

Falmouth University College Woodlane, Falmouth, Cornwall TR11 4RH. Tel 01326 211077; www.falmouth.ac.uk

Harper Adams University College Newport, Shropshire TF10 8NB. Tel 01952 820280; www.harper-adams.ac.uk

Leeds Trinity and All Saints Brownberrie Lane, Horsforth, Leeds LS18 5HD. Tel 0113 283 7100; *Course Enquiries* 0113 283 7150; www.leedstrinityc.ac.uk

Marjon – University College Plymouth Derriford Road, Plymouth, Devon PL6 8BH. Tel 01752 636700; www.marjon.ac.uk

Newman University College Genners Lane, Bartley Green, Birmingham, West Midlands B32 3NT. Tel 0121 476 1181; www.newman.ac.uk

North East Wales Institute of Higher Education Plas Coch Campus, Mold Road, Wrexham, Clwyd, Wales LL11 2AW. Tel 01978 290666; *Student Enquiries* 01978 293439; www.newi.ac.uk

Queen Margaret University College (Now a university: see Section 1)

St Martin's College, Lancaster; Ambleside; Carlisle; London (Now part of University of Cumbria: see Section 1)

St Mary's University College Waldegrave Road, Strawberry Hill, Twickenham, Middlesex TW1 4SX. Tel 020 8240 4000; www.smuc.ac.uk

St Mary's University College 191 Falls Road, Belfast, Northern Ireland BT12 6FE. Tel 028 9032 7678; www.stmarys-belfast.ac.uk (Not in UCAS: applications direct to College)

Stranmillis University College Stranmillis Road, Belfast, Northern Ireland BT9 5DY. Tel 028 9038 1271; www.stran.ac.uk

Suffolk University Campus Ipswich, Suffolk IP4 1LT. Tel 01473 255885; www.suffolk.ac.uk

Swansea Institute (Now Swansea Metropolitan University: see Section 1)

Trinity College Carmarthen College Road, Carmarthen, Wales SA31 3EP. Tel 01267 676767; www.trinity-cm.ac.uk

UHI Millennium Institute (UHI) The UHI is based on a partnership of colleges and research centres, each with its own distinctive character. Full-time undergraduate courses are provided by the following partner colleges (for addresses see Section 6). Institutions are shown by initials in the tables in **Chapter 9**: Argyll College (AC), Highland Theological College (HTC), Inverness College (IC), Lews Castle College (LCC), Lochaber College (LOC), Moray College (MC), Ness Foundation (NF), North Atlantic Fisheries College (NAFC), North Highland College (NHC), Orkney College (OC), Perth College (PC), Sabhal Mor Ostaig (SMO), Scottish Association for Marine Science (SAMS) and Shetland College (SC). (UHI Millennium Institute, Executive Office, Ness Walk, Inverness, Scotland IV3 5SQ. Tel 01463 279000; Course Information 0845 272 3600; www.uhi.ac.uk)

University of Wales Institute, Cardiff PO Box 377, Llandaff Campus, Western Avenue, Cardiff, Wales CF5 2SG. Tel 029 2041 6070; www.uwic.ac.uk

SECTION 3: COLLEGES OF AGRICULTURE AND HORTICULTURE

Some colleges are in the UCAS scheme for some or all of their courses (see the UCAS *Big Guide* for details). Apply direct to colleges for courses outside UCAS.

NB Degree and diploma courses in Agriculture and Horticulture are also offered by some universities and some university colleges (see Sections 1 and 2) and also by some further education colleges (see Section 6).

Askham Bryan College Askham Bryan, York YO23 3FR. Tel 01904 772211; www.askham-bryan.ac.uk

Berkshire College of Agriculture (BCA) Hall Place, Burchetts Green, Maidenhead, Berkshire SL6 6QR. Tel 01628 824444; www.bca.ac.uk

Bicton College East Budleigh, Budleigh Salterton, Devon EX9 7BY. Tel 01395 562400; www.bicton.ac.uk

Bishop Burton College York Road, Bishop Burton, Beverley, East Yorkshire HU17 8QG. Tel 01964 553000; www.bishopburton.ac.uk

Capel Manor College Bullsmore Lane, Enfield, Middlesex EN1 4RQ. Tel 08456 122122; www.capel.ac.uk

College of Agriculture, Food and Rural Enterprise (CAFRE) Greenmount Campus, 22 Greenmount Road, Antrim, Northern Ireland BT41 4PU. Tel 08000 284291; www.cafre.ac.uk

Duchy College Cornwall College Duchy College, Rosewarne Campus, Camborne, Cornwall TR14 0AB. Tel 01209 722100; www.duchy.ac.uk

East Durham and Houghall College Houghall Centre, Durham DH1 3SG. Tel 0191 518 8222; www.edhcc.ac.uk

Harper Adams University College Newport, Shropshire TF10 8NB. Tel 01952 820280; www.harper-adams.ac.uk (See also Section 2)

Hartpury College (an Associate Faculty of Bristol UWE) Hartpury House, Hartpury, Gloucester GL19 3BE. Tel 01452 700283/702132; www.hartpury.ac.uk

Myerscough College (an Associate College of the University of Central Lancashire) Myerscough Hall, St Michael's Road, Bilsborrow, Preston, Lancashire PR3 0RY. Tel 01995 642222; www.myerscough.ac.uk

Otley College Charity Lane, Otley, Ipswich, Suffolk IP6 9EY. Tel 01473 785543; www.otleycollege.ac.uk

Pershore Group of Colleges (includes Pershore College and Holme Lacy College) Pershore Campus, Avonbank, Pershore, Worcestershire WR10 3JP. Tel 01386 552443; www.pershore.ac.uk

Reaseheath College Reaseheath, Nantwich, Cheshire CW5 6DF. Tel 01270 625131; *Course Information* 01270 613242; www.reaseheath.ac.uk

Rodbaston College Penkridge, Staffordshire ST19 5PH. Tel 01785 712209; www.rodbaston.com

Royal Agricultural College Cirencester, Gloucestershire GL7 6JS. Tel 01285 652531; www.rac.ac.uk

Scottish Agricultural College (SAC) Student Recruitment and Admissions Office, SAC Ayr Campus, Auchincruive Estate, Ayr KA6 5HW. Tel 0800 269453; www.sac.ac.uk

Shuttleworth College Old Warden Park, Biggleswade, Bedfordshire SG18 9EA. Tel 01767 626222; www.shuttleworth.ac.uk

Sparsholt College Hampshire Sparsholt, Winchester, Hampshire SO21 2NF. Tel 01962 776441; www.sparsholt.ac.uk

Warwickshire College Warwick New Road, Leamington Spa, Warwickshire CV32 5JE. Tel 01926 318000/0800 783 6767; www.warkscol.ac.uk

Welsh College of Horticulture Northop, Mold, Flintshire, Wales CH7 6AA. Tel 01352 841000; www.wcoh.ac.uk

Writtle College (an Associate College of Essex University) Chelmsford, Essex CM1 3RR. Tel 01245 424200; www.writtle.ac.uk

SECTION 4: COLLEGES OF ART

Many colleges of art are in UCAS for some or all of their courses and some have now merged with universities. Check with the UCAS *Big Guide,* prospectuses and websites. In addition to colleges of art and universities, Art and Design courses are also offered by further education colleges. Apply direct to colleges for courses outside UCAS.

Architectural Association School of Architecture 36 Bedford Square, London WC1B 3ES. Tel 020 7887 4000; www.aaschool.ac.uk

Arts Institute at Bournemouth Wallisdown, Poole, Dorset BH12 5HH. Tel 01202 533011; www.aib.ac.uk

Camberwell College of Arts (University of the Arts London) Peckham Road, London SE5 8UF. Tel 020 7514 6302; www.camberwell.arts.ac.uk

Central Saint Martins College of Art and Design (University of the Arts London) Southampton Row, Holborn, London WC1B 4AP. Tel 020 7514 7022; www.csm.arts.ac.uk

Chelsea College of Art and Design (University of the Arts London) 16 John Islip Street, London SW1P 4JU. Tel 020 7514 7751; www.chelsea.arts.ac.uk

City and Guilds of London Art School 124 Kennington Park Road, London SE11 4DJ. Tel 020 7735 2306; www.cityandguildsartschool.ac.uk

Cleveland College of Art and Design Green Lane, Linthorpe, Middlesbrough TS5 7RJ. Tel 01642 288000; *Student Recruitment* 01642 288888; www.ccad.ac.uk

Creative Arts (UC) University College for the Creative Arts at Canterbury, Epsom, Farnham, Maidstone and Rochester Falkner Road, Farnham, Suffey GU9 7DS. Tel 01372 728811; *Admissions* Canterbury 01227 817312; Epsom and Farnham 01252 892696; Maidstone 01622 620150; Rochester 01634 888717; www.ucreative.ac.uk

Cumbria Institute of the Arts Now part of University of Cumbria (see Section 1)

Dartington College of Arts Dartington Hall Estate, Totnes, Devon TQ9 6EJ. Tel 01803 862224; www.dartington.ac.uk

Dewsbury College (incorporating Batley School of Art and Design) Halifax Road, Dewsbury, West Yorkshire WF13 2AS. Tel 01924 436221; www.dewsbury.ac.uk

Edinburgh College of Art Lauriston Place, Edinburgh, EH3 9DF. Tel 0131 221 6000; www.eca.ac.uk

Glasgow School of Art 167 Renfrew Street, Glasgow, Strathclyde G3 6RQ. Tel 0141 353 4500; www.gsa.ac.uk

Gray's School of Art (Robert Gordon University) School Hill, Aberdeen, Grampian, Scotland AB10 1FR. Tel 01224 262000; www.rgu.ac.uk

Heatherley's School of Fine Art 80 Upcerne Road, London SW10 0SH. Tel 020 7351 4190; www.heatherleys.org

Hereford College of Arts Folly Lane, Hereford HR1 1LT. Tel 01432 273359; www.hereford-art-col.ac.uk

Leeds College of Art and Design Jacob Kramer Building, Blenheim Walk, Leeds LS2 9AQ. Tel 0113 202 8000; www.leeds-art.ac.uk

London College of Communication (University of the Arts London) Elephant and Castle, London SE1 6SB. Tel 020 7514 6500; www.lcc.arts.ac.uk

London College of Fashion (University of the Arts London) 20 John Princes' Street, London W1G 0BJ. Tel 020 7514 7500; www.fashion.arts.ac.uk

Norwich School of Art and Design Francis House, 3–7 Redwell Street, Norwich, Norfolk NR2 4SN. Tel 01603 610561; www.nsad.ac.uk

Plymouth College of Art and Design Tavistock Place, Plymouth, Devon PL4 8AT. Tel 01752 203434; www.pcad.ac.uk

Ravensbourne College of Design and Communication Walden Road, Chislehurst, Kent BR7 5SN. Tel 020 8289 4900; www.rave.ac.uk

Sotheby's Institute of Art 30 Bedford Square, Bloomsbury, London WC1B 3EE. Tel 020 7462 3232; www.sothebysinstitutelondon.com

Wimbledon College of Art (University of the Arts London) Merton Hall Road, London SW19 3QA. Tel 020 7514 9641; *Admissions* 020 7514 9687; www.wimbledon.ac.uk

Winchester School of Art (part of Southampton University) Park Avenue, Winchester, Hampshire SO23 8DL. Tel 023 8059 4741; www.wsa.soton.ac.uk

SECTION 5: COLLEGES OF DANCE, DRAMA, MUSIC AND SPEECH

Some colleges are in UCAS for some or all of their courses (see the UCAS *Big Guide* for details). Apply direct to colleges for courses outside UCAS. Note that Music, Dance and Drama are also offered by universities and higher education colleges.

ALRA (Academy of Live and Recorded Arts) Studio 1 Royal Victoria Patriotic Building, John Archer Way, London SW18 3SX. Tel 020 8870 6475; www.alra.co.uk

Arts Educational Schools London Cone Ripman House, 14 Bath Road, London W4 1LY. Tel for acting 020 8987 6655; for musical theatre 020 8987 6666; www.artsed.co.uk

Birmingham Conservatoire (part of Birmingham City University) Paradise Place, Birmingham B3 3HG. Tel 0121 331 5901/2; www.conservatoire.bcu.ac.uk

Birmingham School of Acting (part of Birmingham City University) Millennium Point, Curzon Street, Birmingham, B4 7XG. Tel 0121 331 7220; www.bssd.ac.uk

Bristol Old Vic Theatre School 1–2 Downside Road, Clifton, Bristol BS8 2XF. Tel 0117 973 3535; www.oldvic.ac.uk

Drama Centre London (part of Central Saint Martins: see University of the Arts London) First Floor, Saffron House, 10 Back Hill, London EC1R 5LQ. Tel 020 7514 8778; www.csm.arts.ac.uk/drama

East 15 Acting School Hatfields, Rectory Lane, Loughton, Essex IG10 3RY. Tel 020 8508 5983; www.east15.ac.uk

GSA Conservatoire Millmead Terrace, Guildford, Surrey GU2 4YT. Tel 01483 560701; www.conservatoire.org

Guildhall School of Music and Drama Silk Street, Barbican, London EC2Y 8DT. Tel 020 7628 2571; www.gsmd.ac.uk

Laban (Trinity Laban) Creekside, London SE8 3DZ. Tel 020 8691 8600; www.laban.org

Leeds College of Music 3 Quarry Hill, Leeds, West Yorkshire LS2 7PD. Tel 0113 222 3400; *Course Enquiries* 0113 222 3416; www.lcm.ac.uk

Liverpool Institute for Performing Arts (LIPA) Mount Street, Liverpool L1 9HF. Tel 0151 330 3000; www.lipa.ac.uk

London Academy of Music and Dramatic Art (LAMDA) 155 Talgarth Road, London W14 9DA. Tel 020 8834 0500; www.lamda.org.uk

Mountview Academy of Theatre Arts Ralph Richardson Memorial Studios, Clarendon Road, Wood Green, London N22 6XF. Tel 020 8881 2201; www.mountview.ac.uk

Northern School of Contemporary Dance 98 Chapeltown Road, Leeds LS7 4BH. Tel 0113 219 3000; www.nscd.ac.uk

Rose Bruford College Lamorbey Park Campus, Burnt Oak Lane, Sidcup, Kent DA15 9DF. Tel 020 8308 2600; www.bruford.ac.uk

Royal Academy of Dance 36 Battersea Square, London SW11 3RA. Tel 020 7326 8000; www.rad.org.uk

Royal Academy of Dramatic Art (RADA) 62–64 Gower Street, London WC1E 6ED. Tel 020 7636 7076; *Prospectus* 020 7908 4710; www.rada.org

Royal Academy of Music Marylebone Road, London NW1 5HT. Tel 020 7873 7373; www.ram.ac.uk

Royal Ballet School 46 Floral Street, Covent Garden, London WC2E 9DA. Tel 020 7845 7073; www.royal-ballet-school.org.uk

Royal College of Music Prince Consort Road, London SW7 2BS. Tel 020 7589 3643; www.rcm.ac.uk

Royal Northern College of Music 124 Oxford Road, Manchester M13 9RD. Tel 0161 907 5200; www.rncm.ac.uk

Royal Scottish Academy of Music and Drama 100 Renfrew Street, Glasgow, Strathclyde, Scotland G2 3DB. Tel 0141 332 4101; www.rsamd.ac.uk

Royal Welsh College of Music and Drama Castle Grounds, Cathays Park, Cardiff, Wales CF10 3ER. Tel 029 2034 2854; www.rwcmd.ac.uk

Trinity College of Music (Trinity Laban) King Charles Court, Old Royal Naval College, Greenwich, London SE10 9JK. Tel 020 8305 4444; www.tcm.ac.uk

SECTION 6: FURTHER EDUCATION AND OTHER COLLEGES OFFERING HIGHER EDUCATION COURSES

The following colleges appear under various subject headings in the tables in **Chapter 9** and some are in UCAS for some of their courses. See prospectuses and websites for application details.

Aberdeen College Gallowgate Centre, Gallowgate, Aberdeen, Grampian AB25 1BN. Tel 01224 612000; *Information and Booking Centre* 01224 612330; www.abcol.ac.uk

Abingdon and Witney College Abingdon Campus, Wootton Road, Abingdon, Oxfordshire OX14 1GG. Tel 01235 555585; www.abingdon-witney.ac.uk

Accrington and Rossendale College Sandy Lane, Accrington, Lancashire BB5 2AW. Tel 01254 389933; *Information and Guidance* 01254 354354; www.accross.ac.uk

Adam Smith College St Brycedale Campus, St Brycedale Avenue, Kirkcaldy, Fife, Scotland KY1 1EX. Tel 01592 268591; *Course Hotline* 0800 413280; www.adamsmith.ac.uk

Andover College (Sparsholt College Hampshire) Charlton Road, Andover, Hampshire SP10 1EJ. Tel 01264 360000; www.andover.ac.uk

Angus College Keptie Road, Arbroath, Angus DD11 3EA. Tel 01241 432600; www.angus.ac.uk

Anniesland College Hatfield Campus, 19 Hatfield Drive, Glasgow G12 0YE. Tel 0141 357 3969; www.anniesland.ac.uk

Argyll College (UHI partner college – see Section 2) West Bay, Dunoon, Argyll PA23 7HP. Tel 08452 309969; www.argyllcollege.ac.uk

Aylesbury College Oxford Road, Aylesbury, Buckinghamshire HP21 8PD. Tel 01296 588588; www.aylesbury.ac.uk

Ayr College Dam Park, Ayr, Strathclyde KA8 0EU. Tel 01292 265184; *Admissions* 0800 199798; www.ayrcoll.ac.uk

Banff and Buchan College Henderson Road, Fraserburgh, Grampian AB43 9GA. Tel 01346 586100; www.banff-buchan.ac.uk

Barnet College Wood Street, Barnet, Hertfordshire EN5 4AZ. Tel 020 8200 8300; *Enrolment/Course Information* 020 8266 4000; www.barnet.ac.uk

Barking College Dagenham Road, Romford, Essex RM7 0XU. Tel 01708 770000; www.barkingcollege.ac.uk

Barnsley University Centre Central Registry, PO Box 266, Church Street, Barnsley, South Yorkshire S70 2AN. Tel 01226 606262; www.barnsley.hud.ac.uk

Barony College Parkgate, Dumfries, Dumfries and Galloway DG1 3NE. Tel 01387 860251; www.barony.ac.uk

Basingstoke College of Technology Worting Road, Basingstoke, Hampshire RG21 8TN. Tel 01256 354141; www.bcot.ac.uk

Bedford College Cauldwell Street, Bedford MK42 9AH. Tel 01234 291000; *Admissions* 08000 740234; www.bedford.ac.uk

Bexley College Tower Road, Belvedere, Kent DA17 6JA. Tel 01322 442331; www.bexley.ac.uk

Bishop Auckland College Woodhouse Lane, Bishop Auckland, County Durham DL14 6JZ. Tel 01388 443000; *Course Enquiries* 08000 926506; www.bacoll.ac.uk

Blackburn College (partner college of East Lancashire (IHE)) Feilden Street, Blackburn, Lancashire BB2 1LH. Tel 01254 55144; *Student Hotline* 01254 292929; www.blackburn.ac.uk

Blackpool and the Fylde College Palatine Road, Blackpool, Lancashire FY1 4DW. Tel 01253 352352; www.blackpool.ac.uk

Borders College Head Office, Melrose Road, Galashiels, Lothian TD1 2AF. Tel 08700 505152; www.borderscollege.ac.uk

Bournemouth and Poole College Customer Enquiry Centre, North Road, Poole, Dorset BH14 0LS. Tel 01202 205205; www.thecollege.co.uk

Bournville College Bristol Road South, Northfield, Birmingham, West Midlands B31 2AJ. Tel 0121 483 1000; *Course Enquiries* 0121 483 1111; www.bournville.ac.uk

Bracknell and Wokingham College College Information Centre, Church Road, Bracknell, Berkshire RG12 1DJ. Tel 0845 330 3343; www.bracknell.ac.uk

Braintree College Church Lane, Braintree, Essex CM7 5SN. Tel 01376 321711; *Course Enquiries* 01376 557020; www.braintree.ac.uk

Boston College Skirbeck Road, Boston, Lincolnshire PE21 6JF. Tel 01205 365701; Course Information 01205 313218; www.boston.ac.uk

Bridgwater College Bath Road, Bridgwater, Somerset TA6 4PZ. Tel 01278 455464; Course Enquiries 01278 441234; www.bridgwater.ac.uk

British College of Osteopathic Medicine Lief House, 120–122 Finchley Road, London NW3 5HR. Tel 020 7435 6464; www.bcom.ac.uk

British School of Osteopathy 275 Borough High Street, London SE1 1JE. Tel 020 7407 0222; *Student Recruitment* 020 7089 5316; www.bso.ac.uk

Brockenhurst College Lyndhurst Road, Brockenhurst, Hampshire SO42 7ZE. Tel 01590 625555; www.brock.ac.uk

Bromley College of Further and Higher Education Rookery Lane, Bromley, Kent BR2 8HE. Tel 020 8295 7000; *Course Enquiries* 020 8295 7001; www.bromley.ac.uk

Brooklands College Church Road, Ashford, Middlesex TW15 2XD. Tel 01784 248666; www.brooklands.ac.uk

Brooksby Melton College Ashfordby Road, Melton Mowbray, Leicestershire LE13 0HJ. Tel 01664 850850; *Course Enquiries* 01664 855444; www.brooksbymelton.ac.uk

Burnley College Shorey Bank, off Ormerod Road, Burnley, Lancashire BB11 2RX. Tel 01282 711200; *Student Services* 01282 711222; www.burnley.ac.uk

Burton College Student Services, Lichfield Street, Burton on Trent, Staffordshire DE14 3RL. Tel 01283 494400; www.burton-college.ac.uk

Bury College Woodbury Centre, Market Street, Bury, Manchester BL9 0BG. Tel 0161 280 8280; *Course Information* 08000 925900; www.burycollege.ac.uk

Calderdale College Francis Street, Halifax, West Yorkshire HX1 3UZ. Tel 01422 399399; www.calderdale.ac.uk

Cambridge Regional College Kings Hedges Road, Cambridge CB4 2QT. Tel 01223 532240; www.camre.ac.uk

Canterbury College New Dover Road, Canterbury, Kent CT1 3AJ. Tel 01227 811111; *Learning Advice/Courses* 01227 811188; www.cant-col.ac.uk

Cardonald College 690 Mosspark Drive, Glasgow, G52 3AY. Tel 0141 272 3333; www.cardonald.ac.uk

Carlisle College Information Unit, Victoria Place, Carlisle, Cumbria CA1 1HS. Tel 01228 822703; www.carlisle.ac.uk

Carmel College Prescot Road, St Helens, Merseyside WA10 3AG. Tel 01744 452200; www.carmel.ac.uk

Carshalton College Nightingale Road, Carshalton, Surrey SM5 2EJ. Tel 020 8544 4444; www.carshalton.ac.uk

Castle College Nottingham Maid Marian Way, Nottingham NG1 6AB. Tel 08458 450500; www.castlecollege.ac.uk

CECOS London College 2–10 Osborn Street, London E1 6TD. Tel 020 7426 0167/8; www.cecos.co.uk

Central College of Commerce 300 Cathedral Street, Glasgow, G1 2TA. *Information Unit* 0141 552 3941; www.centralcollege.ac.uk

Chelmsford College Moulsham Street, Chelmsford, Essex CM2 0JQ. Tel 01245 265611; www.chelmsford-college.ac.uk

Chesterfield College Infirmary Road, Chesterfield, Derbyshire S41 7NG. Tel 01246 500500; www.chesterfield.ac.uk

Chichester College Westgate Fields, Chichester, West Sussex PO19 1SB. Tel 01243 786321; www.chichester.ac.uk

City College, Birmingham Freepost MID 1755, Birmingham B33 0BR. Tel 0121 741 1000; *Course Enquiries* 08450 501144; www.citycol.ac.uk

City College Brighton and Hove Pelham Street, Brighton, East Sussex BN1 4FA. Tel 01273 667788; *Course Advisers* 01273 667759; www.ccb.ac.uk

City of Bristol College Bedminster Centre, Marksbury Road, Bristol BS3 5JL. Tel 0117 312 5000; www.cityofbristol.ac.uk

City College, Coventry Butts, Coventry CV1 3GD. Tel 024 7679 1000; *Course Information* 0800 616202; www.covcollege.ac.uk

City College, Manchester Whitworth Street, Manchester M1 3HB. Tel 0800 013 0123; www.ccm.ac.uk

City College, Norwich Ipswich Road, Norwich, Norfolk NR2 2LJ. Tel 01603 773311; www.ccn.ac.uk

City College, Plymouth (formerly Plymouth College of Further Education) Kings Road, Devonport, Plymouth, Devon PL1 5QG. Tel 01752 305300; www.cityplym.ac.uk

City and Islington College The Marlborough Building, 383 Holloway Road, London N7 0RN. Tel 020 7700 9200; www.candi.ac.uk

City of Bath College Student Advice Centre, Avon Street, Bath, Somerset BA1 1UP. Tel 01225 312191; *Prospectuses* 01225 328666; www.citybathcoll.ac.uk

City of Sunderland College Bede Centre, Durham Road, Sunderland, Tyne and Wear SR3 4AH. Tel 0191 511 6060; *HE Admissions* 0191 511 6260; www.citysun.ac.uk

City of Westminster College 25 Paddington Green, London W2 1NB. Tel 020 7723 8826; www.cwc.ac.uk

City of Wolverhampton College Paget Road Campus, Paget Road, Wolverhampton, West Midlands WV6 0DU. Tel 01902 836000; www.wolverhamptoncollege.ac.uk

Cliff College Calver, Hope Valley, Derbyshire S32 3XG. Tel 01246 584200/20; www.cliffcollege.org

Clydebank College Kilbowie Road, Clydebank, G81 2AA. Tel 0141 952 7771; www.clydebank.ac.uk

Coatbridge College Kildonan Street, Coatbridge, Lanarkshire ML5 3LS. Tel 01236 422316; Admissions 01236 436000; www.coatbridge.ac.uk

Coleg Llandrillo Cymru Llandudno Road, Rhos on Sea, Colwyn Bay, Wales LL28 4HZ. Tel 01492 546666; *Admissions* 01492 542339; www.llandrillo.ac.uk

Coleg Menai Ffriddoedd Road, Bangor, Gwynedd, Wales LL57 2TP. Tel 01248 370125; www.menai.ac.uk

Coleg Sir Gâr Graig Campus, Sandy Road, Pwll, Llanelli, Wales SA15 4DN. Tel 01554 748000; www.colegsirgar.ac.uk

Coleg Ystrad Mynach Twyn Road, Ystrad Mynach, Hengoed, Wales CF82 7XR. Tel 01443 810054; www.ystrad-mynach.co.uk

College of North West London Dudden Hill Lane, London NW10 2XD. Tel 020 8208 5000; *Course Information* 020 8208 5050; www.cnwl.ac.uk

College of West Anglia Tennyson Avenue, King's Lynn, Norfolk PE30 2QW. Tel 01553 761144; www.col-westanglia.ac.uk

CONEL (College of North East London) Tottenham Centre, High Road, Tottenham, London N15 4RU. Tel 020 8802 3111; *Course Information* 020 8442 3055; www.conel.ac.uk

Cornwall College Tregonnisey Road, St Austell, Cornwall PL25 4DJ. Tel 01726 226626; www.cornwall.ac.uk

Craven College High Street, Skipton, North Yorkshire BD23 1JY. Tel 01756 791411; www.craven-college.ac.uk

Crichton Campus (Universities of Glasgow and West Scotland and Dumfries and Galloway College) Rutherford McGowan Buildings, Dumfries, Scotland DG1 4ZL. Tel 01387 702001; *Admissions* 01387 702131; www.crichtoncampus.ac.uk

Croydon College College Road, Croydon CR9 1DX. Tel 020 8760 5914; www.croydon.ac.uk

Cumbernauld College Tryst Road, Cumbernauld, Glasgow, Strathclyde G67 1HU. Tel 01236 731811; www.cumbernauld.ac.uk

Darlington College Central Park, Haughton Road, Darlington DL1 1DR. Tel 01325 503050; *Information* 01325 503030; www.darlington.ac.uk

Dearne Valley College Manvers Park, Wath upon Dearne, Rotherham, South Yorkshire S63 7EW. Tel 01709 513333; www.dearne-coll.ac.uk

Derby College Prince Charles Avenue, Mackworth, Derby DE22 4LR. Tel 01332 520200 or 0800 280289; www.derby-college.ac.uk

Derwentside College Consett Campus, Park Road, Consett, County Durham DH8 5EE. Tel 01207 585900; www.derwentside.ac.uk

Doncaster College (including University Centre Doncaster) The Hub, Chappell Drive, Doncaster DN1 2RF. Tel 01302 553553; *Course Enquiries* 0800 358 7575; www.don.ac.uk

Dudley College The Broadway, Dudley, West Midlands DY1 4AS. Tel 01384 363277; *Course Enquiries* 01384 363319; www.dudleycol.ac.uk

Dumfries and Galloway College Herries Avenue, Heathhall, Dumfries DG1 3QZ. Tel 01387 261261; www.dumgal.ac.uk

Dundee College Kingsway Campus, Old Glamis Road, Dundee, Tayside DD3 8LE. Tel 01382 834834; *Enquiry Service* 01382 834800; www.dundeecoll.ac.uk

Dunstable College Kingsway, Dunstable, Bedfordshire LU5 4HG. Tel 01582 477776; *Enquiries* 0845 355 2525; www.dunstable.ac.uk

Ealing, Hammersmith and West London College Gliddon Road, Barons Court, London W14 9BL. *Course Information Centre* 0800 980 2185; www.westlondoncollege.ac.uk

East Berkshire College Langley Campus, Station Road, Langley, Berkshire SL3 8BX. Tel 01753 793338; *Course Information* 08009 230423; www.eastberks.ac.uk

East Devon College Admissions Department, Bolham Road, Tiverton, Devon EX16 6SH. Tel 01884 235264; www.edc.ac.uk

East Durham and Houghall College Burnhope Way Centre, Burnhope Way, Peterlee, County Durham SR8 1NU. Tel 0191 518 2000; www.edhcc.ac.uk

East Riding College Beverley Campus, Gallows Lane, Beverley, East Riding of Yorkshire HU17 7DT. Tel 0845 120 0037; www.eastridingcollege.ac.uk

East Surrey College Gatton Point North, Claremont Road, Redhill, Surrey RH1 2JX. Tel 01737 788444; www.esc.ac.uk

Eastleigh College Chestnut Avenue, Eastleigh, Hampshire SO50 5FS. Tel 023 8091 1000; www.eastleigh.ac.uk

Easton College Easton, Norwich, Norfolk NR9 5DX. Tel 01603 731200; www.easton.ac.uk

Edinburgh's Telford College 350 West Granton Road, Edinburgh, EH5 1QE. Tel 0131 559 4000; www.ed-coll.ac.uk

Enfield College 73 Hertford Road, Enfield, Middlesex EN3 5HA. Tel 020 8443 3434; www.enfield.ac.uk

European Business School London Regent's College, Inner Circle, Regent's Park, London NW1 4NS. Tel 020 7487 7505; www.ebslondon.ac.uk

European School of Osteopathy Boxley House, The Street, Boxley, Maidstone, Kent ME14 3DZ. Tel 01622 671558; www.eso.ac.uk

Exeter College Exeter Business School, Victoria House, 33–36 Queen Street, Exeter EX4 3SR. Tel 01392 205222; www.exe-col.ac.uk

Fareham College Bishopsfield Road, Fareham, Hampshire PO14 1NH. Tel 01329 815229; www.fareham.ac.uk

Farnborough College of Technology Boundary Road, Farnborough, Hampshire GU14 6SB. Tel 01252 407028; www.farn-ct.ac.uk

Filton College Filton Avenue, Filton, Bristol BS34 7AT. Tel 0117 931 2121; www.filton.ac.uk

Forth Valley College Falkirk Campus, Grangemouth Road, Falkirk FK2 9AD. Tel 01234 403000; www.forthvalley.ac.uk

Furness College Channelside, Barrow-in-Furness, Cumbria LA14 2PJ. Tel 01229 825017; www.furness.ac.uk

Gateshead College Durham Road, Low Fell, Gateshead NE9 5BN. Tel 0191 490 0300; www.gateshead.ac.uk

Glasgow College of Nautical Studies 21 Thistle Street, Glasgow, G5 9XB. Tel 0141 565 2500; www.glasgow-nautical.ac.uk

Glasgow Metropolitan College 60 North Hanover Street, Glasgow, Strathclyde G1 2BP. Tel 0141 566 6222; www.gmc.ac.uk

Gloucestershire College of Arts and Technology Gloucester Campus, Brunswick Road, Gloucester GL1 1HU. Tel 01452 532000; www.gloscat.ac.uk

Grantham College Stonebridge Road, Grantham, Lincolnshire NG31 9AP. Tel 01476 400200; *Course Information* 08000 521577; www.grantham.ac.uk

Great Yarmouth College Southtown, Great Yarmouth, Norfolk NR31 0ED. Tel 01493 655261; www.gyc.ac.uk

Greenwich School of Management Meridian House, Royal Hill, Greenwich, London SE10 8RD. Tel 020 8516 7800; www.greenwich-college.ac.uk

Grimsby Institute of Further and Higher Education Nuns Corner, Laceby Road, Grimsby, North East Lincolnshire DN34 5BQ. Tel 01472 311222; *Course Information* 0800 315002; www.grimsby.ac.uk

Guildford College Stoke Park Campus, Stoke Road, Guildford, Surrey GU1 1EZ. Tel 01483 448500; www.guildford.ac.uk

Hackney Community College Shoreditch Campus, Falkirk Street, London N1 6HQ. Tel 020 7613 9123; www.hackney.ac.uk

Hadlow College Hadlow, Tonbridge, Kent TN11 0AL. Tel 01732 850551; *Course Enquiry Unit* 0500 551434 (free); www.hadlow.ac.uk

Halesowen College Whittingham Road, Halesowen, West Midlands B63 3NA. Tel 0121 602 7777; www.halesowen.ac.uk

Harlow College Valizy Avenue, Harlow, Essex CM20 3LH. Tel 01279 868000; www.harlow-college.ac.uk

Harrow College Harrow on the Hill Campus, Lowlands Road, Harrow, Middlesex HA1 3AQ. Tel 020 8909 6000; www.harrow.ac.uk

Hastings College of Arts and Technology Archery Road, St Leonards on Sea, East Sussex TN38 0HX. Tel 01424 442222; *Student Services* 01424 458458; www.hastings.ac.uk

Havering College Ardleigh Green Road, Hornchurch, Essex RM11 2LL. Tel 01708 462801; www.havering-college.ac.uk

Henley College Coventry Henley Road, Bell Green, Coventry, West Midlands CV2 1ED. Tel 024 7662 6300/0800 252772; www.henley-cov.ac.uk

Herefordshire College of Technology Folly Lane, Hereford HR1 1LS. Tel 08000 321986; www.hereford-tech.ac.uk

Hertford Regional College Scotts Road, Ware, Hertfordshire SG12 9JF. Tel 01922 411411; www.hertreg.ac.uk

Highbury College, Portsmouth Dovercourt Road, Portsmouth, Hampshire PO6 2SA. Tel 023 9231 3373; www.highbury.ac.uk

Highland Theological College (UHI partner college – see Section 2) High Street, Dingwall IV15 9HA. Tel 01349 780000; www.htc.uhi.ac.uk

Hillcroft College South Bank, Surbiton, Surrey KT6 6DF. Tel 020 8399 2688; www.hillcroft.ac.uk

Holborn College Woolwich Road, London SE7 8LN. Tel 020 8317 6000; www.holborncollege.ac.uk

Hopwood Hall College Rochdale Campus, St Mary's Gate, Rochdale OL12 6RY. Tel 01706 345346; www.hopwood.ac.uk

Huddersfield Technical College New North Road, Huddersfield, West Yorkshire HD1 5NN. Tel 01484 536521; www.huddcoll.ac.uk

Hull College The Queen's Gardens Centre, Wilberforce Drive, Hull, East Yorkshire HU1 3DG. Tel 01482 329943; www.hull-college.ac.uk

Huntingdonshire Regional College California Road, Huntingdon PE29 1BL. Tel 01480 379100; www.huntingdon.ac.uk

Inverness College (UHI partner college – see Section 2) 3 Longman Road, Longman South, Inverness, Highland IV1 1SA. Tel 01463 273000; www.inverness.uhi.ac.uk

Islamic College for Advanced Studies 133 High Road, Willesden, London NW10 2SW. Tel 020 8451 9993; www.islamic-college.ac.uk

Isle of Wight College Medina Way, Newport, Isle of Wight PO30 5TA. Tel 01983 526631; www.iwightc.ac.uk

James Watt College Finnart Street, Greenock, Strathclyde PA16 8HF. Tel 01475 724433; *Student Information Centre* 0800 587 2277; www.jameswatt.ac.uk

Jewel and Esk Valley College Eskbank Campus, Newbattle Road, Eskbank, Dalkeith, Midlothian EH22 3AE. Tel 0131 660 1010; *Information Services* 08458 500060; www.jevc.ac.uk

Keighley College (see Park Lane College Keighley below)

Kendal College (The College of the South Lakes) Milnthorpe Road, Kendal, Cumbria LA9 5AY. Tel 01539 814700; *Admissions* 01539 814709; www.kendal.ac.uk

Kidderminster College Market Street, Kidderminster, Worcestershire DY10 1LX. Tel 01562 820811; www.kidderminster.ac.uk

Kilmarnock College Holehouse Road, Kilmarnock, Strathclyde KA3 7AT. Tel 01563 523501; www.kilmarnock.ac.uk

Kingston College Kingston Hall Road, Kingston upon Thames, Surrey KT1 2AQ. Tel 020 8546 2151; www.kingston-college.ac.uk

Kingston Maurward College Kingston Maurward, Dorchester, Dorset DT2 8PY. Tel 01305 215000; *Course Enquiries* 01305 215032/215025; www.kmc.ac.uk

Knowsley Community College Kirkby Campus, Cherryfield Drive, Kirkby L32 8SF. Tel 0151 477 5708/08451 551055; www.knowsleycollege.ac.uk

Lakes College, West Cumbria Hallwood Road, Lillyhall Business Park, Workington, Cumbria CA14 4JN. Tel 01946 839300; www.lcwc.ac.uk

Lambeth College 45 Clapham Common South Side, London SW4 9BL. Tel 020 7501 5010; *Course Information* 020 7501 5000; www.lambeth.ac.uk

Lancaster and Morecambe College Morecambe Road, Lancaster LA1 2TY. Tel 01524 66215; www.lmc.ac.uk

Langside College 50 Prospecthill Road, Glasgow, Strathclyde G42 9LB. Tel 0141 272 3600; *Student Services* 0141 636 6066; www.langside.ac.uk

Lansdowne College 40–44 Bark Place, London W2 4AT. Tel 020 7616 4400; www.lansdownecollege.com

Lauder College Halbeath, Dunfermline, Fife KY11 8DY. Tel 01383 845000; www.lauder.ac.uk

Leeds College of Building North Street, Leeds, West Yorkshire LS2 7QT. Tel 0113 222 6000; *Student Services* 0113 222 6002; www.lcb.ac.uk

Leeds College of Technology Cookridge Street, Leeds, West Yorkshire LS2 8BL. Tel 0113 297 6300; *Course Information* 0113 297 6464; www.lct.ac.uk

Leeds Thomas Danby Roundhay Road, Leeds, West Yorkshire LS7 3BG. Tel 0113 249 4912; www.leedsthomasdanby.ac.uk

Leek College Stockwell Street, Leek, Staffordshire ST13 6DP. Tel 01538 398866; www.leek.ac.uk

Leicester College Freemen's Park Campus, Aylestone Road, Leicester LE2 7LW. Tel 0116 224 2240; www.leicestercollege.ac.uk

Leo Baeck College The Sternberg Centre, 80 East End Road, London N3 2SY. Tel 020 8349 5600; www.lbc.ac.uk

Lewisham College Lewisham Way, London SE4 1UT. Tel 020 8692 0353/0800 834545; www.lewisham.ac.uk

Lews Castle College (Colaisde A' Chaisteil) (UHI partner college – see Section 2) Stornoway, Isle of Lewis HS2 0XR. Tel 01851 770000; www.lews.uhi.ac.uk

Lincoln College Monks Road, Lincoln LN2 5HQ. Tel 01522 876000; www.lincolncollege.ac.uk

Liverpool Community College Bankfield Road, Liverpool L13 0BQ. Tel 0151 709 3079; www.liv-coll.ac.uk

Lochaber College (UHI partner college – see Section 2) An Aird, Fort William, Inverness, Scotland PH33 6AN. Tel 01397 874000; www.lochaber.uhi.ac.uk

London School of Commerce Chaucer House, White Hart Yard, London SE1 1NX. Tel 020 7357 0077; www.lsclondon.co.uk

Loughborough College Radmoor Road, Loughborough, Leicestershire LE11 3BT. Tel 0845 166 2950; www.loucoll.ac.uk

Lowestoft College St Peters Street, Lowestoft, Suffolk NR32 2NB. Tel 0800 854695; www.lowestoft.ac.uk

Macclesfield College Park Lane, Macclesfield, Cheshire SK11 8LF. Tel 01625 410000; *Information/Enrolment* 01625 410002/50; www.macclesfield.ac.uk

Manchester College of Arts and Technology Openshaw Campus, Ashton Old Road, Openshaw, Manchester M11 2WH. Tel 08000 688585; www.mancat.ac.uk

Matthew Boulton College of Further and Higher Education Jennens Road, Birmingham, West Midlands B4 7PS. Tel 0121 446 4545; www.matthew-boulton.ac.uk

Mid-Cheshire College Hartford Campus, Chesterford Road, Northwich, Cheshire CW8 1LJ. Tel 01606 74444; www.midchesh.ac.uk

Mid-Kent College Horsted Centre, Maidstone Road, Chatham, Kent ME5 9UQ. Tel 01634 830633; *Course Information* 01634 402020; www.midkent.ac.uk

Middlesbrough College Roman Road, Linthorpe, Middlesbrough TS5 5JP. Tel 01642 333333; *Course Information* 01642 296600; www.middlesbro.ac.uk

Milton Keynes College Chaffron Way Campus, Woughton Campus West, Leadenhall, Milton Keynes, Buckinghamshire MK6 5LP. Tel 01908 684444; www.mkcollege.ac.uk

Moray College (UHI partner college – see Section 2) Moray Street, Elgin, Moray IV30 1JJ. Tel 01343 576216; www.moray.ac.uk

Moulton College West Street, Moulton, Northampton NN3 7RR. Tel 01604 491131; www.moulton.ac.uk

Nazarene Theological College Dene Road, Didsbury, Manchester M20 2GU. Tel 0161 445 3063; www.nazarene.ac.uk

Neath Port Talbot College Dwr-y-Felin Road, Neath SA10 7RF. Tel 01639 648000; www.nptc.ac.uk

Nelson and Colne College Scotland Road, Nelson, Lancashire BB9 7YT. Tel 01282 440200; www.nelson.ac.uk

Nescot (North East Surrey College of Technology) Reigate Road, Ewell, Epsom, Surrey KT17 3DS. Tel 020 8394 3038; www.nescot.ac.uk

Ness Foundation (UHI partner college – see Section 2) Ness House, Dochfour Business Centre, Dochgarroch, Inverness IV3 8GY. Tel 01463 220407; www.ness-foundation.org.uk

NEW College (North East Worcestershire College) Peakman Street, Redditch, Worcestershire B98 8DW. Tel 01527 570020; www.ne-worcs.ac.uk

New College Durham Framwellgate Moor Campus, Framwellgate Moor, County Durham DH1 5ES. Tel 0191 375 4210; www.newdur.ac.uk

New College Nottingham The Adams Building, Stoney Street, The Lace Market, Nottingham NG1 1NG. Tel 0115 910 0100; www.ncn.ac.uk

New College Stamford Drift Road, Stamford, Lincolnshire PE9 1XA. Tel 01780 484300; www.stamford.ac.uk

New College, Swindon New College Drive, Swindon, Wiltshire SN3 1AH. Tel 01793 611470; www.newcollege.ac.uk

New College, Telford King Street, Wellington, Telford, Shropshire TF1 1NY. Tel 01952 641892; www.newcollegetelford.ac.uk

Newbury College Monks Lane, Newbury, Berkshire RG14 7TD. Tel 01635 845000; www.newbury-college.ac.uk

Newcastle College Rye Hill Campus, Scotswood Road, Newcastle upon Tyne NE4 5BR. Tel 0191 200 4000; www.ncl-coll.ac.uk

Newcastle-under-Lyme College Liverpool Road, Newcastle-under-Lyme, Staffordshire ST5 2DF. Tel 01782 715111; www.nulc.ac.uk

Newham College of Further Education East Ham Campus, High Street South, London E6 6ER. Tel 020 8257 4000; www.newham.ac.uk

North Atlantic Fisheries College (UHI partner college – see Section 2) Port Arthur, Scalloway, Shetland ZE1 0UN. Tel 01595 772000; www.nafc.ac.uk

North East Institute of Further and Higher Education (See Northern Regional College)

North Glasgow College 110 Flemington Street, Springburn, Glasgow G21 4BX. Tel 0141 558 9001; www.north-gla.ac.uk

North Hertfordshire College Monkswood Way, Stevenage, Hertfordshire SG1 1LA. Tel 01462 424239; *Courses* 01462 424239; www.nhc.ac.uk

North Highland College (UHI partner college – see Section 2) Ormlie Road, Thurso, Caithness KW14 7EE. Tel 01847 889000; www.nhcscotland.com

North Lindsey College Kingsway, Scunthorpe, North Lincolnshire DN17 1AJ. Tel 01724 281111; www.northlindsey.ac.uk

North Nottinghamshire College Carlton Road, Worksop, Nottinghamshire S81 7HP. Tel 01909 504504; *Student Services* 01909 504500; www.nnc.ac.uk

North Trafford College (See Trafford College below)

North Warwickshire and Hinckley College Hinckley Road, Nuneaton, Warwickshire CV11 6BH. Tel 024 7624 3000; www.nwhc.ac.uk

Northampton College Booth Lane, Northampton NN3 3RF. Tel 01604 734567/0845 300 4401; www.northamptoncollege.ac.uk

Northbrook College, Sussex West Durrington Campus, Littlehampton Road, Durrington, Worthing, West Sussex BN12 6NU. Tel 08001 836060; www.northbrook.ac.uk

Northern Regional College (formerly North East Institute of Further and Higher Education) Trostan Avenue Building, Ballymena, Co Antrim, Northern Ireland BT43 7BN. Tel 028 2565 2871; www.nrc.ac.uk

Northumberland College College Road, Ashington, Northumberland NE63 9RG. Tel 01670 841200; www.northland.ac.uk

Norton Radstock College South Hill Park, Radstock, Somerset BA3 3RW. Tel 01761 433161; www.nortcoll.ac.uk

Oaklands College St Albans Smallford Campus, Hatfield Road, St Albans, Hertfordshire AL4 0JA. Tel 01727 737000; *Helpline* 01727 737080; www.oaklands.ac.uk

Oatridge College Information Unit, Ecclesmachan, Broxburn, Lothian EH52 6NH. Tel 01506 864800; www.oatridge.ac.uk

Oldham College Rochdale Road, Oldham, Lancashire OL9 6AA. Tel 0161 624 5214/ 0800 269480; www.oldham.ac.uk

Orkney College (UHI partner college – see Section 2) Kirkwall, Orkney KW15 1LX. Tel 01856 569000; www.orkney.uhi.ac.uk

Orpington College The Walnuts, Orpington, Kent BR6 0TE. Tel 01689 899700; www.orpington.ac.uk

Otley College Charity Lane, Otley, Ipswich, Suffolk IP6 9EY. Tel 01473 785543; www.otleycollege.ac.uk

Oxford and Cherwell Valley College Banbury Campus, Broughton Road, Banbury, Oxfordshire OX16 9QA. Tel 01865 551755; www.ocvc.ac.uk

Park Lane College Keighley Cavendish Street, Keighley, West Yorkshire BD21 3DF. Tel 01535 618600; www.keighley.ac.uk

Park Lane College Leeds Park Lane, Leeds LS3 1AA. Admissions 0113 216 2200; *Course/General Enquiries* 0845 045 7275; www.parklanecoll.ac.uk

Pembrokeshire College (Coleg Sir Benfro) FREEPOST, Course Enquiries and Admissions, Pembrokeshire College, Haverfordwest, Pembrokeshire SA61 1SZ. Tel 0800 716236; www.pembrokeshire.ac.uk

Perth College (UHI partner college – see Section 2) Crieff Road, Perth, Scotland PH1 2NX. Tel 01738 877000; *Admissions Office* Freepost, Perth PH1 2BR. Tel 08452 701177; www.perth.ac.uk

Peterborough Regional College Park Crescent, Peterborough, Cambridgeshire PE1 4DZ. Tel 01733 767366; www.peterborough.ac.uk

Plumpton College Ditchling Road, Near Lewes, East Sussex BN7 3AE. Tel 01273 890454; www.plumpton.ac.uk

Plymouth College of Further Education (see City College, Plymouth)

Portsmouth College Tangier Road, Portsmouth, Hampshire PO3 6PZ. Tel 023 9266 7521; www.portsmouth-college.ac.uk

Redbridge College Little Heath, Barley Lane, Romford, Essex RM6 4XT. Tel 020 8548 7484; www.redbridge-college.ac.uk

Redcar and Cleveland College Corporation Road, Redcar TS10 1EZ. Tel 01642 473132; www.cleveland.ac.uk

Regents Business School London Inner Circle, Regent's Park, London NW1 4NS. Tel 020 7477 2990; www.rbslondon.ac.uk

Reid Kerr College Admission Unit, Renfrew Road, Paisley, Renfrewshire PA3 4DR. Tel 0141 581 2222; *Course Enquiries* 08000 527343; www.reidkerr.ac.uk

Richmond upon Thames College Egerton Road, Twickenham, Middlesex TW2 7SJ. Tel 020 8607 8000; www.rutc.ac.uk

Riverside College Halton Kingsway Campus, Kingsway, Widnes, Cheshire WA8 7QQ. Tel 0151 257 2020; www.riverside.ac.uk

Rodbaston College Rodbaston, Penkridge, Stafford ST19 5PH. Tel 01785 712209; www.rodbaston.ac.uk

Rotherham College of Arts and Technology
Town Centre Campus, Eastwood Lane, Rotherham, South Yorkshire S65 1EG. Tel 01709 362111/08080 722777; www.rotherham.ac.uk

Royal Forest of Dean College Five Acres Campus, Bury Hill, Coleford, Gloucestershire GL16 7JT. Tel 01594 833416; www.rfdc.ac.uk

Royal National College for the Blind College Road, Hereford HR1 1EB. Tel 01432 265725; www.rncb.ac.uk

Runshaw College Euxton Lane, Chorley, Lancashire PR7 6AD. Tel 01772 642040; www.runshaw.ac.uk

Ruskin College, Oxford Walton Street, Oxford OX1 2HE. Tel 01865 310713; www.ruskin.ac.uk

Sabhal Mor Ostaig (UHI partner college – see Section 2) Sleat, Isle of Skye, Scotland IV44 8RQ. Tel 01471 888000; www.smo.uhi.ac.uk

SAE Institute United House, North Road, London N7 9DP. Tel 020 7609 2653; www.sae.edu

St Helens College Town Centre Campus, Brook Street, St Helens, Merseyside WA10 1PZ. Tel 01744 733766; www.sthelens.ac.uk

Salford College Worsley Campus, Walkden Road, Worsley M28 7QD. Tel 0161 702 8272; *Central Admissions* 0161 211 5001/2/3; www.salford-col.ac.uk

Salisbury College Southampton Road, Salisbury, Wiltshire SP1 2LW. Tel 01722 344344; www.salisbury.ac.uk

Sandwell College Central Enquiries, Oldbury Campus, Pound Road, Oldbury, West Midlands B68 8NA. Tel 0800 622006; www.sandwell.ac.uk

Scottish Association for Marine Science (UHI partner college – see Section 2) Dunstaffnage Marine Laboratory, Oban, Argyll PA37 1QA. Tel 01631 559000; www.sams.ac.uk

Selby College Abbot's Road, Selby, North Yorkshire YO8 8AT. Tel 01757 211000; www.selby.ac.uk

Sheffield College PO Box 345, Sheffield S2 2YY. Tel 0114 260 3603 (Course Hotline); www.sheffcol.ac.uk

Shetland College (UHI partner college – see Section 2) Gremista, Lerwick, Shetland ZE1 0PX. Tel 01595 771000; www.shetland.uhi.ac.uk

Shrewsbury College of Arts and Technology London Road, Shrewsbury, Shropshire SY2 6PR. Tel 01743 342342; www.shrewsbury.ac.uk

Skelmersdale and Ormskirk Colleges Westbank Campus, Yewdale, Skelmersdale, Lancashire WN8 6JA. Tel 01695 728744; *Enquiries* 01695 52300; www.skelmersdale.ac.uk

Solihull College Blossomfield Road, Solihull, West Midlands B91 1SB. Tel 0121 678 7001/2; www.solihull.ac.uk

Somerset College of Arts and Technology Wellington Road, Taunton, Somerset TA1 5AX. Tel 01823 366331; www.somerset.ac.uk

South Birmingham College Hall Green Campus, Cole Bank Road, Hall Green, Birmingham, West Midlands B28 8ES. Tel 0121 694 5000; www.sbirmc.ac.uk

South Cheshire College Dane Bank Avenue, Crewe, Cheshire CW2 8AB. Tel 01270 654654; www.s-cheshire.ac.uk

South Devon College Newton Road, Torquay, Devon TQ2 5BY. Tel 08000 380123; www.southdevon.ac.uk

South Downs College College Road, Waterlooville, Hampshire PO7 8AA. Tel 023 9279 7979; www.southdowns.ac.uk

South East Derbyshire College Field Road, Ilkeston, Derbyshire DE7 5RS. Tel 0115 849 2020; www.sedc.ac.uk

South East Essex College Luker Road, Southend-on-Sea, Essex SS1 1ND. Tel 01702 220400; www.southend.ac.uk

South Kent College The Grange, Shorncliffe Road, Folkestone, Kent CT20 2NA. Tel 01303 858220; www.southkent.ac.uk

South Lanarkshire College Admissions Unit/Advice Centre, Main Street, East Kilbride G74 4JY. Tel 01355 270750; www.south-lanarkshire-college.ac.uk

South Leicestershire College Station Road, Wigston, Leicestershire LE18 2DW. Tel 0116 288 5051; www.slcollege.ac.uk

South Nottingham College Greythorne Drive, West Bridgford, Nottingham NG2 7GA. Tel 0115 914 6400; www.snc.ac.uk

South Thames College Wandsworth High Street, London SW18 2PP. Tel 020 8918 7000; *Course Enquiries* 020 8918 7777; www.south-thames.ac.uk

South Trafford College (now Trafford College below) Manchester Road, West Timperley, Altrincham, Cheshire WA14 5PQ. Tel 0161 952 4600; *Course Information* 0161 952 4686/7; www.stcoll.ac.uk

South Tyneside College St George's Avenue, South Shields NE34 6ET. Tel 0191 427 3500/3900; www.stc.ac.uk

Southampton City College St Mary Street, Southampton, Hampshire SO14 1AR. Tel 023 8048 4848/023 8057 7400; www.southampton-city.ac.uk

Southern Regional College (Formerly Upper Bann Institute) Portadown Campus, 36 Lurgan Road, Portadown, Armagh, Northern Ireland BT63 5BL. Tel 029 3839 7777; www.src.ac.uk

Southgate College High Street, Southgate, London N14 6BS. Tel 020 8982 5050; www.southgate.ac.uk

Southport College Mornington Road, Southport, Merseyside PR9 0TT. Tel 01704 500606; www.southport.ac.uk

Southwark College Waterloo Centre, The Cut, London SE1 8LE. Tel 020 7815 1600; www.southwark.ac.uk

Spelthorne College (see Brooklands College)

Stafford College Earl Street, Stafford ST16 2QR. Tel 01785 223800; www.staffordcoll.ac.uk

Staffordshire University Regional Federation (SURF) Staffordshire University, College Road, Stoke on Trent ST4 2DE. Tel 01782 292753; www.surf.ac.uk

Stamford College (See New College Stamford)

Stephenson College Coalville Thornborough Road, Coalville, Leicestershire LE67 3TN. Tel 01530 836136; www.stephensoncoll.ac.uk

Stevenson College Edinburgh Bankhead Avenue, Edinburgh, Lothian EH11 4DE. Tel 0131 535 4600; *Course Enquiries* 0131 535 4700; www.stevenson.ac.uk

Stockport College Wellington Road South, Stockport, Greater Manchester SK1 3UQ. Tel 0161 958 3100; *Admissions* 0845 230 3102; www.stockport.ac.uk

Stourbridge College Hagley Road Centre, Hagley Road, Stourbridge, West Midlands DY8 1QU. Tel 01384 344344; www.stourbridge.ac.uk

Stow College Glasgow 43 Shamrock Street, Glasgow, Strathclyde G4 9LD. Tel 0141 332 1786; www.stow.ac.uk

Stratford-upon-Avon College The Willows North, Alcester Road, Stratford-upon-Avon, Warwickshire CV37 9QR. Tel 01789 266245; www.stratford.ac.uk

Strode College Church Road, Street, Somerset BA16 0AB. Tel 01458 844444; www.strode-college.ac.uk

Strode's College High Street, Egham, Surrey TW20 9DR. Tel 01784 437506; www.strodes.ac.uk

Stroud College in Gloucestershire Stratford Road, Stroud, Gloucestershire GL5 4AH. Tel 01453 763424; *Customer Services* 01453 761126; www.stroud.ac.uk

Sussex Downs College Eastbourne Campus, Cross Levels Way, Eastbourne, East Sussex BN21 2UF. Tel 01323 637637; www.sussexdowns.ac.uk

Sutton Coldfield College 34 Lichfield Road, Sutton Coldfield, West Midlands B74 2NW. Tel 0121 362 1121; www.sutcol.ac.uk

Swansea College (Coleg Abertawe) Tycoch Road, Tycoch, Swansea SA2 9EB. Tel 01792 284000/0800 174084; www.swancoll.ac.uk

Swindon College Regent Circus, Swindon, Wiltshire SN1 1PT. Tel 01793 498308/0800 731 2250; www.swindon-college.ac.uk

Tameside College Beaufort Road, Ashton-under-Lyne, Lancashire OL6 6NX. Tel 0161 908 6789; www.tameside.ac.uk

Tamworth and Lichfield College Croft Street, Upper Gungate, Tamworth, Staffordshire B79 8AE. Tel 01827 310202; www.tamworth.ac.uk

Telford College of Arts and Technology Haybridge Road, Wellington, Telford, Shropshire TF1 2NP. Tel 01952 642200; *Student Services* 01952 642237; www.tcat.ac.uk

Thanet College Ramsgate Road, Broadstairs, Kent CT10 1PN. Tel 01843 605040; *Admissions* 01843 605049; www.thanet.ac.uk

Thurrock and Basildon College Woodview, Grays, Essex RM16 2YR. Tel 0845 601 5746; www.tab.ac.uk

Totton College Calmore Road, Totton, Hampshire SO40 3ZX. Tel 023 8087 4874; www.totton.ac.uk

Trafford College Talbot Road, Stretford, Manchester M32 0XH. Tel 0161 886 7000; www.ntc.ac.uk; www.stcoll.ac.uk

Tresham Institute of Further and Higher Education St Mary's, Kettering, Northamptonshire NN15 7BS. Tel 0845 658 8990; www.tresham.ac.uk

Truro College College Road, Truro, Cornwall TR1 3XX. *General Enquiries* 01872 267000; *HE Admissions* 01872 267061; www.trurocollege.ac.uk

Tyne Metropolitan College Embleton Avenue, Wallsend NE28 9NJ. Tel 0191 229 5000; www.tynemet.ac.uk

University Centre Doncaster (see Doncaster College)

Upper Bann Institute (see Southern Regional College)

Uxbridge College Park Road, Uxbridge, Middlesex UB8 1NQ. Tel 01895 853333; www.uxbridge.ac.uk

Wakefield College Margaret Street, Wakefield, West Yorkshire WF1 2DH. Tel 01924 789111; www.wakefield.ac.uk

Walford and North Shropshire College Oswestry Campus, Shrewsbury Road, Oswestry, Shropshire SY11 4QB. Tel 01691 688000; www.wnsc.ac.uk

Walsall College PO Box 4203, St Paul's Street, Walsall, West Midlands WS1 1WY. Tel 01922 657000; www.walcat.ac.uk

Waltham Forest College Forest Building, Forest Road, Walthamstow, London E17 4JB. Tel 020 8501 8000; www.waltham.ac.uk

Warrington Collegiate Winwick Road, Warrington, Cheshire WA2 8QA. Tel 01925 494494; www.warr.ac.uk

West Cheshire College Handbridge Centre, Eaton Road, Handbridge, Chester CH4 7ER. Tel 01244 670600; *Course Information* 0151 356 7800; www.west-cheshire.ac.uk

West Herts College Hempstead Road, Watford, Hertfordshire WD17 3EZ. *Information and Guidance* 01923 812345; www.westherts.ac.uk

West Kent College Brook Street, Tonbridge, Kent TN9 2PW. Tel 01732 358101; www.wkc.ac.uk

West Lothian College Almondvale Crescent, Livingston, West Lothian EH54 7EP. Tel 01506 418181; *Information* 01506 427605; www.west-lothian.ac.uk

West Nottinghamshire College Derby Road, Mansfield, Nottinghamshire NG18 5BH. Tel 01623 627191; *HE Enquiries* 01623 413639/0800 100 3626; www.westnotts.ac.uk

West Suffolk College Out Risbygate, Bury St Edmunds, Suffolk IP33 3RL. Tel 01284 701301; www.westsuffolk.ac.uk

West Thames College London Road, Isleworth, Middlesex TW7 4HS. Tel 020 8326 2000; *Course Enquiries* 020 8326 2020; www.west-thames.ac.uk

Westminster Kingsway College St James's Park Centre, Castle Lane, London SW1E 6DR. Tel 08700 609800; *Course Information* 08700 609801; www.westking.ac.uk

Weston College Knightstone Road, Weston super Mare, Somerset BS23 2AL. Tel 01934 411411; www.weston.ac.uk

Weymouth College Cranford Avenue, Weymouth, Dorset DT4 7LQ. Tel 01305 761100; *Course Applications* 0870 060 9800/1; www.weymouth.ac.uk

Wigan and Leigh College PO Box 53, Parsons Walk, Wigan WN1 1RS. Tel 01942 761600; *Course Enquiries* 01942 761111; www.wigan-leigh.ac.uk

Wiltshire College Cocklebury Road, Chippenham, Wiltshire SN15 3QD. Tel 01249 464644; www.wiltscoll.ac.uk

Wirral Metropolitan College Conway Park Campus, Europa Boulevard, Conway Park, Birkenhead, Wirral, Merseyside CH41 4NT. Tel 0151 551 7777; www.wmc.ac.uk

Worcester College of Technology Deansway, Worcester WR1 2JF. Tel 01905 725555; www.wortech.ac.uk

Yeovil College Mudford Road, Yeovil, Somerset BA21 4DR. Tel 01935 423921; www.yeovil.ac.uk

York College Tadcaster Road, York, North Yorkshire YO24 1UA. Tel 01904 770200; www.yorkcollege.ac.uk

Yorkshire Coast College Lady Edith's Drive, Scarborough, North Yorkshire YO12 5RN. Tel 01723 372105; www.yorkshirecoastcollege.ac.uk

3 | UNIVERSITY COURSE PROFILES

UNIVERSITIES AND THEIR COURSES

Choosing a degree subject is one step of the way to higher education (see **Chapter 1**), choosing a university or college is the next stage (see **Chapter 2**). However, in addition to such features as location, entry requirements, accommodation, students' facilities and the subjects offered, many universities differ in the way they organise and teach their courses. The course profiles which follow aim to identify the main course features of each of the universities and to provide some brief notes about the types of courses they offer and how they differ.

There are five main types of degree courses. Single Honours courses offer one main subject with a range of specialist subject options from which to choose in Years 2 and 3. Joint Honours courses involve the study of two subjects whilst Combined Honours courses may involve a study of two or three subjects. Some institutions also offer Major/Minor courses in which the split between the time spent on each subject may be divided as much as 75/25. Finally, many universities and colleges offer sandwich courses in which students are involved in a work placement often lasting up to a year on full pay (see **Chapter 4**).

The ways in which students are taught differ between universities and often between subjects, even at the same university. Modularisation is now quite common because of the flexibility it offers the student to choose a range of topics within their subject choice. Each course comprises modules of study, some are compulsory, some are optional, and some are 'free units' which allow the student to study a subject totally unrelated to their chosen course, for example a foreign language or management. Each module often has a credit rating and students are awarded this value of credits for each module they successfully complete (ie, they pass the assessment). For a three-year Honours degree students usually need 360 credits. Courses which are not modular are often those for vocational subjects which must conform to the course requirements of professional bodies.

Although universities have their own distinct identities and course characteristics, they have many similarities. Apart from full-time and sandwich courses, one-year Foundation courses are also offered in many subjects which can help the student to either convert or build on existing qualifications to enable them to start an Honours degree programme. All universities also offer one-year International Foundation courses for overseas students to provide a preliminary introduction to courses and often to provide English language tuition.

Foundation courses, however, must not be confused with Foundation degrees which normally require two years' full-time study, or longer for part-time study. They are also often taught in local colleges and may be taken part-time to allow students to continue to work. Successful completion of a Foundation degree can lead into the second or final year of related Honours degree courses when offered by the university validating the Foundation degree. Two-year Higher National Diplomas will also qualify for entry into the second or final year of degree courses. These, too, are often offered at universities as well as colleges of further education and partnership colleges linked to universities.

Part-time degrees and courses in lifelong learning or distance learning are also often available and details of these can be found on university websites and in prospectuses. Some universities publish separate prospectuses for part-time courses.

The following is a list of universities and a brief outline for each of the ways in which their undergraduate courses are structured and provided, and of the range of courses they provide. For full details see university websites and prospectuses.

PROFILES

Aberdeen Students applying for the MA degree in Arts and Social Sciences are admitted to a degree rather than a subject. Students select from a range of courses in the first year, leading up to the final choice of subject and Honours course in the fourth year. The BSc degree is also flexible but within the Science framework. Engineering students follow a common core course in Years 1 and 2, specialising in Year 3. There is less flexibility, however, in some vocational courses such as Accountancy, Law and Medicine. For some degree programmes, highly qualified applicants may be admitted to the second year of the course. Other courses cover Divinity and Religious Studies, Education, Law, Medicine and Sciences.

Abertay Dundee Courses have a strong vocational bias and are offered in the Schools of Computing, Business, Science and Engineering and Social and Health Sciences. Four-year courses are offered on a modular basis. Sandwich courses may be either thick (one-year placement) or thin (two six-month placements) and placements are usually at the end of the second and/or third years.

Aberystwyth The University offers single, joint and major-minor Honours courses on a modular basis. In Part 1 (Year 1) core topics related to the chosen subject are studied alongside optional subjects. This arrangement allows some flexibility for change when choosing final degree subjects in Part 2 (Years 2 and 3). Some students take a year in industry or commerce between Years 2 and 3. Courses include Accountancy and Business, Agriculture, the Arts and Humanities, Computer Science, Education, Law, Mathematics, the Sciences, Sport and Theatre and TV Studies.

American Intercontinental This private university offers courses in Business, Finance, Interior Design, Media Production and Visual Communication.

Anglia Ruskin Courses are modular which enables students to choose from a range of subject topics in addition to the compulsory subject core modules. Single and combined Honours courses are offered, with some opportunities to study abroad; many programmes have a strong vocational focus. Courses include Business Studies, Computer Science, Education, Engineering, Law, Nursing, Psychology, Social Sciences and the Sciences.

Arts London The University is Europe's largest institution offering courses in Art and Design, Communication and Performing Arts, focusing on creativity and practice in a large number of specialist fields.

Aston The University offers modular courses in single Honours degrees (one subject), joint Honours (two subjects, usually in related areas) and in combined Honours and interdisciplinary studies in which programmes are organised across different subjects. Combined Honours courses may be weighted 50%–50%, and major/minor programmes weighted 67% for the major element and 33% for the minor. A distinctive feature of Aston is that most degrees allow students to spend the third year on a one-year sandwich placement; 70% of students follow sandwich courses or study-abroad programmes, leading to a high percentage of employed graduates. Courses are taught in the Schools of Engineering and Applied Science, Languages and European Studies, Life and Health Sciences and in the Aston Business School.

Bangor Modular courses are offered in single and joint Honours programmes. A broad and flexible programme is taken in Level 1 (Year 1) with the opportunity to study modules outside the chosen subject including a language. This is followed by greater specialisation in Levels 2 and 3. Courses include Agriculture and Forestry, Arts subjects, Business and Management, Computer Science and Electronics, Education, Health Studies, Music, Psychology, Sciences, Ocean Sciences, Social Sciences, Sport and

Religious Studies. Contrary to popular belief, two-thirds of the students come from outside Wales and all courses are taught in English.

Bath The academic year is divided into two semesters with single and combined Honours degrees composed of core units and optional units, allowing students some flexibility in shaping their courses with 10–12 units taken each year. A central feature of all programmes is the opportunity to take a sandwich course as part of the degree: this is usually taken as either one 12-month placement or two periods of six months. Courses are offered in the Faculties of Engineering and Design, Humanities and Social Sciences, Science and the Schools of Business and Health.

Bath Spa Most courses – for single awards, specialised awards and combined awards – are part of a flexible modular scheme with students taking six modules each year. Some modules are compulsory but there is a good range of optional modules. Courses on offer include Biology, Business and Management, Creative Studies, Cultural Studies, Dance, Design Technology, Drama, Education, English Literature and Creative Studies in English, Food Studies, Geography, Health Studies, History, Media and Communications, Music, Psychology, Sociology and Study of Religions.

Bedfordshire This university offers BA and BSc undergraduate, Foundation and Extended degrees in Advertising, Marketing and Public Relations, Art and Design, Biosciences, Business, Computing, Language and Communication, Law, Media, Nursing, Psychology, Social Sciences, Sport and Leisure and Tourism. Most of the courses are vocational, some of which offer a placement year in industry or commerce.

Birmingham Courses cover Arts subjects (including Drama), Business and Commerce, Education, Engineering, Law, Medicine and Dentistry and Health Sciences. Single subject and joint Honours courses are offered. In joint Honours courses the two chosen subjects may have common ground or can be very disparate, for example technology and a modern language. Some major/minor combinations are also possible. The modular system provides opportunities for students to study a subject outside their main degree.

Birmingham City Courses are offered through the Birmingham Institute of Art and Design, the Business School, the School of Computing, the School of Jewellery and the Faculties of the Built Environment, Education, Health and Community Care, Law, Humanities and Social Sciences and the Technology Innovation Centre. Many courses have a vocational focus and include sandwich placements. Music is offered through the Birmingham Conservatoire, a music college of international standing. There is also an extensive International Exchange Programme, with many courses abroad being taught in English.

Bolton Courses are offered in Art and Design, Built Environment, Business Studies, Computing and Electronics, Cultural and Creative Studies, Education, Engineering, Health and Social Studies, Product Design, Psychology and Sport, Leisure and Tourism. Teaching and learning take place through a mixture of lectures, practicals, seminars and small tutorial groups. Many courses are based on a modular structure.

Bournemouth The University offers undergraduate degrees leading to BA, BSc and LLB. The programmes, which are mainly vocational and include sandwich placements, often carry professional recognition. The academic schools cover Business, Conservation Sciences, Design, Engineering and Computing, Health and Community Studies, Law and Media.

Bradford Single, joint and major/minor courses are offered, many of which are vocational, leading to professional accreditation, and include sandwich placements in industry and commerce. Other courses offer work-shadowing placements. Language options are available to all students irrespective of their chosen degree course. Subjects are taught in the Schools of Archaeological, Geographical and Environmental Sciences, Engineering Design and Technology, Informatics, Health, Life Sciences, Management, Social and International Studies and Lifelong Learning.

Brighton BA, BSc and BEng courses are offered, 90% with industrial placements including some in

Europe, the USA and Canada. Courses include Art and Architecture, Education and Sport, Health, Management and Information Sciences and Science and Engineering. Brighton and Sussex Medical School students are based at the Falmer campus for the first two years, with academic and clinical studies integrated from Year 1, and thereafter in the education centre at the Royal Sussex County Hospital in Brighton.

Bristol The University offers single and joint Honours programmes, mostly of three or four years and, except for Dentistry, Medicine and Veterinary Science, they are based on a modular structure. Students on single Honours courses have open units allowing optional choices from a range of subjects. Lectures play an important part in teaching and are supported by tutorials and seminars which, in Arts and Social Sciences, tend to dominate the final year. Other subject areas offered in Sciences and Engineering (some courses include a year abroad), Arts, Social Sciences and Law.

Bristol UWE The University offers single and joint Honours courses organised on a modular basis which gives flexibility in the choice of options. Many courses include sandwich placements and, in addition, students have the opportunity to undertake a period of study in another EU country. The language centre is open to all students. Courses cover a full range of subjects in the Faculties of Media and Design, Applied Sciences, Built Environment, Computing, Education, Engineering and Mathematical Sciences, Health and Social Care, Humanities, Law, Languages and Social Sciences, the Bristol Business School and Hartpury College (offering Agricultural and Equine Business courses).

Brunel All courses are made up of self-contained modules enabling students, within their scheme of studies, to choose a broad range of topics or greater specialisation as they prefer. Some modern language modules may be taken, depending on the timetable of the chosen subjects. Almost all degree courses are available in a three-year full-time mode or in four-year thick or thin sandwich courses which combine academic work with industrial experience. Some exchange schemes also operate in Europe and the USA. Degree programmes cover Arts and Humanities subjects, Biological Sciences, Business and Management, Design, Education, Engineering, Health and Social Care, Human Sciences, Law, Mathematical Sciences, Performing Arts and Sport Sciences.

Buckingham The University is an educational charity with its main income provided by the students who pay full tuition fees. A unique feature is the two-year degree programme which starts in January although some courses start in September and may extend to 2¼ years, and some last three years. Courses are offered in Business, Humanities, Law, International Studies and Sciences.

Bucks New BA and BSc courses are offered in the Faculties of Social Sciences and Humanities of this new university created from Buckinghamshire Chilterns University College in 2007. There is also a Business School and a Law School. Subject areas include Accountancy and Finance, Air Transport Management, Animal Studies, Art and Design, Business, Computer Science, Computer Engineering, Creative Writing, Criminology, Drama, English Literature, Equine Studies, Film Studies, Human Resources Management, International Management, Journalism, Law, Marketing, Media, Music Industries Management, Nursing, Photography, Psychology, Social Work, Sociology, Sports Studies and Video Production. The University is a leading centre in furniture design.

Cambridge The University offers undergraduate courses in Arts and Sciences and postgraduate degree programmes. Three-year degree courses (Triposes) provide a broad introduction to the subject followed by options at a later stage, and are divided into Part 1 (one or two years) and Part 2. In some Science and Engineering courses there is a fourth year (Part 3). In college-based teaching sessions (supervisions), essays are set for discussion to support university lectures, seminars and practicals.

Canterbury Christ Church A wide range of BA and BSc courses are on offer in addition to a wide choice of combined courses. Subjects cover American Studies, Applied Criminology, Art, Bioscience, Business, Computing, Digital and Cultural Arts and Media, Early Childhood Studies, English, Film, Radio and TV

Studies, Forensic Investigation, French, Geography, Health Studies, History, Legal Studies, Marketing, Media Studies, Music, Psychology, Religious Studies, Science in the Environment, Social Science, Sport and Exercise Psychology, Sport Science, Theology and Tourism.

Cardiff All students taking the very flexible BA degree study three subjects in the first year and then follow a single or joint Honours course in their chosen subject(s), or a degree in the additional subject. Similarly, BSc Econ courses offer the option to transfer to an alternative degree course at the end of Year 1, depending on the subjects originally chosen. Many degree schemes have a vocational and professional content with a period of attachment in industry, and there are well established links with universities abroad. Degrees schemes are offered by 27 Schools covering Architecture and Planning, Arts and Humanities subjects, Business, Computer Science, Earth, Ocean and Planetary Sciences, Engineering, Healthcare Studies, Law, Media Studies, Medicine, Dentistry and Nursing, Music, Optometry, Pharmacy, Psychology, Religious Studies, Sciences, Social Sciences and Welsh Studies.

Central Lancashire The University has four Faculties – Cultural, Legal and Social Studies, Health, Science, and Design and Technology. Subjects are taught in a series of modules which gives maximum flexibility in the final choice of degree course. Students may specialise or keep their options open with a choice of single Honours, joint or combined Honours, or they can choose three subjects in Year 1 and reduce to two in the second and third years. Some sandwich courses are offered.

Chester Single and combined courses are offered in a wide range of subjects on the Chester campus. Over 60 subjects are offered including Art and Design, Drama and Theatre Studies, Business and Social Studies courses and Nutrition and Health Care. The Warrington campus offers well established courses in Media (Radio, TV, Music) and Journalism in addition to Computer Science and Sports courses.

Chichester Degree subjects can be studied in major, joint or minor programmes. All undergraduate courses comprise a number of individual short course units/modules, taught and assessed separately. Each degree course consists of compulsory and optional modules enabling students to follow their own interests. BA courses are offered in a range of subjects covering Dance, English, Fine Art, History, Media Studies, Music, Performing Arts, Sports Studies and Theology at Chichester, and Business, Education and Tourism at the Bognor Regis campus.

City The University offers a wide range of three-year and four-year programmes leading to degrees in Arts, Business and Management, Computing, Engineering and Mathematical Sciences, Health Sciences, Law and Social Sciences. Some Schools and Departments provide a common first year, allowing students to make a final decision on their degree course at the end of the first year. Some sandwich courses are optional, others compulsory. Students in some subject areas may apply to study abroad.

Coventry Courses are offered in the Schools of Art and Design, Business, Engineering, Health and Social Sciences, Mathematical and Information Sciences and Science and the Environment. Many courses are industry-linked and offer sandwich placements in industry and commerce, with some opportunities to study abroad. Individual programmes of study are usually made up of compulsory modules, core options from a prescribed list and free choice modules.

Cumbria This new university was created in 2007 from a merger of St Martins University College and Cumbria Institute of the Arts. Courses cover Art, Design, Media and Performance, Arts, Humanities and Social Science, Business, IT and Law, Education, Health and Social care, Natural Resources and Outdoor Studies and Sport.

De Montfort The Faculties of Art and Design, Business and Law, Computing Science and Engineering, Health and Life Sciences and Humanities offer single Honours programmes and an extensive joint Honours programme in which two subjects are chosen to be studied equally. Courses are modular, some assessed by coursework only, or by a combination of coursework and examination and a few by examination only. It is possible to change a selected module early in the year.

Derby Courses in Derby are offered across three Schools – Arts, Design and Technology, Business and Education, Health and Sciences, whilst at the Buxton campus Foundation degrees and Higher National Diploma courses are offered as well as some BA and BSc degrees. There is also a comprehensive joint Honours programme offering two subjects and combined Honours courses with a choice of up to three subjects. Major/minor courses are also available.

Dundee Courses are offered in Accountancy, Architecture and Planning, Art and Design, Arts, Education, Engineering, Law, Medicine and Dentistry, Nursing, Sciences and Social Sciences. A flexible modular system is offered in which Arts and Social Science students have a choice of up to three or four subjects in Year 1 leading to greater specialisation as students progress through the next three years. A similar system applies to courses in Life Sciences and Physical Sciences. In Engineering a common core curriculum operates in Level 1 and in the first half of Level 2.

Durham Degree options include single and joint Honours courses to which subsidiary subjects can be added. There are named routes in Natural Sciences and courses in Combined Arts and Social Sciences in which students may design their own degree course by choosing several subjects from a wide range. Courses cover the Arts, Business, Computer Science, Education, Engineering, Law, Medicine, Science and Social Science.

East Anglia There are 18 Schools of Study spanning the Humanities, Social Sciences, Health and professional disciplines. Many Schools are interdisciplinary or multidisciplinary, allowing students to combine a specialist study with complementary subjects and optional units. Some courses include study abroad in Europe, North America and Australasia.

East London The University offers some 130 single Honours degrees and 50 subjects which form part of the combined Honours programme. Courses provide a flexibility of choice and are based on a modular structure with compulsory and optional course units. Courses are offered in Architecture, Art and Design, Business, Computing, Engineering, Health Sciences, Humanities, Law, Media, Social Sciences, Sciences and Sport. A very large number of extended degrees are also available for applicants who do not have the normal university entrance requirements.

Edge Hill This university has three-year programmes in Business, English, Film, Geographical Sciences, History, Law, Media, Midwifery, Nursing, Performance Studies, Social and Psychological Sciences, Sport and Teacher Training.

Edinburgh Courses are offered in Humanities and the Social Sciences, Medicine and Veterinary Medicine and in Science and Engineering. Depending on the choice of degree, three or more subjects are taken in the first year followed by second level courses in at least two of these subjects in Year 2, thus allowing a range of subjects to be studied at degree level. There is a considerable choice of subjects although there may be restrictions in the case of high-demand subjects such as English and Psychology. General or Ordinary degrees take three years and Honours degrees take four years. Joint Honours degrees are also offered.

Essex There are 17 undergraduate departments grouped in Schools of Study covering Humanities and Comparative Studies, Social Sciences, Law and Sciences and Engineering. In Year 1 students take four or five courses including modules for their chosen degree. In Year 2 they may follow their chosen degree or choose another degree, including combined and joint courses. The four-year BA and some Law degrees include a year abroad and/or industrial placements.

Exeter Subjects are offered in the Schools of Biological Sciences, Business and Economics, Classics, Ancient History and Theology, Education and Lifelong Learning, Engineering, Computer Science and Mathematics, English, Geography, Archaeology and Earth Resources, Historical, Political and Sociological Studies, Law, Modern Languages, the Institute of Arab and Islamic Studies and the Peninsula Medical School. In some courses it is possible to study for up to a year in Europe, North America, Australia or New Zealand.

Glamorgan Many of the courses are vocational and can be studied as single or joint Honours courses or major-minor degrees. Courses are offered in the fields of Art and Design, Built Environment, Business, Computing and Mathematics, Education, Engineering, English and Creative Writing, Geography and the Environment, Health Sciences, Life and Physical Sciences, Humanities and Social Sciences, Law, Policing and Crime, Media and Drama Studies and Sport.

Glasgow Applicants choose a Faculty and a degree from the Faculties of Arts, Education, Engineering, Law and Financial Studies, Medicine, Science, Social Science and Veterinary Medicine. Flexible arrangements allow students to build their own degree programme from all the courses on offer. Honours degrees normally take four years, with the decision for Honours taken at the end of Year 2 (not automatic). General degrees take three years except for those involving a foreign language.

Glasgow Caledonian The University offers a wide range of vocational full-time and sandwich courses organised in the Schools of the Built and Natural Environment, Computing and Mathematical Sciences, Engineering Science and Design, Health and Social Care, Law and Social Sciences, Life Sciences, Nursing, Midwifery and Community Health and the Caledonian Business School.

Gloucestershire There are three main Faculties: Arts and Education, Business and Social Sciences and Environment and Leisure. Modular, single and joint courses are offered, many with work placements and some with exchange schemes with institutions in the USA. Many students are home-based.

Greenwich Courses cover Architecture and Construction, Business, Chemical and Life Sciences, Computing and Mathematical Sciences, Earth and Environmental Sciences, Education and Training, Engineering, Languages, Health and Social Care, Humanities and Social Sciences and Law. There is also a flexible and comprehensive combined Honours degree programme offering two joint subjects of equal weight or, alternatively, major-minor combinations.

Heriot-Watt The year is divided into three ten-week terms with four modules taken each term. The six Schools cover the Built Environment, Engineering and Physical Sciences, Management and Languages, Mathematical and Computer Sciences, Textiles and Design and Life Sciences.

Hertfordshire Honours degree courses, including sandwich degrees, are offered in Art and Design, Business, Computer Science, Education, Engineering, Humanities, Law, Life and Physical Sciences, Geography, Music, Sport, Nursing and Health subjects, Psychology and Social Studies and many courses are vocational. There is also an extensive combined modular programme in which students choose three subjects in Year 1, followed by specialisation in Years 2 and 3.

Huddersfield The modular approach to study provides a flexible structure to all courses which are offered as full-time or sandwich options. All students also have the opportunity to study a modern language either as a minor option or by studying part-time through the Modern Languages Centre. Most courses are vocational and include such subjects as Accountancy and Business, Architecture, Art and Design, Computing, Education, Engineering, Geography and Environmental Sciences, Food Sciences, Hospitality and Tourism, Human and Health Sciences, Law, Marketing, Music and Sciences.

Hull The academic year is divided into two semesters with all full-time courses made up of core and optional modules. There is also a free elective scheme which allows students to take one module each year outside their main subject. A 'Languages for All' programme is available for all students irrespective of their degree course subject. The wide range of subjects offered include Arts and Humanities, Business, Computing, Drama, Economics, Education, Engineering, Law, Medicine, Music, Nursing, Physical Sciences, Social Sciences and Sport.

Imperial London The University offers Science and Engineering programmes leading to BSc, BEng, MSci and MEng degrees, and MB, BS and BSc programmes in the School of Medicine. Science courses are offered primarily in one principal subject, but flexibility is provided by the possibility to transfer at the end of the first year and by the choice of optional subjects in the later years of the course. Joint Honours courses are offered in the Departments of Biological Sciences, Chemistry and Mathematics. A Humanities programme is also open to all students with a wide range of options whilst the Tanaka Business School offers Management courses which form an integral part of undergraduate degrees.

Keele Flexibility is provided through either interdisciplinary single Honours degrees, bringing together a number of topics in an integrated form, or dual Honours degrees in which two principal subjects are studied to degree level to the same depth as a single Honours course. In addition, all students take a first-year course in Complementary Studies and may also study a foreign language. Courses are offered in Arts subjects, Biosciences and Physical Sciences, Economics, Education, Law, Management Science, Media, Music and Social Sciences.

Kent Single Honours courses can include the option of taking up to 25% of the degree in another subject, or to change the focus of a degree at the end of the year. Two subjects are studied on a 50/50 basis in joint Honours courses and there are also major/minor Honours degrees. Degrees are offered in Accountancy and Business courses, Arts subjects, Biological and Physical Sciences, Computer Science, Drama and Theatre and Film Studies, Languages, Law, Music Technology, Pharmacy, Psychology, Religious Studies and Social Sciences.

Kingston Single and joint Honours courses are offered within a modular structure, with the opportunity to take a language option in French, German, Italian, Japanese, Mandarin Chinese, Russian or Spanish. Several courses are available as a minor field, for example, Business, which adds an extra dimension to the chosen degree. Subjects are offered in the Faculties of Art, Design and Music, Arts and Social Sciences, Business, Health and Social Care Sciences, Science, Technology and in the School of Education. Exchange schemes are offered with 72 universities in Europe and five in the USA.

Lampeter Single and joint Honours courses are offered, together with combined Honours programmes in which three subjects are taken. All students can apply to study abroad in Canada or the USA during their second year. Over 40 subjects are offered covering Arts, Humanities, Film and Media Studies, the Environment and Business. There is considerable flexibility in course choice. In Year 1 (Part 1) all students take three subjects (two subjects alongside the main subject). In Years 2 and 3 course units can be taken in one subject but two units can be taken in a second subject (not always one studied in the first year). Combined and non-standard degrees are possible including the option to 'choose your own course'.

Leeds A very wide range of courses are on offer in most subject areas (Leeds is a pioneer of joint Honours degrees). In the first year, joint Honours students normally divide their time equally between three subjects, with a wide choice of the third or elective subject in the first year. In many cases, students can transfer to a different course at the end of the first year and delay their final choice of degree. A wide range of subjects is offered in Arts and Humanities, Science and Engineering, Social Sciences and in the Management School.

Leeds Metropolitan Many of the degrees are vocational with links to industry and commerce. Courses are modular with core studies and optional modules. Degree programmes are offered in the Faculties of Arts and Society, Information and Technology, Health, Sport and Recreation, the Leslie Silver International Faculty and the Leeds Business School.

Leicester The single Honours courses are offered in all the main disciplines and are taken by 75% of students. The main subject of study may be supported by one or two supplementary subjects taken in the first, and sometimes the second, year. Joint Honours courses are also offered. A three-year Combined Studies degree is also available in which three subjects are studied, one taken for two years only. Apart from Medicine, all programmes have a common modular structure with compulsory modules and a wide choice of optional modules.

Lincoln Faculties include those of Applied Computing Sciences, Art, Architecture and Design, Business and Law, Health, Life and Social Sciences, Medical Sciences and Media and Humanities. Single and joint subject degrees are offered on a modular basis, with many subjects offering the chance to study abroad.

Liverpool The University offers degrees in the Faculties of Arts, Engineering, Medicine, Science, Social and Environmental Studies and Veterinary Science. Apart from courses with a clinical component, programmes are modular. In some cases they include placements in industry or in another country whilst a 'Languages for All' scheme offers European languages. A combined Honours programme in Arts gives students the chance to choose three subjects in Year 1, reducing to two subjects in Years 2 and 3. A similar combined Honours course in Social and Environmental Studies is also offered.

Liverpool Hope Single Honours courses leading to degrees of BA and BSc are offered and there is also a wide range of options by way of two combined subjects. Course combinations are available in Business, Computing, Dance, Drama, Education, English, Environmental Management, Film Studies, Fine Art and Design, Geography, Health, History, Human Biology, Irish Studies, Law, Leisure, Marketing, Music, Media, Politics, Psychology, Sociology, Sports Studies, Theology and Religious Studies, Tourism, and War and Peace Studies.

Liverpool John Moores Courses are offered in the Faculties of Business and Law, Education, Community and Leisure, Health and Applied Social Sciences, Media, Arts and Social Science, Science and Technology and the Environment. The majority of courses provide the opportunity for work-based learning or for a year-long industrial placement.

London (Birkbeck) Part-time evening courses are offered for mature students wishing to read for first and higher degrees. Courses are offered in the Faculties of Arts, Science, Social Science and Continuing Education.

London (Central School of Speech and Drama) The School offers a broad range of courses in the Theatre Arts. It is also linked to the Webber Douglas Academy of Dramatic Art to provide a range of courses leading to careers in classical and contemporary theatre, film and TV. Courses include Acting, Costume Construction, Stage Design, Prop Making, Puppetry, Stage Management, Theatre Lighting and Sound Design.

London (Goldsmiths) Programmes are offered in Art, Drama and Media, the Arts, Education and Social Sciences. Like most London University degrees, the majority of undergraduate degrees are made up of course units giving some flexibility. Twelve units are taken over three years.

London (Heythrop) Nine BA courses are offered in Philosophy and Theology. The supportive and learning environment is enhanced by one-to-one tutorials for all students throughout their courses.

London (Institute in Paris) A single Honours course in French Studies is offered to English-speaking students, taught almost entirely in French. Students graduate after their three-year course with a University of London BA and study in France for the whole of their course.

London (King's) The College offers more than 200 degree programmes covering Humanities, Law, Physical Sciences and Social Science and Public Policy at the Strand campus, Health and Life Sciences, Nursing and Midwifery and Social Science at Waterloo, and Biomedical Sciences, Medicine and Dentistry at the Guy's or King's Denmark Hill and St Thomas's campuses. The degree course structure varies with the subject chosen and consists of single Honours (one subject), joint Honours (two subjects), combined Honours (a choice of over 60 programmes) and major/minor courses.

London (London School of Economics and Political Science) The School offers courses not only in Economics and Political Science but also in a wide range of Social Science subjects taught in 19 Departments. Programmes are offered as single Honours, joint Honours or major/minor courses. LSE entrance examination may be required (see **Chapter 7**).

London (Queen Mary) The College offers courses in the Arts and Humanities, Biological and Physical Sciences, Business Management and Economics, Computer Science, Engineering, Languages, Materials Science, Mathematics, Medicine and Social Sciences. In most subjects, students choose compulsory and optional course units which allow for some flexibility in planning a course to suit individual interests.

London (Royal Holloway) The College offers single, joint and major/minor Honours degrees in three Faculties – Arts, History and Social Sciences, and Science. Study abroad is a feature of many courses and all students can compete for international exchanges.

London (Royal Veterinary College) Two courses are offered in Veterinary Medicine and Veterinary Sciences, but the latter does not qualify graduates to practise as veterinary surgeons.

London (School of Oriental and African Studies) This is the only higher education institution in the UK specialising in the study of Asia, Africa and the Near and Middle East. Single subject degrees include compulsory and optional units, with two-thirds of the total units studied in the chosen subject and the remaining units or 'floaters' from a complementary course offered at SOAS or another college of the University. In addition, two-subject degrees give great flexibility in the choice of units, enabling students to personalise their degrees to match their interests.

London (School of Pharmacy) The School offers the Master of Pharmacy degree. Except for hospital and extramural projects, all the teaching takes place on the Bloomsbury campus.

London (University College) Subjects are organised in Faculties – Arts and Humanities, Social and Historical Sciences (with a flexible course unit system), Fine Art (the Slade School), Law, Built Environment (the Bartlett), Engineering Sciences, Mathematical and Physical Sciences and Life Sciences. In addition, there is the School of Medicine. The School of Slavonic and East European Studies also offers degrees which focus on developing a high level of proficiency in speaking, writing and understanding the chosen language.

London Metropolitan Single and joint Honours courses are made up of compulsory and optional modules allowing students some flexibility to follow their particular interests. Courses are offered in Accountancy and Business, Art and Architecture, Arts, Humanities and Languages, Computing, Economics and Finance, Education, Health and Human Sciences and Law.

London South Bank Subject areas cover Arts and Human Sciences including Law and Psychology, Business, Computing and Information Management, Engineering, Science and the Built Environment and Health and Social Care. All courses have flexible modes of study and many vocational courses offer sandwich placements.

Loughborough Academic programmes cover Art and Design, Business, Computer Science, Economics, Engineering, European Studies and Politics, Humanities, Sciences, Social Science and Sport. Degree programmes combine compulsory and optional modules and some transfers between courses are possible. Additional language study is possible in French, German or Spanish (including beginners' courses), for students on most courses. Sandwich degree courses with a year's paid work experience in industry result in high graduate employment. World-class sporting facilities and an unrivalled reputation in sporting success attract applicants at junior international level and above.

Manchester The University offers single and joint Honours courses which are divided into course units, some of which are compulsory and others optional, and some are taken from a choice of subjects offered by other Schools and Faculties. A comprehensive Combined Studies degree enables students to choose course units from Arts, Humanities, Social Sciences and Sciences, and this provides the flexibility for students to alter the emphasis of their studies from year to year. Degree programmes are offered in the Faculties of Engineering and Physical Sciences, Humanities, Life Sciences and Medical and Human Sciences.

Manchester Metropolitan Degree programmes are offered in the Faculties of Art and Design, Community Studies and Education, Food, Clothing and Hospitality Management, Humanities, Law and Social Science, Science and Engineering and the Manchester Metropolitan Business School. A large number of courses involve industrial and commercial placements. It is also possible to take combined Honours degrees selecting a combination of two or three subjects. Many programmes have a modular structure with compulsory and optional core modules.

Middlesex Single and joint Honours courses are offered on a modular basis, most programmes having an optional work placement. Courses cover Art and Design, Biological and Health Sciences, Business and Management, Computing and IT, Dance, Drama and Music, English and Mass Communication, Humanities and Cultural Studies, Social Sciences and Teaching and Education.

Napier Students choose between single, joint (two subject) degrees and customised degrees which can include a range of subjects. Courses are offered in Alternative Medicine and Complementary Therapies, Built Environment and Civil Engineering, Business Management and Financial Services, Communication and Creative Industries, Computing and IT, Life Sciences, Nursing and Midwifery and Social Sciences.

Newcastle Degree programmes are available in the Faculties of Arts, Biological Sciences, Business and Law, Engineering, Medical Sciences, Physical Sciences and Social Sciences. Single, joint and combined Honours programmes are offered, in some cases providing students with the opportunity either to defer their choice of final degree or to transfer to other subjects at a later stage. In the Combined Studies BA and BSc courses it is possible to combine the study of up to three different subjects which can be studied over two or three years.

Newport The University consists of seven Schools – Art and Design, Humanities, Business, Computing and Engineering, Social Studies, Education and the Centre for Community and Lifelong Learning. Courses include single and joint Honours and major/minor studies; they vary in structure but many are based on a modular system.

Northampton Courses are offered in seven schools: Applied Sciences (Computing, Mechanical and Electrical/Electronic Engineering), Business, Education, Health, Social Sciences, Arts (including Fine Art and Design) and Land-based subjects at Moulton College. Courses are offered as single, combined and joint Honours programmes.

Northumbria A wide range of courses is offered with an emphasis on vocational studies, covering Art and Design, Arts subjects, Built Environment, Business and Financial Management, Computing, Education and Sport, Engineering, Health and Social Care, Humanities, Languages, Law, Mathematics, Nursing and Midwifery, Psychology and Sciences. Single and joint Honours courses are offered, and a combined Honours course allows a choice of up to three subjects.

Nottingham Single and joint Honours courses are available, with some sandwich courses. Programmes are modular with compulsory and optional modules, the latter giving some flexibility in the selection of topics from outside the chosen subject field. Degree programmes are offered in the Faculties of Arts, Education, Engineering, Law and Social Sciences, Medicine and Health Sciences and Science.

Nottingham Trent Degree programmes are offered in Art and Design, Business, Computing and Technology, Economics, Education, Humanities, Law, Sciences and Social Sciences. Many courses are vocational with industrial and commercial placements and some students are also able to spend a semester (half an academic year) studying at a partner university in Europe, the USA or Australia.

Open University Six hundred degree and diploma courses are offered covering Business, Economics, Education, Engineering, Environmental Studies, Health Studies, Law, Mathematics, Philosophy, Politics, Psychology, Science, Social Sciences and Technology. Students study at home and are sent learning materials by the OU and maintain contact with their tutors by email, post and telephone.

Oxford Candidates apply to a college and for a single or joint Honours programme. Courses are offered with a core element plus a variety of options. Weekly contact with a college tutor assists students to tailor their courses to suit personal interests. Arts students are examined twice, once in the first year (Preliminary examinations) and at the end of the course (Final Honours School). Science students are similarly examined although in some subjects examinations also take place in the second year.

Oxford Brookes Single Honours courses are offered with modules chosen from a field of study or, alternatively, combined Honours courses in which two subjects are chosen. These subjects may be in related or unrelated subjects. There is also a Combined Studies degree in which students 'build' their own degree by taking approved modules from a range of the subjects offered by the University.

Paisley See **West Scotland** below.

Plymouth A broad portfolio of degree courses is available including Medicine at the Peninsula Medical School – a partnership with Exeter University. Other courses cover Agriculture, Art and Design, Biological and Physical Sciences, Built Environment, Business and Financial Management, Computing, Drama, Education, Engineering, Health and Social Sciences, Humanities, Languages, Law, Marine Studies, Mathematics and Sport Studies. Single Honours courses are offered with many vocational programmes offering work placements.

Portsmouth The Faculties of the Environment, Social Sciences, Science, Technology and the Portsmouth Business School offer single and joint Honours courses. Sandwich programmes are also available in many subjects and there is also an opportunity for all students to learn a foreign language. Many courses are planned on a modular basis which allows students to defer specialisation until after their first year.

Queen Margaret The five main areas at this new university (2007) cover Business and Enterprise, Health, Media, Production, Drama and Performance and Social Sciences. All courses focus on vocational careers.

Queen's Belfast The academic year is divided into two semesters of 15 weeks each (12 teaching weeks and three examination weeks), with degree courses (pathways) normally taken over three years of full-time study. Six modules are taken each year (three in each semester) and, in theory, a degree can involve any combination of six Level 1 modules. Single, joint and combined Honours courses are offered and, in addition, major-minor combinations; some courses include sandwich placements. Courses cover Agriculture and Food Science, Education, Engineering, Humanities and Social Sciences, Management and Economics, Law and Medicine and Health Sciences.

Reading Faculties of Arts and Humanities and Economics and Social Sciences provide flexible arrangements for students. A teaching system operates in Year 1 in which students can take modules in their chosen subject and in two or three other subjects. At the end of the first year they may transfer from single Honours to joint Honours courses or change to another subject.

Richmond, The American International University in London Courses in Art, Design and Media, Communication, Computing Engineering, Economics, Engineering (with George Washington University, USA), Finance, History, International Relations, Marketing, Political Science, Psychology and Sociology are offered with entry in September, January, May or June.

Robert Gordon The University offers a wide range of vocational courses including Accountancy and Business, Architecture, Art and Design, Computer Science, Engineering, Law, Nursing, Occupational Therapy, Pharmacy, Physiotherapy, Radiography, Sciences, Social Sciences and Sports Science. Many courses offer work placements and there are some opportunities to study abroad in Europe, Canada and the USA.

Roehampton The University manages its academic programmes in eight Schools – Arts and Business, Social Sciences and Computing, Education Studies, English and Modern Languages, Humanities and Cultural Studies, Initial Teacher Education, Sports Science and Psychological and Therapeutic Studies. All programmes operate within a modular and semester-based structure.

St Andrews A very wide range of subjects is offered across the Faculties of Arts, Divinity, Medicine and Science. A flexible programme is offered in the first two years when students take several subjects. The decision of Honours degree subject is made at the end of Year 2 when students choose between single or joint Honours degrees for the next two years. A broadly-based general degree programme is also offered lasting three years.

Salford The University offers BA, BSc and BEng degrees with teaching methods depending on the degree. There is a wide range of professionally accredited programmes many involving work placements. All undergraduates may study a foreign language. Subjects include Accountancy and Business, Art and Design, Computer Science, Drama, Engineering, Humanities, Journalism, Leisure and Tourism, Languages, Music, Nursing, Physiotherapy, Psychology, Sciences, Social Sciences and Sport Science.

Sheffield The teaching year consists of two semesters (two periods of 15 weeks). Courses are fully modular, with the exceptions of Dentistry and Medicine. Students register for a named degree course which has a number of core modules, some optional modules chosen from a prescribed range of topics and some unrestricted modules chosen from any at the University. Programmes offered include Accounting and Business, Arts and Humanities, Computer Science, Engineering and Materials Science, Languages, Law, Nursing, Psychology, Sciences, Social Sciences and Town and Country Planning.

Sheffield Hallam A large number of vocational courses are offered in addition to those in Arts, Humanities and Social Sciences. The University is the largest provider of sandwich courses in the UK with most courses offering work placements, usually between the second and third years. Most students are able to study an additional language from French, German, Italian, Spanish and Japanese.

Southampton A wide range of courses is offered in the Faculties of Law, Arts and Social Sciences, Engineering, Science and Mathematics and Medicine, Health and Life Sciences. Programmes are generally for three years. All students have the chance to study a language as part of their degree and there are many opportunities for students to study abroad or on Erasmus-Socrates exchange programmes whether or not they are studying modern languages.

Southampton Solent Courses are offered in the Faculties of Technology, Media, Arts and Society and the Southampton Business School. Subjects cover Art and Design, Business and Finance including Accountancy, Marketing and Personnel, Computing, Construction, Engineering and Technology, the Environment, Human and Social Sciences and Law, Leisure, Sport and Tourism, Maritime Studies and Media, Film and Journalism.

Staffordshire The Stafford campus focuses on courses in Computing, Engineering, Technology and Health Studies whilst at Stoke programmes are offered in Art and Design, Law, Business, Humanities, Social Sciences and Science subjects. Single and joint Honours awards are available, some of which are for four years and include a work placement year. Part-time courses are also offered.

Stirling A flexible system operates in which students can delay their final degree choice until midway through the course. The University year is divided into two 15-week semesters, from September to December and February to May with a reading/study block and exams at the end of each semester. Innovative February entry is possible to some degree programmes. There are 250 degree combinations with the opportunity to study a range of disciplines in the first two years. In addition to single and combined Honours degrees, there is a General degree which allows for greater breadth of choice. Subjects range across the Arts, Social Sciences and Sciences.

Strathclyde A credit-based modular system operates with a good degree of flexibility in course choices. The University offers many vocational courses in the Faculties of Engineering, Science and the Strathclyde Business School. There are also degree programmes in Arts subjects, Education, Law and the Social Sciences.

Sunderland There are five Schools of study: Arts, Media and Culture, Business, Computer Science and Technology and single, joint Honours and sandwich courses. A modular programme provides maximum flexibility in choosing appropriate subjects. Some placements are possible in Canada, USA, Australia, New Zealand, India and Europe and there is a large number of mature and local students.

Surrey Degree programmes are offered in the Arts, Biomedical and Molecular Sciences, Electronics and Physical Sciences, Engineering, Health and Medical Sciences, Human Sciences and Management. Some 80% of students spend a professional training year as part of their course and in some cases there are placements abroad. There is also a part-time BSc degree in Professional Development through work based learning.

Sussex Teaching is structured around five Schools of study, the Brighton and Sussex Medical School and the Science and Technology Policy Research Unit. Courses cover a wide range of subjects in Humanities, Life Sciences, Science and Technology, Social Sciences and Cultural Studies. Students are registered in a School depending on the degree taken. The flexible structure allows students to interrupt their degree programme to take a year out.

Swansea Courses are offered in Arts and Social Sciences, Business, Economics and Law, Engineering, Languages, Medicine and Health Sciences and Science. Degree courses are modular with the opportunity to take some subjects outside the chosen degree course. Part-time degrees are available and study-abroad arrangements are possible in several subject areas.

Teesside Single and combined Honours degrees are offered with the major subject occupying two thirds of the course and the minor option one third. There is a wide choice of vocational courses, many with sandwich arrangements in industry, commerce and the professions. Courses are offered in the Arts, Business, Engineering, Law, Media, Social Sciences and Sport with large Schools of Health and Social Care and Computing and Mathematics. There is a high mature student intake.

Thames Valley Subjects offered cover Business, Management and Law, Tourism, Hospitality and Leisure, Music, Media and Creative Technologies and Health and Human Sciences. Credit-rated single and joint Honours courses are offered, many with year-long work placements between Years 2 and 3. There are some study-abroad arrangements in Europe, Canada and the USA and there is a large mature student intake.

Ulster Faculties of Arts, Business and Management, Engineering and Built Environment, Life and Health Sciences and Social Sciences offer a wide range of courses. There are various styles of learning supported by formal lectures and many courses include periods of work placement.

Warwick Courses are offered by Departments in the Faculty of Arts, Science and Social Studies, the Warwick Business School, the Warwick Institute of Education and the Leicester Warwick Medical School. Students may choose single subject degrees or combine several subjects in a joint degree. Options offered in each course provide flexibility in the choice of subjects although courses are not fully modularised. Many degrees offer the opportunity to study abroad and work placements on some science courses.

West Scotland The University (created from the merger of University of Paisley and Bell College in August 2007) is a leading provider of vocational education in the region, offering industry-relevant and career-focused courses, and many programmes include periods of paid work placements. There are also some European and US study opportunities. Courses are offered in the Business School and the Schools of Computing, Education, Engineering and Science, Health, Nursing and Midwifery and Media, Language and Music.

Westminster Courses cover Architecture and the Built Environment, Biosciences, Business Management, Complementary Therapies, Computer Sciences, Electronics, English and Linguistics, Languages, Law, Media and Arts and Design and Psychology and Social Sciences. Undergraduate courses are modular and taught over two semesters. The University has a broad network of partnerships within the EU which enables students to include a period of study abroad as part of their degree.

Winchester Single and two-subject courses are offered consisting of either one subject, or two subjects studied equally (a joint Honours degree) or a 75%–25% split by way of a main and subsidiary Honours degree. Courses are offered in American Studies, Archaeology, Business, Dance, Drama and Performance, Education, English and Creative Writing, Film Studies, History, Horticulture, Journalism and Media Studies, Marketing, Psychology, Sport Science, Theology and Tourism.

Wolverhampton A large number of specialist and joint Honours degrees are offered and many have work placements at home or abroad. Except for courses linked to specific professional requirements, programmes are modular providing flexibility of choice. Courses include Art and Design, Arts and Humanities, Business Studies, Computer Science, Education, Engineering, Environmental Studies, Film and Media, Health Studies, Law, Nursing, Sciences and Social Studies.

Worcester The courses are grouped into six departments: Applied Sciences, Geography and Archaeology, Arts, Humanities and Social Sciences, the Institute of Education, the Institute of Health and Social Care, the School of Sports Science and the Worcester Business School.

York There is a flexible range of subject options in a range of combined courses. The 'Languages for All' programme enables any student to take a course in any one of 14 languages, in addition to which there are several opportunities to build a period abroad into a degree course. Courses are offered in Archaeology, Arts subjects, Computer Science, Economics, Education, Electronics, Health Sciences, Languages, Management, Medicine, Music, Psychology, Sciences and Social Sciences.

York St John Specialist degrees and joint Honours courses are offered in American Studies, Business, Communication, Counselling, Design, Education, English, Film Studies, History, Information Technology, Media Studies, Occupational Therapy, Performance Physiotherapy, Psychology, Sport and Theology.

COLLEGES AND THEIR COURSES

In addition to the large numbers of universities offering degree courses, there are over 100 colleges admitting several thousands of students each on full degree courses. These include University Colleges, Institutes, Colleges of Higher Education, Colleges of Further and Higher Education and specialist colleges of Agriculture and Horticulture, Art, Drama, and Music.

Larger institutions will offer a range of single subject, joint and combined courses leading to BA, BSc and BEd degrees whilst the smaller colleges may only offer one or two degree programmes. A large number, however, also provide Foundation degrees which lead on to full or part-time degree courses. These colleges are listed in the subject tables.

4 | SANDWICH DEGREE COURSES AND PROFESSIONAL PLACEMENTS

EMPLOYMENT AND FINANCIAL BENEFITS

Sandwich courses (or professional or work placements) have been offered for over 30 years. Unfortunately, because the great majority of these placements are still offered by the newer universities, many applicants regard them as 'insurance' choices, considering them to be of less importance than traditional three year Honours degrees. How wrong they are!

You are in the process of considering a degree course which you hope will provide you with employment and a good preparation for a future career. In the end, and depending on your personality, your ability to organise your time, to work in a team, to be able to communicate well and your motivation (all qualities more important than some degrees), you will succeed.

It's true that a three-year Honours degree course may enable you to develop some of these qualities. However, to experience the real demands of your future employers, the only way in which to gain first-hand experience during your degree studies is by following a sandwich course.

There's also another important point to consider: the overall costs of three or four years at university. Together with tuition fees and your annual living costs (see **Chapter 5**) you are investing quite a large amount of money in getting your degree. Consequently, it's worth looking at some of the advantages of spending a year out of your university course working for an employer. It can be quite profitable as well as offering a number of other benefits.

Students report . . .
'I was able to earn £15,000 during my year out and £4000 during my three-month vacation with the same firm.' (**Bath** Engineering)

'There's really no other better way to find out what you want to do for your future career than having tried it for a year.' (**Aston** Human Resources Management)

'It was a welcome break in formal university education: I met some great people including students from other universities.' (**Kingston** Biochemistry)

'Having experienced a year in a working environment, I am more confident and more employable than students without this experience.' (**Aston** Business Studies)

'At Sanolfi in Toulouse, I learned to think on my feet – no two days were the same.' (**Aston** European Studies)

'I have seen how an organisation works at first-hand, learned how academic skills may be applied in a working environment, become proficient in the use of various software, acquired new skills in interpersonal relationships and communications and used my period away to realign my career perspectives.' (**Aston** European Studies)

'I was working alongside graduate employees and the firm offered me a job when I graduated.' (**Bath** Mathematics)

Employers, too, gain from having students . . .
'We meet a lot of enthusiastic potential recruits who bring new ideas into the firm, and we can offer them commercially sponsored help for their final year project.'

'The quality of this student has remained high throughout the year. He will do well for his next employer, whoever that may be. However, I sincerely hope that it will be with us.'

University staff advise . . .

'We refer to sandwich courses as professional placements, not "work experience" which is a phrase we reserve for short non-professional experiences, for example summer or pre-university jobs. The opportunity is available to all students but their success in gaining a good placement depends on academic ability.' (**Bath**)

'Where a placement year is optional, those who opt for it are more likely to be awarded a First or an Upper Second compared to those who don't, not because they are given more marks for doing it, but because they always seem to have added context and motivation for their final year.' (**Aston**)

When choosing your sandwich course, check with the university (a) that the institution will guarantee a list of employers (b) whether placement experience counts towards the final degree result (c) that placements are paid (d) that placements are validated by professional bodies.

Finally, once you start on the course, remember that your first year examination results will count towards placements in those jobs which are closely related to the subject you are studying. It is important to note also that many good firms want students who are heading for a 2i degree.

COURSE AND PLACEMENT DIFFERENCES

The following replies to a questionnaire were received from some universities offering sandwich courses. They give you a useful glimpse of the differences between universities in the ways their sandwich courses and placements are organised.

How many companies are contacted on behalf of students?

Aston (Biol) 15+; (Bus) 1000; (Eng) 150; (Mech Eng) 50. **Bath** (Chem) 150; (Mech Elec Eng) 50; (Mech Eng) 200; (Maths) Many; (Phys) 60. **Brunel** 500–600. **Cardiff (UWIC)** (Yth Work) 40. **Kingston** (Bus Law) Companies contact the University, 33 vacancies currently on the placement website; (Sci) 30–50. **Loughborough** (Civ Eng) 50; (Prod Des) 7.

How many students are placed each year?

Aston (Biol) 20–30; (Bus) c530; (Eng) 118; (Mech Eng) 30–40. **Bath** (Chem) 70 (80%); (Mech Elec Eng) 17 (re-organisation recently taken place); (Mech Eng) 90; (Maths) 40–70; (Phys) 35–40. **Brunel** (All) 900. **Cardiff (UWIC)** (Yth Work) 100; (Leis Mgt) 53; (Teaching) 60. **Kingston** (Bus Law) 75 (decline from 225 a few years ago: possible reason is the introduction of fees, and placements are now optional); (Sci) 30. **Loughborough** (Civ Eng) 140; (Prod Des) 50.

What percentage of students find their own companies?

Aston All attend interviews; (Bus) c20%; (Eng) 10%; (Mech Eng) 40–50. **Bath** (Chem) 5–10%; (Mech Elec Eng) One or two usually sponsored students; (Mech Eng) none; (Maths) Very few; (Phys) About one per year; placement officer makes 50% of applications for students, 50% apply on-line from details provided by the department. **Brunel** 10%. **Cardiff (UWIC)** (Yth Work) 90%. **Kingston** (Bus Law) Very few; (Sci) 590 (approx); **Loughborough** (Civ Eng) None; (Prod Des) 20%.

Which organisations take the most students?

Aston (Biol) NHS in various clinical departments (eg microbiology, biochemistry), Campden and Chorleywood Food Research Association, Merck, Masterfoods, Pfizer; (Bus) Intel, IBM, Microsoft, VW, BMW, Peugeot, Citroen; (Eng) IBM, General Motors, Reuters, BMW; (Mech Eng) Gooch Engine Control Systems. **Bath** (Chem) The major pharmaceutical companies, closely followed by the petrochemical industries; (Mech Eng) Varies from year to year; (Maths) Ernst & Young, PricewaterhouseCoopers, KPMG, IBM, Lloyds TSB, Goldman Sachs, Morgan Stanley, BAE Systems, Pfizer, GlaxoSmithKline, Departments of Work and Pensions, Health, Social Security, Trade and Industry; (Phys) Most organisations take one or two, with few exceptions (eg Rutherford Appleton Laboratory) who might take three or four in a good year. **Brunel** IBM, Walt Disney, British Airways, Xerox, Intel. **Cardiff (UWIC)** (Yth Work) LEA SE Wales, Safer Cardiff, Youth Offending Teams, Grassroots Youth Organisation (Clsrm Asst) Local primary schools. **Kingston** (Sci) Large pharmaceutical companies; (Bus Law) The Walt Disney Company, Toyota (GB) plc, Microsoft, BT. **Loughborough** (Civ Eng) Balfour Beatty, Kier, Laing, Nuttall; (Prod Des) Boots, Masterfoods, Artform International.

What is the duration of a placement?
Aston (Biol) 40–45 weeks; (Bus) 48 wks; (Eng) 44–52 weeks; (Mech Eng) 40–50 weeks. **Bath** (Chem) 44 weeks; (Mech Elec Eng) One year; (Mech Eng) 52–60 weeks; (Maths) 48 weeks; (Phys) 43 weeks min 60 weeks max. **Brunel** 44 weeks. **Cardiff (UWIC)** (Yth Work) Part-time course includes 12 weeks full-time; (Leis Mgt) 48 weeks; (Clsrm Asst) 12 weeks. **Kingston** (Sci) 9–12 months; (Bus Law) 48 weeks. **Loughborough** (Civ Eng) 4 weeks; (Prod Des) 45 weeks.

What do employers stipulate when considering students?
Aston (Biol) Successful second year undergraduates; (Bus) Number of UCAS points, degree programme, any prior experience; (Eng) UCAS points scores and expected degree classification; (Mech Eng) Students interviewed and selected by the company according to student ability, what they are studying and specific needs of the job. **Bath** (Chem) 'Good students': upper second or above and non-international students (those without work visas). Students with strong vivisection views rejected; (Mech Elec Eng) Subject-based, eg electronics, aerospace, computing and electrical engineering; (Mech Eng) Good communication, IT and social skills; (Maths) Interest in positions of responsibility, teamwork, integrity, self-motivation, analytical ability, communication, recent work experience, knowledge of the company, desire to work for the company; GCSE maths/English A/B, AL 300 UCAS points min (excluding general studies), predicted 2.1; (Phys) Many organisations have cut-offs regarding students first-year performance (eg must be heading for a 2i although some require better than this), some need students to be particularly good in some areas (eg lab work, computer programming), many require UK nationality with minimum residency condition. **Brunel** Requirements not usually specified except for IT jobs since they need technical skills. **Cardiff (UWIC)** (Clsrm Asst) Criminal Records Bureau (CRB) checks. **Kingston** (Bus Law) Theoretical knowledge and a stated interest in certain areas (eg finance, human resources, marketing, sales, IT), excellent communication skills, teamwork, ability to prioritise, time management and a professional attitude; (Sci) Grades are rarely mentioned: it's usually a specific module or course requirement undertaken by the students that they are looking for, as well as a good attitude, motivation, initiative: a good all-rounder. **Loughborough** (Civ Eng) Target specific courses.

Are students interviewed prior to placement?
Aston (Biol) Yes: we check their letters of application and review interview technique, working closely with careers advisors at the University; (Bus) No: companies undertake a thorough recruitment and selection processes including interviews; (Eng) No; (Mech Eng) No. **Bath** (Chem) Yes; (Mech Elec Eng) Yes; (Mech Eng) Yes; (Maths) Yes (advice given on CVs); (Phys) Yes. **Brunel** Mock interview service provided for those who need the practice. **Kingston** (Bus Law) Initial meetings; students apply direct and are encouraged to find and use their own contacts; (Sci) Yes. **Loughborough** (Civ Eng) No; (Prod Des) Yes: competitive interviews on receipt of CV and a covering letter.

What percentage of students visit their placement organisation prior to starting?
Aston (Biol) All; (Bus) All; (Eng) Most students except those going abroad; (Mech Eng) 100%. **Bath** (Chem) 40% and falling; (Mech Elec Eng) All; (Mech Eng) All; (Maths) Majority; if interviewed on campus often invited to visit workplace; (Phys) All; employers use interviews to select the best candidates. **Brunel** Students encouraged to see the place of work. **Kingston** (Bus Law) All; (Sci) Nearly all, since they are normally interviewed on the company premises. **Loughborough** (Prod Des) All.

How many students are placed overseas?

Aston (Biol) 2 (2007); (Mech Eng) No; (Bus) Yes; undergraduates taking degrees in International Business and Modern Languages or Management go abroad; (Eng) Europe (Germany, Holland, Belgium) and Asia (Hong Kong). **Bath** (Chem) Europe (most countries), North America, some (rare) Australia, New Zealand, South America; (Mech Elec Eng) Yes, with international companies; (Mech Eng) Some; (Maths) Some placements in Europe; (Phys) A small number, usually three per year, go to Germany, Switzerland, France, USA. (They tend to be paid less since they are regarded as students and get an allowance, whereas in the UK they are employees.) **Brunel** No. **Cardiff (UWIC)** (Leis Mgt) 21 USA, Canada, Brunei, China, Sri Lanka, Hong Kong, France, Bermuda. **Kingston** (Sci) Yes, in Europe on the Erasmus scheme (12 three-month placements) started in 2006/07 by the UK Erasmus Agency); other students may have contacts overseas and set up their own arrangements; (Bus Law) Students find their own placements abroad. **Loughborough** (Prod Des) Occasionally.

Do you receive a report on the student's performance from employers?

Aston (Biol) Yes; (Bus) We ask employers to complete an evaluation questionnaire, 80% do so; (Eng) Yes; (Mech Eng) No. **Bath** (Chem) Yes, several; (Mech Elec Eng) Yes; (Mech Eng) Yes; (Maths) Yes, three-monthly and six-monthly reports; (Phys) Yes. **Brunel** Most subject areas require students to complete a placement report. **Kingston** (Bus Law); Yes (Sci) Yes: once a tutor has visited the student on placement we send a form for completion. **Loughborough** (Civ Eng) Yes; (Prod Des) Yes.

What percentage of students receive payment from their employers?

Aston (Biol) 40–50% (much less than the average as many placements are NHS-related); (Bus) 99%; (Eng) Most are paid except those with charities or universities; (Mech Eng) 98%. **Bath** (Chem) All; (Mech Elec Eng) All; (Mech Eng) All; (Maths) All; (Phys) All. **Brunel** Varies between disciplines: most are paid except those studying Social Sciences and Law. **Kingston** (Bus Law) All; (Sci) 99%; (Prod Des) 99%.

What are the levels of payment?

Aston (Biol) £10,000–£13,000+; (Bus) Up to £32,000; (Eng) £9000–£18,000; (Mech Eng) £10,000–£15,000. **Bath** (Chem) £15,000–£19,000; (Mech Elec Eng) £13,500–£20,000; (Mech Eng) £13,000–£14,500; (Maths) £2000–£30,000 (average for 2006/2007 £17,026); (Phys) £13,000–£24,000 (average for science students £14,000: higher salaries for those working with financial institutions). **Brunel** £9000–£30,000. **Kingston** (Bus Law) £12,000–£16,000; (Sci) Anything from £10,000 to £16,000. **Loughborough** (Civ Eng) £14,000–£23,000; (Prod Des) £7000–£17,000.

What are the advantages of placements to the students?

Aston (Biol) Many take jobs with their placement employers (eg NHS), gaining valuable research and clinical experience; (Bus) Graduate job offers, sponsorship through the final year of the course, gym membership, staff discounts; (Eng) Some students are fast-tracked into full-time employment and, in some cases, have been given higher starting salaries as a result of the placement with the company; (Mech Eng) Offers of full-time employment on graduation, bursaries for their final year of study, final year projects following placements, better class of degree. **Bath** (Chem) Sponsorships for final year project work, offers of full-time employment, PhD offers and work-to-study courses, industrial references, establishment of prizes; (Maths) Sponsorship in the second year, graduate employment, bonuses during placement, travel abroad during placement, sponsorship during final year; (Phys) Job offers on graduation, sponsored final year, improved study skills for final year, job market awareness, career decisions. **Brunel** Higher percentage of students get Firsts, many students get a job offer from the placement provider, higher salaries often paid to sandwich course students, some students get exemptions from professional exams, eg ACCA, ACA and IMechE. **Cardiff (UWIC)** (Clsrm Asst) Good experience in team work, classroom experience, coaching, mentoring: decisions made whether or not to follow a teaching career. **Kingston** (Bus Law) Sponsorships fewer these days but students return with more confidence and maturity and better able to complete their final year; 60% receive job offers on completion of a successful placement; (Sci) Full-time employment on graduation and occasionally part-time work in the final year; many students are encouraged to write their final year dissertation whilst on placement and benefit from the company's support, subject matter and validation. **Loughborough** (Civ Eng) Most students are sponsored by their firms and perform better in their final examinations; (Prod Des) Final year bursary for some students, offer of employment by the sponsor and a final year design project for the sponsor.

Media coverage on student debt and the recent introduction of tuition fees (see **Chapter 5**) highlight the importance of sandwich courses, and the information above from just a few gives you a useful insight into the differences between universities in the ways their sandwich courses and placements are organised. Many sandwich and placement courses are on offer, in which industrial, commercial and public sector placements take place in the third year of a four-year degree course. For example, there is the Work-Based Learning (WBL) programme which Chester University established several years ago, with some other institutions following suit, in which students take a WBL module in the second year of their degree course. This involves a placement lasting a few weeks when students can have the opportunity to try out possible careers. Other universities and colleges may offer longer placements of periods of six months with different employers for students taking vocational courses.

However, the most structured arrangements are known as 'professional placements' which a number of universities offer and which are very advantageous to students. Among the many universities with professional placements in their courses (see the subject tables in **Chapter 9** and university/college websites and prospectuses), **Imperial London** and **Cardiff** have an interesting range of placements in scientific subjects, and **Surrey** has a professional training programme in which most students spend the third year of their degree programme on a work placement. Although placements in some fields such as health, social care, education may be unpaid, in most cases a salary is paid. Where a placement is unpaid the placement period is shorter – 30 weeks – to allow students time to undertake paid work. While students are away from campus they also undertake a series of projects marked during the year by their tutors.

It is important to note that during the placement year students' tuition fees will be reduced by 50% except for those on one-year courses on the Erasmus programme when no fees are paid but student loans will still apply. Many universities in the UK have formal agreements with partner institutions in Europe through the Erasmus programme which enables UK university students to apply for courses in Europe for periods up to one year. Some of these courses are taught in English and students can receive help with accommodation and other expenses through the Erasmus Student Grant scheme. Tuition fees are only paid for courses lasting less than one year.

Once you have chosen your course subject(s) the next step is to find out how much it will cost you and **Chapter 5** provides information to help you do this.

5 | HOW MUCH WILL IT COST?

TUITION FEES AND OTHER COSTS

Tuition fees are now charged for Honours and Ordinary degree courses in England, Wales and Northern Ireland. The level of tuition fees charged for courses is decided annually by each individual university or college.

Most universities have set the annual fees for first degree courses at £3145 for 2008/9. However, the universities listed below have set the following fees:

* Greenwich £2560; £2050 for students from partner schools and colleges; £3000 for Pharmacy degrees
* Leeds Metropolitan £2000
* Northampton £2500
* Thames Valley £2770

Students domiciled in Scotland receive free tuition but Scottish students studying in universities elsewhere in the UK pay up to £3070. Students from England, Wales and Northern Ireland studying in Scotland pay a fee of £1735 (except for Medicine for which the fee is £2700).

Students domiciled in Wales studying in Welsh institutions receive a rebate and pay a fee of £1270 direct to the institution.

You may also have additional charges, depending on your course of study. For example, studio fees for Art courses could reach £250 per year, while for other courses, such as Architecture, Science and Engineering, there could be charges for equipment. Additionally, there could also be charges for fieldwork trips, study abroad and vacation courses. To find out your likely yearly course costs, in addition to your tuition fees, check with your subject department.

It is also important to check your fee status if you are planning a sandwich course involving either unpaid or paid placements. You can receive a salary of up to £12,000 doing a one-year placement but if you earn more than this you'll need to check your fee status carefully with your finance officer and consult the relevant websites listed below.

Useful websites   www.direct.gov.uk/studentfinance
www.saas.gov.uk
www.studentfinancewales.co.uk
www.studentfinanceni.co.uk

HELP TOWARDS TUITION FEES

Loans Students will not have to pay the fees before starting their courses or while they are studying: instead they will be eligible to apply for a student loan. These range from £3145 to £6475 for 2008/9, depending on whether they will live at home or away from home, in or outside London. New, full-time higher education students may also be eligible for a student loan of up to £6475 for 2008/9 to help towards accommodation and other living costs. Loans must be repaid after leaving university when earnings exceed £15,000.

Maintenance grants These government grants are available, depending on the student's household income. They are paid on a sliding scale to students where the family income is between £17,910 and £37,425: the maximum grant is £2835 per annum for 2008/9. These grants are not repayable.

University bursaries These are usually paid in cases of financial need: all universities charging course fees are obliged to offer some bursaries to students receiving maintenance grants. See the list of universities later in this chapter for the value of their bursaries.

Other financial help Some universities also offer additional bursaries to encourage applications from the locality. These may be available to students applying from partner schools or colleges and living in certain postcode areas, in some cases to the brothers and sisters of current students at the university, or to students who have been in care or are homeless. These awards are not repayable.

In addition, students on some Health-related courses, for example Dental Hygiene, Nursing, Occupational Therapy, Physiotherapy, Radiography will be eligible for NHS bursaries. Other bursaries are also payable for programmes funded through the General Social Care Council and also for shortage subjects for those on teacher training courses.

After starting the course, Access to Learning funds are available to help students in financial hardship or through emergency payments for unexpected financial crises. Hardship funds are also offered in very special cases, particularly for students with children or for single parents, mature students and, in particular, students with disabilities who may also claim disability living allowance. These payments are made in instalments or as a lump sum or as a short-term loan.

Scholarships These are usually merit-based and are often competitive although some universities offer valuable scholarships to any new entrant who has achieved top grades at A-level. Scholarships vary considerably and are often subject-specific, offered through faculties or departments, so check the availability of any awards with the subject departmental head. Additionally, there are often music, choral and organ awards, and scholarships and bursaries for sporting achievement.

LIVING COSTS

Most students spend their first year in university accommodation, the costs of which differ between universities. Halls of residence vary in the facilities they provide, and may offer single or shared study bedrooms, in some cases en suite, with meals in some cases included. Average rent prices for one week vary, depending on the location of the university, ranging from £40 in some parts of the country to £70 in London.

The following is a very generalised breakdown of how living expenses might be allocated on a monthly basis:

✱	Rent	£300
✱	Utility bills (water, gas, electricity)	£30
✱	Telephone calls	£30
✱	Food/housekeeping	£170
✱	Local travel	£45
✱	Insurance	£5
✱	Books/stationery	£40
✱	Clothing	£30
✱	Miscellaneous (healthcare etc)	£40
✱	Socialising/leisure	£90
	Monthly total	**£780**
	Total for academic year	**£7800**

Finally, remember that price reductions are available to students at some shops, cinemas, museums and galleries and on local bus and train travel. Contact the National Union of Students for details.

Full details of bursaries and scholarships can be found in *University Scholarships, Awards and Bursaries* (see **Appendix 3**).

UNIVERSITIES' BURSARIES AND AWARDS

The list below gives brief information about the approximate value of bursaries offered to students per year receiving maintenance grants as well as brief notes on the availability of scholarships. An annual 'cost of living' figure is also given although this must only be regarded as approximate since much depends on the individual student's preferences in terms of accommodation and lifestyle. (NB Bursary amounts are continually under review – check websites.)

Aberdeen *Fees:* see www.student-support-saas.gov.uk. *Entrance bursaries:* academic merit £1000. Entrance and subject-specific awards available. *Living costs:* £6000.

Abertay Dundee *Fees:* see www.student-support-saas.gov.uk. *Bursaries:* mature student bursaries. Some financial awards and assistance for mature students. *Living costs:* £5000.

Aberystwyth *Bursaries:* £200–£1000 (see www.studentfinancewales.co.uk). Widening Participation bursaries to students from low-income families. Entrance scholarships and a large number of other awards. *Living costs:* £6000.

Anglia Ruskin *Bursaries:* £305. Academic progress awards £2000 over three years of study. Foundation and sport awards. *Living costs:* £6800.

Arts London *Bursaries:* standard bursaries of £300 and Access bursaries of up to £1000. *Living costs:* £10,000.

Aston *Bursaries:* up to £750; £1000 allowance for students on placement. Subject-specific scholarships for some degree courses £750. *Living costs:* £7000.

Bangor *Bursaries:* £50–£3000 (see www.studentfinancewales.co.uk). Subject-specific and music awards for Welsh students. *Living costs:* £5500. 'One of the cheapest places in Britain to be a student' (*The Independent*).

Bath *Bursaries:* £300–£1500. Several subject-specific, sport and choral awards available. *Living costs:* £7500.

Bath Spa *Bursaries:* up to £1150. Subject-specific scholarships of £1000 for some courses. *Living costs:* £7500.

Bedfordshire *Bursaries:* £305–£800. Living costs £6500.

Birmingham *Bursaries:* £820. Students from low-income backgrounds achieving 340 UCAS points £1230. Subject-specific, music and sport awards. *Living costs:* £7500.

Birmingham City *Bursaries:* £500 for all students receiving a maintenance grant. Music and choral scholarships and several subject-specific awards. *Living costs:* £7500.

Bolton *Bursaries:* £50–£310. Awards for students from partner institutions. *Living costs:* £7000.

Bournemouth *Bursaries:* £305. Some scholarships open to all students. *Living costs:* £8000.

Bradford *Bursaries:* all students on full or partial grants will receive £500 (1st year), £700 (2nd year), £900 (3rd year). Engineering, science and cricket awards. *Living costs:* £7500.

Brighton *Bursaries:* £510–£1020. Disabled athletics scholarships (£1000) and some sports scholarships open to all students. *Living costs:* £8000.

Bristol *Bursaries:* £715–£1125; also bursaries for students from local schools. A large number of subject-specific scholarships are available. *Living costs:* £6500–£8500.

Bristol UWE *Bursaries:* £750–£1250. Access courses students £1250. Memorial bursary for financially restricted students taking Computer Science. Music, sport and a small number of subject-specific awards. *Living costs:* £6500–£8500.

Brunel *Bursaries:* £200–£305 (students on part-time courses £150). Several scholarships open to all students; scholarships also for students from low income or socio-economic groups, ethnic minorities, students with disabilities and for students in the Widening Participation scheme covering schools in local areas. *Living costs:* £8000.

Buckingham *Fees:* £26,500 per degree course (two years or three years). Some awards available for students resident in neighbouring counties. *Living costs:* £7150.

Bucks New *Bursaries:* All students receive £500 per year (non-repayable) for each year of the course. *Living costs:* £7000.

Cambridge *Bursaries:* Up to £3100 per annum. Some funds for students with disabilities. Scholarships and College awards open to all students. *Living costs:* £7500.

Canterbury Christ Church *Bursaries:* £410–£820. Musical scholarships. *Living costs:* £7000.

Cardiff *Bursaries:* £300–£1000 (see www.studentfinancewales.co.uk). Some awards for students with disabilities. Subject-specific scholarships available including Welsh applicant awards. *Living costs:* £7700. 'A low-cost university' (NUS).

Central Lancashire *Bursaries:* £1000 to all students from homes in which the principal earner's income is less than £60,000. Some academic and golf scholarships. *Living costs:* £6500.

Chester *Bursaries:* £1000. Music, choral and sport scholarships available. *Living costs:* £7500.

Chichester *Bursaries:* £250–£1023. Sports scholarships. *Living costs:* £8000.

City *Bursaries:* £1000 for students receiving the full maintenance grant. Some charities award grants for students in need of financial assistance. Some special grants for living costs. Some scholarships available. *Living costs:* £10,000.

Coventry *Bursaries:* £500–£750. Academic awards and 'Star' scholarships for certain courses. *Living costs:* £7000.

Cumbria *Bursaries:* £100–£300. *Living costs:* £7000.

De Montfort *Bursaries:* £300–£500. Some academic and opportunity scholarships available. *Living costs:* £8000.

Derby *Bursaries:* £200–£800. Some Compact bursaries and awards for students living in the DE postcode area from low-income families. *Living costs:* £6800.

Dundee (see www.saas.gov.uk) Several subject-specific scholarships are available. *Living costs:* £7000.

Durham *Bursaries:* £600–£3000. Choral, organ, cricket and subject awards. *Living costs:* £5000 plus college fees.

East Anglia *Bursaries:* £300–£600. Some scholarships available. *Living costs:* £6800.

East London *Bursaries:* £305 for students receiving the full maintenance grant. On completion of the first semester, £500 of vouchers or credits to be spent with a range of agreed suppliers. Achievement and progress bursaries. *Living costs:* £9500.

TIP

Use email rather than mobile phones to contact friends.

Edge Hill *Bursaries:* £510–£1025 for those on state support and £1000 to new students with brothers or sisters already on courses at the university. Also Excellence scholarships. *Living costs:* £5500.

Edinburgh *Fees:* see www.student-support-saas.gov.uk. Subject-related awards and scholarships for Scottish students. *Living costs:* £7500.

Essex *Bursaries:* £1250–£3000. Bursaries for refugees and children of refugees and an award to mature students returning to study after several years and resident in south-east Essex. Mathematics and sport scholarships available. *Living costs:* £8300.

Exeter *Bursaries:* £305–£2000. Several scholarships available for students from the south-west and also choral and organ scholarships. *Living costs:* £7000.

Glamorgan *Bursaries:* £300 (see www.studentfinancewales.co.uk). Widening Participation grants. Several scholarships available. *Living costs:* £7500.

Glasgow *Fees:* see www.student-support-saas.gov.uk. Sport, organ and choral scholarships. *Living costs:* £8000.

Glasgow Caledonian *Fees:* see www.student-support-saas.gov.uk. Sport bursaries. *Living costs:* £8000.

Gloucestershire *Bursaries:* 35% of maintenance grant plus £305 for those on the full grant living outside Gloucestershire. £100 for new students from Compact schools. Annual rebate of 10% of fees to those who progress to the next level of their course. *Living costs:* £6700.

Greenwich *Fees:* MPharm £3000; all other degree programmes £2500. Partner colleges £2000. *Bursaries:* £300 for MPharm students on the full maintenance grant. £500 for mature students and for other students dependent on satisfactory progress. *Living costs:* £9500.

Heriot-Watt *Fees:* see www.student-support-saas.gov.uk. Several scholarships available. *Living costs:* £6300.

Hertfordshire *Bursaries:* 50% of the maintenance grant up to a total of £1350. Academic and Science and Engineering awards for entrants with 280–340 UCAS points. *Living costs:* £6500.

Huddersfield *Bursaries:* £500–£1000. Some subject-specific awards available. *Living costs:* £6000.

Hull *Bursaries:* £500–£1000. Part-time study bursaries. Subject-specific scholarships and awards available to students from local areas. A large number of scholarships available. *Living costs:* £6500.

Imperial London *Bursaries:* £100–£4000. Holligrave scholarships for students from educationally and financially disadvantaged backgrounds. Subject scholarships available. *Living costs:* £10,000.

Keele *Bursaries:* £305 towards fees; bursaries also for students from backgrounds with little or no tradition of higher education and for students from rural areas who need to live on campus because of transport difficulties (£500 for each year of study). Ethnic minority bursaries. Keele-link bursaries for students from partner schools. Some scholarships and bursaries open to all students. *Living costs:* £9000.

Kent *Bursaries:* £250–£1000. Academic excellence, sport and music scholarships. *Living costs:* £8500.

TIP

Get books from the library or secondhand shops.

Kingston *Bursaries:* £305–£1000. Scholarships for students from associate colleges and awards for students taking shortage subjects in the School of Education. *Living costs:* £9000.

Lampeter *Bursaries:* see www.studentfinancewales.co.uk. Scholarships and other awards available. *Living costs:* £5500.

Lancaster *Bursaries:* £500–£1005. Scholarships and subject awards. *Living costs:* £6500.

Leeds *Bursaries:* £310–£1300. Special awards for students in financial difficulties. Further scholarships available. *Living costs:* £9000.

Leeds Metropolitan *Fees:* £2000 per year. Sports bursaries. *Living costs:* £9000.

Leicester *Bursaries:* £100–£1305. First-year and subject-specific scholarships. *Living costs:* £7500.

Lincoln *Bursaries:* up to £600 depending on maintenance support; £500 for each year completed; £500 Faculty award. *Living costs:* £7500.

Liverpool *Bursaries:* £1000–£1300. Attainment scholarships in a range of scientific and engineering subjects. *Living costs:* £7500.

Liverpool Hope *Bursaries:* £700–£1000. £400 for students not entitled to a maintenance grant. Some achievement and excellence awards. *Living costs:* £7500.

Liverpool John Moores *Bursaries:* £410–£1025 for all students in receipt of a maintenance grant. Some A-level and academic awards of £100–£10,000. *Living costs:* £7500.

London (Goldsmiths) *Bursaries:* £100–£1000. Scholarships for students from the London area. Academic and music scholarships. *Living costs:* £10,000.

London (Heythrop) *Bursaries:* £300–£1350. *Living costs:* £10,000.

London (King's) *Bursaries:* £600–£1000. King's myBursary matches 50% of maintenance grant. Scholarships available. *Living costs:* £10,000.

London (London School of Economics and Political Science) *Bursaries:* up to £2500. Some scholarships available. *Living costs:* £10,000.

London (Queen Mary) *Bursaries:* £800–£1000; up to £4000 for high achievers. Some scholarships available. *Living costs:* £10,000.

London (Royal Holloway) *Bursaries:* £500 for all students receiving less than full grants. *Living costs:* £10,000.

London (Royal Veterinary College) *Bursaries:* £1500 for Veterinary Nursing degree. Bursaries for students wishing to join the Royal Army Veterinary Corps. *Living costs:* £8800–£10,000.

London (St George's) *Bursaries:* £150–£1200. *Living costs:* £10,000.

London (School of Oriental and African Studies) *Bursaries:* £400–£700. *Living costs:* £10,000.

London (School of Pharmacy) *Bursaries:* contact the School. *Living costs:* £10,000.

London (University College London) *Bursaries:* Up to £2500 to match 50% of the maintenance grant. Denys Holland scholarship for students experiencing financial difficulty. Academic scholarships available. *Living costs:* £10,000.

London Metropolitan *Bursaries:* pro-rata amounts payable depending on the maintenance grant; minimum bursary £300. Bursary for students with a family member enrolled at the University. *Living costs:* £10,000.

London South Bank *Bursaries:* minimum £300. All students receive £500 in the first year and £750 in Years 2 and 3. Competitive scholarships for students from one of four local colleges and some ethnic minority awards. Science and Engineering scholarships. *Living costs:* £10,000.

Loughborough *Bursaries:* up to £1300 with other bursaries fixed on a sliding scale dependent on the level of the maintenance grant. Higher bursaries for students over 21. Over 100 renewable and merit-based scholarships worth 25% of the tuition fee. Military sponsorships. *Living costs:* £6500.

Manchester *Bursaries:* up to £1000 for students with a family annual income below £26,000. Advantage scholarship of £5000 for all students with three grade As at A-level from households with an annual income of £17,500 or less. Several other scholarships based on academic merit. *Living costs:* £8500.

Manchester Metropolitan *Bursaries:* £305–£1000. *Living costs:* £8500.

Middlesex *Bursaries:* dependent on the level of the maintenance grant; £300 minimum. Merit-based scholarships. *Living costs:* £9000–£10,000.

Napier *Fees:* see www.student-support-saas.gov.uk. Scholarships for students from state schools. *Living costs:* £7000.

Newcastle *Bursaries:* £600–£900. A wide range of merit-based scholarships. *Living costs:* £7600.

Newport *Bursaries:* see www.studentfinancewales.co.uk. Bursaries for some students in the School of Education, partner schools and those seeking childcare support. *Living costs:* £5500.

Northampton *Fees:* £2500. *Bursaries:* Up to £1000 for students paying the full tuition fee depending on family income and/or home postcode. Additional funds are available from the Access to Learning Fund, the Emergency Loan Fund and the Bridging Loan Fund. Awards range from £300 to £3500. Other merit awards are also offered. *Living costs:* £6500.

Northumbria *Bursaries:* minimum £300 for all students receiving the full maintenance grant. Some scholarships available. *Living costs:* £7600.

Nottingham *Bursaries:* £250–£1025 depending on the level of the maintenance grant. 'First in the Family' and other awards and scholarships. *Living costs:* £7600.

Nottingham Trent *Bursaries:* £205–£1025 for students on partial state support plus £250 per annum for those on full state support with a family and an NG postcode; £2000 merit-based scholarships for those on full state support. Part-time and other merit scholarships. *Living costs:* £7000.

Oxford *Bursaries:* £3000 in Year 1 and £2600 in Years 2 and 3 for students on the maximum maintenance grant. Other bursaries for those on partial grants between £2500 and £100. Scholarships and college awards offered. *Living costs:* £9200.

Oxford Brookes *Bursaries:* £200–£1500 depending on the level of the maintenance grant. Some subject scholarships. *Living costs:* £9200.

Paisley See **West Scotland** below.

Plymouth *Bursaries:* £305–£500 for students in schools and colleges receiving educational maintenance allowances; also bursaries for mature students. Some sport scholarships. *Living costs:* £7500.

Portsmouth *Bursaries:* £510–£1120. *Living costs:* £7500.

Queen Margaret *Fees:* see www.student-support-saas.gov.uk. Some partial scholarships for self-funding international students.

Queen's Belfast *Bursaries:* £500–£1000. Entrance, organ, sport and some special awards for students with financial difficulties. *Living costs:* £7500.

Reading *Bursaries:* £330–£1320. Entrance scholarships for some degree courses. *Living costs:* £6000.

Robert Gordon *Fees:* see www.student-support-saas.gov.uk. *Living costs:* £6000.

Roehampton *Bursaries:* up to £870. Some scholarships available. *Living costs:* £8500.

St Andrews *Fees:* see www.student-support-saas.gov.uk. A number of scholarships available. *Living costs:* £7500.

Salford *Bursaries:* £650–£1000. Several scholarships. *Living costs:* £8500.

Sheffield *Bursaries:* £400–£600 for students with high grades at A-level, those from Outreach and Access to Medicine schemes. A range of scholarships available. *Living costs:* £7000.

Sheffield Hallam *Bursaries:* £300–£700. Memorial bursaries for students from South Yorkshire and North Humberside. *Living costs:* £7000.

Southampton *Bursaries:* £500–£1000. Additional bursaries for some students from Hampshire and the Isle of Wight; 30 bursaries of £1000 for students on the six-year BMed programme. Scholarships based on academic excellence. *Living costs:* £7500.

Southampton Solent *Bursaries:* £50–£1025. *Living costs:* £7500.

Staffordshire *Bursaries:* up to £500–£1000. Awards for students from partner colleges in Staffordshire, Cheshire and Shropshire and for some students over 21 enrolling on Level 1 courses. *Living costs:* £7500.

Stirling *Fees:* see www.student-support-saas.gov.uk. Sports scholarships. *Living costs:* £5500.

Strathclyde *Fees:* see www.student-support-saas.gov.uk. Sports scholarships and Engineering awards. *Living costs:* £8000.

Sunderland *Bursaries:* £525. Some Engineering scholarships. *Living costs:* £5500.

Surrey *Bursaries:* £310–£1020. Scholarships for some shortage subjects and/or based on academic criteria. *Living costs:* £7000.

Sussex *Bursaries:* £1000 for students on the full maintenance grant. Several merit-based scholarships available. *Living costs:* £8000.

Swansea *Bursaries:* see www.studentfinancewales.co.uk. New-entrant scholarships and Millennium scholarships based on merit, disability or special needs worth £1125. Subject-specific scholarships. *Living costs:* £5500.

Teesside *Bursaries:* £500–£1300 for students on full or partial maintenance grants. £500 for all new students except those on specially funded courses; 250 subject or merit-based scholarships for Year 1 students up to a maximum of £1000. Elite Athletic bursary. *Living costs:* £5500.

Thames Valley *Fees:* £2700. *Bursaries:* £1000 for students on a maintenance grant, £500 for all other new UK or EU students. *Living costs:* £9000.

Ulster *Bursaries:* up to £1020. Some merit-based scholarships. *Living costs:* £5500.

Warwick *Bursaries:* up to £3000. Music and sports scholarships. *Living costs:* £6500.

TIP

Set a spending limit on your nights out.

West Scotland *Fees:* see www.student-support-saas.gov.uk. A small number of scholarships. *Living costs:* £6500.

Westminster *Bursaries:* £300 (up to £1365 for students with dependants). Some scholarships available for Foundation and part-time courses. *Living costs:* £9400.

Winchester *Bursaries:* £310–£820 plus a Winchester scholarship for all students (£300 to £400 annually). Scholarships for students from partner schools and for those who have been under childcare arrangements since the age of 14. Also awards for living and day-to-day expenses for some students. *Living costs:* £7500.

Wolverhampton *Bursaries:* up to £300–£1500 discount on fees for students on 'Aim Higher' route. Some Excellence scholarships in Science and Engineering. *Living costs:* £6000.

Worcester *Bursaries:* up to £725. Excellence scholarships awarded at the end of Year 1. *Living costs:* £6000.

York *Bursaries:* £600–£1400. Several subject-specific awards. *Living costs:* £6500.

York St John *Bursaries:* £1000–£1500. *Living costs:* £6500.

6 | APPLICATIONS

ENTRY REQUIREMENTS

Before applying to universities and colleges, applicants should check that by the time they plan to start their course they will have the required qualifications. Details of entry requirements are available direct from the universities and colleges. Applicants will need to fulfil:

(i)   the **general** entry requirements for courses;

(ii) any **specific** subject requirements to enter a particular course, for example, study of specified GCE A- and/or AS-levels, Scottish Highers/Advanced Highers, GCSEs, Scottish Standard Grades, or BTEC qualifications (for example, National Diploma, National Certificate). The course requirements are set out in prospectuses and on websites.

(iii) any **age**, **health**, **Criminal Records Bureau (CRB) clearance** or **other** requirements for entry to particular courses and universities and colleges. For entry to some specific courses such as Medicine and Nursing, offers are made subject to health screening for hepatitis B, for example, and immunisation requirements. Owing to recent Government regulations, some universities will now insist on a minimum age at entry of 18 years. Also, for some courses, CRB clearance is required, so check university and college websites and prospectuses for these particular course requirements.

(iv) **admissions tests** which are now required by a number of universities for a range of subjects, including Dentistry, Law, Medicine and Veterinary Science/Medicine. Offers of places made by these universities are dependent on an applicant's performance in the relevant test. It is important to find out full details about universities' course requirements for possible admissions tests well before submitting the UCAS application and to make all the necessary arrangements for registering and taking any required admissions tests. Check university/college and admissions tests websites for the latest information. See also **Chapter 7**.

Potential applicants should ask the advice of teachers, careers advisers and university and college advisers before submitting their application.

APPLICATIONS FOR UNIVERSITY AND COLLEGE COURSES THROUGH UCAS

NB Some changes to the UCAS application process are expected for 2009/2010. Check with the UCAS website (www.ucas.com) and with university/college websites for the latest information.

UCAS, the organisation responsible for managing applications to higher education courses in the UK, deals with applications for admission to full-time and sandwich first degrees, Foundation degrees, Diploma of Higher Education and Higher National Diploma courses and some full-time Higher National Certificate courses in nearly all universities (but not the Open University), university colleges, colleges and institutes of higher education, specialist colleges and some further education colleges.

Full details of application procedures and all course information can be found on the UCAS website www.ucas.com. Information is also available in the UCAS publication *The Big Guide* (available from www.ucasbooks.com or from UCAS Media, PO Box 130, Cheltenham GL52 3ZF, tel 01242 544610).

Applications are usually submitted electronically by using **UCAS Apply**, a secure web-based application system, particularly useful for independent home or international users. Application can also be made by the CD ROM-based Electronic Application System (EAS) available in schools, colleges, Connexions offices or British Council offices. All applications should be made online direct to UCAS, but in some circumstances paper applications can still be made (check with www.ucas.com for the latest information).

Applications are submitted from 1 September (except for Art and Design courses via Route B, see below). The first closing date is 15 October for applications to Oxford or Cambridge Universities and for courses in Medicine, Dentistry and Veterinary Medicine or Veterinary Science. The final closing date for applications (including Art and Design, Route A) from UK and EU students is 15 January. Late applications for all courses may be considered up to 30 June.

On the UCAS application, you may have up to five course choices unless you are applying for Dentistry (courses A200, A203, A204, A205 and A206), Medicine (courses A100, A101, A102, A103, A104 and A106) or Veterinary Science/Medicine (courses D100 and D101). For these courses only four choices are permitted.

It is important to note that some universities (for example Birmingham and Cambridge) now require their applicants to complete a Supplementary Application Questionnaire after they have received your UCAS application. Check the website of your listed universities for their latest application information.

Each university or college makes an offer through the UCAS system. UCAS does not make offers, or recruit on behalf of universities and colleges. It does not advise applicants on their choice of subject although it does publish material which applicants may find useful.

Applicants may receive an 'unconditional' offer in the case of those who already hold the required qualifications, or, for those awaiting examination results, a 'conditional' offer or a rejection. When all replies are received from universities or colleges, applicants may finally hold up to two offers: a first choice (firm) offer and an insurance offer. Those rejected by all universities or who withdraw their applications may decide to use **UCAS Extra**. Applicants are told when they become eligible for **UCAS Extra** and can refer themselves on-line via **UCAS Track** on www.ucas.com from mid March until 12 July. This scheme enables applicants to make additional course choices, one at a time, where vacancies still exist. Courses available on **UCAS Extra** will be highlighted on **Course Search** on www.ucas.com. Applicants not placed through this system will be eligible to re-apply through the Clearing Scheme from mid August.

Confirmation starts on the day when the A-level examination results are released. Clearing vacancy lists are also published on A-level results day. Applicants who have met the conditions of their offers for their firm choice will receive confirmation from their university or college and may still be accepted even if their results are slightly lower than those stipulated in the original offer. If rejected by their firm choice university/college applicants will have their places confirmed by their insurance choice institution providing they have obtained the right grades. Applicants who are unsuccessful with both their institutions will be eligible to go into Clearing in which they can select an appropriate course in the same or a different institution where places are available. Each year up to 40,000 applicants obtain places through Clearing.

UCAS timetable

1 September	UCAS begins accepting applications.
15 October	Deadline for applications to Oxford or Cambridge and courses leading to a professional qualification in Medicine, Dentistry or Veterinary Science to reach UCAS.
15 January	Deadline for UK and EU applications to reach UCAS.
16 January–30 June	Late applications received by UCAS are forwarded to the institutions for consideration at their discretion. Applications received after 30 June (Art and Design Route B after 12 June) are processed through the Clearing Scheme.
14 March	Applicants without offers, who have been rejected by all universities or colleges or who have declined all offers received, will be alerted to a new service by UCAS. They will receive an 'Extra Passport' which will enable them to contact

institutions with vacancies, one at a time. Institutions with vacancies will list courses on the UCAS website. Details of this service will be included in the 'Advice for Applicants' leaflet sent to applicants.

24 March	Applications due at UCAS for Route B Art and Design courses. Applicants are advised to submit these, if possible, by 7 March.
5 May	Applicants who have received all their decisions from universities and colleges by the end of March are asked to reply to their offers by this date.
6 June	Applicants receiving decisions from all their choices by 9 May must reply to their offers by this date.
12 June	Last date for receiving late Route B Art and Design applications.
30 June	Last date for receiving late applications. After this date applications are Clearing only. Mid July Clearing entry forms begin to be issued to eligible applicants.
8 August	Scottish SQA results published.
17 August	GCE A-level and AS-level results published. Clearing vacancy information available. (See **What To Do on Results Day . . . and After** below.)

PLEASE NOTE:

* You are not required to reply to any university/college offers until you have received your last decision.
* Do not send a firm acceptance to more than one offer.
* Do not try to alter a firm acceptance.
* Send a Withdrawal slip to UCAS at once if you decide not to go to university/college this year.
* Remember to tell the institutions and UCAS if you change your address, or change your examination board(s), subjects or arrangements.

APPLICATIONS FOR ART AND DESIGN COURSES

Applications for Art and Design courses are submitted via one or both of two routes which are of equal status.

Route A Courses will be identified on **Course Search** on the UCAS website, by a letter **A** after the course code. Applicants may enter up to **five** choices and the closing date for receipt of applications at UCAS is 15 January although early application is recommended since portfolios have to be inspected. Applications through this route will be considered simultaneously by the institutions listed. Applicants in Route A for Fine Art courses at the Ruskin School of Fine Art, Oxford must submit their application and forms by 15 October. Details from the Ruskin School of Drawing and Fine Art, 74 High Street, Oxford OX1 4BG.

Route B Courses will be identified on **Course Search** on the UCAS website, by a letter **B** after the course code. Additionally **all** Route B course codes have a letter **E** within them. **Three** applications may be submitted between 1 January and 24 March and early application, no later than 8 March, is recommended. Applicants will be asked to indicate on an interview preference form the order in which they wish to be interviewed by the institutions to which they have applied and applications will be considered in that order.

Applicants may apply through both routes if they wish, but can then use no more than three of the maximum five choices on Route B applications.

APPLICATIONS FOR LAW COURSES

Applicants for some specified undergraduate Law programmes at the Universities of Birmingham, Bristol, Cambridge, Durham, Exeter, Glasgow, London (King's), (UCL), Nottingham and Oxford will have to sit the National Admissions Test for Law (LNAT). See **Chapter 7** and see also the LNAT website (www.lnat.ac.uk) for full details of which Law courses require applicants to sit the LNAT and for information about registration fees, sample papers, test dates and test centres. Applicants are advised to fill in their UCAS application before registering or taking the LNAT but it is important to check the deadlines for registering for, and sitting, the test. If you apply for Law at an LNAT-participating university but fail to take the test in time, your application will be rejected by the university. It is important to note that applicants must enter their UCAS number on the LNAT registration form by specified deadlines (check for 2008/2009 dates) and that applicants' LNAT scores cannot be sent to the universities to which they have applied until this has been done and all LNAT fees have been paid.

If you are applying for any other Law courses which are not listed on the LNAT website, or by the universities themselves with the LNAT as a requirement, there is no need for you to sit the LNAT.

APPLICATIONS FOR MEDICINE AND DENTISTRY COURSES

The admissions process for Medicine and Dentistry is currently undergoing change so it is vital that you check university websites for course requirements for their medical and dental schools. Students applying for these subjects are usually required to sit the UK Clinical Aptitude Test (UKCAT) or the BioMedical Admissions Test (BMAT). You will need the most up-to-date information about taking the UKCAT or BMAT admissions tests (for example, about registration deadlines, test dates, test centres, practice papers) by checking their websites frequently (www.ukcat.ac.uk and www.bmat.org.uk). See also **Chapter 7**.

APPLICATIONS FOR VETERINARY SCIENCE/MEDICINE AND PHYSIOLOGICAL SCIENCES COURSES

The BioMedical Admissions Test (BMAT) is required for entry to specified Veterinary Sciences/Medicine courses at the University of Bristol Veterinary School, the University of Cambridge and the Royal Veterinary College. It is also required by the University of Oxford for its Physiological Sciences course.

Applicants have to register for the BMAT and must check the website (www.bmat.org.uk) for the latest information about BMAT entry closing dates, test centres, fees and test dates. See also **Chapter 7**.

APPLICATIONS FOR MUSIC COURSES AT CONSERVATOIRES

The Conservatoires UK Admissions Service (CUKAS) handles applications for practical Music courses. Applications can be made simultaneously to a maximum of six of the conservatoires listed below. Full details of the Service are given on the CUKAS website (www.cukas.ac.uk). The Conservatoires taking part in this online admissions system are:

* Birmingham Conservatoire www.conservatoire.uce.ac.uk
* Leeds College of Music www.lcm.ac.uk
* Royal College of Music www.rcm.ac.uk
* Royal Northern College of Music www.rncm.ac.uk
* Royal Scottish Academy of Music and Drama www.rsamd.ac.uk
* Royal Welsh College of Music and Drama www.rwcmd.ac.uk
* Trinity College of Music www.tcm.ac.uk

See also the **Music** table of interview requirements/tests in **Chapter 7**.

APPLICATIONS FOR NURSING AND MIDWIFERY COURSES

Degree course applications for these subjects are processed by UCAS in the usual way. The Nursing and Midwifery Admissions Service (NMAS) has merged with UCAS and ceases to exist as a separate scheme.

APPLICATIONS FOR SOCIAL WORK COURSES

Applications for courses should be made through UCAS. Details about social work careers and courses are available from www.socialworkcareers.co.uk. See **Appendix 2: Professional Associations** for other relevant websites.

APPLICATIONS FOR TEACHER TRAINING COURSES

From September 2008 applicants intending to start a course of initial teacher training in England leading to Qualified Teacher Status have to be provisionally registered with the General Teaching Council of England (GTCE). Check www.gtce.org.uk for full details, and see also www.tda.gov.uk. Students in Wales and Northern Ireland should also check with this website; Scottish students should check www.infoscotland.com/teaching.

THE UCAS APPLICATION

Two important aspects of the UCAS application concern Sections 3 and 10. In Section 3 all your university/college choices (a maximum of five) are to be listed, but remember that you should not mix your subjects. For example, in popular subject areas such as English, History or Physiotherapy, it is safer to show total commitment by applying for all courses in the same subject and not to include second and/or third subject alternatives on the form. (See advice in separate tables in **Chapter 9** for Medicine, Dentistry and Veterinary Science/Medicine.)

A brief glance at the subject tables in **Chapter 9** will give you some idea of the popularity of various courses. In principle, institutions want the best applicants available so if there are large numbers of applicants the offers made will be higher. For Medicine, offers in terms of A-level grades usually reach AAB or higher, and for Veterinary Science/Medicine AAB. Conversely, for the less popular subjects such as Chemistry or Manufacturing Engineering, the offers can be much lower – down to CC and even CD or equivalent points.

Similarly, some institutions are more popular (not necessarily better) than others. Again, this popularity can be judged easily in the tables in **Chapter 9**: the higher the offer, the more popular the institution. Quite often 'popular' universities are those located in attractive towns or cities such as Bristol, Exeter, Warwick, Bath or York. Additionally, some institutions have established a good 'reputation' for various reasons, for example, Oxford, Cambridge and Durham. Conversely and unfortunately, some universities have confused applicants with unfamiliar names and no immediate identity as to their location, such as De Montfort and Brunel. More applicants would apply to these excellent institutions if their knowledge of geography was more extensive!

When you have chosen your courses and your institutions, look again at the offers the latter usually make and compare these with the grades projected by your teachers on your UCAS reference. *It is most important to maximise your chances of a place by choosing institutions which might make you a range of offers.* When all universities have considered your application you can hold only two offers (one firm and one insurance offer) and naturally it is preferable for one to be lower than the other in case you do not achieve the offer grades or equivalent points for your first choice of university or college.

The other section of the UCAS application that deserves careful thought is Section 10 (*Personal Statement*). This seems simple enough but it is the only part of the application where you can put in a personal bid for a place! In short, you are asked to give relevant background information about yourself, your interests and your choice of course and career. Give yourself plenty of time to prepare Section 10 – if you have a Record of Achievement you could use it as a guide – as this part of your application could make all the difference to getting an offer or not.

Motivation to undertake your chosen course is very important. You can show this by giving details of any work experience and work shadowing you have done (and for History courses, for example, details of visits to places of historical interest). It is a good idea to begin your statement with such evidence explaining how your interest in your chosen subject has developed. In the subject tables in **Chapter 9** under **Advice to applicants and planning the UCAS personal statement**, advice is given on what you might include in Section 10. You should also include various activities in which you have been involved in the last three or four years. Get your parents and other members of the family to refresh your memory – it is easy to forget something quite important. You might consider planning out this section in a series of sub-sections – and if you have a lot to say, be brief. The sub-sections can include:

* **School activities** Are you a prefect, chairperson or treasurer of a society? Are you involved in supervisory duties of any kind? Are you in a school team? Which team? For how long? (Remember, team means any team: sports, chess, debating, even business.)

* **Intellectual activities** Have you attended any field or lecture courses in your main subjects? Where? When? Have you taken part in any school visits? Do you play in the school orchestra or have you taken part in a school drama production – on or off stage? Do you go to the theatre, art galleries or concerts?

* **Out-of-school activities** This category might cover many of the topics above, but it could also include any community work you do, or Duke of Edinburgh's Awards, the Combined Cadet Force (CCF), sport, music and drama activities etc. The countries you have visited might also be mentioned – for example, any exchange visits with friends living abroad.

* **Work experience** Details of part-time, holiday or Saturday jobs could be included here, particularly if they have some connection with your chosen course. Some applicants plan ahead and arrange to visit firms and discuss career interests with various people who already work in their chosen field. For some courses such as Veterinary Science, work experience is essential, and it certainly helps for others, for example Medicine and Business courses.

* **Key Skills** These cover numeracy, communication and information technology (the basics) and also advanced skills involving teamwork, problem solving and improving your own learning. If you are not offering the Key Skills Certificate then evidence of your strengths in these areas may be mentioned in the school or college reference or you may include examples in your personal statement relating to your out-of-school activities.

Finally, plan your UCAS application carefully. You may write short statements if you wish. It is not essential to write in prose except perhaps if you are applying for English or language courses in which case your statement will be judged grammatically! Take a copy to use as a trial and a copy of your complete application to keep by you for reference if you are called for interview. Almost certainly you will be questioned on what you have written. If you are completing a paper application, write legibly and between, not on the lines, preferably printing your statement.

Admissions tutors always stress the importance of the confidential report written by your head teacher or form tutors. Most schools and colleges will make some effort to find out why you want to apply for a particular course, but if they do not ask, do not take it for granted that they will know! Consequently, although you have the opportunity to write about your interests on the form, it is still a good idea to tell your teachers about them. Also, if you have to work at home under difficult conditions or if you have any medical problem, your teachers must be told since these points should be mentioned on the report.

Deferred entry

Although application is usually made in the autumn of the year preceding the proposed year of entry, admissions tutors may be prepared to consider an application made two years before entry, so that the applicant can, perhaps, gain work experience or spend a period abroad. Policies on deferred entry may differ from department to department, so you should check with admissions tutors before applying. Simply remember that there is no guarantee that you will get the grades you need or a place at the university of your first choice at the first attempt! If not, you may need to repeat A-levels and try again. It may be better not to apply for deferred entry until you are certain in August of your grades and your place.

APPLICATIONS TO THE UNIVERSITY OF CAMBRIDGE

The University has recently announced changes to its applications process so you will need to check with its Admissions Office or on www.cam.ac.uk/admissions/undergraduate/apply for the latest information. From 2009, if you are a UK or EU applicant, you need only complete the UCAS application and not the separate additional Cambridge Application Form (CAF) of previous years. You will then receive an email from the University, confirming the arrival of your application and giving you the website address of their online Supplementary Application Questionnaire (SAQ) which you will then need to complete and return by the specified date.

Your UCAS application listing Cambridge as one of your university choices must be sent to UCAS by 15 October. If you are applying for Medicine, Veterinary Medicine and Law you must include your BMAT or LNAT registration with your application. You can indicate your choice of college or make an Open application if you have no preference. Open applicants are allocated by a computer program to colleges that have had fewer applicants per place for your chosen subject.

The Cambridge Special Access Scheme (CSAS) is also available for applicants whose schooling has been disrupted or disadvantaged. You need to complete a CSAS by 15 October but discuss this with your school/college higher education adviser and check with the UCAS website for more information.

Interviews take place in Cambridge in the first three weeks of December, although some may be a little earlier. Many of the University's colleges now use tests as part of the selection process for specific courses and written work also may be requested before interview. See the University website and **Chapter 7** for information you need to know before completing and submitting your application. This practice, however, varies between colleges and subjects (see **Chapter 7**).

In January applicants receive either an offer conditional upon certain grades in examinations to be taken the following summer, or a rejection. Decisions are made on the basis of academic record, reference, personal statement, submitted work/test results and interviews. The conditions set are grades to be obtained in examinations such as A-levels, Scottish Highers/Advanced Highers or the International Baccalaureate. Offers made by some Cambridge University colleges may also include Sixth Term Examination Papers (STEP) in mathematics (see **Chapter 7** under Mathematics). The STEPs are taken in June and copies of past papers and the Regulations and Syllabuses can be obtained from OCR Publications, PO Box 5050, Annersley, Nottingham NG15 0DL; Tel 0870 870 6622.

College policies

All colleges which admit undergraduates use the selection procedures described in **Chapter 7**. However, there will be some minor variations in policy between the various colleges, within each college and also between subjects. Further information about the policies of any particular college can be found in the Cambridge *Undergraduate Prospectus* and may also be obtained from the admissions tutor of the college concerned. No college operates a quota system for any subject except Medicine and Veterinary Medicine, for which there are strict quotas for the University from which places are allocated to each college.

Full details of the admissions procedures are contained in the current Cambridge *Undergraduate Prospectus*. Copies of the prospectus are available from Cambridge Admissions Office, Fitzwilliam House, 32 Trumpington Street, Cambridge CB2 1QY, or via the website www.cam.ac.uk/admissions.

APPLICATIONS TO THE UNIVERSITY OF OXFORD

Application procedures to Oxford are similar to all other universities except that candidates applying to Oxford must submit a UCAS application and an Oxford Application Form by 15 October 2008 for those applying for entry in October 2009 or for deferred entry in October 2010. Admissions are carried out on a college basis: candidates can name a college of preference and may be allocated second and third preference colleges, but if they do not have a specific college in mind, they can make an open application. This means that they will be allocated a college through a computer program which takes account of their chosen course and the approximate number of applicants per place that each college has received that year (and gender in the case of the one women-only college).

For some subjects at some colleges at Oxford, applicants are required to sit aptitude or admissions tests (for example, the History Aptitude Test, the National Admissions Test for Law (LNAT) and the BioMedical Admissions Test (BMAT)) or to provide essays or a portfolio for interview. Specimen test questions are published on the website. See **Chapter 7** for more information and contact the Oxford Colleges Admissions Office for full details. All candidates are considered carefully on their individual merits. Tutors take into account a range of information from the candidate's application including details of their academic record and the reference in order to assess a candidate's suitability and potential for his or her proposed course. Candidates applying for some courses may be required to submit samples of marked school work by early November, and/or to take a short written test when they are in Oxford for interview (see **Chapter 7**). The majority of candidates applying to Oxford are invited for interview at the beginning of December and this is an integral part of the selection procedure. Candidates will be interviewed at their college of preference and also may be interviewed by other colleges. Colleges co-operate and pool candidates to ensure that the most able candidates are offered places. Successful candidates who have not completed their school-leaving examinations will be made conditional offers based on their forthcoming examinations such as A-levels, Scottish Highers, Advanced Highers, International Baccalaureate, European Baccalaureate and other European and international qualifications. Decisions are notified to candidates via UCAS by the end of January. Candidates are welcome to attend Open days which are held at all of the colleges and a number of departments, usually during the summer term or in September.

Common Framework

The University and Colleges have agreed to a Common Framework for Colleges and Faculties (see www.admissions.ox.ac.uk/news/common_framework.shtml) which lays down key principles and procedures for undergraduate admissions. The Common Framework was implemented in October 2007 and is designed to make admissions more transparent, improve methods of assessing candidates and ensure that selection is unaffected by the applicant's choice of college.

Colleges will continue to have the final say over whom they admit but they will be guided by the central banding of candidates by faculties based on the whole range of information arising from the selection process. This information may include results from pre-interview test, written work, school qualifications and/or predicted school-leaving grades, interviews and contextual information about a candidate's educational background.

Where a college wishes to offer a place to a candidate below the 'selection threshold', it will be required to explain the reasons to the relevant faculty with reference to the agreed admissions criteria.

APPLICATIONS TO SCOTTISH UNIVERSITIES

Another point worth noting concerns the older Scottish universities in which admission is generally to a faculty and not to a specific course or department. Students often study three subjects in Year 1 and either two or three in Year 2. Honours courses normally take four years although admission to the second year of the course is sometimes possible (see **Chapter 7**).

MATURE APPLICANTS

There are a great many mature students following first degree courses in UK universities and colleges. The following is a list of key points a group of mature students found useful in exploring and deciding on a university course:

* Check with your nearest university or college to find out about the courses they can offer, for example degrees, diplomas, full-time, part-time.
* Some institutions will require examination passes in some subjects, others may not.
* An age limit may apply for some vocational courses, for example Medicine, Dentistry and Teaching.
* If entry requirements are an obstacle, prospective students should approach their local colleges for information on Access or Open College courses. These courses are fast-growing in number and popularity, offering adults an alternative route into higher education other than A-levels. They are usually developed jointly by colleges of further education and the local higher education institution.
* Demands of the course – how much time will be required for study? What are the assignments and the deadlines to be met? How is your work assessed – unseen examinations, continuous assessment, practicals?
* The demands on finance – cost of the course – loan needed – loss of earnings – drop in income if changing to another career – travel requirements – accommodation – need to work part-time for income?
* The availability and suitability of the course – geographical location – competition for places – where it will lead – student support services, for example childcare, library.
* What benefits will you derive? Fulfilment, transferable skills, social contacts, sense of achievement, enjoyment, self-esteem, career enhancement?
* Why would employers want to recruit you? Ability to adapt to the work scene, realistic and balanced approach, mature attitude to work?
* Why would employers not want to recruit you? Salary expectations, inability to fit in with younger colleagues, limited mobility? However, some employers particularly welcome older graduates: Civil Service, local authorities, Health Service, religious, charitable and voluntary organisations, teaching, social/probation work, careers work, housing.

AND FINALLY . . . BEFORE YOU SEND IN YOUR APPLICATION

CHECK that you have passes at Grade C or higher in the GCSE (or equivalent) subjects required for the course at the institutions to which you are applying. FAILURE TO HAVE THE RIGHT GCSE SUBJECTS OR THE RIGHT NUMBER OF GRADE C PASSES OR HIGHER IN GCSE WILL RESULT IN A REJECTION.

CHECK that you are taking (or have taken) the GCE A- and AS-level (or equivalent) subjects required for the course at the institution to which you are applying. FAILURE TO BE TAKING OR HAVE TAKEN THE RIGHT A-LEVELS WILL ALSO RESULT IN A REJECTION.

CHECK that the GCE A-levels and other qualifications you are taking will be accepted for the course for which you are applying. Some subjects and institutions do not stipulate any specific A-levels, only that you are required to offer two or three subjects at GCE A-level. In the view of some admissions tutors NOT ALL GCE A-LEVELS CARRY THE SAME WEIGHT (see **Chapter 1**).

CHECK that you can meet the requirements for all relevant admissions/interview tests.

CHECK that you have made all the necessary arrangements for sitting any required admissions tests.

CHECK that you can meet any age, health and CRB requirements for entry to your listed courses.

WHAT TO DO ON RESULTS DAY . . . AND AFTER

BE AT HOME! Do not arrange to be away when your results are published. If you do not achieve the grades you require, you will need to follow an alternative course of action and make decisions that could affect your life during the next few years. Do not expect others to make these decisions for you.

If you achieve the grades or points which have been offered you will receive confirmation of a place, but this may take a few days to reach you. Once your place is confirmed contact the accommodation office at the university or college and inform them that you will need a place in a hall of residence or other accommodation.

If you achieve grades or points much higher than you expected – higher than the offer you have received – and you are already holding one or two places, you are not entitled to ignore these offers and try for a place at another 'better' university or college. If, however, you have decided definitely to change courses advise the university or college immediately. (NB Check with www.ucas.com and your school/college adviser for the latest information as changes are expected.)

If your grades or points are higher than you expected and you are not holding any offers you can telephone or e-mail the admissions tutor at the universities and colleges which rejected you and request that they might reconsider you.

If you just miss your offers then telephone or email the universities and colleges to see if they can still offer you a place. ALWAYS HAVE YOUR UCAS REFERENCE NUMBER AVAILABLE WHEN YOU CALL. Their decisions may take a few days. You should check the universities and colleges in your order of preference. Your first choice must reject you before you contact your second choice.

If you have not applied to any university or college earlier in the year then you can apply through the Clearing Scheme which runs from the middle of July. Check the tables in **Chapter 9** to identify which institutions normally make offers matching your results, then telephone or email the institution to see if they have any vacancies before completing your Clearing form.

If you learn finally that you do not have a place you will receive automatically a Clearing form to enable you to re-apply. Before you complete this form follow the instructions above.

If an institution has vacancies they will ask you for your grades. If they can consider you they will ask you for your Clearing form. You can only be considered by one institution at a time.

If you have to re-apply for a place, check the vacancies on the UCAS website (www.ucas.com), in the national press and through your local careers office. If there are vacancies in your subject, check with the university or college that these vacancies have not been taken.

REMEMBER – There are many thousands of students just like you. Admissions tutors have a mammoth task checking how many students will be taking up their places since not all students whose grades match their offers finally decide to do so!

IF YOU HAVE AN OFFER AND THE RIGHT GRADES BUT ARE NOT ACCEPTING THAT OR AN ALTERNATIVE PLACE – TELL THE UNIVERSITY OR COLLEGE. Someone else is waiting for your place!

You may have to make many telephone calls to institutions before you are successful. It may even be late September before you know you have a place so BE PATIENT AND STAY CALM!

TAKING A GAP YEAR

Choosing your course is the first decision you need to make, the second is choosing your university and then, for an increasing number, the third is deciding whether or not to take a gap year. But there lies the problem. Because of the very large number of things to do and places to go, you'll find that you almost need a gap year to choose the right one (although a read through *Your Gap Year* by Susan Griffith (see **Appendix 3**) is a good place to start)!

Planning ahead is important but, in the end, bear in mind that you might be overtaken by events, not least in failing to get the grades you need for a place on the course or at the university you were counting on. This could mean repeating A-levels and re-applying, which in turn could mean waiting for interviews and offers and, possibly, deferring the start of your 'gap' until February or March.

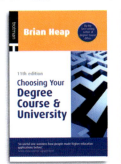

Once you have decided to go, however, it's a question of whether you will go under your own steam or through a gap year agency. Unless you are streetwise, or preferably 'world wise', then an agency offers several advantages. Some agencies may cover a broad field of opportunities whilst others will focus on a specific region and activity, such as the African Conservation Experience, offering animal and plant conservation work in game and nature reserves in southern Africa.

When making the choice, some students will always prefer a 'do-it-yourself' arrangement. However, there are many advantages to going through specialist agencies. They can not only offer a choice of destinations and opportunities but also provide a lot of essential and helpful advice before your departure on issues such as health precautions and insurance. Support is also available in the case of accidents or illnesses when a link can be established between the agency and parents.

Good luck!

7 | ADMISSIONS TESTS, SELECTION OF APPLICANTS AND INTERVIEWS

The selection of applicants takes many forms. The use of predicted A-level grades (and, later, points and AS-grades) has been current practice since 1966. However, with the increase in the number of candidates for places, particularly in the popular subjects, and the rise in the numbers of students achieving higher grades, increasing importance is now attached to other aspects of the application form. The applicant's academic progress through earlier examinations, the school reference and the personal statement now receive greater consideration, particularly in the case of competitive courses, and, in addition, tests and questionnaires to be completed before interview, and further tests at the interview stage are now increasingly used. These include:

ADMISSIONS TESTS FOR LAW, MEDICINE, DENTISTRY AND VETERINARY SCIENCE/MEDICINE

The National Admissions Test for Law (LNAT)

The LNAT is an on-screen test for applicants to specified undergraduate Law programmes at the Universities of Birmingham, Bristol, Cambridge, Durham, Exeter, Glasgow, London (King's), (UCL), Nottingham and Oxford. See **Law** below, and Law in the subject tables in **Chapter 9**. Applicants need to check the universities' websites and the LNAT website (www.lnat.ac.uk) for the UCAS codes for the courses requiring applicants to take the LNAT. Details of the admissions test (which includes multiple-choice and essay questions), practice papers, registration dates, test dates, test centres and fees are all available on the LNAT website (see above). See **Chapter 6** for information about applications for Law courses, and the LNAT website for the latest information.

The UK Clinical Aptitude Test (UKCAT)

The UKCAT is a new clinical aptitude test currently used by the majority of medical and dental schools in the selection of applicants for Medicine and Dentistry, alongside their existing selection processes. The tests are not curriculum-based and do not have a science component. No revision is necessary, there is no textbook and no course of instruction. In the first instance, the UKCAT is a test of cognitive skills involving problem-solving and critical reasoning. With over 150 test centres, it is an on-screen test (not paper-based), and is marked electronically. The cost is £50 and some bursaries are available. Further details (including the most recent list of universities requiring applicants to take the UKCAT) are found on the website www.ukcat.ac.uk. See also the Dentistry and Medicine subject tables in **Chapter 9**, the entries for Dentistry and Medicine below, and **Chapter 6** for application details.

The BioMedical Admissions Test (BMAT)

This is a pen-and-paper admissions test taken by applicants to specified Medicine, Veterinary Medicine and related courses at the Universities of Cambridge, Manchester and Oxford, and at the Royal Veterinary College, Imperial College London and University College London. A list of exactly which courses require the BMAT is available on the BMAT website (www.bmat.org.uk) and also on university websites and in their prospectuses. It is important to note the BMAT early closing date for entries and the test dates. The two-hour test consists of three sections:

* Aptitude and skills
* Scientific knowledge and application
* Writing task.

Applicants sit the test only once and pay one entry fee no matter how many courses they apply for, but if they re-apply to universities the following year they will need to re-take the BMAT and pay another fee. Past question papers are available on the BMAT website, and a study guide is also available on www.heinemann.co.uk/bmat.

Results of the BMAT are first sent to the universities, and then to the BMAT test centres. Candidates need to contact their test centres direct for their results. See Dentistry, Medicine and Veterinary Science below and their subject tables in **Chapter 9**.

DEGREE SUBJECT LISTS OF UNIVERSITIES AND COLLEGES USING TESTS AND ASSESSMENTS

The following list of degree subjects will provide a guide to universities and colleges that use admissions tests and assessments. These may include:

* Questionnaires or tests to be completed by applicants prior to interview and/or offer.
* Examples of school work to be submitted prior to interview and/or offer.
* Written tests at interview.
* Mathematical tests at interview.
* Practical tests at interview.
* A response to a passage at interview.
* Thinking Skills Assessment (TSA) tests. These are aimed at testing critical thinking and problem solving skills and are used by many of the Cambridge University colleges. See www.tsa.ucles.org.uk and www.cam.ac.uk/admissions/undergraduate/tests for further details.
* National Admissions Test for Law (LNAT). See www.lnat.ac.uk for further information and also **Chapter 6** under Applications for Law Courses.
* Mathematics – Sixth Term Examination Papers (STEP), details from www.ocr.org.uk and see **Chapter 6**.
* The UK Clinical Aptitude Test (UKCAT). See above and **Chapter 6** for further information and also under Medicine and Dentistry below. Details also from www.ukcat.ac.uk.
* BioMedical Admissions Test (BMAT). See above for further information and also under Medicine, Dentistry and Veterinary Sciences below and **Chapter 6**. Details also from www.bmat.org.uk.

Cambridge University advises that changes may occur in their selection procedures and that candidates should check for changes at www.cam.ac.uk/admissions/undergraduate/apply.

Specimen tests are on the Oxford University website at www.admissions.ox.ac.uk/interviews/tests.

The information given below in the subject lists has been provided by universities and colleges: **check their prospectuses and websites for full details of their interview and test requirements and if in doubt, contact admissions tutors**.

Accountancy
Buckingham Written test for non-English-speaking applicants.

Anglo Saxon, Norse and Celtic
Cambridge (*Hughes Hall, Lucy Cavendish*): Test at interview; (*Churchill, Fitzwilliam, Girton, Gonville and Caius, Queens', St John's, St Edmund's, Wolfson*): Interview only. All other colleges require essays.

Anthropology
Cambridge See **Archaeology**.
Oxford See **Archaeology**.

Arabic
Salford (Arbc Engl Transl Interp – for native speakers of Arabic) Applicants may be required to sit Arabic or English language tests.

Archaeology
Bournemouth Test for mature applicants.

Cambridge (Arch Anth) (*Clare, Emmanuel, Girton, King's, Robinson, Hughes Hall, Lucy Cavendish*): Test at interview; (*Churchill, Robinson, Trinity*): Preparatory study at interview; (*Fitzwilliam, Gonville and Caius, Jesus, St Edmund's, Wolfson*): Interview only. All other colleges require essays to be submitted before interview.

Oxford (Arch Anth) (*All colleges offering the subject*): Two recently marked essays, preferably in different subjects, plus a statement of no more than 300 words setting out your interests in archaeology and social, cultural and biological anthropology required before interview. No test at interview.

Oxford (Class Arch Anc Hist) (*All colleges offering the subject*): Two recent marked essays. No test at interview.

Architecture
Some universities may require applicants to complete drawing tests at the time of application and prior to interview. Most universities require art portfolios at interview.

Bradford (Coll) Questionnaire and samples of work before interview. Literacy and numeracy test at interview.

Cambridge (*Downing, Emmanuel, Fitzwilliam, Girton, Jesus, King's, Magdalene, Newnham, Peterhouse, Queens', Selwyn, Sidney Sussex, Trinity, Trinity Hall, St Edmund's, Wolfson*): Interview only. Essays to be submitted before interview; (*Lucy Cavendish*): Test at interview. All colleges require a portfolio.

Cardiff Samples of work to be sent before interview.

Dundee Samples of work required before interview.

Huddersfield, **London Met** Portfolio of work required.

Liverpool The interview will be based on the portfolio of work.

London South Bank Samples of work to be sent before interview.

Nottingham Trent Examples of work are required.

Sheffield Art portfolio required for applicants without A-level Art.

Westminster Samples of work required before interview.

Art courses
All institutions will require candidates to provide a portfolio of work for discussion at interview.

Bournemouth (Comp Vis Animat) Maths, logic and life-drawing tests.

Bournemouth (AI) Practical test.

Creative Arts (UC) Tests.

Oxford (Fine Art) (*All colleges offering the subject*): No written work required. Portfolio to be submitted by mid-November (see prospectus). Drawing examination. Two drawings in pencil or pencil and ink from a number of possible subjects. See www.admissions.ox.ac.uk/interview/tests.

Oxford and Cherwell Valley (Coll) A drawing examination is taken by all candidates who are interviewed (two drawings in pencil or pen and ink).

Matthew Boulton (CFHE) Literacy and numeracy tests.

Ravensbourne (CDC) Verbal examination.

Westminster (Fash Mrchnds Mgt) Interview and numeracy test.

Biochemistry
London South Bank Degree subject-based test at interview.

Oxford (*All colleges offering the subject*): No written work required. No written tests.

Biological Sciences
London South Bank Degree subject-based test at interview.
Nottingham Trent Essay set.
Oxford (*St Hilda's*): Practical test, interpreting written work or data. (*All other colleges offering the subject*): No written work required. No written tests.

Biomedical Science
Nottingham Trent Essay.
Portsmouth Test of motivation and knowledge of the subject, the degree and careers to which it leads.

Building/Construction
Bradford (Coll) Questionnaire before interview, literacy and numeracy tests at interview.
London South Bank (Bld Serv Eng) Degree subject-based test and numeracy test at interview**.**

Business Courses
Arts London (CFash) School work to be submitted before interview. Degree subject-based test and numeracy test at interview.
Bath City (Coll) See www.citybathcoll.ac.uk.
Bolton Literacy and numeracy tests.
Buckingham English test for applicants without English as a first language.
Matthew Boulton (CFHE) Literacy and numeracy tests.
Newcastle Some short-listed applicants will be given a variety of assessment tests at interview.
Nottingham Trent Short-listed applicants are invited to a day-long business style assessment.
South Trafford (Coll) Literacy and numeracy tests at interview.
Westminster (Fash Mrchnds Mgt) Interview and numeracy test.

Chemistry
London South Bank Degree subject-based test.
Oxford No written work required. No written tests.

Classical Studies
Birmingham Language aptitude test for students without a language at GCSE.

Classics (See also **Archaeology**)
Cambridge (*St Edmund's, Wolfson*): Interviews only; (*Emmanuel, Jesus, New Hall*): Preparatory study at interview; (*Churchill, Clare, Corpus Christi, Girton, New Hall, Peterhouse, St Catharine's, St John's, Trinity Hall, Hughes Hall, Lucy Cavendish*): Test at interview; (*All colleges* except *Hughes Hall, Lucy Cavendish, St Edmund's, Wolfson*): Essays to be submitted before interview.
Oxford (*All colleges offering the subject*): Two recently marked essays normally in areas related to Classics. Written tests at interview (for details see prospectus) and also www.admissions.ox.ac.uk/interview/tests.

Classics and English
Oxford (*All colleges offering the subject*) Course I: One essay relevant to Classics. (See also **English**) Course II: One essay relevant to Classics or English. Written test at interview (for details see prospectus) and also www.admissions.ox.ac.uk/interview/tests.

Classics and Modern Languages
Oxford (*All colleges offering the subject*): Two Classics essays required. Two modern language essays required, one in the language. See prospectus and also www.admissions.ox.ac.uk/interview/tests.

Communication Studies
Buckingham English test for non-English-speaking applicants.

Computer Science

Abertay Dundee (Comp Arts) Portfolio of work required. Practical tests at interview.

Cambridge (*Gonville and Caius*): Preparatory study at interview; (*Robinson, Trinity, Hughes Hall*): Test at interview; (*St Edmund's, Wolfson*): Interview only; (*all colleges with the exception of Trinity, Hughes Hall, St Edmund's*): TSA tests; (*Churchill*): May use STEP for conditional offers; (*Magdalene*): STEP used for conditional offers.

Central Lancashire Test for Foundation course applicants.

Cumbria Literacy test at interview.

East Lancashire (IHE) Questionnaire and test before interview.

Liverpool John Moores Questionnaire before interview. Literacy test at interview.

London (Gold) Degree subject-based test.

London (QM) Mathematical test at interview.

Manchester (CAT) Literacy and numeracy tests.

Matthew Boulton (CFHE) Literacy and numeracy tests.

Oxford (*All colleges offering the subject*): See **Mathematics** below.

West Thames (Coll) Degree subject-based test and numeracy test.

Dance/Drama

All institutions with courses in which performance is involved will require an audition.

Chichester (Perf Arts) Group practical test.

Liverpool (LIPA) See **Dance/Dance Studies** in **Chapter 9** (Interview advice and questions).

Dentistry

The following universities require UKCAT for specified courses (see **Chapter 6**): **Cardiff**, **Dundee**, **Glasgow**, **London (King's)**, **(QM)**, **Manchester**, **Newcastle**, **Sheffield**.

Bristol Degree subject-based test. (A short ten-minute test on a dental-related subject. No prior knowledge of Dentistry required, merely an awareness of the issues relating to the profession. Clarity of expression is important.)

Manchester BMAT for BDS Pre-dental year entry.

NB Check websites of all universities offering Dentistry courses for their latest admissions requirements: see also www.ukcat.ac.uk and www.bmat.org.uk.

Dietetics

London Met Interview and essay.

Ulster Health Profession Admissions Test: see www.hpat.org.uk and www.ulster.ac.uk before completing the UCAS application.

Drama

London (Gold) Written work required at interview.

Earth Sciences (Geology)

Oxford No essays required. No written tests at interview.

Economics

Buckingham English test for non-English-speaking applicants.

Cambridge (*Churchill, Fitzwilliam, Jesus, Magdalene, Newnham, St John's, Trinity*): Preparatory study at interview; (*Clare, Corpus Christi, Pembroke, Sidney Sussex, Hughes Hall, Lucy Cavendish*): Test at interview; (*Emmanuel, Fitzwilliam, Girton, Gonville and Caius, King's, New Hall, Newnham, St John's, Selwyn, Trinity Hall, Wolfson*): TSA; (*Christ's, Churchill, Downing, Emmanuel, Homerton, Magdalene, Peterhouse*): Essays to be submitted before interview; (*Queens', St Catharine's, St Edmund's*): Interview only. See also TSA tests: www.tsa.cambridgeassessment.org.uk.

Lancaster Workshop.

London (LSE) Has its own admissions test (the LSE Entrance Examination) which is used for some applicants with non-standard backgrounds. The test is not subject or course-specific.

Oxford (Econ Mgt) (*All colleges offering the subject*): Two essays required to be submitted before interview. Applicants should submit essays appropriate to these subjects. One-hour written test at interview (plus 15 minutes' reading time) designed to test comprehension, writing and problem solving skills. See www.admissions.ox.ac.uk/interviews/tests/EM.pdf.

Education Studies (See also **Teacher Training**)

Cambridge (*Christ's, Churchill, Emmanuel, Gonville and Caius, Homerton, Magdalene, Robinson, St John's, Trinity Hall*): Essays to be submitted before interview; (*Churchill, Magdalene, Trinity*): Preparatory study at interview; (*Clare, Girton, Jesus, New Hall, Queens', Selwyn, St Edmund's, Wolfson*): Interview only; (*Hughes Hall, Lucy Cavendish*): Test at interview.

Cumbria (Science and Education) Literacy test.

Durham (Primary Teaching) Key skills tests at interview.

Engineering

Birmingham City Mature students without GCSE English and/or mathematics are required to take a literacy and/or numeracy test.

Bradford (Coll) (Elec Eng; Electron Eng; Instr Contr Eng; Mat Eng; Mech Manuf Eng) Mathematical test at interview.

Bristol (Eng Des) A-level-based test.

Cambridge (*Christ's, Pembroke*): Interview only; (*Churchill, Gonville and Caius, Magdalene, Peterhouse, Robinson, Hughes Hall, Lucy Cavendish, St Edmund's, Wolfson*): Test at interview; (*Trinity*): Essays to be submitted before interview; (*Clare, Corpus Christi, Downing, Emmanuel, Fitzwilliam, Girton, Homerton, Jesus, King's, New Hall, Newnham, Queens', St John's, Selwyn, Sidney Sussex, Trinity Hall, Wolfson*): TSA (www.tsa.cambridgeassessment.org.uk).

East Lancashire (IHE) Questionnaire and tests before interview.

London South Bank (Bld Serv Eng; Civ Eng; Elec Eng; Mech Eng) Degree subject-based test and numeracy test at interview.

Oxford (Eng Sci; Eng Comp Sci; Eng Econ Mgt) No essays required. No written tests. See www.maths.ox.ac.uk.

Southampton Literacy and numeracy tests for Foundation course applicants.

Southampton Solent Mathematical test at interview.

Suffolk (Univ Campus) (Civ Eng, Elec Electron Eng, Mech Eng courses) Interviews.

English

Anglia Ruskin Samples of written work required.

Birmingham City, Bristol Samples of work required.

Blackpool and Fylde (Coll) Samples of work before interview.

Buckingham English test for non-English-speaking applicants.

Cambridge (*All colleges except Downing, King's, Pembroke, Hughes Hall, Lucy Cavendish, St Edmunds, Wolfson*): Essays to be submitted before interview; (*all colleges except Christ's, Gonville and Caius, Queens', St John's, Trinity, Trinity Hall*): Test at interview; (*Emmanuel, Robinson*): Preparatory study at interview.

London (King's) Applicants to prepare a short literary text before interview.

London (UCL) After interview applicants are asked to write a critical commentary on an unseen passage of prose or verse.

Newport (Crea Writ) Samples of creative writing before interview.

Oxford (English) (*All colleges offering the subject*): All candidates taking English Literature, English and Modern Languages, Classics and English (3yr and 4yr courses) take a written test, the English

Literature Admissions Test (ELAT); see www.elat.org.uk. Students taking History and English will not take ELAT but will take the History Aptitude Test (see **History** below).

Oxford (Engl Modn Langs) (*All colleges offering the subject*): See **English** above. A 30-minute test in the foreign language. See www.english.ox.ac.uk.

Portsmouth (Engl Crea Writ; Crea Writ Dr) All applicants will be required to submit a short piece of creative writing to the admissions office. This should be between 400 and 500 words long and should include the following words and use each one twice: shell, flicker, knit, coin, compose, lark, stream, root. All the words must be used and each word must be used in a different context and/or with a different meaning on each occasion. Language should be used imaginatively and accurately.

Southampton Examples of written work required from Access students.

European and Middle Eastern Languages (See **Modern and Medieval Languages**)

Equine Science

Lincoln Applicants are required to show that they can ride to BHS Level 2 or equivalent.
Nottingham Trent (Spo Hrs Mgt) Riding test.

European Studies

London (Gold) Informal conversation in the relevant language (French, German or Spanish).

Film Studies

Bournemouth A 20-page screen-play required before interview.
Bournemouth (AI) Portfolio. Practical test of short film stills.
Creative Arts (UC) Portfolio at interview.
Liverpool John Moores Questionnaire and test before interview.
Newport Portfolio of work.
Roehampton Essays taken to interview and discussed.
Westminster Questionnaire to be completed and samples of work required before interview.

Fine Art

Oxford Specimen drawing examination paper available on website.

French (See also **Modern and Medieval Languages**)

Oxford (*Jesus, St John's, St Hilda's*): Essays to be submitted before interview. (*Jesus*): Response to a passage at interview; (*Jesus, St John's, St Hilda's*): French grammar test.

Geography

Cambridge (*Christ's, Churchill, Clare, Corpus Christi, Emmanuel, Fitzwilliam, Girton, Homerton, Jesus, King's, Magdalene, New Hall, Newnham, Trinity Hall*): Essays to be submitted before interview; (*Downing, Gonville and Caius, Queen's, St John's, Selwyn, Sidney Sussex, Trinity, St Edmund's, Wolfson*): Interview only; (*Churchill, Emmanuel, Robinson, St Catharine's*): Preparatory study at interview; (*Fitzwilliam, New Hall, Hughes Hall, Lucy Cavendish*): Test at interview.
Cardiff Test for some joint courses.
Oxford (*All colleges offering the subject*): Two marked pieces of written work. No written test at interview; (*St Hilda's*): Short written article to discuss.

German (See also **Modern and Medieval Languages**)

Aston, **Liverpool John Moores** Written test at interview.

History

Bangor Samples of work only required from mature applicants without conventional qualifications.
Buckingham English test for non-English-speaking applicants.
Liverpool Test for mature applicants.
Liverpool John Moores Mature students not in education must submit an essay.

London (Gold) Samples of written work from non-standard applicants and from those without academic qualifications.

Oxford (Hist (Anc Modn); Hist Econ; Hist Pol) (*All colleges offering the subject*): All applicants take the History Aptitude Test (www.history.ox.ac). Those called for interview send an essay by the end of November.

Oxford (Hist Modn Langs) Short 30-minute test in the language.

Roehampton Essays taken to interview and discussed.

History of Art

Cambridge (*Christ's, Churchill, Clare, Corpus Christi, Emmanuel, Homerton, King's, Magdalene, New Hall, Newnham, Pembroke, St John's, Sidney Sussex, Trinity, Trinity Hall*): Essays to be submitted before interview; (*Downing, Fitzwilliam, Girton, Gonville and Caius, Jesus, Peterhouse, Queens', Robinson, Selwyn, St Edmund's, Wolfson*): Interview only; (*Hughes Hall, Lucy Cavendish*): Test at interview.

Oxford (*All colleges offering the subject*): Two pieces required: (a) a marked essay from an A-level or equivalent course, and (b) a brief account of no more than 750 words responding to an item of art or design to which the applicant has had first-hand access with a photograph or photocopy of the item provided if possible. No written test at interview although the applicant may be presented with photographs or artefacts for discussion at interview. Submitted written work may also be discussed at interview.

Hospitality Management

Leicester (Coll) Literacy and numeracy test.

Human Sciences

Oxford (*All colleges offering the subject*): Two recent marked essays or project reports, relevant to the Human Sciences course, written as part of the school or college course. No written test at interview.

Italian

Cardiff Test for some joint courses.

Journalism (see also **Media Studies**)

West Scotland Tests on public affairs and writing skills.

Land Economy

Cambridge (*Christ's, Clare, Fitzwilliam, Homerton, King's, Magdalene, Newnham, Peterhouse, Queens'*): Essays to be submitted before interview; (*Downing, Girton, Gonville and Caius, Queens', Robinson, St Catharine's, St John's, Selwyn, Sidney Sussex, Trinity, Trinity Hall, St Edmund's, Wolfson*): Interview only; (*Jesus, Magdalene, Newnham*): Preparatory study at interview; (*Newnham, Lucy Cavendish*): TSA; (*Hughes Hall*): Test at interview.

Law

The following universities require applicants to take the LNAT for specified courses. Check university websites and www.lnat.ac.uk and see also **Chapter 6** and the Law subject table in **Chapter 9**: **Birmingham**, **Bristol**, **Cambridge** (*all colleges*), **Durham**, **Exeter**, **Glasgow**, **London (King's)**, **(UCL)**, **Nottingham**, **Oxford** (*all colleges*) for specified courses: Two hours duration.

Birmingham City Questionnaire to be completed and an IQ test.

Bolton Own diagnostic test used (logic and reasoning).

Bradford (Coll) Academic tests at interview for mature students.

Bristol Check with the Law Department for LNAT requirements.

Cambridge (*Christ's, Corpus Christi, Emmanuel, Homerton, Magdalene, Peterhouse, Robinson, Wolfson*): Essays to be submitted before interview; (*Churchill, Clare, Corpus Christi, Girton, Gonville and Caius, Homerton, Jesus, Pembroke, Robinson, Trinity, St Edmund's*): Test at interview; (*Emmanuel, Jesus,*

Magdalene, New Hall, St Catharine's, Selwyn, Trinity Hall): Preparatory study at interview. All applicants take the LNAT.

Oxford (*All colleges offering the subject*): All applicants take the LNAT. (Law Law St Euro) LNAT plus, at interview, a short oral test in the modern language for students taking a joint language, except for those taking European Legal Studies. No other written work required except for Harris Manchester College.

Materials Science

Oxford (Mat Sci; Mat Econ Mgt) No written work required. No written test at interview.

Mathematics

Cambridge (*All colleges except Homerton, Hughes Hall, Lucy Cavendish, St Edmund's, Wolfson*): Mathematics STEP; (*Churchill (possibly), Corpus Christi, Girton, King's, Magdalene (possibly), New Hall, Peterhouse (possibly), Robinson, Trinity, Hughes Hall*): Test at interview; (*St Edmund's*): Interview only. See www.maths.cam.ac.uk/.

Liverpool John Moores Literacy and numeracy tests.

Oxford (Maths; Maths Comp Sci; Maths Stats) (*All colleges offering the subjects*): Overseas candidates unable to attend for interview may be required to submit written work. A 2½-hour written test is set at interview. See www.admissions.ox.ac.uk/interviews/tests.

Oxford (Maths Phil) (*All colleges offering the subject*): Two essays showing capacity for reasoned argument and clear writing, not expected to be on a philosophical subject. See www.admissions.ox.ac.uk/interviews/tests.

Media Studies

Blackpool and Fylde (Coll) Samples of work before interview.

Bournemouth 250-word essay.

Bournemouth and Poole (Coll) Degree subject-based test at interview.

City, Glasgow Caledonian Written test at interview.

Bolton, **Leicester (Coll)** Samples of work at interview.

Brighton (Spo Jrnl – for those called to interview: contact admissions tutor).

City Spelling, punctuation, grammar, general knowledge tests and an essay assignment. Tests given on current affairs and use of English.

Coventry Interview and portfolio.

Hull (Coll) Essay required before interview.

Liverpool John Moores Questionnaire to be completed before interview. Degree subject-based test at interview.

London Met Mathematics and written English test.

Napier (Journal) Samples of work before interview.

Newport Portfolio of work.

West Scotland (Jrnl) Test covers public affairs and writing ability.

Westminster Questionnaire to be completed before interview.

Medicine

NB Most medical schools require applicants to sit the BioMedical Admissions Test (BMAT) or the UK Clinical Aptitude Test (UKCAT) or, for graduate entry, the Graduate Australian Medical Schools Admissions Test (GAMSAT) for specified Medicine courses. Applicants are advised to check the websites of all universities and medical schools offering Medicine for their latest admissions requirements, including admissions and aptitude tests, and to check www.bmat.org.uk, www.ukcat.ac.uk and www.gamsat.co.uk for the latest information.

BMAT is required by **Cambridge** (*All colleges*), **Imperial London**, **London (RVC)**, **(UCL)**, **Manchester** (for the six-year Medicine and Foundation courses only), **Oxford** (*All colleges*).

GAMSAT is required by **London (St George's)**, **Nottingham, Swansea** (graduate entry).

UKCAT is required by the following universities and medical schools:

> **Aberdeen, Brighton and Sussex Medical School, Cardiff, Dundee, Durham and Newcastle, East Anglia, Edinburgh, Glasgow, Hull York Medical School, Keele, Leeds, Leicester Warwick, London (King's), (QM), (St George's)** (not used for MBBS 5 and MBBS 6), **Manchester, Newcastle, Nottingham, Oxford** (graduate entry Medicine degree only), **Peninsula Medical School, Queen's Belfast, Sheffield, Southampton, St Andrews.**

Modern and Medieval Languages (See also **Oriental Studies** and separate languages)

Bangor Offer may be lowered after interview.

Cambridge (*All colleges except Fitzwilliam, Hughes Hall, Lucy Cavendish, St Edmund's, Wolfson*): Essays to be submitted before interview; (*All colleges except St Edmund's*): Test at interview; (*Emmanuel, New Hall, Robinson, St John's, Trinity*): Preparatory study at interview; (*St Edmund's*): Interview only. See www.mml.cam.ac.uk/prospectus/undergrad/applying/test.html.

Liverpool The interview will last approximately 20 minutes with part of it in the language(s) to be studied. Occasionally the applicant may be asked to sit a short grammar test.

Oxford (*All colleges offering the subjects*): Two marked essays for each language being studied. Two 30-minute tests at interview for each language to be studied (not in languages to be taken from scratch). The tests are designed to assess grammar and not vocabulary. See www.admissions.ox.ac.uk/interviews/tests.

Oxford (Modn Lang Ling) (*All colleges offering the subject*) The essay to be submitted should involve linguistic analysis if the A-level being studied involves this. See www.admissions.ox.ac.uk/interviews/tests.

Oxford (Euro Mid E Langs) (*All colleges offering the subject*): Two recent marked essays, one in the European language. Short written test in the European language at interview. See www.admissions.ox.ac.uk/interviews/tests.

Music

NB See also **Chapter 9 Subject Tables: Music**

All institutions will organise auditions for applicants.

Bangor Candidates offered the option of an audition.

Birmingham City Some subject-based and practical tests.

Cambridge (*All colleges except New Hall, Newnham, Queens', Sidney Sussex, Hughes Hall, Lucy Cavendish, St Edmund's, Wolfson*): Essays to be submitted before interview; (*Churchill, Clare, Fitzwilliam, Girton, Homerton, Jesus, King's, New Hall, Pembroke, Peterhouse, Robinson, St Catharine's, Selwyn, Trinity, Hughes Hall*): Test at interview; (*Clare, Emmanuel, Newnham, Robinson*): Preparatory study at interview; (*Downing, Queens', Sidney Sussex, St Edmund's, Wolfson*): Interview only; (*Lucy Cavendish*): TSA.

Coventry Proforma used prior to interview. Some students rejected at this stage.

Liverpool Candidates may be asked to undertake a variety of aural tests, the performance of a prepared piece of music and some sight-reading when called for interview.

London (Gold) Degree subject-based test.

London Met Performance tests and essay.

Manchester (CAT) Numeracy and literacy test.

Napier Audition and theory test.

Oxford (*All colleges offering the subject*): One marked sample of harmony and/or counterpoint and two marked essays on any areas or aspects of music. Candidates may submit a portfolio of compositions (these are non-returnable). Performance tests at interview; (*St Hilda's*): Performance, keyboard and sight-reading tests. See www.admissions.ox.ac.uk/interviews/tests.

St Helens (Coll) (Mus Tech; Snd Des) Test.

Thames Valley (Mus Tech) Students required to produce a portfolio of work. (Mus Perf) Students attend an audition: see www.tvu.ac.uk.

TABLE OF INTERVIEW REQUIREMENTS FOR MUSIC COURSES

Key
P = Performance
K = Keyboard tests
E = Essay
S = Sight-singing

A = Aural
H = Harmony and Counterpoint (Written)
X = Extracts for analysis or 'guessing the composer', dates etc.

Bangor* PAX (bring example)	**Liverpool Hope** PKH
Barnsley (Coll) A	**London (Gold)** PKH
Bath Spa PKXA	**London (King's)** PASK
Birmingham PSKHXA	**London (RAcMus)** PKHX
Birmingham City PAH	**London (RCMus)** PKEXH
Bristol PSKHEXA	**London (RH)** PHEXA
Cambridge (Hom)* PKE (bring example)	**Manchester (RNCM)** PAX
Cardiff PE	**Newcastle** PHXA
Chichester P	**Oxford** PHAK
City PASKE	**Roehampton** PKH
Colchester (Inst) PKSX	**Royal Scottish (RSAMD)** PSA
Derby PE	**Royal Welsh (CMus/Dr)** PSA
Durham PKXA	**Salford** PKEH
East Anglia PKHEXA	**Sheffield** PEAH
Edinburgh PKHEA	**South Birmingham (Coll)** P
Glasgow PS	**Southampton** P
Huddersfield PH	**Surrey** PH or X
Lancaster PAH	**Ulster** P
Leeds PX	**Wolverhampton** PE
Liverpool PK	**York** PEKHX

* Examples may include essays, harmony and counterpoint compositions. Performance tests/ auditions are standard practice for Music courses in all universities and colleges.

Natural Sciences (Biological)
Cambridge (*Christ's, Fitzwilliam, Gonville and Caius, Jesus, King's, Newnham, Pembroke, St Catharine's, Selwyn*): Interview only; (*Churchill, Clare, Downing, Emmanuel, Girton, Homerton, Queens', St John's, Sidney Sussex, Trinity Hall, Wolfson*): TSA; (*New Hall, Trinity, Hughes Hall, Lucy Cavendish*): Test at interview; (*Corpus Christi, Homerton, Peterhouse, Robinson, St Edmund's*): Essays to be submitted before interview; (*Emmanuel, Magdalene, Robinson*): Preparatory study at interview.

Natural Sciences (Physical)
Cambridge (*Churchill, Clare, Downing, Emmanuel, Fitzwilliam, Girton, Homerton, New Hall, Newnham, Peterhouse, Queens, St John's, Sidney Sussex, Trinity Hall, St Edmund's, Wolfson*): TSA; (*Christ's, Gonville and Caius, Jesus, Magdalene, Pembroke, St Catharine's, Selwyn*): Interview only; (*Corpus Christi, King's, Robinson, Trinity, Hughes Hall, Lucy Cavendish*): Test at interview; (*Emmanuel*): Preparatory study at interview; (*Homerton*): Essays to be submitted before interview. TSA tests, see www.tsa.cambridgeassessment.org.uk.

Nursing
Most institutions will interview.

Birmingham City Literacy and numeracy tests at interview.
Bolton Literacy test.
Bristol UWE Questionnaire/test before interview.
City Written test.
Derby Literacy and numeracy tests at interview.
Dundee Literacy test.
East Anglia Tests.
Liverpool A group of candidates is given a task to undertake during which applicants are assessed for their ability to work in a team, maturity, communication skills and their level of involvement.
London South Bank (Nurs A, C, MH) Literacy and numeracy tests at interview.
Suffolk (Univ Campus) Interview and tests.
Wolverhampton Tests.
York Literacy and numeracy tests.

Occupational Therapy
Bristol UWE Questionnaire/test before interview.
Ulster Health Professions Admissions Test: see www.hpat.org.uk and www.ulster.ac.uk before completing the UCAS application.

Optometry
Bradford (Coll) Literacy and numeracy tests.

Oriental Studies
Cambridge (*Christ's, Churchill, Clare, Downing, Emmanuel, Fitzwilliam, Gonville and Caius, Jesus, Magdalene, New Hall, Newnham, Pembroke, Peterhouse, St Catharine's, St John's, Selwyn, Trinity, Trinity Hall*): Essays to be submitted before interview; (*Churchill, Clare, Corpus Christi, Fitzwilliam, Girton, King's, Magdalene, Peterhouse, Sidney Sussex, Trinity Hall, Hughes Hall, Lucy Cavendish*): Test at interview; (*Homerton, Queens', St Edmund's, Wolfson*): Interview only; (*Robinson, St John's*): Preparatory study at interview.
Oxford (*All colleges offering the subject*): Two essays, preferably of different kinds. Essays in a European language are acceptable. No prior knowledge of Oriental languages required. Occasional written tests. See www.admissions.ox.ac.uk/interviews/tests.

Osteopathy
British Sch of Ost At interview, A-level, literacy, numeracy, logic and reasoning-based tests plus a practical aptitude test.

Paramedic Science
Coventry Stress Test.

Performing Arts (See **Dance/Drama**)

Pharmacology/Pharmaceutical Sciences
Portsmouth Test of motivation, knowledge of the subject, of the degree course and the careers to which it leads.

Pharmacy
Liverpool John Moores Literacy and numeracy tests.
Portsmouth (A-level students) Test of motivation and knowledge of Pharmacy as a profession. (Other applicants) Test of chemistry and biology, plus literacy and numeracy tests.

Philosophy

Cambridge (*All colleges except Lucy Cavendish, St Edmund's, Wolfson*): Test at interview; (*Churchill, Downing, Emmanuel, Homerton, King's, Magdalene, Peterhouse, Trinity, Wolfson*): Essays to be submitted before interview; (*St Edmund's*): Interview only; (*Lucy Cavendish*): TSA.

Leeds, **London (UCL)**, **Oxford**, **Warwick** Written test at interview.

Liverpool Samples of written work may be requested in cases where there is a question of the applicant's ability to cope with the academic skills required of them.

Oxford (Phil Modn Langs) (*All colleges offering the subject*): Two essays required, one in the proposed language unless it is intended to start a language from scratch. A 30-minute test in the modern language at interview. (Phil) A one-hour test to assess the ability to reason analytically and to use language accurately. (Phil Theol) Written work as for Theology (see under **Religious Studies**). Written test at interview as for **Philosophy**. See www.admissions.ox.ac.uk/interviews/tests.

Oxford (PPE) (*All colleges offering the subject*): Two pieces of marked written work. Those studying a related subject (philosophy, politics, economics, sociology, 19th/20th century history) should submit an essay in that subject. If studying more than one of these subjects the essays from two different subjects can be submitted. One-hour written test at interview (plus 15 minutes' reading time). No prior knowledge of philosophy, politics or economics required.

Physical Education

All institutions will require practical tests at interview.

Chichester Physical test.

Liverpool John Moores Literacy and numeracy tests and gym assessment.

Manchester (CAT) Communications test.

Physics

Bristol A-level and degree subject-based tests.

Oxford (*All colleges offering the subject*) Information available at www.physics.ox.ac.uk; (*Corpus Christi, Jesus, St Hilda's*): A-level-based test; (*St John's*): Mathematics-for-Physics test.

Physics and Philosophy

Oxford (*All colleges offering the subject*) Two pieces of written work relating to philosophy or otherwise involving careful, reasoned arguments. No written tests. No philosophy tests.

Physiological Sciences/Physiology

Oxford (*All colleges offering the subject*) BMAT: see www.bmat.org.uk.

Physiotherapy

East Anglia Tests.

Liverpool A group of candidates is given a task to undertake, during which they are assessed for their ability to work in a team, maturity, communication skills and their level of involvement.

Robert Gordon Practical testing varies from year to year.

Ulster Health Professions Admissions Test: see www.hpat.org.uk and www.ulster.ac.uk before completing the UCAS application.

Podiatry

Matthew Boulton (CFHE) Literacy and numeracy tests.

Ulster Health Professions Admissions Test: see www.hpat.org.uk and www.ulster.ac.uk before completing the UCAS application.

Politics (See also **Social and Political Sciences**)

Buckingham English test for non-English-speaking applicants.

Liverpool John Moores Mature students not in education must submit an essay.

London (Gold) Essays from current A/AS-level course to be submitted before interview.
Oxford See (PPE) under **Philosophy** above.

Psychology
Bangor Access course entry students may be asked to submit an essay.
Birmingham Written tests at interview.
Liverpool John Moores Written tests at interview.
London (UCL) Questionnaire to be completed.
Manchester Written tests at interview.
Manchester Met/Manchester (CAT) (Psy p/t) Samples of work before interview, numeracy and literacy tests at interview.
Oxford (Expmtl Psy) (*All colleges offering the subject*): No written work required. One-hour test (15 minutes' reading time) at interview. Applicants comment or answer questions on a scientific article. See www.admissions.ox.ac.uk/interviews/tests.
Oxford (Psy Phil Physiol) To study Philosophy as part of PPP, two pieces of recent written work will be required. Written test at interview (see Expmtl Psy above).
Roehampton Questionnaire before interview; test at interview.

Radiography
Bangor A short essay will be set at interview.
Liverpool (Diag Radiog Radiothera) The group of candidates is given a task to undertake, during which they are assessed for their ability to work in a team, maturity, communication skills and their level of involvement.
Ulster Health Professions Admissions Test: see www.hpat.org.uk and www.ulster.ac.uk before completing the UCAS application.

Religious Studies
Cambridge (Theol Relig St) (*All colleges except Churchill, Clare, Gonville and Caius, Sidney Sussex, Hughes Hall, Lucy Cavendish, St Edmund's*): Essays to be submitted before interview; (*Clare, Corpus Christi, Fitzwilliam, Girton, Peterhouse, Hughes Hall, Lucy Cavendish*): Test at interview; (*Emmanuel, Magdalene, Selwyn*): Preparatory study at interview; (*Gonville and Caius, Sidney Sussex, St Edmund's*): Interview only.
Oxford (Theology) (*All colleges offering the subject*): Two essays to be submitted including one which must be ordinary marked homework of less than 2500 words. If possible, the pieces should reflect work done in Year 13. The work should be prose and should ideally contain evaluative as well as descriptive components.

Russian (See also **Modern and Medieval Languages**)
Oxford (*Jesus*): A-level-based test at interview; (*St John's*): Russian grammar test; (*St Hilda's*): IQ test.

Social and Political Sciences
Cambridge (*All colleges except Clare, Gonville and Caius, Jesus, Queens', St Catharine's, Hughes Hall, Lucy Cavendish*): Essays to be submitted before interview; (*Churchill, Emmanuel, Magdalene, Robinson*): Preparatory study at interview; (*Clare, Gonville and Caius, Hughes Hall, Lucy Cavendish*): Test at interview; (*Jesus, Queens', St Catharine's, St Edmund's*): Interview only.
Manchester Met (Yth Commun Wk).

Social Policy
London (LSE) Two essays to be submitted before interview.

Social Work
Anglia Ruskin Samples of written work required.

Bangor, Birmingham, Brunel, De Montfort, Durham New (Coll), London (Gold), Worcestershire New (Coll) Written test at interview.
Birmingham City Some tests are set at interview.
Bristol UWE Questionnaire before interview.
De Montfort Test.
Derby Literacy and numeracy tests at interview.
Dundee Literacy test.
Durham New (Coll) Test.
East Anglia Test.
London (Gold) Basic mathematics test at interview.
London Met Pre-interview literacy test and if successful, an interview.
London South Bank Literacy and numeracy tests.
NEW (Coll) Test.
Sheffield Literacy and numeracy tests.
Stirling Tests.
Suffolk (Univ Campus) Interview and test.
Wolverhampton Tests.

Sociology
Leeds Copy of written work requested.
London Met Where appropriate separate tests in comprehension and mathematical skills that will be used to help us reach a decision.

Spanish (See also Modern and Medieval Languages)
Oxford (*Jesus*): Essays to be submitted before interview. A-level-based test at interview; (*St John's*): Spanish grammar test.

Speech Sciences
Manchester Met Two essays and a questionnaire.
Sheffield Listening test and problem-solving.
Ulster Health Professions Admissions Test: see www.hpat.org.uk and www.ulster.ac.uk before completing the UCAS application.

Sports Science/Studies
Nottingham Trent (Spo Hrs Mgt) Riding test.

Teacher Training
Anglia Ruskin Literacy test at interview.
Bath Spa, Brighton, Chichester, Cumbria, De Montfort, Gloucestershire, Liverpool John Moores, Nottingham Trent, Plymouth, Roehampton, Sunderland, Trinity Carmarthen (Coll), Worcester, York St John Written test at interview.
Bristol UWE, Newport, St Mary's (UC) Literacy and mathematical tests at interview.
Brunel Literacy, mathematical and practical tests depending on subject.
Chester Literacy and numeracy tests.
Dundee Literacy and numeracy tests.
Durham Key skills test.
Gloucestershire Mathematical test at interview.
Liverpool John Moores Mathematical and diagnostic tests on interview day.
London South Bank Literacy and numeracy tests.
Nottingham Trent Practical presentation.
Plymouth Mathematical test at interview.
St Mary's (UC) Practical tests for PE applicants.

Wigan and Leigh (Coll) Mathematical test at interview.
Winchester Literacy test at interview.

Veterinary Science/Medicine

London (RVC) BMAT (see www.bmat.org.uk).
Cambridge (*All colleges except Homerton, King's, Peterhouse, Hughes Hall*): BMAT; (*Emmanuel, Robinson*): Preparatory study at interview.
Liverpool Candidates are asked to write an essay on a veterinary topic prior to interview.
Myerscough (Coll) (Vet Nurs) Subject-based test at interview.
Nottingham Trent (Vet Nurs) Evidence of 1-2 weeks work experience in a veterinary practice.

SELECTION OF APPLICANTS

University and college departmental admissions tutors are responsible for selecting candidates, basing their decisions on the policies of acceptable qualifications established by each institution and, where required, applicants' performance in admissions tests. There is little doubt that academic achievement, aptitude and promise are the most important factors although other subsidiary factors may be taken into consideration. The outline which follows provides information on the way in which candidates are selected for degree and diploma courses:

* Grades obtained by the applicant in GCE, A-level and AS-level examinations and the range of subjects studied may be considered. In the subject tables of **Chapter 9** some universities have indicated the levels they seek in some subjects.
* Applicant's performance in aptitude and admissions tests, as required by universities and colleges.
* Academic record of the applicant throughout his or her school career, especially up to A-level and AS-levels, Highers, Advanced Highers or other qualifications and the choice of subjects. If you are taking general studies at A-level or AS-level confirm with the admissions tutor that this is acceptable.
* Time taken by the applicant to obtain good grades at GCSE/Standard Grade and A-level and AS-levels/Highers/Advanced Highers.
* Forecast or the examination results of the applicant at A-level and AS-level and head teacher's report.
* The applicant's intellectual development; evidence of ability and motivation to follow the chosen course.
* The applicant's range of interests, both in and out of school; aspects of character and personality.
* The vocational interests, knowledge and experience of the applicant particularly if they are choosing vocational courses.

INTERVIEWS

Fewer applicants are now interviewed than in the past but even if you are not called you should make an effort to visit your chosen universities and/or colleges before you accept any offer. Interviews may be arranged simply to give you a chance to see the institution and the department and to meet the staff and students. Alternatively, interviews may be an important part of the selection procedure for specific courses such as Law, Medicine and Teaching. If they are, you need to prepare yourself well.

Most interviews last approximately 20–30 minutes and you may be interviewed by more than one person. For practical subjects such as Music and Drama almost certainly you will be asked to perform, and for artistic subjects, to take examples of your work. For some courses you may also have a written or other test at interview: see **Degree Subject Lists of Universities and Colleges using Tests and Assessments** above.

How best can you prepare yourself?
Firstly, as one applicant advised, 'Go to the interview – at least you'll see the place.'

Secondly, on the question of dress, try to turn up looking smart (it may not matter, but it can't be wrong). Two previous applicants were more specific: 'Dress smartly but sensibly so you are comfortable for travelling and walking round the campus.'

More general advice was also important:

* 'Prepare well – interviewers are never impressed by applicants who only sit there with no willingness to take part.'
* 'Read up the prospectus and course details. Know how their course differs from any others you have applied for and be able to say why you prefer theirs.'
* 'They always ask if you have any questions to ask them: prepare some!'

Questions which you could ask might focus on the ways in which work is assessed, the content of the course, field work, work experience, teaching methods, accommodation and, especially for vocational courses, contacts with industry, commerce or the professions. However, don't ask questions which are already answered in the prospectus!

These are only a few suggestions and other questions may come to mind during the interview which, above all, should be a two-way flow of information. It is also important to keep a copy of your UCAS application (especially Section 10) for reference since your interview will probably start with a question about something you have written.

Interviewers usually will want to know why you have chosen the subject and why you have chosen their particular institution. They will want to see how motivated you are, how much care you have taken in choosing your subject, how much you know about your subject, what books you have read. If you have chosen a vocational course they will want to find out how much you know about the career it leads to, and whether you have visited any places of work or had any work experience. If your chosen subject is also an A-level subject you will be asked about your course and the aspects of the course you like the most.

Try to relax. For some people interviews can be an ordeal; most interviewers know this and will make allowances. The following extract from the Oxford prospectus will give you some idea of what admissions tutors look for:

* 'Interviews serve various purposes and no two groups of tutors will conduct them in the same way or give them exactly the same weight. Most tutors wish to discover whether a candidate has done more than absorb passively what he/she has been taught. They try to ascertain the nature and strength of candidates' intellectual interests and their capacity for independent development. They are also likely to ask about applicants' other interests outside their school curriculum. This is partly because between two candidates of equal academic merit, preference will be given to the one who has the livelier interests or activities, and partly because it is easier to learn about candidates when they talk about what interests them most.
* 'Interviews are in no sense hostile interrogations. Those candidates who show themselves to be honest, thoughtful and unpretentious will be regarded more favourably than those who try to impress or take the view that it is safest to say as little as possible. We do not expect candidates to be invariably mature and judicious.'

In the tables in **Chapter 9** (**Selection interviews**, **Interview advice and questions** and **Reasons for rejection**) you will also find examples of questions which have been asked in recent years for which you might prepare, and non-academic reasons why applicants have been rejected! You will also find some impressions of applicants' experiences of Open days and interviews they have attended (**Applicants' impressions**). These impressions may not be yours when you visit a university or college, but they do give you an idea of what you might find.

The subject tables in the next chapter represent the core of the book, listing degree courses offered by all UK universities and colleges. These tables are designed to provide you with the information you need so that you can match your abilities and interests with your chosen degree subject, prepare your application and find out how applicants are selected for courses.

At the top of each table there is a brief overview of the subject area, together with a selection of websites for organisations that can provide relevant careers or course information. This is then followed by the subject tables themselves in which information is provided in sequence under the following headings:

Course Offers Information
* Subject requirements/preferences (GCSE/A-level)
* Your target offers
* Alternative offers

Examples of Foundation Degrees in the Subject Field

Choosing Your Course
* Course variations
* Universities and colleges teaching quality
* Top universities and colleges (research)
* Sandwich degree courses

Admissions Information
* Number of applicants per place

* Advice to applicants and planning the UCAS personal statement
* Misconceptions about this course
* Selection interviews
* Interview advice and questions
* Applicants' impressions
* Reasons for rejection (non-academic)

After-Results Advice
* Offers to applicants repeating A-levels

Graduate destinations and employment
* Career note

Other degree subjects for consideration

When selecting a degree course it is important to try to judge the points score or grades that you are likely to achieve and compare them with the offers listed under Your target offers. However, even though you might be capable of achieving the right grades, there is no guarantee that you will receive an offer since other factors in your application, such as the personal statement, will be taken into consideration.

University departments frequently re-adjust their offers, depending on the numbers of candidates applying, so **you must not assume that the offers and policies published now will necessarily apply to courses starting in 2009 or thereafter**. However, you can assume that the offers published in this book represent the general academic levels at which you should aim.

Below are explanations of the information given under the headings in the subject tables. It is important that you read these carefully so that you understand how they can help you to choose and apply for courses that are right for you.

COURSE OFFERS INFORMATION
Subject requirements/preferences
Brief information is given on the GCSE and A-level requirements. Where applicable, details are given on the requirements for the Advanced Extension Awards (AEA) and the Sixth Term Examination Papers

(STEP) as required by certain colleges at Cambridge. Details of STEP can be obtained from OCR, 1 Hills Road, Cambridge CB1 2EU; past papers are available by contacting www.ocr.org.uk. Check prospectuses and websites of universities and colleges for course requirements.

> **NB** A* grades are likely to form part of university offers in the higher ranges for students applying for places in 2008 for entry in 2009.

Your target offers

Universities and colleges offering degree courses in the subject area are listed in descending order according to the number of UCAS tariff points they are likely to require applicants to achieve. The UCAS tariff total is listed down the left-hand side of the page, and to the right appear all the institutions (in alphabetical order) likely to make offers in this region. (More information on the UCAS tariff and how to calculate your offers is provided on page 110 and on the inside back cover of this book. Please also read the information in the **Important Note** box below.)

For each institution listed, the following information may be given:

Name of institution

Note that the name of an institution's university college or campus may be given in brackets after the institution title, for example **London (King's)** or **Kent (Medway)**. Where the institution is not a University, further information about its status may also be given to indicate the type of college – for example **(CHE)** to mean College of Higher Education or **(CAg)** to mean College of Agriculture. This is to help readers to differentiate between the types of colleges and to help them identify any specialisation a college may have – for example art or agriculture. A full list of abbreviations used is given under the heading **Institution Abbreviations** towards the end of this chapter.

Grades/points offer

After the institution name, a line of offers information is given showing the offer likely to be made by the institution for the courses indicated in brackets at the end of the line. Offers, however, may vary between applicants and the published grades and/or points offers should be regarded as targets to aim for and not necessarily the actual grades or points required. Offers may be reduced after the publication of A-level results particularly if a university or college is left with many spare places. However, individual course offers are abridged and should be used as a first source of reference and comparison only. It is not possible to publish all the variables relevant to each offer including the number of units required (see Tip below). **Applicants must check prospectuses and websites for full details of all offers and courses**. Depending on the details given by institutions, the offers may provide information as follows:

* **Grades**: The specific grades, or average grades, required at GCE A-level or at A-level plus AS-level. A-level grades are always presented in capital letters; AS-levels are shown in lower case – so the offer BBBc would indicate three grade Bs at A-level, plus an additional AS-level at grade C. Where necessary, the abbreviation 'AL' is used to indicate A-level; 'AS' to indicate AS-level. Offers are usually shown in terms of three A-level grades although some institutions accept two grades with the same points total or, alternatively, two A-level grades accompanied by AS-level grades. Two AS-levels may generally be regarded as equivalent to one A-level, and one Double Award A-level as equivalent to two standard A-levels.

  NB Unit grade information, introduced into the admissions system for entry in 2007, is most likely to be required by universities where a course is competitive, or where taking a specific unit is necessary or desirable for entry. Check with institutions' websites for their latest information.

* **UCAS Tariff points**: the number (or range) of tariff points. GCE A and AS-levels have a unit value in the UCAS tariff system (see below). Where two sets of tariff points are shown, for example

180–220 points, offers are usually made within this points range. Note that, in some cases, an institution may require a points score which is higher than the specified grade offer given. This can be for a number of reasons – for example, you may not be offering the standard subjects that would have been stipulated in a grades offer. In such cases additional points may be added by way of AS-levels, Key Skills etc. Check with prospectuses and websites or contact the university or college for further information.

In addition to asking for certain grades or points an institution may stipulate the number of units required or preferred, for example, 12 units (= 2AL or 1AL+2AS) or 18 units (= 3AL or 2AL+2AS): see institutions' websites and prospectuses.

The Cambridge Pre-U Diploma, a new examination equivalent to A-levels and the IB, will be offered for the first time in 2010 with coursework starting in 2008. Full details of this examination are given in **Appendix 4**.

Admissions tests for Law, Medicine and Veterinary Science/Medicine: where admissions tests form part of a university's offer for any of these subjects, this is indicated on the offers line in the subject tables for the relevant university. This is shown by '+LNAT' (for Law), '+BMAT' or '+UKCAT' (for Medicine), and '+BMAT' (for Veterinary Science/Medicine). For example, the offers lines could read as follows:

Birmingham – AAA+LNAT (Law; Law Bus St) *(IB 36 pts)*

Edinburgh – AABb+UKCAT (inc chem+1 from maths/phys/biol; AS biol min) (Medicine) *(IB 37 pts H766)*

Imperial London – AABb+BMAT (inc biol/chem+sci/maths) (Medicine) *(IB H655 ST555)*

Entry and admissions tests will be required for 2008/2009 by a number of institutions for a wide range of subjects: see **Chapter 7** for more information and check university websites and prospectuses.

Course title(s)

After the offer, an abbreviated form of the course title(s) to which the offers information refers is provided, also in brackets. The abbreviations used (see **Course abbreviations** below) closely relate to the course titles shown in the institutions' prospectuses. When the course gives the opportunity to study abroad (for example, in Continental Europe, Australia, North America) the abbreviated name of the relevant country is shown after the abbreviated course title. For example:

East Anglia – AAB–ABB (Ecol Aus/N Am) *(IB 31–34 pts)*

When experience in industry is provided as part of the course (not necessarily a sandwich course) this is indicated on the offers line by including 'Ind' after the abbreviated course title. For example:

Bristol – BBB (Pharmacol; Pharmacol Ind) *(IB 32 pts H665 inc 2 sci)*

Southampton – ABBb 370 pts (MEng Civ Eng Ind; Civ Eng Euro St; Env Eng courses; Civ Eng Archit) *(IB 33 pts)*

Sometimes the information in the offers line relates to more than one course (see Southampton above). In such cases, each course title is separated with a semicolon. When a number of joint courses exist in combination with a major subject, they may be presented using a list separated by slashes – for example '(Euro Mgt with Fr/Ger/Ital/Span)' indicates European Management with French or German or Italian or Spanish. Some titles may be followed by the word 'courses' – for example, (Geog courses):

Swansea – 300 pts (Geog courses)

This means that the information on the offer refers not only to the single Honours course in Geography, but also to Geography joint Honours and/or combined courses.

Courses awaiting validation are usually publicised in prospectuses etc., but are not included in these tables since there is no guarantee that they will run. You should check with the university that a non-validated course will be available.

The courses included on the offers line are examples of the courses available at that university or college. You will need to check prospectuses and websites for a complete list of the institution's single, joint, combined or major/minor degree courses available in the subject.

To help you understand the information provided under the 'UCAS tariff points requirements' heading, the box below provides a few examples with their meaning explained underneath.

OFFERS LINES EXPLAINED

320 pts [University/College name] – BBCc **or** BBccc (Fr Ger)
For the joint course in French and German, the University requires grades of BBC (280 pts) at A-level plus AS-level grade c (40 pts) making a total of 320 points or, alternatively, BB (200 pts) at A-level plus AS-level grades ccc (120 pts), making the same total.

220 pts [University/College name] – 220–280 pts (Geography)
For Geography, the University usually requires 220 UCAS tariff points, but offers may range up to 280 UCAS tariff points.

200 pts [University/College name] – 200–240 pts (Env Sci Ecol)
For the course in Environmental Science and Ecology the offer is in the range of 200 to 240 pts; 200 pts may be achieved in a number of ways — for example, with CCE or BDee at A-level or a 12-unit Double Award at CD + an A-level grade D or 2 AS-levels grade dd. Institutions differ in their requirements for the ways in which the points offer can be achieved: check with websites and prospectuses for their exact requirements.

IB offers

A selection of IB points offers appear in italics at the end of some university/subject entries. For comparison of entry requirements, applicants with IB qualifications should check the A-level offers required for their course and then refer to the Equivalent Offers table in this chapter. The figures under this subheading indicate the number or range of International Baccalaureate (IB) Diploma points likely to be requested in an offer. A range of points indicates variations between single and joint Honours courses. Applicants should check with the universities for any requirements for points gained from specific Higher and Standard level subjects.

From 2008 entry onwards, a new UCAS IB tariff has been introduced (see www.ucas.com). However, the **Table of Equivalent Offers** below gives the IB UCAS tariff equivalents currently used by the majority of universities and colleges, but applicants offering the IB should check with prospectuses and websites and, if in doubt, contact admissions tutors for the latest information on IB offers.

Alternative offers

In each of the subject tables, offers are shown in A-level grades or equivalent points, and in some cases as points offers of the International Baccalaureate Diploma (see above). However, applicants taking Scottish Highers, the IB Diploma, the Irish Leaving Certificate, the European Baccalaureate and the French Baccalaureate can compare their results with A-level equivalences by referring to the **Table of Equivalent Offers** below. Students offering the Welsh Baccalaureate Diploma qualify for 120 UCAS tariff points: see www.ucas.com, and also the notes at the bottom of the table (see below). For more information, applicants should compare the grades/tariff information given under **Your target offers** with the equivalents given in the **Table of Equivalent Offers** table below or with the UCAS tariff on www.ucas.com or contact the institution direct.

Scottish offers

Scottish Honours degrees normally take four years. However, students with very good qualifications may be admitted into the second year of courses (Advanced entry). In some cases it may even be possible to enter the third year. The policies at each of the universities are as follows:

Aberdeen Advanced entry possible for many courses, but not for Education, Law or Medicine.
Abertay Dundee No advanced entry.
Dundee Advanced entry possible for many courses, but not Art, Education, Law or Medicine.
Edinburgh Only in very unusual cases is entry to the second year accepted.
Glasgow No advanced entry except in some cases for Engineering and Sciences, but not for Accountancy, Arts or Social Science courses.
Glasgow Caledonian No advanced entry.
Napier Advanced entry to Stages 2, 3 or 4 of a programme, particularly for those with an HNC/HND or those with (or expecting to obtain) good grades in Advanced Highers or A-levels.
St Andrews Advanced entry for some courses.
Stirling Advanced entry for some courses.
Strathclyde Advanced entry for some courses.

IMPORTANT NOTE ON THE COURSE OFFERS INFORMATION

The information provided in **Chapter 9** is presented as a first reference source as to the target levels required. Institutions may alter their standard offers in the light of the qualifications offered by applicants.

The offers they publish do not constitute a contract and are not binding on prospective students: changes may occur between the time of publication and the time of application in line with market and student demand.

The points levels shown on the left-hand side of the offers listings are for ease of reference for the reader: not all universities will be making offers using the UCAS tariff points system and it cannot be assumed that they will accept a points equivalent to the grades they have stipulated.

Check university and college prospectuses, and also their websites, for their latest information before submitting your application.

EXAMPLES OF FOUNDATION DEGREES IN THE SUBJECT FIELD

This section lists examples of universities and colleges offering Foundation degrees in the subject field. Foundation degrees are employment-related higher education qualifications bringing higher education and business closer together to meet the needs of employers. The degrees are at a lower level than Honours degrees and can be studied on a part-time basis or full-time over two years. Entry requirements for these courses vary, but many institutions request between 60 and 100 UCAS tariff points. Full details of institutions offering Foundation degrees can be obtained from www.ucas.com and from Foundation Degree Forward at www.fdf.ac.uk.

CHOOSING YOUR COURSE

The information under this heading (to be read in conjunction with **Chapter 1**) covers factors that are important to consider in order to make an informed decision on which courses to apply for. The information is organised under the following subheadings:

Course variations – Widen your options

The purpose of this section is to widen your minds to appreciate the considerable range of courses available in the subject field. However, they have not been selected on the basis of academic reputation or course quality, only to provide examples of the diversity of courses.

Universities and colleges teaching quality

The Unistats website (www.unistats.com) provides official information for different subjects and universities and colleges in the United Kingdom to help prospective students and their advisers make comparisons between them and so make informed choices about what and where to study. Information is updated anually and is available for each subject taught at each university and college (and for some further education colleges). The Quality Assurance Agency (www.qaa.ac.uk) reviews the quality and standards of all universities and colleges and official reports of their reviews are available on their website but it is important to note their dates of publication.

Top universities and colleges (Research)

In 2001 an assessment exercise was carried out to rate university research on a scale of 1 (lowest) to 5* (highest). The institutions that achieved the highest ratings (5 or 5*) in the relevant subject area have been listed under this heading. However, be aware that some universities may not offer undergraduate courses in these subjects and that the next Research Assessment Exercise will take place in 2008.

Sandwich degree courses

Institutions offering sandwich courses (see **Chapter 4**) are listed here. Check with the institutions too, since new courses may be introduced or withdrawn depending on industrial or commercial arrangements. Further information on sandwich courses with specific information on the placements of students appears at the end of **Chapter 4**.

ADMISSIONS INFORMATION

Under this heading, information gathered from the institutions on their admissions policies has been provided. This should be very useful when planning your application.

Number of applicants per place (approx)

These figures show the approximate number of applicants initially applying for each place before any offers are made. It should be noted that any given number of applicants represents candidates who have also applied for up to four other university and college courses. In some subject areas some universities have provided details of the actual breakdown of numbers of applicants under the following headings: UK, EU (non-UK), non-EU (overseas), mature (over 21).

Advice to applicants and planning the UCAS personal statement

This section offers guidelines on information that could be included in the personal statement section of your UCAS application. In most cases, applicants will be required to indicate why they wish to follow a particular course and, if possible, to provide positive evidence of their interest.

Misconceptions about this course

Admissions tutors are given the opportunity to set the record straight by clarifying aspects of their course they feel are often misunderstood by students, and in some cases, advisers!

Selection interviews

Institutions that normally use the interview as part of their selection procedure are listed here. Those institutions adopting the interview procedure will usually interview only a small proportion of applicants. It is important to use this section in conjunction with **Chapter 7 Admissions Tests, Selection of Applicants and Interviews**.

Interview advice and questions

This section includes information from institutions on what candidates might generally expect the interview to cover, and examples of the types of interview questions posed in recent years. Also refer to **Chapter 7**: this provides information on tests and assessments which are used in selecting students.

Applicants' impressions (A=Open days; B=Interview days)
Extracts are provided, where available, from applicants' reports on visits to Open days and interviews.

Reasons for rejection (non-academic)
Academic ability is the major factor in the selection (or rejection) of applicants. Under this subheading, admissions tutors give other reasons for rejecting applicants.

AFTER-RESULTS ADVICE
Under this heading, information for helping you decide what to do after the examination results are published is provided (see also the section on **What to do on Results Day . . . and After** in **Chapter 6**). Details refer to the main subject area unless otherwise stated in brackets.

Offers to applicants repeating A-levels
This section gives details of whether second-time offers made to applicants repeating their exams may be '**higher**', '**possibly higher**' or the '**same**' as those made to first-time applicants. The information refers to single Honours courses. It should be noted that circumstances may differ between candidates – some will be repeating the same subjects taken in the previous year, while others may be taking different subjects. Offers will also be dictated by the grades you achieved on your first sitting of the examinations. Remember, if you were rejected by all your universities and have achieved good grades, contact them by telephone on results day – they may be prepared to revise their decision. This applies particularly to medical schools.

GRADUATE DESTINATIONS AND EMPLOYMENT
The information under this heading has been provided by the Higher Education Statistics Agency (HESA) and is taken from their report *Destinations of Leavers from Higher Education 2005/6*. The report can be obtained from HESA, 95 Promenade, Cheltenham, Gloucestershire GL50 1HZ; Tel 01242 211155; e-mail customer.services@hesa.ac.uk.

Details are given of the total number of graduates surveyed whose destinations have been recorded – not the total number who graduated in that subject. Employment figures relate to those in full-time permanent paid employment after six months in a variety of occupations not necessarily related to their degree subject (short-term and unpaid employment figures are not included). 'Further Study' includes research into a subject-related field, higher degrees, private study or, alternatively, career training involving work and further study. The 'Assumed unemployed' category refers to those students who were believed to be unemployed for various reasons (eg travelling, personal reasons) or those students still seeking permanent employment six months after graduating.

Career note
Short descriptions of the career destinations of graduates in the subject area are provided.

TIP
The website **www.prospects.ac.uk** also provides information about current career prospects for graduates in their chosen subject.

OTHER DEGREE SUBJECTS FOR CONSIDERATION
This heading includes some suggested alternative courses that have similarities to the courses listed in the subject table.

DECODING THE INFORMATION IN CHAPTER 9

THE UCAS TARIFF SYSTEM

The UCAS tariff system allocates points for grades achieved in a range of qualifications. Detailed information on the tariff system is provided at www.ucas.com/candq/tariff, but a brief outline is given in the table below.

GCEs	Grade	A	B	C	D	E
	AS-level Tariff points	60	50	40	30	20
	A-level (Single Award) Tariff points	120	100	80	60	40
	A-level (Double Award) Tariff points	AA: 240	BB: 200	CC: 160	DD: 120	EE: 80
		AB: 220	BC: 180	CD: 140	DE: 100	
Free-standing mathematics	Grade	A	B	C	D	E
	Tariff points	20	17	13	10	7
Scottish Qualifications	Grade	A	B	C	D	
	Higher Level Tariff points	72	60	48	42	
	Advanced Higher Level Tariff points	120	100	80	72	
Irish Leaving Certificate	Grade	A	B	C	D	
	Higher Level Tariff points	A1: 90	B1: 71	C1: 52	D1: 33	
		A2: 77	B2: 64	C2: 45	D2: 26	
			B3: 58	C3: 39	D3: 20	
Key Skills (number, IT and communication)	Level	4	3	2		
	Tariff points *per unit*	30	20	10		
Advanced Extension Awards	Grade	Distinction		Merit		
	Tariff points	40		20		

Tariff points are also awarded for other qualifications, including:

* **International Baccalaureate**: an IB Diploma ranging from a minimum of 24 points to a maximum of 45 points is equivalent to 280–768 UCAS tariff points but see **IB offers** on page 112.
* **BTEC National Awards, Certificates and Diplomas**: ranging from 40 points for a Pass in a National Award to 360 points for a triple Distinction in a Diploma.
* **CACHE Diploma in Childcare and Education**: ranging from 40 points for an E in Practical to 240 points for AA in Theory.
* **Diploma in Foundation Studies**: Pass=165 points; Merit=225 points; Distinction=285 points.
* **Music qualifications**: ranging from 5 points for a Pass in Grade 6 Theory to 75 points for a Distinction in Grade 8 Practical (as shown in the **Music** table in **Chapter 9**).
* **OCR National Certificates and Diplomas**: ranging from 40 points for a Pass in a Certificate to 360 points for a D1 in an Extended Diploma.

However, although an institution may give an offer in the form of a UCAS tariff total, it may not allow candidates to use points from all the above qualifications to contribute towards the total – always check with the institution direct. For example, it is common for institutions to stipulate to students that the tariff total must be achieved by way of A-levels or from a combination of A-levels and AS-levels – in which case they may specify a number of units using the system outlined below.

GCE AS-level	3 units
GCE A-level	6 units
GCE Double Award A-level	12 units

Most degree courses will require a minimum of 12 units although 15, 18 or 21 units may be stipulated. Key Skills are sometimes, but not always, included: check with the institutions direct for further details.

TIP

The key points are summarised on the **How to calculate your offers** section on the inside back cover of this book. Just fold it out for quick reference while you are looking at **Chapter 9**.

EQUIVALENT OFFERS

There is no nationally agreed set of equivalences as yet between qualifications and across all universities in the UK. Each institution makes its own decisions on the levels of offers in various subjects, depending on the popularity of the course and/or the quality of the individual applicant.

The following table, therefore, must only be used as a general guide to equivalences between A-levels, UCAS tariff points and other qualifications. Applicants should compare the A-level grades/A-level tariff points in the subject tables in **Chapter 9** with the approximate points shown in the International Baccalaureate (IB) (these are not UCAS tariff points), Irish Leaving Certificate and grades in the Scottish Highers columns. It is essential that all applicants contact their chosen institutions to check the specific grades/points to be achieved in the required subjects of the qualifications they expect to offer.

Other Examination Systems
The highest offers made for entry to degree courses, eg **Cambridge**, are as follows:
* Scottish Highers Higher grade AAA plus Advanced Highers.
* Welsh Baccalaureate Applicants are expected to have taken 3 subjects at A-level as part of their qualification.
* German Arbitur Overall score between 1.0 and 1.3 with 13 or 14 in relevant subjects.
* USA SATs and Advanced Placement tests (3) at grades 5.5.5 or 5.5.4.

Cambridge requirements
In addition to the normal A-level offers Advanced Extension Awards (AEAs) and STEP papers may be required by some colleges. See **Chapter 7** and subject tables in **Chapter 9**. AEAs may also be included as part of an offer and applicants are recommended to take one or more Awards if their school or college is happy for them to do so since these are regarded as an excellent preparation for university courses.

TABLE OF EQUIVALENT OFFERS
See overleaf.

GCE A-level	Scottish Highers	IB Diploma	Irish Leaving Certificate Higher Level		EB	French Baccalaureate
Grades and Tariff points	Grades (see Ch.6)	Points	Grades	Points		
AAA (360)	AAAAA	36–42	A1A1A1A1BB	560–570		15
AAB (340)	AAABB	34–36	AAABBB	495–555	85%	14/15
ABB (320)	AABBB	32–34	AABBBB	480–540		13/14
BBB (300)	ABBBC–BBBCC	30–32	BBBBBB	450–510	75%	12/13
BBC (280)	AABB	28–30	BBBBCC	420–480	70%	11/12
BCC (260)	BBBB	28–30	BBBCCC	405–465/360–410	65%	
CCC (240)	ABCC	27–28	BBBCC–CCCCC	345–395	60%	
CCD (220)	BBBC	27–28	BBCCC	330–380		
CDD (200)	BBCC	26–27	BCCCC	315–365		
DDD (180)	BCCC–CCCC	24–26	CCCCC	300–350		
DDE (160)	BBC	22–24	CCCCD	285–335		
DEE (140)	BBC–CCC	22–24	CCCCD	285–335		
DD (120)	BCC–CCC	20	BCCC	255–295		
DE (100)	CCC–CC	18–20	CCC	240–280		
EE (80)	CCC–CC	18	CCC	240–280		

INSTITUTION ABBREVIATIONS

The following abbreviations are used to indicate specific institutions or types of institution:

Ac	Academy
AI	Arts Institute
ALRA	Academy of Live and Recorded Arts
AMD	Academy of Music and Drama
Birk	Birkbeck College (London University)
CA	College of Art(s)
CAD	College of Art and Design
CAFRE	College of Agriculture, Food and Rural Enterprise
CAg	College of Agriculture
CAgH	College of Agriculture and Horticulture
CAST	College of Arts, Science and Technology
CAT	College of Advanced Technology or Arts and Technology
CComm	College of Communication
CDC	College of Design and Communication
CECOS	London College of IT and Management
CFash	College of Fashion
CFE	College of Further Education
CHE	College of Higher Education
CHFE	College of Higher and Further Education
CHort	College of Horticulture
CMus	College of Music
CMusDr	College of Music and Drama
Coll	College

Consv	Conservatoire (Birmingham)
Court	Courtauld Institute (London University)
CT	College of Technology
CTA	College of Technology and Arts
Gold	Goldsmiths (London University)
Hey	Heythrop College (London University)
Hom	Homerton College (Cambridge University)
IA	Institute of Art(s)
IAD	Institute of Art and Design
IFHE	Institute of Further and Higher Education
IHE	Institute of Higher Education
Inst	Institute
King's	King's College (London University)
LIPA	Liverpool Institute of Performing Arts
LSE	School of Economics and Political Science (London University)
Met	Metropolitan
MS	Medical School
QM	Queen Mary (London University)
RAcMus	Royal Academy of Music
RCMus	Royal College of Music
Reg Coll	Regional College
RH	Royal Holloway (London University)
RNCM	Royal Northern College of Music
RSAMD	Royal Scottish Academy of Music and Drama
RVC	Royal Veterinary College (London University)
SA	School of Art
SAD	School of Art and Design
Sch	School
Sch SpDr	School of Speech and Drama
SOAS	School of Oriental and African Studies (London University)
TrCMus	Trinity College of Music
UC	University College
UCL	University College (London University)
Univ	University
UWIC	University of Wales Institute (Cardiff)

COURSE ABBREVIATIONS

The following abbreviations are used to indicate course titles:

Ab	Abrahamic		**Actvt(s)**	Activity/Activities
Abrd	Abroad		**Add**	Additional
Acc	Accountancy/Accounting		**Adlscn**	Adolescence
Accs	Accessories		**Adlt**	Adult
Acoust	Acoustics/Acoustical		**Admin**	Administration/Administrative
Acpntr	Acupuncture		**Adt**	Audit
Acq	Acquisition		**Adv**	Advertising
Act	Actuarial		**Advc**	Advice
Actg	Acting		**Advnc**	Advanced
Actn	Action		**Advntr**	Adventure
Actr	Actor		**Aero**	Aeronautical/Aeronautics

Aerodyn	Aerodynamics		**Aud**	Audio
Aeromech	Aeromechanical		**Audiol**	Audiology
Aerosp	Aerospace		**Audtech**	Audiotechnology
Aeroth	Aerothermal		**Aus**	Australia(n)
Af	Africa(n)		**Auth**	Author/Authoring/Authorship
Affrs	Affairs		**Auto**	Automotive
Age	Ageing`		**Autom**	Automated/Automation
Agncy	Agency		**Automat**	Automatic
Agric	Agriculture/Agricultural		**Autombl**	Automobile
Agrofor	Agroforestry		**AV**	Audio Video
Agron	Agronomy		**Avion**	Avionics
Aircft	Aircraft		**Avn**	Aviation
Airln	Airline		**Ay St**	Ayurvedic Studies
Airpt	Airport			
Am	American		**Bch**	Beach
Amen	Amenity		**Bd**	Based
Analys	Analysis		**Bdwk**	Bodywork
Analyt	Analytical		**Bhv**	Behaviourial
Anat	Anatomy/Anatomical		**Bib**	Biblical
Anim	Animal		**Bio Ins**	Bio Instrumentation
Animat	Animation		**Bioarch**	Bioarchaeology
Animatron	Animatronics		**Bioch**	Biochemistry/Biochemical
Anth	Anthropology		**Biodiv**	Biodiversity
Antq	Antique(s)		**Bioelectron**	Bioelectronics
App(s)	Applied/Applicable/Applications		**Biogeosci**	Biogeoscience
Appr	Appropriate		**Bioinform**	Bioinformatics
Aqua	Aquaculture/Aquatic		**Biokin**	Biokinetics
Ar	Area(s)		**Biol**	Biological/Biology
Arbc	Arabic		**Biom**	Biometry
Arbor	Arboriculture		**Biomed**	Biomedical/Biomedicine
Arch	Archaeology		**Biomol**	Biomolecular
Archit	Architecture		**Biophys**	Biophysics
Aroma	Aromatherapy		**Bioproc**	Bioprocess
Artfcts	Artefacts		**Biorg**	Bio-organic
Artif	Artificial		**Biotech**	Biotechnology
As	Asian		**Bkbnd**	Bookbinding
Ass	Assessment		**Bld**	Build/Building
Assoc	Associated		**Blt**	Built
Asst	Assistant		**Br**	British
Assyr	Assyriology		**Braz**	Brazilian
Ast	Asset		**Brew**	Brewing
Astnaut	Astronautics/Astronautical		**Brit**	British
Astro	Astrophysics		**Brnd**	Brand
Astron	Astronomy		**Broad**	Broadcast
A-Sxn	Anglo-Saxon		**Bty**	Beauty
Ated	Accelerated		**Bulg**	Bulgarian
Atlan	Atlantic		**Bus**	Business
Atmos	Atmospheric		**Byz**	Byzantine
Attrctns	Attractions			
Auc	Auctioneering		**Callig**	Calligraphy

Can	Canada/Canadian	Cntry	Country/Countryside
Cap	Capital	Cntxt	Context
Cardio	Cardiology	Coach	Coaching
Carib	Caribbean	Cog	Cognitive
Cart	Cartography	Col	Colour
Cat	Catering	Comb	Combined
CATS	Credit Accumulation and Transfer Scheme	Combus	Combustion
		Comm(s)	Communication(s)
Cdtng	Conditioning	Commer	Commerce/Commercial
Cell	Cellular	Commun	Community
Celt	Celtic	Comp	Computer/Computerised/ Computing
Cent	Century		
Ceram	Ceramics	Compar	Comparative
Cert	Certificate	Complem	Complementary
Ch Mgt	Chain Management	Comput	Computation/al
Chc	Choice	Con	Context
Chch	Church	Concur	Concurrent
Chem	Chemistry	Cond	Conductive
Cheml	Chemical	Condit	Conditioning
Chin	Chinese	Cons	Conservation
Chld	Child/Children/Childhood	Constr	Construction
Chn	Chain	Consum	Consumer
Chng	Change	Cont	Contour
Choreo	Choreography	Contemp	Contemporary
Chr	Christian(ity)	Contnl	Continental
Chtls	Chattels	Contr	Control
Cits	Cities	Conv	Conveyancing
Civ	Civilisation/Civil	Corn	Cornish
Class	Classical	Corp	Corporate/Corporation
Clim	Climate/Climatic	Cos	Cosmetic
Clin	Clinical	Cosmo	Cosmology
Cllct	Collect/Collecting	Cr	Care
Clnl	Colonial	Crcs	Circus
Cloth	Clothing	Crdc	Cardiac
Clsrm	Classroom	Crea	Creative/Creation
Cmdy	Comedy	Crfts	Crafts/Craftsmanship
Cmn	Common	Crim	Criminal
Cmnd	Command	Crimin	Criminological/Criminology
Cmplrs	Compilers	Crit	Criticism/Critical
Cmpn	Companion	Crm	Crime
Cmpsn	Composition	Cro	Croatian
Cmpste	Composite	Crr	Career
Cmwlth	Commonwealth	Crs	Course
Cncr	Cancer	Crsn	Corrosion
Cnflct	Conflict	Cru	Cruise
Cnma	Cinema/Cinematics	Crypt	Cryptography
Cnslg	Counselling	Cstl	Coastal
Cnsltncy	Consultancy	Cstm	Costume
Cnt	Central	Ctln	Catalan
Cntnt	Content	Ctlys	Catalysis

Ctzn	Citizenship	**Dynmcs**	Dynamics
Culn	Culinary		
Cult	Culture/Cultural	**ECANE**	Early Civilisations of the Aegean and Near East
Cur	Curation		
Cyber	Cybernetics/Cyberspace	**Ecol**	Ecology/Ecological
Cybertron	Cybertronics	**Ecomet**	Econometrics
Cz	Czech	**e-Commer**	E-Commerce
		Econ	Economics/Economies
Dan	Danish	**Ecosys**	Ecosystem(s)
Decn	Decision	**Ecotech**	Ecotechnology
Decr	Decoration/Decorative	**Ecotour**	Ecotourism
Def	Defence	**Ecotox**	Ecotoxicology
Defer	Deferred Choice	**Edit**	Editorial
Deg	Degree	**Educ**	Education
Demcr	Democratic	**Educr**	Educare
Dept	Department	**Efcts**	Effects
Des	Design(er)	**EFL**	English as a Foreign Language
Desr	Desirable	**Egypt**	Egyptian/Egyptology
Dev	Development/Developmental	**Elec**	Electrical
Devsg	Devising	**Elecacoust**	Electroacoustics
Df	Deaf	**Electromech**	Electromechanical
Diag	Diagnostic	**Electron**	Electronics
Diet	Dietetics/Dietitian	**ELT**	English Language Teaching
Dif	Difficulties	**Ely**	Early
Dig	Digital	**Emb**	Embryo
Dir	Direction/Director/Directing	**Embd**	Embedded
Dis	Diseases	**Embr**	Embroidery
Disab	Disability	**Emp**	Employment
Disas	Disaster	**Ener**	Energy
Discip	Disciplinary	**Eng**	Engineering
Diso	Disorders	**Engl**	English
Disp	Dispensing	**Engn**	Engine
Dist	Distributed/Distribution	**Ent**	Enterprise
Distil	Distillation/Distilling	**Enter**	Entertainment
Div	Divinity	**Entre**	Entrepreneur/Entrepreneurship
d/l	distance learning	**Env**	Environment/Environmental
Dlvry	Delivery	**Eql**	Equal
Dnstry	Dentistry	**Eqn**	Equine
Dntl	Dental	**Eqstrn**	Equestrian
Doc	Document/Documentary	**Equip**	Equipment
Dom	Domestic/Domesticated	**Equit**	Equitation
Dr	Drama	**Ergon**	Ergonomics
Drg	Drawing	**Est**	Estate
Dscrt	Discrete	**Eth**	Ethics
Dscvry	Discovery	**Eth-Leg**	Ethico-Legal
Dsply	Display	**Ethn**	Ethnic
Dtbs	Databases	**Ethnol**	Ethnology
Dth	Death	**Ethnomus**	Ethnomusicology
Dvc	Device	**EU**	European Union
Dvnc	Deviance	**Euro**	European

Eval	Evaluation		Furn	Furniture
Evnglstc	Evangelistic		Fut	Futures
Evnts	Events			
Evol	Evolution/Evolutionary		Gael	Gaelic
Ex	Executing		Gam	Gambling
Excl	Excellence		Gdn	Garden
Exer	Exercise		Gem	Gemmology
Exhib	Exhibition		Gen	General
Exp	Export		Genet	Genetics
Explor	Exploration		Geochem	Geochemistry
Explsn	Explosion		Geophys	Geophysical
Expltn	Exploitation		Geosptl	Geospatial
Expmtl	Experimental		Geotech	Geotechnics
Expnc	Experience		Ger	German/Germany
Expr	Expressive		Gerc	Germanic
Ext	Extended		Gk	Greek
Extr	Exterior		GIS	Geographical Information Systems
Extrm	Extreme		Glf	Golf
			Glf Crs	Golf Course
Fac	Faculty		Gllry	Gallery/Galleries
Facil	Facilities		Glob	Global/Globalisation
Fash	Fashion		Gmg	Gaming
Fbr	Fibre		Gmnt	Garment
Fctn	Fiction		Gms	Games
Fd	Food		Gmtc	Geomatic
Fdn	Foundation		Gndr	Gender
Fin	Finance/Financial		Gnm	Genome/Genomics
Finn	Finnish		Gov	Government
Fish	Fisheries		Govn	Governance
Fit	Fitness		Graph	Graphic
Fld	Field		Grgn	Georgian
Flor	Floristry		Grn	Green
FMaths	Further Mathematics		gs	general studies
Fmly	Family			
Fn	Fine		H	IB Higher level
Foot	Footwear		Hab	Habitat
For	Foreign		Hard	Hardware
Foren	Forensic		Haz	Hazard
Foss	Fossil(s)		Heal	Healing
Fr	French		Heb	Hebrew
Frchd	Franchised		Herb	Herbal
Frcst	Forecasting		Herit	Heritage
Frm	Farm		Hisp	Hispanic
Frshwtr	Freshwater		Hist	History/Historical
Frsty	Forestry/Forest		Hlnds	Highlands
Frtlty	Fertility		Hlth	Health
Fst Trk	Fast Track		Hlthcr	Healthcare
Fstvl	Festival		HlthSC	Health and Social Care
Ftbl	Football		Hm	Home
Ftre	Feature(s)		Hol	Holistic

Hom	Homeopathic
Homin	Hominid
Horol	Horology
Hort	Horticulture
Hosp	Hospital
Hous	Housing
HR	Human Resources
Hrdrs	Hairdressing
Hrs	Horse
Hse	House
Hspty	Hospitality
Htl	Hotel
Hum	Human(ities)
Hung	Hungarian
Hydrog	Hydrography
Hydrol	Hydrology
Hyg	Hygiene
Iber	Iberian
Ice	Icelandic
ICT	Information and Communications Technology
Id	Ideas
Idnty	Identity
Illus	Illustration
Imag	Image/Imaging/Imaginative
Immun	Immunology/Immunity
Impair	Impairment
Inc	Including
Incln	Inclusion/Inclusive
Ind	Industrial/Industry
Indep St	Independent Study
Inf	Information
Infec	Infectious/Infection
Infml	Informal
Inform	Informatics
Infra	Infrastructure
Inftq	Informatique
Injry Prvntn	Injury Prevention
Innov	Innovation
Ins	Insurance
Inst	Institution(al)
Instln	Installation
Instr	Instrument/Instrumentation
Int	International
Intcult	Intercultural
Integ	Integrated
Intel	Intelligent/Intelligence
Inter	Interior
Interact	Interactive

Interd	Interdisciplinary
Interp	Interpretation
Intlctl	Intellectual
Intnet	Internet
Intrmdl	Intermodal
Inv	Investment
Invn	Innovation
Invstg	Investigating/Investigation
Ir	Irish
Is	Issues
Isl	Islands
Islam	Islamic
Isrl	Israel/Israeli
IT	Information Technology
Ital	Italian
ITE	Initial Teacher Education
ITT	Initial Teacher Training
Jap	Japanese
Jew	Jewish
Jewel	Jewellery
Jrnl	Journalism
Jud	Judaism
Juris	Jurisprudence
Just	Justice
Kntwr	Knitwear
Knwl	Knowledge
Kor	Korean
Lab	Laboratory
Lang(s)	Language(s)
Las	Laser
Lat	Latin
Lcl	Local
LD	Learning Disabilities
Ldrshp	Leadership
Lea	Leather
Leg	Legal
Legis	Legislative
Leis	Leisure
Lf	Life
Lfstl	Lifestyle
Lgc	Logic
Lib	Library
Lic	Licensed
Lic de Geog	Licence de Geographie
Ling	Linguistics
Lit	Literature/Literary
Litcy	Literacy

Lnd	Land(scape)	MML	Master of Modern Languages
Lndbd	Land-based	Mndrn	Mandarin
Lns	Lens	Mnrts	Minorities
Log	Logistics	Mnstry	Ministry
Lrng	Learning	Mnswr	Menswear
Ls	Loss	Mntl Hlth	Mental Health
Lsr	Laser	Mntn	Mountain
Ltg	Lighting	Mntnce	Maintenance
Ltr	Later	Mny	Money
Lv	Live	Mod	Modular
Lvstk	Livestock	Modl	Modelling/Modelmaking
		Modn	Modern
Mach	Machine(ry)	Modnty	Modernity
Mait	Maitrise Internationale	Mol	Molecular
Mak	Making	Monit	Monitoring
Manuf	Manufacturing	Mov	Movement/Moving
Map	Map/Mapping	Mrchnds	Merchandise
Mar	Marine	Mrchnt	Merchant
Marit	Maritime	Mrl	Moral
Mark	Market(ing)	Mtl	Metal(s)
Masch	Maschinenbau	Mtlsmth	Metalsmithing
Mat	Materials	Mtn	Motion
Mathem	Mathematical	Mtr	Motor
Maths	Mathematics	Mtrcycl	Motorcycle
Mbl	Mobile	Mtrspo	Motorsports
Mdl	Modelling	Multid	Multidisciplinary
Measur	Measurement	Multim	Multimedia
Mech	Mechanical	Mus	Music(ian)
Mecha	Mechatronics	Muscskel	Musculoskeletal
Mechn	Mechanisation	Musl	Musical
Med	Medicine/cal	Musm	Museum
Medcnl	Medicinal		
Mediev	Medieval	N	New
Medit	Mediterranean	N Am	North America
Metal	Metallurgy/Metallurgical	Nano	Nanoscale/Nanoscience
Meteor	Meteorology/Meteorological	Nanotech	Nanotechnology
Meth	Method(s)	Nat	Natural
Mgr	Manager	Navig	Navigation
Mgrl	Managerial	Nclr	Nuclear
Mgt	Management	Nds	Needs
Microbiol	Microbiology/Microbiological	Neg	Negotiated
Microbl	Microbial	Net	Network
Microcomp	Microcomputer/Microcomputing	Neuro	Neuroscience
Microelec	Microelectronics	Neuropsy	Neuropsychology
Midwif	Midwifery	News	Newspaper
Min	Mining	NGO	Non-Governmental Organisation
Miner	Minerals	NI	Northern Ireland/Northern Irish
Mkup	Make-up	NMedia	New Media
Mling	Multilingual	Nnl	National
Mltry	Military	Norw	Norwegian

Nrs	Norse
Nucl	Nuclear
Nurs	Nursing
Nursy	Nursery
Nutr	Nutrition(al)
Nvl	Naval
Objs	Objects
Obs	Observational
Occ	Occupational
Ocean	Oceanography
Ocn	Ocean
Oeno	Oenology
Ofce	Office
Off	Offshore
Offrd	Off-road
Okl	Oklahoma
Onc	Oncology
On-Ln	On-Line
Op(s)	Operation(s)
Oph	Ophthamic
Oprtg	Operating
Opt	Optical
Optim	Optimisation
Optn/s	Optional/Options
Optoel	Optoelectronics
Optom	Optometry
OR	Operational Research
Ord	Ordinary
Org	Organisation
Orgnc	Organic
Orgnsms	Organisms
Orn	Ornithology
Orntl	Oriental
Orth	Orthoptics
Orthot	Orthotics
Oseas	Overseas
Ost	Osteopathy
Out	Outdoor
Out Act	Outdoor Activity
Ovrs	Overseas
P	Primary
P Cr	Primary Care
Pacif	Pacific
Pack	Packaging
PActv	Physical Activity
Pal	Palaeobiology
Palae	Palaeoecology/Palaeontology
Paramed	Paramedic(al)

Parasit	Parasitology
Parl	Parliamentary
Pat	Patent
Path	Pathology
Pathobiol	Pathobiological
Pathogen	Pathogenesis
Patt	Pattern
Pblc	Public
Pce	Peace
PE	Physical Education
Per	Person/Personal
Perf	Performance
Perfum	Perfumery
Pers	Personnel
Persn	Persian
Petrol	Petroleum
Pharm	Pharmacy
Pharmacol	Pharmacology
Pharml	Pharmaceutical
Phil	Philosophy
Philgy	Philology
Phn	Phone
Photo	Photography/Photographic
Photojrnl	Photojournalism
PhotoM	Photomedia
Photon	Photonic(s)
Phys	Physics
Physio	Physiotherapy
Physiol	Physiology/Physiological
Physl	Physical
Pks	Parks
Plan	Planning
Planet	Planetary
Plas	Plastics
Play	Playwork
Plc	Police/Policing
Plmt	Placement
Plnt	Plant
Plntsmn	Plantsmanship
Plt	Pilot
Pltry	Poultry
PMaths	Pure Mathematics
Pntg	Painting
Pod	Podiatry/Podiatric
Pol	Politics/Political/Policy
Polh	Polish
Pollut	Pollution
Poly	Polymer/Polymeric
Pop	Popular
Popn	Population

Port	Portuguese		**Quant**	Quantity/Quantitative
PPE	Philosophy, Politics and Economics **or** Politics, Philosophy and Economics		**Rad**	Radio
			Radiog	Radiography
			Radiothera	Radiotherapy
PPI	Private Pilot Instruction		**Rbr**	Rubber
Ppl	People		**Rce**	Race
Ppr	Paper		**Rcycl**	Recycling
Pptry	Puppetry		**Rdtn**	Radiation
PR	Public Relations		**Realsn**	Realisation
Prac	Practitioner		**Rec**	Recording
Practnr	Practice/Practical		**Reclam**	Reclamation
Prdcl	Periodical		**Recr**	Recreation
Precsn	Precision		**Reg**	Regional
Pref	Preferable/Preferred		**Regn**	Regeneration
Prehist	Prehistory		**Rehab**	Rehabilitation
Prem	Premises		**Rel**	Relations
Proc	Process/Processing		**Relgn**	Religion
Prod	Product/Production/Produce		**Relig**	Religious
Prof	Professional/Professions		**Reltd**	Related
Prog	Programme/Programming		**Rem Sens**	Remote Sensing
Proj	Project		**Ren**	Renaissance
Prom	Promotion		**Renew**	Renewable
Prop	Property/ies		**Reqd**	Required
Pros	Prosthetics		**Res**	Resources
Prot	Protection/Protected		**Resid**	Residential
Prplsn	Propulsion		**Resoln**	Resolution
Prsts	Pursuits		**Resp**	Response
Prt	Print		**Restor**	Restoration
Prtcl	Particle		**Rev**	Revenue
Prtd	Printed		**Rflxgy**	Reflexology
Prtg	Printing/Printmaking		**Rgby**	Rugby
Pst	Post		**Rgstrn**	Registration
Pstrl	Pastoral		**Rl**	Real
Psy	Psychology		**Rlblty**	Reliability
Psybiol	Psychobiology		**Rnwl**	Renewal
Psyling	Psycholinguistics		**Robot**	Robotics
Psysoc	Psychosocial		**Rom**	Roman
p/t	part-time		**Romn**	Romanian
Ptcl	Particle		**Rsch**	Research
Pub	Publishing		**Rsprty**	Respiratory
Pvt	Private		**Rsrt**	Resort
Pwr	Power		**Rstrnt**	Restaurant
Pwrcft	Powercraft		**Rtl**	Retail
			Rts	Rights
Qntm	Quantum		**Rur**	Rural
Qry	Quarry		**Russ**	Russian
Qtrnry	Quaternary			
QTS	Qualified Teacher Status		**S**	Secondary
Qual	Quality		**Sansk**	Sanskrit
Qualif	Qualification			

Sat	Satellite		**SPD**	Surface Pattern Design
Sbstnce	Substance		**Spec**	Special/Specialisms/Specialist
Scand	Scandinavian		**Spec Efcts**	Special Effects
Schlstc	Scholastic		**Sply**	Supply
Schm	Scheme		**Spo**	Sports
Sci	Science/Scientific		**Sprtd**	Supported
Scnc	Scenic		**Sprtng**	Supporting
Scngrph	Scenographic		**Sqntl**	Sequential
Scot	Scottish		**Srf**	Surf/Surfing
Scr	Secure		**Srgy**	Surgery
Script	Scriptwriting		**SS**	Solid-state
Scrn	Screen		**ST**	IB Standard Level
Scrnwrit	Sreenwriting		**St**	Studies
Scrts	Securities		**St Reg**	State Registration
Scrty	Security		**Stats**	Statistics
Sctr	Sector		**Std**	Studio
Sculp	Sculpture		**Stg**	Stage
Sdlry	Saddlery		**Stgs**	Settings
SE	South East		**Stnds**	Standards
Sec	Secretarial		**Str**	Stringed
Semicond	Semiconductor		**Strat**	Strategic
Serb Cro	Serbo-Croat		**Strg**	Strength
Serv	Services		**Struct**	Structural/Structures
Set	Settings		**Stt**	State
Sfc	Surface		**Surf**	Surface
Sfty	Safety		**Surg**	Surgery
Sgnl	Signal		**Surv**	Surveying
Ship	Shipping		**Sust**	Sustainability/Sustainable
Simul	Simulation		**Swed**	Swedish
Sk	Skills		**Sxlty**	Sexuality
Sln	Salon		**Sys**	System(s)
Slov	Slovak/Slovene/Slavonic		**Systmtc**	Systematic
Sls	Sales			
Sml	Small		**Tap**	Tapestry
Smt	Smart		**Tax Rev**	Taxation and Revenue
Smtc	Semitic		**Tcnqs**	Techniques
Snc	Sonic		**Teach**	Teaching
Snd	Sound		**Tech**	Technology/Technician
Sndwch	Sandwich		**Technol**	Technological
Soc	Social		**TEFL**	Teaching English as a Foreign Language
Sociol	Sociology			
SocioLeg	Socio-Legal		**Telecomm**	Telecommunications
Socling	Sociolinguistics		**TESOL**	Teaching English to Speakers of Other Languages
Soft	Software			
Soty	Society		**Testmt**	Testament
Sov	Soviet		**Tex**	Textiles
Sp	Speech		**Thea**	Theatre
Span	Spanish		**Theol**	Theology
Spat	Spatial		**Theor**	Theory/Theoretical
Spc	Space		**Ther**	Therapeutic

Thera	Therapy		**Veh**	Vehicle
Tht	Thought		**Vib**	Vibration
Tiss	Tissue		**Vict**	Victorian
Tm	Time		**Vid**	Video
Tmbr	Timber		**Viet**	Vietnamese
Tnnl	Tunnel/Tunnelling		**Virol**	Virology
Tns	Tennis		**Vis**	Visual/Visualisation
Topog	Topographical		**Vit**	Viticulture
Tour	Tourism		**Vkg**	Viking
Tox	Toxicology		**Vnu**	Venue
Tr	Trade		**Voc**	Vocational
Tr Stands	Trading Standards		**Vol**	Voluntary
Trad	Traditional		**Vrtbrt**	Vertebrate
Trans	Transport(ation)		**Vrtl Rlty**	Virtual Reality
Transl	Translation		**Vsn**	Vision
Trav	Travel		**Vstr**	Visitor
Trfgrs	Turfgrass			
Trg	Training		**Wdlnd**	Woodland
Trnrs	Trainers		**Welf**	Welfare
Trpcl	Tropical		**Wldlf**	Wildlife
Trpl	Triple		**Wls**	Wales
Trstrl	Terrestrial		**Wn**	Wine
Tstmnt	Testament		**Writ**	Writing/Writer
Ttl	Total		**Wrld**	World
Turk	Turkish		**Wrlss**	Wireless
Twn	Town		**Wst**	Waste(s)
Typo	Typographical/Typography		**Wstn**	Western
			Wtr	Water
Ukr	Ukrainian		**Wtrspo**	Watersports
Un	Union		**www**	World Wide Web
Undwtr	Underwater			
Unif	Unified		**Ycht**	Yacht
Up	Upland		**Yng**	Young
Urb	Urban		**Yth**	Youth
USA	United States of America			
Util	Utilities/Utilisation		**Zool**	Zoology
Val	Valuation		**3D**	Three-dimensional
Vcl	Vocal			

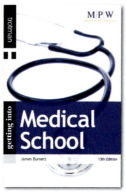

ACCOUNTANCY/ACCOUNTING

(see also **Finance**)

Accounting and Accountancy degree courses include economics, statistics, accounting and law, with some courses emphasising the use of computers. All vocational courses are designed to comply with the regulations of professional bodies. In the case of Accountancy, most degree courses will give partial exemptions from the examinations of some or all the accountancy institutions. Students should check with universities and colleges which professional bodies offer exemptions for their courses before applying. Many graduates entering careers in accountancy will do so after taking degree courses in other subjects although in all cases further study is necessary to qualify as an accountant.

Useful websites www.acca.co.uk; www.cimaglobal.org.uk; www.cipfa.org.uk; www.tax.org.uk; www.icaew.co.uk; www.bized.co.uk.

COURSE OFFERS INFORMATION

Subject requirements/preferences GCSE English and mathematics required: popular universities may specify grades. **AL** Mathematics or accounting required or preferred for some courses. Business studies accepted for some courses. **NB** A* grades are likely to form part of university offers in the higher ranges for students applying for places in 2008 for entry in 2009: check websites.

NB The points totals shown to the left of the institutions are for ease of reference only. It must not be assumed that tariff points are always used by institutions or that they can be substituted for an offer in grades. The level of an offer is not necessarily indicative of the quality of a course.

Your target offers

360 pts **and above**
  Bristol – AAA–ABB (Econ Acc; Acc Fin) *(IB 38 pts)*
  Queen's Belfast – AAA (Law Acc)
  Warwick – AABb **or** AAbbb (Acc Fin) *(IB 36 pts)*

340 pts **Bath** – AAB–ABB (Acc Fin) *(IB 35 pts)*
  Exeter – AAB–BBB 340–300 pts (Acc Fin; Acc Fin Euro; Bus Acc; Bus Acc Euro) *(IB 28–30 pts)*
  Lancaster – AAB (Acc Adt Fin) *(IB 30 pts)*
  London (LSE) – AAB (Acc Fin) *(IB 36 pts)*
  Manchester – AAB–ABB (Acc; Acc Econ; Acc Fin) *(IB 33 pts)*
  Newcastle – AAB (Bus Acc Fin) *(IB 32–35 pts)*
  Queen's Belfast – AAB (Acc; Econ Acc)
  Southampton – AAB–ABBb (Acc Fin; Acc Econ) *(IB 35 pts H 17 pts)*

320 pts **Aston** – 320–340 pts (Acc Mgt) *(IB 34 pts)*
  Birmingham – AAB–ABBc (Acc Fin; Int Acc Fin) *(IB 34 pts)*
  Cardiff – ABB (Acc; Acc Mgt; Acc Econ; Acc Fin)
  Glasgow – ABB (Acc courses) *(IB 30 pts)*
  Kent – 320 pts (Law Acc Fin) *(IB 33 pts H 15 pts)*
  Lancaster – ABB (Acc Econ; Acc Fin; Acc Fin Maths) *(IB 30 pts)*
  Leeds – ABB (Acc Law; Acc Fin; Acc Mgt) *(IB 33 pts H 16 pts)*
  London (RH) – 320–340 pts (Mgt Acc)
  Loughborough – 320 pts (Acc Fin Mgt; Econ Acc; Maths Acc Fin Mgt) *(IB 36 pts)*
  Manchester – ABB (Mgt (Acc Fin)) *(IB 33 pts)*

Newcastle – ABB–BBB (Comp Sci; Acc Maths; Acc Stats) *(IB 33–35 pts)*

Nottingham – ABB (Fin Acc Mgt) *(IB 32 pts)*

Reading – 320–350 pts (Acc Mgt; Acc Econ) *(IB 33 pts)*

Sheffield – ABB–BBB (Acc Fin Mgt; Acc Fin Mgt Bus; Acc Fin Mgt Econ; Acc Fin Mgt Inf Mgt; Acc Fin Mgt Maths) *(IB 33–32 pts)*

Ulster – ABB (Law Acc)

Ulster – 320 pts (Accounting)

300 pts **Aberdeen** – BBB (Law Acc) *(IB 30 pts)*

East Anglia – BBB–BBC 300–280 pts (Acc Fin; Acc Law; Acc Mgt) *(IB 30–32 pts)*

Edinburgh – BBB (Bus St Acc; Econ Acc; Law Acc)

Kent – 300–320 pts (Acc Fin courses) *(IB 33–35 pts)*

Liverpool – BBB 300 pts (Accounting) *(IB 32 pts)*

Strathclyde – ABC–BBB (Acc courses)

280 pts **Aberystwyth** – 280 pts (Acc Fin) *(IB 27 pts)*

Bournemouth – 280 pts (Acc Fin; Acc Tax; Acc Law; Acc Bus)

Brunel – 280 pts or equiv (Fin Acc) *(IB 30 pts)*

City – 280–300 pts (Econ Acc) *(IB 35 pts)*

Durham (Stockton) – BBC (Acc Fin; Bus Fin)

Essex – 280–260 pts (Acc Mgt; Acc Fin) *(IB 30 pts)*

Northumbria – 280 pts (Accounting)

Staffordshire – 280 pts (Foren Acc)

Swansea – 280 pts (Acc courses)

Westminster – 280 pts (Acc Bus Mgt)

260 pts **Aberystwyth** – 260 pts (Acc Fin courses) *(IB 27 pts)*

Coventry – 260 pts (Acc Econ; Acc)

Heriot-Watt – BCC 260 pts (Acc Fin; Acc Bus Law)

Hull – 260 pts (Acc; Acc (Int); Acc (Prof Exp); Acc Fin Mgt)

Keele – 260–320 pts (Acc Fin) *(IB 28–30 pts)*

Kent – 260 pts (Acc Fin courses; BR Fr Acc Fin; Law Acc) *(IB 33 pts H 15 pts)*

Oxford Brookes – BCC (Acc courses)

Westminster – 260–280 pts (Acc Bus Mgt)

240 pts **Aberdeen** – CCC **or** aabb (Acc courses except under **300 pts**) *(IB 30 pts)*

Abertay Dundee – CCC (Acc Fin)

Bangor – 240–280 pts (Acc Fin)

Bradford – CCC 240 pts (Acc Fin)

Bristol UWE – 240–300 pts (Acc courses) *(IB 24–28 pts)*

Buckingham – 240 pts (Acc Fin Mgt)

De Montfort – 240 pts (Acc Fin; Acc Bus; Acc Law)

Dundee – CCC (Acc; Acc (Bus Fin) (Mgt Inf Sys)) *(IB 29 pts)*

Heriot-Watt – CCC (Econ Acc)

Huddersfield – 240 pts (Acc Fin; Acc)

Kingston – 240–280 pts (Acc Fin)

Nottingham Trent – 240 pts (Acc Fin)

Plymouth – 240 pts (Acc Fin)

Portsmouth – 240 pts (Acc; Acc Bus; Acc Bus Law; Acc Fin)

Robert Gordon – CCC (Acc Fin)

Salford – CCC 240–260 pts (Fin Acc) *(IB 28 pts)*

Sheffield Hallam – 240 pts (Acc; Acc Fin Mgt; Bus Acc Mgt)

Staffordshire – 240 pts (Acc; Acc Bus; Acc Econ; Acc Inf Sys) *(IB 26 pts)*

Stirling – CCC (Acc courses) *(IB 30 pts)*

Ulster – 240 pts (Bus Acc)

220 pts **Birmingham City** – 220–200 pts (Acc; Acc joint courses)

Bolton – 220 pts (Acc courses)

Brighton – 220 pts (Acc Fin; Acc Law) *(IB 26 pts)*

Glamorgan – 220 pts (Acc Fin; Acc Mgt; Int Acc)

200 pts **Anglia Ruskin** – 200 pts (Acc Fin)
Edge Hill – 200 pts (Accountancy)
Gloucestershire – 200–280 pts (Acc courses)
Hertfordshire – 200 pts (Acc courses)
Lincoln – 200 pts (Acc courses)
Manchester Met – 200–260 pts (Acc Fin) *(IB 24 pts)*
Napier – 200 pts (Acc courses)
Newport – 200 pts (Acc; Acc Law; PR Acc)
180 pts **Cardiff (UWIC)** – 180 pts (Accounting)
Central Lancashire – 180–220 pts (Acc courses)
Glasgow Caledonian – BC (Accountancy)
Greenwich – 180 pts (Acc Fin)
Northampton – 180–220 pts (Acc courses)
160 pts **Bedfordshire** – 160–200 pts (Acc; Acc Law)
Canterbury Christ Church – 160 pts (Bus St Acc; Mark Acc)
East London – 160 pts (Acc courses)
Liverpool John Moores – 160–220 pts (Acc Fin)
London Met – 160–200 pts (Acc Fin; Acc Bank; Acc Bus; Acc Law)
London South Bank – CC (Acc Fin; Acc Law)
Middlesex – 160–240 pts (Acc courses)
North East Wales (IHE) – 160 pts (Bus Acc)
Southampton Solent – 160–220 pts (Accountancy)
Teesside – 160–220 pts (Acc Fin; Acc Law)
Thames Valley – 160 pts (Acc Fin)
West Scotland – CC (Acc; Bus Acc)
Wolverhampton – 160–220 pts (Acc courses)
Worcester – 160 pts (Bus Mgt (Acc))
140 pts **Derby** – 140–200 pts (Acc courses)
120 pts **Swansea (Inst)** – 120 pts (Accounting)
100 pts **Bradford (Coll)** – 100–140 pts (Acc Law)
80 pts **Croydon (Coll)** – 80–100 pts (Acc Bus)
East Lancashire (IHE) – 80 pts (Bus Acc)
Holborn (Coll) – 80 pts (Accountancy)
London (Birk) – 80 pts (p/t Acc Mgt)
Norwich City (Coll) – 80 pts (Bus Mgt Acc Fin)

Leeds Met – contact University
Regents Bus Sch London – check with Business School (Int Fin Acc)

Alternative offers
See **Chapter 8** for grade/point equivalences and related information for the following examinations: Scottish qualifications, the Welsh Baccalaureate, the IB diploma (approximate points shown also in italics in the table of offers), the Irish Leaving Certificate, the European Baccalaureate and the French Baccalaureate.

EXAMPLES OF FOUNDATION DEGREES IN THE SUBJECT FIELD
Aberdeen (Coll); Adam Smith (Coll); Anniesland (Coll); Ayr (Coll); Banff and Buchan (Coll); Belfast (IHE); Croydon (Coll); Darlington (Coll); Doncaster (Coll); Lambeth (Coll); Langside Glasgow (Coll); London South Bank; Northampton; St Helens (Coll); West Kent (Coll); Westminster Kingsway (Coll).

CHOOSING YOUR COURSE (SEE ALSO CH.1)
Course variations – Widen your options
Accountancy and Entrepreneurship (Aberdeen)
Accountancy and Property (Aberdeen)
Accountancy, Finance and Law (Aberystwyth)
Banking and Accountancy (Bangor)

Accounting and Psychology (Bristol UWE)
Accounting and Criminology (Derby)
Accounting with Leadership (Exeter)
Forensic Accounting (Staffordshire)
CHECK PROSPECTUSES AND WEBSITES FOR OTHER UNIVERSITIES AND COLLEGES OFFERING THESE COURSES.

Universities and colleges teaching quality See www.qaa.ac.uk; www.unistats.com.

Top universities and colleges (Research) Aston; Bangor; Bristol; Bristol UWE; Durham; Edinburgh; Essex; Exeter; Glasgow; London (LSE)*; Manchester; Newcastle; Stirling; Strathclyde; West Scotland.

Sandwich degree courses Abertay Dundee; Aberystwyth; Aston; Birmingham City; Bournemouth; Bradford; Brunel; City; De Montfort; Glamorgan; Gloucestershire; Greenwich; Hertfordshire; Huddersfield; Loughborough; Manchester Met; Northumbria; Plymouth; Portsmouth; Sheffield Hallam; Staffordshire; Ulster; Westminster; Wolverhampton.

ADMISSIONS INFORMATION

Number of applicants per place (approx) Bath 5; Birmingham 9; Bristol 23; Dundee 5; East Anglia 17; Essex 7; Exeter 18; Glasgow 10; Heriot-Watt 7; Hull 8; Kent 10; Lancaster 20; Leeds 25; London (LSE) 16; Loughborough 12; Oxford Brookes 9; Salford 8; Sheffield 40; Southampton 13; Staffordshire 3; Stirling 20; Strathclyde 10; Ulster 10; Warwick 14.

Advice to applicants and planning the UCAS personal statement Universities look for good communication skills, interest in the business and financial world, teamwork, problem-solving and computing experience. On the UCAS application you should be able to demonstrate your knowledge of accountancy and to give details of any work experience or work shadowing undertaken. Try to arrange meetings with accountants, or work shadowing or work experience in accountants' offices, commercial or industrial firms, town halls, banks or insurance companies and describe the work you have done. Obtain information from the main accountancy professional bodies (see **Appendix 2**). Refer to current affairs which have stimulated your interest from articles in the *Financial Times*, *The Economist* or the business and financial sections of the weekend press. **Buckingham** Show commitment to follow the course; details of any extra-curricular activities illustrating personal development are also useful. **London South Bank** There should be no gaps in your chronological history. **Staffordshire** Applicants with two A-levels should contact the Business School.

Misconceptions about this course Many students believe incorrectly that you need to be a brilliant mathematician. However, you do have to be numerate and enjoy numbers (see **Subject requirements/preferences**). Many under-estimate the need for a high level of attention to detail. **Buckingham** Some students think it's a maths course. **Salford** Some applicants believe the course is limited to financial knowledge when it also provides an all-round training in management skills.

Selection interviews Thames Valley; **Some** Aberystwyth, Anglia Ruskin, Bristol, Buckingham, Cardiff, De Montfort, Dundee, East Anglia, Kent, Lincoln, Liverpool John Moores, London (LSE), Staffordshire, Stirling, Sunderland, Wolverhampton.

Interview advice and questions Be prepared to answer questions about why you have chosen the course, the qualities needed to be an accountant, and why you think you have these qualities! You should also be able to discuss any work experience you have had and to describe the differences in the work of chartered, certified, public finance and management accountants. **Buckingham** If students are from a non-English-speaking background, they are asked to write an essay. If their maths results are weak they may be asked to do a simple arithmetic test. Mature students with no formal qualifications are usually interviewed and questioned about their work experience. See also **Chapter 7**.

Reasons for rejection (non-academic) Poor English. Lack of interest in the subject because they realise they have chosen the wrong course! No clear motivation. Course details not researched. **London South Bank** Punctuality, neatness, enthusiasm and desire to come to London South Bank not evident.

For a quick reference offers calculator, fold out the inside back cover.

AFTER-RESULTS ADVICE

Offers to applicants repeating A-levels Higher Brunel, Glasgow (AAA), Hull, Manchester Met; **Possibly higher** Brighton, Central Lancashire, East Anglia, Leeds, Newcastle, Oxford Brookes, Sheffield Hallam; **Same** Aberystwyth, Anglia Ruskin, Bangor, Birmingham City, Bradford, Brighton, Buckingham, Cardiff, De Montfort, Derby, Dundee, Durham, East Anglia, East London, Heriot-Watt, Huddersfield, Liverpool John Moores, Loughborough, Napier, Newcastle, Northumbria, Salford, Staffordshire, Stirling, Thames Valley, Wolverhampton.

GRADUATE DESTINATIONS AND EMPLOYMENT (2005/6 HESA)

Graduates surveyed 2560 **Employed** 1210 **In further study** 195 **Assumed unemployed** 155.

Career note Most Accounting/Accountancy graduates enter careers in finance. Further study is required to qualify as accountants.

OTHER DEGREE SUBJECTS FOR CONSIDERATION

Actuarial Studies; Banking; Business Studies; Economics; Financial Services; Insurance; International Securities and Investment Banking; Mathematics; Quantity Surveying; Statistics.

ACTUARIAL SCIENCE/STUDIES

Actuaries deal with the evaluation and management of financial risks, particularly those associated with insurance companies and pension funds. Although Actuarial Science/Studies degrees are vocational and give full or partial exemptions from some of the examinations of the Institute and Faculty of Actuaries, students are not necessarily committed to a career as an actuary on graduation. However, many graduates go on to be actuary trainees, leading to one of the highest-paid careers.

Useful website www.actuaries.org.uk

NB The points totals shown to the left of the institutions are for ease of reference only. It must not be assumed that tariff points are always used by institutions or that they can be substituted for an offer in grades. The level of an offer is not necessarily indicative of the quality of a course.

COURSE OFFERS INFORMATION

Subject requirements/preferences GCSE Most institutions require grades A or B in mathematics. **AL** Mathematics at a specified grade required. **NB** A* grades are likely to form part of university offers in the higher ranges for students applying for places in 2008 for entry in 2009: check websites.

Your target offers

360 pts **and above**
    City – AAA (Act Sci; Act Sci Ind/Abrd) *(IB 35 pts)*
    London (LSE) – AAA–AAB (Act Sci) *(IB 36 pts)*
340 pts **East Anglia** – AAB–AAC (Act Sci) *(IB 33 pts H maths 6 pts)*
    Southampton – AAB–ABB (Econ Act Sci; Maths Act St) *(IB 35 pts)*
320 pts **Kent** – 320 pts (Act Sci) *(IB 33 pts)*
300 pts **Heriot-Watt** – ABC 1st yr entry (Act Maths Stats) *(IB 34 pts H maths 6 pts)*
280 pts **Swansea** – 280–300 pts (Act St; Act St Acc; Act St Abrd)

Alternative offers

See **Chapter 8** for grade/point equivalences and related information for the following examinations: Scottish qualifications, the Welsh Baccalaureate, the IB diploma (approximate points shown also in italics in the table of offers), the Irish Leaving Certificate, the European Baccalaureate and the French Baccalaureate.

CHOOSING YOUR COURSE (SEE ALSO CH.1)

Course variations – Widen your options
Combined Studies – Actuarial Mathematics (Heriot-Watt)

Actuarial Mathematics (Kingston)

Actuarial Studies with Accounting (Swansea).

CHECK PROSPECTUSES AND WEBSITES FOR OTHER UNIVERSITIES AND COLLEGES OFFERING THESE COURSES.

Universities and colleges teaching quality See www.unistats.com; www.qaa.ac.uk.

Top universities and colleges (Research) Kent; London (LSE); Southampton.

ADMISSIONS INFORMATION

Number of applicants per place (approx) City 6; Heriot-Watt 5; Kent 6; London (LSE) 7; Southampton 5; Swansea 9.

Advice to applicants and planning the UCAS personal statement Demonstrate your knowledge of this career and its training, and mention any contacts you have made with an actuary. (See **Appendix 2** for contact details of professional associations for further information.) Any work experience or shadowing in insurance companies should be mentioned, together with what you have learned about the problems facing actuaries. **Swansea** You must show motivation and sheer determination for training as an actuary which is long and tough (up to three or four years after graduation). Mathematical flair, an ability to communicate and an interest in business are paramount.

Misconceptions about this course There is a general lack of understanding of actuaries' career training and of the career itself.

Selection interviews Some Heriot-Watt, Kent, Southampton, Swansea.

Interview advice and questions In view of the demanding nature of the training, it is important to have spent some time discussing this career with an actuary in practice. Questions, therefore, may focus on the roles of the actuary and the qualities you have to succeed. You should also be ready to field questions about your Advanced Level mathematics course and the aspects of it you most enjoy. **Swansea** The interview does not determine who will be accepted or rejected, only the level of the offer made. See also **Chapter 7**.

Reasons for rejection (non-academic) Kent Poor language skills.

AFTER-RESULTS ADVICE

Offers to applicants repeating A-levels Higher City; **Same** Heriot-Watt, Southampton.

GRADUATE DESTINATIONS AND EMPLOYMENT (2005/6 HESA)

No data available.

Career note Graduates commonly enter careers in finance, many taking further examinations to qualify as actuaries.

OTHER DEGREE COURSE SUBJECTS FOR CONSIDERATION

Accountancy; Banking; Business Studies; Economics; Financial Risk Management; Financial Services; Insurance; Mathematics; Money, Banking and Finance; Statistics.

AFRICAN and CARIBBEAN STUDIES

African Studies courses tend to be multi-disciplinary, covering several subject areas and can include anthropology, history, geography, sociology, social psychology and languages. Most courses focus on Africa and African languages (Amharic (Ethiopia), Hausa (Nigeria), Somali (Horn of Africa), Swahili (Somalia and Mozambique), Yoruba (Nigeria, Sierra Leone, Ghana and Senegal), and Zulu (South Africa)).

Useful websites www.britishmuseum.org.uk; www.africanstudies.org; www.black-history-month.co.uk.

NB The points totals shown to the left of the institutions are for ease of reference only. It must not be assumed that tariff points are always used by institutions or that they can be substituted for an offer in grades. The level of an offer is not necessarily indicative of the quality of a course.

COURSE OFFERS INFORMATION

Subject requirements/preferences GCSE Grade A–C in mathematics and English may be required. **AL** For language courses a language subject or demonstrated proficiency in a language is required. **NB** A* grades are likely to form part of university offers in the higher ranges for students applying for places in 2008 for entry in 2009: check websites.

Your target offers
300 pts Birmingham – BBB–BCC (Af St courses) *(IB 30–32 pts)*
260 pts London (SOAS) – BCC (Af Lang Cult; Af St Ling; Af St Mgt; Hs Arbc; Swhl Mgt) *(IB 30 pts)*
160 pts London Met – 160 pts (Carib St courses)

Alternative offers
See **Chapter 8** for grade/point equivalences and related information for the following examinations: Scottish qualifications, the Welsh Baccalaureate, the IB diploma (approximate points shown also in italics in the table of offers), the Irish Leaving Certificate, the European Baccalaureate and the French Baccalaureate.

CHOOSING YOUR COURSE (SEE ALSO CH.1)

Course variations – Widen your options
African Studies and Media (Birmingham)
American, Canadian and African Studies (Birmingham)
African Studies and History of Art (London (SOAS))
African Studies and Music (London (SOAS))
CHECK PROSPECTUSES AND WEBSITES FOR OTHER UNIVERSITIES AND COLLEGES OFFERING THESE COURSES.

Universities and colleges teaching quality See www.qaa.ac.uk; www.unistats.com.

Top universities and colleges (Research) Birmingham; London (SOAS).

ADMISSIONS INFORMATION

Number of applicants per place (approx) Birmingham 5.

Advice to applicants and planning the UCAS personal statement Describe any visits you have made to African or Caribbean countries, and why you wish to study this subject. Embassies in London may be able to provide information about the history, geography, politics, economics and the culture of the countries in which you are interested. Keep up-to-date with political developments in Africa or Caribbean countries. Discuss any aspects which interest you.

Interview advice and questions Questions are likely on your choice of country or geographical region, your knowledge of it and your awareness of some of the political, economic and social problems that exist. See also **Chapter 7**.

AFTER-RESULTS ADVICE

Offers to applicants repeating A-levels Information not available from institutions.

GRADUATE DESTINATIONS AND EMPLOYMENT (2005/6 HESA)

Graduates surveyed 20 **Employed** 10 **In further study** 5 **Assumed unemployed** 5.

Career note The language skills and knowledge acquired in African Studies courses, particularly when combined with periods of study in Africa, are relevant to a wide range of careers.

OTHER DEGREE SUBJECTS FOR CONSIDERATION

Anthropology; Geography; History; Languages; Sociology.

AGRICULTURAL SCIENCES/AGRICULTURE

(including **Agricultural Business Management, Aquaculture, Countryside Conservation, Crop Science, Rural Resources Management** and **Turf Science;** see also **Animal Sciences, Forestry, Horticulture, Landscape Architecture** and **Surveying**)

Courses in Agriculture recognise that modern farming practice requires sound technical and scientific knowledge, together with appropriate management skills, and most courses focus to a greater or lesser extent on all these skills. Your choice of course depends on your particular interest and aims: some courses will give greater priority than others to practical application. Many students will come from an agricultural background and work experience will be necessary for most institutions.

Useful websites www.defra.gov.uk; www.naturalengland.org.uk; www.ccw.gov.uk; www.rase.org.uk; www.scienceyear.com; www.iah.bbsrc.ac.uk; www.lantra.co.uk; www.nfuonline.com; www.nfyfc.org.uk; www.iagre.org; www.afuturein.com.

NB The points totals shown to the left of the institutions are for ease of reference only. It must not be assumed that tariff points are always used by institutions or that they can be substituted for an offer in grades. The level of an offer is not necessarily indicative of the quality of a course.

COURSE OFFERS INFORMATION

Subject requirements/preferences GCSE English and mathematics usually required. Practical experience may be required. **AL** One or two maths/biological science subjects may be required or preferred. Geography may be accepted as a science subject. Similar requirements apply for Agricultural Business Management courses. (Crop Science) Two science subjects may be required. (Countryside Management) Geography or biology preferred. **NB** A* grades are likely to form part of university offers in the higher ranges for students applying for places in 2008 for entry in 2009: check websites.

NB Many agricultural courses are offered at colleges on sites separate from the universities.

Your target offers

320 pts Newcastle – ABB (Agri-Bus Mgt) *(IB 28 pts)*

300 pts Stirling – BBB 2nd yr entry (Frshwtr Sci; Cons Sci; Aquacult) *(IB 26 pts)*

280 pts Newcastle – BBC–BCC (Agric; Rur Res Mgt; Frm Bus Mgt; Orgnc Fd Prod; Agron) *(IB 28 pts)*
          Queen's Belfast – BBC–BCCb (Lnd Use Env Mgt)
          Reading – 280 pts (Agric Bus Mgt; Rur Res Mgt; Agric) *(IB 29pts)*

260 pts Nottingham – BCC–CCC (Agric; Crop Sci) *(IB 28–30 pts)*

240 pts Aberdeen – CCC (Agric Sci; Agric Bus Mgt) *(IB 28 pts)*
          Bangor – 240–260 pts (Env Cons; Agric Cons Env)
          Queen's Belfast – CCC–BCC (Agric Tech) *(IB 28 pts)*

220 pts Stirling – CCD 1st yr entry (Aquacult; Frshwtr Sci; Cons Sci)

210 pts Aberystwyth – 210 pts (Agric Bus St) *(IB 26 pts)*

200 pts Aberystwyth – 200 pts (Sust Rur Dev; Cntry Recr Tour; Cntry Mgt; Cntry Cons) *(IB 26 pts)*
          Derby – 200 pts (Cons Cntry Mgt)

180 pts Aberystwyth – 180 pts (Agric; Agric Cntry Cons; Agric Cntry Mgt; Agric Mark) *(IB 26 pts)*
          Central Lancashire – 180–220 pts (Up Mntn Mgt; Nnl Pks Prot Ar)
          Nottingham Trent – 180 pts (Env Cons Cntry Mgt)
          Writtle (Coll) – 180 pts (Agric; Agric Bus Mgt; Rur Res Mgt; Cntry Wldlf Mgt; Spo Trf Sci Mgt; Agric Env)

160 pts Bristol UWE (Hartpury) – 160–200 pts (Agric Bus Mgt; Agric Cons; Agric Lnd Mgt; Dy Hrd Mgt) *(IB 28–30 pts)*
          Greenwich – 160 pts (Lnd Mgt; Int Agric)
          Harper Adams (UC) – 160–240 pts (Agric; Agric Anim Sci; Agric Lnd Frm Mgt; Agric Mark; Agric Mechn; Agric Crop Mgt; Agric Env Mgt; Agric Fd Qual Mgt; Rur Ent Lnd Mgt; Cntry Mgt; Cntry Env Mgt; Sust Res Mgt)

Royal (CAg) – 160 pts (Agric; Agric (Orgnc Frm) (Anim Mgt) (Lnd Mgt) (Crop Prod); Agric Frm Mgt; Int Eqn Agric Mgt; Bus Mgt (Agri-Fd)) *(IB 26–28 pts)*

SAC (Scottish CAg) – 160 pts (Agri Sci; Agric; Rur Bus Mgt (Agric))

120 pts **Myerscough (Coll)** – 120 pts (Agriculture)

Sparsholt (Coll) – DD (Aquacult Fish Mgt)

Alternative offers

See **Chapter 8** for grade/point equivalences and related information for the following examinations: Scottish qualifications, the Welsh Baccalaureate, the IB diploma (approximate points shown also in italics in the table of offers), the Irish Leaving Certificate, the European Baccalaureate and the French Baccalaureate.

EXAMPLES OF FOUNDATION DEGREES IN THE SUBJECT FIELD

Aberystwyth; Askham Bryan (Coll); Barony (Coll); Bicton (Coll); Bishop Burton (Coll); Bridgend (Coll); Brighton; Bristol UWE (Hartpury); CAFRE; Capel Manor (Coll); Central Lancashire; Craven (Coll); Derby; Duchy (Coll); Easton (Coll); Elmwood (Coll); Greenwich; Hadlow (Coll); Harper Adams (UC); Kingston Maurward (Coll); Moulton (Coll); Myerscough (Coll); Northampton; Oatridge (Coll); Plumpton (Coll); Reaseheath (Coll); Rodbaston (Coll); Royal (CAg); Sparsholt (Coll); Warwickshire (Coll); Wiltshire (Coll); Wolverhampton; Writtle (Coll).

CHOOSING YOUR COURSE (SEE ALSO CH.1)

Course variations – Widen your options
Agriculture, Conservation and the Environment (Bangor)
International Development with Overseas Experience (East Anglia)
Landscape Technology (Glamorgan)
Landscape Management (Land Use) (Greenwich)
Agri-Food Marketing with Business Studies (Harper Adams (UC))
Agriculture and Mechanisation (Harper Adams (UC))
Agriculture (Organic Farming) (Royal (CAg))
CHECK PROSPECTUSES AND WEBSITES FOR OTHER UNIVERSITIES AND COLLEGES OFFERING THESE COURSES.

Universities and colleges teaching quality See www.qaa.ac.uk; www.unistats.com.

Top universities and colleges (Research) Aberdeen; Bangor; Nottingham; Reading; Stirling.

Sandwich degree courses Aberystwyth; Bangor; Harper Adams (UC); Nottingham Trent; Royal (CAg); Sparsholt (Coll).

ADMISSIONS INFORMATION

Number of applicants per place (approx) Aberystwyth (Agric courses) 2–3; Bangor (Agric Cons Env) 4; Newcastle 6; Nottingham 4; Royal (CAg) (Agric) 2.

Advice to applicants and planning the UCAS personal statement First-hand farming experience is essential for some courses and obviously important for all. Check prospectuses and websites. Describe the work done. Details of experience of work with agricultural or food farms (production and laboratory work), garden centres, even with landscape architects, could be appropriate. Keep up-to-date with European agricultural and fishing policies and mention any interests you have in these areas. Read farming magazines and discuss any articles which have interested you. You may even have had firsthand experience of the serious problems facing farmers. **Bangor** (Agric Cons Env) Evidence of broad interest in land use and conservation. **Derby** (Cons Cntry Mgt) Interest or experience in practical conservation work. Ability to work both independently or as a member of a team is important. (See **Appendix 2**.)

Selection interviews Yes Bristol UWE (Hartpury); **Some** Bangor, Bishop Burton (Coll), Derby, Edinburgh, Harper Adams (UC), Queen's Belfast, Royal (CAg).

Interview advice and questions Agriculture is in the news, especially in relation to the consequences of the considerable problems facing farmers, particularly concerning dairy farmers and milk prices, the consequences of the foot and mouth epidemic, its origins and treatment. You should be up-to-date with political and scientific issues concerning the farming community in general and how these problems might be resolved. You are likely to be questioned on your own farming background (if relevant) and your farming experience. Questions asked in the past have included: What special agricultural interests do you have? What types of farms have you worked on? Farming publications that you read and agricultural shows visited? **Bangor** (Agric Cons Env) No tests at interview; (Rur Res Mgt) What is meant by the term 'sustainable development'? What is the UK Biodiversity Action Plan? Are farmers custodians of the countryside? What are the potential sources of non-fossil-fuel electricity generation? **Derby** (Cons Cntry Mgt) Discussion about fieldwork experience. See also **Chapter 7**.

Reasons for rejection (non-academic) Insufficient motivation. Too immature. Unlikely to integrate well. Lack of practical experience with crops or animals.

AFTER-RESULTS ADVICE

Offers to applicants repeating A-levels **Possibly higher** Newcastle (Agric); **Same** Bangor (Agric Cons Env), Bristol UWE (Hartpury), Derby, Harper Adams (UC), Nottingham, Royal (CAg), Writtle (Coll).

GRADUATE DESTINATIONS AND EMPLOYMENT (2005/6 HESA)

Graduates surveyed 710 **Employed** 400 **In further study** 60 **Assumed unemployed** 50.

Career note The majority of graduates entered the agricultural industry whilst others moved into manufacturing, the wholesale and retail trades and property development.

OTHER DEGREE SUBJECTS FOR CONSIDERATION

Agroforestry; Animal Sciences; Biochemistry; Biological Sciences; Biology; Biotechnology; Chemistry; Conservation Management; Crop Science; Ecology (Biological Sciences); Environmental Sciences; Estate Management (Surveying); Food Science and Technology; Forestry; Horticulture; Land Surveying; Landscape Architecture; Plant Sciences; Veterinary Science; Wood Science; Zoology.

AMERICAN STUDIES

(see also **Latin American Studies**)

Courses normally cover American history, politics and literature, although there are opportunities to study specialist fields such as drama, film studies, history of art, linguistics, politics or sociology. In some universities a year, term or semester spent in the USA (or Canada) is compulsory or optional whilst at other institutions the course lasts three years without a placement abroad.

Useful websites www.historynet.com; www.americansc.org.uk; www.theasa.net.

NB The points totals shown to the left of the institutions are for ease of reference only. It must not be assumed that tariff points are always used by institutions or that they can be substituted for an offer in grades. The level of an offer is not necessarily indicative of the quality of a course.

COURSE OFFERS INFORMATION

Subject requirements/preferences **GCSE** Specific grades in some subjects may be specified by some popular universities. **AL** English, a modern language, humanities or social science subjects preferred. **NB** A* grades are likely to form part of university offers in the higher ranges for students applying for places in 2008 for entry in 2009: check websites.

Your target offers

360 pts   and above
        Manchester – AAA–BBB (Am St courses)
        Warwick – AABb (Engl Am Lit)
        Warwick – ABBc–BBBc (Compar Am St) *(IB 32–36 pts)*

320 pts **Birmingham** – ABB–BBB (Am Can St courses) *(IB 34 pts)*
East Anglia – ABB–BBB 320–300 pts (Am Lit Crea Writ) *(IB 30–31 pts)*
Lancaster – ABB (Am St courses) *(IB 30 pts H 16 pts)*
London (King's) – ABB (Am St; Am St Yr Abrd; Film Am St) *(IB 34 pts)*
Loughborough – 320 pts (Engl N Am Lit Film)
Nottingham – ABB–BBB **or** 3AL+AS (Am St Hist; Am St Lat Am St; Am Engl St) *(IB 32–34 pts)*
Sussex – ABB–BBB **or** 360–340 pts 3AL+1AS (Am St courses) *(IB 32–34 pts)*
300 pts **Dundee** – 300 pts 2nd yr entry (Am St courses; Transat St courses)
East Anglia – BBB–BBC 300–280 pts (Am St) *(IB 30–31 pts)*
Essex – BBB–BBC 280–300 pts (Am (US) St; Am (US St) Film) *(IB 32 pts)*
Leicester – BBB 300 (Am St Yr USA) *(IB 32 pts)*
London (Gold) – 300 pts (Engl Am Lit)
280 pts **Aberystwyth** – 280 pts (Int Pol Am St)
East Anglia – BBC–BCC (Am Hist Engl Hist; Am Hist Pol) *(IB 30–31 pts)*
Hull – BBC–BCC (Am St Hist; Am St Film St; Am St Crea Writ; Am St Engl)
Kent – 280 pts (Am St (Hist) (Lit)) *(IB 31 pts H 14 pts)*
Leicester – BBC (Am St) *(IB 32 pts)*
Liverpool – BBC–BBB 280–300 pts (Compar Am St) *(IB 32 pts)*
Manchester Met – 280 pts (Engl Am Lit)
Northumbria – 280 pts (Br Am Cult)
260 pts **Keele** – 260–320 pts (Am St) *(IB 28–32 pts)*
240 pts **Aberystwyth** – 240 pts (Am St courses) *(IB 29 pts)*
Dundee – 240 pts 1st yr entry (Am St courses; Transat St courses) *(IB 29 pts)*
Kent – 240 pts (Br Am Pol St)
Portsmouth – 240–300 pts (Am St courses)
Swansea – 240–300 pts (Am St)
Ulster – CCC 240 pts (Am St courses)
220 pts **Lincoln** – 220–260 pts (Am St courses)
Winchester – 220 pts (Am St courses; Am Lit courses)
200 pts **Cumbria** – 200 pts (Am St Comb)
Plymouth – 200–280 pts (Am St courses)
Sunderland – 200 pts (Am St courses)
180 pts **Northampton** – 180–220 pts (Am St)
160 pts **Canterbury Christ Church** – CC (Am St courses)
Central Lancashire – 160–240 pts (Am St Comb Hons; Am St)
Liverpool John Moores – 160–260 pts (Am St courses)
London Met – 160–200 pts (Am St courses; Carib St courses)
Wolverhampton – 160–220 pts (Am St courses)
Worcester – 160–200 pts (Am St courses)
York St John – 160 pts (Am St courses)
140 pts **Derby** – 140 pts (Am St courses)

Alternative offers
See **Chapter 8** for grade/point equivalences and related information for the following examinations: Scottish qualifications, the Welsh Baccalaureate, the IB diploma (approximate points shown also in italics in the table of offers), the Irish Leaving Certificate, the European Baccalaureate and the French Baccalaureate.

EXAMPLES OF FOUNDATION DEGREES IN THE SUBJECT FIELD
Northampton.

CHOOSING YOUR COURSE (SEE ALSO CH.1)
Course variations – Widen your options
African and American Studies (Birmingham)

For information on how to read the Subject Tables, see **Chapter 8**.

Geology and Study in North America (Bristol)
American Studies and Early Childhood Studies (Canterbury Christ Church)
American Studies with Popular Music (Derby)
American Studies and International Relations (Dundee)
American Popular Culture (Manchester Met)
American Literature and Drama (Manchester Met)
CHECK PROSPECTUSES AND WEBSITES FOR OTHER UNIVERSITIES AND COLLEGES OFFERING THESE COURSES.

Universities and colleges teaching quality See www.qaa.ac.uk; www.unistats.com.

Top universities and colleges (Research) Keele; Liverpool; Nottingham*; Sussex.

ADMISSIONS INFORMATION

Number of applicants per place (approx) Birmingham 6; Dundee 5; East Anglia 7; Essex 6; Hull 15; Keele 7; Nottingham 12; Swansea 2; Warwick 14;.

Advice to applicants and planning the UCAS personal statement Visits to America should be described, and any knowledge or interests you have of the history, politics, economics and the culture of the USA should be included on the UCAS application. The US Embassy in London may be a useful source of information. American magazines and newspapers are good reference sources and also give a good insight to life in the USA. **Birmingham** (Am Can St) Applicants should demonstrate an intelligent interest in both North American literature and history in their personal statement. We look for enthusiasm about the US Canadian Studies course. Tell us why you are excited and interested in our subject area; at least half of your personal statement should focus on how and why your interest has developed, for example through extra-curricular reading, projects, films, academic study. **East Anglia** Wide-ranging engagement with American culture. **Swansea** We look for well-rounded and motivated students. We also look for strength in the more traditional humanities subjects although we are prepared to be flexible.

Misconceptions about this course Swansea Some candidates feel that American Studies is a soft option. While we study many topics which students find interesting, we are very much a humanities-based degree course incorporating more traditional subjects like history, literature and English. Our graduates also find that they are employable in the same jobs as those students taking other degrees.

Selection interviews Yes Birmingham, Derby, East Anglia, Hull, Sussex, Warwick, Winchester; **Some** Birmingham, Dundee, Kent.

Interview advice and questions Courses often focus on history and literature so expect some questions on any American literature you have read and also on aspects of American history, arts and culture. You may also be questioned on visits you have made to America (or Canada) and your impressions. Current political issues might also be raised, so keep up-to-date with the political scene. **Birmingham** Access course and mature students are interviewed and also those students with strong applications but whose achieved grades do not meet entrance requirements. **Derby** The purpose of the interview is to help applicants understand the interdisciplinary nature of the course. **East Anglia** Admissions tutors want to see how up-to-date is the applicant's knowledge of American culture. **Swansea** Our interviews are very informal, giving students the chance to ask questions about the course. See also **Chapter 7**.

Reasons for rejection (non academic) If personal reasons prevent year of study in America. **Birmingham** Lack of commitment to the course. **Swansea** Lack of knowledge covering literature, history and politics.

AFTER-RESULTS ADVICE

Offers to applicants repeating A-levels Higher Essex, Warwick, Winchester; **Possibly higher** Nottingham; **Same** Birmingham, Derby, Dundee, East Anglia, Hull, Swansea, Wolverhampton.

For a quick reference offers calculator, fold out the inside back cover.

GRADUATE DESTINATIONS AND EMPLOYMENT (2005/6 HESA)
Graduates surveyed 750 **Employed** 400 **In further study** 110 **Assumed unemployed** 55.

Career note All non-scientific careers are open to graduates. Start your career planning during your degree course and obtain work experience.

OTHER DEGREE SUBJECTS FOR CONSIDERATION
Business Studies; Cultural Studies; English Literature; Film Studies; Government; History; International History; International Relations; Latin-American Literature/Studies; Politics.

ANATOMICAL SCIENCE/ANATOMY
(see also **Physiology**)

Anatomy is the study of the structures of living creatures, from the sub-cellular level to the whole individual and relating structure to function in the adult and during embryonic development.

Useful websites www.scienceyear.com; www.innerbody.com; www.instantanatomy.net; www.netanatomy.com.

NB The points totals shown to the left of the institutions are for ease of reference only. It must not be assumed that tariff points are always used by institutions or that they can be substituted for an offer in grades. The level of an offer is not necessarily indicative of the quality of a course.

COURSE OFFERS INFORMATION
Subject requirements/preferences GCSE Mathematics usually required. **AL** One or two mathematics/science subjects usually required; biology and chemistry preferred. **NB** A* grades are likely to form part of university offers in the higher ranges for students applying for places in 2008 for entry in 2009: check websites.

Your target offers
340 pts **Manchester** – AAB–BBB (Anat Sci; Anat Sci Ind Exp Lang)
300 pts **Bristol** – BBB (Anat Sci; Hum Muscskel Sci; Anat Sci Vet Anat) *(IB 32 pts)*
　　　　Cardiff – BBB–ABB (Biomed Sci (Anat))
　　　　Dundee – 300–240 pts (Anat Sci; Anat Physiol Sci) *(IB 26 pts)*
　　　　Liverpool – 300–320 pts (Anat Hum Biol)
280 pts **Glasgow** – BBC–CCC (Anatomy) *(IB 28 pts)*
260 pts **Queen's Belfast** – BCC–CCCc (Anatomy)

Alternative offers
See **Chapter 8** for grade/point equivalences and related information for the following examinations: Scottish qualifications, the Welsh Baccalaureate, the IB diploma (approximate points shown also in italics in the table of offers), the Irish Leaving Certificate, the European Baccalaureate and the French Baccalaureate.

CHOOSING YOUR COURSE (SEE ALSO CH.1)
Course variations – Widen your options
See **Biological Sciences.**

Universities and colleges teaching quality See www.qaa.ac.uk; www.unistats.com.

Top universities and colleges (Research) Birmingham; Bristol*; Leeds; Liverpool*.

Sandwich degree courses: Bristol; Cardiff; Manchester.

ADMISSIONS INFORMATION
Number of applicants per place (approx) Bristol 7; Cardiff 8; Dundee 6; Liverpool 7.

Advice to applicants and planning the UCAS personal statement Give reasons for your interest in this subject (usually stemming from school work in biology). Discuss any articles in medical and other scientific journals which have attracted your attention and any new developments in medicine related to anatomical science. **Liverpool** Genuine interest in a dissection-based course. Motivation to the practical study of anatomy.

Selection interviews Some Cardiff, Dundee.

Interview advice and questions Questions are likely on your particular interests in biology and anatomy, why you wish to study the subject and your future career intentions. See also **Chapter 7**.

Reasons for rejection (non-academic) Liverpool Unfocused applications with no evidence of basic knowledge of the course.

AFTER-RESULTS ADVICE

Offers to applicants repeating A-levels Higher Bristol, Dundee, Sheffield; **Possibly higher** Liverpool; **Same** Cardiff.

GRADUATE DESTINATIONS AND EMPLOYMENT (2005/6 HESA)

(Including **Physiology**)

Graduates surveyed 2620 **Employed** 1380 **In further study** 405 **Assumed unemployed** 190.

Career note The subject leads to a range of careers in various laboratories, in government establishments, the NHS, pharmaceutical and food industries. It can also lead to postgraduate studies in physiotherapy, nursing, osteopathy and, in exceptional cases, in medicine and dentistry.

OTHER DEGREE SUBJECTS FOR CONSIDERATION

Biological Sciences; Biology; Genetics; Microbiology; Neuroscience; Osteopathy; Physiology; Physiotherapy.

ANIMAL SCIENCES

(including **Equine Science/Studies** and **Wildlife Conservation;** see also **Agricultural Sciences/Agriculture, Biological Sciences, Biology, Psychology, Veterinary Science/Medicine, Zoology**)

Animal Sciences is a broad-based subject involving both farm and companion animals. The range of specialisms is reflected in the table of courses above and can focus on animal nutrition and health, animal biology, behaviour, ecology and welfare. In addition, many courses specialise in equine science, studies and management.

Useful websites www.rspca.org.uk; www.iah.bbsrc.ac.uk; www.bhs.org.uk; www.wwf.org.uk; www.bsas.org.uk.

NB The points totals shown to the left of the institutions are for ease of reference only. It must not be assumed that tariff points are always used by institutions or that they can be substituted for an offer in grades. The level of an offer is not necessarily indicative of the quality of a course.

COURSE OFFERS INFORMATION

Subject requirements/preferences GCSE Mathematics/science subjects required. Also check any weight limits on equitation modules. **AL** One or two science subjects required for scientific courses, biology and chemistry preferred. **NB** A* grades are likely to form part of university offers in the higher ranges for students applying for places in 2008 for entry in 2009: check websites.

Your target offers

360 pts and above
   Cambridge – AAA (Nat Sci) *(IB 38–42 pts)*
340 pts Birmingham – AAB–BBB (Anim Biol (Zool))
320 pts Bristol – ABB–BBB (Anim Bhv Welf) *(IB 33 pts)*
   Sheffield – ABB (MBiol Sci Anim Bhv)
300 pts Bristol – BBB or BBbbb (Vet Pathogen; Anat Sci Vet Anat) *(IB 34 pts)*
   Exeter – BBB–BCC (Anim Bhv) *(IB 27–25 pts)*
   London (RVC) – BBB (BSc Vet Sci – **not** a qualification to practise as a vet)
   Newcastle – BBB–BB (Anim Sci (Cmpn Anim St) (Lvstk Tech)) *(IB 32–28 pts)*
   Sheffield – BBB (BSc Anim Bhv)
280 pts Aberystwyth – 280 pts (Anim Bhv)
   Glasgow – BBC–CCC (Anim Biol) *(IB 28 pts)*
   Leeds – 280–300 pts (Zool (Anim Sci))
   Reading – 280 pts 3AL+AS **or** 260 pts 3AL (App Anim Sci) *(IB 30 pts)*
   SAC (Scottish CAg) – 280 pts (Anim Sci)
260 pts Kent – 260 pts (Wldlf Cons)
   Nottingham – BCC–CCC (Anim Sci)
240 pts Aberdeen – CCC (Wldlf Mgt) *(IB 26–28 pts)*
   Aberystwyth – 240 pts (Eqn Sci; Anim Sci; Eqn Hum Spo Sci)
   CAFRE – 240 pts (Eqn Mgt; Eqn St)
   Chester – 240–260 pts (Anim Bhv courses)
   Lincoln – 240 pts (Eqn Sci; Anim Bhv Sci) *(IB 30 pts)*
220 pts Anglia Ruskin – 220 pts (Anim Welf; Anim Bhv; Anim Welf Psy; Eqn Sci)
   Askham Bryan (Coll) – CCD (Anim Mgt Sci)
   Brighton – 220 pts (Eqn Spo Perf) *(IB 26 pts)*
   Liverpool John Moores – 220 pts (Anim Bhv)
   Myerscough (Coll) – 220 pts (Anim Bhv Welf)
   Nottingham Trent (Brackenhurst) – 220 pts (Eqn Spo Sci; Eqn Spo Sci (Eqstrn Psy); Wldlf Cons)
   Stirling – CCD (Anim Biol) *(IB 26 pts)*
200 pts Bristol UWE (Hartpury) – 200–240 pts (Eqn Spo Sci; Eqn Sci; Eqn Dntl Sci)
   Gloucestershire – 200–280 pts (Anim Biol)
   Napier – 200 pts (Anim Biol)
   Plymouth – 200 pts (Anim Sci; Anim Sci (Bhv Welf) (Eqn) (Mgt Welf) (Vet Hlth St))
180 pts Aberystwyth – 180 pts (Agric Anim Sci)
   Lincoln – 180 pts (Eqn Spo Sci)
   Nottingham Trent (Brackenhurst) – DDD 180 pts (Anim Sci courses)
   Oxford Brookes – DDD (Eqn Sci)
   Salford – 180 pts (Wldlf Cons Zoo Biol)
   Staffordshire – 180–240 pts (Anim Biol Cons) *(IB 28 pts)*

For a quick reference offers calculator, fold out the inside back cover.

160 pts **Bristol UWE (Hartpury)** – 160–200 pts (Eqn Bus Mgt; Anim Sci) *(IB 28–30 pts)*
Canterbury Christ Church – CC (Anim Sci)
Greenwich/Hadlow (Coll) – DDE 160 pts (Anim Mgt; Eqn Mgt)
Harper Adams (UC) – 160–240 pts (Anim Bhv Welf; Anim Sci; Agric Anim Sci)
Royal (CAg) – 160 pts (Agric (Anim Mgt); Int Eqn Agric Mgt)
Warwickshire (Coll) – 160 (Eqn Sci; Eqn St; Spo Sci (Eqn Hum); Eqn Bus Mgt; Anim Welf)
Wolverhampton – 160–220 pts (Anim Mgt; Anim Bhv Wldlf Cons)
Worcester – 160 pts (Anim Biol courses)
Writtle (Coll) – 160 pts (Anim Sci; Anim Mgt; Eqn Sci; Eqn St; Eqn Brdng Stud Mgt; Eqn St Bus Mgt)

140 pts **Bishop Burton (Coll)** – 140 pts (Eqn Sci; Env Cons; App Anim Bhv Trg; App Anim Sci)
Liverpool John Moores – 140–180 pts (Wldlf Cons)

120 pts **Sparsholt (Coll)** – 120 pts (Anim Mgt; Eqn St; Wldlf Mgt)

80 pts **Bournemouth** – 80 pts (Anim Sci)

Alternative offers
See **Chapter 8** for grade/point equivalences and related information for the following examinations: Scottish qualifications, the Welsh Baccalaureate, the IB diploma (approximate points shown also in italics in the table of offers), the Irish Leaving Certificate, the European Baccalaureate and the French Baccalaureate.

EXAMPLES OF FOUNDATION DEGREES IN THE SUBJECT FIELD
Aberystwyth; Abingdon and Witney (Coll); Askham Bryan (Coll); Bicton (Coll); Bishop Burton (Coll); Bournemouth; Bridgwater (Coll); Brighton; Bristol UWE (Hartpury); Brooksby Melton (Coll); CAFRE; Capel Manor (Coll); Central Lancashire; Cornwall (Coll); Derby; Duchy (Coll); Easton (Coll); Greenwich; Hadlow (Coll); Harper Adams (UC); Hartpury (Coll); Kingston Maurward (Coll); Moulton (Coll); Myerscough (Coll); Nescot; Northampton; Nottingham Trent; Otley (Coll); Park Lane Leeds (Coll); Plumpton (Coll); Reaseheath (Coll); Shuttleworth (Coll); Solihull (Coll); Sparsholt (Coll); Suffolk (Univ Campus); Warwickshire (Coll); Weston (Coll); Wiltshire (Coll); Writtle (Coll).

CHOOSING YOUR COURSE (SEE ALSO CH.1)
Course variations – Widen your options
Animal Behaviour, Ecology and Conservation (Anglia Ruskin)
Zoology and Animal Behaviour (Bangor)
Animal Science (Bird Biology Foundation degree) (Cornwall (Coll))
Conservation Biology (Lincoln)
Advertising with Equine Studies (Northampton)
Wildlife Conservation (Nottingham Trent)
Animal Biology and Psychology (Worcester)
CHECK PROSPECTUSES AND WEBSITES FOR OTHER UNIVERSITIES AND COLLEGES OFFERING THESE COURSES.

Universities and colleges teaching quality See www.qaa.ac.uk; www.unistats.com.

For information on how to read the Subject Tables, see **Chapter 8**.

142 | Animal Sciences

Top universities and colleges (Research) Sheffield*; see also **Agricultural Sciences/Agriculture**.

Sandwich degree courses Harper Adams (UC); Writtle (Coll).

ADMISSIONS INFORMATION

Number of applicants per place (approx) Aberystwyth 6; Bristol 7; Harper Adams (UC) 5; Leeds 6; Newcastle 9 (all courses); Nottingham 6; Nottingham Trent (Eqn Spo Sci) 4; Reading 10; Royal (CAg) 4.

Advice to applicants and planning the UCAS personal statement Describe any work you have done with animals which generated your interest in this subject. Work experience in veterinary practices, on farms or with agricultural firms would be useful. Read agricultural/scientific journals for updates on animal nutrition or breeding. For Equine courses, details of practical experience with horses (eg BHS examinations, Pony Club tests) should be included. **Bristol** A very rigorous scientific academic course; close contact with horses. **Leeds** Farm experience is helpful but not a requirement. **Lincoln** (Eqn Spo Sci) Give full details of all practical riding experience.

Misconceptions about this course Students are not always aware that horse studies courses cover science, business management, nutrition, health and breeding. **Bishop Burton (Coll)** (Eqn Sci) Some students erroneously believe that riding skills and science background are not required for this course. Animal Management courses also extend to exotic species and livestock. It may also involve difficult decisions, for example for the benefit of the animal or the species rather than for the sensibilities of those involved.

Selection interviews Yes Bristol, Cambridge, Lincoln, Newcastle, Nottingham (depends on application), Plymouth, Royal (CAg), SAC (Scottish CAg), Writtle (Coll); **Some** Bishop Burton (Coll), Bristol UWE (Hartpury), Harper Adams (UC), Stirling.

Interview advice and questions Questions are likely about your experience with animals and your reasons for wishing to follow this science-based subject. Other questions asked in recent years have included: What do your parents think about your choice of course? What are your views on battery hens and the rearing of veal calves? The causes of foot and mouth disease and the on-going BSE question may also feature. **Equine** courses: students should check the level of riding ability expected (eg BHS Level 2 or PC B-test level). Check the amount of riding, jumping and competition work on the course. **Lincoln** (Eqn Spo Sci) Applicants required to show that they can ride to BHS Level 2. Experience with animals in general. See also **Chapter 7**.

Reasons for rejection (non-academic) Uncertainty as to why applicants chose the course. Too immature. Unlikely to integrate well.

AFTER-RESULTS ADVICE

Offers to applicants repeating A-levels Possibly higher Nottingham; **Same** Anglia Ruskin, Bishop Burton (Coll), Bristol UWE (Hartpury), Chester, Harper Adams (UC), Leeds, Liverpool John Moores, Plymouth, Royal (CAg), Stirling.

GRADUATE DESTINATIONS AND EMPLOYMENT (2005/6 HESA)

Graduates surveyed 395 **Employed** 185 **In further study** 75 **Assumed unemployed** 20.

Career note The majority of graduates obtained work with animals whilst others moved towards business and administration careers. This is a specialised subject area and undergraduates should start early to make contacts with organisations and gain work experience.

OTHER DEGREE SUBJECTS FOR CONSIDERATION

Agriculture; Biology; Food Science; Veterinary Science; Zoology.

For a quick reference offers calculator, fold out the inside back cover.

ANTHROPOLOGY

(including **Social Anthropology;** see also **Archaeology**)

Anthropology is the study of people's behaviour, beliefs and institutions and the diverse societies in which they live, and is concerned with the biological evolution of human beings. It also involves our relationships with other primates, the structure of communities and the effects of diet and disease on human groups. Alternatively, social or cultural anthropology covers aspects of social behaviour in respect of family, kinship, marriage, gender, religion, political structures, law, psychology and language.

Useful websites www.british-museum.ac.uk; www.therai.org.uk.

NB The points totals shown to the left of the institutions are for ease of reference only. It must not be assumed that tariff points are always used by institutions or that they can be substituted for an offer in grades. The level of an offer is not necessarily indicative of the quality of a course.

COURSE OFFERS INFORMATION

Subject requirements/preferences GCSE English and mathematics usually required. A foreign language may be required. **AL** Biology and geography preferred for some Biological Anthropological courses. (Social Anthropology) No specific subjects required except **London (LSE)** who stipulate academic subjects. **NB** A* grades are likely to form part of university offers in the higher ranges for students applying for places in 2008 for entry in 2009: check websites.

Your target offers

360 pts and above
- **Cambridge** – AAA (Arch Anth) *(IB 38–42 pts)*
- **Durham** – AAA (Nat Sci (Anth)) *(IB 34 pts H 17–19 pts)*
- **London (UCL)** – AABe–ABBe (Anthropology) *(IB 34–36 pts)*
- **Oxford** – Offers vary eg AAA–AAB (Arch Anth) *(IB 38–42 pts)*

340 pts Bristol – AAB–BBB (Arch Anth) *(IB 32–35 pts H665–666)*
- **Durham** – AAB (Comb Soc Sci (Anth)) *(IB 34 pts H 17–19 pts)*
- **East Anglia** – AAB–BBB (Arch Anth Art Hist) *(IB 32–34 pts)*
- **St Andrews** – AAB–ABB (Soc Anth courses) *(IB 32–36 pts)*

320 pts Durham – ABB (Anthropology) *(IB 34 pts H 17–19 pts)*
- **Glasgow** – ABB (BA Anth)
- **London (LSE)** – ABB (Anth Law) *(IB 36 pts H666)*
- **London (SOAS)** – ABB 320 pts (Soc Anth) *(IB 36 pts)*
- **Manchester** – ABB–BBB (Soc Anth; Soc Anth Sociol; Soc Anth Crimin; Arch Anth) *(IB 34 pts)*
- **Sussex** – ABB–BBB (Anth courses) *(IB 32 pts)*

300 pts Birmingham – BBB–BBC (Anth courses) *(IB 30–32 pts)*
- **Brunel** – 300 pts (Psy Soc Anth)
- **Durham** – BBB (Anth Arch)
- **Edinburgh** – BBB (Soc Anth courses) *(IB 35 pts H555)*
- **Lancaster** – BBB (Anth Relig) *(IB 32–33 pts)*
- **Liverpool** – BBB (Evol Anth) *(IB 34 pts)*
- **London (Gold)** – BBB (Anth; Anth Media; Anth Sociol; Hist Anth) *(IB 32 pts)*
- **London (LSE)** – BBB (Soc Anth) *(IB 36 pts H666)*
- **Oxford Brookes** – BBB–CCC (Anth courses)
- **Queen's Belfast** – BBB–BBCb (Soc Anth courses)

280 pts Durham – BBC (Anth Sociol; Biol Anth; Med Anth)
- **Glasgow** – BBC–CCC (BSc Anth)
- **Southampton** – BBC 280 pts (App Soc Sci (Anth))

260 pts Brunel – 260 pts (Soc Anth courses except under **300 pts**)
- **Dundee** – 260–320 pts (Foren Anth) *(IB 29 pts)*
- **Kent** – 260 pts (Biol Anth; Med Anth) *(IB 28 pts)*

240 pts **Aberdeen** – CCC **or** aabb (Anth courses) *(IB 30 pts)*
Kent – 240 pts (Anthropology) *(IB 27 pts H 13 pts)*
220 pts **Hull** – 220–280 pts (Sociol Anth)
200 pts **Liverpool John Moores** – 200–220 pts (Evol Anth; Foren Anth)
180 pts **Lampeter** – 180–240 pts (Anth courses)
Roehampton – 180–240 pts (Anth; Biol Anth courses)
160 pts **East London** – 160 pts (Anth courses)

Alternative offers
See **Chapter 8** for grade/point equivalences and related information for the following examinations: Scottish qualifications, the Welsh Baccalaureate, the IB diploma (approximate points shown also in italics in the table of offers), the Irish Leaving Certificate, the European Baccalaureate and the French Baccalaureate.

CHOOSING YOUR COURSE (SEE ALSO CH.1)

Course variations – Widen your options
African Studies and Anthropology (Birmingham)
Psychology and Social Anthropology (Brunel)
Social Anthropology and Sociology (Brunel)
Human Sciences (Durham)
Third World Development and Anthropology (East London)
Persian and Social Anthropology (Edinburgh)
Anthropology and Sociology (Glasgow)
Chinese and Anthropology (Lampeter)
Law and Anthropology (Sussex)
CHECK PROSPECTUSES AND WEBSITES FOR OTHER UNIVERSITIES AND COLLEGES OFFERING THESE COURSES.

Universities and colleges teaching quality See www.qaa.ac.uk; www.unistats.com.

Top universities and colleges (Research) Cambridge; Durham; Edinburgh; Kent; London (Gold), (LSE)*, (SOAS), (UCL)*; Manchester; Oxford; Queen's Belfast; Roehampton; St Andrews; Sussex.

Sandwich degree courses Bristol UWE; Brunel.

ADMISSIONS INFORMATION

Number of applicants per place (approx) Cambridge 2; Durham 14; Hull 11; Kent 6; Liverpool John Moores 4; London (Gold) 7, (LSE) (Anth Law) 9, (Soc Anth) 9, (SOAS) 10, (UCL) 3; Oxford Brookes 8; Queen's Belfast 10; Sussex 10.

Advice to applicants and planning the UCAS personal statement Visits to museums should be discussed, for example, museums of anthropology (London, Cambridge). Describe any aspect of the subject which interests you (including books you have read) and how you have pursued this interest. Give details of any overseas travel. Since this is not a school subject, you will need to convince the selectors of your knowledge and interest. **St Andrews** Give reasons for choosing course and evidence of interest, sporting and extracurricular activities and positions of responsibility.

Selection interviews **Yes** Cambridge, Durham, East Anglia, Hull, London (Gold), (UCL) mature students, Oxford, Oxford Brookes; **Some** London (LSE), Roehampton; **No** Bristol.

Interview advice and questions This is a broad subject and questions will tend to emerge as a result of your interests in aspects of anthropology or social anthropology and your comments on your personal statement. Past questions have included: What stresses are there among the nomads of the North African desert? What is a society? What is speech? If you dug up a stone axe what could you learn from it? What are the values created by a capitalist society? Discuss the role of women since the beginning of this century. **Cambridge, Oxford** See **Chapter 7** and **Archaeology**.

Reasons for rejection (non-academic) Lack of commitment. Inability to deal with a more philosophical (less positivist) approach to knowledge.

AFTER-RESULTS ADVICE

Offers to applicants repeating A-levels Possibly higher Durham, Oxford Brookes; **Same** Durham, East Anglia, Liverpool John Moores, London (UCL), Roehampton.

GRADUATE DESTINATIONS AND EMPLOYMENT (2005/6 HESA)

Graduates surveyed 550 **Employed** 250 **In further study** 95 **Assumed unemployed** 50.

Career note All non-scientific careers are open to graduates. However, career planning should start early and efforts made to contact employers and gain work experience.

OTHER DEGREE SUBJECTS FOR CONSIDERATION

Archaeology; Egyptology; Heritage Studies; History; Human Sciences; Political Science; Psychology; Religious Studies; Social Science; Sociology.

ARABIC AND NEAR AND MIDDLE EASTERN STUDIES

Arabic is one of the world's most widely used languages, spoken by more than 300 million people in 21 countries in the Middle East. Links between Britain and Arabic-speaking countries have increased considerably in recent years and most of the larger UK organisations with offices in the Middle East have only a relatively small pool of Arabic-speaking graduates from whom they can recruit future employees each year. Islamic Studies focuses on a faith which has much in common with Christianity and Judaism, is the second largest religion in the world, extending from Africa to the East Indies, and is focused on the Middle East.

Useful websites www.cilt.org.uk; www.iol.org.uk; www.bbc.co.uk/languages; www.languageadvantage.com; www.languagematters.co.uk; www.reed.co.uk/multilingual; www.metimes.com; www.merip.org; www.memri.org; www.mideasti.org.

NB The points totals shown to the left of the institutions are for ease of reference only. It must not be assumed that tariff points are always used by institutions or that they can be substituted for an offer in grades. The level of an offer is not necessarily indicative of the quality of a course.

COURSE OFFERS INFORMATION

Subject requirements/preferences GCSE English, mathematics and a foreign language usually required. A high grade in Arabic may be required. **AL** A modern language is usually required or preferred. **NB** A* grades are likely to form part of university offers in the higher ranges for students applying for places in 2008 for entry in 2009: check websites.

Your target offers

360 pts and above

> **Cambridge** – AAA (Orntl St (Assyr); Orntl St Comb (Arbc) (Assyr) (Persn) (Egypt) (Mid E Islam St Arbc)) *(IB 38–42 pts)*
>
> **Oxford** – Offers vary eg AAA–AAB (Orntl St (Arbc) (Arbc Islam St Hist) (Arbc Lang) (Egypt); Persn Lang; Persn Islam St Hist; Persn Islam Art Arch; Turk courses) *(IB 38–42 pts)*

340 pts St Andrews – AAB–ABB (Mid E St courses; Arbc courses) *(IB 32–36 pts)*

320 pts Exeter – ABB–BBC 320–280 pts (Arbc courses; Mid E St) *(IB 30 pts)*

300 pts Edinburgh – BBB (Arbc courses; Persn Pol, Persn Soc Anth)

> **Swansea** – 300–260 pts (Class Anc Hist Egypt (Egypt))

280 pts Leeds – BBC–BCC (Arbc courses; Mid E St)

> **London (King's)** – BBC+AS (Turk Modn Gk St)
>
> **London (SOAS)** – BBC–BCC (Arbc; Arbc Cult St; Arbc Islam St; Anc Near E St; Persn; Turk; Heb Israeli St) *(IB 32 pts)*
>
> **Manchester** – BBC–BCC (Mid E St; Arbc St; Turk St; Turk Islam St; Persn St; Persn Islam St; Heb Jew St)

For information on how to read the Subject Tables, see **Chapter 8**.

Westminster – 280 pts (Arbc courses)
260 pts Birmingham – BCC 260 pts (Islam St) *(IB 30 pts)*
200 pts Salford – 200 pts (Arbc Engl Transl Interp for Arabic speakers; contact admissions tutor)
180 pts Lampeter – 180–240 pts (Islam St)

London (Birk) – Check with admissions tutor (Arbc courses)

Alternative offers

See **Chapter 8** for grade/point equivalences and related information for the following examinations: Scottish qualifications, the Welsh Baccalaureate, the IB diploma (approximate points shown also in italics in the table of offers), the Irish Leaving Certificate, the European Baccalaureate and the French Baccalaureate.

CHOOSING YOUR COURSE (SEE ALSO CH.1)

Course variations – Widen your options
Arabic and Business Studies (Edinburgh)
Arabic and International Relations (Leeds)
Arabic and Management (St Andrews)
International Business (Arabic) (Westminster)
CHECK PROSPECTUSES AND WEBSITES FOR OTHER UNIVERSITIES AND COLLEGES OFFERING THESE COURSES.

Universities and colleges teaching quality See www.qaa.ac.uk; www.unistats.com.

Top universities and colleges (Research) Cambridge; Edinburgh; London (SOAS); Manchester; Oxford.

ADMISSIONS INFORMATION

Number of applicants per place (approx) Birmingham 3; Cambridge (Orntl St) 3; Leeds 6; London (SOAS) 5; Salford 5.

Advice to applicants and planning the UCAS personal statement Describe any visits to, or your experience of living in, Arabic-speaking countries. Develop a knowledge of Middle Eastern cultures, history and politics and mention these topics on the UCAS application. Provide evidence of language-learning skills and experience. **St Andrews** Reasons for choosing course and evidence of interest. Sporting/extra-curricular activities and positions of responsibility. **Salford** Experience of use and interest in foreign languages. Experience of foreign countries. (Arbc Engl Transl Interp) Arab applicants are normally expected to have passed their secondary school leaving certificate and to demonstrate an acceptable command of English. English and European applicants should also be able to speak Arabic.

Selection interviews **Yes** Cambridge, Exeter, Leeds, Oxford; **Some** Salford.

Interview advice and questions You will need to be able to justify your reasons for wanting to study Arabic or other languages and to discuss your interest in, and awareness of, cultural, social and political aspects of the Middle East. **Cambridge, Oxford** See **Chapter 7** under **Modern and Medieval Languages. Salford** (Arbc/Engl Transl Interp) Applicants may be required to sit Arabic language tests. See also **Chapter 7**.

AFTER-RESULTS ADVICE

Offers to applicants repeating A-levels **Higher** Leeds, St Andrews; **Same** Exeter, Salford.

GRADUATE DESTINATIONS AND EMPLOYMENT (2005/6 HESA)

Graduates surveyed 80 **Employed** 30 **In further study** 15 **Assumed unemployed** 10.

Career note Most graduates entered business and administrative work, in some cases closely linked to their language studies.

OTHER DEGREE SUBJECTS FOR CONSIDERATION

Anthropology; Archaeology; Classical Studies; Hebrew; History; Persian; Politics; Turkish.

For a quick reference offers calculator, fold out the inside back cover.

ARCHAEOLOGY

Courses in Archaeology differ between institutions but the majority focus on the archaeology of Europe, the Mediterranean and Middle Eastern countries and on the close examination of discoveries of prehistoric communities and ancient, medieval and post-medieval societies. Hands-on experience is involved in all courses as well as a close study of the history of the artefacts themselves and, in some courses, an appreciation of the application of science.

Useful websites www.britarch.ac.uk; www.english-heritage.org.uk; www.artefact.co.uk; www.prehistoric.org.uk; www.british-museum.ac.uk; www.archaeologists.net.

NB The points totals shown to the left of the institutions are for ease of reference only. It must not be assumed that tariff points are always used by institutions or that they can be substituted for an offer in grades. The level of an offer is not necessarily indicative of the quality of a course.

COURSE OFFERS INFORMATION

Subject requirements/preferences GCSE English and mathematics or science usually required for BSc courses. **AL** History, geography, English or a science subject may be preferred for some courses and two science subjects for Archaeological Science courses. **NB** A* grades are likely to form part of university offers in the higher ranges for students applying for places in 2008 for entry in 2009: check websites.

Your target offers

360 pts and above

    Cambridge – AAA (Arch Anth) *(IB 38–42 pts)*
    Durham – AAA (Nat Sci (Arch))
    Oxford – Offers vary eg AAA–AAB (Arch Anth; Class Arch Anc Hist) *(IB 38–42 pts)*

340 pts Bristol – AAB–BBB (Arch Anth) *(IB 36 pts H665–666)*
    Durham – AAB (Arch (Comb Soc Sci) (Comb Hons Arts)) *(IB 32 pts)*
    East Anglia – AAB–BBB (Arch Anth Art Hist; Arch Anth Art Hist Aus/N Am) *(IB 32–34 pts)*
    St Andrews – AAB (Anc Hist Arch) *(IB 36 pts)*
    York – AAB–ABB (Arch; Bioarch; Arch Hist) *(IB 34 pts)*

320 pts Glasgow – ABB–BBB (Arch courses) *(IB 28 pts)*
    London (King's) – ABB (Class Arch) *(IB 34 pts)*
    London (UCL) – ABB+AS–BBB+AS (Arch; Class Arch Class Civ; Egypt Arch) *(IB 32–34 pts)*
    Nottingham – ABB (Arch Engl Lang; Arch Geog) *(IB 30–34 pts)*
    Sheffield – ABB–BBC (Arch courses) *(IB 32 pts)*
    Warwick – ABB–BBBc (Anc Hist Class Arch) *(IB 32–36 pts)*

300 pts Bristol – BBB–BCC (Arch; Arch Sci) *(IB 29–32 pts H665–655)*
    Cardiff – BBB (Arch courses) *(IB 30 pts)*
    Durham – BBB (Arch; Anth Arch; Anc Hist Arch) *(IB 32 pts)*

For information on how to read the Subject Tables, see **Chapter 8**.

Edinburgh – BBB (one sitting) (Arch courses) *(IB 34 pts H555)*
Exeter – BBB–BBC **or** BBbb **or** BCcc 300–320 pts (Arch courses) *(IB 30–34 pts)*
Leicester – 300–360 pts (Anc Hist Arch; Hist Arch; Geog Arch)
London (RH) – BBB (Class Arch) *(IB 32 pts)*
London (UCL) – BBB (Vkg St) *(IB 32–34 pts)*
Manchester – BBB (Arch; Anc Hist Arch)
Newcastle – BBB–BCC (Arch; Anc Hist Arch) *(IB 30–32 pts)*
Southampton – BBB (Arch; Arch Geog; Arch Hist) *(IB 28 pts H 13 pts)*
Swansea – 300–260 pts (Egypt courses)

280 pts **Birmingham** – BBC 280 pts (Arch; Arch Anc Hist) *(IB 30–32 pts)*
Glasgow – BBC–CCC (BSc Arch courses) *(IB 28 pts)*
Hull – 280 pts (Geog Arch; Hist Arch)
Kent – 280 pts (Hist Arch St) *(IB 28–29 pts)*
Leicester – 280 pts (Archaeology) *(IB 34 pts)*
Liverpool – BBC 280 pts (Arch; Arch Anc Civ; Egypt Arch; Egypt) *(IB 34 pts)*
Nottingham – BBC (Vkg St; Arch; Arch Art Hist; Arch Class Civ; Arch Hist)
Queen's Belfast – BBC–BBB (Arch courses) *(IB 29 pts H655)*

260 pts **Bradford** – 260–280 pts (Arch Sci; Arch; Bioarch; Foren Arch Sci)
Kent – 260 pts (Class Arch St courses) *(IB 28 pts)*
Leicester – 260–320 pts (Arch Comb courses)
London (SOAS) – BCC (Arch courses) *(IB 30 pts)*
Reading – 260–280 pts 3AL+AS **or** 260 pts 3AL (BSc Archaeology) *(IB 30 pts)*

240 pts **Central Lancashire** – 240 pts (Archaeology)
Chester – 240 pts (Arch; Arch Foren Biol) *(IB 30 pts)*

220 pts **Bangor** – 220–260 pts (Herit Arch Hist)
Winchester – 220 pts (Arch courses)

200 pts **Lampeter** – 200 pts (Arch; Arch (Env) (Prac) (Wrld Cult); Anc Hist Arch; Arch Anth)

180 pts **Portsmouth** – 180 pts (Pal Evol)

160 pts **Bournemouth** – 160 pts (Fld Arch; Mar Arch; Arch; Arch Foren Sci)
Central Lancashire – 160 pts (Comb Hons (Arch))

140 pts **Worcester** – 140–160 pts (Arch Land St; Arch Herit St)

Alternative offers

See **Chapter 8** for grade/point equivalences and related information for the following examinations: Scottish qualifications, the Welsh Baccalaureate, the IB diploma (approximate points shown also in italics in the table of offers), the Irish Leaving Certificate, the European Baccalaureate and the French Baccalaureate.

EXAMPLES OF FOUNDATION DEGREES IN THE SUBJECT FIELD
Bournemouth; Cornwall (Coll).

CHOOSING YOUR COURSE (SEE ALSO CH.1)
Course variations – Widen your options
Combined Honours (Central Lancashire)
Archaeology and Forensic Biology (Chester)
Classical Archaeological Studies (Kent)
Archaeology and Palaeoecology (St Andrews)
Egyptology (Swansea)
CHECK PROSPECTUSES AND WEBSITES FOR OTHER UNIVERSITIES AND COLLEGES OFFERING THESE COURSES.

Universities and colleges teaching quality See www.qaa.ac.uk; www.unistats.com.

Top universities and colleges (Research) Bradford; Cambridge*; Cardiff; Durham; Exeter; Leicester; Liverpool; London (UCL); Oxford*; Queen's Belfast; Reading; Sheffield; Southampton.

Sandwich degree courses Bradford.

ADMISSIONS INFORMATION

Number of applicants per place (approx) Birmingham 7; Bradford 4; Bristol 7; Cambridge 2; Cardiff 6; Durham 6; Lampeter 2; Leicester 4; Liverpool 12, (Egypt) 5; London (UCL) 5; Newcastle 14; Nottingham 11; Sheffield 5; Southampton 9; York 10.

Advice to applicants and planning the UCAS personal statement First-hand experience of 'digs' and other field work should be described. The Council for British Archaeology (see **Appendix 2**) can provide information on where digs are taking place. Describe any interests in fossils and museum visits as well as details of any visits to current archaeological sites. Your local university archaeological department or central library will also provide information on contacts in your local area (each county council employs an archaeological officer). Since this is not a school subject, the selectors will be looking for good reasons for your choice of subject. **Birmingham** Applications from mature students welcome. Although useful, previous experience of archaeology is not necessary. **Bournemouth** Show willingness to participate in excavations. **Bristol** Gain practical field experience and discuss this in the personal statement. A demonstration of serious commitment to the discipline through extra-curricular activities (fieldwork, museum experience) can compensate for exam results that may be less strong than desirable. **Durham** Archaeological experience useful but not necessary. **Lampeter** Experience useful but not essential. **Liverpool** (Egypt) Interest in ancient Egypt developed through reading, TV and the Internet. Course covers archaeology and writings of Ancient Egypt. Be aware of the work of career archaeologists, eg sites and monuments officers, field officers and find researchers (often specialists in particular materials, eg pottery, glass, metalwork). **Oxford** No prior knowledge of archaeology or anthropology required but an enthusiasm for the study of humans and their material culture is expected, preferably from both arts and science viewpoints. (See also **Anthropology**.) **Southampton** Give evidence of practical experience. **York** We look for interested and interesting students. (See also **Appendix 2**.)

Misconceptions about this course Bristol We are not an élitist course: 75% of applicants and students come from state schools and non-traditional backgrounds. **Liverpool** (Egypt) Some students would have been better advised looking at courses in Archaeology or Ancient History and Archaeology which offer major pathways in the study of Ancient Egypt.

Selection interviews Yes Bangor, Bournemouth, Bradford, Cambridge, Durham, East Anglia, Glasgow, Lampeter, Liverpool (Egypt), London (UCL), Newcastle, Nottingham, Oxford, Southampton (mature students), Swansea; **Some** Birmingham, Cardiff; **No** Bristol.

Interview advice and questions Questions will be asked about any experience you have had in visiting archaeological sites or taking part in digs. Past questions have included: How would you interpret archaeological evidence, for example a pile of flints, coins? What is stratification? How would you date archaeological remains? What recent archaeological discoveries have been made? How did you become interested in archaeology? With which archaeological sites in the UK are you familiar? **Birmingham** Questions may cover recent archaeological events. **Cambridge**, **Oxford** (see **Chapter 7**). **Oxford** (Class Arch Anc Hist) Candidates may be shown pictures, objects or other material for discussion. **York** What are your views on the archaeology programmes on TV? What would you do with a spare weekend? See also **Chapter 7**.

Applicants' impressions (A=Open day; B=Interview day) Birmingham (A) A tour of the department, campus and sample lectures. **Liverpool** (B) A talk about the course followed by the interview. I was asked to identify a pot and answer questions on archaeology, such as the treatment of bones. An offer was made at the end of the interview. **Swansea** (B) I had a 30-minute interview (one interviewer) with questions on why I chose the course.

Reasons for rejection (non-academic) (Mature students) Inability to cope with essay-writing and exams. **Bournemouth** Health and fitness important for excavations. **Liverpool** (Egypt) Applicant misguided on choice of course – Egyptology used to fill a gap on the UCAS application.

AFTER-RESULTS ADVICE

Offers to applicants repeating A-levels Same Birmingham, Bradford, Chester, Durham, East Anglia,

Lampeter, Leicester, Liverpool (Egypt), London (UCL), Sheffield, Winchester; **No offers made** Cambridge.

GRADUATE DESTINATIONS AND EMPLOYMENT (2005/6 HESA)
Graduates surveyed 855 **Employed** 465 **In further study** 160 **Assumed unemployed** 60.

Career note Vocational opportunities closely linked to this subject are limited. However, some graduates aim for positions in local authorities, libraries and museums. A number of organisations covering Water Boards, forestry, civil engineering and surveying also employ field archaeologists.

OTHER DEGREE SUBJECTS FOR CONSIDERATION
Ancient History; Anthropology; Classical Studies; Classics; Geology; Heritage Studies; History; History of Art and Architecture; Medieval History.

ARCHITECTURE

(including **Architectural Technology** and **Engineering with Architecture;** see also **Building**)

Courses in Architecture provide a broad education consisting of technological subjects covering structures, construction, materials and environmental studies. Project-based design work is an integral part of all courses and in addition, history and social studies will also be incorporated into degree programmes. After completing the first three years leading to a BA (Hons), students aiming for full professional status take a further two-year course leading to the BA (Arch) degree and after a year in an architect's practice, the final professional examinations are taken.

Useful websites www.ciat.org.uk; www.architecture.com.

NB The points totals shown to the left of the institutions are for ease of reference only. It must not be assumed that tariff points are always used by institutions or that they can be substituted for an offer in grades. The level of an offer is not necessarily indicative of the quality of a course.

COURSE OFFERS INFORMATION
Subject requirements/preferences **GCSE** English and mathematics in some cases at certain grades are required in all cases. A science subject may also be required. **AL** Mathematics and/or physics required or preferred for some courses. Art and design may be preferable to design and technology. Art is sometimes a requirement and many schools of architecture prefer it; a portfolio of art work is often requested and, in some cases, a drawing test will be set. **NB** A* grades are likely to form part of university offers in the higher ranges for students applying for places in 2008 for entry in 2009: check websites.

Your target offers
360 pts and above
> **Bath** – AAA–AAB (Archit St) *(IB 35 pts H art 5 pts)*
> **Cambridge** – AAA (Architecture) *(IB 38–42 pts)*
> **Cardiff** – AAA (Archit St) *(IB 35 pts)*
> **Newcastle** – AAA–ABB (Archit St) *(IB 37 pts H art 6 pts)*
> **Nottingham** – AAA (Architecture) *(IB 36 pts)*
> **Southampton** – ABBb (Civ Eng Archit)

340 pts Sheffield – AAB (Archit; Archit Land) *(IB 35 pts)*
320 pts Heriot-Watt – ABB 2nd yr entry (Archit Eng)
> **Kingston** – 320 pts (Architecture)
> **Liverpool** – ABB 320 pts (Architecture) *(IB 34 pts)*
> **London (UCL)** – ABB+AS (Architecture) *(IB 34 pts)*
> **Manchester** – ABB (Architecture) *(IB 33 pts)*

Plymouth – 320 pts (Architecture) *(IB 32 pts)*
Sheffield – ABB (Struct Eng Archit)

300 pts **Archit Assoc Sch London** – BBB 300 pts (Architecture)
Brighton – 300 pts (Architecture) *(IB 28–30pts)*
City – 300 pts (MEng Civ Eng Archit)
Edinburgh – BBB (Archit Des; Archit Hist; Archit Hist Arch; Archit St) *(IB 34 pts H555)*
Kent – 300 pts (Architecture) *(IB 31 pts)*
Leeds – BBB–CCC (Archit Eng)
Manchester Met – BBB 300 pts (Architecture) *(IB 30 pts)*
Northumbria – 300 pts (Architecture)
Nottingham – BBB (Archit Env Des)
Oxford Brookes – BBB **or** BBe (Architecture)
Queen's Belfast – BBB–BBCb (Struct Eng Archit; Archit) *(IB 29 pts H655)*
Strathclyde – BBB (MEng Archit Eng)
Westminster – 300 pts (Archit; Archit (Archit Eng)) *(IB 33 pts)*

280 pts **Dundee** – BBC (Architecture) *(IB 30 pts)*
Glasgow (SA) – BBC (Archit St)
Nottingham Trent – 280 pts (Architecture) *(IB 28 pts)*
Sheffield Hallam – 280 pts (Archit Env Des; Archit Tech)
Strathclyde – BBC (Archit St; Archit St Euro St)
Ulster – 280 pts (Architecture) *(IB 25 pts)*

260 pts **Anglia Ruskin** – 260 pts (Architecture) *(IB 26 pts)*
Central Lancashire – 260 pts (Archit Tech)
City – 260 pts (BEng Civ Eng Archit)
Creative Arts (UC) – 260 pts (Architecture)
Edinburgh (CA) – 260 pts (Architecture)
Ulster – 260 pts (Archit Tech Mgt)

240 pts **Birmingham City** – 240 pts (Architecture)
Bristol UWE – 240–320 pts (Archit Plan) *(IB 24–28 pts)*
De Montfort – 240 pts (Archit; Archit Des Tech Prod)
Glasgow – CCC (Civ Eng Archit)
Greenwich – 240 pts (Architecture)
Huddersfield – 240 pts (Archit (Int) (Smt Des) (Urb Des); Archit Tech)
Lincoln – 240 pts (Architecture)
Liverpool John Moores – 240 pts (Architecture)
Northumbria – 240 pts (Archit Tech)
Plymouth – 240 pts (Archit Des Struct; Archit Tech Env)
Portsmouth – 240–300 pts (Architecture)
Robert Gordon – CCC (Archit; Archit Tech)

220 pts **Anglia Ruskin** – 220 pts (Archit Tech)
Bolton – 220 pts (Archit Tech)
Heriot-Watt – CCD (Archit Eng)
Napier – CCD (Archit Tech; Archit Des Civ Eng)
Nottingham Trent – 220 pts (Archit Tech)

200 pts **Westminster** – BB 200 pts (Archit Tech)

180 pts **Bristol UWE** – 180–200 pts (Archit Tech Des) *(IB 24–28 pts)*
Cardiff (UWIC) – 180 pts (Archit Des Tech)
Coventry – 180 pts (Archit Des Tech)
Derby – 180–200 pts (Archit Cons courses)
London Met – 180–240 pts (Archit St; Archit)
Northampton – 180–220 pts (Archit Tech)

160 pts **East London** – 160 pts (Architecture)
London South Bank – CC (Archit; Archit Tech; Archit Eng)
Wolverhampton – 160–220 pts (Archit St courses)

For information on how to read the Subject Tables, see **Chapter 8**.

120 pts North East Wales (IHE) – 120 pts (Archit Des Tech)
100 pts Southampton Solent – 120 pts (Archit Tech)

Leeds Met – contact University

Alternative offers
See **Chapter 8** for grade/point equivalences and related information for the following examinations: Scottish qualifications, the Welsh Baccalaureate, the IB diploma (approximate points shown also in italics in the table of offers), the Irish Leaving Certificate, the European Baccalaureate and the French Baccalaureate.

EXAMPLES OF FOUNDATION DEGREES IN THE SUBJECT FIELD
Bolton; Derby; Northumbria; Oldham (Coll); Thames Valley.

CHOOSING YOUR COURSE (SEE ALSO CH.1)
Course variations – Widen your options
Property Surveying (Anglia Ruskin)
Civil and Architectural Engineering (Bath)
Interior Architecture (Brighton)
Built and Natural Environment (Bristol UWE)
Architectural Design and Heritage Conservation (Derby)
Architectural History (Edinburgh)
Quantity Surveying (Glamorgan)
Naval Architecture (Plymouth)
History of Art and Architecture (Reading)
Architectural Glass (Swansea (Inst))
CHECK PROSPECTUSES AND WEBSITES FOR OTHER UNIVERSITIES AND COLLEGES OFFERING THESE COURSES.

Universities and colleges teaching quality See www.qaa.ac.uk; www.unistats.com.

Top universities and colleges (Research) Bath; Cardiff; Heriot-Watt; Sheffield.

Sandwich degree courses Bath; Brighton; Bristol UWE; Cardiff; Edinburgh (CA); Glasgow (SA); Northumbria; Nottingham Trent; Plymouth; Queen's Belfast; Robert Gordon; Sheffield Hallam; Ulster.

ADMISSIONS INFORMATION
Number of applicants per place (approx) Archit Assoc Sch London 2; Bath 22; Cambridge 10; Cardiff 12; Cardiff (UWIC) 2; Creative Arts (UC) 4; Dundee 6; Edinburgh 18; Glasgow 16; London (UCL) 16; London Met 13; Manchester Met 25; Newcastle 11; Nottingham 30; Oxford Brookes 15; Queen's Belfast 9; Robert Gordon 8; Sheffield 20; Strathclyde 10.

Advice to applicants and planning the UCAS personal statement You should describe any visits to historical or modern architectural sites and give your opinions. Contact architects in your area and try to obtain work shadowing or work experience in their practices. Describe any such work you have done. Develop a portfolio of drawings and sketches of buildings and parts of buildings (you will probably need this for your interview). Show evidence of your reading on the history of architecture in Britain and modern architecture throughout the world. Discuss your preferences among the work of leading 20th century world architects. **Archit Assoc Sch London** We look for students with plenty of creativity and motivation. **Cardiff** A good academic base is required, preferably indicating a balance of skills in visual arts, sciences, writing and research. Experience in art and/or design is an advantage. Evidence of work experience in an architect's practice important. **De Montfort** Evidence of work experience and an emphasis on freehand pencil drawing. (See **Appendix 2**.)

Misconceptions about this course Some applicants believe that architectural technology is the same as architecture. Some students confuse architecture with architectural engineering.

Selection interviews The majority of universities and colleges interview or inspect portfolios for Architecture and most require a portfolio of art work. **Yes** Archit Assoc Sch London, Bradford,

Brighton, Cambridge, Cardiff, Coventry, Derby, East London, Edinburgh, Huddersfield, Kingston, Liverpool, London (UCL), London South Bank, Newcastle, Nottingham, Sheffield; **Some** Dundee.

Interview advice and questions Most Architecture departments will expect to see evidence of your ability to draw; portfolios are often requested at interview and, in some cases, drawing tests are set prior to the interview. You should have a real awareness of architecture with some knowledge of historical styles as well as examples of modern architecture. If you have gained some work experience then you will be asked to describe the work done in the architect's office and any site visits you have made. Questions in the past have included the following: What is the role of the architect in society? Is the London Eye an eyesore? Discuss one historic and one 20th century building you admire. Who is your favourite architect? What sort of buildings do you want to design? How do you make a place peaceful? How would you reduce crime through architecture? Do you like the University buildings? Do you read any architectural journals? What are your views on the Millennium Dome? What is the role of an architectural technologist? **Archit Assoc Sch London** The interview assesses the student's potential and ability to benefit from the course. Every portfolio we see at interview will be different; sketches, models, photographs and paintings all help to build up a picture of the student's interests. Detailed portfolio guidelines are available on the website. **Cambridge** How do you make a place peaceful? How do you reduce crime through architecture? **Cambridge (Robinson)** Candidates who have taken, or are going to take, A-level art should bring with them their portfolio of work (GCSE work is not required). All candidates, including those who are not taking A-level art, should bring photographs of any three-dimensional material. Those not taught art should bring a sketch book (for us to assess drawing abilities) and analytical drawings of a new and old (pre-1900) building and a natural and human-made artefact. We are interested to see any graphic work in any medium that you would like to show us – please do not feel you should restrict your samples to only those with architectural reference. All evidence of sketching ability is helpful to us. (**NB** All colleges at Cambridge and other university departments of architecture will seek similar evidence.) **Sheffield** Art portfolio for those without AL/GCSE art. See also **Chapter 7**.

Applicants' impressions (A=Open day; B=Interview day) Bath (A) A four-hour open day. Talks on course and tour of the department, halls and university. Informative – very helpful. **Kingston** (B) A 20-minute interview, very casual. I got a very favourable impression of the teaching quality in the department. The course has an artistic, rather than a maths, emphasis. A good place to study if you want to be near London without being in the city. **Portsmouth** (B) An informal group interview took place and portfolios were discussed.

Reasons for rejection (non-academic) Weak evidence of creative skills. Folio of art work does not give sufficient evidence of design creativity. Insufficient evidence of interest in architecture. Unwillingness to try freehand sketching. **Archit Assoc Sch London** Poor standard of work in the portfolio.

AFTER-RESULTS ADVICE

Offers to applicants repeating A-levels Higher Huddersfield; **Possibly higher** Brighton, De Montfort, Glasgow, Newcastle; **Same** Archit Assoc Sch London, Bath, Birmingham City, Cardiff, Cardiff (UWIC), Creative Arts (UC), Derby, Dundee, Greenwich, Heriot-Watt, Kingston, Liverpool John Moores, London Met, London South Bank, Manchester Met, Nottingham, Nottingham Trent, Oxford Brookes, Queen's Belfast, Robert Gordon, Sheffield; **No offers made** Cambridge.

GRADUATE DESTINATIONS AND EMPLOYMENT (2005/6 HESA)

Graduates surveyed 1530 **Employed** 825 **In further study** 235 **Assumed unemployed** 55.

Career note Further study is needed to enter architecture as a profession but job prospects are good. In 2006 the unemployment rate for architecture, building and planning was below 4%. Opportunities exist in local government or private practice – areas include planning, housing, environmental and conservation fields. Architectural technicians support the work of architects and may be involved in project management, design presentations and submissions to planning authorities.

OTHER DEGREE SUBJECTS FOR CONSIDERATION

Building; Building Surveying; Civil Engineering; Construction; Estate Management; Heritage Management; History of Art and Architecture; Housing; Interior Architecture; Interior Design; Landscape Architecture; Property Development; Quantity Surveying; Surveying; Town and Country Planning; Urban Studies.

ART and DESIGN (General)

(including **Animation, Design Technology** and **Multimedia Design;** see also **Media Studies**)

Art and Design and all specialisms remain one of the most popular subjects. This table provides a list of art and design courses that covers a wide range of creative activities for entry to Foundation studies which are required before embarking on degree courses (check with institution). Many of these courses cover aspects of fine art, graphic or three dimensional design, but to a less specialised extent than those listed in the other Art and Design tables. Travel and visits to art galleries and museums strongly recommended by many universities and colleges.

Useful websites www.artscouncil.org.uk; www.designcouncil.org.uk; www.britart.com; www.theatredesign.org.uk; www.worldofinteriors.co.uk; www.artefact.co.uk; www.arts.ac.uk; www.dandad.org; www.csd.org.uk.

NB The points totals shown to the left of the institutions are for ease of reference only. It must not be assumed that tariff points are always used by institutions or that they can be substituted for an offer in grades. The level of an offer is not necessarily indicative of the quality of a course.

Art and Design degree courses cover a wide range of subjects. These are grouped together in the following six tables:

Art and Design (General)
Art and Design (Fashion and Textiles)
Art and Design (Fine Art)
Art and Design (Graphic Design)
Art and Design (Industrial/Product Design)
Art and Design (Three Dimensional Design)
(**History of Art** and **Photography** are listed in separate tables)

COURSE OFFERS INFORMATION

Subject requirements/preferences Entry requirements for Art and Design courses vary between institutions and courses (check prospectuses and websites). Most courses require an Art and Design Foundation course. **AL** grades or points may be required plus five **GCSE** subjects at grades A–C, or a recognised equivalent. A portfolio of work demonstrating potential and visual awareness will also be required. **AL** (Design Technology) Design technology or a physical science may be required or preferred. (Creative Arts courses) Music/art/drama may be required. **NB** A* grades are likely to form part of university offers in the higher ranges for students applying for places in 2008 for entry in 2009: check websites.

Your target offers
340 pts Reading – AAB–BBB (Art; Art Comb courses)
320 pts Lancaster – ABB–BCC (Crea Arts) (IB 30–33 pts)
300 pts Bournemouth – BBB (Animat Prod – check with admissions tutor)
Manchester – BBB (Art Arch Anc Wrld)
280 pts Leeds – BBC (Contemp Art Prac)
London (Gold) – BBC (Design)
Northumbria – 280 pts (Multim Des)
260 pts Bradford – 260 pts (Comp Animat)
Loughborough – 260–300 pts (Ind Des Tech)
Richmond (Am Int Univ) – 260 pts (Crea Arts Comm)

For a quick reference offers calculator, fold out the inside back cover.

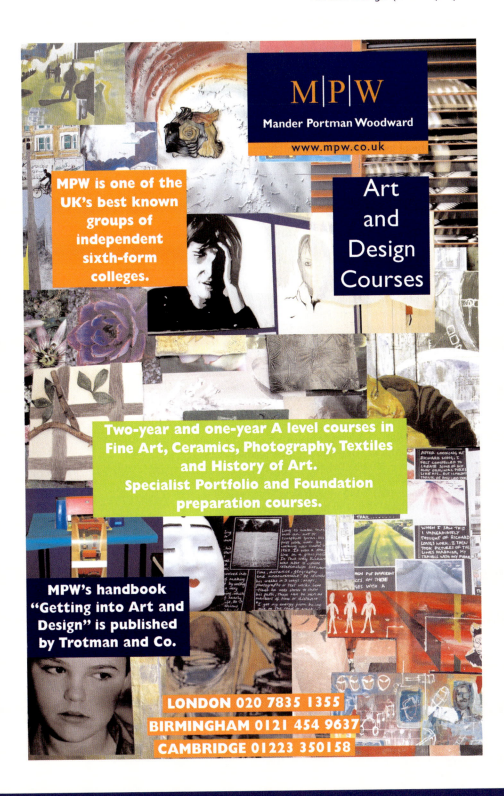

156 | Art and Design (General)

240 pts **Birmingham City/Birmingham (IAD)** – 240–100 pts (Art Des Vis Comm; Animat)
Dundee – 240 pts 1st yr entry (Art Phil Contemp Stes)
Huddersfield – 240 pts (Vrtl Rlty Des)
Lincoln – 240 pts (Animation)
Middlesex – 240 pts (Des Tech courses)
Stranmillis (UC) – CCC (Tech Des Educ)
220 pts **Edge Hill** – 220 pts (Animation)
Teesside – 220–280 pts (Des (Comp Animat))
200 pts **De Montfort** – 200 pts (Animat Des)
Liverpool John Moores – 200 pts (Multim Arts)
Napier – 200 pts (Des Fut)
Newport – 200 pts (Animation)
180 pts **Kingston** – 180–220 pts (Des courses)
Northampton – 180–240 pts (Crea Des Mark)
160 pts **Bishop Grosseteste (Coll)** – CC (Educ St Art QTS)
Bolton – 160 pts (Art Des; Animat Illus)
Cardiff (UWIC) – 160 pts (Art Crea Writ; Art Phil)
Dartington (CA) – 160–200 pts (Art Perf courses; Writ Vis Art Pr)
Glamorgan – 160 pts (Art Prac)
Glasgow (SA) – CC (Vis Comm)
Kingston – 160 pts (Illus Animat)
Lincoln – 160 pts (Cons Restor)
Manchester Met – 160 pts (Des Art Dir; Illus Animat) *(IB 28 pts)*
Middlesex – 160–200 pts (Design)
Newman (UC) – 160–240 pts (Art Educ)
Portsmouth – 160–240 pts (Comp Animat; Animat)
Robert Gordon – 160–180 pts (Des Dig Media; Art Des)
Salford – 160 pts (Des Mgt Crea Ind; Des Fut; Vis Arts)
Thames Valley – 160 pts (Dig Animat courses)
Ulster – 160 pts (Des Vis Comm; Art Des)
Westminster – 160 pts (Animation)
Wolverhampton – 160–220 pts (Des; Animat)
Worcester – 160 pts (Des Comm; Art Des)
York St John – CC 160 pts (Des Prac)
140 pts **Edinburgh (CA)** – 140 pts (Art Des)
Staffordshire – 140–200 pts (Animation) *(IB 28 pts)*
Sunderland – 140 pts (Animat Des)
120 pts **De Montfort** – 120–180 pts (Animat Des)
North East Wales (IHE) – 120–80 pts (Des (Animat))
Southampton Solent – 120 pts (Des St courses; Animat)
100 pts **and below or other selection criteria (Foundation course, interview and portfolio inspection)**
Abertay Dundee; Archit Assoc Sch London; Arts London (Camberwell CA), (Central Saint Martins CAD), (Chelsea CAD), (CFash); Barnsley (Univ Centre); Bedfordshire; Bournemouth (AI); Bradford (Coll); Brighton; Bristol UWE; Cardiff (UWIC); Carmarthenshire (Coll); Chichester; Colchester (Inst); Creative Arts (UC); Cumbria; Dartington (CA); Derby; Dundee; Edinburgh (CA); Falmouth (UC); Forth Valley (Coll); Glamorgan; Glasgow (SA); Hertfordshire; Kingston; Leeds (CAD); Liverpool (LIPA); Liverpool John Moores; London (CMus); London (Gold); London Met; London South Bank; Loughborough; Lowestoft (Coll); Manchester City (Coll); Marjon (UC); Middlesex; Napier; Nescot; Newman (UC); North East Wales (IHE); Northbrook (Coll); Northumbria; Norwich (SAD); Nottingham Trent; Portsmouth; Ravensbourne (CDC); Reading; Robert Gordon; St Helens (Coll); Salford; Solihull (Coll); Southend Campus Essex; Southampton/Winchester (SA); Staffordshire; Suffolk (Univ Campus); Swansea (IHE); Swindon (Coll); Teesside; West Herts (Coll); West Scotland; Westminster; Wiltshire (Coll); Yorkshire Coast (CFHE).

Leeds Met – contact University

Alternative offers

See **Chapter 8** for grade/point equivalences and related information for the following examinations: Scottish qualifications, the Welsh Baccalaureate, the IB diploma (approximate points shown also in italics in the table of offers), the Irish Leaving Certificate, the European Baccalaureate and the French Baccalaureate.

EXAMPLES OF FOUNDATION DEGREES IN THE SUBJECT FIELD

Arts London (Camberwell CA), (CFash), (CComm); Barnet (Coll); Barnfield (Coll); Barnsley (Univ Centre); Bath City (Coll); Bath Spa; Bedfordshire; Bicton (Coll); Blackpool and Fylde (Coll); Bournemouth (AI); Bournemouth and Poole (Coll); Bradford (Coll); Brighton; Brighton and Hove City (Coll); Burnley (Coll); Cardiff (Coll); Cavendish (Coll); Chesterfield (Coll); Cleveland (CAD); Colchester (Inst); Cornwall (Coll); Creative Arts (UC); Croydon (Coll); Darlington (CT); De Montfort; Derby; Dewsbury (Coll); Doncaster (Coll); Dunstable (Coll); East Lancashire (IHE); Grimsby (IFHE); Hastings (Coll); Herefordshire (CAD); Hertfordshire; Hopwood Hall (Coll); Huddersfield; Hull (Coll); Hugh Baird (Coll); Huntingdon (Coll); Leeds (CAD); Leeds Met; Leicester (Coll); London Met; Manchester City (Coll); Mid-Cheshire (Coll); Milton Keynes (Coll); Newcastle (Coll); Newham (Coll); Newport; North East Wales (IHE); North West Kent (Coll); Northumberland (Coll); Norwich (SAD); Nottingham New (Coll); Oldham (Coll); Park Lane Leeds (Coll); Plymouth (CAD); Preston (Coll); Ravensbourne (CDC); Richmond (CmC); Runshaw (Coll); St Helens (Coll); Salisbury (Coll); Shrewsbury (CAT); South Devon (Coll); South Nottingham (Coll); South Tyneside (Coll); Southend Campus Essex; Stafford (Coll); Staffordshire; Suffolk (Univ Campus); Sunderland; Sunderland City (Coll); Sussex Downs (Coll); Tameside (Coll); Teesside; Thames Valley; Truro (Coll); West Anglia (Coll); West Herts (Coll); West Kent (Coll); Weston (Coll); Weymouth (Coll); Wiltshire (Coll); Winchester; Writtle (Coll); York St John; Yorkshire Coast (CFHE).

CHOOSING YOUR COURSE (SEE ALSO CH.1)

Course variations – Widen your options

Computer Animation and Special Effects (Bradford)

History of Design, Culture and Society (Brighton)

Conservation and Restoration (Lincoln)

Contemporary Crafts (Manchester Met)

Design Management for the Creative Industries (Salford).

CHECK PROSPECTUSES AND WEBSITES FOR OTHER UNIVERSITIES AND COLLEGES OFFERING THESE COURSES.

Universities and colleges teaching quality See www.qaa.ac.uk; www.unistats.com.

Top universities and colleges (Research) Bournemouth; Brighton; London (Gold), (UCL); Newport; Sheffield Hallam; Ulster.

ADMISSIONS INFORMATION

Number of applicants per place (approx) Arts London (Camberwell CA) 2; (Chelsea CAD) 2; Birmingham 20; Birmingham City/Birmingham (IAD) (Art Des Vis Comm) 10; Bournemouth (Comp Vis Animat) 16; Canterbury Christ Church 3; Central Lancashire 4; Chichester 3; Colchester (Inst) 4; Cumbria 5; Dartington (CA) 4; Derby 4; Dundee 5; Glamorgan 7; Gloucestershire 8; Kent 3; Leeds (CAD) 5; London (Gold) 10; Manchester Met 10; Newman (UC) 5; Newcastle 23; Northampton (Crea Des Mark) 5; Norwich (SAD) 3; Nottingham Trent (Des Film TV) 25; Portsmouth 3, (Des Interact Media) 13; Robert Gordon 5; Sheffield Hallam 15; Southampton Solent 1; Sunderland 8; Swansea (IHE) 5; Teesside 2; West Herts (Coll) 3; York St John 3.

Advice to applicants and planning the UCAS personal statement Admissions tutors look for a wide interest in aspects of art and design. Discuss the type of work and the range of media you have explored through your studies to date. Refer to visits to art galleries and museums and give your opinions of the styles of painting and sculpture, both historical and present-day. Mention art-related hobbies. **Sunderland** Good drawing skills and sketch book work. Creative and analytical thinking. See also **Appendix 2**.

158 | Art and Design (General)

Misconceptions about this course Kent (Vis Perf Arts) It is not a fine arts course. **Nottingham Trent** School sixth formers are often unaware of the importance of a level zero or Foundation course preceding BA Art and Design courses.

Selection interviews Yes Creative Arts (UC), Liverpool Hope, Nottingham Trent, Thames Valley, and most courses (see under **Interview advice and questions**); **Some** Chester, Lincoln, Staffordshire.

Interview advice and questions All courses require a portfolio inspection. Admissions tutors will want to see both breadth and depth in the applicant's work and evidence of strong self-motivation. They will also be interested to see any sketch books or note books. However, they do not wish to see similar work over and over again! A logical, ordered presentation helps considerably. Large work, especially three-dimensional work, can be presented by way of photographs. Video or film work should be edited to a running time of no more than 15 minutes. Examples of written work may also be provided. Past questions have included: How often do you visit art galleries and exhibitions? Discuss the last exhibition you visited. What are the reactions of your parents to your choice of course and career? How do they link up with art? Do you feel that modern art has anything to contribute to society compared with earlier art? Is a brick a work of art? Show signs of life – no apathy! Be eager and enthusiastic. **Ulster** Candidates should be able to communicate clearly and through discussion, to show an awareness of current developments, and to convey enthusiasm for their chosen subject. See also **Chapter 7**.

Applicants' impressions (A=Open day; B=Interview day) Arts London (Camberwell CA) (B; Art Fdn) A well-organised, friendly 15-minute interview with one interviewer. Why Camberwell? Has your art teacher been supportive? Which contemporary artists do you like? Which recent exhibitions have you seen? (A) Students were present at the Open Day to advise us. **Portsmouth** (B; Art Fdn) A tour of the department in groups of ten took place whilst the staff looked at the portfolios. Two people then interviewed groups of five to seven students. I felt it was a bit inhibiting if you wanted to ask personal questions. A question was asked on 'What do you think we are looking for?' Also random questions about everyday life. **Southampton Solent** (B) A one-to-one interview. An inspection of the portfolio was followed by questions on it. I was asked who won the Turner Prize and to talk about a particular piece of work I had created, my hobbies and my future career hopes.

Reasons for rejection (non-academic) (Des Mgt) Lack of enthusiasm for design issues or to acquire design skills. Poorly presented practical work. Lack of interest or enthusiasm in contemporary visual arts. Lack of knowledge and experience of the art and design industry.

AFTER-RESULTS ADVICE
Offers to applicants repeating A-levels Possibly higher Brighton; **Same** Birmingham City/Birmingham (IAD), Canterbury Christ Church, Chester, Colchester (Inst), Dundee, Leeds, Lincoln, Liverpool Hope, Napier, Newcastle, Nottingham Trent, Richmond (Am Int Univ), Salford, Staffordshire, Suffolk (Univ Campus), Sunderland, Thames Valley, Wolverhampton, York St John.

GRADUATE DESTINATIONS AND EMPLOYMENT (2005/6 HESA)
Graduates surveyed 8460 **Employed** 5095 **In further study** 480 **Assumed unemployed** 755.

Career note Many Art and Design courses are linked to specific career paths which are achieved through freelance consultancy work or studio work. Some enter teaching and many find other areas such as retail, clerical and management fields. Opportunities for Fashion and Graphic Design specialists exceed those of the other areas of art and design. Opportunities in industrial and product design and 3D design are likely to be limited and dependent on the contacts that students establish during their degree courses. Only a very limited number of students committed to painting and sculpture can expect to succeed without seeking alternative employment.

OTHER DEGREE SUBJECTS FOR CONSIDERATION
Animation; Architecture; Art Gallery Management; Communication Studies; Computer Studies; Film Studies; History of Art; Media Studies; Photography; see other **Art and Design** tables.

ART and DESIGN (Fashion and Textiles)

(including **Clothing, Fashion Marketing, Knitwear** and **Surface Decoration**)

Fashion Design courses involve drawing and design, research, pattern cutting and garment construction for clothing for men, women and children. Courses may also cover design for textiles, commercial production and marketing. Some institutions have particularly good contacts with industry and are able to arrange sponsorships for students.

Useful websites www.fashion.net; www.londonfashionweek.co.uk; www.texi.org.

NB The points totals shown to the left of the institutions are for ease of reference only. It must not be assumed that tariff points are always used by institutions or that they can be substituted for an offer in grades. The level of an offer is not necessarily indicative of the quality of a course.

COURSE OFFERS INFORMATION

Subject requirements/preferences AL Textiles or textile science and technology may be required. See also **Art and Design (General)**.

Your target offers

320 pts **Southampton/Winchester (SA)** – ABB (Tex Fash Fbr)

300 pts **Leeds** – BBB–BBC (Fash Des; Des (Tex))

Manchester – BBB (Tex Des Des Mgt courses; Des Mgt Fash Rtl)

240 pts **Birmingham City/Birmingham (IAD)** – 240 pts (Fash Des; Tex Des courses; Fash Rtl Mgt)

De Montfort – 240 pts (Cont Fash; Rtl Buy (Fash) (Tex); Fash Des; Fash Tech; Tex Des)

Dundee – 240 pts (Tex Des)

Huddersfield – 240–320 pts (Fash Media Prom; Fash Des Tex; Tex Des Fash Inter)

Lincoln – 240 pts (Fash St courses)

Northumbria – 240 pts (Fash; Fash Mark)

Nottingham Trent – 240 pts (Fash Tex Mgt; Fash Des; Fash Knit Des Knit Tex; Fash Mark Comm; Tex Des)

Westminster – CCC (Fash Merch Mgt)

220 pts **Falmouth (UC)** – 220 pts (Tex Des)

200 pts **Bolton** – 200 pts (Tex Sfc Des)

Central Lancashire – 200–160 pts (Fash courses)

Coventry – 200–220 pts (Fashion)

Hertfordshire – 200 pts (Fashion)

Swansea (Inst) – 200 pts (Sfc Pattn Tex courses)

180 pts **Anglia Ruskin** – 180 pts (Fash Des)

Edinburgh (CA) – 180 pts (Des App Arts (Fash) (Tex))

Northampton – 180–220 pts (Fashion)

Southampton Solent – 180 pts (Writ Fash Cult)

160 pts **Bedfordshire** – 160 pts (Fash Tex Des)

Bournemouth (AI) – 160 pts (Fash St; Cstm Scrn Stg)

Central Lancashire – 160 pts (Fash; Fash Prom; Tex Innov)

Creative Arts (UC) – 160–200 pts (Fash Innov Mgt; Fash Des; Fash Journal; Tex Des)

Cumbria – CC (Sfc Des)

East London – 160 pts (Fash Des Mark; Fash Des; Prtd Tex Sfc Decr)

Glasgow Caledonian – CC (Fash Mark)

Heriot-Watt (Scottish Borders) – CC (Fash Des Ind; Des Tex; Cloth Des Manuf; Tex Fash Des Mgt)

Hull (Coll) – 160 pts (Tex Des)

Kingston – 160 pts (Fashion)

Liverpool John Moores – 160–200 pts (Fash Tex Des)

London Met – 160 pts (Tex Des Inter Prod)

Manchester Met – 160–200 pts (Tex Des Fash; Fash Des Tech) *(IB 24–28 pts)*

Newport – 160–200 pts (Fash Des)

Portsmouth – 160 pts (Fash Tex Ent)
Robert Gordon – 160 pts (Tex Sfc Des)
Salford – 160–100 pts (Fashion) *(IB 26 pts)*
South East Essex (Coll) – 160–180 pts (Fash Des)
Ulster – 160 pts (Tex Fash Des)
Westminster – CC (Fash Des)
Wolverhampton – 160–220 pts (Fash Accs Tex)

120 pts **Bradford (Coll)** – 120 pts (Fash Des)
Brighton – 120 pts (Fash Des; Fash Des Bus St; Tex Bus St)
Cleveland (CAD) – 120 pts (Fash Ent; Tex Sfc Des)
Derby – 120 pts (Tex Des; Fash St)
Northbrook (Coll) – 120 pts (Fash Des)
Southampton Solent – 120 pts (Des St Fash)
Stockport (CFHE) – 120–240 pts (Des Vis Arts (Tex Fash Inter))

100 pts **and below or other selection criteria (Foundation course, interview and portfolio inspection)**
Arts London (Central Saint Martins CAD), (CFash), (Wimbledon CA); Barnsley (Univ Centre); Basingstoke (CT); Bedfordshire; Bolton; Bournemouth (AI); Bradford (Coll); Brighton; Bristol UWE; Buckinghamshire Chilterns (UC); Cardiff (UWIC); Colchester (Inst); Creative Arts (UC); Croydon (Coll); Dundee; East Lancashire (IHE); Edinburgh (CA); Falmouth (UC); Glasgow Caledonian; Great Yarmouth (Coll); Herefordshire (CAD); Kingston; Leeds (CAD); Leicester (Coll); London (Gold); Loughborough; Mid-Cheshire (Coll); Middlesex; North East Wales (IHE); Northampton; Northbrook (Coll); Norwich (SAD); Oxford and Cherwell Valley (Coll); Plymouth; Portsmouth; Ravensbourne (CDC); Robert Gordon; Rose Bruford (Coll); Somerset (Coll); Southampton/Winchester (SA); Staffordshire (Reg Fed); Sutton Coldfield (Coll); Swansea (Inst); Thames Valley; UHI Millennium Inst (SC); Waltham Forest (Coll); West Thames (Coll); Westminster; Wirral Met (Coll); York (Coll); Yorkshire Coast (CFHE).

Alternative offers
See **Chapter 8** for grade/point equivalences and related information for the following examinations: Scottish qualifications, the Welsh Baccalaureate, the IB diploma (approximate points shown also in italics in the table of offers), the Irish Leaving Certificate, the European Baccalaureate and the French Baccalaureate.

EXAMPLES OF FOUNDATION DEGREES IN THE SUBJECT FIELD
Arts London (CFash); Barnfield (Coll); Bath City (Coll); Bath Spa; Bedfordshire; Bolton; Bournemouth (AI); Chesterfield (Coll); Cleveland (CAD); Creative Arts (UC); Croydon (Coll); Derby; Derby (Coll); Dewsbury (Coll); Dunstable (Coll); East Lancashire (IHE); Hastings (Coll); Havering (CFHE); Herefordshire (CAD); Hull (Coll); Leicester (Coll); Liverpool (CmC); Manchester (CAT); Mid-Cheshire (Coll); Newham (Coll); Plymouth (CAD); South Kent (Coll); Suffolk (Univ Campus); Thurrock and Basildon (Coll); West Herts (Coll); Wolverhampton.

CHOOSING YOUR COURSE (SEE ALSO CH.1)
Course variations – Widen your options
Surface Design (Cumbria)
International Fashion Marketing (Manchester Met)
Fashion Knitwear Design courses (Nottingham Trent)
Textile Fashion and Fibre (Southampton/Winchester (SA))
Fashion Merchandise Management (Westminster).
CHECK PROSPECTUSES AND WEBSITES FOR OTHER UNIVERSITIES AND COLLEGES OFFERING THESE COURSES.

Universities and colleges teaching quality See www.qaa.ac.uk; www.unistats.com.

Top universities and colleges (Research) See **Art and Design (General)**.

Sandwich degree courses Brighton; Central Lancashire; De Montfort; East London; Glasgow Caledonian; Heriot-Watt; Huddersfield; Nottingham Trent.

ADMISSIONS INFORMATION

Number of applicants per place (approx) Arts London (Central Saint Martins CAD) 5, (CFash) (Fash Mgt) 20; Birmingham City/Birmingham (IAD) (Tex Des) 4; Bournemouth (AI) 6; Brighton 6; Bristol UWE 4; Central Lancashire 4; Creative Arts (UC) 8; De Montfort 5; Derby (Tex Des) 2; Heriot-Watt (Scottish Borders) 6; Huddersfield 4; Kingston 5; Leeds (CAD) 4; Liverpool John Moores 6; London (Gold) 5; Loughborough 5; Manchester Met 3; Middlesex 5; Northampton 4; Northumbria 8; Nottingham Trent 8, (Tex Des) 3; Southend Campus Essex 2; Staffordshire 3; Wolverhampton 2.

Advice to applicants and planning the UCAS personal statement A well-written legible statement is sought, clearly stating an interest in fashion and how prior education and work experience relate to your application. You should describe any visits to exhibitions, and importantly, your views and opinions. Describe any work you have done ('making' and 'doing' skills, if any, for example, pattern cutting, sewing) or work observation in textile firms, fashion houses, even visits to costume departments in theatres can be useful. These contacts and visits should be described in detail, showing your knowledge of the types of fabrics and production processes. Give opinions on trends in haute couture, and show awareness of the work of others. Provide evidence of materials handling (see also **Appendix 2**). **Arts London (CFash)** (Fash Comm Prom) Give details of written work (school magazine etc), work placement in media (journalism, broadcasting etc). **Bournemouth (AI)** (Cost Scrn Stg) Ability in sewing, drawing (life and design), knowledge and interest in English literature, theatre and costume for film, TV and theatre. Foundation Art course preferred. **Creative Arts (UC)** Show good knowledge of the contemporary fashion scene. **Huddersfield** (Cost Tex) Interest in historical costume and theatre. See also under **Art and Design (Graphic Design)**.

Misconceptions about this course Creative Arts (UC) Some students expect the Fashion degree to include textiles; (Tex) Some applicants feel that it's necessary to have experience in textiles – this is not the case. The qualities sought in the portfolio are analytical drawing, good colour sense and a sensitivity to materials.

Selection interviews Most institutions interview and require a portfolio of work. You should be familiar with current fashion trends and the work of leading designers. **Brighton** Application route B recommended for students on pre-degree courses.

Interview advice and questions Questions mostly originate from student's portfolio. **Birmingham City/Birmingham (IAD)** (Tex Des) What do you expect to achieve from a degree in Fashion? **Bournemouth (AI)** (Cost Scrn Stg) Questionnaire and project prior to interview. **Creative Arts (UC)** Describe in detail a specific item in your portfolio and why it was selected. See also **Art and Design (General)** and **Chapter 7**.

Reasons for rejection (non-academic) Portfolio work not up to standard. Not enough research. Not articulate at interview. Lack of sense of humour and inflexibility. Narrow perspective. Lack of resourcefulness, self-motivation and organisation. Complacency, lack of verbal, written and self-presentation skills. **Bournemouth (AI)** (Cost Scrn Stg) Not enough experience in designing or making clothes. See also **Art and Design (General)**.

AFTER-RESULTS ADVICE

Offers to applicants repeating A-levels Same Birmingham City/Birmingham (IAD), Bournemouth (AI), Creative Arts (UC), Huddersfield, Manchester Met, Nottingham Trent, South East Essex (Coll), Staffordshire.

GRADUATE DESTINATIONS AND EMPLOYMENT (2005/6 HESA)

See **Art and Design (General)**.

Career note See **Art and Design (General)**.

OTHER DEGREE SUBJECTS FOR CONSIDERATION

History of Art; Retail Management; Theatre Design.

ART and DESIGN (Fine Art)

(including **Printing, Printmaking** and **Sculpture**)

Fine Art courses can involve a range of activities such as painting, illustration and sculpture and often fine art media – electronic media, film, video, photography and print – although course options will vary between institutions. As in the case of most Art degrees, admission to courses usually requires a one-year Foundation Art course before applying.

Useful websites www.artcyclopedia.com; www.fine-art.com; www.nationalgallery.org.uk; www.britisharts.co.uk; www.tate.org.uk.

NB The points totals shown to the left of the institutions are for ease of reference only. It must not be assumed that tariff points are always used by institutions or that they can be substituted for an offer in grades. The level of an offer is not necessarily indicative of the quality of a course.

COURSE OFFERS INFORMATION

Subject requirements/preferences See **Art and Design (General)**.

Your target offers

360 pts and above
> **Oxford** – Offers vary eg AAA–AAB (Fine Art) *(IB 38–42 pts)*

320 pts Southampton – ABB 320 pts (Fine Art)

300 pts Edinburgh – BBB (Fine Art)
> **Leeds** – BBB (Fine Art; Contemp Art Prac)
> **London (UCL/Slade CA)** – BBB+AS minimum (Fine Art) *(IB 32 pts)*
> **Newcastle** – BBB–BCC (Fine Art) *(IB 28–30 pts)*

260 pts Lancaster – BCC (Fine Art)
> **Northumbria** – 260 pts (Fine Art)
> **Reading** – 260 pts (Art Hist Art)

240 pts Aberystwyth – 240 pts (Fine Art courses) *(IB 29 pts)*
> **Birmingham City/Birmingham (IAD)** – 240 pts (Fine Art)
> **Chester** – 240 pts (Fine Art courses)
> **De Montfort** – 240 pts (Fine Art)
> **Huddersfield** – 240 pts (Fine Art courses)
> **Lincoln** – 240 pts (Fine Art)
> **Nottingham Trent** – 240 pts (Fine Art)

230 pts Loughborough – 230 pts (Fine Art)

220 pts Chichester – 220 pts (Fine Art courses) *(IB 28 pts)*
> **East Lancashire (IHE)** – CCD (Fine Art (Integ Media))
> **Falmouth (UC)** – 220 pts (Fine Art)
> **Liverpool Hope** – 220 pts (Fine Art courses)
> **Oxford Brookes** – CCD **or** CDcc 220 pts (Fine Art)
> **Plymouth** – 220–300 pts (Fine Art courses)

205 pts Reading – 205 pts (Fine Art)

200 pts Coventry – 200–220 pts (Fine Art; Fine Art Illus)
> **Cumbria** – 200 pts (Fine Art)
> **Gloucestershire** – 200–280 pts (Fine Art courses)
> **Hertfordshire** – 200 pts (Fine Art)
> **Sheffield Hallam** – 200 pts (Contemp Fine Art)
> **Swansea (Inst)** – 200 pts (Fine Art courses)

180 pts Anglia Ruskin – 180 pts (Fine Art Prtg; Fine Art)
> **Dundee** – 180 pts (Fine Art)
> **Edinburgh (CA)** – 180 pts (Pntg; Sculp)
> **Northampton** – 180–240 pts (Fine Art courses)

For a quick reference offers calculator, fold out the inside back cover.

160 pts **Bedfordshire** – 160 pts (Fine Art)
Blackpool and Fylde (Coll) – 160 pts (Fine Art Prof Prac)
Bolton – 160 pts (Fine Arts courses)
Bournemouth (AI) – 160 pts (Fine Art)
Canterbury Christ Church – CC (Fine Art)
Cardiff (UWIC) – 160 pts (Art Art Hist)
Cleveland (CAD) – 160 pts (Fine Art)
Creative Arts (UC) – 160–220 pts (Fine Art)
Dartington (CA) – 160–200 pts (Fine Art courses)
Derby – 160 pts (Fine Art)
Dewsbury (Coll) – 160 pts (Fine Art Des)
Glasgow (SA) – CC (Fine Art (Env Art Sculp) (Pntg Drgg))
Grimsby (IFHE) – 160 pts (Fine App Arts)
Kingston – 160 pts (Fine Art)
Liverpool John Moores – 160 pts (Fine Art)
London Met – 160 pts (Fine Art)
Manchester Met – 160 pts (Fine Art)
Newport – 160–200 pts (Fine Art)
Portsmouth – 160 pts (Fine Art)
Robert Gordon – 160 pts (Fine Art courses)
South East Essex (Coll) – 160–180 pts (Fine Art)
Southampton Solent – 160 pts (Fine Art; Fine Art Media)
Swindon (Coll) – 160–200 pts (Fine Art)
Ulster – 160 pts (Fine App Arts)
Wolverhampton – 160–220 pts (Fine Art)
York St John – 160 pts (Contemp Fine Art Prac)
Yorkshire Coast (CFHE) – 160–240 pts (Fine Art)

140 pts **Staffordshire** – 140–200 pts (Fine Art) *(IB 28 pts)*
Stamford (Coll) – 140 pts (Fine Art)
Sunderland – 140 pts (Fine Art)

120 pts **Brighton** – 120 pts (Fine Art courses)
Bucks New – 120 pts (Fine Art)
Cleveland (CAD) – 120 pts (Fine Art)
Northbrook (Coll) – 120 pts (Fine Art)

100 pts **and below or other selection criteria (Foundation course, interview and portfolio inspection)**
Arts London (Camberwell CA), (Central Saint Martins CAD), (Chelsea CAD), (Wimbledon CA); Barnsley (Univ Centre); Bath Spa; Bradford (Coll); Bristol UWE; Cardiff (UWIC); Carmarthenshire (Coll); Central Lancashire; Cleveland (CAD); Colchester (Inst); Creative Arts (UC); Croydon (Coll); Doncaster (Coll); Dunstable (Coll); East London; Falmouth (UC); Filton (Coll); Gloucestershire; Herefordshire (CAD); Hertfordshire; Hull (Scarborough); Kingston; Leeds (CAD); Liverpool John Moores; London (Gold), (UCL/Slade SA); London Met; Loughborough; Middlesex; North East Wales (IHE); Northampton; Northbrook (Coll); Norwich (SAD); Oxford and Cherwell Valley (Coll); Robert Gordon; Salford; Solihull (Coll); South East Essex (Coll); South Nottingham (Coll); Southampton/Winchester (SA); Southport (Coll); Suffolk (Univ Campus); Swansea (Inst); Thames Valley; Trinity Carmarthen (Coll); UHI Millennium Inst (MC); Wakefield (Coll); West Thames (Coll); Westminster; Wiltshire (Coll); Wimbledon (CA); Wirral Met (Coll).

Leeds Met – contact University

Alternative offers
See **Chapter 8** for grade/point equivalences and related information for the following examinations: Scottish qualifications, the Welsh Baccalaureate, the IB diploma (approximate points shown also in italics in the table of offers), the Irish Leaving Certificate, the European Baccalaureate and the French Baccalaureate.

For information on how to read the Subject Tables, see **Chapter 8**.

EXAMPLES OF FOUNDATION DEGREES IN THE SUBJECT FIELD

Arts London (Central Saint Martins CAD); Brighton and Hove City (Coll); Canterbury (Coll); Cornwall (Coll); Croydon (Coll); Dunstable (Coll); Hastings (Coll); Havering (Coll); Herefordshire (CAD); Kendal (Coll); Milton Keynes (Coll); Newcastle (Coll); North Devon (Coll); Nottingham New (Coll); Oldham (Coll); Plymouth (CAD); Runshaw (Coll); Somerset (CAT); South Tyneside (Coll); South East Essex (Coll); Suffolk (Univ Campus); Tyne Met (Coll); Yeovil (Coll).

CHOOSING YOUR COURSE (SEE ALSO CH.1)

Course variations – Widen your options
Fine Art and Art History (Aberystwyth)
Fine Art Printmaking (Anglia Ruskin)
Fine Art: New Media (Chester)
Fine Art and Illustration (Coventry)
Contemporary Art Practice (Leeds)
Typography and History of Art (Reading).
CHECK PROSPECTUSES AND WEBSITES FOR OTHER UNIVERSITIES AND COLLEGES OFFERING THESE COURSES.

Universities and colleges teaching quality See www.qaa.ac.uk; www.unistats.com.

Top universities and colleges (Research) See **Art and Design (General)**.

ADMISSIONS INFORMATION

Number of applicants per place (approx) Arts London (Chelsea CAD) 5, Wimbledon (CA) (Sculp) 3; Bath Spa 8; Birmingham City/Birmingham (IAD) 6; Bournemouth (AI) 6; Bristol UWE 3; Cardiff (UWIC) 3; Central Lancashire 4; Cleveland (CAD) 2; Creative Arts (UC) 2; Cumbria 4; De Montfort 5; Derby 3; Dundee 5; Falmouth (UC) 5; Gloucestershire 5; Hertfordshire 6; Hull (Scarborough) 2; Kingston 9; Lincolnshire and Humberside 4; Liverpool John Moores 3; London (Gold) 10, (UCL/Slade SA) 26; London Met 11; Loughborough 4; Manchester Met 4; Middlesex 3; Newcastle 30; Northampton 3; Northumbria 4; Norwich (SAD) 3; Nottingham Trent 5; Oxford (success rate 17%); Portsmouth 6; Robert Gordon 5; Sheffield Hallam 4; Solihull (Coll) 4; Staffordshire 3; Sunderland 3; UHI Millennium Inst (MC) 2; Wirral Met (Coll) 3.

Admissions tutors' advice **Brighton** Application route B recommended for applicants on pre-degree courses.

Advice to applicants and planning the UCAS personal statement Since this is a subject area that can be researched easily in art galleries, you should discuss not only your own style of work and your preferred subjects but also your opinions on various art forms, styles and periods. Keep up-to-date with public opinion on controversial issues. Give your reasons for wishing to pursue a course in Fine Art. **Aberystwyth** If you are not taking the subject at A-level we look for attendance at evening classes for art. Visits to galleries and related hobbies, for example reading, cinema, music, literature should be mentioned. Show the nature of your external involvement in art. Not interested in potted life-history or lists of irrelevant jobs. **Arts London (Chelsea CAD)** We look for visual and plastic skills, conceptual development. **Staffordshire** We look for creativity, problem-solving, cultural awareness, communication skills and commitment. (See also **Appendix 2**.)

Misconceptions about this course That Fine Art is simply art and design. Sixth form applicants are often unaware of the importance of a Foundation Art course before starting a degree programme. **Bournemouth (AI)** Applicants need to make the distinction between fine art and illustration.

Selection interviews Most institutions interview and require a portfolio of work. **Arts London (Chelsea CAD)** Interviews with portfolios and essays. **Oxford** Portfolio to be submitted by 15th November. Drawing examination taken by all interviewed candidates (two drawings in pencil or pen and ink).

Interview advice and questions Questions asked on portfolio of work. Be prepared to answer questions on your stated opinions on your UCAS application and on current art trends and controversial topics reported in the press. Discussion covering the applicant's engagement with contemporary fine art practice. Visits to exhibitions, galleries etc. Ambitions for their own work. Who is your favourite living artist and why? **UHI Millennium Inst (MC)** Applicants are asked to produce a drawing in response to a set topic. See also under **Art and Design (General)**. See also **Chapter 7**.

Reasons for rejection (non-academic) Lack of a fine art specialist portfolio. No intellectual grasp of the subject – only interested in techniques.

AFTER-RESULTS ADVICE
Offers to applicants repeating A-levels **Same** Anglia Ruskin, Arts London (Central Saint Martins CAD), Birmingham City/Birmingham (IAD), Cumbria, Manchester Met, Nottingham Trent, Staffordshire, Sunderland, UHI Millennium Inst (MC).

GRADUATE DESTINATIONS AND EMPLOYMENT (2005/6 HESA)
Graduates surveyed 2535 **Employed** 960 **In further study** 345 **Assumed unemployed** 285.

Career note See **Art and Design (General)**.

OTHER DEGREE SUBJECTS FOR CONSIDERATION
Art Gallery Management; History of Art; see other **Art and Design** tables.

ART and DESIGN (Graphic Design)

(including **Advertising, Graphic Communication, Illustration, Typography and Visual Communication;** see also **Art and Design (General), (Fine Art)** and **Film, Radio, Video and TV Studies**)

Graphic Design ranges from the design of websites, books, magazines and newspapers to packaging and advertisements. Visual communication uses symbols as teaching aids and also includes TV graphics. An Art Foundation course is usually taken before entry to degree courses.

Useful websites www.graphicdesign.about.com; www.graphic-design.com; www.allgraphicdesign.com.

NB The points totals shown to the left of the institutions are for ease of reference only. It must not be assumed that tariff points are always used by institutions or that they can be substituted for an offer in grades. The level of an offer is not necessarily indicative of the quality of a course.

COURSE OFFERS INFORMATION
Subject requirements/preferences See **Art and Design (General)**.

Your target offers

300 pts	**Leeds** – BBB (Graph Comm Des)
	Reading – 300 pts (Des Graph Comm)
280 pts	**Brighton** – 280 pts (Graph Des; Illus)
	Northumbria – 280 pts (Graph Des)
	Reading – 280–340 pts (Typo courses)
240 pts	**Birmingham City** – 240 pts (Vis Comm (Graph Des) (Illus))
	Chester – 240–260 pts (Graph Des courses)
	De Montfort – 240 pts (Graph Des courses)
	Huddersfield – 240 pts (Crea Imag (Graph Des) (Adv) (Illus))
	Lincoln – 240 pts (Graph Des; Illus; Interact Scrnbd Graph Illus; Adv Art Dir Illus)
	Nottingham Trent – 240 pts (Graph Des)
230 pts	**Loughborough** – 230 pts (Vis Comm courses)
220 pts	**Anglia Ruskin** – 220–225 pts (Graph Des; Graph Typo Des; Illus Animat; Graph Web Des)
	Falmouth (UC) – 220 pts (Graph Des; Illus)
	Plymouth – 220–300 pts (Des (Graph Comm Typo) (Illus) (Photo))

200 pts **Bournemouth (AI)** – 200 pts (Graph Des; Illus)
Coventry – 200–220 pts (Illus; Graph Des; Graph Des Illus)
Gloucestershire – 200 pts (Graph Des)
Hull (Coll) – 200 pts (Graph Des; Illus)
Newport – 200 pts (Graph Des; Adv Des)
Westminster – BB (Graph Inf Des)

180 pts **Dundee** – 180 pts (Graph Des)
Northampton – 180 pts (Graph Comm; Illus)

160 pts **Bedfordshire** – 160 pts (Graph Des; Graph Des Adv)
Blackpool and Fylde (Coll) – DDE 160 pts (Graph Des; Inf Illus; Sci Nat Hist Illus)
Bolton – 160–200 pts (Graph Des courses; Animat Illus)
Creative Arts (UC) – 160–200 pts (Graph Des; Illus)
Derby – 160 pts (Graph Des; Illus)
East London – 160 pts (Graph Des; Illus courses)
Glamorgan – 160–180 pts (Graph Comm)
Kingston – 160 pts (Graph Des; Illus Animat; Graph Comm)
Liverpool John Moores – 160–200 pts (Graph Arts)
London Met – 160 pts (Graph Des)
Manchester Met – 160 pts (Illus Animat)
Middlesex – 160 pts (Graph Des; Illus)
Portsmouth – 160–240 pts (Illus; Comm Des)
Robert Gordon – 160 pts (Vis Comm)
Salford – 160–100 pts (Graph Des)
South East Essex (Coll) – 160–180 pts (Graph Des)
Sunderland – 160 pts (Graph Comm Des; Illus Des)
Swindon (Coll) – 160–200 pts (Graph Des; Sqntl Illus)
Teesside – 160–220 pts (Graph Des; Graph Arts)
Ulster – 160 pts (Des Vis Comm)
Wolverhampton – 160–220 pts (Graph Comm; Illus)

140 pts **Greenwich** – 140 pts (Graph Dig Des)
Staffordshire – 140–200 pts (Graph Des)

120 pts **Bradford (Coll)** – 120 pts (Graph Media Comm)
Southampton Solent – 120 pts (Graph Des; Graph Imag Mkg)
Stockport (CFHE) – 120–240 pts (Des Vis Arts (Graph Des) (Illus) (Multim Des))

100 pts **and below or other selection criteria (Foundation course, interview and portfolio inspection)**
Arts London; Barnsley (Univ Centre); Bath Spa; Bedfordshire; Bradford (Coll); Brighton; Bristol UWE; Buckinghamshire Chilterns (UC); Cambridge Reg (Coll); Cardiff (UWIC); Central Lancashire; Colchester (Inst); Creative Arts (UC); Croydon (Coll); Cumbria; Dundee; East Lancashire (IHE); East London; Edinburgh (CA); Falmouth (UC); Filton (Coll); Glasgow Caledonian; Glasgow Met (Coll); Gloucestershire; Herefordshire (CAD); Heriot-Watt; Hertfordshire; James Watt (Coll); Kingston; Leeds (CAD); London Met; Lowestoft (Coll); Menai (Col); Middlesex; North East Wales (IHE); Northbrook (Coll); Norwich (SAD); Oxford and Cherwell Valley (Coll); Ravensbourne (CDC); Robert Gordon; Salisbury (Coll); Solihull (Coll); South Devon (Coll); Southampton/Winchester (SA); Suffolk (Univ Campus); Swansea (Inst); Thames Valley; Trinity Carmarthen (Coll); West Herts (Coll); Westminster; Wiltshire (Coll).

Leeds Met – contact University

Alternative offers

See **Chapter 8** for grade/point equivalences and related information for the following examinations: Scottish qualifications, the Welsh Baccalaureate, the IB diploma (approximate points shown also in italics in the table of offers), the Irish Leaving Certificate, the European Baccalaureate and the French Baccalaureate.

EXAMPLES OF FOUNDATION DEGREES IN THE SUBJECT FIELD

Arts London (CComm); Barnet (Coll); Bedfordshire; Bristol City (Coll); Cleveland (CAD); Cornwall (Coll); Creative Arts (UC); Croydon (Coll); Derby; Dewsbury (Coll); Doncaster (Coll); Dunstable (Coll); Durham New (Coll); Ealing, Hammersmith and West London (Coll); Hastings (Coll); Herefordshire (CAD); Kingston; Milton Keynes (Coll); Newcastle (Coll); North Devon (Coll); Norwich (SAD); Plymouth (CAD); Richmond (Coll); Runshaw (Coll); St Helens (Coll); Sheffield (Coll); Somerset (CAT); South Devon (Coll); Stockport (CFHE); Suffolk (Univ Campus); Thames Valley; West Herts (Coll); Weston (Coll); Weymouth (Coll); Yeovil (Coll).

CHOOSING YOUR COURSE (SEE ALSO CH.1)

Course variations – Widen your options
Graphic and Web Design (Anglia Ruskin)
Scientific and Natural History Illustration (Blackpool and Fylde (Coll))
Advertising Art Direction and Illustration (Lincoln)
Sequential Illustration (Swindon (Coll))
Graphic Arts (Southampton; Teesside)
Graphic Information Design (Westminster).
CHECK PROSPECTUSES AND WEBSITES FOR OTHER UNIVERSITIES AND COLLEGES OFFERING THESE COURSES.

Universities and colleges teaching quality See www.qaa.ac.uk; www.unistats.com.

Sandwich degree courses Glamorgan; Gloucestershire; Huddersfield; Staffordshire.

ADMISSIONS INFORMATION

Number of applicants per place (approx) Anglia Ruskin (Illus) 3; Arts London (Central Saint Martins CAD) 4; Bath Spa 9; Bournemouth (AI) 6; Bristol UWE 4; Cardiff (UWIC) 5; Central Lancashire 5; Colchester (Inst) 3; Coventry 6; Creative Arts (UC) 5; Derby 5; East Lancashire (IHE) 2; Glamorgan 3; Hertfordshire 6; Kingston 8; Lincoln 5; Liverpool John Moores 7; Loughborough 5; Manchester Met 8; Middlesex 3; Napier 7; Northampton 3; Northumbria 8; Norwich (SAD) 4; Nottingham Trent 6; Ravensbourne (CDC) 9; Solihull (Coll) 3; Southend Campus Essex 2; Staffordshire 3; Swansea (Inst) 10; Teesside 5; Wolverhampton 5.

Advice to applicants and planning the UCAS personal statement Discuss your special interest in this field and any commercial applications that have impressed you. Discuss the work you are enjoying at present and the range of media that you have explored. Show your interests in travel, architecture, the arts, literature, film, current affairs (see also **Appendix 2** for contact details of relevant professional associations). **Arts London (Central Saint Martins CAD)** Personality is an important factor. **Creative Arts (UC)** Look for ability to discuss applicant's own work openly and critically (including sketchbooks). Awareness of the place of design in society.

Misconceptions about this course Bath Spa Some students think that they can start the course from A-levels, that a course in Illustration is simply 'doing small drawings' and that Graphic Design is a soft option with little academic work.

Selection interviews All institutions interview and require a portfolio of work.

Interview advice and questions Questions may be asked on recent trends in graphic design from the points of view of methods and designers and, particularly, art and the computer. Questions usually are asked on applicant's portfolio of work. **Nottingham Trent** Why Graphic Design? Why this course? Describe a piece of graphic design which has succeeded. See also **Art and Design (General)**. See also **Chapter 7**.

Reasons for rejection (non-academic) Not enough work in portfolio. Inability to think imaginatively. Lack of interest in the arts in general. Lack of drive. Tutor's statement indicating problems. Poorly constructed personal statement. Inability to talk about your work. Lack of knowledge about the chosen course. See also **Art and Design (General)**.

For information on how to read the Subject Tables, see **Chapter 8**.

AFTER-RESULTS ADVICE

Offers to applicants repeating A-levels Same Bath Spa, Bournemouth (AI), Blackpool and Fylde (Coll), Cardiff (UWIC), Creative Arts (UC), Lincoln, Manchester Met, Nottingham Trent, Salford, South East Essex (Coll), Staffordshire.

GRADUATE DESTINATIONS AND EMPLOYMENT (2005/6 HESA)

See **Art and Design (General).**

Career note Graphic Design students are probably the most fortunate in terms of the range of career opportunities open to them on graduation. These include advertising, book and magazine illustration, film, interactive media design, typography, packaging, photography and work in publishing and television. See also **Art and Design (General).**

OTHER DEGREE SUBJECTS FOR CONSIDERATION

Art Gallery Management; Film and Video Production; History of Art; Multimedia Design, Photography and Digital Imaging. See also other **Art and Design** tables.

ART and DESIGN (Industrial and Product Design)

(including **Design Technology, Footwear Design, Furniture Design, Interior Architecture, Interior Design, Product Design, Museum Design, Theatre Design** and **Transport Design**)

The field of industrial design is extensive and degree studies are usually preceded by an Art Foundation course. Product Design is one of the most common courses in which technological studies (involving materials and methods of production) are integrated with creative design in the production of a range of household and industrial products. Other courses on offer include Furniture Design, Interior, Theatre, Museum and Exhibition, Automotive and Transport Design. It should be noted that some Product Design courses have an engineering bias: see **Subject requirements/preferences below.**

Useful website www.ergonomics.org.uk.

NB The points totals shown to the left of the institutions are for ease of reference only. It must not be assumed that tariff points are always used by institutions or that they can be substituted for an offer in grades. The level of an offer is not necessarily indicative of the quality of a course.

COURSE OFFERS INFORMATION

Subject requirements/preferences AL Check Product Design, Industrial Design and Engineering Design course requirements since these will often require mathematics and/or physics. See also **Art and Design (General).**

Your target offers

320 pts **Glasgow** – ABB (MEng Prod Des Eng)
Nottingham – ABB–BCC (Prod Des Manuf)
Sussex – ABB–BBB 360–330 pts (Prod Des 4 yr)
300 pts **Aston** – BBB–BCC (Eng Prod Des; Ind Prod Des; Sust Prod Des)
Brunel – 300 pts (Multim Tech Des)
Dundee – 300–240 pts (Innov Prod Des)
Leeds – BBB (Prod Des)
Oxford Brookes – BBB/BB (Inter Archit Des Prac)
Queen's Belfast – BBB (MEng Prod Des Dev)
Strathclyde – BBB (Prod Des Eng)
280 pts **Brighton** – 280–260 pts (Prod Des; Inter Archit; Des Tech Educ QTS) *(IB 28–30 pts)*
Cardiff (UWIC) – 280 pts (Inter Archit)
Glasgow (SA) – BBC (Prod Des)

Liverpool – 280–340 pts (Eng Prod Des)
Staffordshire – 280 pts (Prod Des Tech) *(IB 28 pts)*
Sussex – BBC **or** 310 pts (Prod Des 3 yr)
260 pts **Brunel** – 260 pts (Ind Des Tech; Ind Des; Vrtl Prod Des; Prod Des Eng) *(IB 28 pts)*
Coventry – 260 pts (Ind Prod Des; Comp Aid Prod Des)
Loughborough – 260–300 pts (Prod Des Tech; Ind Des Tech) *(IB 30–32 pts)*
Queen's Belfast – BCC–BC (BEng Prod Des Dev)
240 pts **Birmingham City/Birmingham (IAD)** – CCC (Inter Des; Prod Des (Ind Des) (Furn Des);
            Mech Eng Prod Des)
Central Lancashire – 240 pts (Prod Des; Inter Des)
De Montfort – 240 pts (Prod Des; Ind Des; Inter Des; Furn Des; Ftwr Des)
Glasgow – CCC (BEng Prod Des Eng)
Huddersfield – 240 pts (Inter Des; Prod Des; Trans Des; Exhib Rtl Des)
Kent – 240 pts (Inter Des; Inter Archit) *(IB 27 pts)*
Lincoln – 240 pts (Musm Exhib Des; Inter Des; Prod Des; Furn)
London Met – 240 pts (Inter Des Tech)
Northumbria – 240–280 pts (Trans Des; Inter Des; Prod Des Tech)
Nottingham Trent – 240 pts (Furn Prod Des; Prod Des; Inter Archit Des)
Rose Bruford (Coll) – CCC 240 pts (Ltg Des)
Sheffield Hallam – 240 pts (Furn Prod Des; Trans Des; Des Tech)
Strathclyde – CCC (Prod Des Innov)
230 pts **Loughborough** – 230 pts (3D N Prac Des (Furn))
220 pts **Birmingham City/Birmingham (IAD)** – 220 pts (Eng Prod Des)
Bournemouth – 220–300 pts (Prod Des; Ind Des; Inter Des)
Bradford – 220 pts (Ind Des; Auto Des Tech)
Bristol UWE – 220–240 pts (Prod Des Innov) *(IB 28 pts)*
Creative Arts (UC) – 220 pts (Prod Des Sust Fut; Prod Des)
Falmouth (UC) – 220 pts (Spat Des Inter Land) *(IB 24 pts)*
200 pts **Bangor** – 200 pts (Des Tech; Prod Des Manuf)
Bradford – 200–240 pts (Vrtl Des Innov; Ind Des)
Coventry – 200–240 pts (Trans Des; Trans Des Fut; Consum Prod Des; Boat Des; Veh Des;
            Spo Prod Des)
Liverpool John Moores – 200–160 pts (Inter Des; Prod Des; Dig Modl)
Napier – 200 pts (Consum Prod Des; Inter Archit)
Plymouth – 200–300 pts (3D Des (Furn Inter Des))
Portsmouth – 200 pts (Inter Des)
Salford – 200 pts (Prod Des; Spo Eqpmt Des; Inter Des) *(IB 26 pts)*
180 pts **Cardiff (UWIC)** – BC (Prod Des)
Liverpool (LIPA) – 180 pts (Thea Perf Des)
Northampton – 180–220 pts (Prod Des; Inter Des)
160 pts **Bedfordshire** – 160–240 pts (Inter Des)
Glamorgan – 160 pts (Inter Des; Prod Des)
Kingston – 160 pts (Inter Des; Prod Furn Des; Prod Des)
Leeds Met – 160–240 pts (Inter Archit Des)
London Met – 160 pts (Inter Archit Des; Inter Des Tech; Furn Prod Des)
Manchester City (Coll) – 160 pts (Stg Des)
Manchester Met – 160–200 pts (Des Tech; Inter Des; Prod Des Tech)
Middlesex – 160–280 pts (Prod Des; Inter Archit Des; Des Tech)
Robert Gordon – 160–180 pts (Prod Des)
Staffordshire – 160 pts (Prod Des; Prod Innov)
Teesside – 160–200 pts (Inter Archit Des; Prod Des courses)
Ulster – 160 pts (3D Des (Inter Prod Furn))
Wolverhampton – 160–220 pts (Inter Des; Des Tech)
Writtle (Coll) – 160 pts (Inter Des)
140 pts **Bolton** – 140 pts (Consum Prod Des; Auto Prod Des; Des Innov)

For information on how to read the Subject Tables, see **Chapter 8**.

Salford – 140 pts (Inter Des; Prod Des)
Swansea (Inst) – 140 pts (Ind Des; Prod Des)
West Scotland – CD 140 pts (Des Prod Dev)
Wolverhampton – 140–200 pts (Prod Des Innov)

100 pts and below or other selection criteria (Foundation course, interview and portfolio inspection)

Arts London (Central Saint Martins CAD), (Chelsea CAD), (Wimbledon CA); Barking (Coll); Basford Hall; Bath Spa; Bedfordshire; Bolton; Buckinghamshire Chilterns (UC); Cleveland (CAD); Colchester (Inst); Croydon (Coll); Dundee; Easton (Coll); Edinburgh (CA); Falmouth (UC); Farnborough (CT); Forth Valley (Coll); Glasgow (SA); Glasgow Caledonian; Glasgow Met (Coll); Hertfordshire; James Watt (Coll); Kingston; Leeds (CAD); Liverpool (LIPA); Liverpool Hope; London South Bank; Manchester (CAT); Middlesex; North East Wales (IHE); Northbrook (Coll); Northumbria; Plymouth; Ravensbourne (CDC); Robert Gordon; Royal Welsh (CMusDr); Shrewsbury (CAT); South East Essex (Coll); Southampton Solent; Staffordshire; Suffolk (Univ Campus); Trinity Carmarthen (Coll); West Herts (Coll); West Scotland; Worcestershire New (Coll).

Alternative offers

See **Chapter 8** for grade/point equivalences and related information for the following examinations: Scottish qualifications, the Welsh Baccalaureate, the IB diploma (approximate points shown also in italics in the table of offers), the Irish Leaving Certificate, the European Baccalaureate and the French Baccalaureate.

EXAMPLES OF FOUNDATION DEGREES IN THE SUBJECT FIELD

Arts London; Bedfordshire; Belfast (Queen's); Bishop Burton (Coll); Bolton; Bournemouth (AI); Cornwall (Coll); Dewsbury (Coll); East Lancashire (IHE); Farnborough (CT); Gateshead (Coll); London Met; Milton Keynes (Coll); Newcastle (Coll); North Down and Aird (IFHE); Northumberland (Coll); Oxford and Cherwell Valley (Coll); Suffolk (Univ Campus); Truro (Coll).

CHOOSING YOUR COURSE (SEE ALSO CH.1)

Course variations – Widen your options

Transport Design (Coventry)
Interiors and Spatial Design (Hertfordshire)
Product and Furniture Design (Kingston)
Museum and Exhibition Design (Lincoln)
Industrial Design and Technology (Loughborough)
Interior Architecture and Design (Nottingham Trent)
Sport Equipment Design (Salford)
Sustainable Product Design (Sussex).
CHECK PROSPECTUSES AND WEBSITES FOR OTHER UNIVERSITIES AND COLLEGES OFFERING THESE COURSES.

Universities and colleges teaching quality See www.qaa.ac.uk; www.unistats.com.

Top universities and colleges (Research) See **Art and Design (General)**.

Sandwich degree courses Aston; Bournemouth; Bradford; Brighton; Bristol UWE; Brunel; Coventry; De Montfort; Glamorgan; Glasgow Caledonian; Huddersfield; Nottingham Trent; Robert Gordon; Sussex; Wolverhampton.

ADMISSIONS INFORMATION

Number of applicants per place (approx) Abertay Dundee 6; Arts London (Central Saint Martins CAD) 2, (Chelsea CAD) 2; (Wimbledon CA) 2; Aston 6; Bath Spa 4; Birmingham City/Birmingham (IAD) (Furn Des) 4, (Prod Des) 3, (Inter Des) 9; Bolton 1; Brunel 4; Cardiff (UWIC) 6; Central Lancashire 7; Colchester (Inst) 4; Coventry 5; Creative Arts (UC) (Inter Des) 4; De Montfort 5; Derby 2; Lincoln (Musm Exhib Des) 4; Loughborough 9; Manchester Met 2; Middlesex (Inter Archit Des) 4; Napier 6; Northampton (Prod Des) 2; Northumbria 4; Nottingham Trent (Inter Archit Des) 7, (Prod Des) 5; Portsmouth 3; Ravensbourne (CDC) (Inter Des) 4, (Prod Des) 7; Salford 6; Sheffield 4; Shrewsbury (CAT) 6; Staffordshire 3; Swansea (Inst) 3; Teesside 3.

Advice to applicants and planning the UCAS personal statement Your knowledge of design in all fields should be described, including any special interests you may have, for example in domestic, rail and road aspects of design, and visits to exhibitions, motor shows. **School/College reference** Tutors should make it clear that the applicant's knowledge, experience and attitude match the chosen course – not simply higher education in general. **Creative Arts (UC)** (Inter Des) Admissions tutors look for knowledge of interior design and interior architecture, experience in 3D-design projects (which include problem-solving and sculptural demands), model-making experience in diverse materials, experience with 2D illustration and colour work, and knowledge of computer-aided design. Photography is also helpful. **Derby** Basic computer knowledge useful. **Lincoln** (Musm Exhib Des) Drawing (freehand and constructed). Model-making and CAD/computer skills. See also **Art and Design (Graphic Design)**.

Misconceptions about this course Arts London (Wimbledon CA) (Thea Des) The course is sometimes confused with Theatre Architecture or an academic course in Theatre Studies. **Birmingham City/Birmingham (IAD)** (Inter Des) Some applicants believe that it is an interior decoration course (carpets and curtains). **Lincoln** (Musm Exhib Des) This is a design course, not a museum course. **Portsmouth** (Inter Des) Some students think that this is about interior decorating after Laurence Llewelyn-Bowen!

Selection interviews Most institutions will interview and require a portfolio of work. **Some** Salford, Staffordshire.

Interview advice and questions Applicants' portfolios of art work form an important talking-point throughout the interview. Applicants should be able to discuss examples of current design and new developments in the field and answer questions on the aspects of industrial design which interest them. **Creative Arts (UC)** No tests. Discuss any visits to modern buildings and new developments, eg British Museum Great Court or the Louvre Pyramid. See also **Art and Design (General)**. See also **Chapter 7**.

Applicants' impressions (A=Open day; B=Interview day) Bournemouth (Prod Des; B) They inspected the work of those being interviewed. They pinned pieces of my own work on a board and looked at the work of other students. I was tested on maths, design and analytical skills. There was a general talk about the course and the University, but I had no chance to look around. **Portsmouth** (Prod Des; B) There was a brief informal interview, a talk about the course and a tour of the department. A very helpful day.

Reasons for rejection (non-academic) Not hungry enough! Mature students without formal qualifications may not be able to demonstrate the necessary mathematical or engineering skills. Poor quality and organisation of portfolio. Lack of interest. Inappropriate dress. Lack of enthusiasm. Insufficient portfolio work (eg exercises instead of projects). Lack of historical knowledge of interior design. Weak oral communication. **Creative Arts (UC)** Not enough 3D model-making. Poor sketching and drawing. See also **Art and Design (General)**.

AFTER-RESULTS ADVICE
Offers to applicants repeating A-levels Same Birmingham City/Birmingham (IAD), Bournemouth, Creative Arts (UC), Nottingham Trent, Salford, Staffordshire.

NEW GRADUATE DESTINATIONS AND EMPLOYMENT (2005/6 HESA)
See **Art and Design (General).**

Career note See **Art and Design (General)**.

OTHER DEGREE SUBJECTS FOR CONSIDERATION
Architecture; Architectural Studies; Art Gallery Management; Design (Manufacturing Systems); History of Art; Manufacturing Engineering; Multimedia and Communication Design and subjects in other **Art and Design** tables.

ART and DESIGN (3D Design)

(including Ceramics, Design Crafts, Glassmaking, Jewellery, Metalwork, Silversmithing, Plastics and Woodwork; see also Art and Design (General))

This group of courses covers mainly three dimensional design work, focusing on creative design involving jewellery, silverware, ceramics, glass, wood and plastics. Some institutions offer broad three dimensional studies courses while others provide the opportunity to study very specialised subjects such as stained glass, gemology and horology. Students normally take an Art Foundation course before their degree level studies.

Useful website www.ergonomics.org.uk.

NB The points totals shown to the left of the institutions are for ease of reference only. It must not be assumed that tariff points are always used by institutions or that they can be substituted for an offer in grades. The level of an offer is not necessarily indicative of the quality of a course.

COURSE OFFERS INFORMATION

Subject requirements/preferences See **Art and Design (General)**.

Your target offers

240 pts	**Birmingham City/Birmingham (IAD)** – 240 pts (Jewel Silver)
	De Montfort – 240 pts (Des Crfts)
	Hertfordshire – 240 pts (App Arts; 3D Gms Art; 3D Dig Animat)
	Lincoln – 240 pts (Contemp Decr Crfts Fash)
	Nottingham Trent – 240 pts (Decr Arts)
	Sheffield Hallam – 240 pts (Mtl Jewel)
220 pts	**Plymouth** – 220–300 pts (3D Des)
200 pts	**Manchester Met** – 200 pts (Contemp Crfts)
	Salford – 200 pts (Dig 3D Des)
180 pts	**Derby** – 180 pts (Crafts)
160 pts	**Bournemouth (AI)** – 160 pts (Modl Des Media)
	Cumbria – CC (Contemp App Arts)
	Glasgow (SA) – CC (Des (Ceram) (Silver Jewel))
	Manchester Met – 160–300 pts (3D Des)
	Portsmouth – 160–240 pts (3D Des)
	Wolverhampton – 160–220 pts (3D Contemp App Arts (Ceram) (Glass); 3D Des (Wd Mtl Plas) (Jewel Silver) (Furn))
140 pts	**Staffordshire** – 140–200 pts (3D Des (Ceram) (Crfts); Sfc Des)
	Sunderland – 140 pts (Glass Archit Glass Ceram)
120 pts	**Cleveland (CAD)** – 120–80 pts (Enter Des Crfts)
100 pts	**and below or other selection criteria (Foundation course, interview and portfolio inspection)**
	Arts London (Camberwell CA), (Central Saint Martins CAD); Bath Spa; Brighton; Bucks New; Cardiff (UWIC); Central Lancashire; Cleveland (CAD); Colchester (Inst); Coventry; Creative Arts (UC); Croydon (Coll); Cumbria; Dundee; Edinburgh (CA); Falmouth (UC); Herefordshire (CAD); Hertford Reg (Coll); Hertfordshire; London Met; Loughborough; Loughborough (Coll); Menai (Coll); Middlesex; North East Wales (IHE); Northumbria; Oxford and Cherwell Valley (Coll); Portsmouth; Ravensbourne (CDC); Robert Gordon; Staffordshire; Teesside; Thames Valley; West Herts (Coll); Westminster; Worcestershire New (Coll).
	Leeds Met – contact University

Alternative offers

See **Chapter 8** for grade/point equivalences and related information for the following examinations: Scottish qualifications, the Welsh Baccalaureate, the IB diploma (approximate points shown also in

italics in the table of offers), the Irish Leaving Certificate, the European Baccalaureate and the French Baccalaureate.

EXAMPLES OF FOUNDATION DEGREES IN THE SUBJECT FIELD

Barnfield (Coll); Bishop Burton (Coll); Bournemouth and Poole (Coll); Bristol City (Coll); Capel Manor (Coll); Cornwall (Coll); Croydon (Coll); Grimsby (IFHE); Hastings (Coll); Herefordshire (CAD); Hull (Coll); Leeds (CAD); London Arts (CC); London Met; Myerscough (Coll); Newcastle (Coll); North Devon (Coll); Northbrook (Coll); Oxford and Cherwell Valley (Coll); Plymouth (CAD); Salisbury (Coll); Sheffield Hallam; Somerset (CAT); South Devon (Coll); Suffolk (Univ Campus); Truro (Coll); Weymouth (Coll); Writtle (Coll); Yeovil (Coll).

CHOOSING YOUR COURSE (SEE ALSO CH.1)

Course variations – Widen your options
Decorative Arts (Nottingham Trent)
Glass, Architectural Glass and Ceramics (Sunderland)
3D Design (Wood, Metal and Plastics) (Wolverhampton).
CHECK PROSPECTUSES AND WEBSITES FOR OTHER UNIVERSITIES AND COLLEGES OFFERING THESE COURSES.

Universities and colleges teaching quality See www.qaa.ac.uk; www.unistats.com.

ADMISSIONS INFORMATION

Number of applicants per place (approx) Arts London (Camberwell CA) 2, (Ceram) 3, (Central Saint Martins CAD) (Ceram) 2, (Jewel) 2; Bath Spa 3; Birmingham City/Birmingham (IAD) 4, (Jewel) 5; Brighton 3; De Montfort 3; Dundee 5; Creative Arts (UC) 4; Manchester Met 5; Middlesex (3D Des) 4, (Jewel) 4; Nottingham Trent (Decr Arts) 4; Portsmouth 3; Ravensbourne (CDC) 110 first-choice applicants; Staffordshire (Des Crfts) 3; Swansea (Inst) 3; Wolverhampton (3D Des (Wd Mtl Plas)) 4.

Advice to applicants and planning the UCAS personal statement Describe your art studies and your experience of different types of materials used. Discuss your special interest in your chosen field. Compare your work with that of professional artists and designers and describe your visits to museums, art galleries, exhibitions etc. **Bournemouth (AI)** (3D Des) Applicants will be expected to submit a portfolio of recent work to demonstrate drawing skills, visual awareness, creativity and innovation, showing examples of 3D work in photographic or model form. See also **Art and Design (Graphic Design)**.

Selection interviews All institutions will interview and require a portfolio of work.

Interview advice and questions Questions focus on the art work presented in the student's portfolio. See also **Art and Design (General)**. See also **Chapter 7**.

Reasons for rejection (non-academic) Lack of pride in their work. No ideas. See also **Art and Design (General)**.

AFTER-RESULTS ADVICE

Offers to applicants repeating A-levels Same Birmingham City/Birmingham (IAD), Brighton, Creative Arts (UC), Dundee, Manchester Met, Nottingham Trent.

GRADUATE DESTINATIONS AND EMPLOYMENT (2005/6 HESA)

See **Art and Design (General)**.

Career note See **Art and Design (General)**.

OTHER DEGREE SUBJECTS FOR CONSIDERATION

Design Technology; see other **Art and Design** tables.

ARTS
(General/Combined/Humanities/Modular)

(including **Arts Management** and **Cultural Studies**)

Many different subjects are offered in combined or modular arrangements. These courses are particularly useful for those applicants who have difficulty in deciding on one specialist subject to follow, allowing students to 'mix and match' according to their interests and often enabling them to embark on new subjects.

Useful websites www.artscouncil.org.uk; www.scottisharts.org.uk; www.arts.org.uk.

NB The points totals shown to the left of the institutions are for ease of reference only. It must not be assumed that tariff points are always used by institutions or that they can be substituted for an offer in grades. The level of an offer is not necessarily indicative of the quality of a course.

COURSE OFFERS INFORMATION

Subject requirements/preferences GCSE English, mathematics or science and foreign language may be required by some universities. **AL** Some joint courses may require a specified subject. **NB** A* grades are likely to form part of university offers in the higher ranges for students applying for places in 2008 for entry in 2009: check websites.

Your target offers
The offers listed below are average offers. Specific offers will vary depending on the popularity of the subjects in combination.

340 pts **Durham** – AAB (BA Comb Arts) *(IB 34 pts)*
Newcastle – AAB–ABB (BA Comb St) *(IB 34 pts)*
320 pts **Cardiff** – ABB 320 pts (Cult Crit)
Glasgow – ABB–BBB (Arts) *(IB 30 pts)*
St Andrews – ABB–BBC (Arts)
300 pts **Dundee** – BBB–CCC (Arts Soc Sci)
East Anglia – BBB–BBC (Cult Phil Pol; Cult Lit Pol; Soty Cult Media)
Edinburgh – BBB (Hum Soc Sci)
Leeds – BBB (Cult St Jap; Cult St)
Nottingham – ABC–BBB (Soc Cult St)
St Andrews – BBB (MA General)
280 pts **Birmingham** – 280 pts (Media Cult Soty Phil) *(IB 32 pts)*
Essex – 280–260 pts (Joint Comb Hons) *(IB 30–28 pts)*
Leeds – BBC (Cult St Fr/Ger/Ital/Port/Russ)
Liverpool – 280–380 pts (BA Arts Comb Hons) *(IB 30–35 pts)*
260 pts **Leicester** – BCC–BBC 260–320 pts (Comb St/joint courses)
Strathclyde – BCC–BB (Arts Soc Sci)
240 pts **Aberdeen** – CCC (Cult St)
Brighton – 240 pts (Humanities)
Bristol UWE – 240–320 pts (Media Cult St)
Westminster – CCC/BC (Comb Hons)
220 pts **Bath Spa** – 220–260 pts (Crea Art)
Bradford – 220 pts (Comb St)
De Montfort – 220–180 pts (Arts Mgt)
Glamorgan – 220 pts (Cult St Engl St)
Heriot-Watt – CCD (Comb St)
Manchester Met – 220–280 pts (Cult St courses) *(IB 28 pts)*
200 pts **Bath Spa** – 200–240 pts (Cult St)
Central Lancashire – 200–180 pts varies (Comb Hons)
Worcester – CDD–DEE 200–140 pts (Joint Hons)

For a quick reference offers calculator, fold out the inside back cover.

180 pts **Lampeter** – 180 pts (Comb Hons)
Roehampton – 180–220 pts (Hum; Comb Hons)
160 pts **Bournemouth (AI)** – CC (Arts Evnt Mgt)
Canterbury Christ Church – CC (Comb Hons major/minor)
Cumbria – CC 160 pts (Contemp App Arts courses)
Derby – 160–200 pts (Comb Hons)
East London – 160 pts (Cult St courses)
Glamorgan – 160–200 pts (Comb St)
Greenwich – 160 pts (Comb Joint Hons; Comb Hons major/minor)
Hertfordshire – 160–240 pts (Comb Mod courses)
London Met – 160 pts (Hum; Arts Mgt)
London South Bank – CC (Comb Hons; Arts Mgt)
Manchester Met – 160 pts (Contemp Arts)
St Mary's (UC) – 160–180 pts (Cult St courses)
Sunderland – 160 pts (Mod schm)
140 pts **Bath Spa** – CD 140 pts (Comb Hons)
100 pts **and below**
London (Birk) – 80 pts for under 21s (over 21 varies) (p/t Hum Engl/Fr/Ger; Hum Hisp St; Hum Hist Art; Hum Hist; Hum Media St; Hum Phil)
Wigan and Leigh (Coll) – (Comb Hons)
Wirral Met (Coll) – 80 pts (Cult St; Comb St)

Open University – contact University (Humanities)

Alternative offers
See **Chapter 8** for grade/point equivalences and related information for the following examinations: Scottish qualifications, the Welsh Baccalaureate, the IB diploma (approximate points shown also in italics in the table of offers), the Irish Leaving Certificate, the European Baccalaureate and the French Baccalaureate.

EXAMPLES OF FOUNDATION DEGREES IN THE SUBJECT FIELD
Bedfordshire; Canterbury Christ Church; Colchester (Inst); Norwich (SAD); Suffolk (Univ Campus); Truro (Coll).

CHOOSING YOUR COURSE (SEE ALSO CH.1)
Course variations – Widen your options
Culture and Media Studies (Bristol UWE)
Cultural Criticism (Cardiff)
Arts Management (De Montfort)
Combined Honours courses (Durham, Leicester and Newcastle)
Cultural Studies and History (Kent).
CHECK PROSPECTUSES AND WEBSITES FOR OTHER UNIVERSITIES AND COLLEGES OFFERING THESE COURSES.

Universities and colleges teaching quality See www.qaa.ac.uk; www.unistats.com.

ADMISSIONS INFORMATION
Number of applicants per place (approx) Birmingham 5; Dundee 13 (average); Durham (Comb Arts) 7; Heriot-Watt 3; Leeds 15; Liverpool 6; Newcastle 7; Oxford Brookes 14; Staffordshire (Comb St) 5; Strathclyde 9; Swansea (Inst) 3; Thames Valley 4; Trinity Carmarthen (Coll) 3.

Advice to applicants and planning the UCAS personal statement Refer to chosen subject tables.
Bath Spa (Crea Arts) Looks for personal statements which clarify relevant work done outside the school syllabus (eg creative writing). **Bradford** (Interd Hum St) Indications of interest in addressing academic work to contemporary issues. **De Montfort** (Arts Mgt) Give information about practical experience and a personal interest in one or more areas of the arts. Show a mature attitude on arts/culture and be an original thinker. **Liverpool** (Comb Hons Arts) We look for evidence of a broad interest across a range of subjects.

For information on how to read the Subject Tables, see **Chapter 8**.

Misconceptions about this course **Bath Spa** (Crea Arts) Some applicants wish to specialise in one subject not realising it is a joint Honours course. **Liverpool** Some students deterred because they believe that the Combined Honours course is too general. This is not so. The degree certificate shows the names of the two subjects taken to Honours degree level.

Selection interviews **Yes** Aberdeen, Bath Spa, Brighton, Bristol UWE, De Montfort, Dundee, Durham, Gloucestershire, Greenwich, Lincoln, London Met, Manchester Met, Roehampton, St Mary's (UC), Wirral Met (Coll), Worcester; **Some** Birmingham (Comb courses inc Drama), Central Lancashire, Liverpool.

Interview advice and questions Questions will focus on your chosen subjects. See under separate subject tables. **De Montfort** (Arts Mgt) What do you understand to be the role of the Arts Council of England? What recent arts events have you seen/enjoyed? See also **Chapter 7**.

Reasons for rejection (non-academic) Lack of clarity of personal goals.

AFTER-RESULTS ADVICE
Offers to applicants repeating A-levels **Higher** Glamorgan, Huddersfield, St Andrews; **Possibly higher** Bristol UWE, Leeds, Newcastle, Roehampton, St Mary's (UC); **Same** Bath Spa, Birmingham, De Montfort, Derby, Durham, Gloucestershire, Greenwich, Leicester, Liverpool, London Met, Manchester Met, St Mary's (UC), Staffordshire, Wolverhampton, Worcester.

GRADUATE DESTINATIONS AND EMPLOYMENT (2005/6 HESA)
No data available.

Career note Graduates enter a wide range of careers covering business and administration, retail work, education, transport, finance, community and social services. Work experience during undergraduate years will help students to focus their interests.

OTHER DEGREE SUBJECTS FOR CONSIDERATION
See **Social Studies/Science**.

ASIA-PACIFIC STUDIES

(including **East and South Asian Studies;** see also **Chinese, Japanese** and **Languages**)

These courses focus on the study of the cultures and the languages of this region of the world, such as Korean, Sanskrit, Thai, Vietnamese.

Useful website www.dur.ac.uk/oriental.museum.

NB The points totals shown to the left of the institutions are for ease of reference only. It must not be assumed that tariff points are always used by institutions or that they can be substituted for an offer in grades. The level of an offer is not necessarily indicative of the quality of a course.

COURSE OFFERS INFORMATION
Subject requirements/preferences **GCSE** A language subject grade A–C. **AL** A language or a second joint subject may be required. **NB** A* grades are likely to form part of university offers in the higher ranges for students applying for places in 2008 for entry in 2009: check websites.

Your target offers
360 pts **and above**
        Cambridge – AAA (Orntl St)
        Oxford – Offers vary eg AAA–AAB (Sansk; Hindi; Chin; Jap)
300 pts **Edinburgh** – BBB 300 pts (Sansk; Sansk Gk; Sansk Lat; Sansk Ling)
        Leeds – BBB–BBC (As Pacif St Econ; As Pacif St Hist; As Pacif St Mgt; As Pacif St Int Rel; As Pacif St Pol; As Pacif St Lang) *(IB 30 pts)*
        Sheffield – BBB–BBC **or** BBcc **or** BBab (E As S courses; Chin; Jap; Kor) *(IB 33 pts)*

260 pts London (SOAS) – BCC (S As St courses; Sansk; Urdu; Hindi; Nepali; Thai; Viet; Chin; Jap; Kor)
180 pts Central Lancashire – 180–240 pts (As Pacif St)
160 pts London Met – 160–200 pts (As Pacif St Comms)

Alternative offers
See **Chapter 8** for grade/point equivalences and related information for the following examinations: Scottish qualifications, the Welsh Baccalaureate, the IB diploma (approximate points shown also in italics in the table of offers), the Irish Leaving Certificate, the European Baccalaureate and the French Baccalaureate.

CHOOSING YOUR COURSE (SEE ALSO CH.1)
Course variations – Widen your options
Asia-Pacific Studies with Chinese or Japanese (Leeds)
Hindi, Nepali, Urdu and Thai (London (SOAS))
East Asian Studies and Management (Sheffield)
Korean Studies and Japanese (Sheffield)
CHECK PROSPECTUSES AND WEBSITES FOR OTHER UNIVERSITIES AND COLLEGES OFFERING THESE COURSES.

Universities and colleges teaching quality See www.qaa.ac.uk; www.unistats.com.

Top universities and colleges (Research) Cambridge*; Edinburgh; Leeds; London (SOAS); Oxford.

Sandwich degree courses Central Lancashire.

ADMISSIONS INFORMATION
Number of applicants per place (approx) London (SOAS) 4, (Thai) 2, (Burm) 1.

Advice to applicants and planning the UCAS personal statement Connections with, and visits to, South and South East Asia should be mentioned. You should give some indication of what impressed you and your reasons for wishing to study these subjects. An awareness of the geography, culture and politics of the area also should be shown on the UCAS application. **Leeds** Show your skills in learning a foreign language (if choosing a language course), interest in current affairs of the region, experience of travel and self-discipline.

Selection interviews Yes Cambridge, Oxford.

Interview advice and questions General questions are usually asked that relate to applicants' reasons for choosing degree courses in this subject area and to their background knowledge of the various cultures. See also **Chapter 7**.

AFTER-RESULTS ADVICE
Offers to applicants repeating A-levels Information not available from institutions.

GRADUATE DESTINATIONS AND EMPLOYMENT (2005/6 HESA)
Graduates surveyed 10 **Employed** 5 **In further study** none **Assumed unemployed** none.

Career note Graduates enter a wide range of careers covering business and administration, retail work, education, transport, finance, community and social services. Work experience during undergraduate years will help students to focus their interests. Many courses have a language bias or are taught jointly with other subjects. Graduates may have opportunities of using their languages in a range of occupations.

OTHER DEGREE SUBJECTS FOR CONSIDERATION
Anthropology; Development Studies; Far Eastern languages; Geography; History; International Relations; Politics; Social Studies.

ASTRONOMY and ASTROPHYSICS

(including **Planetary Science** and **Space Science**)

All Astronomy-related degrees are built on a core of mathematics and physics which, in the first two years, is augmented by an introduction to the theory and practice of astronomy or astrophysics. Astronomy emphasises observational aspects of the science and includes a study of the planetary system whilst Astrophysics tends to pursue the subject from a more theoretical stand-point. Other courses often combine Mathematics or Physics with Astronomy.

Useful websites www.ras.org.uk; www.scicentral.com.

NB The points totals shown to the left of the institutions are for ease of reference only. It must not be assumed that tariff points are always used by institutions or that they can be substituted for an offer in grades. The level of an offer is not necessarily indicative of the quality of a course.

COURSE OFFERS INFORMATION

Subject requirements/preferences GCSE English and a foreign language may be required by some universities; specified grades may be stipulated for some subjects. **AL** Mathematics and physics usually required. **NB** A* grades are likely to form part of university offers in the higher ranges for students applying for places in 2008 for entry in 2009: check websites.

Your target offers

360 pts **and above**

Cambridge – AAA (Nat Sci (Astro)) *(IB 38–42 pts)*
London (UCL) – AAA–ABB (Planet Sci) *(IB 34–38 pts)*
Manchester – AAA–AAB (Phys Astro)
Sussex – AAA–AAB (MPhys Astro) *(IB 36 pts)*

340 pts **Birmingham** – AAB–ABB (Phys Astro; Phys Prtcl Phys Cosmo; Phys Spc Rsch) *(IB 30–34 pts)*
Durham – AAB (BSc Phys Astron) *(IB 36–40 pts)*
London (QM) – 340 pts (MSci Astro; MSci Astron) *(IB 30–32 pts)*
London (UCL) – AAB–BBB+AS (Astron; Astro) *(IB 32–36 pts)*
St Andrews – AAB 2nd yr entry (Astrophysics) *(IB 36 pts)*
Southampton – AAB–ABB (Phys Astron) *(IB 32 pts)*
Surrey – AAB (MEng Spc Tech Planet Explor)

320 pts **Bristol** – ABB–BBB (Phys Astro) *(IB 34 pts H maths/phys 6 pts)*
Cardiff – ABB (MPhys Phys Astron; MPhys Astro) *(IB 28 pts H maths/phys 6 pts)*
Lancaster – ABB–BBB (Phys Astro Cosmo) *(IB 29–30 pts)*
Leeds – ABB (MPhys Phys Astro)
Leicester – ABB–CCC 320–280 pts (Phys Astro; Maths Astron; Phys Spc Sci Tech) *(IB 28 pts)*
London (RH) - ABB (MPhys Astrophysics) *(IB 34 pts)*
Nottingham – ABB (Phys Astron) *(IB 24 pts H maths/phys 6 pts)*
Queen's Belfast – ABB (MSci Phys Astro)
Sheffield – ABB–BC (Phys Astro; Maths Astron)
Surrey – ABB (BEng Spc Tech Planet Explor; MPhys Phys Nucl Astro)
Sussex – ABB–BBB (BSc Phys Astro)
York – ABB (MPhys Phys Astro) *(IB 30 pts H maths/phys 5 pts)*

300 pts **Cardiff** – ABC (MPhys Phys Astron; MPhys Astro) *(IB 32 pts H maths/phys 6 pts)*
Edinburgh – BBB (Astrophysics)
Exeter – 300 pts (Phys Astro) *(IB 26–28 pts)*
Leeds – BBB (BSc Phys Astro) *(IB 32 pts H 15 pts)*
Liverpool – 300–320 pts (Astro; Phys Astron)
Liverpool John Moores – ABC 300 pts (MPhys Astrophysics)
London (King's) – BBB–BBbbb 260 pts (Phys Astro) *(IB 32 pts)*
London (RH) – BBB (BSc Astro) *(IB 28 pts)*
St Andrews – BBB 1st yr entry (Astrophysics)

York - BBB (BSc) (Phys Astro) *(IB 30 pts H maths/phys 5 pts)*
Surrey – BBB (BSc Phys Nucl Astro)
280 pts **Aberystwyth** – 280 pts (Spc Sci Robot)
Cardiff – BBC (BSc Astrophysics)
Central Lancashire – 280–320 pts (Astro courses)
Glasgow – BBC–CCC (Astron Maths; Astro Phys)
Kent – BBC (Astron Spc Sci; Astro) *(IB 30 pts)*
Liverpool John Moores – BBC (Phys Astron)
London (QM) – 280 pts (BSc Astro; Astron) *(IB 30–32 pts)*
260 pts **Queen's Belfast** – BCC (BSc Phys Astro)
240 pts **Hull** – 240–300 pts (Phys Astro)
Keele – 240–260 pts (Astrophysics) *(IB 26–28 pts)*
Salford – CCC 240 pts (Phys Spc Tech)
220 pts **Hertfordshire** – 220 pts (Astro courses)
Nottingham Trent – 220 pts (Astron courses)

Alternative offers
See **Chapter 8** for grade/point equivalences and related information for the following examinations: Scottish qualifications, the Welsh Baccalaureate, the IB diploma (approximate points shown also in italics in the table of offers), the Irish Leaving Certificate, the European Baccalaureate and the French Baccalaureate.

CHOOSING YOUR COURSE (SEE ALSO CH.1)
Course variations – Widen your options
Physics and Planetary Space Physics (Aberystwyth)
Physics with Astrophysics with Industrial Experience (Bristol)
Geology and Planetary Science (Cardiff)
Astronomy (Natural Sciences) (Durham)
Astrophysics and Computing with a Year in North America (Hertfordshire)
Earth and Planetary Sciences (Leicester)
Planetary Science (London (UCL))
Space Technology and Planetary Exploration (Surrey)
Physics with Particle Physics and Cosmology (Swansea).
CHECK PROSPECTUSES AND WEBSITES FOR OTHER UNIVERSITIES AND COLLEGES OFFERING THESE COURSES.

Universities and colleges teaching quality
See www.qaa.ac.uk; www.unistats.com.

Top universities and colleges (Research)
See **Physics**.

Sandwich degree courses
Hertfordshire.

ADMISSIONS INFORMATION
Number of applicants per place (approx)
Bristol 9; Cardiff 6; Central Lancashire (Astro) 12; Durham 3; Hertfordshire 5; Leicester 12; London (QM) 6, (RH) 6, (UCL) 5; Newcastle 7.

Advice to applicants and planning the UCAS personal statement
Books and magazines you have read on astronomy and astrophysics are an obvious source of information. Describe your interests and why you have chosen this subject. Visits to observatories would also be important. (See also **Appendix 2**.)

Misconceptions about this course
Career opportunities are not as limited as some students think. These courses involve an extensive study of maths and physics, opening many opportunities for graduates such as geodesy, rocket and satellite studies and engineering specialisms.

Selection interviews
Yes Bristol, Cambridge, London (UCL), Newcastle; **Some** Cardiff.

Interview advice and questions
You will probably be questioned on your study of physics and the aspects of the subject you most enjoy. Questions in the past have included: Can you name a recent development in physics which will be important in the future? Describe a physics experiment,

indicating any errors and exactly what it was intended to prove. Explain weightlessness. What is a black hole? What are the latest discoveries in space? See also **Chapter 7**.

AFTER-RESULTS ADVICE

Offers to applicants repeating A-levels **Higher** St Andrews; **Same** Cardiff, Durham, London (UCL), Newcastle; **No offers made** Cambridge.

GRADUATE DESTINATIONS AND EMPLOYMENT (2005/6 HESA)

Graduates surveyed 215 **Employed** 75 **In further study** 85 **Assumed unemployed** 15.

Career note The number of posts for professional astronomers is limited although some technological posts are occasionally offered in observatories. However, degree courses include extensive mathematics and physics so many graduates can look towards related fields including telecommunications and electronics.

OTHER DEGREE SUBJECTS FOR CONSIDERATION

Aeronautical/Aerospace Engineering; Computer Science; Earth Sciences; Geology; Geophysics; Mathematics; Meteorology; Mineral Sciences; Oceanography; Physics.

BIOCHEMISTRY

Biochemistry is the study of life processes at molecular level. Most courses are extremely flexible and have common first years. Modules could include genetics, immunology, blood biochemistry, physiology and biotechnology. The option to choose other courses features at many universities. Many courses allow for a placement in industry in the UK or in Europe or North America.

Useful websites www.biochemistry.org; www.scienceyear.com; www.NewScientistJobs.com/careersguide2007; see also **Biological Sciences** and **Biology**.

NB The points totals shown to the left of the institutions are for ease of reference only. It must not be assumed that tariff points are always used by institutions or that they can be substituted for an offer in grades. The level of an offer is not necessarily indicative of the quality of a course.

COURSE OFFERS INFORMATION

Subject requirements/preferences **GCSE** English, mathematics and science usually required; leading universities often stipulate A-B grades. **AL** Chemistry required and biology usually preferred; one or two mathematics/science subjects required. **NB** A* grades are likely to form part of university offers in the higher ranges for students applying for places in 2008 for entry in 2009: check websites.

Your target offers

360 pts and above
        Cambridge – AAA (Nat Sci (Bioch)) *(IB 38–42 pts)*
        Oxford – Offers vary eg AAA–AAB (Mol Cell Bioch) *(IB 38–42 pts)*
        Warwick – ABBc (Biochemistry) *(IB 34 pts)*

340 pts Bath – AAB (Bioch courses) *(IB 34 pts)*
        Bristol – AAB–ABB (Bioch; Bioch Med Bioch; Bioch Mol Biol Biotech)
        East Anglia – AAB 320 pts (Bioch Aus) *(IB 32 pts H chem 5 pts)*
        London (UCL) – AAB (Biochemistry) *(IB 34–36 pts)*
        Manchester – AAB–BBB (Bioch Ind Exp; Bioch; Med Bioch) *(IB 32–35 pts)*
        Nottingham – AAB–BBB **or** 2AL+2AS (Bioch; Bioch Genet; Bioch Biol Chem; Neuro Bioch) *(IB 32–34 pts)*
        York – AAB–ABB (Bioch; Bioch Yr Euro) *(IB 35 pts)*

320 pts Birmingham – ABB–BBB (Bioch; Bioch Euro; Med Bioch; Bioch Biotech) *(IB 32–34 pts)*
        Cardiff – ABB–BBB 320–280 pts (Biochemistry) *(IB 34 pts)*
        Durham – ABB (Mol Biol Bioch) *(IB 34 pts H chem/biol 5 pts)*
        East Anglia – ABB (Bioch N Am) *(IB 31 pts H chem 5 pts)*

Imperial London – ABB (Bioch; Bioch Mgt; Bioch Rsch Abrd; Bioch Yr Ind) *(IB 38 pts)*
Lancaster – ABB (Bioch N Am/Aus; Bioch Biomed) *(IB 32–34 pts)*
Leeds – ABB (Med Bioch)
Leicester – ABB–BBB 320–300 pts (Biol Sci (Bioch)) *(IB 32–34 pts)*
Newcastle – ABB–BBB (Bioch Immun; Bioch) *(IB 32–35 pts)*
St Andrews – ABB–BBB (Biochemistry) *(IB 31 pts)*
Sheffield – ABB (Bioch; Bioch Genet; Bioch Microbiol; Med Bioch) *(IB 33 pts)*
Southampton – ABB 320 pts (Biochemistry)

300 pts **Dundee** – 300–240 pts (Bioch; Bioch Pharmacol; Bioch Physiol Sci) *(IB 29 pts)*
East Anglia – BBB–BBC (Bioch; Cell Mol Bioch; Bioch Euro) *(IB 31 pts H chem 5 pts)*
Edinburgh – BBB (Biochemistry)
Lancaster – BBB (Bioch; Bioch Biomed; Bioch Genet) *(IB 32–34 pts)*
Leeds – BBB (Bioch Fd Sci; Bioch; Bioch Mol Biol) *(IB 32 pts)*
Leicester – 300–360 pts (Med Bioch) *(IB 32–34 pts)*
London (King's) – BBB **or** BBbb (Bioch; Med Bioch) *(IB 32 pts)*
London (RH) – BBB (Bioch; Bioch Sci Comm; Med Bioch) *(IB 32 pts H biol 6pts)*
Reading – 300 pts (Biochemistry) *(IB 30 pts)*
Sussex – BBB–BBC 330–310 pts (Biochemistry) *(IB 32 pts)*

280 pts **Aberystwyth** – 280 pts (Bioch; Genet Bioch) *(IB 26 pts H chem 5 pts)*
Glasgow – BBC–CCC (Bioch; Med Bioch) *(IB 28 pts)*
Liverpool – BBC–BBB 280–300 pts (Bioch; Bioch Yr Ind) *(IB 28–32 pts)*
London (QM) – 280 pts (Bioch Microbiol; Bioch Foren Sci; Bioch) *(IB 30–32 pts)*
Strathclyde – BBC (Bioch Immun; Bioch Microbiol; Bioch Pharmacol; Nat Sci (Bioch))
Swansea – 280–300 pts (Bioch; Med Bioch)

260 pts **Bradford** – 260 pts (Med Bioch)
Brunel – BCC–BBC 260–280 pts (Biomed Sci (Bioch))
Nottingham – BCC–CCD (Nutr Biochem) *(IB 32–34 pts)*
Queen's Belfast – BCC/AB (Biochemistry) *(IB 28 pts H555)*
Surrey – BCC 260 pts (Bioch; Bioch (Med) (Neuro) (Pharmacol) (Tox)) *(IB 30–32 pts)*

240 pts **Aberdeen** – 240 pts (Bioch; Bioch Yr Ind) *(IB 28 pts)*
Heriot-Watt – CCC 2nd yr entry (Biochemistry)
Keele – 240–260 pts (Bioch courses) *(IB 26–28 pts)*
Kent – CCC (Bioch; Bioch Euro) *(IB 28 pts)*
Portsmouth – 240–280 pts (Bioch; Bioch Microbiol)

220 pts **Liverpool John Moores** – 220 pts (Bioch; App Bioch Foren Sci; Bioch App Bioch Microbiol)
200 pts **Hertfordshire** – 200 pts (Bioch; Bioch Euro/N Am)
Huddersfield – 200 pts (Bioch; Med Bioch)
Kingston – 200–240 pts (Bioch; Med Bioch)
Nottingham Trent – 200 pts (Biochemistry)
Salford – 200 pts (Bioch Sci; Bioch Sci USA) *(IB 34 pts)*

180 pts **Essex** – 180–160 pts (Biochemistry)
Heriot-Watt – DDD 1st yr entry (Biochemistry)
Staffordshire – 180–240 pts (Bioch Microbiol) *(IB 28 pts)*

160 pts **Bristol UWE** – 160–200 pts (App Bioch Mol Biol)
London Met – 160 pts (Biochemistry)
London South Bank – CC (Biosci (Bioch))
Westminster – CC (Biochemistry)
Wolverhampton – 160–220 pts (Bioch; Medcnl Bioch; Bioch Fd Sci; Bioch Mol Biol)

120 pts **East London** – 120 pts (Biochemistry)
West Scotland – DD **or** bbc (Biol Bioch)

80 pts **London (Birk)** – 80 pts for under 21s (over 21s offer varies) (p/t Bioch Sci)

Alternative offers

See **Chapter 8** for grade/point equivalences and related information for the following examinations:
Scottish qualifications, the Welsh Baccalaureate, the IB diploma (approximate points shown also in

italics in the table of offers), the Irish Leaving Certificate, the European Baccalaureate and the French Baccalaureate.

EXAMPLES OF FOUNDATION DEGREES IN THE SUBJECT FIELD
Ealing, Hammersmith and West London (Coll); Riverside Halton (Coll); St Andrews; Truro (Coll).

CHOOSING YOUR COURSE (SEE ALSO CH.1)
Course variations – Widen your options
Biochemistry with Study in Continental Europe (Bradford)
Biochemistry and Nutrition (Kingston)
Biochemistry and Forensic Science (London (QM))
Biochemistry with Science Communication (London (RH))
Biochemistry with Immunology (Newcastle)
Biochemistry (Neuroscience) (Surrey)
Medicinal Biochemistry (Wolverhampton)
CHECK PROSPECTUSES AND WEBSITES FOR OTHER UNIVERSITIES AND COLLEGES OFFERING THESE COURSES.

Universities and colleges teaching quality See www.qaa.ac.uk; www.unistats.com.

Top universities and colleges (Research) Bristol; Cambridge*; Durham; Edinburgh; Imperial London; Leeds; Leicester; London (King's); Manchester; Oxford; Sussex.

Sandwich degree courses Aston; Bath; Bristol; Bristol UWE; Cardiff; Coventry; East London; Essex; Huddersfield; Kent; Kingston; Liverpool John Moores; London (King's); London South Bank; Manchester; Northumbria; Nottingham Trent; Sheffield Hallam; Surrey; Sussex; York.

ADMISSIONS INFORMATION
Number of applicants per place (approx) Aberystwyth 5; Bath 7; Birmingham 5; Bradford 7; Bristol 8; Cardiff 6; Central Lancashire 9; Coventry 10; Dundee 6; Durham 6; East Anglia 10; East London 5; Edinburgh 8; Essex 5; Imperial London 6; Keele 7; Leeds 10; London (RH) 8, (UCL) 8; Newcastle 7; Nottingham 14; Oxford (success rate 57%); Salford 4; Southampton 5; Staffordshire 6; Strathclyde 7; Surrey 3; Warwick 6; York 10.

Advice to applicants and planning the UCAS personal statement It is important to show by reading scientific journals that you have interests in chemistry and biology beyond the exam syllabus. Focus on one or two aspects of biochemistry that interest you. Attend scientific lectures (often arranged by universities on open days), find some work experience if possible, and use these to show your understanding of what biochemistry is. Give evidence of your communication skills and time management. Further information may be obtained from the Institute of Biology and the Royal Society of Chemistry (see **Appendix 2**). **Bath** Internal transfer between degree programmes possible; do not make multiple applications (contact admissions tutor). **Oxford** Candidates are expected to have an informed interest in the subject, originating from news items or magazine articles. **St Andrews** Evidence of interest and reasons for choosing the course; sport and extra-curricular activities, posts of responsibility. **Southampton** Evidence of work experience. **Surrey** More about applicants' interests and aspirations, less about what they think the subject is. **Swansea** Evidence of interest in the subject beyond their formal studies and that some thought has been given to their future career. **Wolverhampton** Good communication skills and motivation.

Misconceptions about this course York Students feel that being taught by two departments could be a problem but actually it increases their options.

Selection interviews **Yes** Birmingham (Clearing only), Bradford, Brunel, Cambridge, East Anglia, East London, Keele (mature students only), Kingston, Leeds, London (RH), (UCL), London South Bank, Oxford, Portsmouth (mature students only), Surrey, Warwick; **Some** Aberystwyth (mature students only), Bath, Cardiff, East Anglia, Liverpool John Moores, Salford, Sheffield, Staffordshire, Wolverhampton.

Interview advice and questions Questions will be asked on your study of chemistry and biology and any special interests. They will also probe your understanding of what a course in Biochemistry involves and the special features offered by the university. In the past questions have been asked covering Mendel, genetics, RNA and DNA. **Liverpool John Moores** Informal interviews. It would be useful to bring samples of coursework to the interview. See also **Chapter 7**.

Reasons for rejection (non-academic) Borderline grades plus poor motivation. Failure to turn up for interviews or answer correspondence. Inability to discuss subject. Not compatible with A-level predictions or references. **Birmingham** Lack of total commitment to Biochemistry, for example intention to transfer to Medicine without completing the course.

AFTER-RESULTS ADVICE

Offers to applicants repeating A-levels Higher East Anglia, Leeds, Leicester, Nottingham, St Andrews, Strathclyde, Surrey, Warwick; **Possibly higher** Bath, Bristol, Brunel, Central Lancashire, Keele, Kent, Lancaster, Newcastle; **Same** Aberystwyth, Aston (Comb Hons), Birmingham, Bradford, Cardiff, Dundee, Durham, East Anglia, Heriot-Watt, Hull, Liverpool, Liverpool John Moores, London (RH), (UCL), Salford, Sheffield, Staffordshire, Wolverhampton, York; **No offers made** Cambridge.

GRADUATE DESTINATIONS AND EMPLOYMENT (2005/6 HESA)

Graduates surveyed 1220 **Employed** 445 **In further study** 450 **Assumed unemployed** 90.

Career note Biochemistry courses involve several specialities which offer a range of job opportunities. These include the application of biochemistry in industrial, medical and clinical areas with additional openings in pharmaceuticals and agricultural work, environmental science and in toxicology.

OTHER DEGREE SUBJECTS FOR CONSIDERATION

Agricultural Sciences; Agriculture; Biological Sciences; Biology; Biotechnology; Botany; Brewing; Chemistry; Food Science; Genetics; Medical Sciences; Medicine; Microbiology; Neuroscience; Nursing; Nutrition; Pharmaceutical Sciences; Pharmacology; Pharmacy; Plant Science.

BIOLOGICAL SCIENCES

(Including **Biomedical Science, Ecology, Forensic Science, Immunology, Neurosciences** and **Virology;** see also **Anatomical Science/Anatomy, Biochemistry, Biology, Biotechnology, Genetics, Human Sciences, Microbiology, Plant Sciences, Zoology**)

Biological Sciences (in some universities referred to as Biosciences) cover a very wide subject field and, as for Biochemistry and Biology courses, many modular programmes are offered with a common first year allowing final decisions to be made later in the course. Since most subjects are research-based, students undertake their own projects in the final year.

Useful websites www.immunology.org; www.ibms.org; www.scienceyear.com; www.scicentral.com; www.forensic.gov.uk; www.bbsrc.ac.uk; www.NewScientistJobs.com/careersguide2007; see also **Biochemistry** and **Biology**.

NB The points totals shown to the left of the institutions are for ease of reference only. It must not be assumed that tariff points are always used by institutions or that they can be substituted for an offer in grades. The level of an offer is not necessarily indicative of the quality of a course.

COURSE OFFERS INFORMATION

Subject requirements/preferences GCSE English, mathematics and science usually required. Grades A-B often stipulated by popular universities. **AL** Chemistry required plus one or two other mathematics/science subjects, biology preferred. (Ecology) Biology and one other science subject may be required or preferred. (Neuroscience) Mathematics/science subjects with chemistry and/or biology required or preferred. **NB** A* grades are likely to form part of university offers in the higher ranges for students applying for places in 2008 for entry in 2009: check websites.

Your target offers

360 pts **and above**

>**Cambridge** – AAA (Nat Sci (Biol Biomed Sci) (Neuro) (Path) (Plant Sci); Biol Sci Educ St) *(IB 38–42 pts)*
>**Imperial London** – AAA (Biomed Sci)
>**Oxford** – Offers vary eg AAA–AAB (Biol Sci) *(IB 38–42 pts)*
>**Warwick** – ABBc (Biol Sci) *(IB 34 pts)*

340 pts **East Anglia** – AAB–ABB (Biol Sci N Am/Aus; Ecol N Am/Aus)
>**London (UCL)** – AAB+AS–BBB+AS (Biomed Sci; Neuro) *(IB 36 pts)*
>**Manchester** – AAB–BBC (Neuro; Cog Neuro Psy; Biomed Sci; Biol Comp Sci; Lf Sci; Foren Sci)

320 pts **Aberdeen** – ABB 2nd yr entry (Biomed Sci)
>**Birmingham** – ABB–BBC (Biol Sci courses; Bioinform; Med Sci; Neuro)
>**Cardiff** – ABB–BBB (Biomed Sci (Neuro); Biomed Sci; Mol Biosci; Ecol)
>**Durham** – ABB (Ecol; Mol Biol Bioch)
>**East Anglia** – ABB 320 pts (Ecol with N Am/Aus; Biol Sci with N Am/Aus)
>**Exeter** – ABB–BBB (Biol Sci) *(IB 30–34 pts)*
>**Imperial London** – ABB (Ecol Env Biol)
>**Lancaster** – ABB (Ecol N Am/USA; Biol Sci N Am/USA) *(IB 32–34 pts)*
>**Leicester** – ABB 320 pts (MBiol Biol Sci)
>**London (RH)** – ABB–BBB 320–300 pts (Biomed Sci) *(IB 34 pts)*
>**Manchester** – ABB (MEng Biomed Mat Sci Ind) *(IB 32–35 pts)*
>**Newcastle** – ABB–BBB (Biomed Sci; Med Microbiol Immun; Biol Sci) *(IB 32–35 pts)*
>**Nottingham** – ABB–BBB (Neuro Bioch; Neuro Pharmacol) *(IB 30–34 pts)*
>**St Andrews** – ABB–BBB (Biomol Sci; Ecol Cons)
>**Sheffield** – ABB or ABab (Biomed Sci; Biomed Sci Ent; Neuro) *(IB 33 pts)*
>**Sussex** – ABB–BBB (Med Neuro; Cog Neuro)
>**York** – ABB (Ecol Cons Env) *(IB 34 pts)*

300 pts **Aberdeen** – BBB 2nd yr entry (Ecol; Immun; Neuro Psy; Cons Biol) *(IB 32 pts)*
>**Aston** – BBB–BBC (Biomed Sci)
>**Bristol** – BBB (Neuro; Immun; Virol Immun) *(IB 33 pts)*
>**Dundee** – 300–240 pts (Spo Biomed; Foren Anth; Neuro; Biomed Sci)
>**Durham** – BBB (Biomed Sci) *(IB 28 pts)*
>**East Anglia** – BBB–BBC 300–280 pts (Ecol; Ecol Euro; Biol Sci; Biol Sci Euro; Ecol Biol) *(IB 30 pts)*
>**Edinburgh** – BBB (Biol Sci; Neuro; Biol Sci Mgt; Ecol Sci; Ecol; Immun)
>**Lancaster** – BBB–BBC 300–280 pts (Biol Sci; Biol Sci Biomed; Biomed Med Stats; Ecol) *(IB 32–34 pts)*
>**Leeds** – BBB 300 pts (Neuro; Hum Physiol; Nanotech; Med Sci; Biol Sci) *(IB 32 pts)*
>**Leicester** – BBB 300 pts (BSc Biol Sci courses; Biomed Sci) *(IB 32 pts)*
>**London (King's)** – BBB **or** BBbb **or** ACac (Biomed Sci; Biomol Sci; Neuro) *(IB 32 pts)*
>**London (QM)** – 300–280 pts (Biomed Sci) *(IB 30–32 pts)*
>**London (RVC)** – BBB (Vet Sci – **not** a qualification to practise as a vet)
>**Reading** – 300 pts (Biol Sci; Biol Sci Ind; Biomed Sci; App Ecol Cons) *(IB 30–32 pts)*
>**Sheffield** – BBB (Ecology)
>**Southampton** – BBB 300 pts (Biomed Sci) *(IB 30 pts)*
>**Stirling** – BBB 2nd yr entry (Ecol; Cons Biol; Aquacult; Frshwtr Sci)
>**Surrey** – BBB–BCC 300–260 pts (Biomed Sci; Biomed Sci+Fdn Yr; Bioch (Neuro)) *(IB 30–32 pts)*

280 pts **Aberystwyth** – 280 pts (Lf Sci) *(IB 26 pts)*
>**Anglia Ruskin** – 280 pts (Foren Sci courses)
>**Aston** – BBC 280 pts (Infec Immun)
>**Birmingham** – BBC 280 pts (Biomed Mat Sci) *(IB 32–34 pts)*
>**Bournemouth** – 280 pts (Foren Crime Scn Sci)
>**Brunel** – 280 pts (Biomed Sci; Biomed Sci (Foren)) *(IB 30 pts)*

Essex – BBC–CCC 280–240 pts (Biol Sci; Biomed Sci; Ecol) *(IB 30 pts)*
Glasgow – BBC–CCC (App Biosci; Biomed Sci; Immun; Neuro) *(IB 28 pts)*
Hull – BBC–BCC (Biomed Sci)
Lincoln – 280 pts (Biovet Sci)
Liverpool – BBC–BBB 280–300 pts (Biol Sci; Biol Med Sci; Lf Sci App Med) *(IB 28–32 pts)*
Manchester – BBC (BSc Biomed Mat Sci)
Queen's Belfast – BBC–BCC (Biomed Sci; Biol Sci)
Strathclyde – BBC (Biol Sci; Biomed Sci; Immun Microbiol; Immun Pharmacol)
Swansea – 280–300 pts (Biol Sci joint courses)
Ulster – 280 pts (Biomed Sci)

260 pts **Aberdeen** – BCC 1st yr entry (Biomed Sci; Neuro Psy) *(IB 32 pts)*
Bradford – 260 pts (Clin Sci; Biomed Sci; Biosci; Foren Sci; Foren Med Sci; Bioarch)
Central Lancashire – 260 pts (Foren Biol; Biomed Sci; Biol Sci)
Hull – 260–300 pts (Biomed Sci)
Keele – 260–300 pts (Foren Sci) *(IB 26–28 pts)*
Kent – 260 pts (Biol Anth; Foren Sci courses; Biomed Sci)
London (St George's) – BCC 260 pts (Biomed Sci)
Northumbria – 260 pts (Foren Sci)
Oxford Brookes – BCC **or** BCbc (Biomed Sci; Ecol)
Staffordshire – 260 pts (Biol Sci; Biomed Sci; Foren Biol) *(IB 28 pts)*
Teesside – 260 pts (Foren Psy)
Wolverhampton – 260–320 pts (Biol Sci; Biomed Sci; App Biomed Sci)

240 pts **Aberdeen** – CCC 1st yr entry (Immun; Ecol; Neuro Psy; Cons Biol)
Abertay Dundee – CCC 240 pts (Foren Sci)
Bangor – 240–280 pts (App Trstrl Mar Ecol; Biomed Sci; Ecol; Neuro)
Bristol UWE – 240–260 pts (Foren Sci)
Cardiff (UWIC) – 240 pts (Spo Biomed Nutr; Biomed Sci (Mol Biol) (Foren Tox))
Central Lancashire – 240 pts (Neuro; Biomed Sci)
Heriot-Watt – CCC 240 pts 2nd yr entry (Biol Sci; Brew Distil)
Keele – 240–260 pts (Biomed Sci; Neuro)
Lincoln – 240 pts (Foren Sci; Neuro)
London (St George's) – 240 pts (Biomed Inform)
Northumbria – 240 pts (Biomed Sci)
Nottingham Trent – 240 pts (Foren Sci courses except under **220 pts**; App Biomed Sci; Neuro)
Robert Gordon – CCC (Foren Sci)
Salford – 240 pts (Env Biol)

220 pts **Bangor** – 220–200 pts (Env Foren)
Bradford – 220 pts (App Ecol)
Brighton – CCD–BCD 240–280 pts (Biol Sci; App Biomed Sci)

For information on how to read the Subject Tables, see **Chapter 8**.

Chester – 220 pts (Foren Biol courses; Biomed Sci) *(IB 30 pts)*
Coventry – 220–240 pts (Biol Foren Sci; Foren Invstg St; Biol Sci; Biomed Sci)
De Montfort – 220–240 pts (Biomed Sci)
Glamorgan – 220–260 pts (Foren Sci)
Kingston – 220–200 pts (Biomed Sci; Foren Sci Invstg Analys)
Liverpool John Moores – 220–260 pts (Foren Sci courses; Biomed Sci)
London Met – 220 pts (Biomed Sci)
Nottingham Trent – 220 pts (Foren Sci (Ecol))
Sheffield Hallam – 220 pts (Biomed Sci; Foren Biosci)
Stirling – CCD/BC 1st yr entry (Ecol; Aquacult; Cons Biol; Frshwtr Sci) *(IB 26 pts)*

200 pts **Abertay Dundee** – CDD (Biomed Sci)
Anglia Ruskin – 200 pts (Biomed Sci; Biol Sci; Ecol Cons)
Derby – 200 pts (Ecol; Foren Sci)
Glasgow Caledonian – CDD (Foren Invstg)
Hertfordshire – 200 pts (Bioscience)
Huddersfield – 200 pts (Foren Analyt Sci)
Lincoln – 200 pts (Biomed Sci; App Biomed Sci)
Manchester Met – 200–280 pts (Ecol; Foren Sci; Biol Biomed Psy; Foren Sci Comb) *(IB 28 pts)*
Napier – 200 pts (Biol Sci; Immun Tox; Biomed Sci)
North East Wales (IHE) – 200 pts (Foren Sci; Foren Sci Crim Just)
Plymouth – 200 pts (Biol Sci; Foren Sci; Mar Ecol)
Portsmouth – 200–280 pts (Biomed Sci; Foren Sci)
Salford – 200 pts (Biol Sci; Biol Sci Fr/USA; Biomol Sci Pharm Sci; Biomed Sci; Env Biosci) *(IB 24 pts)*
Sheffield Hallam – 200 pts (Foren Eng)
Teesside – 200–260 pts (Crim Scn Sci; Foren Biol)

180 pts **Bristol UWE** – 180–220 pts (App Biol Sci; Biomed Sci) *(IB 26–28 pts)*
De Montfort – 180–160 pts (Foren Sci) *(IB 24 pts)*
Glasgow Caledonian – DDD (Biomed Sci; Hum Biosci; Foren Invstg; Cell Mol Biol)
Greenwich – 180 pts (Biol Sci; Biomed Sci)
Heriot-Watt – DDD 180 pts 1st yr entry (Brew Distil)
Liverpool Hope – 180 pts (Foren Sci)
Napier – 180 pts (Foren Sci)
Northampton – 180–220 pts (Biol Cons)
Nottingham Trent – 180 pts (Biol Sci)
Teesside – 180–240 pts (Foren Crim Scn Invst Consum Law)

160 pts **Bedfordshire** – 160 pts (Biomed Sci)
Canterbury Christ Church – 160 pts (Biosci courses)
Greenwich – 160 pts (Biosci (Biol Sci))
Leeds Trinity & All Saints (UC) – 160–240 pts (Foren (Psy))
London Met – 160 pts (Biol Sci; Foren Sci)
London South Bank – CC (Foren Sci)
SAC (Scottish CAg) – CC (App Biosci)
Staffordshire – 160 pts (Foren Sci Crimin Fdn Yr)
Sunderland – 160 pts (Biomed Sci)
Westminster – CC (Biol Sci; Biomed Sci; Foren Sci; Neuro)
Wolverhampton – 160–220 pts (Foren Sci; Foren Mol Biol; Ecol; Biolt Sci)

140 pts **Liverpool** – 140 pts (Biol Sci Fdn)
Thames Valley – 140–160 pts (Foren Sci)
Worcester – 140 pts (Ecology)

120 pts **East London** – 120 pts (Biomed Sci; Foren Sci)
Essex – 120 pts (Biol Sci 4 yrs; Ecol 4 yrs; Cell Mol Biol 4 yrs)
Nescot – 120–160 pts (Biomed Sci)

Roehampton – 120–200 pts (Biol Sci; Biomed Sci)
UHI Millennium Inst – 120 pts (Biomed Sci)
West Scotland – DD **or** bbc (Foren Sci; Biomed Sci; App Biomed Sci)
80 pts **London (Birk)** – 80 pts for under 21s (over 21 varies) (p/t Biol Sci Biomed)

Leeds Met – contact University

Alternative offers

See **Chapter 8** for grade/point equivalences and related information for the following examinations: Scottish qualifications, the Welsh Baccalaureate, the IB diploma (approximate points shown also in italics in the table of offers), the Irish Leaving Certificate, the European Baccalaureate and the French Baccalaureate.

EXAMPLES OF FOUNDATION DEGREES IN THE SUBJECT FIELD

Askham Bryan (Coll); Bedford (Coll); Bedfordshire; Blackpool & Fylde (Coll); Bournemouth; Bridgwater (Coll); Brighton; Brighton & Hove City (Coll); Bromley (CFHE); Central Lancashire; City and Islington (Coll); Coventry; Ealing, Hammersmith & West London (Coll); Easton (Coll); Gloucestershire; Hertfordshire; London (QM); Myerscough (Coll); Nescot; North Devon (Coll); North East Wales (IHE); Nottingham Trent; Plymouth City (Coll); Preston (Coll); Riverside Halton (Coll); Sheffield (Coll); Staffordshire; Thames Valley; Truro (Coll); Weymouth (Coll); Wigan and Leigh (Coll); Worcester; York (Coll).

CHOOSING YOUR COURSE (SEE ALSO CH.1)

Course variations – Widen your options

Biomedical Materials Science (Birmingham, Manchester)
Immunology Sciences (Manchester)
Combined Studies (Newcastle)
Functional Genomics and Stem Cell Science (Sheffield)
Forensic Science and Criminology (Staffordshire)
CHECK PROSPECTUSES AND WEBSITES FOR OTHER UNIVERSITIES AND COLLEGES OFFERING THESE COURSES.

Universities and colleges teaching quality See www.qaa.ac.uk; www.unistats.com.

Top universities and colleges (Research) Aberdeen; Aston; Bath; Birmingham; Bradford; Brighton; Bristol; Cambridge; Cardiff; Dundee*; Durham; East Anglia; Edinburgh; Glasgow; Imperial London; Leeds; Leicester*; Liverpool; London (King's), (RH), (UCL); Manchester*; Newcastle*; Nottingham; Oxford; St Andrews; Sheffield*; Southampton; Sussex; Ulster*; Warwick; York.

Sandwich degree courses See **Biology**.

ADMISSIONS INFORMATION

Number of applicants per place (approx) Aston (Biomed Sci) 8; Bristol 8, (Neuro) 10; Cardiff 8; Durham 11; East Anglia (Biol Sci) 15; Edinburgh 8; Essex 8; Lancaster (Biol Sci) 12; Leeds (Med Sci) 25; Leicester 7; London (King's) 7, (QM) 8, (St George's) 15; Newcastle 14; Nottingham 11; Oxford (success rate 43%); Portsmouth (Biomed Sci) 4; Southampton 5; Stirling 7; York 9.

Advice to applicants and planning the UCAS personal statement Read scientific journals and try to extend your knowledge beyond the A-level syllabus. Discuss your special interests, for example, microbiology, genetics or zoology (read up thoroughly on your interests since questions could be asked at interview). **Birmingham** (Biomed Mat Sci) Applicants should show a genuine interest in medicine. They should be able to demonstrate good oral and written communication skills and be competent at handling numerical data. **De Montfort** Evidence of outgoing personality (sport, community work, part-time job). Statement of interest simply in a 'pure' science career is a negative factor. (Foren Sci) Meticulous interest in the law. An ability to keep going under pressure. **Surrey** Voluntary attendance on courses, work experience, voluntary work, holiday jobs. See **Appendix 2**.

Misconceptions about this course **Anglia Ruskin** (Foren Sci) Students are not aware that modules in management and quality assurance are taken as part of the course. **Birmingham** We offer a range of degree labels each with different UCAS codes, for example Biol Sci Genet, Biol Sci Microbiol: all have the same first year and students can freely transfer between them. It is not necessary to apply for more than one except Biol Sci Euro. (Med Sci) Applicants often use this course as an insurance for a vocational course (usually Medicine). If they are unsuccessful for their first choice, they occasionally find it difficult to commit themselves to Medical Sciences and do not perform as well as their academic performance would predict. **Cardiff** Some students mistakenly believe that they can transfer to Medicine. **De Montfort** (Foren Sci) Students are often unaware of how much of the work is analytical biology and chemistry: they think they spend their time visiting crime scenes. **London (St George's)** It is not possible to transfer to Medicine after the first year of the Biomedical Science course. Students may be able to transfer to Year 3 of the Medical course on completion of the BSc degree. **Swansea** (Med Sci) Some applicants think the course is a form of medical training – it isn't. Alternatively, some think that they can transfer after only two years of study with us to the Medical School at Cardiff. They can't but it is possible to take a special final (third) year in our degree and then be accepted into the second year of the Cardiff Medical School (subject to Cardiff's admissions procedure). (Biol Sci deferred entry) Some applicants think that this is a degree in its own right. In fact, after the first year, students have to choose one of the other degrees offered by the School of Biological Sciences. However, this course allows students an extra year in which to consider their final specialisation.

Selection interviews Yes Bangor, Bristol, Bristol UWE, Durham, East Anglia, Essex, Greenwich, Hull, London (RH), (UCL), London South Bank, Manchester, Newcastle, Nottingham, Nottingham Trent, Oxford, Oxford Brookes, Stirling, Strathclyde, Sunderland, Surrey (Biomed Sci), Sussex, Swansea (Med Sci), Warwick; **Some** Aston, Birmingham, Cardiff, De Montfort, Derby, East Anglia, Kent, Liverpool John Moores, London (St George's), Roehampton, Salford, Sheffield, Sheffield Hallam, Staffordshire, Wolverhampton, York.

Interview advice and questions You are likely to be asked about your main interests in biology and your choice of specialisation in the field of biological sciences or, for example, about the role of the botanist, specialist microbiologist in industry, your understanding of biotechnology or genetic engineering. Questions likely to be asked on field courses attended. If you have a field course workbook, take it to interview. **Birmingham** (Biomed Sci) Applicants are invited to interview to assess their suitability for the chosen course. Basic questions relating to the content of their current course will be asked. Those with strong enthusiasm for the subject and considered to be an ideal candidate may be given a reduced points offer. **London (St George's)** (Biomed Sci) What career path do you envisage for yourself with this degree? **Oxford** Applicants are expected to demonstrate their ability to understand whatever facts they have encountered and to discuss a particular aspect of biology in which they are interested (interviews rigorous but sympathetic). What problems does a fish face under water? Are humans still evolving? See also **Chapter 7**.

Applicants' impressions (A=Open day; B=Interview day) Oxford (B) There were three interviews, very daunting. I felt fairly pressurised with constant questions and with little time to think about the answers. I didn't have much time to look around the department, only the College. The interview process seemed fairly rushed, with not too much time to meet undergraduates. Oxford is worth a try if your grades are good enough, even if it's only to prove you can get an interview at one of the top universities. **Oxford** (Worcester) (B) There were two interviewers at the first interview and one at the second. The first interview lasted half an hour with questions relating to my specific interests in biology. The second interview lasted 15 minutes with questions involving problem-solving and interpreting graphs. Both interviews were very well organised and, although I felt under pressure, staff were all very friendly and approachable. I was able to meet students who were also very helpful.

AFTER-RESULTS ADVICE

Offers to applicants repeating A-levels Higher Bristol, Bristol UWE, Durham, Hull, London (St George's), Newcastle, St Andrews, Sheffield; **Possibly higher** Aston, Essex, Lancaster, Manchester Met; **Same** Anglia Ruskin, Birmingham, Cardiff, Chester, De Montfort, Derby, Durham, East Anglia, Exeter, Heriot-Watt, Kingston, Leeds, Lincoln, Liverpool Hope, Liverpool John Moores, London (RH), Napier,

Oxford Brookes, Plymouth, Robert Gordon, Roehampton, Salford, Sheffield Hallam, Stirling, Thames Valley, Wolverhampton, Worcester, York; **No offers made** Cambridge.

GRADUATE DESTINATIONS AND EMPLOYMENT (2005/6 HESA)
See **Biology**.

Career note Degrees in Biological Science subjects often lead graduates into medical, pharmaceutical, veterinary, food and environmental work, research and education, in both the public and private sectors (see also **Biology**). Sandwich courses are offered at many institutions enabling students to gain paid experience in industry and commerce, often resulting in permanent employment on graduation. However, students should be warned that the ever-popular Forensic Science courses may not always pave the way to jobs in this highly specialised field. Its popularity is reflected in a 32% rise in applicants in the past year.

OTHER DEGREE SUBJECTS FOR CONSIDERATION
Biochemistry; Biology; Biotechnology; Botany; Chemistry; Consumer Sciences; Ecology; Environmental Health; Environmental Science; Genetics; Genomics; Immunology; Microbiology; Pharmaceutical Sciences; Pharmacology; Pharmacy; Physiology; Plant Sciences; Psychology; Sport and Exercise Science; Toxicology; Virology; Zoology.

BIOLOGY

(including **Applied, Cancer, Environmental, Forensic, Human, Marine, Molecular** and **Plant Biology;** see also **Biological Sciences, Biotechnology, Microbiology** and **Zoology**)

The science of biology is a broad and rapidly developing subject that increasingly affects our lives. Biologists address the challenges faced by human populations such as disease, conservation and food production, and the continuing advances in such areas as genetics and molecular biology that have applications in medicine and agriculture.

Useful websites www.iob.org; www.scienceyear.com; www.bbsrc.ac.uk; www.NewScientistJobs.com/careersguide2007; see also **Biochemistry**.

NB The points totals shown to the left of the institutions are for ease of reference only. It must not be assumed that tariff points are always used by institutions or that they can be substituted for an offer in grades. The level of an offer is not necessarily indicative of the quality of a course.

COURSE OFFERS INFORMATION
Subject requirements/preferences **GCSE** Mathematics and English stipulated in some cases. **AL** Biology and chemistry important, other science subjects may be accepted. Two and sometimes three mathematics/science subjects required including biology. **NB** A* grades are likely to form part of university offers in the higher ranges for students applying for places in 2008 for entry in 2009: check websites.

Your target offers

360 pts **and above**
    Bath – AAA–AAB (MBiol Mol Cell Biol) *(IB 34 pts)*
    Cambridge – AAA varies between colleges (Nat Sci (Biol Biomed Sci)) *(IB 38–42 pts)*
    Durham – AAA (Nat Sci (Biol))
    London (UCL) – AAA+AS–AAB+AS (Palaeobiology) *(IB 34–38 pts)*
    Warwick – ABBc (Cell Biol; Chem Biol) *(IB 34 pts)*

340 pts **Manchester** – AAB–BBC (Biol courses; Cell Biol courses; Dev Biol courses) *(IB 32–35 pts)*
    Reading – AAB (Psy Biol)

320 pts **Birmingham** – ABB–BBB 320–300 pts (Hum Biol; Env Biol; Plant Biol) *(IB 32–34 pts)*
    Bristol – ABB–BBB (Biol; Geol Biol; Biol Maths; Palae Evol) *(IB 33 pts H665)*
    Cardiff – ABB–BBB 320–300 pts (Biology)

For a quick reference offers calculator, fold out the inside back cover.

Durham – ABB (Biol; Cell Biol; Biol Ind) *(IB 34 pts)*
Exeter (Cornwall) – ABB–BBC (Biol Anim Bhv; Mol Biol; Evol Biol) *(IB 26–29 pts)*
Imperial London – ABB (Biol; Biol Mgt; Biol Yr Euro/Ind/Rsch; Biol Microbiol)
Lancaster – ABB (Cell Biol; Env Biol N Am/Aus)
London (RH) – ABB–BBB (Biol; Biol Psy) *(IB 34 pts)*
London (UCL) – ABB+AS (Biol; Env Biol)
Nottingham – ABB–BBB (Biology) *(IB 31–32 pts)*
Sheffield – ABB–BBB **or** ABbb (Biol courses; Dev Cell Biol) *(IB 32–36 pts)*
Sussex – ABB (Biology) *(IB 32 pts)*
York – ABB–BBB (Biol; Biol Yr Ind/Euro; Mol Cell Biol; Biol Educ) *(IB 34 pts)*

300 pts Aberdeen – BBB 2nd yr entry (Mar Biol; Cons Biol; Biol)
Bath – BBB (Biology)
Birmingham – BBB–BCC (Geol Biol)
Bristol – BBB (Cncr Biol; Immun; Virol Immun)
Dundee – 300 2nd yr entry (Biol; Mol Biol; Microbiol; Zool) *(IB 29 pts)*
East Anglia – BBB–BBC (Cell Biol; Genet Mol Biol Microbiol; Plnt Biol) *(IB 30 pts)*
Edinburgh – BBB (Dev Biol; Med Biol; Repro Biol)
Lancaster – BBB–BBC (Env Biol; Cell Biol Biomed)
Leeds – BBB (Biol courses)
Leicester – BBB–BBC (Psy Biol)
Loughborough – 300–320 pts (Hum Biol)
Newcastle – ABB–BBB (Biol; App Biol; Biol Chem; Biol Psy; Mar Biol) *(B 32–35 pts)*
Reading – 300 pts (Env Biol)
St Andrews – ABC–BBB (Biol courses) *(IB 31 pts)*
Southampton – BBB (Mar Biol Ocean; Biol) *(IB 30 pts)*
Stirling – BBB 2nd yr entry (Biol courses) *(IB 26 pts)*
Strathclyde – BBB (Foren Biol)

280 pts Aberystwyth – 280 pts (Biol; Env Biol; Mar Frshwtr Biol) *(IB 26 pts)*
Aston – BBC 280 pts (Cell Mol Biol; Infec Immun; Hum Biol; Biol joint courses)
Essex – 280–240 pts (Mar Frshwtr Biol; Mol Cell Biol) *(IB 26–30 pts)*
Exeter (Cornwall) – BBC (Cons Biol Ecol)
Glasgow – BBC–CCC (Hum Biol; Infec Biol; Mar Frshwtr Biol; Anim Biol) *(IB 28 pts)*
Liverpool – BBC–BBB 280–300 pts (Mar Biol; Trpcl Dis Biol; Env Biol) *(IB 28–32 pts)*
London (QM) – 280 pts (Biol; Env Biol; Evol Biol; Mar Frshwtr Biol) *(IB 30–32 pts)*
Plymouth – 280–260 pts (Mar Biol; Mar Biol Cstl Ecol; Mar Biol Ocean; Env Biol)
Swansea – 280–300 pts (Biol; Mar Biol)

260 pts Bangor – 260–320 pts (Mar Biol; App Mar Biol)
Nottingham – BCC–CCC (App Biol; Env Biol)
Oxford Brookes – BCC **or** BCbc (Biol courses; Hum Biol; Cell Mol Biol)
Queen's Belfast – BCC/AB (Env Biol; Mar Biol)
Ulster – 260 pts (Biology) *(IB 28 pts)*
Wolverhampton – 260–320 pts (Hum Biol Microbiol)

240 pts Aberdeen – CCC 1st yr entry (Biol; Cons Biol; Mar Biol) *(IB 28 pts)*
Bangor – 240–280 pts (Biol; Mol Biol) *(IB 28 pts)*
Bristol UWE – 240–260 pts (Foren Biol)
Central Lancashire – 240 pts (Foren Biol)
Chester – 240 pts (Foren Biol courses) *(IB 30 pts)*
Dundee – 240 pts 1st yr entry (Mol Biol) *(IB 29 pts)*
Hull – 240–260 pts (Biol; Hum Biol; Mar Frshwtr Biol)
Keele – CCC 240–260 pts (Biol courses) *(IB 26–28 pts)*
Kent – CCC (Foren Biol; Biol) *(IB 26 pts)*
Northumbria – 240 pts (App Biol; Biol Foren Biol)
Portsmouth – 240–280 pts (Biol; Foren Biol)
Salford – 240 pts (Hum Biol Infec Dis) *(IB 24 pts)*

220 pts **Brighton** – 220 pts (App Biol)

Chester – 220 pts (Biol courses except under 240 pts)

Gloucestershire – 220 pts (Biol courses; Anim Biol)

Hull – 220 pts (Cstl Mar Biol)

Liverpool John Moores – 220 pts (Biol; Psy Biol)

Sheffield Hallam – 220 pts (Hum Biol; Biol)

Stirling – CCD/BC (Biol; Mar Biol; Aquacult; Frshwtr Sci) *(IB 26 pts)*

200 pts **Anglia Ruskin** – 200–140 pts (Med Biol; Mar Biol courses; Nat Hist Wldlf Biol)

Bath Spa – 200–240 pts (Biol courses)

Bolton – 200 pts (Biol courses)

Central Lancashire – 200–260 pts (Mol Cell Biol)

Heriot-Watt – CDD 1st yr entry (Brew Distil; App Mar Biol)

Hertfordshire – 200 pts (App Biol; Hum Biol courses)

Huddersfield – 200 pts (Med Biol; Mol Cell Biol)

Lincoln – 200 pts (Cons Biol (Anim Bhv))

Manchester Met – 200–280pts (Biol courses; Cell Mol Biol; Hum Biol) *(IB 28 pts)*

Napier – 200 pts (Env Biol; Mar Frshwtr Biol; Foren Biol)

180 pts **Bristol UWE** – 180–220 pts (Hum Biol; Spo Biol; Cons Biol; Env Biol) *(IB 26–28 pts)*

Derby – 180–200 pts (Biol courses)

Edge Hill – 180 pts (Biology)

Glamorgan – 180–220 pts (Biol; Hum Biol)

Glasgow Caledonian – DDD (Hum Biol Sociol Psy)

Greenwich – 180–120 pts (App Biol)

Kingston – 180–220 pts (Biol; Mar Frshwtr Biol; Foren Biol; Hum Biol; Cell Mol Biol)

Middlesex – 180 pts (Med Biol)

Northampton – 180–220 pts (Biol; Biol Cons courses; Hum Biol)

Nottingham Trent – 180 pts (Biology)

Roehampton – 180–200 pts (Biol courses)

Salford – 180 pts (Hum Biol Hlth)

Staffordshire – 180–240 pts (Biol courses; Hum Biol) *(IB 28 pts)*

Teesside – 180–240 pts (App Biol)

160 pts **Bournemouth** – 160 pts (App Biol; Env Cons Biol)

Canterbury Christ Church – CC (Env Biol courses)

London South Bank – CC (Biosci (Hum Biol); App Biol)

Newman (UC) – CC 160 pts (BEd/BSc Biol)

Queen Margaret – 160 pts (Hum Biol)

St Mary's (UC) – 160–200 pts (Hum Biol courses)

Westminster – CC (Microbiol; Foren Biol; Mol Biol Genet)

Wolverhampton – 160–220 pts (Biol courses)

120 pts **Bedfordshire** – 120–160 pts (Hum Biol)

Cardiff (UWIC) – 120 pts (Psy Hum Biol; Mol Biol)

East London – 120 pts (App Biol; Hum Biol courses)

Strathclyde – DD (Nat Sci (Biol))

Suffolk (Univ Campus) – 120–180 pts (Hum Biol courses)

West Scotland – DD **or** bbc (Biol courses; Env Biol)

Worcester – 120–200 pts (Hum Biol courses)

80 pts **London (Birk)** – 80 pts for under 21s (over 21 varies) (p/t Mol Biol)

Leeds Met – contact University

Alternative offers

See **Chapter 8** for grade/point equivalences and related information for the following examinations: Scottish qualifications, the Welsh Baccalaureate, the IB diploma (approximate points shown also in italics in the table of offers), the Irish Leaving Certificate, the European Baccalaureate and the French Baccalaureate.

EXAMPLES OF FOUNDATION DEGREES IN THE SUBJECT FIELD

Anglia Ruskin; Bedfordshire; Blackpool & Fylde (Coll); Bournemouth; Cornwall (Coll); Harlow (Coll); Nottingham Trent; Truro (Coll).

CHOOSING YOUR COURSE (SEE ALSO CH.1)

Course variations – Widen your options

Marine Biology and Oceanography (Bangor)
Biology and Food Studies (Bath Spa)
Applied Biology and Health Science (Bournemouth)
Genetics and Molecular Biology (East Anglia)
Evolutionary Biology (Edinburgh)
Biology with Ornithology (Hull)
Environmental Biology (London (UCL))
Behavioural Biology (St Andrews)
Forensic Biology (Strathclyde)
Chemical Biology (Warwick)
CHECK PROSPECTUSES AND WEBSITES FOR OTHER UNIVERSITIES AND COLLEGES OFFERING THESE COURSES.

Universities and colleges teaching quality See www.qaa.ac.uk; www.unistats.com.

Top universities and colleges (Research) Bristol; Cambridge; Cardiff; Durham; Edinburgh; Imperial London; Leeds; Leicester; London (King's), (UCL); Manchester; Oxford; Sheffield*.

Sandwich degree courses Aston; Bath; Bradford; Bristol; Bristol UWE; Coventry; East London; Glamorgan; Greenwich; Hertfordshire; Huddersfield; Kent; Kingston; Liverpool John Moores; London South Bank; Manchester; Oxford Brookes; Surrey; Sussex; Ulster; Wolverhampton; York.

ADMISSIONS INFORMATION

Number of applicants per place (approx) Aberdeen 8; Aberystwyth 5; Aston 6; Bath 7; Birmingham 7; Bradford 7; Bristol 7; Cardiff 8; Dundee 6; Durham 11; Exeter 6; Hull 4; Imperial London 4; Kent 10; Leeds 6; Leicester 15; London (King's) 5; (RH) 5; Newcastle (Mar Biol) 15, (App Biol) 9; Nottingham 9; Oxford Brookes 13; Salford 3; Southampton 14, (Mar Biol) 8; Stirling 15; Sussex 4; Swansea (Mar Biol) 8, (Env Biol) 3, (Biol) 4; York 9.

Advice to applicants and planning the UCAS personal statement **Bath** Internal transfer between degree programmes possible; do not make multiple applications (contact admissions tutor). **Bristol** (Geol Biol) Looks for experience in the ecological field. **Swansea** Evidence needed of subject interest beyond formal studies and that some thought has been given to their future careers (see **Appendix 2**). See also **Biochemistry** and **Biological Sciences**.

Misconceptions about this course **Sussex** Many students think that a Biology degree limits you to being a professional scientist which is not the case. **York** Some fail to realise that chemistry beyond GCSE is essential. Mature students often lack the confidence to consider the course.

Selection interviews **Yes** Bangor, Bath, Birmingham, Bradford (informal, after offer), Cambridge, Durham, East Anglia, Essex, Hertfordshire, Kent, Kingston, London (RH), (UCL), London South Bank, Nottingham (depends on application), Oxford (see **Biological Sciences**), SAC (Scottish CAg), Sheffield Hallam, Southampton, Staffordshire, Surrey, Swansea, Writtle (Coll); **Some** Aston, Bath Spa, Derby, Dundee, Liverpool John Moores, London (King's), Roehampton, Salford, Sheffield, Stirling, Wolverhampton, York.

Interview advice and questions Questions are likely to focus on your studies in biology, on any work experience or any special interests you may have in biology outside school. In the past, questions have included: Is the computer like a brain and, if so, could it ever be taught to think? What do you think the role of the environmental biologist will be in the next 40–50 years? Have you any strong views on vivisection? You have a micro-organism in the blood: you want to make a culture. What conditions should be borne in mind? What is a pacemaker? What problems will a giraffe experience? How does water enter a flowering plant? Compare an egg and a potato. Discuss a family tree of human genotypes. Discuss fish farming in Britain today. **Liverpool John Moores** Informal interview. It is useful to bring samples of coursework to the interview. **York** Why biology? How do you see your future? See also **Chapter 7**.

Applicants' impressions (A=Open day; B=Interview day) **Bath** (B) There was only one 30-minute interview with a few probing questions on why I had chosen the course and what my interests were. The department seemed well-organised, well-equipped and high quality. There were no opportunities to speak to students. I would strongly recommend this department: but the interview is important, so read around the subject. **Durham** (A) The open day consisted of a talk by the master of the college and a tour by student union reps. A further three-day visit was planned. **London (UCL)** (B) There was one 20-minute fairly relaxed interview with questions on 'What makes you tick?' and 'What do you see yourself doing in 10 years' time?' A second-year student took us on a tour of the university.

Reasons for rejection (non-academic) Mainly academic. **Bath Spa** Poor mathematical and scientific knowledge. **Oxford** He appeared to have so much in his head that he tended to express his ideas in too much of a rush. He needs to slow down a bit and take more time to select points that are really pertinent to the questions.

AFTER-RESULTS ADVICE

Offers to applicants repeating A-levels **Higher** Cardiff, East London, London (King's), St Andrews, Strathclyde; **Possibly higher** Aston, Bath, Bradford, Durham, Leeds, London (RH), Nottingham, Portsmouth; **Same** Aberystwyth, Anglia Ruskin, Bangor, Bedfordshire, Brunel, Chester, Derby, Dundee, Heriot-Watt, Hull, Liverpool John Moores, London (UCL), London South Bank, Manchester Met, Napier, Newcastle, Oxford Brookes, Plymouth, Roehampton, St Mary's (UC), Salford, Sheffield, Southampton, Staffordshire, Stirling, Teesside, Ulster, Wolverhampton, York.

GRADUATE DESTINATIONS AND EMPLOYMENT (2005/6 HESA)

Graduates surveyed 2980 **Employed** 1305 **In further study** 735 **Assumed unemployed** 245.

Career note Some graduates go into research, but many will go into laboratory work in hospitals, food laboratories, agriculture, the environment and pharmaceuticals. Others go into teaching, management and other professional and technical areas. In 2004/5 the main career destinations were health and social work, education, wholesale and retail trade and social and pastoral services.

OTHER DEGREE SUBJECTS FOR CONSIDERATION

Anatomy; Biochemistry; Biological Sciences; Biotechnology; Chemistry; Dentistry; Ecology; Environmental Health; Environmental Science/Studies; Food Science; Genomics; Health Studies; Medicine; Midwifery; Nursing; Nutrition; Optometry; Orthoptics; Pharmaceutical Sciences; Pharmacology; Pharmacy; Physiology; Physiotherapy; Plant Sciences; Radiography; Speech and Language Therapy; Zoology.

BIOTECHNOLOGY

(including **Medical Engineering**)

Biotechnology is a multidisciplinary subject which can include chemistry, biological sciences, microbiology, genetics and chemical engineering. Medical engineering involves the design, installation, maintenance and provision of technical support for diagnostic, therapeutic and other clinical equipment used by doctors, nurses and other clinical healthcare workers.

Useful websites www.bbsrc.ac.uk; www.scienceyear.com.

NB The points totals shown to the left of the institutions are for ease of reference only. It must not be assumed that tariff points are always used by institutions or that they can be substituted for an offer in grades. The level of an offer is not necessarily indicative of the quality of a course.

For information on how to read the Subject Tables, see **Chapter 8**.

COURSE OFFERS INFORMATION

Subject requirements/preferences **GCSE** Mathematics and science subjects required. **AL** Courses vary but one, two or three subjects from chemistry, biology, physics and mathematics may be required. **NB** A* grades are likely to form part of university offers in the higher ranges for students applying for places in 2008 for entry in 2009: check websites.

Your target offers

340 pts **Bath** – AAB (MEng Med Eng) *(IB 36 pts)*
Bristol – AAB (Bioch Mol Biol Biotech) *(IB 35 pts H666)*
Imperial London – AAB (Biomed Eng)
Leeds – AAB (MEng Med Eng) *(IB 35 pts)*
London (UCL) – AAB+AS–ABB+AS (Biotech; Bioch Eng (Proc Biotech))
Manchester – AAB–BBB (Biotech (Ent) (Ent Ind)) *(IB 32–35 pts)*
Newcastle – AAB–ABB (Biotech; Bioproc Eng) *(IB 30–32 pts)*

320 pts **Birmingham** – ABB–BBB (Bioch Biotech; Biomed Eng) *(IB 32–34 pts)*
Cardiff – ABB–BBB 320–300 pts (Biotech; MEng Med Eng)
Imperial London – ABB (BSc Biotech; Biotech Yr Ind/Rsch; Biomat Tiss Eng) *(IB 38 pts H chem/biol 6 pts)*
Liverpool – ABB–BBB (Microbl Biotech; MEng Med Electron Instr) *(IB 28–32 pts)*
London (QM) – 320–260 pts (MEng/BEng Med Eng; Biomed Mat Sci Eng) *(IB 30–32 pts)*
Surrey – ABB–BBC (MEng Med Eng)

300 pts **Bradford** – 300 pts (MEng Med Eng)
Edinburgh – BBB (Biotechnology) *(IB 35 pts H666)*
Leeds – BBB 300 pts (Biotech; BEng Med Eng) *(IB 32 pts)*
Nottingham – BBB (Biomed Mat Sci) *(IB 32 pts)*
Reading – 300 pts (Biotechnology) *(IB 30 pts)*
Sheffield – ABB–BBC (Med Sys Eng; Biomat Sci Tiss Eng; Biomed Eng)

280 pts **Aston** – BBC–CCC (Biosci Tech)
Cardiff – BBC 280 pts (BEng Med Eng)
Glasgow – BBC–CCC (Biotechnology) *(IB 28 pts)*
Oxford Brookes – BBC **or** BBbc (Biotechnology)
Reading – 280 pts (Biomed Eng Cyber) *(IB 30 pts)*
Strathclyde – BBC (Pros Orth)
Surrey – BBC (BEng Med Eng)

260 pts **Bradford** – 260 pts (BEng Med Eng)
Nottingham – BCC–CCC (Biotechnology) *(IB 24–30 pts)*
Salford – 260 pts (Pros Orth)

240 pts **Bradford** – 240 pts (BEng Med Eng; Med Tech Spo; Clin Tech)
City – CCC (BEng Biomed Eng) *(IB 25–28 pts)*
London (QM) – 240 pts (BSc Biomed Mat Sci Eng)
Northumbria – 240 pts (Biotechnology) *(IB 28 pts)*
Ulster – CCC–DDD 240–180 pts (Biomed Eng)

220 pts **Liverpool John Moores** – 220–260 pts (Biotechnology)

200 pts **Abertay Dundee** – CDD (Biotechnology)
Bradford – 200 pts (Clin Tech)
Hertfordshire – 200 pts (Biotech; Biotech Euro/N Am)
Napier – 200 pts (Microbiol Biotech)

180 pts **City** – DDD (BSc Biomed Eng App Phys)

160 pts **SAC (Scottish CAg)** – CC (App Biosci)
Wolverhampton – 160–220 pts (Biotechnology)

140 pts **West Scotland** – CD 140 pts (App Biosci)

120 pts **West Scotland** – DD **or** bb (Phys Med Tech)

Alternative offers

See **Chapter 8** for grade/point equivalences and related information for the following examinations: Scottish qualifications, the Welsh Baccalaureate, the IB diploma (approximate points shown also in

italics in the table of offers), the Irish Leaving Certificate, the European Baccalaureate and the French Baccalaureate.

EXAMPLES OF FOUNDATION DEGREES IN THE SUBJECT FIELD
Napier.

CHOOSING YOUR COURSE (SEE ALSO CH.1)
Course variations – Widen your options
Medical and Biological Chemistry (Edinburgh)
Biotechnology with a Year in North America (Hertfordshire)
Biotechnology with a Year in Industry (Imperial London)
Biochemical Engineering (London (UCL))
Applied Bioscience (SAC (Scottish CAg))
CHECK PROSPECTUSES AND WEBSITES FOR OTHER UNIVERSITIES AND COLLEGES OFFERING THESE COURSES.

Universities and colleges teaching quality See www.qaa.ac.uk; www.unistats.com.

Sandwich degree courses Aberdeen; Aston; Bradford; Bristol; Cardiff; Hertfordshire; Manchester; Napier; Reading; Sussex.

ADMISSIONS INFORMATION
Number of applicants per place (approx) Cardiff 4; Imperial London 4; Leeds 7; London (UCL) 4; Strathclyde 4.

Advice to applicants and planning the UCAS personal statement See **Biological Sciences** and **Biochemistry**. See also **Appendix 2**.

Selection interviews Yes Leeds, Sheffield Hallam, Strathclyde, Surrey; **Some** Cardiff, Liverpool John Moores, Wolverhampton.

Interview advice and questions See **Biology** and **Biological Sciences**. See also **Chapter 7**.

AFTER-RESULTS ADVICE
Offers to applicants repeating A-levels Possibly higher Nottingham; **Same** Cardiff, Leeds, Liverpool John Moores, Wolverhampton.

GRADUATE DESTINATIONS AND EMPLOYMENT (2005/6 HESA)
See **Biological Sciences**.

Career note Biotechnology, biomedical and biochemical engineering opportunities exist in medical, agricultural, food science and pharmaceutical laboratories.

OTHER DEGREE SUBJECTS FOR CONSIDERATION
Agriculture; Biochemistry; Biological Sciences; Biology; Chemistry; Food Science; Health Studies; Materials Science and Technology; Microbiology; Nanotechnology; Pharmacology.

BUILDING

(including **Building Design, Building Services Engineering, Building Surveying, Construction, Fire Risk Engineering, Fire Safety Management;** for **Architectural Technology** see **Architecture;** see also **Property Management/Development**)

The building industry covers a wide range of activities and is closely allied to civil, municipal and structural engineering and quantity surveying. One branch of the industry covers building services engineering, a career which involves specialised areas such as heating, acoustics, lighting, refrigeration and air conditioning. Many Building courses include industrial placements.

Useful websites www.ciob.org.uk; www.cibse.org; www.cskills.org.

For information on how to read the Subject Tables, see **Chapter 8**.

NB The points totals shown to the left of the institutions are for ease of reference only. It must not be assumed that tariff points are always used by institutions or that they can be substituted for an offer in grades. The level of an offer is not necessarily indicative of the quality of a course.

COURSE OFFERS INFORMATION

Subject requirements/preferences GCSE English, mathematics and science usually required. **AL** Physics, mathematics or a technical subject may be required for some courses. **NB** A* grades are likely to form part of university offers in the higher ranges for students applying for places in 2008 for entry in 2009: check websites.

Your target offers

300 pts **Leeds** – BBB (Civ Eng Constr Mgt)
London (UCL) – BBB+AS (Proj Mgt Constr) *(IB 32 pts)*
Loughborough – 300 pts (Commer Mgt Quant Surv)
Ulster – 300 pts (Bld Surv) *(IB 32 pts)*

280 pts **Glasgow Caledonian** – BBC (Fire Rsk Eng)
Northumbria – 280 pts (Bld Surv) *(IB 30 pts)*
Nottingham Trent – 280 pts (Bld Surv) *(IB 31 pts)*
Ulster – 280 pts (Constr Eng Mgt)

270 pts **Glasgow Caledonian** – 270 pts (Bld Contr Surv; Bld Surv; Constr Mgt)
Sheffield Hallam – 270 pts (Bld Surv)

260 pts **Anglia Ruskin** – 260 pts (Bld Surv)
Aston – BCC–CCC 260–240 pts 3AL **or** 2AL+2AS (Constr Mgt; Constr Proj Mgt) *(IB 29 pts)*
Bristol UWE – 260–300 pts (Bld Surv)
Brunel – 260 pts (Mech Eng Bld Serv)
Heriot-Watt – BCC (Constr Mgt Bld Serv; Constr Mgt; Bld Surv; Constr Mgt (Proj Mgt)) *(IB 28 pts)*
Loughborough – 260 pts (Constr Eng Mgt)
Oxford Brookes – BCC (Bld; Constr Mgt)
Reading – 260–280 pts (3AL+AS) 260 pts (3AL) (Bld Constr Mgt; Bld Surv; Constr Mgt Surv)
Salford – BCC 260 pts (Bld Surv)

250 pts **Kingston** – 250 pts (Bld Surv) *(IB 28 pts)*

240 pts **Anglia Ruskin** – 240 pts (Constr Mgt)
Central Lancashire – 240–220 pts (Bld Serv Eng; Bld Surv; Constr Proj Mgt; Facil Mgt)
Brighton – CCC–BCD 240–280 pts (Bld Surv; Bld St; Constr Mgt; Proj Mgt Constr) *(IB 28 pts)*
Glamorgan – 240 pts (Bld Serv Eng)
Northumbria – 240 pts (Bld Des Mgt; Constr Mgt; Bld Serv Eng; Bld Proj Mgt) *(IB 30 pts)*
Nottingham – CCC (Sust Blt Env)
Plymouth – 240 pts (Constr Mgt Env)
Salford – 240 pts (Constr Mgt; Constr Proj Mgt)
Westminster – 240 pts (Bld Surv)

230 pts **Birmingham City** – 230 pts (Bld Surv)
Bristol UWE – 230–260 pts (Bld Surv) *(IB 24–28 pts)*
Coventry – 230 pts (Bld Surv)
Liverpool John Moores – 230 pts (Bld Surv) *(IB 25 pts)*
Napier – 230 pts (Bld Surv)
Plymouth – 230 pts (Bld Surv Env)
Sheffield Hallam – 230 pts (Constr Mgt)
Wolverhampton – 230 pts (Bld Surv)

220 pts **Bolton** – 220–80 pts (Constr Mgt; Bld Surv Prop Mgt; Constr)
Bristol UWE – 220–260 pts (Blt Nat Env; Bld Serv Eng; Constr Commer Mgt; Constr Mgt)
Coventry – 220 pts (Constr Mgt)
Napier – 220 pts (Constr Proj Mgt)
Newport – 220 pts (Bld St)
Nottingham Trent – 220 pts (Constr Mgt)
Plymouth – 220 pts (Constr Mgt Env)

Westminster – 220 pts (Constr Surv; Bld Eng; Constr Mgt)
180 pts **Anglia Ruskin** – 180–240 pts (Constr Des; Prop Surv)
Birmingham City – 180 pts (Constr Mgt Econ; Prop Constr)
Cardiff (UWIC) – 180 pts (Bld Mntnce Mgt)
Derby – 180 pts (Constr Mgt)
Glamorgan – 180 pts (Constr Mgt)
Greenwich – 180 pts (Bld Surv; Des Constr Mgt; Constr Bus Mgt)
Kingston – 180 pts (Constr Mgt)
Liverpool John Moores – 180 pts (Bld Des Tech Mgt; Constr Mgt)
Plymouth – 180 pts (Env Constr Surv)
Portsmouth – 180–240 pts (Constr Eng Mgt)
160 pts **Central Lancashire** – 160 pts (Fire Sfty courses)
Glasgow Caledonian – CC (Bld Serv Eng)
London South Bank – CC (Constr Mgt; Bld Serv Eng)
Robert Gordon – CC (Constr Des Mgt)
Wolverhampton – 160–220 pts (Comp Aid Des Constr; Constr Mgt)
120 pts **North East Wales (IHE)** – 120 pts (Constr Mgt)
Swansea (Inst) – 120 pts (Bld Cons Mgt; Proj Constr Mgt)
100 pts **Southampton Solent** – 100 pts (Constr Mgt)

Leeds Met – contact University

Alternative offers
See **Chapter 8** for grade/point equivalences and related information for the following examinations: Scottish qualifications, the Welsh Baccalaureate, the IB diploma (approximate points shown also in italics in the table of offers), the Irish Leaving Certificate, the European Baccalaureate and the French Baccalaureate.

EXAMPLES OF FOUNDATION DEGREES IN THE SUBJECT FIELD
Anglia Ruskin; Barnfield (Coll); Barnsley (Univ Centre); Bedford (Coll); Bedfordshire; Bolton; Bolton (CmC); Bournemouth; Bracknell & Wokingham (Coll); Bradford (Coll); Brighton; Central Lancashire; Colchester (Inst); Derby; East Down (IFHE); East Lancashire (IHE); Exeter (Coll); Glamorgan; Hastings (CAT); Highbury (Coll); Kingston; Lambeth (Coll); London South Bank; Manchester (CAT); Mid-Kent (CFHE); North East Wales (IHE); North West London (Coll); Northumbria; Oldham (Coll); Peterborough (Coll); Portsmouth; St Helens (Coll); Sir Gar (Col); Somerset (CAT); South Kent (Coll); Stockport (CFHE); Stoke on Trent (Coll); Suffolk (Univ Campus); Swansea (Inst); West Nottinghamshire (Coll); Westminster City (Coll); Weymouth (Coll).

CHOOSING YOUR COURSE (SEE ALSO CH.1)
Course variations – Widen your options
Building Studies (Architectural Technology) (Bolton)
Built and Natural Environments (Bristol UWE)
Quantity Surveying Consultancy (Kingston)
Building Services Engineering (London South Bank)
Commercial Management and Quantity Surveying (Loughborough)
Civil and Timber Engineering (Napier)
Fire Engineering (Newport)
Property Asset Management (Wolverhampton)
CHECK PROSPECTUSES AND WEBSITES FOR OTHER UNIVERSITIES AND COLLEGES OFFERING THESE COURSES.

Universities and colleges teaching quality
See www.qaa.ac.uk; www.unistats.com.

Top universities and colleges (Research)
Loughborough; Reading; Salford.

Sandwich degree courses
Aston; Bath; Bristol UWE; Brunel; Central Lancashire; Glamorgan; Kingston; Liverpool John Moores; London South Bank; Loughborough; Northumbria; Nottingham Trent; Oxford Brookes; Plymouth; Portsmouth; Sheffield Hallam; Ulster; Westminster; Wolverhampton.

200 | Business Courses

ADMISSIONS INFORMATION

Number of applicants per place (approx) Bristol UWE (Constr Mgt) 5; Glamorgan 3; Glasgow Caledonian 6; Heriot-Watt 6; Kingston 4; London (UCL) 4; Loughborough 4; Napier 8; Northumbria 6; Salford (Bld Surv) 6; Sheffield Hallam (Bld Surv) 7; Strathclyde 5.

Advice to applicants and planning the UCAS personal statement Details of work experience with any levels of responsibility should be included. Make contact with any building organisation to arrange a meeting with staff to discuss careers in building. Building also covers civil engineering, surveying, quantity surveying etc and these areas should also be explored. **Birmingham City** We look for evidence of work experience in the construction industry. **London South Bank** (Bld Serv Eng) Knowledge of the profession. **Loughborough** Ability to work in a team. **Salford** Personal achievement in technological areas, work experience. See also **Appendix 2.**

Misconceptions about this course Loughborough Some students fail to realise that the degree includes law, finance, economics and management plus constructional technology.

Selection interviews Yes Brunel, Derby, Glamorgan, Glasgow Caledonian, Greenwich, Kingston, Liverpool John Moores, London South Bank, Loughborough, Plymouth, Robert Gordon, Sheffield Hallam, Staffordshire, Westminster; **Some** Birmingham City, Brighton, Salford.

Interview advice and questions Work experience in the building and civil engineering industries is important and you could be expected to describe any building project you have visited and any problems experienced in its construction. A knowledge of the range of activities to be found on a building site will be expected, for example the work of quantity and land surveyors and of the various building trades. **Loughborough** The applicant should show an understanding of the role of the quantity surveyor. See also **Chapter 7.**

Reasons for rejection (non-academic) Inability to communicate. Lack of motivation. Indecisiveness about reasons for choosing the course. **Loughborough** Applicant more suited to hands-on rather than an academic course.

AFTER-RESULTS ADVICE

Offers to applicants repeating A-levels Higher Liverpool John Moores, Strathclyde; **Possibly higher** Bristol UWE; **Same** Birmingham City, Bolton, Brighton, Coventry, Heriot-Watt, Huddersfield, Kingston, London (UCL), Loughborough, Northumbria, Robert Gordon.

GRADUATE DESTINATIONS AND EMPLOYMENT (2005/6 HESA)
Graduates surveyed 945 **Employed** 675 **In further study** 25 **Assumed unemployed** 30.

Career note There is a wide range of opportunities within the building and construction industry for building technologists and managers particularly stemming from the construction projects for the 2012 Olympic Games in London. This subject area also overlaps into surveying, quantity surveying, civil engineering, architecture and planning and graduates from all these subjects commonly work together as members of construction teams.

OTHER DEGREE SUBJECTS FOR CONSIDERATION
Architecture; Civil Engineering; Quantity Surveying; Surveying.

BUSINESS COURSES

(**Section A:** Business and Management Courses; **Section B:** International and European Business and Management Courses, Business and Management Courses with Languages; **Section C:** Specialised Business and Management Courses including Advertising, E-Commerce, Entrepreneurship, Operations Management, Public Relations and Publishing; see also **Hospitality and Hotel Management, Human Resource Management, Leisure and Recreation Management/Studies, Marketing, Retail Management** and **Tourism and Travel**)

This subject attracts more applicants than any other degree course, with a further rise in the past year for places on a wide range of programmes. Financial studies form part of most courses, in addition to sales, marketing, human resources management and general management. Since this is a vocational subject, some work experience in the field is generally required prior to application. Many courses offer industrial placements, in some cases in the USA, Australia and New Zealand and, for those students with an A-level in a language (and in some cases a good GCSE), placements abroad in Europe are possible.

Useful websites www.faststream.gov.uk; www.bized.co.uk; www.icsa.org.uk; www.oft.gov.uk; www.adassoc.org.uk; www.cipr.co.uk; www.ismm.co.uk; www.export.org.uk; www.ipsos-mori.com; www.capitaras.co.uk; www.tax.org.uk; www.hmrc.gov.uk; www.camfoundation.com; www.shell-livewire.org/mentor; www.imc.co.uk; www.managers.org.uk; www.cipd.co.uk; www.iqps.org; www.managementhelp.com.

NB The points totals shown to the left of the institutions are for ease of reference only. It must not be assumed that tariff points are always used by institutions or that they can be substituted for an offer in grades. The level of an offer is not necessarily indicative of the quality of a course.

COURSE OFFERS INFORMATION
Subject requirements/preferences GCSE Mathematics and English often at grade A or B required. **AL** Mathematics required for some courses and a language will be stipulated for most courses in Section B. In some cases grades A, B or C may be required. (Publishing) English required for some courses. **NB** A* grades are likely to form part of university offers in the higher ranges for students applying for places in 2008 for entry in 2009: check websites.

SECTION A: BUSINESS AND MANAGEMENT COURSES
(Refer to **Section B** and **Section C** for other Business courses)

Your target offers

360 pts **and above**
       Bath – AAA–AAB (Bus Admin) *(IB 35 pts)*
       Cambridge – competitive entry after 2 or 3 yrs **or** another Cambridge Tripos course (Mgt St) *(IB 38–42 pts)*
       London (King's) – AABb (Bus Mgt) *(IB 36 pts)*
       Warwick – AABb **or** AAbbb (Management) *(IB 36 pts)*
340 pts **Birmingham** – AAB–ABB (Bus Mgt courses) *(IB 34 pts)*
       City – AAB (Bus St; Mgt) *(IB 35 pts)*
       Exeter – AAB–BBB (Bus Mgt) *(IB 32–35 pts)*
       London (LSE) – AAB **or** AAbbb (Mgt Sci) *(IB 36 pts)*
       Loughborough – 340–320 pts (Spo Sci Spo Mgt) *(IB 36 pts)*
       Manchester – AAB–BBB (Bus St; Mgt courses) *(IB 33–35 pts)*
       Southampton – AAB 340 pts (Mgt; Mgt Sci courses) *(IB 35 pts)*
320 pts **Aston** – ABB–AAB 320–340 pts (Bus courses) *(IB 34 pts)*
       Cardiff – ABB (Bus St)
       Glasgow – ABB–AAA (Bus Mgt courses) *(IB 30 pts)*
       Kent – 320 pts (MSci App Bus Mgt courses) *(IB 27–33 pts)*
       Lancaster – ABB (Bus St (Acc) (Fin); Org St courses; Bus St; Mgt courses) *(IB 34–36 pts)*
       Leeds – ABB (Mgt Trans St)
       Liverpool – 320 pts (Bus St) *(IB 30–32 pts)*
       London (QM) – 320–300 pts (Bus Mgt) *(IB 32 pts)*
       London (RH) – ABB (Management) *(IB 33 pts)*
       Loughborough – ABB (Mgt Sci)
       Newcastle – ABB (Bus Mgt) *(IB 33–35 pts)*
       Northumbria – 320 pts ABB (Bus St; Bus Mgt)
       Nottingham – ABB (Mgt St) *(IB 32 pts)*
       Reading – ABB (Mgt Bus Admin; Acc Mgt) *(IB 33 pts)*

202 | Business Courses

      St Andrews – ABB (Mgt courses) *(IB 32 pts)*
      Sheffield – ABB–BBC (Bus courses) *(IB 30–32 pts)*
      Surrey – 320 pts (Bus Mgt) *(IB 34 pts)*
      Sussex – ABB **or** 360 pts 3AL+AS (Bus Mgt St) *(IB 34 pts)*
      York – ABB (Mgt courses) *(IB 36 pts)*

300 pts **Bournemouth** – 300 pts (Bus St)
      East Anglia – BBB–BBC (Bus Mgt) *(IB 30–32 pts)*
      Edinburgh – BBB (Bus St courses)
      Keele – BBB–BCC 300–260 pts (Bus Admin courses) *(IB 28–32 pts)*
      Queen's Belfast – BBB (Management)

280 pts **Brunel** – 280 pts (Bus Mgt; Bus Mgt (Acc); Bus St Spo Sci)
      Durham (Stockton) – BBC (Bus Fin; Bus)
      Leicester – 280–320 pts (Mgt St) *(IB 30 pts)*
      Loughborough – 280–320 pts (Geog Mgt; Maths Mgt; Phys Mgt)
      Strathclyde – BBC/AB (Bus; Bus Ent)
      Swansea – 280–300 pts (Bus Mgt courses; Mgt Sci courses)

260 pts **Aberystwyth** – 260 pts (Bus Mgt courses) *(IB 29 pts)*
      Coventry – 260 pts (Bus St; Bus Mgt; Bus Admin) *(IB 24 pts)*
      Kent – 260–280 pts (Bus joint courses)
      Leeds – BCC (Bus courses)
      London (SOAS) – BCC (Mgt courses) *(IB 30 pts)*
      Loughborough – 260–280 pts (Trans Bus Mgt)
      Oxford Brookes – BCC–BBB (Bus courses)
      Richmond (Am Int Univ) – 260 pts (Bus Admin courses)
      Stranmillis (UC) – BCC 260 pts (Bus St Educ)
      Westminster – BCC 260–280 pts (Bus Mgt courses; Bus St courses; Bus courses)

240 pts **Aberdeen** – CCC **or** aabb (Mgt St) *(IB 30 pts)*
      Bangor – 240–280 pts (Bus St courses; Mgt courses) *(IB 28 pts)*
      Brighton – 240–260 pts (Bus St; Bus St E–Commer; Bus St Fin; Law Bus; Bus Mark; Bus Mgt courses) *(IB 28 pts)*
      Bristol UWE – 240–260 pts (Bus courses; Mgt) *(IB 26–32 pts)*
      Chester (Warrington) – 240 pts (Bus courses; Mgt courses) *(IB 30 pts)*
      De Montfort – 240–280 pts (Bus courses)
      Huddersfield – 240 pts (Bus St courses)
      Hull – 240 pts (Bus courses)
      Northumbria – 240 pts (Bus joint courses)
      Plymouth – 240 pts (Bus St courses; Marit Bus courses)
      Portsmouth – 240 pts (Bus Admin; Bus St)
      Robert Gordon – CCC (Mgt courses)
      Salford – 240–260 pts (Bus Mgt St) *(IB 28–32 pts)*
      Sheffield Hallam – 240 pts (Bus courses)
      Ulster – 240–200 pts (Bus courses)

220 pts **Abertay Dundee** – CCD (Bus St; Fin Bus)
      Bolton – 220 pts (Bus St courses
      Buckingham – 220–240 pts (Bus Mgt; Bus Ent)
      Glamorgan – 220–260 pts (Bus courses)
      Heriot-Watt – CCD (Bus Mgt Ind; Bus Admin)
      Hertfordshire – 220–260 pts (Bus St; Mgt Sci)
      Kingston – 220–280 pts (Bus courses)
      Liverpool Hope – 220 pts (Bus St)
      Manchester Met – 220–280 pts (Mgt Sys Comb Hons)
      Nottingham Trent – 220–240 pts (Bus courses)
      Stirling – CCD–BCC (Bus St courses) *(IB 28–30 pts)*
      Winchester – 220 pts (Bus Mgt courses)

For a quick reference offers calculator, fold out the inside back cover.

BUSINESS SCHOOL

TOP 10
2007
The Guardian League Tables
2007
The Guardian League Tables
UNIVERSITY

TOP 6
UNIVERSITY
The Times Good Uni Guide
2007

Loughborough University Business School runs outstanding degree programmes in business and management. From part-time programmes for working professionals to conversion programmes for non-business graduates, the Business School offers a wealth of career-enhancing courses to fuel your ambition.

For high-flyers in business:
The Loughborough MBA

For non-business graduates:
MSc in Management
MSc in Business Analysis and Management
MSc in Finance and Management
MSc in International Management
MSc in Marketing and Management

For graduates seeking higher education:
Postgraduate Research Programmes

For working managers seeking career advancement:
Certificates, Diplomas and MSc's in Management

Invest in your future and transform your career prospects

Loughborough University Business School
T: +44 (0)1509 223140 (MBA & short coures),
    223291 (MSc's) or 228276 (PhD)
F: +44 (0)1509 223963 E: pmdc@lboro.ac.uk
www.lboro.ac.uk/businessschool

"LOUGHBOROUGH OFFERS SO MUCH: APART FROM DEGREE COURSES, LOUGHBOROUGH HOLDS ONE OF THE HIGHEST EMPLOYABILITY RATINGS FOR ITS GRADUATES. WOULD I HAVE CHOSEN ANY OTHER UNIVERSITY? NO."

OLUSEGUN CADMUS, IM GRADUATE

OPEN DAYS

Held throughout the year –
consult our website for details

Loughborough
University

Ref: BS/4019

204 | Business Courses

200 pts **Anglia Ruskin** – 200 pts (Bus Mgt)
Bath Spa – 200–240 pts (Bus Mgt courses)
Birmingham City – 200 pts (Bus courses)
Bradford – 200–220 pts (Bus Mgt St 3 yrs; Bus courses)
Cumbria – 200 pts (Bus courses)
Derby – 200–240 pts (Bus St)
Edge Hill – 200 pts (Bus Mgt St)
Gloucestershire – 200–280 pts (Bus Mgt courses)
Kent (Medway) – 200 pts (Bus IT Yr Ind)
Lincoln – 200 pts (Bus St; Mgt)
Manchester Met – 200–260 pts (Bus courses) *(IB 24–28 pts)*
Napier – 200 pts (Bus St courses)
Sunderland – 200–220 pts (Bus Mgt courses)

180 pts **Cardiff (UWIC)** – BC 180 pts (Bus St courses)
Central Lancashire – 180–220 pts (Bus joint courses)
Chichester – 180–220 pts (Bus St courses) *(IB 28 pts)*
De Montfort – 180–220 pts (Bus Mgt)
Greenwich – 180 pts (Bus Admin; Bus St)
Lampeter – 180–240 pts (Bus Mgt)
Liverpool John Moores – 180–220 pts (Bus St)
Marjon (UC) – 180–240 pts (Mgt courses)
Northampton – 180–220 pts (Bus; Bus St; Bus Bus Entre; Mgt)
Queen Margaret – 180 pts (Bus Mgt)
Staffordshire – 180–240 pts (Bus St courses) *(IB 26 pts)*

160 pts **Bedfordshire** – 160–240 pts (Bus St courses)
Canterbury Christ Church – CC (Bus St joint courses)
Doncaster (Coll) – 160 pts (Bus courses)
East London – 160 pts (Bus St courses)
Farnborough (CT) – 160–200 pts (Bus Mgt)
Glasgow Caledonian – CC (Bus Mgt; Bus St)
Harper Adams (UC) – 160–240 pts (Bus courses)
Leeds Trinity and All Saints (Coll) – CC 160 pts (Bus Mgt; Bus)
London Met – 160–200 pts (Bus courses)
Middlesex – 160–280 pts (Bus courses)
Newman (UC) – 160–240 pts (Mgt St courses)
North East Wales (IHE) – 160 pts (Bus Mgt courses)
Roehampton – 160–280 pts (Bus Mgt courses)
Royal (CAg) – 160–220 pts (Bus Mgt courses)
St Mary's (UC) – 160–200 pts (Mgt St)
Southampton Solent – 160 pts (Bus St courses)

For a quick reference offers calculator, fold out the inside back cover.

South East Essex (Coll) – 160 pts (Bus St)
Teesside – 160 pts (Bus Mgt; Bus St)
Thames Valley – 160 pts (Bus St)
West Scotland – CC (Bus; Ent St)
Wolverhampton – 160–220 pts (Bus; Bus Mgt; Bus Inf Sys)
Worcester – 160 pts (Bus Mgt)
Writtle (Coll) – 160 pts (Bus Mgt)
York St John – CC 160 pts (Bus Mgt)

140 pts **Newport** – 140–160 pts (Bus courses)
Trinity Carmarthen (Coll) – 140 pts (Bus St)

120 pts **Bucks New** – 120–180 pts (Bus Mgt courses)
Grimsby (IFHE) – 120 pts (Bus Psy; Tour Bus Mgt)
London South Bank – DD–CC (Bus St; Bus Admin; Mgt Comb)
Northbrook (Coll) – 120 pts (Bus Admin)
Norwich City (Coll) – 120 pts (Bus Mgt)
Peterborough Reg (Coll) – 120 pts (Bus courses)
Swansea (Inst) – 120 pts (Bus St)

100 pts **Bradford (Coll)** – 100–140 pts (Bus St)
Suffolk (Univ Campus) – 100–120 pts (Bus Mgt courses)

80 pts **CECOS** – 80 pts (Business)
Croydon (Coll) – 80–100 pts (Management)
East Lancashire (IHE) – 80 pts (Bus St)
Greenwich (Sch Mgt) – 80–120 pts (Bus Mgt IT)
Holborn (Coll) – 80 pts (Bus Admin)
Kensington Bus (Coll) – 80 pts (Bus St)
Llandrillo Cymru (Coll) – 80 pts min (Mgt Bus)
London (Birk) – 80 pts under 21s (over 21 varies) (p/t Mgt)
UHI Millennium Inst (IC) – 80 pts (Bus Mgt)
West Anglia (Coll) – 80 pts (Bus Mgt)

Euro Bus Sch London – contact School
Leeds Met – contact University
Open University – contact University
Regents Bus Sch London – check with School (Bus courses)

SECTION B: INTERNATIONAL AND EUROPEAN BUSINESS AND MANAGEMENT COURSES, BUSINESS AND MANAGEMENT COURSES WITH LANGUAGES

(Refer to **Section A** and **Section C** for other Business courses)

Your target offers

360 pts **and above**
Lancaster – AAA (Bus St N Am/Aus; Ops Mgt N Am/Aus; Mgt N Am/Aus)
Manchester – AAA (Int Mgt Am Bus St)

340 pts **Bath** – AAB 340 pts (Int Mgt Fr/Ger/Span)
Birmingham – AAB–ABB 320 pts (Int Bus Lang courses)
Manchester – AAB (Int Bus Fin Econ)
Southampton – AAB 340 pts (Mgt Sci Fr/Ger/Span)
Warwick 340 pts (Int Bus)

320 pts **Aston** – ABB 320–300 pts (Int Bus Mgt; Int Bus Fr/Ger/Span)
Cardiff – ABB–BBB (Bus Mgt (Int Mgt); Bus Mgt Euro Lang)
Lancaster – ABB (Euro Mgt Fr/Ger/Ital/Span)
London (RH) – ABB 320 pts (Mgt Fr/Ger/Ital/Span)
Loughborough – ABB (Int Bus)
Newcastle – ABB–BBB (Modn Lang Mgt St; Bus St Fr/Ger/Span)
Nottingham – ABB (Mgt St Chin St/Fr/Ger/Span; Mgt Chin St/As St/Fr/Ger/Span; Int Bus – China campus)

206 | Business Courses

Reading – ABB 320–350 pts (Int Mgt Bus Admin Fr/Ger/Ital)
Sheffield – ABB (Mgt Jap St; Kor St Mgt; E As St Mgt; Chin St Mgt; Fr/Ger/Russ Mgt)

300 pts **Bournemouth** – 300 pts (Bus St Langs)
Dundee – 300 pts 4 yrs (Int Bus; Int Bus Fr/Ger/Span)
Edinburgh – BBB (Bus St Fr/Ger/Span; Int Bus; Int Bus Langs)
Liverpool – BBB 280–300 pts (Bus St Fr/Ger/Ital; Bus St Hisp St; Int Bus)
Manchester – BBB (Int Mgt; Bus Mgt Chin/Fr/Ger/Ital/Port/Russ/Span)
Queen's Belfast – BBB–BCC (Mgt Fr/Ger/Span)
Stirling – BBB 2nd yr entry (Bus St Fr/Span)
Surrey – BBB–BCC 300–260 pts (Bus Mgt Fr)

280 pts **Brunel** – 280 pts (Int Bus)
Essex – 280–260 pts (Int Ent Bus Dev; Bus Mgt Mdn Lang)
Heriot-Watt – BBC 280 pts (Int Mgt Fr/Ger/Span)
Northumbria – 280 pts (Int Bus Mgt)
Oxford Brookes – BBC (Int Bus Mgt)
Strathclyde – BBC (Int Bus Modn Lang; Int Bus)
Westminster – BBC 280 pts (Int Bus Arbc/Chin/Fr/Span; Int Bus)

260 pts **Aberystwyth** – 260 pts (Bus Mgt Fr/Ger)
Heriot-Watt – BCC 260 pts 1st yr entry (Int Mgt)
Keele – 260–280 pts (Bus Admin Fr)
Kent – 260–320 pts (Bus Admin (Euro Mgt); Hisp St Bus Admin; Euro Mgt Sci)
London (QM) – 260 pts (Bus Mgt Fr/Ger/Hisp St/Russ)
Richmond (Am Int Univ) – 260 pts (Bus Admin (Int Bus))
Swansea – 260–300 pts (Int Bus Econ; Int Mgt Sci N Am/Euro; Int Mgt Sci Lang)

240 pts **Aberdeen** – CCC (Entre Fr)
Bangor – 240 pts (Bus St Fr/Ger/Ital/Span)
Bradford – 240 pts (Int Bus Mgt)
Bristol UWE – 240 pts (Int Bus St Modn Lang; Int Bus St)
Central Lancashire – 240–280 pts (Bus Mgt Chin)
Chester – 240 pts (Bus Fr/Ger/Span)
Coventry – 240 pts (Int Bus Mgt)
De Montfort – 240 pts (Int Bus Glob; Int Mark Bus)
Dundee – 240–300 pts 3 yrs (Int Bus; Int Bus Fr/Ger)
Huddersfield – 240 pts (Int Bus; Glob Pol Int Bus)
Nottingham Trent – CCC 240 pts (Int Bus; Int Bus Admin)
Plymouth – 240 pts (Int Bus; Int Bus Fr/Ger/Span; Marit Bus Fr/Ger/Span)
Portsmouth – 240 pts (Int Bus St)
Salford – 240–260 pts (Bus St Int Bus Mgt; Mgt Modn Lang; Mgt Sci N Am)
Sheffield Hallam – 240 pts (Int Bus St)
Stirling – CCC (Int Mgt St)
Swansea – 240 pts (Bus St Fr/Ger; Int Bus Mgt)
Ulster – CCC (Bus St Fr/Ger/Span)

220 pts **Abertay Dundee** – 220 pts (Int Mgt)
Brighton – 220 pts (Int Bus)
Glamorgan – 220 pts (Int Bus Excl)
Kingston – 220–320 pts (Int Bus; Int Bus Fr/Span)

200 pts **Anglia Ruskin** – 200 pts (Int Bus courses; Int Mgt)
Derby – 200 pts (Int Bus Mgt)
Gloucestershire – 200–280 pts (Int Bus Mark)
Hertfordshire – 200–260 pts (Int Bus; Euro Bus Mgt Sci; Euro Bus Fr/Ger/Ital/Span)
Hull – 200–220 pts (Int Bus; Bus Fr/Ger/Ital/Span)
Lincoln – 200 pts (Euro Bus; Bus Fr/Ger/Span)
Liverpool John Moores – 200 pts (Int Bus St Chin/Fr/Ger/Jap/Span)
Manchester Met – 200–260 pts (Int Bus; Euro St Int Bus; Int Bus Lang)
Napier – 200 pts (Bus St Lang)

For a quick reference offers calculator, fold out the inside back cover.

208 | Business Courses

Westminster – 200 pts (Euro Mgt)
180 pts **Cardiff (UWIC)** – 180 pts (Bus St Lang) *(IB 28 pts)*
Central Lancashire – 180–220 pts (Int Bus)
Greenwich – 180–200 pts (Int Bus; Bus Fr/Ger/Ital/Span)
Northampton – 180 pts (Bus Fr/Ger)
Roehampton – 180 pts (Int Bus)
Staffordshire – 180–240 pts (Int Bus Mgt)
160 pts **Canterbury Christ Church** – CC (Int Bus Mgt; Bus St Fr)
East London – 160 pts (Int Bus courses)
Glasgow Caledonian – CC (Int Bus)
London Met – 160–200 pts (Int Bus)
Middlesex – 160–200 pts (Bus St Fr/Ger/Ital/Span)
Southampton Solent – 160 pts (Int Bus Mgt; Int Bus Mgt Engl; Bus Euro St)
Teesside – 160 pts (Int Bus)
Wolverhampton – 160–220 pts (Int Bus Mgt; Bus Fr)
140 pts **Cardiff (UWIC)** – CD 140 pts (Int Bus Mgt)
120 pts **Bedfordshire** – 120–160 pts (Int Bus St)
Bucks New – 120–180 pts (Bus Mgt Fr/Ital/Span)
80 pts **Euro Bus Sch London** – contact School (Int Bus courses)
Regents Bus Sch London – check with Sch (Int Bus; Int Bus Des Mgt)

Leeds Met – contact University

SECTION C: SPECIALISED BUSINESS AND MANAGEMENT COURSES INCLUDING:

Advertising, Air Transport Management, Arts Management, Entrepreneurship, Industrial Relations, Operations Management, Public Relations, Publishing, Quality Management. (Refer to **Section A** and **Section B** for other Business courses); see also **Art and Design (Graphic Design)** for other **Advertising** courses, and **Events Management** under **Hospitality and Hotel Management**.

Your target offers
340 pts **Southampton** – AAB 340 pts (Mgt Entre)
Ulster – AAB 340 pts (Comm Adv Mark)
320 pts **Lancaster** – ABB (Ops Mgt N Am/Aus)
Newcastle – ABB (Agri-Bus Mgt)
300 pts **Bournemouth** – 300 pts (PR; Adv Mark Comm)
Lancaster – BBB **or** AAac/bb **or** ABaa 300 pts (Adv Mark)
280 pts **Birmingham City** – 280 pts (Media Comm (PR))
City – BBC (Air Op Mgt) *(IB 28 pts)*
Coventry – 280 pts (Crea Ind Mgt)
Liverpool – BBC–BBB (E-Business)
Loughborough – 280 pts (Pub Engl)
Surrey – 280 pts (Entre Tech IT Bus)
Swansea – 280 pts (Pblc Media Rel)
260 pts **Aston** – BCC–CCC (Tech Ent Mgt)
Chester (Warrington) – 260 pts (Adv courses)
Coventry – 260 pts (Adv Bus; Adv Mark)
Loughborough – 260–280 pts (Air Trans Mgt) *(IB 30 pts)*
Oxford Brookes – BCC **or** BCcc (Publishing)
Sunderland – 260 pts (PR)
240 pts **Aberdeen** – CCC (Entrepreneurship)
Huddersfield – 240–320 pts (Adv Mark Comm; PR Pol; Adv Media Des Mgt)
London Met – 240 pts (Avn Mgt)
Portsmouth – 240 pts (Bus Ent Dev)
Robert Gordon – CCC (Pub Jrnal)
220 pts **Abertay Dundee** – 220 pts (Op Mgt)
Central Lancashire – 220–260 pts (PR Mgt)

MPW is one of the UK's best known groups of independent sixth-form colleges. We offer a range of specialist services to those who have chosen a career in Business.

Business and Management Courses
Consult the Specialist

Two-year and one-year A level courses
Detailed UCAS advice
Seminars on applications procedures
Interview training

London 020 7835 1355
Birmingham 0121 454 9637
Cambridge 01223 350158

MPW's handbook "Getting into Business and Management Courses" is published by Trotman Group

De Montfort – 220 pts (Arts Mgt)
Gloucestershire – 220 pts (Evnts Mgt)
Liverpool John Moores – 220 pts (Mgt Trans Log)
Southampton Solent – 220–240 pts (Wtrspo St Mgt)

200 pts **Birmingham City** – 200 pts (Bus PR; Adv Mgt)
Central Lancashire – 200–260 pts (Adv Mgt)
Coventry – 200–260 pts (Disas Mgt; Spa Mgt)
De Montfort – 200 pts (Des Mgt Innov)
Lincoln – CDD 200 pts (Adv PR; Adv Mark)
London Met – 200 pts (Avn Mgt)
Manchester Met – 200–260 pts (Adv Mgt Brnd Mgt)
Plymouth – 200 pts (Cru Op Mgt; Evnt Mgt)
Salford – 200 pts (Des Mgt Crea Ind)
Southampton Solent – 200 pts (Adv; PR Comm)
Staffordshire – 200 pts (Adv Brnd Mgt)

180 pts **Birmingham (CFTCS)** – 180–200 pts (Spa Mgt; Evnt Mgt)
Greenwich – 180 pts (Adv Mark Comm)
Liverpool (LIPA) – BC 180 pts (Mus Thea Enter Mgt)
Marjon (UC) – 180–240 pts (PR courses)
Northampton – 180–220 pts (Bus Entre; Adv Des; Adv PR)
Queen Margaret – DDD (PR Media; PR Mark)
Swansea (Inst) – 180–120 pts (Sply Chn Mgt)
Teesside – 180–240 pts (Disas Mgt)
Thames Valley – 180 pts (Airln Airpt Mgt)

160 pts **Central Lancashire** – 160 pts (Fire Sfty Mgt)
Derby – 160–200 pts (Evnts Mgt)
London Met – 160 pts (PR; Arts Mgt; Bus Ent; Adv Mark Commun)
London South Bank – CC (Arts Mgt)
Middlesex – 160–200 pts (Pub Media)
Thames Valley – 160 pts (Adv; PR)
West Scotland – CC (Ent St)
Wolverhampton – 160–220 pts (PR)

140 pts **Trinity Carmarthen (Coll)** – 140 pts (Adv courses)

120 pts **Bedfordshire** – 120–160 pts (PR)
Bucks New – 120 pts (Bus Adv Mgt; Adv Prom Mgt; PR Mgt)

Leeds Met – contact University

Alternative offers

See **Chapter 8** for grade/point equivalences and related information for the following examinations: Scottish qualifications, the Welsh Baccalaureate, the IB diploma (approximate points shown also in italics in the table of offers), the Irish Leaving Certificate, the European Baccalaureate and the French Baccalaureate.

EXAMPLES OF FOUNDATION DEGREES IN THE SUBJECT FIELD

Abingdon and Witney (Coll); Amersham (Coll); Anglia Ruskin; Arts London (CComm); Askham Bryan (CAg); Barnet (Coll); Barnfield (Coll); Barnsley (Univ Centre); Bath Spa; Bedfordshire; Bexley (Coll); Birmingham (CFTCS); Bishop Auckland (Coll); Blackpool and Fylde (Coll); Bolton; Bournemouth; Bournemouth and Poole (Coll); Bracknell & Wokingham(Coll); Bradford; Bradford (Coll); Bridgend (Coll); Brighton; Bristol City (Coll); Bromley (CFHE); Bucks New; Burnley (Coll); Central Lancashire; Central Sussex (Coll); Chesterfield (Coll); Colchester (Inst); Cornwall (Coll); Coventry; Coventry City (Coll); Craven (Coll); Croydon (Coll); Cumbria; De Montfort; Dearne Valley (Coll); Derby; Doncaster (Coll); Duchy (Coll); Dunstable (Coll); Durham New (Coll); Ealing, Hammersmith and West London (Coll); East Devon (Coll); East Lancashire (IHE); Eccles (Coll); Edge Hill; Essex; Farnborough (CT); Glamorgan; Grantham (Coll); Guildford (Coll); Gwent (Coll); Halesowen (Coll); Harper Adams (UC); Hartpury (Coll); Hastings (Coll); Havering (Coll); Hertford Reg (Coll); Hertfordshire; Highbury (Coll);

Huddersfield; Hugh Baird (Coll); Hull (Coll); Huntingdonshire Reg (Coll); Joseph Priestley (Coll); Kendal (Coll); Kensington Bus (Coll); Kingston; Kingston (Coll); Knowsley (Coll); Lakes (Coll); Leeds (CAD); Leeds (CAT); Leeds Met; Liverpool (CmC); Llandrillo Cymru (Coll); London (Birk); London Met; London South Bank; Loughborough (Coll); Macclesfield (Coll); Manchester (CAT); Manchester City (Coll); Manchester Met; Matthew Boulton (Coll); Merthyr Tydfll (Coll); Mid-Cheshire (Coll); Middlesbrough (Coll); Middlesex; Milton Keynes (Coll); Morgannwg (Col); Myerscough (Coll); Neath Port Talbot (Coll); Nelson and Colne (Coll); Newcastle (Coll); North Devon (Coll); North East Wales (IHE); North Herts (Coll); North Warwickshire (Coll); North West Kent (Coll); Northampton; Northumbria; Northbrook (Coll); Nottingham Castle (Coll); Nottingham Trent; Oaklands (Coll); Oldham (Coll); Oxford Brookes; Park Lane Leeds (Coll); Penwith (Coll); Plymouth; Plymouth (CFE); Portsmouth; Powys (Coll); Preston (Coll); Redcar (Coll); Richmond upon Thames (Coll); Riverside Halton (Coll); Royal (CAg); Runshaw (Coll); St Helens (Coll); St Martin's (Coll); Salford; Salisbury (Coll); Sheffield (Coll); Sheffield Hallam; Somerset (CAT); South Cheshire (Coll); South Devon (Coll); South Kent (Coll); South Thames (Coll); South Tyneside (Coll); Southampton Solent; Southend Campus Essex; Staffordshire Reg (Coll); Stockton Riverside (Coll); Suffolk (Univ Campus); Sunderland; Sunderland City (Coll); Teesside; Telford (CAT); Thames Valley; Thomas Danby (Coll); Thurrock (Coll); Trinity Carmarthen (Coll); Truro (Coll); Tyne Met (Coll); Wakefield (Coll); Warrington (Coll); Warwickshire (Coll); West Anglia (Coll); West Herts (Coll); West Nottinghamshire (Coll); West Thames (Coll); Westminster Kingsway (Coll); Weston (Coll); Weymouth (Coll); Wigan and Leigh (Coll); Winchester; Wolverhampton; Worcester; Worcester (CT); Worcestershire New (Coll); Writtle (Coll); Yeovil (Coll); York (Coll).

CHOOSING YOUR COURSE (SEE ALSO CH.1)

Course variations – Widen your options
International Business (Berlin) (Anglia Ruskin)
Optical Management (Anglia Ruskin)
Advertising and Economics (Birmingham City)
Arts and Event Management (Bournemouth AI)
Fashion Design and Business Studies (Brighton)
Property Management and Investment (Bristol UWE)
Business Studies and Japanese (Cardiff)
Business Management in China (Central Lancashire)
Air Transport Operations (City)
Business with Sport and Leisure (Leeds Trinity and All Saints)
Health Studies Management (Lincoln)
Maritime Business (Liverpool John Moores)
Air Transport Management (Loughborough)
Music and Arts Management (Middlesex)
Waste Management (Northampton)
Creative Music Production and Business (Westminster)
CHECK PROSPECTUSES AND WEBSITES FOR OTHER UNIVERSITIES AND COLLEGES OFFERING THESE COURSES.

Universities and colleges teaching quality See www.qaa.ac.uk; www.unistats.com.

Top universities and colleges (Research) Aston; Bath; Cambridge; Cardiff; City; Imperial London; Lancaster*; Leeds; London (LSE); Manchester; Nottingham; Oxford; Reading; Warwick*.

Sandwich degree courses Abertay Dundee; Aberystwyth; Arts London; Aston; Bath; Bedfordshire; Birmingham (CFTCS); Birmingham City; Bournemouth; Bradford; Brighton; Bristol UWE; Brunel; Central Lancashire; City; Coventry; De Montfort; Derby; East London; Glamorgan; Glasgow Caledonian; Gloucestershire; Greenwich; Harper Adams (UC); Hertfordshire; Huddersfield; Hull; Kingston; Lancaster; Leeds Met; Lincoln; Liverpool John Moores; London South Bank; Loughborough; Manchester Met; Middlesex; Napier; Newcastle; Northumbria; Nottingham Trent; Plymouth; Portsmouth; Queen's Belfast; Royal (CAg); Sheffield Hallam; Southampton Solent; Staffordshire; Sunderland; Surrey; Teesside; Thames Valley; Ulster; Warwickshire (Coll); West Scotland; Westminster; Wolverhampton.

ADMISSIONS INFORMATION

Number of applicants per place (approx) Abertay Dundee (Bus St) 4; Aberystwyth 3; Anglia Ruskin 5; Aston (Bus Mgt) 12, (Int Bus) 6, (Mgt) 5, (Int Bus Econ) 8; Bangor 4; Bath (Bus Admin) 13, (Int Mgt Lang) 14; Birmingham 7; Birmingham (CFTCS) 5; Blackpool and Fylde (Coll) 2; Bolton 3; Bournemouth 30, (Adv) 20, (PR) 10; Bradford 12; Bristol 28; Brunel 12; Canterbury Christ Church 20; Cardiff 8; Central Lancashire 15; City (Bus St) 17, (Mgt Sys) 6; Colchester (Inst) 2; De Montfort (Bus St) 5, (Adv Mark Comm) 6; Derby (Int Bus) 4; East Anglia (Bus Fin) 18; Edge Hill 4; Glasgow Caledonian 18; Heriot-Watt 5; Hertfordshire 10; Huddersfield 5; Hull (Bus St) 19, (Mgt) 10; Hull (Scarborough) 3; Kent 30; Kingston 50; Leeds 27, (Mgt St) 16; Leeds Trinity and All Saints (Coll) 3; Liverpool John Moores (Int Bus) 16; Llandrillo Cymru (Col) 2; London (King's) 25, (LSE) (Mgt) 23, (Mgt Sci) 19, (RH) 9; London Met 10; London South Bank 4; Loughborough 5; Manchester Met (Bus St) 26, (Int Bus) 8; Mid-Kent (CFHE) 2; Middlesex 12; Napier (Pub) 7; Newcastle 27, (Euro Bus Mgt) 54, (Int Bus Mgt) 25, (Bus Mgt) 40; Northumbria 10; Oxford Brookes 40; Plymouth 4; Portsmouth 10; (Bus Admin) 7, (Bus St) 6, (Int Bus) 5, (Euro Bus) 3; Regents Bus Sch London 25; Robert Gordon 5; Salford (Bus St) 9, (Mgt Sci) 2; Sheffield Hallam (Int Bus) 6; Southampton Solent 13; Strathclyde 12, (Int Bus Lang) 6; Sunderland 20; Surrey (Bus Mgt) 6; Swansea (Inst) 7; Teesside (Bus St) 4; Thames Valley 4; Warwick 22; West Scotland 5; Westminster 12; Winchester 4; Wolverhampton 7; York 7; York St John 3.

Advice to applicants and planning the UCAS personal statement There are many different kinds of businesses and any work experience is almost essential for these courses. This should be described in detail: for example, size of firm, turnover, managerial problems, sales and marketing aspects, customers' attitudes. Any special interests in business management should also be included, for example, personnel work, purchasing, marketing. Give details of travel or work experience abroad and, for international courses, language expertise and examples of leadership and organising skills. Reference can be made to any particular business topics you have studied in the *Financial Times*, *The Economist* and the business sections in the weekend press. Don't say 'I enjoy socialising with my friends'. **Bournemouth** (Adv Mark Comm) Focus required on marketing. **Cardiff (UWIC)** Applicants need to be sociable, ambitious, team players. **Derby** (Int Bus) Interest in working outside the UK or with a multinational company. Students need an understanding of the objectives and practice of the EU. **Leeds** Mention your interests and ambitions. **Salford** Tell us why you are interested in the course, identify your academic strengths, your personal strengths and interests. **Staffordshire** Applicants with two A-levels contact the Business School. **Surrey** Further information could be obtained from the Chartered Institute of Public Relations, the Chartered Institute of Marketing and the Chartered Institute of Personnel and Development. **Warwick** One year preparatory courses for non-EU students failing to get the right grades. See **Appendix 2**; see also **Accountancy/Accounting**.

Misconceptions about this course **Aberystwyth** Students are unaware that the course addresses practical aspects of business. **Aston** (Int Bus Fr) Not two separate disciplines – the two subjects are integrated involving the study of language in a business and management context. **Loughborough** (Pub Engl) That this is a course in Journalism: it is not! **Salford** (Mgt Sci) Students should appreciate that the courses are fairly mathematical. **York** A previous study of management, IT or languages at A-level is necessary.

Selection interviews **Yes** Abertay Dundee, Birmingham City, Bradford, Carmarthenshire (Coll), Coventry, Doncaster (Coll), Durham, Edge Hill, Euro Bus Sch London, Glamorgan, Glasgow Caledonian, Hull, Kent (mature and Access students), Lampeter, London Met, Middlesex, Northumbria, Nottingham Trent, Plymouth, Robert Gordon, Roehampton, Sheffield Hallam, Strathclyde, Swansea, Teesside, Thames Valley, Warwick, West Thames (Coll), York; **Some** Aberystwyth, Anglia Ruskin, Bath, Blackpool and Fylde (Coll), Brighton, Buckingham, Cardiff (UWIC), Chichester, City, De Montfort, Derby (Int Bus), East Anglia, Greenwich, Kent, Leeds, Lincoln, Liverpool John Moores, Manchester Met, Salford, South Kent (Coll), Staffordshire, Stirling, Sunderland, Winchester, Wolverhampton.

Interview advice and questions Any work experience you describe on the UCAS form probably will be the focus of questions which could include topics covering marketing, selling, store organisation and management and customer problems. Personal qualities are naturally important in a career in business, so be ready for such questions as: What qualities do you have which are suitable and important for this course? Describe your strengths and weaknesses. Why should we give you a place on this course? Is advertising fair? What qualities does a person in business require to be successful? What makes a good manager? What is a cash-flow system? What problems can it cause? How could supermarkets improve customer relations? **Int Bus courses** Why can you be expected to be sent to China by your company when you only have French as a second language? Do you consider that knowing a foreign language makes you a good international manager? **Buckingham** Why Business? How do you see yourself in five years' time? Have you had any work experience? If so, discuss. **Loughborough** (Pub Engl) No tests at interview. We seek students with an interest in information issues within society. **Manchester Met** (Fash Buy) Be able to discuss in detail experience working with a fashion retailer. Knowledge of garment manufacture an advantage. **Wolverhampton** Mature students with no qualifications will be asked about their work experience. See also **Chapter 7**.

Applicants' impressions (A=Open day; B=Interview day) Bath Spa (A; Bus St Media Comm) There was a tour of the campus, a talk on student finance and a chance to talk to the subject lecturers. **Exeter** (A; Bus Mgt) The open day included a talk by a business expert. We then toured the campus and spoke to the students. **Portsmouth** (A; 1) There were no interviews, but a lot of good information on the induction course structure and good supporting information. (A; 2) I was sent a map of buildings and a plan of activities for the day. Most of the day was spent in the lecture theatre listening to talks, by the end of which everyone wanted to go home. It would have been useful to have a variety of activities and a tour of the campus. (A; 3) Coach tour round Portsmouth. Brief presentation. Tour of halls and departments. Free lunch and a chance to ask questions. (A; 4) A really good day with talks on the course, finance and the grades needed. There was also an opportunity to talk to current students. This was very encouraging and gave a better insight into the course and made it more appealing. **Reading** (A) The open day consisted of a talk about the course and a tour of the halls, facilities and union. **Surrey** (A) We met lecturers and were given an overview of the course and shown round the campus by a student. We didn't get to see the accommodation which would have been useful. **Warwickshire (Coll)** (B) There was an informal interview about my career plans and what the college expected of me. **Winchester** (A; Bus Media) We had a campus tour, a one-hour talk on finance and a meeting with subject tutors. There was a lot of friendly, good advice.

Reasons for rejection (non-academic) Hadn't read the prospectus. Lack of communication skills. Limited commercial interest. Weak on numeracy and problem-solving. Lack of interview preparation (no questions). Lack of outside interests. Inability to cope with a year abroad. The candidate brought his parent who answered all the questions. **Aberystwyth** Would have trouble fitting into the unique environment of Aberystwyth. Casual approach to learning. **Bournemouth** The Business Studies course is very popular. **Surrey** Hesitation about the period abroad. See also **Marketing**.

AFTER-RESULTS ADVICE
Offers to applicants repeating A-levels Higher Bradford, Bristol UWE, Brunel, Greenwich, Hertfordshire, Kingston, Lancaster, Liverpool, Manchester Met, St Andrews, Sheffield, Strathclyde, Teesside; **Same** Aberystwyth, Anglia Ruskin, Aston, Bath, Birmingham City, Blackpool and Fylde (Coll), Bournemouth, Brighton, Buckingham, Cardiff, Cardiff (UWIC), Chester, Chichester, De Montfort, Derby, Durham, East Anglia, Gloucestershire, Huddersfield, Hull, Kent, Leeds, Lincoln, Liverpool Hope, Liverpool John Moores, Llandrillo Cymru (Coll), Loughborough, Northumbria, Oxford Brookes, Richmond (Am Int Univ), Robert Gordon, Roehampton, Royal (CAg), St Mary's (UC), Salford, Sheffield Hallam, Staffordshire, Stirling, Sunderland, Suffolk (Univ Campus), Surrey, Thames Valley, Ulster, Winchester, Wolverhampton, Worcester, York, York St John; **Rare** Queen Margaret, Warwick.

GRADUATE DESTINATIONS AND EMPLOYMENT (2005/6 HESA)
Graduates surveyed 13195 **Employed** 8380 **In further study** 885 **Assumed unemployed** 860.
Publishing graduates surveyed 175 **Employed** 120 **In further study** 10 **Assumed unemployed** 10.

Career note The majority of graduates enter trainee management roles in business-related and administrative careers, many specialising in some of the areas listed below. In 2005/6 the main graduate destinations were in finance, property development, wholesale, retail and manufacturing.

OTHER DEGREE SUBJECTS FOR CONSIDERATION

Accountancy; Banking; Business Information Technology; E-Business; Economics; Estate Management; Finance; Hospitality Management; Housing Management; Human Resource Management; Insurance; Leisure Management; Logistics; Marketing; Public Administration; Retail Management; Sports Management; Surveying; Transport Management; Tourism.

CHEMISTRY

There is a shortage of applicants for this subject despite the fact that it is the basis of a wide range of careers in the manufacturing industries. These focus on such areas as pharmaceuticals, medicine, veterinary science and health, agriculture, petroleum, cosmetics, plastics, the food industry, colour chemistry and aspects of the environment such as pollution and recycling.

Useful websites www.rsc.org; www.NewScientistJobs.com/careersguide2007; www.chem.ox.ac.uk/vrchemistry.

NB The points totals shown to the left of the institutions are for ease of reference only. It must not be assumed that tariff points are always used by institutions or that they can be substituted for an offer in grades. The level of an offer is not necessarily indicative of the quality of a course.

COURSE OFFERS INFORMATION

Subject requirements/preferences GCSE English, mathematics/science subjects usually required. A/B grades often stipulated by popular universities. **AL** Two science subjects including chemistry required. **NB** A* grades are likely to form part of university offers in the higher ranges for students applying for places in 2008 for entry in 2009: check websites.

Your target offers

360 pts **and above**

Cambridge – AAA (Nat Sci (Chem)) *(IB 38–42 pts)*

Durham – AAA (Nat Sci (Chem))

London (UCL) – ABBe–BBBe (Chem courses) *(IB 32–36 pts)*

Oxford – Offers vary eg AAA–AAB (Chemistry) *(IB 38–42 pts)*

350 pts **Southampton** – BBBb–BBCc (BSc Chem; Chem Medcnl Sci; Chem Ocn Earth Sci)

340 pts **Cardiff** – AAB–BBB (MChem Chem; Chem Ind; Chem Abrd) *(IB 30pts)*

Edinburgh – AAB 2nd yr entry (Chem Phys Ind)

Manchester – AAB–ABC (Chem; Chem Ind Exp; Chem Euro/N Am; Chem Bus Mgt; Chem Pat Law; Medcnl Chem) *(IB 32–35 pts)*

Sheffield – AAB–ABB (Chem Chem Eng)

320 pts **Bristol** – ABB–BBC (Cheml Phys; Chem courses)

Durham – ABB–BBB (MChem Chem; Chem Ind; Chem Int)

East Anglia – ABB (MChem Chem N Am; Chem Ind; Chem Analyt Foren Sci; Chem Euro; Biol Medcnl Chem; Env Chem) *(IB 32–33 pts)*

Imperial London – AAB–ABB (MSci/BSc Chem; Chem Rsch Abrd; Chem Mgt; Chem Cons Sci; Chem Fr Sci; Chem Fn Cheml Proc; Chem Medcnl Chem; Chem Ind)

Leeds – ABB (Nanotechnology)

Newcastle – ABB (MChem Chem courses) *(IB 32 pts)*

Nottingham – ABB–BBB (Chem Mol Phys; Chem Ind; Medcnl Biol Chem) *(IB 32 pts)*

St Andrews – ABB 2nd yr entry (Chem courses) *(IB 31–34 pts)*

Sussex – ABB (MChem Chem; Chem Foren Sci)

Strathclyde – ABB–AAC (Foren Analyt Chem; App Chem Chem Eng; Chem Drug Dscvry)

Warwick – 320–350 pts (Chem; Chem Mgt; Chem Medcnl Chem; Biomed Chem; Chem Biol) *(IB 34 pts)*

300 pts **Aston** – 300 pts (MChem Chem courses; Biol Chem)

Bath – BBB–ABB 300–320 pts (Chem; Chem Mgt; Chem Drug Dscvry) *(IB 34 pts)*

Birmingham – BBB–BBC (Chem; Chem Analyt Sci; Chem Bio-org Chem; Chem Fr; Chem Euro; Chem Abrd; Chem Bus Mgt; Chem Env Sci; Chem Pharmacol; Chem Psy) *(IB 31 pts)*

Cardiff – BBB–BBC 300–280 pts (BSc Chem courses)

Dundee – 300 pts 1st yr entry (Pharml Chem 3yrs)

East Anglia – BBB (BSc Chem; Chem N Am; Chem Analyt Sci; Biol Medcnl Chem; Env Chem; Chem Phys) *(IB 31–33 pts)*

Edinburgh – BBB (Chem; Chem Analyt Chem; Chem Col Sci)

Leeds – BBB (Chem courses except under **320 pts**; Chem joint courses; Medcnl Chem) *(IB 30 pts H chem 6 pts)*

Queen's Belfast – BBB–BBCb (Medcnl Chem; MSci Chem) *(IB 30 pts H655)*

St Andrews – BBB 1st yr entry (Chem Geosci; Chem Comp Sci; Chem Fr/Ger/Span; Chem Sci) *(IB 31–34 pts)*

Sheffield – BBB (Chem Comput Drug Des; Chem Ent Mgt; Chem Ind; Chem Euro; Chem Maths; Chem Jap; Chem USA) *(IB 29–35 pts)*

Sussex – BBB (BSc Chem; Chem Foren Sci) *(IB 32 pts)*

York – BBB (Chem; Chem Biol Medcnl Chem; Chem Mgt Ind; Chem Res Env) *(IB 32 pts)*

290 pts Leicester – 290–320 pts (MChem Chem; Chem USA; Chem Euro)

Reading – 290–320 pts (MChem Chem courses)

280 pts Bangor – 280–340 pts (MChem Chem)

Glasgow – BBC–CCC (Chem; Chem Foren St; Chem Medcnl Chem; Chem Maths; Chem Euro) *(IB 28 pts)*

Liverpool – 280 pts (Chem Nano; MChem Chem; Chem Bus St; Chem Ind; Medcnl Chem Pharmacol) *(IB 28–32 pts)*

London (QM) – 280 pts (Pharml Chem)

Loughborough – 280 pts (MChem: Chem Analyt Chem; Medcnl Pharml Chem; Chem Foren Analys; Chem Spo Sci; Chem IT) *(IB 30 pts)*

Newcastle – BBC (BSc Chem courses)

Northumbria – 280 pts (MChem Chem)

Strathclyde – BBC (Chem; Chem Teach) *(IB 28 pts)*

260 pts Aberdeen – 260 pts (MChem Chem) *(IB 30 pts)*

Bradford – BCC 260 pts (Chem Pharml Foren Sci)

Dundee – 260 pts 2nd yr entry (Pharm Chem)

Heriot-Watt – BCC 2nd yr entry (Chem courses)

Kent – 260 pts (Foren Chem)

Northumbria – 260 pts (Chem Foren Chem; Chem Biomed Sci; Pharm Chem; App Chem)

Nottingham – BCC (Chem courses except under **320 pts**)

Plymouth – 260–300 pts (Analyt Chem)

Queen's Belfast – BCC–CCC (BSc Chem) *(IB 28 pts)*

Reading – 260–290 pts (BSc Chem courses)

Surrey – BCC–CCC 260–240 pts (MChem Chem; Chem Foren Invstg; Medcnl Chem; Comp Aid Chem) *(IB 30 pts)*

240 pts Aberdeen – CCC (BSc Chem; Env Chem; Med Chem)

Aston – 240–280 pts (App Chem; Chem courses)

Hull – CCC–BBB 240–300 pts (Chem courses)

Leicester – CCC (BSc Chem) *(IB 30–28 pts)*

Loughborough – 240 pts (BSc Chem: Chem Analyt Chem; Chem Foren Analys; Chem Spo Sci; Medcnl Pharml Chem; Chem IT)

220 pts Bangor – 220–280 pts (BSc Chem; Env Chem; Mar Chem; Chem Euro; Chem Ind; Chem Comp Sci; Chem Biomol Sci)

Glamorgan – 220–260 pts (Chem; Chem Biol)

Heriot-Watt – CCD 220 pts 1st yr entry (Chem courses)

Keele – 220–260 pts (Chem courses) *(IB 26–28 pts)*

Liverpool John Moores – 220–240 pts (Pharml Chem)

Plymouth – 220 pts (App Chem)

200 pts **Brighton** – 200 pts (Pharm Chem Sci)

Kingston – 200–260 pts (MChem Chem; Chem Ind; App Chem; Chem Hum Biol; Chem Bus; Medcnl Chem)

Nottingham Trent – 200 pts (Chem courses; Pharm Medcnl Sci)

Sunderland – 200 pts (Chem Pharml Sci)

180 pts **Greenwich** – 180 pts (Chem; Pharm Chem; Analyt Chem)

160 pts **Huddersfield** – 160–280 pts (Chem; Chem Ind)

Liverpool John Moores – 160 pts (Medcnl Chem)

London Met – 160 pts (Chem; Biol Medcnl Chem)

Manchester Met – 160–220 pts (Chem; Chem Euro; Medcnl Biol Chem; Analyt Chem; Foren Chem) *(IB 24 pts)*

140 pts **Teesside** – 140–200 pts (Foren Chem)

120 pts **London Arts** – 120 pts (Cos Sci)

London Met – 120 pts (Cos Sci)

West Scotland – DD **or** bbc (Chem; Medcnl Chem)

80 pts **London (Birk)** – 80 pts under 21s (over 21s varies) (p/t Chemistry)

Alternative offers

See **Chapter 8** for grade/point equivalences and related information for the following examinations: Scottish qualifications, the Welsh Baccalaureate, the IB diploma (approximate points shown also in italics in the table of offers), the Irish Leaving Certificate, the European Baccalaureate and the French Baccalaureate.

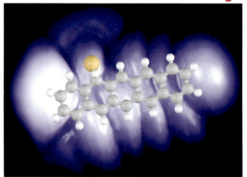
For a quick reference offers calculator, fold out the inside back cover.

EXAMPLES OF FOUNDATION DEGREES IN THE SUBJECT FIELD
Nottingham Trent; Sunderland City (Coll).

CHOOSING YOUR COURSE (SEE ALSO CH.1)
Course variations – Widen your options
Environmental Chemistry (Bangor)
Marine Chemistry (Bangor)
Pharmaceutical Chemistry (East Anglia)
Chemistry with Conservation Science (Imperial London)
Medicinal Chemistry and Music (Keele)
Colour and Polymer Chemistry (Leeds)
Chemistry and Archaeology (Reading)
Medicinal Chemistry (Surrey)
CHECK PROSPECTUSES AND WEBSITES FOR OTHER UNIVERSITIES AND COLLEGES OFFERING THESE COURSES.

Universities and colleges teaching quality See www.qaa.ac.uk; www.unistats.com.

Top universities and colleges (Research) Bristol*; Cambridge*; Cardiff; Durham*; East Anglia; Edinburgh; Imperial London*; Leeds; Liverpool; London (UCL)*; Manchester; Nottingham; Oxford*; St Andrews; Sheffield; Southampton; Sussex; Warwick; York.

Sandwich degree courses Aston; Bangor; Bath; Bradford; Cardiff; Coventry; Glamorgan; Huddersfield; Kingston; Leicester; Liverpool John Moores; Loughborough; Manchester; Northumbria; Nottingham Trent; Plymouth; Queen's Belfast; St Andrews; Surrey; Teesside; West Scotland.

ADMISSIONS INFORMATION
Number of applicants per place (approx) Bangor (Mar Chem) 3, (Chem) 6; Bradford (Chem Pharm Foren Sci) 10; Bristol 5; Durham 6; Edinburgh 5; Glasgow Caledonian 4; Heriot-Watt 6; Hull 7; Imperial London 3; Kingston 4; Leeds 3; London (QM) 3, (UCL) 5; Newcastle 5; Nottingham (Chem Mol Phys) 4, (Chem) 8; Oxford (success rate 63%); Southampton 12; Surrey 3; York 5.

Advice to applicants and planning the UCAS personal statement Extend your knowledge beyond your exam studies by reading scientific journals and keeping abreast of scientific developments in the news. Discuss any visits to chemical firms and laboratories, for example, pharmaceutical, food science, rubber and plastic, paper, photographic, environmental health. **Bath** We look for good communication skills, a positive personality and a mature outlook. **St Andrews** Reasons for choosing the course and evidence of interest. Sport and extra-curricular activities, positions of responsibility. **Sheffield** Some students feel that they should be doing a similar number of lectures as their friends doing Arts courses without realising just how much time Arts students are required to be in the library or studying at home. Some students are not prepared for the freedom they enjoy at university and, without the pressure of parents, they fall behind in their work. Often it is the ones who have had less parental pressure that perform the best because they are self-motivated. **Southampton** We value the individuality of students. The style of personal statement should reflect this. **Surrey** We look for work experience, language skills, travel, computing, business experience. See also **Appendix 2**.

Misconceptions about this course Many students do not fully appreciate the strengths of a chemistry degree for ANY career despite the fact that graduates regularly go into a diverse range of careers. **Durham** Students fail to realise that they require mathematics and that physics is useful.

Selection interviews Yes Bangor, Bath, Bristol, Cambridge, Coventry, Durham, East Anglia, Glasgow Caledonian, Greenwich, Huddersfield, Hull, Keele (mature students only), Kingston, London (UCL), London Met, London South Bank, Loughborough, Newcastle, Northumbria, Nottingham, Nottingham Trent, Oxford (success rate 66%), Sheffield, Southampton, Surrey, Warwick, York; **Some** Aston, Cardiff, Dundee, East Anglia, Liverpool John Moores, Plymouth.

Interview advice and questions Be prepared for questions on your chemistry syllabus and aspects that you enjoy the most. In the past a variety of questions have been asked, for example: Why is carbon a special element? Discuss the nature of forces between atoms with varying intermolecular distances. Describe recent practicals. What is acid rain? What other types of pollution are caused by the human race? What is an enzyme? What are the general properties of benzene? Why might sciences be less popular among girls at school? What can a mass spectrometer be used for? What would you do if a river turned bright blue and you were asked how to test a sample? What would be the difference between metal and non-metal pollution? **Bath** Why Chemistry? Discuss the practical work you are doing. **Oxford** Evidence required of motivation and further potential and a capacity to analyse and use information to form opinions and a willingness to discuss them. **York** Discuss your favourite areas of chemistry, some of your extracurricular activities, your preferred learning styles – for example, small tutorials of four or fewer, lectures. See also **Chapter 7**.

Applicants' impressions (A=Open day; B=Interview day) Aston (A) We had a talk by members of staff, a tour of the campus with students and a group interview. **Bristol** (B) We had a short talk about the course, lunch, tour and an informal 15-minute interview. Quite useful. **London (UCL)** (B) Short tour and lunch, followed by an informal interview. It was useful to see the department. **Nottingham** (B) We had a tour of the campus and department, lunch, a talk on the course and an informal interview. **Nottingham Trent** (B) There was a tour of the department, interview and a chance to talk to students. **Southampton** (A) There was a tour and a very informal interview (really only a chance to ask questions). (B) A tour of department, halls, lunch, talk with current students, followed by an informal interview.

Reasons for rejection (non-academic) Didn't attend interview. Rude and unco-operative. Arrived under influence of drink. Poor attitude and poor commitment to chemistry. Incomplete, inappropriate, illegible, illiterate personal statements. **Southampton** Applicants called for interview are not normally rejected.

AFTER-RESULTS ADVICE

Offers to applicants repeating A-levels Higher Bangor, Dundee, Hull, Leeds, Loughborough, Northumbria, Nottingham, St Andrews, Warwick; **Possibly higher** Coventry, East Anglia, Edinburgh, Newcastle; **Same** Aston, Bath, Bristol (no offer if first-time grades are low), Cardiff, Derby, Durham, East Anglia, Greenwich, Heriot-Watt, Huddersfield, Keele, Kingston, Liverpool John Moores, London (UCL), London Met, Plymouth, Robert Gordon, Sheffield, Surrey; **No offers made** Cambridge.

GRADUATE DESTINATIONS AND EMPLOYMENT (2005/6 HESA)

Graduates surveyed 1790 **Employed** 710 **In further study** 655 **Assumed unemployed** 110.

Career note A large number of chemistry graduates chose to go on to further study as well as into scientific careers in research, analysis or development. Significant numbers also follow careers in a wide range of areas in management, teaching and retail work.

OTHER DEGREE SUBJECTS FOR CONSIDERATION

Agriculture; Biochemistry; Biological Sciences; Biomedical Science; Chemical Engineering; Environmental Science; Forensic Science; Genetics; Materials Science; Medicine; Microbiology; Oceanography; Pharmacology; Pharmacy.

CHINESE

(including **Korean;** see also **Asia-Pacific Studies, Business Courses** and **Languages**)

Oriental languages are not necessarily difficult languages but they differ considerably in their writing systems which present their own problems for the new student. Even so, Chinese is not a language to be chosen for its novelty and students should have a strong interest in China and its people. It is a country with a high economic growth rate and there are good opportunities for graduates, an increasing number being recruited by firms based in East Asia. Other opportunities exist in diplomacy, aid work and tourism throughout China, Taiwan and Mongolia as well as most non-scientific career areas in the UK.

Useful websites www.cilt.org.uk; www.iol.org.uk; www.bbc.co.uk/languages; www.chinaonline.com; www.china.org.cn/english; www.languageadvantage.com; www.languagematters.co.uk; www.reed.co.uk/multilingual; www.chinadaily.com.cn.

NB The points totals shown to the left of the institutions are for ease of reference only. It must not be assumed that tariff points are always used by institutions or that they can be substituted for an offer in grades. The level of an offer is not necessarily indicative of the quality of a course.

COURSE OFFERS INFORMATION

Subject requirements/preferences GCSE A language is required. **AL** A modern language is usually required. **NB** A* grades are likely to form part of university offers in the higher ranges for students applying for places in 2008 for entry in 2009: check websites.

Your target offers

360 pts **and above**
        Cambridge – AAA (Orntl St (Chin St)) *(IB 38–42 pts)*
        Oxford – Offers vary eg AAA–AAB (Chinese) *(IB 38–42 pts)*

340 pts **Birmingham** – AAB–ABB (Int Bus Chin)

320 pts **Newcastle** – ABB–BBB (Chin/Jap Cult St; Chin Comb Hons; Ling Jap Chin) *(IB 32 pts)*

300 pts **Edinburgh** – BBB (Chin; Econ Chin; Hist Art Chin St) *(IB 34 pts H555)*
        Manchester – BBB–BBC (Chin courses) *(IB 35–33 pts)*
        Sheffield – BBB–BBC (Chin St Mgt; Chin St Fr/Ger/Jap/Russ/Span; E As St Hist (Chin); Mus Chin St; Kor St courses)

280 pts **Leeds** – BBC **or** Bbbcc (Chin courses)
        London (SOAS) – BBC 280 pts (Chin courses; Kor courses) *(IB 32 pts)*
        Nottingham – BBC (Contemp Chin St; Am St Chin St; Econ St Chin St; Film TV St Chin St; Geog Chin St; Mgt Chin St; Fr Contemp Chin St)

240 pts **Central Lancashire** – 240–280 pts (Bus Mgt Chin)
        Westminster – 240–280 pts (Chin joint courses)

200 pts **Sheffield Hallam** – 200 pts (Int Bus Chin)

180 pts **Lampeter** – 180 pts (Chin St Anth; Chin St Arch; Chin St Class St; Chin St Engl; Chin St Phil; Chin St Relig St; Chin St Welsh St)
        Liverpool John Moores – 180–200 pts (Int Bus St Chin; App Langs (Fr Chin) (Span Chin); Tour Leis Chin; PR Chin)

160 pts **Central Lancashire** – 160 pts (Chin Comb courses)
        London (Birk) – check with admissions tutor (Chin Hist Art; Chin Ling)

Alternative offers

See **Chapter 8** for grade/point equivalences and related information for the following examinations: Scottish qualifications, the Welsh Baccalaureate, the IB diploma (approximate points shown also in italics in the table of offers), the Irish Leaving Certificate, the European Baccalaureate and the French Baccalaureate.

CHOOSING YOUR COURSE (SEE ALSO CH.1)

Course variations – Widen your options
Business and Management in China (Central Lancashire)
Public Relations and Chinese (Liverpool John Moores)
Tourism and Leisure and Chinese (Liverpool John Moores)
Chinese and Japanese (Manchester)
Traditional Chinese Medicine (Middlesex)
Korean Studies and Management (Sheffield)
CHECK PROSPECTUSES AND WEBSITES FOR OTHER UNIVERSITIES AND COLLEGES OFFERING THESE COURSES.

Universities and colleges teaching quality See www.qaa.ac.uk; www.unistats.com.

Sandwich degree courses Westminster.

For information on how to read the Subject Tables, see **Chapter 8**.

ADMISSIONS INFORMATION

Number of applicants per place (approx) Leeds 5; London (SOAS) 8; Westminster 18.

Advice to applicants and planning the UCAS personal statement It will be necessary to demonstrate a knowledge of China, its culture, political and economic background. Visits to the Far East should be mentioned, with reference to any features which have influenced your choice of degree course. See also **Appendix 2** under **Languages**.

Selection interviews Yes Cambridge, Leeds, London (SOAS), Oxford.

Interview advice and questions You will be expected to convince the admissions tutor why you wish to study the language. Your knowledge of Chinese culture, politics and society in general, and of Far Eastern problems, could also be tested. See also **Chapter 7**.

Reasons for rejection (non-academic) Oxford His language background seemed a little weak and his written work not as strong as that of other applicants. At interview he showed himself to be a dedicated hard-working young man but lacking in the imagination, flexibility and the intellectual liveliness needed to succeed on the course.

AFTER-RESULTS ADVICE

Offers to applicants repeating A-levels Higher Leeds; **No offers made** Cambridge.

GRADUATE DESTINATIONS AND EMPLOYMENT (2005/6 HESA)

Graduates surveyed 65 **Employed** 35 **In further study** 16 **Assumed unemployed** 10.

Career note See **Languages**.

OTHER DEGREE SUBJECTS FOR CONSIDERATION

Traditional Chinese Medicine; other Oriental languages.

CLASSICAL STUDIES/CLASSICAL CIVILISATION

(see also **Archaeology, Classics** and **History (Ancient)**)

Classical Studies and Classical Civilisation courses cover the literature, history, philosophy and archaeology of Ancient Greece and Rome. A knowledge of Latin or Greek is not necessary for many courses.

Useful websites www.britishmuseum.org; see also **History** and **History (Ancient)**.

NB The points totals shown to the left of the institutions are for ease of reference only. It must not be assumed that tariff points are always used by institutions or that they can be substituted for an offer in grades. The level of an offer is not necessarily indicative of the quality of a course.

COURSE OFFERS INFORMATION

Subject requirements/preferences GCSE English and a foreign language often required. **AL** A modern language is required for joint language courses. Relevant subjects include classical civilisation, English literature, archaeology, Latin, Greek. **NB** A* grades are likely to form part of university offers in the higher ranges for students applying for places in 2008 for entry in 2009: check websites.

Your target offers

360 pts Warwick – AAB–ABBb (Phil Class Civ; Class Civ) *(IB 36–32 pts)*
340 pts Exeter – AAB–BBB 340–300 pts (Class St; Class St Engl/Fr/Ger/Ital/Russ/Span; Class St Phil; Class St Theol) *(IB 34–30 pts)*
　　　　St Andrews – AAB (Class St courses) *(IB 36 pts)*
320 pts Bristol – ABB (Class St; Class St Euro; Class St Phil; Engl Class St) *(IB 34 pts)*
　　　　Durham – ABB (Class Past; Class Past Euro St)

Glasgow – ABB–BBB (Class Civ courses) *(IB 30 pts)*
London (UCL) – ABB+AS (Anc Wrld St)
Manchester – ABB–ABC (Class St; Class Civ Art Hist courses)
Newcastle – ABB (Class St courses) *(IB 32 pts)*
Nottingham – ABB (Class Civ Engl St)

300 pts Edinburgh – BBB (Class St)
Leeds – BBB (Class Civ; Rom Civ courses; Gk Civ courses)
London (King's) – BBB+AS **or** BBbbc (Class St courses) *(IB 32 pts)*
London (RH) – BBB 300 pts (Class St; Engl Class St; Class St Fr; Class St Ger; Class St Ital; Class St Dr) *(IB 32 pts)*
Nottingham – ABC–BBB (Class Civ; Class Civ Fr/Ger; Class Civ Phil)

280 pts Birmingham – 280 pts (Class Lit Civ; Anth Class Lit Civ) *(IB 30 pts)*
Liverpool – BBC 280 pts (Class St; Class St Modn Lang) *(IB 30 pts)*
Reading – 280 pts (Class St courses) *(IB 30 pts)*

260 pts Kent – 260–280 pts (Class Arch St; Dr Thea Class Arch St; Engl Am Lit Class Arch St; Class Arch St Comp; Class Arch St Hist Phil Art)
Swansea – 260–300 pts (Class Civ joint courses; Egypt Class Civ)

180 pts Lampeter – 180 pts (Class St courses)
Roehampton – 180–200 pts (Class Civ courses)

80 pts London (Birk) – 80 pts for under 21s (over 21s varies) (p/t Class St)

Alternative offers

See **Chapter 8** for grade/point equivalences and related information for the following examinations: Scottish qualifications, the Welsh Baccalaureate, the IB diploma (approximate points shown also in italics in the table of offers), the Irish Leaving Certificate, the European Baccalaureate and the French Baccalaureate.

CHOOSING YOUR COURSE (SEE ALSO CH.1)

Course variations – Widen your options

Anthropology and Classical Literature and Civilisation (Birmingham)
Classical Studies and Study in Continental Europe (Bristol)
Classical Studies and Philosophy (Exeter)
Classical and Archaeological Studies (Kent)
Classical Studies and Ancient History (Lampeter)
Byzantine Studies (Queen's Belfast)
Egyptology and Classical Civilisation (Swansea)
CHECK PROSPECTUSES AND WEBSITES FOR OTHER UNIVERSITIES AND COLLEGES OFFERING THESE COURSES.

Universities and colleges teaching quality See www.qaa.ac.uk; www.unistats.com.

Top universities and colleges (Research) Bristol; Durham; Leeds; London (RH); Nottingham; Warwick.

ADMISSIONS INFORMATION

Number of applicants per place (approx) Birmingham 3; Bristol 10; Durham 15; Exeter 3; Lampeter 2; Leeds 7; London (RH) 4; Newcastle 8; Nottingham 10; Reading 10; Swansea 5; Warwick 23.

Advice to applicants and planning the UCAS personal statement Discuss any A-level work and what has attracted you to this subject. Describe visits to classical sites or museums and what impressed you. **Birmingham** (Class Lit Civ) The course is appropriate for students who enjoy books and the ideas behind them and who are fascinated by other cultures and different ways of observing the world. What do you most enjoy reading? **St Andrews** Reasons for choosing course. Evidence of interest. Sport/extra-curricular activities. Posts of responsibility.

Misconceptions about this course **Birmingham** (Class Lit Civ) A study of Classics at school is not necessary although while many people catch the classics bug by doing classical civilisation at A-level, others come to classics through reading the myths or seeing the plays and being fascinated by them. For others the interdisciplinary nature of the subject attracts them – literature, drama, history, politics and philosophy. **Exeter** (Class St) This is not a language degree. There is no requirement for either A-level Latin or Greek.

Selection interviews **Yes** Birmingham, Durham, Kent, Lampeter, London (RH), Newcastle, Nottingham, Warwick; **No** Bristol.

Interview advice and questions In the past questions have included: What special interests do you have in Classical Studies/Classics? Have you visited Greece, Rome or any other classical sites or museums and what were your impressions? These are the types of questions to expect, along with those to explore your knowledge of the culture, theatre and architecture of the period. **Birmingham** (Class Lit Civ) The programme includes some language study and, if applicants do not have a GCSE in a foreign language, we ask them to do a short language aptitude test. Interview questions are likely to focus on your reading interests (not necessarily classical texts!) and your own reflections on them. We are interested in your ability to think for yourself and we want to be sure that you are someone who will enjoy three years of reading and talking about books. **Swansea** Reasons for choosing the subject and how the student hopes to benefit from the course. See also **Chapter 7**.

Applicants' impressions (A=Open day; B=Interview day) **Birmingham** (A) A group talk about the course and tour was followed by individual interviews. **Exeter** (A) There was a lecture on gladiators, a tour, a lecture on the course and questions with current students and staff. **Warwick** (A) A talk about the course and finance, a tour of the campus and a question-and-answer session.

Reasons for rejection (non-academic) **Birmingham** Lukewarm interest in the subject. Lack of clear idea why they wanted to do this degree.

AFTER-RESULTS ADVICE

Offers to applicants repeating A-levels **Higher** Nottingham, St Andrews, Warwick; **Same** Birmingham, Bristol, Durham, Exeter, Leeds, London (RH), Newcastle.

GRADUATE DESTINATIONS AND EMPLOYMENT (2005/6 HESA)
Graduates surveyed 585 **Employed** 250 **In further study** 155 **Assumed unemployed** 30.

Career note As with other non-vocational subjects graduates enter a wide range of careers. In a small number of cases this may be subject-related with work in museums and art galleries. However, much will depend on how the student's interests develop during the undergraduate years and career planning should start early.

OTHER DEGREE SUBJECTS FOR CONSIDERATION
Archaeology; Ancient History; Classics; Greek; History; History of Art; Latin; Philosophy.

CLASSICS

(see also **Classical Studies/Classical Civilisation, Greek** and **Latin**)

Classics courses focus on a study of Greek and Latin but may also include topics related to ancient history, art and architecture, drama and philosophy. These subjects are also frequently offered in joint courses.

Useful websites www.classicspage.com; www.classics.ac.uk; www.cambridgescp.com. www.bbc.co.uk/history/ancient/greeks; www.bbc.co.uk/history/ancient/romans;

NB The points totals shown to the left of the institutions are for ease of reference only. It must not be assumed that tariff points are always used by institutions or that they can be substituted for an offer in grades. The level of an offer is not necessarily indicative of the quality of a course.

COURSE OFFERS INFORMATION

Subject requirements/preferences GCSE English and a foreign language usually required. Grades A*/A/B may be stipulated. **AL** Check courses for Latin/Greek requirements. **NB** A* grades are likely to form part of university offers in the higher ranges for students applying for places in 2008 for entry in 2009: check websites.

Your target offers

360 pts and above

    Cambridge – AAA (Class Gk Lat; Class Educ St; Modn Mediev Langs (Class Lat) (Class Gk)) *(IB 38–42 pts)*

    Oxford – Offers vary eg AAA–AAB (Class Engl; Class Modn Langs; Class I; Class II) *(IB 38–42 pts)*

340 pts Bristol – AAB–ABB (Class; Class Euro) *(IB 34–33 pts)*

    St Andrews – AAB (Class courses) *(IB 36 pts)*

320 pts Durham – ABB (Classics)

    Exeter – ABB–BBB (Classics)

    London (UCL) – ABB+AS–BBB+AS (Class; Class Abrd) *(IB 34 pts)*

    Newcastle – ABB–BBC (Classics) *(IB 32 pts)*

    Warwick – ABB–BBBc **or** AB–BBbbc (Classics) *(IB 36–32 pts)*

300 pts Edinburgh – BBB (Class; Class Engl Lang; Class Ling)

    Leeds – BBB (Classics)

    London (King's) – BBB+AS **or** BBbbc (Classics) *(IB 32 pts)*

    London (RH) – BBB 300 pts (Classics) *(IB 32 pts)*

    Manchester – BBB (Class; Class Anc Hist) *(IB 32 pts)*

    Nottingham – ABC–BBB (Class (Gk Lat))

280 pts Liverpool – BBC 280 pts (Classics) *(IB 30 pts)*

    Reading – 280 pts (Classics) *(IB 30 pts)*

260 pts Swansea – 260–300 pts (Classics)

180 pts Lampeter – 180 pts (Classics)

** 80 pts London (Birk)** – 80 pts for under 21s (over 21s varies) (p/t Classics)

Alternative offers

See **Chapter 8** for grade/point equivalences and related information for the following examinations: Scottish qualifications, the Welsh Baccalaureate, the IB diploma (approximate points shown also in italics in the table of offers), the Irish Leaving Certificate, the European Baccalaureate and the French Baccalaureate.

CHOOSING YOUR COURSE (SEE ALSO CH.1)

Course variations – Widen your options

Classics with Education Studies (Cambridge)

Classics: Greek and Latin (Cambridge)

Classics and English Language (Edinburgh)

Combined Honours (Liverpool)

Classics and Modern Languages (Oxford)
Classics and Philosophy (London (RH))
Classics and Management (St Andrews)
CHECK PROSPECTUSES AND WEBSITES FOR OTHER UNIVERSITIES AND COLLEGES OFFERING THESE COURSES.

Universities and colleges teaching quality See www.qaa.ac.uk; www.unistats.com.

Top universities and colleges (Research) (including Ancient History and Modern Greek Studies) Bristol; Cambridge*; Durham; Exeter; London (King's)*, (RH), (UCL)*; Manchester; Oxford*; Reading; St Andrews; Warwick.

ADMISSIONS INFORMATION

Number of applicants per place (approx) Bristol 12; Cambridge 2; Durham (Class) 8, (Class Past) 10; Lampeter 5; Leeds 4; London (King's) 6, (RH) 6; Newcastle 14; Nottingham 10; Oxford 2; Swansea 6.

Advice to applicants and planning the UCAS personal statement Describe any visits made to classical sites or museums, or literature which you have read and enjoyed. Discuss any significant aspects which impressed you. **Birmingham** Classics is an interdisciplinary subject and we are looking for people who are versatile, imaginative and independently minded, so all types of extra-curricular activities (drama, music, philosophy, creative arts, politics, other languages and cultures) will be relevant. See also **Classical Studies/Classical Civilisation**.

Misconceptions about this course While Classics can appear irrelevant and elitist, universities aim to assist students to leave with a range of transferable skills that are of importance to employers.

Selection interviews Yes Cambridge, London (RH), (UCL), Newcastle, Oxford, Swansea; **No** Durham, Leeds, St Andrews.

Interview advice and questions What do you think it means to study Classics? Do you think Classics is still a vital and central cultural discipline? What made you apply to study Classics at this university? There are often detailed questions on the texts which the students have read, to find out how reflective they are in their reading. **Cambridge** What would happen if the Classics department burned down? Do you think feminism is dead? 'Emma has become a different person since she took up yoga. Therefore she is not responsible for anything she did before she took up yoga'. Discuss. **Oxford** (Class Engl) What is fate? See also **Classical Studies/Classical Civilisation**. See also **Chapter 7**.

Applicants' impressions (A=Open day; B=Interview day) Oxford (B; Classics and English) There were two interviewers and a 30-minute interview. I felt nervous but not pressurised, the interviewers were rather detached and not particularly friendly. The questions related to English Literature – the sources of Chaucer's *The Miller's Tale* and Shakespeare's *A Midsummer Night's Dream*. I was also asked to comment on an unseen poem and asked several questions about my personal statement. I was able to meet a number of undergraduates and discussed student life in detail. I also attended an unofficial 'open day' hosted by the students which covered these topics in more detail.

Reasons for rejection (non-academic) Did not demonstrate a clear sense of why they wanted to study Classics rather than anything else.

AFTER-RESULTS ADVICE

Offers to applicants repeating A-levels Higher Leeds, Nottingham, St Andrews; **Same** Durham, Newcastle; Swansea; **No offers made** Cambridge.

GRADUATE DESTINATIONS AND EMPLOYMENT (2005/6 HESA)

See **Classical Studies/Classical Civilisation**.

Career note See **Classical Studies/Classical Civilisation**.

OTHER DEGREE SUBJECTS FOR CONSIDERATION

See **Classical Studies/Classical Civilisation**.

COMMUNICATION STUDIES/COMMUNICATIONS

(see also **Art and Design (General), Business Courses (Section C), Computer Courses, Engineering (Communications), Film, Radio, Video and TV Studies, Media Studies** and **Speech Pathology/Sciences/Therapy**)

Some courses combine academic and vocational studies, whilst others may be wholly academic or strictly vocational. The subject thus covers a very wide range of approaches concerning 'communication' which should be carefully researched before applying.

Useful websites www.camfoundation.com; www.coi.gov.uk; www.aejmc.org.

NB The points totals shown to the left of the institutions are for ease of reference only. It must not be assumed that tariff points are always used by institutions or that they can be substituted for an offer in grades. The level of an offer is not necessarily indicative of the quality of a course.

COURSE OFFERS INFORMATION

Subject requirements/preferences GCSE English and mathematics grade A–C may be required. **AL** No specific subjects required. **NB** A* grades are likely to form part of university offers in the higher ranges for students applying for places in 2008 for entry in 2009: check websites.

Your target offers

360 pts **and above**
　　　　　London (UCL) – AABe–BBBe (Sci Comm Pol)
340 pts **Liverpool** – AAB (Engl Comm St) *(IB 36 pts H Engl 7 pts)*
320 pts **London (Gold)** – ABB (Media Comm)
300 pts **Birmingham** – BBB 300 pts approx (Cult Soty Comm (Euro))
　　　　　Bournemouth – 300 pts (Adv Mark Comm; PR)
　　　　　Cardiff – BBB (ABB joint hons) (Comm; Engl Lang Comm) *(IB 32 pts)*
　　　　　Leeds – BBB (Comm St)
　　　　　Leicester – BBB 300 pts (Comm Media Soty) *(IB 30 pts)*
　　　　　Loughborough – BBB **or** BBbb (Comm Media St)
　　　　　Newcastle – BBB–BBC (Media Comm Cult St)
　　　　　Sheffield – BBB (Hum Comm Sci)
280 pts **Aberystwyth** – 280 pts (Media Comm St) *(IB 28 pts)*
　　　　　Birmingham City – 280 pts (Media Comm)
　　　　　Bournemouth – BBC 280 pts (Comm Media)
　　　　　De Montfort – 280 pts (Hum Comm (Sp Lang Thera))
　　　　　Liverpool – 280–300 pts (Comm Media Pop Mus; Comm Bus St; Pol Comm St) *(IB 30 pts)*
　　　　　London (King's) – BBC (Engl Lang Comm)
　　　　　London (RH) – BBC (Sci Comm courses)
　　　　　Manchester – BBC–BCC (Lang Litcy Comm)
　　　　　Oxford Brookes – BBC (Comm Media Cult)
260 pts **Brunel** – 260 pts (Comm Media St)
　　　　　Chester – 260 pts (Comm St courses) *(IB 30 pts)*
　　　　　Glasgow Caledonian – BCC (Media Comm)
　　　　　Huddersfield – 260 pts (Adv Mark Comm)
　　　　　Keele – 260 pts (Media Comm Cult courses)
　　　　　Northumbria – BCC 260 pts (Comm PR)
　　　　　Oxford Brookes – BCC (Publishing)
　　　　　Ulster – BCC 260 pts (Comm courses) *(IB 24 pts)*
240 pts **Abertay Dundee** – 240 pts (Corp Comm)
　　　　　Brighton – 240 pts (Comm Dig Media; Comm Media St) *(IB 30 pts)*
　　　　　Robert Gordon – CCC (Corp Comm; Comm PR)
220 pts **Bath Spa** – 220–260 pts (Media Comm courses)

Glamorgan – 220–260 pts (Comm Media)
Lincoln – 220–240 pts (Media Cult Comm courses)
Nottingham Trent – 220 pts (Media Comm Soty)
200 pts **Buckingham** – 200–240 pts (Comm Media St)
Chester – 200–240 pts (Mark Commun St)
Coventry – 200–260 pts (Comm Cult Media)
Gloucestershire – 200–260 pts (Mark Adv Comm)
Napier – 200 pts (Communication)
Southampton Solent – 200 pts (Media Comm)
180 pts **Anglia Ruskin** – 180–220 pts (Comm St courses)
Sheffield Hallam – 180–240 pts (Comm St)
160 pts **Canterbury Christ Church** – 160 pts (Comm St courses)
Central Lancashire – 160–200 pts (Fash Brnd Prom Jrnl; Comm St courses)
East London – 160 pts (Comm St)
Greenwich – CC 160 pts (Media Cult Comm)
London Met – 160–200 pts (Comm courses)
Manchester Met – 160 pts (Communication)
Middlesex – 160–200 pts (Comm Media St)
Wolverhampton – 160–220 pts (Media Comm St)
York St John – 160 pts (Comm courses)
140 pts **Richmond (Am Int Univ)** – 140 pts (Crea Arts Comm)

Leeds Met – contact University
Newman (UC) – contact the College

Alternative offers

See **Chapter 8** for grade/point equivalences and related information for the following examinations: Scottish qualifications, the Welsh Baccalaureate, the IB diploma (approximate points shown also in italics in the table of offers), the Irish Leaving Certificate, the European Baccalaureate and the French Baccalaureate.

EXAMPLES OF FOUNDATION DEGREES IN THE SUBJECT FIELD

Blackpool and Fylde (Coll); Derby; East Lancashire (IHE); Leicester; Oxford Brookes.

CHOOSING YOUR COURSE (SEE ALSO CH.1)

Course variations – Widen your options
Information and Library Studies (Aberystwyth)
Creative Writing and Media Communications (Bath Spa)
Advertising and Marketing Communications (Bedfordshire)
Media and Communications (Radio) (Birmingham City)
Public Relations (Central Lancashire)
Media Communications and Culture (Keele)
Islamic Studies and Media Studies (Lampeter)
Advertising (Lincoln)
Graphic and Media Design (London Arts)
Publishing (Loughborough)
CHECK PROSPECTUSES AND WEBSITES FOR OTHER UNIVERSITIES AND COLLEGES OFFERING THESE COURSES.

Universities and colleges teaching quality See www.qaa.ac.uk; www.unistats.com.

Top universities and colleges (Research) See **Media Studies**.

Sandwich degree courses Brighton; Brunel; De Montfort; London Met; Loughborough; Ulster.

ADMISSIONS INFORMATION

Number of applicants per place (approx) Brunel 9; Cardiff 6.

For a quick reference offers calculator, fold out the inside back cover.

Advice to applicants and planning the UCAS personal statement Applicants should be able to give details of any work experience/work shadowing/discussions they have had in the media including, for example, in newspaper offices, advertising agencies, local radio stations or film companies (see also **Media Studies**). **Huddersfield** Critical awareness. Willingness to develop a range of communication skills including new technologies. **London (Gold)** Interest in a study in depth of media theory plus some experience in media practice. **Manchester Met** Motivation more important than grades.

Selection interviews Yes Brighton, Brunel, Buckingham, Coventry, Glamorgan, Glasgow Caledonian, Leicester, London Met, Manchester Met, Middlesex, Southampton Solent, Ulster; **Some** Anglia Ruskin, Cardiff, Chester, Huddersfield (rarely), London (Gold) (mature students), Sheffield Hallam (mature students).

Interview advice and questions Courses vary in this subject and, depending on your choice, the questions will focus on the type of course, either biased towards the media, or towards human communication by way of language, psychology, sociology or linguistics. See also separate subject tables. See also **Chapter 7**.

Applicants' impressions (A=Open day; B=Interview day) Bournemouth (A) Applicants had a chance to wander round the campus (but not the accommodation since it was term time). There was a talk on Media and Communications courses, followed by questions and a guided tour with the students.

Reasons for rejection (non-academic) Unlikely to work well in groups. Poor writing. Misguided application, for example more practical work wanted. Poor motivation. Inability to give reasons for choosing the course. More practice needed in academic writing skills. Wrong course choice, wanted more practical work.

AFTER-RESULTS ADVICE
Offers to applicants repeating A-levels Possibly higher Coventry; **Same** Brunel, Cardiff, Chester, Huddersfield, Loughborough, Nottingham Trent, Richmond (Am Int Univ), Robert Gordon, Sheffield Hallam.

GRADUATE DESTINATIONS AND EMPLOYMENT (2005/6 HESA)
Graduates surveyed 210 **Employed** 120 **In further study** 20 **Assumed unemployed** 20.

Career note Graduates have developed a range of transferable skills in their courses which open up opportunities in several areas. There are obvious links with openings in the media, public relations and advertising.

OTHER DEGREE SUBJECTS FOR CONSIDERATION
Art and Design; Film, Radio, Video and TV Studies; Information Studies; Media Studies; Psychology.

COMMUNITY STUDIES

(see also **Health Sciences/Studies, Nursing and Midwifery** and **Social Work**)

These courses cover aspects of social problems, for example housing, food, health, the elderly, welfare rights and counselling. Work experience is very important. Most courses will lead to professional qualifications.

Useful websites www.csv.org.uk; www.infed.org/community.

NB The points totals shown to the left of the institutions are for ease of reference only. It must not be assumed that tariff points are always used by institutions or that they can be substituted for an offer in grades. The level of an offer is not necessarily indicative of the quality of a course.

For information on how to read the Subject Tables, see **Chapter 8**.

COURSE OFFERS INFORMATION

Subject requirements/preferences **GCSE** English and mathematics grade A–C may be required at some institutions. **AL** No specific subjects required. **Other** Minimum age 19 plus youth work experience for some courses. **NB** A* grades are likely to form part of university offers in the higher ranges for students applying for places in 2008 for entry in 2009: check websites.

Your target offers

320 pts **Birmingham** – ABB–BBB (Spo PE Commun St)

300 pts **Durham** – 300 pts (Sociol Commun – check with admissions tutor)

280 pts **Oxford Brookes** – BBC (Bus Perf Arts: Commun Educ)

240 pts **Bangor** – 240–280 pts (Commun Dev)

220 pts **Dundee** – 220 pts 2nd yr entry (Commun Educ) *(IB 29 pts)*
Gloucestershire – 220 pts (Hlth Commun Soc Cr courses)

200 pts **Coventry** – 200 pts (Soc Welf Commun St)
Manchester Met – 200 pts (Commun Arts courses)
Ulster – 200 pts (Commun Yth Wk)

180 pts **Bolton** – 180 pts (Commun St courses)
Bournemouth – 180 pts (Commun Wk)
Derby – 180 pts (App Commun Yth St)
Manchester Met – 180 pts (Yth Commun Wk)

160 pts **Cardiff (UWIC)** – 160 pts (Commun Educ)
Central Lancashire – 160 pts (Cr Commun Ctzn)
De Montfort – 160 pts (Yth Commun Dev)
Edinburgh – CC (Commun Educ)
Greenwich – 160 pts min (Educ Commun Dev)
Liverpool John Moores – CC (App Commun Soc St; Commun Hlth Soc Welf)
London (Gold) – CC (App Soc Sci Commun Dev Yth Wk)
London Met – 160 pts (Commun Sctr Mgt)
Newport – 160 pts (Yth Commun St)
Sheffield Hallam – CC (Community)
Strathclyde – CC (Commun Arts; Commun Educ)
Sunderland – 160 pts (Commun Yth Wk)

150 pts **Dundee** – 150 pts 1st yr entry (Commun Educ)

140 pts **Bishop Grosseteste (UC)** – 140 pts (Dr Commun)
Marjon (UC) – 140–200 pts (Commun Prac courses; Commun Wk; Yth Commun Wk)
Trinity Carmarthen (Coll) – 140 pts (Chr Commun St; Commun Dev; Yth Commun Wk)

120 pts **Huddersfield** – 120–140 pts (Hlth Commun St)
North East Wales (IHE) – 120–80 pts (Yth Commun St)

100 pts **Bradford (Coll)** – 100–140 pts (Yth Commun Dev)

80 pts **Canterbury Christ Church** – 80 pts (Inf Commun Educ)
Cumbria – 80 pts (Yth Commun Dev Wk)
East London – 80 pts (Educ Commun Dev)
Oxford Brookes – EE (Yth Commun Wk App Theol)
St Mary's (UC) – 80 pts (PE Commun courses)

Alternative offers

See **Chapter 8** for grade/point equivalences and related information for the following examinations: Scottish qualifications, the Welsh Baccalaureate, the IB diploma (approximate points shown also in italics in the table of offers), the Irish Leaving Certificate, the European Baccalaureate and the French Baccalaureate.

EXAMPLES OF FOUNDATION DEGREES IN THE SUBJECT FIELD

Bangor; Bradford; Bradford (Coll); Bury (Coll); De Montfort; Derby; Glamorgan; Grimsby (IFHE); Leeds Met; Newcastle (Coll); North East Wales (IHE); North Warwickshire (Coll); Truro (Coll); Winchester; Wolverhampton.

CHOOSING YOUR COURSE (SEE ALSO CH.1)

Course variations – Widen your options
Planning, Housing and Renewal (Bristol UWE)
Community Education (Edinburgh)
Crime and Community Justice (Huddersfield)
Community Development (London (Gold))
Community Arts (Manchester Met)
Youth Work (Nottingham Trent)
Primary and Community Health Care (Oxford Brookes)
Crime, Deviance, Society and Legal Studies (Staffordshire)
CHECK PROSPECTUSES AND WEBSITES FOR OTHER UNIVERSITIES AND COLLEGES OFFERING THESE COURSES.

Universities and colleges teaching quality See www.qaa.ac.uk; www.unistats.com.

ADMISSIONS INFORMATION

Number of applicants per place (approx) Bradford (Coll) 5; Liverpool John Moores 2; Manchester Met 8; Marjon (UC) 7; Strathclyde 6.

Advice to applicants and planning the UCAS personal statement You should describe any work you have done with people, particularly in a caring capacity, such as social work, or with the elderly or young children in schools, nursing, hospital work, youth work, community or charity work. You should also describe any problems arising when dealing with such people and how staff overcame these difficulties. **Derby** Experience and the ability to express oneself in written and spoken form. Relevant experience of work with the elderly or young people in the 11–25 age range. See **Appendix 2**.

Advice for overseas applicants Marjon (UC) Strong multi-cultural policy. English as a Foreign Language teaching offered.

Selection interviews Yes Bradford (Coll), Derby, Huddersfield (in groups), Manchester Met, Strathclyde; **Some** Liverpool John Moores.

Interview advice and questions This subject has a vocational emphasis and work experience, or even full-time work in the field, will be expected. Community work varies considerably so, depending on your experiences, you could be asked about the extent of your work and how you would solve the problems which occur. **Derby** Take us through your experience of youth and community work. What are the problems facing young people today? See also **Chapter 7**.

Reasons for rejection (non-academic) Insufficient experience. Lack of understanding of community and youth work. Uncertain career aspirations. Incompatibility with values, methods and aims of the course. No work experience.

AFTER-RESULTS ADVICE
Offers to applicants repeating A-levels Same Bradford (Coll), Liverpool John Moores, Marjon (UC).

GRADUATE DESTINATIONS AND EMPLOYMENT (2005/6 HESA)
See **Social Work**.

Career note Social and welfare areas of employment provide openings for those wishing to specialise in their chosen field of social work. Other opportunities will also exist in educational administration, leisure and outdoor activities.

OTHER DEGREE SUBJECTS FOR CONSIDERATION
Communication Studies; Education; Nursing; Politics; Psychology; Social Policy and Administration; Social Work; Sociology; Youth Studies.

COMPUTER COURSES

(including **Artificial Intelligence, Business Information Systems, Computer Networks, Computer Science, Digital Computing, E-Commerce, Information Technology, Technology, Virtual Reality** and **Web Management;** see also **Engineering (Computer, Control, Software and Systems)** and **Technology**)

Computer courses are extremely popular and provide graduates with very good career prospects. Courses vary in content and in the specialisations offered which may include software engineering, programming languages, artificial intelligence, data processing and graphics. Many universities offer sandwich placements in industry and commerce.

Useful websites www.bcs.org; www.intellectuk.org; www.e-skills.com; www.iap.org.uk.

NB The points totals shown to the left of the institutions are for ease of reference only. It must not be assumed that tariff points are always used by institutions or that they can be substituted for an offer in grades. The level of an offer is not necessarily indicative of the quality of a course.

COURSE OFFERS INFORMATION

Subject requirements/preferences GCSE Mathematics usually required. A*/A/B grades may be stipulated for some subjects. **AL** Mathematics, a science subject or computer science required for some courses. **Cambridge** (Churchill, Magdalene) Uses STEP as part of offers; (Gonville and Caius) AEA mathematics required (see **Chapter 7**). **NB** A* grades are likely to form part of university offers in the higher ranges for students applying for places in 2008 for entry in 2009: check websites.

Your target offers

360 pts and above

Cambridge – AAA (Comp Sci) *(IB 38–42 pts)*

Durham – AAA (Nat Sci (Comp Sci))

Imperial London – AAA (Maths Comp Sci)

Manchester – AAA (MEng: Comp Sci; Artif Intel; Soft Eng) *(IB 35–37 pts)*

Manchester – AAA–AAB (BSc: Comp Sci Ind; Comp Sci; Artif Intel; Comp Sci Maths; Comp Sci Bus Mgt; Comp Sci Soft Eng)

Oxford – Offers vary eg AAA–AAB (Comp Sci) *(IB 38–42 pts)*

Southampton – 390 pts (MEng Comp Sci; Comp Sci Artif Intel; Soft Eng) *(IB 33 pts)*

Strathclyde – AAA 2nd yr entry (MEng Comp Sci)

Warwick – AABb **or** AAbbb (Comp Sci; Comp Bus St; Comp Mgt Sci; Phil Comp Sci; Maths Comp) *(IB 36 pts)*

340 pts Bath – AAB 340 pts (Comp Sci; Comp Inf Sys; Comp Sci Bus; Comp Sci Maths) *(IB 35 pts)*

Bristol – AAB (Comp Sci; Comp Sci Euro) *(IB 36 pts)*

Durham – AAB–BBC (Comp Sci) *(IB 30 pts)*

Imperial London – AAB (Comp; Comp (Artif Intel) (Comput Mgt)) *(IB 38 pts)*

Lancaster – AAB (Comp Sci Innov)

Nottingham – AAB–BBC (Comp Sci courses) *(IB 30 pts H maths/comp 5 pts)*

St Andrews – AAB–ABB (Comp Sci Econ; Comp Sci Phys; Comp Sci Lang; Comp Sci Lgc Phil Sci; Comp Sci Mgt; Comp Sci Maths; Comp Sci Stats; Intnet Comp Sci courses) *(IB 36–31 pts)*

York – AAB (Comp Sys Soft Eng; Comp Sci; Comp Sci Maths) *(IB 36 pts)*

320 pts Aston – ABB 320 pts (Bus Comp IT)

Birmingham – ABB–BBC (Comp Sci; Comp Sci Bus Mgt; Artif Intel Comp Sci) *(IB 34–32 pts)*

Cardiff – ABB–BBC (Comp Sci; Comp Sci Comp Vis Comp Graph; Comp Sci Dist (Knwl Inf Sys) (Mbl Sys); Comp Phys; Comp Maths; Inf Sys) *(IB 32 pts)*

East Anglia – ABB (Comp Sci N Am/Aus) *(IB 30–32 pts)*

Essex – 320–300 pts (Comp Maths; Maths Crypt Net Scrty)

Exeter – ABB–BBC (IT Mgt Bus; Comp Sci Intnet Comp) *(IB 34–28 pts)*

Glasgow – ABB–BBB (BA Comp Sci courses) *(IB 28 pts)*

Kent – 320 pts (Comp Sci courses)

Lancaster – ABB (Bus Comp Inf Sys) *(IB 33–35 pts)*

Leeds – ABB (Artif Intel Phil; Artif Intel Phys; Artif Intel Maths; Artif Intel Mus; Comp Sci courses; Comp courses)

London (King's) – ABB **or** AAC **or** ABbb (Comp Sci; Comp Sci Mgt; Comp Sci Abrd; Comp Sci Ind) *(IB 34–30 pts)*

London (QM) – ABB (IT Org Mgt) *(IB 30 pts)*

London (UCL) – ABB+AS (Comp Sci; Comp Sci Int) *(IB 34 pts)*

Loughborough – ABB (MEng Electron Soft Eng) *(IB 30–32 pts)*

Reading – 320 pts (MEng: Artif Intel Cyber; Cyber; Comp Sci Cyber) *(IB 33 pts)*

Sheffield – ABB (MComp courses: Comp Sci; Artif Intel Comp Sci; Comp Bus Fin; MEng Soft Eng; Soft Eng Mgt; Soft Eng Bus) *(IB 33 pts)*

Southampton – ABB (Comp Sci; Comp Sci Artif Intel) *(IB 33 pts)*

Sussex – ABB–BBB 360–340 pts (MComp: IT E-Comm; Comp Sci; Comp Artif Intel; BA/BSc: Comp Sci; Intnet Comp; Multim Dig Sys; Mus Inform)

300 pts **Aberdeen** – BBB (Comp Sci; Intnet Inf Sys; Comp E-Bus; Comp Sci (Biomed Comp) (Bus Comp)) *(IB 30 pts)*

Aston – BBB–BCC (Comp Sci; Comp Bus) *(IB 31 pts)*

Bournemouth – 300 pts (Comp Vis Animat)

City – BBB–BBC (Comp Sci; Comp Sci Artif Intel; Comp Sci Dist Sys; Comp Sci Gms Tech; Comp Sci Mus Tech; Bus Comp Sys) *(IB 30 pts)*

Dundee – BBB–CCC (App Comp; E-Comm Comp) *(IB 28 pts)*

Durham – BBB–AAB (Comp Sci; Comp Sci Euro St)

East Anglia – BBB (Bus Inf Sys) *(IB 30–32 pts)*

Edinburgh – ABC–BBB (Comp Sci; Comp Sci Mgt Sci; Comp Sci Phys; Comp Sci Maths; Artif Intel Comp Sci; Inform)

Essex – 300 pts (Comp Sci; Embd Comp Sys; Comp Net; Intnet Tech; Scr Comp Sys) *(IB 32–30 pts)*

Heriot-Watt – ABC 2nd yr entry (Comp Electron)

Kent – BBB (Comp Psy) *(IB 28–32 pts)*

Lancaster – BBB (Comp Sci; Comp Sci Maths; Comp Sci Mus; Comp Sci Multim Sys; Comp Euro Lang) *(IB 29 pts H 15 pts)*

Leicester – 300–340 pts (Maths Comp Sci; Comp Sci; Comp Sci (Euro)) *(IB 28–30 pts)*

Liverpool – BBB 300 pts (MEng Comp Sci; Comp Inf Sys; Comp Sci; Intnet Comp; Soft Dev)

London (Gold) – BBB (Comp Sci; Comp Inf Sys) *(IB 28 pts)*

London (QM) – 300–260 pts (Comp Sci Bus Mgt; Fr/Ger/Russ Ling Comp Sci; Bus Comp courses)

London (RH) – ABC–BBB 300 pts (Comp Sci; Comp Sci Artif Intel; Comp Sci Cmplrs; Comp Sci Mgt; Comp Sci Fr; Comp Sci Maths; Comp Sci Phys; Comp Sci Bioinform)

Newcastle – ABC–BBB (Comp Sci courses; Inf Sys courses) *(IB 32–30 pts)*

Queen's Belfast – BBB (Mgt Inf Sys; MEng Comp Sci; Bus IT)

Reading – 300–340 pts (Comput Sci; App Comp Sci; IT courses)

St Andrews – BBB (Intnet Comp Sci) *(IB 31–36 pts)*

Sheffield – BBB **or** ABbb/BBbb (BSc: Comp Sci; Comp Sci Maths; Comp Sci Fr/Ger; Artif Intel Comp Sci) *(IB 33 pts)*

Sheffield – BBB 300 pts (BEng Soft Eng; Soft Eng Bus)

Strathclyde – BBB–ABB 1st yr entry (Comp Sci; Bus Inf Sys; Comp Sci Law; MEng Des Comp; Intnet Comp) *(IB 28 pts)*

Surrey – BBB (Comp IT; Comp Comm; Comp Modl Simul; Comp Sci Eng)

Swansea – 300 pts (MEng Computing)

280 pts **Abertay Dundee** – BBC (Comp Arts; Comp Gms Tech; Comp)

Aberystwyth – 280 pts (Comp Sci; Comp Graph Vsn Gms; Comp Sci Artif Intel; Artif Intel Robot) *(IB 26–28 pts)*

Brunel – BBC 280 pts (Comp Sci; Inf Sys; Interact Comp; Net Comp; Multim Tech Des)

East Anglia – BBC (Comp Sci; App Comp Sci) *(IB 30–32 pts)*

For information on how to read the Subject Tables, see **Chapter 8.**

Heriot-Watt – BBC 2nd yr entry (IT; Comp Sci courses)
Kent – 280 pts (Multim Tech Des) *(IB 28–32 pts)*
Lancaster – BBC (IT Media Comm) *(IB 33–35 pts)*
Lincoln – 280 pts (MComp Comp; Intnet Comp; Gms Comp; Comp Cyber; Comp Inf Sys; Web Tech)
Reading – 280 pts (BSc Artif Intel Cyber courses)
St Andrews – BBC (Comp Sci; Comp Sci Lang; Comp Comm; Maths Comp Sci)
Westminster – 280 pts (Bus IT)

260 pts **Aston** – BCC–CCC (Multim Comp; Intnet Eng; Intnet Sys)
Brunel – BCC 260 pts (Fin Comp; Mbl Comp) *(IB 28–30 pts)*
Coventry – 260–280 pts (Crea Comp; Gms Tech)
Glasgow – BCC–CCC (BSc Comp Sci courses)
Heriot-Watt – BCC 260 pts 2nd yr entry (Chem Comp Sci)
Hertfordshire – 260–220 pts (Bus Inf Sys)
Kingston – 260 pts (Bus IT; Comp Sci courses; Mbl Comp; Intnet Comp)
Lancaster – BCC (Comm Comp Sys)
London (Gold) – BCC (Comp Des WWW; Intnet Comp; IT)
Loughborough – 260–340 pts (MComp Comp Sci; Comp Sci E–Bus; Comp Sci Artif Intel; BSc Comp Sci) *(IB 30–32 pts)*
Napier – 260 pts (Comp; Comp Net Distr Sys; Hum Comp Sys; Inf Sys; Inf Sys (Mgt); Intnet Comp; Multim Sys; Soft Eng)
Northumbria – 260 pts (Bus Inf Sys)
Queen's Belfast – BCC (BEng Comp Sci)
Richmond (Am Int Univ) – 260 pts (Comp Inf Sys)
Stirling – BCC (Bus Comp) *(IB 26–30 pts)*
Swansea – 260 pts (Intnet Tech; Mbl Comm Intnet Tech)
Ulster – 260–280 pts (Comp Sci; Comp; Comp Gms Dev)

240 pts   **Abertay Dundee** – CCC (Gms Prod Mgt)

        Bangor – 240–260 pts (Comp Sci; Comp Sys Bus St; Comp Sys Psy; Intnet Sys E Commer)

        Bournemouth – 240 pts (Comp; Soft Prod Des; Soft Eng Mgt)

        Bradford – 240 pts (Comp Sci; Comp Inf Sys; Intnet Comp; Mbl Comp; Bus Comp; Multim Comp; Cyber Vrtl Wrlds; ICT courses; Comp Animat)

        Brighton – 240 pts (Intnet Comp; Comp Inf Sys; Comp Sci; Bus Inf Sys) *(IB 28 pts)*

        Bristol UWE – 240–260 pts (Comp Sci; Bus Intnet Sys; Intnet Tech courses; Comp courses) *(IB 28–30 pts)*

        Buckingham – 240 pts (Comp; Bus Mgt IT)

        Chester – 240–260 pts (Multim Tech; Intnet Tech; Inf Sys Mgt; Comp Sci courses) *(IB 30 pts)*

        Coventry – 240 pts (Net Mbl Comp)

        De Montfort – 240 pts (Comp joint Hons)

        Glamorgan – 240 pts (Comp Foren; Net Mgt Scrty; Bus IT)

        Greenwich – 240 pts (BEng Comp Sys Soft Eng; Comp Net; Intnet Tech; Bus Comp)

        Hull – 240–300 pts (Comp Sci Gms Dev; Comp Sci Ind Exp; Comp Sci)

        Keele – 240–260 pts (Comp Sci courses; Inf Sys courses) *(IB 26–28 pts)*

        Kent – 240 pts (IT courses) *(IB 28–32 pts)*

        Lincoln – 240 pts (BSc Comp Inf Sys; Comp; Web Tech; Gms Comp)

        Loughborough – 240 pts (Chem IT)

        Northumbria – 240 pts (Multim Dig Enter; Intnet Comp; Comp Sci; Comp Gms Soft Eng; Comp Foren; Comp Bus)

        Nottingham Trent – 240 pts (Comp Sci courses; Comp St; Inf Sys; Bus Inf Mgt)

        Oxford Brookes – CCC (Inf Sys; Comp; Comp Sci)

        Plymouth – 240 pts (Comp Sys Net; Comp Inform)

        Portsmouth – 240 pts (Bus Inf Sys; Comp Net Mgt Des; Intnet Tech; Ent Enter Tech; Ent Comp Net)

        Roehampton – 240 pts (Comp St)

For information on how to read the Subject Tables, see **Chapter 8**.

Salford – 240 pts (Comp Sci; Comp Sci Inf Sys; Intnet Comp; Mbl Comp; e-Commer Sys) *(IB 25–30 pts)*

Strathclyde – CCC (Des Comp)

Sunderland – 240 pts (BSc Net Comp; Comp)

220 pts **Glamorgan** – 220–260 pts (Comp Sci; Inf Sys; IT; Intnet Comp)

Gloucestershire – 220 pts (Bus IT; Comp courses; IT; Intnet Sys Dev)

Heriot-Watt – CCD 1st yr entry (Chem Comp Sci; Comp Sci courses)

Liverpool Hope – 220 pts (IT; Intnet Tech)

Manchester Met – 220–280 pts (Comp; Inf Sys; Multim Comp; Intnet Comp; Comp Sys; Mbl Comp Tech) *(IB 26 pts)*

Stirling – CCD/BC (Comp Sci courses; Inf Sys)

Sunderland – 220 pts (Foren Comp)

Teesside – 220–260 pts (IT; Bus Inf Sys; Bus Comp; Comp Gms Des; Comp Gms Sci; Comp Gms Prog; Comp Graph Sci; Web Dev; Crea Multim; Comp St; Dig Foren)

200 pts **Abertay Dundee** – CDD (Web Des Dev)

Aberystwyth – 200 pts (Intnet Comp)

Anglia Ruskin – 200 pts (Comp Sci; Bus Inf Sys)

Bolton – 200 pts (Multim Web Dev; Comp courses; Comp Gms Soft Dev; Intnet Comm Net)

Bournemouth – 200–240 pts (Comp; Net Sys Mgt)

Central Lancashire – 200 pts (Comp Gms Dev; Comp courses)

Coventry – 200–280 pts (Comp; Bus IT; Net Mbl Comp; Comp Sci; Bus Inf Sys)

De Montfort – 200 pts (Comp Inf Mgt)

Derby – 200 pts (Comp Gms Prog)

Dundee – CDD 200 pts (App Comp without Hons)

Edge Hill – 200 pts (Web Sys Dev; Comp courses)

Hertfordshire – 200–240 pts (Inf Sys courses; Comp courses; Soft Eng)

Huddersfield – 200–240 pts (Soft Dev courses; Intnet Sys Dev; Comp; Bus Comp; Multim Comp)

Hull – CDD–BBC 200–280 pts (Comp Bus Inform)

Hull (Scarborough) – 200–280 pts (Intnet Comp courses)

Liverpool John Moores – 200 pts (Comp St; Multim Sys)

Manchester Met – 200–260 pts (Bus Inf Sys; Bus IT; Comp Gms Tech; Comp Sci)

Middlesex – 200–220 pts (Comp Sci; Bus Inf Sys; Comp Net; IT; Comp Comm IT; Comp Mus Tech)

Napier – 200 pts (Bus Inf Sys)

Portsmouth – 200 pts (Comp; e-Commer Intnet Sys)

Sheffield Hallam – 200 pts (Comp courses)

190 pts **London Met** – 190 pts (Bus IT Mgt)

180 pts **Bournemouth** – 180–280 pts (Multim Comm Sys)

Bristol UWE – 180–240 pts (Computing)

Central Lancashire – 180–200 pts (Bus Inf Sys)

Chichester – 180–220 pts (IT Mgt Bus) *(IB 28 pts)*

Derby – 180 pts (2AL) 200 pts (3AL) (Comp Net; Comp)

Huddersfield – 180 pts (ICT)

Lampeter – 180 pts (Bus IT; IT)

Liverpool John Moores – 180 pts (Bus Inf Sys)

Newport – 180 pts (Computing)

Northampton – 180–220 pts (Bus Comp Sys; Comp; Comp (Comp Comm))

Plymouth – 180 pts (Intnet Tech Apps; Multim Prod Tech)

Staffordshire – 180–240 pts (Comp Sci; Bus Comp; Bus IT; Foren Comp; Intnet Tech courses; Mbl Comp; Net Comp; Comp Gms Prog)

Sunderland – 180–200 pts (Bus Comp; Comp)

160 pts **Bedfordshire** – 160–120 pts (Comp Sci courses; Inf Sys; Intnet Comp; Comp Gms Dev; Comp Graph)

Birmingham City – 160–180 pts (Comp; Comp Multim; Comp Net Scrty; Bus IT)

Canterbury Christ Church – CC (Comp courses; Dig Cult Arts media courses; Intnet Comp courses; Bus Comp courses)
Cumbria – CC 160 pts (Bus IT courses)
De Montfort – 160–240 pts (Bus Inf Sys; Foren Comp; Multim Comp; Inf Sys Mgt; Comp Sci; Comp; Comp Gms Prog)
Derby – 160–200 pts (Web Sys courses)
East London – 160 pts (Bus Inf Sys; IT; Comp Net; Multim Tech; Soft Eng)
Farnborough (CT) – 160–200 pts (Computing)
Glasgow Caledonian – CC (Comp; Gms Soft Dev; E-Bus; Intnet Soft Dev)
London Met – 160 pts (Comp Sci; Comp; Bus IT; Comp Net; Comp Animat)
Manchester Met – 160–180 pts (Bus IT)
Newman (UC) – CC 160 pts (IT courses)
North East Wales (IHE) – 160 pts (Comp Net; Comp; Intnet Multim Comp; IT; Comp)
Robert Gordon – CC (Comp Sci; Comp Graph Animat; Inf Sys Tech)
Roehampton – 160–180 pts (Comp courses)
South East Essex (Coll) – 160–180 pts (Net Tech; Intnet Tech)
Swansea (Inst) – 160 pts (Bus IT)
Thames Valley – 160 pts (Bus Inf Sys; Comp Net Mgt; Comp Sci; Comp Inf Sys)
West Scotland – CC-DD/cdd (Bus IT courses; Comp Sci; Comp Gms Tech; Multim Tech; IT; Comp Net)
Westminster – CC (Comp Sci; Comp; Bus Comp; Inf Sys; Comp Comm Net; Intnet Comp; Multim Comp; Comp Gms; Comp Vis)
Wolverhampton – 160–220 pts (Comp Sci courses; Comp courses; Bus Comp)
Worcester – 160 pts (Bus IT; Comp)
York St John – 160 pts (IT courses)

For information on how to read the Subject Tables, see **Chapter 8**.

140 pts **Anglia Ruskin** – 140 pts (Comp Aid Vis)
Blackpool and Fylde (Coll) – 140 pts (Intnet Media Tech)
Cardiff (UWIC) – 140 pts (Bus Inf Sys courses)
Marjon (UC) – 140–200 pts (Comp IT courses)
Trinity Carmarthen (Coll) – 140 pts (Inf Sys courses; IT Mgt; Comp)
120 pts **Bradford (Coll)** – 120 pts (Bus (IT))
Bucks New – 120–180 pts (Bus IT; Comp; Multim Tech)
London South Bank – DD (Comp; Bus IT)
Peterborough Reg (Coll) – DD (Comp Inf Sys)
Southampton Solent – 120 pts (Comp Net Web Des; Comp Vid Gms; Comp St; Bus IT; ICT; Intnet Comp)
100 pts **Suffolk (Univ Campus)** – 100 pts (Comp Gms courses)
Swansea (Inst) – 100–160 pts (Comp Net)
 80 pts **and below**
London (Birk) – 80 pts for under 21s (over 21s varies) (p/t Inf Sys Mgt; Comp Biol/Chem)
UHI Millennium Inst (LCC) – (Computing)

Leeds Met – contact University
Open University – contact University (Comp; Comp Stats; Comp Sys; Inf Comm Tech)

Alternative offers
See **Chapter 8** for grade/point equivalences and related information for the following examinations: Scottish qualifications, the Welsh Baccalaureate, the IB diploma (approximate points shown also in italics in the table of offers), the Irish Leaving Certificate, the European Baccalaureate and the French Baccalaureate.

EXAMPLES OF FOUNDATION DEGREES IN THE SUBJECT FIELD
Abingdon (Coll); Arts London; Barnet (Coll); Barnsley (Univ Centre); Bath; Bath City (Coll); Bath Spa; Bedford (Coll); Bedfordshire; Birmingham City; Blackpool and Fyde (Coll); Bournemouth; Bournemouth and Poole (Coll); Bracknell (Coll); Bradford (Coll); Bridgend (Coll); Brighton; Brighton City (Coll); Bristol City (Coll); Bromley (CFHE); Bucks New; Burnley (Coll); Canterbury Christ Church; Castlereagh (CFE); Central Lancashire; Central Sussex (Coll); Colchester (Inst); Cornwall (Coll); Darlington (CAT); De Montfort; Derby (Coll); Dewsbury (Coll); Doncaster (Coll); Dunstable (Coll); Durham New (Coll); East Anglia; East Berkshire (Coll); East Lancashire (IHE); East London; Edge Hill; Enfield (Coll); Exeter (Coll); Farnborough (CT); Furness (Coll); Gateshead (Coll); Glamorgan; Gloucestershire; Grimsby (IFHE); Hastings (Coll); Herefordshire (CAD); Hertford Reg (Coll); Hertfordshire; Huddersfield; Huntingdonshire Reg (Coll); Isle of Man (Coll); Joseph Mason Sixth Form (Coll); Kidderminster (Coll); Kingston; Kingston (Coll); Knowsley (CmC); Leeds (CAT); Leeds Met; Lewisham (Coll); Limavady (CFHE); Lincoln (Coll); Llandrillo Cymru (Coll); London (Birk); London Elect (Coll); London Met; London South Bank; Luton Barnfield (Coll); Manchester (CAT); Manchester Met; Merton (Coll); Mid-Cheshire (Coll); Mid-Kent (Coll); Nescot; Newbury (Coll); Newcastle (Coll); Newman (UC); Newport; Newry (IFHE); North Devon (Coll); North East Wales (IHE); North Hertfordshire (Coll); North West (IFHE); Northampton; Northbrook (Coll); Norwich City (Coll); Oaklands (Coll); Oldham (Coll); Omagh (CFE); Park Lane Leeds (Coll); Portsmouth; Powys (Coll); Preston (Coll); Queen's Belfast; Ravensbourne (CDC); Richmond Adult (Coll); Riverside Halton (Coll); Runshaw (Coll); St Helens (Coll); Salford; Salisbury (Coll); Selby (Coll); Sheffield (Coll); Sheffield Hallam; Shrewsbury (Coll); Sir Gar (Coll); Skelmersdale (Coll); Somerset (CAT); South Birmingham (Coll); South East Essex (Coll); South Kent (Coll); Southampton Solent; Southport (Coll); Staffordshire; Staffordshire (Univ Fed); Stockport (CFHE); Stockton Riverside (Coll); Stoke on Trent (Coll); Stratford-upon-Avon (Coll); Strodes (Coll); Suffolk (Univ Campus); Sunderland; Sunderland City (Coll); Sussex Downs (Coll); Sutton Coldfield (Coll); Swansea (Inst); Tameside (Coll); Thames Valley; Thurrock (Coll); Trinity Carmarthen (Coll); Truro (Coll); Tyne Met (Coll); Uxbridge (Coll); Wakefield (Coll); Warwickshire (Coll); West Cheshire (Coll); West Herts (Coll); West Kent (Coll); West Nottinghamshire (Coll); West Thames (Coll); Weston (Coll); Wigan and Leigh (Coll); Wiltshire (Coll); Wolverhampton; Yeovil (Coll); York (Coll); Yorkshire Coast (CFHE).

CHOOSING YOUR COURSE (SEE ALSO CH.1)
Course variations – Widen your options
Computer Science and Human Psychology (Aston)
Oceanography and Computing (Bangor)
Financial Computing (Brunel)
Dance with Computer Science (Chester)
English and Creative Writing with IT Management (Chichester)
Health Informatics (De Montfort)
Natural Sciences (Computer Science) (Durham)
Artificial Intelligence (Edinburgh)
Adaptive and Robotic Systems (Hertfordshire)
Geographical Information Systems (Kingston)
Computer Games Production (Lincoln)
Health and IT (Liverpool Hope)
Database Technologies (Portsmouth)
European Computing (Sheffield Hallam)
Forensic Computing (Staffordshire)
Digital Forensics (Teesside)
Mobile and Wireless Computing (Westminster)
CHECK PROSPECTUSES AND WEBSITES FOR OTHER UNIVERSITIES AND COLLEGES OFFERING THESE COURSES.

Universities and colleges teaching quality See www.qaa.ac.uk; www.unistats.com.

Top universities and colleges (Research) Aston; Bristol; Cambridge*; Cardiff; Edinburgh; Glasgow; Imperial London; Lancaster; Leeds; Liverpool; London (RH), (UCL); Manchester; Newcastle; Nottingham; Oxford; Plymouth; St Andrews; Sheffield; Southampton*; Sussex; Warwick; York*.

Sandwich degree courses Aberystwyth; Aston; Bath; Bournemouth; Bradford; Brighton; Bristol UWE; Brunel; Central Lancashire; City; Coventry; De Montfort; Derby; East London; Glamorgan; Glasgow Caledonian; Gloucestershire; Hertfordshire; Huddersfield; Kent; Kingston; Leeds Met; Liverpool John Moores; London South Bank; Loughborough; Manchester; Manchester Met; Napier; Nescot; Northumbria; Nottingham Trent; Oxford Brookes; Plymouth; Portsmouth; Queen's Belfast; Reading; Sheffield Hallam; Southampton Solent; Staffordshire; Surrey; Teesside; Ulster; West Scotland; Westminster; Wolverhampton; York.

ADMISSIONS INFORMATION
Number of applicants per place (approx) Abertay Dundee 2; Aberystwyth 8; Aston (Bus Comp IT) 12; Bath 10; Birmingham 7; Bournemouth 8; Bradford 13; Bristol 9; Bristol UWE 4; Brunel 10; Buckingham 6; Cambridge 3; Cardiff 5; City 10; Coventry 10; Derby 3; Dundee 6; Durham 10; East Anglia (Comp Maths) 7; Edinburgh 4; Essex 2; Exeter 10; Glasgow Caledonian 8; Heriot-Watt 6; Hull (Comp Sci) 6; Imperial London 6; Kent 8; Kingston 10; Lampeter 1; Lancaster 5; Leeds 10; Leicester 22; Lincoln 5; Liverpool John Moores 3; London (King's) 20, (QM) 6, (RH) 5; Loughborough (CT) 2; Manchester Met 10, (Bus IT) 8; Newcastle 7; North East Wales (IHE) 3; Northumbria 4; Nottingham Trent 4; Oxford (success rate 23%); Oxford Brookes 18; Plymouth 12; Portsmouth 6; Richmond (Am Int Univ) 3; Robert Gordon 3; Roehampton 3; Sheffield Hallam 5; Southampton 9; Staffordshire 4; Stirling 6; Strathclyde 16; Surrey 9; Swansea 5; Teesside 4; Trinity Carmarthen (Coll) 2; Warwick 11; York 9.

Advice to applicants and planning the UCAS personal statement Your interest in, and use of computers, programming etc outside school or college should be described. It is also useful to give details of any visits, work experience and work shadowing relating to industrial or commercial organisations and their computer systems. (See **Appendix 2**.) **Birmingham** Little previous experience required, opportunity to study abroad or have a year in industry. **City** We are interested in applicants with an interest in the IT industry, the underlying principles and technology and how computers are applied to real world problems. **De Montfort** (Multim Comp) Interest in hardware and software. Prior experience should be included in the use of multimedia packages and your knowledge of computer usage and programming. **London (QM)** We are looking for applicants who are comfortable with formal reasoning and abstract concepts. This is more important than experience with computers. **Portsmouth** Evidence needed that applicants can work with people. Contact the British Computer Society for information. **St Andrews** Give reasons for choosing the course and evidence of interest and include details of sport and extra-curricular activities and positions of responsibility. **Sunderland** Provide an example of when you have worked as part of a team or met a deadline or worked on your own. **York** Be interested and articulate, think why you want to come to this University and why study Computer Science (have answers to these questions at interview).

Misconceptions about this course That anyone who plays computer games or uses a word processor can do a degree in Computer Studies. Some think Computing degrees are just about programming; in reality, programming is only one, albeit essential, part of computing. **Aston** (Bus Comp IT) 60% business, 40% computing and IT; compulsory placement year in industry. **City** (Bus Comp Sys) Some applicants think that it is a Business degree: it is a Computing degree focused on computing in business. **London (QM)** There are many misconceptions – among students, teachers and careers advisers – about what computer science entails. The main one is to confuse it with what schools call information and communication technology which is about the use of computer applications. Computer science is all about software – ie programming – and will generally only cover a limited study of hardware.

Selection interviews Yes Abertay Dundee, Bath, Bradford, Bristol, Bristol UWE, Brunel, Buckingham, Cambridge, Cardiff, City, Coventry, Cumbria, Durham, East Lancashire (IHE), Edinburgh, Glamorgan, Hertfordshire, Hull, Kingston, Liverpool Hope, London (Gold), (QM), (UCL), London South Bank, Loughborough, Newcastle, Newport, Northampton, Northbrook (Coll), Nottingham, Nottingham Trent, Oxford, Plymouth, Portsmouth, Sheffield Hallam, Southampton, Surrey, Thames Valley, Warwick, Wigan and Leigh (Coll), York; **Some** Aberystwyth, Anglia Ruskin, Birmingham City, Blackpool and Fylde (Coll), Brighton, Chichester, Dundee, East Anglia, Exeter, Liverpool John Moores, London Met, Manchester Met, Napier, Salford, Staffordshire, Sunderland.

Interview advice and questions Whilst A-level computer studies is not usually required, you will be questioned on your use of computers and aspects of the subject which interest you. How do you organise your homework/social life? What are your strengths and weaknesses? Do you have any idea of the type of career you would like? **Cambridge** Why is the pole-vaulting world record about 6.5m and why can't it be broken? **City** The aim of the interview is to obtain a full picture of the applicant's background, life experiences etc, before making an offer. **York** No tests. Questions for discussion at the whiteboard are usually mathematical or are about fundamental computer science such as sorting. See also **Chapter 7**.

Applicants' impressions (A=Open day; B=Interview day) Imperial London (B) There was a 45-minute talk on the College and the course structure and content with free refreshments. We were then split into small groups for a tour, followed by a brief interview. I had to demonstrate that I could understand simple mathematical problems clearly but there was no opportunity to ask questions. The offer was made after the interview. **Portsmouth** (A) I was sent a map and details of the open day. We had an interesting coach tour of the city, followed by lunch and then course talks, tea and coffee. At the end of the day students had private discussions with the staff.

Reasons for rejection (non-academic) Little practical interest in computers/electronics. Inability to work as part of a small team. Mismatch between referee's description and performance at interview. Unsatisfactory English. Can't communicate. Inability to convince interviewer of the candidate's worth. Incoherent, unmotivated, arrogant and without any evidence of good reason. **London (QM)** Misunderstanding of what computer science involves as an academic subject – especially in personal statements where some suggest that they are interested in a course with business and secretarial skills. Lack of sufficient mathematics. Computer science is a mathematical subject and we cannot accept applicants who are unable to demonstrate good mathematical skills. **Southampton** Lack of motivation; incoherence; carelessness.

AFTER-RESULTS ADVICE

Offers to applicants repeating A-levels Higher Brighton, De Montfort, Greenwich, Kingston, St Andrews, Surrey, Sussex, Warwick; **Possibly higher** Bath, Bristol UWE, Edinburgh, Lancaster, Leeds, Newcastle, Oxford Brookes, Portsmouth, Sheffield, Teesside; **Same** Anglia Ruskin, Aston, Blackpool and Fylde (Coll), Brunel, Buckingham, Cardiff, Chichester, City, Derby, Dundee, Durham, East Anglia, Exeter, Farnborough (CT), Huddersfield, Hull, Kent, Lincoln, Liverpool, Liverpool Hope, Liverpool John Moores, London (RH), (UCL), London South Bank, Loughborough, Manchester Met, Newman (UC), Northumbria, Nottingham Trent, Richmond (Am Int Univ), Robert Gordon, Salford, Sheffield Hallam, Staffordshire, Sunderland, Suffolk (Univ Campus), Thames Valley, Ulster, Wolverhampton, Worcester, York; **No offers made** Cambridge.

GRADUATE DESTINATIONS AND EMPLOYMENT (2005/6 HESA)

Computer Science graduates surveyed 6995 **Employed** 4295 **In further study** 655 **Assumed unemployed** 790.

Information Systems graduates surveyed 2415 **Employed** 1490 **In further study** 200 **Assumed unemployed** 225.

Artificial Intelligence graduates surveyed 75 **Employed** 45 **In further study** 15 **Assumed unemployed** 10.

Career note A high proportion of graduates go to work in the IT sector with some degrees leading towards particular fields (usually indicated by the course title). Significant areas include software design and engineering, web and internet-based fields, programming, systems analysis and administration.

OTHER DEGREE SUBJECTS FOR CONSIDERATION

Business Studies; Communications Engineering; Computer Engineering; Electrical and Electronic Engineering; Geographical Information Systems; Information Studies; Mathematics; Physics; Software Engineering.

CONSUMER STUDIES/SCIENCES

(including **Consumer Product Design;** see also **Food Science/Studies, Technology** and **Hospitality and Hotel Management**)

Consumer Studies courses involve topics such as food and nutrition, shelter, clothing, community studies and consumer behaviour and marketing.

Useful websites www.which.co.uk; www.blackwellpublishing.com/ijc.

NB The points totals shown to the left of the institutions are for ease of reference only. It must not be assumed that tariff points are always used by institutions or that they can be substituted for an offer in grades. The level of an offer is not necessarily indicative of the quality of a course.

COURSE OFFERS INFORMATION

Subject requirements/preferences GCSE Mathematics and English usually required. **AL** No specific subjects required. **NB** A* grades are likely to form part of university offers in the higher ranges for students applying for places in 2008 for entry in 2009: check websites.

Your target offers
300 pts **Reading** – 300 pts (Consum Bhv Mark)
260 pts **Ulster** – BCC 260 pts (Consum St)
240 pts **Coventry** – 240–200 pts (Consum Prod Des)
        Glasgow Caledonian – CCC (Psy (Consum Sci))
        Manchester Met – 240 pts (Consum Law; Law Tr Stnds)

200 pts **Abertay Dundee** – CDD 200 pts (Fd Consum St)

Bath Spa – 200–240 pts (Fd Nutr Consum Prot)

Manchester Met – 200 pts (Consum Prot; Int Consum Mark; Consum Mark; Consum Mark
Prod Dev) *(IB 24 pts)*

Teesside – 200 pts (Foren Invstg Consum Law)

180 pts **Napier** – BC (Consum Prod Des)

Queen Margaret – DDD/BC 180 pts (Consum St Mgt; Consum St Mark; Consum St Rtl)

160 pts **Birmingham (CFTCS)** – 160 pts (Fd Consum Mgt) *(IB 24 pts)*

Liverpool John Moores – 160 pts (Consum St Mark)

140 pts **Bolton** – 140 pts (Consum Prod Des)

Cardiff (UWIC) – 140 pts approx (Consum Tr Stnds) *(IB 28 pts)*

120 pts **Harper Adams (UC)** – 120 pts (Fd Consum St)

London Met – 120 pts (Fd Consum St; Biol Sci Consum St; Consum St Foren Sci; Consum St
Hum Nutr; Consum St Mark; Consum St Rtl Mgt; Consum St Spo Sci)

Leeds Met – contact University

Alternative offers

See **Chapter 8** for grade/point equivalences and related information for the following examinations:
Scottish qualifications, the Welsh Baccalaureate, the IB diploma (approximate points shown also in
italics in the table of offers), the Irish Leaving Certificate, the European Baccalaureate and the French
Baccalaureate.

CHOOSING YOUR COURSE (SEE ALSO CH.1)

Course variations – Widen your options

Food Product Innovation (CAFRE)

Psychology (Food Science) (Glasgow Caledonian)

Consumer Studies and Forensic Science (London Met)

Consumer Law (Manchester Met).

CHECK PROSPECTUSES AND WEBSITES FOR OTHER UNIVERSITIES AND COLLEGES OFFERING THESE COURSES.

Universities and colleges teaching quality See www.qaa.ac.uk; www.unistats.com.

ADMISSIONS INFORMATION

Number of applicants per place (approx) Bath Spa 6; Birmingham (CFTCS) 2; Cardiff (UWIC) 5;
Liverpool John Moores 3; London Met 5; Manchester Met 4; Queen Margaret 3.

Advice to applicants and planning the UCAS personal statement Relevant work experience or
work shadowing in, for example, business organisations, restaurants, cafes, or the school meals
service, would be appropriate. **Liverpool John Moores** Discuss consumer studies on your UCAS form.
(See also **Hospitality and Hotel Management** and **Dietetics**.) Details may be obtained from the
Institute of Consumer Sciences – see **Appendix 2**.

Selection interviews Bath Spa; **Some** Manchester Met.

Interview advice and questions Questions will stem from your special interests in this subject and
in the past have included: What interests you in consumer behaviour? What are the advantages and
disadvantages? What is ergonomics? What do you understand by the term 'sustainable consumption'?
What world or national news has annoyed, pleased or upset you? What relevance do textiles and
dress have to home economics? How would you react in a room full of fools? **Manchester Met** A
general discussion – no tests. **Queen Margaret** Very informal interviews covering work experience
and career aspirations. See also **Chapter 7**.

AFTER-RESULTS ADVICE

Offers to applicants repeating A-levels **Same** Bath Spa, Liverpool John Moores, Manchester Met,
Queen Margaret, Ulster.

GRADUATE DESTINATIONS AND EMPLOYMENT (2005/6 HESA)
No data available.

Career note The various specialisms involved in these courses will allow graduates to seek openings in several career areas, for example, food quality assurance, trading standards, consumer education and advice. Many graduates will enter business administration, particularly retailing, evaluating new products and liaising with the public.

OTHER DEGREE SUBJECTS FOR CONSIDERATION
Biological Sciences; Business Studies; Dietetics; Environmental Health; Food Science; Health Studies; Hospitality Management; Marketing; Nutrition; Psychology; Retail Management.

DANCE/DANCE STUDIES
(see also **Drama**)

Every aspect of dance can be studied in the various courses on offer as well as the theoretical, educational, historical and social aspects of the subject.

Useful websites www.arts.org.uk; www.cdet.org.uk; www.ballet.co.uk; www.ndta.org.uk.

NB The points totals shown to the left of the institutions are for ease of reference only. It must not be assumed that tariff points are always used by institutions or that they can be substituted for an offer in grades. The level of an offer is not necessarily indicative of the quality of a course.

COURSE OFFERS INFORMATION
Subject requirements/preferences **GCSE** English usually required. Practical dance experience essential. **AL** No specific subjects required. **NB** A* grades are likely to form part of university offers in the higher ranges for students applying for places in 2008 for entry in 2009: check websites.

Your target offers
300 pts Surrey – BBB–BBC (Dance Cult; Dance Cult Prof Trg) *(IB 30–28 pts)*
280 pts Leeds – BBC (Perf Des; Thea Perf)
　　　　Roehampton – 280 pts (Dance St courses)
260 pts Hull – BCC–CCC (Crea Mus Tech Dance)
　　　　Northumbria – 260 pts (Dance Choreo)
240 pts Chester – 240 pts (Dance courses; Perf New Media Dance) *(IB 30 pts)*
　　　　Dartington (CA) – 240–280 pts (Choreography)
　　　　Edge Hill – 240 pts (Dance)
　　　　Hull (Scarborough) – 240–260 pts (Thea Dance)
　　　　Kingston – 240 pts (Dance courses)
　　　　Oxford Brookes – CCC (Perf Arts courses)
　　　　Salford – CCC 240 pts (Perf Arts)
220 pts Chichester – 220–240 pts (Dance courses) *(IB 28 pts)*
　　　　Liverpool Hope – 220 pts (Dance courses; Crea Perf Arts)
　　　　Winchester – 220 pts (Choreo Dance St courses)
200 pts Bath Spa – 200–240 pts (Dance; Crea Writ Dance; Perf Arts; Dance Comb Hons)
　　　　Cardiff (UWIC) – BB (Dance)
　　　　Central Lancashire – 200 pts (Dance Perf Teach)
　　　　Coventry – 200–220 pts (Dance Thea; Dance Prof Prac)
　　　　Liverpool John Moores – 200 pts (Dance St)
　　　　Manchester Met – 200 pts (Dance joint courses; Contemp Arts) *(IB 28 pts)*
　　　　Middlesex – 200–240 pts (Dance St; Dance Contemp Perf Arts; Dance Perf)
　　　　Sunderland – 200 pts (Dance courses)
180 pts Bedfordshire – 180 pts (Perf Arts)
　　　　De Montfort – 180–200 pts (Dance courses; Perf Arts)

For information on how to read the Subject Tables, see **Chapter 8**.

Liverpool (LIPA) – BC 180 pts (Dance (Perf Arts))
Northampton – 180–220 pts (Dance courses; Perf)

160 pts **Canterbury Christ Church** – CC (Dance Educ)
Colchester (Inst) – 160 pts (Mus Thea)
Cumbria – 160 pts (Dance Perf Tech Thea; Dance Perf Musl Thea Perf; Dance Perf Dr Perf; Dance Perf Contemp Cult)
Derby – 160 pts (Dance Mov St Thea St; Dance Mov St Heal Arts; Dance Mov St Mark)
East London – 160 pts (Dance)
Laban – CC (Dance Thea – apply early)
London Met – 160 pts (Perf Arts)
Wolverhampton – 160–220 pts (Dance Prac Perf courses)
Ulster – 160 pts (Dance courses)
York St John – 160 pts (Perf Dance)

80 pts **and below**
Brighton – 80 pts (Vis Art Perf (Thea) (Dance))
Doncaster (Coll) – 80 pts (Dance Prac Dig Perf)
Greenwich – 80–120 pts (Dance Thea Perf)
Grimsby (IFHE) – 80 pts (Perf Dance)
London (Arts Educ Sch) – (Musl Thea)
London (RAc Dance) – 80 pts (Ballet Educ)
Northern (Sch Contemp Dance) – (Dance)

Alternative offers
See **Chapter 8** for grade/point equivalences and related information for the following examinations: Scottish qualifications, the Welsh Baccalaureate, the IB diploma (approximate points shown also in italics in the table of offers), the Irish Leaving Certificate, the European Baccalaureate and the French Baccalaureate.

EXAMPLES OF FOUNDATION DEGREES IN THE SUBJECT FIELD
Bristol City (Coll); Bucks New; Coventry; London Studio; Newcastle (Coll); Northbrook (Coll); Truro (Coll).

CHOOSING YOUR COURSE (SEE ALSO CH.1)
Course variations – Widen your options
Dance and Food Studies (Bath Spa)
Archaeology and Dance (Chester)
Dance and Drama Performance (Cumbria)
Choreography (Dartington (CA))
Music with Dance (Kingston)
Dance and War and Peace Studies (Liverpool Hope)
Abuse Studies and Dance (Manchester Met)
Ballet Education (London (RAc Dance))
CHECK PROSPECTUSES AND WEBSITES FOR OTHER UNIVERSITIES AND COLLEGES OFFERING THESE COURSES.

Universities and colleges teaching quality See www.qaa.ac.uk; www.unistats.com.

Top universities and colleges (Research) See **Drama**.

ADMISSIONS INFORMATION
Number of applicants per place (approx) Chichester 6; De Montfort (Dance) 13, (Perf Arts) 9; Derby 12; Hull (Scarborough) 2; Laban 5; Liverpool (LIPA) 24; Liverpool John Moores 3; Middlesex 12; Northern (Sch Contemp Dance) 6; Roehampton 17; Surrey 5; York St John 3.

Advice to applicants and planning the UCAS personal statement Full details should be given of examinations taken and practical experience in contemporary dance or ballet. Refer to your visits to the theatre and your impressions. You should list the dance projects in which you have worked, productions in which you have performed and the roles. State any formal dance training you have had and the grades achieved. See **Appendix 2**. **De Montfort** (Perf Arts) A good balance of interests, both theoretical and practical; strengths in both dance and theatre. **Laban** We look for dedication, versatility, inventiveness and individuality. **Liverpool (LIPA)** Applicants should be educated to A-level standard with good communication and entrepreneurial skills and experience in dance projects/productions, and should give details of the roles they have played. **Surrey** Personal and intellectual maturity. Make sure you can demonstrate practical experience of dance, theoretical ability and language competency. **Winchester** Mature students with relevant experience considered.

Misconceptions about this course That Performing Arts is only an acting course: it also includes music. **Wolverhampton** The course focuses on the practical study of dance technique, performance and choreography with theoretical study and practical experience of teaching and community work.

Interview advice and questions All institutions will require auditions. The following scheme required by **Liverpool (LIPA)** may act as a guide:

1 Write a short essay (500 words) on your own views and experience of dance. You should take into account the following:
   * Your history and how you have developed physically and intellectually in your run-up to applying to LIPA.
   * Your main influences and what inspires you.
   * What you want to gain from training as a dancer.
   * Your ideas on health and nutrition as a dancer, taking into account gender and physicality.

2 All candidates must prepare **two** practical audition pieces:
   * Whatever you like, in whatever style you wish, as long as the piece does not exceed two minutes (please note: panel will stop anyone exceeding this time-limit). There will be no pianist at this part of the session, so if you're using music please bring it with you on a cassette tape. This devised piece should be created through you and this means that you should feel comfortable with it and that it expresses something personal about you. You should wear your regular practice clothes for your presentation.
   * You must prepare a song of your own choice. An accompanist is provided, but you must provide the sheet music for your song, fully written out for piano accompaniment and in the key you wish to sing (the accompanist will **not** transpose at sight). **Important:** Do NOT choreograph your song. You should expect to sit on a high stool or stand when singing for the audition.

3 Additionally, all candidates will participate in a class given on the day of audition:
   * Please ensure that you are dressed appropriately for class with clothing you are comfortable in but allows your movement to be seen. In preparing the practical elements of the audition, please remember that audition panels are not looking for a 'polished' performance. The panel will be looking for candidates' ability to make a genuine emotional and physical connection with the material that they are presenting which shows clear intent and focus.

Remember that it is in your best interest to prepare thoroughly. Nerves inevitably play a part in any audition and can undermine even the best-prepared candidate. Your best defence is to feel confident in your preparation. **De Montfort** (Perf Arts) Practical workshops in dance and theatre plus a written paper. **Salford** (Perf Arts) Audition and interview. **Surrey** Applicants invited to spend a day at the university for interview and a practical class to assess dance skills. An audition fee may be charged. **Wolverhampton** Audition in the form of a dance class. See also **Chapter 7**.

Reasons for rejection (non-academic) Applicants more suitable for an acting or dance school course than a degree course. No experience of dance on the UCAS application. Limited dance skills. **Surrey** Inadequate dance background. Had not seen/read about/done any dance.

AFTER-RESULTS ADVICE
Offers to applicants repeating A-levels Same Chester, Chichester, De Montfort (Perf Arts), Laban, Liverpool John Moores, Salford, Surrey, Winchester, Wolverhampton, York St John.

GRADUATE DESTINATIONS AND EMPLOYMENT (2005/6 HESA)

Graduates surveyed 440 **Employed** 205 **In further study** 65 **Assumed unemployed** 15.

Career note Teaching is the most popular career destination for the majority of graduates. Other opportunities exist as dance animators working in education or in the community to encourage activity and participation in dance. There is a limited number of openings for dance or movement therapists who work with the emotionally disturbed, the elderly or physically disadvantaged.

OTHER DEGREE SUBJECTS FOR CONSIDERATION

Arts Management; Drama; Education (Primary); Performance Studies; Physical Education; Sport and Exercise Science.

DENTISTRY/DENTAL SURGERY

(including **Dental Technology, Dental Hygiene, Equine Dental Science**
and **Oral Health Science**)

Courses in Dentistry cover the basic medical sciences, human disease, clinical studies and clinical dentistry. The amount of patient contact will vary between institutions but will be considerable in all Dental Schools. Intercalated courses in other science subjects are offered on most courses.

Useful websites www.bda.org.uk; www.bdha.org.uk; www.dla.org.uk; www.gdcuk.org.

NB The points totals shown to the left of the institutions are for ease of reference only. It must not be assumed that tariff points are always used by institutions or that they can be substituted for an offer in grades. The level of an offer is not necessarily indicative of the quality of a course.

COURSE OFFERS INFORMATION

Subject requirements/preferences **GCSE** English, mathematics and science subjects required in most cases. A*/A/B grades stipulated in certain subjects by many Dental Schools. Evidence of non-infectivity or hepatitis-B immunisation required and all new dental students screened for hepatitis-C. Completion of a criminal record disclaimer required and consent to police record check. **AL** Chemistry plus biology or a science subject usually required: see offers lines below. Some Dental Schools use admissions tests (eg UKCAT: see **Chapter 7**). **Dental Technology, Oral Health Sciences** AL science subject required or preferred. **NB** A* grades are likely to form part of university offers in the higher ranges for students applying for places in 2008 for entry in 2009: check websites.

Your target offers
360 pts and above

    Dundee – AAA +UKCAT (inc biol+2 subj from chem/phys/maths) (Dentistry)

    Liverpool – AABb 390–340 pts (inc 2AL AA–AB inc chem/biol+1 subj from chem, biol, maths, phys, stats) (Dntl Srgy) *(IB 36 pts H chem/biol 6 pts)*

    London (King's) – ABBb +UKCAT (inc AL chem/biol) (Dentistry) *(IB 36 pts H665)*

    Queen's Belfast – AAAa (inc AL/AS chem A+1 subj from biol, maths, phys (must inc AS biol)) (Dentistry) *(IB 37 pts H666)*

340 pts Birmingham – AAB–ABB 340–320 pts (inc 300 pts 3AL inc 2AL AB chem+biol) (Dentistry) *(IB 36 pts)*

    Bristol – AAB (inc chem+biol pref+biol if 3rd AL is non-sci) (Dentistry A206) *(IB 36 pts H666)*

    Bristol – AAB (inc 3 non-sci subjs **or** 1 sci+2 non-sci) (Dentistry A204) *(IB 36 pts H666)*

    Cardiff – AAB +UKCAT 340 pts +UKCAT (inc chem/biol+2 sci subj (5yr course); inc no more than one sci subj from chem/biol/phys (6yr course)) (Dentistry; Fdn Dentistry) *(IB 34 pts H chem 5 pts)*

    Glasgow – AAB +UKCAT (inc chem+phys/maths/biol) (Dentistry) *(IB 34 pts)*

    Leeds – AAB (inc AL chem, biol) (Dentistry) *(IB 35 pts H666)*

London (QM) – AAB +UKCAT (inc 2ALs chem/biol/sci subj **or** chem/biol bb) (Dentistry) *(IB 36 pts H665)*

Manchester – AAB +UKCAT (inc AL chem+biol+1 sci from phys/maths/comp sci) (Dentistry)

Manchester – ABB (2 arts+sci subj) (Dentistry pre-dental entry)

Newcastle – AAB +UKCAT (inc AL chem and/or biol) (Dentistry) *(IB 35 pts H chem/biol 6 pts)*

Sheffield – AAB **or** ABaa/ab +UKCAT (inc AL chem AB+1 sci B) (Dentistry) *(IB 35 pts)*

300 pts **London (QM)** – BBB–BCC (Dntl Mat)

280 pts **Birmingham** – BBC (Dntl Hyg Ther inc St Reg) *(IB 30 pts)*

240 pts **Dundee** – 240 pts (Oral Hlth Sci)

Manchester – CCC (Oral Hlth Sci)

Portsmouth – 240 pts (Dntl Hyg Dntl Thera)

200 pts **Bristol UWE** – 200–240 pts (Eqn Dntl Sci)

160 pts **Cardiff (UWIC)** – 160 pts (inc sci subj) (Dntl Tech)

Manchester Met – 160–220 pts (inc sci/tech) (Dntl Tech)

Central Lancashire – graduate entry only (contact university)

Alternative offers

See **Chapter 7** for grade/point equivalences and related information for the following examinations: Scottish qualifications, the Welsh Baccalaureate, the IB diploma (approximate points shown also in italics in the table of offers), the Irish Leaving Certificate, the European Baccalaureate and the French Baccalaureate.

EXAMPLES OF FOUNDATION DEGREES IN THE SUBJECT FIELD

Cardiff (UWIC); De Montfort; Lambeth (Coll); Liverpool (CmC); Nottingham Castle (Coll).

Diploma courses

160 pts **Cardiff** – CC (Dntl Hyg; Dntl Thera)

London (King's) – CC (Dntl Hyg)

CHOOSING YOUR COURSE (SEE ALSO CH.1)

Mature students A-level standard necessary. Graduates require 2:1 degree plus A-level grades close to the normal requirement.

Course variations – Widen your options

Dental Hygiene and Therapy (Birmingham)

Oral Health Sciences (Dundee)

Dental Technology (Manchester Met)

Dental Materials (London (QM))

CHECK PROSPECTUSES AND WEBSITES FOR OTHER UNIVERSITIES AND COLLEGES OFFERING THESE COURSES.

Universities and colleges teaching quality See www.qaa.ac.uk; www.unistats.com.

Top universities and colleges (Research) Bristol*; Dundee; Leeds; London (King's)*, (QM); Newcastle; Sheffield.

ADMISSIONS INFORMATION

Number of applicants per place (approx) Birmingham 10; Bristol 16; Cardiff 14; Cardiff (UWIC) (Dntl Tech) 1; Dundee 8, (Pre-dental) 5; Glasgow 7; Leeds 11.5; Liverpool 15; London (King's) 162 places, (QM) 18, (300 interviewed and 200 offers made); Manchester 24; Manchester Met 16; Newcastle 12; Portsmouth 2; Queen's Belfast 5; Sheffield 16 (interviews not held for non-EU students: 3 accepted each year). **International applicants** Birmingham 129 (no quota).

Number of applicants (a UK b EU (non-UK) c non-EU d mature) Bristol **ab**633 **c**83 **d**148; Glasgow **a**437 **b**45 **c**70 **d**79; Leeds **a**877 **b**42 **c**97 **d**158; Liverpool **a**704 **b**46 **c**73 **d**143; London (King's) **ab**137 **c**25; Manchester **a**1290 **b**81 **c**152 **d**331.

Advice to applicants and planning the UCAS personal statement UCAS applications listing four choices only should be submitted by 15 October. Applicants may add up to two alternative (non-Dentistry) courses. However, if they receive offers for these courses and are rejected for Dentistry, they will not be considered for Dentistry courses in Clearing if they perform better than expected in the examinations.

On your UCAS application show evidence of your manual dexterity, work experience and awareness of problems experienced by dentists. Details should be provided of discussions with dentists and workshadowing in dental surgeries. Employment (paid or voluntary) in any field, preferably dealing with people in an environment widely removed from your home or school, could be described. Discuss any specialised fields of dentistry in which you might be interested. See also **Appendix 2**. **Cardiff** Expects students to have had work experience. Needs evidence of, and potential for, high academic achievement; a caring and committed attitude towards people; an understanding of the demands of dental training and practice; the ability to communicate effectively; a willingness to accept responsibility; evidence of broad social, cultural or sporting interests, good manual dexterity. **Cardiff (UWIC)** (Dntl Tech) Evidence of manual dexterity. **London (King's)** The personal statement is a significant factor in our assessment. We would expect that you will have undertaken some work experience in a caring environment. Communication skills and the ability to work in a team are important. Approximately 25% of applicants are invited to interview after initial UCAS screening.

Misconceptions about this course **Cardiff (UWIC)** (Dntl Tech) Some think that the course allows them to practise as a dentist. Some think the degree is entirely practical.

Selection interviews Birmingham (400–450 applicants and only 50% of applicants get through the initial sort); Bristol; Cardiff; Dundee; Glasgow; Leeds; London (King's), (QM); Newcastle; Sheffield.

Interview advice and questions Work shadowing in a dental surgery is essential and, as a result, questions will be asked on your reactions to the work and your understanding of the different types of treatment that a dentist can offer. In the past questions at interview have included: What is conservative dentistry? What does integrity mean? Do you think the first-year syllabus is a good one? What qualities are required by a dentist? What are prosthetics, periodontics, orthodontics? What causes tooth decay? Questions asked on the disadvantages of being a dentist, the future of dentistry and how you could show that you are manually dexterous. Other questions on personal attributes and spare time activities. What are the careers within the profession open to dentists? Questions on the future of dentistry (preventative and cosmetic dentistry), the problems facing dentists, the skills needed and the advantages and disadvantages of fluoride in water. How do you relax? How do you cope with stress? **Leeds** The interview assesses personality, verbal and communication skills and knowledge of dentistry. See also **Chapter 7**.

Applicants' impressions (A=Open day; B=Interview day) **Cardiff** (B) There were two interviewers (one male, one female). They were very helpful although I was not always sure whether they were smiling because they agreed with me or whether they were just being polite. It was a well-organised interview but there was no opportunity to meet any students. **Sheffield** (A) The facilities looked impressive and the Dental School was quite new: it's a 15-minute walk from the city centre.

Reasons for rejection (non-academic) Lack of evidence of a firm commitment to Dentistry. Lack of breadth of interests. Lack of motivation for a health care profession. Unprofessional attitude. Poor manual dexterity. Poor communication skills. Poor English. Lack of evidence of ability to work in groups. Not for the faint-hearted! More interested in running a business and making money than in caring for people. **Cardiff (UWIC)** (Dntl Tech) Target numbers need to be precise so the course fills at a late stage.

AFTER-RESULTS ADVICE
Offers to applicants repeating A-levels **Higher** Bristol, Cardiff (preference given to students who previously applied), Dundee, Leeds (very few); **Same** Cardiff (UWIC) (Dntl Tech), Queen's Belfast.

GRADUATE DESTINATIONS AND EMPLOYMENT (2005/6 HESA)
Graduates surveyed 630 **Employed** 520 **In further study** none **Assumed unemployed** 5.

Career note The great majority of Dental Technology graduates gain employment in this career with job opportunities excellent in both the UK and Europe. There are openings in the NHS, commercial dental laboratories and armed services.

OTHER DEGREE SUBJECTS FOR CONSIDERATION

Anatomy; Biochemistry; Biological Sciences; Chemistry; Medicine; Nursing; Optometry; Pharmacy; Physiology; Physiotherapy; Radiography; Speech Therapy/Sciences; Veterinary Medicine/Science.

DEVELOPMENT STUDIES

Development Studies courses are multi-disciplinary and cover a range of subjects including economics, geography, sociology, social anthropology, politics, natural resources, with special reference to countries overseas.

Useful websites www.devstud.org.uk; www.dfid.gov.uk; www.ids.ac.uk; see also **Politics**.

NB The points totals shown to the left of the institutions are for ease of reference only. It must not be assumed that tariff points are always used by institutions or that they can be substituted for an offer in grades. The level of an offer is not necessarily indicative of the quality of a course.

COURSE OFFERS INFORMATION

Subject requirements/preferences **GCSE** Mathematics, English and a foreign language may be required. **AL** Science or social science subjects may be required or preferred for some courses. **NB** A* grades are likely to form part of university offers in the higher ranges for students applying for places in 2008 for entry in 2009: check websites.

Your target offers
340 pts **Bath** – AAB (Econ Int Dev)
Manchester – AAB–ABB (Dev St courses) *(IB 32–34 pts)*
320 pts **Liverpool** – ABB (Int Dev)
300 pts **Birmingham** – BBB–BCC (Af St Dev)
East Anglia – BBB (Dev Langs; Int Dev Ovrs Exp; Int Dev) *(IB 32 pts)*
Leeds – BBB (Int Dev)
London (King's) – BBB+AS (Dev Geog)
St Andrews – BBB (BSc Sust Dev)
Sussex – BBB 3AL+AS (Dev St)
280 pts **Bradford** – 280 pts (Dev Pce St)
London (SOAS) – BBC (Dev St courses) *(IB 31 pts)*
240 pts **Chester** – 240 pts (Int Dev St courses) *(IB 30 pts)*
Kingston – 240 pts (Dev Sust)
200 pts **London Met** – 200 pts (Dev St courses)
Middlesex – 200–240 pts (Dev St courses)
Portsmouth – 200–280 pts (Lat Am Dev St)
180 pts **Northampton** – 180–220 pts (Third Wrld Dev courses)

Alternative offers
See **Chapter 8** for grade/point equivalences and related information for the following examinations: Scottish qualifications, the Welsh Baccalaureate, the IB diploma (approximate points shown also in italics in the table of offers), the Irish Leaving Certificate, the European Baccalaureate and the French Baccalaureate.

CHOOSING YOUR COURSE (SEE ALSO CH.1)

Course variations – Widen your options
Sustainable Rural Development (Bangor)
Economics and International Development (Bath)
African Studies and Development (Birmingham)

Development and Peace Studies (Bradford)
Property Development (Bristol UWE)
Natural Hazards Management and International Development (Chester)
Third World Development (East London)
International Development with Overseas Experience (East Anglia)
Sustainable Development (St Andrews)
CHECK PROSPECTUSES AND WEBSITES FOR OTHER UNIVERSITIES AND COLLEGES OFFERING THESE COURSES.

Universities and colleges teaching quality See www.qaa.ac.uk; www.unistats.com.

Top universities and colleges (Research) East Anglia.

ADMISSIONS INFORMATION

Number of applicants per place (approx) Bradford 6; East Anglia 8; Leeds 8.

Advice to applicants and planning the UCAS personal statement Discuss aspects of development studies which interest you, for example in relation to geography, economics, politics. Interests in Third World countries should be mentioned. **East Anglia** Knowledge of current events.

Misconceptions about this course Some students think that Development Studies has something to do with property, with plants or with childhood. It is none of these and is about international processes of change, development, progress and crisis.

Interview advice and questions Since this is a multi-disciplinary subject, questions will vary considerably. Initially they will stem from your interests and the information given on your UCAS application and your reasons for choosing the course. In the past, questions at interview have included: Define a Third World country. What help does the United Nations provide in the Third World? Could it do too much? What problems does the United Nations face in its work throughout the world? Why Development Studies? What will you do in your gap year, and what do you want to achieve? See also **Chapter 7**.

AFTER-RESULTS ADVICE

Offers to applicants repeating A-levels Same East Anglia.

GRADUATE DESTINATIONS AND EMPLOYMENT (2005/6 HESA)

No data available.

Career note The range of specialisms offered on these courses will encourage graduates to make contact with and seek opportunities in a wide range of organisations, not necessarily limited to the Third World and government agencies.

OTHER DEGREE SUBJECTS FOR CONSIDERATION

Economics; Environmental Science/Studies; Geography; Government; International Relations; Politics; Sociology.

DIETETICS

(see also **Food Science/Studies and Technology** and **Nutrition**)

In addition to the scientific aspects of dietetics covering biochemistry, human physiology, food and clinical medicine, students are also introduced to health promotion, psychology, counselling and management skills. (See **Appendix 2**.)

Useful websites www.eatright.org; www.bda.uk.com; www.dietetics.co.uk.

NB The points totals shown to the left of the institutions are for ease of reference only. It must not be assumed that tariff points are always used by institutions or that they can be substituted for an offer in grades. The level of an offer is not necessarily indicative of the quality of a course.

COURSE OFFERS INFORMATION

Subject requirements/preferences **GCSE** English, mathematics and science usually required. **AL** Biology and/or chemistry may be required. **NB** A* grades are likely to form part of university offers in the higher ranges for students applying for places in 2008 for entry in 2009: check websites.

Your target offers

300 pts **Nottingham** – BBB–BBC (Nutr (Diet))
      Surrey – BBB–BBC (Nutr Diet) *(IB 30 pts)*
280 pts **Hertfordshire** – 280 pts (Dietetics)
      London (King's) – BBC+AS (Nutr Diet)
      Plymouth – 280 pts (Dietetics)
240 pts **Coventry** – 240 pts (Dietetics)
      Ulster – 240 pts (Dietetics) (see **Ch 7**)
220 pts **Bath Spa** – 220–260 pts (Diet Hlth)
      Cardiff (UWIC) – 220 pts (Hum Nutr Diet)
200 pts **London Met** – 200 pts (Hum Nutr Diet)
180 pts **Queen Margaret** – 180 pts (Dietetics)
160 pts **Glasgow Caledonian** – CC (Hum Nutr Diet)
      Robert Gordon – CC (Nutr Diet)

      Leeds Met – contact University

Alternative offers

See **Chapter 7** for grade/point equivalences and related information for the following examinations: Scottish qualifications, the Welsh Baccalaureate, the IB diploma (approximate points shown also in italics in the table of offers), the Irish Leaving Certificate, the European Baccalaureate and the French Baccalaureate.

CHOOSING YOUR COURSE (SEE ALSO CH.1)

Course variations – Widen your options
Human Nutrition and Dietetics (Cardiff (UWIC))
Nutrition and Psychology (Chester)
Public Health Nutrition (Oxford Brookes)
Coaching Science and Nutrition (St Mary's (UC))
Nutrition, Health and Fitness (Westminster)
CHECK PROSPECTUSES AND WEBSITES FOR OTHER UNIVERSITIES AND COLLEGES OFFERING THESE COURSES.

Universities and colleges teaching quality See www.qaa.ac.uk; www.unistats.com.

Sandwich degree courses Cardiff (UWIC); Glasgow Caledonian; Surrey.

ADMISSIONS INFORMATION

Number of applicants per place (approx) Glasgow Caledonian 11; Queen Margaret 5; Surrey 1.

Advice to applicants and planning the UCAS personal statement Discuss the work with a hospital dietitian and describe fully work experience gained in hospital dietetics departments or with the schools meals services, and the problems of working in these fields. Contact the British Dietetic Association (see **Appendix 2**).

Selection interviews All institutions.

Interview advice and questions Your knowledge of a career in dietetics will be fully explored and questions will be asked on your work experience and how you reacted to it. See also **Chapter 7**.

AFTER-RESULTS ADVICE

Offers to applicants repeating A-levels **Possibly higher** Glasgow Caledonian.

For a quick reference offers calculator, fold out the inside back cover.

GRADUATE DESTINATIONS AND EMPLOYMENT (2005/6 HESA)
No data available.

Career note Dietitians are professionally trained to advise on diets and aspects of nutrition and many degree courses combine both subjects. They may work in the NHS as hospital dietitians collaborating with medical staff on the balance of foods for patients, or in local health authorities working with GPs, or in health centres or clinics dealing with infant welfare and ante-natal problems. In addition, dietitians advise consumer groups in the food industry and government and may be involved in research. Courses can lead to professional registration: check with admissions tutors.

OTHER DEGREE SUBJECTS FOR CONSIDERATION
Biological Sciences; Biochemistry; Biology; Consumer Studies; Food Science; Health Studies; Hospitality Management; Nursing; Nutrition.

DRAMA

(including **Performing Arts/Studies, Theatre Arts, Theatre Studies** and **Theatre Design;** see also **Art and Design (General)**)

Drama courses are popular, with twice as many women as men applying each year. Lack of confidence in securing appropriate work at the end of the course, however, tends to encourage many applicants to bid for joint courses although these are usually far more competitive since there are fewer places available. Most Schools of Acting and Drama provide a strong vocational bias whilst University Drama departments offer a broader field of studies combining theory and practice. The choice of course will depend on personal preferences, either practical or theoretical, or a combination of both.

Useful websites www.equity.org.uk; www.abtt.org.uk; www.thestage.co.uk; www.uktw.co.uk; www.netgain.org.uk; www.arts.org.uk; www.stagecoach.co.uk.

NB The points totals shown to the left of the institutions are for ease of reference only. It must not be assumed that tariff points are always used by institutions or that they can be substituted for an offer in grades. The level of an offer is not necessarily indicative of the quality of a course.

COURSE OFFERS INFORMATION
Subject requirements/preferences GCSE English usually required. **AL** English, drama, theatre studies may be required or preferred. (Theatre Arts) English, theatre studies or drama may be required for some courses. **NB** A* grades are likely to form part of university offers in the higher ranges for students applying for places in 2008 for entry in 2009: check websites.

Your target offers

360 pts and above
    Cambridge – AAA (Engl Dr Educ)
    Exeter – AAA–BBB (Drama)
    Warwick – ABBb–ABabb (Thea Perf St; Engl Thea St) *(IB 36 pts)*

340 pts Birmingham – AAB–ABB (Dr Thea Arts) *(IB 34 pts)*
    Leeds – AAB (Engl Lit Thea St)
    Manchester – AAB–ABB (Dr; Dr Engl Lit; Dr Scrn St) *(IB 32–35 pts)*

320 pts East Anglia – ABB 320 pts (Engl Lit Dr; Dr) *(IB 32 pts)*
    Glasgow – ABB–BBB (Thea St)
    Kent – 320 pts (Dr Thea St) *(IB 28–34 pts)*
    Lancaster – ABB (Thea St; Thea St Engl Lit; Fr St Thea St; Span St Thea St)
    London (RH) – ABB 320 pts (Dr Thea St; Dr Mus; Dr Ger/Ital; Dr Crea Writ; Engl Dr; Class St Dr; Int Thea (Aus) (Fr))
    Loughborough – 320–300 pts (Dr; Dr Engl) *(IB 32–35 pts)*

Sheffield – ABB (Engl Dr)

Sussex – ABB **or** 360 pts 3AL+AS (Dr St courses)

300 pts **Birmingham** – BBB (Modn Langs Thea St; Dr joint courses)

Bristol – BBB (Dr; Dr Engl; Dr Fr/Ger/Ital/Port/Span) *(IB 32 pts)*

Essex – 300 pts (Dr; Dr Lit; Dr Modn Lang) *(IB 32 pts)*

Hull – BBB–BBC 300–280 pts (Dr; Dr Engl; Dr Lang; Dr Mus; Dr Theol; Dr Hist Art; Dr Film St)

Kent – 300 pts (Engl Am Lit Dr Thea St; Film St Dr Thea St) *(IB 28–34 pts)*

London (Gold) – BBB (Dr Thea Arts)

London (QM) – 300–370 pts (Dr; Engl Dr; Fr Dr; Ger Dr; Russ Dr; Hisp St Dr; Film St Dr) *(IB 32 pts)*

Queen's Belfast – BBB–BBCb (Dr courses)

Reading – 300 pts (TV Film Thea)

280 pts **Aberystwyth** – 280 pts (Dr; Perf St courses; Scnograph St Dr; Dr joint courses)

Bristol UWE – 280–300 pts (Dr; Dr joint courses) *(IB 28–32 pts)*

Brunel – 280 pts (Modn Dr St; Dr Engl; Dr Film TV St) *(IB 30 pts)*

Kent – 280 pts (Dr Hist; Dr Phil; Dr Relig St)

Kingston – 280–320 pts (Dr courses)

Leeds – BBC (Thea Perf)

Liverpool John Moores – BBC (Dr courses)

Queen Margaret – BBC (Thea Prod; Dr Thea Arts)

Salford – 280 pts (Perf Arts) *(IB 28 pts)*

260 pts **Central Lancashire** – 260–240 pts (Mus Thea; Actg)

Kent – 260 pts (Dr Thea St Fr/Ger/Ital; Dr Hisp St) *(IB 28–34 pts)*

London (Central Sch SpDr) – BCC (Dr App Thea Educ)

Northumbria – BCC (Dr; Script Dr; Perf)

Roehampton – 260–240 pts (Dr Thea Perf St courses)

Salford – 260 pts (Contemp Thea Prac)

240 pts **Bangor** – 240–280 pts (Engl Thea St; Thea Media St)

Chester – 240 pts (Dr Thea S courses; Perf NMedia courses) *(IB 30 pts)*

Chichester – 240–280 pts (Perf Arts) *(IB 28–30 pts)*

Dartington (CA) – 240–280 pts (Thea courses)

Edge Hill – 240 pts (Dr Physl Thea Dance)

Glamorgan – 240–300 pts (Ltg Tech; Live Evnt Tech)

Huddersfield – 240 pts (Dr; Mus Dr; Dr Engl; Dr Media)

Oxford Brookes – CCC **or** CCcc (Perf Arts)

Portsmouth – 240–300 pts (Engl Dr)

Ulster – CCC 240 pts (Drama)

220 pts **Bath Spa** – 220–260 pts (Dr St; Perf Arts (Actg) (Dir) (Perf Mgt); Dr St joint courses)

Brighton – 220 pts approx (Perf Vis Arts)

Central Lancashire – 220 pts (Engl Thea St)

De Montfort – 220 pts (Dr St; Arts Mgt Dr St)

Edge Hill – 220–240 pts (Dr; Dr Comb courses)

Lincoln – 220 pts (Drama)

Liverpool Hope – 220 pts (Dr Thea St courses; Crea Perf Arts)

Plymouth – 220 pts (Thea Perf)

Queen Margaret – CCD (Perf Prod Mgt; Cstm Des Constr)

Southampton Solent – 220 pts (Cmdy (Writ Perf))

Winchester – 220–240 pts (Dr courses)

200 pts **Anglia Ruskin** – 200 pts (Dr; Dr Engl; Dr Film; Media St Dr; Mus Dr; Phil Dr; Writ Dr)

Birmingham City – CDD–BB (Engl Dr; Dr P Educ)

Central Lancashire – 200 pts (Contemp Thea Perf)

Coventry – 200–220 pts (Thea Prof Prac)

Cumbria – 200 pts (Drama)

Glamorgan – 200–240 pts (Dr (Thea Media) courses; Media Perf; Media Prod)

Manchester Met – 200 pts (Contemp Thea Perf) *(IB 32–35 pts)*
Middlesex – 200–240 pts (Dr Thea Perf; Dr Tech Thea Arts)
Newport – 200 pts (Perf Arts)
180 pts **Bedfordshire** – 180 pts (Media Perf)
Cardiff (UWIC) – BC (Dr S Educ)
Central Lancashire – 180–160 pts (Thea Prac)
De Montfort – 180–200 pts (Dr St Engl; Perf Arts)
Doncaster (Coll) – 180–240 pts (Perf Arts courses)
Edge Hill – 180–220 pts (Educ St Dr)
Liverpool (LIPA) – BC 180 pts (Actg (Perf Arts); Commun Dr; Perf Arts (Mus))
London (Central Sch SpDr) – 180 pts (Thea Prac (Stg Mgt) (Pptry) (Cstm Constr) (Thea Snd)
(Scnce Art))
Northampton – 180–220 pts (Dr courses)
Staffordshire – 180–240 pts (Thea Arts Film St; Dr Perf Thea Arts; Thea St Script)
160 pts **Central Lancashire** – 160 pts (Dr Thea St Comb Hons)
Cumbria – CC 160 pts (Dr Crea Writ; Dr Mus Thea; Dr Tech Thea)
East London – 160 pts (Perf Arts courses)
Greenwich – 160 pts (Dr Comb courses)
London (Central Sch SpDr) – CC (Actg courses)
London Met – 160 pts (Perf Arts; Thea St courses)
London South Bank – CC (Actg; Dr Perf St; Thea Prac)
Manchester City (Coll) – 160 pts (Actg St; Stg Des Mgt St)
Manchester Met – 160 pts (Dr courses)
Newman (UC) – CC 160 pts (Dr courses)
Queen Margaret – CC (Actg Perf)
Reading – 160 pts (Thea Arts Educ Df St)
Rose Bruford (Coll) – 160 pts min approx; indiv interview/audition (Actg; Dir; Thea Des;
Stg Mgt; Actr Mus; Am Thea Arts; Euro Thea Arts; Ltg Des; Scnc Arts; Cstm Prod)
St Mary's (UC) – 160–200 pts (Dr Perf St; Physl Thea courses)
Wolverhampton – 160 pts (Dr Perf)
Worcester – 160 pts (Dr Perf St)
York St John – CC 160 pts (Perf Thea; Thea Engl Lit)
140 pts **Bishop Grosseteste (UC)** – 140–160 pts (Dr Commun; Educ St Dr)
Derby – 140–180 pts (Thea St Comb; Thea Arts)
Sunderland – 140–160 pts (Perf Arts St)
Thames Valley – 140–160 pts (Acting)
120 pts **Birmingham City** – EEE–EE (Acting)
Bucks New – 120–180 pts (Dr courses)
North East Wales (IHE) – 120–80 pts (Thea Perf)

For information on how to read the Subject Tables, see **Chapter 8**.

Peterborough Reg (Coll) – 120 pts (Perf Arts)
Royal Welsh (CMusDr) – 120–200 pts (Actg; Stg Mgt; Thea Des)
Southampton Solent – 120 pts (Live Perf Mkup Des (Stg Thea))
Suffolk (Univ Campus) – 120–180 pts (Performance)
Swansea (Inst) – 120 pts (Perf Arts Thea St)
Trinity Carmarthen (Coll) – 120 pts (Thea St; Thea Des Prod; Actg)

100 pts **Birmingham (Sch Actg)** – 100 pts (Actg; Actg (Musl Thea))
80 pts **and below**

ARLA – (Acting)
Arts Educ London – entry by audition (Actg; Musl Thea)
Arts London (Central Saint Martins CAD) – 80 pts audition (Actg; Dir; Thea; Des Perf)
Arts London (CFash) – 80 pts (Cstm Tech Effct Mkup)
Arts London (Wimbledon CA) – interview+portfolio (Thea Ltg Des Prac; Thea Set Des Stg
Scrn; Tech Arts Spec Efcts)
Bournemouth (AI) – 80 pts (Actg Thea Film TV)
Essex – 80 pts+audition (Actg; Contemp Thea; Tech Thea St)
Greenwich – 80 pts (Drama)
Grimsby (IFHE) – (Dr St)
GSA (Cons) – audition (Actg; Musl Thea)
Laban – (Dance Thea)
London (Arts Educ Sch) – (Acting)
London (RADA) – audition (BA Dr)
London Mountview (Ac Thea Arts) – audition (Musl Thea; Actg; Tech Thea)
Manchester Met – 80 pts (Acting)
Royal Scottish (RSAMD) – 80 pts (Contemp Thea Prac; Actg; Tech Prod Arts)

Alternative offers
See **Chapter 8** for grade/point equivalences and related information for the following examinations:
Scottish qualifications, the Welsh Baccalaureate, the IB diploma (approximate points shown also in
italics in the table of offers), the Irish Leaving Certificate, the European Baccalaureate and the French
Baccalaureate.

EXAMPLES OF FOUNDATION DEGREES IN THE SUBJECT FIELD

Arts London (Wimbledon CAD); Bath Spa; Bedford (Coll); Bedfordshire; Bournemouth and Poole (Coll);
Bridgwater (Coll); Brooklands (Coll); Burnley (Coll); Canterbury Christ Church; Coventry; Croydon (Coll);
Cumbria; De Montfort; East Durham (CmC); East 15 Acting (Sch); Grimsby (IFHE); Guildford (Coll);
Herefordshire (CAD); Hull (Coll); Leeds (CMus); Leeds Met; London Met; Nescot; Newcastle (Coll);
North Devon (Coll); North East Wales (IHE); Northbrook (Coll); Nottingham New (Coll); Oldham (Coll);
Oxford and Cherwell Valley (Coll); Park Lane Leeds (Coll); Preston (Coll); Rotherham (CAT); St Helens
(Coll); Sheffield Hallam; Sheffield New (Coll); South Birmingham (Coll); South Cheshire (Coll);
Staffordshire (Univ Fed); Stockton Riverside (Coll); Stratford-upon-Avon (Coll); Suffolk (Univ Campus);
Sunderland; Teesside; Thames Valley; Truro (Coll); West Herts (Coll); West Kent (Coll); Weston (Coll);
Weymouth (Coll); Worcestershire New (Coll); Yeovil (Coll).

CHOOSING YOUR COURSE (SEE ALSO CH.1)

Course variations – Widen your options
Writing and Drama (Anglia Ruskin)
Drama and Food Studies (Bath Spa)
Theatre, Performance and Event Design (Birmingham City)
Acting for Theatre, Film and TV (Bournemouth (AI))
Drama and Music Technology (Bristol UWE)
Contemporary Theatre (Essex)
Drama and Screen Studies (Liverpool John Moores)
Theatre Practice: Puppetry (London (Central Sch SpDr))
Drama and Scriptwriting (Northumbria)

DRAMA CENTRE LONDON

BA (Hons) Acting Course
Accredited by the National Council for Drama Training

BA (Hons) Directing Course

Foundation in Performance

MA Screen: Acting, Directing, Writing

MA in European Classical Acting

Information Office
Central Saint Martins College of Art & Design
Southampton Row
London
WC1B 4AP
Tel: +44 (0)20 7514 7022
E-mail: info@csm.arts.ac.uk
Website: www.csm.arts.ac.uk/drama

University of the
Arts London
Central
Saint Martins

European Theatre Arts (Rose Bruford (Coll))
French, Irish and Drama (Ulster)
CHECK PROSPECTUSES AND WEBSITES FOR OTHER UNIVERSITIES AND COLLEGES OFFERING THESE COURSES.

Universities and colleges teaching quality See www.qaa.ac.uk; www.unistats.com.

Top universities and colleges (Research) (including Dance and Performing Arts) Aberystwyth; Bristol*; Kent; London (RH); Manchester; Nottingham Trent; Reading; Warwick*.

ADMISSIONS INFORMATION
Number of applicants per place (approx) Aberystwyth 10; Arts London (Central Saint Martins CAD) (Actg) 32, (Dir) 10, (Wimbledon (CA) (Tech Arts Spec Efcts) 3; Birmingham 15; Bishop Grosseteste (UC) 4; Bristol 40; Brunel 9; Chester 14; Cumbria 4; Dartington (CA) 8; De Montfort (Perf Arts) 5; East Anglia 13; Edge Hill 8; Essex 15; Exeter 20; Glamorgan 6; Huddersfield 5; Hull 16; Hull (Scarborough) 2; Kent 24; Lancaster 18; Leeds 10; Liverpool (LIPA) (Perf Arts (Actg)) 48; Liverpool John Moores 10; London (Central Sch SpDr) (Thea Prac) 5, (Actg) 50, (Gold) 28, (RH) 10; London Met 20; London Mountview (Ac Thea Arts) (Mus Thea) 8; Loughborough 6; Manchester City (Coll) 10; Manchester Met 48; Middlesex 26; Northampton 3; Northumbria 25; Nottingham Trent 4; Queen Margaret 4; Reading 17; Roehampton 6; Royal Welsh (CMusDr) (Actg) 50, (Stg Mgt) 10; Warwick 18; Winchester (Dr) 6; Worcester 4; York St John 9.

Advice to applicants and planning the UCAS personal statement List the plays in which you have performed and specify the characters played. Indicate any experience in other areas of theatre, especially directing or writing. Add any information on projects you have initiated or developed or experienced in theatre craft, such as set design, costume design, lighting design, prop-making, scene painting. List any community arts projects such as work with youth clubs, hospital radio, amateur dramatics, music/drama workshops and voluntary work within the arts. **Arts London (Central Saint Martins CAD)** Only apply if you wish to pursue professional careers in acting or directing. **De Montfort** Strengths in both dance and theatre. **East Anglia** An all-round commitment to drama in all its aspects. **Leeds** Offers one, two or three-year diploma courses which provide an individually designed programme of study and do not have standard entry requirements. These give an opportunity for overseas students to work alongside honours degree students in a very rich arts context. **Liverpool (LIPA)** We look for communication and entrepreneurial skills; (Perf Arts (Actg)) Details of performance and specific characters played; **Loughborough** The course combines both theory and practice. **Nottingham Trent** Art portfolio required. See Chapter 6 and also **Appendix 2**.

Misconceptions about this course That a Theatre Studies course is a training for the stage: it is not. **Arts London (Central Saint Martins CAD)** provides a long-established classical conservatoire-type training for actors, and not Theatre Studies or Performance Arts courses, contrary to the views of some students. It is no longer a private school and home and EU students pay the standard degree fee. **De Montfort** (Perf Arts) Unaware that the course involves music. **Huddersfield** This is not a performing course. **Kent** This is not like an acting school. **Salford** (Contemp Thea Prac) This course does not include musical theatre. **Staffordshire** We stress to applicants that this is not a drama school course. **Sunderland** (Perf Arts St) Applicants often think the course only involves one subject but in fact they are required to study two. **Winchester** This is not an Acting course although practical work is involved. **York St John** This is not a course for intending actors.

Selection interviews **Yes** Most institutions, usually with auditions which are likely to involve solo and group tests; **Some** Chester, St Mary's (UC).

Interview advice and questions **Arts London (Central Saint Martins CAD)** (Actg) Two three-minute speeches or scenes, one of which must be from the classical repertoire. (Dir) Interview and practical workshop which may involve directing actors. **Bristol** Assesses each case on its merits, paying attention to candidate's educational and cultural opportunities. Particularly interested in applicants who have already shown some evidence of commitment in their approach to drama in practical work, theatre-going, film viewing or reading. One fifth of applicants are called for interview and take part in practical sessions. They may present any art work, photography or similar material. (London Board Practical Music not acceptable for Drama/Music unless offered with theoretical music + one other A-level.) **Brunel** All applicants to whom an offer may be made will be auditioned, involving a practical workshop, voice, movement improvisation and a short prepared speech. Offers unlikely to be made to those with less than a grade B in drama or theatre studies. **De Montfort** (Perf Arts) What do you hope to gain on a three-year course in Performing Arts? Interviews involve practical workshops in drama and theatre and a written paper. **East Anglia** Looks for candidates with a sound balance of academic and practical skills. Applicants will be expected to analyse performance and to understand what is entailed in the production of a drama. **Hull** Interviews two groups of 18 for whole day which presents a mini-version of the course, with entire staff and number of current students present. Offers then made to about half. Selection process is all-important. More applicants for the joint honours courses with English, Theology, Classical Studies, American Studies or Modern Language who have a conventional half-hour interview. Drama/English is the most popular combination and the offer includes a B in English. **Kent** No single honours candidate accepted without interview. Emphasis equally on academic and practical abilities. Questions asked to probe the applicant's creative and analytical grasp of theatre. **Lancaster** (Thea St) Candidates invited for interview and should be prepared to take part in a workshop with other candidates. We are just as interested in backstage people as actors and now have an arts administration option. **Liverpool (LIPA)** (Perf Arts (Actg)) Applicants will be expected to perform one devised piece, one Shakespearean piece and a song plus a short review of a performance they have seen recently. **London (Central Sch SpDr), Central Lancashire, De Montfort, London (RH)** Written papers and/or tests. **London (RH)** At interview we look for students who are mentally agile and versatile who enjoy reading as well as taking part in productions. **London Mountview (Ac Thea Arts)** Voice, movement and singing sessions plus acting pieces. **Loughborough** Offers in terms of A-levels not set.

Candidates judged as individuals. Applicants with unconventional subject combinations and mature students considered. Final selection based on interview and audition. Applicants ought to show experience of practical drama, preferably beyond school plays. **Royal Welsh (CMusDr)** Written papers and/or tests. BA Acting – audition; BA Stage Management – interview; BA Theatre Design – interview and portfolio presentation. All applicants are charged an audition/interview fee. **Warwick** Interview is important to assess academic potential and particularly commitment to, and suitability for, teaching; offers therefore variable. See also **Chapter 7**.

Applicants' impressions (A=Open day; B=Interview day) **London (Gold)** (B) There was one interviewer, who was fairly aggressive and forceful and who made me feel intimidated. I was asked what I thought about Goldsmiths, why I wanted to do Drama, would I rather go to a drama school and who was the most influential person of the 20th century? It was a well-organised visit. The teachers were very enthusiastic and the students thought it was a good course.

Reasons for rejection (non-academic) Poor ambition. Wrong expectations of the course. Several students clearly want a drama school acting training rather than a degree course. Not enough background reading. **Arts London (Central Saint Martins CAD)** Insufficient clarity about career aims. **De Montfort** (Perf Arts) Candidate more suitable for a drama or dance school than for a degree course. No genuine engagement with the subject. Evidence of poor attendance at school.

AFTER-RESULTS ADVICE
Offers to applicants repeating A-levels **Higher** Hull, Warwick; **Possibly higher** London (RH); **Same** Brunel, Chichester, De Montfort (Perf Arts), East Anglia, GSA (Cons), Huddersfield, Kent, Leeds (further audition required), Liverpool Hope, Liverpool John Moores, Loughborough, Manchester City (Coll), Newman (UC), Nottingham Trent, Roehampton, Royal Welsh (CMusDr), St Mary's (UC), Staffordshire, Sunderland, Winchester, York St John.

GRADUATE DESTINATIONS AND EMPLOYMENT (2005/6 HESA)
Graduates surveyed 2945 **Employed** 1665 **In further study** 275 **Assumed unemployed** 210.

Career note Some graduates develop careers in performance, writing, directing and producing as well as wider roles within the theatre. Others go on to careers such as teaching, media management and retail where their creativity and communication skills are valued.

OTHER DEGREE SUBJECTS FOR CONSIDERATION
Art and Design (Costume Design, Stage Design); Arts Management; Dance; Education (Primary); English; Performance Studies.

ECONOMICS

Economics is about how society makes good use of the limited resources available. Degree courses cover all aspects of finance, taxation and monetary union between countries, aiming to equip the student to analyse economic problems in a systematic way and thus acquire an understanding of how economic systems work. Applicants without economics at A- or AS-level should be prepared for a study involving some mathematics and statistics, depending on which course they choose.

Useful websites www.bized.co.uk; www.iea.org.uk; www.res.org.uk; see also **Finance**.

NB The points totals shown to the left of the institutions are for ease of reference only. It must not be assumed that tariff points are always used by institutions or that they can be substituted for an offer in grades. The level of an offer is not necessarily indicative of the quality of a course.

COURSE OFFERS INFORMATION
Subject requirements/preferences **GCSE** English, mathematics and occasionally a foreign language required. A*/A/B may be stipulated by some universities. **AL** Mathematics, economics or business studies may be required or preferred. Business studies may be preferred if economics is not offered.

NB A* grades are likely to form part of university offers in the higher ranges for students applying for places in 2008 for entry in 2009: check websites.

Your target offers

360 pts and above

Bristol – AAA–AAB (Econ; Econ Euro; Econ Economet; Econ Fin; Econ Hist; Econ Maths; Econ Pol; Econ Sociol; Phil Econ; Econ Mgt) *(IB 34–38 pts)*

Cambridge – AAA (Econ; Land Econ (Env Law Econ)) *(IB 38–42 pts)*

Durham – AAA (Nat Sci Econ) *(IB 36 pts)*

Lancaster – AAA (Econ N Am/Aus) *(IB 34–36 pts)*

London (LSE) – AAA (Econ; Econ Econ Hist; Env Pol Econ; Geog Econ; Gov Econ; Maths Econ; Phil Econ; Soc Pol Econ; Economet Mathem Econ) *(IB 38 pts)*

London (UCL) – AAA+AS–AAB+AS (Econ; Econ Stats; Econ Geog; Phil Econ) *(IB 36–39 pts)*

Nottingham – AAA–AABB (Econ courses; Int Econ) *(IB 38 pts)*

Oxford – Offers vary eg AAA–AAB (Econ Mgt; Hist Econ; Mat Econ Mgt; Eng Econ Mgt; PPE) *(IB 38–42 pts)*

Warwick – AABb (Econ; Ind Econ; Econ Pol Int St; Econ Econ Hist; Maths Econ; PPE) *(IB 38 pts)*

340 pts **Aston** – 340 pts (2AL+2AS) **or** 320 pts (3AL) (Int Bus Econ)

Bath – AAB (Econ; Econ Pol; Econ Int Dev; Pol Econ) *(IB 38 pts)*

Durham – AAB (Econ; Bus Econ; PPE; Econ Fr; Comb Soc Sci; Nat Sci Joint Hons)

Essex – 340–280 pts (PPE)

Exeter – AAB–BBB (Econ; Econ Fin; Econ Economet; Econ Pol; Bus Econ) *(IB 32–35 pts)*

Manchester – AAB (Econ; PPE) *(IB 34 pts)*

St Andrews – AAB (App Econ; Econ courses) *(IB 34–36 pts)*

Southampton – AAB 340 pts (Econ; Econ Act Sci; Econ Fin; Econ Mgt Sci; Maths Econ; Econ Phil; Pol Econ; Acc Econ) *(IB 35 pts)*

York – AAB (Econ; Econ Fin; Econ Economet Fin; Econ Econ Hist; PPE) *(IB 36 pts H666)*

320 pts **Aston** – 320 pts (Econ Mgt)

Birmingham – ABB (Mathem Econ Stats; Econ; Econ Lang; Pol Econ)

Cardiff – ABB (Bus Econ; Econ; Econ Mgt St; Econ Euro Lang; Bus Econ Euro Lang; Sociol Econ; Econ Fin)

Glasgow – ABB (Econ courses; Bus Econ courses) *(IB 36 pts)*

Kent – 320 pts (Law Econ) *(IB 34 pts H 16 pts)*

Lancaster – ABB (Econ; Econ Maths; Econ Geog; Adv Econ Mark; Fin Econ; Econ Lang)

Leeds – ABB (Econ courses; Bus Fin Econ; Bus Econ) *(IB 33 pts H econ/bus/Engl/maths 5 pts)*

Leicester – ABB (BA Econ Law; Econ; Fin Econ; Bus Econ) *(IB 32 pts)*

London (RH) – ABB–BBB (Econ; Fin Bus Econ; Econ Fr/Ger/Ital/Span; Econ Mgt; Econ Maths; Econ Mus) *(IB 33–35 pts)*

London (SOAS) – ABB (Econ; Dev Econ)

London (UCL) – ABB+AS (Econ Bus E Euro St)

Loughborough – ABB–AAC (Econ; Bus Econ Fin; Int Econ; Econ Acc; Econ Pol; Econ Fr/Ger/Span; Geog Econ; Econ Soc Pol; Econ Sociol) *(IB 34 pts)*

Manchester – ABB–BBB (BA Econ; Econ Pol; Econ Sociol; Econ Fin; Econ Crim; Econ Econ Soc Hist) *(IB 34 pts)*

Newcastle – ABB–BBB (Econ courses) *(IB 33–35 pts)*

Nottingham – ABB (Ind Econ; Ind Econ Ins) *(IB 38 pts)*

Queen's Belfast – ABB–BBBb (Econ Acc)

Reading – 320 (3AL+AS) **or** 300 pts (3AL) (Econ; Bus Econ; Econ Economet)

Sheffield – ABB–BBB (Econ; Econ Geog; Econ Phil; Econ Pol; Econ Soc Pol; Fr/Ger/Russ Econ; Mgt Econ; Acc Fin Mgt Econ) *(IB 32 pts)*

300 pts **City** – 300–320 pts (Econ; Econ Acc; Journal Econ; Mathem Sci Fin Econ; Sociol Econ) *(IB 28–30 pts)*

Dundee – 300 pts (Bus Econ Mark courses; MA Econ; MA Fin Econ) *(IB 29 pts)*

East Anglia – BBB–BBC (Econ; Econ Acc; Econ Phil; Bus Econ; Bus Fin Econ; PPE) *(IB 32–35 pts)*

Edinburgh – BBB (Econ; Econ Acc; Econ Chin; Econ Law; Econ Econ Hist; Econ Pol; Econ Sociol; Econ Env St; Econ Mgt Sci) *(IB 34 pts H555)*

Essex – BBB 300 pts (Econ; Econ Euro; Econ Fr/Ger/Ital/Span; Econ Pol; Econ Maths; Acc Econ; Hist Econ; Int Econ; Fin Econ) *(IB 32 pts)*

Kent – 300 pts (PPE Euro; PPE) *(IB 32 pts)*

Lancaster – BBB (Econ Int Rel; Econ Pol; PPE) *(IB 34–36 pts)*

Leeds – BBB (Chin Econ)

Leicester – ABC (BSc Bus Econ; Econ; Fin Econ) *(IB 32 pts)*

Liverpool – BBB–ABB 300–320 pts (Fin Econ; Econ; Bus Econ) *(IB 32 pts)*

London (QM) – 300 pts (Econ courses) *(IB 34 pts)*

Queen's Belfast – BBB (Bus Econ; Econ Mgt; Econ Fin; Econ Fr/Ger/Span; Econ) *(IB 35 pts H655)*

Strathclyde – ABC–BBB (Economics)

Surrey – 300 pts (Bus Econ Fin; Econ; Bus Econ) *(IB 32 pts)*

Sussex – BBB **or** 340 pts 3AL+AS (Econ courses)

Swansea – 300 pts (Economics)

280 pts **Brunel** – 280–260 pts (Econ Bus Fin; Econ Mgt; Bus Econ)

Kent – BBC 280 pts (Econ; Econ Comp; Euro Econ (Fr) (Ger) (Span); Soc Anth Econ; App Econ Sociol) *(IB 32 pts)*

Swansea – 280 pts (BSc: Fin Econ; Int Bus Econ; Fin Econ Acc; Fin Econ Comp)

Westminster – 280 pts (Bus Econ)

260 pts **Aberystwyth** – 260 pts (Econ; Bus Econ; Econ joint courses)

Bradford – 260 pts (Econ; Econ Dev St; Econ Int Rel; Econ Mark; Econ Sociol; Econ Psy; Int Econ; Bus Econ)

Coventry – 260–320 pts (Econ; Econ joint courses; Fin Econ; Bus Econ)

Heriot-Watt – BCC–CCC 260 pts (Econ courses)

Hull – 260 pts (Econ; Int Econ; Bus Econ courses)

Keele – 260–280 pts (Bus Econ; Econ courses) *(IB 28–30 pts)*

Kingston – 260 pts (Econ; Bus Econ; Fin Econ; App Econ courses)

London (Gold) – BCC (Pol Econ; Econ Pol Pblc Pol)

Oxford Brookes – BCC–CCC (Econ courses; Bus Econ)

Richmond (Am Int Univ) – 260 pts (Economics)

Swansea – 260 pts (BSc Bus Econ; BA: Econ; Bus Econ; Bus Econ Acc)

240 pts **Aberdeen** – CCC (Econ courses)

Bangor – 240–280 pts (Bus Econ; Econ joint courses) *(IB 28 pts)*

Dundee – 240 pts (Econ; Bus Econ Mark; Fin Econ; Econ joint courses)

Manchester Met – CCC 240 pts (Econ courses; Bus Econ courses) *(IB 28 pts)*

Northumbria – 240 pts (Bus Econ)

Nottingham Trent – 240 pts (Econ; Bus Econ)

Portsmouth – 240–200 pts (Econ Fin Bank; Econ; Bus Econ; Bus Econ Bus Law; App Econ)

Robert Gordon – CCC (Mgt Econ)

Salford – 240–260 pts (Econ; Bus Econ; Bus Econ Gam St) *(IB 30 pts)*

Sheffield Hallam – 240 pts (Bus Econ)

Stirling – CCC/BC (Econ; PPE)

Ulster – CCC 240 pts (Econ; Econ Pol)

230 pts **Buckingham** – 230 pts (Econ; Econ Bus Law; Econ Bus Jrnl; Econ Hist; Econ Inf Sys; Econ Pol; Econ Fr/Span)

220 pts **Abertay Dundee** – 220 pts (Bus St (Econ))

Glamorgan – 220 pts (Maths Bus Econ)

200 pts **Anglia Ruskin** – 200 pts (Bus Econ)

Aston – 200–300 pts (Econ joint courses)

Birmingham City – 200 pts (Acc Econ; Adv Econ; Bus Econ; Constr Mgt Econ; Econ Comp; Mark Econ; Econ Fin)

For information on how to read the Subject Tables, see **Chapter 8**.

Bristol UWE – 200–240 pts (Int Bus Econ; Econ; Econ Mny Bank Fin) *(IB 24–28 pts)*
Central Lancashire – 200–240 pts (Econ courses)
Hertfordshire – 200–240 pts (Econ courses; Bus Econ courses)
London Met – 200 pts (Econ; Econ St; Econ (Int Bus); Int Econ; Bus Econ)
Middlesex – 200–240 pts (Bus Econ courses)
Napier – 200 pts (Bus Econ; Acc Econ)
Newport – 200 pts (Econ Law; Acc Econ)
Plymouth – 200 pts (Econ courses; Bus Econ courses)

180 pts **Cardiff (UWIC)** – 180 pts (Acc Econ)
Glasgow Caledonian – BC (Soc Sci (Econ))
Northampton – 180–220 pts (Econ courses)
Southampton Solent – 180 pts (App Econ courses)
Staffordshire – 180–240 pts (Bus Fin Econ; Bus Econ)

160 pts **East London** – 160 pts (Econ courses)
Greenwich – 160 pts (Bus Econ; Econ; Int St Econ)
Liverpool John Moores – 160–200 pts (Economics)
West Scotland – CC–CD (Bus Econ App Econ; Econ)
Winchester – 160 pts (Bus Fin Econ)

100 pts **Bradford (Coll)** – 100 pts (Bus St (Econ))

80 pts **CECOS** – 80 pts (Econ Mgt)
London (Birk) – 80 pts for under 21s (over 21 varies) (p/t Econ Soc Pol; Fin Econ)
Worcester – 80–160 pts (Bus Mgt (Econ))
European Bus Sch London – contact admissions tutor

Leeds Met – contact University
Open University – contact University (Econ Maths Sci)

Alternative offers
See **Chapter 8** for grade/point equivalences and related information for the following examinations: Scottish qualifications, the Welsh Baccalaureate, the IB diploma (approximate points shown also in italics in the table of offers), the Irish Leaving Certificate, the European Baccalaureate and the French Baccalaureate.

CHOOSING YOUR COURSE (SEE ALSO CH.1)
Course variations – Widen your options
Land Economy (Cambridge)
International Business and Economics (Central Lancashire)
Economics and Trade (Coventry)
Philosophy, Politics and Economics (Durham)
Economics and Management (Edinburgh)
Economics (European Exchange) (Essex)
Business Economics and Financial Management (Hull)
European Economics (French) (Kent)
Medical Statistics and Applied Economics (Kingston)
Industrial Economics (Nottingham)
CHECK PROSPECTUSES AND WEBSITES FOR OTHER UNIVERSITIES AND COLLEGES OFFERING THESE COURSES.

Universities and colleges teaching quality See www.qaa.ac.uk; www.unistats.com.

Top universities and colleges (Research) Aston; Cambridge; Essex*; Exeter; Leicester; London (LSE)*, (QM), (UCL)*; Nottingham; Oxford; Southampton; Warwick*; York.

Sandwich degree courses Abertay Dundee; Aberystwyth; Aston; Bath; Brunel; City; Hertfordshire; Kingston; Lancaster; Loughborough; Middlesex; Newcastle; Oxford Brookes; Plymouth; Portsmouth; Reading; Staffordshire; Surrey; Ulster; West Scotland; Westminster.

ADMISSIONS INFORMATION

Number of applicants per place (approx) Abertay Dundee 3; Aberystwyth 3; Anglia Ruskin 10; Aston 8; Bangor 4; Bath 12; Birmingham 10; Birmingham City 16; Bradford 5; Bristol 11; Brunel 12; Buckingham 4; Cambridge 7; Cardiff 8; Central Lancashire 5; City 18, (Econ Acc) 12; Coventry 10; Derby 3; Dundee 5; Durham (Econ) 10; East Anglia 15; Essex 6; Exeter 12; Greenwich 8; Heriot-Watt 4; Hull 15; Kent 11; Kingston 9; Lancaster 14; Leeds 16; Leicester 10; Liverpool 4; Liverpool John Moores 8; London (LSE) (Econ) 10, (Econ Econ Hist) 8, (Economet Mathem Econ) 20, (UCL) 12; Loughborough 15; Manchester Met 5; Middlesex (Econ) 8; Newcastle 11, (Econ Bus Mgt) 27, (Fin Bus Econ) 16; Northampton 8; Northumbria 16; Nottingham 15; Nottingham Trent 2; Oxford (success rate Econ Mgt 16%, PPE 29%); Oxford Brookes 51; Plymouth 4; Portsmouth 6; Queen's Belfast 10; St Andrews 5; Salford 6; Sheffield 10; Southampton 8; Staffordshire 4; Stirling 6; Sunderland 8; Surrey 5; Swansea 7; Warwick 16; West Scotland 7; York 17.

Number of applicants (a UK **b** EU (non-UK) **c** non-EU **d** mature) Aston **a**300 **b**30 **c**50 **d**20; Leeds **a**433 **b**5 **c**70 **d**33.

Advice to applicants and planning the UCAS personal statement Visits, work experience and work shadowing in banks, insurance companies, accountants' offices etc should be described. Keep up-to-date with economic issues by reading *The Economist* and *Financial Times* and find other sources of information. Describe any particular aspects of economics which interest you – and why. Make it clear on the statement that you know what economics is and why you want to study it. **Hull** Interests and ambitions. **Kent** Take three A-levels and optionally one AS. **St Andrews** Evidence of interest and reasons for choosing the course. Sport/extra-curricular activities. Positions of responsibility. Applicants should note that (a) it is not a disadvantage not to have studied economics and (b) an MA degree is not better than a BSc – they are both first degrees in the Scottish system. **Southampton** Clearly written statement of academic and non-academic strengths and interests. **York** We look for diligent, highly motivated students.

Misconceptions about this course Bradford That the course is very mathematical and that students will not get a good job, eg management. **Kent** That the course is mathematical, has a high failure rate and has poorer job prospects than Business Studies courses. **London (UCL)** Some think the Economics course is a Business course. **York** That PPE is a degree taken mainly by male students! That it is dry and overly abstract. Applicants should note that many courses will accept students without economics (check prospectuses and websites).

Selection interviews Yes Bristol, Bristol UWE, Brunel, Cambridge, Coventry, East London, Edinburgh, Essex, Keele, London (RH), (UCL), Manchester Met, Middlesex, Nottingham Trent, Oxford, Southampton (Econ Acc) (interviews influence level of offer), Surrey; **Some** Aberystwyth, Anglia Ruskin, Bangor, Buckingham, Dundee, East Anglia, Kent, Leeds, London (LSE), London Met (mature students), Staffordshire, Swansea, York (PPE).

Interview advice and questions If you have studied economics at A-level or in other examinations, expect to be questioned on aspects of the subject. This is a subject which is constantly in the news, so keep abreast of developments and be prepared to be asked questions such as: What is happening to sterling at present? What is happening to the dollar? How relevant is economics today? What are your views of the Government's economic policy? Do you think that the family is declining as an institution? Discuss Keynesian economics. Is the power of the Prime Minister increasing? What is a recession? How would you get the world out of recession? What causes a recession? **Cambridge** What is the point of using NHS money to keep old people alive? What would you say if Gordon Brown were to take a report which shows that people who go to university earn more than those who did not and then proclaim that university causes you to earn more? **Oxford** (Econ Mgt) Two samples of work required relating to economics or management (if studied at A-level). One-hour written test covering comprehension, writing, problem-solving skills. 'I was asked questions on a newspaper article I had been given to read 45 minutes beforehand, followed by a few maths problems and an economics question.' Explain why teachers might be changing jobs to become plumbers. (Econ Mgt) What is the difference between the buying and selling of slaves and the buying and selling of football players? Should a Wal-Mart store be opened in the middle of Oxford? See also **Chapter 7**.

For information on how to read the Subject Tables, see **Chapter 8**.

Applicants' impressions (A=Open day; B=Interview day) **Bath** (A) An informal day. We were able to pick and choose talks and tours. I went to talks about the course and student life and a tour of the campus and accommodation. **Birmingham** (B) There was a talk about the course, a free lunch and a tour of the campus. **Oxford** (B) All three interviewers were kind and helpful. They would re-route me if I went wrong and hint at the right answer. I was a bit apprehensive since I hadn't done any economics previously. The interview lasted 30 minutes.

Reasons for rejection (non-academic) Lack of knowledge about the course offered and the subject matter. Lack of care in preparing personal statement. Poor written English. The revelation on the statement that they want a course different from that for which they have applied! **Aberystwyth** Would have trouble fitting into the unique environment at Aberystwyth.

AFTER-RESULTS ADVICE

Offers to applicants repeating A-levels **Higher** Birmingham City, City, Derby, East Anglia, Essex, Leeds, Newcastle, Northumbria, Nottingham, Queen's Belfast, St Andrews, Warwick, York; **Possibly higher** Bradford, Brunel, Durham, Lancaster, Oxford Brookes; **Same** Aberystwyth, Anglia Ruskin, Bangor, Bath, Buckingham, Cardiff, Coventry, Dundee, East London, Heriot-Watt, Hull, Kingston, Liverpool, Liverpool John Moores, London (RH), London Met, Loughborough, Napier, Nottingham Trent, Salford, Sheffield, Staffordshire, Surrey, Swansea, Ulster; **No offers made** Cambridge.

GRADUATE DESTINATIONS AND EMPLOYMENT (2005/6 HESA)
Graduates surveyed 3420 **Employed** 1725 **In further study** 485 **Assumed unemployed** 230.

Career note Most graduates work within areas of business and finance in a range of jobs including management and administration posts across both public and private sectors.

OTHER DEGREE SUBJECTS FOR CONSIDERATION
Accountancy; Actuarial Studies; Administration; Banking; Business Studies; Development Studies; Estate Management; Financial Services; Government; Politics; Property Development; Quantity Surveying; Social Sciences; Sociology; Statistics.

EDUCATION STUDIES and TEACHER TRAINING
(see also **Social Studies/Science**)

Abbreviations P – Primary Teaching; S – Secondary Teaching; QTS – Qualified Teacher Status.

There are two types of degree courses in Education – those which cover the history, philosophy and theory of education but which are not necessarily teacher training courses, and those which prepare the student for a career in the teaching profession. Read prospectuses carefully. For the latter, candidates should be well motivated towards teaching and education – the interview is important. Interview panels look for candidates with confidence in their own ability, a lively personality, patience and optimism. Experience of working with children is important. Students planning to follow a degree with a Postgraduate Certificate in Education (PGCE) are advised that problems may arise if their first degree subject is not a National Curriculum subject.

Teacher training courses are offered in the following subject areas: Art and Design (P); Biology (P S); Business Studies (S); Chemistry (P S); Childhood (P); Computer Education (P); Creative and Performing Arts (P); Dance (P S); Design and Technology (P S); Drama (P S); English (P S); Environmental Science (P S); Environmental Studies (P); French (P S); General Primary; Geography (P S); History (P S); Maths (P S); Music (P S); Physical Education/Movement Studies (P S); Religious Studies (P); Science (P S); Sociology (P); Textile Design (P); Welsh (P). Two-year BEd courses are also offered for holders of HND or equivalent qualifications (minimum age in some cases 23–25) in the following subject areas: Business Studies (S); Chemistry (S); Design and Technology (S); English (P); French (S); General Primary; German (S); Language Studies (P); Mathematics (S); Music (S); Physics (S); Science (S); Spanish (S); Welsh (S). For further information on teaching as a career see websites below and

Appendix 2 for contact details. Over 50 taster courses are offered each year to those considering teaching as a career. Early Childhood Studies has been introduced in recent years by a number of universities. The courses focus on child development, from birth to eight years of age, and the provision of education for children and their families. It is a multi-disciplinary subject and can cover social problems and legal and psychological issues.

Useful websites www.tda.gov.uk; www.gtcs.org.uk; www.gttr.ac.uk; www.teachertrainingwales.org; wwwdcsf.gov.uk.

NB The points totals shown to the left of the institutions are for ease of reference only. It must not be assumed that tariff points are always used by institutions or that they can be substituted for an offer in grades. The level of an offer is not necessarily indicative of the quality of a course.

COURSE OFFERS INFORMATION

Subject requirements/preferences GCSE English, mathematics and a science subject for those born after 1 September 1979. **AL** One A-level is usually required in the main subject of choice plus one or two other subjects **NB** A* grades are likely to form part of university offers in the higher ranges for students applying for places in 2008 for entry in 2009: check websites.

The following table is divided into two sections: **Education Studies** including Childhood Studies and **Teacher Training Courses**.

EDUCATION STUDIES

Your target offers

360 pts **and above**
Cambridge – AAA (Educ St courses) *(IB 38–42 pts)*

340 pts **Cardiff** – AAB–BCC 340–260 pts (Educ joint Hons)

320 pts **Bath** – ABB (Coach Educ Spo Dev)
Durham – ABB (Educ St (Biol Sci) (Engl St) (Geog) (Hist) (Maths) (Mus) (Psy)) *(IB 34 pts)*
Lancaster – ABB (Psy Educ)
Warwick – BBCc **or** BBccc (Ely Chld St) *(IB 30 pts)*

300 pts **Birmingham** – BBB (Engl Lang Lit Educ; Hist Herit Educ) *(IB 32 pts)*
Cardiff – BBB–BCC (Educ single Hons)
Exeter – BBB–BCC (Educ St; Chld Yth St) *(IB 28–33 pts)*
Liverpool – 300–320 pts (Maths Educ)

280 pts **Birmingham** – BBC 280 pts (Chld Cult Educ) *(IB 32 pts)*
Bristol – BBC (Ely Chld St)
Glasgow – BBC (Commun Dev)
Leeds – BBC (Chld St)
Manchester – BBC–BCC (Lrn Disab St)
Oxford Brookes – BBC (Ely Chld St courses; Educ Hum Dev courses)
York – BBC–BCC (Educ St)

260 pts **Aberystwyth** – 260 pts (Educ joint major courses) *(IB 30 pts)*
Keele – 260–280 pts (Educ St courses) *(IB 28–30 pts)*
London (Gold) – BCC (Educ Cult Soty) *(IB 28 pts)*
Stirling – BCC–CCC (Phil Relig St Prof Educ)
Stranmillis (UC) – BCC (Ely Chld St)
Sussex – 260–300 pts approx (Educ St courses)
Swansea – BCC 260 pts (Ely Chld St)

240 pts **Aberdeen** – 240 pts (Educ courses)
Bristol – CCC (Df St)
Bristol UWE – 240–280 pts (Ely Chld St courses; Educ courses) *(IB 32 pts)*
Chester – 240 pts (Ely Chld St; Educ St courses) *(IB 30 pts)*
Liverpool Hope – 240 pts (Dishab St courses; Ely Chld St; Educ St courses)
Plymouth – 240 pts (Ely Chld St)
Ulster – 240 pts (Educ courses)

220 pts **Bangor** – CCD 220–260 pts (Child St (Addysg; Astudiaethau Plentyndod joint Hons))
Brighton – 220 pts (Education) *(IB 28 pts)*
Dundee – 220 pts 3 yr entry (Commun Educ)
Edge Hill – 220 pts (Ely Chld St)
Glamorgan – 220 pts (Ely Yrs Dev Educ; Educ courses)
Hull – 220–280 pts (Educ St courses)
Strathclyde – CCD (Commun Educ)
Winchester – 220 pts (Educ St courses)
200 pts **Bangor** – 200–240 pts (Chld St)
Bath Spa – 200–260 pts (Educ courses; Ely Yrs Educ courses)
Bolton – 200 pts (Educ St Comb courses)
Central Lancashire – 200 pts (Psy Educ St)
Cumbria – 200 pts (Educ St)
Edge Hill – 200–220 pts (Chld Yth St)
Gloucestershire – 200 pts (Educ courses)
Heriot-Watt – 200 pts (Chem Prof Educ; Prof Educ Maths; Phys Educ)
Lincoln – 200 pts (Chld Yth St)
Manchester Met – 200 pts (Ely Chld St; Chld Yth St) *(IB 28 pts)*
Newport – 200 pts (Education)
Northumbria – 200 pts (Disab St Chld St; Chld St Prof Prac St; Cr Educ courses)
Nottingham Trent – 200 pts (Chld St)
180 pts **Bedfordshire** – 180 pts (Educ St; Educ St Engl; Chld Yth St)
Chichester – 180–220 pts (Chld St; Chld Yth Soty) *(IB 26–28 pts)*
De Montfort – 180–200 pts (Educ St courses)
Derby – 180 pts (Ely Chld St)
Hertfordshire – 180 pts (Educ St)
Liverpool John Moores – 180 pts (Out Educ Env Educ)
Middlesex – 180–200 pts (Educ St courses; Ely Chld St)
Newport – 180 pts (Ely Yrs)
Northampton – 180–220 pts (Educ St courses; Ely Chld St)
Plymouth – 180 pts (Educ St)
Roehampton – 180 pts (Ely Chld St; Educ; Chld Soty courses)
Sheffield Hallam – 180 pts (Educ St; Educ Disab St)
Sunderland – 180 pts (Chld St; Educ courses; TESOL Educ)
160 pts **Anglia Ruskin** – CC (Educ St; Educ St Ely Chld St)
Birmingham (CFTCS) – 160 pts (Ely Chld St)
Bishop Grosseteste (UC) – 160 pts (Ely Chld St; Educ courses)
Canterbury Christ Church – CC (Ely Chld St; Infml Commun Educ)
Central Lancashire – 160–200 pts (Df St Educ; Educ courses)
East London – 160 pts (Educ Commun Dev; Lang Educ; Ely Chld St; Spec Educ Nds)
Edinburgh – CC (Commun Educ)
Greenwich – 160 pts (Chld St; Educ courses)
Hull – 160–220 pts (Educ St Urb Lrng)
Hull (Scarborough) – 160–220 pts (Educ St Ely Chld St; Educ St Env Sci; Educ St Engl St; Educ St ICT)
Leeds Trinity and All Saints (Coll) – 160–240 pts (Chld Yth)
Liverpool John Moores – 160 pts (Ely Child St; Educ St courses)
London Met – 160 pts (Educ St courses)
Newman (UC) – CC 160 pts (Ely Yrs Educ St; Educ St courses)
Reading – 160 pts (Thea Arts Educ Df St)
St Mary's (UC) – CC 160 pts (Educ Emp courses)
Sheffield Hallam – 160 pts (Ely Chld St)
Wolverhampton – 160–220 pts (Df St Educ; Educ St joint courses; Cond Educ; Ely Chld St; Interp (Brit Sign Lang))
Worcester – 160 pts (Ely Chld)

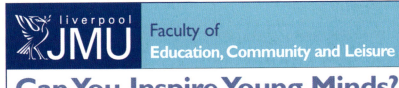
For information on how to read the Subject Tables, see **Chapter 8**.

York St John – 160 pts (Educ St)
150 pts Dundee – 150 pts 4 yr entry (Commun Educ)
140 pts Cardiff (UWIC) – 140 pts (Educ St Ely Chld St; Educ St Hum; Educ St Welsh)
Derby – 140 pts (Educ St)
Guildford (Coll) – 140 pts (Ely Chld St)
Marjon (UC) – 140–200 pts (Educ St courses)
Trinity Carmarthen (Coll) – 140 pts (Ely Yrs Educ; Educ St courses)
120 pts Bradford (Coll) – 120 pts (Educ St)
North East Wales (IHE) – 120–80 pts (Ely Chld St courses; Educ St courses)
Suffolk (Univ Campus) – 120–180 pts (Ely Chld)
UHI Millennium Inst (NHC) – 120 pts (Chld Yth St)
Worcester – 120 pts (Educ St)
100 pts Cardiff (UWIC) – 100 pts (Commun Educ)
80 pts South East Essex (Coll) – 80 pts (Ely Yrs Educ; Spec Educ Nds)
Stockport (CFHE) – 80 pts (Ely Chld St)

Leeds Met – contact University
Open University – contact University (Chld Yth St)

TEACHER TRAINING

Subjects attracting the most applicants include Drama, History, Physical Education, Social Science, English and Art. Subjects attracting the fewest applicants include Modern Languages, Sciences, Craft Design and Technology, Music, Religious Education, Mathematics and Home Economics. The choice of subject will affect the level of the offer made. See also separate subject tables.

Subject requirements/preferences GCSE Grades A–C in English, mathematics and a science subject. **AL** One subject is usually required in the main subject of choice. **NB** A* grades are likely to form part of university offers in the higher ranges for students applying for places in 2008 for entry in 2009: check websites.

Your target offers
360 pts and above
Cambridge – AAA (BA Educ (Biol Sci) (Class) (Engl) (Engl Dr) (Geog) (Hist) (Maths) (Modn Langs) (Mus) (Phys Sci) (Relig St))
320 pts Stranmillis (UC) – ABB (Engl Educ; Geog Educ; Hist Educ; Relig St Educ)
300 pts Sussex – BBB–BBC **or** 340–310 pts 3AL+AS (Engl Lang Teach joint courses)
Stranmillis (UC) – BBB (Art Des Educ; PE Educ; Sci Educ)
280 pts Durham (Stockton) – 280 pts (BA/BSc P Teach Gen; P Teach ICT)
Edinburgh – BBC–BCC (BEd P; Des Tech BEd; PE BEd)
Northumbria – 280 pts (BA P)
Stirling – BBC–CCD (Prof Educ Comb courses BA/BSc P S)
Stranmillis (UC) – BBC (Mus Educ)

UNIVERSITY OF CAMBRIDGE
Faculty of Education

Tel: 01223 767678

www.educ.cam.ac.uk/ugrad/

Education Studies at Cambridge

We offer a BA which combines the study of the history, philosophy, psychology and sociology of education with one of the following subjects; Biological or Physical Sciences, Classics, English, English with Drama, Geography, History, Mathematics, Modern languages, Music, Religious Studies. The degree (the Education Tripos) prepares students for a wide range of careers in education and related areas and, for those going into teaching, a place on a PGCE course.

For a quick reference offers calculator, fold out the inside back cover.

260 pts **Nottingham Trent** – BCC 260 pts (BA P)
Stranmillis (UC) – BCC (Bus St Educ)

240 pts **Anglia Ruskin** – 240 pts (BA P (ITT))
Brunel – 240 pts (BSc S PE)
Chester – 240 pts (BEd P)
Glasgow – CCC (BEd P)
Glasgow (RSAMD) – AA–DD (Mus BEd)
Hertfordshire – 240 pts (BEd P)
Hull – 240 pts (BA P; BA P Engl)
Liverpool John Moores – 240 pts (BA Spo Dev PE; BA P S)
Manchester Met – CCC (BA P)
Oxford Brookes – CCC **or** CCcc (BA P)
Roehampton – 240 pts (BA P Key Stgs 1 and 2)
Sheffield Hallam – 240 pts (Ely Yrs Educ QTS; BA P S)
Stranmillis (UC) – CCC (Tech Des Educ)
Swansea – 240–300 pts (TEFL Engl/Fr/Ger/Ital/Span/Welsh; TEFL (Lang St))

220 pts **Aberdeen** – 220 pts (BA P)
Bedfordshire – 220 pts (BA PE S)
Brighton – 220 pts (BA P QTS (3–7) (5–11); S Educ QTS; PE QTS; Des Tech Educ QTS)
Edge Hill – 220 pts (BA P)
Essex – 220–280 pts (TEFL)
Glasgow – CCD (MA Relig Phil Educ S)
Huddersfield – 220 pts (BA P)
Hull (Scarborough) – 220–240 pts (BA P ICT)
Liverpool Hope – 220 pts (BA P QTS)
Nottingham Trent – 220 pts (TESOL (Fr) (Ger) (Span) (Euro St) (Int Rel))
Strathclyde – CCD/BB (BEd P)
West Scotland – CCD (BEd P)
Winchester – 220 pts (BA P)
York St John – 220 pts (BA P)

200 pts **Bangor** – CDD 200–240 pts (BEd P; BSc Des Tech)
Birmingham City – 200 pts (BA P)
Bristol UWE – 200–260 pts (BA P ITE/Ely Yrs Chld Educ)
Chichester – 200–240 pts (PE Educ S QTS; BA P Educ (Maths) (ICT))
Cumbria – 200 pts (BA/BSc QTS S P)
Dundee – 200–230 pts (BEd P Educ)
Gloucestershire – 200–260 pts (BEd P Educ)
Liverpool John Moores – 200 pts (TESOL (Chin) (Fr) (Jap) (Span); BA P; BA S PE)
Northampton – 200–220 pts (BA P Educ; Ely Yrs Educ)
Nottingham Trent – 200 pts (Des Tech Educ QTS)
Plymouth – 200 pts (TESOL Langs)
Sunderland – 200 pts (BA P Educ)
Swansea (Inst) – 200 pts (BA P Educ)
Worcester – 200 pts (BA Ely Yrs P)

180 pts **Bedfordshire** – 180–260 pts (BA/BSc PE S)
Buckingham – 180–290 pts (Engl EFL)
Chichester – 180–220 pts (P Educ)
Coventry – DDD 180 pts (TEFL (Engl) (Fr) (Span))
Edge Hill – 180 pts (BSc S QTS (Des Tech) (ICT) (Maths) (Sci))
Huddersfield – 180–220 pts (BEd S (Des Tech))
Hull (Scarborough) – 180 pts (BSc Biol St)
Kingston – 180 pts (BA P QTS)
Newport – 180 pts (BA P St QTS)
Plymouth – 180–240 pts (Steiner–Waldorf Educ)
Reading – 180 pts (BEd Educ St P)

For information on how to read the Subject Tables, see **Chapter 8**.

St Mary's (UC) – 180 pts (PE S)

160 pts **Bishop Grosseteste (UC)** – CC (BA Educ St P)
Canterbury Christ Church – CC (BA QTS P Educ)
Cardiff (UWIC) – CC (BA P; BA S (Dr); 2yr Welsh/Mus/Modn Langs – applicants over 21)
Central Lancashire – 160–200 pts (Df St courses; TESOL (Fr) (Ger) (Span); Brit Sign Lang)
East London – 160 pts (Spec Educ Nds)
Edinburgh – CC (BEd Des Tech; PE; P Educ)
Glasgow – CC (Technol Educ)
Greenwich – 160 pts (BA S Des Tech Educ; BA P Educ)
Leeds Trinity and All Saints (Coll) – 160–240 pts (BA P Educ)
Liverpool John Moores – 160 pts (BA/BSc P (Maths) (PE))
London (Gold) – CC (Educ Des Tech)
Manchester Met – CC 160 pts (BSc S Educ)
Middlesex – 160–200 pts (BA P Educ)
Newman (UC) – 160–240 pts (BA/BEd P S (Art) (Biol) (Engl) (Geog) (Hist) (IT) (PE Spo Sci) (Theol))
Newport – 160–200 pts (BA S (Des Tech) (Maths ICT) (Maths Sci))
North East Wales (IHE) – 160 pts (BA P Educ)
Plymouth – 160–240 pts (BEd P)
St Mary's (UC) – 160–200 pts (BA P Educ ITT)
Sheffield Hallam – 160 pts (BSc QTS S (Des Tech) (Sci) (Maths))
Sunderland – 160 pts (BA S (Engl Educ) (Geog Educ))
Wolverhampton – 160–220 pts (BEd P)
York St John – 160–220 pts (BA P Educ)
140 pts **Royal Welsh (CMusDr)** – 140 pts (BA S)
Trinity Carmarthen (Coll) – 140 pts (BA Educ P QTS)
120 pts **Bradford (Coll)** – 120 pts (BA P)
Marjon (UC) – 120–180 pts (BEd P S (Maths) (PE))

Leeds Met – contact University

Alternative offers

See **Chapter 8** for grade/point equivalences and related information for the following examinations: Scottish qualifications, the Welsh Baccalaureate, the IB diploma (approximate points shown also in italics in the table of offers), the Irish Leaving Certificate, the European Baccalaureate and the French Baccalaureate.

EXAMPLES OF FOUNDATION DEGREES IN THE SUBJECT FIELD

Abingdon (Coll); Accrington and Rossendale (Coll); Anglia Ruskin; Bangor; Barnet (Coll); Barnsley (Univ Centre); Bath Spa; Bedfordshire; Beverley (CFE); Bicton (Coll); Birmingham (CFTCS); Birmingham City (Coll); Bishop Grosseteste (UC); Blackpool and Fylde (Coll); Bolton; Bolton (CmC); Boston (Coll); Bournemouth and Poole (Coll); Bournville (CFHE); Bracknell (Coll); Bradford; Bradford (Coll); Bridgwater (Coll); Brighton City (Coll); Bristol City (Coll); Bromley (Coll); Burnley (Coll); Cambridge Reg (Coll); Canterbury Christ Church; Cardiff (UWIC); Carshalton (Coll); Central Lancashire; Chester; Cirencester (Coll); City and Islington (Coll); Colchester (Inst); Coventry City (Coll); Craven (Coll); Croydon (Coll); Cumbria; Darlington (Coll); Derby; Dewsbury (Coll); Doncaster (Coll); Duchy (Coll); Dunstable (Coll); Ealing, Hammersmith and West London (Coll); East Antrim (IFHE); East Berkshire (Coll); East Lancashire (IHE); East London; Edge Hill; Evesham (Coll); Exeter (Coll); Farnborough (CT); Gateshead (Coll); Glamorgan; Gloucester (CAT); Gloucestershire; Grantham (Coll); Grimsby (IFHE); Hartlepool (CFE); Havering (CFHE); Herefordshire (CAD); Herefordshire (CT); Hertford Reg (Coll); Hertfordshire; Holy Cross (Coll); Hopwood Hall (Coll); Hugh Baird (Coll); Hull; Hull (Coll); Huntingdonshire Reg (Coll); Josiah Mason Sixth Form (Coll); Kendal (Coll); Kensington (Coll); Kent; Kingston; Kingston (Coll); Lambeth (Coll); Leeds Met; Leeds Trinity and All Saints (Coll); Leicester; Leicester (Coll); Lewisham (Coll); Liverpool (CmC); Liverpool Hope; Llandrillo (Coll); London Met; Macclesfield (Coll); Manchester Met; Mid-Kent (Coll); Middlesbrough (Coll); Milton Keynes (Coll); Myerscough (Coll); Nescot; New (Coll); Newcastle (Coll); Newman (UC); Norland (Coll); North Devon

(Coll); North East London (Coll); North East Wales (IHE); North East Worcestershire (Coll); North Hertfordshire (Coll); North Lindsey (Coll); North Trafford (Coll); Northampton; Nottingham Castle (Coll); Nottingham Trent; Oaklands (Holl); Oldham (Coll); Open University; Oxford Brookes; Park Lane Leeds (Coll); Peterborough Reg (Coll); Plumpton (Coll); Plymouth; Plymouth (CFE); Portsmouth; Preston (Coll); Redcar (Coll); Riverside Halton (Coll); Runshaw (Coll); St Helens (Coll); St Mary's (UC); Selby (Coll); Sheffield (Coll); Sheffield Hallam; Shrewsbury (CAT); Solihull (Coll); Somerset (CAT); South Cheshire (Coll); South Devon (Coll); South East Essex (Coll); Southampton; Southampton Solent; Southport (Coll); Sparsholt (Coll); Spelthorne (Coll); Staffordshire (Reg Fed); Stamford (Coll); Stockport (CFHE); Stockton Riverside (Coll); Stratford-upon-Avon (Coll); Suffolk (Univ Campus); Sunderland; Swansea (Inst); Swindon (Coll); Thames Valley; Thomas Danby (Coll); Thurrock (Coll); Trinity Carmarthen (Coll); Truro (Coll); Wakefield (Coll); Walsall (Coll); Warwick; West Anglia (Coll); West Cheshire (Coll); West Herts (Coll); West Kent (Coll); West Nottinghamshire (Coll); West Thames (Coll); Weston (Coll); Weymouth (Coll); Wigan and Leigh (Coll); Wiltshire (Coll); Winchester; Wirral Met (Coll); Wolverhampton; Worcester; Worcester (CT); Worcestershire New (Coll); Yeovil (Coll); York St John.

CHOOSING YOUR COURSE (SEE ALSO CH.1)

Course variations – Widen your options
International Education (Bath Spa)
Childhood Culture and Education (Birmingham)
Education and Psychology (Bristol UWE)
Art with Early Childhood Studies (Canterbury Christ Church)
Instrumental and Vocational Music Teaching (Chichester)
Special Educational Needs (East London)
Educational Studies and Neuroscience (Keele)
Conductive Education (Wolverhampton)
CHECK PROSPECTUSES AND WEBSITES FOR OTHER UNIVERSITIES AND COLLEGES OFFERING THESE COURSES.

Top teacher training providers See www.tda.gov.uk (England); www.shefc.ac.uk (Scotland); www.elwa.org.uk (Wales); www.unistats.com.

Top universities and colleges (Research) Aston (Audiology); Bath; Birmingham; Cambridge; Cardiff; Durham; Exeter; Lancaster; London (King's); Oxford; Sheffield; Sussex.

ADMISSIONS INFORMATION

Number of applicants per place (approx) Aberystwyth 6; Anglia Ruskin 1; Bangor 5; Bath 17; Bath Spa 5; Birmingham 8; Bishop Grosseteste (UC) 12; Bristol (Df St) 2, (Ely Chld Dt) 9; Bristol UWE 20; Brunel (PE) 5; Cambridge 2.5; Canterbury Christ Church 15; Cardiff (Educ) 8; Cardiff (UWIC) 3; Central Lancashire 5; Chester 25; Chichester 12; Cumbria 5; Derby 13; Dundee 5; Durham 8; Edge Hill 17; Edinburgh (P) 3; Exeter 10, (S PE) 13; Gloucestershire 20; Greenwich 3; Hull 7; Hull (Scarborough) 4; Kingston 9; Leeds 4; Liverpool Hope 5; Liverpool John Moores 3, (TEFL) 10; London (Gold) 5, (Des Tech) 4; Manchester Met 23, (Maths) 4; Marjon (UC) 5; Middlesex 7; Newman (UC) (S Engl) 3, (Theol) 3, (Ely Yrs) 5, (Biol) 7, (Geog) 3, (PE) 6, (Sci) 1; North East Wales (IHE) 15; Northampton 7; Northumbria 8; Nottingham Trent 11; Oxford Brookes 6; Plymouth 14; Roehampton 6; St Mary's (UC) 19; Sheffield Hallam 7, (PE) 60; Strathclyde 7; Swansea (Inst) 10; Trinity Carmarthen (Coll) 10; West Scotland 7; Winchester 4; Wolverhampton 4; Worcester 21, (Engl) 51; York 3; York St John (Mus) 3, (Maths) 2, (Biol) 10, (Engl) 5, (Theol Relig St) 4, (Fr) 12, (Des Tech) 10, (IT) 4.

Advice to applicants and planning the UCAS personal statement Any application for teacher training courses requires candidates to have experience of observation in schools and with children relevant to the choice of age range. Describe what you have learned from this. Any work with young people should be described in detail, indicating any problems which you may have seen which children create for the teacher. Applicants are strongly advised to have had some teaching practice prior to interview and should give evidence of time spent in primary school and give an analysis of activity undertaken with children. Give details of music qualifications, if any. **Anglia Ruskin** (Educ St) Experience of working with children. **De Montfort** (Educ St) Mature applicants welcome; the course is interdisciplinary and multidisciplinary. **Kingston** Precise, succinct, well-reasoned, well-written statement (no mistakes!). **Liverpool John Moores** (TESOL) We look for an interest in the language and culture of other countries. **Newman (UC)** Classroom placements an advantage. Be prepared for hard work throughout the course. **Winchester** We look for students who are curious about the uses and abuses of educational processes. **York** (Educ St) Experience with children and young people useful but not essential. See also **Appendix 2**.

Misconceptions about this course That Childhood Studies is a childcare, child health or teaching course: it is not. That Educational Studies leads to a teaching qualification – it does not. **Bath Spa** (Educ St) Applicants should note that this is not a teacher training course – it leads on to PGCE teacher training (this applies to other Education Studies courses). **Newman (UC)** That the Theology course only concentrates on the Christian/Catholic religions (all major religions are covered). **UHI Millennium Inst (NHC)** Candidates are unaware that on-line methods form a significant part of the course delivery.

Selection interviews Yes Bangor, Bishop Grosseteste (UC), Brighton, Bristol, Bristol UWE, Cambridge, Chichester, Derby, Kingston, London (Gold), Manchester Met (group interviews), Nottingham Trent, Oxford Brookes, Plymouth, Stockport (CFHE), Worcester, York St John. Check all institutions. It is a requirement that all candidates for teacher education are interviewed. Many institutions offering education studies also interview selected applicants. Additionally, candidates are asked to compose a short written statement on a given topic at interview in order to ensure an acceptable standard of written English; **Some** Bangor, Cardiff, Dundee, Lincoln, Liverpool John Moores, Marjon (UC), Roehampton, West Scotland, Winchester, York.

Interview advice and questions Questions invariably focus on why you want to teach and your experiences in the classroom. In some cases you may be asked to write an essay on these topics. Questions in the past have included: What do you think are important issues in education at present? Discussion of course work will take place for Art applicants. **Bath Spa** Short essay on an aspect of education. **Brighton** 200-word essay. **Cambridge** The stage is a platform for opinions or just entertainment? **Derby** Applicants are asked about an aspect of education. **Liverpool John Moores** Discussion regarding any experience the applicant has had with children. **Nottingham Trent** English test. **Sunderland** (BA S Des Tech) Applicants will be asked to complete a short piece of written work and to discuss their Des Tech curriculum. **Worcester** Interviewees are asked to write a statement concerning their impressions of the interview. **York St John** A short piece of written work is set on arrival for interview. See also **Chapter 7**.

Applicants' impressions (A=Open day; B=Interview day) Brighton (B) Talks on the course and the University were followed by individual interviews. **Bristol UWE** (B) There was a group interview and a tour of the campus and halls. Questions included 'What inspires you to become a teacher?' and 'What do you think you could contribute to the profession?' **Chichester** We had a group information session, individual interviews and a 30-minute essay test. **De Montfort** (B) There was a literacy test. Questions on health and safety and recent developments in education. **Gloucestershire** (B) There were individual interviews with maths and English tests, followed by a talk on the course and the University. **Nottingham Trent** (B) There was an English test, a talk on the University and the course, individual interviews and debate. **Plymouth** (B; Science) There was a group discussion and interviews in pairs, written and number tests and marking. (B) There were two literacy tests and a numeracy test. There were group interviews in subject groups and questions on our understanding of the role of the subject teacher in a primary school. **Winchester** (B) There was a group information session, group interviews (eight students) with a 10-minute essay task. Then followed a tour of the accommodation.

Reasons for rejection (non-academic) Unable to meet the requirements of written standard English. Ungrammatical personal statements. Lack of research about teaching at primary or secondary levels. Lack of experience in schools. Insufficient experience of working with people; tendency to be racist.

AFTER-RESULTS ADVICE
Offers to applicants repeating A-levels Higher Oxford Brookes, Warwick; **Possibly higher** Cumbria; **Same** Anglia Ruskin, Aston, Bangor, Bishop Grosseteste (UC), Brighton, Brunel, Canterbury Christ

Church, Cardiff, Chester, Chichester, De Montfort, Derby, Dundee, Durham, East Anglia, Lincoln, Liverpool Hope, Liverpool John Moores, London (Gold), Manchester Met, Marjon (UC), Newman (UC), Northumbria, Nottingham Trent, Roehampton, St Mary's (UC), Stirling, Sunderland, UHI Millennium Inst (NHC), Winchester, Wolverhampton, Worcester, York, York St John; **Not considered** Kingston; **No offers made** Cambridge.

GRADUATE DESTINATIONS AND EMPLOYMENT (2005/6 HESA)
Teacher graduates surveyed 5005 **Employed** 3850 **In further study** 110 **Assumed unemployed** 150.

Academic graduates surveyed 2190 **Employed** 970 **In further study** 530 **Assumed unemployed** 95.

Career note Education Studies degrees prepare graduates for careers in educational administration although many will move into more general areas of business or into aspects of work with Social Services. Providing courses in Education include Qualified Teacher Status (QTS), graduates can enter the teaching profession. Prospects are generally very good. Course in Childhood Studies could lead to work in health or childcare-related posts, in social work or administration.

OTHER DEGREE SUBJECTS FOR CONSIDERATION
Psychology; Social Policy; Social Sciences; Social Work.

ENGINEERING/ENGINEERING SCIENCES

(including **General Engineering, Integrated Engineering, Engineering Product Design** and **Robotics;** see also **Art and Design (Industrial/Product Design)** and **Technology**)

Many of these Engineering courses enable students to delay their decision on their final Engineering specialism. Mathematics and physics provide the basis of all Engineering courses although several universities and colleges now provide one-year Foundation courses for applicants without science A-levels. Many institutions offer sandwich courses and firms also offer sponsorships. Throughout prospectuses it will be noted that some courses are 'subject to approval'. The problem which can arise is that the examinations taken on these courses may not be accepted by the professional body overseeing that particular branch of engineering and examinations set by these professional bodies (see **Appendix 2**) will have to be retaken in order that graduates can obtain Chartered Engineer status.

Useful websites www.setwomenresource.org.uk; www.ergonomics.org.uk; www.scicentral.com; www.engc.org.uk; www.noisemakers.org.uk; www.yini.org.uk; www.enginuity.org.uk.

NB The points totals shown to the left of the institutions are for ease of reference only. It must not be assumed that tariff points are always used by institutions or that they can be substituted for an offer in grades. The level of an offer is not necessarily indicative of the quality of a course.

ENGINEERING COUNCIL UK (ECUK) STATEMENT
Recent developments in the engineering profession and the regulations that govern registration as a professional engineer (UK-SPEC) mean that MEng and Bachelors degrees are the typical academic routes to becoming registered.

Chartered Engineers (CEng) develop solutions to engineering problems, using new or existing technologies, through innovation, creativity and change. They might develop and apply new technologies, promote advanced designs and design methods, introduce new and more efficient production techniques, marketing and construction concepts, and pioneer new engineering services and management methods.

The typical academic qualifications for CEng are a BEng (Hons) with subsequent 'further learning' or an integrated MEng degree.

Indicative entry requirements are:

MEng GCE A-levels ABC–BBB
(SQA Highers AABB; SQA Advanced Highers ABC–BBB; IB 32–36 pts; Irish Leaving Certificate AABB)

BEng (Hons) GCE A-levels CCC–BCD
(SQA Highers BBBC; SQA Advanced Highers CCC–BCD; IB 26–30 pts; Irish Leaving Certificate BBBC)

All applicants should check the offers for MEng, BEng and BSc courses in each of the Engineering tables unless otherwise stated.

Incorporated Engineers (IEng) act as exponents of today's technology through creativity and innovation. They maintain and manage applications of current and developing technology, and may be involved in engineering design, development, manufacture, construction and operation.

Both Chartered and Incorporated Engineers are variously engaged in technical and commercial leadership and possess effective interpersonal skills.

The typical academic qualifications for IEng are an accredited Bachelor's degree.

Indicative entry requirements are: GCE A-levels CD/EE–DDE; SQA Highers BCC–CCCC; IB 24 pts; Irish Leaving Certificate BCC–CCC.

You should confirm with universities whether their courses are accredited for CEng or IEng by relevant professional engineering institutions. There are 21 institutions licensed by the ECUK to accredit engineering degree programmes.

To become a Chartered or Incorporated Engineer, you will have to demonstrate competence and commitment appropriate to the registration category. On top of your academic knowledge, you will also need to demonstrate your professional development and experience. Most of this will come after you graduate but placements in industry during your degree course are also available.

Both Chartered and Incorporated Engineers usually progress to become team leaders or to take other key management roles. Chartered Engineers earn an average salary of £53,067 (2005) and the top 10% over £80,000. Incorporated Engineers earn an average salary of £40,533 and the top 10% over £60,000. More information on registering as a professional engineer can be found on the ECUK website www.engc.org.uk.

COURSE OFFERS INFORMATION

Subject requirements/preferences **GCSE** English, mathematics and a science subject required. **AL** Mathematics and/or physics, engineering or another science usually required. Design technology may be acceptable or in some cases required. **Cambridge** (Churchill, Peterhouse) May use STEP as part of conditional offer; (Trinity) If not further mathematics then a merit in AEA mathematics is required. **Oxford** Maths mechanics modules recommended, further mathematics helpful. (See **Chapter 6**.) **NB** A* grades are likely to form part of university offers in the higher ranges for students applying for places in 2008 for entry in 2009: check websites.

Your target offers

360 pts **and above**
Cambridge – AAA (Engineering) *(IB 38–42 pts)*
Oxford – Offers vary eg AAA–AAB (Eng Sci; Eng Econ Mgt) *(IB 38–42 pts)*

340 pts **Bath** – AAB (Innov Eng Des; Innov Eng Des Fr/Ger; Spo Eng) *(IB 36 pts)*
Bristol – AAB–ABB (Eng Des) *(IB 36 pts)*
Durham – AAB (MEng Gen Eng; New Renew Ener) *(IB 38 pts)*
Leeds – AAB (Qntm Sci Eng)
Liverpool – AAB (MEng Eng; Eng Prod Des)
London (UCL) – AAB+AS–BBB+AS (Eng Bus Fin)
Warwick – AAB–ABB (MEng Eng) *(IB 35–37 pts)*

320 pts **Birmingham** – ABB–BBC (Eng Bus Mgt) *(IB 32–36 pts)*
Bristol – ABB (Eng Maths)
Brunel – ABB 320 pts (MEng Des Eng)
Cardiff – ABB–BBB 320–300 pts (MEng Integ Eng)
Exeter – ABB–BBC (MEng Eng Mgt; Eng) *(IB 30–34 pts)*
Lancaster – ABB–AAB (MEng Eng Yr in USA/Aus) *(IB 32–34 pts)*
Leicester – 320 pts (MEng Gen Eng; Gen Eng Ind/Euro/USA)
London (King's) – ABB+AS **or** ABbb (Eng Bus Mgt) *(IB 34 pts)*
Loughborough – 320 pts (Prod Des Manuf)
Nottingham – ABB–BCC (Integ Eng; Prod Des Manuf) *(IB 33 pts)*
Reading – 320 pts (Cybernetics)
Sussex – ABB–BBB 360–330 pts (MEng Eng Des; Prod Des 4yr; Eng Soty)
Swansea – 320 pts (MEng Prod Des Eng)

300 pts **Aberdeen** – BBB 2nd yr entry (MEng Eng; Eng Sfty Rlblty Eng)
Bath – BBB (BEng Spo Eng)
Dundee – 300 pts 2nd yr entry (Innov Prod Des) *(IB 28 pts)*
Durham – BBB (BEng Gen Eng)
Edinburgh – BBB (Engineering)
London (UCL) – BBB+AS (BEng Geoinform; Eng Bus Fin) *(IB 34 pts)*
Queen's Belfast – BBB (MEng Prod Des Dev)
Strathclyde – BBB (MEng Eng Ent Mgt; Prod Des Eng)
Sussex – BBB–BBC (BEng Eng Des)
Ulster – 300 pts (MEng Eng)
Warwick – BBB–BBC (BEng/BSc Eng (Bus Mgt); Robot Eng; Eng Bus St)

280 pts **Aberdeen** – BBC 1st yr entry (BEng Integ Eng Euro St; Integ Eng)
Aston – 280–240 pts (Eng Prod Des; Auto Prod Des; Des Eng) *(IB 31–32 pts)*
Brighton – 280 pts (Prod Des Tech Prof Expnc)
Cardiff – BBC 280 pts (BEng Integ Eng; Integ Eng Ind; Integ Eng Fr/Ger/Span)
Exeter – BBC–CCC (BEng Eng; Eng Mgt) *(IB 26–30 pts)*
Heriot-Watt – BBC 2nd yr entry (Eng Mgt; Integ Prod Des)
Lancaster – BBC (BEng Eng; Eng N Am/Aus) *(IB 30–32 pts)*
Liverpool – 280 pts (BEng Eng; Eng Prod Des)
Queen's Belfast – BBC (BEng Prod Des Dev)
Staffordshire – 280 pts (Prod Des Tech; Robot Tech; Robot Eng; Des Tech)
Sussex – BBC **or** 310 pts 3AL+AS (Prod Des 3yr)

260 pts **Brunel** – BCC 260 pts (Prod Des Eng; Vrtl Prod Des; Prod Des)
Coventry – 260 pts (Disas Mgt Eng)
Glasgow – BCC 260 pts (MEng Prod Des Eng)
Leicester – BCC 260 pts (BEng Gen Eng; Gen Eng Ind/Euro/USA) *(IB 30–32 pts)*
London (QM) – 260–340 pts (Eng Sci; Eng; Eng Bus Mgt; Des Innov; Spo Eng) *(IB 30–32 pts)*
Loughborough – 260–300 pts (Prod Des Tech; Ind Mgt Tech)
Swansea – 260–300 pts (BEng Prod Des Eng)

240 pts **Bradford** – 240 pts (Eng Mgt; Ind Eng)
Dundee – 240 pts 1st yr entry (Innov Prod Des) *(IB 28 pts)*
Glasgow – CCC 240 pts (BEng Prod Des Eng)
Greenwich – 240 pts (Ind Autom)
Hull – 240 pts (Med Prod Des)
Kingston – 240 pts (Prod Des)
Manchester Met – 240–220 pts (Eng; Eng IT; Vrtl Des Eng) *(IB 26 pts)*
Middlesex – 240–260 pts (Eng Prod Des)
Northumbria – 240 pts (Prod Des Tech; Eng Bus St)
Nottingham Trent – 240 pts (Comp Aid Prod Des; Ind Des Innov)
Salford – 240 pts (Pros Orthot) *(IB 28 pts)*
Strathclyde – CCC (BEng Prod Des Eng; Pros Orthot; Eng Ent Mgt)

220 pts **Aberdeen** – CCD 2nd yr entry (BEng Integ Eng Euro St)

Birmingham City – 220–240 pts (Eng Prod Des)
Bournemouth – 220–300 pts (Prod Des)
Bristol UWE – 220–300 pts (Robot; Prod Des Innov; Eng)
Central Lancashire – 220 pts (Comp Aid Eng)
Heriot-Watt – CCD 1st yr entry (Integ Prod Des; Eng; BSc Eng Mgt)
Hull – CCD–BBC 220–280 pts (Prod Innov)
Napier – 220 pts (Eng Mgt; Prod Des Eng)
Robert Gordon – CCD (Engineering)
Staffordshire – 220–280 pts (Foren Eng courses)
Ulster – 220 pts (Eng Mgt)

200 pts **Bradford** – 200 pts (Ind Des; Tech Mgt; Vrtl Des Innov)
Coventry – 200 pts (Vrtl Eng)
Liverpool – 200 pts (Eng Prod Des)
Sheffield Hallam – 200 pts (Foren Eng)
Sunderland – 200 pts (Prod Des; Auto Eng Des)

180 pts **Cardiff (UWIC)** – 180 pts (Prod Des courses)
Huddersfield – 180 pts (Prod Innov Des Dev; Eng Tech Mgt)
Leicester – 180–240 pts (Fdn Eng)
Manchester Met – 180 pts (Robot Auto; Prod Des Tech)
Northampton – 180–220 pts (BSc Eng; Prod Des; Eng Bus St)
Plymouth – 180 pts (Robotics)

160 pts **Anglia Ruskin** – 160–180 pts (Integ Eng)
Bournemouth – 160–220 pts (Des Eng)
Coventry – 160 pts (Eng St)
De Montfort – 160 pts (BSc Eng; Des Tech)
Derby – 160 pts (Prod Des Innov Mark)
East London – 160–180 pts (BSc Prod Des courses)

Engineering

The University of Nottingham

School of Mechanical, Materials and Manufacturing Engineering

As one of the UK's premier engineering schools, we have an international reputation for high quality research, teaching and graduates. Our courses are accredited by professional institutions and are consistently well-ranked in league tables.

For 2008, we offer the following courses as BEng or MEng:

Mechanical Engineering, with specialist streams in manufacturing, aerospace, automotive, modern languages, bioengineering, management and materials

Design Engineering, with specialist streams in mechanical, materials and manufacture

Manufacturing Engineering and Management, with a specialist stream in aerospace

Product Design and Manufacture

In addition, we also offer the following BSc course:

Biomedical Materials Science

Specialist streams provide a route to developing a career in a particular industry. They are supported by academic staff with particular research interests relevant to the industry. For more detailed information, please refer to our website: www.nottingham.ac.uk/schoolm3 or send an email to m3-courses@nottingham.ac.uk

Glamorgan – 160 pts (Prod Des)
Greenwich – 160 pts (Eng Bus Mgt)
Harper Adams (UC) – 160 pts (Eng Des Dev)
140 pts **Glamorgan** – 140–180 pts (Eng Tech Mgt)
Wolverhampton – 140 pts (Eng Tech Prod Des Tech)
120 pts **Aberdeen** – DD (BSc Eng Gen)
Bradford – 120 pts (Fdn Eng)
Brighton – 120 pts (Fdn Eng)
Huddersfield – 120 pts (Fdn Eng)
London South Bank – DD (Eng Prod Des; Prod Des Comp; Prod Des Env; Eng)
Southampton Solent – 120 pts (Eng Bus)
Ulster – 120 pts (Eng Integ Fdn Yrs)
West Scotland – DD (Prod Des Dev; Eng Mgt)
100 pts **Southampton Solent** – 100 pts (Prod Des)
80 pts **City** – EE 80 pts (Fdn Eng)

Open University – contact University

Alternative offers
See **Chapter 8** for grade/point equivalences and related information for the following examinations: Scottish qualifications, the Welsh Baccalaureate, the IB diploma (approximate points shown also in italics in the table of offers), the Irish Leaving Certificate, the European Baccalaureate and the French Baccalaureate.

EXAMPLES OF FOUNDATION DEGREES IN THE SUBJECT FIELD
Birmingham City (Coll); Bishop Auckland (Coll); Blackpool & Fylde (Coll); Bradford (Coll); Central Lancashire; Colchester (Inst); Coventry City (Coll); Exeter (Coll); Farnborough (CT); Harper Adams (UC); Lincoln (Coll); Loughborough (Coll); Newcastle (Coll); Newport; Northampton; Plymouth (CAD); Somerset (CAT); Suffolk (Univ Campus); Sutton Coldfield (Coll); Wakefield (Coll); Warwickshire (Coll); Wolverhampton; Yeovil (Coll).

CHOOSING YOUR COURSE (SEE ALSO CH.1)
Course variations – Widen your options
Smart Systems (Abertay Dundee)
Automotive Engineering (Bath)
Innovation Engineering Design (Bath)
Industrial Engineering (Bradford)
Vehicle Technology (Bradford)
Integrated Engineering (Cardiff)
New and Renewable Energy (Durham)
Railtrack and Rolling Stock (Kingston)
Materials Science and Engineering (London (QM))
Forensic Engineering and Applied Statistics (Staffordshire)
CHECK PROSPECTUSES AND WEBSITES FOR OTHER UNIVERSITIES AND COLLEGES OFFERING THESE COURSES.

Universities and colleges teaching quality www.qaa.ac.uk; www.unistats.com.

Top universities and colleges (Research) Aston; Birmingham; Brunel; Cambridge*; Cardiff; Durham; Edinburgh; Glasgow; Leeds; Leicester; Liverpool John Moores; Manchester; Oxford*; Sheffield; Strathclyde; Sussex; Warwick.

Sandwich degree courses Aston; Bath; Birmingham City; Bournemouth; Bradford; Brighton; Bristol; Cardiff; Coventry; De Montfort; Glamorgan; Hertfordshire; Huddersfield; Leeds Met; Leicester; London South Bank; Loughborough; Manchester Met; Northumbria; Queen's Belfast; Sheffield Hallam; Sunderland; Surrey; Teesside; Ulster; Wolverhampton.

ADMISSIONS INFORMATION

Number of applicants per place (approx) Aberdeen 6; Abertay Dundee 2; Aston 8; Bath 15; Blackburn (Coll) 1; Birmingham 6; Bournemouth 5; Bristol (Eng Des) 5; Brunel (Ind Des Eng) 10; Cambridge 4; Cardiff 5; City 3; Coventry 6, (Fdn) 2; Durham 9; Edinburgh 5; Exeter 6; Glasgow Caledonian 10; Hertfordshire 2; Hull 6; Kingston 5; Lancaster 15; Leicester 12; London (UCL) 5; Loughborough 9; Manchester Met 2; Northampton 3; Oxford (success rate 45%); Robert Gordon 2; Salford (Pros Orthot) 3; Sheffield Hallam 6; Strathclyde 5; Warwick 10.

Advice to applicants and planning the UCAS personal statement Details of careers in the various engineering specialisms should be obtained from the relevant engineering institutions (see **Appendix 2**). This will enable you to describe your interests in various aspects of engineering. Contact engineers to discuss their work with them. Try to arrange a visit to an engineering firm relevant to your choice of specialism. **Bristol** (Eng Maths) Skills, work experience.

Selection interviews Yes Bristol (Eng Maths), Brunel, Cambridge, Coventry, Durham, Lancaster, Leeds, Leicester, London (QM), (UCL), Loughborough, Manchester Met, Oxford, Oxford Brookes (English test for overseas students), Portsmouth, Robert Gordon, Salford, Sheffield Hallam, Strathclyde, Thames Valley; **Some** Cardiff.

Applicants' impressions (A=Open day; B=Interview day) Oxford (B) I had two interviews, the first at Keble. They asked me why Engineering and why Oxford? How could you increase the force on a car without changing its acceleration or mass? I also had to work through equations to do with force on a whiteboard. They helped me along to work out what it was to do with – the grip of the tyres and the friction caused by the road surface. The second interview was at St Anne's, where they asked me an integration question and other topics such as graphic interpretations. However, the theme of the interview was aeronautics and they asked me a question about the fuel needed for an aircraft to take off from a given point at a certain speed and the pressure changes in the engine. Throughout the interview they were hinting a lot of things to me and so I felt I didn't do too well, but I must have done something right, because I got the offer!

Interview advice and questions Since mathematics and physics are important subjects, it is probable that you will be questioned on the applications of these subjects to, for example, the transmission of electricity, nuclear power, aeronautics, mechanics etc. Past questions have included: Explain the theory of an arch; what is its function? What is the connection between distance and velocity and acceleration and velocity? How does a car ignition work? **Nottingham Trent** What is Integrated Engineering? **Oxford** No written work required and no written test at interview. See also separate **Engineering** tables and **Chapter 7**.

Reasons for rejection (non-academic) Made no contribution whatsoever to the project discussions during the UCAS interview. Forged reference! Poor work ethic. Lack of motivation towards the subject area. Better suited to an alternative Engineering course. Failure to attend interview. Poor interview preparation. **Salford** (Pros Orthot) Lack of sympathy with people with disabilities.

AFTER-RESULTS ADVICE

Offers to applicants repeating A-levels Higher Loughborough, Warwick; **Possibly higher** Coventry, Edinburgh, Lancaster, Manchester Met, Robert Gordon, Sheffield Hallam; **Same** Birmingham City, Brunel (good reasons needed for repeating), Cardiff, Derby, Durham, Exeter, Harper Adams (UC), Heriot-Watt, Huddersfield, Hull, Leeds, Liverpool, London (UCL), Napier, Nottingham Trent, Suffolk (Univ Campus), Thames Valley; **No offers made** Cambridge.

GRADUATE DESTINATIONS AND EMPLOYMENT (2005/6 HESA)

Graduates surveyed 895 **Employed** 525 **In further study** 115 **Assumed unemployed** 70.

Career note A high proportion of engineering graduates go into industry as engineers, technicians, IT specialists or managers irrespective of their engineering speciality. However the transferable skills gained during their courses are also valued by employers in other sectors.

OTHER DEGREE SUBJECTS FOR CONSIDERATION
Computer Science; Materials Science; Mathematics; Physics; Technology; all branches of Engineering (see also following **Engineering** tables).

ENGINEERING (ACOUSTICS)

(including **Audio Engineering** and **Sound Technology;** see also **Film, Radio, Video and TV Studies** and **Media Studies**)

Apart from the scientific aspect of sound, these courses also involve the measurement of sound, hearing, environmental health and legal aspects of sound and vibration. Acoustics topics are also included in some Music and Media Technology courses.

Useful websites www.ioa.org.uk; www.engc.org.uk; www.enginuity.org.uk.

NB The points totals shown to the left of the institutions are for ease of reference only. It must not be assumed that tariff points are always used by institutions or that they can be substituted for an offer in grades. The level of an offer is not necessarily indicative of the quality of a course.

Engineering Council Statement: See **Engineering/Engineering Sciences**.

COURSE OFFERS INFORMATION
Subject requirements/preferences AL mathematics and physics usually required; music is also required for some courses. See also **Engineering/Engineering Sciences. NB** A* grades are likely to form part of university offers in the higher ranges for students applying for places in 2008 for entry in 2009: check websites.

Your target offers

340 pts **Surrey** – AAB (MEng Aud Media Eng)

320 pts **Southampton** – ABB 320 pts (MEng/BEng Acoust Eng) *(IB 34 pts)*

300 pts **Southampton** – BBB 300 pts (Acoust Mus) *(IB 34 pts)*
Surrey – BBB (BEng Aud Media Eng)

260 pts **Birmingham** – 260 pts approx (Electron Audio Eng)
Brighton – 260 pts (Audio Electron)
Glasgow – BCC (AV Eng)
London (QM) – 260 pts (Aud Sys Eng)

240 pts **Lincoln** – 240 pts (Aud Tech)
Salford – 240 pts (Phys Acoust)

220 pts **Birmingham City** – 220 pts (Snd Eng Prod)
Bristol UWE – 220–240 pts (Aud Mus Tech)

200 pts **Bolton** – 200 pts (Snd Eng Des)
Salford – 200 pts (Acoust; AV Broad Tech; Aud Tech) *(IB 27 pts)*

180 pts **Liverpool (LIPA)** – 180 pts (Snd Tech)
Oxford Brookes – contact admissions tutor (Snd Tech Dig Mus)

160 pts **Anglia Ruskin** – 160 pts (Aud Mus Tech)
London Met – 160 pts (Mus Tech (Aud Sys))
Southampton Solent – 160 pts (Snd Eng)

120 pts **North East Wales (IHE)** – 140 pts (Snd Broad Eng; Std Rec Perf Tech)

Leeds Met – contact University

Alternative offers
See **Chapter 8** for grade/point equivalences and related information for the following examinations: Scottish qualifications, the Welsh Baccalaureate, the IB diploma (approximate points shown also in italics in the table of offers), the Irish Leaving Certificate, the European Baccalaureate and the French Baccalaureate.

EXAMPLES OF FOUNDATION DEGREES IN THE SUBJECT FIELD
Bolton; Glamorgan; North East Wales (IHE); Thames Valley.

CHOOSING YOUR COURSE (SEE ALSO CH.1)
Course variations – Widen your options
Audio Music Technology (Anglia Ruskin)
Sound Engineering (Glamorgan)
Physics and Acoustics (Salford)
Audio Media Engineering (Surrey)
CHECK PROSPECTUSES AND WEBSITES FOR OTHER UNIVERSITIES AND COLLEGES OFFERING THESE COURSES.

Universities and colleges teaching quality See www.qaa.ac.uk; www.unistats.com.

Top universities and colleges (Research) Southampton.

ADMISSIONS INFORMATION
Number of applicants per place (approx) Anglia Ruskin 5; Salford 4; Southampton 4–5.

Advice to applicants and planning the UCAS personal statement See **Engineering/Engineering Sciences**. See also **Appendix 2**.

Misconceptions about this course Anglia Ruskin Failure to appreciate the emphasis that the course gives to science and technology.

Selection interviews Salford, Southampton.

Interview advice and questions What interests you about Acoustics Engineering? What career do you have in mind on graduating? See also **Chapter 7**.

Reasons for rejection (non-academic) See **Engineering/Engineering Sciences**.

AFTER-RESULTS ADVICE
Offers to applicants repeating A-levels Same Anglia Ruskin, Salford.

GRADUATE DESTINATIONS AND EMPLOYMENT (2005/6 HESA)
No data available.

Career note Specialist topics on these courses will enable graduates to make decisions as to their future career destinations.

OTHER DEGREE SUBJECTS FOR CONSIDERATION
Audiology; Broadcast Engineering; Communications Engineering; Computer Engineering; Computer Science; Media Technology; Music; Radio and TV; Technology; Telecommunications Engineering and Electronic Engineering.

ENGINEERING (AERONAUTICAL and AEROSPACE)

Courses cover the manufacture of military and civil aircraft, theories of mechanics, thermodynamics, electronics, computing and engine design. Avionics courses include flight and energy control systems, airborne computing, navigation, optical and TV displays, airborne communications, and radar systems for navigation and power.

Useful websites www.raes.org.uk; www.engc.org.uk; www.enginuity.org.uk.

NB The points totals shown to the left of the institutions are for ease of reference only. It must not be assumed that tariff points are always used by institutions or that they can be substituted for an offer in grades. The level of an offer is not necessarily indicative of the quality of a course.

Engineering Council statement: See **Engineering/Engineering Sciences**.

For information on how to read the Subject Tables, see **Chapter 8**.

COURSE OFFERS INFORMATION

Subject requirements/preferences See **Engineering/Engineering Sciences**. **NB** A* grades are likely to form part of university offers in the higher ranges for students applying for places in 2008 for entry in 2009: check websites.

Your target offers

360 pts **and above**

Cambridge – AAA (Aerosp Aeroth Eng) *(IB 38–42 pts)*

340 pts **Bath** – AAB (Aerosp Eng; Aerosp Eng Fr; Aerosp Eng Ger) *(IB 36 pts)*

Bristol – AAB–BBB 340 pts (Avion Sys; Aero Eng; Aero Eng Euro) *(IB 36 pts)*

Brunel – AAB 340 pts (MEng Spc Eng; Aerosp Eng; Avn Eng; Avn Eng Plt St) *(IB 28–34 pts)*

Durham AAB (MEng Aeronautics) *(IB 38 pts)*

Imperial London – AAB 340 pts 3AL **or** 2AL+2AS (Aero Eng; Aero Eng Euro)

Leeds – AAB–BBB (MEng/BEng Aero Aerosp Eng) *(IB 32 pts)*

Liverpool – AAB (MEng Aerosp Eng; Aerosp Eng Plt St; Avion Sys; Avion Sys Plt St) *(IB 36 pts)*

Loughborough – AAB (MEng Aero Eng) *(IB 30–36 pts)*

Sheffield – AAB 340 pts (MEng Aerosp Eng; Aerosp Eng PPI) *(IB 32 pts H maths/phys 6 pts)*

Southampton – AAB–ABB 340 pts (Aero Astro; Aerosp Eng (Eng Mgt); Aerosp Eng Advnc Mat; Aerosp Eng Euro; Spc Sys Eng) *(IB 34 pts)*

Strathclyde – AAB (MEng Aero Mech Eng)

Surrey – AAB–BBB (Aerosp Eng)

320 pts **Brunel** – ABB 320 pts (MEng Avn Eng; Avn Eng Plt St) *(IB 32 pts H maths/phys 5 pts)*

Hertfordshire – 320 pts (MEng Aerosp Eng; Aerosp Sys Eng)

Imperial London – ABB (MEng Aerosp Mat)

London (QM) – 320 pts (MEng Aerosp Eng; Avion Spc Sys) *(IB 30–32 pts)*

Manchester – ABB (MEng Aerosp Eng; Aerosp Eng Ind; Aerosp Eng Mgt; Aerosp Eng Euro) *(IB 34–36 pts)*

Queen's Belfast – ABB–BBB (MEng Aero Eng)

Sheffield – ABB 320 pts (BEng Aerosp Eng; Aerosp Eng PPI) *(IB 31–32 pts)*

Swansea – 320–360 pts (MEng Aerosp Eng; Aerosp Eng Mat; Aerosp Eng Mgt; Aerosp Eng Prplsn)

300 pts **Brunel** – BBB 300 pts (Mech Eng Aero)

City – 300 pts (MEng Aero Eng; Air Trans Eng) *(IB 30 pts)*

Kingston – BBB 300 pts (MEng Aerosp Eng; Aerosp Eng Astnaut)

Leeds – BBB (Avn Tech Plt St; Avn Tech Mgt; BEng Aero Aerosp Eng)

Liverpool – BBB (BEng Aerosp Eng courses; Avion Sys Plt St) *(IB 30–33 pts)*

Loughborough – BBB–ABC (BEng Aero Eng) *(IB 30–36 pts)*

Manchester – BBB (BEng Aerosp Eng)

Salford – 300 pts (MEng Mech Eng (Aerosp)) *(IB 27–32 pts)*

Strathclyde – BBB (BEng Aero Mech Eng)

280 pts **Brunel** – BBC 280 pts (BEng Aerosp Eng)

City – 280–240 pts (Air Trans Ops; Air Trans Eng; Aero Eng)

Glasgow – BBC (Aero Eng)

Queen's Belfast – BBC–BCC (BEng Aero Eng)

Staffordshire – 280 (Aero Tech)

260 pts **Brighton** – 260 pts (Aero Eng)

Brunel – BCC 260 pts (BEng Avn Eng; Avn Eng Plt St; Spc Eng)

Coventry – 260 pts (Aerosp Sys Eng)

Hertfordshire – 260 pts (BEng Aerosp Eng; Aerosp Sys Eng)

Imperial London – BCC (BEng Aerosp Mat)

London (QM) – 260 pts (BEng Aerosp Eng) *(IB 30–32 pts)*

Swansea – 260 pts (BEng Aerosp Eng; Aerosp Eng Mat)

240 pts	**Bristol UWE** – 240–280 pts (Aerosp Sys Eng)
	Coventry – 240 pts (Aerosp Tech; Avion Tech)
	Kingston – 240 pts (BEng Aerosp Eng Astnaut; Aerosp Eng)
	London (QM) – 240 pts (Avionics)
	Salford – 240 pts (BEng Aero Eng; Aircft Eng Plt St; Mech Eng (Aerosp))
220 pts	**Bristol UWE** – 220–260 (MEng/BEng Aerosp Manuf Eng)
200 pts	**Glasgow** – BB 200 pts (Avionics)
	Hertfordshire – 200 pts (Aerosp Tech Mgt; Aerosp Tech Plt St)
	Staffordshire – 200–240 pts (Aero Robot Tech)
160 pts	**Farnborough (CT)** – 160–200 pts (Aero Eng)
	Salford – 160 pts (BSc Aerosp Bus Sys; Avn Tech Plt St; Mech Eng (Aerosp))
140 pts	**Glamorgan** – 140 pts (Aircrft Mntnc Eng; Aerosp Eng)
	Kingston – 140 pts (BEng Aerosp Eng Des; Air Eng)
	North East Wales (IHE) – 140 pts (Aero Electron Eng (Avion); Aero Mech Eng; Aero (Avion))
120 pts	**Kingston** – 120 pts (Fdn Aerosp Eng)
80 pts	**UHI Millennium Inst (PC)** – 80 pts (Aircrft Eng)
	London Met – contact University (Avn Mgt)

Alternative offers
See **Chapter 8** for grade/point equivalences and related information for the following examinations: Scottish qualifications, the Welsh Baccalaureate, the IB diploma (approximate points shown also in italics in the table of offers), the Irish Leaving Certificate, the European Baccalaureate and the French Baccalaureate.

EXAMPLES OF FOUNDATION DEGREES IN THE SUBJECT FIELD
Bedford (Coll); Bristol City (Coll); Farnborough (CT); Hertfordshire; Kingston; London Met; Macclesfield (Coll); North East Wales (IHE).

CHOOSING YOUR COURSE (SEE ALSO CH.1)
Course variations – Widen your options
Avionic Systems (Bristol)
Aviation Engineering with Pilot Study (Brunel)
Air Transport Engineering (City)
Aircraft Maintenance Engineering (Glamorgan)
Aerospace Engineering with Astronautics (Kingston)
Aviation Technology with Pilot Study (Salford)
Space Systems Engineering (Southampton)
Aeronautical and Robotics Technology (Staffordshire)
CHECK PROSPECTUSES AND WEBSITES FOR OTHER UNIVERSITIES AND COLLEGES OFFERING THESE COURSES.

Universities and colleges teaching quality See www.qaa.ac.uk; www.unistats.com.

Top universities and colleges (Research) See **Engineering (Mechanical)**.

Sandwich degree courses Bath; Brunel; City; Coventry; Glamorgan; Hertfordshire; Kingston; Liverpool; London (QM); Loughborough; Queen's Belfast; Salford; Staffordshire; Surrey.

ADMISSIONS INFORMATION
Number of applicants per place (approx) Bath 13, (MEng) 18; Bristol 11; Bristol UWE 4; City 17; Coventry 7; Farnborough (CT) 7; Hertfordshire 17; Imperial London 7; Kingston 9; London (QM) 8; Loughborough 10; North East Wales (IHE) 5; Queen's Belfast 6; Salford 6; Southampton 10.

Advice to applicants and planning the UCAS personal statement **Bristol** Interest in engineering and aerospace. Work experience in engineering. Flying experience. Personal attainments. **London (QM)** Practical experience. Relevant hobbies. Membership of Air Training Corps. See also **Engineering/Engineering Sciences**. See also **Appendix 2**.

Misconceptions about this course That Aeronautical Engineering is not a highly analytical subject: it is.

Selection interviews **Yes** Bristol, Cambridge, Farnborough (CT), Hertfordshire, Kingston, London (QM), Loughborough, Salford, Southampton.

Interview advice and questions Why Aeronautical Engineering? Questions about different types of aircraft and flight principles of helicopters. Range of interests in engineering. See also **Chapter 7**.

Reasons for rejection (non-academic) See **Engineering/Engineering Sciences**.

AFTER-RESULTS ADVICE
Offers to applicants repeating A-levels **Higher** Bristol, Queen's Belfast; **Possibly higher** Hertfordshire; **Same** Bath, City, Farnborough (CT), Kingston, Liverpool, Loughborough, Salford, Southampton, York; **No offers made** Cambridge.

GRADUATE DESTINATIONS AND EMPLOYMENT (2005/6 HESA)
Graduates surveyed 725 **Employed** 405 **In further study** 60 **Assumed unemployed** 55.

Career note Specialist areas of study on these courses will open up possible career directions. See also **Engineering/Engineering Sciences**.

OTHER DEGREE SUBJECTS FOR CONSIDERATION
Astronomy; Astrophysics; Computer Science; Electronics and Systems Engineering; Materials Science; Mathematics; Naval Architecture; Physics.

ENGINEERING (CHEMICAL)
(Including **Fire Engineering** and **Fire Safety**)

Courses cover chemistry, microbiology, physics and mathematics. Management, economics, process dynamics, process design and safety are introduced in Years 2 and 3.

Useful websites www.icheme.org; www.engc.org.uk; www.enginuity.org.uk; www.whynotchemeng.com.

NB The points totals shown to the left of the institutions are for ease of reference only. It must not be assumed that tariff points are always used by institutions or that they can be substituted for an offer in grades. The level of an offer is not necessarily indicative of the quality of a course.

Engineering Council Statement See **Engineering/Engineering Sciences**.

COURSE OFFERS INFORMATION
Subject requirements/preferences **AL** Mathematics and chemistry required. See also **Engineering/Engineering Sciences**. NB A* grades are likely to form part of university offers in the higher ranges for students applying for places in 2008 for entry in 2009: check websites.

Your target offers
360 pts **and above**
      Cambridge – (Chem Eng 2nd yr entry only via Eng or Nat Sci) *(IB 38–42 pts)*
      Oxford – Offers vary eg AAA–AAB (Chem Eng) *(IB 38–42 pts)*
340 pts **Imperial London** – AAB–ABB (Chem Eng; Chem Eng Yr Abrd; Chem Fn Chem Proc) *(IB 38 pts H maths/chem/phys 6 pts)*
320 pts **Birmingham** – ABB–BBB 320–300 pts (Chem Eng; Chem Eng Bus Mgt; Chem Eng Int St; Chem Eng Ind Exp) *(IB 32–34 pts)*
      London (UCL) – ABB–BBB (Chem Eng courses; Chem Bioch Eng) *(IB 32–36 pts)*
      Manchester – ABB (MEng Chem Eng; Chem Eng Ind; Chem Eng Euro; Chem Eng Biotech; Chem Eng Chem; Chem Eng Env Tech; Chem Eng (Bus Mgt)) *(IB 35 pts)*
      Newcastle – ABB–BBB (MEng Chem Eng; Bioproc Eng) *(IB 30–34 pts)*

Biochemical Engineering –
the challenge to sixth formers in creating health and wealth from new life science discoveries

The discovery of penicillin was a momentous achievement. It took 15 years and an international effort to find a way to produce it in the quantities needed for medical treatment and led to the birth of the discipline of biochemical engineering.

The medicines of the future – human proteins, therapeutic vaccines and human tissue for repair – are even more complex than penicillin. They address previously intractable conditions and are generating many opportunities spanning the initial discovery, to point of care. Those who are numerate and have gained engineering team and leadership skills are translating these opportunities into new medicines. It is also such people who are managing the billions of pounds of investment required and who are dealing with the social and environmental issues that all big endeavours must address.

Those seeking a professional career in a subject that is demanding, and who want a life at the cutting edge that is highly rewarded, should consider the excitement of biochemical engineering as a degree option.

Information on courses can be found in UCAS guides both under biochemical engineering and chemical engineering and more information is on the web. Visits can be arranged to explore in more detail the A level requirements, the courses and the careers available.

Nottingham – ABB (MEng/BEng Chem Eng; Chem Eng Env Eng)
Sheffield – ABB (MEng Chem Eng Chem) *(IB 34 pts)*
Strathclyde – ABB (MEng Chem Eng)
300 pts **Aston** – BBB–ABB 300–320 pts (MEng Chem Eng; Chem Eng App Chem) *(IB 32 pts)*
Bath – BBB–ABC 300 pts (MEng Chem Eng; Bioch Eng) *(IB 34 pts)*
Edinburgh – BBB (BEng Chem Eng; Chem Eng Mgt; Struct Fire Sfty Eng)
Leeds – BBB (Chem Eng Chem) *(IB 32 pts)*
Loughborough – 300–320 pts (MEng Chem Eng courses; Chem Eng Mgt) *(IB 30–32 pts)*
Newcastle – BBB–BBC (BEng Chem Eng courses)
Queen's Belfast – BBB (MEng Chem Eng)
Sheffield – BBB–BCC (BEng Chem Eng Chem; Chem Eng Modn Lang; Chem Eng Fuel Tech; Chem Eng Mgt; Chem Chem Eng)
Surrey – BBB–BBC 300–280 pts (Chem Eng; Chem Biosys Eng)
Swansea – 300 pts (MEng Chem Bioproc Eng)
280 pts **Aston** – BBC–CCC (BEng Chem Eng; Chem Eng App Chem)
Heriot-Watt – BBC 2nd yr entry (Chem Eng; Chem Eng Ener Eng; Chem Eng Oil Gas Tech; Chem Eng Pharm Chem)
260 pts **Bath** – 260 pts (BEng Chem Eng; Chem Bioproc Eng)
Glasgow Caledonian – BCC (Fire Risk Eng)
Leeds – BCC (Fire Explsn; Chem Eng)
Loughborough – 260–280 pts (BEng Chem Eng; Chem Eng Env Prot)
Queen's Belfast – BCC (BEng Chem Eng)
Strathclyde – BCC (BEng Chem Eng; Chem Eng Bioproc Biotech)
Swansea – 260 pts (BEng Chem Bioproc Eng)
240 pts **Central Lancashire** – 240 pts (Fire Eng)
Heriot-Watt – CCC 2nd yr entry (Brew Distil)
Loughborough – 240 pts (Proc Tech Mgt)
200 pts **Heriot-Watt** – CDD–CCD 1st yr entry (Brew Distil; Chem Eng; Chem Eng Pharm Chem; Chem Eng Env; Chem Eng Ener Eng; Chem Eng Oil Gas Tech)
180 pts **Glamorgan** – 180–240 pts (Fire Sfty Eng)
Huddersfield – DDD 180 pts (Chem Chem Eng)
Teesside – 180–240 pts (Chem Eng)
160 pts **Central Lancashire** – 160 pts (Fire Sfty Risk Mgt)
London South Bank – CC (Chem Proc Eng; Petrol Eng)
Newport – 160 pts (Fire Eng)
120 pts **London Met** – 120 pts (Poly Eng joint courses)
West Scotland – DD **or** bbc (BSc Chem Eng)

Alternative offers
See **Chapter 7** for grade/point equivalences and related information for the following examinations: Scottish qualifications, the Welsh Baccalaureate, the IB diploma (approximate points shown also in italics in the table of offers), the Irish Leaving Certificate, the European Baccalaureate and the French Baccalaureate.

EXAMPLES OF FOUNDATION DEGREES IN THE SUBJECT FIELD
Central Lancashire; Teesside.

CHOOSING YOUR COURSE (SEE ALSO CH.1)
Course variations – widen your options
Medical Product Design (Aston)
Fire Engineering (Central Lancashire)
Oil and Gas Technology (Edinburgh)
Food Science Technology and Management (Edinburgh)
Fire and Explosion (Leeds)
CHECK PROSPECTUSES AND WEBSITES FOR OTHER UNIVERSITIES AND COLLEGES OFFERING THESE COURSES.

Universities and colleges teaching quality See www.qaa.ac.uk; www.unistats.com.

Top universities and colleges (Research) Aston; Birmingham*; Cambridge; Imperial London*; London (UCL)*; Newcastle; Surrey.

Sandwich degree courses Aston; Bath; London South Bank; Loughborough; Manchester; Paisley; Queen's Belfast; Surrey; Teesside.

ADMISSIONS INFORMATION

Number of applicants per place (approx) Aston 4; Bath 6; Birmingham 8; Heriot-Watt 8; Huddersfield 7; Imperial London 4, (MEng) 4; Leeds 9; London (UCL) 8; Loughborough 7; Newcastle (MEng/BEng) 6; Nottingham 6; Sheffield 14; Strathclyde 6; Surrey 5; Swansea 3.

Misconceptions about this course Surrey That chemical engineering is chemistry on a large scale: physics is as applicable as chemistry.

Selection interviews Yes Bath, Cambridge, Leeds, London (UCL), London South Bank, Newcastle, Nottingham, Oxford, Surrey, Sussex, Teesside.

Interview advice and questions Past questions have included the following: How would you justify the processing of radioactive waste to people living in the neighbourhood? What is public health engineering? What is biochemical engineering? What could be the sources of fuel and energy in the year 2020? Discuss some industrial applications of chemistry. Regular incidents occur in which chemical spillage and other problems affect the environment. Be prepared to discuss these social issues. See also **Chapter 7**.

Reasons for rejection (non-academic) See **Engineering/Engineering Sciences**.

AFTER-RESULTS ADVICE

Offers to applicants repeating A-levels Higher Swansea; **Possibly higher** Bath, Leeds, London South Bank, Queen's Belfast; **Same** Aston, Birmingham, Loughborough, Newcastle, Nottingham, Sheffield, Surrey, Teesside; **No offer made** Cambridge.

GRADUATE DESTINATIONS AND EMPLOYMENT (2005/6 HESA)

Graduates surveyed 400 **Employed** 240 **In further study** 70 **Assumed unemployed** 40.

Career note Chemical Engineering is involved in many aspects of industry and scientific development. In addition to the oil and chemical-based industries, graduates enter a wide range of careers including the design and construction of chemical process plants, food production, pollution control, environmental protection, energy conservation, waste recovery and recycling, medical science, health and safety, and alternative energy sources.

OTHER DEGREE SUBJECTS FOR CONSIDERATION

Biochemistry; Biotechnology; Chemistry; Colour Chemistry; Cosmetic Science; Environmental Science; Food Science and Technology; Materials Science; Mathematics; Nuclear Engineering; Physics.

ENGINEERING (CIVIL)

(including **Architectural, Coastal, Disaster Management, Environmental, Offshore, Structural** and **Transportation Engineering**)

Civil engineering is concerned with the science and art of large-scale projects. This involves the planning, design, construction, maintenance and environmental assessment of roads, railways, bridges, airports, tunnels, docks, offshore structures, dams, high rise buildings and other major works. Specialist courses may also involve water, drainage, irrigation schemes and waste engineering, traffic and public health engineering.

Useful websites www.ice.org.uk; www.engc.org.uk; www.enginuity.org.uk.

NB The points totals shown to the left of the institutions are for ease of reference only. It must not be assumed that tariff points are always used by institutions or that they can be substituted for an offer in grades. The level of an offer is not necessarily indicative of the quality of a course.

Engineering Council statement See **Engineering/Engineering Sciences**.

COURSE OFFERS INFORMATION

Subject requirements/preferences See **Engineering/Engineering Sciences**. **NB** A* grades are likely to form part of university offers in the higher ranges for students applying for places in 2008 for entry in 2009: check websites.

Your target offers

360 pts and above

Cambridge – AAA (Civ Struct Env Eng) *(IB 38–42 pts)*

Oxford – Offers vary eg AAA–AAB (Civ Eng) *(IB 38–42 pts)*

Southampton – ABBb 370 pts (MEng Civ Eng Ind; Civ Eng Euro St; Env Eng courses; Civ Eng Archit) *(IB 33 pts)*

350 pts Southampton – BBBb 350 pts (BEng Civ Eng; Env Eng courses) *(IB 31–33 pts)*

340 pts Bath – 340 pts AAB (MEng Civ Eng; Civ Archit Eng) *(IB 35–36 pts)*

Durham – AAB (MEng Civ Eng) *(IB 38 pts)*

Imperial London – AAB–BBB (Civ Eng; Civ Env Eng; Civ Eng Yr Abrd) *(IB 36 pts H maths/phys 6 pts)*

London (UCL) – AAB–BBB (MEng/BEng Civ Eng; Env Eng) *(IB 36–38 pts)*

Sheffield – AAB–BBB **or** AAbb–BBbb (MEng Civ Eng; Struct Eng Archit; Civ Struct Eng; Civ Eng Modn Lang; Civ Eng Bus Mgt; Eng (Civ Mat Mech)) *(IB 32–34 pts)*

Warwick – AAB–ABB (MEng Civ Eng; Civ Eng (Bus Mgt) (Eng Sust)) *(IB 35–37 pts)*

320 pts Birmingham – ABB–BBC (MEng Civ Eng; Civ Eng Ind; Civ Eng Int; Civ Eng Bus Mgt)

Bristol – ABB–BBB (Civ Eng; Civ Eng Euro) *(IB 35 pts H666)*

Cardiff – ABB 320–300 pts (MEng Civ Eng; Civ Env Eng; Archit Eng; Archit Eng Euro)

Dundee – 320–260 pts (MEng Civ Eng; Civ Eng Mgt; Civ Eng Des Mgt)

Edinburgh – ABB 2nd yr entry (Civ Eng; Civ Eng Constr Mgt; Struct Fire Sfty Eng; Struct Eng Archit; Civ Env Eng) *(IB 30 pts)*

Exeter – ABB–BBC (MEng Civ Eng) *(IB 30–34 pts)*

Heriot-Watt – 320 pts 2nd yr entry (MEng/BEng Civ Eng; Struct Eng Archit Des; Civ Env Eng)

Manchester – ABB (MEng Civ Eng N Am; Civ Eng Ent; Civ Eng Euro; Civ Eng Ind) *(IB 34–36 pts)*

Newcastle – ABB–BBB (MEng Civ Eng; Civ Struct Eng; Off Eng) *(IB 34–36 pts)*

Nottingham – ABB–BBC (Civ Eng; Civ Eng Fr/Ger) *(IB 32 pts)*

Swansea – 320 pts (MEng Civ Eng)

300 pts Aberdeen – BBB 2nd yr entry (MEng Civ Eng; Civ Struct Eng; Civ Eng Euro St; Civ Eng Mgt)

Bath – BBB (BEng Civ Eng) *(IB 32 pts)*

Bradford – 300 pts (MEng Civ Struct Eng)

Brighton – 300 pts (MEng Civ Eng) *(IB 32 pts)*

Brunel – 300 pts (Mech Eng Bld Serv)

City – 300 pts (MEng Civ Eng; Civ Eng Surv; Civ Eng Archit)

Coventry – 300 pts (MEng Civ Eng)

Dundee – 300–240 pts (BEng Civ Eng; Civ Eng Mgt; Civ Eng Des Mgt) *(IB 28 pts)*

East London – 300 pts (MEng Civ Eng)

Edinburgh – BBB 1st yr entry (Civ Eng; Civ Eng Constr Mgt; Struct Fire Sfty Eng; Struct Eng Archit; Civ Env Eng) *(IB 30 pts)*

Glasgow – BBB (Civ Eng Archit)

Leeds – BBB (MEng Civ Struct Eng; Civ Env Eng; Civ Eng Constr Mgt; Archit Eng)

Liverpool – 300 pts (MEng Civ Env Eng; Civ Eng; Civ Marit Eng; Civ Struct Eng) *(IB 30 pts)*

Liverpool John Moores – 300 pts (MEng Civ Eng)

Loughborough – 300 pts (MEng Civ Eng) *(IB 30–32 pts)*

Manchester – BBB (BEng Civ Eng; Civ Struct Eng) *(IB 30–34 pts)*

Newcastle – BBB–BBC (BEng Civ Eng; Env Eng; Civ Struct Eng Archit) *(IB 30–32 pts)*
Nottingham – BBB–BCC (Archit Env Eng; Env Eng)
Plymouth – 300 pts (MEng Civ Eng; Civ Cstl Eng)
Portsmouth – 300 pts (MEng Civ Eng)
Queen's Belfast – BBB (MEng Civ Eng; Env Civ Eng; Struct Eng Archit)
Salford – 300 pts (MEng Civ Eng) *(IB 27–32 pts)*
Strathclyde – BBB (MEng Civ Eng; Civ Eng Euro St; Civ Eng Env Mgt; Archit Eng)
Surrey – ABC–BBB (MEng Civ Eng)
Warwick – BBB–BBC (BEng Civ Eng; Civ Eng (Bus Mgt) (Eng Sust)) *(IB 34 pts)*

280 pts **Aberdeen** – BBC (BEng 2nd yr entry CCD 1st yr entry) (Civ Eng; Civ Eng Euro St; Civ Struct Eng; Civ Env Eng; Civ Eng Mgt; Off Eng)
Cardiff – BBC 280 pts (BEng Archit Eng; Civ Eng; Civ Env Eng)
Nottingham Trent – 280 pts (BEng Civ Eng)

260 pts **Coventry** – 260 pts (BEng Civ Eng; Civ Struct Eng; Civ Eng Mgt; Disas Mgt)
Exeter – BCC–CCC (BEng Civ Eng) *(IB 26–30 pts)*
Glasgow – BCC–CCC (Civ Eng)
Glasgow Caledonian – BCC (Env Civ Eng)
Heriot-Watt – BCC 260 pts 1st yr entry (MEng/BEng Civ Eng; Struct Eng Archit Des; Civ Env Eng)
Liverpool – 260 pts (BEng Civ Eng) *(IB 30 pts)*
Liverpool John Moores – 260 pts (BEng Civ Eng)
Loughborough – 260 pts (Constr Eng Mgt; Archit Des Mgt; BEng Civ Eng) *(IB 28 pts H maths/phys 5 pts)*
Queen's Belfast – BCC (BSc/BEng Civ Eng; Env Civ Eng; Struct Eng Archit)
Strathclyde – BCC (BEng Civ Eng; Civ Eng Env Mgt; Archit Eng)
Surrey – BCC (BEng Civ Eng; Fdn Civ Eng)
Swansea – 260 pts (BEng Civ Eng)
Ulster – BCC 260 pts (BEng Civ Eng)

240 pts **Anglia Ruskin** – 240 pts (Civ Eng)
Bradford – 240 pts (BEng Civ Struct Eng)
Brighton – 240 pts (BEng Civ Eng; Civ Env Eng)
Glamorgan – 240 pts (BEng Civ Eng)
Greenwich – 240 pts (BEng Civ Eng; Civ Eng Proj Mgt; Civ Eng Wtr Env Mgt)
Plymouth – 240 pts ((BEng Civ Eng; Civ Cstl Eng)
Portsmouth – 240 pts (BEng Civ Eng)
Salford – 240 pts (BEng Civ Eng; Struct Eng Comp Sci)

230 pts **City** – 230 pts (BEng Civ Eng; Civ Eng Surv; Civ Eng Archit)
Napier – 230 pts (BEng Civ Trans Eng; Civ Eng)

220 pts **Bristol UWE** – 220 pts (BSc Civ Eng)
Dundee – 220–260 pts (BEng Civ Eng; Civ Eng Des Mgt)
East London – 220 pts (BEng Civ Eng)
Kingston – 220 pts (BEng Civ Eng; Env Haz Disas Mgt)
Nottingham Trent – 220 pts (BSc Civ Eng St)
Swansea – 220 pts (BEng Civ Eng Mgt)

200 pts **Abertay Dundee** – CDD 200 pts (Civ Eng)
Bolton – 200 pts (Civ Eng)
Coventry – 200 pts (BEng/BSc Civ Eng Constr; Civ Eng Des)
Napier – 200 pts (BSc Civ Eng; Civ Tmbr Eng)

180 pts **Greenwich** – 180 pts (BSc Civ Eng)

160 pts **East London** – 160 pts (BEng Civ Eng; Civ Eng Surv)
London South Bank – CC (BEng/BSc Civ Eng; Archit Eng)
Newport – 160 pts (Civ Constr Eng)
Plymouth – 160 pts (BSc Civ Eng; Civ Cstl Eng)
Salford – 160 pts (BSc Civ Eng)
Teesside – 160–240 pts (Civ Eng; Disas Mgt)

For information on how to read the Subject Tables, see **Chapter 8.**

West Scotland – DDE (BEng Civ Eng)
Wolverhampton – 160–220 pts (Civ Eng; Civ Eng Mgt)
140 pts **Glamorgan** – 140 pts (BSc Civ Eng; Civ Eng Int St)
120 pts **Aberdeen** – DD (BSc Civ Eng)
East London – 120 pts (BSc Civ Eng)
Kingston – 120 pts (BSc Civ Eng)
West Scotland – DD (BSc Civ Eng)
80 pts **Swansea (Inst)** – 80 pts (Civ Eng Env Mgt)

Leeds Met – contact University

Alternative offers
See **Chapter 8** for grade/point equivalences and related information for the following examinations: Scottish qualifications, the Welsh Baccalaureate, the IB diploma (approximate points shown also in italics in the table of offers), the Irish Leaving Certificate, the European Baccalaureate and the French Baccalaureate.

EXAMPLES OF FOUNDATION DEGREES IN THE SUBJECT FIELD
Bolton; Bristol UWE; Central Lancashire; Derby; East Lancashire (IHE); Glamorgan; Kent; Mid-Kent (Coll); Northampton; Nottingham Trent; Suffolk (Univ Campus); Swansea (Inst).

CHOOSING YOUR COURSE (SEE ALSO CH.1)
Course variations – Widen your options
Disaster Management Technology (Birmingham)
Water and Land Management (Bradford)
Architectural Engineering (Cardiff)
Civil and Timber Engineering (Napier)
Civil and Coastal Engineering (Plymouth)
CHECK PROSPECTUSES AND WEBSITES FOR OTHER UNIVERSITIES AND COLLEGES OFFERING THESE COURSES.

Universities and colleges teaching quality See www.qaa.ac.uk; www.unistats.com.

Top universities and colleges (Research) (See also **Building**) Birmingham; Bristol*; Cardiff*; Dundee; Imperial London*; Leeds; London (UCL); Newcastle; Nottingham; Queen's Belfast; Sheffield; Southampton*.

Sandwich degree courses Bath; Bradford; Brighton; Cardiff; City; Coventry; East London; Glamorgan; Kingston; London South Bank; Loughborough; Nottingham Trent; Portsmouth; Queen's Belfast; Salford; Surrey; Teesside; Ulster; West Scotland.

ADMISSIONS INFORMATION
Number of applicants per place (approx) Abertay Dundee 8; Bath 5; Birmingham 6; Bradford (BEng) 5; Bristol 10; Brunel 4; Cardiff 5; City 11; Coventry 10, (Civ Eng) 11; Dundee 5; Durham 8; Glamorgan 6; Glasgow Caledonian 4; Greenwich 11; Heriot-Watt 7; Imperial London 4; Kingston 8; Leeds 10; Liverpool John Moores 16; London (UCL) 5; London South Bank 5; Loughborough 6; Napier 4; Newcastle 11, (Off Eng) 9; Nottingham 6; Nottingham Trent 11; Plymouth 3; Portsmouth 3; Queen's Belfast 6; Salford 5; Sheffield 7; Southampton 9; Strathclyde 4; Surrey 5; Swansea 3; Teesside 6; West Scotland 4; Wolverhampton 3.

Advice to applicants and planning the UCAS personal statement **Portsmouth** Evidence of mathematical skills. See **Engineering/Engineering Sciences**. Also read the magazine *The New Civil Engineer* and discuss articles which interest you on your application. See also **Appendix 2**.

Selection interviews **Yes** Bath, Brighton, Bristol, Brunel, Cambridge, Coventry, Durham, Glamorgan, Greenwich, Heriot-Watt, Kingston, Leeds, London (UCL), London South Bank, Loughborough, Napier, Newcastle, Nottingham, Oxford, Queen's Belfast, Southampton, Surrey, Sussex, Warwick; **Some** Cardiff, Dundee, Nottingham Trent, Salford.

Interview advice and questions Past questions have included: Why have you chosen Civil

Engineering? Have you contacted the Institution of Civil Engineers? How would you define the difference between the work of a civil engineer and the work of an architect? What would happen to a concrete beam if a load were applied? Where would it break and how could it be strengthened? The favourite question: Why do you want to be a civil engineer? What would you do if you were asked to build a concrete boat? Do you know any civil engineers? What problems have been faced in building the Channel Tunnel? **Cambridge** Why did they make mill chimneys so tall? See also **Chapter 7**.

Reasons for rejection (non-academic) Lack of vitality. Lack of interest in buildings, the built environment or in civil engineering. Poor communication skills. See also **Engineering/Engineering Sciences**.

AFTER-RESULTS ADVICE
Offers to applicants repeating A-levels Higher East London, Kingston, Liverpool John Moores, Nottingham, Queen's Belfast, Teesside, Warwick; **Possibly higher** Portsmouth, Southampton; **Same** Bath, Birmingham, Bradford, Brighton, Bristol, Cardiff, City, Coventry, Dundee, Durham, Greenwich, Heriot-Watt, Leeds, London (UCL), London South Bank, Loughborough, Newcastle, Nottingham Trent, Salford, Sheffield, Wolverhampton; **No offers made** Cambridge.

GRADUATE DESTINATIONS AND EMPLOYMENT (2005/6 HESA)
Graduates surveyed 1080 **Employed** 775 **In further study** 70 **Assumed unemployed** 40.

Career note The many aspects of this subject will provide career directions for graduates with many openings with local authorities and commercial organisations.

OTHER DEGREE SUBJECTS FOR CONSIDERATION
Architecture; Building; Surveying; Town and Country Planning.

ENGINEERING (COMMUNICATIONS)
(Including **Mobile Communications;** see also **Engineering (Computer, Control, Software and Systems)** and **Engineering (Electrical and Electronic)**)

Communications Engineering impacts on many aspects of the engineering and business world. Courses overlap considerably with Electronic Engineering and provide graduates with expertise in such fields as telecommunications, mobile communications and microwave engineering, optoelectronics, radio engineering and internet technology. Sandwich courses and sponsorships are offered by several universities.

Useful websites See **Computer Courses** and **Engineering (Electrical and Electronic)**.

NB The points totals shown to the left of the institutions are for ease of reference only. It must not be assumed that tariff points are always used by institutions or that they can be substituted for an offer in grades. The level of an offer is not necessarily indicative of the quality of a course.

Engineering Council Statement See **Engineering/Engineering Sciences**.

COURSE OFFERS INFORMATION
Subject requirements/preferences See **Engineering/Engineering Sciences. NB** A* grades are likely to form part of university offers in the higher ranges for students applying for places in 2008 for entry in 2009: check websites.

Your target offers
360 pts and above
> **London (UCL)** – AAA+AS–AAB+AS (Electron Eng Comm Eng)
> **Strathclyde** – AAA (Dig Comm Multim Sys)
> **Warwick** – AABc **or** ABbbb (MEng Electron Eng (Comm))

340 pts **Bristol** – AAB–BBC (Comm Multim Eng; Electron Comm Eng)

Durham – AAB (MEng Comm Eng)

Sheffield – AAB–ABB **or** ABab–BBaa (Electron Comms Eng; Data Comms Eng)

Southampton – AAB (Electron Eng Wrlss Comms)

Surrey – AAB (MEng Telecomm Sys; Electron Sat Eng)

320 pts **Bath** – ABB (MEng Electron Comm Eng; Comp Electron Comm) *(IB 32–34 pts)*

Lancaster – ABB (Telecomm Mgt)

Leeds – ABB–BBB (Electron Comm Eng)

Leicester – 320 pts (MEng Comm Electron Eng courses)

Liverpool – ABB 320 pts (MEng Electron Comm Eng; Wrls Comm 3G Tech)

London (QM) – 320 pts (MEng Comm Eng) *(IB 30–36 pts)*

Newcastle – ABB (MEng Electron Comm) *(IB 32–34 pts)*

Surrey – ABB (BEng Telecomm Sys; Electron Sat Eng)

300 pts **Bangor** – 300–320 pts (MEng Comm Comp Sys)

Bath – BBB (BEng Electron Comm Eng; Comp Electron Comm)

Birmingham – 300–340 pts (Comm Sys Eng; Comp Comm Sys Eng; Comp Comm Sys Eng Int St; Comp Comm Sys Eng Bus Mgt; Electron Comm Eng) *(IB 32–36 pts)*

Bradford – BBB 300 pts (MEng Electron Telecomm Intnet Eng)

Dundee – 300 pts 2nd yr entry (Electron Comp (Comm Eng))

Edinburgh – BBB (Electron Elec Eng Comm)

Essex – 300 pts (MEng Telecomm Eng)

Hertfordshire – 300 pts (MEng Dig Comm Electron)

London (King's) – BBB+AS **or** BBbb (Telecomm Eng; Telecomm Eng Ind) *(IB 30 pts)*

Loughborough – BBB 300 pts (Wrlss Comm Eng)

Newcastle – BBB (BEng Electron Comm)

Portsmouth – 300 pts (MEng Comm Sys Eng)

Strathclyde – BBB (BEng Dig Comm Multim Sys)

Swansea – 300 pts (MEng Comm Sys)

Warwick – BCCc **or** BCccc (BEng Electron Eng (Comm))

York – BBB–BBC (Electron Comm Eng)

280 pts **Aberdeen** – BBC (Electron Eng Comm)

Hull – 280–300 pts (MEng Mbl Telecomm Tech)

Liverpool – BBC 280 pts (BEng Electron Comm Eng; Wrls Comm 3G Tech)

260 pts **Aston** – BCC–CCC 260–240 pts (Comm Eng)

Brunel – 260 pts (Electron Elec Eng (Comm Sys))

Glamorgan – 260 pts (Electron Comm Eng)

Kent – 260 pts (Electron Comm Eng)

Leicester – 260 pts (BEng Comm Electron Eng) *(IB 32 pts)*

London (QM) – 260 pts (BEng Telecomm; Comm Eng)

Robert Gordon – BCC (Electron Comm Eng; Comm Comp Net Eng; Artif Intel Comm Eng)

Swansea – 260 pts (BEng Comm Sys; Mbl Comm Intnet Tech; Comm Sys Euro; Comm Sys Aus; Comm Sys N Am; Comm Sys Ind Exp)

Westminster – BCC (Dig Comm Eng)

240 pts **Bangor** – 240–260 pts (BEng Comm Comp Sys)

Bradford – CCC 240 pts (BEng Electron Telecomm Intnet Eng)

Brighton – 240 pts (Dig Electron Comp Comm)

Bristol UWE – 240 pts (Mbl Tech)

City – CCC (BEng Media Comm Sys; Multim Intnet Sys Eng; Comm) *(IB 28 pts)*

Greenwich – 240 pts (Comm Sys Soft Eng)

Liverpool John Moores – 240 pts (Comp Net Telecomm Eng)

Northumbria – 240 pts (Comm Electron Eng)

Plymouth – 240 pts (BEng Comm Eng)

Portsmouth – 240 pts (BEng Comm Sys Eng; Comm Eng)

220 pts	**Birmingham City** – 220–240 pts (Telecomm Net)
	East London – 220 pts (Elec Electron Eng Comm St)
	Hertfordshire – 220 pts (BEng Dig Comm Electron)
	Hull – 220–280 pts (BEng Mbl Telecomm Tech)
	Napier – 220 pts (Electron Comm Eng)
200 pts	**Central Lancashire** – 200 pts (Dig Sgnl Imag Proc)
	Coventry – 200 pts (Comp Net Comm Tech; Comm Eng)
	Manchester Met – 200–240 pts (Comm Electron Eng) *(IB 26 pts)*
	Oxford Brookes – CDD or CDdd (Telecommunications)
	Portsmouth – 200 pts (BEng Comm Eng)
	Westminster – 200–260 pts (Mbl Comm; Net Comm Eng)
180 pts	**Plymouth** – 180 pts (Electron Comm Sys)
160 pts	**Kingston** – 160 pts (Comm Sys)
	London Met – 160 pts (Comm Sys)
	London South Bank – CC (Telecomm Comp Net Eng)
140 pts	**Cardiff (UWIC)** – 140 pts (Electron Comm Sys)
	Glasgow Caledonian – CD (Telecomm Eng)
	Wolverhampton – 140 pts (Electron Comm Eng)
120 pts	**West Scotland** – DD (Comm Tech)
80 pts	**UHI Millennium Inst** – 80 pts (Eng (Telecomm))
	Leeds Met – contact University

Alternative offers

See **Chapter 8** for grade/point equivalences and related information for the following examinations: Scottish qualifications, the Welsh Baccalaureate, the IB diploma (approximate points shown also in italics in the table of offers), the Irish Leaving Certificate, the European Baccalaureate and the French Baccalaureate.

EXAMPLES OF FOUNDATION DEGREES IN THE SUBJECT FIELD

Barnfield (Coll); East Antrim (IFHE); East Lancashire (IHE); Plymouth (CAD).

CHOOSING YOUR COURSE (SEE ALSO CH.1)

Course variations – Widen your options

Electronic, Telecommunications and Internet Engineering (Bradford)
Digital Communications with Electronics (Hertfordshire)
Wireless Communications and 3G Technology (Liverpool)
Networks and Telecommunications Engineering (Liverpool John Moores)
Mobile Communication and Internet Technology (Swansea).
CHECK PROSPECTUSES AND WEBSITES FOR OTHER UNIVERSITIES AND COLLEGES OFFERING THESE COURSES.

Universities and colleges teaching quality See www.qaa.ac.uk; www.unistats.com.

Sandwich degree courses See under **Engineering (Electrical and Electronic)**.

ADMISSIONS INFORMATION

Number of applicants per place (approx) Bradford 9; Bristol 2; Coventry 7; Hull 8; London Met 5; London South Bank 3; Northumbria 7; Plymouth 4.

Advice to applicants and planning the UCAS personal statement See **Engineering (Electrical and Electronic)**. See also **Appendix 2**.

Selection interviews Yes Bradford, Bristol, Hertfordshire, Kent, London Met, London South Bank, Sunderland.

Interview advice and questions See **Engineering (Electrical and Electronic)**.

Reasons for rejection (non-academic) See **Engineering (Electrical and Electronic)**.

AFTER-RESULTS ADVICE

Offers to applicants repeating A-levels **Same** Loughborough.

GRADUATE DESTINATIONS AND EMPLOYMENT (2005/6 HESA)

See **Engineering (Electrical and Electronic)** and **Engineering/Engineering Sciences**.

Career note Many commercial organisations offer opportunities in the specialist areas described at the top of this table. Work placements by way of sandwich courses result in over 60% of graduates gaining employment with their firms.

OTHER DEGREE SUBJECTS FOR CONSIDERATION

Computer Science; Engineering (Computer, Control, Electrical, Electronic Systems); Physics.

ENGINEERING (COMPUTER, CONTROL, SOFTWARE and SYSTEMS)

(see also **Computer Courses** and **Engineering (Electrical and Electronic)**)

The design and application of modern computer systems is fundamental to a wide range of disciplines which also include electronic, software and computer-aided engineering. Most courses give priority to reinforcing the essential 'transferable skills' consisting of management techniques, leadership skills, literacy, presentation skills, business skills and time management. At many universities Computer Engineering is offered as part of a range of Electronics degree programmes when the first and even the second year courses are common to all students who choose to specialise later. A year in industry is a common feature of many of these courses.

Useful websites See **Computer Courses** and **Engineering/Engineering Sciences**.

NB The points totals shown to the left of the institutions are for ease of reference only. It must not be assumed that tariff points are always used by institutions or that they can be substituted for an offer in grades. The level of an offer is not necessarily indicative of the quality of a course.

Engineering Council statement See **Engineering/Engineering Sciences**.

COURSE OFFERS INFORMATION

Subject requirements/preferences See **Engineering/Engineering Sciences**. **NB** A* grades are likely to form part of university offers in the higher ranges for students applying for places in 2008 for entry in 2009: check websites.

Your target offers

360 pts **and above**

Cambridge – AAA (Eng (Inf Comp Eng) yrs 3 and 4 specialisation via Engineering Tripos) *(IB 38–42 pts)*

Imperial London – AAA (Inf Sys Eng; Inf Sys Eng Abrd)

Manchester – AAA–AAB (Comp Sys Eng; Soft Eng)

Oxford – Offers vary eg AAA (Inf Eng) *(IB 38–42 pts)*

Strathclyde – AAA (MEng Comp Electron Sys; Dig Comm Multim Sys)

340 pts **Bristol** – AAB (Comp Sys Eng; Comp Sys Eng Euro) *(IB 34 pts)*

Reading – 340 pts (MEng Comp Eng)

Sheffield – AAB–ABB (Electron Contr Sys Eng; Sys Contr Eng; Med Sys Eng; Sys Eng) *(IB 32–35 pts)*

Southampton – AAB 340 pts (MEng/BEng Comp Eng; MEng Soft Eng) *(IB 34 pts)*

Surrey – AAB (MEng Dig Media Eng)

Warwick – AAB–ABB (MEng Sys Eng; Comp Eng) *(IB 35–37 pts)*

York – AAB (Electron Comp Eng; Comp Sys Soft Eng)

320 pts **Bath** – ABB (MEng Comp Electron Comm) *(IB 34–36 pts)*
Cardiff – ABB 320–300 pts (MEng Comp Sys Eng)
Essex – 320–300 pts (4yr Electron Comp; Comp Sys Eng)
Lancaster – ABB (MEng Comp Sys Eng) *(IB 32–34 pts)*
Leeds – ABB (Electron Comp Eng)
Leicester – 320 pts (MEng Embd Sys Eng)
Liverpool – 320 pts (MEng Comp Sci Electron Eng)
London (QM) – 320 pts (MEng Comp Eng; E–Commer Eng; Intnet Comp)
Loughborough – ABB 320 pts (MEng Comp Sys Eng; Sys Eng; Electron Soft Eng)
Newcastle – ABB (MEng Electron Comp Sys Eng) *(IB 34 pts)*
Sussex – ABB–BBB 360–330 pts (MEng Comp Sys Eng)

300 pts **Bangor** – 300–320 pts (MEng Comm Comp Sys)
Bath – BBB (BEng Comp Electron Comm)
Birmingham – 300 pts (Comp Sys Eng courses; Comp Comm Sys Eng courses) *(IB 32–36 pts)*
Bradford – 300–280 pts (Electron Telecomm Intnet Eng)
Brunel – BBB 300 pts (Multim Tech Des) *(IB 28–30 pts)*
Dundee – 300 pts 2nd yr entry (Electron Comp)
Durham – BBB 300 pts check with admissions tutor (Comp Eng)
Edinburgh – BBB (Comp Sci Electron; Soft Eng)
Essex – 300 pts (Comp Net; Comp Sys Eng; Soft Eng; Embd Comp Sys; Dig Media Eng; Scr Comp Sys)
Heriot-Watt – ABC 2nd yr entry (Comp Electron Inf Sys Eng)
Hertfordshire – 300 pts (MEng Dig Sys Comp Eng)
Lancaster – BBB (BEng Comp Sys Eng) *(IB 32–34 pts)*
Newcastle – BBB (BEng Comp Sci (Soft Eng))
Portsmouth – 300 pts (MEng Comp Eng)
Reading – 300 pts (BSc Comp Eng; Cyber Contr Eng; Sys Eng) *(IB 30 pts)*
Surrey – BBB–BBC (BEng Dig Media Eng; Comp Sci Eng)
Strathclyde – BBB (BEng Comp Electron Sys; Dig Comm Multim Sys)
Sussex – BBB–BBC (BEng Comp Sys Eng)
Warwick – BBB–BBC+AS (BEng Sys Eng; Electron Eng (Comp Eng))

280 pts **Aston** – 280 pts (Intnet Sys; Multim Dig Sys)
Bath – BBC (BEng Comp Electron Comm)
Bristol UWE – 280–300 pts (MEng/BEng Dig Sys Eng)
Cardiff – BBC 280 pts (BEng Comp Sys Eng)
Exeter – BBC (Intnet Eng)
Liverpool – 280 pts (Comp Sci Electron Eng)

260 pts **Aberystwyth** – 260–310 pts (Soft Eng)
Brunel – BCC 260 pts (Intnet Eng; Comp Sys Eng) *(IB 28–30 pts)*
Glamorgan – 260 pts (Comp Sys Eng)
Glasgow – BCC (Electron Soft Eng; Microcomp Sys Eng)
Heriot-Watt – BCC 260 pts 1st yr entry (Comp Electron (Inf Sys Eng))
Huddersfield – 260–320 pts (Comp Contr Sys)
Kent – 260 pts (BEng Comp Sys Eng)
Leicester – 260 pts (BEng Embd Sys Eng)
London (QM) – 260–300 pts (BEng Comp Eng; Aud Sys Eng; Multim Sys Tech; Dig Aud Mus Sys Eng) *(IB 30–36 pts)*
Loughborough – 260 pts (BEng Sys Eng)
Reading – 260 pts (Sys Eng) *(IB 30 pts)*
Richmond (Am Int Univ) – 260 pts (Comp Aid Eng)
Robert Gordon – BCC 2nd yr entry (Electron Comp Eng courses)
Westminster – 260 pts (Comp Sys Eng)

For information on how to read the Subject Tables, see **Chapter 8**.

240 pts **Bangor** – 240–260 pts (BEng Comp Sys)
Bradford – 240 pts (BEng Soft Eng)
Brighton – 240 pts (Dig Electron Comp Comm)
Bristol UWE – 240–260 pts (Soft Eng) *(IB 28–30 pts)*
City – CCC (BEng Sys Contr Eng; Multim Intnet Sys Eng; Comp Sys Eng) *(IB 25–28 pts)*
Glamorgan – 240 pts (Comp Sys Eng)
Greenwich – 240 pts (Comp Sys Soft Eng; Contr Instr Eng)
Hertfordshire – 240 pts (BEng Dig Sys Comp Eng; Aud Vid Broad Eng)
Liverpool John Moores – 240 pts (Comp Eng)
Manchester Met – 240 pts (Comp Electron Eng; Auto Contr) *(IB 26 pts)*
Northumbria – 240 pts (Comp Aid Eng)
Oxford Brookes – CCC (Comp Sys)
Plymouth – 240 pts (Robot Auto Sys)
Portsmouth – 240 pts (BEng Comp Eng)
Ulster – 240 pts (Electron Comp Sys)

220 pts **Aberdeen** – CCD (Electron Comp Eng)
Birmingham City – 220–240 pts (Soft Des Net; Comp Electron)
East London – 220–180 pts (Comp Electron)
Essex – 220–200 pts (Electron Comp)
Hull – 220–280 pts (Comp Sys Eng)
Napier – 220 pts (Electron Comp Eng)
Robert Gordon – CCD 1st yr entry (Electron Comp Eng)
Staffordshire – 220–280 pts (Comp Sys Net Eng; Net Comp Robot Tech; Soft Eng)

200 pts **Bolton** – 200 pts (Electron Comp Eng)
Coventry – 200 pts (Comp Net Comm Tech)
Heriot-Watt – CDD (BEng Comp Electron (Inf Sys Eng))
Manchester Met – 200–240 pts (Comp Net Tech; Comp Electron Eng)

180 pts **Aberdeen** – BC (Eng (Electron Comp Eng))
Anglia Ruskin – 180 pts (Electron Intnet Tech)
Central Lancashire – 180–200 pts (Comp Eng)
Greenwich – 180 pts (Intnet Eng Web Mgt)
Sheffield Hallam – 180 pts (Comp Electron Sys)
Teesside – 180–240 pts (Soft Eng; Instr Contr Eng)

160 pts **Bournemouth** – 160–180 pts (Electron Comp Tech)
Greenwich – CC (Contr Instr Eng)
North East Wales (IHE) – 160 pts (Comp Net; Intnet Multim Comp)
Westminster – CC (Comp Sys Tech; Mbl Comm)
Wolverhampton – 160–220 pts (Comp Sci (Soft Eng))

140 pts **Cardiff (UWIC)** – 140 pts (Electron Contr Sys)
Glasgow Caledonian – CD/DDE (Comp Eng)

120 pts **Bradford** – 120 pts (Fdn Cyber)
London South Bank – DD (Intnet Comp; Comp Aid Eng)

100 pts **West Scotland** – DE (Comp Net; Intnet Tech)

80 pts **Swansea (Inst)** – 80 pts (Comp Sys Electron)

Alternative offers

See **Chapter 8** for grade/point equivalences and related information for the following examinations: Scottish qualifications, the Welsh Baccalaureate, the IB diploma (approximate points shown also in italics in the table of offers), the Irish Leaving Certificate, the European Baccalaureate and the French Baccalaureate.

EXAMPLES OF FOUNDATION DEGREES IN THE SUBJECT FIELD

Bedfordshire; Bournemouth & Poole (Coll); Bradford (Coll); Ealing, Hammersmith and West London (Coll); East Lancashire (IHE); Glamorgan; Hull (Coll); North East Wales (IHE); Preston (Coll); Runshaw (Coll).

CHOOSING YOUR COURSE (SEE ALSO CH.1)

Course variations – Widen your options
Digital Electronics, Computing and Communications (Brighton)
Animatronics (Central Lancashire)
Digital Forensics and System Security (Coventry)
Secure Computer Systems (Essex)
Artificial Intelligence (Manchester)
Medical Systems Engineering (Sheffield)
CHECK PROSPECTUSES AND WEBSITES FOR OTHER UNIVERSITIES AND COLLEGES OFFERING THESE COURSES.

Universities and colleges teaching quality See www.qaa.ac.uk; www.unistats.com.

Top universities and colleges (Research) See **Computer Courses**.

Sandwich degree courses See **Engineering (Electrical and Electronic)**.

ADMISSIONS INFORMATION

Number of applicants per place (approx) Aberystwyth 6; Aston 6; Bangor 5; Birmingham 10; Birmingham City 6; Bournemouth 3; Bradford 6; Bristol 4; Bristol UWE 12; Cardiff 6; Central Lancashire 12; Coventry 2; Durham 6; East Anglia 4; Edinburgh 3; Huddersfield 2; Imperial London 5; Kent 5; Lancaster 12; Liverpool John Moores 2; London South Bank 3; Loughborough 17; Sheffield 10; Sheffield Hallam 8; Southampton 4; Staffordshire 5; Stirling 7; Strathclyde 7; Suffolk (Univ Campus) 1; Surrey (MEng, BEng) 3; Swansea (Inst) 4; Teesside 3; Westminster 5.

Advice to applicants and planning the UCAS personal statement See **Computer Courses** and **Engineering (Electrical and Electronic)**. See also **Appendix 2**.

Selection interviews Aston, Bath, Bradford, Cardiff, Durham, East Anglia, Glamorgan, Hertfordshire, Huddersfield, Kent, Liverpool John Moores, London South Bank, Nottingham Trent, Sheffield Hallam, Swansea (Inst), Westminster, York; **Some** Aberystwyth, Exeter, Manchester.

Interview advice and questions Southampton (B; Soft Eng) Free transport was provided from the railway station and free refreshments. There was a 45-minute talk on the University and tariff points and a brief outline of the courses on offer. There was a brief tour with a member of staff, lunch and a tour with students. The interview was really an informal chat about the personal statement and the teacher's reference. See also **Computer Courses** and **Engineering (Electrical and Electronic)** and **Chapter 7**.

Reasons for rejection (non-academic) Lack of understanding that the course involves engineering. See also **Computer Courses** and **Engineering (Electrical and Electronic)**.

AFTER-RESULTS ADVICE

Offers to applicants repeating A-levels Higher Bristol, Strathclyde, Warwick, York; **Possibly higher** City, Huddersfield, Sheffield; **Same** Aston, Bath, Birmingham, Coventry, East Anglia, Exeter, Lancaster, Liverpool John Moores, London South Bank, Salford, Teesside, Ulster; **No offers made** Cambridge.

GRADUATE DESTINATIONS AND EMPLOYMENT (2005/6 HESA)

Software Engineering graduates surveyed 655 **Employed** 440 **In further study** 45 **Assumed unemployed** 80.

Career note Career opportunities extend right across the whole field of electronics, telecommunications, control and systems engineering.

OTHER DEGREE SUBJECTS FOR CONSIDERATION

Computer Science; Computing; Engineering (Aeronautical, Aerospace, Communications, Electrical and Electronic); Mathematics; Physics.

ENGINEERING (ELECTRICAL and ELECTRONIC)

Electrical and Electronic Engineering courses provide a sound foundation for those looking for a career in electricity generation and transmission, communications or control systems, including robotics. All courses cater for students wanting a general or specialist Engineering education and options should be considered when choosing degree courses. These could include optoelectronics and optical communication systems, microwave systems, radio frequency engineering and circuit technology. Many courses have common first years, allowing transfer in Year 2. Most universities and colleges have good industrial contacts and can arrange industrial placements, in some cases abroad.

Useful websites www.theiet.org; www.engc.org.uk; www.enginuity.org.uk.

NB The points totals shown to the left of the institutions are for ease of reference only. It must not be assumed that tariff points are always used by institutions or that they can be substituted for an offer in grades. The level of an offer is not necessarily indicative of the quality of a course.

Engineering Council statement See **Engineering/Engineering Sciences**.

COURSE OFFERS INFORMATION

Subject requirements/preferences See **Engineering/Engineering Sciences**. **NB** A* grades are likely to form part of university offers in the higher ranges for students applying for places in 2008 for entry in 2009: check websites.

Your target offers

360 pts and above

> **Cambridge** – AAA (Eng (Elec Inf Sci) (Elec Electron Eng)) *(IB 38–42 pts)*
>
> **Imperial London** – AAA (MEng/BEng Elec Electron Eng; Inf Sys Eng; Inf Sys Eng Yr Abrd; Elec Electron Eng Mgt; Elec Electron Eng Yr Abrd) *(IB 38 pts)*
>
> **London (UCL)** – AAA+AS–AAB+AS (Electron Elec Eng; Electron Eng Comm Eng; Electron Eng Comp Sci; Electron Elec Int; Electron Eng Nanotech) *(IB 34–38 pts)*
>
> **Oxford** – Offers vary eg AAA–AAB (Elec Eng) *(IB 38–42 pts)*
>
> **Strathclyde** – AAA (MEng Elec Mech Eng; Elec Ener Sys; Electron Dig Sys; Electron Elec Eng Euro)

340 pts Bristol – AAB (Electron Eng; Elec Electron Eng; Elec Electron Eng Euro; Electron Comm Eng; Elec Electron Mgt) *(IB 36 pts)*

> **Durham** – AAB (MEng Electron Eng) *(IB 38 pts)*
>
> **Nottingham** – AAB–BCC (MEng/BEng Elec Eng; Elec Electron Eng courses; Electron Eng courses) *(IB 30–32 pts)*
>
> **Sheffield** – AAB–ABB **or** ABab **or** BBaa (Elec Eng courses; Electron Eng courses) *(IB 33 pts)*
>
> **Southampton** – AAB 340 pts (MEng Electron Eng courses) *(IB 34 pts)*
>
> **Surrey** – AAB (MEng Electron Eng; Electron Comp Eng; Dig Media Eng; Aud Media Eng)
>
> **Warwick** – AAB–ABB (MEng Electron Eng) *(IB 35–37 pts)*
>
> **York** – AAB–ABB (MEng Electron Eng; Electron Eng Bus Mgt; Electron Comm Eng; Electron Comp Eng; Electron Eng Media Tech; Electron Eng Mus Tech Sys; Rad Freq Eng)

320 pts Aston – ABB–BBB (MEng Electron Sys Eng Mgt St; Electron Sys Eng) *(IB 29 pts)*

> **Bath** – ABB (MEng Elec Electron Eng; Comp Electron Comm; Electron Comm Eng; Electron Spc Sci Tech)
>
> **Birmingham** – ABB–BBC (Electron Eng; Electron Comp Eng; Electron Comm Eng; Electron Eng Bus Mgt; Electron Elec Eng Int St; Electron Elec Eng) *(IB 32–36 pts)*
>
> **Cardiff** – ABB–BBB 320–300 pts (MEng Elec Electron Eng; Electron Comm Eng)
>
> **Dundee** – 320–260 pts (MEng Electron Elec Eng; Electron Eng Mgt; Electron Eng Microcomp Sys; Electron Eng Phys) *(IB 32 pts)*
>
> **Exeter** – ABB–BBC (MEng Electron Eng) *(IB 30–34 pts)*
>
> **Lancaster** – ABB (MEng Electron Sys Eng; Mecha) *(IB 32–34 pts)*
>
> **Leeds** – ABB–BBB (MEng Electron Elec Eng; Electron Eng; Electron Comm Eng; Nano)
>
> **Leicester** – 320 pts (MEng Elec Electron Eng courses) *(IB 32 pts)*

Schools of
Electronic Engineering
and Computer Science
University of Wales, Bangor

· PRIFYSGOL CYMRU ·
UNIVERSITY OF WALES
BANGOR
1884

Electronics and Computer Science at Bangor will provide you with the Science and Engineering training for the job you want. Our up-to-date courses are taught in a friendly and supportive atmosphere with well-equipped laboratories & teaching facilities, situated between the beaches of Anglesey and the mountains of Snowdonia.

Undergraduate Honours Courses:
MEng Electronic Engineering (4 years, H601)   BEng Electronic Engineering (3 years, H610)
MEng Communications and Computer Systems (4 years, H655)
BEng Communications and Computer Systems (3 years, H654)
BSc Creative Technologies (3 years, GW49)
BSc Computer Systems with Business Studies (3 years, H6N1)
BSc Computer Systems with Psychology (3 years, H6C8)
BSc Internet Systems and E-Commerce (3 years, NGC5)
BSc Computer Science with Mathematics (3 years, G4G1)
BSc Computer Science (3 years, G400)

NEW Courses, see www.seecs.bangor.ac.uk for further details:
3 year BSc Honours degrees in
  Electronics with Computer Science, Electronics with Finance, Electronics with Management

Further Information:
Please contact Admissions Tutor, Schools of Electronic Engineering and Computer Science, University of Wales, Bangor, Dean Street, Bangor, Gwynedd LL57 1UT.
Tel: 01248 382686   www.seecs.bangor.ac.uk
Email: admissions@informatics.bangor.ac.uk

Liverpool – 320 pts (MEng Elec Eng Electron courses; Med Electron Instr)
Loughborough – 320 pts (Electron Soft Eng; Electron Elec Eng) *(IB 30–34 pts)*
Manchester – ABB (MEng/BEng Elec Electron Eng; Electron Sys Eng) *(IB 33 pts)*
Newcastle – ABB–BBB (MEng Electron Comm; Elec Electron Eng) *(IB 32–34 pts)*
Reading – 320 pts (MEng Electron Eng courses; Cyber) *(IB 29–32 pts)*
Southampton – ABB 320 pts (MEng/BEng Elec Eng; Electromech Eng)
Sussex – ABB–BBB 360–330 pts (MEng Elec Electron Eng; Electron Comm Eng)
300 pts **Aberdeen** – BBB 2nd yr entry (MEng Elec Electron Eng; Elec Electron Eng Euro St; Electron Eng Comm; Elec Electron Eng Contr; Elec Electron Eng Mgt; Electron Comp Eng)
Bangor – 300–320 pts (MEng Electron Eng)
Bradford – 300 pts (MEng Elec Electron Eng; Electron Telecomm Intnet Eng)
City – 300–280 pts (MEng Elec Electron Eng) *(IB 28–32 pts)*
Dundee – 300–240 pts (BEng Electron Elec Eng; Electron Eng Mgt; Electron Eng Microcomp Sys; Electron Eng Phys; Electron Comp) *(IB 28 pts)*
Edinburgh – BBB (MEng/BEng Electron Elec Eng (Comm); Elec Eng; Electron; Electron Elec Mgt) *(IB 30 pts)*
Essex – 300 pts (Telecomm Eng; Electron Eng) *(IB 32–34 pts)*
Heriot-Watt – ABC 2nd yr entry (MEng Elec Electron Eng)
Hull – 300 pts (MEng Electron Eng)
Kent – 300 pts (MEng Electron Comm Eng) *(IB 28 pts)*
Lancaster – BBB (BEng Electron Sys Eng; Mecha)
London (King's) – BBB+AS **or** BBbb (Electron Eng; Electron Eng Ind; Mecha) *(IB 30 pts)*
London (QM) – 300–340 pts (MEng Electron Eng courses) *(IB 30–36 pts)*
Newcastle – BBB–BBC (BEng Elec Electron Eng; Electron Comm)
Portsmouth – 300 pts (MEng Electron Elec Eng)
Queen's Belfast – BBB (MEng Elec Electron Eng; Electron Soft Eng)
Robert Gordon – BBB (MEng Electron Elec Eng)
Strathclyde – BBB–AAA 2nd yr entry (BEng Elec Ener Sys; Electron Dig Sys; Electron Elec Sys)

Sussex – BBB (BEng Elec Electron Eng; Electron Eng) *(IB 30–32 pts)*

Swansea – BBB (MEng Electron Elec Eng; Electron Comp Sci)

Warwick – BBB–BBC (BEng Electron Eng) *(IB 34 pts)*

Westminster – 300 pts (MEng Electron Eng)

York – BBB–BBC (BEng Electron Eng) *(IB 32 pts)*

280 pts **Aberdeen** – BBC 2nd yr entry (BEng Elec Electron Eng; Elec Electron Eng Euro St; Electron Eng Comm; Elec Electron Eng Contr; Electron Eng Soft Eng; Electron Eng Comp Eng; Electron Eng Mgt)

Bath – BBC **or** 2AL+2AS (BEng Elec Electron Eng; Electron Spc Sci Tech; Electron Comm Eng; Comp Electron Comm)

Brighton – 280 pts (Elec Electron Eng) *(IB 30 pts)*

Cardiff – BBC 280 pts (BEng Electron Eng; Elec Electron Eng)

Exeter – BBC–CCC (BEng Electron Eng) *(IB 26–30 pts)*

Glasgow – BBC (Electron Mus; Electron Elec Eng Euro; Electron Elec Eng Int)

Liverpool – 280 pts (BEng Elec Eng Electron; Med Electron Instr)

Reading – 280 pts (BEng Electron Eng courses)

Staffordshire – 280 pts (Electron Eng; Electron Sys Des)

Surrey – BBC–BBB (BEng Electron Eng; Electron Comp Eng; Dig Media Eng)

260 pts **Aberdeen** – BCC 1st yr entry (MEng Elec Electron Eng; Elec Electron Eng Euro St; Electron Eng Comm; Electron Eng Comp)

Aston – BCC–CCC (BEng Elec Electron Eng; Electron Eng Mgt St; Electron Eng Comp Sci; Electromech Eng; Multim Dig Sys; Electron Prod Des)

Brunel – BCC 260 pts (Electron Elec Eng courses; Electron Microelec Eng) *(IB 28 pts)*

Glamorgan – 260–220 pts (BEng Elec Electron Eng courses)

Glasgow – BCC (Electron Soft Eng; Electron Elec Eng)

Heriot-Watt – BCC 260 pts (Elec Electron Eng courses; Robot Cybertron; Comp Electron)

Huddersfield – 260–320 pts (MEng/BEng Electron Eng)

Kent – 260 pts (BEng Electron Comm Eng) *(IB 28 pts)*

London (QM) – 260–300 pts (BEng Elec Electron Eng courses)

Leicester – 260 pts (BEng Elec Electron Eng)

Loughborough – 260 pts (BEng Electron Elec Eng)

Queen's Belfast – BCC (BEng Elec Electron Eng; Electron Soft Eng)

Robert Gordon – BCC–CCC (BEng Electron Comm Eng; Electron Elec Eng; Electron Comp Eng; Artif Intel Electron Eng)

Swansea – BCC 260 pts (BEng Electron Elec Eng; Electron Comp Sci)

Ulster – 260 pts (Electron Comp Sys)

Westminster – BCC (BEng Electron Eng)

240 pts **Bangor** – 240–260 pts 2AL (BEng Electron Eng)

Bradford – 240 pts (BEng Elec Electron Eng; Electron Telecomm Intnet Eng)

Brighton – 240 pts (Dig Electron Comp Comm; Aud Electron)

City – CCC (Elec Electron Eng)

Greenwich – 240 pts (BEng Electron Eng; Elec Eng; Elec Electron Eng; Electron Comp Sys)

Hull – 240–300 pts (BEng Electron Eng; Electron Gmg Sys)

Liverpool John Moores – 240 pts (Elec Electron Eng; Electron Broad Eng)

Manchester Met – 240 pts (Elec Electron Eng; Elec Electron Eng Euro; Comp Electron Eng) *(IB 24 pts)*

Northumbria – 240 pts (Elec Electron Eng; Comm Electron Eng)

Plymouth – 240 pts (BEng Elec Electron Sys; Robot Auto Sys)

Portsmouth – 240 pts (BEng Electron Elec Eng)

Sheffield Hallam – 240 pts (Elec Electron Eng)

Strathclyde – CCC (BEng Electron Elec Eng courses)

Surrey – 240 pts (Fdn Electron Comp Eng)

220 pts **Birmingham City** – 220 pts (Electron Eng)

Bristol UWE – 220–260 pts (Mus Sys Eng; Elec Electron Eng) *(IB 24–30 pts)*

East London – 220–260 pts (BEng Elec Electron Eng; Elec Electron Eng (Contr) (Comm))

For a quick reference offers calculator, fold out the inside back cover.

Glamorgan – 220–300 pts (Elec Electron St; Electron; Electron IT St; Electron Comm Eng)
Hertfordshire – 220 pts (BEng Elec Electron Eng; AV Dig Broad Eng)
Huddersfield – 220–260 pts (Electron Des; Electron Mus Tech)
Napier – 220 pts (Electron Elec Eng; Mecha)
Oxford Brookes – CCD **or** CCcc (BEng Electron Sys Des)
Staffordshire – 220–280 pts (Electron Eng)
Ulster – 220–180 pts (Electron Comms Soft)

200 pts **Anglia Ruskin** – 200 pts (Aud Tech Electron; Electron Comp Sci)
Central Lancashire – 200 pts (Electron Eng; Robot Mecha)
Coventry – 200 pts (Electron Eng)
De Montfort – 200–280 pts (Electron Eng)
Glasgow Caledonian – AC (BEng Electron Eng)
Heriot-Watt – CDD 1st yr entry (BEng Elec Electron Eng courses; Electron Photon Eng; Robot Cybertron)
Liverpool – CDD 200 pts (Fdn Elec Eng Electron)
Liverpool John Moores – 200 pts (Broad Tech; Des Electron)
Oxford Brookes – CDD (BSc Electron Sys Des)
Portsmouth – 200 pts (BEng Electron Eng)
Reading – 200 pts (Fdn Electron Eng)
Westminster – CDD/EE (Dig Sig Proc; Electron Eng; Electron Comp)

180 pts **Derby** – 180 pts CC **or** DDee (Elec Electron Eng; Electron)
Glasgow Caledonian – BC (Elec Pwr Eng)
Leicester – 180–240 pts (Fdn Eng)
Plymouth – 180 pts (Electron Comm Sys)
Sheffield Hallam – 180 pts (Electron Eng)
Teesside – 180–240 pts (Elec Electron Eng)

160 pts **City** – DDE (BSc Elec Electron Eng)
De Montfort – 160–240 pts (Electron Gms Tech)
Greenwich – 160 pts (Elec Electron Eng Tech)
Kent – 160 pts (Fdn Electron Eng)
London Met – 160 pts (Electron Comm Eng; Aud Electron)
London South Bank – CC (Elec Electron Eng)
Loughborough – CC (Fdn Elec Electron Eng)
Newport – 160 pts (Elec Eng; Electron Eng)

140 pts **Bolton** – 140–160 pts (Electronics)
Cardiff (UWIC) – 140 pts (Electron Microcomp Sys; Electron Comm Sys; Electron Contr Sys)
Glasgow Caledonian – CD (BSc Electron Eng; Mecha)
North East Wales (IHE) – 140 pts (Elec Electron Eng; Aero Electron Eng)
Robert Gordon – CD–CEE (BSc Electron Elec Eng)

120 pts **Aberdeen** – DD (BSc Electron courses)
Bradford – 120 pts (Fdn Cyber)
Southampton Solent – 120 pts (Electron Eng)
Swansea (Inst) – 120–180 pts (Comp Sys Electron; Auto Electron Sys)

80 pts **East Lancashire (IHE)** – 80 pts (Elec Eng)
Glamorgan – 80–140 pts (Elec Electron Eng)
Greenwich – 80 pts (Ext Mecha)
Portsmouth – 80 pts (Ext Eng)
UHI Millennium Inst (IC) (NHC) – 80 pts (Elec Electron Eng)

Leeds Met – contact University

Alternative offers
See **Chapter 8** for grade/point equivalences and related information for the following examinations: Scottish qualifications, the Welsh Baccalaureate, the IB diploma (approximate points shown also in italics in the table of offers), the Irish Leaving Certificate, the European Baccalaureate and the French Baccalaureate.

For information on how to read the Subject Tables, see **Chapter 8**.

EXAMPLES OF FOUNDATION DEGREES IN THE SUBJECT FIELD

Birmingham City (Coll); Bolton; Bournemouth and Poole (Coll); Brighton City (Coll); Bristol City (Coll); De Montfort; East Lancashire (IHE); Farnborough (CT); Glamorgan; Hastings (Coll); Huddersfield; Leeds Met; London Electron (Coll); Mid-Kent (Coll); Newcastle (Coll); Northampton; Plymouth City (Coll); Portsmouth; Somerset (CAT); Southampton Solent; Staffordshire Reg (Fed); Suffolk (Univ Campus); Thames Valley; Walsall (Coll); York (Coll).

CHOOSING YOUR COURSE (SEE ALSO CH.1)

Course variations - Widen your options

Electronics with Space Science Technology (Bath)
Music, Audio and Electronic Systems (Cardiff (UWIC))
Electrical Power Engineering (Glasgow Caledonian)
Electronics and Nanotechnology (Leeds)
Medical Electronics and Instrumentation (Liverpool)
Cybernetics (Southampton)
Digital Media Engineering (Surrey)
CHECK PROSPECTUSES AND WEBSITES FOR OTHER UNIVERSITIES AND COLLEGES OFFERING THESE COURSES.

Universities and colleges teaching quality See www.qaa.ac.uk; www.unistats.com.

Top universities and colleges (Research) Aston; Birmingham; Bristol; Cardiff; Edinburgh*; Essex; Glasgow; Heriot-Watt; Imperial London; Leeds*; Liverpool; London (King's), (UCL); Loughborough; Newcastle; Queen's Belfast; Reading; Sheffield*; Southampton*; Strathclyde; Surrey*; Ulster.

Sandwich degree courses Aston; Bath; Birmingham City; Bournemouth; Bradford; Brighton; Bristol UWE; Brunel; Cardiff; Central Lancashire; City; Coventry; De Montfort; East London; Glamorgan; Glasgow Caledonian; Greenwich; Hertfordshire; Huddersfield; Kingston; Leicester; Liverpool John Moores; London Met; London South Bank; Loughborough; Manchester; Manchester Met; Middlesex; Northumbria; Nottingham Trent; Oxford Brookes; Plymouth; Portsmouth; Queen's Belfast; Reading; Sheffield Hallam; Southampton Solent; Staffordshire; Surrey; Teesside; Ulster; York.

ADMISSIONS INFORMATION

Number of applicants per place (approx) Aston 6; Bath 8; Birmingham 7; Birmingham City 11; Bolton 3; Bournemouth 3; Bradford (Electron Eng) 8; Bristol 5; Bristol UWE 8; Cardiff 7; Central Lancashire 4; City 10; Coventry 8; De Montfort 1; Derby 8; Dundee 5; Glamorgan 2; Glasgow Caledonian 5; Greenwich 10; Hertfordshire 7; Heriot-Watt 6; Huddersfield 5; Hull 8; Kent 5; Kingston 8; Leeds 15; Lancaster 7; Leicester 15; Lincoln 8; Liverpool John Moores 2; London (King's) 8, (UCL) 9; London South Bank 5; Manchester Met 5; Napier 8; Newcastle 9; North East Wales (IHE) 3; Northumbria 7; Nottingham 6, (Fdn courses) 6, (BEng/MEng) 8; Plymouth 22; Portsmouth 4; Robert Gordon 3; Salford 5; Sheffield 15; Sheffield Hallam 2; Southampton 10; Staffordshire 7; Strathclyde 7; Sunderland 6; Surrey (BEng) 6, (MEng) 3; Swansea 3; Teesside 4; UHI Millennium Inst (IC) 1; Westminster 5; Warwick 8; York 5.

Advice to applicants and planning the UCAS personal statement **Liverpool John Moores** Enthusiasm for the subject, for example career ambitions, hobbies, work experience, attendance at appropriate events, competitions etc. **York** Our top priority is evidence of good ability in mathematics and also a scientific mind. Applicants should show that they can think creatively and have the motivation to succeed on a demanding course. See also **Engineering/Engineering Sciences** and **Appendix 2**.

Selection interviews Aston, Bangor (Electron Eng only), Bath, Bournemouth, Bradford, Bristol, Bristol UWE, Cambridge, Central Lancashire, De Montfort, Derby, Durham, East Anglia (Electron Eng), Essex, Heriot-Watt, Hertfordshire, Huddersfield, Hull, Kingston, Lancaster, Liverpool, London (UCL), London South Bank, Loughborough, Newcastle, Nottingham, Oxford, Plymouth, Portsmouth, Queen's Belfast, Southampton, Strathclyde, Sunderland, Surrey, Thames Valley, Westminster, York; **Some** Anglia Ruskin, Brighton, Cardiff, Dundee, Kent, Leicester, Liverpool John Moores, Salford, Staffordshire.

Interview advice and questions Past questions have included: How does a combustion engine work? How does a trumpet work? What type of position do you hope to reach in five to ten years' time? Could you sack an employee? What was your last physics practical? What did you learn from it? What are the methods of transmitting information from a moving object to a stationary observer? Wire bending exercise – you are provided with an accurate diagram of a shape that could be produced by bending a length of wire in a particular way. You are supplied with a pair of pliers and the exact length of wire required and you are given 10 minutes to reproduce as accurately as possible the shape drawn. How does a transistor work? A three-minute talk had to be given on one of six subjects (topics given several weeks before the interview); for example, the best is the enemy of the good. Is there a lesson here for British industry? 'I was asked to take my physics file and discuss some of my conclusions in certain experiments.' Explain power transmission through the National Grid. How would you explain power transmission to a friend who hasn't done physics? **York** Questions based on a mathematical problem. See also **Chapter 7**.

Reasons for rejection (non-academic) Poor English. Inability to communicate. Frightened of technology or mathematics. Poor motivation and work ethic. Better suited to a less specialised engineering/science course. Some foreign applicants do not have adequate English. **Surrey** Can't speak English (it has happened!). See also **Engineering/Engineering Sciences**.

AFTER-RESULTS ADVICE

Offers to applicants repeating A-levels Higher Brighton, Central Lancashire, Greenwich, Huddersfield, Kingston, Newcastle, Queen's Belfast, Strathclyde, Warwick; **Possibly higher** Aston, City, De Montfort, Derby, Glasgow, Hertfordshire, London Met, Portsmouth, Sheffield; **Same** Anglia Ruskin, Bangor, Bath, Birmingham, Bolton, Bradford, Cardiff, Coventry, Dundee, Durham, Hull, Kent, Leeds, Liverpool, Liverpool John Moores, London South Bank, Loughborough, Northumbria, Nottingham (usually), Nottingham Trent, Robert Gordon, Salford, Southampton, Staffordshire, Surrey, Thames Valley, Wolverhampton, York; **No offers made** Cambridge.

GRADUATE DESTINATIONS AND EMPLOYMENT (2005/6 HESA)

Graduates surveyed 2120 **Employed** 1270 **In further study** 255 **Assumed unemployed** 220.

Career note Electrical and Electronic Engineering is divided into two main fields – heavy current (electrical machinery, distribution systems, generating stations) and light current (computers, control engineering, telecommunications). Opportunities exist with many commercial organisations.

OTHER DEGREE SUBJECTS FOR CONSIDERATION

Computer Science; Engineering (Aeronautical, Communications, Computer, Control); Mathematics; Physics.

ENGINEERING (MANUFACTURING)

Manufacturing Engineering is sometimes referred to as production engineering. It is a branch of the subject concerned with management aspects of engineering such as industrial organisation, purchasing, and the planning and control of operations. Manufacturing Engineering courses are therefore geared to providing the student with a broad-based portfolio of knowledge in both the technical and business areas.

Useful websites www.engc.org.uk; www.imeche.org.uk; www.enginuity.org.uk.

NB The points totals shown to the left of the institutions are for ease of reference only. It must not be assumed that tariff points are always used by institutions or that they can be substituted for an offer in grades. The level of an offer is not necessarily indicative of the quality of a course.

Engineering Council statement See **Engineering/Engineering Sciences**.

COURSE OFFERS INFORMATION

Subject requirements/preferences See **Engineering/Engineering Sciences**. **NB** A* grades are likely to form part of university offers in the higher ranges for students applying for places in 2008 for entry in 2009: check websites.

Your target offers

360 pts **and above**
      Cambridge – AAA (Manuf Eng) *(IB 38–42 pts)*
340 pts **Bath** – AAB (Manuf; Manuf Fr/Ger; Spo Eng) *(IB 34–36 pts)*
      Durham – AAB (MEng Des Manuf Mgt) *(IB 38 pts)*
      Warwick – AAB–ABB (MEng Manuf Mech Eng) *(IB 35–37 pts)*
320 pts **London (King's)** – BBB (Eng Bus Mgt)
      Loughborough – 320 pts (Innov Manuf Tech)
      Newcastle – ABB (Mech Manuf Eng) *(IB 34 pts)*
      Nottingham – ABB–BCC (MEng Manuf Eng Mgt; Manuf Eng Mgt Fr/Ger/Ital/Jap/Span; Prod Des Manuf) *(IB 30 pts)*
300 pts **London (QM)** – 300 pts (Innov Entre Mgt Advnc Tech)
      Loughborough – BBB–BCC (MEng Prod Des Manuf; Manuf Eng Mgt) *(IB 34 pts)*
      Queen's Belfast – BBB (MEng Manuf Eng; Mech Manuf Eng)
      Strathclyde – BBB–CCC (Manuf Eng Tech courses)
      Warwick – BBB–BBC (BEng Manuf Mech Eng)
280 pts **Queen's Belfast** – BBC–BCC (BEng Manuf Eng)
260 pts **Loughborough** – 260 pts (BEng Prod Des Manuf; Manuf Eng Mgt) *(IB 34 pts)*
240 pts **Aston** – CCC (Eng Prod Des; Ind Prod Des; Prod Des Mgt; Sust Prod Des) *(IB 30–32 pts)*
      Greenwich – 240 pts (BEng Manuf Sys Eng)
      Hertfordshire – 240–280 pts (Manuf Eng)
220 pts **Birmingham City** – 220 pts (Mgt Manuf Sys)
      Huddersfield – 220 pts (Manuf Ops Mgt)
180 pts **Glamorgan** – 180 pts (BSc Mech Manuf Eng)
      Glasgow Caledonian – BC (Manuf Sys Eng)
160 pts **Blackpool & Fylde (Coll)** – 160 pts (Mech Prod Eng)
      Portsmouth – 160 pts (Mech Manuf Eng)
      Southampton Solent – 160 pts (Ycht Prod Surv)
140 pts **Liverpool John Moores** – 140 pts (Robotics)
100 pts **Greenwich** – 100 pts (Ext Manuf Sys Eng)
 80 pts **Swansea (Inst)** – 80–340 pts (Mech Manuf Eng; Manuf Sys Eng)

      Leeds Met – contact University

Alternative offers

See **Chapter 8** for grade/point equivalences and related information for the following examinations: Scottish qualifications, the Welsh Baccalaureate, the IB diploma (approximate points shown also in italics in the table of offers), the Irish Leaving Certificate, the European Baccalaureate and the French Baccalaureate.

EXAMPLES OF FOUNDATION DEGREES IN THE SUBJECT FIELD

Bristol City (Coll); Darlington (Coll); Derby (Coll); Glamorgan; Havering (Coll); Huddersfield; Huddersfield (TC); Swansea (Inst); York (Coll).

CHOOSING YOUR COURSE (SEE ALSO CH.1)

Course variations – Widen your options
Industrial Product Design (Aston)
Innovation Engineering Design and French (Bath)
Aerospace Manufacturing Engineering (Bristol UWE)
Robotics (Liverpool John Moores)
Innovative Manufacturing Technology (Loughborough)

Psychology and Ergonomics (Loughborough)
Yacht Production and Surveying (Southampton Solent)
CHECK PROSPECTUSES AND WEBSITES FOR OTHER UNIVERSITIES AND COLLEGES OFFERING THESE COURSES.

Universities and colleges teaching quality See www.qaa.ac.uk; www.unistats.com.

Top universities and colleges (Research) Aston; Bath*; London (King's), (QM); Loughborough; Nottingham; Strathclyde.

Sandwich degree courses See under **Engineering (Mechanical)**.

ADMISSIONS INFORMATION
Number of applicants per place (approx) Aston 6; Bath 18; Hertfordshire 1; Huddersfield 1; Loughborough 6; Nottingham 6; Strathclyde 8; Warwick 8.

Advice to applicants and planning the UCAS personal statement Work experience shadowing in industry should be mentioned. See **Engineering/Engineering Sciences**. See also **Appendix 2**.

Selection interviews Yes Cambridge, Hertfordshire, Loughborough, Nottingham, Strathclyde.

Interview advice and questions Past questions include: What is the function of an engineer? Describe something interesting you have recently done in your A-levels. What do you know about careers in manufacturing engineering? Discuss the role of women engineers in industry. Why is a disc brake better than a drum brake? Would you be prepared to make people redundant to improve the efficiency of a production line? See also **Chapter 7**.

Reasons for rejection (non-academic) Mature students failing to attend interview are rejected. One applicant produced a forged reference and was immediately rejected. See also **Engineering/ Engineering Sciences**.

AFTER-RESULTS ADVICE
Offers to applicants repeating A-levels Higher Strathclyde; **Possibly higher** Hertfordshire; **Same** Huddersfield, Nottingham; **No offers made** Cambridge.

GRADUATE DESTINATIONS AND EMPLOYMENT (2005/6 HESA)
Graduates surveyed 580 **Employed** 360 **In further study** 65 **Assumed unemployed** 45.

Career note Graduates with experience in both technical and business skills have the flexibility to enter careers in technology or business management.

OTHER DEGREE SUBJECTS FOR CONSIDERATION
Business Studies; Computer Science; Engineering (Electrical, Mechanical); Physics; Technology.

ENGINEERING (MECHANICAL)
(including **Agricultural Engineering, Automotive Engineering** and **Motorsport Engineering**)

Mechanical Engineering is one of the most wide-ranging engineering disciplines. All courses involve the design, installation and maintenance of equipment used in industry. Several universities include a range of Engineering courses with a common first year allowing students to specialise from Year 2. Agricultural Engineering involves all aspects of off-road vehicle design and maintenance of other machinery used in agriculture.

Useful websites www.imeche.org.uk; www.engc.org.uk; www.iagre.org.

NB The points totals shown to the left of the institutions are for ease of reference only. It must not be assumed that tariff points are always used by institutions or that they can be substituted for an offer in grades. The level of an offer is not necessarily indicative of the quality of a course.

Engineering Council statement See **Engineering/Engineering Sciences**.

COURSE OFFERS INFORMATION

Subject requirements/preferences (Product Design courses) Design technology or art may be required or preferred. See also **Engineering/Engineering Sciences**. **NB** A* grades are likely to form part of university offers in the higher ranges for students applying for places in 2008 for entry in 2009: check websites.

Your target offers

360 pts **and above**

Bristol – AAA (Mech Eng; Mech Eng Euro) *(IB 38 pts)*

Cambridge – AAA (Eng (Mech Eng)) *(IB 38–42 pts)*

Oxford – Offers vary eg AAA–AAB (Mech Eng) *(IB 38–42 pts)*

340 pts **Bath** – AAB (Auto Eng; Mech Eng; Innov Eng Des; Auto Eng Fr/Ger; Mech Eng Fr/Ger; Innov Eng Des Fr/Ger; Spo Eng) *(IB 36 pts)*

Brunel – 340 pts (Mech Eng Auto Des) *(IB 28–30 pts)*

Imperial London – AAB 3AL **or** 2AL+2AS (MEng Mech Eng; Mech Eng Yr Abrd) *(IB 38 pts H maths/phys 6 pts)*

Leeds – AAB (MEng Mech Eng) *(IB 30 pts)*

Liverpool – AAB (MEng Mech Eng; Mech Sys Des Eng; Mecha Robot Sys; Mech Eng Bus)

London (UCL) – AAB+AS–ABB+AS (MEng Mech Eng) *(IB 34–36 pts)*

Loughborough – 340 pts (MEng Auto Eng; Spo Tech; Mech Eng) *(IB 34 pts)*

Nottingham – AAB–BBB (MEng/BEng Mech Eng; Mech Eng Fr/Ger/Span; Mech Eng Mat Manuf; Mech Eng Maths; Mech Eng (Aerosp) (Auto) (Bioeng) (Bus)) *(IB 33 pts)*

Sheffield – 340 pts (MEng Mech Eng; Mech Eng Ind Mgt; Mech Eng N Am; Mtrspo Eng Mgt; Spo Eng; Mech Eng Lang) *(IB 32 pts)*

Southampton – AAB 340 pts (MEng/BEng Mech Eng courses) *(IB 34 pts)*

Strathclyde – AAB (MEng Mech Eng; Mech Eng Aero; Mech Eng Int St)

Warwick – AAB–ABB (MEng Mech Eng; Manuf Mech Eng; Auto Eng) *(IB 35–37 pts)*

320 pts **Birmingham** – ABB–BBC (MEng Mech Eng; Mech Eng Bus Mgt; Mech Auto Eng) *(IB 32–34 pts)*

Cardiff – ABB (MEng Mech Eng) *(IB 30 pts)*

City – ABB–BBB (MEng Auto Mtrspo Eng; Mech Eng) *(IB 28–30 pts)*

Durham – ABB–AAC 3AL **or** 2AL+2AS (MEng Mech Eng) *(IB 38 pts)*

Exeter – ABB–BBC (MEng Mech Eng; Min Eng) *(IB 30–34 pts)*

Glasgow – ABB (MEng Mech Eng (fast track); Mech Eng Aero; Mech Eng Euro)

Hertfordshire – 320 pts (MEng Auto Eng; Auto Eng Mtrspo)

Lancaster – ABB (MEng Eng (Mech); Mecha) *(IB 30 pts)*

Leicester – 320 pts (MEng Mech Eng) *(IB 30–32 pts)*

London (QM) – 320 pts (MEng Mech Eng courses; Spo Eng) *(IB 30–32 pts)*

Manchester – ABB (MEng Mech Eng courses; Mecha Eng courses) *(IB 34–36 pts)*

Newcastle – ABB (MEng Mech Eng courses) *(IB 30–34 pts)*

Queen's Belfast – ABB–BBB (MEng Mech Manuf Eng) *(IB 34 pts)*

Sheffield – 320 pts (BEng Mech Eng) *(IB 30 pts)*

Sussex – ABB–BBB (MEng Auto Eng; Mech Eng)

Swansea – 320 pts (MEng Mech Eng)

300 pts **Aberdeen** – BBB (MEng Mech Eng courses)

Aston – BBB or 2AL+2AS (MEng Electromech Eng; Mech Eng) *(IB 32 pts)*

Bradford – 300 pts (MEng Mech Eng; Mech Auto Eng)

Brunel – 300 pts (MEng Mech Eng Bld Serv; Mech Eng Auto Des; Mech Eng Aero; Mech Eng)

Dundee – 300–240 pts (BEng Mech Eng) *(IB 28 pts)*

Edinburgh – BBB (Mech Eng; Mech Eng Mgt; Mech Eng Renew Ener; Elec Mech Eng) *(IB 30 pts)*

Exeter – BBB–BCC (BEng Mech Eng; Min Eng) *(IB 26–30 pts)*

Hull – 300 pts (MEng Mech Eng; Mech Med Eng)

Lancaster – BBB (BEng Eng (Mech); Mecha) *(IB 30 pts)*

Leeds – BBB–BBC (Auto Eng; Mech Eng; Mecha Robot; Med Eng)

For a quick reference offers calculator, fold out the inside back cover.

Engineering

The University of Nottingham

School of Mechanical, Materials and Manufacturing Engineering

As one of the UK's premier engineering schools, we have an international reputation for high quality research, teaching and graduates. Our courses are accredited by professional institutions and are consistently well-ranked in league tables.

For 2008, we offer the following courses as BEng or MEng:

Mechanical Engineering, with specialist streams in manufacturing, aerospace, automotive, modern languages, bioengineering, management and materials

Design Engineering, with specialist streams in mechanical, materials and manufacture

Manufacturing Engineering and Management, with a specialist stream in aerospace

Product Design and Manufacture

In addition, we also offer the following BSc course:

Biomedical Materials Science

Specialist streams provide a route to developing a career in a particular industry. They are supported by academic staff with particular research interests relevant to the industry. For more detailed information, please refer to our website: www.nottingham.ac.uk/schoolm3 or send an email to m3-courses@nottingham.ac.uk

London (King's) – BBB+AS **or** BBbb (Mecha; Mech Eng) *(IB 30 pts)*
London (UCL) – BBB+AS–BBC+AS (BEng Mech Eng) *(IB 32 pts)*
Loughborough – BBB–ABC 300 pts (BEng Auto Eng) *(IB 30 pts)*
Manchester – BBB (BEng Mech Eng courses)
Oxford Brookes – BBB–DD (Mech Eng; Auto Eng; Mtrspo Eng)
Portsmouth – 300 pts (MEng Mech Eng)
Robert Gordon – BBB/ABC 300 pts (MEng Mech Eng)
Salford – 300 pts (MEng Mech Eng (Aerosp)) *(IB 27–32 pts)*
Sheffield – BBB–ABC 300 pts (Fdn Mech Eng; Mech Sys Eng; Mecha)
Sheffield Hallam – 300 pts (MEng Mech Eng)
Strathclyde – BBB (BEng Mech Eng; Mech Eng Int St)
Surrey – BBB (MEng Mech Eng; Sust Sys Eng)
Sussex – BBB–BBC (BEng Mech Eng; Auto Eng) *(IB 30–32 pts)*
Warwick – BBB–BBC+AS (BEng Manuf Mech Eng; Mech Eng; Auto Eng) *(IB 34 pts)*
280 pts Aberdeen – BBC 2nd yr entry (CCD 1st yr entry) (BEng Mech Eng; Mech Eng Comp Aid Eng; Mech Eng Contr; Mech Eng Euro St; Mech Eng Mgt; Mech Eng Oil Gas St)
Birmingham – 280–320 pts (BEng Mech Eng; Mech Mat Eng)
Brighton – 280 pts (MEng Mech Eng) *(IB 30 pts)*
Brunel – 280 pts (BEng Mtrspo Eng)
Cardiff – BBC (BEng Mech Eng) *(IB 28 pts)*
Harper Adams (UC) – 280–300 pts (Agric Eng; Off Rd Veh Des)
Heriot-Watt – BBC 2nd yr entry (Mech Eng; Mech Eng Comp Aid Eng; Mech Ener Eng; Auto Eng; Robot Cyber)
Liverpool – 280 pts (BEng Mech Eng; Mech Sys Des Eng; Mecha Robot Sys; Mech Eng Bus) *(IB 28 pts)*
London (UCL) – BBC+AS–BCC+AS (BEng Mech Eng)
Newcastle – BBC (BEng Mech Eng courses) *(IB 30 pts)*
Staffordshire – 280–200 pts (Mech Eng Spo Tech; Mecha; Mech Eng; Foren Comp Mech Eng)

260 pts **Aston** – BCC–CCC (BEng Mech Eng; Electromech Eng; Eng Prod Des)

Brighton – 260 pts (Mech Eng; Auto Eng)

Coventry – 260 pts (BEng Mech Eng; Auto Eng; Auto Eng Des)

Edinburgh – BCC (BEng Mech Eng courses)

Glasgow – BCC (BEng Prod Des Eng; Mech Eng; Mech Eng Aero; Mech Eng Euro; Mech Des Eng)

Hertfordshire – 260 pts (BEng Auto Eng; Mech Eng; Auto Eng Mtrspo)

Huddersfield – 260 pts (MEng Auto Eng; Auto Des; Mech Eng; Eng Des (Mech); Mtrspo Eng)

Leicester – 260 pts (BEng Mech Eng; Prod Des) *(IB 30–32 pts)*

London (QM) – 260–340 pts (BEng Mech Eng courses; Spo Eng)

Loughborough – 260 pts (Mech Eng) *(IB 30 pts)*

Queen's Belfast – BCC–BBC (BEng Mech Eng) *(IB 30–32 pts)*

Robert Gordon – BCC (BEng Mech Eng; Mech Off Eng; Mech Env Eng; Mech Eng Ener Eng)

Surrey – BCC (BEng Mech Eng)

Swansea – 260 pts (BEng Mech Eng courses)

240 pts **Bradford** – 240 pts (BEng Mech Eng; Mech Auto Eng)

Brunel – 240 pts (BEng Mech Eng Bld Serv; Mech Eng; Mech Eng Auto Des; Mech Eng Aero)

Central Lancashire – 240 pts (Mtrspo Eng)

City – BCD–CCD (BEng Auto Mtrspo Eng; Mech Eng)

Glamorgan – 240–260 pts (BEng Mech Eng; Mecha Eng)

Glasgow – CCC (BEng Mech Eng; Mech Eng Aero; Mech Eng Euro; Prod Des Eng; Mech Des Eng)

Greenwich – 240 pts (BEng Mech Eng; Ind Autom; Mecha)

Hull – 240 pts (BEng Mech Eng; Prod Innov)

Kingston – 240 pts (BEng Mech Eng)

Liverpool John Moores – 240 pts (Mecha; Auto Eng; Mech Eng; Mech Mar Eng)

Northumbria – 240 pts (Mech Eng)

Plymouth – 240 pts (BEng Mech Eng)

Portsmouth – 240 pts (Mech Eng)

Salford – 240 pts (BEng Mech Eng (Aerosp))

Sheffield Hallam – 240 pts (Mech Comp Aid Eng)

Strathclyde – CCC (Spo Eng)

Surrey – CCC (BEng Mech Eng; Fdn Mech Eng)

220 pts **Birmingham City** – 220–240 pts (Mech Eng; Auto Eng)

Bradford – 220 pts (Auto Des Tech; Veh Tech)

Bristol UWE – 220–260 pts (Mech Eng; Mtrspo Eng) *(IB 24–30 pts)*

Heriot-Watt – CCD 1st yr entry (Mech Eng; Mech Eng Comp Aid Eng; Auto Eng; Mech Eng Ener Eng; Robot Cybertron)

Huddersfield – 220 pts (BEng Auto Des; Auto Eng; Eng Des Mech; Mech Eng; Mtrspo Eng)

Napier – 220 pts (Mech Eng; Mecha)

Ulster – 220 pts (BEng Mech Eng)

200 pts **Bolton** – 200 pts (Auto Eng; Mech Eng)

Coventry – 200–240 pts (Mtrspo Eng; Veh Des; Mtrspo Mtrcycl Eng; Auto Eng Des; Mtrspo Pwrtrn Eng)

Dundee – 200 pts (BEng Mech Eng without Hons)

Hertfordshire – 200 pts (BSc Auto Tech Mgt; Mtrspo Tech)

Liverpool – 200 pts (BEng Fdn Mech Eng)

Manchester Met – 200–240 pts (Mech Eng; Autom Contr; Auto Eng) *(IB 26 pts)*

Portsmouth – 200 pts (Prod Des Innov; Prod Des Modn Mats)

Queen's Belfast – BB–BC (BSc Agric Tech)

Sheffield Hallam – 200 pts (Spo Equip Des)

Sunderland – 200 pts (Auto courses; Mech Eng Des)

Swansea – 200 pts (Fdn Mech Eng)

180 pts **Central Lancashire** – 180–200 pts (Mtrspo Ops; Robot Mecha)

Dundee – 180–200 pts (BSc Mech Eng)

For a quick reference offers calculator, fold out the inside back cover.

Glamorgan – 180 pts (Mech Manuf Eng)
Glasgow Caledonian – 180 pts (Mech Electron Sys Eng)
Leicester – 180–240 pts (Fdn Eng)
Manchester Met – 180–220 pts (BSc Mech Eng; Mech Eng Tech Auth)
Sheffield Hallam – 180 pts (Mech Eng)
Teesside – 180–240 pts (Mech Eng)

160 pts Blackpool and Fylde (Coll) – 160 pts (Mech Prod Eng; Mecha)
Greenwich – 160 pts (Mech Eng Tech)
Harper Adams (UC) – 160 pts (Eng Des Dev; Agric Eng Mark Mgt; Agric Eng; Offrd Veh Des)
Plymouth – 160 pts (BSc Mech Des Manuf; Mech Des Manuf Bus St; Mech Eng Comp Aid Des)
Portsmouth – 160 pts (Mech Manuf Eng)
Salford – 160 pts (BSc Mech Eng (Aerosp))
Wolverhampton – 160–200 pts (Auto Sys Eng; Mech Eng; Mecha)

140 pts Bolton – 140 pts (Auto Mbl Tech)
Cardiff (UWIC) – 140 pts (Mech Sys Eng)
Glamorgan – 140–180 pts (BSc Mech Manuf Eng)
Glasgow Caledonian – CD/DDE (Mechatronics)
Kingston – 140 pts (Mtrcycl Eng Des; Mech Eng Des; Auto Eng Des; Mtrspo Eng)
North East Wales (IHE) – 140 pts (Auto Electron Tech; Mtrspo Des Mgt)
Robert Gordon – CD (BSc Mech Eng)
Sheffield Hallam – 140 pts (Auto Tech)
Swansea (Inst) – 140 pts (Auto Eng; Mech Manuf Eng; Mtrspo Eng manuf)
West Scotland – CD (Mech Eng)

120 pts Aberdeen – DD (BSc Mech Eng)
London South Bank – DD (Mech Eng; Mecha)
Southampton Solent – 120 pts (Mech Des)

100 pts Coventry – 100 pts (Fdn Mtrspo Eng)
Hull – 100 pts (BEng Mech Eng 4 yrs)

80 pts East Lancashire (IHE) – 80 pts (Mech Eng)
Greenwich – 80 pts (Ext Mech Eng)
Hertfordshire – 80 pts (BEng Eng Ext)
Stockport (CFHE) – 80 pts (Mech Eng)
UHI Millennium Inst (NHC) – 80 pts (Mech Eng)

Alternative offers

See **Chapter 8** for grade/point equivalences and related information for the following examinations: Scottish qualifications, the Welsh Baccalaureate, the IB diploma (approximate points shown also in italics in the table of offers), the Irish Leaving Certificate, the European Baccalaureate and the French Baccalaureate.

EXAMPLES OF FOUNDATION DEGREES IN THE SUBJECT FIELD

Blackpool and Fylde (Coll); Bolton; Bournemouth; Bridgwater (Coll); Brighton & Hove City (Coll); Brooklands (Coll); Central Lancashire; Colchester (Inst); Coventry; Derby; East Lancashire (IHE); Exeter (Coll); Farnborough (CT); Glamorgan; Hastings (Coll); Havering (Coll); Kingston; Myerscough (Coll); Newcastle (Coll); Northampton; Oxford Brookes; Plymouth City (Coll); Sheffield Hallam; Somerset (CAT); Southampton Solent; Swansea (Inst); Tameside (Coll); Warwickshire (Coll); West Nottinghamshire (Coll). **Agricultural Engineering** Bicton (Coll); Harper Adams (UC).

CHOOSING YOUR COURSE (SEE ALSO CH.1)

Course variations – Widen your options

Electromechanical Engineering (Aston)
Sports Engineering (Bath)
Mechanical Engineering and Business Management (Birmingham)
Motorsport Engineering (Brunel)

Off-road Vehicle Design (Harper Adams (UC))
Robotics and Cybertronics (Heriot-Watt)
Motorcycle Engineering Design (Kingston)
Medical Engineering (Leeds)
Automotive Engineering (Loughborough)
CHECK PROSPECTUSES AND WEBSITES FOR OTHER UNIVERSITIES AND COLLEGES OFFERING THESE COURSES.

Universities and colleges teaching quality See www.qaa.ac.uk; www.unistats.com.

Top universities and colleges (Research) (Engineering, including Aeronautical and Manufacturing Engineering) Aston; Bath*; Bristol; Brunel; Glasgow; Imperial London*; Leeds*; London (King's), (QM), (UCL); Loughborough; Manchester; Nottingham; Sheffield; Southampton; Strathclyde.

Sandwich degree courses Aston; Bath; Birmingham City; Bradford; Brighton; Bristol UWE; Brunel; Cardiff; Central Lancashire; City; Coventry; East London; Glamorgan; Glasgow Caledonian; Greenwich; Harper Adams (UC); Hertfordshire; Huddersfield; Kingston; Leicester; Liverpool John Moores; London (QM); London South Bank; Loughborough; Manchester Met; Northumbria; Nottingham Trent; Oxford Brookes; Plymouth; Portsmouth; Queen's Belfast; Salford; Sheffield Hallam; Staffordshire; Sunderland; Surrey; Teesside; Ulster; West Scotland.

ADMISSIONS INFORMATION

Number of applicants per place (approx) Abertay Dundee 4; Aston 8; Bath (MEng) 13; Birmingham 8; Blackpool and Fylde (Coll) 1; Bradford 4; Brighton 10; Bristol 8; Bristol UWE 17; Brunel 12; Cardiff 8; Coventry 8; City 13; Dundee 5; Durham 8; Glamorgan 6; Hertfordshire 10; Heriot-Watt 9; Huddersfield 1; Hull 11; Kingston 8; Lancaster 8; Leeds 15; Leicester 11; Liverpool 6; Liverpool John Moores (Mech Eng) 2; London (King's) 8, (QM) 6; London South Bank 4; Loughborough 8, (Mech Eng) 12, (Auto Eng) 7; Manchester Met 6, (Mecha) 2, (Mech Eng) 6; Newcastle 10; North East Wales (IHE) 4; Northumbria 4; Nottingham 8; Plymouth 6; Portsmouth 6; Sheffield 10; Southampton 8; Staffordshire 6; Strathclyde 6; Surrey 9; Teesside 7; Warwick 8; Westminster 11.

Advice to applicants and planning the UCAS personal statement **Cardiff** Work experience; hands-on skills; self-starter. **Liverpool** An interest in solving mathematical problems related to physical concepts. Enjoyment in designing mechanical devices or components. Interest in engines, structures, dynamics or fluid flow and efficient use of materials or energy. **London (UCL)** We encourage applicants to apply for the Year in Industry Scheme (www.yini.org.uk) for placement. Scholarships are available to supplement the scheme. Students have the opportunity to work in industry for a year during their degree course. See **Engineering/Engineering Sciences**. See also **Appendix 2**.

Misconceptions about this course **Loughborough** Although organised by the Wolfson School of Manufacturing and Mechanical Engineering, the degree does not include manufacturing.

Selection interviews **Yes** Aston, Birmingham, Bolton, Bradford, Brighton, Bristol, Brunel, Cambridge, Cardiff, Durham, Harper Adams (UC), Hertfordshire, Huddersfield, Kingston, Lancaster, Leeds, Leicester, Liverpool John Moores, London (QM), London South Bank, Loughborough, Manchester Met, Newcastle, Nottingham, Oxford, Queen's Belfast, Sheffield, Sheffield Hallam, Strathclyde, Sunderland, Surrey, Sussex; **Some** Blackpool and Fylde (Coll), Dundee, Liverpool, Staffordshire.

Interview advice and questions Past questions include: What mechanical objects have you examined and/or tried to repair? How do you see yourself in five years' time? What do you imagine you would be doing (production, management or design engineering)? What engineering interests do you have? What qualities are required to become a successful mechanical engineer? Do you like sixth form work? Describe the working of parts on an engineering drawing. How does a fridge work? What is design in the context of mechanical engineering? What has been your greatest achievement to date? What are your career plans? **Hertfordshire** All interviewees receive a conditional offer. **Sunderland** Provide an example of working as part of a team, meeting a deadline, working on your own. See also **Engineering/Engineering Sciences** and **Chapter 7**.

Reasons for rejection (non-academic) See **Engineering/Engineering Sciences**.

For a quick reference offers calculator, fold out the inside back cover.

AFTER-RESULTS ADVICE

Offers to applicants repeating A-levels **Higher** Brighton, Dundee, Kingston, Loughborough, Newcastle, Queen's Belfast, Swansea, Warwick; **Possibly higher** City, Huddersfield; **Same** Aston, Bath, Blackpool and Fylde (Coll), Bradford, Bristol, Brunel, Coventry, Derby, Durham, East London, Harper Adams (UC), Heriot-Watt, Leeds (usually), Lincoln, Liverpool, Liverpool John Moores, London South Bank, Manchester Met, Napier, Northumbria, Nottingham, Nottingham Trent, Oxford Brookes, Sheffield, Sheffield Hallam, Southampton, Staffordshire, Sunderland, Surrey, Teesside, Wolverhampton; **No offers made** Cambridge.

GRADUATE DESTINATIONS AND EMPLOYMENT (2005/6 HESA)

Graduates surveyed 1855 **Employed** 1150 **In further study** 220 **Assumed unemployed** 155.

Career note Mechanical Engineering graduates have a wide choice of career options. Apart from design and development of plant and machinery, they are also likely to be involved in production processes and working at various levels of management. Mechanical engineers share interests such as structures and stress analysis with civil and aeronautical engineers, and electronics and computing with electrical and software engineers.

OTHER DEGREE SUBJECTS FOR CONSIDERATION

Engineering (Building, Manufacturing, Marine); Materials Science; Mathematics; Physics.

ENGLISH

(including **Creative Writing**)

English courses continue to be extremely popular and competitive. They are an extension of school studies in literature and language and may cover topics ranging from Anglo-Saxon literature to writing in the present day. Most courses, however, will focus on certain areas such as the Medieval or Renaissance periods of literature or on English language studies. Admissions tutors will expect students to have read widely outside their A-level syllabus.

Useful websites www.bl.uk; www.lrb.co.uk; www.literature.org; www.bibliomania.com; www.onlineliterature.com.

NB The points totals shown to the left of the institutions are for ease of reference only. It must not be assumed that tariff points are always used by institutions or that they can be substituted for an offer in grades. The level of an offer is not necessarily indicative of the quality of a course.

COURSE OFFERS INFORMATION

Subject requirements/preferences GCSE English language, literature required and a foreign language may be preferred. Grades may be stipulated. **AL** English with specific grades usually stipulated. Modern languages required for joint courses with languages. **NB** A* grades are likely to form part of university offers in the higher ranges for students applying for places in 2008 for entry in 2009: check websites.

Your target offers

360 pts **and above**

Bristol – AAA–ABB no pts offer (Engl; Engl Phil; Dr Engl) *(IB 38 pts)*
Cambridge – AAA (Engl; A–Sxn Nrs Celt; Engl Dr Educ St; Engl Educ) *(IB 38–42 pts)*
Durham – AAA (Engl Lit) *(IB 34 pts)*
Exeter – AAA–AAB (Engl; Engl Film St; Engl N Am) *(IB 34–36 pts)*
London (UCL) – AAA+AS–AAB+AS (Engl; Engl Ger) *(IB 36–38 pts)*
Manchester – AAA (Engl Lit)
Oxford – Offers vary eg AAA–AAB (Engl Lang Lit; Class Engl; Engl Modn Langs; Hist Engl) *(IB 38–42 pts)*
Sussex – AAA–AAB (Engl courses; Engl Langs)

Warwick – AABb **or** AAaab (Engl Lit; Engl Am Lit; Engl Lit Crea Writ; Engl Fr Lit; Eng Ger Lit; Eng It Lit; Eng Lat Lit; Engl Lit Thea St) *(IB 36 pts)*

York – AAA–AAB (Engl; Engl Educ; Engl Hist Art; Engl Pol; Engl Hist; Engl Phil; Engl Lang Ling) *(IB 36 pts)*

340 pts Birmingham – AAB (English) *(IB 34–36 pts)*

Cardiff – AAB (Engl Lit courses)

Durham – AAB (Engl Lit Phil; Engl Comb Hons)

East Anglia – AAB (Engl Lit Crea Writ; Engl Lit)

Exeter – AAB–ABB (Engl Fr/Ger/Ital/Russ/Span) *(IB 34–36 pts)*

Leeds – AAB (Engl; Engl Lang; Engl Lit Thea St)

Liverpool – AAB 340 pts (Engl Lang Lit; Engl Comm St; Engl Modn Hist; Engl Phil) *(IB 36 pts)*

Newcastle – AAB–ABB (Engl Lit; Engl Lang Lit; Engl Lang; Class St Engl)

Nottingham – AAB–ABB (Engl St courses) *(IB 34–36 pts)*

St Andrews – AAB (Engl courses) *(IB 36 pts)*

Sheffield – AAB–AAbb (Engl Hist; Engl Lit) *(IB 29–35 pts)*

Southampton – AAB–ABB (Engl courses) *(IB 33–36 pts)*

320 pts Cardiff – ABB (Cult Crit Engl Lit)

Durham – ABB (Educ St (Engl St))

East Anglia – ABB–BBB (Engl Am Lit; Engl Lit Dr)

Glasgow – ABB (Engl Lit; Engl Lang; Scot Lit)

Keele – 320–260 pts (Engl courses) *(IB 30–32 pts)*

Lancaster – ABB–BBB (Engl Lang courses; Engl Lit courses; Engl Lit Crea Writ) *(IB 32–34 pts)*

Leeds – ABB–BBC (Engl joint courses)

London (King's) – ABB+AS (Engl Lang Lit; Engl Film; Fr Engl)

Loughborough – 320–280 pts (Engl; Engl N Am Lit Film; Pub Engl) *(IB 32–35 pts)*

Manchester – ABB–BBB (Engl Lang courses; Engl Lit courses except under **360 pts**)

Stranmillis (UC) – ABB (Engl Educ)

300 pts Birmingham – BBB (Modn Langs Engl Lit; Mediev Engl Hist; Engl Lang Lit Educ; Engl courses)

Bournemouth – 300 pts (Scrptwr Film TV)

Dundee – BBB–CCC (Engl courses)

East Anglia – BBB–ABB (Engl Compar Lit; Cult Lit Pol; Script Perf)

Edinburgh – BBB (Engl Lang courses; Engl Lit courses; Scot Lit courses)

Essex – 300 pts (Engl Lit; Lit Myth; Crea Writ) *(IB 30–32 pts)*

Liverpool – BBB–BBC (Engl Fr/Ger; Engl Hisp St) *(IB 34–36 pts)*

London (Gold) – ABC–BBB (Engl; Media Modn Lit; Engl Am Lit; Engl Hist; Engl Compar Lit; Engl Dr)

London (King's) – BBB (Gk Engl; Hisp St Engl; Lat Engl; Port Braz St Engl)

London (QM) – 300–370 pts (Engl courses) *(IB 32 pts)*

London (RH) – ABC–ABB (Engl courses; Engl Crea Writ) *(IB 34 pts)*

Manchester – BBB (Engl Lit Fr/Ger/Ital/Jap/Port/Port/Russ/Span; Engl Lang Ger/Ital/Span/Russ)

Queen's Belfast – BBB (Engl courses)

Reading – 300–340 pts (Engl Comb courses) *(IB 31–32 pts)*

Sheffield – BBB–ABB (Engl courses except under **340 pts**)

Surrey – 300–320 pts (Engl Lit courses; Engl Crea Writ)

280 pts Aberystwyth – 280 pts (Engl Lit courses; Engl Lit Crea Lit) *(IB 30 pts)*

Aston – 280–300 pts (Engl Lang courses)

Brighton – 280 pts (Engl Sociol) *(IB 28–30 pts)*

Essex – 280 pts (Engl Lang Ling; Engl Lang Lit) *(IB 30–32 pts)*

Exeter (Cornwall) – 280–320 pts (Engl Corn St)

Kent – 280–320 pts (Engl Am Lit courses)

Leicester – 280–320 pts (Engl; Engl Am St; Engl Hist) *(IB 32 pts)*

Nottingham – BBC (Vkng St)

Oxford Brookes – BBC–CDD (Engl courses)
Plymouth – 280 pts (Engl Am St; Media Arts Engl; Engl Hist; Engl Pop Cult)
Salford – 280 pts (Engl Lit; Engl Crea Writ; Engl Journal)
Sheffield Hallam – 280 pts (Engl St)
Strathclyde – BBC (Jrnl Crea Writ)
Swansea – 280–300 pts (Engl single Hons courses)

260 pts **Coventry** – 260 pts (Engl; Jrnl Engl; Engl Jrnl St; Engl TEFL)
Huddersfield – 260 pts (Engl St; Engl Lang courses; Engl Lit courses; Engl Crea Writ)
Hull – 260–300 pts (Engl Crea Writ; Engl courses)
Leeds – BCC–BBB (Engl courses except under **340 pts**)
Leicester – 260–320 pts (Engl Comb courses) *(IB 32 pts)*
Lincoln – 260–280 pts (English)
Liverpool – 260 pts (Irish St Engl Lang Lit)
Northumbria – 260–280 pts (Engl Crea Writ; Engl Lang St)
Sheffield Hallam – 260 pts (Engl Hist)
Stirling – BCC (Engl St courses; Scot Lit) *(IB 30 pts)*
Strathclyde – BCC/BB (English)
Swansea – 260–280 pts (Engl joint Hons courses)
Ulster – BCC 260 pts (English)
Westminster – BCC (Engl courses; Engl Crea Writ)

240 pts **Aberdeen** – CCC (Engl courses; Engl Scot Lit)
Bangor – 240–280 pts (Engl courses; Engl Lang Crea Writ; Engl Jrnl; Engl Am Lit Cult; Engl Lang courses)
Bradford – 240 pts (Engl courses; Crea Writ)
Brighton – 240 pts (Engl St Engl Lit; Engl Lang Engl Lit; Engl St Ling; Engl St Media)
Bristol UWE – 240–300 pts (Engl courses; Dr Eng Langl; EFL courses)
Brunel – 240–300 pts (Engl; Dr Engl; Engl Crea Writ)
Central Lancashire – CCC (Jrnl Engl Lit)
Chester – 240 pts (Engl Comb courses; Crea Writ courses; Dr Engl) *(IB 30 pts)*
Kingston – 240–320 pts (Crea Writ courses)
Liverpool Hope – 240 pts (Engl Lang courses; Engl Lit courses)
Nottingham Trent – 240–220 pts (Engl; Engl Crea Writ)
Portsmouth – 240–300 pts (Engl courses; Crea Writ Dr)
Roehampton – 240–320 pts (Engl Lit courses; Engl Lang courses; Crea Writ courses)
Ulster – 240–260 pts (Engl Comb courses)
Winchester – 240–280 pts (Engl courses; Engl Lit courses; Crea Writ courses) *(IB 24–26 pts)*

220 pts **Bath Spa** – 220–260 pts (Engl Lit courses; Crea Writ Engl; Engl Media St)
Chichester – 220–240 pts (Engl courses; Engl Crea Writ courses) *(IB 28 pts)*
Edge Hill – 220 pts (Crea Writ Media)
Falmouth (UC) – 220–280 pts (Engl Crea Writ; Engl Media St)

Glamorgan – 220–260 pts (Engl Lit; Crea Prof Writ; Engl St)
Gloucestershire – 220–280 pts (Engl Lit; Engl Lang Crea Writ)
Hull (Scarborough) – 220–240 pts (Educ St Engl St; Thea Engl)
Kingston – 220–320 pts (Engl Lang courses; Engl Lit courses)
Manchester Met – 220–200 pts (Crea Writ courses) *(IB 28 pts)*
Napier – 220 pts (Engl Jrnl; Engl Pub; Engl Comm Adv PR; Engl Film)
Nottingham Trent – 220 pts (Engl joint courses)

200 pts **Anglia Ruskin** – 200–240 pts (Engl courses; Writ courses)
Birmingham City – 200 pts (Engl Lit; Engl Dr; Engl Lang St)
Blackpool and Fylde (Coll) – 200 pts (Engl Lang Lit Writ)
Bolton – 200 pts (Crea Writ; Engl; Media Writ Prod; Engl courses)
Central Lancashire – 200–240 pts (Engl Lang St; Engl Lit; Engl Lang Lit)
East Lancashire (IHE) – 200–240 pts (Engl Lang Lit St)
Edge Hill – 200 pts (Engl courses; Engl Lit courses; Crea Writ courses)
Hertfordshire – 200–240 pts (Engl Lang courses; Engl Lit courses; Crea Writ courses)
Lampeter – 200–300 pts (Engl Lit courses)
London Met – 200–240 pts (Crea Writ; Engl Lang St; Engl Lit)
Manchester Met – 200–220 pts (Engl courses; Crea Writ courses)
Newport – 200 pts (Engl; Engl Crea Writ)
Plymouth – 200–240 pts (Engl courses except under **280 pts**)
Sunderland – 200–260 pts (Engl courses)

190 pts **Buckingham** – 190 pts (Engl Lit courses)
180 pts **Anglia Ruskin** – 180–220 pts (EFL courses)
Dartington (CA) – 180 pts (Writ courses)
De Montfort – 180–200 pts (Engl joint Hons; Crea Writ joint hons)
East London – 180 pts (Engl Lang; Engl Lit Crea Prof Writ)
Lampeter – 180–240 pts (Engl Modn Lit courses)
Liverpool John Moores – 180–280 pts (Imgntv Writ; Engl courses)
Northampton – 180–220 pts (Engl; Crea Writ courses)
Southampton Solent – 180–200 pts (Scrnwrit; TV Prod (Writ); Writ Pop Fctn; Cmdy Writ Perf)
Worcester – 180 pts (Engl Lit St)

160 pts **Canterbury Christ Church** – CC (Engl courses; Engl Lang Comm courses)
Cardiff (UWIC) – 160 pts (Art Crea Writ)
Cumbria – 160–200 pts (Engl; Engl Am St; Engl Crea Writ; Engl Dr; Engl Hist)
Doncaster (Coll) – 160 pts (English)
Greenwich – 160 pts (Engl; Crea Writ courses)
Grimsby (IFHE) – 160–240 pts (Prof Writ)
Leeds Trinity and All Saints (Coll) – CC–CCC (Engl; Engl Hist; Engl Media; Engl Film St; Engl Writ)

For a quick reference offers calculator, fold out the inside back cover.

London South Bank – CC–CCC (Engl; Crea Writ Engl)
Middlesex – 160–200 pts (Engl Lit courses; Crea Media Writ; Engl St; Crea Writ Engl Lit)
Newman (UC) – 160–240 pts (Engl; Engl Lit courses; Crea Writ courses)
North East Wales (IHE) – 160–200 pts (Engl; Engl Crea Writ)
Norwich City (Coll) – 160 pts (Engl courses)
St Mary's (UC) – 160–220 pts (Engl courses)
Staffordshire – 160–240 pts (Engl Lit courses; Crea Writ courses) *(IB 28 pts)*
Wolverhampton – 160–220 pts (Engl courses; Engl Lang; Crea Prof Writ courses; Lit St)
York St John – 160 pts (Engl courses)

140 pts   **Bishop Grosseteste (UC)** – 140 pts (Engl Lit)
Derby – 140–160 pts (Engl courses; Crea Writ courses)
Marjon (UC) – 140–200 pts (Engl Lit; Engl Lang Ling; Crea Writ courses)
Suffolk (Univ Campus) – 140–200 pts (Engl; Engl Hist; Engl Film Media St; Engl Sociol)
Teesside – 140–160 pts (Engl St; Engl St Media St; Engl Hist; Engl St Sociol)
Trinity Carmarthen (Coll) – 140 pts (Engl; Crea Writ courses)

120 pts   **Bucks New** – 120–240 pts (Crea Writ courses; Engl Lit courses; Engl Lit Dr)
Peterborough Reg (Coll) – 120 pts (Hist Engl; Engl Sociol)

100 pts   **Bournemouth (Yeovil Coll)** – 100 pts (Engl Hist)
Swansea (Inst) – 100 pts (Engl St courses)

80 pts   **London (Birk)** – 80 pts for under 21s (over 21s varies) (p/t English)
North Lindsey (Coll) – 80 pts (Engl Hist)
Norwich (SAD) – 80 pts (Crea Writ)
South Devon (Coll) – 80 pts check with Inst (Arts (Engl Hist))
West Anglia (Coll) – 80–160 pts (Engl Hist; Engl Sociol)

Leeds Met – contact University

Alternative offers
See **Chapter 8** for grade/point equivalences and related information for the following examinations: Scottish qualifications, the Welsh Baccalaureate, the IB diploma (approximate points shown also in italics in the table of offers), the Irish Leaving Certificate, the European Baccalaureate and the French Baccalaureate.

EXAMPLES OF FOUNDATION DEGREES IN THE SUBJECT FIELD
Arts London; Bedfordshire; North West Kent (Coll); St Helens (Coll); Truro (Coll).

CHOOSING YOUR COURSE (SEE ALSO CH.1)
Course variations – Widen your options
English and Gaelic Studies (Aberdeen)
English Literature and Library Studies (Aberystwyth)
EFL and European Studies (Bristol UWE)
English Language and Communication (Cardiff)
English and Creative Writing (Chester)
Fashion Journalism (Creative Arts (UC))
Literature and Myth (Essex)
Media and Modern Literature (London (Gold))
Portuguese and Brazilian Studies with English (London (King's))
Journalism and English (Northumbria)
Typography and English (Reading)
Advertising and English (Trinity Carmarthen (Coll))
CHECK PROSPECTUSES AND WEBSITES FOR OTHER UNIVERSITIES AND COLLEGES OFFERING THESE COURSES.

Universities and colleges teaching quality See www.qaa.ac.uk; www.unistats.com.

Top universities and colleges (Research) Anglia Ruskin; Birmingham; Bristol; Cambridge*; Cardiff*;
De Montfort; Durham*; East Anglia; Edinburgh*; Exeter; Glasgow*; Hull; Keele; Kent; Lampeter; Lancaster; Leeds*; Leicester; Liverpool*; London (Birk), (Gold), (QM), (RH), (UCL); Loughborough;

Manchester; Newcastle; Nottingham; Nottingham Trent; Oxford*; Oxford Brookes; Queen's Belfast; Reading; St Andrews*; Sheffield; Southampton; Stirling; Strathclyde; Sussex; Warwick*; York*.

Sandwich degree courses Brighton; East London; Glamorgan; Huddersfield; Lancaster; Loughborough; Nottingham Trent; Oxford Brookes; Westminster.

ADMISSIONS INFORMATION

Number of applicants per place (approx) Aberystwyth 7; Anglia Ruskin 5; Bangor 5; Bath Spa 8; Birmingham 7; Birmingham City 9; Blackpool and Fylde (Coll) 2; Bristol 28, (Engl Dr) 45; Bristol UWE 4; Brunel 10; Buckingham 2; Cambridge (A-Sxn Nrs Celt) 2, (Engl) 4.9; Cardiff (Engl Lit) 6; Central Lancashire 10; Chester 20; Chichester 4; Cumbria 24; De Montfort 7; Derby 6; Dundee 6; Durham 20; East Anglia (Engl Lit Dr) 22, (Engl Lit Crea Writ) 17, (Engl St) 12, (Engl Compar Lit) 13; Edge Hill (CHE) 4; Exeter 13; Glamorgan 8; Gloucestershire 35; Hertfordshire 6; Huddersfield 5; Hull 14; Hull (Scarborough) 1; Kingston 6; Lampeter 4; Lancaster 12; Leeds 10; Leeds Trinity and All Saints (Coll) 7; Leicester 7; Liverpool (Engl Comm St) 7; London (Gold) 9, (King's) 15, (QM) 9, (RH) 9, (UCL) 13; Loughborough 40; London South Bank 5; Manchester Met 7; Middlesex 8; Newman (UC) 3; North East Wales (IHE) 2; Northampton 3; Nottingham 22; Nottingham Trent 21; Oxford (success rate 25%), (Magdalen) 15; Oxford Brookes 15; Portsmouth 8; Reading 11; Roehampton 5; Salford 12; Sheffield 12; Sheffield Hallam 4; Southampton 5; Stirling 9; Sunderland 10; Swansea (Inst) 4; Teesside 5; Warwick 15, (Engl Thea) 26; Winchester 3; York 16; York St John 3.

Advice to applicants and planning the UCAS personal statement Applicants should read outside their subject. Details of any writing you have done (for example poetry, short stories) should be provided. Theatre visits and play readings are also important. Keep up to date by reading literary and theatre reviews in the national newspapers (keep a scrapbook of reviews for reference). Evidence is needed of a good writing style. **Birmingham** Independence of mind, wit! **Bristol** Very popular course – not enough places to make offers to all those whose qualifications are deserving of a place. **Bristol UWE** Favourite authors, spare-time reading. **Cardiff** (Engl Lit) Ability to write lucidly, accurately and succinctly. Evidence of literary enthusiasm. **Derby** We seek a literate and accurate statement. **Durham** Background reading about linguistics essential. **East Anglia** (Crea Writ) Aims and objectives in their own writing. (Engl Lit Dr) Commitment to drama in all its aspects. **Leeds** 'Tell me why you read and, more importantly, what you think about what you read.' **Liverpool** General interest in communications – verbal, visual, media. Intellectual curiosity. Read everything from the classics to contemporary literature and the daily newspaper. For non-EU students – limited places; English language competence essential. **London (Gold)** Some interests should reflect chosen course. **London (QM)** Evidence of commitment to literature; also for Dr Engl, evidence of acting and production experience. **Nottingham Trent** Ability to write accurately and clearly. **St Andrews** Evidence of interest and reasons for choosing the course. Sport/extracurricular activities. Posts of responsibility. **Sheffield Hallam** (Engl St) Applicants do not need previous experience in literature, language or creative writing. **Stirling** What has the student done between school and university? Literary and linguistic interests. **Warwick** Oxbridge decisions awaited before offers made. Reading beyond the syllabus. (Engl St Thea) Synopsis of theatre experience (viewing and/or practical).

Misconceptions about this course Birmingham City The study of English language means descriptive linguistics – the course won't necessarily enable students to speak or write better English. **Buckingham** Native speakers of English often do not realise that the EFL degree courses are restricted to non-native speakers of English. **East Anglia** (Engl Lit Crea Writ) This is not simply a creative writing course: English literature is the predominant element. **Liverpool** (Engl Comm St) The course is not a training in journalism, although some students go on to work in the press, radio or TV.

Selection interviews Yes Anglia Ruskin, Bangor (mature students), Brunel, Cambridge, Canterbury Christ Church, Exeter, Gloucestershire, Huddersfield, Hull, Hull (Scarborough), Kingston, Lampeter, Lancaster, Leeds Trinity and All Saints (Coll), London (Gold), (RH), London South Bank, Loughborough, Middlesex, Newcastle, Newport, Oxford, Portsmouth, Reading, Roehampton, Warwick; **Some** Aberystwyth, Bangor, Bath Spa, Birmingham City, Blackpool and Fylde (Coll), Bristol, Chester, De Montfort, Derby, Dundee, East Anglia, East Lancashire (IHE), Leeds, Liverpool (Engl Comm St), London (King's), London Met, Salford, Southampton, Swansea (Inst), Truro (Coll), Wolverhampton.

For a quick reference offers calculator, fold out the inside back cover.

Interview advice and questions Questions will almost certainly be asked on set A-level texts and any essays which have been submitted prior to the interview. You will also be expected to have read outside your A-level subjects and to answer questions about your favourite authors, poets, dramatists etc. Questions in the past have included: Do you think that class discussion plays an important part in your English course? What is the value of studying a text in depth rather than just reading it for pleasure? What is the difference between satire and comedy? Are books written by women different from those written by men? Why would you go to see a production of *Hamlet*? What are your views on the choice of novels for this year's Booker Prize? Short verbal tests and a précis may be set. **Buckingham** It is useful to know if there is any particular reason why students want a particular programme; for example, for the TEFL degree is a member of the family a teacher? **Cambridge** We look for interviewees who respond positively to ideas, can think on their feet, engage intelligently with critical issues and sustain an argument. If they don't evince any of these we reject them. What books are bad for you? **East Anglia** (Am Lit Crea Writ) Compare your writing trends with other examples. How does a study of English literature contribute to your critical attitude to your own work? (Engl Lit Dr) How do you reconcile yourself to an academic interest in literature on the one hand and the belief in practical performance on the other? Interviews are accompanied by auditions. **Leeds** Academic ability; current reading interests. **Liverpool** (Engl Comm St) General questions only. Reading interests, general interests, career ambitions. **Oxford** Is there a difference between innocence and naivety? If you could make up a word, what would it be? Why? Do you think *Hamlet* is a bit long? No? Well I do. Is the Bible a fictional work? Was Shakespeare a rebel? **Roehampton** Samples of work taken to interview and discussed. **Warwick** We may ask students to sight-read or to analyse a text. See also **Chapter 7**.

Applicants' impressions (A=Open day; B=Interview day) Cambridge (B) There was one half-hour interview with questions on my A-level subjects and specific questions on English, plays and books I had read. It was a formal interview but not intimidating. (B) I was asked how I chose my reading material and to respond to a set poem. **Exeter** (B) There were three interviewers, all helpful, friendly, encouraging and welcoming. We had a comprehensive discussion on the areas which interest me, why I had applied to Exeter and what I felt it would offer me. **Lancaster** (A) There was a mini-lecture and tour. We were introduced to all the lecturers and had a talk and presentation on the social life of the university and of Lancashire. **Oxford** (B) I was asked to discuss a text I had mentioned in my personal statement and to comment on a set poem. **(St Hilda's)** (B) There were two interviewers, with the interview lasting 40 minutes. The questions were demanding but I was treated helpfully. There was a very friendly atmosphere and beautiful surroundings. I was able to meet students to discuss various problems concerning studying and living in college. Strongly recommended. **(Magdalen)** (B) There were two interviews, one of 15 minutes and the other of 30 minutes. The questioning was intense and I felt I had been 'laid bare'! The students were overwhelmingly friendly and there was a really happy atmosphere; pity I was rejected! The department was very high-powered and dynamic – the best of the best! But I wasn't aware that it was the most popular college! **Sussex** (A) The open day consisted of a talk on the course. It would be useful to have some questions prepared before you go. **Warwick** (B) (Engl Thea St) One 20-minute pressurised interview with one person. I was unable to meet the students. **York** (A) The open day consisted of a mini-lecture, an introduction to the lecturers and a campus tour.

Reasons for rejection (non-academic) Some are well-informed about English literature – others are not. Inability to respond to questions about their current studies. Lack of enthusiasm for the challenge of studying familiar subjects from a different perspective. Must be able to benefit from the course. Little interest in how people communicate with each other. They don't know a single thing about our course. **Bangor** We reject those who decline interviews. **Bristol** Not enough places to make offers to all those whose qualifications deserve one. **Cambridge** See **Interview advice and questions**. **Oxford** (1) The essay she submitted was poorly written, careless and reductive and, in general, lacking in attention to the subject. She should be encouraged to write less and think more about what she is saying. She seems to put down the first thing that comes into her head. (2) We had the feeling that he rather tended to dismiss texts which did not satisfy the requirements of his personal canon and that he therefore might not be happy pursuing a course requiring the study of texts from all periods. (3) In her essay on Brontë she took a phrase from Arnold which was metaphorical (to do with hunger) and applied it literally, writing at length about the diet of the characters. **East Anglia** (Am Engl Lit) Personal statement unconvincing in its commitment to American literature. (Other courses) Poor examples of work submitted. **Leeds** Unsuitable predictions. **Liverpool** (Engl Comm St) Student more suited to a practical course. Ungrammatical Personal Statement. **Reading** None. If they have reached the interview we have already eliminated all other factors. **Sheffield Hallam** Apparent lack of eagerness to tackle all three strands of the course (literature, language and creative writing). **Southampton** Insufficient or patchy academic achievement. Applicants coming from non-standard academic backgrounds are assessed in terms of their individual situations.

AFTER-RESULTS ADVICE

Offers to applicants repeating A-levels Higher Aberystwyth, Sheffield Hallam, Southampton (varies), Warwick; **Possibly higher** Lancaster, Newcastle, Oxford Brookes; **Same** Anglia Ruskin, Bangor, Birmingham City, Blackpool and Fylde (Coll), Bristol, Cardiff, Chester, Chichester, Cumbria, De Montfort, Derby, Dundee, Durham, East Anglia, Edge Hill, Hull, Lampeter, Leeds, Leeds Trinity and All Saints (Coll), Liverpool, Liverpool Hope, London (Gold), (RH), Loughborough (varies), Manchester Met, Newman (UC), Newport, Nottingham, Nottingham Trent, Portsmouth, Reading, Roehampton, St Mary's (UC), Salford, Sheffield, Staffordshire, Stirling, Suffolk (Univ Campus), Ulster, Winchester, Wolverhampton, York, York St John; **No offers made** Cambridge.

GRADUATE DESTINATIONS AND EMPLOYMENT (2005/6 HESA)

English graduates surveyed 7380 **Employed** 3495 **In further study** 1635 **Assumed unemployed** 465.

Creative Writing graduates surveyed 350 **Employed** 165 **In further study** 40 **Assumed unemployed** 45.

Career note English graduates work in the media, management, public and social services, business, administration and IT, sales retail, the cultural industries and the teaching profession. Those who have undertaken courses in creative writing could aim for careers in advertising, public relations, journalism or publishing.

OTHER DEGREE SUBJECTS FOR CONSIDERATION

Communication Studies; Drama; Language courses; Linguistics; Literature; Media Studies.

ENVIRONMENTAL SCIENCE/STUDIES

(including **Conservation, Ecology, Environmental Health** and **Environmental Management;** see also **Biological Sciences, Geography** and **Geology/Geological Sciences**)

Environmental Science/Studies courses need to be considered with care as, depending on their content and specialisms, they lead to very different careers. Environmental Health courses usually focus on the training of environmental health officers whilst Environmental Studies or Science degrees cover a range of subjects with options which may include biology, geography, geology, oceanography, chemistry, legal, social and political issues.

Useful websites www.cieh.org; www.ends.co.uk; www.enn.com; www.iagre.org.uk; www.defra.gov.uk; www.socenv.org.uk; www.ies-uk.org.uk; www.noc.soton.ac.uk.

NB The points totals shown to the left of the institutions are for ease of reference only. It must not be assumed that tariff points are always used by institutions or that they can be substituted for an offer in grades. The level of an offer is not necessarily indicative of the quality of a course.

COURSE OFFERS INFORMATION

Subject requirements/preferences GCSE English, mathematics and a science (often chemistry or biology) usually required. **AL** One or two science subjects are usually stipulated; mathematics may be required. (Meteorology) Mathematics, physics and another science may be required sometimes with specified grades, eg **Reading** mathematics and physics grade B. **NB** A* grades are likely to form part of university offers in the higher ranges for students applying for places in 2008 for entry in 2009: check websites.

Your target offers

360 pts **and above**
      Cambridge – AAA (Ener Env; Lnd Econ; Nat Sci (Geol Sci)) *(IB 38–42 pts)*
      East Anglia – AAA–AAB (Env Sci N Am/Aus; Env Earth Sci N Am/Aus; Env Geog Int Dev; Meteor Ocean Aus/N Am) *(IB 31–34 pts)*
      Leeds – AAA (MGeol Env Geol Int)

340 pts **East Anglia** – AAB–ABB (Ecol Aus/N Am) *(IB 31–34 pts)*
      Imperial London – AAB–ABB (Ecol; Env Geosci)
      London (UCL) – AAB–BBB+AS (Env Biol; Env Geog) *(IB 32–36 pts)*
      Manchester – AAB–BBC (Blt Nat Env courses)
      Reading – 340 pts (Meteor; Meteor Yr Okl) *(IB 31 pts)*

320 pts **Cardiff** – ABB–BBB (Ecology) *(IB 32 pts)*
      Durham – ABB (Ecol; Env Geosci; Earth Sci) *(IB 34 pts)*
      East Anglia – ABB (Env Earth Sci Euro; Env Sci Euro; Env Chem; Meteor Ocean Euro) *(IB 31–34 pts)*
      Lancaster – ABB (Env Sci N Am/Aus; Env Biol N Am/Aus; Env Chem N Am/Aus; Earth Env Sci N Am/Aus) *(IB 32–34 pts)*
      London (LSE) – ABB (Env Pol Econ; Env Pol) *(IB 32 pts)*
      Newcastle – ABB (Env Sci) *(IB 28–30 pts)*
      St Andrews – ABB (MA Sust Dev)
      Sheffield – ABB (MBioch Ecol; Env Sci; Env Maths)
      Sheffield – ABB–ABbb (Env Sci 4 yrs)
      Southampton – ABB 320 pts (MEnvSci Env Sci; Ocean courses)
      Southampton – ABB–BBB (BSc Env Sci) *(IB 31–32 pts)*
      Ulster – 320 pts (Env Hlth)

300 pts **Aberdeen** – BBB 300 pts 2nd yr entry (Env Sci; Ecol; Cons Biol)
      Birmingham – BBB–BCC 300–260 pts (Env Geosci; Env Mgt; Env Sci; Env Sci Abrd) *(IB 32 pts)*
      Bristol – BBB (Env Geosci)
      Dundee – BBB–CCC 300–240 pts (Env Mgt; Env Sci; Env Sci Geog; Renew Ener) *(IB 26 pts)*
      Durham – BBB (New Renew Ener)
      Edinburgh – BBB (Ecol Sci; Ecol Sci (Cons Ecol Mgt) (Ecol) (Env Sci) (Frsty); Geog Env St) *(IB 30 pts)*
      Exeter (Cornwall) – BBB–BCC 300–260 pts (Renew Ener)
      Lancaster – BBB (Env Chem; Env Biol; Ecol)
      Leeds – BBB 300 pts (Ener Env Eng; Env Mgt; Ecol Env Biol)
      Manchester – ABC (Env Sci; Env Res Geol; Env St)
      Nottingham – BBB–BBC (Env Sci Chin St; Env Sci Euro)
      Queen's Belfast – BBB–BCC (Env Plan)
      Reading – 300 pts (Env Biol; Env Sci)
      Sheffield – BBB **or** BBbb (BSc Ecol; Env Sci 3 yrs) *(IB 29 pts)*
      Stirling – BBB 2nd yr entry (Env Sci; Env Geog; Ecol; Cons Sci; Cons Mgt Cons Biol; Frshwtr Sci)
      Strathclyde – BBB (Civ Eng Env Mgt)
      Sussex – BBB–BBC 330–310 pts (Ecol Cons; Env Sci Dev St)
      York – BBB (Env Sci; Env Econ Env Mgt) *(IB 30 pts)*

280 pts **Aberystwyth** – 280 pts (Env Sci; Env Earth Sci) *(IB 30 pts)*
      Coventry – 280 pts (Cons Geog; Nat Haz)
      East Anglia – BBC 280 pts (Env Sci; Env Sci Ind; Env Earth Sci; Meteor Ocean; Meteor Ocean Ind)

For information on how to read the Subject Tables, see **Chapter 8**.

Edinburgh – BBC (Env Geosci)
Essex – 280–240 pts (Env Lf Hlth; Ecol) *(IB 26–30 pts)*
Glasgow – BBC–CCC (Env Chem Geog; Env Biogeochem)
Glasgow (Crichton) – BBC (Env St)
Lancaster – BBC (Env Sci)
Leeds – BBC (Env Biogeosci; Env Cons; BSc Env Geol; Env Bus; Env Trans Plan; Env Sci; Env Sust)
Liverpool – BBC–BBB 280–300 pts (Env Biol)
London (QM) – 280–320 pts (Env Sci; Env Geog) *(IB 30 pts)*
Loughborough – 280 pts (Chem Eng Env Prot)
Stirling – BBC (Env Sci Film Media St) *(IB 26 pts)*

260 pts
Abertay Dundee – BCC (Nat Res Mgt)
Coventry – 260 pts (Disas Mgt courses)
Lancaster – BCC (BSc Env Chem; Env Maths; Env Chem)
Liverpool – BCC 280 pts (Env Plan)
Manchester – BCC (Env Mgt)
Northumbria – 260 pts (Env Mgt; Env Hlth)
Nottingham – BCC (Env Biol) *(IB 24–30 pts)*
Oxford Brookes – BCC (Env Sci courses)
Portsmouth – 260–300 pts (Env Biol)
Queen's Belfast – BCC/AB (Env Biol)
Strathclyde – BCC (Env Hlth)

240 pts
Aberdeen – CCC 1st yr entry (Env Sci; Ecol; Cons Biol)
Anglia Ruskin – 240 pts (Env Plan)
Bangor – 240–280 pts (Env Cons; Env Sci; Ecol; Env Mgt; Sust Dev)
Brighton – CCC–BCD (Env Haz; Ecol Biogeog; Env Sci)
Bristol UWE – 240–300 pts (Env Sci Euro St; Env Sci Law; Env Sci Robot; Env Foren)
Glasgow Caledonian – CCC (Env Mgt Plan)
Hertfordshire – 240 pts (Env St; Env Mgt)
Keele – CCC 240 pts (App Env Sci) *(IB 26–28 pts)*
Kent – 240 pts (Env Soc Sci) *(IB 27 pts)*
Kingston – 240–260 pts (Env Haz Disas Mgt)
Liverpool Hope – 240 pts (Env Mgt)
Manchester Met – 240 pts (Env Hlth) *(IB 24–28 pts)*
Middlesex – 240 pts (Env Hlth)
Nottingham Trent – 240 pts (Env Des Mgt; Hlth Env)
Oxford Brookes – CCC or BCcc (Cits Env Des Dev)
SAC (Scottish CAg) – CCC (Env Prot)
Salford – 240 pts (Env Biosci)
Staffordshire – 240 pts (Hum Env Geog; Anim Biol Cons)

230 pts
Sheffield Hallam – 230 pts (Env Mgt; Env Cons; Env St)

220 pts
Bangor – 220–260 pts (Mar Env St)
Bath Spa – 220–260 pts (Env Sci)
Bradford – 220 pts (Env Sci; App Ecol; Geog Env Mgt)
Bristol UWE – 220–260 pts (Blt Nat Env)
Gloucestershire – 220 pts (Env Mgt; Env Sci)
Hull (Scarborough) – 220–280 pts (Ecol; Env Sci; Cstl Mar Biol)
Liverpool John Moores – 220 pts (Env Sci; Wldlf Cons)
Nottingham Trent – 220 pts (Wldlf Cons)
Portsmouth – 220–280 pts (Mar Env Sci; Env Biol; Env Haz; Env Foren Sci; Env Sci)
Stirling – CCD 1st yr entry (Env Sci; Cons Biol; Cons Mgt; Cons Sci; Env Geog; Ecol; Frshwtr Sci)
Ulster – 220 pts (Env Sci courses)

200 pts
Aberystwyth – 200 pts (Sust Rur Dev; Cntry Cons; Cntry Mgt) *(IB 28 pts)*
Bolton – 200 pts (Env St courses)

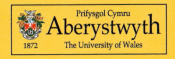

Bradford – 200 pts (Wtr Lnd Mgt)
Central Lancashire – 200–240 pts (Env Haz; Ener Sust Des; Env Mgt; Env Mgt Geog)
Kingston – 200 pts (Env St courses)
Napier – 200 pts (Env Biol; Ecotour)
Salford – 200 pts (Env Hlth)

180 pts **Bristol UWE** – 180–220 pts (Env Hlth; Env Biol; Hlth Sfty Env; Env Sci) *(IB 24–26 pts)*
Lampeter – 180 pts (Env Arch)
Liverpool John Moores – 180 pts (Out Env Educ)
Manchester Met – 180–200 pts (Env Mgt; Env Sci; Env St; Sust Dev; Ecol; Ecol Cons; Env Ent)
Northampton – 180–200 pts (Env Mgt; Wst Mgt courses)
Nottingham Trent – 180 pts (Env Cons Cntry Mgt; Wldlf Cons Env Sci)
Salford – 180 pts (Env Mgt; Aqua Sci; Wldlf Prac Cons; Env St; Env Hlth; Env Geog)
Wolverhampton – 180–220 pts (Env Sci Mgt; Wtr Sci Mgt)

160 pts **Bournemouth** – 160 pts (Env Prot; Env Cons Biol; Env Cstl Mgt; Env Geog; Env Foren)
Canterbury Christ Church – CC (Env Biol; Env Sci courses)
Cardiff (UWIC) – 160 pts (Env Hlth)
Derby – 160–200 pts (Env Mgt; Env Sci; Ecol)
Greenwich – 160–240 pts (Env Sci courses)
Harper Adams (UC) – 160–240 pts (Agric Env Mgt)
Plymouth – 160–240 pts (Env Sci; Env Sci (Biodiv Cons) (Env Chng) (Env Sust) (Env Hlth) (Mar Cons))
SAC (Scottish CAg) – CC (Sust Env Mgt; Env Prot)
Southampton Solent – 160–180 pts (Cstl Cons Mgt; Mar Env Sci; Geog Sust)

140 pts **Anglia Ruskin** – 140–200 pts (Ecol Cons; Nat Hist)
Worcester – 140–120 pts (Env Mgt; Wtr Env Mgt)
Writtle (Coll) – 140–160 pts (Cons Env; Wldlf Mgt)

120 pts **North East Wales (IHE)** – 120 pts (Env St; Env St (Sci) (Mgt))
Paisley – DD (Env Biol; Earth Sci Env Mgt)
Worcester – 120–140 pts (Env Mgt courses)
Southampton Solent – 120 pts (Geog Env St)

100 pts **Southampton Solent** – 100 pts (Ship Mar Env)
Swansea (Inst) – 100 pts (BA/BSc Env Cons)

80 pts **London (Birk)** – 80 pts for under 21s (over 21s varies) (p/t Env Cons; Env Sci; Env Mgt; Env Geol)
UHI Millennium Inst (IC) (NHC) – 80 pts (Env Herit St)

Leeds Met – contact University
Open University – contact University

Alternative offers

See **Chapter 8** for grade/point equivalences and related information for the following examinations: Scottish qualifications, the Welsh Baccalaureate, the IB diploma (approximate points shown also in italics in the table of offers), the Irish Leaving Certificate, the European Baccalaureate and the French Baccalaureate.

EXAMPLES OF FOUNDATION DEGREES IN THE SUBJECT FIELD

Blackpool and Fylde (Coll); Bournemouth; Cornwall (Coll); Dudley (Coll); East Lancashire (IHE); Kingston Maurward (Coll); Myerscough (Coll); Northampton; Nottingham Trent; Park Lane Leeds (Coll); Suffolk (Univ Campus); Swansea (Inst); Wigan and Leigh (Coll); Writtle (Coll).

CHOOSING YOUR COURSE (SEE ALSO CH.1)

Course variations – Widen your options

Tropical Environmental Science (Aberdeen)
Applied Terrestrial and Marine Ecology (Bangor)
Environmental Studies and Philosophy (Bolton)
Environmental Hazards (Brighton)

Environmental Earth Science in Australasia (East Anglia)
Meteorology and Atmospheric Science (Leeds)
Environmental Policy (London (LSE))
Environmental Health (Salford)
Shipping and Marine Environment (Southampton Solent)
Water and Environmental Management (Worcester)
CHECK PROSPECTUSES AND WEBSITES FOR OTHER UNIVERSITIES AND COLLEGES OFFERING THESE COURSES.

Universities and colleges teaching quality See www.qaa.ac.uk; www.unistats.com.

Top universities and colleges (Research) East Anglia*; Leeds; Reading*; Southampton.

Sandwich degree courses Aston; Bradford; Brighton; Bristol UWE; Coventry; Glasgow Caledonian; Greenwich; Harper Adams (UC); Hertfordshire; Kingston; Liverpool John Moores; Manchester Met; Nottingham Trent; Oxford Brookes; Paisley; Plymouth; Reading; Salford; Staffordshire; Ulster; Wolverhampton.

ADMISSIONS INFORMATION

Number of applicants per place (approx) Abertay Dundee 5; Aberystwyth 3; Aston 6; Bangor 3; Bath Spa 2; Birmingham 5; Bournemouth 4; Bradford 3; Bristol UWE 1, (Env Hlth) 7; Cardiff (UWIC) 4; Coventry 9; De Montfort 9; Dundee 6; Durham 5; East Anglia 7; Edinburgh 1; Essex 3; Glamorgan 1; Glasgow Caledonian 1; Greenwich 2; Gloucestershire 11; Harper Adams (UC) 5; Hertfordshire 5; Hull 8; Kingston 3; Lampeter 3; Lancaster 11; Leeds (Env Sci Ener) 2; Liverpool John Moores 5; London (King's) 5, (LSE) 4, (RH) 8; Manchester Met (Env Mgt) 16, (Env Sci) 5; North East Wales (IHE) 3; Northampton 4; Northumbria 8; Nottingham 6; Nottingham Trent 3; Oxford Brookes 13; Plymouth 8; Portsmouth 5; Roehampton 3; Salford 8; Sheffield Hallam 8; Southampton 5; Stirling 10; Strathclyde 1; Ulster 16; Wolverhampton 2; Worcester 7; York 3.

Advice to applicants and planning the UCAS personal statement 'We want doers, not just thinkers' is one comment from an admissions tutor. Describe any field courses which you have attended; make an effort to visit one of the National Parks. Discuss these visits and identify any particular aspects which impressed you. Outline travel interests. Give details of work as a conservation volunteer and other outside-school activities. Strong communication skills, people-oriented work experience. **Bangor** Competence in science and watch your spelling and grammar! **Bath Spa** Evidence of a good science background and willingness to undertake fieldwork. **East Anglia** What sparked your interest in Environmental Science? Discuss your field trips. **Leeds** Give details of outside activities, career interests. **Nottingham Trent** (Hlth Env) A basic knowledge of environmental health as opposed to environmental sciences. Work experience in an environmental health department is looked upon very favourably. **Southampton** See www.envsci.soton.ac.uk/study/skills.htm. Problem-solving ability, resilience and self-management. See also **Appendix 2**.

Misconceptions about this course **Bangor** Students should note that only simple mathematical skills are required for this course. **Leeds** (Ener Env Sci) Note that the course is closer to environmental technology than to environmental science. **Nottingham Trent** (Hlth Env) Too many are influenced by what is shown on TV, for example some aspects of food safety, pest control and work in mortuaries! The work also involves health and safety, housing, public health and environmental management. **Southampton** This is not just a course for environmentalists, for example links with BP, IBM etc. **Wolverhampton** This is a course in Environmental Science, not Environmental Studies: there is a difference. **York** (Env Econ) Some students worry that the economics part of the course will be too difficult which is not the case.

Selection interviews **Yes** Bradford, Bristol UWE, Cambridge, Coventry, Durham, Glamorgan, Gloucestershire, Greenwich, Harper Adams (UC) (advisory), Hertfordshire, Kingston, Lampeter, Manchester Met, Newcastle, Newport, Nottingham, Nottingham Trent, Oxford Brookes, Sheffield Hallam, Strathclyde, Sussex; **Some** Bangor, Bath Spa, Birmingham, Derby, Dundee, East Anglia, London (King's), Plymouth, Salford, Southampton, Staffordshire, York.

Interview advice and questions Environmental issues are constantly in the news, so keep abreast of developments. You could be asked to discuss any particular environmental problems in the area in which you live and to justify your stance on any environmental issues on which you have strong opinions. **Bath Spa** Questions on school work, current affairs and field courses. **East Anglia** Can you display an informed interest in any aspect of environmental science? See also **Chapter 7**.

Applicants' impressions (A=Open day; B=Interview day) **Bangor** (A) A very interesting open day with talks on the course content, a tour of the University and also a coach tour of the surrounding countryside, including glacial features, which made the day all the more interesting. **Bristol** (B) It was an informal interview with questions about my personal statement and an environmental problem near my home and how I thought it could be managed or prevented. **East Anglia** (A) There was a general talk on the University and the course content. Go to open days, they give a good idea of what to expect. **London (UCL)** (B) It was a hard interview. I was asked challenging questions on all the subjects I was studying.

Reasons for rejection (non-academic) Inability to be aware of the needs of others.

AFTER-RESULTS ADVICE
Offers to applicants repeating A-levels **Higher** Greenwich, Lancaster, London (King's), Nottingham, Nottingham Trent, Strathclyde; **Possibly higher** Aberystwyth, Bradford, Northumbria; **Same** Aston, Bangor, Brighton, Cardiff (UWIC), Derby, Dundee, East Anglia, Leeds, Liverpool John Moores, Manchester Met, Plymouth, SAC (Scottish CAg), Salford, Southampton, Ulster, Wolverhampton.

GRADUATE DESTINATIONS AND EMPLOYMENT (2005/6 HESA)
Graduates surveyed 5435 **Employed** 2690 **In further study** 1130 **Assumed unemployed** 285.

Career note Some graduates find work with government departments, local authorities, statutory and voluntary bodies in areas like land management and pollution control. Others go into a range of non-scientific careers.

OTHER DEGREE SUBJECTS FOR CONSIDERATION

Biological Sciences; Biology; Chemistry; Earth Sciences; Environmental Engineering; Geography; Geology; Meteorology; Ocean Sciences/Oceanography; Town and Country Planning.

EUROPEAN STUDIES

(see also **Business Courses, Languages** and **Russian and East European Studies**)

European Studies is an increasingly popular subject and in many cases offers the language student an opportunity to study modern languages within the context of a European country (for example, economics, politics, legal, social and cultural aspects). In these courses there is usually a strong emphasis on the written and spoken word. It is important to note, also, that many courses in other subjects offer the opportunity to study in Europe.

Useful websites www.europa.eu; www.uaces.org; see also **Languages**.

NB The points totals shown to the left of the institutions are for ease of reference only. It must not be assumed that tariff points are always used by institutions or that they can be substituted for an offer in grades. The level of an offer is not necessarily indicative of the quality of a course.

COURSE OFFERS INFORMATION

Subject requirements/preferences GCSE English and a foreign language for all courses and possibly mathematics. Grades may be stipulated. **AL** A modern language usually required. **NB** A* grades are likely to form part of university offers in the higher ranges for students applying for places in 2008 for entry in 2009: check websites.

Your target offers

360 pts **and above**
　　　　London (UCL) – AAA+AS (Euro Soc Pol St) *(IB 38 pts)*
340 pts **Durham** – AAB (Geog (Euro St))
　　　　Exeter – AAB–BBB (Euro courses)
320 pts **Bath** – ABB–BBB (Modn Lang Euro St) *(IB 36 pts)*
　　　　East Anglia – ABB–BBB (Euro St Pol; Euro St Lang)
　　　　Kingston – 320 pts (Law Euro St 4 yrs)
　　　　Lancaster – ABB (Euro Lang Mgt)
　　　　London (King's) – ABB+AS **or** ABaaa (Euro St)
　　　　Manchester – ABB–BBB (Euro St Fr/Ger/Ital/Port/Russ/Span)
　　　　Southampton – ABB 320 pts (Contemp Euro) *(IB 32 pts)*
300 pts **Aston** – 300 pts (Euro St Fr/Ger/Span; Euro St Sociol; Euro St Engl Lang)
　　　　Birmingham – 300 pts (Modn Langs Euro St (Soty Cult Hist)) *(IB 32 pts)*
　　　　Cardiff – BBB (EU St)
　　　　Dundee – BBB–CCC 300–240 pts (Euro St courses) *(IB 29 pts)*
　　　　Edinburgh – BBB (Modn Euro Lang EU St)
　　　　Glasgow – BBB (Slav St Cnt E Euro St)
　　　　Hull – 300 pts (Euro Gov Pol)
　　　　Leeds – BBB–BBC (Euro St courses)
　　　　Lancaster – BBB (Euro St; Euro Pol Soty Cult) *(IB 33 pts)*
　　　　London (RH) – ABC–BBB (Euro St Fr/Ger/Ital/Span)
　　　　Nottingham – BBB–BBC (Modn Euro St)
　　　　Queen's Belfast – BBB (Euro St)
　　　　Reading – 300–320 pts (Euro St; Engl Euro Lit Cult; Hist Euro Lit Cult)
280 pts **Aberystwyth** – 280 pts (Euro Lang; Euro Pol; Euro St joint courses) *(IB 29 pts)*
　　　　Kingston – 280 pts (Law Euro St 3 yrs)
　　　　Leicester – 280–300 pts (Euro St) *(IB 28–30 pts)*
　　　　Newcastle – BBC (Gov EU St)

260 pts	**Essex** – 260 pts (Euro St; Euro St Fr/Ger/Ital/Span; Euro St Pol) *(IB 32 pts)*
	Kent – 260–280 pts (Euro St courses; Euro Cult Tht courses) *(IB 28–32 pts)*
	London (Gold) – BCC (Euro St)
	London (QM) – 260 pts (Euro St courses)
	London (RH) – BCC (Euro Lit Cult St) *(IB 32 pts)*
	Loughborough – 260–280 pts (Euro St) *(IB 30 pts)*
	Northumbria – 260 pts (Euro Int Pol)
	Stirling – BCC (Euro Soc Pol) *(IB 30 pts)*
	Swansea – 260 pts (Geog Euro St)
240 pts	**Aberdeen** – CCC (Euro St; Euro Mgt St)
	Bristol UWE – 240–300 pts (Euro St joint courses) *(IB 26–32 pts)*
	Ulster – CCC–CCD 240 pts (Euro St courses)
220 pts	**Nottingham Trent** – 220 pts (Euro St courses)
200 pts	**Glamorgan** – 200–240 pts (Modn Euro)
	Manchester Met – 200–220 pts (Euro St courses) *(IB 26 pts)*
	Portsmouth – 200–280 pts (Euro St courses)
180 pts	**Liverpool John Moores** – 180–220 pts (Euro St Fr/Ger/Span)
	Southampton Solent – 180–200 pts (Euro St courses)
160 pts	**London South Bank** – CC (Euro Pol St Int Soc Pol)

Alternative offers

See **Chapter 8** for grade/point equivalences and related information for the following examinations: Scottish qualifications, the Welsh Baccalaureate, the IB diploma (approximate points shown also in italics in the table of offers), the Irish Leaving Certificate, the European Baccalaureate and the French Baccalaureate.

EXAMPLES OF FOUNDATION DEGREES IN THE SUBJECT FIELD

Canterbury Christ Church.

CHOOSING YOUR COURSE (SEE ALSO CH.1)

Course variations – Widen your options

European Union Studies (Cardiff)
European Politics (Leeds)
European Social and Political Studies (London (UCL))
Government and European Union Studies (Newcastle)
Contemporary Europe (Southampton)
CHECK PROSPECTUSES AND WEBSITES FOR OTHER UNIVERSITIES AND COLLEGES OFFERING THESE COURSES.

Universities and colleges teaching quality See www.qaa.ac.uk; www.unistats.com.

Top universities and colleges (Research) Aston; Bath; Birmingham*; Cardiff; Glasgow*; Lancaster; London (UCL); Loughborough; Portsmouth; Queen's Belfast; Southampton*.

ADMISSIONS INFORMATION

Number of applicants per place (approx) Aberystwyth 10; Aston 5; Cardiff 5; Dundee 6; Durham 2; East Anglia 11; Hull 6; Kent 11; Lancaster 9; Leicester 15; London (King's) 7, (UCL) 2; London South Bank 6; Loughborough 4; Northumbria 7; Nottingham 23; Nottingham Trent 12; Portsmouth 5.

Advice to applicants and planning the UCAS personal statement Try to identify an interest you have in the country relevant to your studies. Visits to that country should be described. Read the national newspapers and magazines and keep up to date with political and economic developments. Interest in the culture and civilisation of Europe as a whole. **Leeds** Motivation for choosing the course; personal achievements; future career plans, if any; travel. **Loughborough** Broad range of interests and experience. **Portsmouth** International awareness and perspective.

Selection interviews **Yes** Durham, East Anglia, Hull, London (Gold), London Met, London South Bank, Stirling, Sussex; **Some** Cardiff, Dundee, Kent (not usually), Liverpool John Moores, Loughborough, Portsmouth.

Interview advice and questions Whilst your interest in studying a language may be the main reason for applying for this subject, the politics, economics and culture of European countries are constantly in the news. You should keep up-to-date with any such topics concerning your chosen country and be prepared for questions. A language test may occupy part of the interview. **Loughborough** No tests. Interview designed to inform students about the course. See also **Chapter 7**.

Reasons for rejection (non-academic) Poor powers of expression. Lack of ideas on any issues. Lack of enthusiasm.

AFTER-RESULTS ADVICE

Offers to applicants repeating A-levels **Higher** Aberystwyth, East Anglia; **Same** Aston, Cardiff, Dundee, Liverpool John Moores, London South Bank, Loughborough.

GRADUATE DESTINATIONS AND EMPLOYMENT (2005/6 HESA)

No data available. See under **Languages** and separate Language tables.

Career note See **Languages**.

OTHER DEGREE SUBJECTS FOR CONSIDERATION

Business and Management; History; International Relations; Politics; Language courses.

FILM, RADIO, VIDEO and TV STUDIES

(see also **Communication Studies, Media Studies** and **Photography**)

A wide range of courses in this field are on offer although applicants should be aware that many courses cover theoretical or historical aspects of the subject. Students wishing to follow courses with practical applications must check with the institution beforehand to determine how much time in the course is spent on actual film-making or video production.

Useful websites www.bfi.org.uk; www.film.com; www.allmovie.com; www.bksts.com; www.imdb.com; www.fwfr.com; www.bafta.org; www.movingimage.us; www.britfilms.com; www.filmsite.org; www.festival-cannes.fr; www.bbc.co.uk/jobs; http://rogerebert.suntimes.com; www.radiostudiesnetwork.org.uk.

NB The points totals shown to the left of the institutions are for ease of reference only. It must not be assumed that tariff points are always used by institutions or that they can be substituted for an offer in grades. The level of an offer is not necessarily indicative of the quality of a course.

COURSE OFFERS INFORMATION

Subject requirements/preferences **GCSE** English usually required. Courses vary, check prospectuses. **AL** English may be stipulated for some courses. **NB** A* grades are likely to form part of university offers in the higher ranges for students applying for places in 2008 for entry in 2009: check websites.

Your target offers

360 pts **and above**
London (UCL) – ABBa–BBBe (Fr Film St; Russ Film St)
Warwick – AABb **or** AAaab–BBBc (Film TV St; Film Lit) *(IB 36 pts)*

340 pts East Anglia – AAB–BBB 340–300 pts (Film TV St; Film Engl St; Film Am St; Film St Art Hist)
St Andrews – AAB–ABB (Film St courses) *(IB 32 pts)*
Southampton – AAB–ABB (Film courses) *(IB 33 pts)*

320 pts **Cardiff** – ABB (Jrnl Film Media; Journal Film Media joint courses)

Exeter – ABB–BBB 320–300 pts (Film St (Cnma Prac); Film St Fr/Ger/Ital/Russ/Span) *(IB 32–34 pts)*

Glasgow – ABB (Film TV St courses)

Kent – 320 pts (Film St)

Lancaster – ABB–BBB (Film St courses) *(IB 34 pts)*

London (King's) – ABB–BBC+AS (Film courses)

London (RH) – ABB–ABbb (Film TV)

Manchester – ABB–BBB (Film St courses)

Sussex – ABB–BBB **or** 360 pts 3AL+AS see 2nd subj (Film St courses)

300 pts **Aberdeen** – BBB–BBC 2nd yr entry (Film St courses)

Bournemouth – 300 pts (Script Film TV; TV Prod)

Essex – BBB–BBC 300–280 pts (Film St courses) *(IB 28–30 pts)*

Leeds – BBB (Broad Jrnl; TV Prod)

Nottingham – ABC/BBB (Film Am St)

Queen's Belfast – BBB–BBCb (Film St)

Reading – 300–340 pts (Film Thea courses; TV Engl)

280 pts **Birmingham City** – 280 pts (Media Comm (TV))

Chester – 280 pts (TV Prod; Rad Prod)

Hull – 280 pts (Film St)

Northumbria – 280 pts (Engl Film St)

Reading – 280 pts (TV Film Thea) *(IB 32 pts)*

Stirling – BBC (Film Media St; Euro Film Media) *(IB 32 pts)*

Westminster – BBC (Film TV Prod)

260 pts **Brunel** – 260 pts (Film TV St courses) *(IB 28 pts)*

Kent – 260–300 pts (Film St joint courses) *(IB 29–33 pts)*

Leicester – BCC **or** 260–340 pts (Film St Vis Arts) *(IB 30 pts)*

Liverpool – 260 pts (inc B/C lang) (Euro Film St Modn Lang)

London (QM) – 260–300 pts (Film St courses) *(IB 32 pts)*

Northumbria – 260–280 pts (Film TV St)

Oxford Brookes – BCC (Film St)

Sunderland – 260 pts (Film Media St; Media Prod (TV Rad))

Surrey – 260–300 pts (Film St courses)

240 pts **Aberdeen** – CCC (Film St)

Bangor – 240–280 pts (Film St courses)

Bradford – 240 pts (TV Prod)

Bristol UWE – 240–320 pts (Film St courses)

Chester (Warrington) – 240 pts (Film St courses)

For a quick reference offers calculator, fold out the inside back cover.

           Dundee – 240–300 pts (Engl Film St)
           Hertfordshire – 240 pts (Film Comb courses; Film TV (Fctn) (Doc) (Enter))
           Lincoln – 240 pts (Contemp Lns Media)
           Northumbria – 240 pts (Film St Sociol)
           Portsmouth – 240–300 pts (Film St; Film St Crea Writ; Film St Enter Tech; Film St Dr)
           Roehampton – 240–320 pts (Film St)
           Sheffield Hallam – 240–260 pts (Film courses)
           Southampton Solent – 240 pts (Film)
           Swansea – 240–280 pts (Scrn St joint courses)
           Winchester – 240–280 pts (Film St courses)
           York St John – 240 pts BCC (Film TV Prod)
220 pts **Aberystwyth** – 220–280 pts (Film TV St courses; Scngrph St courses) *(IB 28 pts)*
           Anglia Ruskin – 220 pts (Film TV Prod)
           Bath Spa – 220–260 pts (Film Scrn St courses)
           Birmingham City – 220–240 pts (TV Tech Prod; Broad Tech Prod)
           Brighton – 220 pts (Scrn St; Mov Imag) *(IB 28 pts)*
           Central Lancashire – 220 pts (Film Media St)
           De Montfort – 220–240 pts (Film St; Film St Media St)
           Falmouth (UC) – 220 pts (Film St)
           Glamorgan – 220 pts (Film St Media Prod)
           Liverpool Hope – 220 pts (Film St)
           Queen Margaret (UC) – 220 pts (Film Media)
200 pts **Bolton** – 200 pts (Film Media St)
           Central Lancashire – 200 pts (Film Media St)
           Creative Arts (UC) – 200 pts (Film Prod; Dig Scrn Arts)
           Edge Hill – 200 pts (Film St courses)
           Hull (Coll) – 200 pts (TV Film Des)
           Liverpool John Moores – BB (Scrn St courses)
           Manchester Met – CDD 200–220 pts (Film TV St courses)
           Napier – 200 pts (Photo Film Imag)
           Newport – 200 pts (Film Vid; Doc Film TV)
           Staffordshire – 200–240 pts (Film Prod Tech)
           Swansea (Inst) – 200 pts (Vid courses)
180 pts **Derby** – 180 pts (Film TV St; Film St)
           Huddersfield – 180 pts (Dig Film Vis Efcts Prod)
           Kingston – 180–240 pts (Film St courses)
           Lampeter – 180–300 pts (Film Media; Film St courses)
           Northampton – 180 pts (Film TV St)
           West Scotland – BC–CC (Film Scrnwrit; Broad Prod; Cnma)
160 pts **Bedfordshire** – 160 pts (TV Prod)
           Bournemouth (AI) – 160 pts (Film Prod; Animat Prod)
           Canterbury Christ Church – CC (Film Rad TV St courses)
           De Montfort – 160–240 pts (Rad Prod)
           East London – 160 pts (Film St Photo; Film Vid Theor Prac)
           Gloucestershire – 160–280 pts (Film St courses)
           Leeds Trinity and All Saints (Coll) – 160–240 pts (Film St; Engl Film St)
           London Met – 160–240 pts (Film St; Dig Media; Film Broad Prod)
           London South Bank – CC (Film St; Dig Film Vid)
           Middlesex – 160–280 pts (TV Prod; Film St)
           Portsmouth – 160–240 pts (Vid Prod)
           St Mary's (UC) – 160–200 pts (Film TV courses)
           Southampton Solent – 160 pts (Film Vid Tech)
           Thames Valley – 160 pts (Film Vid Prod)
           Wolverhampton – 160–220 pts (Film St courses)
           Worcester – 160 pts (Film St Jrnl)

For information on how to read the Subject Tables, see **Chapter 8**.

140 pts **Teesside** – 140 pts (TV Prod Prof Prac)
120 pts **Bucks New** – 120 pts (Film St courses; Vid Prod courses)
North East Wales (IHE) – 120–80 pts (Des (Mov Imag))
Suffolk (Univ Campus) – 120–180 pts (Film Media St)
Trinity Carmarthen (Coll) – 120 pts (Film St courses)
100 pts **St Helens (Coll)** – 100–120 pts (TV Vid Prod)
Swansea (Inst) – 100–340 pts (Engl St Film TV St)
 80 pts **Arts London** – 80 pts (Film Vid)
Havering (Coll) – 80 pts (Mov Imag)
Ravensbourne (CDC) – 80–240 pts (Des Mov Imag)
Royal Scottish (RSAMD) – 80 pts (Film TV)
South East Essex (Coll) – 80–160 pts (TV Prod Scrn Media)

Leeds Met – contact University

Alternative offers
See **Chapter 8** for grade/point equivalences and related information for the following examinations: Scottish qualifications, the Welsh Baccalaureate, the IB diploma (approximate points shown also in italics in the table of offers), the Irish Leaving Certificate, the European Baccalaureate and the French Baccalaureate.

EXAMPLES OF FOUNDATION DEGREES IN THE SUBJECT FIELD
Bournemouth and Poole (Coll); Bristol City (Coll); Cleveland (CAD); Dewsbury (Coll); Farnborough (CT); Herefordshire (Coll); Leeds Met; Leicester (Coll); Manchester (CAT); Newcastle (Coll); Norwich (SAD); St Helens (Coll); Solihull (Coll); South East Essex (Coll); Teesside.

CHOOSING YOUR COURSE (SEE ALSO CH.1)
Course variations – Widen your options
Divinity and Film Studies (Aberdeen)
Entertainment Industries and English (Bangor)
Journalism, Film and Media (Cardiff)
Animation (Creative Arts (UC))
Film Studies and the Visual Arts (Leicester)
European Film Studies – Combined Honours (Liverpool)
Imaginative Writing and Film Studies (Liverpool John Moores)
Documentary Film and TV (Newport)
Video Production (Portsmouth)
Make-up and Hair Design for Music, Film and Photography (Southampton Solent)
CHECK PROSPECTUSES AND WEBSITES FOR OTHER UNIVERSITIES AND COLLEGES OFFERING THESE COURSES.

Universities and colleges teaching quality See www.qaa.ac.uk; www.unistats.com.

Top universities and colleges (Research) Warwick.

Sandwich degree courses See under **Media Studies**.

ADMISSIONS INFORMATION
Number of applicants per place (approx) Anglia Ruskin 3; Bournemouth 30; Bournemouth (AI) 9; Brunel 10; Canterbury Christ Church 50; Cardiff 11; Central Lancashire 5; East Anglia (Film Engl St) 7, (Film Am St) 5; Kent 30; Liverpool John Moores 17; London Met 7; Portsmouth 20; Ravensbourne (CDC) 9; Sheffield Hallam 60; Southampton 5; Southampton Solent 7; Staffordshire 31; Stirling 12; Warwick 18; Westminster 41; York St John 6.

Advice to applicants and planning the UCAS personal statement Any experience in film-making (beyond home videos) should be described in detail. Knowledge and preferences of types of films and the work of some producers should be included on the UCAS application. Read film magazines and other appropriate literature to keep informed of developments. Show genuine interest in film and be knowledgeable about favourite films, directors and give details of work experience or film projects undertaken. **De Montfort** A genuine interest in a range of film genres. **East Anglia** Applicants need to discuss the ways in which films relate to broader cultural phenomena, social, literary, historical. **Staffordshire** Are you fascinated by film, inspired by television or devoted to radio and keen to know more? See also **Appendix 2**.

Misconceptions about this course That an A-level film or media studies is required; it is not. That it's Film so it's easy! That the course is all practical work. Some applicants believe that these are Media courses. Some applicants believe that Film and TV Studies is a training for production work. **Bournemouth (AI)** (Animat Prod) This is not a Film Studies course but a course based on traditional animation with supported computer image processing. **De Montfort** Some believe that this is a course in practical film-making: it is not, it is for analysts and historians. **Winchester** That graduation automatically leads to a job in broadcasting!

Selection interviews Most institutions will interview some applicants in this subject. **Yes** Bournemouth, Bournemouth (AI), Brunel, Canterbury Christ Church, Chichester, Liverpool John Moores, Newport, York St John; **Some** Anglia Ruskin, East Anglia, Staffordshire, Wolverhampton.

Interview advice and questions Questions will focus on your chosen field. In the case of films be prepared to answer questions not only on your favourite films but on the work of one or two directors you admire and early Hollywood examples. **Anglia Ruskin** We ask for an original review of a film recently seen. **Bournemouth** (Script Film TV) Successful applicants will be required to submit a 20-page screenplay; (TV Prod) A good applicant will have the ability to discuss media issues in depth, to have total commitment to TV and video production and will have attempted to make programmes. **Bournemouth (AI)** Written piece prior to interview. Questions at interview relevant to the portfolio/reel. **Staffordshire** We assess essay-writing skills. See also **Chapter 7**.

Reasons for rejection (non-academic) Not enough drive or ambition. No creative or original ideas. Preference for production work rather than practical work. Inability to articulate the thought process behind the work in the applicant's portfolio. Insufficient knowledge of media affairs. Lack of knowledge of film history. Wrong course choice, wanted more practical work.

AFTER-RESULTS ADVICE
Offers to applicants repeating A-levels **Higher** Bournemouth (AI), Glasgow, Manchester Met; **Same** Anglia Ruskin, De Montfort, East Anglia, Liverpool Hope, St Mary's (UC), Staffordshire, Stirling, Winchester, Wolverhampton, York St John.

GRADUATE DESTINATIONS AND EMPLOYMENT (2005/6 HESA)
Cinematics and Photography graduates surveyed 1945 **Employed** 1010 **In further study** 125 **Assumed unemployed** 240.

Career note Although this is a popular subject field, job opportunities in film, TV and radio are limited. Successful graduates have frequently gained work experience with companies during their undergraduate years. The transferable skills (verbal communication etc) will open up other career opportunities.

OTHER DEGREE SUBJECTS FOR CONSIDERATION
Animation; Communication Studies; Creative Writing; Media Studies; Photography.

FINANCE
(including **Banking, Financial Services, Insurance;** see also **Accountancy/Accounting**)

Financial Services courses provide a comprehensive view of the world of finance and normally cover banking, insurance, investment, building societies, international finance, accounting and economics. Major banks offer sponsorships for some of the specialised Banking courses.

For information on how to read the Subject Tables, see **Chapter 8**.

330 | Finance

Useful websites www.cii.co.uk; www.sii.org.uk; www.fsa.gov.uk; www.efinancialnews.com; www.worldbank.org; www.ifslearning.com; www.ft.com.

NB The points totals shown to the left of the institutions are for ease of reference only. It must not be assumed that tariff points are always used by institutions or that they can be substituted for an offer in grades. The level of an offer is not necessarily indicative of the quality of a course.

COURSE OFFERS INFORMATION

Subject requirements/preferences GCSE Most institutions will require English and mathematics grade C minimum. **AL** Mathematics may be required or preferred. **NB** A* grades are likely to form part of university offers in the higher ranges for students applying for places in 2008 for entry in 2009: check websites.

Your target offers

360 pts **and above**
    London (UCL) – AAAb–BBBe (Eng Bus Fin)
340 pts **City** – AAB (Bank Int Fin; Invest Fin Risk Mgt; Rl Est Fin Invest; Risk Analys Ins) *(IB 35 pts)*
    Newcastle – AAB (Fin Maths)
    Sheffield – AAB–AAbb (Fin Maths)
320 pts **Birmingham** – ABB 320 pts (Mny Bank Fin) *(IB 32–34 pts)*
    Heriot-Watt – ABB 320 pts 2nd yr entry (Fin Maths)
    Lancaster – ABB (Fin Econ; Fin Maths; Fin)
    Leeds – ABB (Maths Fin)
    Loughborough – ABB (Bank Fin Mgt)
    Manchester – ABB–ABC (Fin; Econ Fin)
    Nottingham – ABB (Ind Econ Ins; Fin Acc Mgt)
    Queen's Belfast – ABB–BCCb (Finance)
    Reading – 320–360 pts (Invest Fin Prop; Int Scrts Inv Bank) *(IB 33 pts)*
    Surrey – 320 pts (Fin Maths)
300 pts **Aberystwyth** – 300 pts (Fin Maths) *(IB 29 pts)*
    Bristol – 300 pts (Econ Fin)
    Cardiff – BBB (Bank Fin; Bank Fin Euro Lang)
    East Anglia – BBB–BBC (Bus Fin Econ)
    Exeter – 300–320 pts (Econ Fin; Econ Fin Euro)
    Heriot-Watt – ABC 1st yr entry (Fin Maths)
    Heriot-Watt – BBB 2nd yr entry (Econ Fin; Fin Bus Law)
    Leicester – 300 pts (Fin Maths)
    Liverpool – 300 pts (Maths Fin)
    London (QM) – 300 pts (Econ Fin)
    Loughborough – 300 pts (Bus Econ Fin)
    Sheffield – BBB 300 pts (Acc Fin Mgt courses)
    Strathclyde – ABC–BBC (Fin courses)
280 pts **Abertay Dundee** – BBC 2nd yr entry (Fin Bus)
    Bournemouth – 280 pts (Fin Bus; Fin Serv)
    Durham – BBC (Bus Fin) *(IB 30 pts)*
    Essex – 280–260 pts (Fin Mgt; Fin; Fin Maths; Fin Econ)
    Swansea – 280 pts (Fin Econ Acc; Fin Econ)
260 pts **Brunel** – 260–280 pts (Fin courses) *(IB 30 pts)*
    Coventry – 260–320 pts (Fin Serv; Fin Econ)
    Heriot-Watt – BCC 260 pts 1st yr entry (Econ Fin; Fin Bus Law)
    Keele – 260–320 pts (Fin courses) *(IB 28–30 pts)*
    Kent – 260 pts (Fin Maths)
    Kingston – 260 pts (Fin Econ)
    Nottingham Trent – 260 pts (Fin Maths)
    Richmond Am Int – 260 pts (Bus Admin (Fin))

For a quick reference offers calculator, fold out the inside back cover.

Cass Business School
City of London

Unlock your career in finance

At City University's Cass Business School, we give you what it takes to succeed in a career in the City of London, the world's foremost financial centre.

Our highly specialised courses include Actuarial Science, Banking & International Finance, Investment & Financial Risk Management, Real Estate Finance & Investment and Risk Analysis & Insurance.

And with our location on the doorstep of the City, there's nowhere better to prepare for your career in finance. You'll have access to real-world expertise, excellent career opportunities and an optional professional placement or study abroad year.

Our students cite our reputation, location and courses as excellent reasons to study here, so why not find out more or arrange a visit? Call 020 7040 8613, email cass-ug-programme@city.ac.uk or visit www.cass.city.ac.uk/dco

www.cass.city.ac.uk/dco

Salford – BCC–CCC (Fin Acc)
Westminster – 260–280 pts (Fin Serv; Bus Mgt (Fin))
Winchester – 260–300 pts (Bus Mgt Fin Econ)
240 pts **Aberdeen** – CCC (Fin courses)
Bangor – 240–280 pts (Bank Fin)
Brighton – CCC–BCD 240–280 pts (Fin Invest)
Buckingham – CCC (Acc Fin Mgt)
De Montfort – 240–220 pts (Bus Fin)
Dundee – CCC 240 pts (Finance) *(IB 29 pts)*
Huddersfield – 240 pts (Bus St Fin Serv)
Northumbria – 240 pts (Bus Fin)
Portsmouth – 240 pts (Fin Bus; Int Fin Tr)
Robert Gordon – CCC (Mgt Fin)
Salford – 240–260 pts (Bus St Fin Mgt)
Sheffield Hallam – 240 pts (Bank Fin; Bus Fin Serv)
Stirling – CCC (Fin courses; Mny Bank Fin) *(IB 30 pts)*
Ulster – 240 pts (Bus Fin Invest)
220 pts **Abertay Dundee** – CCD 1st yr entry (Fin Bus)
Aberystwyth – 220–280 pts (Bus Fin)
Sunderland – 220 pts (Bus (Fin Mgt))
200 pts **Birmingham City** – 200 pts (Bus Fin)
Hertfordshire – 200–240 pts (Finance)
Lincoln – 200–220 pts (Fin courses)
Liverpool John Moores – 200 pts (Int Bank Fin; Bus Fin)
Manchester Met – 200–260 pts (Fin Serv; Fin Mgt courses)
Napier – 200 pts (Fin Serv)
Plymouth – 200 pts (Bank Fin)
180 pts **Greenwich** – 180–220 pts (Fin Fin Inf Sys)
Northampton – 180–220 pts (Fin Inf Mgt; Fin Serv)
Staffordshire – 180–240 pts (Finance)
160 pts **London Met** – 160–200 pts (Fin Maths; Fin Serv; Bank Fin; Inves courses; Ins; Euro Bank Fin)
Middlesex – 160–200 pts (Mny Bank Fin)
Southampton Solent – 160 pts (Bus Fin Mgt)
York St John – 160 pts (Bus Mgt Fin)
120 pts **Bucks New** – 120–140 pts (Fin courses)
Northbrook (Coll) – 120 pts (Bus Admin Fin)
Norwich City (Coll) – 120 pts (Bus Mgt (Acc Fin))
100 pts **Bradford (Coll)** – 100–140 pts (Fin Serv)
80 pts **London Sch Bus Comp** – 80 pts (Bank Fin)
Regents Bus Sch London – 80 pts (Int Fin Acc)

Leeds Met – contact University

Alternative offers

See **Chapter 8** for grade/point equivalences and related information for the following examinations: Scottish qualifications, the Welsh Baccalaureate, the IB diploma (approximate points shown also in italics in the table of offers), the Irish Leaving Certificate, the European Baccalaureate and the French Baccalaureate.

EXAMPLES OF FOUNDATION DEGREES IN THE SUBJECT FIELD

Bournemouth and Poole (Coll); Bromley (CFHE); Grimsby (IFHE); Leicester; London Met; North West Kent (Coll); Northampton (Coll); Stratford-upon-Avon (Coll); Suffolk (Univ Campus); Sutton Coldfield (Coll); Swansea (Inst); Thames Valley; West Kent (Coll); Weymouth (Coll).

For a quick reference offers calculator, fold out the inside back cover.

CHOOSING YOUR COURSE (SEE ALSO CH.1)

Course variations – Widen your options
Accounting for Management (Aston)
Banking and Finance (Bangor)
Money, Banking and Finance (Birmingham)
International Finance (Birmingham City)
Finance and Investment (Brighton)
Financial Mathematics (Brunel)
Real Estate Finance and Investment (City)
Business Finance and Economics (East Anglia)
Financial Economics (Essex)
Marketing and Financial Management (International) (Hull)
Financial Services (Manchester Met)
Investment and Finance in Property (Reading)
CHECK PROSPECTUSES AND WEBSITES FOR OTHER UNIVERSITIES AND COLLEGES OFFERING THESE COURSES.

Universities and colleges teaching quality See www.qaa.ac.uk; www.unistats.com.

ADMISSIONS INFORMATION

Number of applicants per place (approx) Aberystwyth 4; Bangor 30; Birmingham 17; Birmingham City 13; Bristol UWE 4; Buckingham 4; Cardiff 10; Central Lancashire 6; City 10; Dundee 5; Durham 4; Glamorgan 3; Loughborough 35; Middlesex 3; Northampton 3; Portsmouth 4; Sheffield Hallam 4.

Advice to applicants and planning the UCAS personal statement Visits to banks or insurance companies should be described, giving details of any work experience or work shadowing done in various departments. Discuss any particular aspects of finance etc which interest you. **City** Give details of sport, voluntary work, skills etc. See also **Appendix 2**.

Misconceptions about this course Many applicants believe that they can only enter careers in banking and finance when they graduate.

Selection interviews Yes Buckingham (pref), Huddersfield; **Some** Dundee, Staffordshire, Stirling; **No** City.

Interview advice and questions Banking involves both high street and merchant banks, so a knowledge of banking activities in general will be expected. In the past mergers have been discussed and also the role of the Bank of England in the economy. The work of the accountant may be discussed. See also **Chapter 7**.

Reasons for rejection (non-academic) Lack of interest. Poor English. Lacking in motivation and determination to complete the course.

AFTER-RESULTS ADVICE

Offers to applicants repeating A-levels Higher Glasgow; **Possibly higher** Bangor; **Same** Birmingham, Birmingham City, Bradford, Cardiff, City, Dundee, London Met, Loughborough, Napier, Northumbria, Stirling.

GRADUATE DESTINATIONS AND EMPLOYMENT (2005/6 HESA)

Graduates surveyed 840 **Employed** 435 **In further study** 70 **Assumed unemployed** 45.

Career note Most graduates entered financial careers. Further study is required to qualify as an accountant and to obtain other professional qualifications, eg Institute of Banking.

OTHER DEGREE SUBJECTS FOR CONSIDERATION

Accountancy; Actuarial Studies; Business Studies; Economics.

FOOD SCIENCE/STUDIES and TECHNOLOGY

(see also **Agricultural Sciences/Agriculture, Consumer Studies, Dietetics, Nutrition**)

Biochemistry, microbiology, dietetics, human nutrition, food processing and technology are components of Food Science courses as well as being degree courses in their own right (and appropriate alternative courses). The study depends for its understanding on a secure foundation of several pure sciences – chemistry and two subjects from physics, mathematics, biology, botany or zoology. Only students offering subjects from these fields are likely to be considered. Food Technology covers the engineering aspects of food processing and management. A number of bursaries are offered by the food industry. Check with admissions tutors. See also **Appendix 2**.

Useful websites www.scienceyear.com; www.sofht.co.uk; www.ifst.org; www.defra.gov.uk; www.iagre.org.

NB The points totals shown to the left of the institutions are for ease of reference only. It must not be assumed that tariff points are always used by institutions or that they can be substituted for an offer in grades. The level of an offer is not necessarily indicative of the quality of a course.

COURSE OFFERS INFORMATION

Subject requirements/preferences GCSE English, mathematics and a science. **AL** One or two mathematics/science subjects; chemistry may be required. **NB** A* grades are likely to form part of university offers in the higher ranges for students applying for places in 2008 for entry in 2009: check websites.

Your target offers

320 pts Newcastle – ABB (Fd Hum Nutr) *(IB 32 pts)*

300 pts Leeds – BBB (Fd Sci Microbiol; Biol Fd Sci; Bioch Fd Sci)

280 pts Leeds – BBC 280–260 pts (Fd St Nutr; Fd Sci; Fd Mgt)
Nottingham – BBC (Fd Sci) *(IB 24–30 pts)*
Queen's Belfast – BBC (Fd Qual Sfty Nutr)
Reading – 280 pts (Fd Sci; Fd Sci Bus; Fd Tech; Fd Mark Bus Econ) *(IB 30 pts)*

260 pts Northumbria – 260 pts (Fd Sci Nutr)
Surrey – 260–300 pts (Fd Sci Microbiol; Nutr Fd Sci) *(IB 30–32 pts)*

240 pts Brighton – CCC (Vit Oeno; Mark Fd Drink)
Nottingham – CCC (Fd Microbiol)
Ulster – 240 pts (Fd Nutr)

220 pts Coventry – 220 pts (Fd Sci Nutr)

200 pts Abertay Dundee – CDD (Fd Consum Sci; Fd Nutr Hlth; Fd Prod Des)
Bath Spa – 200–240 pts (Fd Nutr Consum Prot; Fd St courses)
Cardiff (UWIC) – 200 pts (Fd Sci Tech)
Glamorgan – 200–240 pts (Nutr Fd Tech Hlth)
Huddersfield – 200–240 pts (Fd Nutr Hlth; Fd Nutr)
London Met – 200 pts (Fd Consum St courses)
Manchester Met – 200 pts (Fd Nutr; Fd Mgt; Fd Tech) *(IB 28 pts)*
Sheffield Hallam – 200 pts (Fd Nutr; Fd Mark)

180 pts Birmingham (UC) – 180 pts (Fd Rtl Mgt; Culn Arts Mgt; Fd Mark Mgt; Fd Prod Dev Mgt; Fd Media Comm Mgt)
Bournemouth – 180 pts (Fd Mark)
Glasgow Caledonian – DDD–CC (Fd Biosci)
Heriot-Watt – DDD–CCC (Fd Sci Tech Mgt; Brew Distil)
Liverpool John Moores – 180–200 pts (Fd Nutr; Home Econ (Fd Des Tech); Consum St Mark)
Teesside – 180–240 pts (Fd Nutr Hlth Sci)

160 pts CAFRE – CC 160 pts (Fd Tech; Sply Mgt (Fd))
Harper Adams (UC) – CC (Fd Rtl Mgt; Fd Qual Bus Mgt; Fd Consum St; Frsh Prod Mgt)
London South Bank – CC–EE (Orgnc Fd St; Fd courses)

Royal (CAg) – 160–220 pts (Bus Mgt (Agri–Fd); Fd Sply Chn Mgt)
SAC (Scottish CAg) – CC (Rur Bus Mgt (Fd); App Biosci (Fd Sci))

Alternative offers
See **Chapter 8** for grade/point equivalences and related information for the following examinations: Scottish qualifications, the Welsh Baccalaureate, the IB diploma (approximate points shown also in italics in the table of offers), the Irish Leaving Certificate, the European Baccalaureate and the French Baccalaureate.

EXAMPLES OF FOUNDATION DEGREES IN THE SUBJECT FIELD

Birmingham (UC); Bridgwater (Coll); Brighton; Bristol UWE; CAFRE; Duchy (Coll); Harper Adams (UC); Hartpury (Coll); Pershore (Coll); Plumpton (Coll); Reaseheath (Coll).

CHOOSING YOUR COURSE (SEE ALSO CH.1)

Course variations – Widen your options
Food Studies and Music (Bath Spa)
Food and Retail Management (Birmingham (UC))
Food Marketing (Bournemouth)
Food Science and Technology (Cardiff (UWIC))
Food Industry and Management (Harper Adams (UC))
Food and Nutrition (Huddersfield)
Food and Consumer Studies (London Met)
Culinary Arts Management (Thames Valley)
CHECK PROSPECTUSES AND WEBSITES FOR OTHER UNIVERSITIES AND COLLEGES OFFERING THESE COURSES.

Universities and colleges teaching quality See www.qaa.ac.uk; www.unistats.com.

Top universities and colleges (Research) Leeds*; Nottingham; Reading.

Sandwich degree courses Birmingham (UC); Bournemouth; Coventry; Glasgow Caledonian; Harper Adams (UC); Huddersfield; Leeds Met; London South Bank; Manchester Met; Newcastle; Northumbria; Queen's Belfast; Reading; Sheffield Hallam; Surrey; Teesside; Ulster; Wolverhampton.

ADMISSIONS INFORMATION

Number of applicants per place (approx) Bath Spa 4; Bournemouth 5; Cardiff (UWIC) 1; Dundee 3; Huddersfield (Fd Nutr Hlth) 4; Leeds 5; Liverpool John Moores 2; London Met 5; London South Bank 3; Manchester Met 3; Newcastle 13; Nottingham 7; Oxford Brookes 20; Queen's Belfast 10; Robert Gordon 4; Sheffield Hallam 4; Surrey 17.

Advice to applicants and planning the UCAS personal statement Visits, work experience or work shadowing in any food manufacturing firm, or visits to laboratories, should be described on your UCAS application. Keep up-to-date with developments by reading journals relating to the industry. See also **Appendix 2**.

Misconceptions about this course Some applicants confuse food technology with catering or hospitality management. Applicants under-estimate the job prospects. There are approximately 300 vacancies per month advertised by food manufacturers. **Leeds** (Fd Sci) Food Science is NOT food technology, catering or cooking. It aims to understand WHY food materials behave in the way they do, in order to improve the nutritive value, safety and quality of the food we eat.

Selection interviews Yes London South Bank, Nottingham (depends on application), Queen's Belfast, Reading, Surrey; **Some** Bath Spa, Leeds (applicants with non-standard qualifications), Liverpool John Moores, Manchester Met, Salford.

Interview advice and questions This is a specialised field and admissions tutors will want to know your reasons for choosing the subject. You will be questioned on any experience you have had in the food industry. More general questions may cover the reasons for the trends in the popularity of certain types of food, the value of junk food and whether scientific interference with food is justifiable. **Leeds** Questions asked to ensure that the student understands, and can cope with, the science content of the course. See also **Chapter 7**.

Reasons for rejection (non-academic) Too immature. Unlikely to integrate well. Lack of vocational commitment.

AFTER-RESULTS ADVICE

Offers to applicants repeating A-levels **Higher** Leeds; **Possibly higher** Nottingham; **Same** Liverpool John Moores, Manchester Met, Queen's Belfast, Salford, Sheffield Hallam, Surrey, Wolverhampton.

GRADUATE DESTINATIONS AND EMPLOYMENT (2005/6 HESA)
Graduates surveyed 285 **Employed** 180 **In further study** 40 **Assumed unemployed** 20.

Career note Employment levels for food graduates are high mainly in manufacturing and retailing and increasingly with large companies.

OTHER DEGREE SUBJECTS FOR CONSIDERATION

Biochemistry; Biological Sciences; Biology; Biotechnology; Chemistry; Consumer Studies; Dietetics; Health Studies; Hospitality Management; Nutrition.

FORESTRY

(see also **Agricultural Sciences/Agriculture**)

Forestry is concerned with the establishment and management of forests for timber production, environmental, conservation and amenity purposes.

Useful websites www.iagre.org.uk; www.forestry.gov.uk; www.rfs.org.uk; www.charteredforesters.org; www.iwsc.org.uk; www.british-trees.com; www.woodland-trust.org.uk.

NB The points totals shown to the left of the institutions are for ease of reference only. It must not be assumed that tariff points are always used by institutions or that they can be substituted for an offer in grades. The level of an offer is not necessarily indicative of the quality of a course.

COURSE OFFERS INFORMATION

Subject requirements/preferences **GCSE** English, Mathematics or science usually required. Check prospectuses. **AL** Two science subjects are usually stipulated which can include mathematics, geography or geology. **NB** A* grades are likely to form part of university offers in the higher ranges for students applying for places in 2008 for entry in 2009: check websites.

Your target offers
300 pts Edinburgh – BBB (Ecol Sci (Frsty))
240 pts Aberdeen – CCC (Frsty; Frsty Sci; Frst Cons)
          Bangor – 240 pts (Cons Frsty Ecosys; Frsty) *(IB 28 pts)*
140 pts Worcester – 140 pts (Sust Wdlnd Mgt)
120 pts UHI Millennium Inst (IC) – 120 pts (Sust Frsty Mgt)
 80 pts Myerscough (Coll) – 80 pts (Arboriculture)

Alternative offers
See **Chapter 8** for grade/point equivalences and related information for the following examinations: Scottish qualifications, the Welsh Baccalaureate, the IB diploma (approximate points shown also in italics in the table of offers), the Irish Leaving Certificate, the European Baccalaureate and the French Baccalaureate.

EXAMPLES OF FOUNDATION DEGREES IN THE SUBJECT FIELD

Central Lancashire; Plumpton (Coll); Sparsholt (Coll); Sunderland; Warwickshire (Coll).

CHOOSING YOUR COURSE (SEE ALSO CH.1)

Course variations – Widen your options
Forest Conservation (Aberdeen)
Countryside Management (Aberystwyth)
Conservation and Forest Ecosystems (Bangor)
Ecological Science (Edinburgh)
Sustainable Woodland Management (UHI Millennium (IC))
CHECK PROSPECTUSES AND WEBSITES FOR OTHER UNIVERSITIES AND COLLEGES OFFERING THESE COURSES.

Universities and colleges teaching quality See www.qaa.ac.uk; www.unistats.com.

Sandwich degree courses Aberdeen; Bangor.

ADMISSIONS INFORMATION

Number of applicants per place (approx) Bangor 2; Edinburgh 9.

Advice to applicants and planning the UCAS personal statement Contact the Forestry Training Council and Commission and try to arrange visits to forestry centres, local community forests and nature trails. Discuss the work with forest officers and learn about future plans for specific forest areas and describe any visits made. **Bangor** Mention any experience of forestry or wood processing industries (for example, visits to forests and mills, work experience in relevant organisations). See **Appendix 2**.

Advice to overseas (non-EU) applicants Bangor Good proportion of overseas students on course.

Misconceptions about this course Bangor The course does not provide practical training in forestry (eg use of chainsaws and pesticides) or wood processing. It is intended to educate future managers, for example, not to train forestry or mill workers.

Selection interviews Most institutions.

Interview advice and questions Work experience or field courses attended are likely to be discussed and questions asked such as: What is arboriculture? On a desert island how would you get food from wood? How do you see forestry developing in the next hundred years? What aspects of forestry are the most important? **Bangor** Why are you interested in forestry/forest products? See also **Chapter 7**.

AFTER-RESULTS ADVICE

Offers to applicants repeating A-levels Same Bangor.

GRADUATE DESTINATIONS AND EMPLOYMENT (2005/6 HESA)

Graduates surveyed 40 **Employed** 25 **In further study** 5 **Assumed unemployed** 5.

Career note Opportunities exist with the Forestry Commission as supervisors, managers and in some cases, scientists. Other employers include private landowners (especially in Scotland), co-operative forest societies, local authorities and commercial firms.

OTHER DEGREE SUBJECTS FOR CONSIDERATION

Agriculture; Biological Sciences; Countryside Management; Ecology; Environmental Sciences; Woodland and Wildlife Management

FRENCH

(see also **European Studies** and **Languages**)

Applicants should select courses according to the emphasis which they prefer. Courses could focus on literature or language (or both), or on the written and spoken word, as in the case of interpreting and translating courses, or on the broader study of French culture, political and social aspects found on European Studies courses.

For information on how to read the Subject Tables, see **Chapter 8**.

Useful websites www.europa.eu; www.visavis.org; www.bbc.co.uk/languages;
www.languageadvantage.com; www.languagematters.co.uk; www.iol.org.uk;
www.reed.co.uk/multilingual; www.cilt.org.uk; www.lemonde.fr; www.institut-francais.org.uk;
www.academie-francaise.fr; www.institut-de-france.fr; www.sfs.ac.uk; fs.oxfordjournals.org.

*NB The points totals shown to the left of the institutions are for ease of reference only. It must not
be assumed that tariff points are always used by institutions or that they can be substituted for an
offer in grades. The level of an offer is not necessarily indicative of the quality of a course.*

COURSE OFFERS INFORMATION

Subject requirements/preferences **GCSE** French, mathematics (for business courses), grade levels
may be stipulated. **AL** French is usually required at a specific grade and in some cases a second
language may be stipulated. **NB** A* grades are likely to form part of university offers in the higher
ranges for students applying for places in 2008 for entry in 2009: check websites.

Your target offers
360 pts and above

Birmingham – AAA (Law Fr) *(IB 30–32 pts)*
Bristol – AAA–BBC (Hist Art Fr; Law Fr; Phil Fr; Pol Fr) *(IB 30 pts)*
Cambridge – AAA (Modn Mediev Lang (Fr)) *(IB 38–42 pts)*
London (King's) – AAA (Fr Maths) *(IB 36 pts)*
Newcastle – AAA (Law Fr) *(IB 32 pts H Fr 6 pts)*
Oxford – Offers vary eg AAA–AAB (Modn Lang (Fr)) *(IB 38–42 pts)*
St Andrews – AAA (Fr Int Rel) *(IB 32 pts)*
Warwick – ABBb–BBBb (Fr courses) *(IB 34–35 pts)*

340 pts **Bath** – AAB–ABBb (Int Mgt Fr)
Birmingham – AAB–ABB (Int Bus Fr) *(IB 30–32 pts)*
Durham – AAB (Econ Fr)
Exeter – AAB (Engl Fr; Int Rel Fr) *(IB 30–32 pts)*
Lancaster – AAB (Euro Mgt (Fr))
Leicester – 340–400 pts (Law Fr Law Fr)
Liverpool – AAB (Engl Fr Law Fr)
Manchester – AAB (Fr Ger; Fr Ital; Fr Span; Fr Russ; Fr Chin) *(IB 32 pts)*
Nottingham – AAB (Law Fr; Mech Eng Fr)
Queen's Belfast – AAB (Acc Fr)
St Andrews – AAB (Fr Psy; Engl Fr; Class Fr; Maths Fr)
Sheffield – AAB (Law Fr)
Southampton – AAB–ABB (Fr courses)
Surrey – AAB–BBB (Law Fr Law)

320 pts **Aston** – ABB 320 pts (Int Bus Fr)
Bath – ABB–BBB 3AL+AS (Modn Lang Euro St (Fr Ital) (Fr Russ) (Fr Ger) (Fr Span))
Birmingham – ABB–BBB (Fr courses)
Bristol – ABB–BBB (Fr courses except under **360/300 pts**) *(IB 30–33 pts)*
Cardiff – ABB–BBC (Fr; Fr joint courses except under **280 pts**)
Exeter – ABB–BBB (Fr courses except under **340 pts**) *(IB 33–34 pts)*
Glasgow – ABB–BBB (Fr courses) *(IB 30 pts)*
Imperial London – ABB (Chem Fr Sci)
Kingston – 320 pts (Law Fr St)
Lancaster – ABB (Fr St Engl Lit; Fr St Psy)
Leeds – ABB (Comp Fr; Engl Fr; Fr Hist; Fr Maths; Fr Phys; Fr Stats)
Liverpool – 320 pts (Fr Maths) *(IB 30 pts)*
London (Inst in Paris) – ABB (Fr St)
London (King's) – ABB (Fr courses except under **360/300** pts) *(IB 36 pts)*
London (RH) – ABB–BBB (Fr courses) *(IB 32 pts H Fr 6 pts)*
London (UCL) – ABB+AS–BBB+AS (Fr courses) *(IB 32–34 pts)*
Loughborough – 320 pts (Econ Fr)

Newcastle – ABB–BBB (Fr courses)
Nottingham – ABB (Civ Eng Fr; Manuf Eng Mgt Fr; Mgt St Fr) *(IB 30–32 pts)*
St Andrews – ABB–BBB (Fr courses except under **360/340 pts**)
Sheffield – ABB–BBB (Fr courses) *(IB 30–35 pts)*
York – ABB (Fr Ger; Fr Ling) *(IB 34 pts)*

300 pts **Aston** – 300 pts (Fr courses except under **320 pts**; Transl St Fr/Ger)
Bristol – BBB (Dr Fr) *(IB 30–33 pts)*
Buckingham – 300 pts (Law Fr)
East Anglia – 300–260 pts (Interp Transl 2 Langs Modn Lang)
Edinburgh – BBB (Fr courses)
Essex – 300 pts (Econ Fr)
Lancaster – BBB (Fr Comb courses except under **340/320 pts**)
Leeds – BBB–BBC (Fr courses except under **320 pts**)
Liverpool – BBB–BBC (Fr courses except under **340/320 pts**)
London (King's) – BBB (Fr Ger)
London (QM) – 300 pts (Engl Fr; Fr St; Econ Fr; Fr Pol) *(IB 32 pts H Fr 6 pts)*
Manchester – BBB (Fr courses except under **340 pts**)
Northumbria – 300 pts (Fr Ger Trpl Qualif)
Nottingham – BBB–BBC (Fr courses except under **340/320 pts**) *(IB 30–32 pts)*
Oxford Brookes – BBB–BBC (Fr courses)
Queen's Belfast – BBB–BBCb (Fr courses except under **340 pts**)
Reading – 300–320 pts (Fr courses) *(IB 28 pts)*
Surrey – BBB–BCC 300–260 pts (Bus Mgt Fr; Engl Lit Fr) *(IB 34 pts)*
Sussex – BBB (Fr courses)

280 pts **Cardiff** – 280 pts (Fr Jap)
Coventry 280 pts (Law Fr)
Heriot-Watt – 280 pts (Fr courses except under **240** pts inc App Langs Transl)
Kingston – 280 pts (Dr Fr; Int Bus Fr)
Plymouth – 280 pts (Geog Fr)
Stirling – BBC–CCC (Fr courses) *(IB 28 pts)*
Swansea – 280–300 pts (Law Fr)

260 pts **Aberystwyth** – 260 pts (Fr courses)
Brighton – BCC–CCC (Fr St courses) *(IB 28 pts)*
Bristol UWE – 260–300 pts (LLB Fr)
Essex – 260 pts (Euro St Fr; Fr St Modn Lang)
Hull – 260–280 pts (Fr courses except under **220 pts**)
Kent – 260 pts (Fr courses) *(IB 28–34 pts)*
Leicester – 260–300 pts (Fr courses except under **340 pt**s)
London (QM) – 260–280 pts (Fr courses except under **300 pts**)
Strathclyde – BCC–BB (Fr courses)

240 pts **Aberdeen** – CCC (Fr courses)
Bangor – 240–260 pts (Fr courses)
Bristol UWE – 240–300 pts (Fr courses except under **260 pts**) *(IB 26–32 pts)*
Buckingham – 240 pts (Econ Fr; Int St Fr)
Chester – 240 pts (Fr courses) *(IB 30 pts)*
Coventry – 240–260 pts (Fr courses except under **280 pts**)
Dundee – 240–300 pts (Fr courses)
Heriot-Watt – CCC (Maths Fr)
Kingston – 240–320 pts (Engl Lit Fr; TV New Broad Media Fr)
Plymouth – 240 pts (Fr courses except under **280 pts**)
Portsmouth – 240–280 pts (Fr courses)
Salford – 240–300 pts (Modn Lang Transl Interp (Fr); Modn Lang Ling courses)
Swansea – 240–300 pts (Fr courses except under **280 pts**)
Ulster – 240–280 pts (Fr courses)

220 pts **Hull** – 220 pts (Soc Anth Fr)
Nottingham Trent – 220 pts (Fr courses)
Westminster – CCD (Fr courses)
200 pts **Buckingham** – 200 pts (Psy Fr)
Central Lancashire – 200 pts (Fr Bus Fr)
Hertfordshire – 200–240 pts (Fr; Fr Comb courses)
Kingston – 200–240 pts (Fr courses except under **320/280/240 pts**)
Lincoln – 200 pts (Bus Fr)
London Met – 200–240 pts (Fr St courses)
Middlesex – 200–240 pts (Fr courses)
Napier – 200 pts (Fr Mark Mgt)
Roehampton – 200–280 pts (Fr courses)
Sheffield Hallam – 200 pts (Int Bus Fr; Fr Mark; Fr Tour)
190 pts **Buckingham** – 190 pts (Engl Lit Fr)
180 pts **Greenwich** – 180 pts (Fr courses)
Liverpool John Moores – 180–200 pts (Fr courses)
Manchester Met – 180–200 pts (Fr courses) *(IB 26 pts)*
Northampton – 180–220 pts (Fr courses)
160 pts **Canterbury Christ Church** – CC (Fr courses)
West Scotland – CC (French)
Wolverhampton – 160–220 pts (Fr courses)
120 pts **Bucks New** – 120–240 pts (Fr courses)
80 pts **London (Birk)** – 80 pts for under 21s (p/t Fr Ger; Fr Span; Fr Mgt; Fr St)

Bradford – French modules in 'Languages for All' offered
Leeds Met – contact University
London (LSE) – optional course offered by the language centre: check with admissions tutor
(Fr/Ger/Span/Russ)

Alternative offers
See **Chapter 8** for grade/point equivalences and related information for the following examinations:
Scottish qualifications, the Welsh Baccalaureate, the IB diploma (approximate points shown also in
italics in the table of offers), the Irish Leaving Certificate, the European Baccalaureate and the French
Baccalaureate.

CHOOSING YOUR COURSE (SEE ALSO CH.1)
Course variations
European Studies French and German (Aston)
International Business and French (Aston)
Medical Engineering and French (Bath)
LLB with French (Bristol UWE)
Tourism with French (Canterbury Christ Church)
Scots Law and French (Dundee)
Translation Media and French (East Anglia)
Two Modern Languages with Business (Hull)
Combined Studies French (Leicester)
Translation and TEFL (Middlesex)
CHECK PROSPECTUSES AND WEBSITES FOR OTHER UNIVERSITIES AND COLLEGES OFFERING THESE COURSES.

Universities and colleges teaching quality See www.qaa.ac.uk; www.unistats.com.

Top universities and colleges (Research) Aberdeen*; Aston; Birmingham*; Bristol; Cambridge*;
Durham; Edinburgh; Glasgow; Liverpool; London (King's), (QM), (RH)*, (UCL); Manchester; Nottingham;
Oxford*; Oxford Brookes; Reading; Stirling; Warwick.

ADMISSIONS INFORMATION
Number of applicants per place (approx) Aston 6; Bangor 4; Birmingham 10; Bradford 3; Bristol 6;

Cardiff 6; Central Lancashire 5; Durham 8; Exeter 8; Huddersfield 3; Hull 12; Kent 10; Kingston 4; Lancaster 7; Leeds (joint Hons) 8; Leicester (Fr Ital) 5; Liverpool 5; Liverpool John Moores 8; London (Inst in Paris) 9, (King's) 9, (RH) 5, (UCL) (Fr Phil) 7, (Fr Span) 8, (Fr Ital) 4, (Fr Hist Art) 8; Manchester Met 13; Middlesex 6; Newcastle (Fr) 17, (Fr minor) 16, (Fr Span) 22, (Fr Ger) 20; Northampton 3; Nottingham 16; Oxford Brookes 8; Portsmouth 20; Roehampton 5; Warwick 7; York 8.

Advice to applicants and planning the UCAS personal statement Visits to France (including exchange visits) should be described, with reference to any particular cultural or geographical features of the region visited. Contacts with French friends and experience in speaking the language are also important. Willingness to work/live/travel abroad. Interests in French life and culture. Read French newspapers and magazines and keep up-to-date with news stories etc. **Hull** We look for dynamism – students looking for a challenge. **Leeds** See **Languages**. **St Andrews** Evidence of interest and reasons for choosing the course. Sport/extra-curricular activities. Posts of responsibility. **Sheffield** Applicants should state if French is their first language. **Swansea** Applicants with AS French grades A or B will be considered for joint courses. We are interested to read about extra-curricular activities involving France and French culture. See also **Appendix 2**.

Misconceptions about this course **Leeds** See **Languages**. **Swansea** Some applicants are not aware of the range of subjects which can be combined with French in our flexible modular system. They sometimes do not know that linguistics and area studies options are also available as well as literature options in French.

Selection interviews **Yes** Bangor, Birmingham, Cambridge, Canterbury Christ Church, Durham, East Anglia (after offer), Essex, Exeter, Heriot-Watt, Huddersfield, Hull, Kingston, Lancaster, Liverpool, Liverpool John Moores, London (RH), (UCL), Oxford, Portsmouth, Reading, Surrey, Sussex, Warwick; **Some** Brighton, Leeds.

Interview advice and questions Questions will almost certainly be asked on your A-level texts, in addition to your reading outside the syllabus – books, magazines, newspapers etc. Part of the interview may be conducted in French and written tests may be involved (see **Chapter 7**). **Leeds** See under **Languages**.

Applicants' impressions (A=Open day; B=Interview day) **London (Inst in Paris)** (B) There were two interviewers, both nice and not intimidating. They explained about the course and the department. The interview started in English, then suddenly changed to French. The interview was in London. The course in Paris lasts three years with a small department of 30 students. No students' union as such and accommodation in Paris very expensive. It's a good course if you want to be independent and wish to become fluent quickly, but the student life is different from that in a large British university. **Manchester** (B; Fr Span) A well organised interview, very friendly and supportive. The department was impressive and well equipped. There was an opportunity to meet the students to discuss various aspects of student life. I was not interviewed in the foreign languages. (B; Fr Ital) The interview lasted 15 minutes with one interviewer. More like an informal chat, but there was no warning when he would start speaking French. Not impressed with the university buildings but the students recommended the department, the teaching and the facilities. **Oxford** (B; Modn Lang (Fr/Span)) Questions were asked in the target language. The French interview seemed fairly well organised and the interviewer seemed very sympathetic which made it feel more like a chat.

Reasons for rejection (non-academic) Unstable personality. Known alcoholism. Poor motivation. Candidate unenthusiastic, unmotivated, ill-informed about the nature of the course (had not read the prospectus). Not keen to spend a year abroad.

AFTER-RESULTS ADVICE

Offers to applicants repeating A-levels **Higher** Aberystwyth, Bristol (Fr), Glasgow, Leeds, Oxford Brookes, Warwick; **Possibly higher** Aston (Fr; Fr Ger); **Same** Aston, Bradford, Brighton, Bristol (Phil Fr; Fr Lat), Chester, Durham, East Anglia, Lancaster, Liverpool, London (RH), Newcastle, Nottingham (Fr Ger; Fr Lat), Roehampton, Sheffield, Surrey, Sussex, Ulster; **No offers made** Cambridge.

GRADUATE DESTINATIONS AND EMPLOYMENT (2005/6 HESA)

Graduates surveyed 1310 Employed 690 In further study 270 Assumed unemployed 60.

Career note See Languages.

OTHER DEGREE SUBJECTS FOR CONSIDERATION

European Studies; International Business Studies; Literature; other language tables.

GENETICS

(see also Biological Sciences)

Over the years genetics has developed into a detailed and wide-ranging science. It involves, on the one hand, population genetics, and on the other, molecular interactions. Studies may therefore cover microbial, plant, animal and human genetics.

Useful websites www.genetics.org; www.nature.com/genetics; www.genetics.org.uk; see also Biological Sciences.

NB The points totals shown to the left of the institutions are for ease of reference only. It must not be assumed that tariff points are always used by institutions or that they can be substituted for an offer in grades. The level of an offer is not necessarily indicative of the quality of a course.

COURSE OFFERS INFORMATION

Subject requirements/preferences GCSE English, mathematics and science subjects. AL Chemistry and/or biology are usually required or preferred. NB A* grades are likely to form part of university offers in the higher ranges for students applying for places in 2008 for entry in 2009: check websites.

Your target offers

360 pts and above
Cambridge – AAA (Nat Sci (Genet)) *(IB 38–42 pts)*

350 pts Warwick – BBBb (Biol Sci (Mol Genet))

340 pts London (UCL) – AAB+AS–BBB+AS (Genet; Hum Genet) *(IB 32–36 pts)*
Manchester – AAB–BBB (Genet; Genet Ind; Genet Modn Lang)

320 pts Birmingham – ABB–BBB (Biol Sci (Genet)) *(IB 32–34 pts)*
Cardiff – ABB–AAB 320–340 pts (Genetics) *(IB 34 pts)*
Leicester – ABB (Med Genet; Biol Sci (Genet)) *(IB 32 pts)*
Liverpool – ABB–BBB (Genet; Genet Ind; Genet Comb Hons) *(IB 28–30 pts)*
London (King's) – ABB (Mol Genet) *(IB 34 pts)*
Newcastle – ABB–BBB (Hum Genet; Genet) *(IB 30–32 pts)*
Nottingham – ABB–BBB (Genet; Hum Genet) *(IB 32 pts)*
Sheffield – ABB or ABbb (Genet; Genet Microbiol; Genet Mol Cell Biol; Med Genet) *(IB 33 pts)*
York – ABB (Genet; Genet Euro; Genet Ind) *(IB 34 pts)*

300 pts Dundee – 300–240 pts (Mol Genet) *(IB 26 pts)*
East Anglia – BBB–BBC (Genet Mol Biol)
Edinburgh – BBB (Genetics) *(IB 30 pts)*
Lancaster – BBB (Bioch Genet)
Leeds – 300 pts (Genet; Hum Genet) *(IB 32 pts)*
Sussex – BBB–BBC 330–300 pts (Mol Genet)

280 pts Brunel – BBC 280 pts (Biomed Sci (Genet))
Glasgow – BBC–CCC (Genetics)
London (QM) – 280–300 pts (Genet; Genet Microbiol) *(IB 30 pts)*
Swansea – 280–300 pts (Genet; Med Genet)

260 pts Portsmouth – 260–300 pts (Gnm Sci)
Queen's Belfast – BCC/AB (Genetics) *(IB 28 pts)*

240 pts **Aberdeen** – CCC (Genet; Genet (Immun))
Aberystwyth – 240–280 pts (Genet Hum Hlth; Genet; Genet Bioch) *(IB 26 pts)*
Essex – 240–280 pts (Genetics) *(IB 26–28 pts)*
220 pts **Liverpool John Moores** – 220–260 pts (App Mol Biol Genet)
200 pts **Anglia Ruskin** – 200 pts (Genet Med Biol; Genet Microbiol)
Huddersfield – 200–280 pts (Med Genet)
180 pts **Bristol UWE** – 180–220 pts (App Genet)
Hertfordshire – 180–220 pts (Mol Biol Genet courses)
160 pts **Westminster** – CC (Mol Biol Genet) *(IB 26 pts)*
Wolverhampton – 160–220 pts (Genet Mol Biol)

Alternative offers
See **Chapter 8** for grade/point equivalences and related information for the following examinations: Scottish qualifications, the Welsh Baccalaureate, the IB diploma (approximate points shown also in italics in the table of offers), the Irish Leaving Certificate, the European Baccalaureate and the French Baccalaureate.

CHOOSING YOUR COURSE (SEE ALSO CH.1)
Course variations – Widen your options
Genetics and Human Health (Aberystwyth)
Biological Science (Genetics) (Birmingham)
Applied Genetics (Bristol UWE)
Medical Genetics (Huddersfield)
Human Genetics (Leeds)
Genetics and a Year in Industry (Liverpool)
Genetics in Industry (Manchester)
Genome Science (Portsmouth)
Medical Genetics (Swansea)
Genetics and a Year in Europe (York)
CHECK PROSPECTUSES AND WEBSITES FOR OTHER UNIVERSITIES AND COLLEGES OFFERING THESE COURSES.

Universities and colleges teaching quality See www.qaa.ac.uk; www.unistats.com.

Top universities and colleges (Research) Cambridge; Leicester; Nottingham.

Sandwich degree courses Bristol UWE; Brunel; Cardiff; Huddersfield; Sussex; York; see also **Biological Sciences**.

ADMISSIONS INFORMATION
Number of applicants per place (approx) Cardiff 8; Dundee 5; Leeds 7; Leicester (for all Biol Sci courses) 10; Newcastle 8; Nottingham 13; Swansea 7; Wolverhampton 4; York 9.

Advice to applicants and planning the UCAS personal statement See **Biological Sciences**.

Misconceptions about this course York Some fail to realise that chemistry (beyond GCSE) is essential to an understanding of genetics.

Selection interviews Yes Cambridge, Liverpool, Swansea; **Some** Cardiff, Dundee, Wolverhampton, York.

Interview advice and questions Likely questions will focus on your A-level science subjects, particularly biology, why you wish to study genetics, and on careers in genetics. See also **Chapter 7**.

AFTER-RESULTS ADVICE
Offers to applicants repeating A-levels Higher Aberystwyth, Leeds, Newcastle, Nottingham, Swansea; **Same** Anglia Ruskin, Cardiff, Dundee, London (UCL), Wolverhampton, York; **No offers made** Cambridge.

GRADUATE DESTINATIONS AND EMPLOYMENT (2005/6 HESA)
Graduates surveyed 320 **Employed** 115 **In further study** 120 **Assumed unemployed** 25.

Career note See **Biological Sciences**.

OTHER DEGREE SUBJECTS FOR CONSIDERATION
Anatomy; Biochemistry; Biological Sciences; Biology; Biotechnology; Human Sciences; Life Sciences; Medicine; Microbiology; Molecular Biology; Natural Sciences; Physiology; Plant Sciences.

GEOGRAPHY
(including **Meteorology**)

Students following BA and BSc Geography courses often choose options from the same range of modules, but the choice of degree will depend on the arts or science subjects taken at A-level. The content and focus of courses will vary between universities and could emphasise the human, physical, economic or social aspects of the subject.

Useful websites www.metoffice.gov.uk; www.ccw.gov.uk; www.rgs.org; www.ordnancesurvey.co.uk; www.geographical.co.uk; www.nationalgeographic.com; www.cartography.org.uk; www.countryside.gov.uk; www.geography.org.uk; www.thepowerofgeography.co.uk; www.spatial-literacy.org; www.geographynetwork.com; www.gis.com.

NB The points totals shown to the left of the institutions are for ease of reference only. It must not be assumed that tariff points are always used by institutions or that they can be substituted for an offer in grades. The level of an offer is not necessarily indicative of the quality of a course.

COURSE OFFERS INFORMATION
Subject requirements/preferences **GCSE** Geography usually required. Mathematics/sciences often required for BSc courses. **AL** Geography is usually required for most courses. Mathematics/science subjects required for BSc courses. (Meteorology) Mathematics, physics and another science may be required sometimes with specified grades, eg **Reading** mathematics and physics grade B. **NB** A* grades are likely to form part of university offers in the higher ranges for students applying for places in 2008 for entry in 2009: check websites.

Your target offers
360 pts and above
    Bristol – AAA–AAB (Geog; Geog Euro) *(IB 38 pts)*
    Cambridge – AAA (Geography) *(IB 38–42 pts)*
    Durham – AAA (Nat Sci Geog)
    East Anglia – AAA–AAB (Env Geog Int Dev; Meteor Ocean N Am/Aus)
    Leeds – AAA (Meteor Atmos Sci Int)
    London (King's) – AAA–AAB (Geog Hist) *(IB 34 pts)*
    London (SOAS) – AAA (Law Geog; Pol Geog)
    Nottingham – AAA–AAB (Geog; Geog Bus Env) *(IB 34–36 pts)*
    Oxford – Offers vary eg AAA–AAB (Geography) *(IB 38–42 pts)*
    Southampton – AAA–BBC (Geol Physl Geog; Ocean Physl Geog) *(IB 33 pts)*
340 pts **Durham** – AAB (BA/BSc Geog; Geog (Euro St); Geog Comb Soc Sci)
    Lancaster – AAB (Physl Geog Aus; Geog N Am)
    Leeds – AAB (BA Geog)
    London (LSE) – AAB (Geog Econ) *(IB 35 pts)*
    London (UCL) – AAB+AS–ABB+AS (Geog; Env Geog; Econ Geog) *(IB 34–36 pts)*
    Manchester – AAB–ABB (Geog courses)
    Nottingham – AAB–ABB (Arch Geog; Geog Chin St)
    Reading – 340 pts (Meteor Yr Okl)
    St Andrews – AAB (MA Geog courses) *(IB 32–36 pts)*

320 pts **Birmingham** – ABB–BBB 320–300 pts (Am St Geog; Geog Econ) *(IB 32–34 pts)*
Durham – ABB (Educ St (Geog))
East Anglia – ABB (Meteor Ocean Euro)
Exeter – ABB–ACC (Geog; Geog Euro) *(IB 30–34 pts)*
Exeter (Cornwall) – ABB–BBC (Geog; Geog Earth Sys Sci; Geog Env Mgt; Geog Env Soty)
Glasgow – ABB–BBB (BA Geog courses) *(IB 28–30 pts)*
Hull – 320 pts (MPhysl Geog)
Lancaster – ABB–BBB (Geog; Physl Geog; Hum Geog; Econ Geog)
Leeds – ABB (BSc Geog; Geog Hist; Geog Mgt; Geog Maths)
Liverpool – ABB–BBB (Geog; Geog Mgt; Geol Physl Geog; Ocns Clim Physl Geog; Geog Arch)
(IB 30 pts)
London (LSE) – ABB (Geography) *(IB 35 pts)*
London (RH) – ABB 320 pts (Geog; Hum Geog; Physl Geog; Physl Geog Sci Comm) *(IB 34
pts)*
Loughborough – 320–340 pts (Geog Spo Sci; Geog) *(IB 30 pts)*
Newcastle – ABB (BA Geog; Geog Maths; Geog Stats) *(IB 30–38 pts)*
Oxford Brookes – ABB–CCD (Geog Law; Geog Psy)
Reading – 320 pts (Meteor; Maths Meteor) *(IB 33–34 pts)*
St Andrews – ABB (BSc Geog courses)
Sheffield – ABB **or** ABbb (BA Geog; Econ Geog; Geog Pol; Geog Sociol; Geog Plan) *(IB 33
pts)*
Southampton – ABB 320 pts (BSc Geog; Geog Ocean)
Stranmillis (UC) – ABB (Geog Educ)
300 pts **Birmingham** – BBB–BCC (Geol Geog; Geog courses except under **320 pts**) *(IB 32–34 pts)*
Cardiff – 300 pts BBB (Hum Geog Plan; Mar Geog)
Dundee – 300 pts (Geog courses 3 yr)
East Anglia – BBB (Meteor Ocean; Meteor Ocean Ind)
Edinburgh – BBB (MA Geog courses; BSc Geog courses; Geophys Meteor)
Keele – 300 pts (Crim Geog) *(IB 26–28 pts)*
Leicester – BBB 260–320 pts (Geog; Geog Arch; Geog Geol; Physl Geog; Hum Geog) *(IB 30
pts)*
London (King's) – BBB+AS **or** BBbbc (Dev Geog; Geog; Geog Film) *(IB 32 pts)*
London (SOAS) – 300–260 pts (Geog courses except under **360 pts**)
London (UCL) – BBB+AS (Geoinform) *(IB 34–36 pts)*
Loughborough – 300 pts (BSc Geog; Geog Econ; Geog Mgt; Geog Spo Leis Mgt)
Manchester – BBB (Geog Arch)
Newcastle – BBB–BCC (Geog Plan; Geog Inf Sci; Physl Geog; BSc Geog) *(IB 30–38 pts)*
Reading – 300 pts (Hum Geog; Physl Geog; Hum Physl Geog; Geog Econ (Reg Sci)) *(IB
28–31 pts)*
Southampton – BBB (Popn Sci; Arch Geog)
Stirling – BBB 2nd yr entry (Env Geog)
Sussex – BBB **or** 340 pts 3AL+AS (Geog courses)
Swansea – 300 pts (Geog; Geog Euro St)
280 pts **Coventry** – 280 pts (Geog courses)
Glasgow – BBC–CCC (BSc Geog; Geog Chem Env)
Lancaster – BBC (Geog courses except under **340/320 pts**)
Leeds – BBC (Geog courses except under **340/320 pts**; Meteor Atmos Sci)
London (QM) – 280–320 pts (BA/BSc Geog; Hum Geog; Physl Geog; Env Geog; Geog Bus
Mgt; Hisp St Geog; Russ Geog; Cits Econ Soc Ch; Geog Env Haz) *(IB 32 pts)*
London (RH) – BBC (Physl Geog Geol)
Oxford Brookes – BBC (Geog Spo Coach St; Env Mgt Geog; Bus Geog; Biol Geog)
Plymouth – 280 pts (BA/BSc Geog courses)
Portsmouth – 280 pts (BA/BSc Geog; Hum Geog; Physl Geog; Geog Inf Sci)
Queen's Belfast – BBC **or** BCCb (Arch Palae Geog; Geog Euro; Geog)
Sheffield Hallam – 280 pts (Hum Geog)

260 pts **Aberystwyth** – 260–320 pts (Geog courses) *(IB 30 pts)*
Brighton – BCC–CCC (Geog; Hum Geog courses) *(IB 28 pts)*
Bristol UWE – 260–300 pts (Geog; Geog Env Mgt; Geog Plan; Geog Trans) *(IB 26–32 pts)*
Keele – 260–280 pts (Geog; Hum Physl Geog; Physl Geog) *(IB 26–28 pts)*
Northumbria – 260 pts (Geog; Geog Env Mgt; Geog Spo St) *(IB 28 pts)*
Oxford Brookes – BCC–CCD (Geog courses except under **320/280 pts**)
Strathclyde – BCC–BB (Geography)
Winchester – 260–300 pts (P Educ Geog)

240 pts **Aberdeen** – CCC (BA/BSc Geog)
Bangor – 240–320 pts (Geog courses) *(IB 28 pts)*
Bradford – 240 pts (Geog Arch)
Chester – 240 pts (Geog courses) *(IB 30 pts)*
Cumbria – 240 pts (Geography)
Dundee – 240 pts (Geog courses 4 yr)
Hull – 240–300 pts (Geog Arch; Geog Ecol; Geog Spo Sci; BSc Physl Geog)
Kingston – 240–200 pts (Geog courses; Hum Geog courses; Geog Inf Sys courses)
Liverpool Hope – 240 pts (Geog courses)
Sheffield Hallam – 240 pts (Geog Plan; Geog Trans)
Swansea – 240–300 pts (Geog courses except under **300 pts**)
Westminster – CCC (Hum Geog)

220 pts **Bath Spa** – 220–260 pts (Film Scrn St Geog; Geog Phil Eth)
Bradford – 220 pts (Geog Env Mgt; Physl Env Geog)
Glamorgan – 220 pts (Geog Inf Sci)
Hertfordshire – 220–260 pts (Geog courses)
Liverpool John Moores – 220 pts (Physl Geog)
Manchester Met – 220 pts (Geog GIS; Physl Geog; Hum Geog; Comb Geog courses) *(IB 24 pts)*
Nottingham Trent – 220 pts (Geog courses)
Stirling – CCD 1st yr entry (Env Geog) *(IB 26 pts)*
Ulster – 220–240 pts (Geography)

200 pts **Glamorgan** – 200 pts (Physl Geog courses)
Gloucestershire – 200–280 pts (Hum Geog; Geog; Physl Geog courses)
Plymouth – 200–240 pts (Physl Geog Geol)
Staffordshire – 200–280 pts (Geog; Physl Env Geog; Hum Env Geog; Geog Mntn Ldrshp; Geog joint courses) *(IB 28 pts)*
Sunderland – 200 pts (Geog courses)

180 pts **Edge Hill** – 180 pts (Geog; Hum Geog; Physl Geog)
Greenwich – 180–240 pts (Geog; Geog Geog Inf Sys)
Liverpool John Moores – 180–240 pts (Geography)
Northampton – 180–220 pts (Hum Geog; Physl Geog; Hum Geog)
Nottingham Trent – 180 pts (Physl Geog)
Salford – 180 pts (Env Geog; Geog)

160 pts **Bishop Grosseteste (UC)** – 160 pts (Educ St Geog)
Bournemouth – 160 pts (App Geog)
Canterbury Christ Church – CC (Geog courses)
Central Lancashire – 160–200 pts (Geog courses)
Derby – 160–240 pts (Geog courses)
East London – 160 pts (Geog Inf Sci)
Glamorgan – 160 pts (Hum Geog)
Newman (UC) – 160–240 pts (Geography)
St Mary's (UC) – 160–200 pts (Geog courses)
Southampton Solent – 160 pts (Geog Env St; Mar Geog; Geog Sustr)
Wolverhampton – 160–200 pts (Geog courses)

140 pts **Worcester** – 140–200 pts (Geog; Hum Geog; Physl Geog)

100 pts **Wigan and Leigh (Coll)** – 100 pts (Geog Comb Hons)
 80 pts **London (Birk)** – 80 pts for under 21s (over 21s varies) (p/t Geog Env)

Leeds Met – contact University

Alternative offers

See **Chapter 8** for grade/point equivalences and related information for the following examinations: Scottish qualifications, the Welsh Baccalaureate, the IB diploma (approximate points shown also in italics in the table of offers), the Irish Leaving Certificate, the European Baccalaureate and the French Baccalaureate.

EXAMPLES OF FOUNDATION DEGREES IN THE SUBJECT FIELD

Truro (Coll).

CHOOSING YOUR COURSE (SEE ALSO CH.1)

Course variations – Widen your options

Coastal Geography (Bangor)
Geography and Environment (Bournemouth)
Ecology and Biogeography (Brighton)
Marine Geography (Cardiff)
Natural Hazards (Coventry)
Social Sciences Combined (Durham)
Flexible Combined Honours (Exeter)
Applied Environmental Sciences and Human Geography (Keele)
Earth Science and Geography (Lancaster)
Development Geography (London (King's))
Geography and Business Management (London (QM))
Town Planning (Newcastle)
Geography and Environmental Management (Northumbria)
Urban Studies (Sheffield)
CHECK PROSPECTUSES AND WEBSITES FOR OTHER UNIVERSITIES AND COLLEGES OFFERING THESE COURSES.

Universities and colleges teaching quality See www.qaa.ac.uk; www.unistats.com.

Top universities and colleges (Research) Bristol*; Cambridge; Durham*; Edinburgh*; Hull; Leeds; London (LSE), (QM), (RH), (UCL)*; Loughborough; Newcastle; Nottingham; Sheffield; Southampton.

Sandwich degree courses Aberystwyth; Bradford; Cardiff; Coventry; Glamorgan; Hertfordshire; Kingston; Loughborough; Manchester Met; Nottingham Trent; Oxford Brookes; Plymouth; Queen's Belfast; Salford; Ulster; Wolverhampton.

ADMISSIONS INFORMATION

Number of applicants per place (approx) Aberystwyth 3; Birmingham 6; Bristol 9; Bristol UWE 10; Cambridge 3; Cardiff 5; Central Lancashire 3; Chester 10; Coventry 12; Cumbria 5, (Comb) 10, (QTS) 11; Derby 4; Dundee 5; Durham 8; East Anglia (Meteor Ocean) 7; Edge Hill 8; Edinburgh 8; Exeter 10; Glamorgan 5; Gloucestershire 40; Greenwich 2; Hull 10; Kent 15; Kingston 7; Lancaster 13; Leeds 12; Leicester (BA) 19, (BSc) 17; Liverpool 3; Liverpool John Moores 6; London (King's) 5, (LSE) (Geog) 5 (Geog Econ) 4, (QM) 5, (RH) 7, (SOAS) 5; Loughborough 6, (Geog Spo Sci) 20; Newcastle 14; Newman (UC) 2; Northampton 4; Northumbria 16; Nottingham 12; Oxford (success rate 41%); Plymouth 10; Portsmouth (Geog) 5; St Mary's (UC) 4; Salford 3; Sheffield (BA) 13, (BSc) 10; Southampton (Geog) 7; Staffordshire 10; Strathclyde 8; Swansea 5; Wolverhampton 2; Worcester 5.

Advice to applicants and planning the UCAS personal statement Visits to, and field courses in, any specific geographical region should be fully described. Study your own locality in detail and get in touch with the area Planning Office to learn about any future developments. Read geographical magazines and describe any special interests you have – and why. **Durham** Interview essential for overseas students. **Liverpool** We look for evidence of interest in geography or at least in a particular part of the subject, for example field trips, travel, books or magazines read, and also for evidence of interests beyond academic work. **London (King's)** Awareness of world issues. **Loughborough** Geography interest, travel experience, voluntary work and, for the Geography and Sports Science course a very high level of sports experience. **St Andrews** Reasons for choosing course and evidence of interest; sport/extracurricular activities and posts of responsibility.

Misconceptions about this course Birmingham Some students think that the BA and BSc Geography courses are very different: in fact they do not differ from one another. All course options are available for both degrees. **East Anglia** (Meteor Ocean) Some applicants don't realise that the course is a very mathematical and physics subject. **Liverpool** Some applicants assume that a BSc course restricts them to physical geography modules. This is not so since human geography modules can be taken. Some students later specialise in human geography. **Southampton** (Popn Sci) No previous knowledge of population science is necessary for this course and we positively welcome applications from mature students, with considerable flexibility in the entrance requirements for such candidates.

Selection interviews Yes Bristol UWE, Cambridge, Central Lancashire, Coventry, Durham (essential for overseas applicants), East Anglia, Edge Hill, Greenwich, Kingston, London (King's), (QM), (RH), (SOAS), (UCL), Manchester Met, Northumbria, Oxford, Warwick (BA QTS); **Some** Aston, Bath Spa, Bristol, Cardiff, Chichester, Dundee, Liverpool, Loughborough, Newcastle, Nottingham, Salford, Southampton, Staffordshire.

Interview advice and questions Geography is a very broad subject and applicants can expect to be questioned on their syllabus and those aspects which they find of special interest. Some questions in the past have included: What fieldwork have you done? What are your views on ecology? What changes in the landscape have you noticed on the way to the interview? Explain in simple meteorological terms today's weather. Why are earthquakes almost unknown in Britain? What is the value of practical work in geography to primary school children? (BEd course) What do you enjoy about geography and why? Are there any articles of geographical importance in the news at present? Discuss the current economic situation in Britain and give your views. Questions on the Third World, on world ocean currents and drainage and economic factors world-wide. Expect to comment on local geography and on geographical photographs and diagrams. **Cambridge** What do you think about those who regard global warming as nonsense? Are Fair-Trade bananas really fair? Imagine you are hosting the BBC radio show on New Year's day, what message would you send to listeners? **Liverpool** Looks for why students have chosen Geography and the aspects of the subject they enjoy. **Oxford** Is nature natural? **Southampton** Applicants selected on academic ability only. See **Chapter 7**.

Applicants' impressions (A=Open day; B=Interview day) Bath Spa (B; Geog Sociol) I had interviews with both heads of department followed by a tour of the University. **Cambridge (Emmanuel)** (B) There were two interviews, each with one interviewer. I was asked why Geography and why Emmanuel? I was also asked whether there was much of a distinction between human and physical geography. At the second interview the essays I had previously submitted were discussed. The visit was well organised. We were able to discuss life in Cambridge and in the college with some of the students. **Oxford (St Edmund Hall)** (B) There were two 20-minute interviews with two interviewers asking questions on physical geography and human geography respectively. I was asked why I wanted to do Geography, about the formation of hurricanes in Bermuda, about the geographical aspects of my holiday in Singapore and questions on my AS- and A-level coursework investigations. The interviews were well organised and although fairly informal, I felt under pressure. **Southampton** (B) There was an informal interview and a talk on the human and physical aspects of the courses. There was also a tour of the campus and halls.

Reasons for rejection (non-academic) Lack of awareness of the content of the course. Failure to attend interview. Poor general knowledge. Lack of geographical awareness. **Hull** (BSc) Usually insufficient science background. **Liverpool** Personal statement gave no reason for choosing Geography.

AFTER-RESULTS ADVICE

Offers to applicants repeating A-levels Higher Bournemouth, Glasgow, Hull, Kingston, Nottingham, St Andrews, Sussex (Geog Lang); **Possibly higher** Edinburgh; **Same** Aberystwyth, Birmingham,

Bradford, Brighton, Bristol, Cardiff, Chester, Chichester, Coventry, Cumbria, Derby, Dundee, Durham, East Anglia, Edge Hill, Lancaster, Leeds (applicants consider which A-levels to resit for the BSc course), Liverpool, Liverpool Hope, Liverpool John Moores, London (RH), (SOAS), Loughborough, Manchester Met, Newcastle, Newman (UC), Newport, Northumbria, Oxford Brookes, Plymouth, St Mary's (UC), Salford, Southampton, Staffordshire, Ulster, Wolverhampton; **No offers made** Cambridge.

GRADUATE DESTINATIONS AND EMPLOYMENT (2005/6 HESA)
Human and Social Geography graduates surveyed 2325 **Employed** 1190 **In further study** 480 **Assumed unemployed** 90.

Career note Geography graduates enter a wide range of occupations, many in business and administrative careers. Depending on specialisations, areas could include agriculture, forestry, hydrology, transport, market research and retail. Teaching is also a popular option.

OTHER DEGREE SUBJECTS FOR CONSIDERATION
Agriculture; Anthropology; Countryside Management; Development Studies; Environmental Science/Studies; Forestry; Geology; Surveying; Town Planning; Urban Land Economics; Urban Studies.

GEOLOGY/GEOLOGICAL SCIENCES
(including **Earth Sciences and Engineering (Mining), Geophysics** and **Geoscience**)

Topics in Geology courses include the physical and chemical constitution of the earth, exploration geophysics, oil and marine geology (oceanography) and seismic interpretation. Earth Sciences cover geology, environmental science, physical geography and can also include business studies and language modules. No previous knowledge of geology is required for most courses.

Useful websites www.geolsoc.org.uk; www.bgs.ac.uk; www.noc.soton.ac.uk; www.scicentral.com.

NB The points totals shown to the left of the institutions are for ease of reference only. It must not be assumed that tariff points are always used by institutions or that they can be substituted for an offer in grades. The level of an offer is not necessarily indicative of the quality of a course.

COURSE OFFERS INFORMATION
Subject requirements/preferences GCSE English, mathematics and a science required. **AL** One or two mathematics/science subjects usually required. Geography may be accepted as a science subject. **NB** A* grades are likely to form part of university offers in the higher ranges for students applying for places in 2008 for entry in 2009: check websites.

Your target offers
360 pts and above
    Birmingham – AAA–AAB (MSci Geol Int Yr; Res App Geol Int Yr; Env Geosci) *(IB 30–32 pts)*
    Cambridge – AAA (Nat Sci (Geol Sci)) *(IB 38–42 pts)*
    East Anglia – AAA–AAB (Env Earth Sci N Am/Aus; Geophys Sci N Am/Aus)
    Leeds – AAA (Geophys Sci Int; MGeol Env Geol Int)
    London (UCL) – AAA–AAB+AS (Geol; Earth Sci; Geophys; Env Geosci; Pal; Planet Sci)
    Oxford – Offers vary eg AAA–AAB (Earth Sci; Geol) *(IB 38–42 pts)*
    Southampton – AAA–BBC (Geol courses)
340 pts **Imperial London** – AAB (Geol; Env Geosci Geophys; Geol Geophys; Geol Geophys Abrd)
    Liverpool – AAB 340 pts (MSci Geophys N Am) *(IB 31 pts)*
    London (RH) – AAB (Geosci Int St)
320 pts **Durham** – ABB (Nat Sci (Earth Sci))
    East Anglia – ABB–BBC (Geophys Sci Euro; Env Earth Sci Euro; see also **360 pts**)
    Lancaster – ABB–BBC (Earth Sci courses)
    Liverpool – ABB 320 pts (MSci Geol; Geol Geophys) *(IB 31 pts)*
    St Andrews – ABB–BBB (Geosci courses; Env Geosci courses) *(IB 30–32 pts)*

300 pts **Birmingham** – BBB–BCC 300–260 pts (Geol; Geol Biol; Env Geosci; Res App Geol)
Bristol – ABB (Env Geosci; Geol Biol; Geol; Geol N Am/Euro; Env Geosci N Am/Euro; Palae Evol) *(IB 32 pts)*
Durham – BBB (Geol; Earth Sci; Env Geosci; Geophys Geol)
Edinburgh – BBB (Geol; Env Geosci; Geol Physl Geog; Geophys)
Exeter – BBB–BCC (Min Eng; App Geol; Eng Geol Geotech; Geotech) *(IB 25–27 pts)*
Leeds – BBB (Geol Sci courses; Env Geol courses except under **360 pts**)
Leicester – BBB–ABB 300–320 pts (MGeol Geol courses; MGeol App Env Geol; MGeol Geol Geophys; Geol Pal; Earth Planet Sci) *(IB 28–30 pts)*
Liverpool – BBB 300 pts (BSc Geol; Geophys; Geol Physl Geog; Geophys (Phys); Ocn Earth Sci; Ocn Clim; Chem Ocean)
London (RH) – 300–280 pts (Geol courses; Env Geol courses; Env Geosci; Geosci) *(IB 35 pts)*
Manchester – ABC (Geol; Env Res Geol; Geol Planet Sci; Geochem; Earth Sci)
Southampton – BBB 300 pts (MGeol Geol; MGeophys Geophys courses) *(IB 30–38 pts)*
280 pts **Aberystwyth** – 280 pts (Env Earth Sci)
Cardiff – BBC 280–320 pts (BSc Geol; Explor Res Geol; Env Geosci; Earth Sci courses)
East Anglia – BBC (Geophys Sci; Env Earth Sci)
Leicester – BBC 280 pts (BSc Geol; App Env Geol; Geol Geophys; BSc Geol Pal; Geog Geol; Earth Planet Sci) *(IB 28–30 pts)*
260 pts **Glasgow** – BCC–CCC (Earth Sci; Env Biogeochem) *(IB 28 pts)*
Lancaster – BCC (Earth Env Sci)
240 pts **Aberdeen** – CCC (Geol Petrol Geol; Geosci; Geol Phys)
Brighton – 240 pts (Geol; Geog Geol) *(IB 28 pts)*
Plymouth – 240–280 pts (MGeol Geol)
Portsmouth – 240–280 pts (Eng Geol Geotech; Earth Sci; Geol; Geol Haz; Pal Evol)

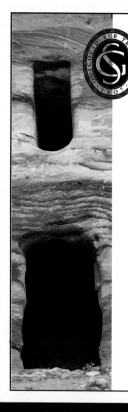

220 pts **Bangor** – 220–260 pts (Geol Ocean)

Keele – 220–260 pts (Geol courses; Earth Sys Sci) *(IB 26–30 pts)*

Liverpool John Moores – 220 pts (Geol; Haz Geosci)

200 pts **Glamorgan** – 200–240 pts (Geology)

Kingston – 200–240 pts (Earth Sys Sci; Geol courses)

Plymouth – 200–240 pts (Ocn Sci; App Geol; Geol; Physl Geog Geol; Ocn Explor)

180 pts **Edge Hill** – 180 pts (Geol courses; Geol Sci courses)

Northampton – 180–220 pts (Earth Sci courses)

160 pts **Derby** – 160–240 pts (Earth Sys Sci courses; Geol courses)

120 pts **West Scotland** – DD (Earth Sci)

80 pts **Eastleigh (Coll)** – 80 pts (Fdn Sci)

London (Birk) – 80 pts for under 21s (over 21s varies) (p/t Geol; Env Geol; Earth Sci; dist learn)

Alternative offers

See **Chapter 8** for grade/point equivalences and related information for the following examinations: Scottish qualifications, the Welsh Baccalaureate, the IB diploma (approximate points shown also in italics in the table of offers), the Irish Leaving Certificate, the European Baccalaureate and the French Baccalaureate.

CHOOSING YOUR COURSE (SEE ALSO CH.1)

Course variations – Widen your options

Geology and Petroleum Geology (Aberdeen)

Geological Oceanography (Bangor)

Geology and Geography (Brighton)

Palaeontology and Evolution (Bristol)

Exploration and Resource Geology (Cardiff)

Mining Engineering (Exeter Cornwall Campus)

Earth and Planetary Science (Leicester)

Marine Geoscience (Plymouth)

CHECK PROSPECTUSES AND WEBSITES FOR OTHER UNIVERSITIES AND COLLEGES OFFERING THESE COURSES.

Universities and colleges teaching quality See www.qaa.ac.uk; www.unistats.com.

Top universities and colleges (Research) (including Environmental Sciences) Bristol*; Cambridge*; Cardiff; Edinburgh; Leeds; Liverpool; London (RH), (UCL); Manchester; Newcastle; Oxford*.

Sandwich degree courses Glamorgan; Greenwich; Kingston; West Scotland.

ADMISSIONS INFORMATION

Number of applicants per place (approx) Aberystwyth 5; Bangor 4; Birmingham 4; Bristol 7; Cardiff 7; Derby 4; Durham 4; East Anglia 7; Edinburgh 5; Exeter 5; Greenwich 2; Kingston 19, (Earth Sys Sci) 3; Imperial London 5; Leeds 8; Liverpool 5; Liverpool John Moores 6; London (RH) 5, (UCL) 3; Northampton 7; Oxford 1.2; Plymouth 7; Portsmouth (Eng Geol Geotech) 2, (Geol) 2; Southampton 5.

Advice to applicants and planning the UCAS personal statement Visits to any outstanding geological sites and field courses you have attended should be described in detail. Apart from geological formations, you should also be aware of how geology has affected humankind in specific areas in the architecture of the region and artefacts used. Evidence of social skills could be given. **Bristol** Apply early. **Leeds** Solid maths and science background required. See also **Appendix 2**.

Misconceptions about this course East Anglia Many applicants fail to realise that environmental earth science extends beyond geology to the links between the solid earth and its behaviour and society in general. **London (UCL)** Environmental geoscience is sometimes mistaken for environmental science; they are two different subjects.

Selection interviews Yes Birmingham, Cambridge, Durham, Edinburgh, Exeter, Greenwich, Kingston, Liverpool, London (RH), Oxford, Southampton, Sunderland; **Some** Aberystwyth (mature students only), Cardiff, Derby, East Anglia.

Interview advice and questions Some knowledge of the subject will be expected and applicants could be questioned on specimens of rocks and their origins. Past interviews have included questions on the field courses attended, and the geophysical methods of exploration in the detection of metals. How would you determine the age of this rock (sample shown)? Can you integrate a decay curve function and would it help you to determine the age of rocks? How many planes of crystallisation could this rock have? What causes a volcano? What is your local geology? **Oxford** (Earth Sci) Candidates may be asked to comment on specimens of a geological nature, based on previous knowledge of the subject. See **Chapter 7**.

Applicants' impressions (A=Open day; B=Interview day) Bristol (B) There was an overview of the course, a tour of the department and accommodation and an informal interview when I was asked questions about my personal statement.

Reasons for rejection (non-academic) Misconceptions about the course. **Exeter** Outright rejection uncommon but some applicants advised to apply for other programmes.

AFTER-RESULTS ADVICE

Offers to applicants repeating A-levels Higher Bristol, St Andrews; **Possibly higher** Portsmouth; **Same** Aberystwyth, Cardiff, Derby, Durham, East Anglia, Leeds, Liverpool John Moores, London (RH), Plymouth, Southampton; **No offers made** Cambridge.

GRADUATE DESTINATIONS AND EMPLOYMENT (2005/6 HESA)

Geology graduates surveyed 445 **Employed** 55 **In further study** 245 **Assumed unemployed** 70. **Mining Engineering graduates surveyed** 50 **Employed** 30 **In further study** 5 **Assumed unemployed** 5.

Career note Areas of employment include mining and quarrying, the oil and gas industry, prospecting and processing.

OTHER DEGREE SUBJECTS FOR CONSIDERATION

Archaeology; Civil and Mining Engineering; Environmental Science; Geography; Physics.

GERMAN

(see also **European Studies** and **Languages**)

Language, literature, practical language skills or a broader study of Germany and its culture (European Studies) are alternative study approaches. See also **Appendix 2** under **Languages**.

Useful websites www.cilt.org.uk; www.goethe.de; www.bbc.co.uk/languages; www.iol.org.uk; www.languageadvantage.com; www.languagematters.co.uk; www.reed.co.uk/multilingual; www.deutsch-online.com; www.faz.net; www.sueddeutsche.de; www.europa.eu; www.gslg.org.uk; www.amgs.org.uk; www.wigs.ac.uk.

NB The points totals shown to the left of the institutions are for ease of reference only. It must not be assumed that tariff points are always used by institutions or that they can be substituted for an offer in grades. The level of an offer is not necessarily indicative of the quality of a course.

COURSE OFFERS INFORMATION

Subject requirements/preferences GCSE English and German are required. **AL** German required usually at a specified grade. **NB** A* grades are likely to form part of university offers in the higher ranges for students applying for places in 2008 for entry in 2009: check websites.

Your target offers

360 pts **and above**

Birmingham – AAA (Law Ger)

Bristol – AAA–AAB (Law Ger; Hist Ger) *(IB 29 pts)*

Bristol – AAA–ABB (Phil Ger; Pol Ger) *(IB 29 pts)*

Bristol – AAA–BBC (Hist Art Ger) *(IB 29 pts)*

Cambridge – AAA (Modn Mediev Lang (Ger))

London (UCL) – AAA+AS–BBB+AS (Ger courses) *(IB 32–36 pts)*

Nottingham – AAA–AABB (Econ Ger) *(IB 30–32 pts)*

Oxford – Offers vary eg AAA–AAB (Modn Lang (Ger))

Southampton – AAA–ABB (Maths Ger) *(IB 32 pts)*

340 pts **Bristol** – AAB–BBC (Cz Ger; Fr Ger; Ger Ital/Port/Russ/Span) *(IB 29 pts)*

Cardiff – AAB (Engl Lit Ger)

Durham – AAB (Comb St)

Lancaster – AAB (Euro Mgt Ger)

London (King's) – AAB (Ger Hist; Ger Mus; Ger Phil; Ger War St) *(IB 32 pts)*

Manchester – AAB (Fr Ger; Engl Lang Ger; Ger Chin/Jap/Russ/Span) *(IB 30–35 pts)*

Nottingham – AAB (Law Ger; Mech Eng Ger; Ger Mus)

Queen's Belfast – AAB (Acc Ger)

St Andrews – AAB–ABB (Ger courses) *(IB 32–36 pts)*

Sheffield – AAB–BBC (Ger courses)

Southampton – AAB (Engl Ger) *(IB 32 pts)*

Surrey – AAB (Law Ger Law)

320 pts **Bath** – ABB–BBBb (Int Mgt Ger)

Birmingham – ABB–BBB (Ger St courses; Ger courses except under **360 pts**) *(IB 32–34 pts)*

Bristol – ABB (Mus Ger) *(IB 29 pts)*

Exeter – ABB (Ger courses) *(IB 32–33 pts)*

Glasgow – ABB (Ger courses) *(IB 30 pts)*

Hull – 320 pts (Law Ger Law Lang)

Imperial London – ABB (Chem Ger Sci)

Lancaster – ABB (Ger St Psy; Ger St Engl Lit)

Leeds – ABB (Ger Pol; Ger Stats; Ger Mus)

Loughborough – 320 pts (Econ Ger)

Newcastle – ABB–BBB (Ger; Ger Bus St)

Reading – ABB (Int Mgt Bus Admin Ger)

Southampton – ABB (Ger courses except under **360/340 pts**) *(IB 32 pts)*

York – ABB–BBB (Ger Ling; Fr Ger (Lang Ling)) *(IB 34 pts)*

300 pts **Aston** – 300 pts (Ger courses)

Cardiff – BBB–ABC–BBC (Ger courses)

Dundee – 300 pts (Law Ger)

Durham – ABC–BBB (Modn Lang)

Edinburgh – BBB (Ger courses)

Essex – 300 pts (Econ Ger)

Lancaster – BBB (Ger St; Ger St courses except under **340/320 pts**)

Leeds – BBB (Chem Ger; Engl Ger; Euro St Ger; Ger Maths; Ger Span)

Liverpool – BBB–BBC (Ger courses) *(IB 30 pts)*

London (King's) – 300 pts (Ger courses except under **340 pts**) *(IB 32 pts)*

London (LSE) – optional course offered by language centre (check with admissions tutor) (Fr/Ger/Russ/Span)

London (RH) – 300–320 pts (Ger courses) *(IB 32 pts)*

Manchester – BBB–BBC (Ger courses except under **340 pts**)

Newcastle – ABC–BBB (Ling Ger) *(IB 32 pts)*

Northumbria – 300 pts (Fr Ger)

Nottingham – AAB–BBC (Ger courses except under **360 pts**) *(IB 30–32 pts)*

Queen's Belfast – BBB–BBC (Ger courses except under **340 pts**)

For information on how to read the Subject Tables, see **Chapter 8**.

Reading – 300–320 pts (Ger courses) *(IB 28 pts)*
Sheffield – BBB-BBC (Ger courses) *(IB 32–35 pts)*
Warwick – 300–340 pts (Ger courses)
280 pts **Bangor** – 280 pts (Law Ger)
Heriot-Watt – BBC (Ger courses except under **260 pts**)
Hull – 280 pts (Phil Ger)
Leeds – BBC-BCC (Ger courses except under **320/300** pts)
Plymouth – 280 pts (Geog Ger)
260 pts **Brighton** – BCC-CCC (Ger St Engl Lit; Ger St Ling; Ger St Media) *(IB 28 pts)*
Essex – 260 pts (Euro St Ger; Modn Lang Ger St)
Heriot-Watt – BCC (Chem Ger)
Kent – 260 pts (Ger courses) *(IB 28 pts)*
Leicester – BCC 260–300 pts (Ital Ger; Span Ger; Fr Ger)
London (QM) – 260–300 pts (Ger courses) *(IB 32–36 pts)*
Strathclyde – BCC/BB (Arts Soc Sci (Ger))
Surrey – 260 pts (Film St Ger; Media St Ger)
240 pts **Aberdeen** – CCC (Ger courses)
Aberystwyth – 240–260 pts (Ger courses) *(IB 29 pts)*
Bangor – 240–260 pts (Ger courses except under **280 pts**)
Chester – 240 pts (Ger courses) *(IB 30 pts)*
Dundee – 240–300 pts (Ger courses except under **300 pts**)
Heriot-Watt – CCC (Maths Ger)
Salford – 240–300 pts (Ger with 2nd Lang)
Swansea – 240–300 pts (Ger courses)
Ulster – 240 pts (Ger courses)
220 pts **Hull** – 220–280 pts (Ger courses except under **320/280 pts**)
Nottingham Trent – 220 pts (Ger courses)
200 pts **Anglia Ruskin** – 200 pts (Int Bus Ger)
Central Lancashire – 200 pts (Ger Bus Ger)
Hertfordshire – 200–240 pts (Mgt Sci Ger)
Lincoln – 200 pts (Bus Ger)
Manchester Met – 200 pts (Fr Ger; Ger Ital/Span) *(IB 28 pts)*
Napier – 200 pts (Ger courses)
Plymouth – 200–260 pts (Ger courses except under **280 pts**)
Portsmouth – 200–280 pts (Ger St)
Sheffield Hallam – 200 pts (Int Bus Ger; Ger Mark; Ger Tour)
180 pts **Greenwich** – 180 pts (Ger courses)
Manchester Met – 180 pts (Ger Cult St; Ger Engl; Ger Intnet Mgt) *(IB 28 pts)*
Northampton – 180–220 pts (Ger courses)
160 pts **Wolverhampton** – 160–220 pts (Ger courses)
80 pts **London (Birk)** – 80 pts (p/t Ger Mgt; Modn Grmny St)

Leeds Met – contact University

Alternative offers

See **Chapter 8** for grade/point equivalences and related information for the following examinations: Scottish qualifications, the Welsh Baccalaureate, the IB diploma (approximate points shown also in italics in the table of offers), the Irish Leaving Certificate, the European Baccalaureate and the French Baccalaureate.

CHOOSING YOUR COURSE (SEE ALSO CH.1)

Course variations – Widen your options
International Business and German (Aston)
German and Japanese (Cardiff)
Combined courses (Central Lancashire)
International Business and German (Greenwich)

Accounting and German (Hertfordshire)
German and Management (Hull)
German Studies and Economics (Lancaster)
German and Hispanic Studies (Liverpool)
German and Digital Humanities (London (King's))
German and Music (Nottingham)
English and German Literature (Warwick)
Linguistics and German (Wolverhampton).
CHECK PROSPECTUSES AND WEBSITES FOR OTHER UNIVERSITIES AND COLLEGES OFFERING THESE COURSES.

Universities and colleges teaching quality See www.qaa.ac.uk; www.unistats.com.

Top universities and colleges (Research) Aston; Birmingham*; Bristol; Cambridge; Edinburgh; Exeter*; Liverpool; London (King's)*, (QM), (RH)*, (UCL)*; Manchester*; Nottingham*; Oxford*; Swansea; Warwick.

ADMISSIONS INFORMATION

Number of applicants per place (approx) Aston 4; Bangor 6; Birmingham 6; Bradford 6; Bristol 3; Cardiff 6; Central Lancashire 2; Durham 4; East Anglia 4; Exeter 4; Heriot-Watt 10; Hull 12; Kent 10; Lancaster 7; Leeds (joint hons) 8; Leicester 4; London (King's) 5, (QM) 6, (RH) 5, (UCL) 4; Newcastle 6; Nottingham 14; Portsmouth 5; Salford 5; Staffordshire 5; Stirling 6; Surrey 2; Swansea 4; Warwick (Ger Bus St) 16, (Ger) 8; York 6.

Advice to applicants and planning the UCAS personal statement Describe visits to Germany or a German-speaking country and the particular cultural and geographical features of the region. Contacts with friends in Germany and language experience should also be mentioned, and if you are bilingual, say so. Read German newspapers and magazines and keep up-to-date with national news. **Leeds** See **Languages. Nottingham** We are looking for a high degree of competence in using and understanding German, a genuine determination to develop skills in linguistic comprehension and analysis, a love of literature, an imaginative approach to it and a keen interest in German affairs. **Portsmouth** Experience of German-speaking countries not necessary. **St Andrews** Evidence of interest and reasons for choosing the course. **Swansea** We like students who have been to Germany or are planning to go.

Misconceptions about this course Leeds See **Languages. Swansea** Some students are afraid of the year abroad, which is actually one of the most enjoyable parts of the course.

Selection interviews Yes Bangor, Birmingham (short conversation in German), Bradford, Cambridge, Durham, East Anglia, Exeter, Heriot-Watt, Huddersfield, Hull, Kingston, Liverpool, Liverpool John Moores, London (RH), (UCL), Newcastle, Oxford, Sheffield, Southampton, Surrey (always); **Some** Cardiff, Leeds, Portsmouth, Staffordshire, Swansea.

Interview advice and questions Questions asked on A-level syllabus. Part of the interview may be in German. What foreign newspapers and/or magazines do you read? Questions on German current affairs, particularly politics and reunification problems, books read outside the course, etc. **Leeds** See **Languages**. See **Chapter 7**.

Reasons for rejection (non-academic) Unstable personality. Poor motivation. Insufficient commitment. Unrealistic expectations. Not interested in spending a year abroad.

AFTER-RESULTS ADVICE

Offers to applicants repeating A-levels Higher Birmingham, Glasgow, Leeds, Warwick; **Same** Aston, Bradford, Brighton, Cardiff, Chester, Durham, East Anglia, London (RH), Newcastle (not always), Nottingham, Salford, Staffordshire, Surrey, Swansea, Ulster, York; **No offers made** Cambridge.

GRADUATE DESTINATIONS AND EMPLOYMENT (2005/6 HESA)

Graduates surveyed 510 **Employed** 275 **In further study** 100 **Assumed unemployed** 30.

Career note See **Languages**.

OTHER DEGREE SUBJECTS FOR CONSIDERATION
East European Studies; European Studies; International Business Studies.

GREEK
(see also **Classical Studies/Classical Civilisation** and **Classics**)

Courses are offered in Ancient and Modern Greek, covering the language and literature from ancient times to present day.

Useful websites www.greek-language.com; www.arwhead.com/Greeks; www.greekmyth.org; www.fhw.gr; www.culture.gr; www.greeklanguage.gr.

NB The points totals shown to the left of the institutions are for ease of reference only. It must not be assumed that tariff points are always used by institutions or that they can be substituted for an offer in grades. The level of an offer is not necessarily indicative of the quality of a course.

COURSE OFFERS INFORMATION
Subject requirements/preferences **GCSE** English and a foreign language required. Greek required by some universities. **AL** Latin, Greek or a foreign language may be specified by some universities. **NB** A* grades are likely to form part of university offers in the higher ranges for students applying for places in 2008 for entry in 2009: check websites.

Your target offers
360 pts and above
Cambridge – AAA (Modn Mediev Lang (Class Gk) (Modn Gk); Class Gk Lat; Orntl St (ECANE)) *(IB 38–42 pts)*
340 pts Durham – AAB–BBB (Class (Gk lang option); Comb St Gk)
Newcastle – AAB (Comb St (Gk))
St Andrews – AAB (Gk courses) *(IB 36 pts)*
320 pts Glasgow – ABB (Gk courses)
Leeds – ABB (Gk courses)
London (UCL) – ABB+AS–BBB+AS (Gk Lat)
Manchester – ABB (Gk; Gk Engl Lit)
300 pts Edinburgh – BBB (Gk St; Class Arch Gk)
London (King's) – BBB (Gk Engl) *(IB 32 pts)*
London (RH) – BBB (Gk courses)
280 pts London (King's) – BBC (Modn Gk St Ling)
240 pts Swansea – 240–280 pts (Gk joint courses)
200 pts Lampeter – 200–300 pts (Gk joint courses)

Alternative offers
See **Chapter 8** for grade/point equivalences and related information for the following examinations: Scottish qualifications, the Welsh Baccalaureate, the IB diploma (approximate points shown also in italics in the table of offers), the Irish Leaving Certificate, the European Baccalaureate and the French Baccalaureate.

CHOOSING YOUR COURSE (SEE ALSO CH.1)
Course variations – Widen your options
Classics (Bristol)
Arts Combined – Greek (Durham)
Philosophy and Greek (Edinburgh)
Modern Greek Studies with Linguistics (London (King's))
Classics (Greek and Latin) (Nottingham)
CHECK PROSPECTUSES AND WEBSITES FOR OTHER UNIVERSITIES AND COLLEGES OFFERING THESE COURSES.

Universities and colleges teaching quality See www.qaa.ac.uk; www.unistats.com.

Top universities and colleges (Research) See **Classics**.

ADMISSIONS INFORMATION
Number of applicants per place (approx) Lampeter 1; Leeds 2; London (King's) 3.

Advice to applicants and planning the UCAS personal statement See **Classical Studies/Classical Civilisation**.

Selection interviews **Yes** Cambridge, Lampeter, London (RH).

Interview advice and questions Questions asked on A-level syllabus. Why do you want to study Greek? What aspects of this course interest you? (Questions will develop from answers.) See also **Chapter 7**.

Reasons for rejection (non-academic) Poor language ability.

AFTER-RESULTS ADVICE
Offers to applicants repeating A-levels **Higher** St Andrews; **Same** Leeds; **No offers made** Cambridge.

GRADUATE DESTINATIONS AND EMPLOYMENT (2005/6 HESA)
Graduates surveyed 5 **Employed** 5 **In further study** none **Assumed unemployed** none.

Career note See **Languages**.

OTHER DEGREE SUBJECTS FOR CONSIDERATION
Ancient History; Classical Studies; Classics; European Studies; Philosophy.

HEALTH SCIENCES/STUDIES
(including **Audiology, Chiropractic** and **Osteopathy;** see also **Community Studies, Environmental Science/Studies, Nursing and Midwifery, Optometry, Physiotherapy, Podiatry, Radiography, Social Work** and **Sports Science/Studies**)

Health Sciences/Studies is a broad subject-field which offers courses covering both practical applications concerning health and well-being (some of which border on nursing) and also the administrative activities involved in the promotion of health in the community. Also included are some specialised careers which include **Chiropractic**, involving the healing process by way of manipulation, mainly in the spinal region, and **Osteopathy** in which joints and tissues are manipulated to correct abnormalities. **Audiology** is concerned with the treatment and diagnosis of hearing and balance disorders while **Prosthetics** and **Orthotics** involve the provision and fitting of artificial limbs.

Useful websites www.riph.org.uk; www.bmj.com; www.reflexology.org; www.baap.org.uk; www.chiropractic-uk.co.uk; www.osteopathy.org.uk; www.who.int; www.i-cm.org.uk; www.csp.org.uk; www.scienceyear.com; www.intute.ac.uk.

NB The points totals shown to the left of the institutions are for ease of reference only. It must not be assumed that tariff points are always used by institutions or that they can be substituted for an offer in grades. The level of an offer is not necessarily indicative of the quality of a course.

COURSE OFFERS INFORMATION
Subject requirements/preferences **GCSE** English, mathematics and a science important or essential for some courses. **AL** Mathematics, chemistry or biology may be required for some courses. **NB** A* grades are likely to form part of university offers in the higher ranges for students applying for places in 2008 for entry in 2009: check websites.

For information on how to read the Subject Tables, see **Chapter 8**.

Your target offers

350 pts Southampton – BBBb (Audiology) *(IB 34 pts)*

300 pts Bristol – BBB–ABB (Audiology) *(IB 32–34 pts)*
Essex – 300–260 pts (Hlth Hum Sci) *(IB 28–30 pts)*
Glamorgan – 300–340 pts (Chiropractic)
Oxford Brookes – BBB (Osteopathy – check with University)
Sheffield – BBB or BBbb (Orthoptics) *(IB 29 pts)*

280 pts Aberdeen – BBC 2nd yr entry (Hlth Sci; Hlth Sci (Hlth Soty) (Hlth Spo) (Hlth Nutr); Hlth Serv Rsch)
Aston – BBC (Audiology) *(IB 30 pts)*
Bangor – 280 pts (Hlth Soc Cr)
Brighton – 280 pts (Hlth Soc Cr) *(IB 28 pts)*
British Sch Ost – BBC (Osteopathy)
Hertfordshire – 280 pts (Paramed Sci)
London (UCL) – BCCe (Audiology) *(IB 32 pts)*
Manchester – BBC (Audiology)
Queen Margaret – BBC 280 pts (Audiology)

260 pts Oxford Brookes – BCC (Exer Nutr Hlth joint courses)
Sheffield – BCC (Hlth Hum Sci) *(IB 29 pts)*

240 pts Aberdeen – CCC 1st yr entry (Hlth Sci; Hlth Sci (Hlth Nutr) (Hlth Spo) (Hlth Soty); Hlth Serv Rsch)
Aberystwyth – 240 pts (Genet Hum Hlth)
Bournemouth Anglo Euro (Coll) – 240 pts (Chiropractic – apply direct, not in UCAS scheme)
Bristol – CCC (Df St) *(IB 30 pts)*
De Montfort – 240 pts (Audiology)
Dundee – 240 pts (Oral Hlth Sci)
Essex – 240–260 pts (Env Lf Health)
Greenwich – 240 pts (Osteopathy)
Kent – 240–260 pts (Hlth Soc Cr Prac) *(IB 27 pts)*
Leeds – CCC–CC (Audiology)
Manchester – CCC (Oral Hlth Sci)
Manchester Met – CCC (Hlth Soc Cr + Fdn Yr)
Nescot – 240 pts (Ost Med)
Northumbria – 240 pts (Cr Educ (Ely Yrs Disab St) (Ely Yrs Prof Prac); Hlth Soc Cr)
Nottingham Trent – 240 pts (Hlth Env)
Queen Margaret – BCD 240 pts (Hlth Psy)
Salford – 240 pts (Pros Orthot)
Strathclyde – CCC/BCD (Env Hlth; Pros Orthot)
Swansea – 240 pts (Audiology)
Teesside – 240 pts (Hlth Psy)

220 pts Anglia Ruskin – 220 pts (Hlth Psy)
Bath Spa – 220 pts (Diet Hlth; Hlth St courses)
Birmingham City – 220 pts (Hlth St; Hlth Pol Mgt)
British Coll Ost Med – 220–260 pts (Ost Med)
Coventry – 220 pts (Hlth Lfstl Mgt)
Hertfordshire – 220 pts (Radiothera Onc)
Liverpool Hope – 220 pts (Hlth Comb Hons)

200 pts Abertay Dundee – CDD (Hlth Sci; Mntl Hlth Cnslg)
Bedfordshire – 200 pts (Exer Fit Prac)
Gloucestershire – 200 pts (Commun Hlth St; Exer Hlth Sci Psy)
Huddersfield – 200–220 pts (Hlth Commun St; Hlth Soc Welf)
Kent – 200 pts (Hlth Soc Cr)
Lincoln – 200 pts (Hlth St courses; Acpntr; Herb Med)

Manchester Met – CDD 200 pts (Env Hlth; Hlth St courses)
Middlesex – 200–240 pts (Env Hlth)
Napier – 200 pts (Complem Thera; Herb Med; Hlth Soty)
Plymouth – 200 pts (Hlth Soc Cr St)
Southampton Solent – 200 pts (Hlth Psy)
Sunderland – 200 pts (Hlth St; Hlth Soc Cr; Commun Hlth Inform)
Thames Valley – 200 pts (Hlth St Sci)
UHI Millennium Inst – 200 pts (Hlth St)

180 pts **Bolton** – 180 pts (Commun Hlth)
Bristol UWE – 180–220 pts (Hlth Sfty Env)
Cardiff (UWIC) – 180 pts (Complem Thera)
Greenwich – 180 pts (Pblc Hlth)
Liverpool John Moores – 180 pts (Commun Hlth Soc Welf; Pblc Hlth)
Northampton – 180–220 pts (Hlth St courses)
Salford – 180–200 pts (Hlth Sci Soc Pol; Hlth Sci; Exer Hlth Sci; Trad Chin Med; Complem Med Hlth Sci)
Sheffield Hallam – 180–200 pts (Pblc Hlth Nutr)
Southampton Solent – 180 pts (Hlth Fit Mgt; Hlth Exer Physl Actvt)
Teesside – 180–240 pts (Fd Nutr Hlth Sci; Pblc Hlth)
Trinity Carmarthen (Coll) – 180 pts (Hlth Exer; Hlth Exer Out Educ; Hlth Exer Spo St)

160 pts **Anglia Ruskin** – 160 pts (Complem Med (Aroma) (Rflxgy))
Bedfordshire – 160–240 pts (Hlth Soc Cr; Hlth Psy)
Canterbury Christ Church – CC (Hlth St)
Central Lancashire – 160–200 pts (Hlth St courses; Exer Nutr Hlth; Df St; Herb Med; Hom Med)
Derby – 160–180 pts (Complem Thera)
East London – 160 pts (Fit Hlth; Pblc Hlth; Hlth Prom courses; Hlth Serv Mgt; Complem Med; Herb Med)
European Sch Ost – CC 160–280 pts flexible approach (Osteopathy)
Greenwich – 160 pts (Hlth courses; Complem Thera)
London Met – 160 pts (Hlth Prom; Herb Medicin Sci)
North East Wales (IHE) – 160 pts (Occ Hlth Sfty Env Mgt; Complem Med Prac)
St Mary's (UC) – 160–200 pts (Hlth Exer)
Westminster – CC (Hlth Sci (Complem Thera) (Herb Med) (Hom) (Nutr Thera) (Ther Bdwk); Trad Chin Med)
Wolverhampton – 160–220 pts (Complem Thera; Hlth St; Df St)
Worcester – 160 pts (Hlth St Psy)

140 pts **Suffolk (Univ Campus)** – 140–200 pts (Nutr Hlth)

120 pts **Bradford (Coll)** – DD 120 pts (Hlth Soc Welf)
Brighton – 120 pts check with admissions tutor (Orntl Med (Acpnctr))
Derby – 120 pts (Heal Arts courses)
Gloucestershire – 120 pts (Hlth Commun Soc Cr)
London South Bank – 120 pts (Hlth Prot)
Roehampton – 120 pts (Hlth St; Nutr Hlth)
Sheffield Hallam – 120 pts (Hlth Inform)
West Scotland – DD (Hlth Sci; Occ Sfty Hlth)

80 pts **Arts London (CFash)** – 80 pts (Cos Sci)
Kingston – 80 pts (Acupuncture)
Swansea (Inst) – 80 pts (Hlth St courses)
Worcester – EE 80 pts (Hlth Sci)

Leeds Met – contact University
Middlesex – contact University (Trad Chin Med)
Open University – contact University

Alternative offers

See **Chapter 8** for grade/point equivalences and related information for the following examinations: Scottish qualifications, the Welsh Baccalaureate, the IB diploma (approximate points shown also in italics in the table of offers), the Irish Leaving Certificate, the European Baccalaureate and the French Baccalaureate.

EXAMPLES OF FOUNDATION DEGREES IN THE SUBJECT FIELD

(See also **Social and Public Policy and Administration**)

Abingdon (Coll); Arts London (CFash); Barnet (Coll); Barnfield (Coll); Bath City (Coll); Bath Spa; Bedford (Coll); Bedfordshire; Bexley (Coll); Bishop Auckland (Coll); Bolton; Bolton (CmC); Bournemouth and Poole (Coll); Bradford; Bradford (Coll); Brighton; Brighton & Hove City (Coll); Bristol City (Coll); Bristol UWE; Bucks New; Bromley (Coll); Burnley (Coll); Calderdale (Coll); Canterbury (Coll); Canterbury Christ Church; Cardiff (UWIC); Central Lancashire; Chesterfield (Coll); Cirencester (Coll); City; Colchester (Inst); Coleg Sir Gar; Cornwall (Coll); Cumbria; Derby; Dewsbury (Coll); Dunstable (Coll); Durham New (Coll); East Berkshire (Coll); East London; Edge Hill; Exeter (Coll); Farnborough (CT); Gateshead (Coll); Glamorgan; Gloucestershire (CAT); Great Yarmouth (Coll); Greenwich; Grimsby (IFHE); Hartpury (Coll); Herefordshire (CAT); Hopwood Hall (Coll); Hugh Baird (Coll); Hull (Coll); Kendal (Coll); Kingston; Kingston (Coll); Leeds Thomas Danby (Coll); London Met; Loughborough (Coll); Manchester (CAT); Manchester Met; Matthew Boulton (CFHE); Middlesex; Myerscough (Coll); Newcastle (Coll); Newman (UC); North East London (Coll); North East Wales (IHE); Northumberland (Coll); Norwich City (Coll); Open University; Park Lane Leeds (Coll); Penwith (Coll); Peterborough Reg (Coll); Plymouth (CT); Portsmouth; Preston (Coll); Redcar (Coll); Richmond upon Thames (Coll); Riverside Halton (Coll); St Helens (Coll); St Mary's (UC); Salisbury (Coll); Sheffield (Coll); Shipley (Coll); Shrewsbury (CAT); Somerset (CAT); South Birmingham (Coll); South Downs (Coll); Southampton; Stratford-upon-Avon (Coll); Stockport (Coll); Stockton Riverside (Coll); Suffolk (Univ Campus); Sunderland; Sunderland City (Coll); Sussex Downs (Coll); Sutton Coldfield (Coll); Swansea (Coll); Swindon New (Coll); Teesside; Telford (CAT); Thames Valley; Totton (Coll); Trinity Carmarthen (Coll); Truro (Coll); Tyne Met (Coll); Wakefield (Coll); Walsall (Coll); Warwickshire (Coll); West Anglia (Coll); West Herts (Coll); West Kent (Coll); West Nottinghamshire (Coll); Weston (Coll); Weymouth (Coll); Wigan and Leigh (Coll); Wolverhampton City (Coll); Worcester; Worcester (CT); Yeovil (Coll); York (Coll); York St John.

CHOOSING YOUR COURSE (SEE ALSO CH.1)

Course variations – Widen your options

Genetics and Human Health (Aberystwyth)

Exercise and Fitness Practice (Bedfordshire)

Diagnostic Radiotherapy (Birmingham City)

Occupational Therapy (Bournemouth)

Complementary Healthcare (Brighton)

Environmental Health (Bristol UWE)

Health and Lifestyle Management (Coventry)

Women's Health (Edge Hill)

Health and Child Development (Greenwich)

Podiatry (Huddersfield)

Health and Social Care Practice (Kent)

Exercise, Nutrition and Health (Kingston)

Audiology (Leeds)

Oral Health Science (Manchester)

Occupational Health (North East Wales (IHE))

Clinical Physiology (Portsmouth)

Homeopathy (Westminster)

CHECK PROSPECTUSES AND WEBSITES FOR OTHER UNIVERSITIES AND COLLEGES OFFERING THESE COURSES.

Universities and colleges teaching quality See www.qaa.ac.uk; www.unistats.com.

Top universities and colleges (Research) Aston (Audiology).

ADMISSIONS INFORMATION

Number of applicants per place (approx) Bangor 2; Bath Spa 1; Bournemouth 4; Bournemouth Anglo Euro (Coll) 1; British Sch Ost 5; Brunel 2; Central Lancashire 6; Chester 6; Chichester 5; Cumbria 4; European (Sch Ost) 3; Huddersfield (Hlth Spo St) 4; Liverpool John Moores 10; London Met 7; Manchester Met 10; Middlesex 4; Northampton 3; Portsmouth 12; Roehampton 10; Salford 8; Southampton 4; Swansea 1; Worcester 3.

Advice to applicants and planning the UCAS personal statement You should describe any work with people you have done, particularly in a caring capacity, for example, working with the elderly, nursing, hospital work. Give evidence of why you wish to study this subject. Evidence of people orientated work experience. (Chiropractic) You should provide clear evidence of why you wish to follow this career. Give evidence of talking to a chiropractor and details of any work using your hands. (Osteopathy) Evidence required for motivation to study Osteopathy through work experience or general hobbies/activities, communication skills, a caring nature and people orientation. **Bangor** (Hlth Soc Cr) Applicants should be able to communicate and work in a group. They should also have an interest in the non-nursing side of health authorities. Evidence needed to indicate that applicants have an understanding of the NHS and health care systems. **European Sch Ost** Evidence of interest in the caring professions. Some work experience in an osteopathic practice preferable. **Liverpool John Moores** Information on relevant experience, reasons for wanting to do this degree and the types of careers sought would be useful.

Misconceptions about this course There is a mistaken belief that all courses cover nursing. **Bangor** (Hlth Soc Cr) This is an administration course, not a nursing course. **Brit Coll Ost Med** Some students think that we offer an orthodox course in medicine. **European Sch Ost** We do not teach in French although we do have a franchise with a French school based in St Etienne and a high percentage of international students. All lectures are in English. Applicants should note that cranial osteopathy – one of our specialisms – is only one aspect of the programme.

Selection interviews Yes Aston, Bristol, Central Lancashire, Chichester, Coventry, European Sch Ost, Glamorgan, Middlesex, Nottingham Trent, Worcester **Some** Bath Spa, Canterbury Christ Church, Derby, Huddersfield (mature students), Liverpool John Moores, Salford, Swansea.

Interview advice and questions Courses vary considerably and you are likely to be questioned on your reasons for choosing the course at that university or college. If you have studied biology then questions are possible on the A-level syllabus and you could also be asked to discuss any work experience you have had. (Chiropractic) Interview questions are likely to arise about your reasons for choosing this career and your discussions with a chiropractor. Be aware of the differences between the work of chiropractors, osteopaths and physiotherapists. (Osteopathy) What personal qualities would you need to be a good osteopath? What have you done that you would feel demonstrates a sense of responsibility? What would you do if you were not able to secure a place on an Osteopathy course this year? International applicants will be verbally tested on their ability in spoken English at interview. **Liverpool John Moores** Interviews are informal. It would be useful for you to bring samples of coursework to the interview. See **Chapter 7**.

Reasons for rejection (non-academic) Some students are mistakenly looking for a professional qualification in, for example, occupational therapy, nursing. Inability to be aware of the needs of others (in the environmental health field). **Coventry** Inadequate mathematics. **Salford** (Trad Chn Med) No experience of communicating with people. No knowledge of Chinese Medicine.

AFTER-RESULTS ADVICE

Offers to applicants repeating A-levels Same Aston, Bangor, Brighton, Chester, Derby, European Sch Ost, Huddersfield, Lincoln, Liverpool John Moores, Nottingham Trent (Hlth Env), Roehampton, Salford, Surrey, Swansea.

GRADUATE DESTINATIONS AND EMPLOYMENT (2005/6 HESA)
Complementary Medicine graduates surveyed 445 **Employed** 270 **In further study** 25 **Assumed unemployed** 20. See also **Dentistry, Medicine, Nursing and Midwifery, Nutrition, Optometry, Physiotherapy, Podiatry** and **Radiography**.

Career note Graduates enter a very broad variety of careers depending on their specialism. Opportunities exist in the public sector, eg management and administrative positions with health and local authorities and in health promotion. Others enter many other careers recruiting graduates in any subjects.

OTHER DEGREE SUBJECTS FOR CONSIDERATION
Audiology; Biological Sciences; Biology; Community Studies; Consumer Studies; Dentistry; Dietetics; Medicine; Nursing; Occupational Therapy; Optometry; Physiotherapy; Psychology; Podiatry; Radiography; Speech Therapy; Sport Science.

HISTORY

(including **Heritage Management** and **Medieval Studies; see also **History (Ancient)**, **History (Economic and Social)** and **History of Art**)

Degrees in History cover a very broad field with many courses focusing on British and European history. However, specialised History degrees are available which cover other regions of the world and, in addition, all courses will offer a wide range of modules.

Useful websites www.english-heritage.org.uk; www.historytoday.com; www.genhomepage.com; www.historynet.com; www.archives.org.uk; www.rhs.ac.uk; www.nationalarchives.gov.uk; www.historesearch.com.

NB The points totals shown to the left of the institutions are for ease of reference only. It must not be assumed that tariff points are always used by institutions or that they can be substituted for an offer in grades. The level of an offer is not necessarily indicative of the quality of a course.

COURSE OFFERS INFORMATION
Subject requirements/preferences **GCSE** English and a foreign language may be required or preferred. **AL** History usually required at a specified grade. (Medieval Studies) History or English literature required for some courses. (Viking Studies) English or history. **NB** A* grades are likely to form part of university offers in the higher ranges for students applying for places in 2008 for entry in 2009: check websites.

Your target offers
360 pts and above

    Bristol – AAA–AAB (Hist St Ger; Econ Hist; Hist) *(IB 36–38 pts)*

    Cambridge – AAA (Hist; Hist Educ St) *(IB 38–42 pts)*

    Durham – AAA (Hist; Modn Langs Hist; Engl Lit Hist; Anc Mediev Modn Hist) *(IB 40 pts)*

    Exeter – AAA–AAB 360–340 pts (Hist; Hist Pol; Hist Euro; Hist Int Rel)

    London (King's) – AAAb (Hist courses) *(IB 36–37 pts)*

    London (UCL) – AAA–AAB+AS (Hist courses) *(IB 36–39 pts)*

    Manchester – AAA–BBB (Hist courses) *(IB 32–37 pts)*

    Oxford – Offers vary eg AAA–AAB (Hist Econ; Anc Modn Hist; Hist Engl; Hist Modn Lang; Hist Pol) *(IB 38–42 pts)*

    Sussex – AAA (Contemp Hist Lang)

    Warwick – AABc (Hist (Modn) (Ren Modn); Hist Cult courses; Hist Pol) *(IB 37–38 pts)*

340 pts **Birmingham** – AAB (Hist courses) *(IB 34–36 pts)*

    Durham – AAB (Hist Comb Hons Soc Sci)

    East Anglia – AAB–BBB (Hist; Modn Hist; Hist Pol; Hist Land Arch; Euro Hist Lang; Hist Hist Med) *(IB 31–33 pts)*

Exeter – AAB–ABB 340–320 pts (Hist courses except under **360 pts**)
Leeds – AAB–ABB (Hist courses) *(IB 30–31 pts)*
Liverpool – AAB (Hist; Engl Modn Hist)
London (King's) – AAB (War St courses) *(IB 36–37 pts)*
London (LSE) – AAB (Gov Hist)
London (RH) – AAB–ABB (Hist courses) *(IB 35 pts)*
Newcastle – AAB (Hist; Pol Hist; Arch Hist) *(IB 35 pts)*
Nottingham – AAB (Hist; Hist Pol) *(IB 37 pts)*
St Andrews – AAB (Mediev Hist courses; Modn Hist courses; Scot Hist courses; Mediev St)
     (IB 36–38 pts)
Sheffield – AAB–BBB (Hist courses) *(IB 32–35 pts)*
Sussex – AAB–BBB (Hist; Hist Anth; Hist Film St; Hist Lang; Intlctl Hist)
York – AAB (Hist courses) *(IB 37 pts)*

320 pts **Cardiff** – ABB–BBB (Hist courses)
Durham – ABB (Educ St (Hist))
Glasgow – ABB–BBB (Hist courses; Scot Hist) *(IB 30 pts)*
Lancaster – ABB (Hist; Mediev Ren St; Engl Lit Hist)
Leicester – ABB–BBB 320–300 pts (Hist; Engl Hist) *(IB 34 pts)*
Liverpool – ABB (Modn Hist Pol) *(IB 33 pts)*
London (LSE) – ABB (Hist; Int Rel Hist) *(IB 37 pts)*
London (QM) – 320 pts (Hist; Jrnl Contemp Hist; Film St Hist; Fr Hist; Hist Ger Lang; Modn
     Contemp Hist) *(IB 30 pts)*
Nottingham – ABB (Hist courses; Hist Contemp Chin St)
Southampton – ABB–BBB (Hist courses) *(IB 32 pts)*
Stranmillis (UC) – ABB (Hist Educ)

300 pts **Dundee** – 300 pts 2nd yr entry (Hist; Scot Hist St)
Edinburgh – BBB (Hist courses) *(IB 34 pts)*
Essex – 300–260 pts (Hist courses) *(IB 28–32 pts)*
Hull – BBB–BBC (Hist courses)
Kent – 300–280 pts (Hist courses except under **260/280 pts**) *(IB 28–32 pts)*
Lancaster – BBB (Hist courses except under **320 pts**)
Leicester – BBB–BBC 300 pts (Contemp Hist; Hist Pol; Hist Arch; Int Rel Hist; Engl Hist) *(IB
     34 pts)*
Liverpool – BBB–BBC (Hist Fr/Ger; Hist Hisp St)
London (Gold) – BBB–BBC (Hist; Hist Hist Ideas; Hist Sociol; Hist Anth; Hist Pol)
Queen's Belfast – BBB–BBC (Modn Hist; Byz St courses; Hist Sci)

280 pts **East Anglia** – BBC–BCC (Am Hist Engl Hist; Am Hist Pol)
Glasgow (Crichton) – BBC (Scot St)
Huddersfield – 280 pts (Hist courses)
Kent – 280–260 pts (Hist joint courses; Hist Arch St) *(IB 28–32 pts)*
Lincoln – 280 pts (Film TV Hist)
Northumbria – 280 pts (Br Am Cult; Engl Hist; Hist)
Nottingham – BBC (Viking St)
Oxford Brookes – BBC–BCC (Hist joint courses)
Reading – 280–300 pts (3AL+AS) (Hist; Modn Hist Int Rel; Hist Euro Lit Cult; Modn Hist Pol)
     (IB 32 pts)
Stirling – BBC–CCC (Hist courses; Scot Hist) *(IB 28 pts)*

260 pts **Aberystwyth** – 260–300 pts (Hist courses; Musm Gllry St; Welsh Hist) *(IB 28–30 pts)*
Brunel – 260 pts (Hist; Pol Hist) *(IB 28 pts)*
Keele – 260–280 pts (Am St Hist; Hist courses) *(IB 28–30 pts)*
Kent – 260 pts (Ger Hist; Fr Hist; Engl Lang St Hist) *(IB 28–32 pts)*
Leicester – 260–320 pts BCC (Hist Comb courses) *(IB 30–34 pts)*
London (SOAS) – BCC (Hist courses) *(IB 30–32 pts)*
Northumbria – 260 pts (Hist Pol; Hist Sociol)

Richmond (Am Int Univ) – 260 pts (History)
Strathclyde – BCC–BB (History)
240 pts **Aberdeen** – CCC (Hist courses; Scot St; Celt Civ Hist Art)
Bradford – 240 pts (Hist Law; Hist Pol; Hist Phil; Modn Euro Hist)
Brighton – CCC (Cult Hist St) *(IB 28 pts)*
Bristol UWE – 240–300 pts (Hist courses) *(IB 28–30 pts)*
Cardiff (UWIC) – 240 pts (Modn Hist Pol; Modn Hist Pop Cult)
Chester – 240–260 pts (Hist courses) *(IB 30 pts)*
Coventry – 240–260 pts (Hist courses)
Cumbria – 240 pts (Educ Hist)
Dundee – 240 pts 1st yr entry (Hist; Scot Hist St)
Glasgow Caledonian – 240 pts (Psy (Hist))
Hertfordshire – 240 pts (Hist courses)
Liverpool Hope – 240 pts (Hist courses)
Portsmouth – 240–300 pts (Hist; Am St Hist; Hist Pol; Int Rel Hist; Hist joint courses)
Roehampton – 240–300 pts (Hist courses)
Sheffield Hallam – 240 pts (Hist; Engl Hist)
Swansea – 240–300 pts (Mediev St courses; Hist courses)
Ulster – CCC 240 pts (Irish Hist; Hist courses)
Westminster – CCC (Modn Hist)
Winchester – 240–280 pts (Hist courses)
220 pts **Bangor** – 220–260 pts (Hist joint courses; Herit Arch Hist; Mediev Ely Modn Hist; Welsh Hist courses)
Bath Spa – 220–260 pts (History)
Central Lancashire – 220 pts (Hist Mus Herit; Modn Wrld Hist; Hist)
Chichester – 220–240 pts (Hist courses) *(IB 26 pts)*
De Montfort – 220–240 pts (Hist; Hist joint courses)
Gloucestershire – 220 pts (Hist; Herit Mgt; Herit Mgt Hist)
Kingston – 220–320 pts (Hist; Hist joint courses)
Lincoln – 220 pts (History)
Manchester Met – 220 pts (Hist courses) *(IB 24–26 pts)*
Nottingham Trent – 220 pts (Hist courses)
200 pts **Anglia Ruskin** – 200 pts (Hist; Hist Engl; Hist Sociol)
Bolton – 200–240 pts (Hist courses)
Central Lancashire – 200 pts (Hist Am St; Hist Engl Lit; Hist Law)
Cumbria – 200 pts (Hist; Hist Am St)
Glamorgan – 200–240 pts (Hist; Modn Euro)
Huddersfield – 200–280 pts (Pol Contemp Hist)
London Met – 200–240 pts (Hist courses)

Newport – 200 pts (Hist courses)
Plymouth – 200–240 pts (Hist courses)
Sunderland – 200 pts (Hist courses)
180 pts **Buckingham** – 180 pts (Engl Lit Hist)
Greenwich – 180 pts (History)
Lampeter – 180–300 pts (Hist courses; Mediev St; Modn Hist St; Welsh St; Ch Hist Anc Hist)
Northampton – 180–220 pts (Hist courses)
Salford – 180–200 pts (Contemp Hist Pol; Contemp Mltry Int Hist)
160 pts **Bishop Grosseteste (UC)** – 160 pts (Educ St Hist)
Bournemouth – 160 pts (Arch Prehist; Herit Cons)
Canterbury Christ Church – CC (Hist courses)
Derby – 160–240 pts (Hist courses)
East London – 160 pts (Hist courses)
Edge Hill – 160–180 pts (Hist courses)
Leeds Trinity and All Saints (Coll) – 160–240 pts (Hist; Engl Hist)
Liverpool John Moores – 160–240 pts (Hist courses)
Newman (UC) – 160–240 pts (Hist courses)
North East Wales (IHE) – 160–200 pts (Hist courses)
SAC (Scottish CAg) – CC (Rur Recr Tour Mgt Herit St)
St Mary's (UC) – 160–200 pts (Hist courses)
Staffordshire – 160–200 pts (Modn Hist courses)
Wolverhampton – 160–220 pts (App Hist St; Hist; War St Hist)
Worcester – 160–200 pts (Hist courses)
York St John – 160 pts (Hist courses)
140 pts **Bishop Grosseteste (UC)** – 140 pts (Herit St)
Suffolk (Univ Campus) – 140–200 pts (Hist courses)
Teesside – 140 pts (Hist; Modn Contemp Euro Hist; Soc Cult Hist; Hist Media St)
120 pts **Bradford (Coll)** – 120 pts (Humanities)
Peterborough Reg (Coll) – 120 pts (Engl Hist; Hist Sociol)
South Devon (Coll) – 120 pts (Arts (Engl Hist))
80 pts **Bournemouth** – 80 pts (Engl Hist)
East Lancashire (IHE) – 80 pts (Hist courses)
Havering (Coll) – 80 pts (Hist courses)
Lincoln – 80–240 pts (Cons Restor)
London (Birk) – 80 pts for under 21s (over 21s varies) (p/t Hist; Hist Arch)
North Lindsey (Coll) – 80 pts (History)
UHI Millennium Inst – 80 pts (Scot Hist)
West Anglia (Coll) – 80 pts (Engl Hist; Sociol Hist)
Wigan and Leigh (Coll) – 80 pts (Hist Comb Hons)

Leeds Met – contact University

Alternative offers
See **Chapter 8** for grade/point equivalences and related information for the following examinations: Scottish qualifications, the Welsh Baccalaureate, the IB diploma (approximate points shown also in italics in the table of offers), the Irish Leaving Certificate, the European Baccalaureate and the French Baccalaureate.

EXAMPLES OF FOUNDATION DEGREES IN THE SUBJECT FIELD
Bath Spa; Blackpool and Fylde (Coll); Cumbria; Truro (Coll); Winchester.

CHOOSING YOUR COURSE (SEE ALSO CH.1)
Course variations – Widen your options
Scientific and Natural History Illustration (Blackpool & Fylde (Coll))
Archaeology and Pre-history (Bournemouth)

For information on how to read the Subject Tables, see **Chapter 8**.

Fashion and Dress History (Brighton)
Ancient and Medieval History (Cardiff)
Race and Ethnic Studies and History (Central Lancashire)
Forensic Biology and History (Chester)
Scottish History (Edinburgh)
Marine and Natural History Photography (Falmouth (UC))
Church History (Lampeter)
International History and Politics (Leeds)
Government and History (London (LSE))
Contemporary History (Sussex)
European History (Swansea)
History and Culture (Warwick)
CHECK PROSPECTUSES AND WEBSITES FOR OTHER UNIVERSITIES AND COLLEGES OFFERING THESE COURSES.

Universities and colleges teaching quality See www.qaa.ac.uk; www.unistats.com.

Top universities and colleges (Research) Birmingham; Cambridge*; Cardiff; Dundee; Durham*; East Anglia*; Edinburgh; Essex; Exeter; Glasgow; Hertfordshire; Huddersfield; Hull; Keele; Leeds; Leicester; Liverpool; London (King's)*, (LSE)*, (QM), (RH), (SOAS)*, (UCL); Manchester; Oxford; Oxford Brookes*; Queen's Belfast; Roehampton; St Andrews; Sheffield; Sheffield Hallam; Southampton; Stirling; Teesside; Warwick; York.

Sandwich degree courses Bangor (workplace modules).

ADMISSIONS INFORMATION

Number of applicants per place (approx) Aberystwyth 6; Anglia Ruskin 4; Bangor 6; Bath Spa 6; Birmingham 7, (E Medit Hist) 3; Bournemouth (Herit Cons) 3; Bristol 25; Bristol UWE 6; Brunel 6; Buckingham 10; Cambridge 4; Cardiff 7; Central Lancashire 5; Chichester 4; Cumbria 5; De Montfort 10; Dundee 6; Durham 15; East Anglia 8; Edge Hill 8; Exeter 9; Gloucestershire 26; Huddersfield 4; Hull 5; Kent 12; Kingston 6; Lampeter 6; Lancaster 11; Leeds 12; Leeds Trinity and All Saints (Coll) 14; Leicester 7; Liverpool 6; London (Gold) 6, (King's) 10, (LSE) 10, (Gov Hist) 10, (QM) 5, (RH) 9, (UCL) 13; London Met 2; Manchester Met 8; Middlesex 10; Newcastle 13; Newman (UC) 2; North East Wales (IHE) 2; Northampton 4; Nottingham 20; Oxford (success rate 39%); Oxford Brookes 25; Portsmouth 5; Richmond (Am Int Univ) 2; Roehampton 3; St Mary's (UC) 5; Sheffield Hallam 21; Southampton 12; Staffordshire 8; Stirling 2; Teesside 4; Warwick 17; York 10; York St John 3.

Advice to applicants and planning the UCAS personal statement Show your passion for the past! Visits to places of interest should be mentioned, together with any particular features which impressed you. Read historical books and magazines outside your A-level syllabus. Mention these and describe any special areas of study which interest you. (Check that these areas are covered in the courses for which you are applying!) **Bangor** Clear commitment to history/archaeological studies through, for example, work experience, travel. **Birmingham** An interest in the past above and beyond school work. **London (King's)** History books read and enjoyed – why? **(UCL)** We are impressed by a genuine academic passion for the subject for which you are applying. We are looking for teachable, committed students who will contribute to class discussion. **Nottingham** Active engagement with history and enthusiasm for the subject. **Portsmouth** Write clearly and concisely. **St Andrews** Reasons for choosing the course. Evidence of interest. **Southampton** Demonstrate through the personal statement an enthusiasm to study a range of periods, approaches and geographical areas.

Misconceptions about this course Students sometimes under-estimate the amount of reading required. **Lincoln** Some students expect the subject to be assessed only by exams and essays. It is not – we use a wide range of assessment methods. **Liverpool John Moores** Some applicants think that they have to study ancient and medieval history as well as modern; we actually only cover post-1750 history. **Stirling** Some applicants think that we only teach British history. We also cover European, American, African and Environmental History.

Selection interviews Yes Bangor, Birmingham (Mediev St) (all), (E Medit Hist), Bishop Grosseteste

(UC), Brighton, Bristol, Brunel, Cambridge, Edge Hill, Essex, Hertfordshire, Hull, Lancaster, Leeds Trinity and All Saints (Coll), Lincoln (Cons Restor), London (King's), (QM), (RH), (UCL), London Met, London South Bank, Middlesex, Oxford, Oxford Brookes, Portsmouth, Roehampton, Sussex, Warwick; **Some** Anglia Ruskin, Bath Spa, Buckingham, Cardiff, Chichester, De Montfort, Dundee, Exeter, Huddersfield, Kent, Lampeter, Lincoln, Liverpool, London (LSE) (rarely), Salford, Sheffield Hallam, Southampton, Staffordshire, Winchester, Wolverhampton, York.

Interview advice and questions Questions are almost certain to be asked on those aspects of the history A-level syllabus which interest you. Examples of questions in previous years have included: Why did imperialism happen? If a Martian arrived on Earth what aspect of life would you show him/her to sum up today's society? Has the role of class been exaggerated by Marxist historians? What is the difference between power and authority and between patriotism and nationalism? Did Elizabeth I have a foreign policy? What is the relevance of history in modern society? Who are your favourite monarchs? How could you justify your study of history to the taxpayer? **Cambridge** How would you compare Henry VIII to Stalin? In the 1920s did the invention of the Henry Ford car lead to a national sub-culture or was it just an aspect of one? Is there such a thing as 'race'? Should historians be allowed to read sci-fi novels? **Cumbria** Questions about interest in research, analysis, argument, information gathering, future plans after study, motivation. **De Montfort** Why History? Why is history important? **Oxford** Questions on submitted work and the capacity to think independently. **Oxford** What are the origins of your name? Why are you sitting in this chair? **Swansea** We ask applicants to explain something – a hobby, an historical problem or a novel. The subject is less important than a coherent and enthusiastic explanation. See **Chapter 7**.

Applicants' impressions (A=Open day; B=Interview day) Bristol (A) The open day consisted of a tour of the city, accommodation and a talk to lecturers and current students. **Cardiff** (A) There was a tour of halls, the students' union and the History department. There was also a talk by staff and the opportunity to speak to the students. **Exeter** (A) There was a well-planned tour, a talk about the course and chance to speak to students. **Reading** (A) We were given a talk by the History department staff and a tour of the campus, halls and students' union. We also had the opportunity to speak to staff and students.

Reasons for rejection (non-academic) Personal statements which read like job applications, focusing extensively on personal skills and saying nothing about the applicant's passion for history. Poor use of personal statement combined with predicted grades. Little commitment and enthusiasm. No clear reason for choice of course. Little understanding of history. Absence or narrowness of intellectual pursuits. Deception or concealment on the UCAS application. His knowledge of 19th century history (his chosen subject) did not have any depth. Unwillingness to learn. Narrow approach to subject. Failure to submit requested information. **Birmingham** Commitment insufficient to sustain interest over three years. **London (King's)** Inability to think analytically and comparatively. **(UCL)** The vast majority of applications are of a very high standard, many applicants being predicted AAA grades. We view each application as a complete picture, taking into account personal statement, reference and performance at any interview as well as actual and predicted academic performance. There is no single rule by which applicants are selected and therefore no single reason why they are rejected. **Nottingham** No discrimination against Oxbridge applicants.

AFTER-RESULTS ADVICE
Offers to applicants repeating A-levels Higher Exeter, Glasgow, Huddersfield, Lampeter, Leeds, Liverpool, St Andrews, Warwick; **Possibly higher** Aberystwyth, Birmingham, Cambridge, Portsmouth; **Same** Anglia Ruskin, Bangor, Buckingham, Bristol, Cardiff, Chester, Chichester, De Montfort, Dundee, Durham, East Anglia, Edge Hill, Hull, Kent, Lancaster, Lincoln, Liverpool Hope, Liverpool John Moores, London (QM), (RH), (SOAS), Newcastle, Newman (UC), Newport, Nottingham Trent, Oxford Brookes, Richmond (Am Int Univ), Roehampton, St Mary's (UC), Staffordshire, Stirling, Suffolk (Univ Campus), Winchester, Wolverhampton, York, York St John.

GRADUATE DESTINATIONS AND EMPLOYMENT (2005/6 HESA)
Graduates surveyed 6930 **Employed** 3125 **In further study** 1590 **Assumed unemployed** 450.

For information on how to read the Subject Tables, see **Chapter 8**.

Career note Graduates enter a broad spectrum of careers. Whilst a small number seek positions with museums and galleries, most will enter careers in management, public and social services and retail as well as the teaching profession.

OTHER DEGREE SUBJECTS FOR CONSIDERATION
Ancient History; Anthropology; Archaeology; Economic and Social History; Government; History of Art; International Relations; Medieval History; Politics.

HISTORY (ANCIENT)
(see also **History**)

Ancient History covers the Greek and Roman world, the social, religious, political and economic changes taking place in the Byzantine period and the medieval era which followed.

Useful websites www.rhs.ac.uk; www.guardians.net; www.arwhead.com/Greeks; www.ancientworlds.com; www.bbc.co.uk/history/ancient; www.historesearch.com/ancient.html.

NB The points totals shown to the left of the institutions are for ease of reference only. It must not be assumed that tariff points are always used by institutions or that they can be substituted for an offer in grades. The level of an offer is not necessarily indicative of the quality of a course.

COURSE OFFERS INFORMATION
Subject requirements/preferences **GCSE** A foreign language or classical language may be required. **AL** History or classical civilisation may be preferred subjects. **NB** A* grades are likely to form part of university offers in the higher ranges for students applying for places in 2008 for entry in 2009: check websites.

Your target offers

360 pts and above
London (UCL) – AABe–BBBe (Anc Hist; Anc Hist Egypt)
Oxford – Offers vary eg AAA–AAB (Anc Modn Hist; Class Arch Anc Hist)
Warwick – ABBc–BBBc (Anc Hist Class Arch)

340 pts Durham – AAB (Anc Mediev Modn Hist)
Exeter – AAB–BBB (Anc Hist; Anc Hist Arch)
St Andrews – AAB (Anc Hist courses) *(IB 36 pts)*

320 pts Bristol – ABB (Anc Hist; Anc Hist Arch) *(IB 32 pts)*
Cardiff – ABB–BBB (Anc Hist courses)
Leeds – ABB (Gk Civ Hist)
London (King's) – ABB+AS (Anc Hist) *(IB 32 pts)*
Manchester – ABB (Anc Hist courses)
Newcastle – ABB–BBC (Anc Hist courses)

300 pts Durham – BBB (Anc Hist Arch)
Edinburgh – BBB (Anc Hist; Anc Hist Class Arch; Anc Hist Gk; Anc Hist Lat)
Leicester – BBB 300–360 pts (Anc Hist Hist; Anc Hist Arch; Comb St)
Liverpool – BBB (Anc Hist Arch; Anc Hist Comb Hons; Egypt; Arch Anc Civ; Egypt Arch)
London (RH) – BBB (Anc Hist)
Nottingham – ABC–BBB (Anc Hist; Anc Hist Arch; Anc Hist Hist; Anc Hist Lat)
Queen's Belfast – BBB–BBC (Anc Hist courses; Byz St)

280 pts Birmingham – BBC (Hist Anc Mediev; Anc Hist; Arch Anc Hist Hist E Medit) *(IB 33- 34 pts)*
Reading – 280–300 pts (Anc Hist) *(IB 30 pts)*

240 pts Swansea – 240–280 pts (Anc Hist courses)

180 pts Lampeter – 180–200 pts (Anc Mediev Hist; Anc Hist Arch; Anc Hist)

Alternative offers
See **Chapter 8** for grade/point equivalences and related information for the following examinations:

Scottish qualifications, the Welsh Baccalaureate, the IB diploma (approximate points shown also in italics in the table of offers), the Irish Leaving Certificate, the European Baccalaureate and the French Baccalaureate.

CHOOSING YOUR COURSE (SEE ALSO CH.1)
Course variations – Widen your options
Ancient History and Archaeology (Bristol)
Ancient and Medieval History (Lampeter)
Greek Civilisation and History (Leeds)
Byzantine Studies (Queen's Belfast)
Egyptology and Ancient History (Swansea)
CHECK PROSPECTUSES AND WEBSITES FOR OTHER UNIVERSITIES AND COLLEGES OFFERING THESE COURSES.

Universities and colleges teaching quality See www.qaa.ac.uk; www.unistats.com.

Top universities and colleges (Research) See **Classics**.

ADMISSIONS INFORMATION
Number of applicants per place (approx) Birmingham 8; Bristol 11; Cardiff 4; Durham 12; Leicester 32; London (RH) 3; Newcastle 10; Nottingham 10; Oxford 2.

Advice to applicants and planning the UCAS personal statement Any information about experience of excavation or museum work should be given. Visits to Greece and Italy to study archaeological sites should be described. **Liverpool** (Egypt) Interest in Ancient Egypt developed through, for example reading, television and the Internet. Course covers archaeology and the writings of Ancient Egypt. Be aware of the work of the career archaeologist, for example, sites and measurement officers, field officers and field researchers (often specialists in pottery, glass, metalwork). See also **History**.

Misconceptions about this course **Liverpool** (Egypt) Some students would have been better advised looking at V400 Archaeology or VV16 Ancient History and Archaeology, both of which offer major pathways in the study of Ancient Egypt.

Selection interviews **Yes** Birmingham, Durham, Leeds, London (RH), Oxford; **Some** Cardiff, Newcastle.

Interview advice and questions See **History**.

Applicants' impressions (A=Open day; B=Interview day) **Bristol** (A) There were sample lectures, a question-and-answer session and a tour of halls. **London (RH)** (B) I had a relatively informal interview followed by a session on finance and a talk about the course. **(UCL)** A 30-minute interview, quite intellectually demanding. **Swansea** (B) Nice interview. I was asked general questions, testing my knowledge, but it was mainly structured round my personal statement.

Reasons for rejection (non-academic) **Liverpool** (Egypt) Egyptology used to fill a gap on the UCAS application. Applicant misguided in choice of subject.

AFTER-RESULTS ADVICE
Offers to applicants repeating A-levels **Same** Birmingham, Cardiff, Durham, Newcastle.

GRADUATE DESTINATIONS AND EMPLOYMENT (2005/6 HESA)
See **History**.

Career note See **History**.

OTHER DEGREE SUBJECTS FOR CONSIDERATION
Anthropology; Archaeology; Classical Studies; Classics; Greek; History of Art; Latin.

HISTORY (ECONOMIC and SOCIAL)

(see also **History**)

Economic and Social History is a study of societies and economies and explores the changes that have taken place in the past and the causes and consequences of those changes. The study can cover Britain, Europe and other major powers.

Useful websites www.rhs.ac.uk; www.ehs.org.uk; see also **Economics** and **History**.

NB The points totals shown to the left of the institutions are for ease of reference only. It must not be assumed that tariff points are always used by institutions or that they can be substituted for an offer in grades. The level of an offer is not necessarily indicative of the quality of a course.

COURSE OFFERS INFORMATION

Subject requirements/preferences **GCSE** Mathematics usually required and a language may be preferred. **AL** History preferred. **NB** A* grades are likely to form part of university offers in the higher ranges for students applying for places in 2008 for entry in 2009: check websites.

Your target offers

360 pts and above

   Warwick – AAAb (Econ Econ Hist)

340 pts London (LSE) – AAB (Econ Hist; Econ Hist Econ; Econ Econ Hist) *(IB 36 pts)*

   York – AAB (Econ Econ Hist)

320 pts Birmingham – ABB (Econ Soc Hist)

   Glasgow – ABB (Econ Soc Hist)

300 pts Edinburgh – BBB (Econ Hist; Econ Soc Hist; Econ Soc Hist Env St)

   Essex – 300 pts (Soc Cult Hist)

   Lancaster – BBB (Soc Hist)

   Manchester – BBB (Econ Hist Econ) *(IB 32–34 pts)*

280 pts Hull – 280 pts (Hist Soc Hist; Hist Econ)

   Liverpool – BBC 320 pts (Hist (Soc Econ)) *(IB 30 pts)*

260 pts Aberystwyth – 260–300 pts (Econ Soc Hist; Econ Soc Hist Bus Mgt; Hist Econ Soc Hist) *(IB 29 pts)*

240 pts Swansea – 240–300 pts (Econ Soc Hist courses)

220 pts Manchester Met – 220 pts (Bus Econ Soc Hist)

Alternative offers

See **Chapter 8** for grade/point equivalences and related information for the following examinations: Scottish qualifications, the Welsh Baccalaureate, the IB diploma (approximate points shown also in italics in the table of offers), the Irish Leaving Certificate, the European Baccalaureate and the French Baccalaureate.

CHOOSING YOUR COURSE (SEE ALSO CH.1)

Course variations – Widen your options

Business Management and Economic and Social History (Aberystwyth)

Political Economy (Birmingham)

Social and Cultural History (Essex)

Modern History – Politics (London (RH))

CHECK PROSPECTUSES AND WEBSITES FOR OTHER UNIVERSITIES AND COLLEGES OFFERING THESE COURSES.

Universities and colleges teaching quality See www.qaa.ac.uk; www.unistats.com.

Top universities and colleges (Research) Birmingham; Edinburgh; Glasgow; Hull; London (LSE).

ADMISSIONS INFORMATION

Number of applicants per place (approx) Birmingham 10; Hull 4; Liverpool 3; London (LSE) (Econ Hist) 3, (Econ Hist Econ) 5; York 8.

Advice to applicants and planning the UCAS personal statement See **History**.

Selection interviews Yes Aberystwyth, Birmingham, Liverpool, Warwick.

Interview advice and questions See **History**.

AFTER-RESULTS ADVICE
Offers to applicants repeating A-levels Higher Warwick, York; **Possibly higher** Liverpool; **Same** Hull.

GRADUATE DESTINATIONS AND EMPLOYMENT (2005/6 HESA)
See **History**.

Career note See **History**.

OTHER DEGREE SUBJECTS FOR CONSIDERATION
Economics; Government; History; Politics; Social Policy and Administration; Sociology.

HISTORY OF ART

History of Art (and Design) courses differ slightly between universities although most will focus on the history and appreciation of European art and architecture from the 14th to 20th centuries. Some courses also cover the Egyptian, Greek and Roman periods and, in the case of London (SOAS), Asian, African and European Art. The history of all aspects of design and film can also be studied in some courses. There has been an increase in the popularity of these courses in recent years.

Useful websites www.artchive.com; www.artcyclopedia.com; www.artguide.org; www.artefact.co.uk; www.fine-art.com; www.nationalgallery.org.uk; www.britisharts.co.uk; www.tate.org.uk.

NB The points totals shown to the left of the institutions are for ease of reference only. It must not be assumed that tariff points are always used by institutions or that they can be substituted for an offer in grades. The level of an offer is not necessarily indicative of the quality of a course.

COURSE OFFERS INFORMATION
Subject requirements/preferences GCSE English required and a foreign language usually preferred. **AL** History is preferred for some courses. **NB** A* grades are likely to form part of university offers in the higher ranges for students applying for places in 2008 for entry in 2009: check websites.

Your target offers

360 pts and above
    Bristol – AAA–BBC (Hist Art; Hist Art St Abrd; Hist Art Fr/Ger/Ital/Port/Russ/Span) *(IB 32–38 pts)*
    Cambridge – AAA (Hist Art) *(IB 38–42 pts)*
    London (UCL) – AABe–BBBe (Hist Art courses)
    Oxford – Offers vary eg AAA–AAB (Hist Art) *(IB 38–42 pts)*
    Warwick – ABBc–BBBc (Hist Art; Hist Art Fr St) *(IB 32–34 pts)*

340 pts **East Anglia** – AAB–BBB (Hist Art; Hist Art Aus/N Am; Hist Art Hist; Art Hist Phil; Hist Art Lit; Hist Art Hist Euro Lit; Arch Anth Art Hist)
    St Andrews – AAB (Art Hist Class St; Art Hist; Art Hist Engl; Art Hist Gk; Art Hist Int Rel; Art Hist Mediev Hist; Art Hist Modn Hist; Art Hist Psy)
    York – AAB (Hist Hist Art) *(IB 32–34 pts)*

320 pts **Birmingham** – ABB–BBB 300–320 pts (Hist Art; Hist Art Ital St; Hist Art Port; Hist Art Russ St; Hist Art Phil; Hist Art Theol; Hist Art Am Can St; Modn Lang Hist Art) *(IB 34 pts)*
    Glasgow – ABB–BBB (Hist Art) *(IB 30 pts)*
    St Andrews – ABB (Art Hist courses except under **340 pts**) *(IB 32–36 pts)*
    Sussex – ABB–BBB **or** 340 pts 3AL+AS (Art Hist courses) *(IB 32–34 pts)*
    York – ABB (Engl Hist Art)

300 pts **Edinburgh** – BBB (Hist Art; Hist Art Archit Hist; Hist Art Chin St; Hist Art Engl Lit; Hist Art Hist Mus)

Essex – 300–340 pts (Hist Art; Hist Modn Contemp Art; Lit Hist Art; Film St Hist Art; Hist Art Modn Lang)

Hull – 300 pts (Hist Art courses)

Kent – 300 pts (Hist Phil Art (Art Hist); Hist Phil Art)

London (Court) – BBB (Hist Art)

London (SOAS) – 300 pts (Hist Art; Hist Art Arch) *(IB 30 pts)*

Manchester – BBB (Art Arch Anc Wrld; Hist Art)

Nottingham – ABC–BBB (Art Hist; Arch Art Hist; Art Hist Class Civ; Art Hist Ger)

Oxford Brookes – BBB–BBC (Hist Art courses)

Reading – 300–280 pts (Art Hist Art; Anc Hist Hist Art; Arch Hist Art; Class St Hist Art; Engl Hist Art; Film Thea Hist Art; Hist Hist Art; Fr/Ger/Ital Hist Art; Typo Hist Art Archit) *(IB 30 pts)*

York – BBB (Hist Art) *(IB 32 pts)*

280 pts **Leeds** – BBC–ABB (Hist Art; Hist Art Musm St) *(IB 32 pts)*

London (Gold) – BBC (Hist Art)

260 pts **Aberystwyth** – 260 pts (Art Hist; Art Hist Fine Art; Musm Gllry St) *(IB 27–29 pts)*

Leicester – BCC–BBC 260–340 pts (Hist Art) *(IB 30 pts)*

Northumbria – 260 pts (Hist Modn Art Des Film)

240 pts **Aberdeen** – CCC 1st yr entry (Hist Art courses)

Brighton – CCC (Musm Herit St; Hist Decr Arts Crfts; Hist Des Cult Soty; Vis Cult) *(IB 28 pts)*

220 pts **Kingston** – 220–320 pts (Hist Art Des Film courses)

Manchester Met – 220 pts (Hist Art Des)

Plymouth – 220–300 pts (Fine Art Art Hist)

200 pts **Central Lancashire** – 200 pts (Art Hist Vis Cult courses)

Middlesex – 200–240 pts (Hist Art courses)

Roehampton – 200–280 pts (Art Hist courses)

180 pts **Liverpool John Moores** – 180–260 pts (Hist Art Musm St)

Northampton – 180 pts (Hist Art Des courses)

Plymouth – 180–220 pts (Art Hist)

160 pts **Cardiff (UWIC)** – 160 pts (Art Art Hist)

East London – 160 pts (Vis Theor)

Lincoln – 160 pts (Cons Restor)

120 pts **Northbrook (Coll)** – 120 pts (Hist Vis Cult)

80 pts **London (Birk)** – 80 pts for under 21s (over 21s varies) (p/t Hist Art)

Alternative offers

See **Chapter 8** for grade/point equivalences and related information for the following examinations: Scottish qualifications, the Welsh Baccalaureate, the IB diploma (approximate points shown also in italics in the table of offers), the Irish Leaving Certificate, the European Baccalaureate and the French Baccalaureate.

CHOOSING YOUR COURSE (SEE ALSO CH.1)

Course variations

Art History and Fine Art (Aberystwyth)

Museum and Gallery Studies (Aberystwyth)

Archaeology, Anthropology and Art History (East Anglia)

Architectural History (Edinburgh)

History of Modern and Contemporary Art (Essex)

History and Philosophy of Art (Kent)

History of Art, Design and Film (Kingston)

Creative Arts (Lancaster)

History of Art and Museum Studies (Liverpool John Moores)

For a quick reference offers calculator, fold out the inside back cover.

History of Art and Architecture and Tibetan (London (SOAS))
History of Modern Art, Design and Film (Northumbria)
CHECK PROSPECTUSES AND WEBSITES FOR OTHER UNIVERSITIES AND COLLEGES OFFERING THESE COURSES.

Universities and colleges teaching quality See www.qaa.ac.uk; www.unistats.com.

Top universities and colleges (Research) Birmingham; Cambridge; East Anglia; Essex; Glasgow; London (UCL); Manchester; Middlesex; St Andrews; Sussex; Warwick.

ADMISSIONS INFORMATION
Number of applicants per place (approx) Aberystwyth 9; Birmingham 6; Brighton 8; Bristol 10; Cambridge 4; East Anglia 7; Essex 5; Kent 3; Kingston 4; Leeds 29; Leicester 10; Liverpool John Moores 2; London (Gold) 10, (SOAS) 4; Manchester Met 10; Northampton 2; Nottingham 10; Portsmouth 8; York 6.

Advice to applicants and planning the UCAS personal statement Applicants for History of Art courses should have made extensive visits to art galleries, particularly in London, and should be familiar with the main European schools of painting. Evidence of lively interest required. Discuss your preferences and say why you prefer certain types of work or particular artists. You should also describe any visits to museums and any special interests in furniture, pottery or other artefacts (see also **Appendix 2**). **Aberystwyth** Attendance at evening classes in art history (if not at A-level). Related hobbies and interests, for example, reading, literature, music, cinema. **Kent** An interest in Modern Period (especially). An interest in all the arts. **London (Gold)** Art enthusiasms, influences, passions. **St Andrews** Reasons for choosing the course and evidence of interest. Sport/extra-curricular activities and positions of responsibility. **York** Visit art galleries, read books on the subject.

Misconceptions about this course Kent The History of Art is not a practical course in fine arts. **York** Students do not need a background in art or art history. It is not a course with a studio element in it.

Selection interviews Yes Brighton, Cambridge, East Anglia (majority), London (UCL), Manchester Met, Warwick; **Some** Bristol, Buckingham, Central England, Kent.

Interview advice and questions Some universities set slide tests on painting and sculpture. Those applicants who have not taken history of art at A-level will be questioned on their reasons for choosing the subject, their visits to art galleries and museums and their reactions to the art work which has impressed them. **Kent** Do they visit art galleries? Have they studied art history previously? What do they expect to get out of the degree? Sometimes they are given images to compare and discuss. See **Chapter 7**.

Applicants' impressions (A=Open day; B=Interview day) East Anglia (B) I had a 25-minute informal chat with one interviewer who made me feel at ease. It was a well-organised interview and she knew what she wanted to find out. It's a modern campus with a good art collection. Students took prospective students on tours round the campus and advised us on university life. I strongly recommend the course.

Reasons for rejection (non-academic) Poorly presented practical work. Students who do not express any interest or enthusiasm in contemporary visual arts are rejected.

AFTER-RESULTS ADVICE
Offers to applicants repeating A-levels Possibly higher Oxford Brookes, St Andrews; **Same** Aberystwyth, East Anglia, Huddersfield, Kent, Leeds, Warwick, York; **No offers made** Cambridge.

GRADUATE DESTINATIONS AND EMPLOYMENT (2005/6 HESA)
No data available.

Career note Work in galleries, museums and collections will be the objective of many graduates who should try to establish contacts by way of work placements and experience during their undergraduate years. The personal skills acquired during their studies however, open up many opportunities in other careers.

For information on how to read the Subject Tables, see **Chapter 8**.

OTHER DEGREE SUBJECTS FOR CONSIDERATION
Art; Archaeology; Architecture; Classical Studies; Photography.

HORTICULTURE
(including **Garden Design;** see also **Landscape Architecture**)

Horticulture is a broad subject area which covers commercial horticulture and the provision of recreational and leisure facilities (amenity horticulture).

Useful websites www.iagre.org; www.rhs.org.uk; www.horticulture.org.uk.

NB The points totals shown to the left of the institutions are for ease of reference only. It must not be assumed that tariff points are always used by institutions or that they can be substituted for an offer in grades. The level of an offer is not necessarily indicative of the quality of a course.

COURSE OFFERS INFORMATION
Subject requirements/preferences **GCSE** Mathematics sometimes required. **AL** A science subject may be required or preferred for some courses.

Your target offers
240 pts **Aberdeen** – 240 pts (Plant Soil Sci)
220 pts **Reading** – 220 pts (Horticulture) *(IB 27 pts)*
160 pts **Bristol UWE** – 160 pts (Amen Hort Mgt) *(IB 28 pts)*
         SAC (Scottish CAg) – CC (Hort Plntsmn; Hort)
140 pts **Writtle (Coll)** – 140 pts (Hort; Hort Bus Mgt; Land Amen Mgt; Hort Crop Prod; Int Hort)
120 pts **Greenwich** – 120 pts (Hort (Commer); Medcnl Hort)
         Worcester – DD 120 pts (Horticulture)
  80 pts **Myerscough (Coll)** – 80 pts (Anim Hort Thera)

Alternative offers
See **Chapter 8** for grade/point equivalences and related information for the following examinations: Scottish qualifications, the Welsh Baccalaureate, the IB diploma (approximate points shown also in italics in the table of offers), the Irish Leaving Certificate, the European Baccalaureate and the French Baccalaureate.

EXAMPLES OF FOUNDATION DEGREES IN THE SUBJECT FIELD
Askham Bryan (Coll); Bicton (Coll); Bishop Burton (Coll); Bournemouth; Bristol UWE; CAFRE; Duchy (Coll); Falmouth (UC); Greenwich; Harper Adams (UC); Hartpury (Coll); Moulton (Coll); Myerscough (Coll); Northampton; Nottingham Trent; Pershore (Coll); Plumpton (Coll); Plymouth; SAC (Scottish CAg); Sparsholt (Coll); Warwickshire (Coll); Welsh Hort (Coll); Wolverhampton; Worcester; Writtle (Coll).

CHOOSING YOUR COURSE (SEE ALSO CH.1)
Course variations – Widen your options
Amenity Horticulture Management (Bristol UWE)
Garden Design and Environment (Falmouth (UC))
Commercial Horticulture (Greenwich)
Medicinal Horticulture (Greenwich)
Retail Horticultural Management (Myerscough (Coll))
CHECK PROSPECTUSES AND WEBSITES FOR OTHER UNIVERSITIES AND COLLEGES OFFERING THESE COURSES.

Sandwich degree courses Greenwich; Nottingham Trent.

ADMISSIONS INFORMATION
Number of applicants per place (approx) Greenwich 4; SAC (Scottish CAg) 1; Writtle (Coll) 3.

Advice to applicants and planning the UCAS personal statement Practical experience is important and visits to botanical gardens (the Royal Botanic Gardens, Kew or Edinburgh and the Royal Horticultural Society gardens at Wisley) could be described. Contact your local authority offices for details of work in parks and gardens departments. **Greenwich** An enthusiasm for horticulture, plants, science, technology and the land-based industries on a scale from worldwide to organic smallholdings. See also **Appendix 2**.

Misconceptions about this course Greenwich (Hort (Commer)) Students are unaware of the scope of this degree. The course covers commercial horticulture – plants, plant products, ornamentals, bedding plants, hardy trees and shrubs, salads, vegetables, fruit and organic crops from production to marketing.

Selection interviews Yes Greenwich, SAC (Scottish CAg), Worcester.

Interview advice and questions Past questions have included: How did you become interested in horticulture? How do you think this course will benefit you? Could you work in all weathers? What career are you aiming for? Are you interested in gardening? Describe your garden. What plants do you grow? How do you prune rose trees and fruit trees? Are there any EU policies at present affecting the horticulture industry? Topics relating to the importance of science and horticulture. See **Chapter 7**.

AFTER-RESULTS ADVICE
Offers to applicants repeating A-levels Same Greenwich, SAC (Scottish CAg).

GRADUATE DESTINATIONS AND EMPLOYMENT (2005/6 HESA)
See **Agricultural Sciences/Agriculture**.

Career note Graduates seeking employment in horticulture will look towards commercial organisations for the majority of openings. These will include positions as growers and managers with fewer vacancies for scientists involved in research and development and advisory services for which degree courses are primarily aimed.

OTHER DEGREE SUBJECTS FOR CONSIDERATION
Agriculture; Crop Science; Landscape Architecture; Plant Sciences.

HOSPITALITY and HOTEL MANAGEMENT
(including **Events Management;** see also **Business Courses, Consumer Studies/Sciences, Food Science/Studies and Technology, Leisure and Recreation Management Studies** and **Tourism and Travel**)

Courses cover the full range of skills required for those working in the industry. Specific studies include management, food and beverage supplies, equipment design, public relations and marketing. Depending on the course, other topics may include events management, tourism and the international trade.

Useful websites www.baha.org.uk; www.cordonbleu.net; www.instituteofhospitality.org; www.people1st.co.uk.

NB The points totals shown to the left of the institutions are for ease of reference only. It must not be assumed that tariff points are always used by institutions or that they can be substituted for an offer in grades. The level of an offer is not necessarily indicative of the quality of a course.

COURSE OFFERS INFORMATION
Subject requirements/preferences GCSE English and mathematics usually required together with a foreign language for International Management courses. **AL** No specified subjects. **NB** A* grades are likely to form part of university offers in the higher ranges for students applying for places in 2008 for entry in 2009: check websites.

280 pts **Surrey** – 280 pts (Int Hspty Mgt; Int Hspty Tour Mgt) *(IB 30–32 pts)*

240 pts **Bournemouth** – 240 pts (Evnts Mgt)

Brighton – 240 pts (Entre Hspty; Int Hspty Mgt; Hspty Evnt Mgt; Mark Fd Drnk) *(IB 28 pts)*

Chester – 240 pts (Evnts Mgt)

Oxford Brookes – BCD (Hspty Mgt courses; Int Hspty Mgt)

Ulster – CCC–CCD (Int Hspty Mgt; Leis Evnts Cult Mgt; Int Hspty St Fr/Ger/Span; Int Htl Tour Mgt)

Winchester – 240 pts (Evnt Mgt)

220 pts **Central Lancashire** – 220–240 pts (Hspty Mgt Int Hspty Mgt)

Gloucestershire – 220 pts (Hspty Mgt; Int Hspty Mgt; Evnt Mgt) *(IB 26–30 pts)*

Liverpool John Moores – 220 pts (Evnts Mgt)

Strathclyde – CCD/BC (Hspty Mgt)

200 pts **Central Lancashire** – 200–260 pts (Evnt Mgt)

London Met – 200 pts (Evnts Mgt Spo Mgt; Int Hspty Mgt)

Manchester Met – 200 pts (Hspty Mgt; Hspty Mgt Tour; Hspty Mgt Culn Arts; Int Hspty Mgt; Hspty Lic Rtl Mgt; Evnts Mgt) *(IB 28 pts)*

Napier – 200 pts (Hspty Mgt courses; Fstvl Evnts Mgt)

Plymouth – 200 pts (Hspty Mgt; Int Hspty Mgt; Cru Op Mgt; Evnts Mgt) *(IB 24 pts)*

Portsmouth – 200 pts (Hspty Mgt; Hspty Mgt Tour)

Sheffield Hallam – 200 pts (Hspty Bus Mgt courses; Int Htl Mgt; Evnts Mgt courses)

Staffordshire – BB (Evnts Mgt)

180 pts **Birmingham (UC)** – 180–200 pts (Hspty Bus Mgt; Hspty Fd Mgt; Hspty Tour Mgt; Culn Arts Mgt; Fd Rtl Mgt; Hspty Leis Mgt; Mark Evnts Mgt; Mark Hspty Mgt; Hspty Lic Rtl Mgt)

Bournemouth – 180 pts (Hspty Mgt)

East London – 180 pts (Evnts Mgt)

Glamorgan – 180–220 pts (Evnt Mgt)

Greenwich – 180 pts (Evnts Mgt)

Huddersfield – 180–200 pts (Hspty Mgt Modn Lang; Hspty Mgt Tour Leis; Hspty Mgt; Evnts Mgt)

Northampton – 180–220 pts (Evnts Mgt)

Queen Margaret – BC/DDD (Hspty Tour Mgt; Int Hspty Mgt; Evnts Mgt)

Salford – DDD 180 pts (Hspty Mgt; Hspty Tour Mgt; Hspty Leis Mgt) *(IB 26 pts)*

160 pts **Bedfordshire** – 160 pts (Evnts Mgt)

Canterbury Christ Church – 160 pts (Evnt Mgt)

Derby – 160–80 pts (Hspty Mgt; Hspty Advntr Mgt)

Glasgow Caledonian – CC (Hspty Mgt; Enter Evnts Mgt)

London Met – 160 pts (Evnts Mgt)

Robert Gordon – CC 160 pts (Int Hspty Mgt)

Thames Valley – 160–180 pts (Culn Arts Mgt; Hspty Mgt; Hspty Mgt Fd St; Media Evnts Mgt) *(IB 28 pts)*

West Scotland – CC (Evnts Mgt)

Wolverhampton – 160–220 pts (Int Hspty Mgt; Evnts Vnu Mgt Mgt courses)

140 pts **Bishop Grosseteste (UC)** – 140 pts (Arts Evnts Mgt)

Blackpool and Fylde (Coll) – DEE 140 pts (Hspty Mgt; Hspty Mgt (Int Htl Mgt))

Bournemouth (AI) – 140 pts (Arts Evnt Prod)

Cardiff (UWIC) – CD 140 pts (Hspty Mgt courses; Evnts Mgt)

Derby – 140–160 pts (Evnts Mgt)

Southampton Solent – 140 pts (Evnt Mgt; Hspty Mgt)

Suffolk (Univ Campus) – 140 pts (Evnt Mgt)

120 pts **Bucks New** – 120 pts (Evnt Fstvl Mgt)

Colchester (Inst) – DD 120 pts (Hspty Mgt)

Llandrillo Cymru (Col) – 120–80 pts (Htl Hspty Mgt; Evnts Mgt)

Leeds Met – contact University

Alternative offers

See **Chapter 8** for grade/point equivalences and related information for the following examinations: Scottish qualifications, the Welsh Baccalaureate, the IB diploma (approximate points shown also in italics in the table of offers), the Irish Leaving Certificate, the European Baccalaureate and the French Baccalaureate.

EXAMPLES OF FOUNDATION DEGREES IN THE SUBJECT FIELD

Accrington and Rossendale (Coll); Bedford (Coll); Birmingham (UC); Bishop Grosseteste (UC); Blackpool and Fylde (Coll); Bournemouth; Bradford (Coll); Brighton; Brighton and Hove City (Coll); Bristol City (Coll); Bromley (CFHE); Bucks New; Central Lancashire; Cirencester (Coll); Colchester (Inst); Cornwall (Coll); Croydon (Coll); Darlington (CT); Derby; Doncaster (Univ Centre); Gloucestershire; Gloucestershire (CAT); Greenwich; Herefordshire (CAD); Kendal (Coll); Liverpool (CmC); Llandrillo Cymru (Col); Loughborough (Coll); Manchester City (Coll); Middlesbrough (Coll); Newcastle (Coll); North Down and Ards (IFHE); North West Kent (Coll); Northbrook (Coll); Norwich City (Coll); Nottingham New (Coll); Oxford Brookes; Plymouth (CFE); Preston (Coll); Riverside Halton (Coll); Rose Bruford (Coll); Runshaw (Coll); Salford; Sheffield (Coll); Solihull (Coll); South Devon (Coll); Southampton City (Coll); Southampton Solent; Stratford-upon-Avon (Coll); Suffolk (Univ Campus); Thames Valley; Ulster; Westminster Kingsway (Coll); Worcestershire New (Coll); Yorkshire Coast (CFHE).

CHOOSING YOUR COURSE (SEE ALSO CH.1)

Course variations – Widen your options

Hospitality and Food Management (Birmingham (UC))
Hospitality and Leisure Management (Birmingham (UC))
Hospitality and Tourism (Birmingham (UC))
International Food and Hospitality Management (Bournemouth)
Hospitality – Licensed Premises (Cardiff (UWIC))
Event Management (Central Lancashire)
Hospitality and Spa Management (Derby)
Hospitality Management with a Modern Language (Huddersfield)
Religion, Culture and Ethics and Hospitality Management (Oxford Brookes)
Hospitality Management and Culinary Arts (Sheffield Hallam)
CHECK PROSPECTUSES AND WEBSITES FOR OTHER UNIVERSITIES AND COLLEGES OFFERING THESE COURSES.

Sandwich degree courses Birmingham (UC); Bournemouth; Brighton; Cardiff (UWIC); Central Lancashire; Derby; Gloucestershire; Huddersfield; Leeds Met; London Met; Manchester Met; Oxford Brookes; Portsmouth; Plymouth; Sheffield Hallam; Surrey; Ulster; Wolverhampton.

ADMISSIONS INFORMATION

Number of applicants per place (approx) Blackpool and Fylde (Coll) 3; Bournemouth 9; Cardiff (UWIC) 12; Central Lancashire 8; London Met 10; Manchester Met (Hspty Mgt) 12, (Hspty Mgt Tour) 20; Middlesex 4; Napier 17; Oxford Brookes 9; Plymouth 5; Portsmouth 10; Robert Gordon 3; Strathclyde 8; Surrey 12.

Advice to applicants and planning the UCAS personal statement Experience in dealing with members of the public is an important element in this work which, coupled with work experience in cafés, restaurants or hotels, should be described fully. Admissions tutors are likely to look for experience in industry and for people who are ambitious, sociable and team players. **Bournemouth**, **London Met**, **Middlesex** (non-EU students) Ability required in spoken and written English. See also **Appendix 2**.

Misconceptions about this course Cardiff (UWIC) (Hspty Mgt) The course is not about cookery! We are looking to create managers, not chefs.

Selection interviews Yes Manchester Met, Portsmouth, Robert Gordon, Surrey; **Some** Blackpool and Fylde (Coll), Salford.

For information on how to read the Subject Tables, see **Chapter 8**.

Interview advice and questions What books do you read? What do you know about hotel work and management? What work experience have you had? What kind of job do you have in mind when you have qualified? How did you become interested in this course? Do you eat in restaurants? What types of restaurants? Discuss examples of good and bad restaurant organisation. What qualities do you have which make you suitable for management? All applicants are strongly recommended to obtain practical experience in catering or hotel work. See **Chapter 7**.

Reasons for rejection (non-academic) Lack of suitable work experience or practical training. Inability to communicate. Lack of awareness of work load, for example shift working, weekend work. **Cardiff (UWIC)** Students looking specifically for licensed trade courses or a cookery course. **Oxford Brookes** Lack of commitment to the hotel and restaurant industry.

AFTER-RESULTS ADVICE
Offers to applicants repeating A-levels **Higher** Bournemouth, Huddersfield, Oxford Brookes, Surrey; **Same** Blackpool and Fylde (Coll), Brighton, Cardiff (UWIC), Manchester Met, Salford, Strathclyde, Suffolk (Univ Campus), Surrey (BSc Ord), Thames Valley, Ulster, Wolverhampton.

GRADUATE DESTINATIONS AND EMPLOYMENT (2005/6 HESA)
No data available.

Career note These business-focused hospitality programmes open up a wide range of employment and career opportunities in both hospitality and other business sectors. The demand for employees is extremely high and the industry's professional body (Hotel, Catering and International Management Association (HCIMA)) currently estimates that the demand for managers exceeds supply by a factor of eight. Events Management is currently a growth area with graduates working in sports and the arts, tourist attractions, hospitality, business and industry.

OTHER DEGREE SUBJECTS FOR CONSIDERATION
Business; Consumer Studies; Dietetics; Food Science; Health Studies; Leisure and Recreation Management; Management; Tourism and Travel.

HOUSING

(see also **Building, Community Studies, Consumer Studies/Sciences, Property Management/Development** and **Town and Country Planning**)

These courses prepare students for careers in housing management although topics covered will also be relevant to other careers in business and administration. Modules will be taken in housing, law, finance, planning policy, public administration and construction.

Useful websites www.housingcorp.gov.uk; www.communities.gov.uk/housing.

NB The points totals shown to the left of the institutions are for ease of reference only. It must not be assumed that tariff points are always used by institutions or that they can be substituted for an offer in grades. The level of an offer is not necessarily indicative of the quality of a course.

COURSE OFFERS INFORMATION
Subject requirements/preferences **GCSE** English and mathematics required. **AL** No specified subjects. **NB** A* grades are likely to form part of university offers in the higher ranges for students applying for places in 2008 for entry in 2009: check websites.

Your target offers
240 pts **Bristol UWE** – 240–280 pts (Plan Hous Renew)
230 pts **Sheffield Hallam** – 230 pts (Hous Prof St)
220 pts **Ulster** – CCD 220 pts (Hous Mgt)
200 pts **Anglia Ruskin** – 200 pts (Housing)
180 pts **Birmingham City** – 180 pts (Prof Hous St)

160 pts **London South Bank** – CC–CD (Hous St)
       Middlesex – 160–200 pts (Housing)
140 pts **Cardiff (UWIC)** – CD 140 pts (Hous (Supptd); Hous Pol Prac)
       North East Wales (IHE) – 140 pts (p/t Hous St)

       Bristol UWE – contact University (Hous Dev Mgt)
       Leeds Met – contact University
       Southampton Solent – contact University (Soc Hous)

Alternative offers
See **Chapter 8** for grade/point equivalences and related information for the following examinations: Scottish qualifications, the Welsh Baccalaureate, the IB diploma (approximate points shown also in italics in the table of offers), the Irish Leaving Certificate, the European Baccalaureate and the French Baccalaureate.

EXAMPLES OF FOUNDATION DEGREES IN THE SUBJECT FIELD
Anglia Ruskin; Birmingham City; East Lancashire (IHE); Leeds Met; Middlesex; North East London (Coll); St Helens (Coll); Swansea (Inst).

CHOOSING YOUR COURSE (SEE ALSO CH.1)
Course variations – Widen your options
Real Estate Management (Birmingham City)
Housing Policy and Practice (Cardiff (UWIC))
Care, Community and Citizenship (Central Lancashire)
Social Housing (Southampton Solent)
CHECK PROSPECTUSES AND WEBSITES FOR OTHER UNIVERSITIES AND COLLEGES OFFERING THESE COURSES.

ADMISSIONS INFORMATION
Number of applicants per place (approx) Anglia Ruskin 2; Bristol UWE 4; Cardiff (UWIC) 1; Sheffield Hallam 2.

Advice to applicants and planning the UCAS personal statement An interest in people, housing problems, social affairs and the built environment is important for this course. Contacts with local housing managers (through local authority offices or housing associations) are important. Describe any such contacts and your knowledge of the housing types and needs in your area. The planning department in your local council office will be able to provide information on the various types of developments taking place in your locality and how housing needs have changed during the past 50 years. See also **Appendix 2**.

Misconceptions about this course Applicants do not appreciate that the course is very close to social work/community work and is most suitable for those wishing to work with people.

Selection interviews **Some** Birmingham City.

Interview advice and questions Since the subject is not studied at school, questions are likely to be asked on reasons for choosing this degree. Other past questions include: What is a housing association? Why were housing associations formed? In which parts of the country would you expect private housing to be expensive and, by comparison, cheap? What is the cause of this? Have estates of multi-storey flats fulfilled their original purpose? If not, why not? What causes a slum? What is an almshouse? **Sheffield Hallam** An informal discussion of the course focusing on the student's interest in housing and any experience of working with the public. See **Chapter 7**.

Reasons for rejection (non-academic) Lack of awareness of current social policy issues.

AFTER-RESULTS ADVICE
Offers to applicants repeating A-levels **Same** Birmingham City, Bristol UWE, Cardiff (UWIC), London South Bank, Sheffield Hallam.

GRADUATE DESTINATIONS AND EMPLOYMENT (2005/6 HESA)
No data available.

Career note Graduates aiming for openings in housing will be employed mainly as managers with local authorities; others will be employed by non-profit-making housing associations and trusts and also by property companies owning blocks of flats.

OTHER DEGREE SUBJECTS FOR CONSIDERATION
Architecture; Building; Business Studies; Community Studies; Environmental Planning; Estate Management; Property Development; Social Policy and Administration; Social Studies; Surveying; Town Planning; Urban Regeneration.

HUMAN RESOURCE MANAGEMENT
(see also **Business Courses**)

This is one of the many branches of the world of business and has developed from the role of the personnel manager. HR managers may be involved with the induction and training of staff, disciplinary and grievance procedures, redundancies and equal opportunities issues. In large organisations some HR staff may specialise in one or more of these areas. Work experience dealing with the public should be stressed in the UCAS personal statement.

Useful websites www.hrmguide.co.uk; www.humanresourcemanagement.co.uk.

NB The points totals shown to the left of the institutions are for ease of reference only. It must not be assumed that tariff points are always used by institutions or that they can be substituted for an offer in grades. The level of an offer is not necessarily indicative of the quality of a course.

COURSE OFFERS INFORMATION
Subject requirements/preferences GCSE English and mathematics at C or above. **AL** No subjects specified. **NB** A* grades are likely to form part of university offers in the higher ranges for students applying for places in 2008 for entry in 2009: check websites.

Your target offers
340 pts **Manchester** – AAB–ABB (Mgt HR)
320 pts **Aston** – ABB 320–340 pts (HR Mgt) (IB 35 pts)
Cardiff – ABB (Bus Mgt (HR))
Lancaster – ABB (Mgt Org (HR Mgt)) (IB 30 pts)
Leeds – ABB (HR Mgt) (IB 33 pts)
London (LSE) – ABB (HR Mgt Emp Rel) (IB 37 pts)
300 pts **Bath** – BBB (Sociol HR Mgt) (IB 36 pts)
Bournemouth – 300 pts (Bus St (HR Mgt))
Liverpool – BBB (HR Mgt) (IB 32 pts)
Stirling – BBB 2nd yr entry (HR Mgt)
Strathclyde – BBB–ABC (HR Mgt)
Ulster – 300 pts (HR Mgt)
280 pts **Kingston** – 280 pts (HR Mgt) (IB 31 pts)
Northumbria – 280–240 pts (HR Mgt) (IB 28 pts)
Oxford Brookes – BBC 280 pts (HR Mgt Bus) (IB 28–30 pts)
260 pts **Coventry** – 260 pts (HR Mgt)
Heriot-Watt – BCC 260 pts (Mgt HR Mgt) (IB 28–30 pts)
Keele – 260–280 pts (HR Mgt courses) (IB 28–30 pts)
Kent – 260–280 pts (Ind Rel HR Mgt courses) (IB 30 pts)
Stirling – BCC 1st yr entry (HR Mgt) (IB 30 pts)
Westminster – 260–280 pts (Bus HR Mgt) (IB 28 pts)
Winchester – 260–300 pts (Bus Mgt HR Mgt) (IB 26 pts)

240 pts **Bradford** – 240 pts (HR Mgt)
Central Lancashire – CCC (HR Mgt courses) *(IB 28 pts)*
De Montfort – 240 pts (HR Mgt courses)
Middlesex – 240 pts (HR Mgt)
Plymouth – 240 pts (HR Mgt)
Portsmouth – 240 pts (HR Mgt; HR Mgt Psy)
Robert Gordon – 240 pts (Mgt HR Mgt)
Salford – 240 pts (Bus St HR Mgt)
Sheffield Hallam – 240 pts (Bus HR Mgt)
Staffordshire – 240 pts (HR Mgt)
Ulster – 240 pts (HR Mgt Mark; Bus St HR Mgt)
230 pts **Napier** – 230 pts (HR Mgt; Hspty HR Mgt)
220 pts **Bolton** – 220 pts (HR Mgt courses)
Glamorgan – 220 pts (Psy HR Mgt)
Huddersfield – 220–200 pts (HR Mgt)
Liverpool John Moores – 220 pts (HR Mgt)
Sunderland – 220 pts (Bus HR Mgt)
Teesside – 220 pts (HR Mgt)
200 pts **Birmingham City** – 200 pts (PR HR Mgt) *(IB 28 pts)*
Bristol UWE – 200–280 pts (Bus St HR Mgt)
Cumbria – 200 pts (Bus HR Mgt)
Gloucestershire – 200–280 pts (HR Mgt courses)
Hertfordshire – 200 pts (HR Mgt; HR courses)
Lincoln – CDD 200 pts (HR Mgt courses)
Manchester Met – 200–260 pts (HR Mgt courses)
Worcester – 200 pts (HR Mgt courses)
York St John – 200 pts (Bus Mgt HR Mgt)
180 pts **Abertay Dundee** – DDD (HR Mgt)
Cardiff (UWIC) – 180 pts (Bus St HR)
Derby – 180–200 pts (HR Mgt courses)
Greenwich – 180 pts (HR Mgt)
Northampton – 180–220 pts (HR Mgt courses)
160 pts **Anglia Ruskin** – 160–200 pts (HR Mgt)
Bedfordshire – 160–240 pts (HR Mgt)
Canterbury Christ Church – 160 pts (Bus St HR Mgt; Mark HR Mgt)
East London – 160 pts (HR Mgt)
Leeds Trinity and All Saints (Coll) – 160 pts (Bus HR Mgt)
London Met – 160–240 pts (HR Mgt courses; Int HR Mgt)
London South Bank – CC (HR Mgt courses)
Roehampton – 160 pts (Bus Mgt HR Mgt)
Southampton Solent – 160 pts (HR Mgt courses)
South East Essex (Coll) – 160 pts (Bus St (HR))
Thames Valley – 160 pts (Bus St HR Mgt)
West Scotland – 160 pts (HR Mgt)
Wolverhampton – 160 pts (Bus Law HR Mgt; Bus HR Mgt)
140 pts **Suffolk (Univ Campus)** – 140–200 pts (HR Mgt)
120 pts **Bradford (Coll)** – 120 pts (HR Mgt)
Bucks New – 120 pts (HR Mgt courses)
Newport – 120 pts (Bus (HR Mgt))
North East Wales (IHE) – 120 pts (Bus HR Mgt)
Swansea (Inst) – 120 pts (HR Mgt)
80 pts **Euro Bus Sch London** – 80 pts (Int Bus HR Mgt Lang)
Norwich City (Coll) – 80 pts (Bus Mgt (HR))

Leeds Met – contact University

For information on how to read the Subject Tables, see **Chapter 8**.

Alternative offers
See **Chapter 8** for grade/point equivalences and related information for the following examinations: Scottish qualifications, the Welsh Baccalaureate, the IB diploma (approximate points shown also in italics in the table of offers), the Irish Leaving Certificate, the European Baccalaureate and the French Baccalaureate.

EXAMPLES OF FOUNDATION DEGREES IN THE SUBJECT FIELD
Barry (Coll); Bridgend (Coll); Croydon (Coll); Glamorgan; Gwent (Coll); Hertfordshire; Northampton; Powys (Coll); Truro (Coll); West Herts (Coll); West Kent (Coll); Wolverhampton.

CHOOSING YOUR COURSE (SEE ALSO CH.1)
Course variations – Widen your options
Sociology and Human Resource Management (Bath)
Public Relations and Human Resource Management (Birmingham)
Combined Studies Human Resource Management (Bucks New)
Human Resource Management and Marketing (De Montfort)
Human Resource Management and Law (Keele)
Industrial Relations and Human Resource Management (Kent)
Human Resource Management with Psychology (Portsmouth)
CHECK PROSPECTUSES AND WEBSITES FOR OTHER UNIVERSITIES AND COLLEGES OFFERING THESE COURSES.

Universities and colleges teaching quality See www.qaa.ac.uk; www.unistats.com.

Top universities and colleges (Research) Aston; Bath; Lancaster.

Sandwich degree courses Aston; Bath; Bradford; Central England; Coventry; De Montfort; East London; Glamorgan; Gloucestershire; Hertfordshire; Lincoln; Liverpool John Moores; London Met; Napier; Plymouth; Portsmouth; Sheffield Hallam; Staffordshire; Sunderland; Swansea (Inst); Teesside; Ulster; West Scotland; Westminster.

ADMISSIONS INFORMATION
Number of applicants per place (approx) Aston 10; Anglia Ruskin 10; London (LSE) 13; see also **Business Courses**.

Advice to applicants and planning the UCAS personal statement See under **Business Courses**.

Selection interviews **Yes** De Montfort; see also **Business Courses**.

Interview advice and questions See **Business Courses**.

Reasons for rejection (non-academic) See **Business Courses (A).**

AFTER-RESULTS ADVICE
Information not available from institutions.

GRADUATE DESTINATIONS AND EMPLOYMENT (2005/6 HESA)
Graduates surveyed 565 **Employed** 375 **In further study** 35 **Assumed unemployed** 35.

Career note See **Business Courses**.

OTHER DEGREE SUBJECTS FOR CONSIDERATION
Business Studies; Information Systems; Management Studies/Sciences; Marketing; Psychology; Retail Management; Sociology; Sports Management.

HUMAN SCIENCES/HUMAN BIOSCIENCES

Human Sciences is a multi-disciplinary study relating to biological and social sciences. Topics range from genetics and evolution to health, disease, social behaviour and industrial societies.

For a quick reference offers calculator, fold out the inside back cover.

Useful websites www.scienceyear.com; www.becominghuman.org; see also **Biology** and **Geography**.

NB The points totals shown to the left of the institutions are for ease of reference only. It must not be assumed that tariff points are always used by institutions or that they can be substituted for an offer in grades. The level of an offer is not necessarily indicative of the quality of a course.

COURSE OFFERS INFORMATION

Subject requirements/preferences GCSE Science essential and mathematics usually required. **AL** Chemistry/biology usually required or preferred for some courses. **NB** A* grades are likely to form part of university offers in the higher ranges for students applying for places in 2008 for entry in 2009: check websites.

Your target offers

360 pts and above
Oxford – Offers vary eg AAA–AAB (Hum Sci) *(IB 38–42 pts)*
340 pts London (UCL) – AAB+AS–ABB+AS (Hum Sci) *(IB 34–36 pts)*
320 pts Exeter – ABB–BBB (Hum Biosci)
London (King's) – ABB+AS (Hum Sci) *(IB 34 pts)*
Sussex – ABB–BBB 360–340 pts (Hum Sci) *(IB 34–36 pts)*
300 pts Sheffield – BBB (Hum Comm Sci) *(IB 29 pts)*
280 pts Loughborough – 280 pts (Ergonomics) *(IB 30 pts)*
Plymouth – 280 pts (Hum Biosci)
260 pts Essex – 260–300 pts (Hlth Hum Sci) *(IB 27–29 pts)*
240 pts Northumbria – 240 pts (Hum Biosci)
200 pts Bolton – 200 pts (Hum Sci courses)
Thames Valley – 200 pts (Hum Sci – pre-Med Yr 1 optional transfer to Medicine at London (UCL)) *(IB 30 pts)*
160 pts Roehampton – 160–200 pts (Hum Biosci courses)
Westminster – CC (Hum Med Sci) *(IB 26 pts)*

Alternative offers
See **Chapter 8** for grade/point equivalences and related information for the following examinations: Scottish qualifications, the Welsh Baccalaureate, the IB diploma (approximate points shown also in italics in the table of offers), the Irish Leaving Certificate, the European Baccalaureate and the French Baccalaureate.

CHOOSING YOUR COURSE (SEE ALSO CH.1)

Course variations – Widen your options
Clinical Science – Medicine Foundation (Bradford)
Interdisciplinary Human Studies (Bradford)
Scottish Ethnology (Edinburgh)
Health and Human Sciences (Essex)
Ergonomics (Human Factors Design) (Loughborough)
Anatomical Sciences (Manchester)
Biological Anthropology and Human Biosciences (Roehampton)
Human and Medical Science (Westminster)
CHECK PROSPECTUSES AND WEBSITES FOR OTHER UNIVERSITIES AND COLLEGES OFFERING THESE COURSES.

ADMISSIONS INFORMATION

Number of applicants per place (approx) Bradford 7; Oxford 4–5.

Advice to applicants and planning the UCAS personal statement See **Biology** and **Anthropology**. See also **Appendix 2**.

Selection interviews Yes London (UCL), Oxford.

Interview advice and questions Past questions have included: What do you expect to get out of a degree in Human Sciences? Why are you interested in this subject? What problems do you think you will be able to tackle after completing the course? Why did you drop PE as an A-level given that it's relevant to Human Sciences? How do you explain altruism, given that we are surely programmed by our genes to be selfish? How far is human behaviour determined by genes? What do you think are the key differences between animals and human beings? **Oxford** Are there too many people in the world? See **Chapter 7**.

AFTER-RESULTS ADVICE
Information not available from institutions.

GRADUATE DESTINATIONS AND EMPLOYMENT (2005/6 HESA)
No data available for this subject area.

Career note As a result of the multi-disciplinary nature of these courses, graduates could focus on openings linked to their special interests or look in general at the scientific and health sectors. Health administration and social services work and laboratory-based careers are some of the more common career destinations of graduates.

OTHER DEGREE SUBJECTS FOR CONSIDERATION
Anthropology; Biology; Community Studies; Environmental Sciences; Life Sciences; Psychology; Sociology.

INFORMATION MANAGEMENT
(including **Librarianship**)

Information Management and Library Studies covers the very wide field of information. Its organisation, retrieval, indexing, computer and media technology, classification and cataloguing are all included in these courses.

Useful websites www.aslib.co.uk; www.ukoln.ac.uk; www.cilip.org.uk; www.bl.uk.

NB The points totals shown to the left of the institutions are for ease of reference only. It must not be assumed that tariff points are always used by institutions or that they can be substituted for an offer in grades. The level of an offer is not necessarily indicative of the quality of a course.

COURSE OFFERS INFORMATION
Subject requirements/preferences **GCSE** English, mathematics and occasionally a foreign language. **AL** No specified subjects. **NB** A* grades are likely to form part of university offers in the higher ranges for students applying for places in 2008 for entry in 2009: check websites.

Your target offers
320 pts London (UCL) – ABB+AS (Inf Mgt Bus) *(IB 34 pts)*
300 pts Loughborough – 300 pts (Inf Mgt Bus St; Inf Mgt Comp) *(IB 30 pts)*
         Sheffield – BBB (Inf Mgt) *(IB 32 pts)*
260 pts Aberystwyth – 260 pts (Musm Gllry St) *(IB 26 pts)*
         Chester – 260 pts (Inf Sys Mgt)
         Northumbria – 260 pts (Electron Pub Inf Mgt) *(IB 24 pts)*
240 pts Plymouth – 240 pts (Bus Econ Inf Mgt)
220 pts De Montfort – 220 pts (Soty Inf)
         Wolverhampton – 220–280 pts (Bus Inf Sys)
200 pts Bradford – 200 pts (IT Mgt)
         Kingston – 200 pts (Inf Sys; Inf Mgt Acc)
         Manchester Met – 200 pts (Librarianship)
         Napier – 200 pts (Inf Sys courses)
         Southampton Solent – 200–260 pts (LLB Inf Mgt)
         Westminster – 200–240 pts (Bus St (Inf Mgt))

For a quick reference offers calculator, fold out the inside back cover.

180 pts **Aberystwyth** – 180 pts (Inf Mgt; Inf Lib St)
160 pts **Glasgow Caledonian** – CC (Bus Inf Mgt)
West Scotland – CC (Inf Mgt)

Leeds Met – contact University

Alternative offers
See **Chapter 8** for grade/point equivalences and related information for the following examinations: Scottish qualifications, the Welsh Baccalaureate, the IB diploma (approximate points shown also in italics in the table of offers), the Irish Leaving Certificate, the European Baccalaureate and the French Baccalaureate.

EXAMPLES OF FOUNDATION DEGREES IN THE SUBJECT FIELD
Peterborough Reg (Coll).

CHOOSING YOUR COURSE (SEE ALSO CH.1)
Course variations – Widen your options
Information and Library Studies and History (Aberystwyth)
Society and Information (De Montfort)
Design for Exhibitions and Museums (Lincoln)
Librarianship (Manchester Met)
Electronic Publishing and Information Management (Northumbria)
CHECK PROSPECTUSES AND WEBSITES FOR OTHER UNIVERSITIES AND COLLEGES OFFERING THESE COURSES.

Universities and colleges teaching quality See www.qaa.ac.uk; www.unistats.com.

Top universities and colleges (Research) Loughborough; Sheffield*.

Sandwich degree courses Loughborough; Napier; West Scotland.

ADMISSIONS INFORMATION
Number of applicants per place (approx) Aberystwyth 4; London (UCL) 7; Loughborough 5; Manchester Met 4; Sheffield 30.

Advice to applicants and planning the UCAS personal statement Work experience or work shadowing in local libraries is important but remember that reference libraries provide a different field of work. Visit university libraries and major reference libraries and discuss the work with librarians. Describe your experiences on the form. **Loughborough** It might be helpful to have numerate ability. A-level business studies helpful but not a requirement. AS-level maths, physics, economics or biology could be useful. See also **Appendix 2**.

Misconceptions about this course Read the prospectus carefully. The course details can be confusing. Some courses have a bias towards the organisation and retrieval of information, others towards computing.

Selection interviews Yes London (UCL), Loughborough.

Interview advice and questions Past questions include: What is it about librarianship that interests you? Why do you think you are suited to be a librarian? What does the job entail? What is the role of the library in school? What is the role of the public library? What new developments are taking place in libraries? Which books do you read? How often do you use a library? What is the Dewey number for the history section in the library? (Applicant studying A-level History.) See **Chapter 7**.

AFTER-RESULTS ADVICE
Offers to applicants repeating A-levels Higher Loughborough; **Same** Sheffield.

GRADUATE DESTINATIONS AND EMPLOYMENT (2005/6 HESA)
Graduates surveyed 205 **Employed** 135 **In further study** 15 **Assumed unemployed** 20.

Career note Graduates in this subject area and in communications enter a wide range of public and private sector jobs where the need to process information as well as to make it easily accessible and user-friendly, is very high. Areas of work could include web content, design and internet management and library management.

OTHER DEGREE SUBJECTS FOR CONSIDERATION

Business Information Systems; Communication Studies; Computer Science; Geographic Information Systems; Media Studies.

INTERNATIONAL RELATIONS

(including **International Development, Peace Studies** and **War Studies;** see also **European Studies** and **Politics**)

A strong interest in international affairs is a pre-requisite for these courses which often allow students to focus on a specific area such as African, Asian, West European politics.

Useful websites www.sipri.org; www.un.org; www.un.int; www.irc-online.org; see also **Politics**.

NB The points totals shown to the left of the institutions are for ease of reference only. It must not be assumed that tariff points are always used by institutions or that they can be substituted for an offer in grades. The level of an offer is not necessarily indicative of the quality of a course.

COURSE OFFERS INFORMATION

Subject requirements/preferences **GCSE** English; a foreign language usually required. **AL** No specified subjects. (War Studies) History may be required. **NB** A* grades are likely to form part of university offers in the higher ranges for students applying for places in 2008 for entry in 2009: check websites.

Your target offers

360 pts and above
> **St Andrews** – AAA (Int Rel courses) *(IB 38 pts)*
> **Warwick** – AABb (Econ Pol Int St; Pol Int St)

340 pts Bath – AAB (Econ Int Dev) *(IB 31 pts)*
> **London (King's)** – AAB+AS (War St; War St Film St) *(IB 36–37 pts)*
> **London (LSE)** – AAB–ABB (Int Rel; Int Rel Hist) *(IB 37 pts)*
> **Sheffield** – AAB (Int Rel Pol)
> **Surrey** – AAB–BBB (Law Int St) *(IB 32 pts)*

320 pts Birmingham – ABB (Int Rel) *(IB 34 pts)*
> **Cardiff** – ABB–BBB (Euro Pol Int Rel) *(IB 35 pts)*
> **East Anglia** – ABB–BBB (Int Rel Modn Hist) *(IB 31–32 pts)*
> **Exeter** – ABB–BBB (Int Rel courses) *(IB 32–34 pts)*
> **Liverpool** – ABB 320 pts (Int Dev) *(IB 30 pts)*
> **London (RH)** – ABB (Hist Int Rel; Ger Int Rel)
> **Manchester** – ABB (Pol Int Rel)
> **Southampton** – ABB 320 pts (Int Rel courses) *(IB 33 pts)*
> **Sussex** – ABB **or** 360 pts 3AL+AS (Int Rel courses)

300 pts Aston – 300 pts (Int Rel courses)
> **Bath** – 300 pts (Pol Int Rel)
> **Dundee** – 300 pts 2nd yr entry (Int Rel courses)
> **Edinburgh** – BBB (Int Rel) *(IB 34 pts)*
> **Essex** – 300–340 pts (Int Rel Pol) *(IB 29–31 pts)*
> **Hull** – 300 pts (Glob Gov; Pol Int Rel) *(IB 34–36 pts)*
> **Lancaster** – BBB **or** 2AL+2AS 280–260 pts (Int Rel Strat St; Pol Int Rel) *(IB 29 pts)*
> **Leeds** – BBB–BBC (Int Rel courses; Int Dev)

        Leicester – BBB (Int Rel Hist)
        Liverpool – BBB (Int Pol Pol)
        Oxford Brookes – BBB–CCC (Int Rel courses)
        Queen's Belfast – BBB–BBCb (Int St)
        Reading – 300–320 pts (War Pce Int Rel; Int Rel courses) *(IB 31 pts)*

280 pts **Aberdeen** – BBC 2nd yr entry (Pol Int Rel)
        Aberystwyth – 280 pts (Int Rel) *(IB 28 pts)*
        Bradford – 280 pts (Pce St; Cnflct Resoln; Dev Pce St; Int Rel Scrty St) *(IB 30 pts)*
        Kent – 280 pts (Int Rel courses; Pol Int Rel; Cnflct Pce Scrty) *(IB 32 pts)*
        Leicester – 280–300 pts (Int Rel)
        Surrey – BBC 280 pts (Pol Int St)

260 pts **London (Gold)** – BCC (Int St) *(IB 28 pts)*
        Loughborough – 260–300 pts (Int Rel)
        Richmond (Am Int Univ) – 260 pts (Soc Sci (Int Rel))

240 pts **Aberdeen** – CCC 1st yr entry (Pol Int Rel courses)
        Bristol UWE – 240–280 pts (Int Rel courses) *(IB 26–32 pts)*
        Coventry – 240–260 pts (Int Rel courses)
        Dundee – 240 pts 1st yr entry (Int Rel Pol)
        Keele – 240–280 pts (Int Rel) *(IB 28–30 pts)*
        Plymouth – 240 pts (Int Rel)
        Portsmouth – 240–280 pts (Int Rel Hist)
        Salford – 240 pts (Int Rel Pol)
        Swansea – 240–280 pts (Int Rel single Hons courses; Int Rel joint courses)

230 pts **Buckingham** – 230 pts (Int St; Int St EFL; Int St Fr/Span; Int St Jrnl)

220 pts **Nottingham Trent** – 220 pts (Int Rel Chin)
        Westminster – CCD (Int Rel courses)

200 pts **Chester** – 200–240 pts (Int Dev St)
        Huddersfield – 200–280 pts (Int St)
        Lincoln – CDD 200 pts (Int Rel courses)
        London Met – 200–240 pts (Int Rel courses)

180 pts **De Montfort** – 180–220 pts (Int Rel courses)

160 pts **Greenwich** – 160 pts (Int St courses)
        Middlesex – 160–200 pts (Int Pol St Dev)
        Wolverhampton – 160–220 pts (War St Pol; War St Phil)

140 pts **Derby** – 140–200 pts (Int Rel Glob Dev; Third Wrld Dev)

        Leeds Met – contact University

Alternative offers

See **Chapter 8** for grade/point equivalences and related information for the following examinations: Scottish qualifications, the Welsh Baccalaureate, the IB diploma (approximate points shown also in italics in the table of offers), the Irish Leaving Certificate, the European Baccalaureate and the French Baccalaureate.

CHOOSING YOUR COURSE (SEE ALSO CH.1)

Course variations – Widen your options

International Politics and Military History (Aberystwyth)
Economics and International Development (Bath)
International Studies and Politics (Birmingham)
European Politics and International Relations (Cardiff)
Banking and International Finance (City)
Flexible Combined Honours (Exeter)
Peace Studies and International relations (Lancaster)
International Development (Liverpool)
European Studies (Loughborough)

Media and International Relations (Nottingham Trent)
American Studies with International Development (Ulster)
CHECK PROSPECTUSES AND WEBSITES FOR OTHER UNIVERSITIES AND COLLEGES OFFERING THESE COURSES.

Top universities and colleges (Research) See **Politics**.

Sandwich degree courses Aston; Loughborough; Nottingham Trent; Oxford Brookes; Plymouth; Portsmouth; Surrey.

ADMISSIONS INFORMATION

Number of applicants per place (approx) Aberystwyth 6; Birmingham 4; De Montfort 6; Derby 3; Exeter 8; Leeds 13; London (King's) 6, (LSE) (Int Rel) 17, (Int Rel Hist) 12; Portsmouth 2; Reading 5; Richmond (Am Int Univ) 5.

Advice to applicants and planning the UCAS personal statement Describe any special interests you have in the affairs of any particular country. Contact embassies for information on cultural, economic and political developments. Follow international events through newspapers and magazines. Give details of any voluntary work you have done. **London (King's)** Substantial experience in some area of direct relevance to War Studies. **St Andrews** Reasons for choice of course. Evidence of interest.

Misconceptions about this course Some students think that this degree will give direct entry into the Diplomatic Service. **Richmond (Am Int Univ)** Applicants should note that this is a UK/US validated degree.

Selection interviews **Yes** Birmingham, London (King's), London Met, Nottingham Trent; **Some** Buckingham, De Montfort, Kent, Wolverhampton.

Interview advice and questions Applicants are likely to be questioned on current international events and crises between countries. **Nottingham Trent** Be prepared to be challenged on your existing views! See **Chapter 7**.

AFTER-RESULTS ADVICE

Offers to applicants repeating A-levels **Same** Buckingham, Chester, De Montfort, Exeter, Lincoln, Richmond (Am Int Univ), Wolverhampton.

GRADUATE DESTINATIONS AND EMPLOYMENT (2005/6 HESA)
See **Politics**.

Career note See **Politics**.

OTHER DEGREE SUBJECTS FOR CONSIDERATION
Development Studies; Economics; European Studies; Government; Politics.

ITALIAN
(see also **Languages**)

The language and literature of Italy will feature strongly on most Italian courses. The majority of applicants have no knowledge of Italian. They will need to give convincing reasons for their interest and to show that they have the ability to assimilate language quickly. See also **Appendix 2** under **Languages**.

Useful websites www.europa.eu; www.italia.gov.it; www.bbc.co.uk/languages; www.languageadvantage.com; www.sis.ac.uk; www.italianstudies.org; www.languagematters.co.uk; www.reed.co.uk/multilingual; see also **Languages**.

NB The points totals shown to the left of the institutions are for ease of reference only. It must not be assumed that tariff points are always used by institutions or that they can be substituted for an offer in grades. The level of an offer is not necessarily indicative of the quality of a course.

COURSE OFFERS INFORMATION

Subject requirements/preferences GCSE English and a foreign language required. **AL** Italian may be required for some courses. **NB** A* grades are likely to form part of university offers in the higher ranges for students applying for places in 2008 for entry in 2009: check websites.

Your target offers

360 pts **and above**
Cambridge – AAA (Modn Mediev Lang (Ital)) *(IB 38–42 pts)*
Oxford – Offers vary eg AAA–AAB (Modn Lang) *(IB 38–42 pts)*
340 pts **Bristol** – AAB–BBC (Ital; Ital Port/Russ/Span; Cz Ital; Fr Ital; Ger Ital) *(IB 30–35 pts)*
Durham – AAB (Arts Comb) *(IB 33–34 pts)*
Manchester – AAB (Ital Jap/Russ/Span)
St Andrews – AAB–ABB (Ital courses) *(IB 32 pts)*
Warwick – BBBc–Cbbc (Ital courses) *(IB 32–34 pts)*
320 pts **Bath** – ABB (Euro St Modn Lang)
Birmingham – ABB–BBB (Ital St) *(IB 32–34 pts)*
Cardiff – ABB–BBB (Ital courses) *(IB 30–32 pts)*
Exeter – ABB–BBB (Int Rel Ital; Ital Comb courses) *(IB 29 pts)*
Glasgow – ABB (Italian) *(IB 30 pts)*
Lancaster – ABB (Ital St Engl Lit; Ital St Psy) *(IB 29–30 pts)*
London (RH) – ABB–BBB (Ital courses) *(IB 32 pts)*
Manchester – ABB–BBB (Ital Ling)
300 pts **Bath** – BBB 3AL+AS (Modn Langs Euro St (Ital Fr/Ger/Span))
Durham – ABC–BBB (Modn Lang)
Edinburgh – BBB (Ital courses) *(IB 34 pts)*
Lancaster – BBB (Ital courses except under **320 pts**) *(IB 29–30 pts)*
Liverpool – BBB–BBC (Ital Comb Hons)
London (UCL) – BBB+AS (Ital courses) *(IB 32 pts)*
Manchester – BBB–BBC (Ital courses except under **340 pts**) *(IB 30–35 pts)*
Reading – 300–320 pts (Ital courses)
Sussex – BBB (Ital courses)
280 pts **Bangor** – 280 pts (Law Ital)
Cardiff – BBC–BCC 280–260 pts (Ital Jap; Ital Pol; Ital Relig St; Ital Welsh)
Leeds – BBC (Ital courses)
260 pts **Essex** – 260–300 pts (Ital courses) *(IB 28 pts)*
Kent – 260–280 pts (Ital courses) *(IB 28 pts)*
Leicester – 260–300 pts (Ital courses) *(IB 30 pts)*
Strathclyde – BCC/BB (Ital courses)
240 pts **Bangor** – 240–280 pts (Bus St Ital; Mark Ital; Span Ital)
Hertfordshire – 240 (Ital joint courses)
Hull – 240–300 pts (Ital courses)
Portsmouth – 240–300 pts (App Lang; Comb Modn Langs)
Salford – 240–300 pts (Ital courses)
Swansea – 240–300 pts (Ital courses)
220 pts **Nottingham Trent** – 220 pts (Ital courses)
200 pts **European Bus Sch London** – CDD 200 pts (Int Bus Ital)
Middlesex – 200–240 pts (Ital courses)
Napier – 200 pts (Lang joint courses)
Sheffield Hallam – 200 pts (Int Bus St Ital)

For information on how to read the Subject Tables, see **Chapter 8**.

180 pts **Manchester Met** – 180 pts (Ital courses) *(IB 26 pts)*
160 pts **Greenwich** – 160–200 pts (Ital courses)
120 pts **Bucks New** – 120–240 pts (Ital courses)

Alternative offers
See **Chapter 8** for grade/point equivalences and related information for the following examinations: Scottish qualifications, the Welsh Baccalaureate, the IB diploma (approximate points shown also in italics in the table of offers), the Irish Leaving Certificate, the European Baccalaureate and the French Baccalaureate.

CHOOSING YOUR COURSE (SEE ALSO CH.1)
Course variations – Widen your options
International Management (Italian) (Bucks New)
Arts Combined (Durham)
Advertising and Marketing with Italian (Greenwich)
Tourism and Italian (Hertfordshire)
Classical and Archaeological Studies and Italian (Kent)
Modern Languages and Translation and Interpreting – Italian (Salford)
Law and Italian (Swansea)
CHECK PROSPECTUSES AND WEBSITES FOR OTHER UNIVERSITIES AND COLLEGES OFFERING THESE COURSES.

Universities and colleges teaching quality See www.qaa.ac.uk; www.unistats.com.

Top universities and colleges (Research) Birmingham*; Bristol; Cambridge*; Leeds*; London (UCL)*; Manchester; Oxford*; Reading*; Warwick.

ADMISSIONS INFORMATION
Number of applicants per place (approx) Birmingham 5; Bristol 4; Cardiff 3; Hull 8; Lancaster 8; Leeds 3; London (RH) 4.

Advice to applicants and planning the UCAS personal statement Describe any visits to Italy and experience of speaking the language. Interests in Italian art, literature, culture, society and architecture could also be mentioned. Read Italian newspapers and magazines and give details if you have a bilingual background. **Leeds** See **Languages**. **St Andrews** Evidence of interest. Reasons for choosing the course. See also **Appendix 2** under **Languages**.

Misconceptions about this course **Leeds** See **Languages**.

Selection interviews **Yes** Birmingham (majority receive offers), Cambridge, London (RH), Oxford.

Interview advice and questions Past questions include: Why do you want to learn Italian? What foreign newspapers or magazines do you read (particularly if the applicant has taken A-level Italian)? Have you visited Italy? What do you know of the Italian people, culture, art? **Leeds** See **Languages**. See **Chapter 7**.

AFTER-RESULTS ADVICE
Offers to applicants repeating A-levels **Higher** Birmingham, Glasgow, Warwick; **Same** Cardiff, Hull, Leeds; **No offers made** Cambridge.

GRADUATE DESTINATIONS AND EMPLOYMENT (2005/6 HESA)
Graduates surveyed 255 Employed 130 In further study 40 Assumed unemployed 15.

Career note See **Languages**.

OTHER DEGREE SUBJECTS FOR CONSIDERATION
European Studies; International Business Studies; other languages.

JAPANESE

(see also **Asia-Pacific Studies, Business Courses** and **Languages**)

A strong interest in Japan and its culture is expected of applicants. A number of four-year joint courses are now offered, all of which include a period of study in Japan. Potential employers are showing an interest in Japanese. Students report that 'it is not a soft option'. They are expected to be firmly committed to a Japanese degree (for example, by listing only Japanese on the UCAS application), to have an interest in using their degree in employment and to be prepared for a lot of hard work. See **Appendix 2** under **Languages**.

Useful websites www.cilt.org.uk; www.iol.org.uk; www.bbc.co.uk/languages; www.languageadvantage.com; www.languagematters.co.uk; www.reed.co.uk/multilingual; www.japanese-online.com; www.japaneselifestyle.com.au; www.thejapanesepage.com; www.japanesestudies.org.uk.

NB The points totals shown to the left of the institutions are for ease of reference only. It must not be assumed that tariff points are always used by institutions or that they can be substituted for an offer in grades. The level of an offer is not necessarily indicative of the quality of a course.

COURSE OFFERS INFORMATION

Subject requirements/preferences GCSE Edinburgh: English and a foreign language usually required. **AL** Modern language required for some courses. **NB** A* grades are likely to form part of university offers in the higher ranges for students applying for places in 2008 for entry in 2009: check websites.

Your target offers

360 pts and above
　　　　　Cambridge – AAA (Orntl St (Jap St)) *(IB 38–42 pts)*
　　　　　Oxford – Offers vary eg AAA–AAB (Japanese) *(IB 38–42 pts)*
340 pts Birmingham – AAB–ABB (Jap courses) *(IB 32–34 pts)*
　　　　　Newcastle – AAB–BBB (Jap courses) *(IB 34 pts)*
300 pts Cardiff – ABC–BBC (Fr Jap; Ger Jap; Ital Jap; Jap Span) *(IB 32 pts)*
　　　　　Cardiff – BBB (Bus St Jap) *(IB 32 pts)*
　　　　　Edinburgh – BBB (Jap; Jap Ling) *(IB 34 pts)*
　　　　　Leeds – BBB (Jap courses)
　　　　　London (SOAS) – 300 pts (Jap courses) *(IB 32 pts)*
　　　　　Manchester – BBB (Jap courses)
　　　　　Nottingham – BBB 300 pts (Manuf Eng Mgt Jap)
　　　　　Sheffield – BBB–BBC **or** BBcc (Jap courses) *(IB 32 pts)*
260 pts Oxford Brookes – BCC **or** BCbc (Jap Lang Contemp Soty; Jap minor courses)
200 pts Central Lancashire – 200 pts (Jap Comb courses) *(IB 26 pts)*
　　　　　Liverpool John Moores – 200 pts (Jap courses) *(IB 26 pts)*
180 pts European Bus Sch – DDD 180 pts (Int Bus Jap)

Alternative offers

See **Chapter 8** for grade/point equivalences and related information for the following examinations: Scottish qualifications, the Welsh Baccalaureate, the IB diploma (approximate points shown also in italics in the table of offers), the Irish Leaving Certificate, the European Baccalaureate and the French Baccalaureate.

CHOOSING YOUR COURSE (SEE ALSO CH.1)

Course variations – Widen your options

Economics and Japanese (Birmingham)
Business Studies and Japanese (Cardiff)
Politics and International Relations with a Year in Japan (Kent)
Applied Languages – French and Japanese (Liverpool John Moores)

Chinese and Japanese (Manchester)
Combined Studies (Newcastle)
CHECK PROSPECTUSES AND WEBSITES FOR OTHER UNIVERSITIES AND COLLEGES OFFERING THESE COURSES.

Universities and colleges teaching quality See www.qaa.ac.uk; www.unistats.com.

Sandwich degree courses Oxford Brookes.

ADMISSIONS INFORMATION

Number of applicants per place (approx) Cardiff 8; London (SOAS) 9; Sheffield 10.

Advice to applicants and planning the UCAS personal statement Discuss your interest in Japan and your reasons for wishing to study the language. Know Japan, its culture and background history. Discuss any visits you have made or contacts with Japanese nationals. **Leeds** See **Languages**. See also **Appendix 2** under **Languages**.

Misconceptions about this course **Leeds** See **Languages**.

Selection interviews **Yes** Cambridge, Oxford; **Some** Leeds.

Interview advice and questions Japanese is an extremely demanding subject and applicants are most likely to be questioned on their reasons for choosing this degree. They will be expected also to have some knowledge of Japanese culture, history and current affairs. See **Chapter 7**.

Reasons for rejection (non-academic) Insufficient evidence of genuine motivation.

AFTER-RESULTS ADVICE

Offers to applicants repeating A-levels **No offers made** Cambridge.

GRADUATE DESTINATIONS AND EMPLOYMENT (2005/6 HESA)

Graduates surveyed 65 **Employed** 40 **In further study** 5 **Assumed unemployed** 5.

Career note See under **Languages**.

OTHER DEGREE SUBJECTS FOR CONSIDERATION

Asia-Pacific Studies; International Business Studies; Oriental Languages; South East Asia Studies.

LANDSCAPE ARCHITECTURE

(including **Garden Design** and **Landscape Design and Management;** see also **Art and Design (Industrial/Product Design)** and **Horticulture**)

Landscape architecture is a specialised branch of architecture for which an ability in art and design is sought and for some of these courses a portfolio of art work may be required. Courses focus on the design of the environment and surrounding buildings. Landscape architecture should not be confused with the work of a garden centre.

Useful websites www.landscape.co.uk; www.laprofession.org.

NB The points totals shown to the left of the institutions are for ease of reference only. It must not be assumed that tariff points are always used by institutions or that they can be substituted for an offer in grades. The level of an offer is not necessarily indicative of the quality of a course.

COURSE OFFERS INFORMATION

Subject requirements/preferences **GCSE** English, geography, art and design, mathematics and at least one science usually required. **AL** Preferred subjects for some courses include biology, geography, environmental science. **NB** A* grades are likely to form part of university offers in the higher ranges for students applying for places in 2008 for entry in 2009: check websites.

Your target offers

340 pts Sheffield – AAB **or** AAbb (Archit Land) *(IB 29–35 pts)*
320 pts Kingston – 320 pts (Land Archit; Land Plan) *(IB 28 pts)*
260 pts Sheffield – BCC (Land Archit Plan; Land Archit Ecol) *(IB 29–35 pts)*
240 pts Edinburgh (CA) – CCC (Land Archit) *(IB 30 pts)*
        Greenwich – 240 pts (Land Archit)
        Manchester Met – 240–280 pts (Land Archit) *(IB 24 pts)*
        Nottingham Trent – 240 pts (Land Inter Des)
230 pts Birmingham City – 230 pts (Land Archit)
200 pts Gloucestershire – 200 pts (Gard Des Land Mgt; Land Des Land Mgt; Land Gard Des; Land Archit)
160 pts Bristol UWE – 160–200 pts (Blt Nat Env)
        Greenwich – 160 pts (Land Mgt)
140 pts Writtle (Coll) – 140 pts (Land Gard Des; Gard Des Restor Mgt; Land Amen Mgt)
100 pts Greenwich – 100 pts (Gard Des)
  80 pts Bournemouth – 80 pts (Land Gard Des Mgt)
        Myerscough (Coll) – 80 pts (Land Mgt)

        Falmouth (UC) – contact College (Gard Des)
        Leeds Met – contact University

Alternative offers

See **Chapter 8** for grade/point equivalences and related information for the following examinations: Scottish qualifications, the Welsh Baccalaureate, the IB diploma (approximate points shown also in italics in the table of offers), the Irish Leaving Certificate, the European Baccalaureate and the French Baccalaureate.

EXAMPLES OF FOUNDATION DEGREES IN THE SUBJECT FIELD

Askham Bryan (Coll); Bishop Burton (Coll); Bournemouth; Bridgwater (Coll); Brighton; Capel Manor (Coll); East Anglia; Harper Adams (UC); Herefordshire (CA); Myerscough (Coll); Northampton; Plumpton (Coll); Reading; Reaseheath (Coll); SAC (Scottish CAg); Sparsholt (Coll); Suffolk (Univ Campus); Warwickshire (Coll); Welsh (CHort); Writtle (Coll).

CHOOSING YOUR COURSE (SEE ALSO CH.1)

Course variations – Widen your options

Landscape and Garden Management (Askham Bryan (Coll))
Built and Natural Environments (Bristol UWE)
History with Landscape Archaeology (East Anglia)
Environment Design and Management (Nottingham Trent)
Landscape Architecture with Ecology (Sheffield)
Garden Design, Restoration and management (Writtle (Coll))
CHECK PROSPECTUSES AND WEBSITES FOR OTHER UNIVERSITIES AND COLLEGES OFFERING THESE COURSES.

Universities and colleges teaching quality See www.qaa.ac.uk; www.unistats.com.

Top universities and colleges (Research) Gloucestershire; Sheffield.

Sandwich degree courses Gloucestershire; Nottingham Trent; Writtle (Coll).

ADMISSIONS INFORMATION

Number of applicants per place (approx) Gloucestershire 9; Greenwich 3; Edinburgh (CA) 7; Kingston 4; Manchester Met 9; Writtle (Coll) 5.

Advice to applicants and planning the UCAS personal statement Knowledge of the work of landscape architects is important. Arrange a visit to a landscape architect's office and try to organise some work experience. Read up on historical landscape design and visit country house estates with examples of outstanding designs. Describe these visits in detail and your preferences. Membership of the National Trust could be useful. **Sheffield** Portfolio of work required. A-level art not necessary. See also **Appendix 2**.

Selection interviews **Yes** Gloucestershire, Greenwich, Manchester Met, Sheffield, Writtle (Coll); **Some** Birmingham City.

Interview advice and questions Applicants will be expected to have had some work experience and are likely to be questioned on their knowledge of landscape architectural work and the subject. Historical examples of good landscaping could also be asked for. See **Chapter 7**.

Reasons for rejection (non-academic) Lack of historical knowledge and awareness of current developments. Poor portfolio.

AFTER-RESULTS ADVICE
Offers to applicants repeating A-levels **Same** Birmingham City, Greenwich, Edinburgh (CA), Manchester Met.

GRADUATE DESTINATIONS AND EMPLOYMENT (2005/6 HESA)
Graduates surveyed 140 **Employed** 90 **In further study** 10 **Assumed unemployed** 5.

Career note Opportunities at present in landscape architecture are good. Openings exist in local government or private practice and may cover planning, housing, environmental and conservation.

OTHER DEGREE SUBJECTS FOR CONSIDERATION
Architecture; Art and Design; Environmental Planning; Forestry; Horticulture.

LANGUAGES

(including **Hebrew** and **Modern Languages;** see also **African and Caribbean Studies, Arabic and Near and Middle Eastern Studies, Asia-Pacific Studies, Chinese, English, French, German, Greek, Italian, Japanese, Latin, Linguistics, Russian and East European Studies, Scandinavian Studies, Spanish** and **Welsh (Cymraeg) and Celtic**)

Modern Language courses usually offer three main options: a single subject degree commonly based on literature and language, a European Studies course, or two-language subjects which can often include languages different from those available at school (such as Scandinavian Studies, Russian and the languages of Eastern Europe, the Middle and Far East).

Useful websites www.iol.org.uk; www.iti.org.uk; www.europa.eu; www.cilt.org.uk; www.bbc.co.uk/languages; www.languageadvantage.com; www.omniglot.com; www.languagematters.co.uk; www.reed.co.uk/multilingual; www.thelanguageshow.co.uk.

NB The points totals shown to the left of the institutions are for ease of reference only. It must not be assumed that tariff points are always used by institutions or that they can be substituted for an offer in grades. The level of an offer is not necessarily indicative of the quality of a course.

COURSE OFFERS INFORMATION
Subject requirements/preferences **GCSE** English and a modern language required. In some cases grades A and/or B may be stipulated. **AL** A modern foreign language required usually with specified grades. **NB** A* grades are likely to form part of university offers in the higher ranges for students applying for places in 2008 for entry in 2009: check websites.

Your target offers
360 pts and above
        Cambridge – AAA (Modn Mediev Lang; Orntl St (Heb St)) *(IB 38–42 pts)*
        London (UCL) – AAA+AS–ABB+AS (Lang Cult; Modn Lang courses) *(IB 32–38 pts)*
        Oxford – Offers vary eg AAA–AAB (Euro Mid E Lang; Class Modn Lang; Engl Modn Lang; Modn Langs; Modn Lang Ling; Phil Modn Langs; Hist Modn Langs; Heb) *(IB 38–42 pts)*

York – AAA–AAB (Ling Lit)

340 pts **Bristol** – AAB–BCC (see also separate language tables) (Cz; Fr; Ger; Ital; Port; Russ; Span)

Durham – AAB (Modn Euro Langs Hist)

Leeds – AAB–BCC (Modn Langs joint Hons (see separate language tables))

St Andrews – AAB–ABB (Modn Lang courses; Heb courses) *(IB 32–36 pts)*

320 pts **Bath** – ABB–BBB (Modn Lang Euro St Fr/Ger/Ital/Russ/Span)

Birmingham – ABB 320 pts (Modn Langs) *(IB 32–34 pts)*

Cardiff – ABB (Lang Comm)

Durham – ABB (Modn Langs; Modn Lang comb Hons)

Lancaster – ABB (Euro Lang Mgt)

London (RH) – ABB–BBB (Euro Lit Cult St; Multiling St; Modn Lang courses)

Manchester – ABB (Modn Lang Bus Mgt Fr; Lang St courses; Heb St; Heb Jew St)

Newcastle – ABB (Modn Langs; Modn Lang Ling; Modn Langs Mgt St) *(IB 32 pts)*

Nottingham – ABB (Modn Langs Bus) *(IB 32 pts)*

Southampton – ABB 320 pts (Modn Langs; Lang Learn; Lang Soty; Ling St Fr/Ger/Span) *(IB 33 pts)*

York – ABB (Engl Ling)

300 pts **Birmingham** – BBB 300 pts (Modn Lang Euro St (Pol) (Soty Cult Hist)) *(IB 32–34 pts)*

East Anglia – ABC (Fst Trk: Modn Langs; Lang Mgt)

Edinburgh – BBB (Modn Euro Langs; Modn Euro Langs Euro St – 2 from Fr/Ger/Ital/Russ St/Scand St/Span) *(IB 34 pts)*

Essex – 300–260 pts (Modn Lang; Lang St; Modn Lang Fr/Ger/Ital/Span) *(IB 27 pts)*

Leeds – BBB (SE As St Span)

London (UCL) – BBB (Dutch courses)

Manchester – BBB (Modn Lang Bus Mgt Chin/Ger/Ital/Span/Port/Russ) *(IB 28–30 pts)*

Nottingham – ABC–BBB (Modn Langs St; Modn Euro St) *(IB 32 pts)*

Sheffield – BBB–BBC **or** BBbb (Modn Langs; Modn Langs Interp) *(IB 32 pts)*

Surrey – 300–280 pts (Comb Langs; Bus Mgt Lang; Modn Lang Transl)

Sussex – BBB or 340 pts 3AL+AS (Fr/Ger/Ital/Span courses; Lang Cult St; Lang Contemp Euro St; Lang Ling; Lang Phil)

York – BBB–ABB (Modn Lang Ling; Lang Ling; Ling Lit; Ling Phil; Maths Ling) *(IB 34 pts)*

280 pts **Aberystwyth** – 280 pts (Euro Lang) *(IB 29 pts)*

Aston – 280–300 pts (Transl St Fr/Ger/Span; Modn Langs courses; Modn Lang Abrd)

East Anglia – BBC (Transl Interp (double Hons Langs))

Exeter – BBC–BCC (see separate language tables) (Comb Lang courses)

Heriot-Watt – BBC (App Langs Transl; Langs (Interp Transl)) (For Langs Teach Engl (TESOL))

Lancaster – BBC (Euro Langs)

Liverpool – BBC–BBB 280–300 pts (Modn Euro Langs) *(IB 30 pts)*

London (King's) – BBC+AS **or** BBcc (Modn For Lang Educ)

London (SOAS) – BBC–BCC (Amharic; Bengali; Burmese; Georgian; Gujarati; Hausa; Hindi; Indonesian; Jap; Korean; Nepali; Sanskrit; Sinhala; Swahili; Tamil; Thai; Tibetan; Turkish; Urdu; Vietnamese; Anc Nr E Langs; Heb Isrl St) *(IB 30 pts)*

Strathclyde – BBC (Int Bus Modn Lang)

260 pts **East Anglia** – BCC (Lang(s) Mgt St; Modn Lang Yr Abrd)

Essex – 260 pts (Modn Lang courses) *(IB 27 pts)*

Hull – 260–220 pts (Modn Lang St; Two Modn Langs Bus/Mgt/Mark)

Leicester – 260–300 pts (Modn Lang St courses; Modn Lang Mgt) *(IB 28–30 pts)*

London (QM) – 260 pts 3AL **or** 2AL+2AS (joint courses Euro St Fr/Ger/Russ; Modn Langs Hisp St)

Northumbria – 260 pts (Contemp Lang St; Modn Lang; Modn Lang Bus)

Salford – 260–300 pts (Euro Lang Fr/Ger/Ital/Span/Port) *(IB 28 pts)*

Strathclyde – BCC (Modn Lang)

Ulster – 260 pts inc BC (Lang Ling; Lang Comm; Lang PR)

Westminster – BCC (Lang Soc Sci; Lang St; Modn Langs Arbc/Chin/Fr/Span)

For information on how to read the Subject Tables, see **Chapter 8**.

240 pts **Aberdeen** – CCC (Euro Langs 20th Cent Cult; Lang Ling courses; Langs Lit Scot)

Bangor – 240–260 pts (Three Langs course Fr/Ger/Ital/Span; joint Hons Lang)

Chester – 240 pts (Modn Langs) *(IB 30 pts)*

Portsmouth – 240–300 pts (Comb Modn Lang; Langs Am St; Langs Crea Writ; Langs Euro St; Langs Film St; Langs Int Tr)

Salford – 240–300 pts (Modn Lang Transl Interpret St (Fr/Ger/Ital/Port/Span); Modn Langs St; Media Lang Bus; Modn Lang Ling) *(IB 28 pts)*

Stirling – CCC (Modn Lang (Fr/Ger/Span); Modn Lang Bus St; Modn Lang Int Pol; Modn Lang Mark) *(IB 28 pts)*

Swansea – 240–280 pts (Lang courses)

Ulster – CCC 240 pts (Langs Bus Comp; Irish Euro St)

220 pts **Hull** – 220–280 pts (Comb Langs)

Leo Baeck (Coll) – by interview (Heb Jew St)

Nottingham Trent – 220 pts (Modn Langs courses; Fr/Ger/Ital/Span courses)

200 pts **Bristol UWE** – 200–260 pts (Int Bus Modn Langs)

Cardiff (UWIC) – 200 pts (Tour Mgt Langs)

Hertfordshire – 200–300 pts (Langs (Comb Mod Schm))

Lincoln – 200 pts (Bus Langs)

Liverpool John Moores – 200–180 pts (App Lang St (Chin/Fr/Ger/Ital/Jap/Span); App Lang Euro)

Manchester Met – 200–280 pts (Comb Hons Langs)

Middlesex – 200–240 pts (Modn Langs Transl)

Napier – 200 pts (Lang joint courses; Euro Bus Langs)

Plymouth – 200 pts (Modn Langs courses; Modn Lang St) *(IB 24 pts)*

Sheffield Hallam – 200 pts (Langs (Fr/Ger/Ital/Span) Tour/Mark/Int Bus St)

180 pts **Anglia Ruskin** – 180–220 pts (Intercult Comm)

Central Lancashire – 180 pts (Modn Lang 4yr course)

Coventry – 180 pts (Modn Langs)

Manchester Met – 180 pts (Langs Mgt Sys)

Roehampton – 180 pts (Translation)

160 pts **Anglia Ruskin** – 160–180 pts (Comb Langs (Fr/Ger/Span))

East London – 160 pts (Lang Educ)

London Met – 160 pts (App Transl)

West Scotland – CC (Langs Fr/Ger/Span)

Wolverhampton – 160–220 pts (Interp (Brit Sign Lang Engl))

Leeds Met – contact University

Alternative offers

See **Chapter 8** for grade/point equivalences and related information for the following examinations: Scottish qualifications, the Welsh Baccalaureate, the IB diploma (approximate points shown also in italics in the table of offers), the Irish Leaving Certificate, the European Baccalaureate and the French Baccalaureate.

CHOOSING YOUR COURSE (SEE ALSO CH.1)

Course variations – Widen your options

Translation Studies French/German (Aston)

Joint courses with Languages (Birmingham)

Modern Languages and Music (Durham)

Interpreting and Translating with Double Honours Language (East Anglia)

Translation and Media (East Anglia)

Georgian joint courses (London (SOAS))

Hebrew and Jewish Studies (Manchester)

Contemporary Language Studies (Northumbria)

French and Canadian Studies (Nottingham)
Communication, Sociology and French (Nottingham Trent)
Creative Writing and Language (Roehampton)
Languages, Business and Computing (Ulster)
Linguistics and Literature (York).
CHECK PROSPECTUSES AND WEBSITES FOR OTHER UNIVERSITIES AND COLLEGES OFFERING THESE COURSES.

Universities and colleges teaching quality See www.qaa.ac.uk; www.unistats.com.

Top universities and colleges (Research) See separate language tables.

ADMISSIONS INFORMATION

Number of applicants per place (approx) Aston 4; Bangor 5; Birmingham 8; Brighton 4; Bristol 15; Bristol UWE 4; Cambridge 3, (Orntl St) 3; Cardiff 6; Durham 6; East Anglia 15; Heriot-Watt 5; Huddersfield 12; Lancaster 10; Leeds (joint Hons) 8; Leicester 5; Liverpool 5; Liverpool John Moores 12; Newcastle 22; Northumbria 4; Oxford (success rate 55%); Roehampton 3; Salford 6; Swansea 4; Wolverhampton 10.

Advice to applicants and planning the UCAS personal statement Leeds Many languages can be started from scratch. See separate language tables. **Oxford** Students can embark on language courses in which they have no previous knowledge (Italian, Portuguese, Modern Greek, Czech, Celtic, Russian). However, they would be expected to have done a considerable amount of language work on their own in their chosen language before starting the course. See also **Appendix 2**.

Misconceptions about this course Leeds (joint Hons) Some applicants think that studying languages means studying masses of literature – wrong. At Leeds, generally speaking, it's up to you; you study as much or as little literature as you choose. Residence abroad does not inevitably mean a university course (except where you are taking a language from scratch). Paid employment is usually another option. **Liverpool John Moores** (App Langs) Applicants often assume that this course involves the study of literature.

Selection interviews Yes Aston, Cambridge, Coventry, Durham, East Anglia, Heriot-Watt, Hertfordshire, Huddersfield, Liverpool (Open day invitation), Oxford (success rates (Euro Mid E Lang) 46%, (Modn Lang) 52%, (Modn Lang Ling) 27%, (Orntl St) 45%), Roehampton, Salford; **Some** Brighton, Bristol UWE, Leeds, Liverpool John Moores, Salford, Swansea.

Interview advice and questions Bangor All applicants invited for interview after offer when a lower offer may be made. **Cambridge** Think of a painting of a tree. Is the tree real? **Leeds** (joint Hons) Give an example of something outside your studies that you have achieved over the past year. See **Chapter 7**.

Reasons for rejection (non-academic) Lack of commitment to spend a year abroad. Poor references. Poor standard of English. No reasons for why the course has been selected. Poor communication skills. Incomplete applications, for example missing qualifications and reference.

AFTER-RESULTS ADVICE

Offers to applicants repeating A-levels Higher Bristol UWE; **Possibly higher** Aston; **Same** Bangor (usually), Birmingham, Bristol, Durham, East Anglia, Leeds, Liverpool, Liverpool Hope, Liverpool John Moores, Newcastle, Nottingham Trent, Salford, Stirling, Wolverhampton, York; **No offers made** Cambridge.

GRADUATE DESTINATIONS AND EMPLOYMENT (2005/6 HESA)

See separate language tables.

Career note The only career-related fields for language students are teaching which attracts some graduates and the demanding work of interpreting and translating to which only a small number aspire. The majority will be attracted to work in management and administration, financial services and a host of other occupations which may include the social services, law and property development.

OTHER DEGREE SUBJECTS FOR CONSIDERATION

Communication Studies; Linguistics.

LATIN

(see also **Classical Studies/Classical Civilisation** and **Classics**)

Latin courses provide a study of the language, art, religion and history of the Roman world. This table should be read in conjunction with the **Classical Studies/Classical Civilisation** and **Classics** tables.

Useful websites www.thelatinlibrary.com; www.la.wikipedia.org.

NB The points totals shown to the left of the institutions are for ease of reference only. It must not be assumed that tariff points are always used by institutions or that they can be substituted for an offer in grades. The level of an offer is not necessarily indicative of the quality of a course.

COURSE OFFERS INFORMATION

Subject requirements/preferences **GCSE** English, a foreign language and Latin may be stipulated. **AL** Check courses for Latin requirement. **NB** A* grades are likely to form part of university offers in the higher ranges for students applying for places in 2008 for entry in 2009: check websites.

Your target offers

360 pts **and above**
　　　　　Cambridge – AAA (Class; Modn Mediev Lang (Class Gk Lat)) *(IB 38–42 pts)*
　　　　　Oxford – Offers vary between candidates (Classics) *(IB 38–42 pts)*
340 pts **St Andrews** – AAB (Lat courses) *(IB 36 pts)*
320 pts **Exeter** – ABB 320 pts (Latin) *(IB 29 pts)*
　　　　　Glasgow – ABB–BBB (Latin) *(IB 30 pts)*
　　　　　London (UCL) – ABB+AS–BBC+AS (Lat Gk)
　　　　　Manchester – ABB (Lat; Lat Fr/Ital/Span; Lat Engl Lit; Lat Ling)
300 pts **Edinburgh** – BBB (Lat St; Anc Hist Lat) *(IB 34 pts)*
　　　　　Leeds – BBB (Latin)
　　　　　London (King's) – BBB+AS **or** BBbbc (Lat Engl)
　　　　　London (RH) – BBB (Latin) *(IB 32 pts)*
　　　　　Nottingham – ABC–BBB (Anc Hist Lat; Lat; Engl St Lat) *(IB 32 pts)*
　　　　　Warwick – BBB (Engl Lat Lit)
260 pts **Swansea** – 260–300 pts (Lat joint courses)
200 pts **Lampeter** – 200–300 pts (Lat courses) *(IB 24 pts)*

Alternative offers
See **Chapter 8** for grade/point equivalences and related information for the following examinations: Scottish qualifications, the Welsh Baccalaureate, the IB diploma (approximate points shown also in italics in the table of offers), the Irish Leaving Certificate, the European Baccalaureate and the French Baccalaureate.

CHOOSING YOUR COURSE (SEE ALSO CH.1)

Course variations – Widen your options
Classics (Cambridge)
Latin and Greek (London (UCL))
Ancient History and Latin (Nottingham)
English and Latin Literature (Warwick)
See also **Classics**.
CHECK PROSPECTUSES AND WEBSITES FOR OTHER UNIVERSITIES AND COLLEGES OFFERING THESE COURSES.

Universities and colleges teaching quality See www.qaa.ac.uk; www.unistats.com.

Top universities and colleges (Research) See **Classics**.

ADMISSIONS INFORMATION

Number of applicants per place (approx) Lampeter 3; Leeds 2; Nottingham 3.

Advice to applicants and planning the UCAS personal statement See **Classical Studies/Classical Civilisation** and **Classics**.

Selection interviews Yes Cambridge, Exeter, Lampeter, London (RH), (UCL), Nottingham, Oxford.

Interview advice and questions See **Classical Studies/Classical Civilisation** and **Classics**.

AFTER-RESULTS ADVICE

Offers to applicants repeating A-levels Higher Leeds, St Andrews, Warwick.

GRADUATE DESTINATIONS AND EMPLOYMENT (2005/6 HESA)

Graduates surveyed 15 **Employed** 5 **In further study** 5 **Assumed unemployed** None.

Career note Graduates enter a broad range of careers within management, the media, commerce and tourism as well as social and public services. Some graduates choose to work abroad and teaching is a popular option.

OTHER DEGREE SUBJECTS FOR CONSIDERATION

Ancient History; Archaeology; Classical Studies; Classics.

LATIN AMERICAN STUDIES

(including **Hispanic Studies;** see also **American Studies** and **Spanish**)

Latin American courses provide a study of Spanish and of Latin American republics, covering both historical and present-day conditions and problems. Normally a year is spent in Latin America.

Useful websites www.iol.org.uk; www.bbc.co.uk/languages; www.languageadvantage.com; www.languagematters.co.uk; www.reed.co.uk/multilingual; www.cilt.org.uk; www.latinworld.com; www.wola.org; www.latinamericalinks.com; see also **Languages** and **Spanish**.

NB The points totals shown to the left of the institutions are for ease of reference only. It must not be assumed that tariff points are always used by institutions or that they can be substituted for an offer in grades. The level of an offer is not necessarily indicative of the quality of a course.

COURSE OFFERS INFORMATION

Subject requirements/preferences GCSE Aberdeen: English, mathematics or science and a foreign language. English and a foreign language required by most universities. **AL** Spanish may be required for some courses. **NB** A* grades are likely to form part of university offers in the higher ranges for students applying for places in 2008 for entry in 2009: check websites.

Your target offers

320 pts Glasgow – ABB (Hisp St courses)
London (UCL) – ABB+AS (Modn Iber Lat Am Reg St; Hisp St)
Newcastle – ABB–BBB (Span Port Lat Am St)
Southampton – ABB 320 pts **or** 400 pts 4AL (Span Lat Am St)
300 pts Leeds – BBB (Hisp Lat Am St) *(IB 32 pts)*
London (King's) – BBB+AS **or** BBbbb (Port Braz St courses; Hisp St joint courses)

Manchester – BBB (Am Lat Am St)
Sheffield – BBB–BBC (Hisp St courses)
280 pts **Birmingham** – 280–320 pts (Hisp St courses)
Essex – 280–260 pts (Lat Am St; Lat Am St Hum Rts; Lat Am St Bus Mgt)
Liverpool – BBC–BBB 280–300 pts (Lat Am Hisp St) *(IB 32 pts)*
London (QM) – BBC–BCD (Hisp St Ling; Hisp Compar Lit)
Nottingham – BBC (Am St Lat Am St; Hisp St courses)
260 pts **Kent** – 260 pts (Hisp St)
240 pts **Aberdeen** – CCC (Hisp St courses) *(IB 30 pts)*
220 pts **Hull** – 220–280 pts (Hisp St Theol)
200 pts **London Met** – 200 pts (Span Lat Am St) *(IB 28 pts)*
Middlesex – 200–240 pts (Lat Am St minor subj joint Hons)
Portsmouth – 200–280 pts (Lat Am Dev St; Span Lat Am St)

Alternative offers
See **Chapter 8** for grade/point equivalences and related information for the following examinations: Scottish qualifications, the Welsh Baccalaureate, the IB diploma (approximate points shown also in italics in the table of offers), the Irish Leaving Certificate, the European Baccalaureate and the French Baccalaureate.

CHOOSING YOUR COURSE (SEE ALSO CH.1)
Course variations – Widen your options
Latin American Studies with Business Management with a Year in Latin America (Essex)
Portuguese and Brazilian Studies (London (King's))
Modern Iberian and Latin American Regional Studies (London (UCL))
CHECK PROSPECTUSES AND WEBSITES FOR OTHER UNIVERSITIES AND COLLEGES OFFERING THESE COURSES.

Top universities and colleges (Research) Birmingham.

ADMISSIONS INFORMATION
Number of applicants per place (approx) Essex 3; Liverpool 3; Newcastle 25; Portsmouth 5.

Advice to applicants and planning the UCAS personal statement Visits and contacts with Spain and Latin American countries should be described. An awareness of the economic, historical and political scene of these countries is also important. Information may be obtained from respective embassies.

Selection interviews **Yes** Newcastle; **Some** Portsmouth.

Interview advice and questions Past questions include: Why are you interested in studying Latin American Studies? What countries related to the degree course have you visited? What career are you planning when you finish your degree? Applicants taking Spanish are likely to be asked questions on their syllabus and should also be familiar with some Spanish newspapers and magazines. See **Chapter 7**.

AFTER-RESULTS ADVICE
Offers to applicants repeating A-levels **Higher** Essex; **Same** Newcastle, Portsmouth.

GRADUATE DESTINATIONS AND EMPLOYMENT (2005/6 HESA)
No data available.

Career note See **Languages**.

OTHER DEGREE SUBJECTS FOR CONSIDERATION
American Studies; Brazilian; Portuguese; Spanish.

LAW

(for **Criminology and Criminal Justice** courses see also **Social Studies/Science**)

Law courses are usually divided into two parts. Part I occupies the first year and introduces the student to criminal and constitutional law and the legal process. Thereafter many different specialised topics can be studied in the second and third years. The course content is very similar for most courses. Applicants are advised to check with universities as to their current policies concerning their use of the National Admissions Test for Law (LNAT). See **Subject requirements/preferences** below and also **Chapter 7**.

Useful websites www.barcouncil.org.uk; www.ilex.org.uk; www.lawcareers.net; www.lawsociety.org.uk; www.cps.gov.uk; www.hmcourts-service.gov.uk; www.lawscot.org.uk; www.lawsoc-ni.org; www.rollonfriday.com; www.lnat.ac.uk.

NB The points totals shown to the left of the institutions are for ease of reference only. It must not be assumed that tariff points are always used by institutions or that they can be substituted for an offer in grades. The level of an offer is not necessarily indicative of the quality of a course.

COURSE OFFERS INFORMATION

Subject requirements/preferences GCSE Many universities will expect high grades. **AL** Arts, humanities, social sciences and sciences plus languages for courses combined with a foreign language. **All universities** Applicants offering art and music A-levels should check whether these subjects are acceptable. **NB** A* grades are likely to form part of university offers in the higher ranges for students applying for places in 2008 for entry in 2009: check websites. The National Admissions Test for Law (LNAT) may be required by universities other than those listed below – check university websites and prospectuses and see also **Chapter 7**.

Your target offers

360 pts **and above**

Birmingham – AAA +LNAT (Law; Law Bus St) *(IB 36 pts)*

Bristol – AAA–AAB +LNAT (Law; Law Fr/Ger; Chem Law) *(IB 37 pts)*

Cambridge – AAA +LNAT (Law; Land Econ; Law (Double Maîtrise Cambridge/Paris)) *(IB 38–42 pts)*

Cardiff – AAA (Law; Law Crim)

Durham – AAA–AAB +LNAT (Law; Euro Leg St) *(IB 38–40 pts)*

East Anglia – AAA (Law Am Law) *(IB 36 pts)*

Exeter – AAA–AAB +LNAT (Law; Euro Law; Hist Law; Pol Law) *(IB 30–31 pts)*

Lancaster – AAA–AAB (Law (Int)) *(IB 31–32 pts H 17–18 pts)*

Leeds – AAA (Law; Law Fr) *(IB 38 pts H 18 pts)*

London (King's) – AABb–ABBb +LNAT (Law; Engl Fr Law) *(IB 38 pts H555/5544)*

London (LSE) – AAA–AAB (Law) *(IB 38 pts H766/666)*

London (SOAS) – AAA (Law courses) *(IB 40 pts)*

London (UCL) – AAA+AS +LNAT (Law; Law Advnc St; Law Fr Law; Law Ger Law; Law Ital Law; Law Hisp Law; Engl Fr Law; Engl Ger Law)

Manchester – AAA (Law; Engl Law Fr Law; Law Crim)

Newcastle – AAA (Law; Law Fr) *(IB 38 pts H666)*

Nottingham – AAA–AAB +LNAT (Law; Law Fr; Law Ger) *(IB 40 pts)*

Oxford – Offers vary eg AAA–AAB +LNAT (Law; Law Law St Euro) *(IB 38–42 pts)*

Queen's Belfast – AAA–AABa (Law; Law Acc; Law Pol) *(IB 34 pts H666)*

Sheffield – AAA–AAB (Law; Euro Int Compar Law; Law joint courses) *(IB 35 pts)*

Southampton – AAA–AAB +LNAT 360 pts +LNAT (Law) *(IB 36 pts H 18 pts)*

Warwick – AAAc–AAB +LNAT (Law 3yr/4yr) *(IB 36–38 pts)*

Warwick – AABb–AAAc (Euro Law; Law Bus St)

Warwick – ABBc (Law Sociol)

York – AAA–AAB (Law)

340 pts **Aston** – AAB–ABB 340–320 pts (Law Mgt)
Cardiff – AAB–BBB (Law Pol; Law Sociol)
Durham – AAB (Sociol Law)
East Anglia – 340–360 pts (Law; Law Euro Leg Sys)
Essex – 340–320 pts (Law; Engl Fr Law; Phil Law; Law Pol; Law Hum Rts; Engl Euro Law)
Glasgow – AAB +LNAT (Law courses)
Lancaster – AAB (Law; Law Crim; Euro Leg St) *(IB 31 pts H 17 pts)*
Leeds – AAB (Law Mgt; Law Fr)
Leicester – AAB 340–400 pts (Law; Law Fr Law Lang; Engl Fr Law (LLB Maîtrise))
Liverpool – 340–390 pts (Engl Fr Law Fr; LLB Law)
London (King's) – AAB–AAA +LNAT **or** AAbbb–ABaab +LNAT (Law Ger Law)
Manchester – AAB (Law Pol)
Reading – AAB (Law; Law Leg St Euro)
Sheffield – AAB (Law Fr; Law Ger; Law Span; Law Crim)
Strathclyde – AAB (Scots Law)
Surrey – AAB–BBB (Law; Law Fr Law; Law Ger Law; Law Span Law; Law Int St)
Sussex – AAB–ABB **or** 360 pts 3AL+AS (Law courses) *(IB 34–36 pts)*
Westminster – AAB (Commer Law)
320 pts **Brunel** – ABB–AAC 320 pts (Law) *(IB 34 pts)*
City – ABB 320 pts (Law; Law Prop Val; Engl Fr Law) *(IB 32 pts)*
East Anglia – ABB (Law Fr Law Lang)
Kent – 320 pts (Law; Engl Fr Law; Engl Ger Law; Engl Ital Law; Engl Span Law; Law joint courses; Euro Leg St) *(IB 34 pts)*
Leeds – ABB (Acc Law)
London (LSE) – ABB (Anth Law)
London (QM) – ABB–BBB (Law; Engl Euro Law; Law Ger)
Northumbria – ABB 320 pts (Law (exempting)) *(IB 32 pts)*
Oxford Brookes – ABB–CCD (Law Comb Hons)
Ulster – ABB (Law; Law Econ; Law Int Pol; Law Pol; Law Fr/Ger/Irish/Span)
Westminster – ABB/AA (Euro Leg St; LLB Law; Law Fr) *(IB 32 pts)*
300 pts **Aberdeen** – BBB (Law; Law Acc; Law Econ; Law Mgt; Law Gael; Law Mus; Law Belg Law; Law Fr Law; Law Ger Law; Law Span Law) *(IB 36 pts)*
Aston – 300 pts (Pol Law)
Bradford – 300 pts (Law)
Buckingham – 300 pts (Law; Law Fr; Law Bus Fin; Law Econ; Law Engl Lang St (EFL); Law Mgt St; Law Pol; Law Span)
Cardiff – BBB (Law Ger/Fr/Welsh)
Derby – 300 pts (Law; Law Crim; Law (Bus Law) (Int Law) (Soc Pblc Law))
Dundee – BBB 300 pts (Scots Law; Law (Engl NI); Law Fr/Ger/Span)
Edinburgh – BBB (Law courses)
Glasgow Caledonian – BBB (LLB Law)
Hull – BBB 320 pts (Law; Law Fr Law Lang; Law Ger Law Lang; Law Crim; Law Phil; Law Pol)
Kent – 300 pts (Law Fr/Ger)
Liverpool – 300 pts (Leg Bus St)
Manchester Met – BBB 300 pts (Law; Law Fr) *(IB 30 pts)*
Oxford Brookes – BBB **or** BBbb (Law)
Portsmouth – 300 pts (Law Crim)
Swansea – 300–320 pts (Law)
280 pts **Aberystwyth** – 280 pts (Law; Law joint courses) *(IB 32 pts)*
Bangor – 280 pts (Law) *(IB 28 pts)*
Birmingham City – 280 pts (Law; Law Am Leg St; Law Crim)
Bournemouth – 280 pts (Law; Law Tax; Acc Law)
Central Lancashire – BBC (Law)
Coventry – 280 pts (Law; Law Bus; Law Fr/Span)

De Montfort – 280 pts (Law Crim Just; Law)
Glamorgan – 280 pts (Law; Commer Law; Euro Law; Law Crim)
Kingston – 280–320 pts (Law; Commer Law; Int Bus Law; Law Fr Law; Law Fr St)
Liverpool John Moores – 280 pts (Law) *(IB 30 pts)*
Nottingham Trent – 280 pts (Law) *(IB 24 pts)*
Salford – 280 pts (Law)
Strathclyde – BBC (Bus Law)

260 pts Abertay Dundee – BCC (LLB Hons Law)
East Lancashire (IHE) – 260 pts (Law)
Heriot-Watt – BCC (Bus Law courses)
Keele – 260–360 pts (Law; Law Dual Hons)
Sheffield Hallam – 260 pts (Law; Law Crim; Law Psy; Law Maîtrise Fr; Bus Law)

240 pts Aberdeen – CCC (Leg St courses)
Bolton – 240–200 pts (Law courses)
Bradford – 240 pts (Bus St Law; Hist Law; ICT Law; Pharm Sci Law)
Brighton – 240 pts (Law Bus)
Bristol UWE – 240–300 pts (Law; Commer Law; Euro Int Law; Law Fr/Ger/Span/EFL)
Chester – 240 pts (Law courses)
Edge Hill – 240 pts (Law; Law Crim)
Glamorgan – 240–280 pts (Bus Law; Crim Crim Just)
Greenwich – 240 pts (Law)
Hertfordshire – 240 pts (Law; Law joint courses)
Huddersfield – 240–300 pts (Law; Bus Law; Euro Leg St; Law Acc)
Liverpool Hope – 240 pts (Law)
London South Bank – CCC (Law courses)
Manchester Met – 240 pts (Consum Law; Law Tr Stnds)

For information on how to read the Subject Tables, see **Chapter 8**.

Napier – 240–200 pts (LLB Law)
Plymouth – 240–300 pts (Law courses)
Portsmouth – 240–280 pts (Law Acc; Law Bus; Law Int Rel; Law Fr; Law Euro St)
Robert Gordon – CCC (Law; Law Mgt)
Salford – 240–260 pts (Bus Mgt St Law)
Stirling – CCC (Bus St Law)
Swansea – 240–300 pts (Law joint courses)
Teesside – 240 pts (Law)
Thames Valley – 240 pts (Law) *(IB 24 pts)*

220 pts **Anglia Ruskin** – 220–260 pts (Law Crim; Bus Law)
Central Lancashire – 220–200 pts (Law Crim; Law Psy)
Lincoln – CCD 220 pts (Law)
Northampton – 220–240 pts (LLB Law)
Sunderland – 220 pts (Law) *(IB 33 pts)*

200 pts **Birmingham City** – 200 pts (Bus Bus Law; Bus Law joint courses) *(IB 30 pts)*
East London – 200–180 pts (Law; Crim Law; Acc Law; Bus St Law)
Gloucestershire – 200–260 pts (Law)
London Met – 200–280 pts (LLB (Soc Just) (Bus Law); Law; Int Law Int Pol)
Middlesex – 200–280 pts (Law)
Napier – 200 pts (BA Law)
Northampton – 200–240 pts (BA/BSc Law)
Plymouth – 200–220 pts (Law joint courses)
Southampton Solent – 200–260 pts (Law; Commer Law)
Staffordshire – 200–300 pts (LLB Law; LLB (Crim) (Hum Rts) (Bus Law) (Spo Law) (Intnet Commer))

180 pts **Bradford (Coll)** – BC–CC 180–160 pts (LLB Law)
Derby – 180–220 pts (Law Comb)
Glasgow Caledonian – BC (Bus Law)
Greenwich – 180 pts (Law joint courses)

160 pts **Bedfordshire** – 160–240 pts (Law; Acc Law)
Canterbury Christ Church – CC (Leg St courses)
Central Lancashire – 160 pts (Law Bus; Law Engl Lit; Law Pol)
Leeds Trinity and All Saints (Coll) – CC (Bus Law)
London Met – 160–200 pts (Leg Econ St; BA Bus Law)
London South Bank – CC (Law Comb)
North East Wales (IHE) – 160 pts (Law Bus)
St Mary's (UC) – CC 160 pts (Bus Law courses)
Staffordshire – 160–200 pts (Advc Wk Law)
West Scotland – CC (Law; Law Pol)
Wolverhampton – 160–220 pts (LLB Law; BA Law; Bus Law; Soc Welf Law Sociol)

120 pts **Bucks New** – 120–180 pts (Law; Bus Law)
Grimsby (IFHE) – 120 pts (Law)
Peterborough Reg (Coll) – 120 pts (Bus Law)

100 pts **Bradford (Coll)** – 100–140 pts (Acc Law; Mark Law)

80 pts **Croydon (Coll)** – 80 pts (Law)
Holborn (Coll) – 80 pts (Law)
Lansdowne (Coll) – 80 pts (Law)

Leeds Met – contact University
London (Birk) – degree reqd (not Law) interview+reasoning test (p/t Accelerated Law)
London Regents Bus Sch – check with admissions tutor (Law)
Open University – contact University

Alternative offers
See **Chapter 8** for grade/point equivalences and related information for the following examinations:
Scottish qualifications, the Welsh Baccalaureate, the IB diploma (approximate points shown also in

italics in the table of offers), the Irish Leaving Certificate, the European Baccalaureate and the French Baccalaureate.

EXAMPLES OF FOUNDATION DEGREES IN THE SUBJECT FIELD
Bradford; Croydon (Coll); Kingston; Peterborough Reg (Coll); Portsmouth; Shrewsbury (Coll); Truro (Coll); Walsall (Coll); Weston (Coll).

CHOOSING YOUR COURSE (SEE ALSO CH.1)
Course variations – Widen your options
Human Rights (Aberystwyth)
Law and Taxation (Bournemouth)
Law (4-year thin sandwich) (Brunel)
Forensic Biology and Law (Chester)
English and French Law (City)
Scots Law (Dundee)
Business Studies and Law (Edinburgh)
European Law (French Maîtrise/German Magister) (Essex)
Commercial Law (Hull)
Law with another Legal System – Australia/Hong Kong/Singapore (London (UCL))
Law and Trading Standards (Manchester Met)
Maritime Business and Law (Plymouth)
European, International and Comparative Law (Sheffield)
Law and Spanish Law (Surrey)
European Law including a Year Abroad (Warwick)
CHECK PROSPECTUSES AND WEBSITES FOR OTHER UNIVERSITIES AND COLLEGES OFFERING THESE COURSES.

Universities and colleges teaching quality See www.qaa.ac.uk; www.unistats.com.

Top universities and colleges (Research) Aberdeen; Birmingham; Bristol; Brunel; Cambridge*; Cardiff; City; Dundee; Durham*; East Anglia; Edinburgh; Essex; Exeter; Glasgow; Hull; Keele*; Kent; Lancaster; Leeds; Leicester; London (King's), (LSE)*, (QM)*, (SOAS), (UCL)*; Manchester; Newcastle; Nottingham; Oxford*; Queen's Belfast; Reading; Sheffield; Southampton*; Strathclyde; Ulster; Warwick; Westminster.

Sandwich degree courses Aston (compulsory); Birmingham City; Bournemouth; Bradford; Brighton; Brunel; City; Coventry; De Montfort; Hertfordshire; Huddersfield; Lancaster; Nottingham Trent; Oxford Brookes; Plymouth; Portsmouth; Staffordshire; Surrey; Teesside; Westminster.

ADMISSIONS INFORMATION
Number of applicants per place (approx) Abertay Dundee 3; Aberystwyth 8; Anglia Ruskin 10; Aston 10; Bangor 3; Birmingham 7; Birmingham City 20; Bournemouth 9; Bradford (Coll) 2; Bristol 20; Bristol UWE 27; Brunel 2; Buckingham 3; Cambridge 7; Cardiff 12; Central Lancashire 36; City 23; Coventry 15; De Montfort 6; Derby 7; Dundee 6; Durham 14; East Anglia 14; East London 13; Edinburgh 5; Essex 26; Exeter 15; Glamorgan 3; Glasgow 8; Glasgow Caledonian 10; Huddersfield 10; Hull 15; Kent 11; Kingston 25; Lancaster 8; Leeds 15; Leicester 14; Liverpool 10; Liverpool John Moores 10; London (King's) 14, (LSE) 14, (QM) 17, (SOAS) 8, (UCL) 21; London Met 13; London South Bank 4; Manchester Met 21; Middlesex 25; Napier 7; Newcastle 13; Northampton 4; Northumbria 12; Nottingham 25; Nottingham Trent 15; Oxford (success rate 25%, (Law Law St Euro) 10%); Oxford Brookes 18; Plymouth 14; Robert Gordon 4; Sheffield 16; Sheffield Hallam 6; Southampton 8; Southampton Solent 5; Staffordshire 16; Strathclyde (Law) 10; Sussex 10; Teesside 3; Thames Valley 18; Warwick 20; Westminster 29; Wolverhampton 12.

Advice to applicants and planning the UCAS personal statement Visit the law courts and take notes on cases heard. Follow leading legal arguments in the press. Read the law sections in *The Independent*, *The Times* and *The Guardian*. Discuss the career with lawyers and, if possible, obtain work shadowing in lawyers' offices. Describe these visits and experiences and indicate any special areas of law which interest you. (Read *Learning the Law* by Glanville Williams.) **Birmingham** We look for commitment to the study of law as an academic discipline (not necessarily to taking up a career in it) and for a commitment to study in Birmingham. When writing to admissions tutors, especially by email, take care to present yourself well. Text language is not acceptable. You should use communication as an opportunity to demonstrate your skill in the use of English. Spelling mistakes, punctuation errors and bad grammar suggest that you will struggle to develop the expected writing ability (see **Misconceptions about this course**) and may lead to your application being rejected. When writing to an admissions tutor do not demand an answer 'immediately' or 'by return' or 'urgently'. If your query is reasonable the tutor will respond without such urging. Adding these demands is bad manners and suggests that you are doing everything at the last minute and increases your chances of a rejection. **Bournemouth** Good command of English required. **Bristol** Make sure you submit a detailed statement which includes evidence that you have researched what the study of law entails. **Brunel** Intermediate London External LLB may enable direct entry to year 2. **Glamorgan** Fluency in English required. **Oxford** Criteria for admission: motivation and capacity for sustained and intense work; the ability to analyse and solve problems using logical and critical approaches; the ability to draw fine distinctions, to separate the relevant from the irrelevant; the capacity for accurate and critical observation, for sustained and cogent argument; creativity and flexibility of thought and lateral thinking; competence in English; willingness and the ability to express ideas clearly and effectively, to listen and to be able to give considered responses. (It should be assumed that these criteria will also apply to other Law courses.) **Oxford Brookes** Work experience very important, particularly for mature students. **Sheffield Hallam** Experience with a law firm, strong academic profile and interest in current affairs. **Southampton** Evidence that the applicant has given serious thought to the career; reading, work experience, court visits. See also **Appendix 2**.

Misconceptions about this course **Aberystwyth** Some applicants believe that all Law graduates enter the legal profession – this is incorrect. **Birmingham** Applicants do not necessarily have to be predicted to obtain the grades in our standard offer in order to receive an offer; after all, predictions are frequently inaccurate. Students tend to believe that success in the law centres on the ability to learn information. Whilst some information does necessarily have to be learnt, the most important skills involve (a) developing an ability to select the most relevant pieces of information and (b) developing the ability to write tightly argued, persuasively reasoned essays on the basis of such information. **Bristol** Many applicants think that most of our applicants have been privately educated: the reverse is true. **Derby** Many applicants do not realise the amount of work involved to get a good degree classification.

Selection interviews Approximately four well-qualified candidates apply for every place on undergraduate Law courses in the UK and the National Admission Test for Law (LNAT) has been introduced by a number of universities (see **Chapter 7**). Only candidates performing well in this test will be called for interview at universities requiring LNAT, but a good performance in this test, however, does not guarantee an interview or admission (see www.lnat.ac.uk). **Yes** Aberystwyth, Bristol, Bristol UWE, Buckingham, Cambridge, Central Lancashire, Coventry, Durham, East London, Essex, Glasgow, Lancaster, Liverpool, Liverpool John Moores, London (UCL), London South Bank, Napier, Northumbria, Nottingham, Oxford, Queen's Belfast, Southampton Solent, Surrey, Teesside, Warwick; **Some** Anglia Ruskin, Bangor, Birmingham, Cardiff, Derby, Dundee, East Anglia, Exeter, Huddersfield, Kent (mature/Access students), Nottingham Trent (mature students), Oxford Brookes (mature students), Sheffield Hallam, Southampton (mature students), Staffordshire, Sunderland; **No** Sussex.

Interview advice and questions Law is a highly competitive subject and applicants will be expected to have a basic awareness of aspects of law and to have gained some work experience, on which they are likely to be questioned. It is almost certain that a legal question will be asked at interview and applicants will be tested on their responses. Questions in the past have included: What interests you in the study of law? What would you do to overcome the problem of prison overcrowding if you were (a) a judge (b) a prosecutor (c) the Prime Minister? What legal cases have you read about recently? What is jurisprudence? What are the causes of violence in society? A friend bought a bun which, unknown to him, contained a stone. He gave it to you to eat and you broke a tooth. Could you sue anyone? Have you visited any law courts? What cases did you see? A person arrives in

England unable to speak the language. He lights a cigarette in a non-smoking compartment of a train. Can he be charged and convicted? What should be done in the case of an elderly person who steals a bar of soap? What, in your opinion, would be the two basic laws in Utopia? Describe, without using your hands, how you would do the butterfly stroke. What would happen if there were no law? Should we legalise euthanasia? If you could change any law, what would it be? How would you implement the changes? If a person tries to kill someone using black magic, are they guilty of attempted murder? If a jury uses a ouija board to reach a decision, is it wrong? If so, why? Jane attends an interview. As she enters the building she sees a diamond brooch on the floor. She hands it to the interviewer who hands it to the police. The brooch is never claimed. Who is entitled to it? Jane? The interviewer? The police? The university authorities? The Crown? Mr Grabbit who owns the building? **Cambridge** Logic questions. If I returned to the waiting room and my jacket had been taken and I then took another one, got home and actually discovered it was mine, had I committed a crime? If the interviewer pulled out a gun and aimed it at me, but missed as he had a bad arm, had he committed a crime? If the interviewer pulled out a gun and aimed it at me, thinking it was loaded but, in fact, it was full of blanks and fired it at me with the intention to kill, had he committed a crime? Which of the three preceding situations are similar and which is the odd one out? If a law is immoral, is it still a law and must people abide by it? For example, when Hitler legalised the systematic killing of Jews, was it still law? For joint courses: what academic skills are needed to succeed? Why a joint degree? Where does honesty fit into law? **Oxford** Should the use of mobile phones be banned on public transport? Is wearing school uniform a breach of human rights? If you could go back in time to any period of time, when would it be and why? Would you trade your scarf for my bike, even if you have no idea what state it's in or if I even have one? Is someone guilty of an offence if they did not set out to commit a crime but ended up doing so? Does a girl-scout have a political agenda? See also **Chapter 7**.

Applicants' impressions (A=Open day; B=Interview day) **Brunel** (A) Tour of the campus, a sample lecture and a chat with the tutors. **Kent** (A) The Open day included a tour of the campus, talks on the course, finance and accommodation. **Reading** (A) We attended a lecture and a seminar, toured the halls and had lunch. **Southampton** (A) We were set a series of tasks, followed by talks, and visited halls of residence.

Reasons for rejection (non-academic) 'Dreams' about being a lawyer! Poorly informed about the subject. Badly drafted application. Under-estimate of work load. Poor communication skills. **Manchester Met** Some were rejected because they were obviously more suited to Psychology.

AFTER-RESULTS ADVICE
Offers to applicants repeating A-levels **Higher** Aberystwyth, Bristol UWE, Coventry, Dundee, Essex, Glamorgan, Glasgow, Hull, Leeds, London Met, Manchester Met, Newcastle, Nottingham, Oxford Brookes, Queen's Belfast, Sheffield, Sheffield Hallam, Strathclyde, Warwick; **Possibly higher** Liverpool; **Same** Anglia Ruskin, Bangor, Birmingham, Bradford (Coll), Brighton, Bristol, Brunel, Cardiff, De Montfort, Derby, Durham, East Anglia, Huddersfield, Kingston, Lincoln, Liverpool Hope, Liverpool John Moores, Northumbria, Nottingham Trent, Staffordshire, Stirling, Sunderland, Surrey, Wolverhampton; **No offers made** Cambridge.

GRADUATE DESTINATIONS AND EMPLOYMENT (2005/6 HESA)
Graduates surveyed 8010 **Employed** 2445 **In further study** 3645 **Assumed unemployed** 305.

Career note Many graduates seek to practise in the legal profession after further training. However, a law degree provides a good starting point for many other careers in industry, commerce and the public services. Consumer protection can lead to specialisation and qualification as a trading standards officer.

OTHER DEGREE SUBJECTS FOR CONSIDERATION
Criminology; Economics; Government; History; International Relations; Politics; Social Policy and Administration; Sociology.

LEISURE and RECREATION MANAGEMENT/STUDIES

(see also **Sports Sciences/Studies** and **Tourism and Travel**)

The courses cover various aspects of leisure and recreation. Specialist options include recreation management, tourism and countryside management, all of which are offered as individual degree courses in their own right. There is also an obvious link with Sports Studies and Physical Education courses. See also **Appendix 2**.

Useful websites www.ispal.org.uk; www.bized.co.uk; www.leisuremanagement.co.uk; www.baha.org.uk; www.leisureopportunities.co.uk; www.recmanagement.com; www.isrm.co.uk; www.uksport.gov.uk; www.london2012.org.

NB The points totals shown to the left of the institutions are for ease of reference only. It must not be assumed that tariff points are always used by institutions or that they can be substituted for an offer in grades. The level of an offer is not necessarily indicative of the quality of a course.

COURSE OFFERS INFORMATION

Subject requirements/preferences GCSE Normally English and mathematics grades A–C. **AL** No specified subjects. **NB** A* grades are likely to form part of university offers in the higher ranges for students applying for places in 2008 for entry in 2009: check websites.

Your target offers

340 pts Loughborough – 340 pts (Spo Leis Mgt; Geog Spo Leis Mgt)
280 pts Manchester – BBC (Mgt Leis)
260 pts Brighton – 260 pts (Spo Leis Mgt) *(IB 30 pts)*
240 pts Bangor – 240–280 pts 2AL (Leis Tour Res Mgt; Leis Mgt) *(IB 26 pts)*
        Coventry – 240 pts (Leis Mgt)
        Hull – 240 pts (Spo Leis Mgt)
        Ulster – CCC 240 pts (Leis Evnts Cult Mgt)
230 pts Napier – 230 pts (Fstvl Evnts Mgt courses)
220 pts Bournemouth – 220 pts (Leis Mark)
        Cumbria – 220–200 pts (Advntr Recr Mgt; Out St; Out Ldrshp)
        Liverpool Hope – 220 pts (Leis Comb Hons)
        Liverpool John Moores – 220 pts (Tour Leis Mgt) *(IB 25 pts)*
        Staffordshire – CCD 220 pts (Spo Leis Mgt)
        Winchester – 220–280 pts (Leis Mgt courses)
200 pts Aberystwyth – 200 pts (Cntry Rec Tour)
        Cardiff (UWIC) – BB 200 pts (Leis Mgt courses)
        Central Lancashire – 200–240 pts (Leis Mgt) *(IB 28 pts)*
        Gloucestershire – 200–280 pts (Advntr Leis Mgt courses; Leis Spo Mgt courses)
        Manchester Met – 200 pts (Leis St joint Hons; Leis Mgt)
        Salford – 200pts (Leis Tour Mgt; Spo Leis Mgt) *(IB 26 pts)*
180 pts Bedfordshire – 180–240pts (Leis Mgt)
        Birmingham (UC) – 180 pts (Advntr Tour Mgt) *(IB 24 pts)*
        Chichester (UC) – 180–220 pts (Advntr Educ) *(IB 28 pts)*
        Kingston – 180 pts (Out Educ)
        Liverpool John Moores – 180 pts (Tour Leis Lang)
        Marjon (UC) – 180 pts (Out Advntr courses)
        Portsmouth – 180–200 pts (Leis Mgt Mark)
        Teesside – 180–220 pts (Leis Mgt; Leis Tour Mgt) *(IB 24 pts)*
160 pts Canterbury Christ Church – CC (Spo Leis Mgt)
        Central Lancashire – 160–180 pts (Out Ldrshp courses)
        Glasgow Caledonian – CC (Enter Evnts Mgt)
        Manchester Met – 160 pts (Leis Mgt; Leis Mgt (Out Actvts)) *(IB 28 pts)*
        SAC (Scottish CAg) – CC (Advntr Tour Out Prsts; Rur Recr Tour Mgt; Leis Mgt (Spo Recr))

140 pts **Blackpool and Fylde (Coll)** – 140 pts (Leis Evnts Enter Mgt)
Derby – 140 pts (Out Recr courses)
Suffolk (Univ Campus) – 140 pts (Leis Mgt)

120 pts **Bucks New** – 120–180 pts (Spo Leis Mgt)
Southampton Solent – 120 pts (Out Advntr Mgt)
Swansea (Inst) – 120–180 pts (Leis Mgt)
Writtle (Coll) – 120 pts (Leis Tour Mgt; Advntr Tour; Out Recr Cons)

Leeds Met – contact University

Alternative offers

See **Chapter 8** for grade/point equivalences and related information for the following examinations: Scottish qualifications, the Welsh Baccalaureate, the IB diploma (approximate points shown also in italics in the table of offers), the Irish Leaving Certificate, the European Baccalaureate and the French Baccalaureate.

EXAMPLES OF FOUNDATION DEGREES IN THE SUBJECT FIELD

(see also **Tourism and Travel**) Bicton (Coll); Blackpool and Fylde (Coll); Bolton; Bournemouth; Chichester; Cornwall (Coll); Cumbria; Derby; Edge Hill; Harper Adams (UC); Kingston Maurward (Coll); Leeds Park Lane (Coll); Liverpool (CmC); Loughborough (Coll); Myerscough (Coll); Newcastle (Coll); Oxford Brookes; Plymouth; Sheffield (Coll); Shuttleworth (Coll); Solihull (Coll); South Birmingham (Coll); Teesside; West Nottinghamshire (Coll); Weymouth (Coll); Wolverhampton; Writtle (Coll); Yorkshire Coast (Coll).

CHOOSING YOUR COURSE (SEE ALSO CH.1)

Course variations – Widen your options

Hospitality and Leisure Management (Birmingham (UC))
Marine Leisure Management (Bournemouth)
Sport and Leisure Management (Brighton)
Leisure Management (Licensed Premises) (Cardiff (UWIC))
Outdoor Leadership (Central Lancashire)
Adventure Leisure Management (Gloucestershire)
Sport and Leisure Management (Loughborough)
Entertainment Management (Leeds Met)
Exercise, Physical Activity and Leisure Management (Manchester Met)
Festival and Events Management (Napier)
Rural Recreation and Tourism Management (SAC (Scottish CAg)).
CHECK PROSPECTUSES AND WEBSITES FOR OTHER UNIVERSITIES AND COLLEGES OFFERING THESE COURSES.

Sandwich degree courses
Brighton; Gloucestershire; Loughborough; Ulster.

ADMISSIONS INFORMATION

Number of applicants per place (approx)
Brighton 10; Cardiff (UWIC) 3; Coventry 14; Gloucestershire 7; Hull 3; Liverpool John Moores 3; Loughborough 25; Portsmouth 3; SAC (Scottish CAg) 4; Swansea (Inst) 8; Writtle (Coll) 8.

Advice to applicants and planning the UCAS personal statement
Work experience, visits to leisure centres and national park centres and any interests you have in particular aspects of leisure should be described, for example, art galleries, museums, countryside management, sport. An involvement in sports and leisure as a participant or employee is an advantage. See also **Appendix 2**.

Misconceptions about this course
The level of business studies in leisure management courses is higher than many students expect.

Selection interviews
Yes Coventry, Writtle (Coll); **Some** Blackpool and Fylde (Coll), Liverpool John Moores, Salford.

Interview advice and questions
In addition to sporting or other related interests, applicants will be

expected to have had some work experience and can expect to be asked to discuss their interests. What do you hope to gain by going to university? See **Chapter 7**.

Reasons for rejection (non-academic) Poor communication or presentation skills. Relatively poor sporting background or knowledge.

AFTER-RESULTS ADVICE
Offers to applicants repeating A-levels Same Blackpool and Fylde (Coll), Cardiff (UWIC), Liverpool John Moores, Salford.

GRADUATE DESTINATIONS AND EMPLOYMENT (2005/6 HESA)
No data available.

Career note Career opportunities exist in public and private sectors within leisure facilities, health clubs, the arts, leisure promotion, marketing and events management. Some graduates work in sports development and outdoor activities.

OTHER DEGREE SUBJECTS FOR CONSIDERATION
Business Studies; Hospitality Management; Sports Studies; Tourism.

LINGUISTICS
(see also **English**)

Linguistics covers the study of language in general, and also includes areas such as children's language, slang, language handicap, advertising language, language styles and the learning of foreign languages.

Useful websites www.iol.org.uk; www.cal.org; http://web.mit.edu/linguistics; www.applij.oxfordjournals.org; www.aclweb.org; www.lsadc.org; www.sil.org; www.baal.org.uk.

NB The points totals shown to the left of the institutions are for ease of reference only. It must not be assumed that tariff points are always used by institutions or that they can be substituted for an offer in grades. The level of an offer is not necessarily indicative of the quality of a course.

COURSE OFFERS INFORMATION
Subject requirements/preferences GCSE English required and a foreign language preferred. **AL** English may be required or preferred for some courses. **NB** A* grades are likely to form part of university offers in the higher ranges for students applying for places in 2008 for entry in 2009: check websites.

Your target offers
360 pts **and above**
    Cambridge – AAA (Ling (Part II subject, taken after Part I in another usually language-related subject)) *(IB 38–42 pts)*
    London (UCL) – AABe–BBBe (Ling courses) *(IB 32–34 pts)*
    Oxford – AAA–AAB (Modn Lang Ling) *(IB 38–42 pts)*
340 pts **St Andrews** – AAB (Engl Ling)
320 pts **Lancaster** – ABB–BBB (Ling; Socioling; Ling Psy; Ling N Am; Engl Lang Ling; Engl Lit Ling)
    London (King's) – ABB–BBC (Ling courses)
    Manchester – ABB–BBB (Ling; Ling Sociol; Ling Soc Anth; Ling Port/Russ/Span; Ling Mid E Lang; Engl Lit Ling; Ling Jap) *(IB 32–33 pts)*
    St Andrews – ABB–BBC (Ling courses except under **340 pts**)
    Sheffield – ABB–BBB (Ling courses)
    Southampton – ABB (Fr/Ger/Span Ling St) *(IB 32 pts)*
    Sussex – ABB–BBB 360–340 pts 3AL+AS (Ling courses) *(IB 32–34 pts)*
    York – ABB–BBB (Engl Ling; Fr/Ger Ling; Langs Ling; Phil Ling; Maths Ling) *(IB 34 pts)*

300 pts **Edinburgh** – BBB (Ling; Ling Artif Intel; Comput Ling; Ling Soc Anth; Ling Modn Lang) *(IB 34 pts H555)*

Lancaster – BBB (Ling Phil) *(IB 30 pts H 16 pts)*

Leeds – BBB–BBC (Ling courses) *(IB 32 pts)*

Newcastle – ABC–BBB (Ling courses) *(IB 32 pts H Engl 5 pts)*

Queen's Belfast – BBB–BBCb (Ling courses)

280 pts **Essex** – 280 pts (Engl Lang Ling; Engl Lang Socioling) *(IB 28 pts)*

Oxford Brookes – BBC (Engl Lang Ling courses)

260 pts **London (QM)** – 260–300 pts (Ling courses) *(IB 32 pts)*

London (SOAS) – 260–300 pts (Ling courses) *(IB 30 pts)*

Ulster – 260 pts (Ling Adv; Ling Comm; Ling Hlth Comm; Ling PR) *(IB 24 pts)*

Westminster – BCC (Ling courses) *(IB 30 pts)*

240 pts **Aberdeen** – CCC (Lang Ling courses)

Bangor – 240–260 pts (Ling Engl Lang; Ling Engl Lit)

Brighton – CCC (Engl Lang Ling; Fr St/Ger St Ling)

Bristol UWE – 240–300 pts (Ling joint courses) *(IB 26–32 pts)*

Salford – 240–300 pts (Ling Fr/Ger/Ital/Port/Span)

220 pts **Nottingham Trent** – 220–240 pts (Ling courses)

200 pts **Central Lancashire** – 200 pts (Engl Lang Ling Comb Hons)

Manchester Met – 200–220 pts (Ling courses)

Roehampton – 200–280 pts (Engl Lang Ling)

Sunderland – 200 pts (Ling courses)

180 pts **Wolverhampton** – 180–220 pts (Ling courses)

160 pts **East London** – 160 pts (App Ling)

Greenwich – 160 pts (ELT Ling)

140 pts **Marjon (UC)** – 140–200 pts (Engl Lang Ling courses)

80 pts **London (Birk)** – no A-level reqs (p/t Ling Lang)

Alternative offers

See **Chapter 8** for grade/point equivalences and related information for the following examinations: Scottish qualifications, the Welsh Baccalaureate, the IB diploma (approximate points shown also in italics in the table of offers), the Irish Leaving Certificate, the European Baccalaureate and the French Baccalaureate.

CHOOSING YOUR COURSE (SEE ALSO CH.1)

Course variations – Widen your options

English Studies with Linguistics (Brighton)
History and Linguistics (Bristol UWE)
Linguistics and Artificial Intelligence (Edinburgh)
Language and Communication (Essex)
Socio-Linguistics (Lancaster)
Public Relations with English Language and Linguistics (Marjon (UC))
German (Linguistic Studies) (Southampton)
The Spanish-speaking World (Southampton)
Linguistics and Cognitive Science (Sussex)
CHECK PROSPECTUSES AND WEBSITES FOR OTHER UNIVERSITIES AND COLLEGES OFFERING THESE COURSES.

Universities and colleges teaching quality
See www.qaa.ac.uk; www.unistats.com.

Top universities and colleges (Research)
Cambridge*; Edinburgh; Essex; Lancaster; London (QM)*, (UCL)*; Manchester; Newcastle; Oxford*; Westminster; York.

ADMISSIONS INFORMATION

Number of applicants per place (approx)
Bangor 3; East London 3; Essex 1; Lancaster 12; Leeds 12; York 11.

Advice to applicants and planning the UCAS personal statement
Give details of your interests in

language and how it works, and about your knowledge of languages and their similarities and differences.

Selection interviews Yes Brighton, Cambridge, East London, Essex, Lancaster, Newcastle, Reading; **Some** Salford, Sheffield.

Interview advice and questions Past questions include: Why do you want to study Linguistics? What does the subject involve? What do you intend to do at the end of your degree course? What answer do you give to your parents or friends when they ask why you want to study the subject? How and why does language vary according to sex, age, social background and regional origins? See **Chapter 7**.

Reasons for rejection (non-academic) Lack of knowledge of linguistics. Hesitation about the period to be spent abroad.

AFTER-RESULTS ADVICE
Offers to applicants repeating A-levels Higher Essex, Sussex; **Same** Brighton, Leeds, Newcastle, Salford, York.

GRADUATE DESTINATIONS AND EMPLOYMENT (2005/6 HESA)
Graduates surveyed 470 **Employed** 210 **In further study** 95 **Assumed unemployed** 35.

Career note Students enter a wide range of careers, with information management and editorial work in publishing offering some interesting and useful outlets.

OTHER DEGREE SUBJECTS FOR CONSIDERATION
Communication Studies; English; Speech Sciences.

LITERATURE
(see also **English**)

This is a very broad subject introducing many aspects of the study of literature and aesthetics. Courses will vary in content. Degree courses in English and foreign languages will also include a study of literature.

Useful websites www.lrb.co.uk; www.literature.org; www.bibliomania.com; www.bl.uk; www.acla.org; http://icla.byu.edu.

NB The points totals shown to the left of the institutions are for ease of reference only. It must not be assumed that tariff points are always used by institutions or that they can be substituted for an offer in grades. The level of an offer is not necessarily indicative of the quality of a course.

COURSE OFFERS INFORMATION
Subject requirements/preferences GCSE English and a foreign language usually required. **AL** English may be required or preferred for some courses. **NB** A* grades are likely to form part of university offers in the higher ranges for students applying for places in 2008 for entry in 2009: check websites.

Your target offers

360 pts **and above**
        Warwick – AABb (Film Lit)

340 pts **East Anglia** – AAB (Engl Lit Crea Writ)
        East Anglia – AAB–ABB (Engl Lit)

320 pts **East Anglia** – ABB–BBB (Engl Am Lit; Cult Lit Pol; Lit Hist)
        Glasgow – 320 pts ABB–BBB (Scot Lit courses; Compar Lit) *(IB 30 pts)*
        London (King's) – ABB+AS (Compar Lit; Compar Lit Film St) *(IB 35 pts)*
        London (RH) – ABB–BBB (Euro Lit Cult St)

Manchester – ABB–BBC (Lit St courses)

York – ABB–BBB (Ling Lit)

300 pts **Edinburgh** – BBB (Scot Ethnol Scot Lit)

Essex – BBB–BBC 300–280 pts (Compar Lit; Lit Myth; Engl US Lit; Engl Lang Lit; Lit Sociol; Lit Hist Art; Hist Lit; Phil Lit; Lit Modn Lang; Dr Lit) *(IB 29 pts)*

London (Gold) – BBB (Engl Compar Lit) *(IB 32 pts)*

Reading – 300–280 pts (Euro Lit Cult; Engl Lit courses)

260 pts **Kent** – 260–300 pts (Compar Lit St courses) *(IB 28 pts)*

Stirling – BCC 1st yr entry (Scot Lit)

240 pts **Aberdeen** – CCC (Engl Scot Lit; Lang Lit Scot)

Ulster – 240 pts (Irish Irish Lit Engl)

200 pts **Sunderland** – 200 pts (Engl Lang Lit)

Worcester – 200 pts (Engl Lit St)

180 pts **Lampeter** – 180 pts (Welsh St; Engl Modn Lit; Engl Lit)

Alternative offers

See **Chapter 8** for grade/point equivalences and related information for the following examinations: Scottish qualifications, the Welsh Baccalaureate, the IB diploma (approximate points shown also in italics in the table of offers), the Irish Leaving Certificate, the European Baccalaureate and the French Baccalaureate.

EXAMPLES OF FOUNDATION DEGREES IN THE SUBJECT FIELD

Bath Spa; Truro (Coll); Winchester.

CHOOSING YOUR COURSE (SEE ALSO CH.1)

Course variations – Widen your options

Classical Literature and Civilisation (Birmingham)

Cultural Criticism and English Literature (Cardiff)

English Literature and Creative Writing (East Anglia)

Scottish Ethnology and Scottish Literature (Edinburgh)

Comparative Literature (Essex)

Creative Writing and English Literature (Kingston)

Media and Modern Literature (London (Gold))

European Literature (London (RH))

English with minor North American Literature and Film (Loughborough)

Language, Literature and Communication (Manchester)

Combined Studies – English Literature (Newcastle)

English and Post-colonial Literature (Stirling)

Film and Literature (Warwick)

CHECK PROSPECTUSES AND WEBSITES FOR OTHER UNIVERSITIES AND COLLEGES OFFERING THESE COURSES.

ADMISSIONS INFORMATION

Number of applicants per place (approx) East Anglia 12; Essex 4.

Advice to applicants and planning the UCAS personal statement **Kent** Interest in literatures other than English. See **English**.

Misconceptions about this course **Kent** Some students think that a foreign language is required – it is not.

Selection interviews **Yes** Lampeter.

Interview advice and questions **Kent** Which book would you take on a desert island, and why? What is the point of doing a Literature degree in the 21st century? See **English**. See also **Chapter 7**.

Reasons for rejection (non-academic) **Kent** Perceived inability to think on their feet.

For information on how to read the Subject Tables, see **Chapter 8**.

AFTER-RESULTS ADVICE
Information not available from institutions.

GRADUATE DESTINATIONS AND EMPLOYMENT (2005/6 HESA)
Graduates surveyed 145 Employed 70 In further study 30 Assumed unemployed 5.

Career note See English.

OTHER DEGREE SUBJECTS FOR CONSIDERATION
Arts; English; Linguistics; Welsh and Celtic Studies.

MARINE/MARITIME STUDIES

(including **Oceanography;** see also **Biology** (for **Marine Biology** courses) and **Naval Architecture**)

Marine and Maritime Studies can involve a range of subjects such as marine business, technology, navigation, nautical studies, underwater rescue and transport.

Useful websites www.bized.co.uk; www.british-shipping.org; www.uk-sail.org.uk; www.rya.org.uk; www.royalnavy. mod.uk; www.sstg.org; www.noc.soton.ac.uk; www.nautinst.org; www.mcsuk.org; www.nmm.ac.uk; www.imo.org; www.mcga.gov.uk.

NB The points totals shown to the left of the institutions are for ease of reference only. It must not be assumed that tariff points are always used by institutions or that they can be substituted for an offer in grades. The level of an offer is not necessarily indicative of the quality of a course.

COURSE OFFERS INFORMATION
Subject requirements/preferences **GCSE** Mathematics and science are required for several courses. **AL** Science or mathematics will be required or preferred for some courses. **NB** A* grades are likely to form part of university offers in the higher ranges for students applying for places in 2008 for entry in 2009: check websites.

Your target offers

360 pts **East Anglia** – AAA–ABB (Meteor Ocean courses except under **280 pts**) *(IB 32 pts H66 inc maths)*
　　　Southampton – AAA (MOcean Ocean N Am)
320 pts **Liverpool** – 320 pts (Mar Biol) *(IB 38 pts)*
　　　Newcastle – ABB (MEng Mar Tech; Mar Eng; Off Eng; Nvl Archit; Sml Crft Tech) *(IB 35 pts)*
300 pts **Aberdeen** – BBB (Mar Cstl Res Mgt; Mar Biol) *(IB 28 pts)*
　　　Liverpool – BBB 300 pts (Ocean Chem; Ocn Earth Sys; Ocn Clim; Civ Marit Eng) *(IB 31 pts)*
　　　Southampton – BBB 300 pts (MOcean Ocean; Ocean Fr; Ocn Earth Sys Sci) *(IB 30–32 pts)*
280 pts **East Anglia** – BBC (Meteor Ocean)
　　　Essex – 280–240 pts (Mar Frshwtr Biol) *(IB 26–28 pts)*
　　　London (QM) – 280 pts (Mar Frshwtr Biol)
　　　Newcastle – BBC (BEng Mar Tech; Mar Eng; Off Eng; Nvl Archit; Sml Crft Tech)
　　　Plymouth – 280 pts (Mar Biol Cstl Ecol; Mar Biol Ocean) *(IB 24 pts)*
　　　Southampton – BBC 280 pts (BSc Ocean; Ocean Physl Geog; Ocean Geol; Ocn Phys; Ocn Chem; Ocn Earth Sys Sci) *(IB 30–32 pts)*
260 pts **Bangor** – 260–320 pts (App Mar Biol; Mar Biol Zool; Mar Biol Ocean) *(IB 28 pts)*
　　　Cardiff – BCC–CCC (Mar Geog) *(IB 32 pts)*
　　　Hull – 260–300 pts (Aqua Zool; Mar Frshwtr Biol)
　　　Plymouth – BCC 260 pts (BEng Mar Tech)
240 pts **Bangor** – 240–280 pts (Mar Biol Ocean; Mar Biol Vrtbrt Zool)
　　　Portsmouth – 240–280 pts (Mar Biol)

FALMOUTH
MARINE
SCHOOL

CORNWALL'S COLLEGE
OF THE OCEAN

A BLOCKBUSTER FUTURE

We offer:
▌ Expert coaches
▌ Excellent links with industry
▌ Opportunities for jobs abroad

Foundation Degrees in:
▌ Boat Design Production FdSc
▌ Marine Environmental Management FdSc
▌ Marine Leisure Management FdSc
▌ Marine Sports Science FdSc
▌ Marine Science FdSc
▌ Operational Yacht Science FdSc

With expert lecturers on hand to give you all the advice
and support you need, you really cannot ask for more.

Courses validated by the University of Plymouth.

* £2000 annual fees with £500 fee waiver (full-time courses)

Tuition fees
from just
£1500*

Part of The **CORNWALL COLLEGE** GROUP

For further details contact:
Tel: 01326 310310
Email: falenquiries@cornwall.ac.uk
www.falmouthmarineschool.ac.uk
Falmouth Marine School, Killigrew Street, Falmouth, TR11 3QS

CHARITY BY STATUTE

UNIVERSITY
OF PLYMOUTH · COLLEGES
CORNWALL COLLEGE

COMBINED UNIVERSITIES
IN CORNWALL

416 | Marine/Maritime Studies

220 pts **Bangor** – 220–260 pts (Ocn Sci; Geol Ocean; Ocean Comp; Cstl Geog; Geol Ocean; Mar Env St) *(IB 28 pts)*

Hull – 220–280 pts (Cstl Mar Biol)

Ulster – CCD (Mar Sci) *(IB 24 pts)*

200 pts **Coventry** – 200–240 pts (Boat Des)

Plymouth – 200 pts (Ocn Explor; Surf Sci Tech; Marit Bus; Marit Bus Log; Marit Bus Marit Law; Ocn Sci; App Mar Spo Sci; Mar St (Ocn Ycht) (Navig))

Portsmouth – 200 pts (Mar Spo Tech)

Southampton Solent – 200 pts (Wtrspo St Mgt)

Strathclyde/Glasgow – BB–CCC (BSc Hons Naut Sci) *(IB 30 pts)*

180 pts **Greenwich** – 180 pts (Naut Sci Tech)

Heriot-Watt – DDD (App Mar Biol)

Kingston – 180 pts (Mar Frshwtr Biol)

Portsmouth – 180–240 pts (Mar Env Sci)

Southampton Solent – 180 pts (BEng Ycht Manuf Surv; Ycht Pwrcrft Des)

160 pts **Bournemouth** – 160 pts (Mar Arch; Env Cstl Mgt)

Glamorgan – 160–180 pts (Boat Des)

Plymouth – 160 pts (Mar Spo Tech; Env Sci (Mar Cons); Mar Cmpste Tech)

Southampton Solent – 160 pts (Geog Mar St)

Strathclyde/Glasgow – CC–DDD (BSc Naut Sci) *(IB 26 pts)*

140 pts **Blackpool and Fylde (Coll)** – 140 pts (Cstl Cons Mar Biol)

Liverpool John Moores – 140–200 pts (Marit St; Marit Bus Mgt; Navig Mar Tech; Naut Sci)

120 pts **South Tyneside (Coll)** – 120–180 pts (Mar Ops; Mar Eng)

Southampton Solent – 120 pts (Marit Bus; Marit St; Mar Ship Port Mgt; Ship Mar Eng)

100 pts **Hull (Scarborough)** – 100 pts (Fdn Cstl Mar Biol)

Pembrokeshire (Coll) – 100 pts (Cstl Zn Mar Env St)

80 pts **and below**

Eastleigh (Coll) – (Fdn Sci)

UHI Millennium Inst (NHC) – check with admissions tutor (Mar Sci)

Alternative offers

See **Chapter 8** for grade/point equivalences and related information for the following examinations: Scottish qualifications, the Welsh Baccalaureate, the IB diploma (approximate points shown also in italics in the table of offers), the Irish Leaving Certificate, the European Baccalaureate and the French Baccalaureate.

EXAMPLES OF FOUNDATION DEGREES IN THE SUBJECT FIELD

Blackpool and Fylde (Coll); Bournemouth; Bournemouth & Poole (Coll); Cornwall (Coll).

CHOOSING YOUR COURSE (SEE ALSO CH.1)

Course variations – Widen your options

Marine and Freshwater Biology (Aberystwyth)
Applied Terrestrial and Marine Ecology (Bangor)
Coastal Geography (Bangor)
Ocean Science (Bangor)
Marine Archaeology (Bournemouth)
Marine and Natural History Photography (Falmouth (UC))
Navigation and Marine Technology (Liverpool John Moores)
Naval Architecture (London (UCL))
Marine Engineering (Newcastle)
Applied Marine Sport Science (Plymouth)
Marine Studies (Merchant Shipping) (Plymouth)
Marine Studies (Ocean Yachting) (Plymouth)
Surf Science and Technology (Plymouth)
Ship Science and Marine Systems Engineering (Southampton)

CHECK PROSPECTUSES AND WEBSITES FOR OTHER UNIVERSITIES AND COLLEGES OFFERING THESE COURSES.

Universities and colleges teaching quality See www.qaa.ac.uk; www.unistats.com.

Sandwich degree courses Liverpool John Moores; Plymouth; Southampton Solent.

ADMISSIONS INFORMATION
Number of applicants per place (approx) Glasgow 2; Liverpool John Moores (Marit St) 3.

Advice to applicants and planning the UCAS personal statement This is a specialised field and, in many cases, applicants will have experience of marine activities. Describe these experiences, for example, sailing, snorkelling, fishing. **UHI Millennium Inst (NHC)** Small intake, high staff/student ratio. Mature students welcome. See also **Appendix 2**.

Selection interviews Yes UHI Millennium Inst (NHC).

Interview advice and questions Most applicants will have been stimulated by their studies in science or will have strong interests or connections with marine activities. They are likely to be questioned on their reasons for choosing the course. See **Chapter 7**.

AFTER-RESULTS ADVICE
Offers to applicants repeating A-levels Same Bangor, Liverpool John Moores, Plymouth, UHI Millennium Inst (NHC).

GRADUATE DESTINATIONS AND EMPLOYMENT (2005/6 HESA)
Maritime Technology graduates surveyed 80 **Employed** 50 **In further study** 5 **Assumed unemployed** 5.

Ocean Sciences graduates surveyed 170 **Employed** 75 **In further study** 35 **Assumed unemployed** 15.

Career note This subject area covers a very wide range of vocational courses, each offering graduates an equally wide choice of career openings in either purely scientific or very practical areas.

OTHER DEGREE SUBJECTS FOR CONSIDERATION
Biology; Civil Engineering; Environmental Studies/Sciences; Marine Engineering; Marine Transport; Naval Architecture; Oceanography.

MARKETING

(including **Public Relations;** see also **Art and Design (Fashion), Business Courses,** and **Food Sciences/Studies and Technology**)

Marketing courses are very popular and applications should include evidence of work experience or work shadowing. Marketing is a subject also covered in most Business Studies courses and in specialist (and equally relevant) courses such as Leisure Marketing and Food Marketing for which lower offers are often made. Most courses offer the same subject content.

Useful websites www.adassoc.org.uk; www.cim.co.uk; www.camfoundation.com; www.ipa.co.uk; www.ipsos-mori.com; www.marketingstudies.net; www.marketingtoday.com.

NB The points totals shown to the left of the institutions are for ease of reference only. It must not be assumed that tariff points are always used by institutions or that they can be substituted for an offer in grades. The level of an offer is not necessarily indicative of the quality of a course.

COURSE OFFERS INFORMATION
Subject requirements/preferences GCSE English and mathematics. **AL** No specified subjects required. **NB** A* grades are likely to form part of university offers in the higher ranges for students applying for places in 2008 for entry in 2009: check websites.

360 pts **and above**

Lancaster – AAA (Mark N Am/Aus) *(IB 32 pts)*

Leeds – AAA (Mgt Mark) *(IB 38 pts)*

340 pts Lancaster – AAB (Mark Mgt; Adv Mark) *(IB 32 pts)*

Manchester – AAB (Mgt (Mark))

Ulster – 340 pts (Comm Adv Mark)

320 pts Aston – ABB 320 pts (Marketing) *(IB 34 pts H665)*

Cardiff – ABB (Bus Mgt (Mark))

Lancaster – ABB (Marketing)

London (RH) – 320–340 pts (Mgt Mark)

Newcastle – ABB (Mark; Mark Mgt) *(IB 34 pts)*

Northumbria – ABB–BBC (Mark Mgt; Adv Mgt)

300 pts Bournemouth – 300 pts (Adv Mark Comm)

Hull – 300 pts (Mgt Mark)

Liverpool – BBB (Marketing) *(IB 32 pts)*

Reading – 300 pts (Consum Bhv Mark)

Stirling – BBB 2nd yr entry (Rtl Mark)

280 pts Bournemouth – 280–260 pts (Mark; Int Mark) *(IB 30 pts)*

Brunel – 280 pts (Bus Mgt (Mark))

Essex – 280 pts (Mark Innov)

Kingston – 280 pts (Mark Mgt)

Reading – 280 pts (Fd Mark Bus Econ)

Strathclyde – BBC/ABC (Mark; Mark Modn Langs)

Swansea – 280 pts (Bus Mgt (Mark); Mgt Sci (Mark))

Ulster – 280 pts (Marketing)

260 pts Aberystwyth – 260 pts (Mark courses) *(IB 27 pts)*

Coventry – 260 pts (Mark Mgt; Bus Mark; Adv Mark; Mark Acc)

Heriot-Watt – BCC (Mgt Mark)

Hertfordshire – 260 pts (Marketing)

Keele – 260–320 pts (Mark courses)

Kent – 260 pts (Bus St Mark) *(IB 33 pts)*

Oxford Brookes – BCC–BBC (Mark Mgt courses)

Richmond (Am Int Univ) – 260 pts (Bus Admin (Mark))

Staffordshire – BCC (Mark Mgt)

Stirling – BCC 2nd yr entry (Mark; Rtl Mark)

Westminster – 260–280 pts (Bus Mark Mgt; Mark Comm; Int Mark Glob Mark)

240 pts Bangor – 240–280 pts (Mark Fr/Ger/Ital/Span)

Bradford – 240–300 pts (Marketing)

Brighton – 240 pts (Rtl Mark; Bus Mgt Mark; Mark Fd Drink; Int Evnt Mark)

Bristol UWE – 240–300 pts (Mark courses)

Buckingham – 240 pts (Mark Fr/Span; Mark Media Comm; Mark Psy)

Central Lancashire – 240 pts (Mark Bus; Mark Int Bus; Mark Mgt; Mark PR) *(IB 28 pts)*

Chester – 240–260 pts (Marketing)

Coventry – 240 pts (Spo Mark; Tour Mark)

De Montfort – 240 pts (Mark; Int Mark Bus; Bus Mark)

Huddersfield – 240–260 pts (Mark courses)

Hull – 240–280 pts (Mark; Mark (Int) (Prof Exp); Mark Bus Econ)

Liverpool Hope – 240 pts (Mark courses)

Liverpool John Moores – 240 pts (Marketing)

Manchester Met – 240 pts (Consum Mark)

Northumbria – CCC (Mark Lang; Bus Mark)

Nottingham Trent – 240 pts (3AL or Art Fdn) (Fash Mark Comm)

Plymouth – 240–260 pts (Marketing)

Portsmouth – 240–200 pts (Mark; Mark Psy; Mark joint courses)

For a quick reference offers calculator, fold out the inside back cover.

Robert Gordon – 240 pts (Mgt Mark)
Salford – 240–300 pts (Bus St Mark Mgt)
Sheffield Hallam – 240 pts (Bus Mark)
Stirling – CCC (Modn Lang Mark)
Winchester – 240–280 pts (Bus Mgt Mark)
Worcester – 240 pts (Bus Mgt Mark; PR courses)

220 pts **Abertay Dundee** – CCD (Mark Bus)
Bolton – 220 pts (Marketing)
Bournemouth – 220 pts (Fd Mark; Leis Mark)
Dundee – 220–300 pts (Bus Econ Mark)
Glamorgan – 220–280 pts (Mark courses)
Napier – 220–240 pts (Mark Mgt)
Roehampton – 220–160 pts (Mark; Mark Fr/Span)
Sunderland – 220 pts (Bus Mark)

200 pts **Anglia Ruskin** – 200 pts (Marketing)
Birmingham City – 200–240 pts (Mark courses)
Coventry – 200–260 pts (Adv Mark; Mark courses)
Cumbria – 200 pts (Bus Mark)
Edge Hill – 200 pts (Marketing)
Gloucestershire – 200–280 pts (Mark Mgt Brnd; Int Bus Mark)
Lincoln – 200–220 pts (Mark courses)
Liverpool John Moores – 200 pts (PR courses)
London Met – 200–240 pts (Mark; Mark Bus Mgt)
Manchester Met – 200 pts (Fd Mark; Int Fash Mark; Rtl Mark Mgt; Mark Mgt)
Sheffield Hallam – 200 pts (Fd Mark)

180 pts **Birmingham (UC)** – 180 pts (Mark Mgt; Mark Evnts Mgt; Mark Tour Mgt; Mark Hspty Mgt)
Cardiff (UWIC) – 180 pts (Mark; Bus St Mark)
Derby – 180–240 pts (Mark Mgt)
Greenwich – 180 pts (Adv Mark Comm; Glob Mark; Glob Mark Langs; Mark)
Marjon (UC) – 180–240 pts (PR courses)
Northampton – 180–220 pts (Mark; Mark Psy; Enter Mark; Fash Mark; Rtl Mark)
Queen Margaret – 180 pts (Mark courses; PR)
Southampton Solent – 180 pts (Mark courses)
Writtle (Coll) – 180 pts (Mark Sply Chn Mgt)

160 pts **Arts London** – CC (Fash Mark Prom; Mark Adv)
Bedfordshire – 160–240 pts (Mark; Adv Mark Comm; Mark Media Prac)
Canterbury Christ Church – CC (Mark courses)
Creative Arts (UC) – 160 pts (Des Brnd Mark)
Doncaster (Coll) – 160–240 pts (Bus Mark)
East London – 160 pts (Mark; Fash Des Mark)
Farnborough (CT) – 160–200 pts (Mark courses)
Glasgow Caledonian – CC (Mark; Fash Mark)
Leeds Trinity and All Saints (Coll) – 160–240 pts (Mark; Media Mark; Bus Mark)
London South Bank – CC (Mark; Mark Comb courses)
Middlesex – 160–280 pts (Mark; Mark Mgt; Mark Comm)
North East Wales (IHE) – 160 pts (Marketing)
Royal (CAg) – 160 pts (Bus Mgt (Mark))
South East Essex (Coll) – 160–180 pts (Bus St (Mark))
Staffordshire – 160 pts (Adv Brnd Mgt)
Swansea (Inst) – 160 pts (Marketing)
Teesside – 160 pts (Mark; Mark Rtl Mgt; Mark Adv Mgt; PR; Prod Des (Mark))
Thames Valley – 160 pts (Mark Adv; Mark Bus)
West Scotland – CC (Mark Int Mark)
Wolverhampton – 160–220 pts (Mark; PR)

For information on how to read the Subject Tables, see **Chapter 8**.

140 pts **Harper Adams (UC)** – 140–280 pts (Agri-Fd Mark courses; Agric Mark)
          Suffolk (Univ Campus) – 140–200 pts (Mark Mgt)
120 pts **Bradford (Coll)** – 120 pts (Mark Sls; Mark Law)
          Bucks New – 120–180 pts (Mark courses)
          Roehampton – 120–200 pts (Marketing)
          Southampton Solent – 120 pts+Art Fdn (Prod Des Mark)
  80 pts **and below**
          Arts London (CComm) – 80 pts (Mark Adv; PR)
          Arts London (CFash) – 2AL contact admission tutor (Mark Adv)
          Croydon (Coll) – 80 pts (Bus (Mark))
          European Bus Sch London – 80 pts (Int Bus Mark Lang)
          Regents Bus Sch London – 80 pts (Int Mark)

          Leeds Met – contact University

Alternative offers

See **Chapter 8** for grade/point equivalences and related information for the following examinations: Scottish qualifications, the Welsh Baccalaureate, the IB diploma (approximate points shown also in italics in the table of offers), the Irish Leaving Certificate, the European Baccalaureate and the French Baccalaureate.

EXAMPLES OF FOUNDATION DEGREES IN THE SUBJECT FIELD

Arts London (CComm); Barry (Coll); Birmingham (UC); Bournemouth; Bournemouth and Poole (Coll); Brighton; Croydon; Dewsbury (Coll); Glamorgan; Gwent (Coll); Leeds (CAD); Manchester City (Coll); Merthyr Tydfil (Coll); Newcastle (Coll); Northampton; Sheffield (Coll); South East Essex (Coll); Southampton Solent; West Herts (Coll).

CHOOSING YOUR COURSE (SEE ALSO CH.1)

Course variations – Widen your options

Food Marketing (Birmingham (UC))
International Marketing (Bournemouth)
Marketing Food and Drink (Brighton)
Retail Marketing (Cardiff (UWIC))
Fashion and Brand Promotion Marketing (Central Lancashire)
Advertising and Media (Coventry)
Marketing and Innovation (Essex)
Agri-Food Marketing (Harper Adams (UC))
Marketing with Professional Experience (Hull)
Sports Development (Leeds Trinity and All Saints (Coll))
Public Relations (Middlesex)
Property Marketing Design and Development (Portsmouth)
Consumer Behaviour and Marketing (Reading)
CHECK PROSPECTUSES AND WEBSITES FOR OTHER UNIVERSITIES AND COLLEGES OFFERING THESE COURSES.

Universities and colleges teaching quality See www.qaa.ac.uk; www.unistats.com.

Top universities and colleges (Research) Aston.

Sandwich degree courses Aston; Bournemouth; Bradford; Brighton; Bristol UWE; Brunel; Central England; Central Lancashire; Coventry; De Montfort; East London; Glamorgan; Glasgow Caledonian; Gloucestershire; Greenwich; Harper Adams (UC); Hertfordshire; Huddersfield; Hull; Lancaster; Leeds Met; Liverpool John Moores; London South Bank; Manchester; Manchester Met; Middlesex; Napier; Northumbria; Oxford Brookes; Plymouth; Portsmouth; Royal (CAg); Sheffield Hallam; Staffordshire; Sunderland; Swansea (Inst); Teesside; West Scotland; Westminster.

ADMISSIONS INFORMATION

Number of applicants per place (approx) Abertay Dundee 6; Aberystwyth 3; Anglia Ruskin 5; Aston

9; Birmingham 4; Bournemouth 10; Brunel 10; Central England 15; Central Lancashire 13; De Montfort 3; Derby 5; Glasgow Caledonian 15; Harper Adams (UC) 3; Huddersfield 7; Lancaster 28; Lincoln 3; London Met 10; Northampton 4; Northumbria 8; Nottingham Trent 2; Plymouth 12; Portsmouth 4; Staffordshire 6; Stirling 10; Teesside 3.

Advice to applicants and planning the UCAS personal statement See **Business Courses.** See also **Appendix 2**.

Selection interviews Yes Harper Adams (UC) (advisory), Manchester Met, Middlesex, Northbrook (Coll), Writtle (Coll); **Some** Aberystwyth, Anglia Ruskin, Aston, Buckingham, De Montfort, Queen Margaret, Staffordshire.

Interview advice and questions Past questions include: What is marketing? Why do you want to take a Marketing degree? Is sales pressure justified? How would you feel if you had to market a product which you considered to be inferior? **Buckingham** What job do you see yourself doing in five years' time? See **Chapter 7**.

Reasons for rejection (non-academic) Little thought of reasons for deciding on a Marketing degree. Weak on numeracy and problem-solving. Limited commercial awareness. Poor inter-personal skills. Lack of leadership potential. No interest in widening their horizons, either geographically or intellectually. 'We look at appearance and motivation and the applicant's ability to ask questions.' Not hungry enough. Limited understanding of the career. No clear reasons for wishing to do the course.

AFTER-RESULTS ADVICE
Offers to applicants repeating A-levels Same Aberystwyth, Anglia Ruskin, Aston, Buckingham, De Montfort, Lincoln, Manchester Met, Queen Margaret, Staffordshire.

GRADUATE DESTINATIONS AND EMPLOYMENT (2005/6 HESA)
Graduates surveyed 2100 **Employed** 1450 **In further study** 75 **Assumed unemployed** 140.

Career note See under **Business Courses**.

OTHER DEGREE SUBJECTS FOR CONSIDERATION
Advertising; Art and Design; Business Studies; Communications; Graphic Design; Psychology; Public Relations.

MATERIALS SCIENCE/METALLURGY
(including **Polymer Engineering**)

Materials Science is a subject which covers physics, chemistry and engineering at one and the same time! From its origins in metallurgy, materials science has now moved into the processing, structure and properties of materials – ceramics, polymers, composites and electrical materials. Materials science and metallurgy are perhaps the most misunderstood of all careers and applications for degree courses are low with very reasonable offers. Valuable bursaries and scholarships are offered by the Institute of Materials, Minerals and Mining (check with Institute – see **Appendix 2**). Polymer Science is a branch of materials science and is often studied in conjunction with Chemistry and covers such topics as polymer properties and processing relating to industrial applications with, for example, plastics, paints, adhesives. See also **Appendix 2**.

Useful websites www.scienceyear.com; www.uksteel.org.uk; www.iom3.org.uk; www.noisemakers.org.uk; www.imm.org.

NB The points totals shown to the left of the institutions are for ease of reference only. It must not be assumed that tariff points are always used by institutions or that they can be substituted for an offer in grades. The level of an offer is not necessarily indicative of the quality of a course.

COURSE OFFERS INFORMATION

Subject requirements/preferences **GCSE** Science/mathematics subjects. **AL** Mathematics, physics and/or chemistry required for most courses. (Polymer Science) Mathematics and/or physics usually required; design technology encouraged. **NB** A* grades are likely to form part of university offers in the higher ranges for students applying for places in 2008 for entry in 2009: check websites.

Your target offers

360 pts **and above**
    Cambridge – AAA varies between colleges (Nat Sci (Mat Sci Metal)) *(IB 38–42 pts)*
    Oxford – Offers vary eg AAA–AAB (Mat Sci; Mat Econ Mgt) *(IB 38–42 pts)*

340 pts **London (UCL)** – ABBe (Hist Art Mat St) *(IB 34 pts)*
    Manchester – AAB–ABC (Mat Sci Eng; Biomed Mat Sci) *(IB 32–35 pts)*
    Sheffield – AAB **or** AAbb (MEng Eng (Civ Mat Mech)) *(IB 30–32 pts)*
    Southampton – AAB 340 pts (MEng Mech Eng Advnc Mat) *(IB 34 pts)*
    Strathclyde – AAB (Mech Eng Mat Eng)

320 pts **Imperial London** – ABB (MEng Mat Sci Eng; Biomat Tiss Eng; Aerosp Mat)
    Leeds – ABB (Chem Mat Eng)
    Liverpool – ABB 320 pts (MEng Mat Eng; Mat Sci Eng) *(IB 26–30 pts)*
    Newcastle – ABB–BBB (MEng Mech Mat Eng; Mat Proc Eng) *(IB 34 pts)*
    Nottingham – ABB (MEng Mech Des Mat Manuf) *(IB 30–32 pts)*
    St Andrews – ABB 2nd yr entry (Mat Sci; Chem Mat Chem) *(IB 31 pts)*
    Sheffield – ABB **or** ABbb (MEng Mat Sci Eng courses; Metal; Biomat Sci Tiss Eng) *(IB 30–33 pts)*

300 pts **Birmingham** – BBB–BBC (Mech Mat Eng; Mat Sci Tech Mat Eng; Metal Mat Eng; Biomed Mat Sci; Spo Sci Mat Tech; Mat Sci Eng Bus Mgt) *(IB 30 pts)*
    Edinburgh – BBB (Chem Mat Chem) *(IB 30 pts)*
    Leeds – BBB 3AL (MEng Mat Sci Eng) *(IB 30 pts)*
    London (QM) – 300 pts (MEng Aerosp Mat Tech; Dntl Mat; Env Mat Tech; Mat Foren Sci; Mat Bus; Biomat; Biomed Mat Sci Eng; Spo Mat)
    Loughborough – 300 pts (MEng Mat Eng; Auto Mat) *(IB 32 pts)*
    Newcastle – BBB–BBC **or** BBcc (BEng Mech Mat Eng; Mat Proc Eng) *(IB 30 pts)*
    Nottingham – BBB (Biomed Mat Sci) *(IB 30–32 pts)*
    St Andrews – BBB 1st yr entry (Mat Sci)

280 pts **Aberdeen** – BBC 280 pts 2nd yr entry (Eng (Mech Mat)) *(IB 22 pts)*
    Imperial London – BBC (BEng Mat Sci Eng; Mat Yr Abrd; Mat Mgt; Mat Mgt Yr Abrd)
    Liverpool – BBC 280 pts (BEng Mat Sci Eng; Mat Des Manuf) *(IB 26 pts)*
    Sheffield – BBC (BEng Mat Sci Eng; Biomat Sci Tiss Eng; Aerosp Mat; Mat Sci Eng Modn Lang) *(IB 30–33 pts)*

260 pts **London (QM)** – 260 pts (BEng Biomed Mat Sci Eng; Mat Sci Eng; Mat For Sci; Env Mat Tech; Mat Bus; Poly Tech; Mat Eng Med; Biomat; Dntl Mat; Spo Mat) *(IB 26–32 pts)*
    Nottingham – BCC (BSc Mech Des Mat Manuf) *(IB 30–32 pts)*

240 pts **Leeds** – CCC (BEng Mat Sci Eng; Spo Mat Tech)
    London (QM) – 240 pts (BSc Biomat; Mat Sci Eng; Mat Eng Med) *(IB 26–32 pts)*
    Loughborough – 240 pts (BEng Mat Eng; Auto Mat; Des Eng Mat)
    Swansea – 240–300 pts (Mat Sci Eng)

220 pts **Aberdeen** – CCD 1st yr entry (Eng (Mech Mat))
    Napier – 220 pts (Poly Eng)

200 pts **Liverpool** – CDD 200 pts (BEng Fdn Mat Sci)

180 pts **Northampton** – 180 pts (Mat Tech (Lea))

160 pts **Plymouth** – 160 pts (Mar Cmpste Tech)

120 pts **London Met** – 120 pts (Poly Eng)

Alternative offers

See **Chapter 8** for grade/point equivalences and related information for the following examinations: Scottish qualifications, the Welsh Baccalaureate, the IB diploma (approximate points shown also in

italics in the table of offers), the Irish Leaving Certificate, the European Baccalaureate and the French Baccalaureate.

EXAMPLES OF FOUNDATION DEGREES IN THE SUBJECT FIELD
Bradford (Coll); Capel Manor (Coll); Plymouth City (Coll); Staffordshire (Reg Fed); West Nottinghamshire (Coll).

CHOOSING YOUR COURSE (SEE ALSO CH.1)
Course variations – Widen your options
Biomedical Materials Science (Birmingham)
Sports Science and Materials Technology (Birmingham)
Sport Technology (Tennis) (Cycling) (Golf) (Central Lancashire)
Aerospace Materials (Imperial London)
Nanotechnology (Leeds)
Dental Materials (London (QM))
Polymer Engineering (London Met)
Materials Technology (Leather) (Northampton)
Maritime and Composites Technology (Plymouth)
CHECK PROSPECTUSES AND WEBSITES FOR OTHER UNIVERSITIES AND COLLEGES OFFERING THESE COURSES.

Universities and colleges teaching quality See www.qaa.ac.uk; www.unistats.com.

Top universities and colleges (Research) Birmingham*; Cambridge*; Imperial London; Liverpool; Manchester*; Oxford*; Sheffield*.

Sandwich degree courses Plymouth.

ADMISSIONS INFORMATION
Number of applicants per place (approx) Birmingham 8; Imperial London 3; Liverpool 3; Manchester Met 7; Nottingham 7; Oxford (success rate 62%); Swansea 4.

Advice to applicants and planning the UCAS personal statement Read scientific and engineering journals and describe any special interests you have. Try to visit chemical or technological installations (rubber, plastics, glass etc) describing any such visits. See also **Appendix 2**.

Misconceptions about this course Students are generally unaware of what this subject involves or the opportunities within the industry.

Selection interviews Yes Birmingham, Oxford; **Some** Leeds.

Interview advice and questions Questions are likely to be based on A/AS-level science subjects. Recent examples include: Why did you choose Materials Science? How would you make each part of this table lamp (on the interviewer's desk)? Identify this piece of material. How was it manufactured? How has it been treated? (Questions related to metal and polymer samples.) What would you consider the major growth area in materials science? **Birmingham** We try to gauge understanding; for example, an applicant would be unlikely to be questioned on specific facts, but might be asked what they have understood from a piece of coursework at school. **Oxford** Tutors look for an ability to apply logical reasoning to problems in physical science and an enthusiasm for thinking about new concepts in science and engineering. See **Chapter 7**.

AFTER-RESULTS ADVICE
Offers to applicants repeating A-levels Higher Swansea; **Same** Birmingham, Leeds, Liverpool, Manchester Met; **No offers made** Cambridge.

GRADUATE DESTINATIONS AND EMPLOYMENT (2005/6 HESA)
Materials Science graduates surveyed 270 **Employed** 125 **In further study** 65 **Assumed unemployed** 30.

Materials Technology graduates surveyed 236 **Employed** 110 **In further study** 55 **Assumed unemployed** 25.

Metallurgy graduates surveyed 20 **Employed** 10 **In further study** 5 **Assumed unemployed** none.

Polymer Science/Engineering graduates surveyed 260 **Employed** 185 **In further study** 15 **Assumed unemployed** 15.

Ceramics graduates surveyed 10 **Employed** 5 **In further study** none **Assumed unemployed** 5.

Career note Materials scientists are involved in a wide range of specialisms in which openings are likely in a range of industries. These include manufacturing processes in which the work is closely linked with that of mechanical, chemical, production and design engineers.

OTHER DEGREE SUBJECTS FOR CONSIDERATION
Aerospace Engineering; Biotechnology; Chemistry; Engineering Sciences; Mathematics; Mechanical Engineering; Plastics Technology; Physics; Product Design and Materials; Sports Technology.

MATHEMATICS
(including **Applied/Applicable Mathematics** and **Mathematical Sciences/Studies**)

Mathematics at degree level is an extension of A-level mathematics, covering pure and applied mathematics, statistics, computing, mathematical analysis and mathematical applications. Mathematics is of increasing importance and is used in the simplest of design procedures and not only in applications in the physical sciences and engineering. It also plays a key role in management, economics, medicine and the social and behavioural sciences.

Useful websites www.ima.org.uk; www.gchq.gov.uk/codebreaking; www.orsoc.org.uk; www.scienceyear.com; www.m-a.org.uk; www.mathscareers.org.uk; www.imo.math.ca; www.bmoc.maths.org; www.maths.org; www.ukmt.org.uk.

NB The points totals shown to the left of the institutions are for ease of reference only. It must not be assumed that tariff points are always used by institutions or that they can be substituted for an offer in grades. The level of an offer is not necessarily indicative of the quality of a course.

COURSE OFFERS INFORMATION
Subject requirements/preferences **GCSE** English often required and mathematics is obviously essential at a high grade for leading universities. **AS** further mathematics may be required. **AL** Mathematics, in several cases with a specified grade, required for all courses. **NB** A* grades are likely to form part of university offers in the higher ranges for students applying for places in 2008 for entry in 2009: check websites.

Your target offers
360 pts   and above

> **Bath** – AAA–AAB (Maths; BSc Maths; Mathem Sci; Maths Stats; Comp Sci Maths; Maths Phys) *(IB 36 pts H maths 6 pts)*
>
> **Bristol** – AAA–AAB (Maths; Maths Stats; Maths Euro; Maths Comp Sci; Maths Phil; Maths Phys; Biol Maths; Econ Maths) *(IB 36 pts H666)*
>
> **Cambridge** – AAA+STEP varies between colleges (Maths; Maths Phys; Maths Educ St) *(IB 38–42 pts)*
>
> **Durham** – AAA (Nat Sci (Maths)) *(IB 35 pts H maths 7 pts)*
>
> **Imperial London** – AAA (Maths Comp Sci) *(IB 38 pts)*
>
> **London (King's)** – AAA–AAB (Maths courses) *(IB 38 pts H maths 6 pts)*
>
> **London (LSE)** – AAA–AAB (Bus Maths Stats)
>
> **London (UCL)** – AAA+AS–AAB+AS (Maths courses) *(IB 36–38 pts H766)*
>
> **Nottingham** – AAA–AAB (Maths; Mathem Phys; Maths Comp Sci; Maths Chin St; Maths Econ; Maths Mgt St; Maths Phil) *(IB 35 pts H maths 6 pts)*

Oxford – Offers vary eg AAA–AAB (Maths; Maths Phil; Maths Comp Sci; Maths Stats) *(IB 38–42 pts)*

Sheffield – AAA (Maths Aus/N Am)

Southampton – AAA–ABB 360 pts (MMaths Maths)

Warwick – AAAa–AABa (Maths; Maths Bus St; Maths Econ; Maths Phil; Maths Comp; Maths Phys; MORSE) *(IB 34 pts H maths 6 pts)*

340 pts **Aberystwyth** – 340 pts (MMaths Maths) *(IB 31 pts)*

Birmingham – AAB–ABB 320 pts (Mathem Sci; Mathem Eng; Maths (Euro); Maths Bus Mgt; Maths Arts subjs) *(IB 34 pts H maths 6 pts)*

Durham – AAB; AAA joint Hons (Maths; Maths (Euro St); Maths Educ St; Comb Arts) *(IB 35 pts H maths 7 pts)*

East Anglia – AAB (MMath Maths; Maths Euro; Maths N Am)

Imperial London – 340 pts (MSci/BSc Maths; Maths Euro; Maths Stats; Maths Stats Fin; Maths App Maths; Maths Mathem Comput) *(IB 38 pts)*

Lancaster – AAB (Maths N Am/Aus; Maths Stats OR) *(IB 30–31 pts)*

Leeds – AAB (Maths; Maths Fin)

London (LSE) – AAB (Maths Econ)

London (QM) – 340 pts (MSci Maths courses) *(IB 32 pts H maths 6 pts)*

Manchester – AAB (Maths; Maths Bus Mgt; Maths Fin Maths; Maths Stats; Maths Modn Lang; Maths Phil; Maths Mgt)

Newcastle – AAB–ABB (MMaths Maths; MMaths Maths Stats; Maths Mgt; Maths Stats; Fin Maths; Fin Maths Mgt) *(IB 34–36 pts)*

Reading – 340 pts (Maths Psy)

St Andrews – AAB–ABB (Maths courses)

Southampton – AAB 340 pts (BSc Maths)

Surrey – AAB (MMaths Maths; Fin Maths) *(IB 30–32 pts)*

Sussex – AAB–ABB (Maths courses)

York – AAB–ABB (Maths courses) *(IB 34 pts H maths 6 pts)*

320 pts **Birmingham** – ABB–ABC 300 pts (Maths Comp Sci; Maths Phil; Maths Psy; Maths Spo Sci)

Bristol – ABB (Eng Maths Abrd)

Cardiff – ABB–ABC 300 pts (Maths; Maths App; Maths OR Stats; Phys Maths; Comp Maths; Maths Hum courses) *(IB 32 pts H maths 6 pts)*

East Anglia – ABB (BSc Maths; Maths Meteor; Maths Mgt St; Maths Econ; Maths Env Sci; Maths Stats; Maths Comp) *(IB 32 pts H maths 6 pts)*

Exeter – ABB–BBB (Maths; Maths Phys; Maths Comp Sci; Maths Acc; Maths Econ; Maths Fin; Maths Mgt) *(IB 29 pts H maths 6 pts)*

Glasgow – ABB–BBB (BA Maths) *(IB 28 pts)*

Lancaster – ABB (Mathematics) *(IB 30–31 pts)*

Leicester – 320–420 pts (MMaths Maths; MMaths Maths USA; Comput Maths; Maths Astron) *(IB 28–32 pts)*

Liverpool – ABB 320 pts (Maths; Mathem Sci; PMaths; Maths Stats; Maths joint courses)

London (RH) – ABB–ABC (Maths courses) *(IB 33 pts H maths 6 pts)*

Loughborough – 320 pts (Maths Spo Sci; Maths Econ)

Newcastle – ABB (Mathem Sci; Comp Sci Maths; Econ Maths; Geog Maths; Acc Maths; Maths Psy)

Nottingham – ABB (Maths Eng)

Queen's Belfast – ABB (App Maths Phys)

Reading – 320 pts (MMaths courses)

St Andrews – ABB (Maths courses except under **340 pts**)

Sheffield – ABB (Geog Maths; Env Maths; Maths Phil) *(IB 32 pts H maths 5 pts)*

Southampton – ABB 320 pts (Mathem St; Maths Fr/Ger; Maths Act St; Maths Astron; Maths Mus; Maths Mgt Sci) *(IB 33 pts H 16 pts)*

Strathclyde – ABB–BBB 2nd yr entry (MSci/BSc Maths courses)

Surrey – ABB (BSc Maths; Maths Stats; Maths Comp Sci; Maths Mus; Fin Maths)

Swansea – ABB 320 pts (MMaths courses)

For information on how to read the Subject Tables, see **Chapter 8**.

300 pts **Aberystwyth** – 300 pts (BSc Maths; PMaths Stats; App Maths joint courses; Fin Maths) *(IB 27 pts)*

Aston – BBB 300 pts (Maths; Maths Comb; Comp Sci Maths) *(IB 32 pts)*

Brunel – 300 pts (Mathematics) *(IB 32 pts H maths 6 pts)*

City – BBB (Maths Fin)

Dundee – BBB 300 pts 2nd yr entry (Maths courses) *(IB 28 pts)*

Edinburgh – ABC (Maths; PMaths; Maths Stats; Maths Mgt; Maths Phys; Maths Bus St; Maths Mus) *(IB 33 pts H maths 6 pts)*

Essex – 300–320 pts (Maths; Maths USA; Acc Maths; Maths Comp; Maths Econ; Fin Maths; Mgt Maths; Maths Crypt Net Scrty) *(IB 29–32 pts)*

Glasgow – BBB–BCC (BSc Maths; App Maths; Maths Stats)

Heriot-Watt – BBB–ABC 2nd yr entry (Act Maths Stats; Fin Maths)

Lancaster – BBB (Maths Phil)

Leeds – BBB–ABC (Mathem St)

Leicester – 300 pts (Maths courses except under **320 pts**)

Loughborough – BBB–ABC 300 pts (BSc Maths; Maths Comp; Maths Acc Fin Mgt; Maths Mgt; Fin Maths) *(IB 32 pts H maths 5 pts)*

Queen's Belfast – ABC (MSci Maths courses)

Reading – 300 pts (BSc Maths; Maths App Stats; Maths Meteor; Comput Maths)

Sheffield – BBB–BBC (Chem Maths; Comp Sci Maths; Econ Maths; Mgt Maths; Acc Fin Mgt Maths)

Stranmillis (UC) – BBB (Maths Educ)

Surrey – ABC 300 pts (BSc Maths Bus St; Maths Mgt)

280 pts **Aberdeen** – BBC 2nd yr entry (BSc Maths)

Brunel – 280 pts (Fin Maths)

Central Lancashire – BBC (Mathematics)

Lancaster – BBC (Maths Stats)

London (QM) – BBC 280 pts (BSc Maths courses)

Northumbria – 280 pts (Maths; Maths Bus) *(IB 30 pts)*

Oxford Brookes – BBC–CD (Maths courses)

Queen's Belfast – BBC–BCC (BSc Maths; Maths Euro; Comput Maths; App Maths Phys; Maths Stats OR)

Swansea – 280–300 pts (Maths courses except under **320 pts**)

260 pts **Brighton** – 260 pts (Maths; Maths Fin; Maths Bus; Maths Comp) *(IB 28 pts)*

Brunel – 260–300 pts (Maths Comp; Mathem Mgt St; Maths Stats Mgt)

Canterbury Christ Church – BCC (Maths Educ QTS)

City – BCC (Mathem Sci; Mathem Sci Comp Sci) *(IB 28 pts)*

Keele – 260–300 pts (Mathematics)

Kent – 260–280 pts (MMaths/BSc/BA Maths; Bus Maths; Fin Maths; Maths Stats; App Quant Fin) *(IB 28 pts)*

Kingston – 260 pts (Mathem Sci; Maths Bus Mgt; Act Maths Stats; Maths Med Stats) *(IB 26–28 pts)*

Lancaster – BCC (Env Maths)

Strathclyde – BCC–BBC (Maths courses)

240 pts **Aberdeen** – CCC (BA Maths)

Bristol UWE – 240–300 pts (Maths; Euro St Maths; Lat Am St Maths; Intnet Sys Maths) *(IB 24–28 pts)*

Central Lancashire – 240 pts (Maths Comb Hons; Maths Astron; Maths Psy)

Chester – 240 pts (Mathematics)

Dundee – 240 pts 1st yr entry (Maths courses)

Glamorgan – 240–280 pts (Maths; Maths Educ QTS)

Heriot-Watt – CCC 1st yr entry (Maths courses except under **300 pts**)

Liverpool Hope – 240 pts (Educ St (Maths))

Portsmouth – 240 pts (Maths; Maths Stats; Maths Fin Mgt; Maths Comp)

Reading – 240 pts (BSc Mathem St)

Winchester – 240–280 pts (Maths P Educ)
230 pts **Bolton** – 230 pts (Mathematics)
220 pts **Aberdeen** – CCD 1st yr entry (BSc Maths)
Central Lancashire – 220 pts (Maths Bus Inf Sys; Maths Educ)
Edge Hill – 220 pts (Maths Educ)
Manchester Met – 220–280 pts (BA/BSc Bus Maths Comb courses)
Stirling – CCD–CCC (Maths Apps; Maths courses)
200 pts **Coventry** – 200–260 pts (Mathem Sci; Maths courses)
Cumbria – 200 pts (Maths courses)
Liverpool John Moores – 200–240 pts (Maths courses)
London Met – 200–240 pts (Bus Maths)
Manchester Met – 200–260 pts (Maths courses)
Nottingham Trent – 200–280 pts (Maths courses)
Plymouth – 200 pts (Maths courses)
Sheffield Hallam – 200 pts (Maths; Maths Comp Apps; Maths Stats)
Staffordshire – 200–240 pts (Maths courses)
180 pts **Greenwich** – 180–220 pts (Maths; Maths Stats Comp)
Hertfordshire – 180 pts (Maths; Maths Comb St)
Northampton – 180–220 pts (Maths courses)
160 pts **Bishop Grosseteste (UC)** – 160 pts (Educ St Maths Tech)
Chichester – DDE 160–240 pts (Maths Educ QTS)
Derby – 160–240 pts (Mathem St; Mathem St Educ; Mathem Comp St)
Oxford Brookes – CC (Mathem Sci; Bus Stats Maths; Maths Stats)
140 pts **Wolverhampton** – 140–220 pts (Mathem Sci; Mathem Bus Analys; Mathem Sci Spo St)
120 pts **West Scotland** – DD **or** bbc (Mathem Sci courses)
80 pts **Aberystwyth** – 80 pts (Maths Ord)
London (Birk) – 80 pts for under 21s (over 21s varies) (p/t Maths Stats)

Open University – contact University

For information on how to read the Subject Tables, see **Chapter 8**.

Alternative offers
See **Chapter 8** for grade/point equivalences and related information for the following examinations: Scottish qualifications, the Welsh Baccalaureate, the IB diploma (approximate points shown also in italics in the table of offers), the Irish Leaving Certificate, the European Baccalaureate and the French Baccalaureate.

EXAMPLES OF FOUNDATION DEGREES IN THE SUBJECT FIELD
Nottingham Trent.

CHOOSING YOUR COURSE (SEE ALSO CH.1)
Course variations – Widen your options
Engineering Mathematics (Bristol)
Business Decision Mathematics (Bristol UWE)
Financial Mathematics (Brunel)
Mathematics, Cryptography and Network Security (Essex)
Decision Science (Greenwich)
Pure Mathematics (Imperial London)
Actuarial Mathematics (Kingston)
Biomedicine and Medical Statistics (Lancaster)
Computational Mathematics (Leicester)
Econometrics and Mathematical Economics (London (LSE))
Mathematical Physics (Nottingham)
Applied Mathematics (Swansea)
Mathematics, Operational Research, Statistics and Economics (MORSE) (Warwick)
CHECK PROSPECTUSES AND WEBSITES FOR OTHER UNIVERSITIES AND COLLEGES OFFERING THESE COURSES.

Universities and colleges teaching quality See www.qaa.ac.uk; www.unistats.com.

Top universities and colleges (Research) Aberdeen; Bath*; Birmingham; Bristol*; Brunel; Cambridge*; Cardiff; Dundee; Durham*; East Anglia; Edinburgh*; Exeter; Glasgow; Heriot-Watt; Imperial London*; Keele; Kent; Leeds; Leicester; Liverpool; London (King's), (QM), (RH), (UCL); Manchester; Newcastle; Nottingham; Oxford*; St Andrews; Sheffield; Southampton; Strathclyde; Surrey; Warwick*; York.

Sandwich degree courses Aston; Bath; Brighton; Brunel; Cardiff; Coventry; Derby; Glamorgan; Glasgow Caledonian; Greenwich; Hertfordshire; Kent; Kingston; Lancaster; Liverpool John Moores; Loughborough; Manchester Met; Northumbria; Nottingham Trent; Oxford Brookes; Portsmouth; Queen's Belfast; Reading; Sheffield Hallam; Staffordshire; Surrey; West Scotland; Wolverhampton; York.

ADMISSIONS INFORMATION
Number of applicants per place (approx) Aberystwyth 8, (App Maths) 5; Anglia Ruskin 6; Aston 8; Bangor 4; Bath 10; Birmingham 7; Bristol 7; Brunel 5; Cambridge 4; Cardiff 5; Central Lancashire 7; City 6; Coventry 8; Cumbria 9; Derby 4; Dundee 5; Durham 5; East Anglia 5; East London 2; Edinburgh 4; Exeter 6; Glamorgan 3; Greenwich 2; Hertfordshire 9; Heriot-Watt 5; Kent 8; Lancaster 12; Leeds (Maths) 5, (Maths Fin) 4; Leicester 8; Liverpool 5; London (Gold) 5, (King's) 8, (LSE) (Maths Econ) 10, (Bus Maths Stats) 10, (QM) 5, (RH) 8, (UCL) 8; London Met 3; Manchester Met 3; Middlesex 5; Newcastle 7; Northumbria 7; Nottingham 15; Oxford (success rate 43%); Oxford Brookes 21; Plymouth 8; Portsmouth 7; Sheffield 5; Sheffield Hallam 3; Southampton 8; Strathclyde 6; Surrey 7; Warwick 6; Westminster 3; York 10.

Advice to applicants and planning the UCAS personal statement Any interests you have in careers requiring mathematical ability could be mentioned – for example, engineering, computers (hardware and software) and business applications. Show determination, love of mathematics and an appreciation of the rigour of the course. **Bristol** (Eng Maths) Skills, work experience, positions of responsibility. **Coventry** (for non-EU students) Fluency in oral and written English required. **St Andrews** Reasons for course choice. Evidence of interest. **Southampton** A variety of non-academic interests to complement the applicant's academic abilities. See also **Appendix 2**.

Misconceptions about this course **London (QM)** Some believe that a study of mechanics is compulsory – it is not. **Surrey** Maths is not just about calculations: it focuses on reasoning, logic and applications. **York** Further maths is not required for this course.

Selection interviews **Yes** Aberystwyth, Bath, Birmingham, Bishop Grosseteste (UC), Bristol UWE, Brunel, Cambridge, Cardiff, Central Lancashire, City, Coventry, Durham, East London, Essex, Exeter, Glamorgan, Heriot-Watt, Kent, Kingston, Lancaster, Leeds, Liverpool, Liverpool John Moores, London (Gold), (King's), (RH), (UCL), London Met, Manchester Met, Newcastle, Northampton, Northumbria, Nottingham, Oxford, Reading, Salford, Sheffield, Southampton, Sussex, Warwick, York; **Some** Brighton, Bristol, East Anglia, Greenwich, London (LSE) (rarely), Loughborough.

Interview advice and questions Questions are likely to be asked arising from the information you have given in your UCAS application and about your interests in the subject. Questions in recent years have included: How many ways are there of incorrectly setting up the back row of a chess board? A ladder on a rough floor leans against a smooth wall. Describe the forces acting on the ladder and give the maximum possible angle of inclination possible. There are three particles connected by a string; the middle one is made to move – describe the subsequent motion of the particles. What mathematics books have you read outside your syllabus? Why does a ball bounce? Discuss the work of any renowned mathematician. Balance a pencil on your index fingers and then try to move both towards the centre of the pencil. Explain what is happening in terms of forces and friction. **Cambridge** If you could spend half an hour with any mathematician past or present, who would it be? **Oxford** (Maths Phil) What makes you think I'm having thoughts? What was the most beautiful proof in A-level mathematics? I am an oil baron in the desert and I need to deliver oil to four different towns which happen to lie in a straight line. In order to deliver the correct amount to each town I must visit each town in turn, returning to my warehouse in between each visit. Where would I position my warehouse in order to drive the shortest possible distance? Roads are no problem since I have a friend who will build me as many roads as I like for free. **Southampton** Personal statements generate discussion points. Our interviews are informal chats and so technical probing is kept low key. See **Chapter 7**.

Applicants' impressions (A=Open day; B=Interview day) **Cambridge** (B) The first interview (five minutes) was relaxed with a very helpful interviewer. The second interview (10 minutes) was intimidating, almost aggressive, and I felt under a lot of pressure. The course is very theoretical and the professors seemed very distant. There was no real chance to talk to the students. **Exeter** (B) There was one informal interview of 30 minutes with one interviewer. General questions were asked on why I wanted to study maths, what aspects of the subject interested me the most and questions on my personal statement. It is a pleasant campus, with the library and shops all fairly central. A friendly male-dominated department. We had a chance to meet and talk to students about the course and the University. **Oxford (St Hugh's)** (B) There were two interviews of 20 minutes, each with one interviewer. Very few questions were asked about why I wanted to study the subject and my extra-curricular activities. Most of the questions related to maths problems. The interviewers were friendly and helped me when I had difficulty with a problem. I felt under pressure but they helped me relax. The College is spacious and the buildings and grounds attractive. The small community atmosphere about the College impressed me. Being a student there would be a challenging and beneficial experience. No chance to talk to any students.

Reasons for rejection (non-academic) Usually academic reasons only. Lack of motivation. We were somewhat uneasy about how much mathematics he will remember after a gap year running a theatre in South Africa. **Birmingham** A poorly written and poorly organised personal statement.

AFTER-RESULTS ADVICE
Offers to applicants repeating A-levels **Higher** Brighton, Coventry, Essex, Glasgow, London Met, Salford, Strathclyde, Swansea, Surrey, Warwick; **Possibly higher** Cambridge (Hom), Durham, Lancaster, Leeds, Newcastle, Sheffield; **Same** Aberystwyth, Aston, Bath, Birmingham, Bristol, Brunel, Chester, East Anglia, Liverpool, Liverpool Hope, London (RH), Loughborough (usually), Manchester Met, Nottingham, Nottingham Trent, Oxford Brookes, Sheffield Hallam, Southampton, Stirling, Ulster, Wolverhampton, York; **No offers made** Cambridge.

For information on how to read the Subject Tables, see **Chapter 8**.

GRADUATE DESTINATIONS AND EMPLOYMENT (2005/6 HESA)

Mathematics graduates surveyed 3150 **Employed** 1325 **In further study** 795 **Assumed unemployed** 175.

Operational Research graduates surveyed 70 **Employed** 45 **In further study** 5 **Assumed unemployed** none.

Career note Graduates enter a range of careers. Whilst business, finance and retail areas are popular options, mathematicians also have important roles in the manufacturing industries. Mathematics offers the pleasure of problem-solving, the satisfaction of a rigorous argument and the most widely employable non-vocational degree subject. A student's view: 'Maths trains you to work in the abstract, to think creatively and to come up with concrete conclusions'. These transferable skills are much sought-after by employers. Employment prospects are excellent with high salaries.

OTHER DEGREE SUBJECTS FOR CONSIDERATION

Accountancy; Actuarial Studies; Astronomy; Astrophysics; Computer Science; Economics; Engineering Sciences; Operational Research; Physics; Statistics.

MEDIA STUDIES

(including **Broadcasting and Journalism;** see also **Art and Design (General), Communication Studies/Communications, Computer Courses, Engineering (Acoustics)** and **Film, Radio, Video and TV Studies**)

Intending Media applicants need to check course details carefully since this subject area can involve graphic design, illustration and other art courses as well as the media in the fields of TV, radio and journalism. Courses in Journalism include block and day release, pre-academic year, pre-entry calendar year, evening/weekend magazine journalism, and photo-journalism. Full details can be obtained by referring to www.nctj.com/courses.

Useful websites www.bbc.co.uk/jobs; www.newspapersoc.org.uk; www.ppa.co.uk; www.reuters.com/careers; www.arts.org.uk; www.nctj.com; www.ipa.co.uk; www.camfoundation.com; www.mediastudies.com.

NB The points totals shown to the left of the institutions are for ease of reference only. It must not be assumed that tariff points are always used by institutions or that they can be substituted for an offer in grades. The level of an offer is not necessarily indicative of the quality of a course.

COURSE OFFERS INFORMATION

Subject requirements/preferences **GCSE** English and mathematics often required. **AL** No specified subjects required. **NB** A* grades are likely to form part of university offers in the higher ranges for students applying for places in 2008 for entry in 2009: check websites.

Your target offers
360 pts and above
        London (UCL) – AABe–BBBe (Sci Comm Pol)
340 pts Surrey – AAB (MEng Dig Media Eng; Aud Media Eng; Media Eng)
        York – AAB–BBB (Media Tech) *(IB 32 pts)*
320 pts Birmingham – ABB–BBB (Media Cult Soty courses) *(IB 32–34 pts)*
        Cardiff – ABB 320 pts (Jrnl Film Media; Jrnl Media Cult Crit; Jrnl Media Soc Pol; Jrnl Media Sociol) *(IB 36 Perf)*
        East Anglia – ABB–BBB (Scrpt Perf; Soty Cult Media; Pol Media) *(IB 31–32 pts)*
        Glasgow – ABB–BBB (Arts Media Inform; Film TV) *(IB 30 pts)*
        London (Gold) – ABB (Media Comm) *(IB 34 pts)*
        London (QM) – 320 pts (Jrnl Contemp Hist) *(IB 30–36 pts)*

London (RH) – ABB 320 pts (Media Arts) *(IB 34 pts)*
Loughborough – ABB (Comm Media St) *(IB 32 pts)*
Newcastle – ABB (Media Comm Cult St) *(IB 30–32 pts)*
Surrey – ABB (BEng Dig Media Eng; Media Eng)
Surrey – ABB–BBC 320–280 pts (Media St Mus; Media St Lang; Media St Dance)
Sussex – ABB–BBB **or** 360–340 pts 3AL+AS (Media Prac Theor; Media St Fr/Ger/Ital/Span; Media St Anth; Media Cult St)

300 pts **Bournemouth** – 300 pts (Multim Jrnl)
Central Lancashire – BBB 300 pts (Jrnl; Interact Dig Media; Spo Jrnl)
City – BBB (Jrnl Sociol; Jrnl Psy; Jrnl Econ)
Hull – 300 pts (Media Cult Soc)
Lancaster – BBB (Media Cult St) *(IB 29 pts)*
Leeds – BBB (Broad Jrnl; Broad; Comm St; New Media)
Leicester – BBB (Comm Media Soty) *(IB 30 pts)*
Liverpool – BBB (Comm Media Pop Mus)
London (Gold) – BBB (Media joint courses)
Sheffield – BBB **or** ABbb **or** BBbb (Jrnl St; Jrnl Gerc St; Jrnl Fr/Russ; Jrnl Hisp St)
Westminster – BBB (Media St (Jrnl)) *(IB 30 pts)*

280 pts **Bournemouth** – 280 pts (Interact Media Prod; Comm Media; Script Film TV) *(IB 32–34 pts)*
Brighton – BBC–BBB (Spo Jrnl)
Brunel – BBC (Multim Tech Des)
Central Lancashire – 280 pts (Web Multim; Media Prod Tech; TV Prod)
Essex – 280–300 pts (Sociol Media St) *(IB 28–29 pts)*
Huddersfield – 280 pts (Mus Jrnl Media; Jrnl Media; Rad Jrnl Media)
Kent – BBC (Journalism)
Kingston – 280–320 pts (Journalism)
Lincoln – BBC 280 pts (Media Prod)
London (Gold) – BBC (Int Media; Media Sociol)
Northumbria – 280 pts (Jrnl; Jrnl Engl; Media Jrnl)
Oxford Brookes – BBC–BCC (Comm Media Cult courses)
Salford – BBC 280 pts (Jrnl Des St; Jrnl Engl Lit; Jrnl Pol; Jrnl Sociol; Jrnl Broad joint courses; Media Perf) *(IB 28 pts)*
Sheffield Hallam – 280 pts (Media St)
Stirling – BBC (pre-application experience req) (Jrnl St; Film Media St courses)
Strathclyde – BBC–BBB (Jrnl Crea Writ courses)
Swansea – 280 pts (3AL) 200 pts (2AL) (Media St courses)

260 pts **Bangor** – 260–300 pts (Cyfathrebu a' Cyfryngau; Jrnl Media St; Thea Media St)
Brunel – 260 pts (Comm Media St)
Glasgow Caledonian – BCC (Jrnl; Media Comm)

For information on how to read the Subject Tables, see **Chapter 8**.

Lincoln – 260 pts (Journalism)
Northumbria – 260 pts (Media Cult Soty)
Nottingham Trent – 260–300 pts (Broad Jrnl)
Wolverhampton – 260–320 pts (Jrnl Edit Des)

240 pts **Bolton** – 240 pts (Media Writ Prod)
Bradford – 240 pts (Media St courses)
Brighton – 240 pts (Comm Dig Media; Comm Media St)
Bristol UWE – 240–280 pts (Media Cult St Pol; Media Cult St Sociol; Media Cult St EFL; Media Cult St Fr/Ger/Span) *(IB 28 pts)*
Central Lancashire – 240 pts (Int Jrnl)
Chester – 240 pts (Media St courses; Multim Tech; Jrnl)
City – CCC (Sociol Media St)
Coventry – 240–280 pts (Comm Cult Media; Jrnl Engl; Jrnl Media)
Edge Hill – 240 pts (Media (Adv) (Film TV); Jrnl)
Glamorgan – 240–280 pts (Journalism)
Hertfordshire – 240 pts (Jrnl Media Cult Comb St; Scrn Cult Media Prac)
Huddersfield – 240 pts (Multim Des)
Keele – 240–280 pts (Media Comm Cult courses) *(IB 28–32 pts)*
Kingston – 240–320 pts (Media Cult St)
Napier – 240 pts (Journalism)
Nottingham Trent – 240–220 pts (Media courses; Comm Soty)
Portsmouth – 240–300 pts (Media St joint courses; Dig Media)
Robert Gordon – CCC (Pub Jrnl)
Roehampton – 240 pts (Media Cult; Jrnl News Media courses)
Salford – 240 pts (Media Lang Bus; Media Tech)
Sheffield Hallam – 240–260 pts (Jrnl St; Media St)
Staffordshire – 240–280 pts (Jrnl; Broad Jrnl; Spo Jrnl)
Ulster – 240–280 pts (Media St; Media Arts)

220 pts **Aberystwyth** – 220–260 pts (Media Comm St)
Central Lancashire – 220 pts (Media Prod Tech Jrnl)
De Montfort – 220–240 pts (Media St; Jrnl St)
Falmouth (UC) – CCD 220 pts (Broad; Engl Media St; Jrnl)
Lampeter – CCD–CDD 220–200 pts (Media St; Media Prod)
Lincoln – 220 pts (Media Cult Comm courses)
Liverpool Hope – 220 pts (Media courses)
Manchester Met – 220–280 pts (Media Tech)
Middlesex – 220 pts (Journalism)
Plymouth – 220–240 pts (Media Prac Soty)
Queen Margaret – 220 pts (Media; Media Cult; PR Media)

Salford – 220 pts (Multim Intnet Tech)
Southampton Solent – 220 pts (Spo Writ; Spo Media; TV Prod; Jrnl)
Staffordshire – 220 pts (TV Rad Doc)
Winchester – 220–240 pts (Media Prod; Jrnl; Media St Comb courses) *(IB 26–28 pts)*
200 pts **Bath Spa** – 200–240 pts (Media Comm courses)
Birmingham City – 200–280 pts (Media Comm (Mus Ind) (Jrnl) (Rad) (PR) (Media Photo) (TV); Multim Tech; Multim Dev courses)
Birmingham City – 200 pts (Multim Tech; Multim Dev)
Central Lancashire – 200 pts (Media Prod Tech; Web Multim Comb Hons)
Coventry – 200–220 pts (Media Prod)
Creative Arts (UC) – 200 pts (Vid Media Arts)
Edge Hill – 200–240 pts (Crea Writ Media)
Gloucestershire – 200–280 pts (Media Comm joint courses)
Kingston – 200–260 pts (Media Tech)
London Met – 200 pts (Media St; Dig Media courses; Mass Comm courses)
Napier – 200 pts (Pub Media)
Roehampton – 200 pts (Media Cult; Jrnl News Media)
Sunderland – 200–300 pts (Broad Jrnl; Media St courses; Jrnl courses)
Swansea (Inst) – 200 pts (Photojournalism)
190 pts **Buckingham** – 190–240 pts (Comm Media St; Jrnl Comm St; Engl Lit Jrnl; Jrnl Int St)
180 pts **Anglia Ruskin** – 180–220 pts (Comm St courses; Media St)
Chichester – 180–240 pts (Media St; Media Prod Media St) *(IB 28 pts)*
Greenwich – 180 pts (Jrnl PR)
Liverpool John Moores – 180–280 pts (Jrnl; Int Jrnl; Media Cult St courses)
Marjon (UC) – 180–240 pts (Crea Writ Media; Media courses; Crea Media Prac; Contemp Cult Media Soty)
Northampton – 180–220 pts (Media St; Jrnl)
Southampton Solent – 180–280 pts (Jrnl; Mag Jrnl FtreWrit; Media Comm; Media Cult Prod)
Staffordshire – 180–240 pts (Media St courses; Mus Broad)
Teesside – 180–240 pts (Media Prod Prof Prac; Multim Prof Prac; Media St; Crea Multim)
West Scotland – BC–CC (Media; Multim Tech)
160 pts **Abertay Dundee** – CC (Media Cult Soty)
Arts London – 160 pts (Jrnl; Media Cult St)
Bedfordshire – 160–240 pts (Media Prod; Media Prac; Jrnl)
Canterbury Christ Church – CC (Film Rad TV St; Media Cult St joint courses; Jrnl courses)
Cardiff (UWIC) – 160–280 pts (Media St Vis Cult)
Cumbria – CC 160 pts (Media Prod; Jrnl)
De Montfort – 160–240 pts (Media Tech; Arts Mgt Media Sth)
Derby – 160–180 pts (Broad Media; Jrnl; Media St)
East London – 160 pts (Media St; Jrnl; Multim St)
Glamorgan – 160–260 pts (Media Prod; Media Prod (Rad); Media St courses; Multim Tech)
Grimsby (IFHE) – 160–240 pts (Jrnl; Multim)
Leeds Trinity and All Saints (Coll) – 160–240 pts (Spo Jrnl; Media; Engl Media; Media Mark; Spo Hlth Leis Media)
London South Bank – CC (Media Soty; Writ Media Arts)
Middlesex – 160–240 pts (Crea Media Writ; Media Cult St; Jrnl Comm; Pub Media)
Newman (UC) – 160 pts (Media Comm courses)
North East Wales (IHE) – 160 pts (Media St courses; Perf Media Comm Writ; Rad Prod Media Comm)
St Mary's (UC) – CC (Media Arts; Prof Crea Writ Media Arts)
South East Essex (Coll) – 160–180 pts (Jrnl; Dig Imag Interact Media)
Southampton Solent – 160 pts (Media Tech)
Swansea (Inst) – 160 pts (Multimedia)
Thames Valley – 160–180 pts (Media Sts; Dig Media Prod NMedia Jrnl courses)

For information on how to read the Subject Tables, see **Chapter 8.**

West Scotland – CC–DDD (Multim Tech)
Wolverhampton – 160–220 pts (Media Comm St; Media Cult St; Dig Media Cult St)
Worcester – 160 pts (Media Cult St; Crea Dig Media)
York St John – 160 pts (Media)

140 pts **Liverpool John Moores** – 140–220 pts (Broad Tech)
Suffolk (Univ Campus) – 140–200 pts (Dig Media)
Teesside – 140–220 pts (Media St; TV Prod Prof Prac; Crea Dig Media)

120 pts **Bucks New** – 120–240 pts (Media Prod; Jrnl courses; Media Dr)
London Met – (Jrnl via Fdn course only)
Northbrook (Coll) – 120 pts (Dig Jrnl)
Trinity Carmarthen (Coll) – 120–160 pts (Media St)

80 pts **Creative Arts (UC) (F)** – (Jrnl; Fash Jrnl)
Farnborough (CT) – 80–160 pts (Media Prod)
Havering (Coll) – 80 pts (Media Mus)
Wirral Met (Coll) – 80 pts (Media St)

Leeds Met – contact University

Alternative offers

See **Chapter 8** for grade/point equivalences and related information for the following examinations: Scottish qualifications, the Welsh Baccalaureate, the IB diploma (approximate points shown also in italics in the table of offers), the Irish Leaving Certificate, the European Baccalaureate and the French Baccalaureate.

EXAMPLES OF FOUNDATION DEGREES IN THE SUBJECT FIELD

Arts London (CComm); Barnet (Coll); Barnfield (Coll); Barnsley (Univ Centre); Bedfordshire; Blackpool and Fylde (Coll); Bradford (Coll); Brighton; Cornwall (Coll); Croydon (Coll); Darlington (Coll); Farnborough (CT); Lambeth (Coll); Liverpool John Moores; Llandrillo Cymru (Coll); London (Birk); London Met; Milton Keynes (Coll); Nescot; Newham (Coll); North East Wales (IHE); Peterborough Reg (Coll); Plymouth (CAD); Ravensbourne (CDC); St Helens (Coll); Solihull (Coll); South Devon (Coll); South East Essex (Coll); Suffolk (Univ Campus); Teesside; Truro (Coll); Weston (Coll); Wolverhampton.

CHOOSING YOUR COURSE (SEE ALSO CH.1)

Course variations – Widen your options
Media Communications (Music Industries) (PR) (TV) (Birmingham City)
Internet Media Technologies (Blackpool and Fylde (Coll))
Entertainment Technology (Bournemouth)
Broadcast Media (Brighton)
Journalism, Film and Media (Cardiff)
Wildlife and Media (Cumbria)
Media and Sports Journalism (Huddersfield)
Religious Media and Society (Hull)
New Media (Leeds)
Communication, Media and Popular Music (Liverpool)
Art Media and Design (London Met)
Writing for the Media (Marjon (UC))
Publishing (Oxford Brookes)
Media Studies and Russian (Surrey)
CHECK PROSPECTUSES AND WEBSITES FOR OTHER UNIVERSITIES AND COLLEGES OFFERING THESE COURSES.

Universities and colleges teaching quality See www.qaa.ac.uk; www.unistats.com.

Top universities and colleges (Research) (including Communication and Cultural Studies)
Birmingham; Bristol UWE; East Anglia; East London; London (Gold), (RH); Stirling; Sussex; Westminster.

For a quick reference offers calculator, fold out the inside back cover.

Sandwich degree courses Birmingham City; Bradford; Brunel; Huddersfield; Salford; Ulster.

ADMISSIONS INFORMATION

Number of applicants per place (approx) Birmingham 10; Bournemouth (Interact Media Prod) 24, (Multim Jrnl) 30; Bradford 13; Bristol UWE 20; Canterbury Christ Church 23; Cardiff 11; Cardiff (UWIC) 3; Central Lancashire 33; Chichester 6; City 50; Creative Arts (UC) 3; Cumbria 4; De Montfort 11; East London 27; Falmouth (UC) 4; Gloucestershire 25; Greenwich 12; Lincoln 4; London (Gold) 13, (RH) 11; London South Bank 11; Newport 12; Northampton 4; Northumbria 14; Nottingham Trent 5; Plymouth (Coll) 33; Portsmouth 5; Sheffield Hallam 56; South East Essex (Coll) 10; Southampton Solent (Jrnl) 20, (Media Tech) 6; Swansea (Inst) 5; Teesside 33; Winchester 7; West Scotland 6; Westminster 44.

Advice to applicants and planning the UCAS personal statement Work experience or work shadowing is important. Contact local newspaper offices to meet journalists and to discuss their work. Contact local radio stations and advertising agencies, read newspapers (all types) and be able to describe the different approaches of newspapers. Watch TV coverage of news stories and the way in which the interviewer deals with politicians or members of the public. Give your opinions on the various forms of media. School magazine and/or any published work should be mentioned. **Birmingham City** A balance of academic and practical skills. **Bournemouth** (Non-EU students) Fluency in written and spoken English required. **Staffordshire** Creativity, problem-solving, cultural awareness, communication skills and commitment. See also **Communication Studies/ Communications** and **Appendix 2**.

Misconceptions about this course Birmingham City That Media courses are soft options: they are not! **Cardiff (UWIC)** Some applicants believe that the course will automatically lead to a job in the media – it won't. This depends on the student developing other employment skills and experience. **Cumbria** This is not a Media Studies course: it is a highly practical media production course. **Lincoln** (Media Prod) BTEC applicants may think that this is a technology based course.

Selection interviews Yes Bournemouth, Brunel, Creative Arts (UC), East Anglia, Glamorgan, Huddersfield, Liverpool John Moores, London (Gold), (RH), London South Bank, Marjon (UC), Portsmouth, Sheffield Hallam, Solihull (Coll), South East Essex (Coll), Staffordshire, Swansea (IHE), Thames Valley (group interview), Wakefield (Coll), York; **Some** Cardiff, Cardiff (UWIC), Chichester, City, Nottingham Trent, Salford, Sunderland, West Herts (Coll), Wolverhampton.

Interview advice and questions Past questions include: Which newspapers do you read? Discuss the main differences between the national daily newspapers. Which radio programmes do you listen to each day? Which television programmes do you watch? Why do you think that ITV needs to spend £32 million advertising itself? Should the BBC broadcast advertisements? What do you think are the reasons for the popularity of *EastEnders*? Film or video work, if required, should be edited to a running time of 15 minutes unless otherwise stated. **Cardiff (UWIC)** What is your favourite area in respect of popular culture? Are you considering taking up the work placement module? If so where would you plan to go? **Cumbria** Role of journalism in society. What is today's main news story? Who is Rupert Murdoch? **Lincoln** Give a written or verbal critique of a media product. See **Chapter 7**.

Reasons for rejection (non-academic) No clear commitment (to Broadcast Journalism) plus no evidence of experience (now proving to be essential). Mistaken expectations of the nature of the course. Can't write and doesn't work well in groups. Too specific and narrow areas of media interest, for example, video or script-writing. Lack of knowledge of current affairs. **Cardiff (UWIC)** Lack of experience in the field. Application arrived too late. **City** Inadequate English language.

AFTER-RESULTS ADVICE

Offers to applicants repeating A-levels Same Birmingham City, Cardiff, Cardiff (UWIC), Chester, Chichester, City, De Montfort, Huddersfield, Lincoln, Loughborough, Manchester Met, Nottingham Trent, St Mary's (UC), Salford, South East Essex (Coll), Staffordshire, Sunderland, Winchester, Wolverhampton.

436 | Medicine

GRADUATE DESTINATIONS AND EMPLOYMENT (2005/6 HESA)
Graduates surveyed 3725 **Employed** 2265 **In further study** 230 **Assumed unemployed** 330.
Journalism graduates surveyed 970 **Employed** 580 **In further study** 20 **Assumed unemployed** 20.

Career note See **Film, Radio, Video and TV Studies**.

OTHER DEGREE SUBJECTS FOR CONSIDERATION
Advertising; Communications; English; Film, Radio and TV Studies; Journalism; Photography; Public Relations.

MEDICINE

(see also **Medical Sciences** under **Health Sciences/Studies**)

Medicine is still a highly popular choice with a further rise of six per cent in the past year. All courses listed below under Your target offers include the same areas of study and training and all lead to a qualification and career in medicine. Methods of teaching may vary slightly, depending on the medical school. To achieve these aims, some medical schools adopt the system of self-directed learning (SDL) in which objectives are set to assess your progress, and problem-based learning (PBL) which helps you to develop critical thinking and clinical problem-solving skills.

Methods of teaching may vary slightly, depending on the medical school. Medical schools aim to produce doctors who are clinically competent, who are able to see patients as people and have a holistic and ethical approach (including the ability to understand and manage each patient's case in a family and social context as well as in the hospital), who treat patients and colleagues with respect, dignity and sensitivity, are skilled at teamwork and prepared for continual learning. These aims in several ways reflect the qualities which selectors seek when interviewing applicants. In all cases, close attention will be paid to the confidential report on the UCAS application to judge the applicant's personality, communication skills, academic potential and commitment to a medical career. Whilst there is a core curriculum of knowledge, the first three years integrate scientific and clinical experience, and there are fewer formal lectures than before, with more group and individual work. For outstanding students without science A-levels, some pre-medical courses are available. Thereafter for all, a period of pre-clinical studies leads on to clinical studies. Intercalated courses of one year leading to a BSc are also offered and elective periods abroad in the final years can sometimes be taken.

Useful websites www.scicentral.com; www.ipem.org.uk; www.bmj.com; www.bmat.org.uk; www.gmc-uk.org; www.nhscareers.nhs.uk.

Applicants for places in Medicine may select only four universities or medical schools.

COURSE OFFERS INFORMATION
Subject requirements/preferences **GCSE** In all cases a good spread of science and non-science subjects will be expected at high grades.

Aberdeen English, mathematics, biology, physics or dual award science. Combinations of AB grades, especially in sciences.

Birmingham Chemistry, English language and mathematics normally at grade A. Dual science award grade A acceptable as an alternative to physics and biology.

Brighton and Sussex (MS) Mathematics and English at grade B, biology and chemistry.

Bristol Wide spread of subjects including mathematics, English language and the sciences at grade B.

Cambridge Mathematics, physics, chemistry or dual science award.

Cardiff English or Welsh at grade B, mathematics at grade B or above, grades AA in dual science or AAA in three sciences.

438 | Medicine

Dundee Chemistry and biology or human biology essential.

East Anglia Science subjects, English and mathematics at high grades. NB chemistry A-level not a requirement (contact the Medical School).

Edinburgh English, mathematics, biology, chemistry or dual science award at grade B or higher.

Glasgow English, chemistry, biology (preferred), mathematics and physics.

Hull York (MS) Six subjects grades A*-C: English and mathematics at grade B or higher plus chemistry and biology.

Imperial London Chemistry, biology, physics (or dual science award) plus mathematics and English. At least three subjects are required at grade A, and two subjects at grade B.

Keele Chemistry, physics, biology (dual science award acceptable, grades BB minimum), English language and mathematics at grade B minimum. A broad spread of subjects is expected with a minimum of four at grade A.

Leeds Six subjects at grade B minimum including English, mathematics, chemistry and biology or dual science award.

Leicester Warwick English language and sciences (including chemistry) or dual science award.

London (King's) Grade B (minimum) in chemistry, biology and physics (or dual science award), English and mathematics.

London (QM) Six subjects at AB minimum grades including English, mathematics and science subjects.

London (St George's) Eight subjects including English, mathematics, physics, chemistry, biology (or dual science award) at grade B minimum.

London (UCL) Chemistry, biology, English and mathematics at grade B minimum.

Manchester Seven subjects with five at grades A/A*. Chemistry, biology and physics required with English and mathematics at grade B minimum.

Newcastle and Durham At least five subjects with grades AAAAB to include English, mathematics and either biology, chemistry, physics or dual science award.

Nottingham Six subjects at grade A/A* to include biology, chemistry and physics or dual science award. (Grade A AS physics can compensate for a B at GCSE.)

Oxford Chemistry, mathematics, biology and physics or dual science award acceptable.

Peninsula (MS) Seven subjects at grades A/B including biology, chemistry or physics or dual science award, English and mathematics or dual science award..

Queen's Belfast Chemistry, biology, mathematics and either physics or dual science award.

Sheffield At least four subjects at grade A and grade C and above in English, mathematics, chemistry and preferably biology and physics.

Southampton Seven subjectss at grade B or above including English, mathematics and dual science award or equivalent. (Widening Access course BM6) Five GCSEs at grade C including English, mathematics and dual science award or equivalent. (Students join the five-year programme on completion of Year Zero.)

St Andrews Chemistry, biology, mathematics and physics. If mathematics and biology are not offered at A2 then each must have been passed at grade B or higher. English is required at grade B or higher.

AL See **Your target offers** below. Candidates applying for A104 courses at **Bristol**, **Cardiff**, **Dundee**, **East Anglia**, **Edinburgh**, **London (King's)**, **Manchester**, **Sheffield** and **Southampton** are not accepted if they are offering more than one laboratory-based subject (check with University).

For a quick reference offers calculator, fold out the inside back cover.

Cambridge (Emmanuel) AEA in one science subject when only two are taken may be required. **London (UCL)** Mathematics and further mathematics will not both be counted towards three AL subjects. **NB** A* grades are likely to form part of university offers in the higher ranges for students applying for places in 2008 for entry in 2009: check websites. **Other requirements** See Health Requirements below; CRB clearance is also required.

NB Home and EU-funded students applying for entry to Medicine are required by many universities to sit either the UKCAT or BMAT tests before applying. See Your target offers **below, Chapter 6 and Chapter 7 for further information.**

NB The points totals shown to the left of the institutions are for ease of reference only. It must not be assumed that tariff points are always used by institutions or that they can be substituted for an offer in grades. The level of an offer is not necessarily indicative of the quality of a course.

Your target offers

360 pts and above

Cambridge – AAA +BMAT (inc AL biol/chem/maths/phys; chem reqd at least at AS; some colleges may require 3 sci ALs) (Medicine) *(IB 38–42 pts)*

Cardiff – 370 pts from 21u +UKCAT (inc 2 subjs from chem, biol, phys, stats inc chem/biol at AS if not at AL) (Medicine) *(IB 36 pts H 18 pts)*

Dundee – AAA +UKCAT (inc chem +any sci +any subj at grade A) (Medicine) *(IB 34 pts H766)*

Dundee – AAA (inc not more than 1 sci) (Medicine Pre-Med Year) *(IB 34 pts H766)*

Durham and Newcastle – See **Newcastle and Durham** below

Edinburgh – AAAb +UKCAT (inc AL chem+1 from maths/phys/biol; AS biol min) (Medicine 5/6 yrs) *(IB 37 pts H766)*

Hull York (MS) – AABb +UKCAT (inc chem, biol) (Medicine) *(IB 36 pts H766)*

Imperial London – AAAb +BMAT (inc AL biol/chem+sci/maths) (Medicine) *(IB H655 ST555)*

Liverpool – AABb 390 pts (inc chem+biol at AL/AS) (Medicine) *(IB 38 pts H776)*

London (King's) – AABb +UKCAT (inc AL chem/biol **or** AS b chem/biol) (Medicine) *(IB 38 pts H655)*

London (King's) – AABb +UKCAT (Med Conv Entry Prog)

London (St George's) – AABb +UKCAT (BBCb for schools with AL average 245 pts and below) (inc AL chem+biol **or** AS chem/biol b) (Medicine)

London (UCL) – AABa +BMAT (inc AL chem+biol; some pref to applicants offering a contrasting 3rd subj, eg English, music, history) (Medicine) *(IB 36 pts H665)*

Newcastle and Durham – AAA +UKCAT (inc AL chem/biol pref 1 non-sci at AL/AS) (Medicine) *(IB 38 pts)*

Oxford – AAA +BMAT (inc AL chem+1 from biol/phys/maths) (Medicine) *(IB 38–42 pts)*

Peninsula (MS) – 370–400 pts +UKCAT (inc biol/chem/phys +2AL inc 1 non-sci pref) (Medicine)

Queen's Belfast – AAAa +UKCAT (inc AL chem+sci/maths subj; AS biol b min) (Medicine) *(IB 37 pts H666)*

340 pts Aberdeen – AAB +UKCAT (chem desirable+1 from biol/maths/phys+1 other) (Medicine) *(IB 36 pts H666)*

Birmingham – AAB 340–360 pts (inc AL chem+1 from biol/maths/phys; AS biol grade b if not offered at AL: hum biol acceptable) (Medicine) *(IB 36 pts)*

Brighton and Sussex (MS) – 340 pts AL+UKCAT (inc AS biol/chem+AL) (Medicine) *(IB 37 pts H 17 pts)*

Bristol – AAB (A106: chem +2 subj biol pref inc 4AS; A104: 3AL 1 sci accepted) (Medicine; 1st/2nd MB) *(IB 36 pts H666)*

East Anglia – AAB +UKCAT (inc AL A biol) (Medicine) *(IB 34 pts)*

Glasgow – AAB +UKCAT (inc AL chem+1 subj from maths/phys/biol; biol/hum biol pref; 4AS in yr 12; pts not accepted) (Medicine) *(IB 36 pts)*

Keele – AAB +UKCAT (inc AL chem+1 from biol/phys/maths+1 from a rigorous academic subj if only 2 sci subjs are offered) (Medicine) *(IB 34 pts)*

Understanding How to Make the New Medicines – 5th/6th UCAS Choices

The discovery of penicillin was a huge achievement. It took 15 years and an international effort to find a way to produce it in the quantities needed for medical treatment and led to the birth of the discipline of biochemical engineering.

The medicines of the future – human proteins, therapeutic vaccines, human cells and tissue for repair – are much more complex than penicillin. The challenges to biochemical engineers in understanding how to bring such new discoveries to fruition have never been greater, nor the rewards higher.

All who apply for a medical place through UCAS are asked to choose additional fifth and sixth places in other fields. Those seeking a professionally recognised qualification in a subject that is demanding, and who want a life at the cutting edge that is highly regarded, should consider the excitement of biochemical engineering as a degree option.

Details of courses can be found in UCAS guides, or on the web and visits can be arranged to explore in more detail the A level requirements, the courses and the careers available.

Leeds – AAB +UKCAT 3AL **or** ABaa (inc AL chem) (Medicine) *(IB 36 pts H666)*
Leicester Warwick – AAB +UKCAT 3AL **or** 340–400 pts +UKCAT (inc 4AS in yr 12 inc A chem, biol at AL/AS) (Medicine) *(IB 36 pts H chem biol 6 pts)*
London (QM) – AAB +UKCAT (inc chem and/or biol to at least AS b with 1 of these (or both) to A2 +1 other sci) (Medicine) *(IB 36 pts H665)*
Manchester – AAB+AS +UKCAT (inc AL chem+1 from biol/hum biol/phys/maths +1 other subj; not 2AS for 1AL) (Medicine)
Nottingham – AAB+AS +UKCAT (inc AL chem+biol) (Medicine) *(IB 38 pts)*
St Andrews – AAB +UKCAT (inc AL chem+biol/maths/phys) (Medicine) *(IB 37 pts H766)*
Sheffield – AAB +UKCAT (inc AB chem+sci subjs) (Medicine) *(IB 34 pts H666)*
Southampton – AAB 340 pts +UKCAT (inc AS chem+biol or AL chem) (Medicine 5yrs)
Warwick – See **Leicester Warwick** above

320 pts **Manchester** – ABB (Medicine 6 yrs)
260 pts **Brighton and Sussex (MS)** – BCC (biol/chem pref) (Pre-Med Prog)
240 pts **Southampton** – CCC or equiv +UKCAT (inc chem+biol+1 subj) (Medicine 6yr)
220 pts **Thames Valley** – CCD (inc C min chem) (Hum Sci – Pre-Med option)
200 pts **London (St George's)** – min age 21 GCSE sci, Engl, maths (Fdn Med)

Alternative offers
See **Chapter 8** for grade/point equivalences and related information for the following examinations: Scottish qualifications, the Welsh Baccalaureate, the IB diploma (approximate points shown also in italics in the table of offers), the Irish Leaving Certificate, the European Baccalaureate and the French Baccalaureate.

OTHER HIGHER EDUCATION COURSES IN THE SUBJECT FIELD
Foundation and other courses (contact the institutions for details) Bradford (Clin Sci Fdn 200 pts); Brighton and Sussex (MS) 260 pts; Cardiff (370 pts); Coventry; Hertfordshire (Paramed Sci); London (King's) (St George's) (Nat Sci ABBc); Portsmouth.

Six-year Pre-Medicine courses Brighton and Sussex (MS); Bristol; Cardiff; Dundee; Edinburgh; London (King's) (St George's); Manchester; Sheffield; Southampton; Sussex. Most of these courses are open to students with a high academic potential who have not taken science subjects or have combination of subjects that include not more than one subject from biology, chemistry or physics.

CHOOSING YOUR COURSE (SEE ALSO CH.1)
NB See Chapter 7 for details of admissions tests to be taken before application.
Course variations – Widen your options
Medical Microbiology (Aberdeen)
Medical Product Design (Aston)
Medical Engineering (Bath)
Biomedical Materials Science (Birmingham)
Oriental Medicine (Brighton)
Medical Technology (Cardiff (UWIC))
Pharmacy (Central Lancashire)
Medical Anthropology (Durham)
History and History of Medicine (East Anglia)
Herbal Medicine (East London)
Sports Medicine (Glasgow)
Medicinal Horticulture (Greenwich)
Medicinal Chemistry (Keele)
Medical Statistics (Keele)
Medical Physics (Leeds)
Chinese Medicine (Middlesex)
Complementary Health Science (Middlesex)
Osteopathic Medicine (Nescot)
Acupuncture (Salford)

For a quick reference offers calculator, fold out the inside back cover.

Medical Genetics (Sheffield)
Medical Neuroscience (Sussex)
Medical Sciences (Sussex)
Clinical Physiology (Swansea)
CHECK PROSPECTUSES AND WEBSITES FOR OTHER UNIVERSITIES AND COLLEGES OFFERING THESE COURSES.

Universities and colleges teaching quality See www.qaa.ac.uk; www.unistats.com.

Top universities and colleges (Research) Cardiff; Dundee*; Liverpool; London (King's)*; Newcastle*; Queen's Belfast.

ADMISSIONS INFORMATION

Number of applicants per place and places (**a** UK **b** EU (non-UK) **c** non-EU **d** mature). Note that numbers quoted of applicants per place are approximate, and that all medical schools have a limited quota of places for non-EU applicants.

Aberdeen ab1513 for 162 places; **c**270 for 13 places (preference given to applicants from countries unable to provide a medical training); **Birmingham a**5, **c**25 Grad entry 12; **Brighton and Sussex (MS) a**10; **Bristol** 10; **Cambridge a**5; **Cardiff a**20 (6-year course) **c**22 (preference given to applicants from countries not providing a medical training); **Dundee a**7 (Pre-Med yr 11); **East Anglia a**7; **Edinburgh a**11 (international applicants not normally called for interview); **Glasgow a**6, **c**20; **Hull York (MS) a**13; **Imperial London a**7 **c**25; **Leeds a**2156 **b**97 **c**352 **d**488; **Leicester Warwick a**7; **Liverpool a**8; **London (King's) ab**311 places **c**25 places; **London (QM) a**8 **c**20; **London (St George's)** 19 (**a**3200 **b**250 **c**260 **d**1950: total places 292); **London (UCL) a**8 **c**14; **Manchester a**8 **c**10; **Newcastle and Durham a**10 (Pre-Med yr 27) **c**14; **Nottingham a**9 **c**15; **Oxford a**26% success rate **c**10; **Peninsula (MS) a**9; **Queen's Belfast a**4 **c**(a small number of places are allocated); **St Andrews a**8; **Sheffield a**17. (For six-year courses the number of applicants per place averages 30)

Admissions tutors' advice Policies adopted by all medical schools are very similar. However, a brief outline of the information provided by admissions tutors is given below. Further information should be obtained direct from institutions. Applicants wishing to contact medical schools should do so either by letter or by telephone and not by e-mail.

Aberdeen Interviews for some applicants. Overseas applicants may be interviewed abroad. Interviews last about 15 minutes. Most offers made in March. Points equivalent results not accepted. Re-sits not normally accepted. International students English language entry requirement (or equivalent): IELTS 7.0. Minimum age on entry 17 years 5 months. Clinical teaching and patient contact in Year 2.

Birmingham Non-academic interests and extra-curricular activities noted in addition to academic factors. General studies not accepted, but points equivalent results may be accepted. Interviews last about 15 minutes with three interviewers – a GP, a surgeon and a student. Approximately 1000 called for interview; 10% take a year off which does not jeopardise the chances of an offer but candidates must be available for interview. Re-sit candidates who failed by a small margin are only considered in exceptional circumstances. Transfers of undergraduates from other medical schools not considered. Clinical studies from Year 3.

Brighton and Sussex (MS) General studies not accepted. No offers without an interview. Interviews last about 15 minutes with three selectors. Students are members of both universities. Years 3–5 take place in the new Medical Education Centre at the Royal Sussex Hospital in Brighton. Clinical experience from Year 1.

Bristol Selection in stages. Top 10% of applicants called for interview, remainder grouped into three categories: 'high reserve', 'hold' and 'unsuccessful' – some from the first two categories will be interviewed. Widening participation panel considers appropriate candidates, 50 of whom will be interviewed. Criteria for selection: realistic and academic interest in medicine, commitment to helping others, wide range of interests, contribution to school/college activities, personal achievements. Interview criteria: reasons for wanting to study Medicine, awareness of current developments, communication skills, self-confidence, enthusiasm and determination to study, ability to cope with

444 | Medicine

stress, awareness of the content of the course and career. Gap year acceptable but applicants must be available for interview. Points equivalent results not accepted. International students English language requirement (or equivalent): IELTS 7.0. Clinical practice from Year 4.

Cambridge Some colleges insist on three science/maths subjects. Normally two interviews, each of 20 minutes each. Films of interviews on www.cam.ac.uk/admissions/undergraduate/interviews. Gap year acceptable but for positive reasons. Clinical studies from Year 4; 50% of students continue at the Cambridge Clinical School (Addenbrooke's Hospital).

Cardiff Great emphasis placed on evidence of a caring nature and exposure to hospital/health environments. Applicant's comment: 'Two interviewers and a 15-minute interview. Mainly questions on "Why Medicine?" Very helpful students'. Points equivalent results not accepted. Clinical studies from Year 1.

Dundee Preference given to candidates who achieve the right grades at the first sitting. Interviews – 20 minutes. Deferred entry acceptable. Clinical attachments in Year 4.

Durham (see also **Newcastle**) The medical course is offered in partnership with Newcastle University. Study is at Queen's Campus, Stockton. Preference given to applicants with relevant work experience in caring environment, hospital, voluntary capacity or through previous employment. Particular interest in recruiting local students, either school leavers or mature students. Interviews at Stockton with two selectors; may include a written personal qualities assessment test (PQA). Applicants from non-EU countries must apply to Newcastle where there is a quota of places for overseas students. Clinical contact begins in Year 1.

East Anglia Screening of applications done by two selectors. Criteria include academic requirements, capacity to cope with self-directed learning, team work, responsibility, motivation. Interview regarded as the acid test; lasts 30–45 minutes including two scenarios (examples online at www.med.uea.ac.uk/mbbs/mbbs_application). Clinical experience from Year 1.

Edinburgh All examination grades must be achieved at the first sitting; only in extenuating circumstances will re-sits be considered. Equal weighting given to academic and non-academic criteria. Non-academic criteria score based on personal qualities and skills, evidence of career exploration prior to application, breadth and level of non-academic achievements and interests. Work experience and work shadowing viewed positively but the admissions panel recognise that not all applicants have equal opportunities to gain such experience. Most school-leaving applicants interviewed, also shortlisted graduate and mature applicants. International applicants not normally called for interview. Clinical experience from Year 1.

Glasgow Formal work experience expected. (Work experience scheme operated by staff at Monklands Hospital, Lanarkshire.) All interviews held in Glasgow including those for overseas students. interviews assess candidates' performance on five points (i) knowledge of the medical course and experience of self-directed learning, (ii) experience of teamwork, (iii) communication skills, (iv) understanding of a medical career, (v) enthusiasm and commitment to medicine. Only in extenuating circumstances (family illness etc) will second-time applications be considered. Points equivalent results not accepted. Feedback available to all candidates who fail to achieve admission. Transfers from other medical schools not accepted. Clinical experience from Year 1.

Hull York (MS) Students allocated places at Hull or York by ballot in Years 1 and 2. Non-EU applicants English language (or equivalent requirement) IELTS 7.0. Transfers from other medical schools not accepted. Disabilities listed on UCAS application do not affect the assessment of the application. Formally structured interviews exploring academic ability, motivation, understanding of healthcare issues, communication skills, conscientiousness, empathy, tolerance and maturity. Questions are drawn from a bank of possible topics (available online prior to interview). Re-sits acceptable but with higher grades. Feedback to unsuccessful candidates not possible. Clinical placements from Year 1.

Imperial London Fifteen-minute interviews with panel of four or five selectors. Not aimed at being an intimidating experience – an evaluation of motivation, capacity to deal with stress, evidence of working as a leader and team member, ability to multitask, likely contribution to university life, communication skills and maturity. Admissions tutor's comment: 'We look for resourceful men and women with wide interests and accomplishments, practical concern for others and those who will make a contribution to the life of the school and hospital.' Results within two weeks. Re-sit candidates must have applied to Imperial School of Medicine previously, have achieved at least CCC and have predictions of AAA in the winter re-sit examinations and have extenuating circumstances to explain previous failure in the referee's statement. Candidates may also write directly to the School. Clinical contact in Year 1.

Keele (see also **Manchester**) Keele is in partnership with the Manchester Medical School. Years 1 and 2 take place in Manchester, Years 3–5 in Keele. All applications are submitted to Manchester showing one of three study preferences – Manchester, Keele or either.

Leeds Admissions tutors' comment: 'Consider your motivation carefully – we do!' Good verbal, non-verbal and presentational skills required. Candidates should: (i) be able to report on some direct experience of what a career in medicine is about; (ii) show evidence of social activities on a regular basis (eg, part-time employment, organised community experiences); (iii) show evidence of positions of responsibility and interests outside medical and school activities. Gap years encouraged but candidates must be available for interview, 20% of all applicants interviewed. Points equivalent results not accepted. International students English language requirement (or equivalent): IELTS 7.5. Re-applications from students who have achieved the right grades accepted. Re-sits only considered in exceptional circumstances and with good supporting evidence; offer AAA. Transfers from other medical schools not encouraged. Clinical practice commences in Year 4.

Leicester Warwick Students resident in Leicester. Final award is a combined degree from both universities. Interview lasts 20 minutes with two selectors (one doctor and one final-year medical student; both have had interview training). Interview not an academic test. Selectors each score independently on motivation, communication skills and suitability for a career in medicine. Gap years acceptable. Re-sits considered only in exceptional circumstances; offer AAA. Transfers from other medical schools not accepted. Clinical work commences in Year 1.

Liverpool Gap years acceptable for positive reasons but applicants must be available for interview. Gap year not possible for overseas students. First year Foundation programme offered for under-qualified international students. English language requirement (or equivalent): IELTS 7.5. Clinical contact from Year 1.

London (King's) Personal statement a significant factor in selection. Emphasis placed on appreciation of academic, physical and emotional demands of the course, commitment, evidence of working in a caring environment, communication skills and interaction with the general public. Approximately 1200 applicants (35%) called for interview. Clinical contact in Year 1.

London (QM) Personal statement a significant factor in selection. 'You are expected to write your own, with an honest reflection of your strengths and interests and you will be closely questioned on this statement at interview. We don't want people who are simply good at science. High grades are no guarantee of a place.' Interview of 15–20 minutes. Re-sits only considered in exceptional cases; offer AAA. Clinical experience from Year 1.

London (St George's) Applicants must be taking A-level chemistry and biology (or one to A-level and the other to AS-level). They will be required to complete their A-levels within two years of study and be predicted between BBC and AAA and have taken a fourth distinct AS-level in which they have achieved (or are predicted) a B. If not, your application will be unsuccessful. However, if you are predicted AABb and have at least 416 pts from 8 subjects at GCSE including mathematics, English and dual award science (ie average of grade A) then you will be called for interview. All applicants expected to have undertaken work experience in a medical environment. No offers without an interview – predicted grades important in selecting candidates for interview. Four selectors and an interview of 15–20 minutes. Some students who are not predicted to get the grades of our offer are also interviewed and considered for a place. Transfers from other medical schools rare. International students English language requirement (or equivalent): IELTS 7.0. Clinical experience commences in Year 3. (Fdn Med) This course is for mature non-graduate students only.

446 | Medicine

London (UCL) Three selectors interview applicants, each interview lasting 15–20 minutes; 30% of applicants interviewed. Qualities sought include motivation, awareness of scientific and medical issues, ability to express and defend opinions, maturity and individual strengths. Deferred entry for good reason is acceptable. Repeat applications only considered if candidate has previously received and held a firm offer from Royal Free or University College Medical School. Minimum age of entry: 18 years. Transfers from other medical schools not accepted. International students may take the University Preparation Certificate for Science and Engineering (UPCSE) which is the minimum entry requirement for entry to Medicine. Clinical attachments commence in Year 3.

Manchester (see also **Keele**) 341 places at Manchester/55 places at Keele. Minimum age of entry 17 years. Interviews with three selectors last about 15 minutes. If you feel unwell before the interview inform the admissions tutor and the interview will be re-scheduled; pleas of infirmity cannot be accepted after the interview! Candidates should be aware of the advantages and disadvantages of problem-based learning and opinions may be asked. Ethical questions may be raised. Decisions will be made by the end of March. Re-sit offers only made to applicants who received an offer after interview the previous year and who marginally failed to achieve the required grades; increasingly such offers are only made in the light of extenuating circumstances. Clinical attachments from Year 3.

Newcastle (see also **Durham**) 220 places at Newcastle; 95 places at Durham. Applicants' comments (Durham): 'Two interviewers and a 25 minute interview. Very relaxed interview. Stockton campus small. Good community spirit but some way from Durham'; (Newcastle): 'I had an interview with two selectors who had a gentle, helpful manner. I didn't feel under pressure but felt stretched'. Retakes not considered except in special circumstances. Deferred entry accepted. Consideration given to candidates who have overcome significant disadvantages (eg caring for parents with ill health). Clinical experience from Year 3.

Nottingham Candidates receive preliminary online questionnaire to be completed. Interviews 15 minutes with two selectors. Re-sit applicants who have previously applied will be reconsidered but only in extenuating circumstances. Deferred entry acceptable. International students English language requirement (or equivalent): IELTS 7.0. No transfers accepted from other medical schools. Clinical experience from Year 1. **Applicant's comment** I had one interview. There were two interviewers: the first asked me questions based on my personal statement, the second asked no scientific questions, focussing on the problems of the NHS and asking how I would deal with certain problems. He finally asked me to convince him why he should offer me a place.

Oxford Applicants called for interview on the basis of academic performance, test score and information on the application form. Ratio of interviewees to places approximately 2.5 to 1. No student admitted without an interview. All colleges use a common set of selection criteria. Candidates comment (Lincoln College): 'Two interviewers and two interviews. Questions covered my hobbies and social life, and scientific topics to test my logical train of thought. A great university, but it's not the be-all and end-all if you don't get in'. Clinical experience commences in Year 4.

Peninsula (MS) In the first two years students will be based at either the Universities of Exeter or Plymouth, selection taking place on a random basis. Qualities sought on the application and at interview: (i) integrity and honesty; (ii) motivation and commitment; (iii) empathy and non-judgemental attitudes; (iv) communication and listening skills; (v) teamwork; (vi) ability to cope with stress; (vii) problem-solving skills; (viii) awareness of one's strengths and weaknesses; (ix) reflectiveness; (x) suitable approach to life and people. Applicant's comment: 'I was asked to stand in the middle of the room and to demonstrate my commitment to Medicine in one minute! They then asked me to write my responses to a series of questions.' Clinical skills training commences in the first year.

Queen's Belfast Majority of applicants are school-leavers; 95% from Northern Ireland. A proportion of candidates will be called for interview. Interviews last about 15 minutes. A small number of places are allocated to non-EU applicants. Offer for repeating applicants AAA: number of places restricted for re-sit applicants who have narrowly missed an offer at Queen's. Clinical experience from Year 1.

St Andrews Medical Science students take full three-year programme leading to BSc (Hons), followed by clinical studies at Manchester University. Interviews last about 20 minutes with two or three selectors. Special attention given to international students and those who achieve qualifications at more than one sitting. As far as possible the interview panel will reflect the gender and ethnic distribution of candidates for interview.

Sheffield Applications processed between October and end of March. Candidates may send additional information concerning extenuating circumstances or health problems. Interviews last 20 minutes with up to three selectors. Candidates re-sitting for the first time may be considered: offer AAA. Gap year acceptable; medicine-related work very helpful. Clinical experience from Year 1.

Southampton In the personal statement and at interview applicants should be able to demonstrate that they are (i) self-motivated and have initiative, (ii) literate and articulate, (iii) able to interact successfully with others, (iv) able to demonstrate that they have learnt from their experiences with people in health and social care settings. Interviews normally last 20 minutes with two selectors. Deferred entry accepted. Candidates who wish to change their year of entry should submit requests before mid-March. Patient contact from Year 1.

Warwick – See **Leicester Warwick**

Advice to applicants and planning the UCAS personal statement (See also **Admissions Tutors' advice**).
NB Nearly all universities now require either the UKCAT or BMAT entry tests to be taken before applying for Medicine. Check websites (www.ukcat.ac.uk; www.bmat.org.uk) for details of test dates and test centres and with universities for their requirements. The medical admission process is changing fast and it is essential that you check for the latest information before applying and that you give yourself plenty of time to make arrangements for sitting these tests (see also **Chapter 7**).

Four Medicine choices only may be listed on the UCAS application which must be submitted by 15 October. Applicants may add up to two alternative courses. However, if they receive offers for these courses and perform better than expected, they will not be able to request medical schools to reconsider their application in Clearing. 'Don't rush around doing things just for your CV. If you are a boring student, be an incredibly well-read boring student! You can play netball, rugby, hockey, make beautiful music and paint with your feet, but if you fail to get the grades you'll be rejected.' Some 13,000 applications are submitted for Medicine each year, with approximately 4,700 candidates being successful. Admissions tutors obviously look for certain personal qualities and these will emerge in your personal statement, at the interview and on your school or college reference. There should be evidence of scientific interest, commitment, enthusiasm, determination, stability, self-motivation, ability to organise your own work, interest in the welfare of others, communication skills, modesty (arrogance and over-confidence could lead to rejection!), breadth of interest, leadership skills, stamina, good physical and mental health.

Some kind of first-hand experience in a medical setting is almost obligatory for those applying for Medicine (see also under **Admissions tutors' advice**). Depending on your personal contacts in the medical profession, this could include observing operations (for example, orthopaedic surgery), working in hospitals and discussing the career with your GP. Remember that your friends and relatives may have medical conditions that they would be willing to discuss with you – and all this will contribute to your knowledge and show that you are informed and interested. Read medical and scientific magazines and keep up-to-date with important current issues – AIDS, avian 'flu, euthanasia, abortion. Community work, clubs, societies, school and social activities should be mentioned. Show that you have an understanding of the role of health professionals in society and the social factors that influence health and disease.

Misconceptions about this course Liverpool Some applicants think that three science subjects at A-level are required to study Medicine. **London (St George's)** That you should be white, middle class and male: 60% of medical students are now female and 53% of our students are not white.

Selection interviews See **Admissions tutors' advice**. See also **Chapter 7**.

Interview advice and questions Questions will vary between applicants, depending on their UCAS statements and their A/AS-level subjects. Questions are likely to relate to A-level specific subjects, general medicine topics and unconnected topics (see also under **Admissions tutors' advice**). The following questions will provide a guide to the range of topics covered in past interviews. Outline the structure of DNA. What is meant by homeostasis? Is a virus a living organism? What has been the most important advance in biology in the last 50 years? What interests you about (i) science, (ii) biology, (iii) chemistry? Why did you choose the particular AS/A-level subjects you are doing? Why do you want to study Medicine/become a doctor? Do you expect people to be grateful? Why do you want to study here? Why should we take you? Do you agree with the concept of Foundation hospitals? Do you think NHS doctors and staff should be able to take private patients? If you were in charge of finances for a large health authority, what would be your priorities for funding? If you had to decide between saving the life of a young child and that of an old person, what would you do? Would you treat lung cancer patients who refuse to give up smoking? What do you understand by 'gene therapy'? Can you give any examples? In your opinion what is the most serious cause for concern for the health of the UK? What do you want to do with your medical degree? What do you think the human genome project can offer medicine? Should we pay for donor organs? Where do you see yourself in 15 years' time? What was the last non-technical book you read? What is your favourite piece of classical music? List your top five novels. What is your favourite play? What politician do you admire the most? Who made the most valuable contribution to the 20th century? Why do you think research is important? Why is teamwork important? What do you think about the NHS's problems? What do you think about euthanasia, cloning, etc? Do you think that sport is important? What did you gain from doing work experience in a nursing home? What were the standards like? How does the medical profession deal with social issues? What societies will you join at university? How could you compare your hobby of rowing with medicine? Do you agree that it is difficult to balance the demands of being a doctor with those of starting a family? In doing a medical course, what would you find the most emotionally challenging aspect? How would you cope with emotional strain? What do you think about going to war with Iraq? Who should have priority for receiving drugs in an avian 'flu epidemic/pandemic? How would you deal with the death of a patient? What are stem cells? Why are they controversial? How is cloning done? What constitutes a human being? Describe an egg. How can you measure intelligence? How do we combat genetic diseases? How are genes actually implanted? What do you want to talk about? If you were a cardiothoracic surgeon, would you perform a heart by-pass operation on a smoker? What are the negative aspects of becoming a doctor? At some interviews essays may be set, eg (i) 'A Scientific Education is a Good Basis for a Medical Degree: discuss'; (ii) 'Only Drugs that are Safe and Effective should be prescribed to Patients: discuss'. Occasionally applicants at interview may be given scenarios to discuss (see **East Anglia** under **Admissions tutors' advice**). **Oxford** Tell me about drowning. What do you think of assisted suicide? Would you give a 60-year-old woman IVF treatment? When are people dead? See **Chapter 7**.

Applicants' impressions See **Admissions tutors' advice**.

Reasons for rejection (non-academic) Insufficient vocation demonstrated. No steps taken to gain practical experience relevant to medicine. Doubts as to the ability to cope with the stress of a medical career. Not enough awareness about the career. Lack of knowledge about the course. Applicant appears dull and lacking in enthusiasm and motivation. Lacking in a caring, committed attitude towards people. No evidence of broad social, cultural or sporting interests or of teamwork. Poor or lack of communication skills. Uncaring attitude. Arrogance. Over-confident at interview. Unrealistic expectations about being a doctor.

Age at entry Applicants must be 17 years old on 30 September of the year of entry. However, some medical schools stipulate 17 years 6 months, and a small number stipulate 18 years. Those considering entry at 17 would probably be advised to take a gap year.

Health requirements Medical schools require all students to have their immunity status for hepatitis B, tuberculosis and rubella checked on entry. Offers are usually made subject to satisfactory health screening for hepatitis B. In line with advice from the General Medical Council, students will not be admitted to courses who are found to be e-antigen positive when screened within the first week of the course. Candidates accepting offers should assure themselves of their immunity status. **Dyslexia** Applicants with dyslexia should contact the admissions office prior to application. It is expected that most students will have successfully adapted to their medical condition. Whilst some medical schools may allow a limited amount of extra time for purely academic examinations, eg essays and multiple choice questions, the British Dyslexia Association and medical schools generally take the view that absolutely no concessions should be made in the conduct of clinical examinations.

Advice to mature students Medical schools usually accept a small number of mature students each year. However, several, if not the majority, reject applicants over 30 years of age. Some medical schools accept non-graduates although A-level passes at high grades are usually stipulated. The majority of applicants accepted are likely to be graduates with a first or upper second honours degree. **Birmingham**, **Bristol**, **Leeds** Maximum age at entry is 30 years. **Leeds** Applicants should hold the required A-level grades or a high class science degree; 15–20 places. **Southampton** 36 places available, maximum age 40; GCSE mathematics, physics, biology or double science required. Applicants with nursing qualifications should hold two grade B A-levels including chemistry. Mature students taking Access courses must achieve 70% in A2 chemistry.

Advice to graduate applicants Graduate applicants are considered by all medical schools. At some medical schools the Graduate Australian Medical Schools Admission Test (GAMSAT) and the Medical Schools Admissions Test (MSAT) are now being used to assess the aptitude of prospective applicants. Applicants, for example, at **Peninsula (MS)**, are selected on the basis of three criteria: (i) an honours degree at 2.2 or above; (ii) the GAMSAT score; (iii) performance at interview. All applicants must be EU students. **London (St George's)** Some students think that science graduates are the only ones to do well in GAMSAT: 40% of those on the course do not have a science degree or A-levels; however, work experience is essential.

GRADUATE DESTINATIONS AND EMPLOYMENT (2005/6 HESA)
Graduates surveyed 4790 **Employed** 4735 **In further study** 5 **Assumed unemployed** 5.

Career note The current problems facing newly qualified doctors have been widely reported in the press. It is unlikely, however, that such reports will affect the numbers of determined students who wish to enter the medical profession. Furthermore, this year's applicants will not graduate until 2014 when the picture could have changed radically. Applicants should also bear in mind that while most doctors do work in the NHS either in hospital services or in general practice, not a few choose to work in other fields such as public health, pharmacology, the environment, occupational medicine with industrial organisations, the armed services and opportunities abroad.

OTHER DEGREE SUBJECTS FOR CONSIDERATION
Anatomy; Biochemistry; Biological Sciences; Biology; Biomedical/Medical Materials Science; Biology; Biotechnology; Clinical Sciences; Dentistry; Dietetics; Genetics; Health Sciences; Medical Physics; Medical Sciences; Midwifery; Nursing; Nutrition; Occupational Therapy; Optometry; Pharmacology; Pharmacy; Physiology; Physiotherapy; Psychology; Radiography; Speech Sciences – and Law! (The work of doctors and lawyers is similar in that both are required to identify the relevant information – symptoms or legal issues!)

MICROBIOLOGY

(see also **Biological Sciences, Biology, Biotechnology** and **Genetics**)

Microbiology is a branch of biological science specialising in the study of micro-organisms: bacteria, viruses and fungi. The subject covers the relationship between these organisms and disease and industrial applications such as food and drug production, waste-water treatment and future biochemical uses.

Useful websites www.scienceyear.com; www.sgm.ac.uk; www.nature.com/micro; www.microbes.info; www.asm.org; www.microbiol.org; see also **Biochemistry**, **Biological Sciences** and **Biology**.

NB The points totals shown to the left of the institutions are for ease of reference only. It must not be assumed that tariff points are always used by institutions or that they can be substituted for an offer in grades. The level of an offer is not necessarily indicative of the quality of a course.

COURSE OFFERS INFORMATION

Subject requirements/preferences **GCSE** English and mathematics and science subjects. **AL** One or two mathematics/science subjects including chemistry and/or biology, required or preferred; grades sometimes specified. **NB** A* grades are likely to form part of university offers in the higher ranges for students applying for places in 2008 for entry in 2009: check websites.

Your target offers

340 pts **Imperial London** – AAB–ABB 340–320 pts (Microbiology) *(IB 36 pts H66)*
Manchester – AAB–BBB (Microbiol; Microbiol Ind; Microbiol Modn Lang)

320 pts **Birmingham** – ABB–BBB (Biol Sci (Microbiol)) *(IB 32–34 pts)*
Cardiff – ABB–BBB (Microbiology) *(IB 32 pts H biol chem 55)*
Liverpool – ABB–BBB (Microbiol; Microbl Biotech) *(IB 28–30 pts)*
Newcastle – ABB–BBB (Med Microbiol Immun)
Sheffield – ABB–ABbb (Microbiol courses)

300 pts **Bristol** – BBB (Path Microbiol; Med Microbiol; Microbiol) *(IB 32 pts H655)*
Dundee – 300 pts 2nd yr entry (Microbiology)
East Anglia – BBB–BBC (Microbiology) *(IB 31 pts H555)*
Edinburgh – BBB (Microbiol Infec)
Leeds – BBB–BBC (Microbiol; Med Microbiol; Microbiol Immun; Microbiol Virol) *(IB 32 pts H 15 pts)*
Leicester – BBB (Biol Sci (Microbiol)) *(IB 32 pts H66)*
Nottingham – BBB (Microbiology) *(IB 24–30 pts)*
Surrey – BBB–BCC (Microbiol; Microbiol (Med); Microbl Genet; Fd Sci Microbiol; Bioch (Tox)) *(IB 28 pts)*
Warwick – BBB (Microbiol Virol) *(IB 32 pts)*

280 pts **Aston** – BBC 280 pts (Infec Immun)
Glasgow – BBC–CCC (Microbiology) *(IB 28 pts)*
London (QM) – 280 pts (Bioch Microbiol; Genet Microbiol)
Reading – 280 pts (Med Microbiol)
Strathclyde – BBC (Bioch Microbiol; Immun Microbiol)

260 pts **Bradford** – 260 pts (Med Microbiol)
Nottingham – BCC–CCC (Fd Microbiol)
Portsmouth – 260–300 pts (Microbiology)
Queen's Belfast – BCC/AB (Microbiology) *(IB 28 pts H555)*

240 pts **Aberdeen** – CCC (Microbiology)
Aberystwyth – 240–280 pts (Microbiology) *(IB 26 pts H biol 5 pts)*
Dundee – 240 pts 1st yr entry (Microbiology)

220 pts **Liverpool John Moores** – 220–260 pts (Microbiol; App Microbiol)

200 pts **Anglia Ruskin** – 200 pts (Microbiology)
Heriot-Watt – CDD (Microbiology)
Huddersfield – 200–280 pts (Microbl Sci)
Manchester Met – 200–240 pts (Med Env Microbiol)
Napier – 200 pts (Microbiol Biotech)
Nottingham Trent – 200 pts (Microbiol courses)
Staffordshire – 200–260 pts (Bioch Microbiol)

180 pts **Bristol UWE** – 180–220 pts (App Microbiol)
Glamorgan – 180–220 pts (Microbiology)
Glasgow Caledonian – DDD (Microbiology)
Hertfordshire – 180–200 pts (Microbiology)

For a quick reference offers calculator, fold out the inside back cover.

160 pts **London Met** – 160 pts (Microbiology)
London South Bank – CC–CCC (Biosci (Microbiol))
Westminster – CC (Microbiology)
Wolverhampton – 160–220 pts (Microbiol; Microbiol Genet Mol Biol)

Alternative offers
See **Chapter 8** for grade/point equivalences and related information for the following examinations: Scottish qualifications, the Welsh Baccalaureate, the IB diploma (approximate points shown also in italics in the table of offers), the Irish Leaving Certificate, the European Baccalaureate and the French Baccalaureate.

EXAMPLES OF FOUNDATION DEGREES IN THE SUBJECT FIELD
St Helens (Coll).

CHOOSING YOUR COURSE (SEE ALSO CH.1)
Course variations – Widen your options
Infection and Immunity (Aston)
Medical Microbiology (Bradford)
Pathology and Microbiology (Bristol)
Microbiology Sciences (Huddersfield)
Microbial Biotechnology (Liverpool)
Microbiology with Industrial Experience (Manchester)
Medical and Environmental Microbiology (Manchester Met)
Food Microbiology (Nottingham)
Microbiology and Virology (Warwick)
CHECK PROSPECTUSES AND WEBSITES FOR OTHER UNIVERSITIES AND COLLEGES OFFERING THESE COURSES.

Universities and colleges teaching quality See www.qaa.ac.uk; www.unistats.com.

Top universities and colleges (Research) Leeds; see also **Biological Sciences**.

Sandwich degree courses Aston; Bristol; Bristol UWE; Cardiff; Glamorgan; Leeds; Liverpool John Moores; London South Bank; Nottingham Trent. See also **Biochemistry** and **Biological Sciences**.

ADMISSIONS INFORMATION
Number of applicants per place (approx) Aberystwyth 5; Bradford 6; Bristol 6; Cardiff 4; Dundee 5; Leeds 7; Liverpool 3; Strathclyde 10; Surrey 4; Swansea 5; Wolverhampton 4.

Advice to applicants and planning the UCAS personal statement Relevant experience, particularly for mature students. See **Biological Sciences**. See also **Appendix 2**.

Selection interviews Yes Bristol, London South Bank, Nottingham (depends on application), Surrey, Swansea; **Some** Aberystwyth (mature applicants only), Cardiff, Leeds, Liverpool John Moores, Wolverhampton.

Interview advice and questions Examples of past questions include: Is money spent on the arts a waste? How much does the country spend on research and on the armed forces? Discuss reproduction in bacteria. What do you particularly like about your study of biology? What would you like to do after your degree? Do you have any strong views on vivisection? Discuss the differences between the courses you have applied for. What important advances have been made in the biological field recently? How would you describe microbiology? Do you know anything about the diseases caused by micro-organisms? What symptoms would be caused by which particular organisms? See **Chapter 7**.

AFTER-RESULTS ADVICE
Offers to applicants repeating A-levels Higher Bristol, Strathclyde, Swansea, Warwick; **Possibly higher** East Anglia, Nottingham; **Same** Aberystwyth, Anglia Ruskin, Bradford, Cardiff, Leeds, Liverpool, Wolverhampton.

GRADUATE DESTINATIONS AND EMPLOYMENT (2005/6 HESA)
Graduates surveyed 485 **Employed** 205 **In further study** 140 **Assumed unemployed** 40.

Career note See **Biology**.

OTHER DEGREE SUBJECTS FOR CONSIDERATION
Animal Sciences; Biochemistry; Biological Sciences; Biology; Biotechnology; Genetics; Medical Sciences; Medicine; Pharmacology; Physiology.

MUSIC

Theory and practice are combined to a greater or lesser extent in most university Music courses and from which about 50 per cent or more of graduates will go on to non-music careers. However, courses are also offered by Conservatoires and Schools of Music where the majority of applicants are aiming to become professional musicians. For these courses the ability to perform on an instrument is more important than academic ability and offers are therefore likely to be lower. See also **Appendix 2**.

Useful websites www.arts.org.uk; www.communitymusic.org; www.ism.org; www.bpi-med.co.uk; www.royalopera.org; www.nyo.org.uk; www.bbc.co.uk/youngmusican; www.cukas.ac.uk.

NB The points totals shown to the left of the institutions are for ease of reference only. It must not be assumed that tariff points are always used by institutions or that they can be substituted for an offer in grades. The level of an offer is not necessarily indicative of the quality of a course.

COURSE OFFERS INFORMATION

Subject requirements/preferences GCSE A foreign language and mathematics may be required. A good range of As and Bs for popular universities. **AL** Music plus an instrumental grade usually required. **NB** A* grades are likely to form part of university offers in the higher ranges for students applying for places in 2008 for entry in 2009: check websites.

NB Some applications are made through the Conservatoires Admissions Service (CUKAS): see **Chapter 6** for details.

Music examinations Additional points will be awarded for Music examinations from the Associated Board of the Royal Schools of Music (ABRSM), the Guildhall School of Music and Drama, the London College of Music Examinations (LCMM) and Trinity College of Music music examinations at grades 6, 7, 8 (D=Distinction; M=Merit; P=Pass).

Practical:	Grade 6 – D 45 pts; M 40 pts; P 25 pts.
	Grade 7 – D 60 pts; M 55 pts; P 40 pts.
	Grade 8 – D 75 pts; M 70 pts; P 55 pts.
Theory:	Grade 6 – D 15 pts; M 10 pts; P 5 pts.
	Grade 7 – D 20 pts; M 15 pts; P 10 pts.
	Grade 8 – D 30 pts; M 25 pts; P 20 pts.

Your target offers

360 pts and above
        Cambridge – AAA (Music) *(IB 38–42 pts)*
        Imperial London – AAA (Phys St Musl Perf) *(IB 38 pts H666)*
        Manchester – AAA–AAB (Mus; Mus Dr)
        Oxford – Offers vary eg AAA–AAB (Music) *(IB 38–42 pts)*

340 pts **Birmingham** – AAB–ABB (Mus courses) *(IB 34 pts)*

Cambridge (Hom) – AAB–ABB (BA Mus Educ St) *(IB 38–42 pts)*

Durham – AAB (Mus Comb Arts)

London (King's) – AAB+AS **or** AAaab (Mus; Mus Dig Hum; Ger Mus) *(IB 36 pts H mus 7 pts)*

Nottingham – AAB (Music) *(IB 32 pts H mus 6 pts)*

Surrey – AAB (inc gr 7) (Mus Snd Rec (Tonmeister))

320 pts **Bristol** – 320 pts ABB (inc ABRSM gr 5 piano) (Mus; Mus Fr/Ger/Ital) *(IB 34 pts)*

Cardiff – ABB–BBC gr 8 theor+gr 8 prac (BA/BMus courses) *(IB 30 pts)*

Durham – ABB (Mus; Mus Educ) *(IB 30 pts)*

Glasgow – ABB (+ gr 8 for BMus) (Music) *(IB 30 pts)*

Liverpool – ABB 320 pts (Mus; Mus Pop Mus; Pop Mus) *(IB 31 pts)*

London (RH) – ABB (inc gr 7 instr) (Mus Fr/Ger/Ital/Span; Mus Pol St) *(IB 35 pts H mus 6 pts)*

Newcastle – ABB (BA Mus/BMus Folk Trad Mus; Pop Contemp Mus) *(IB 35 pts H mus 5 pts)*

Sheffield – ABB–BBC (Mus courses)

Southampton – ABB 320 pts (Mus courses)

Surrey – ABB–BBB (Music) *(IB 32 pts)*

Sussex – ABB–BBB 3AL+AS (inc gr 7) (Mus; Mus Cult St; Mus Film St; Mus Fr/Ger/Ital/Span; Mus Inform) *(IB 32–34 pts)*

York – ABB (Music) *(IB 34 pts H mus 6 pts)*

300 pts **East Anglia** – BBB–BBC (Mus; Mus Comp; Mus Maths) *(IB 30 pts)*

Edinburgh – BBB (Mus; Mus Tech) *(IB 34 pts H555)*

Lancaster – BBB–BBC (Mus; Mus Tech) *(IB 28–29 pts)*

Leeds – ABC (inc ABRSM gr 5 not prac mus/mus tech) (Mus courses) *(IB 33 pts)*

London (Gold) – BBB (Mus; Pop Mus St) *(IB 32 pts)*

Queen's Belfast – BBB–BBCb (Mus; Ethnomus courses) *(IB 29 pts H655)*

Stranmillis (UC) – BBB (Mus Educ)

York – BBB–BBC (BEng Mus Tech)

280 pts **Birmingham City** – 280 pts (Media Comm (Mus Ind))

Brunel – 280 pts (inc gr 6/7 instr/vocal) (Engl Mus; Dr Mus; Film TV St Mus; Crea Mus) *(IB 32 pts)*

Coventry – 280 pts (Mus Tech)

Hull – BBC–BBB (inc gr 7 or above on 1st study instr/voice) (Mus Fr/Ger/Ital/Span)

Kent – 280 pts (Mus Tech)

Leeds – BBC (Mus Multim Electron; Pop Wrld Mus) *(IB 33 pts)*

Liverpool – BBC–BBB 280–300 pts (Comm Media Pop Mus) *(IB 31 pts)*

Ulster – 280 pts (Music)

260 pts **Bangor** – 260–280 pts (Music) *(IB 28 pts)*

Cardiff – BCC (Phys Mus)

City – 260–300 pts (inc gr 7) (Wrld Mus St)

Huddersfield – 260–320 pts (Mus Tech courses; Pop Mus Prod; Mus; Mus Jrnl; Mus Lang; Mus Dr; Mus Engl; Mus Hist)

Keele – 260–320 pts (Mus courses; Mus Tech)

Liverpool (LIPA) – BCC (Music)

London (SOAS) – BCC/BB (Mus courses)

Oxford Brookes – BCC–CCD (joint Hons)) (Mus; Snd Tech Dig Music)

Winchester – 260 pts (Perf Arts Mus Thea)

240 pts **Aberdeen** – CCC/BB (BMus Mus; Mus St courses)

Brighton – CCC (Dig Mus)

Chester – 240–260 pts (Commer Mus Prod; Pop Mus courses)

Glasgow – AA–DD (Mus BEd)

Hertfordshire – 240 pts+pts from graded mus exams (inc gr 5 theor) (Mus Commer Cmpsn Tech; Snd Des Tech; Mus Tech; Mus Enter Ind Mgt)

Hull – 240–300 pts (BA/BMus Mus)

Hull (Scarborough) – CCC–BBB 240–300 pts (Crea Mus Tech; Crea Mus Tech Bus Mgt)

Leeds (CMus) – 240 pts (Mus; Jazz; Pop Mus St; Mus Prod)

Liverpool Hope – 240 pts (Mus; Mus Tech)

Portsmouth – 240 pts (Mus Snd Tech)

220 pts **Bath Spa** – 220–260 pts (+ gr 8) (Mus; Crea Mus Tech)

Birmingham City – 220–240 pts (Mus Tech; Snd Multim Tech)

Bristol UWE – 220–240 pts (Mus Sys Eng; Crea Mus Tech)

Chichester – 220 pts (Perf Arts Mus)

De Montfort – 220 pts (Mus Tech Innov)

London (RAcMus) – AB–BC (BMus Mus)

Swansea (Inst) – 220 pts (Mus Tech)

200 pts **Anglia Ruskin** – 200–240 pts (Mus; Mus Dr; Mus Engl; Crea Mus Tech; Crea Mus Tech Mus)

Coventry – 200–220 pts (Mus Prof Prac; Mus Cmpsn Prof Prac)

Cumbria – BB–CC (Educ Mus; Mus QTS Perf courses; Musl Thea)

Glamorgan – 200 pts (Pop Mus)

Kingston – 200–240 pts (Mus; Mus joint courses)

Lincoln – 200 pts (Aud Tech)

Manchester Met – 200 pts (Mus courses; Pop Mus courses; Snc Arts courses)

Middlesex – 200–240 pts (Mus Arts Mgt; Jazz; Mus Commun)

Napier – 200 pts (Mus; Pop Mus)

Roehampton – 200–280 pts (Mus courses)

Salford – 160–200 pts (Music) *(IB 24 pts)*

Staffordshire – 200–280 pts (Crea Mus Tech; Mus Tech Mgt)

Sunderland – 200–260 pts (Mus courses)

190 pts **London Met** – 190 pts (Mus Media Mgt)

180 pts **Doncaster (Coll)** – 180 pts (Crea Mus Tech; App Mus; NMus Prod)

Liverpool John Moores – 180–280 pts (Pop Mus St)

Liverpool (LIPA) – BC 180 pts (Snd Tech)

Northampton – 180–220 pts (Pop Mus courses)

Plymouth – 180 pts (Mus; Mus Educ St)

Reading – 180 pts (Educ St Mus)

Royal Welsh (CMusDr) – 180–260 pts (Mus (gr 8 principal instrument); Pop Mus; Perf Prod; apply direct)

Southampton Solent – 180–200 pts (Pop Mus Rec Prod; Dig Mus courses; Urb Electron Mus)

Teesside – 180–240 pts (Dig Mus Crea; Mus Soft Dev)

160 pts **Bedfordshire** – 160 pts (Mus Tech)

Bishop Grosseteste (UC) – DDE 160 pts (Educ St Mus)

Canterbury Christ Church – CC (Music)

Central Lancashire – 160 pts+audition (Mus Prac)

Chichester – 160–200 pts/gr 8+C (Mus; Mus joint courses)

Colchester (Inst) – BD 160 pts (Mus; Mus (Educ) (Mus Tech) (Perf St))

Dartington (CA) – 160–200 pts (Mus (Cmpsn); Mus (Perf))
Derby – 160–240 pts (Mus joint courses)
East London – 160 pts (Mus Cult (Theor Prod); Perf Arts)
London Met – 160–200 pts (Mus Tech (Aud Sys); Mark Musl Instr; Mus Media Mgt)
Newcastle (Coll) – 160 pts (BMus Pop Jazz Commer Mus)
South East Essex (Coll) – 160 pts (Mus Prod)
Southampton Solent – 160 pts (Aud Tech)
Strathclyde – CC (App Mus)
Thames Valley – 160 pts (Mus Perf Comp; Mus Tech; Pop Mus Perf)
Truro (Coll) – 160 pts (Contemp Wrld Jazz)
West Scotland – CC (Commer Mus)
Westminster – CC (Commer Mus; Commer Mus Perf)
Wolverhampton – 160–220 pts (Mus; Mus Tech Pop Mus; Pop Mus)
York St John – 160 pts (Perf Mus; Mus)
140 pts **Bath Spa** – 140 pts (Commer Mus)
Thames Valley – 140 pts (Mus Media; Mus Evnt Mgt)
120 pts **Bucks New** – 120–180 pts (Mus Ind Mgt)
RCMus – 120 pts (Music)
100 pts **and below**
Arts Educ (Sch) – 2AL (Mus Thea)
Arts London – 80 pts (Snd Arts Des)
Arts London (CComm) – 100 pts (Music)
Birmingham City/Birmingham Consv – 80 pts (Mus; Jazz)
Guildhall (Sch Mus Dr) – 100 pts (Mus; Thea)
Manchester (RNCM) – 80–120 pts (BMus; Mus)
Northbrook (Coll) – 100 pts (Mus Cmpsn Prof Media)
Rose Bruford (Coll) – 100 pts individual interview/audition (Act Mus; Mus Tech)
Royal Scottish (RSAMD) – (Mus; BA Scot Mus; Scot Mus Piping)
Trinity (CMus) – (inc gr 8) (BMus (Perf); MMus (Perf St))
UHI Millennium Inst (PC) – (Mus Perf)
West Scotland – DE (Mus Tech)
Weston (Coll) – 80 pts **or** mus tech qual (Crea Mus Tech)

Leeds Met – contact University

Alternative offers

See **Chapter 8** for grade/point equivalences and related information for the following examinations: Scottish qualifications, the Welsh Baccalaureate, the IB diploma (approximate points shown also in italics in the table of offers), the Irish Leaving Certificate, the European Baccalaureate and the French Baccalaureate.

EXAMPLES OF FOUNDATION DEGREES IN THE SUBJECT FIELD

Barnsley (Univ Centre); Bath Spa; Bedfordshire; Blackpool and Fylde (Coll); Bournemouth and Poole (Coll); Burnley (Coll); Chichester; Colchester (Inst); Coventry; Cumbria; Durham New (Coll); Farnborough (CT); Gateshead (Coll); Glamorgan; Hull (Coll); Isle of Wight (Coll); Kendal (Coll); Leeds (CMus); London Met; Manchester (RNCM); Manchester City (Coll); Newcastle (Coll); North Devon (Coll); North East London (Coll); Northbrook (Coll); Park Lane Leeds (Coll); Peterborough Reg (Coll); Plymouth; Preston (Coll); St Helens (Coll); South Thames (Coll); Suffolk (Univ Campus); Sussex Downs (Coll); Teesside; Thames Valley; Truro (Coll); West Anglia (Coll); West Kent (Coll); West Thames (Coll); Westminster City (Coll); Weston (Coll); Weymouth (Coll); York St John.

CHOOSING YOUR COURSE (SEE ALSO CH.1)

Course variations – Widen your options

Business Management and Music (Bath Spa)
Film Sound Technology (Birmingham City)
Music Technology and Robotics (Bristol UWE)

Music Composition (Brunel)
Music Industry Management (Bucks New)
Music joint courses (Canterbury Christ Church)
Combined Arts (Durham)
Electronic Music and Business (Hertfordshire)
Creative Music Technology (Hull (Scarborough))
Popular and World Musics (Leeds)
Music Technology (Liverpool Hope)
Popular Music Studies (London (Gold))
Folk and Traditional Music (Newcastle)
Popular Music Recording (Salford)
Music and Sound Recording (Surrey)
Music Informatics (Sussex)
CHECK PROSPECTUSES AND WEBSITES FOR OTHER UNIVERSITIES AND COLLEGES OFFERING THESE COURSES.

Universities and colleges teaching quality See www.qaa.ac.uk; www.unistats.com.

Top universities and colleges (Research) Bangor; Birmingham*; Bristol; Cambridge*; Cardiff; City*; Huddersfield; Hull; London (Gold), (King's), (RH), (SOAS); Manchester*; Newcastle*; Nottingham*; Oxford*; Queen's Belfast; Sheffield; Southampton*; Sussex; York.

Sandwich degree courses Brunel; Hertfordshire; Huddersfield; Leeds Met; London Met; Staffordshire; Surrey; Teesside; UCE Birmingham.

ADMISSIONS INFORMATION

Number of applicants per place (approx) Aberystwyth 5; Anglia Ruskin 5; Bangor (BA) 4; Bath Spa 8; Birmingham 12; Bristol 8; Brunel 7; Cambridge 3; Cambridge (Hom) 4; Cardiff 6; Chichester 4; City 7; Colchester (Inst) 4; Cumbria 7; Dartington (CA) 8; Durham 5; East Anglia 12; Edinburgh 11; Glasgow 4; Huddersfield 2; Hull 21; Kingston 18; Lancaster 8; Leeds 18; Liverpool 9; Liverpool (LIPA) 12; London (Gold) 7, (King's) 10, (RAcMus) 7, (RH) 7, (SOAS) 4; London Met 10; Manchester (RNCM) 8; Middlesex 23; Napier 3; Newcastle 24; Northampton 3; Northern (Coll) 3; Northumbria 12; Nottingham 35; Oxford (success rate 61%); Oxford Brookes 12; Queen's Belfast 6; Roehampton 4; Rose Bruford (Coll) 15; RCMus 10; Royal Scottish (RSAMD) 6; Salford 5; Southampton 5; Strathclyde 15; Surrey average 6, (Tonmeister) 12; TrCMus 4; Ulster 8; Worcester 8; York 11; York St John 2.

Interview advice and questions
NB See also **Chapter 7** under **Music.**

Anglia Ruskin In addition to A-levels, we also require Grade 7 (good pass, first study) plus Grade 5 minimum keyboard standard.

Bangor Offer depends on proven ability in historical or compositional fields plus acceptable performance standard. Options include music therapy, recording techniques, jazz.

Bath Spa Some candidates interviewed. Required to perform and sight-read on main instrument, and given aural and critical listening tests. Discussion of previous performing, composing and academic experience. (Fdn Commer Mus) All applicants must submit a self-composed audio prior to interview.

Bristol (Mus Modn Lang) No in-depth interviews; candidates invited to Open days.

Cambridge (Hom) Tests will also include busking accompaniments to children's songs on keyboard. Questions on stylistic features of piece performed.

Cambridge (St Catharine's) At interview candidates may have to undergo some simple keyboard or aural tests (such as harmonisation of an unseen melody or memorisation of a rhythm). More importantly, they will have to comment on some unseen musical extracts from a stylistic and analytical point of view. Candidates are asked to submit some examples of work before the interview, from the fields of harmony and counterpoint, history, and analysis; they are also encouraged to send any other material such as compositions, programme notes or an independent essay on a subject of interest to the candidate. (Taking the STEP examination is not a requirement for admission.) Above all this, though, the main pre-requisite for reading Music at St Catharine's is an academic interest in the subject itself.

Canterbury Christ Church Associated Board examinations in two instruments (or one instrument and voice); keyboard competence essential, particularly for the BEd course.

Colchester (Inst) Great stress laid on candidate's ability to communicate love of the subject.

Cumbria Admission by live performance or on tape. QTS applicants interviewed for teaching suitability. See **Chapter 6**.

Durham We also require Grade 6 piano (Associated Board) and a foreign language (GCSE grade A–C), A-level music grade B.

East Anglia Only unusual and mature candidates are interviewed. Applicants are expected to perform music with insight and show genuine intellectual curiosity about music and its cultural background. At interview candidates will be asked to perform on their principal instrument. Those who play orchestral instruments or sing will also be expected to play simple music on the piano. At interview we look for applicants with proficiency in instrumental or vocal performance (preferably at Grade 8 standard or above), range of experience of music of many types and an intelligent attitude towards discussion.

Edinburgh Most candidates are called for interview, although very well qualified candidates may be offered a place without interview. All are asked to submit samples of their work. Associated Board Grade 7 on piano is usually expected.

Glasgow The BA (Mus Educ) course is for students aiming at a career in school music and is largely keyboard-orientated. The BA (Music Performance) course is for those wanting a career in professional performance (Instrument and Voice).

Huddersfield Have an open and inquisitive outlook with regard to all aspects of music from performing to composing, musicology to listening. Candidates auditioned on their principal instrument or voice. They will be asked about playing technique, interpretation and interests.

Hull Good instrumental grades can improve chances of an offer and of confirmation in August. Students are not normally required to attend an audition/interview. Decisions will be made according to the information supplied on the UCAS application. Successful applicants will be invited to attend a departmental open day. We welcome applications from mature students and those with unconventional qualifications: in such cases an interview may be required.

Kingston Associated Board Grade 8 on main instrument is required, with at least Grade 4 on a keyboard instrument (where this is not the main instrument). Audition and interview may be required. Candidates with non-standard qualifications are interviewed and asked to bring samples of written work.

Lancaster Grade 8 Associated Board required on an instrument or voice and some keyboard proficiency (grade 6) usually expected. We do not accept candidates without interview. For the Music degree, instrumental or vocal skills equivalent to Grade 8 required. For Music Technology, applicants should hold music theory grade 5 or be able to demonstrate the ability to read a score. Applicants wishing to take practical studies will need instrumental or vocal skills equivalent to Grade 8.

Leeds Intending students should follow an academic rather than practical-oriented A-level course. The University is experimenting with abandoning the formal interview in favour of small group open days for those holding offers made on the UCAS information, to focus on a practical exchange of information relevant to the applicant's decision to accept or reject the offer. Grade 8 Associated Board on an instrument is a normal expectation.

Leeds (CMus) There will be an audition and an essay on music theory.

Liverpool (LIPA) In addition to performing in orchestras etc, give details of any compositions you have completed (the number and styles). Instrumentalists (including vocalists) should describe any performance/gig experience together with any musical instrument grades achieved. (Mus) Candidates should prepare two pieces of contrasting music to play on their chosen instrument. Candidates who have put song-writing/composition as either first or second choice should have a cassette, CD or minidisc of their work to play to the panel. (Snd Tech) Applicants must prepare a critical review of a sound recording of their choice which highlights the technical and production values that they think are the most important. Examples of recorded work they have undertaken should also be available at interview eg on CD, cassette or DAT.

London (Gold) The interview will include an aural discussion of music and the personal interests of the applicant.

London (RAcMus) All candidates are called for audition, and those who are successful are called for a further interview; places are offered later, subject to the minimum GCSE requirements being achieved.

London (RH) Candidates are tested with an aural test, a harmony/counterpoint test, a conceptual essay, and a *viva* at which they are asked questions and asked to perform. On the basis of the results in these tests we make offers. There is a tradition of caring for each individual and we strive to give each applicant a fair hearing. Musicality, a good intellect and real enthusiasm are the qualities we look for.

London (SOAS) Candidates are judged on individual merits. Applicants are expected to have substantial practical experience of musical performance, but not necessarily Western music.

Manchester (RNCM) All applicants are called for audition. Successful applicants proceed to an academic interview which will include aural tests and questions on music theory and history. Student comment: 'A 45-minute interview with a panel of three. Focus was on portfolio of compositions sent in advance. Prior to interview was asked to harmonise a short passage and study an orchestral excerpt followed up at interview. Aural test waived.'

Newcastle We expect a reasonable background knowledge of musical history, basic harmony and counterpoint and keyboard skills of approximately Grade 8 standard; if the main instrument is not piano or organ – Grade 5. While practical skills are important, academic ability is the primary requisite. Practical Music or Music Technology accepted in place of Music.

Nottingham A high standard of aural ability is expected. Interviewees take two short written papers, intellectual enquiry and attainment are looked for, together with a good range of knowledge and sense of enterprise. No places are offered without interview – each offer is tailored to the student at interview: we do not just use the points system. Only borderline/mature students are interviewed, successful applicants are invited to an open day.

Nottingham Trent Music students require Grade 6 on two instruments. Candidates submit a marked sample of harmony and/or counterpoint and two marked essays on any areas or aspects of music. Candidates may also submit a portfolio of compositions if they wish, but it is not possible to return any copies. Candidates will take the following tests at interview: (i) A one-hour harmony or counterpoint written test (candidates will not have access to a piano); there is no composition option; (ii) A 40-minute aural test in three parts: dictation of a Bach chorale (bass given)/melodic dictation, and identification of errors heard in a twopart piece; (iii) Performance of a prepared piece on the candidate's principal instrument or voice (organists, percussionists and candidates requiring an accompanist should inform the Faculty in advance of the interview period); (iv) Keyboard skills in three parts: score reading of a string quartet; keyboard harmony; and sight-reading (sight-reading examples will take into account candidates' keyboard proficiency).

RCMus All UK and Eire candidates are required to attend for audition in person but tapes are acceptable from overseas applicants. It must be stressed, however, that personal audition is preferable and those students offered places on the basis of a tape audition may be required to take a confirmatory audition on arrival. Candidates are required to perform on the principal study instrument as well as undertaking sight-reading, aural tests and paperwork. There is also an interview. Potential scholars sometimes proceed to a second audition, usually on the same day. The academic requirement for the BMus (RCM) course is two A-levels at pass grades. Acceptance is ultimately based on the quality of performance at audition, performing experience and perceived potential as a performer. As a guide, applicants should be of at least Grade 8 distinction standard.

Royal Welsh (CMus Dr) All UK and Eire applicants are called to audition in person; overseas candidates may audition by tape. Candidates are required to perform on their sight-reading ability. Candidates who are successful in the audition proceed to interview in which there will be a short aural test. Candidates for the BA (Music) course are required to bring recent examples of harmony, counterpoint and essays.

Surrey (Music) Applicants may expect to be questioned in the interview about their musical experience, enthusiasm and any particular compositions they have studied. They will also be asked to perform on their first instrument. (Mus Snd Rec) Applicants can expect to be questioned about their recording interests and motivation and show an ability to relate A-level scientific knowledge to simple recording equipment. They may be asked to perform on their first instrument.

TrCMus Applicants for the BMus degree must attend an audition and show that they have attained a certain level of competence in their principal and second studies, musical subjects and in musical theory. Grade 8 practical and theory can count as one A-level, but not if the second A-level is in music. Overseas applicants may submit a tape recording in the first instance when a place may be offered for one year. Thereafter they will have to undergo a further test. They must also show evidence of good aural perception in musical techniques and musical analysis.

Wolverhampton The audition will involve playing/singing a piece of own-choice music (up to five minutes – no longer). Accompanists may be brought along or the department may be able to provide one if requested in advance. Candidates will be requested to produce a short piece of written work. It would be helpful to see any music certificates and a Record of Achievement if available, together with examples of recent work in music (an essay, harmony, composition etc).

Advice to applicants and planning the UCAS personal statement In addition to your ability and expertise with your chosen musical instrument(s), it is also important to know your composers and to take a critical interest in various kinds of music. Reference should be made to these, visits to concerts listed and any special interests indicated in types of musical activity, for example, opera, ballet. Work with orchestras, choirs and other musical groups should also be included and full details given of any competitions entered and awards obtained. **London (Gold)** We encourage students to bring examples of their written and creative work. **Royal Welsh (CMus Dr)** Evidence of performance-related experience, eg youth orchestras, solo work, prizes, scholarships etc. Our course is a conservatoire course as opposed to a more academic university course. We offer a very high standard of performance tuition balanced with academic theory modules. **Surrey** (Music Snd Rec (Tonmeister)) Demonstration of motivation towards professional sound recording. See also **Appendix 2**.

Misconceptions about this course Cardiff Some mistakenly think that the BMus scheme is either performance-based or something inferior to the principal music-based degree. **Leeds (CMus)** (Mus St) This is not a performing course: it is a classical performance degree. No pop music on any of our courses. **SAE (Inst)** Some applicants think that this is only a practical course – there is a strong theoretical element. That contemporary music means pop. **Salford** (Pop Mus Rec) This is not a specialised music technology degree, it is a music degree with specialisation in music technology and production. Specialisation can be significant in Year 3. BTEC Popular Music students must be prepared for the rigours of an academic degree. Some students expect the course to make them famous! **Surrey** Some believe that the Music course is exclusively performance-based (the course includes substantial academic and compositional elements).

Selection interviews Yes Most institutions, plus audition to include a performance of a prepared piece (or pieces) on main instrument or vocal study; **Some** Anglia Ruskin, Bath Spa, Cardiff, Coventry (Proforma used prior to interview – some students rejected at this stage), Liverpool (LIPA), Staffordshire (Mus Tech Mgt), Surrey. See also **Chapter 7** under **Music**.

Applicants' impressions (A=Open day; B=Interview day) Bath Spa (B) A formal interview, an audition and a tour of the campus. **Bristol** (A) On the Open day we were split into small groups for the talk and tour which included the accommodation. **Cardiff** (B) There was a tour, a 45-minute examination, an audition, but no formal interview (the audition and interview are combined). **Chichester** (B) I had a short informal interview, an audition on one instrument and a course talk. I didn't see the accommodation. **Salford** (B; Mus Tech) There was a performance, theory test and interview. **Southampton** (A) On the Open day we had a course talk, a tour of the department and halls and a short chat with head of department. **York** (B) There was one interviewer and one interview of 25 minutes which seemed to be a little haphazard although quite friendly. I was asked questions about my special interests and future career options and also where else I had applied and what was the likelihood of me accepting a place! The course looks good as does the department. Go to the Open day or interview before deciding whether or not to accept an offer.

Reasons for rejection Usually academic (auditions, practical, aural/written test). Dull, unenthusiastic students, ignorant about their subject, showing lack of motivation and imagination. **Cambridge** Her harmony was marred by elementary technical errors and her compositions lacked formal and stylistic focus. **London (King's)** Apparent lack of interest, performance not good enough, lack of music history knowledge. Foreign students: language skills inadequate. **Royal Welsh (CMus Dr)** Performing/ technical ability not of the required standard.

AFTER-RESULTS ADVICE

Offers to applicants repeating A-levels **Higher** Aberystwyth, Leeds; **Possibly higher** Cambridge (Hom); **Same** Anglia Ruskin, Bath Spa, Bristol, Cardiff, City, Colchester (Inst), De Montfort, Durham, East Anglia, Huddersfield, Hull, Kingston, Leeds (CMus), London Guildhall (Sch Mus), London (RAcMus), (RH), Nottingham, Rose Bruford (Coll), Royal Welsh (CMus Dr), SAE (Inst), Salford, Staffordshire, Surrey, York, York St John.

GRADUATE DESTINATIONS AND EMPLOYMENT (2005/6 HESA)

Graduates surveyed 2605 **Employed** 1160 **In further study** 640 **Assumed unemployed** 150.

Career note Some graduates go into performance-based careers, many enter the teaching profession and others go into a wide range of careers requiring graduate skills.

OTHER DEGREE COURSES FOR CONSIDERATION

Acoustics; Drama; Musical Theatre; Performance Arts.

NATURAL SCIENCES

(see also **Biological Sciences** and **Science**)

Natural Sciences degrees allow the student to obtain a broad view of the origins and potential of science in general, and then to focus on one specialist area of scientific study.

Useful websites www.scienceyear.com; www.scicentral.com; www.nature.com; see also **Biology**, **Chemistry** and **Physics**.

NB The points totals shown to the left of the institutions are for ease of reference only. It must not be assumed that tariff points are always used by institutions or that they can be substituted for an offer in grades. The level of an offer is not necessarily indicative of the quality of a course.

COURSE OFFERS INFORMATION

Subject requirements/preferences **GCSE Cambridge** Mainly grade As. **AL** Science subjects required. **Cambridge** (Emmanuel) One AEA science may be required when only two sciences taken; (Peterhouse) STEP may be used as part of conditional offer (see **Chapter 7**). **NB** A* grades are likely to form part of university offers in the higher ranges for students applying for places in 2008 for entry in 2009: check websites.

Your target offers
360 pts **and above**
       Bath – AAA (Nat Sci; Nat Sci Yr Ind; Nat Sci Yr Abrd) *(IB 36 pts H666)*

Cambridge – AAA (Nat Sci courses) *(IB 38–42 pts)*
Durham – AAA (Nat Sci courses) *(IB 30–40 pts)*
London (King's) – ABBc **or** ABbbc (Fdn Nat Sci (Dntstry) (Med)) *(IB 36 pts H665)*
London (UCL) – AAA+AS–ABB+AS (Nat Sci) *(IB 34–38 pts)*
340 pts **Birmingham** – AAB–ABB (Nat Sci; Nat Sci Euro) *(IB 34 pts)*
Leeds – AAB (Nat Sci)
320 pts **East Anglia** – ABB (Nat Sci) *(IB 32–36 pts)*
Lancaster – ABB (Nat Sci N Am) *(IB 30 pts)*
Newcastle – ABB (Nat Sci) *(IB 34 pts)*
Reading – ABB–BBB (Nat Sci)
280 pts **Essex** – 280 pts (Nat Sci) *(IB 28 pts)*
Lancaster – BBC (Nat Sci) *(IB 28 pts)*
London (QM) – 280 pts (Nat Sci) *(IB 30–32 pts)*
Strathclyde – BBC–CCC (BSc Hons Nat Sci courses)
260 pts **Leicester** – 260 pts (Interd Sci) *(IB 28 pts)*
200 pts **UHI Millennium Inst** – 200 pts check with admissions tutor (Nat Env Sci)
180 pts **Bristol UWE** – 180–220 pts check with admissions tutor (Nat Sci)
Strathclyde – DDD/CC (BSc Pass Nat Sci)

Liverpool John Moores – check with admissions tutor (Nat Sci)

Alternative offers
See **Chapter 8** for grade/point equivalences and related information for the following examinations: Scottish qualifications, the Welsh Baccalaureate, the IB diploma (approximate points shown also in italics in the table of offers), the Irish Leaving Certificate, the European Baccalaureate and the French Baccalaureate.

EXAMPLES OF FOUNDATION DEGREES IN THE SUBJECT FIELD
Liverpool John Moores.

CHOOSING YOUR COURSE (SEE ALSO CH.1)
Course variations – Widen your options
See separate science tables.
CHECK PROSPECTUSES AND WEBSITES FOR OTHER UNIVERSITIES AND COLLEGES OFFERING THESE COURSES.

Sandwich degree courses Bath.

ADMISSIONS INFORMATION
Number of applicants per place (approx) Bath 8; Birmingham 11; Cambridge 3; Durham 5.

Advice to applicants and planning the UCAS personal statement See **Biology**, **Chemistry** and **Physics**. See also **Appendix 2**.

Selection interviews Yes Bath, Cambridge.

Interview advice and questions **Cambridge** Questions are dependent on subject choices and studies at A-level and past questions have included the following: Discuss the setting up of a chemical engineering plant and the probabilities of failure of various components. Questions on the basic principles of physical chemistry, protein structure and functions and physiology. Questions on biological specimens. Comment on the theory of evolution and the story of the Creation in Genesis. What are your weaknesses? Questions on electro-micrographs. What do you talk about with your friends? How would you benefit from a university education? What scientific magazines do you read? Questions on atoms, types of bonding and structures. What are the problems of being tall? What are the differences between metals and non-metals? Why does graphite conduct? Questions on quantum physics and wave mechanics. How could you contribute to life here? What do you see yourself doing in five years' time? Was the Second World War justified? If it is common public belief that today's problems, for example industrial pollution, are caused by scientists, why do you wish to become one? Questions on the gyroscopic motion of cycle wheels, the forces on a cycle in motion and the

design of mountain bikes. What do you consider will be the most startling scientific development in the future? What do you estimate is the mass of air in this room? If a carrot can grow from one carrot cell, why not a human? See **Chapter 7**.

Applicants' impressions (A=Open day; B=Interview day) **Cambridge** I was asked why Cambridge? And why I had chosen their college? I had an interview with the Biology professors. They asked me questions on my personal statement and on biology and what were my views on genetic engineering. I was also asked to design a mammal – challenging but fun! It was a great experience – even though I didn't get an offer!

AFTER-RESULTS ADVICE
Offers to applicants repeating A-levels **No offers made** Cambridge.

GRADUATE DESTINATIONS AND EMPLOYMENT (2005/6 HESA)
See separate science subjects.

Career note These courses offer a range of science and in some cases non-scientific subjects, providing students with the flexibility to develop particular interests as they progress through the course.

OTHER DEGREE SUBJECTS FOR CONSIDERATION
Anatomy; Anthropology; Archaeology; Astrophysics; Biochemistry; Biological Sciences; Biology; Chemistry; Earth Sciences; Ecology; Genetics; Geology; History and Philosophy of Science; Neuroscience; Pharmacology; Physics; Plant Sciences; Psychology; Zoology.

NAVAL ARCHITECTURE
(including **Marine Engineering** and **Ship Science;** see also **Marine/Maritime Studies**)

There is a shortage of applicants for Naval Architecture and Ship Science courses and a shortage of well qualified naval architects. Naval Architecture is also an option at **Newcastle** in the Marine Technology course. Studies involve marine structures, transport and operations, design, propulsion and mathematics. Ship design has many similarities to the design of aircraft. See **Appendix 2**.

Useful website www.rina.org.uk.

NB The points totals shown to the left of the institutions are for ease of reference only. It must not be assumed that tariff points are always used by institutions or that they can be substituted for an offer in grades. The level of an offer is not necessarily indicative of the quality of a course.

COURSE OFFERS INFORMATION
Subject requirements/preferences **GCSE** Grades A–C in mathematics and physics are normally required. **AL** Mathematics and physics usually required. **NB** A* grades are likely to form part of university offers in the higher ranges for students applying for places in 2008 for entry in 2009: check websites.

Your target offers

320 pts London (UCL) – ABB+AS (MEng Nvl Archit Mar Eng) *(IB 34 pts H655)*

Newcastle – ABB (MEng Mar Tech; Mar Eng; Off Eng; Nvl Archit; Sml Crft Tech) *(IB 34 pts)*

Southampton – ABB 320 pts (MEng Ship Sci Nvl Archit; Ship Sci Advnc Mats; Ship Sci Mar Sys Eng; Ship Sci Ycht Sml Crft; Ship Sci (Eng Mgt); BEng Ship Sci) *(IB 34 pts H 17 pts)*

Strathclyde/Glasgow – ABB 2nd yr entry (MEng Nvl Archit Mar Eng; Nvl Archit; Nvl Archit Ocn Eng; Nvl Archit Sml Crft Eng) *(IB 34 pts)*

300 pts Newcastle – BBB–BBC (BEng Mar Tech; Mar Eng; Nvl Archit; Off Eng; Sml Crft Tech) *(IB 30 pts H maths phys 5 pts)*

280 pts London (UCL) – BBC+AS (BEng Nvl Archit Mar Eng) *(IB 32 pts H555)*

Strathclyde/Glasgow – BBC 2nd yr entry (BEng Nvl Archit Mar Eng; Nvl Archit Ocn Eng; Nvl Archit Sml Crft Eng) *(IB 30 pts)*

Strathclyde/Glasgow – BBC 1st yr entry (MEng Nvl Archit Mar Eng; Nvl Archit; Nvl Archit Ocn Eng; Nvl Archit Sml Crft Eng) *(IB 34 pts)*

260 pts **Liverpool** – 260 pts (Civ Marit Eng)

Plymouth – 260 pts (Mar Tech)

240 pts **Liverpool John Moores** – 240–200 pts (Mech Mar Eng; Naut Sci)

Strathclyde/Glasgow – CCC 1st yr entry (BEng Nvl Archit Mar Eng; Nvl Archit Ocn Eng; Nvl Archit Sml Crft Eng; BSc Hons Naut Sci) *(IB 30 pts)*

200 pts **Coventry** – 200–240 pts (Boat Des)

180 pts **Greenwich** – 180 pts (Naut Sci Tech)

South Tyneside (Coll) – 180 pts (Mar Eng)

Southampton Solent – 180 pts (Ycht Prod Surv; Ycht Pwrcrft Des)

160 pts **Plymouth** – 160 pts (Mar Spo Tech; Mar Cmpste Tech)

Strathclyde/Glasgow – CC–DDD (BSc Naut Sci) *(IB 30 pts)*

Alternative offers

See **Chapter 8** for grade/point equivalences and related information for the following examinations: Scottish qualifications, the Welsh Baccalaureate, the IB diploma (approximate points shown also in italics in the table of offers), the Irish Leaving Certificate, the European Baccalaureate and the French Baccalaureate.

EXAMPLES OF FOUNDATION DEGREES IN THE SUBJECT FIELD

Cornwall (Coll); Liverpool John Moores; Plymouth (CFE); Southampton Solent.

CHOOSING YOUR COURSE (SEE ALSO CH.1)

Course variations – Widen your options

Boat Design (Coventry)
Naval Architecture and Marine Engineering (London (UCL))
Offshore Engineering (Newcastle)
Marine Composites Technology (Plymouth)
Ship Science (Southampton)
Yacht and Powercraft Design (Southampton Solent)
Small Craft Technology (Strathclyde/Glasgow).
CHECK PROSPECTUSES AND WEBSITES FOR OTHER UNIVERSITIES AND COLLEGES OFFERING THESE COURSES.

Top universities and colleges (Research) Southampton.

ADMISSIONS INFORMATION

Number of applicants per place (approx) Newcastle 9; Southampton 6.

Advice to applicants and planning the UCAS personal statement Special interests in this subject area should be described fully. Visits to shipyards and awareness of ship design from the *Mary Rose* in Portsmouth to modern speed boats should be fully explained and the problems noted. See also **Engineering/Engineering Sciences** and **Marine/Maritime Studies**. See also **Appendix 2**.

Selection interviews **Yes** Newcastle, Southampton.

Interview advice and questions Because of the highly vocational nature of this subject, applicants will naturally be expected to discuss any work experience and to justify their reasons for choosing the course. See **Chapter 7**.

AFTER-RESULTS ADVICE

Offers to applicants repeating A-levels **Higher** Newcastle.

GRADUATE DESTINATIONS AND EMPLOYMENT (2005/6 HESA)

Graduates surveyed 35 **Employed** 30 **In further study** 5 **Assumed unemployed** 0.

Career note A small proportion of naval architects work in the shipbuilding and repair industry, others are involved in the construction of oil rigs or may work for ship-owning companies. There are also a number of firms of marine consultants employing naval architects as managers or consultants.

OTHER DEGREE SUBJECTS FOR CONSIDERATION

Aeronautical Engineering; Civil Engineering; Electrical/Electronic Engineering; Geography; Marine Biology; Marine Engineering; Marine/Maritime Studies; Marine Technology; Mechanical Engineering; Oceanography; Physics; Shipping Operations; Transport Management.

NURSING and MIDWIFERY

(including **Paramedic Science; see also Biological Sciences, Community Studies** and **Health Sciences/Studies**)

Nursing and Midwifery courses are designed to equip students with the scientific and caring skills demanded by medical science in the 21st century. Courses follow a similar pattern with an introductory programme of study covering clinical skills, nursing practice and the behavioural and social sciences. Thereafter, specialisation starts in adult, child or mental health nursing, or with patients with learning disabilities. Throughout the three-year course students gain extensive clinical experience in hospital wards, clinics, accident and emergency and high-dependency settings.

Useful websites www.scicentral.com; www.nhscareers.nhs.uk; www.nursingtimes.net; see also **Health Sciences/Studies** and **Medicine**.

NB The points totals shown to the left of the institutions are for ease of reference only. It must not be assumed that tariff points are always used by institutions or that they can be substituted for an offer in grades. The level of an offer is not necessarily indicative of the quality of a course.

Applications for Nursing and Midwifery UCAS now handles applications for Nursing degree and diploma courses.

COURSE OFFERS INFORMATION

Subject requirements/preferences GCSE English and a science subject. Mathematics required at several universities. **AL** Science subjects required for some courses. **NB** A* grades are likely to form part of university offers in the higher ranges for students applying for places in 2008 for entry in 2009: check websites.

Other requirements All applicants holding firm offers will require an occupational health check and Criminal Records Bureau clearance and are required to provide documentary evidence that they have not been infected with hepatitis-B.

Abbreviations used in the following table A Adult; C Child; LD Learning Disability; MH Mental Health.

Your target offers

320 pts **Southampton** – 320 pts (Midwifery)

300 pts **Edinburgh** – BBB (Nursing) *(IB 34 pts H555)*
Cumbria – 300 pts (Nurs A)
Southampton – BBB–BBC 300–280 pts (Nurs A/C/MH/LD)

280 pts **Bradford** – 280 pts (Midwif St)
Hertfordshire – 280–300 pts (Paramed Sci)
Leeds – BBC (Midwifery)
London (King's) – BBC (Midwif; Nurs A/C/LD/MH)
Manchester – BBC–BBB (Nurs; Midwif)
Ulster – 280 pts (Nurs A/MH)

260 pts **Birmingham** – BCC–CCC 260–240 pts (Nurs A/MH) *(IB 28–30 pts)*
Coventry – 260 pts check with admissions tutor (Midwifery)

For a quick reference offers calculator, fold out the inside back cover.

East Anglia – BCC 260 pts (Nurs A/C/LD/MH; Midwif)
Liverpool – 260 pts (Nursing) *(IB 30 pts)*
Northumbria – 260 pts (Midwif St; Nurs A/C/LD/MH) *(IB 26 pts)*
Nottingham – BCC (Nurs Sci A/C/MH) *(IB 30 pts H55 biol 6 pts)*
Surrey – BCC or 300 pts (Midwif St; Nurs St A/C/MH)
York – BCC/CCC (Nurs Prac A/C/LD/MH) *(IB 28 pts)*

240 pts **Birmingham City** – 240 pts (Midwifery)
Cardiff – CCC 240 pts (Nurs A/C/MH; Midwif) *(IB 26 pts)*
Central Lancashire – 240–220 pts (Nurs A/C/MH; Midwif; Paramed Prac)
Chester – 240 pts (Nurs A/C/LD/MH; Midwif)
Coventry – 240 pts (Nurs A/LD/MH)
De Montfort – 240–260 pts (Nurs A/C/MH; Midwif)
Glasgow – CCC (Nurs A/C/LD/MH) *(IB 28 pts)*
Huddersfield – 240 pts (Midwif St)
Leeds – CCC (Nurs A/C/LD/MH)
London (King's) – CCC+AS **or** BCccc (Nurs St A/C/MH) *(IB 30 pts H sci 5pts)*
Queen's Belfast – CCC/BB (Nurs A/C/MH/LD; Midwif)
Robert Gordon – CCC–BC (Nurs A/C/MH)
Salford – 240 pts (Midwifery) *(IB 26 pts)*
Staffordshire – 240 pts (Midwif Prac)
Swansea – 240 pts (Nurs A/C/MH; Midwif)

220 pts **Bournemouth** – 220 pts (Midwifery)
City (St Bartholomew's) – 220 pts (Nurs A/C/MH; Midwif)
Edge Hill – 220 pts (Nurs A/C/MH/LD; Midwif)
Hull – 220–240 pts (Nurs A/C/MH/LD)
Robert Gordon – 220–240 pts (Nurs A)

For information on how to read the Subject Tables, see **Chapter 8**.

210 pts **Kingston (London St George's)** – 210 pts (Nurs A/C/LD/MH) *(IB 27 pts)*
200 pts **Abertay Dundee** – CDD (Mntl Hlth Cnslg)
Bangor – 200 pts 2AL (Nurs A/C/MH/LD)
Bedfordshire – 200 pts (Nurs A/C/MH; Midwif)
Birmingham City – BB 200 pts (Nurs A/C/LD/MH)
Bristol UWE – 200–240 pts (Midwif; Nurs A/C/MH/LD) *(IB 24 pts)*
Cumbria – 200 pts (Nurs MH)
Glamorgan – 200–240 pts (Nurs A/C/LD/MH; Midwif)
Hertfordshire – 200 pts (Midwif; Nurs LD Soc Wk; Nurs A/C/LD/MH) *(IB 26–28 pts)*
Huddersfield – 200–240 pts (Nurs A/C/LD/MH)
Lincoln – 200 pts (Nurs A)
Liverpool John Moores – 200 pts (Nurs A/MH; Midwif)
Middlesex – 200 pts (Nurs A/C/MH; Euro Nurs; Midwif)
North East Wales (IHE) – 200 pts (Nursing)
Oxford Brookes – BB (Midwifery)
Plymouth – 200 pts (Midwif; Nurs A/C/MH; Paramed Practnr)
Queen Margaret – CDD (Nursing)
Staffordshire – 200 pts (Nurs Prac A/C/MH)
Teesside – 200 pts (Midwif; Nurs St A/C/MH)
Wolverhampton – 200 pts (Nurs; Midwif)
180 pts **Brighton** – 180 pts (Midwif; Nurs A/C/MH) *(IB 28 pts)*
Greenwich – 180 pts (Nurs A/C/LD/MH; Midwif)
Napier – 180 pts (Nurs A/C/MH/LD; Midwif)
Northampton – 180–220 pts (Midwif; Nurs A/C/MH/LD)
Sheffield Hallam – 180 (Nurs St A/C/MH; App Nurs Soc Wk LD)
160 pts **Anglia Ruskin** – 160–180 pts (Nurs A/C/LD/MH; Midwif)
Bournemouth – 160–240 pts (Nurs A/MH/LD/C)
Bradford – 160–200 pts (Nurs A/C/LD/MH)
Canterbury Christ Church – CC (Nurs A/C/MH; Midwif)
Derby – 160 pts (Nurs A/MH)
Essex – CC (Nurs St A/MH)
Glasgow Caledonian – CC (Nurs St A/LD/MH; Midwif)
Keele – 160 pts (Nurs A/C/MH/LD; Midwif)
London South Bank – CC (Nurs St A/C/MH; Nurs Soc Wk St (LD))
Manchester Met – 160 pts (Nurs A/MH)
Oxford Brookes – CC (Nurs A/C/LD/MH)
Salford – CC 160 pts (Nurs A/C/MH; Prof St Nurs Soc Wk) *(IB 26 pts)*
Sheffield Hallam – 160 pts (Oprtg Dpt Prac)
Suffolk (Univ Campus) – 160 pts (Nurs A)
Worcester – CC–EE (Midwifery)
120 pts **Bucks New** – 120 pts (Nurs A/C/MH)
Robert Gordon – DD (Midwifery)
80 pts **Worcester** – 80 pts (Nurs A/C/MH)

Leeds Met – contact University

Alternative offers
See **Chapter 8** for grade/point equivalences and related information for the following examinations: Scottish qualifications, the Welsh Baccalaureate, the IB diploma (approximate points shown also in italics in the table of offers), the Irish Leaving Certificate, the European Baccalaureate and the French Baccalaureate.

EXAMPLES OF FOUNDATION DEGREES IN THE SUBJECT FIELD
Bournemouth; Bristol UWE; Cornwall (Coll); Coventry; Greenwich; Halton Riverside (Coll); Kingston (London St George's); Liverpool John Moores; Northampton; Sheffield Hallam.

For a quick reference offers calculator, fold out the inside back cover.

UNIVERSITY OF
Southampton
School of Nursing and Midwifery

Study nursing or midwifery at the University of Southampton

The University of Southampton offers some of the best nursing and midwifery training in the country.

Because we offer training across Hampshire and the Isle of Wight, we can offer you a huge range of experiences in all areas of healthcare.

We are now looking for high-quality nursing students to start next year. We have state-of-the-art teaching facilities where students learn to become the nurses of tomorrow.

We offer:	You can study in:
• Adult nursing	• Basingstoke
• Children's nursing	• Isle of Wight
• Learning disability nursing	• Portsmouth
• Mental health nursing	• Southampton
• Midwifery	• Winchester

There are no tuition fees to pay and you may receive a bursary of around £6,500 per year while you study. We also welcome applications from mature students as there is no age limit to training.

If you think you have what it takes, call us now on **023 8059 5500** or visit **www.southampton.ac.uk/nursing** for a prospectus and to find out more.

CHOOSING YOUR COURSE (SEE ALSO CH.1)
Course variations – Widen your options
Mental Health and Counselling (Abertay Dundee)
Paramedic Science (Hertfordshire)
Applied Nursing and Social Work (Sheffield Hallam)
Operating Department Practice (Sheffield Hallam)
CHECK PROSPECTUSES AND WEBSITES FOR OTHER UNIVERSITIES AND COLLEGES OFFERING THESE COURSES.

Universities and colleges teaching quality See www.qaa.ac.uk; www.unistats.com.

Top universities and colleges (Research) Manchester; Newcastle; Sheffield; York.

ADMISSIONS INFORMATION
Number of applicants per place (approx) Abertay Dundee 10; Anglia Ruskin 10; Bangor 10; Birmingham 8; Birmingham City 15; Bournemouth 9; Brighton 3; Bristol UWE 27; Cardiff 12, (non-EU) 6; Central Lancashire (Midwif) 14; City (Nurs MH) 4, (Nurs C) 8, (Midwif) 5; Cumbria 8; De Montfort 10; Glasgow Caledonian 12; Huddersfield (Midwif) 10; Hull 10; Leeds (Midwif) 12; Liverpool John Moores (Nurs) 5; London (King's) 4; London South Bank 16; Middlesex 10; North East Wales (IHE) 4; Northampton 17; Northumbria 16; Queen Margaret 3; Salford 10, (Midwif) 11; Sheffield Hallam 8; Staffordshire (Midwif) 10; Surrey 10; Swansea 10; York (Nurs) 6, (Midwif) 2.

Advice to applicants and planning the UCAS personal statement Experience of care work – for example in hospitals, old people's homes, children's homes – is important. Describe what you have done and what you have learned. Read nursing journals in order to be aware of new developments in the treatment of illnesses. Note, in particular, the various needs of patients and the problems they experience. Try to compare different nursing approaches with, for example, children, people with learning disabilities, old people and terminally ill people. If you under-performed at GCSE, give reasons. If you have had work experience or a part-time job, describe how your skills have developed, for example responsibility, communication, team-building, organisational skills. How do you spend your spare time? Explain how your interests help with stress and pressure. **City** (Midwif) Some experience of care is very valuable (paid or voluntary). **De Montfort** A financially demanding course (37 hours per week) with no time for part-time work. See also **Appendix 2**. Admission is subject to eligibility for an NHS bursary. Contact NHS Student Grants Unit, tel 01253 655655.

Misconceptions about this course That Nursing programmes are not demanding. Midwives and nurses don't do shift work and are not involved in travelling! **City** Midwives are not only involved at the birth stage but ante-natal, post-natal, in education and support.

Selection interviews **Yes** Most institutions, Birmingham, Bournemouth (Midwif), Brighton, Cardiff, City, East Anglia, Hertfordshire, Sheffield Hallam, Swansea, Thames Valley, Wolverhampton, York; **Some** Salford.

Interview advice and questions Past questions have included: Why do you want to be a nurse? What experience have you had in nursing? What do you think of the nurses' pay situation? Should nurses go on strike? What are your views on abortion? What branch of nursing most interests you? How would you communicate with a foreigner who can't speak English? What is the nurse's role in the community? How should a nurse react in an emergency? How would you cope with telling a patient's relative that the patient was dying? Admissions tutors look for communication skills, team interaction and the applicant's understanding of health/society-related subjects. (Some applicants have difficulty with maths – multiplication and division – used in calculating dosage for medicines.) **London South Bank** What do you understand by equal opportunities? **Swansea** What is your perception of the role of the nurse? What qualities do you have that would be good for nursing? See **Chapter 7**.

Applicants' impressions (A=Open day; B=Interview day) **Bournemouth** (B) Talk on the course. My reasons for choosing adult nursing and aspects of my current studies (AVCE). **Nottingham** (B) I was interviewed by two members of staff who asked me why I thought I would make a good nurse and what I would find the most challenging part of the work. They were obviously looking for real commitment and were particularly interested in my attitude and personality. We were taken round the medical centre by a student and I would strongly recommend students to apply here. The only problem seemed to be the difficulty of changing from children's to adults' nursing.

Reasons for rejection (non-academic) Insufficient awareness of the roles and responsibilities of a midwife or nurse. Lack of motivation. Poor communication skills. Lack of awareness of nursing developments through the media. (Detailed knowledge of the NHS or nursing practice not usually required.) Failed medical. Unsatisfactory health record. Not fulfilling the hepatitis B requirements or police check requirements. Poor preparation for the interview. Too shy. Only wants nursing as a means to something else, for example commission in the armed forces. Too many choices on the UCAS application, for example Midwifery, Physiotherapy, Occupational Therapy. No care experience. **Birmingham** No work experience. **De Montfort** No insight as to nursing as a career or the various branches of nursing. **Swansea** Poor communication skills.

AFTER-RESULTS ADVICE
Offers to applicants repeating A-levels **Higher** Bristol UWE, Cardiff, Hull, Liverpool John Moores (Midwif); **Same** De Montfort, Huddersfield, Liverpool John Moores, London South Bank, Queen Margaret, Salford, Staffordshire, Stirling, Suffolk (Univ Campus), Surrey, Swansea, Thames Valley, Wolverhampton.

GRADUATE DESTINATIONS AND EMPLOYMENT (2005/6 HESA)
Graduates surveyed 5010 **Employed** 3605 **In further study** 350 **Assumed unemployed** 80.

Career note The majority of graduates aim to enter the nursing profession.

OTHER DEGREE SUBJECTS FOR CONSIDERATION
Audiology; Biological Sciences; Biology; Community Studies; Dietetics; Education; Health Studies; Medicine; Nutrition; Occupational Therapy; Optometry; Pharmacology; Pharmacy; Physiotherapy; Podiatry; Psychology; Radiography; Social Policy and Administration; Social Work; Sociology; Speech Therapy; Veterinary Nursing.

NUTRITION
(see also **Dietetics** and **Food Science/Studies and Technology**)

Nutrition attracts a great deal of attention in society and whilst controversy, claim and counter-claim seem to focus daily on the merits and otherwise of food and its value, it is, nevertheless, a scientific study in itself. Courses involve topics relating to diet, health, nutrition and food policy and are designed to prepare students to enter careers as specialists in nutrition and dietetics.

Useful websites www.nutrition.org.uk; see also under **Dietetics**.

NB The points totals shown to the left of the institutions are for ease of reference only. It must not be assumed that tariff points are always used by institutions or that they can be substituted for an offer in grades. The level of an offer is not necessarily indicative of the quality of a course.

COURSE OFFERS INFORMATION
Subject requirements/preferences **GCSE** Mathematics and science usually required. **AL** Science subjects required for most courses, biology and/or chemistry preferred. **NB** A* grades are likely to form part of university offers in the higher ranges for students applying for places in 2008 for entry in 2009: check websites.

Your target offers
320 pts **Newcastle** – ABB (Fd Hum Nutr) *(IB 32 pts)*
Surrey – 320–260 pts (Nutr Fd Sci; Nutr Diet) *(IB 30–32 pts)*
300 pts **London (King's)** – BBB (Nutr Diet)
Nottingham – BBB–BCC (Nutr courses)

280 pts **Glasgow** – BBC–CCC (Physiol Spo Sci Nutr)
Leeds – BBC 280 pts (Fd St Nutr)
Nottingham – BBC (MNutr Nutr+Diet St Reg)
Plymouth – 280 pts (Dietetics)
Queen's Belfast – BBC–BCCb (Fd Qual Sfty Nutr)
Reading – 280 pts (Nutr Fd Sci)
Robert Gordon – 280 pts (Nutr Diet)
260 pts **Cardiff (UWIC)** – 260 pts (Hum Nutr Diet)
Chester – 260 pts (Hum Nutr)
London (King's) – BCC (Nutrition)
London Met – 260 pts (Hum Nutr Diet)
Northumbria – 260 pts (Hum Nutr; Fd Sci Nutr)
Oxford Brookes – BCC (Nutr; Pblc Hlth Nutr)
240 pts **Aberdeen** – 240 pts (Hlth Sci (Hlth Nutr))
Cardiff (UWIC) – 240 pts (Pblc Nutr Hlth; Spo Biomed Nutr)
Central Lancashire – 240–280 pts (Exer Nutr Hlth)
Chester – 240 pts (Nutr courses; Hum Nutr) *(IB 30 pts)*
Manchester Met – 240 pts (Hum Nutr)
Nottingham Trent – 240 pts (Exer Nutr Hlth)
Staffordshire – 240 pts (Spo Exer Nutr)
Ulster – CCC 240 pts (Hum Nutr; Fd Nutr)
220 pts **Bath Spa** – 220–260 pts (Fd Nutr Consum Prot)
Liverpool Hope – 220 pts (Nutr Hlth Prom) *(IB 25 pts)*
Liverpool John Moores – 220 pts (Nutrition)
200 pts **Glamorgan** – 200 pts (Nutr Fd Tech Hlth)
Huddersfield – 200 pts (Fd Nutr; Fd Nutr Hlth; Nutr Pblc Hlth)
Kingston – 200–240 pts (Nutr courses)
London Met – 200 pts (Hum Nutr)
Sheffield Hallam – 200 pts (Pblc Hlth Nutr)
180 pts **Abertay Dundee** – 180–160 pts (Fd Nutr Hlth)
Bournemouth – 180 pts (Nutrition)
Greenwich – 180 pts (Hum Nutr)
Queen Margaret – 180–160 pts (Nutr; Diet)
Teesside – 180–240 pts (Fd Nutr Hlth Sci)
160 pts **Glasgow Caledonian** – CC (Hum Nutr Diet)
Leeds Trinity and All Saints (Coll) – 160–240 pts (Spo Hlth Exer Nutr)
London South Bank – CC–EE (Fd Nutr; Biosci (Nutr))
Robert Gordon – CC (Nutrition)
St Mary's (UC) – CC 160 pts (Hlth Exer Nutr courses; Nutr courses)
Westminster – CC (Hum Nutr; Hlth Sci (Nutr Thera))
120 pts **Roehampton** – 120–200 pts (Exer Nutr Hlth; Nutr Hlth)

Leeds Met – contact University

Alternative offers

See **Chapter 8** for grade/point equivalences and related information for the following examinations: Scottish qualifications, the Welsh Baccalaureate, the IB diploma (approximate points shown also in italics in the table of offers), the Irish Leaving Certificate, the European Baccalaureate and the French Baccalaureate.

EXAMPLES OF FOUNDATION DEGREES IN THE SUBJECT FIELD
Duchy (Coll); Glamorgan.

CHOOSING YOUR COURSE (SEE ALSO CH.1)
Course variations – Widen your options
Diet and Health (Bath Spa)

Food, Nutrition and Consumer Protection (Bath Spa)
Consumer and Nutrition Psychology (Cardiff (UWIC))
Public Health Nutrition (Cardiff (UWIC))
Health Sciences and Nutrition (Chester)
Dietetics (Coventry)
Physiology, Sports Science and Nutrition (Glasgow)
Human Biology and Nutrition (Kingston)
Nutrition and Health Promotion (Liverpool Hope)
Nutritional Biochemistry (Nottingham)
Environmental Science and Nutrition (Oxford Brookes)
Coaching Science and Nutrition (St Mary's (UC))
CHECK PROSPECTUSES AND WEBSITES FOR OTHER UNIVERSITIES AND COLLEGES OFFERING THESE COURSES.

Top universities and colleges (Research) London (King's).

Sandwich degree courses Cardiff (UWIC); Glasgow Caledonian; Leeds Met; London South Bank; Manchester Met; Northumbria; Oxford Brookes; Queen's Belfast; Reading; Sheffield Hallam; Surrey; Teesside; Ulster.

ADMISSIONS INFORMATION

Number of applicants per place (approx) Cardiff (UWIC) 5; Glasgow Caledonian 8; Liverpool John Moores 10; London (King's) 6; London Met 9; London South Bank 5; Newcastle 5; Robert Gordon 4; Surrey 5.

Advice to applicants and planning the UCAS personal statement Liverpool John Moores
Information on relevant experience, reasons for wanting to do the degree and careers sought would be useful. **Surrey** Overseas students not eligible for Nutrition and Dietetics course. See also **Dietetics** and **Appendix 2**.

Misconceptions about this course Some applicants do not realise that this is a science course.

Selection interviews Yes London Met, London South Bank, Nottingham (depends on application), Robert Gordon, Surrey; **Some** Liverpool John Moores, Roehampton.

Interview advice and questions Past questions have focused on scientific A-level subjects studied and aspects of subjects enjoyed by the applicants. Questions then arise from answers. Extensive knowledge expected of nutrition as a career and candidates should have talked to people involved in this type of work, for example dieticians. They will also be expected to discuss wider problems such as food supplies in developing countries and nutritional problems resulting from famine. **Liverpool John Moores** Interviews are informal. It would be useful for you to bring samples of coursework to the interview. See **Chapter 7**.

AFTER-RESULTS ADVICE

Offers to applicants repeating A-levels Possibly higher Nottingham; **Same** Liverpool John Moores, Manchester Met, Roehampton, St Mary's (UC), Surrey.

GRADUATE DESTINATIONS AND EMPLOYMENT (2005/6 HESA)

Graduates surveyed 405 **Employed** 205 **In further study** 50 **Assumed unemployed** 35.

Career note Nutritionists work in retail, health promotion and sport whilst others specialise in dietetics.

OTHER DEGREE SUBJECTS FOR CONSIDERATION

Biological Sciences; Biology; Consumer Studies; Dietetics; Food Sciences; Health Studies/Sciences.

OCCUPATIONAL THERAPY

Contrary to common belief, occupational therapy is not an art career although art and craftwork may be involved as a therapeutic exercise. Occupational therapists assess the physical, mental and social needs of ill or disabled people and help them regain lost skills and manage their lives to the best of their circumstances. Most courses include anatomy, physiology, physical rehabilitation, psychology, sociology, mental health and ethics. Selectors look for maturity, initiative, enterprise, tact, sound judgement and organising ability.

Useful websites www.cot.co.uk; www.otdirect.co.uk.

NB The points totals shown to the left of the institutions are for ease of reference only. It must not be assumed that tariff points are always used by institutions or that they can be substituted for an offer in grades. The level of an offer is not necessarily indicative of the quality of a course.

COURSE OFFERS INFORMATION

Subject requirements/preferences GCSE English, mathematics and science grade A–C. **AL** A social science or science subjects required or preferred for most courses. **NB** A* grades are likely to form part of university offers in the higher ranges for students applying for places in 2008 for entry in 2009: check websites. **Other requirements** All applicants need to pass an occupational health check and obtain Criminal Records Bureau (CRB) clearance.

Your target offers

320 pts **Bradford** – ABB (Occ Thera)
300 pts **Cardiff** – 300 pts (Occ Thera) *(IB 28 pts)*
      Cumbria – 300 pts (Occ Thera)
      Southampton – BBB 300 pts (Occ Thera) *(IB 28 pts)*
      Ulster – BBB 300 pts (Occ Thera) (See **Ch.7**)
280 pts **Northumbria** – 280 pts (Occ Thera) *(IB 26 pts)*
260 pts **Brunel** – 260 pts (Occ Thera) *(IB 26 pts)*
      East Anglia – BCC (Occ Thera) *(IB 30 pts)*
240 pts **Coventry** – 240 pts (Occ Thera)
      Derby – CCC **or** CCcc 240 pts (Occ Thera)
      Huddersfield – CCC (Occ Thera)
      Liverpool – 240 pts (Occ Thera) *(IB 26 pts)*
      Northampton – 240 pts (Occ Thera)
      Oxford Brookes – CCC **or** CCcc (Occ Thera)
      Queen Margaret – 240 pts (Occ Thera)
      Robert Gordon – 240 pts (Occ Thera)
      Salford – 240 pts CCC (Occ Thera) *(IB 24 pts)*
      Sheffield Hallam – 240 pts (Occ Thera)
      Teesside – CCC 240 pts (Occ Thera)
      York St John – CCC 240 pts (Occ Thera)
220 pts **Bournemouth** – 220 pts (Occ Thera)
      Bristol UWE – 220–280 pts (Occ Thera) *(IB 24–28 pts)*
180 pts **Plymouth** – 180 pts (Occ Thera)
160 pts **Canterbury Christ Church** – CC (Occ Thera)
      Glasgow Caledonian – CC (Occ Thera)

Alternative offers

See **Chapter 8** for grade/point equivalences and related information for the following examinations: Scottish qualifications, the Welsh Baccalaureate, the IB diploma (approximate points shown also in italics in the table of offers), the Irish Leaving Certificate, the European Baccalaureate and the French Baccalaureate.

EXAMPLES OF FOUNDATION DEGREES IN THE SUBJECT FIELD

Salford.

CHOOSING YOUR COURSE (SEE ALSO CH.1)

Course variations – Widen your options
See **Health Sciences/Studies**.
CHECK PROSPECTUSES AND WEBSITES FOR OTHER UNIVERSITIES AND COLLEGES OFFERING THESE COURSES.

Universities and colleges teaching quality See www.qaa.ac.uk; www.unistats.com.

ADMISSIONS INFORMATION

Number of applicants per place (approx) Canterbury Christ Church 5; Cardiff 10; Coventry 15; Cumbria 20; Derby 5; East Anglia 5; Northampton 4; Northumbria 4; Oxford Brookes 12; Queen Margaret 7; Robert Gordon 6; Salford 5; Sheffield Hallam 7; Southampton 7; Ulster 13; York St John 5.

Advice to applicants and planning the UCAS personal statement Contact your local hospital and discuss this career with the occupational therapists. Try to obtain work shadowing experience and make notes of your observations. Describe any such visits in full (see **Reasons for rejection**). Applicants are expected to have visited two occupational therapy departments, one in a physical or social services setting, one in the mental health field. Good interpersonal skills. **Brunel** Breadth and nature of health-related work experience. Also skills, interests (for example, sports, design). **Sheffield Hallam** Applicants should have a high standard of communication skills and experience of working with people with disabilities. **York St John** Contact with the profession essential; very competitive course. See also **Appendix 2**.

Selection interviews East Anglia; most institutions.

Interview advice and questions Since this a vocational course, work experience is nearly always essential and applicants are likely to be questioned on the types of work involved and the career. Some universities may use admissions tests: check websites and see **Chapter 7**.

Reasons for rejection (non-academic) Poor communication skills. Lack of knowledge of occupational therapy. Little evidence of working with people. Uncertain about their future career. Lack of maturity. Indecision regarding the profession. **Salford** Failure to function well in groups and inability to perform practical tasks.

AFTER-RESULTS ADVICE

Offers to applicants repeating A-levels Same Derby, Salford, York St John.

GRADUATE DESTINATIONS AND EMPLOYMENT (2005/6 HESA)

No data available.

Career note Occupational therapists (who work mostly in hospital departments) are involved in the rehabilitation of those who have required medical treatment and involve the young, aged and, for example, people with learning difficulties.

OTHER DEGREE SUBJECTS FOR CONSIDERATION

Audiology; Community Studies; Dietetics; Education; Health Studies/Sciences; Nursing; Nutrition; Physiotherapy; Podiatry; Psychology; Radiography; Social Policy and Administration; Social Work; Sociology; Speech Sciences.

OPTOMETRY (OPHTHALMIC OPTICS)

(including **Ophthalmic Dispensing** and **Orthoptics**)

Optometry courses lead to qualification as an optometrist (previously known as an ophthalmic optician). Courses provide training in detecting defects and diseases in the eye and in prescribing treatment with, for example, spectacles, contact lenses and other appliances to correct or improve vision. Optometry has become an increasingly popular course. **Orthoptics** includes the study of general anatomy, physiology and normal child development and leads to a career as an orthoptist.

This involves the investigation, diagnosis and treatment of binocular vision and other eye conditions. The main components of degree courses include the study of the eye, the use of diagnostic and measuring equipment and treatment of eye abnormalities. See also **Appendix 2**.

Useful websites www.optical.org; www.orthoptics.org.uk.

NB The points totals shown to the left of the institutions are for ease of reference only. It must not be assumed that tariff points are always used by institutions or that they can be substituted for an offer in grades. The level of an offer is not necessarily indicative of the quality of a course.

COURSE OFFERS INFORMATION

Subject requirements/preferences **GCSE** Good grades in English and science subjects usually required. **AL** Science subjects required for all Optometry courses. Mathematics usually acceptable. **NB** A* grades are likely to form part of university offers in the higher ranges for students applying for places in 2008 for entry in 2009: check websites.

Your target offers

340 pts **Aston** – AAB–AAA (Optometry) *(IB 35 pts)*
Cardiff – AAB (Optometry) *(IB 34 pts)*
Ulster – AAB 340 pts (Optometry) *(IB 37 pts)*
320 pts **Anglia Ruskin** – ABB (Optometry) *(IB 33 pts H chem biol maths 6 pts)*
Bradford – 320 pts (Optometry) *(IB 33 pts)*
City – ABB (Optometry) *(IB 30 pts)*
Glasgow Caledonian – ABB (Optometry)
Manchester – ABB (Optometry)
300 pts **Sheffield** – BBB or BBbb (Orthoptics) *(IB 32 pts)*
240 pts **Liverpool** – CCC 240 pts (Orthoptics) *(IB 26 pts)*
200 pts **Anglia Ruskin** – 200–160 pts (Oph Disp)
120 pts **Bradford (Coll)** – 120–160 pts (Oph Disp Mgt)
Glasgow Caledonian – DD (Oph Disp)

Alternative offers
See **Chapter 8** for grade/point equivalences and related information for the following examinations: Scottish qualifications, the Welsh Baccalaureate, the IB diploma (approximate points shown also in italics in the table of offers), the Irish Leaving Certificate, the European Baccalaureate and the French Baccalaureate.

EXAMPLES OF FOUNDATION DEGREES IN THE SUBJECT FIELD

Anglia Ruskin; City and Islington (Coll).

CHOOSING YOUR COURSE (SEE ALSO CH.1)

Course variations – Widen your options
Optical Management (Anglia Ruskin)
Ophthalmic Dispensing with Management (Bradford (Coll))
Orthoptics (Liverpool; Sheffield)
See also **Biology**, **Chemistry**, **Physics**.
CHECK PROSPECTUSES AND WEBSITES FOR OTHER UNIVERSITIES AND COLLEGES OFFERING THESE COURSES.

Universities and colleges teaching quality See www.qaa.ac.uk; www.unistats.com.

Top universities and colleges (Research) Aston; City.

ADMISSIONS INFORMATION

Number of applicants per place (approx) Anglia Ruskin 12; Aston 7; Bradford 6; Cardiff 13; City 11; Glasgow Caledonian 9.

Number of applicants (a UK b EU (non-UK) c non-EU d mature) Anglia Ruskin **ab**431; Aston **a**700 **b**50 **c**70 **d**10; Bradford **ab**600 **c**90; Glasgow Caledonian **a**548 **c**23

Advice to applicants and planning the UCAS personal statement For Optometry courses contact with optometrists is essential, either work shadowing or gaining some work experience. Make notes of your experiences and the work done and report fully on the UCAS application on why the career interests you. See also **Appendix 2**.

Selection interviews **Yes** Bradford, City, Glasgow Caledonian; **Some** Anglia Ruskin, Aston, Cardiff.

Interview advice and questions Optometry is a competitive subject requiring applicants to have had some work experience on which they will be questioned. **Anglia Ruskin** Why will you make a good optometrist? Describe the job. See **Chapter 7**.

AFTER-RESULTS ADVICE
Offers to applicants repeating A-levels **Higher** City; **Possibly higher** Aston; **Same** Anglia Ruskin, Cardiff.

GRADUATE DESTINATIONS AND EMPLOYMENT (2005/6 HESA)
Optometry graduates surveyed 520 **Employed** 325 **In further study** 10 **Assumed unemployed** 15.

Career note The great majority of graduates enter private practice either in small businesses or in larger organisations (which have been on the increase in recent years). A small number work in eye hospitals. Orthoptists tend to work in public health and education dealing with children and the elderly.

OTHER DEGREE SUBJECTS FOR CONSIDERATION
Health Studies; Nursing; Occupational Therapy; Physics; Physiotherapy; Radiography; Speech Studies.

PHARMACOLOGY

(including **Toxicology;** see also **Biological Sciences, Health Sciences/Studies** and **Pharmacy**)

Pharmacology is the study of drugs and medicines and courses focus on physiology, biochemistry, toxicology, immunology, microbiology and chemotherapy. Pharmacologists are not qualified to work as pharmacists. Toxicology involves the study of the adverse effects of chemicals on living systems. See also **Appendix 2** under **Pharmacology**.

Useful websites www.thebts.org; www.scienceyear.com; www.pharmacology.com.

NB The points totals shown to the left of the institutions are for ease of reference only. It must not be assumed that tariff points are always used by institutions or that they can be substituted for an offer in grades. The level of an offer is not necessarily indicative of the quality of a course.

COURSE OFFERS INFORMATION
Subject requirements/preferences **GCSE** English, science and mathematics. **AL** Chemistry and/or biology required for most courses. **NB** A* grades are likely to form part of university offers in the higher ranges for students applying for places in 2008 for entry in 2009: check websites.

Your target offers
360 pts **and above**
    Cambridge – AAA (Nat Sci (Pharmacol)) *(IB 38–42 pts)*
340 pts **Manchester** – AAB–ABB (Pharmacol Physiol Ind; Pharmacol; Pharmacol Ind; Pharmacol Modn Lang) *(IB 33 pts)*
    Sheffield – AAB **or** ABab (Physiol Pharmacol) *(IB 33 pts)*
320 pts **Bath** – ABB (Pharmacology) *(IB 32 pts H chem biol 6 pts)*
    Cardiff – ABB–BBB 320–300 pts (Biomed Sci (Pharmacol)) *(IB 32 pts)*
    London (King's) – ABB (Pharmacol; Pharmacol Mol Gnm; Physiol Pharmacol) *(IB 34 pts H5 chem biol)*
    London (UCL) – ABB–BBB+AS (Pharmacology) *(IB 32–36 pts)*

Newcastle – ABB (Pharmacology) *(IB 30–32 pts H5 chem)*
St Andrews – ABB–BBB (Chem Pharmacol) *(IB 31–24 pts)*
300 pts **Aberdeen** – BBB 2nd yr entry (Pharmacology)
Birmingham – BBB (Chem Pharmacol) *(IB 31 pts H chem 5 pts)*
Bristol – BBB (Pharmacol; Pharmacol Ind) *(IB 32 pts H665 inc 2 sci)*
Dundee – 300 pts 2nd yr entry (Pharmacol; Bioch Pharmacol; Pharmacol Physiol Sci)
Edinburgh – BBB (Pharmacology) *(IB 30 pts)*
Leeds – BBB 300 pts (Pharmacology) *(IB 32 pts)*
Leicester – BBB 300 pts (Biol Sci (Physiol Pharmacol))
Middlesex – 300–240 pts (Trad Chin Med)
Nottingham – BBB (Neuro Pharmacol)
Southampton – BBB 300 pts (Pharmacol; Pharmacol Yr Ind) *(IB 32 pts H 15 pts)*
Strathclyde – BBB–BBC (Bioch Pharmacol; Immun Pharmacol)
Ulster – 300 pts (Pharmacology)
280 pts **Glasgow** – BBC–CCC (Pharmacology)
Liverpool – BBC–BBB 280–300 pts (Pharmacol; Medcnl Chem Pharmacol) *(IB 26 pts)*
260 pts **Bradford** – 260 pts (Pharmacology)
Surrey – BCC 260 pts (Bioch (Pharmacol) (Tox)) *(IB 30–32 H5 chem biol)*
240 pts **Aberdeen** – CCC 1st yr entry (Pharmacology) *(IB 28 pts)*
Central Lancashire – 240 pts (Physiol Pharmacol)
Dundee – 240 pts 1st yr entry (Pharmacol; Bioch Pharmacol; Pharmacol Physiol Sci)
220 pts **Coventry** – 220 pts (Med Pharmacol Sci)
Middlesex – 220–180 pts (Herb Med)
Napier – 220 pts (Tox; Immun Tox)
200 pts **Hertfordshire** – 200 pts (Pharmacol courses)
Kingston – 200–240 pts (Pharmacology)
Manchester Met – 200–240 pts (Physiol Pharmacol St)
Nottingham Trent – 200 pts (Pharmacology)
Portsmouth – 200–280 pts (Pharmacology)
Sunderland – 200 pts (Pharmacology)
180 pts **Bristol UWE** – DDD–CCD 180–220 pts (App Physiol Pharmacol)
160 pts **East London** – 160 pts (Pharmacol courses; Tox courses)
London Met – 160 pts (Pharmacol; Herb Medicin Sci)
Queen Margaret – 160 pts (App Pharmacol)
Westminster – CC (Physiol Pharmacol; Hlth Sci (Hom))
Wolverhampton – 160–200 pts (Pharmacol; Pharmacol Hum Biol)

Leeds Met – contact University

Alternative offers

See **Chapter 8** for grade/point equivalences and related information for the following examinations: Scottish qualifications, the Welsh Baccalaureate, the IB diploma (approximate points shown also in italics in the table of offers), the Irish Leaving Certificate, the European Baccalaureate and the French Baccalaureate.

CHOOSING YOUR COURSE (SEE ALSO CH.1)

Course variations – Widen your options

Biomedical Sciences (Bradford)
Pharmacology with a Year in Industry (Bristol)
Biomedical Sciences (Forensic Toxicology) (Cardiff (UWIC))
Medical and Pharmacological Sciences (Coventry)
Chemical Engineering – Pharmaceutical Chemistry (Heriot-Watt)
Pharmacology with a Year in North America (Hertfordshire)
Human Physiology (Leeds)
Medicinal Chemistry with Pharmacology (Liverpool)

For a quick reference offers calculator, fold out the inside back cover.

Neuroscience and Pharmacology (Nottingham)
CHECK PROSPECTUSES AND WEBSITES FOR OTHER UNIVERSITIES AND COLLEGES OFFERING THESE COURSES.

Universities and colleges teaching quality See www.qaa.ac.uk; www.unistats.com.

Top universities and colleges (Research) Cambridge; Liverpool; London (UCL)*.

Sandwich degree courses (including **Pharmaceutical Sciences**, **Pharmacology** and **Pharmacy**) Bath (Pharmacol); Bradford (Pharm); Bristol (Pharmacol); Bristol UWE (Pharm Sci); Cardiff (Pharmacol); Coventry (Pharm Sci); De Montfort (Pharm Sci); East London (Pharmacol); Greenwich (Pharm Sci); Hertfordshire (Pharm Sci); Huddersfield (Pharm Sci); Kingston (Pharm Sci; Pharmacol); London Met (Pharmacol); Manchester (Pharmacol); Manchester Met (Physiol Pharmacol St); Napier (Tox); Nottingham Trent (Physiol Pharmacol); Salford (Pharm Sci); Sheffield Hallam (Pharm Sci); Southampton (Pharmacol); Sunderland (Pharmacol).

ADMISSIONS INFORMATION
Number of applicants per place (approx) Bath 12; Birmingham 6; Bradford 20; Bristol 8; Cardiff 8; Dundee 5; East London 4; Hertfordshire 10; Leeds 7; Liverpool 5; London (King's) 6; Portsmouth 4; Southampton 8; Strathclyde 10; Sunderland 12, Wolverhampton 4.

Advice to applicants and planning the UCAS personal statement Contact with the pharmaceutical industry is important in order to be aware of the range of work undertaken. Read pharmaceutical journals (although note that Pharmacology and Pharmacy courses lead to different careers). **Bath** Interests outside A-level studies. Evidence that there is more to the student than A-level ability. **Bristol** Be aware that a Pharmacology degree is mainly biological rather than chemical although both subjects are important. See also **Pharmacy**.

Misconceptions about this course Mistaken belief that Pharmacology and Pharmaceutical Sciences is the same as Pharmacy and that a Pharmacology degree will lead to work as a pharmacist.

Selection interviews Yes Bath, Birmingham (Don't be anxious – this is an opportunity for you to see us!), Cambridge, Newcastle; **Some** Cardiff, Dundee, Sunderland.

Interview advice and questions Past questions include: Why do you want to do Pharmacology? Why not Pharmacy? Why not Chemistry? How are pharmacologists employed in industry? What are the issues raised by anti-vivisectionists on animal experimentation? Questions relating to the A-level syllabus in chemistry and biology. See **Chapter 7**.

Reasons for rejection (non-academic) Confusion between Pharmacology, Pharmacy and Pharmaceutical Sciences. One university rejected two applicants because they had no motivation or understanding of the course (one had A-levels at AAB!). Insurance against rejection for Medicine. Lack of knowledge about pharmacology as a subject.

AFTER-RESULTS ADVICE
Offers to applicants repeating A-levels Higher Bristol, Glasgow, Leeds; **Same** Bath, Bradford, Cardiff, Dundee, Portsmouth, Sunderland.

GRADUATE DESTINATIONS AND EMPLOYMENT (2005/6 HESA)
Pharmacology, Toxicology and Pharmacy graduates surveyed 1745 **Employed** 1195 **In further study** 150 **Assumed unemployed** 35.

Career note The majority of pharmacologists work with the large pharmaceutical companies involved in research and development. A small number are employed by the NHS in medical research and clinical trials. Some will eventually diversify and become involved in marketing, sales and advertising.

OTHER DEGREE SUBJECTS FOR CONSIDERATION
Biochemistry; Biological Sciences; Biology; Biotechnology; Chemistry; Life Sciences; Microbiology; Natural Sciences; Pharmaceutical Sciences; Pharmacy; Physiology; Toxicology.

PHARMACY

(including **Herbal Medicine, Pharmaceutical Management** and **Pharmaceutical Sciences**)

Pharmacy is the science of medicines, involving research into chemical structures and natural products of possible medicinal value, the development of dosage and the safety testing of products. This table also includes information on courses in Pharmaceutical Science (which should not be confused with Pharmacy) which is a multi-disciplinary subject covering chemistry, biochemistry, pharmacology and medical issues. Pharmaceutical scientists apply their knowledge of science and the biology of disease to the design and delivery of therapeutic agents. **Note** All Pharmacy courses leading to MPharm are now four years. Recommended reading: *Pharmacy: Effective Caring* Royal Pharmaceutical Society, www.rpsgb.org.uk. See also **Appendix 2**.

Useful websites www.pharmweb.net; www.scienceyear.com; www.pharmacycareers.org; www.dotpharmacy.com.

NB The points totals shown to the left of the institutions are for ease of reference only. It must not be assumed that tariff points are always used by institutions or that they can be substituted for an offer in grades. The level of an offer is not necessarily indicative of the quality of a course.

Not all courses lead to qualification as a pharmacist; check prospectuses and websites.

COURSE OFFERS INFORMATION

Subject requirements/preferences **GCSE** English, mathematics and science subjects. **AL** Chemistry and one or two other sciences required for most courses. **NB** A* grades are likely to form part of university offers in the higher ranges for students applying for places in 2008 for entry in 2009: check websites.

Your target offers

350 pts London (King's) – BBBb–ABB (MPharm Pharm) *(IB 34 pts H655)*

340 pts Manchester – AAB–ABB (MPharm) *(IB 34 pts H666)*

Queen's Belfast – AAB–ABBa (MPharm Pharm)

320 pts Aston – ABB–BBB (MPharm Pharm) *(IB 32 pts)*

Bath – ABB (MPharm Pharm) *(IB 34 pts H6 chem+ 1 sci)*

Brighton – ABB (MPharm Pharm) *(IB 32 pts H5 chem)*

Cardiff – ABB–BBB (MPharm Pharm) *(IB 34 pts H6 chem+1 sci)*

East Anglia – ABB–BBB (MPharm Pharm) *(IB 31–32 pts)*

Hertfordshire 320 pts check with admissions tutor (MPharm Pharm)

Liverpool John Moores – ABB–BBC 320–280 pts (MPharm Pharm)

London (Sch Pharm) – ABB (MPharm Pharm) *(IB 32 pts H655)*

Nottingham – ABB (MPharm Pharm) *(IB 34 pts H655–555)*

Reading – 320 pts (Pharm)

Strathclyde – ABB–BBB (MPharm Pharm)

300 pts Central Lancashire – 300 pts (Pharmacy) *(IB 32 pts)*

De Montfort – 300–320 pts (MPharm Pharm)

Dundee – 300–240 pts (Pharml Chem)

East Anglia – BBB (Pharml Chem)

Hull – 300 pts (Pharmacy) *(IB 30 pts)*

Keele – BBB (MPharm Pharm) *(IB 32 pts)*

Kent (Medway Sch Pharm) – 300 pts (MPharm Pharm) *(IB 30 pts)*

Kingston – 300 pts (MPharm Pharm)

Portsmouth – BBB 300 pts (MPharm Pharm) *(IB 30 pts)*

Robert Gordon – 300 pts (MPharm Pharm)

Sunderland – 300 pts (MPharm Pharm)

Wolverhampton – 300 pts (Pharmacy)

280 pts **Bradford** – 280 pts (MPharm Pharm) *(IB 30 pts)*
260 pts **Leicester** – 260 pts (Pharml Chem) *(IB 30 pts)*
240 pts **Bradford** – 240 pts (Pharml Mgt; Pharml Sci Law; Chem Pharml Foren Sci)
Brighton – CCC (Pharml Chem Sci) *(IB 28 pts)*
Liverpool John Moores – 240–280 pts (Pharml Sci Biol Chem; Pharml Sci Clin Rsch; Pharml Analys)
Northumbria – 240 pts (Pharml Chem)
220 pts **Middlesex** – 220–180 pts (Herb Med)
200 pts **Central Lancashire** – 200 pts (Hom Med; Herb Med)
Hertfordshire – 200 pts (Pharml Sci)
Kingston – 200–240 pts (Pharml Sci)
Nottingham Trent – 200–220 pts (Pharml Medicin Sci)
Portsmouth – 200–280 pts (Pharm Sci)
180 pts **Bristol UWE** – 180–220 pts (Pharml Sci) *(IB 24–26 pts)*
De Montfort – 180–220 pts (Pharml Sci (Drug Dlvry) (Cosmet Prod)) *(IB 28 pts)*
Greenwich – 180 pts (Pharml Sci)
Sheffield Hallam – 180 pts (Pharml Sci)
Sunderland – 180 pts (Chem Pharml Sci)
160 pts **Huddersfield** – 160–280 pts (Pharml Sci)
Westminster – CC (Hlth Sci (Herb Med) (Hom))
Wolverhampton – 160–220 pts (Pharml Sci)
120 pts **London Met** – 120 pts (Pharml Sci; Herb Medicin Sci)
West Scotland – DD (Pharml Sci)

Alternative offers
See **Chapter 8** for grade/point equivalences and related information for the following examinations: Scottish qualifications, the Welsh Baccalaureate, the IB diploma (approximate points shown also in italics in the table of offers), the Irish Leaving Certificate, the European Baccalaureate and the French Baccalaureate.

EXAMPLES OF FOUNDATION DEGREES IN THE SUBJECT FIELD
Aston; Kent (Medway Sch Pharm); Kingston; Matthew Boulton (CFHE); Merton (Coll); Preston (Coll); Sunderland City (Coll).

CHOOSING YOUR COURSE (SEE ALSO CH.1)
Course variations – Widen your options
Pharmaceutical Science (Drug Delivery) (Cosmetic Products) (De Montfort)
Herbal Medicinal Science (London Met)
Pharmaceutical and Medicinal Sciences (Nottingham Trent)
Health Sciences (Homeopathy) (Westminster)
See also **Pharmacology**.
CHECK PROSPECTUSES AND WEBSITES FOR OTHER UNIVERSITIES AND COLLEGES OFFERING THESE COURSES.

Universities and colleges teaching quality See www.qaa.ac.uk; www.unistats.com.

Top universities and colleges (Research) Aston; Bath*; Cardiff; London (King's), (Sch Pharm); Manchester*; Nottingham; Strathclyde.

Sandwich degree courses See **Pharmacology**.

ADMISSIONS INFORMATION
Number of applicants per place (approx) Aston 10; Bath 6; Bradford 10; Brighton 24 (apply early); Cardiff 5; De Montfort 14; Liverpool John Moores (Pharm) 7, (Pharml Sci Biol Chem) 2; London (King's) 15, (Sch Pharm) 6; Nottingham 11; Portsmouth 20; Robert Gordon 11; Strathclyde 10; Sunderland 20.

Number of applicants (**a** UK **b** EU (non-UK) **c** non-EU **d** mature) Aston **a**1400 **b**100 **c**300 **d**180; Bradford **ab**1200 **c**200.

Advice to applicants and planning the UCAS personal statement Work experience and work shadowing with a retail and/or hospital pharmacist is important and essential for Pharmacy applicants. Read pharmaceutical journals, extend your knowledge of well known drugs and antibiotics. Read up on the history of drugs. Attendance at open days or careers conference. See also **Appendix 2**.

Misconceptions about this course That a degree in Pharmaceutical Science is a qualification leading to a career as a pharmacist. It is not: it is a course which concerns the application of chemical and biomedical science to the design, synthesis and analysis of pharmaceuticals for medicinal purposes. See also **Pharmacology**.

Selection interviews Yes Bath, Bradford, Brighton, Bristol, De Montfort, East Anglia, Liverpool John Moores, London (Sch Pharm), Nottingham, Robert Gordon, Strathclyde, Wolverhampton; **Some** Aston, Cardiff.

Interview advice and questions As work experience is essential for Pharmacy applicants, questions are likely to focus on this and what they have discovered. Other relevant questions could include: Why do you want to study Pharmacy? What types of work do pharmacists do? What interests you about the Pharmacy course? What branch of pharmacy do you want to enter? Name a drug – what do you know about it (formula, use etc)? Name a drug from a natural source and its use. Can you think of another way of extracting a drug? Why do fungi destroy bacteria? What is an antibiotic? Can you name one and say how it was discovered? What is insulin? What is its source and function? What is diabetes? What type of insulin is used in its treatment? What is a hormone? What drugs are available over the counter without prescription? What is the formula of aspirin? What is genetic engineering? **Bath** Informal and relaxed; 400 approx selected for interview – very few rejected at this stage. **Cardiff** Interviews cover both academic and vocational aspects; candidates must reach a satisfactory level in both areas. **Liverpool John Moores** What are the products of a reaction between an alcohol and a carboxylic acid? See **Chapter 7**.

Applicants' impressions (A=Open day; B=Interview day) Nottingham (B) I had a 20–30 minute interview with two interviewers. They asked me why Pharmacy? And why is geography (one of my A-level subjects) useful for pharmacy? I felt the interview intimidating but I would strongly recommend to others to apply. They regarded their course very highly.

Reasons for rejection (non-academic) Poor communication skills. Poor knowledge of pharmacy and the work of a pharmacist.

AFTER-RESULTS ADVICE

Offers to applicants repeating A-levels Higher Bradford, Cardiff, De Montfort, Liverpool John Moores, London (Sch Pharm), Nottingham (offers rarely made), Portsmouth, Queen's Belfast, Strathclyde; **Possibly higher** Aston, Robert Gordon; **Same** Bath, Brighton, East Anglia, Sunderland, Wolverhampton.

GRADUATE DESTINATIONS AND EMPLOYMENT (2005/6 HESA)

See under **Pharmacology**.

Career note The majority of Pharmacy graduates proceed to work in the commercial and retail fields, although opportunities also exist with pharmaceutical companies and in hospital pharmacies. There are also opportunities in agricultural and veterinary pharmacy.

OTHER DEGREE SUBJECTS FOR CONSIDERATION

Biochemistry; Biological Sciences; Biology; Biotechnology; Chemistry; Life Sciences; Microbiology; Natural Sciences; Pharmacology; Physiology.

PHILOSOPHY

Philosophy is one of the oldest and most fundamental disciplines which examines the nature of the universe and humanity's place in it. Philosophy seeks to discover the essence of the mind, language and physical reality and discusses the methods used to investigate these topics.

Useful websites www.iep.utm.edu; www.philosophypages.com; www.philosophy.eserver.org; see also **Religious Studies**.

NB The points totals shown to the left of the institutions are for ease of reference only. It must not be assumed that tariff points are always used by institutions or that they can be substituted for an offer in grades. The level of an offer is not necessarily indicative of the quality of a course.

COURSE OFFERS INFORMATION

Subject requirements/preferences GCSE English and mathematics. A foreign language may be required. **AL** No specific subjects except for joint courses. **NB** A* grades are likely to form part of university offers in the higher ranges for students applying for places in 2008 for entry in 2009: check websites.

Your target offers

360 pts and above
 Bristol – AAA–ABB (Phil courses) *(IB 34–37 pts H665)*
 Cambridge – AAA (Philosophy) *(IB 38–42 pts)*
 Durham – AAA (Nat Sci (Phil); Phil Psy) *(IB 38 pts)*
 Exeter – AAA–ABB (Phil Hist)
 London (King's) – AAA–AAB (Phil; War St Phil; Relig Phil Eth; Ger Phil; Maths Phil; Phil Hisp St)
 London (LSE) – AAA (Phil Econ)
 Nottingham – AAA (Econ Phil)
 Oxford – Offers vary eg AAA–AAB (Maths Phil; Phys Phil; PPE; Phil Theol; Psy Phil; Phil Modn Lang; Physiol Phil) *(IB 38–40 pts)*
 Warwick – AABb (Phil; Phil Lit; Phil Class Civ; Phil Comp Sci; Phil Psy; PPE) *(IB 34–38 pts)*

340 pts Durham – AAB (PPE) *(IB 38 pts)*
 Durham – AAB–ABB (Phil; Phil Pol; Phil Theol) *(IB 38 pts)*
 Essex – AAB (Law Phil)
 London (LSE) – AAB (Phil Lgc Sci Meth) *(IB 36 pts H666)*
 London (UCL) – AAB+AS–ABB+AS (Phil; Phil Gk; Phil Econ; Phil Hist Art; Fr Phil) *(IB 36 pts)*
 Manchester – AAB–BBC (Phil Sci Psy; Phil Class Civ Art Hist; Phil Relig St Compar Relig; Phil Jew St; Phil Ling Engl Lang; Phil Langs; Phil Blt Nat Env; Phil Pol)
 Manchester – AAB (PPE)
 St Andrews – AAB (Phil Scot Hist; Phil Psy; Lgc Phil Sci Phys) *(IB 32 pts)*

For information on how to read the Subject Tables, see **Chapter 8**.

Sheffield – AAB–BBB (Phil courses) *(IB 35 pts)*

Sussex – AAB–ABB (Phil courses) *(IB 34–36 pts)*

York – AAB–ABB (Phil courses) *(IB 34 pts)*

320 pts **Birmingham** – ABB–BBB (Philosophy) *(IB 32–34 pts)*

Cardiff – ABB–BBB (Phil; Hist Ideas Phil; Hist Ideas Hum courses) *(IB 32 pts)*

East Anglia – ABB–BBB (PPE) *(IB 31–32 pts)*

East Anglia – ABB–ABC (Philosophy) *(IB 31–32 pts)*

Exeter – ABB–BBB (Phil Fr/Ger/Ital/Russ/Span; Phil Pol; Phil Sociol; Phil Theol) *(IB 28–29 pts)*

Glasgow – ABB–BBB (BA Philosophy) *(IB 30 pts)*

Leeds – ABB (Artif Intel Phil)

Liverpool – ABB 320 pts (Phil; Phil Pol) *(IB 34 pts H555)*

London (RH) – ABB–BBB (Phil courses)

Manchester – ABB (Philosophy)

Newcastle – ABB (Phil St)

Nottingham – ABB (Mus Phil)

St Andrews – ABB (Phil Langs)

Southampton – ABB 320 pts (Phil; Econ Phil; Phil Maths; Phil Pol; Phil Sociol) *(IB 33 pts H 16 pts)*

300 pts **Dundee** – BBB 2nd yr entry (Philosophy)

East Anglia – BBB–BBC (Phil Hist; Phil Pol)

Edinburgh – BBB (Phil courses; Scot Ethnol) *(IB 34 pts H555)*

Essex – 300 pts (Phil; Phil Hist; Phil Lit; Phil Pol; Phil Sociol; Phil Law) *(IB 29 pts)*

Keele – 300–320 pts (Law Phil)

Lancaster – BBB 300 pts (Phil; Phil Pol; Phil Relig St; Film St Phil; Phil Fr/Ger/Span/Ital; Hist Phil; Ling Phil; Eth Phil Relig)

Lancaster – ABC (Engl Lit Phil) *(IB 29 pts H 15 pts)*

Leeds – BBB (Phil courses except under **320 pts**)

London (UCL) – BBB+AS (Hist Phil Sci)

Nottingham – ABC–BBC (Phil; Phil Theol) *(IB 32 pts)*

Queen's Belfast – BBB–BBCb (Phil courses; Schlstc Phil courses) *(IB 29 pts H655)*

Reading – 300–320 pts (Phil; Art Phil)

280 pts **Bolton** – 280 pts (Phil courses)

Hull – BBC 280 pts (Phil; Phil Film St; Phil Crea Writ; Phil Lang; Phil Sociol; Phil Pol; Phil Psy) *(IB 30 pts)*

Kent – 280 pts (Phil; Phil Yr Abrd; Phil Pol; Phil Relig St; Phil Soc Anth; Phil Soc Bhv; Phil Sociol)

Liverpool – BBC 280 pts (Phil Fr/Ger; Phil Hisp St)

London (Hey) – 280–320 pts (Phil; Phil Relig Eth; Phil Theol; Psy Phil)

Oxford Brookes – BBC (Phil courses)

Stirling – BBC–CCC (Phil; Comp Sci Phil; Phil Psy; PPE)

260 pts **Keele** – 260–320 pts (Phil courses except under **300 pts**)

240 pts **Aberdeen** – CCC (Phil courses) *(IB 30 pts H 15 pts)*

Bradford – 240 pts (Phil courses) *(IB 24 pts)*

Bristol UWE – 240–300 pts (Phil courses)

Dundee – 240 pts 1st yr entry (Philosophy)

Liverpool Hope – 240 pts (Phil Eth courses)

Manchester Met – 240 pts (Philosophy)

220 pts **Bath Spa** – 220–260 pts (Bus Mgt Phil)

Glamorgan – 220–260 pts (Phil courses)

200 pts **Anglia Ruskin** – 200 pts (Phil; Phil Dr; Phil Engl; Phil Film St)

Gloucestershire – 200 pts (Relig Phil Eth)

Hertfordshire – 200–240 pts (Phil (Mod Schm); Phil Comb courses)

London Met – 200 pts (Pol Phil Econ; Phil courses)

For a quick reference offers calculator, fold out the inside back cover.

Newport – 200 pts (Relig St Phil courses)
Nottingham Trent – 200 pts (Phil courses)
Roehampton – 200 pts (Phil courses)
Staffordshire – 200–160 pts (Phil courses)
180 pts **Central Lancashire** – 180–200 pts (Phil courses)
Greenwich – 180 pts (Phil courses)
Lampeter – 180–220 pts (Philosophy)
Northampton – 180 pts (Phil courses)
160 pts **Cardiff (UWIC)** – 160 pts (Art Phil)
Cumbria – 160 pts (Phil Eth)
Glamorgan – 160–200 pts (Phil Contemp Tht)
Middlesex – 160–200 pts (Phil courses)
Newman (UC) – 160 pts (Phil Relig Eth; Phil Theol courses)
St Mary's (UC) – 160–200 pts (Phil courses)
Wolverhampton – 160–220 pts (Phil courses)
140 pts **Marjon (UC)** – 140–200 pts (Phil courses)
 80 pts **London (Birk)** – 80 pts for under 21s (over 21s varies) (p/t Philosophy)

Leeds Met – contact University
Open University – contact University

Alternative offers

See **Chapter 8** for grade/point equivalences and related information for the following examinations: Scottish qualifications, the Welsh Baccalaureate, the IB diploma (approximate points shown also in italics in the table of offers), the Irish Leaving Certificate, the European Baccalaureate and the French Baccalaureate.

CHOOSING YOUR COURSE (SEE ALSO CH.1)

Course variations – Widen your options

Art, Philosophy and Contemporary Practices (Dundee)
Philosophy and Social Behaviour (Kent)
Artificial Intelligence and Philosophy (Leeds)
Combined Studies (Newcastle)
Philosophy, Politics and Economics (Oxford)
Biblical Studies and Philosophy (Sheffield)
Ethics, Philosophy and Society (Staffordshire)
CHECK PROSPECTUSES AND WEBSITES FOR OTHER UNIVERSITIES AND COLLEGES OFFERING THESE COURSES.

Universities and colleges teaching quality See www.qaa.ac.uk; www.unistats.com.

Top universities and colleges (Research) Bristol; Cambridge; Durham; East Anglia; Edinburgh*; Essex; Leeds; London (King's), (LSE)*, (UCL); Middlesex; Nottingham; Oxford*; Reading; St Andrews; Sheffield; Stirling; Warwick; York.

ADMISSIONS INFORMATION

Number of applicants per place (approx) Birmingham 6; Bradford 7; Bristol 20; Cambridge 6; Cardiff 8; Dundee 6; Durham 14 (all courses); East Anglia 6; Hull 19; Kent 9; Lampeter 4; Lancaster 6; Leeds 10; Liverpool 5; London (Hey) 4, (King's) 6, (LSE) (Phil Lgc Sci Meth) 4, (Phil Econ) 32; London Met 3; Middlesex 8; Northampton 3; Nottingham 11; Oxford (success rate 44%, (PPE) 29%); Sheffield 6; Southampton 7; Staffordshire 8; Warwick 9; York 11.

Advice to applicants and planning the UCAS personal statement Read Bertrand Russell's *Problems of Philosophy*. Refer to any particular aspects of philosophy which interest you (check that these are offered on the courses for which you are applying). Since Philosophy is not a school subject, selectors will expect applicants to have read around the subject. **Bristol** Explain what you know about the nature of studying philosophy. **East Anglia** (non-EU students) Pre-sessional courses in English and study skills. **Lampeter** Books which have influenced you. **Staffordshire** We look for an interest in some of the most basic and universal questions about human nature and our experience of the world. **York** Say what you have read in philosophy and give an example of a philosophical issue that interests you. We do not expect applicants to have a wide knowledge of the subject, but evidence that you know what the subject is about is important.

Misconceptions about this course Applicants are sometimes surprised to find what wide-ranging Philosophy courses are offered. **York** That PPE is a degree taken only by male students and that it is dry and overly abstract!

Selection interviews **Yes** Bangor, Birmingham, Bristol (mature students), Cambridge, Durham, Kingston, Lampeter, Lancaster, Leeds, Liverpool, London (Hey), (UCL), Newcastle, Oxford, Southampton, Staffordshire, Warwick; **Some** Cardiff, Dundee, Hull, London (LSE) (rare), York.

Interview advice and questions Philosophy is a very wide subject and initially applicants will be asked for their reasons for their choice and their special interests in the subject. Questions in recent years have included: Is there a difference between being tactless and being insensitive? Can you be tactless and thin-skinned? Define the difference between knowledge and belief. Was the vertical distortion of El Greco's paintings a product of a vision defect? What is the point of studying philosophy? What books on philosophy have you read? Discuss the work of a renowned philosopher. What is a philosophical novel? Who has the right to decide your future – yourself or another? What do you want to do with your life? What is a philosophical question? John is your husband, and if John is your husband then necessarily you must be his wife; if you are necessarily his wife then it is not possible that you could not be his wife; so it was impossible for you not to have married him – you were destined for each other. Discuss. What is the difference between a man's entitlements, his deserts and his attributes? What are morals? A good understanding of philosophy is needed for entry to degree courses, and applicants are expected to demonstrate this if they are called to interview. As one admissions tutor stated, 'If you find Bertrand Russell's *Problems of Philosophy* unreadable – don't apply!' **Cambridge** If you were to form a government of philosophers what selection process would you use? Is it moral to hook up a psychopath (whose only pleasure is killing) to a really stimulating machine so that he can believe he is in the real world and kill as much as he likes? **Leeds** A 500 word essay. **Oxford** If you entered a teletransporter and your body was destroyed and instantly recreated on Mars in exactly the same way with all your memories intact etc, would you be the same person? (PPE) Tutors are not so much concerned with what you know as how you think about it. Evidence required concerning social and political topics and the ability to discuss them critically. **Oxford** (PPE) Is being hungry the same thing as wanting to eat? Why is there not a global government? What do you think of teleport machines? Should there be an intelligence test to decide who should vote? **York** Do human beings have free will? Do we perceive the world as it really is? See also **Chapter 7**.

Applicants' impressions (A=Open day; B=Interview day) **London (UCL)** (B) There were no individual interviews. All candidates were given a lecture on free will problems and had 30 minutes in which to write an essay on the subject. **Oxford** (PPE; B) There were interviews with one–four interviewers lasting 20 to 30 minutes. The more interviewers present, the less intimidating the interviews; the one-to-one interviews were quite intense. In Politics, I was questioned on current affairs, and for Economics I was given a sheet with questions and was asked to prepare the answers. In Philosophy I was asked 'If God is all-powerful could He create a rock too heavy for Him to lift?' The whole process was tough but it was worth it and was good experience. **(Magdalen)** (B) I had three separate interviews, each lasting about 15 minutes and each with one interviewer. In Philosophy I had a question on time travel and in Economics I was asked which part of my A-level course I enjoyed the most and was given a topic to discuss. For Politics I had to answer questions on political parties and on power and expertise.

Reasons for rejection (non-academic) Evidence of severe psychological disturbance, criminal activity, drug problems (evidence from referees' reports). Lack of knowledge of philosophy. **Oxford** He was not able to explore his thoughts deeply enough or with sufficient centrality. **York** No evidence of having read any philosophical literature.

AFTER-RESULTS ADVICE

Offers to applicants repeating A-levels Higher Bristol (Phil Econ), Essex, Glasgow, Leeds, Nottingham (in some cases), Warwick, York (PPE); **Same** Bangor, Birmingham, Bristol, Cardiff, Dundee, Durham, East Anglia, Hull, Liverpool Hope, Newcastle, Newport, Nottingham (for previous applicants), Nottingham Trent, Southampton, St Mary's (UC), Staffordshire, Stirling, Wolverhampton, York; **No offers made** Cambridge.

GRADUATE DESTINATIONS AND EMPLOYMENT (2005/6 HESA)

Graduates surveyed 1470 **Employed** 670 **In further study** 120 **Assumed unemployed** 325.

Career note Graduates have a wide range of transferable skills that can lead to employment in many areas, eg management, public administration, publishing, banking and social services.

OTHER DEGREE SUBJECTS FOR CONSIDERATION

Divinity; History of Art; History and Philosophy of Science; Human Sciences; Psychology; Religious Studies; Science; Theology.

PHOTOGRAPHY

(see also **Film, Radio, Video and TV Studies** and **Media Studies**)

Photography courses offer a range of specialised studies involving commercial, industrial and still photography, portraiture and film, digital and video work. Increasingly this subject is featuring in Graphic Design courses. See also **Appendix 2**.

Useful websites www.the-aop.org; www.rps.org; www.bjphoto.co.uk.

NB The points totals shown to the left of the institutions are for ease of reference only. It must not be assumed that tariff points are always used by institutions or that they can be substituted for an offer in grades. The level of an offer is not necessarily indicative of the quality of a course.

COURSE OFFERS INFORMATION

Subject requirements/preferences GCSE Art and/or a portfolio usually required. **AL** One or two subjects may be required, including an art/design or creative subject. **NB** A* grades are likely to form part of university offers in the higher ranges for students applying for places in 2008 for entry in 2009: check websites.

Your target offers

300 pts	**Leeds** – BBB 300 pts (Cnma Photo TV St)
260 pts	**Northumbria** – 260 pts 2AL Fdn art+portfolio (Contemp Photo Prac)
240 pts	**Birmingham City** – 240 pts (Media Comm (Media Photo))
	Chester – 240 pts (Photo Comb courses)
	De Montfort – 240 pts (Photo courses)
	Huddersfield – 240 pts (Art Des (Photo))
	Lincoln – 240 pts (Contemp Lns Media courses)
	Nottingham Trent – 240 pts (Photo Photo Euro)
220 pts	**Anglia Ruskin** – 220 pts (Photography)
	Falmouth (UC) – 220 pts (Photo; Press Photo; Mar Nat Hist Photo)
	Glamorgan – 220 pts (Media Prod (Photo))
	Robert Gordon – CCD (Photo Electron Media)
200 pts	**Bristol UWE** – 200 pts check with admissions tutor (Photography)
	Gloucestershire – 200–240 pts (Photojrnl; Photo Edit Adv)
	Napier – 200 pts (Photo Film Imag)
	Newport – 200 pts (Doc Photo; Photo Art)
	Sunderland – 200 pts (Photo courses except under **140 pts**)
	Swansea (Inst) – 200 pts (Photo Arts)

180 pts	**East London** – 180 pts (Photography)
	Kingston – 180 pts (Graph Des Photo; Photo)
	Northampton – 180 pts (Photo Prac)
	Northbrook (Coll) – 180 pts (Photo Arts)
	Roehampton – 180–200 pts (Photo courses)
160 pts	**Blackpool and Fylde (Coll)** – 160 pts (Photo; Wldlf Photo)
	Bolton – 160–200 pts (Photo Vid courses)
	Central Lancashire – 160–200 pts (Photo; Photo Jrnl; Photo Fash Brnd Prom)
	Creative Arts (UC) – 160–200 pts (Photography)
	Cumbria – CC 160 pts (Photography)
	Derby – 160 pts (Photography)
	Dewsbury (Coll) – 160 pts (Contemp Photo Arts)
	Glasgow (SA) – CC (Fine Art (Photo))
	Grimsby (IFHE) – 160 pts (Commer Photo)
	Hertfordshire – 160 pts (Dig Lens Media)
	London South Bank – CC (Dig Film Vid; Dig Photo)
	Manchester Met – 160 pts+Fdn art (Photography)
	Middlesex – 160–280 pts (Photography)
	Portsmouth – 160–240 pts Fdn art (Photo; Vid Prod)
	Thames Valley (London CMusMedia) – 160 pts (Photo Dig Imag; Photo St)
	Westminster – CC (Photo Arts)
	Wolverhampton – 160–220 pts (Photo; Photo Film St)
140 pts	**Edinburgh (CA)** – DEE 140 pts (Vis Comm (Photo))
	Great Yarmouth (Coll) – 140–200 pts (Photo Dig Imag)
	Staffordshire – 140 pts (Photography)
	Sunderland – 140–160 pts (Photo Vid Dig Imag)
120 pts	**Bournemouth (AI)** – 120 pts (Photography)
	Southampton Solent – 120 pts (Fash Photo)
	Stockport (CFHE) – 120–240 pts (Photography)
	Suffolk (Univ Campus) – 120 pts (Photo Dig Imag)
100 pts	**Arts London (CComm)** – contact Univ (Photography)
80 pts	**Bedfordshire** – contact Univ (Dig Photo Vid Art)
	Carmarthenshire (Coll) – 80 pts (Photography)
	Cleveland (CAD) – 80–120 pts (Photography)
	Croydon (Coll) – 80 pts (Photomedia)
	Leeds Met – contact University

Alternative offers

See **Chapter 8** for grade/point equivalences and related information for the following examinations: Scottish qualifications, the Welsh Baccalaureate, the IB diploma (approximate points shown also in italics in the table of offers), the Irish Leaving Certificate, the European Baccalaureate and the French Baccalaureate.

EXAMPLES OF FOUNDATION DEGREES IN THE SUBJECT FIELD

Anglia Ruskin; Bournemouth (AI); Croydon (Coll); Derby; Dewsbury (Coll); Dunstable (Coll); East Lancashire (IHE); Farnborough (CT); Guildford (CFHE); Herefordshire (CAD); Hull (Coll); Leeds (CAD); Leicester (Coll); Mid Cheshire (Coll); Nescot; Newcastle (Coll); Plymouth; St Helens (Coll); South East Essex (Coll); South Nottingham (Coll); Swindon New (Coll); Truro (Coll); Westminster City (Coll).

CHOOSING YOUR COURSE (SEE ALSO CH.1)

Course variations – Widen your options

Film and TV Studies (Aberystwyth)
Digital Photography and Video Art (Bedfordshire)
Wildlife Photography (Blackpool and Fylde (Coll))
Photography, Film and TV Multimedia (Bournemouth)

Marine and Natural History Photography (Falmouth (UC))
Photojournalism (Gloucestershire)
Cinema, Photography and TV Studies (Leeds)
Contemporary Lens Media (Lincoln)
Documentary Photography (Newport (UWIC))
Photographic Practice (Northampton)
Fashion with Photography (Southampton Solent)
Criminology with Photography (Sunderland)
CHECK PROSPECTUSES AND WEBSITES FOR OTHER UNIVERSITIES AND COLLEGES OFFERING THESE COURSES

Universities and colleges teaching quality See www.qaa.ac.uk; www.unistats.com.

Sandwich degree courses Birmingham City; Portsmouth; Staffordshire.

ADMISSIONS INFORMATION
Number of applicants per place (approx) Arts London 10; Birmingham City 6; Blackpool and Fylde (Coll) 3; Bournemouth (AI) 7; Cleveland (CAD) 2; Croydon (Coll) 15; Derby 20; Falmouth (UC) 3; Napier 33; Newport 2; Nottingham Trent 4; Plymouth 2; Plymouth (CAD) 7; Portsmouth 4; Staffordshire 3; Stockport (CFHE) 6; Swansea (Inst) 12.

Advice to applicants and planning the UCAS personal statement Discuss your interest in photography and your knowledge of various aspects of the subject, for example, digital, 35mm, video, landscape, medical, wildlife and portrait photography. Read photographic journals to keep up-to-date on developments, particularly in photographic technology. You will also need first-hand experience of photography and be competent in basic skills. **Croydon (Coll)** Broad range of interests. **Derby** (Non-EU students) Fluency in written and spoken English important. Portfolio of work essential. See also **Appendix 2**.

Misconceptions about this course Some believe that courses are all practical work with no theory. **Cumbria** They didn't realise the facilities were so good! **Dewsbury (Coll)** Some applicants think that it's a traditional photography course. It's as digital as the individual wants it to be.

Selection interviews Yes Most institutions will interview applicants and expect to see a portfolio of work.

Interview advice and questions Questions relate to the applicant's portfolio of work which, for these courses, is of prime importance. Who are your favourite photographers? What is the most recent exhibition you have attended? Have any leading photographers influenced your work? Questions regarding contemporary photography. Written work sometimes required. See **Chapter 7**.

Reasons for rejection (non-academic) Lack of passion for the subject. Lack of exploration and creativity in practical work. Poorly presented portfolio.

AFTER-RESULTS ADVICE
Offers to applicants repeating A-levels Same Birmingham City, Blackpool and Fylde (Coll), Chester, Cumbria, Manchester Met, Nottingham Trent, Staffordshire.

GRADUATE DESTINATIONS AND EMPLOYMENT (2005/6 HESA)
See **Film, Radio, Video and TV Studies**.

Career note Opportunities for photographers exist in a range of specialisms including advertising and editorial work, fashion, medical, industrial, scientific and technical photography. Some graduates also go into photojournalism and other aspects of the media.

OTHER DEGREE SUBJECTS FOR CONSIDERATION
Animation; Art and Design; Film, Radio, Video and TV Studies; Media Studies; Moving Image.

PHYSICAL EDUCATION

(see also **Sports Sciences/Studies**)

Physical Education courses are very popular and unfortunately restricted in number. Ability in gymnastics and involvement in sport are obviously important factors. See also **Appendix 2**.

Useful websites www.afpe.org.uk; www.uksport.gov.uk; see also **Education Studies and Teacher Training**.

NB The points totals shown to the left of the institutions are for ease of reference only. It must not be assumed that tariff points are always used by institutions or that they can be substituted for an offer in grades. The level of an offer is not necessarily indicative of the quality of a course.

Abbreviations: P – Primary Teaching; S – Secondary Teaching; QTS – Qualified Teacher Status.

COURSE OFFERS INFORMATION

Subject requirements/preferences **GCSE** English, mathematics and a science. **AL** PE, sports studies and science are preferred subjects and for some courses one of these may be required. **NB** A* grades are likely to form part of university offers in the higher ranges for students applying for places in 2008 for entry in 2009: check websites.

Your target offers

320 pts **Birmingham** – ABB–BBB (Spo PE Commun St)
Exeter – ABB–BBB (Exer Spo Sci Educ) *(IB 28–29 pts)*

300 pts **Edinburgh** – BBB (BEd PE)
Queen's Belfast – BBB (Educ (PE))
Stranmillis (UC) – BBB (PE Educ)

280 pts **Brighton** – BBC (PE QTS)
Brunel – 280 pts (Spo Sci (PE))
Cardiff (UWIC) – 280 pts (Spo PE) *(IB 28 pts)*
Cumbria – 280 pts (PE Educ)
Stirling – BBC (Spo St PE)

260 pts **Brunel** – 260 pts (PE S) *(IB 26 pts)*
Sheffield Hallam – 260 pts (PE Yth Spo)
Winchester – 260 pts (P PE QTS)

240 pts **Hull** – 240–280 pts (PE Spo Sci Psy; PE Spo Sci Mgt)
Liverpool John Moores – 240–260 pts (Spo Dev PE; PE P S; Physl Actvt Exer Hlth)
Roehampton – 240 pts (P Educ (PE) QTS)
Worcester – 240 pts (PE Spo Coach Sci; PE)

220 pts **Edge Hill** – 220 pts (PE)

200 pts **Cumbria** – 200 pts (PE)
Manchester Met – 200 pts (Educ St Spo; Coach Spo Dev; PE)
York St John – CDD–DDD 200–180 pts (Spo St)

180 pts **Bangor** – 180–240 pts (Spo Hlth PE)
Liverpool Hope – DDD 180–160 pts (Educ St Spo St)
Marjon (UC) – 180–240 pts (Coach PE)
St Mary's (UC) – 180–200 pts (PE courses)
Trinity Carmarthen (Coll) – 180 pts (PE)

160 pts **Canterbury Christ Church** – CC 160 pts (PE Spo Exer Sci) *(IB 24 pts)*
Chichester – 160–220 pts (PE QTS S; Advntr Educ)
Leeds Trinity and All Saints (Coll) – 160–240 pts (Spo Dev PE)
Newman (UC) – 160–180 pts (Educ St Spo St; PE P Spo Sci)
Plymouth – 160–200 pts (PE P)
St Mary's (UC) – 160–200 pts (Spo Sci PE Commun)
Wolverhampton – 160–220 pts (PE non-QTS)

For a quick reference offers calculator, fold out the inside back cover.

Leeds Met – contact University

Alternative offers

See **Chapter 8** for grade/point equivalences and related information for the following examinations: Scottish qualifications, the Welsh Baccalaureate, the IB diploma (approximate points shown also in italics in the table of offers), the Irish Leaving Certificate, the European Baccalaureate and the French Baccalaureate.

CHOOSING YOUR COURSE (SEE ALSO CH.1)

Course variations – Widen your options
Sport, Physical Education and Community Studies (Birmingham)
Sport Sciences (Physical Education) (Brunel)
Biology and Sport and Exercise Science (Chester)
Adventure Education (Chichester)
Physical Education and Education (Cumbria)
Sport Development and PE (Leeds Trinity and All Saints (Coll))
Outdoor Education with Physical Education (Liverpool John Moores)
Geography and Sport Science (Loughborough)
Health and Exercise with PE in the Community (St Mary's (UC))
CHECK PROSPECTUSES AND WEBSITES FOR OTHER UNIVERSITIES AND COLLEGES OFFERING THESE COURSES.

Top universities and colleges (Research) See under **Sports Sciences/Studies**.

ADMISSIONS INFORMATION

Number of applicants per place (approx) Bangor 19; Birmingham 5; Brunel 10; Chichester 5; Edge Hill 40; Leeds Trinity and All Saints (Coll) 33; Liverpool John Moores 4; Marjon (UC) 18; Newman (UC) 5; St Mary's (UC) 9; Sheffield Hallam 60; Worcester 31.

Advice to applicants and planning the UCAS personal statement Ability in gymnastics, athletics and all sports and games is important. Full details of these activities should be given on the UCAS application – for example, teams, dates and awards achieved, assisting in extra-curricular activities. Involvement with local sports clubs, health clubs, summer camps, gap year. Relevant experience in coaching, teaching, community and youth work. **Liverpool John Moores** Commitment to working with children and a good sports background.

Selection interviews Yes Most institutions. In most cases, applicants will take part in physical education practical tests and games/gymnastics, depending on the course. The results of these tests could affect the level of offers. See **Chapter 7**.

Interview advice and questions The applicant's interests in physical education will be discussed, with specific questions on, for example, sportsmanship, refereeing, umpiring and coaching. Questions in the past have also included: What qualities should a good netball goal defence possess? How could you encourage a group of children into believing that sport is fun? Do you think that physical education should be compulsory in schools? Why do you think you would make a good teacher? What is the name of the education minister? **Liverpool John Moores** Questions on what the applicant has gained or learned through experiences with children.

Reasons for rejection (non-academic) Poor communication and presentational skills. Relatively poor sporting background or knowledge. Lack of knowledge about the teaching of physical education and the commitment required. Lack of ability in practicalities, for example, gymnastics, dance when relevant. Poor self-presentation. Poor writing skills.

AFTER-RESULTS ADVICE

Offers to applicants repeating A-levels Same Liverpool John Moores, Newman (UC), St Mary's (UC).

NEW GRADUATE DESTINATIONS AND EMPLOYMENT (2005/6 HESA)

No data available.

For information on how to read the Subject Tables, see **Chapter 8**.

Career note The majority of graduates go into education although, depending on any special interests, they may also go on to posts in sport and leisure industry.

OTHER DEGREE SUBJECTS FOR CONSIDERATION

Coach Education; Exercise and Fitness; Exercise Physiology; Human Biology; Leisure and Recreation; Physiotherapy; Sport and Exercise Science; Sport Health and Exercise; Sport Studies/Sciences; Sports Development; Sports Engineering; Sports Psychology; Sports Therapy.

PHYSICS

(see also **Astronomy/Astrophysics**)

There is a considerable shortage of applicants for Physics courses. Many courses have flexible arrangements to enable students to follow their own interests and specialisations, for example circuit design, microwave devices, cosmology, medical physics, solid state electronics.

Useful websites www.scienceyear.com; www.scicentral.com; www.ipem.org.uk; www.iop.org; www.noisemakers.org.uk; www.NewScientistJobs.com/careersguide2007; www.physics.org; www.nature.com/physics.

NB The points totals shown to the left of the institutions are for ease of reference only. It must not be assumed that tariff points are always used by institutions or that they can be substituted for an offer in grades. The level of an offer is not necessarily indicative of the quality of a course.

COURSE OFFERS INFORMATION

Subject requirements/preferences **GCSE** English, mathematics and science. **AL** Physics and mathematics are required for most courses. **NB** A* grades are likely to form part of university offers in the higher ranges for students applying for places in 2008 for entry in 2009: check websites.

Your target offers

360 pts and above

Cambridge – AAA (Nat Sci (Phys Expmntl Theor) (Physl Sci); Astro) *(IB 38–42 pts)*

Durham – AAA (Nat Sci Phys) *(IB 38–40 pts H6/7 maths phys)*

Durham – AAA–AAB (Phys; Phys Astron; Theor Phys) *(IB 36–40 pts)*

Imperial London – AAA (Phys; Phys St Musl Perf; Phys Yr Euro; Phys Theor Phys) *(IB 38 pts H666)*

London (King's) – AAA–AAB (Maths Phys)

Manchester – AAA–AAB (Phys; Phys Euro; Phys Technol Phys; Phys Astro; Phys Bus Mgt; Phys Phil)

Oxford – Offers vary eg AAA–AAB (Phys; Phys Phil) *(IB 38–42 pts)*

Sussex – AAA (Phys Astro; Phys Foren Sci; Theor Phys)

Warwick – AAA–AAB (Maths Phys) *(IB 36 pts)*

340 pts Birmingham – AAB–ABB (Phys; Theor Phys; Phys Astro; Phys Bus Mgt; Phys Astro Int; Phys Spc Rsch; Phys Prtcl Phys Cosmo) *(IB 32–34 pts)*

Edinburgh – AAB 2nd yr entry (Astro; Phys; Comput Phys; Phys Meteor; Phys Mus) *(IB 30 pts)*

Liverpool – AAB–BBB (MPhys Phys; Mathem Phys; Phys Maths; Astro; Theor Phys) *(IB 33 pts)*

London (King's) – AAB–ABB (Phys; Phys Phil; Phys Mgt; Phys Med Apps; Maths Phys) *(IB 34 pts H5 maths phys)*

London (QM) – 340 pts (MPhys Phys)

London (UCL) – AAB+AS–BBB+AS (Phys; Chem Phys; Theor Phys; Med Phys) *(IB 32–36 pts H6 maths phys)*

St Andrews – AAB 2nd yr entry (Phys courses) *(IB 36 pts)*

Sussex – AAB–ABB (MPhys Phys; Phys Astro; Phys Foren Sci; Theor Phys) *(IB 34–36 pts)*

Warwick – AAB–ABB (Phys; Phys Bus St) *(IB 36 pts)*

York – AAB (MPhys Phys; Phys Astro; Phys Bus Mgt; Maths Phys; Phys Phil courses)
320 pts **Bath** – AAC (MPhys Phys; Maths Phys) *(IB 32 pts)*
Bristol – ABB–BBB (Cheml Phys; Cheml Phys Ind Exp; Phys courses) *(IB 32–34 pts H665 maths phys chem)*
Cardiff – ABB (MPhys Astro; Phys Astron; Phys; Phys Mus; Theor Comput Phys) *(IB 32 pts H6 maths phys)*
Glasgow – ABB–CCC (Phys courses)
Lancaster – ABB–BBB (MPhys Phys; MSci Phys N Am; Phys Astro Cosmo; Phys Med Phys; Phys (Comput Phys); Theor Phys; Theor Phys Maths) *(IB 30 pts H 16 pts)*
Leeds – ABB (MPhys Phys; Phys Astro; Phys Nano; Theor Phys) *(IB 33 pts H 16 pts maths phys)*
Leicester – ABB 320 pts (MPhys Phys; Phys Astro; Phys Spc Sci Tech; Phys Nanotech) *(IB 34 pts)*
Nottingham – ABB–BBB (Chem Mol Phys; Mathem Phys; Phys; Phys Euro Lang; Phys Astron; Phys Med Phys; Phys Theor Astro; Phys Theor Phys) *(IB 35 pts)*
Queen's Belfast – ABB (MSci Phys; Phys Euro) *(IB 30 pts H655)*
Sheffield – ABB–ABC (MPhys Theor Phys; Phys Aus/N Am; Phys Phil) *(IB 30 pts)*
Southampton – ABB 320 pts (Phys; Phys Astron; Phys Nano; Phys Photon; Phys Spc Sci) *(IB 32 pts)*
Surrey – ABB–BBB (MPhys Phys; Phys Fin; Phys Med Phys; Phys Nclr Astro; Phys Sat Tech) *(IB 28 pts)*
Sussex – ABB–BBB (BSc Phys; Phys Astron; Phys Foren Sci; Theor Phys)
300 pts **Bath** – ABC (BSc Maths Phys; Phys Comp) *(IB 30 pts H5 maths phys)*
East Anglia – BBB (Cheml Phys) *(IB 31 pts)*
Edinburgh – BBB 1st yr entry (Phys; Comput Phys; Phys Meteor; Phys Mus)
Exeter – BBB (Phys Euro/Aus/N Am/NZ; Phys Astro; Phys Med Apps; Phys Qntm Las Tech; Qntm Sci Lsr) *(IB 28 pts)*

Department of Physics

Durham University

B.Sc. and M.Phys/M.Sci. degrees in Physics, Physics & Astronomy, Theoretical Physics and Mathematics & Physics, Chemistry & Physics and E-science & Physics

Specialised courses include particle physics, cosmology and photonics

Excellent laboratory facilities include 4 modern telescopes

Supportive college system

Learning based on lectures, tutorials, labs and projects

Internationally renowned research department

http://www.dur.ac.uk/physics
Email: physics.admissions@durham.ac.uk
Tel: +44(0)191 334 3726

Ogden Centre for Fundamental Physics

physics
AT BRISTOL

▶▶ Live and study in one of the most dynamic and exciting cities in the UK

▶▶ Choose from programmes in Physics, Physics & Astrophysics, Mathematics & Physics, and Physics & Philosophy

▶▶ Enjoy excellent teaching with world-class researchers and facilities - 15 new lecturers and £10M new teaching lab

Glasgow – BBB–BBC (BSc Phys; Astron Phys; Cheml Phys)

Heriot-Watt – 300 pts 2nd yr entry (MPhys Phys courses)

Lancaster – BBB (BSc Phys; Phys Med Phys; Theor Phys; Phys (Cosmo))

Leeds – BBB (BSc Phys; Phys Astro; Phys Nanotech)

Liverpool – BBB (BSc Phys Ocn Clim St; Mathem Phys; Phys Med Appl; Phys Astron)

Liverpool John Moores – 300–320 pts (Phys Astron; Astro)

London (RH) – 300–320 pts (MSci Phys; App Phys; Theor Phys; Phys Mus; Phys Prtcl Phys; Phys Mgt; Astro) *(IB 30 pts)*

Loughborough – 300–280 pts (MPhys Eng Phys; Phys Maths) *(IB 30 pts)*

Strathclyde – BBB–BBC (Biophys; App Phys; Phys Mathem Fin; Phys Vis Simul; Lsr Phys Optoel; Phys)

Swansea – 300–320 pts (Theor Phys; Phys joint Hons)

York – BBB (BSc Phys courses) *(IB 36 pts)*

280 pts **Aberdeen** – BBC 2nd yr entry (Phys; Physl Sci)

Aberystwyth – 280 pts (Spc Sci Robot) *(IB 27 pts H5 phys comp-sci maths)*

Cardiff – BBC (BSc Phys Astron; Astro; Phys Med Phys)

Central Lancashire – BBC (MPhys Phys)

Kent – BBC–BCC (MPhys/BSc Phys; Phys Foren Sci; Phys Spc Sci Sys; Phys Astro) *(IB 30 pts)*

Leicester – BBC 280 pts (BSc Phys; Phys Astro; Phys Spc Sci Tech; Phys Nano Tech; Phys Planet Sci)

London (QM) – 280 pts (Phys; Phys Comp; Phys Comp Sci; Phys Env; Phys Bus Mgt) *(IB 30–32 pts)*

London (RH) – BBC (Phys Sci Comm)

Loughborough – 280 pts (BSc Phys; Phys Mgt; Spo Sci Phys; Phys Maths; Eng Phys) *(IB 30 pts)*

Swansea – 280 pts (Phys courses except under **300 pts**)

For a quick reference offers calculator, fold out the inside back cover.

260 pts **Belfast (Queen's)** – BCC (BSc Phys; Theor Phys)
Heriot-Watt – 260 pts 1st entry (MPhys Phys)
Heriot-Watt – 260 pts 2nd yr entry (BSc Phys)
Hull – 260–300 pts (MSci Phys Med Tech; Phys Lsr Phot; Phys Astro; Phys; App Phys)
London (RH) – BCC–BBC (BSc Phys courses)
Surrey – BCC (BSc Phys; Phys Med Phys; Phys Nclr Astro; Phys Sat Tech; Phys Fin)

240 pts **Aberdeen** – CCC (Nat Phil (Phys); Phys)
Aberystwyth – 240–300 pts (Phys courses)
Dundee – 240–300 pts (Phys courses)
Hertfordshire – 240–280 pts (Phys Sci Comp)
Hull – 240–280 pts (BSc App Phys; Phys Astro; Phys Lsr Phot; Phys Med Tech; Phys Phil)
Keele – 240–260 pts (Physics)
Surrey – CCC (Fdn Phys)

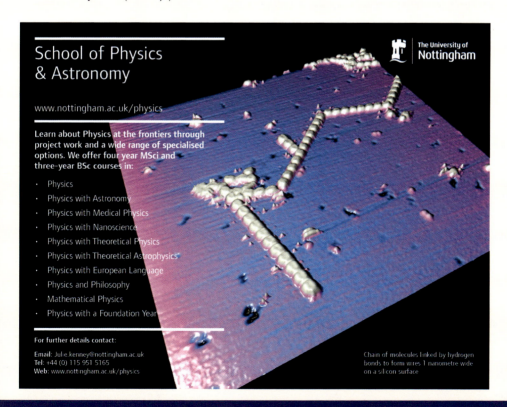
For information on how to read the Subject Tables, see **Chapter 8**.

220 pts **Central Lancashire** – 220–240 pts (Phys Media Prod Tech; Phys Mgt; Phys Mark; Phys Phil; Phys Maths)
Nottingham Trent – 220–240 pts (Phys; Phys Astro; Astron Phys)
200 pts **Dundee** – 200 pts 1st yr entry (BSc Phys 4 yr; MSci Phys 5 yr)
180 pts **Salford** – 180–260 pts (Phys; Phys N Am; Phys Acoust; Phys Euro; Phys Avn St; Phys Spc Tech)
160 pts **Heriot-Watt** – CC 1st yr entry (BSc Phys)
Strathclyde – CC (Phys QTS)
120 pts **West Scotland** – DD **or** bbc (Phys courses)
100 pts **London (Birk)** – 100 pts (p/t Phys)
 80 pts **Aberystwyth** – 80 pts (Phys + Fdn)

Alternative offers
See **Chapter 8** for grade/point equivalences and related information for the following examinations: Scottish qualifications, the Welsh Baccalaureate, the IB diploma (approximate points shown also in italics in the table of offers), the Irish Leaving Certificate, the European Baccalaureate and the French Baccalaureate.

EXAMPLES OF FOUNDATION DEGREES IN THE SUBJECT FIELD
Hull; Nottingham Trent.

CHOOSING YOUR COURSE (SEE ALSO CH.1)
Course variations – Widen your options
Space Science and Robotics (Aberystwyth)
Physics and Space Research (Birmingham)
Physics with Study in Continental Europe (Bristol)
Astrophysics (Central Lancashire)
Natural Sciences with a Year in Australasia (East Anglia)
Computational Physics (Edinburgh)
Physics with Nanotechnology (Hull)
Music Technology and Physics (Keele)
Astronomy, Space Science and Astrophysics with a Year in USA (Kent)
Theoretical Physics (Liverpool)
Engineering Physics (Loughborough)
Ocean Physics (Southampton)
Physics with Satellite Technology (Surrey)
CHECK PROSPECTUSES AND WEBSITES FOR OTHER UNIVERSITIES AND COLLEGES OFFERING THESE COURSES.

Universities and colleges teaching quality See www.qaa.ac.uk; www.unistats.com.

Top universities and colleges (Research) Birmingham; Bristol; Cambridge*; Cardiff; Durham; Edinburgh; Exeter; Glasgow; Imperial London*; Lancaster*; Leeds; Leicester; Liverpool; London (QM), (RH), (UCL); Manchester; Nottingham; Oxford*; Queen's Belfast; St Andrews; Sheffield; Southampton; Surrey; Sussex; Swansea; Warwick.

Sandwich degree courses Aston; Bath; Bristol; Loughborough; Nottingham Trent; Salford; Surrey.

ADMISSIONS INFORMATION
Number of applicants per place (approx) Bath 8; Birmingham 6; Bristol 9; Cardiff 4, (Phys Astron) 6; Dundee 5; Durham 6; Edinburgh 9; Exeter 5; Heriot-Watt 5; Hull 7; Imperial London 3; Kent 8; Lancaster 8; Leeds 7; Leicester 7; Liverpool 4; London (King's) 7, (QM) 6, (RH) 9, (UCL) 6; Loughborough 6; Nottingham 9; Oxford (success rate 46%); Salford 5; Southampton 5; Strathclyde 5; Surrey 5; Swansea 3; Warwick 8; York 9.

Advice to applicants and planning the UCAS personal statement Work experience should be mentioned, together with interests in maths and physics. Admissions tutors look for potential, enthusiasm and interest in the subject. The Institute of Physics can provide information on the work of the physicist. An awareness of the range of careers in which physics is involved should also be mentioned on the UCAS application, together with an explanation of any particular interests and details of books read on physics or mathematics (not science fiction!), and attendance at courses on physics or engineering. See **Appendix 2**.

Selection interviews **Yes** Bath, Birmingham, Cambridge, Durham, Exeter, Heriot-Watt, Hull, Lancaster, Liverpool, London (QM), (RH), Loughborough, Nottingham, Oxford, Sheffield, Strathclyde, Surrey, Swansea, Warwick, York; **Some** Cardiff, Dundee, East Anglia, Salford.

Interview advice and questions Questions will almost certainly focus on those aspects of the physics A/AS-level course which the student enjoys. **Bristol** Why Physics? Questions on mechanics, physics and pure maths. Given paper and calculator and questions asked orally; best to take your own calculator. Tutors seek enthusiastic and highly motivated students and the physicist's ability to apply basic principles to unfamiliar situations. See **Chapter 7**.

Applicants' impressions (A=Open day; B=Interview day) **Bath** (B) We had a tour of the campus and department, followed by an informal interview with questions based on my personal statement. **Bristol** (B) There was a tour of the city, the department and accommodation. A formal interview followed. **London (RH)** (Astro; B) There was a tour of the campus with an opportunity to see the telescope. The interviewer asked questions about star gazing and web design and some ideas about the solar system. **London (UCL)** (B) There was a tour and talk about the course. I was asked questions only on physics during the interview. **Oxford** (B) I had a formal physics interview, going through problems and explaining points which I had mentioned in my personal statement. **Southampton** (Phys Astron; A) The Open day consisted of a tour of the campus and labs and talks about the course. Seems a really good university. **Warwick** (B) No interview as such, just small group discussions.

Royal Holloway
University of London

The Department of Physics at Royal Holloway is one of the major centres for physics teaching and research in the University of London. Our research programmes cover the fundamental properties of matter from the lowest temperatures up to the highest energies, as well as nanotechnology, defects in solids and advanced industrial applications of physics. In the QAA review (the national review of teaching quality) the Department was rated excellent with a score of 23 out of 24. In the most recent Research Assessment Exercise (RAE) the Department was rated 5, placing us among the top Physics departments in the UK.

- BSc and MSci programmes including Physics, Astrophysics and Combined Honours courses
- Friendly department with a high level of student-staff contact
- Excellence in teaching and research

- Beautiful campus set in 135 acres of parkland
- Easy access to London in a more affordable location
- Excellent sports facilities, and a thriving Students' Union
- Computer Centre open 24 hours
- Accommodation guaranteed to all first year students

Royal Holloway
University of London

To apply please contact:
The Admissions Tutor, Department of Physics,
Royal Holloway, University of London, Egham, Surrey TW20 0EX
Tel: +44 (0)1784 443506 or email: physics@rhul.ac.uk
www.rhul.ac.uk/physics

For information on how to read the Subject Tables, see **Chapter 8**.

AFTER-RESULTS ADVICE

Offers to applicants repeating A-levels **Higher** Bristol, Glasgow, St Andrews, Warwick; **Possibly higher** Aberystwyth, Hull, Leeds, Loughborough, York; **Same** Birmingham, Cardiff, Dundee, Durham, East Anglia, Exeter, Lancaster, Leicester, Liverpool, Salford, Swansea; **No offers made** Cambridge.

GRADUATE DESTINATIONS AND EMPLOYMENT (2005/6 HESA)

Graduates surveyed 1755 **Employed** 615 **In further study** 570 **Assumed unemployed** 140.

Career note Many graduates go into scientific and technical work in the manufacturing industries. However, in recent years, financial work, management and marketing have also attracted many seeking alternative careers.

OTHER DEGREE SUBJECTS FOR CONSIDERATION

Astronomy; Astrophysics; Computer Science; Earth Sciences; Engineering subjects; Geophysics; Materials Science and Metallurgy; Mathematics; Meteorology; Natural Sciences; Oceanography; Optometry; Radiography.

PHYSIOLOGY

(see also **Animal Sciences**)

Physiology is a study of body function. Courses in this wide-ranging subject will cover the central nervous system, special senses and neuro-muscular mechanisms, and body-regulating systems such as exercise, stress and temperature regulation.

Useful websites www.scienceyear.com; www.physoc.org; www.physiology.org; see also **Biological Sciences**.

NB The points totals shown to the left of the institutions are for ease of reference only. It must not be assumed that tariff points are always used by institutions or that they can be substituted for an offer in grades. The level of an offer is not necessarily indicative of the quality of a course.

COURSE OFFERS INFORMATION

Subject requirements/preferences **GCSE** Science and mathematics at grade A. **AL** Two science subjects are usually required; chemistry and biology are the preferred subjects. **NB** A* grades are likely to form part of university offers in the higher ranges for students applying for places in 2008 for entry in 2009: check websites. **Other requirements Oxford** (Physiol Sci) Applicants take the BioMedical Admissions Test (BMAT) (see **Chapter 7**).

Your target offers

360 pts and above
    Cambridge – AAA (Nat Sci (Physiol Dev Neuro)) *(IB 38–42 pts)*
    Oxford – Offers vary eg AAA–AAB +BMAT (Physiol Sci; Physiol Psy; Physiol Phil) *(IB 38–42 pts)*

340 pts **Manchester** – AAB–BBB (Physiol; Physiol Ind; Physiol Modn Lang)
320 pts **Cardiff** – ABB–BBB 320–300 pts (Biomed Sci (Physiol)) *(IB 34 pts)*
    Leicester – ABB (Med Physiol) *(IB 32–34 pts)*
    London (King's) – ABB (Physiol; Physiol Pharmacol) *(IB 34 pts)*
    Newcastle – ABB (Physiol Sci) *(IB 30–32 pts)*
    Sheffield – ABB–ABab (Physiol Pharmacol)
300 pts **Bristol** – BBB (Physiol Sci) *(IB 32 pts H6/5 inc sci)*
    Dundee – 300 pts 2nd yr entry (Physiol Sci; Physiol Spo Biomed; Bioch Physiol Sci)
    Edinburgh – BBB (Physiology) *(IB 30 pts)*
    Leeds – BBB 300 pts (Hum Physiol) *(IB 32 pts)*
    Liverpool – BBB–BBC (Physiology)
    St Andrews – BBB (Physiology) *(IB 31 pts)*

280 pts **Aberdeen** – BBC 2nd yr entry (Physiology)
  Glasgow – BBC–BCC (Physiol; Physiol Spo Sci; Physiol Psy)
260 pts **Essex** – 260–240 pts (Clin Physiol (Cardio))
  Queen's Belfast – BCC–CCCc (Physiology) *(IB 28 pts H555)*
  Wolverhampton – 260–320 pts (Hum Physiol joint hons)
240 pts **Central Lancashire** – 240 pts (Physiol Pharmacol)
  Dundee – 240 pts 1st yr entry (Physiol Sci; Physiol Spo Biomed; Bioch Physiol Sci)
  Leeds – CCC (Clin Physiol (Cardio))
  Swansea – 240 pts (Clin Physiol Rsprty Physiol; Clin Physiol Clin Tech; Clin Physiol Cardiol)
220 pts **Napier** – 220 pts (Spo Exer Sci (Exer Physiol))
200 pts **Aberdeen** – CDD 1st yr entry (Physiology)
  Manchester Met – 200–240 (Physiol Pharmacol)
180 pts **Bristol UWE** – 180–220 pts (App Physiol Pharmacol)
  Greenwich – 180 pts (Hlth Physiol)
  Hertfordshire – 180–220 pts (Physiol; Physiol N Am)
  Salford – 180–200 pts (Physiol Bioch)
160 pts **East London** – 160 pts (Clin Physiol)
  Westminster – CC (Physiol Pharmacol)
140 pts **Portsmouth** – 140 pts (Clin Physiol)
  Wolverhampton – 140 pts (Physiol Pharmacol)

  Leeds Met – contact University

Alternative offers
See **Chapter 8** for grade/point equivalences and related information for the following examinations: Scottish qualifications, the Welsh Baccalaureate, the IB diploma (approximate points shown also in italics in the table of offers), the Irish Leaving Certificate, the European Baccalaureate and the French Baccalaureate.

EXAMPLES OF FOUNDATION DEGREES IN THE SUBJECT FIELD
Nescot.

CHOOSING YOUR COURSE (SEE ALSO CH.1)
Course variations – Widen your options
See **Biological Sciences**
CHECK PROSPECTUSES AND WEBSITES FOR OTHER UNIVERSITIES AND COLLEGES OFFERING THESE COURSES.

Universities and colleges teaching quality See www.qaa.ac.uk; www.unistats.com.

Top universities and colleges (Research) Aberdeen; Leeds; Liverpool*; Newcastle; Oxford.

Sandwich degree courses Bristol UWE; Coventry; Hertfordshire; London (King's); Salford.

ADMISSIONS INFORMATION
Number of applicants per place (approx) Birmingham 9; Bristol 8; Cardiff 8; Dundee 5; Leeds 4; Liverpool 10; London (King's) 5; Newcastle 6; Oxford (success rate 41%); Sheffield 25.

Advice to applicants and planning the UCAS personal statement See **Anatomical Science/ Anatomy** and **Biological Sciences**.

Selection interviews Yes Birmingham, Cambridge, Leeds, Newcastle, Oxford, Sheffield; **Some** Bristol, Cardiff, Dundee.

Interview advice and questions Past questions include: What made you decide to do a Physiology degree? What experimental work have you done connected with physiology? What future career do you have in mind? What is physiology? Why not choose Medicine instead? What practicals do you do at school? **Cardiff** Interviewer expects to see outside interests and ability to mix with people as well as an interest in biological sciences. **Oxford** Over 85% of applicants interviewed. What food (out of choice) was the best to eat before an interview? See **Chapter 7**.

For information on how to read the Subject Tables, see **Chapter 8**.

AFTER-RESULTS ADVICE

Offers to applicants repeating A-levels **Higher** Bristol, Glasgow, Leeds, Leicester, Newcastle, St Andrews, Sheffield; **Same** Cardiff, Dundee; **No offers made** Cambridge.

GRADUATE DESTINATIONS AND EMPLOYMENT (2005/6 HESA)

(including **Anatomy/Anatomical Science**) **Graduates surveyed** 2620 **Employed** 1380 **In further study** 405 **Assumed unemployed** 190.

Career note See **Biology**.

OTHER DEGREE SUBJECTS FOR CONSIDERATION

Anatomy; Biochemistry; Biological Sciences; Biotechnology; Dentistry; Genetics; Health Studies; Medicine; Microbiology; Nursing; Optometry; Pharmacology; Radiography; Sports Science.

PHYSIOTHERAPY

Physiotherapists work as part of a multi-disciplinary team with other health professionals and are involved in the treatment and rehabilitation of patients of all ages and with a wide variety of medical problems. On successful completion of the three-year course, graduates are eligible for State Registration and Membership of the Chartered Society of Physiotherapy. (See **Appendix 2**)

Useful websites www.csp.org.uk; www.thephysiotherapysite.co.uk; www.nhscareers.nhs.uk; www.physiotherapy.co.uk.

NB The points totals shown to the left of the institutions are for ease of reference only. It must not be assumed that tariff points are always used by institutions or that they can be substituted for an offer in grades. The level of an offer is not necessarily indicative of the quality of a course.

COURSE OFFERS INFORMATION

Subject requirements/preferences **GCSE** English, mathematics and science subjects. Many universities stipulate A/B grades in specific subjects. **AL** One or two science subjects are required. **NB** A* grades are likely to form part of university offers in the higher ranges for students applying for places in 2008 for entry in 2009: check websites. **Other requirements** Occupational health check and Criminal Records Bureau (CRB) clearance.

Your target offers

360 pts **and above**
    Southampton – ABBb 370 pts (Physiotherapy) *(IB 33 pts)*
340 pts **Cardiff** – AAB (Physiotherapy) *(IB 30 pts H6 in 1 sci)*
    London (King's) – BBBc (Physiotherapy) *(IB 34 pts H5 in 2 sci)*
320 pts **Birmingham** – ABB 320 pts (Physiotherapy) *(IB 34 pts)*
    Brighton – 320 pts (Physiotherapy) *(IB 32 pts)*
    Keele – ABB (Physiotherapy) *(IB 27 pts)*
    Northumbria – 320 pts (Physiotherapy) *(IB 32 pts)*
    Nottingham – ABB (Physiotherapy) *(IB 32 pts H6 biol)*
    Queen Margaret – ABB (Physiotherapy)
300 pts **Bradford** – 300 pts **or** BBB (Physiotherapy)
    Brunel – 300 pts (Physiotherapy) *(IB 30 pts)*
    Central Lancashire – BBB (Physiotherapy) *(IB 30 pts)*
    Coventry – 300 pts (Physiotherapy)
    Cumbria – 300 pts (Physiotherapy
    East Anglia – 300 pts (Physiotherapy) *(IB 32 pts H555)*
    East London – 300 pts (Physiotherapy)
    Glasgow Caledonian – BBB (Physiotherapy)
    Hertfordshire – BBB–ABB (Physiotherapy)

        Liverpool – 300 pts (Physiotherapy) *(IB 32 pts H666 inc biol)*
        London (St George's) – 300 pts (Physiotherapy)
        Manchester Met – BBB (Physiotherapy)
        Oxford Brookes – BBB **or** BBbb (Physiotherapy)
        Plymouth – 300 pts (Physiotherapy)
        Robert Gordon – BBB (Physiotherapy)
        Salford – BBB 300 pts (Physiotherapy) *(IB 32 pts)*
        Sheffield Hallam – 300 pts (Physiotherapy)
        Teesside – 300–320 pts (Physiotherapy)
        Ulster – BBB (Physiotherapy) (See **Ch.7**)
        York St John – 300 pts (Physiotherapy)
280 pts **Bristol UWE** – 280–340 pts (Physiotherapy)
        Kingston – 280–300 pts (Physiotherapy)
260 pts **Bournemouth** – 260 pts (Physiotherapy)
        Huddersfield – BCC 260 pts (Physiotherapy)
240 pts **Keele** – 240 pts (Physio with Hlth Fdn Yr)
160 pts **and below**
        Colchester (Inst) – part–time; contact Inst (Physiotherapy)
        London South Bank – min age 21 (Physiotherapy)
        York St John – Part–time courses for physiotherapy assistants, min age 21; A-levels or equiv
          reqd.

        Leeds Met – contact University

Alternative offers

See **Chapter 8** for grade/point equivalences and related information for the following examinations: Scottish qualifications, the Welsh Baccalaureate, the IB diploma (approximate points shown also in italics in the table of offers), the Irish Leaving Certificate, the European Baccalaureate and the French Baccalaureate.

EXAMPLES OF FOUNDATION DEGREES IN THE SUBJECT FIELD
Salford.

CHOOSING YOUR COURSE (SEE ALSO CH. 1)
Course variations – Widen your options
Science and Management of Exercise and Health (Farnborough (CT))
Osteopathy (Greenwich)
Sports Therapy (Hertfordshire)
Exercise, Nutrition and Health (Kingston)
Sports Science and Physiology (Leeds)
Sports and Exercise Science (Oxford Brookes)
Podiatry (Plymouth)
Sports Rehabilitation (Salford)
CHECK PROSPECTUSES AND WEBSITES FOR OTHER UNIVERSITIES AND COLLEGES OFFERING THESE COURSES.

Universities and colleges teaching quality See www.qaa.ac.uk; www.unistats.com.

Sandwich degree courses Glasgow Caledonian.

ADMISSIONS INFORMATION
Number of applicants per place (approx) Birmingham 15; Bradford 22; Brighton 30 (6 places for overseas candidates); Bristol UWE 12; Brunel 11; Cardiff 17; Coventry 15; East Anglia 14; East London 10; Glasgow Caledonian 12; Hertfordshire 13; Huddersfield 18; Kingston 9; Liverpool 20; London (King's) 16; Manchester 18; Northumbria 37; Nottingham 48; Queen Margaret 11; Robert Gordon 13; Salford 28; Sheffield Hallam 12; Southampton 20; Teesside 33; Ulster 12.

Advice to applicants and planning the UCAS personal statement Visits to, and work experience in, hospital physiotherapy departments are important although many universities publicly state that this is not necessary. However, with the level of competition for this subject I would regard this as doubtful (see Reasons for rejection). Applicants must demonstrate a clear understanding of the nature of the profession. Give details of voluntary work activities. Take notes of the work done and the different aspects of physiotherapy. Explain your experience fully on the UCAS application. Outside interests and teamwork are considered important. Good communication skills. Observation placement within a physiotherapy department. **Manchester Met** We need to know why you want to be a physiotherapist. We also look for work shadowing a physiotherapist or work experience in another caring role. Evidence is also required of good communication skills, ability to care for people and of teamwork and leadership. **Salford** Essential for applicants to seek experience in as wide a range of settings as possible. See also **Appendix 2**.

Advice to overseas (non-EU) applicants Places for students from overseas are limited and applicants must be able to read, speak and write English fluently. Information on the minimum educational qualifications required by overseas students and details concerning grants and funding are available from the Chartered Society of Physiotherapy (see **Appendix 2**). **Brunel, Glasgow Caledonian** Proficiency in English essential. **Queen Margaret** Several overseas students recruited each year. **Ulster** Exams and continuous assessment.

Misconceptions about this course Some applicants think that physiotherapy has a sports bias.

Selection interviews **Yes** Most institutions including Birmingham, Bradford, Brighton, Coventry, East Anglia, East London, Huddersfield, Nottingham, Robert Gordon, Salford, Sheffield Hallam; **Some** Brunel (mature students), Cardiff (mature students), Kingston, Queen Margaret, Southampton (mature students, who are asked to write about their life experience).

Interview advice and questions Physiotherapy is one of the most popular courses at present and work experience is very important, if not essential. A sound knowledge of the career, types of treatment used in physiotherapy and some understanding of the possible problems experienced by patients will be expected. Past interview questions include: How does physiotherapy fit into the overall health care system? If one patient was a heavy smoker and the other not, would you treat them the same? What was the most emotionally challenging thing you have ever done? Give an example of teamwork in which you have been involved. Why should we make you an offer? What is chiropractic? What is osteopathy? See **Chapter 7**.

Applicants' impressions (A=Open day; B=Interview day) **Nottingham** (B) The interviewers were helpful and not aggressive. It was a modern department with good facilities. There was no chance to talk to the students.

Reasons for rejection (non-academic) Lack of knowledge of the profession. Failure to convince the interviewers of a reasoned basis for following the profession. Failure to have visited a hospital physiotherapy unit. Lack of awareness of the demands of the course. Other subjects listed on the UCAS application. **Birmingham** Poor communication skills. Lack of career insight. **Bristol UWE** Applicants re-sitting A-levels are not normally considered. **Cardiff** Lack of knowledge of physiotherapy; experience of sports injuries only.

AFTER-RESULTS ADVICE

Offers to applicants repeating A-levels **Higher** Bristol UWE (candidates who fail at interview will not normally be reconsidered), East Anglia, East London, Glasgow Caledonian, Kingston, Teesside; **Same** Coventry, Queen Margaret, Salford, Southampton.

GRADUATE DESTINATIONS AND EMPLOYMENT (2005/6 HESA)

No data available.

Career note The professional qualifications gained on graduation enable physiotherapists to seek posts in the Health Service where the majority are employed. A small number work in the community health service, particularly in rural areas, whilst others work in residential homes. In addition to private practice, there are also some opportunities in professional sports clubs.

For a quick reference offers calculator, fold out the inside back cover.

OTHER DEGREE SUBJECTS FOR CONSIDERATION

Anatomy; Audiology; Biological Sciences; Health Studies; Leisure and Recreation; Nursing; Occupational Therapy; Osteopathy; Physical Education; Psychology; Sport Science/Studies.

PLANT SCIENCES

(including **Botany;** see also **Biological Sciences** and **Biology**)

Plant Sciences cover such areas as plant biochemistry, plant genetics, plant conservation and plant geography. Botany encompasses all aspects of plant science and also other subject areas including agriculture, forestry and horticulture. Botany is basic to these subjects and others including pharmacology and water management. As with other biological sciences, some universities introduce Plant Sciences by way of a common first year with other subjects.

Useful websites www.kew.org; www.anbg.gov.au; www.scienceyear.com; www.botany.net; www.botany.org.

NB The points totals shown to the left of the institutions are for ease of reference only. It must not be assumed that tariff points are always used by institutions or that they can be substituted for an offer in grades. The level of an offer is not necessarily indicative of the quality of a course.

COURSE OFFERS INFORMATION

Subject requirements/preferences GCSE Mathematics if not offered at A-level. **AL** One or two science subjects are usually required. **NB** A* grades are likely to form part of university offers in the higher ranges for students applying for places in 2008 for entry in 2009: check websites.

Your target offers

360 pts **and above**
  Cambridge – AAA (Nat Sci (Plnt Sci)) *(IB 38–42 pts)*
340 pts **Manchester** – AAB–BBB (Plnt Sci; Plnt Sci Modn Lang; Plnt Sci Ind)
320 pts **Birmingham** – ABB–BBC (Biol Sci (Plnt Biol))
  Bristol – ABB–BBB (Botany) *(IB 33 pts H665 inc 2 sci)*
  Durham – ABB (Plnt Sci; Plnt Sci Ind) *(IB 34 pts H55 inc biol +1 sci)*
  Sheffield – ABB (MBS Plnt Sci) *(IB 33 pts)*
  Sheffield – ABB–BBB (BSc Plnt Sci)
300 pts **East Anglia** – BBB–BBC (Plnt Biol)
  Edinburgh – BBB (Plnt Sci) *(IB 30 pts)*
  Glasgow – BBB–BCC (Plnt Sci)
280 pts **Aberdeen** – BBC 2nd yr entry (Plnt Biol; Plnt Soil Sci)
  Nottingham – BBC–CCC (Plnt Sci; Plnt Sci Euro St) *(IB 24–30 pts)*
260 pts **Reading** – 260 pts (Bot Zool; Bot)
240 pts **Aberystwyth** – 240–280pts (Plnt Biol)
200 pts **Aberdeen** – CDD 1st yr entry (Plnt Biol; Plnt Soil Sci)
160 pts **Worcester** – 160–120 pts (Ecol Plnt Sci; Plnt Sci courses)

Alternative offers

See **Chapter 8** for grade/point equivalences and related information for the following examinations: Scottish qualifications, the Welsh Baccalaureate, the IB diploma (approximate points shown also in italics in the table of offers), the Irish Leaving Certificate, the European Baccalaureate and the French Baccalaureate.

CHOOSING YOUR COURSE (SEE ALSO CH.1)

Course variations – Widen your options

See **Biology** and **Horticulture**.
CHECK PROSPECTUSES AND WEBSITES FOR OTHER UNIVERSITIES AND COLLEGES OFFERING THESE COURSES.

Top universities and colleges (Research) Aberdeen; Cambridge; Reading; see also **Biological Sciences**.

Sandwich degree courses Durham; Glasgow; Manchester.

ADMISSIONS INFORMATION

Number of applicants per place (approx) Bristol 5; Edinburgh 6; Glasgow 4; Nottingham 5; Reading 3; Sheffield 5.

Advice to applicants and planning the UCAS personal statement Visit botanical gardens. See **Biological Sciences**. See also **Appendix 2**.

Selection interviews **Yes** Cambridge, Durham, Nottingham (depends on application).

Interview advice and questions You are likely to be questioned on your biology studies, your reasons for wishing to study Plant Sciences and your ideas about a possible future career. In the past questions have been asked about Darwin's theory of evolution, photosynthesis and DNA and the value of gardening programmes on TV! See **Chapter 7**.

AFTER-RESULTS ADVICE

Offers to applicants repeating A-levels **Possibly higher** Nottingham; **Same** Birmingham, Sheffield; **No offer made** Cambridge.

GRADUATE DESTINATIONS AND EMPLOYMENT (2005/6 HESA)

Graduates surveyed 40 **Employed** 15 **In further study** 15 **Assumed unemployed** 5.

Career note See **Biology** and **Horticulture**.

OTHER DEGREE COURSES FOR CONSIDERATION

Agriculture; Biochemistry; Biological Sciences; Biology; Crop Science (Agronomy); Food Science; Forestry; Herbal Medicine; Homeopathy; Horticulture; Landscape Architecture; Traditional Chinese Medicine.

PODIATRY (CHIROPODY)

Students on health-related courses are required to have Criminal Records Bureau (CRB) clearance. Podiatry is a relatively new term for chiropody and deals with the management of disease and disorders of the ankle and foot. Podiatrists diagnose nail, skin and movement problems, devise treatment plans and carry out treatment for all age groups. Courses lead to state registration and some work shadowing prior to application is preferred by admissions tutors.

Useful websites www.feetforlife.org; www.nhscareers.nhs.uk; www.podiatrynetwork.com; www.podiatrytoday.com; www.podiatrychannel.com.

NB The points totals shown to the left of the institutions are for ease of reference only. It must not be assumed that tariff points are always used by institutions or that they can be substituted for an offer in grades. The level of an offer is not necessarily indicative of the quality of a course.

COURSE OFFERS INFORMATION

Subject requirements/preferences **GCSE** Mathematics and science subjects. **AL** Biology usually required or preferred. **NB** A* grades are likely to form part of university offers in the higher ranges for students applying for places in 2008 for entry in 2009: check websites. **Other requirements** Hepatitis B, tuberculosis and tetanus immunisation; Criminal Records Bureau (CRB) clearance (a pre-existing record could prevent a student from participating in the placement component of the course and prevent the student from gaining state registration).

Your target offers
300 pts Southampton – BBB (Podiatry) *(IB 28 pts)*
 Ulster – BBB (Podiatry) (See **Ch.7**)

For a quick reference offers calculator, fold out the inside back cover.

240 pts   **Brighton** – CCC (Podiatry) *(IB 28 pts)*
          East London – 240 pts (Pod Med)
          Plymouth – 240–260 pts (Podiatry)
          Salford – 240 pts (Podiatry) *(IB 24 pts)*
220 pts   **Huddersfield** – 220 pts (Podiatry)
200 pts   **Cardiff (UWIC)** – 200 pts (Podiatry)
180 pts   **Northampton** – 180 pts (Podiatry)
160 pts   **Durham New (Coll)** – 160 pts (Podiatry)
          Glasgow Caledonian – CC (Podiatry)
          Matthew Boulton (CFHE) – 160 pts (Podiatry)
          Queen Margaret – DDE (Podiatry)
  80 pts   **Sunderland** – contact University (Podiatry – course is run in association with the Durham School of Podiatric Medicine at New College Durham)

Alternative offers
See **Chapter 8** for grade/point equivalences and related information for the following examinations: Scottish qualifications, the Welsh Baccalaureate, the IB diploma (approximate points shown also in italics in the table of offers), the Irish Leaving Certificate, the European Baccalaureate and the French Baccalaureate.

EXAMPLES OF FOUNDATION DEGREES IN THE SUBJECT FIELD
Salford.

CHOOSING YOUR COURSE (SEE ALSO CH.1)
Course variations - Widen your options
See **Health Sciences/Studies**.
CHECK PROSPECTUSES AND WEBSITES FOR OTHER UNIVERSITIES AND COLLEGES OFFERING THESE COURSES.

Universities and colleges teaching quality See www.qaa.ac.uk; www.unistats.com.

ADMISSIONS INFORMATION
Number of applicants per place (approx) Cardiff (UWIC) 8; Huddersfield 2–3; Matthew Boulton (CFHE) 4; Northampton 2; Salford 3; Southampton 3.

Advice to applicants and planning the UCAS personal statement Visit a podiatrist's clinic to gain work experience/work shadowing experience. Discuss your knowledge of the work fully on your UCAS application. **Cardiff (UWIC)** Applicants need the ability to communicate with all age ranges, to work independently, to be resourceful and to possess a focussed approach to academic work. **Huddersfield** Admissions tutors look for evidence of an understanding of podiatry, some work experience, good people skills, and effective communication. Mature applicants must include an academic reference (not an employer reference). See also **Appendix 2**.

Misconceptions about this course Cardiff (UWIC) Prospective students are often not aware of the demanding requirements of the course: 1000 practical clinical hours augmented by a rigorous academic programme. Applicants are often unaware that whilst the elderly are a significant sub-population of patients with a variety of foot problems, increasingly the role of the podiatrist is the diagnosis and management of biomechanical/developmental disorders as well as the management of the diabetic or rheumatoid patient and those who require surgical intervention for nail problems. **Huddersfield** Many people think that podiatry is limited in its scope of practice to treating toe nails, corns and calluses – FALSE. As professionals, we do treat such pathologies but the scope of practice is much wider. It now includes surgery, biomechanics, sports injuries, treating children and high risk patients. Because offers are low it is considered an easier course than, for example, Physiotherapy – FALSE. The course is academically demanding in addition to the compulsory clinical requirement.

Selection interviews Yes Most institutions; Huddersfield, Southampton; **Some** Cardiff (UWIC).

Interview advice and questions Past questions include: Have you visited a podiatrist's surgery? What do your friends think about your choice of career? Do you think that being a podiatrist could cause you any physical problems? With which groups of people do podiatrists come into contact? What are your perceptions of the scope of practice of podiatry? What transferable skills do you think you will need? **Cardiff (UWIC)** What made you consider podiatry as a career? Have you researched your career choice and where did you find the information? What have you discovered and has this altered your original perception of podiatry? What personal characteristics do you think you possess which might be useful for this work? See **Chapter 7**.

Reasons for rejection (non-academic) Unconvincing attitude; poor communication and inter-personal skills; lack of motivation; medical condition or physical disabilities which are incompatible with professional practice; no knowledge of chosen profession; lack of work experience.

AFTER-RESULTS ADVICE
Offers to applicants repeating A-levels **Same** Cardiff (UWIC), Huddersfield, Salford.

GRADUATE DESTINATIONS AND EMPLOYMENT (2005/6 HESA)
No data available.

Career note Many state-registered podiatrists are employed by the NHS whilst others work in private practice or commercially-run clinics.

OTHER DEGREE SUBJECTS FOR CONSIDERATION
Audiology; Biological Sciences; Health Studies; Nursing; Occupational Therapy; Osteopathy; Physiotherapy.

POLITICS

(including **Government;** see also **Development Studies** and **International Relations**)

Politics is often described as the study of 'who gets what, where, when and how'. Courses have become increasingly popular in recent years and usually cover the politics and government of the major powers. Because of the variety of degree courses on offer, it is possible to study the politics of almost any country in the world.

Useful websites www.europa.eu; www.fco.gov.uk; www.psa.ac.uk; www.parliament.uk; www.whitehouse.gov; www.amnesty.org; www.direct.gov.uk; www.un.org; www.un.int.

NB The points totals shown to the left of the institutions are for ease of reference only. It must not be assumed that tariff points are always used by institutions or that they can be substituted for an offer in grades. The level of an offer is not necessarily indicative of the quality of a course.

COURSE OFFERS INFORMATION
Subject requirements/preferences **GCSE** English, mathematics and a foreign language may be required. **AL** No subjects specified; history useful but an arts or social science subject an advantage. **NB** A* grades are likely to form part of university offers in the higher ranges for students applying for places in 2008 for entry in 2009: check websites.

Your target offers
360 pts and above
    Bristol – AAA–AAB (Pol courses) *(IB 34–38 pts)*
    Cambridge – AAA (Soc Pol Sci) *(IB 38–42 pts)*
    Durham – AAA (Hist Pol) *(IB 36 pts H 17 pts)*
    London (UCL) – AAA+AS (Euro Soc Pol St) *(IB 38 pts)*
    Oxford – Offers vary eg AAA–AAB (Hist Pol; PPE) *(IB 38–40 pts)*
    Queen's Belfast – AAA (Law Pol)
    St Andrews – AAA–AAB (Int Rel courses) *(IB 38 pts)*
    Warwick – ABBb (Pol; Pol Int St; Pol Fr) *(IB 36 pts)*

340 pts **Bath** – AAB–ABB (Pol Econ) *(IB 34 pts)*
Durham – AAB (Pol; Pol (Euro St); PPE; Econ Pol; Hist Pol; Phil Pol; Comb Soc Sci)
Essex – 340–280 pts (Pol; Pol Hum Rts; Econ Pol; Pol Sociol; Int Rel Pol; PPE) *(IB 32–36 pts)*
Hull – 340 pts (Brit Pol Legis St)
London (King's) – AAB+AS **or** AAbb (War St courses)
London (SOAS) – 340–360 pts (Pol courses) *(IB 34 pts)*
Manchester – AAB–ABB (Pol Modn Hist)
Newcastle – AAB–ABB (Pol Econ; Pol Hist)
Nottingham – AAB (Pol; Int Rel Glob Is; Pol Am St)
Sheffield – AAB (Politics)
Surrey – AAB (Law Int St)
York – AAB–ABB (Hist Pol; Engl Pol; Econ Pol; Pol Sociol; Pol Soc Pol)
320 pts **Birmingham** – ABB 320 pts (Pol Sci; Econ Pol Sci; Int St Pol Sci) *(IB 32 pts)*
Cardiff – ABB–BBB (Pol; Euro Pol Int Rel; Modn Hist Pol; Pol Econ; Pol Sociol) *(IB 35 pts)*
Durham – ABB (Pol Sociol) *(IB 36 pts H 17 pts)*
East Anglia – ABB–BBB–BBC (Pol; Pol Sociol Contemp Cult; Pol Media; PPE) *(IB 35 pts)*
Exeter – ABB–BBB 320–300 pts (Pol; Pol Fr/Ger/Ital/Russ/Span; Pol Arbc St) *(IB 28–29 pts)*
Glasgow – ABB–BBB (Pol courses)
Kent – 320 pts (PPE Euro)
Lancaster – ABB (Pol N Am)
Leeds – ABB (Pol Parl St; Pol St)
Liverpool – ABB (Hist (Modn) Pol; Phil Pol)
London (LSE) – ABB (Gov; Gov Econ; Gov Hist; Int Rel Hist) *(IB 37 pts)*
London (RH) – ABB–BBB (Pol courses) *(IB 34 pts)*
London (UCL) – ABB (Pol E Euro St) *(IB 34 pts)*
Loughborough – ABB–AAC (Econ Pol) *(IB 34 pts)*
Manchester – ABB–BBB (Pol Sociol; Pol Econ Soc Hist; Pol Crim)
Newcastle – ABB–BBB (Pol courses except under **340 pts**) *(IB 35–37 pts)*
Oxford Brookes – ABB (Law Pol)
Sheffield – ABB (Pol Phil; Int Hist Int Pol) *(IB 35 pts)*
Southampton – ABB–BBB (Pol courses) *(IB 33 pts)*
Sussex – ABB **or** 360 pts 3AL+AS (Pol courses) *(IB 34 pts)*
Ulster – ABB (Law Int Pol)
300 pts **Aston** – BBB 300 pts (Pol courses)
Brighton – BBB (Pol courses)
Dundee – BBB 2nd yr entry (Pol; Euro Pol courses; Int Rel Pol)
East Anglia – BBB–BBC (Pol Econ)
Edinburgh – BBB (Pol; Pol Econ Soc Hist; Geog Pol) *(IB 34 pts H555)*
Hull – 300 pts (Pol; Pol Int Rel; PPE; War Scrty St; Glob Gov; Euro Gov Pol)
Kent – 300 pts (Pol Int Rel Jap) *(IB 32 pts)*
Lancaster – BBB (Pol; Pol Int Rel; Glob Pol; Pce St Int Rel; Euro Pol Soty Cult) *(IB 29 pts)*
Leicester – BBB (Hist Pol)
Liverpool – BBB (Pol; Int Pol Pol; Pol Int Bus; Pol Comm St)
London (LSE) – BBB (Soc Pol Gov)
London (QM) – 300 pts (Pol courses) *(IB 32 pts)*
Nottingham – BBB (Fr Pol; Ger Pol; Euro Pol) *(IB 34 pts)*
Queen's Belfast – BBB–BBCb (Politics) *(IB 29 pts H655)*
Reading – 300 pts (3AL+AS) 280 pts (3AL) (Pol Econ; Pol Int Rel; War Pce Int Rel)
Sheffield – BBB–BBC (Pol courses except under **340/320/280 pts**)
280 pts **Aberystwyth** – 280–240 pts (Pol St; Int Pol; Euro Pol; Int Pol Intel St)
Bradford – 280 pts (Pol courses)
Kent – 280 pts (Pol; Pol Int Rel courses except under **320/300 pts**) *(IB 32 pts)*
Leeds – BBC (Pol Russ; Pol Russ Civ; Pol Span)
Leicester – BBC 280–340 pts (Politics) *(IB 28 pts)*
Sheffield – BBC **or** BBcc (Ger Pol; Russ Pol)

For information on how to read the Subject Tables, see **Chapter 8**.

Surrey – 280 pts (Pol; Pol Int St; Pol Citz St; Pol Pol St)

260 pts **Brunel** – 260 pts (Int Pol; Pol courses) *(IB 28 pts)*

Keele – BCC–BBC 260–280 pts (Pol courses)

London (Gold) – BCC (Pol; Pol Econ; Econ Pol Pblc Pol; Int St) *(IB 28 pts)*

Loughborough – 260–300 pts (Pol with minor subj)

Northumbria – 260 pts (Pol courses)

Richmond (Am Int Univ) – 260 pts (Soc Sci (Int Rel) (Pol Sci))

Stirling – BCC (PPE; Pol; Int Pol Lang)

Strathclyde – BCC–BB (Pol courses)

240 pts **Aberdeen** – CCC 240 pts (Pol courses; Pol Int Rel)

Bradford – 240 pts (Pce St; Pol Pce St)

Bristol UWE – 240–300 pts (Pol courses)

Buckingham – 240 pts (Pol Econ Law)

Cardiff (UWIC) – 240 pts (Politics)

City – 240–260 pts (Int Pol; Int Pol Sociol) *(IB 26 pts)*

Coventry – 240–260 pts (Pol courses)

Dundee – 240 pts 1st yr entry (Pol courses; Euro Pol courses; Int Rel Pol)

Liverpool Hope – 240 pts (Politics)

Oxford Brookes – CCC–BBC (Pol courses)

Plymouth – 240 pts (Pol courses)

Portsmouth – 240–300 pts (Pol; Pol Sociol)

Robert Gordon – 240 pts (Pol Mgt)

Salford – 240–200 pts (Pol; E W Euro Pol St; Crim Pol)

Sheffield Hallam – 240 pts (Pol courses)

Swansea – 240–300 pts (Pol joint courses; War Soty; Fr Euro Pol)

Ulster – CCC 240 pts (Pol; Int Pol courses; Econ Pol) *(IB 24 pts)*

Westminster – CCC/BC (Politics)

Winchester – 240 pts (Pol Glob St courses)

220 pts **Bangor** – 220–260 pts (Pol Soc Sci)

De Montfort – 220–240 pts (Pol joint courses)

Kingston – 220–320 pts (Pol courses)

Nottingham Trent – 220 pts (Pol courses)

200 pts **Anglia Ruskin** – 200 pts (Pol courses)

Central Lancashire – 200 pts (Pol; Pol Phil; Pol Soc Pol; Pol Hist)

Huddersfield – 200–240 pts (Pol; Pol Contemp Hist; Pol Media)

Lincoln – 200–260 pts (Pol courses)

London Met – 200 pts (Pol Sociol; Pol Soc Pol; Pol)

Manchester Met – 200–220 pts (Pol courses; Int Pol courses)

Sunderland – 200–300 pts (Pol courses)

180 pts **Greenwich** – 180 pts (Politics)

Liverpool John Moores – 180–240 pts (Pol courses)

Northampton – 180–220 pts (Pol courses)

160 pts **Canterbury Christ Church** – CC (Pol courses)

East London – 160 pts (Int Pol)

Glamorgan – 160–200 pts (Pol courses)

London Met – 160 pts (Pol courses)

London South Bank – CC (Int Pol courses)

Middlesex – 160–200 pts (Int Pol St)

West Scotland – CC (Law Pol)

Wolverhampton – 160–220 pts (Pol courses)

Worcester – 160 pts (Pol courses)

140 pts **West Scotland** – CD (Politics)

120 pts **Roehampton** – 120–220 pts (Hum Rts courses)

80 pts **London (Birk)** – 80 pts for under 21s (over 21s varies) (p/t Pol Soc; Pol Phil Hist)

For a quick reference offers calculator, fold out the inside back cover.

East Lancashire (IHE) – check with admissions tutor (Politics)
Leeds Met – contact University
Newport – check with admissions tutor (Pol St)
Open University – contact University

Alternative offers

See **Chapter 8** for grade/point equivalences and related information for the following examinations: Scottish qualifications, the Welsh Baccalaureate, the IB diploma (approximate points shown also in italics in the table of offers), the Irish Leaving Certificate, the European Baccalaureate and the French Baccalaureate.

CHOOSING YOUR COURSE (SEE ALSO CH.1)

Course variations – Widen your options

International Politics and Intelligence Studies (Aberystwyth)
History and Political Science (Birmingham)
Peace Studies (Bradford)
Culture, Philosophy and Politics (East Anglia)
Politics and Human Rights (Essex)
Politics with Arabic Studies (Exeter)
Political Communication (Greenwich)
Politics and Journalism (Kingston)
Politics and Parliamentary Studies (Leeds)
CHECK PROSPECTUSES AND WEBSITES FOR OTHER UNIVERSITIES AND COLLEGES OFFERING THESE COURSES.

Universities and colleges teaching quality See www.qaa.ac.uk; www.unistats.com.

Top universities and colleges (Research) Aberystwyth*; Birmingham; Bradford; Bristol; De Montfort; Essex*; Exeter; Glasgow; Hull; Keele; London (King's) (War St)*, (LSE); Manchester; Newcastle; Oxford*; Queen's Belfast; Reading; St Andrews; Sheffield*; Strathclyde; Sussex; Warwick; York.

Sandwich degree courses Aston; Brunel; De Montfort; Lancaster; Loughborough; Oxford Brookes; Plymouth; Surrey.

ADMISSIONS INFORMATION

Number of applicants per place (approx) Aberystwyth 4; Aston 4; Bath 2; Birmingham 6; Bradford 10; Bristol 18; Brunel 5; Buckingham 2; Cambridge (Soc Pol Sci) 5; Cardiff 14; Cardiff (UWIC) 3; De Montfort 6; Dundee 6; Durham 11 (all courses); East Anglia 15; Exeter 8; Hull 11, (PPE) 20; Kent 14; Lancaster 14; Leeds 18; Leicester 10; Liverpool 9; Liverpool John Moores 6; London (LSE) (Gov) 17, (Gov Econ) 10, (Gov Hist) 17, (QM) 10, (SOAS) 5; London Met 5; Loughborough 4; Newcastle 9; Northampton 4; Nottingham 12; Nottingham Trent 3; Oxford (PPE) 7; Oxford Brookes 12; Portsmouth 6; Salford 7; Southampton 10; Staffordshire 10; Stirling 9; Swansea 3; Warwick 10; York 8.

Advice to applicants and planning the UCAS personal statement Study the workings of government in the UK, Europe and other areas of the world, such as the Middle East, the Far East, America and Russia. Describe visits to the Houses of Commons and Lords and the debates taking place. Attend council meetings – county, town, district, village halls. Describe these visits and agendas. Read current affairs avidly. Be aware of political developments in the major countries (UK, Europe, USA, China, Korea, and Russia and the Commonwealth of Independent States). Keep abreast of developments in theatres of war. Explain your interests in detail. **Aberystwyth** We look for degree candidates with a strong interest in political and social issues and who want to inquire into the way in which the world is organised politically, socially and economically. **De Montfort** Demonstration of active interest in current affairs and some understanding of how politics affects our daily lives.

Misconceptions about this course Aberystwyth Many students believe that they need to study politics at A-level for Politics courses – this is not the case. **Cardiff (UWIC)** Some consider that Politics is a narrow subject, only relevant to those who want a political career. **De Montfort** Some applicants believe that a Politics course only covers the mechanics of government and parliament.

Selection interviews **Yes** Bath (mature students), Birmingham, Cambridge, Durham, Exeter, Huddersfield, Hull, Leeds (Pol Parl St), Leicester, Liverpool, London (Gold), (SOAS), London Met, London South Bank, Nottingham, Oxford, Portsmouth, Sheffield, Sussex, Swansea, Ulster, Warwick; **Some** Aberystwyth, Bristol, Cardiff (UWIC), De Montfort, Dundee, Liverpool John Moores, London (LSE), Loughborough, Salford, Staffordshire, York.

Interview advice and questions Questions may stem from A/AS-level studies but applicants will also be expected to be up-to-date in their knowledge and opinions of current events. Questions in recent years have included: What constitutes a 'great power'? What is happening at present in the Labour Party? Define capitalism. What is a political decision? How do opinion polls detract from democracy? Is the European Union a good idea? Why? What are the views of the present government on the European Union? What is a 'spin doctor'? Are politicians hypocrites? **De Montfort** Why Politics? What political issues motivate your interests, for example environmentalism, human rights? For PPE course see **Philosophy**. See also **Chapter 7**.

Applicants' impressions (A=Open day; B=Interview day) **Cardiff** (Modn Hist Pol; A) We were shown a video of the University and visited the departments of politics and history and the students' union. It was very informative and interesting. **Exeter** (A) A very well-organised day with lunch and a detailed and well-presented guided tour. **Nottingham** (A) A well-organised and informative Open day. **Oxford (Keble)** (B) I had three one-to-one interviews. In the Politics interview I was asked to name the positions of ten current and former politicians. I also had a difficult written examination with questions based on a specific test, whilst in Philosophy I had to answer questions on work I had previously submitted.

AFTER-RESULTS ADVICE
Offers to applicants repeating A-levels **Higher** Essex, Glasgow, Leeds, Newcastle, Nottingham, Warwick, York; **Possibly higher** Hull, Lancaster, Oxford Brookes, Swansea; **Same** Aberystwyth, Birmingham, Bristol, Buckingham, Cardiff (UWIC), De Montfort, Dundee, Durham, East Anglia, Lancaster, Lincoln, Liverpool Hope, Liverpool John Moores, London (SOAS), London Met, London South Bank, Loughborough, Nottingham Trent, Portsmouth, Richmond (Am Int Univ), Salford, Staffordshire, Stirling, Sussex, Wolverhampton; **No offer made** Cambridge.

GRADUATE DESTINATIONS AND EMPLOYMENT (2005/6 HESA)
Graduates surveyed 3400 **Employed** 1720 **In further study** 645 **Assumed unemployed** 240.

Career note The transferable skills gained in this degree open up a wide range of career opportunities. Graduates seek positions in management, public services and administration and in some cases in political activities.

OTHER DEGREE SUBJECTS FOR CONSIDERATION
Development Studies; Economics; Government; History; International Relations; Public Policy and Administration; Social Policy and Administration; Sociology.

PROPERTY MANAGEMENT/DEVELOPMENT

(including **Estate, Land and Valuation Surveying;** see also **Building Surveying** (under **Building**), **Housing** and **Quantity Surveying**)

Property degree courses cover a wide range of subjects relevant to careers in managing, planning and implementing the development of property and regeneration of cities. Surveying is also a very broad subject (and career) and includes several specialisms, for example building surveying, quantity surveying, land valuation, surveying and architecture: this table focuses on degrees in general surveying, land and valuation surveying.

Useful website www.rics.org/careers.

NB The points totals shown to the left of the institutions are for ease of reference only. It must not be assumed that tariff points are always used by institutions or that they can be substituted for an offer in grades. The level of an offer is not necessarily indicative of the quality of a course.

COURSE OFFERS INFORMATION

Subject requirements/preferences GCSE English and mathematics required and for some institutions, a science subject (for Chartered Surveyor registration). **AL** No subjects specified. **NB** A* grades are likely to form part of university offers in the higher ranges for students applying for places in 2008 for entry in 2009: check websites.

Your target offers

360 pts **Cambridge** – AAA (Lnd Econ)

320 pts **City** – ABB (Rl Est Fin Invest; Law Prop Val) *(IB 32 pts)*
Reading – 320 pts 3AL or 350 pts 3AL+AS (Rl Est; Invest Fin Prop; Rur Prop Mgt)

300 pts **Newcastle** – BBB–BCC (Surv Map Sci)
Oxford Brookes – BBB (Rl Est Mgt)
Ulster – 300 pts (Prop Invest Dev)

280 pts **Kingston** – 280 pts (Rl Est Mgt; Prop Plan Dev) *(IB 28 pts)*
Northumbria – 280 pts (Est Mgt; Plan Dev Surv) *(IB 30 pts)*
Nottingham Trent – 280 pts (Rl Est Mgt; Plan Prop Dev) *(IB 31 pts)*

270 pts **Portsmouth** – 270 pts (Prop Dev; Prop Dev Quant Surv; Prop Mark Des Dev) *(IB 28 pts)*
Sheffield Hallam – 270 pts (Bus Prop Mgt; Prop Dev; Urb Lnd Econ)

260 pts **Anglia Ruskin** – 260 pts (Rl Est Mgt)
Bristol UWE – 260–300 pts (Bus Prop; Prop Mgt Invest; Plan Prop Dev) *(IB 24–28 pts)*
Heriot-Watt – 260 pts (Rl Est Mgt; Plan Prop Dev)
Westminster 260–280 pts (Bus Prop)

240 pts **Aberdeen** – CCC (Prop Spat Plan)
Glasgow Caledonian – CCC (Prop Mgt Val)
London South Bank – 240 pts (Surveying)
Napier – 240 pts (Prop Dev Val)
Robert Gordon – CCC (Surveying)
Salford – 240 pts (Prop Mgt Invest)

220 pts **Royal (CAg)** – 220–240 pts (Prop Agncy Mark)

200 pts **Anglia Ruskin** – 200 pts (Prop Surv)
Bristol UWE – 200–240 pts (Rl Est (Val Mgt))

180 pts **Glamorgan** – 180 pts (Surveying)
Liverpool John Moores – 180 pts (Prop Mgt; Rl Est Mgt; Rl Est Mgt Bus)

160 pts **East London** – 160 pts (Surv courses)
Wolverhampton – 160–220 pts (Prop Ast Mgt; Surv)

140 pts **Harper Adams (UC)** – 140–280 pts (Rur Ent Lnd Mgt)

120 pts **North East Wales (IHE)** – 120–80 pts (Est Agncy; Est Mgt)
Southampton Solent – 120 pts (Prop Dev)

Alternative offers
See **Chapter 8** for grade/point equivalences and related information for the following examinations: Scottish qualifications, the Welsh Baccalaureate, the IB diploma (approximate points shown also in italics in the table of offers), the Irish Leaving Certificate, the European Baccalaureate and the French Baccalaureate.

EXAMPLES OF FOUNDATION DEGREES IN THE SUBJECT FIELD

Anglia Ruskin; Birmingham City; Bradford; Glamorgan; Middlesex; Moulton (Coll); North East Wales (IHE); Northampton; Northumbria; Royal (CAg).

CHOOSING YOUR COURSE (SEE ALSO CH.1)

Course variations – Widen your options
Built and Natural Environment (Bristol UWE)
Environmental Design Management (Nottingham Trent)

For information on how to read the Subject Tables, see **Chapter 8**.

Cities and Environmental Design (Oxford Brookes)
Business Property Management (Sheffield Hallam)
Property Investment (Ulster)
CHECK PROSPECTUSES AND WEBSITES FOR OTHER UNIVERSITIES AND COLLEGES OFFERING THESE COURSES.

Universities and colleges teaching quality See www.qaa.ac.uk; www.unistats.com.

Top universities and colleges (Research) Cambridge.

Sandwich degree courses Bristol UWE; Glasgow Caledonian; Heriot-Watt; Kingston; Northumbria; Portsmouth; Salford; Sheffield Hallam.

ADMISSIONS INFORMATION

Number of applicants per place (approx) Bristol UWE 11; Cambridge 4; City 20; Glamorgan 6; Harper Adams (UC) 4; Heriot-Watt 6; Kingston 22; Liverpool John Moores 15; London South Bank 2; Newcastle 6; North East Wales (IHE) 3; Northumbria 17; Nottingham Trent 3; Portsmouth 5; Royal (CAg) 3; Salford 3; Sheffield Hallam 5; Westminster 10.

Advice to applicants and planning the UCAS personal statement There are different specialisms in this subject area. If you have any special interests, list and discuss them. Give details of all the contacts you have made, especially with, for example, property developers or surveying practices in your locality. Discuss the careers and try to arrange work experience or work shadowing.
Nottingham Trent Candidates should demonstrate that they have researched the employment opportunities in the property and construction sectors and should have sought some practical experience. **Oxford Brookes** (Non-EU students) Written and spoken English must be good.

Misconceptions about this course Students under-estimate the need for numerical competence.

Selection interviews Yes Bristol UWE, Cambridge, Glamorgan, Harper Adams (UC), Heriot-Watt, Newcastle, Royal (CAg); **Some** East London, Nottingham Trent, Salford.

Applicants' impressions (A=Open day; B=Interview day) Cambridge (Land Econ; B) The interview was well organised but I felt under pressure with difficult taxing questions followed by a debate. I didn't meet any students.

Interview advice and questions Some work experience will be expected and questions will be asked on the applicants' course and career interests. **Cambridge** Questions on subsidies and the euro, economics, dynamic efficiency. Who owns London? How important is the modern-day church in town planning? How important are natural resources to a country? Is it more important to focus on poverty at home or abroad? Is the environment a bigger crisis than poverty? Do you think that getting involved with poverty abroad is interfering with others' 'freedoms'? (Questions based on information given in the personal statement.) See **Chapter 7**.

Reasons for rejection (non-academic) Nottingham Trent Incoherent and badly written application forms.

AFTER-RESULTS ADVICE

Offers to applicants repeating A-levels Same Nottingham Trent, Salford.

GRADUATE DESTINATIONS AND EMPLOYMENT (2005/6 HESA)

No data available.

Career note Property development is a rapidly expanding field and attracts graduates from a range of disciplines. These courses, however, provide exemptions in many cases from the examinations of the Royal Institution of Chartered Surveyors, opening up a wide range of opportunities.

OTHER DEGREE SUBJECTS FOR CONSIDERATION

Architecture; Building Surveying; Civil Engineering; Construction; Estate Management; Housing; Quantity Surveying; Town Planning; Urban Studies.

PSYCHOLOGY

(including **Behavioural Science, Cognitive Sciences, Counselling** and **Neuroscience;** see also **Biological Sciences**)

Psychology is a very popular subject, with the number of applications rising by 40,000 in the last ten years. The study attracts three times more women than men. It covers studies in development, behaviour, perception, memory, language, learning, personality as well as social relationships and abnormal psychology. Psychology is a science and you will be involved in experimentation and statistical analysis. The degree is usually offered as a BSc or a BA course and there are many similarities between them. The differences are in the elective subjects which can be taken in the second and third years. It is not a training to enable you to psycho-analyse your friends – psychology is not the same as psychiatry!

To qualify as a chartered psychologist (for which a postgraduate qualification is required) it is necessary to obtain a first degree (or equivalent) qualification which gives eligibility for both Graduate Membership (GM) **and** the Graduate Basis for Registration (GBR) of the British Psychological Society (BPS). A full list of courses accredited by the British Psychological Society can be viewed at www.bps.org.uk/careers/accredited-courses/accreditedcourses_ home.cfm. The Society also publishes a booklet *So You Want to be a Psychologist*? which can be downloaded from www.bps.org.uk/careers/careers_home.cfm. Full details about careers in psychology can also be obtained from the British Psychological Society (see **Appendix 2**).

Behavioural Science covers the study of animal and human behaviour and offers an overlap between Zoology, Sociology, Psychology and Biological Sciences. Psychology, however, also crosses over into Education, Management Sciences, Human Resource Management, Counselling, Public Relations, Advertising, Artificial Intelligence, Marketing, Sales and Social Studies.

Useful websites www.psychology.org; www.bps.org.uk; www.socialpsychology.org; www.psych-central.com.

NB The points totals shown to the left of the institutions are for ease of reference only. It must not be assumed that tariff points are always used by institutions or that they can be substituted for an offer in grades. The level of an offer is not necessarily indicative of the quality of a course.

COURSE OFFERS INFORMATION

Subject requirements/preferences GCSE English, mathematics and a science. **AL** A science subject is usually required. **NB** A* grades are likely to form part of university offers in the higher ranges for students applying for places in 2008 for entry in 2009: check websites.

Your target offers

360 pts and above

Bath – AAAb–AAA (Psychology) *(IB 36 pts)*
Cambridge – AAA (Nat Sci (Psy)) *(IB 38–42 pts)*
Cardiff – AAA (Psy; App Psy; Psy Crim; Educ Psy)
Durham – AAA (Nat Sci (Psy)) *(IB 38–40 pts)*
Exeter – AAA–AAB (Psychology)
London (UCL) – AAAe–AABe (Psychology) *(IB 36–38 pts)*
Oxford – Offers vary eg AAA–AAB (Expmtl Psy; Psy Phil; Physiol Psy) *(IB 38–40 pts)*
Reading – AAA–AAB (Psy Chld Age; Psy (Mntl Phys Hlth))
Warwick – AABb (Phil Psy) *(IB 36 pts)*
Warwick – ABBb–BBBb (Psychology)

340 pts **Birmingham** – AAB–ABB (Psychology) *(IB 34 pts)*
Bristol – AAB–ABB (Psy; Psy Phil; Psy Zool) *(IB 34–36 pts)*
Durham – AAB (Psy Comb Soc Sci; Comb Arts; Psy; Phil Psy) *(IB 36 pts)*
Leeds – AAB–ABB (Psy; Cog Sci) *(IB 35 pts)*
Leicester – AAB–ABB (Psy courses) *(IB 33 pts)*

London (RH) – AAB–ABB (Psy; Maths Psy; Mus Psy; Biol Psy)
Loughborough – AAB (Psy; Psy Ergon)
Manchester – AAB–ABB (Psychology)
Newcastle – AAB–ABB (Psy; Psy Stats; Maths Psy) *(IB 34 pts)*
Nottingham – AAB (Psy; Psy Phil; Psy Cog Neuro) *(IB 36 pts)*
Queen's Belfast – AAB–ABBb (Psychology)
Reading – 340 pts (Psy; Art Psy; Psy Phil; Psy Biol; Maths Psy)
St Andrews – AAB (Psy courses) *(IB 36 pts)*
Sheffield – AAB (Psy; Phil Psy) *(IB 35 pts)*
Southampton – AAB 340 pts (Psychology)
Strathclyde – AAB–BBB (Biomed Sci Psy)
Sussex – AAB–ABB (Psy; Psy Am St; Psy Cog Sci; Psy Sociol; Psy Neuro) *(IB 34–36 pts)*
York – AAB–ABB (Psychology) *(IB 36 pts)*

320 pts **Aston** – ABB 320 pts (Bus Hum Psy)
Cardiff – ABB (Physiol Psy) *(IB 33 pts)*
City – ABB (Psychology)
Durham – ABB (Educ St (Psy))
Glasgow – ABB–BBB (BA Psy) *(IB 30 pts)*
Kent – 320 pts (App Soc Psy Clin Psy; App Psy Clin Psy; Psy Clin Psy; Soc Psy Clin Psy) *(IB 35 pts)*
Lancaster – ABB–BBB (Psy; Psy Educ; Fr St Psy; Ger St Psy; Ital St Psy; Span St Psy; Org St Psy) *(IB 30 pts)*
Leeds – ABB (Psy Sociol) *(IB 35 pts)*
Liverpool – ABB 320 pts (Psychology)
London (LSE) – ABB approx (Soc Psy – optional subject, check with admissions tutor)
Loughborough – ABB (Soc Psy)
Oxford Brookes – ABB offers vary depending on 2nd subj (Psy Comb courses)
Surrey – ABB (Psychology) *(IB 32 pts)*

300 pts **Aston** – BBB 300 pts (Psy courses except under **320 pts**) *(IB 32 pts)*
Bangor – 300–260 pts (Psy; Psy Neuropsy; Psy Clin Hlth Psy; Psy Chld Lang Dev; Psy joint courses) *(IB 28 pts)*
Brighton – 300 pts (App Psy Sociol; Crim App Psy; Pol App Psy) *(IB 28 pts)*
Bristol – BBB (Neuroscience)
Brunel – 300 pts (Psy; Psy Soc Anth; Psy Sociol)
City – BBB (Jrnl Psy)
Dundee – BBB 300 pts (MA Psy 3 yr; BSc Psy 3 yr)
Durham (Stockton) – BBB (App Psy)
East Anglia – BBB (Psysoc Sci) *(IB 32 pts)*
Edinburgh – BBB (Psy; Psy Bus St; Psy Ling) *(IB 34 pts)*
Essex – 300 pts (Psy; Soc Psy Sociol) *(IB 29 pts)*
Keele – BBB **or** 300 pts (Psy courses)
Kent – BBB 300 pts (Psy; Euro Soc Psy; App Psy; App Soc Psy; Psy (Euro); Soc Psy)
Lancaster – BBB (Biol Psy; Psy Stats)
Leeds – BBB (Neuroscience)
London (Hey) – 300–340 pts (Psy Phil)
Manchester Met – 300 pts (Psy Sp Path)
Newcastle – BBB (Biol Psy)
Northumbria – 300 pts (Psy; Psy Spo Sci) *(IB 32 pts)*
Oxford Brookes – BBB **or** BBbb (Psychology)
Portsmouth – 300 pts (Psy; Foren Psy; Psy Crim) *(IB 30 pts)*
Sheffield Hallam – 300 pts (Psychology)
Stirling – BBB 2nd yr entry (Psychology)
Surrey – BBB–BBC (App Psy Sociol)
Swansea – 300–320 pts (Psy; Psy Law)
Ulster – 300–240 pts (Psy courses)

For a quick reference offers calculator, fold out the inside back cover.

Westminster – BBB (Psychology)

280 pts **Coventry** – 280 pts (Psychology)

Glasgow – BBC–BCC (BSc Psy; Neuro)

Hertfordshire – 280 pts (Psychology)

Hull – BBC–BCC 280–260 pts (Psy; Psy Cnslg; Psy Crim; Psy Phil; Psy Sociol; Psy Spo Sci)

Lincoln – BBC 280 pts (Psychology)

London (Gold) – BBC (Psychology) *(IB 30 pts)*

Manchester Met – 280 pts (Psychology)

Nottingham Trent – BBC 280 pts (Psy; Psy Crim; Psy Educ Dev; Psy Sociol)

Salford – BBC (Psychology)

Southampton – 280–330 pts (App Soc Sci (Crim Psy St))

Sheffield – BBC–BB+bc (Hum Comm Sci)

260 pts **Bournemouth** – 260 pts (Spo Psy Coach Sci)

Bristol UWE – 260–300 pts (Psychology) *(IB 24–28 pts)*

Central Lancashire – 260 pts (Psy; App Psy; Neuropsy)

Coventry – 260 pts (Psy joint courses)

Kingston – BCC 260 pts (Psychology) *(IB 30 pts)*

Liverpool John Moores – 260 pts (App Psy)

London (Hey) – 260–300 pts (Psy Theol)

Richmond (Am Int Univ) – 260 pts (Soc Sci (Psy))

Salford – 260–280 pts (Psy St Cnslg St; Psy St Hlth Sci) *(IB 27 pts)*

Stirling – BCC 1st yr entry (Psy courses)

Strathclyde – BCC/BB (Psy courses except under **340 pts**)

240 pts **Aberdeen** – CCC (Neuro Psy; Psy courses))

Birmingham City – 240 pts (Psy courses)

Bolton – 240 pts (Psy; Cnslg Psy; Crim Foren Psy; Spo Exer Psy)

For information on how to read the Subject Tables, see **Chapter 8**.

Bradford – 240 pts (Psy courses)
Bristol UWE – 240–300 pts (Psy Foren Sci; Psy joint Hons)
Buckingham – 240 pts (Mark Psy)
Chester – 240 pts (Psy; Cnslg Sk Psy)
City – 240–260 pts (Sociol Psy)
Dundee – CCC 240 pts (MA Psy 4 yr; BSc Psy 4 yr)
Edge Hill – 240 pts (Psychology)
Glasgow Caledonian – CCC (Psy courses)
Heriot-Watt – CCC 240 pts (Spo Exer Sci Psy; Maths Psy; App Psy)
Huddersfield – 240 pts (Psy; Spo Exer Sci Psy; Psy Cnslg)
Keele – 240–260 pts (Neuroscience)
Liverpool Hope – 240 pts (Psychology)
London Met – 240 pts (Psy; Hlth St Psy)
Nottingham Trent – 240 pts (Psy Spo Sci)
Portsmouth – 240–300 pts (Engl Psy; Mark Psy; HR Mgt Psy) *(IB 30 pts)*
Queen Margaret – CCC 240 pts (Hlth Psy; Psy)
Sheffield Hallam – 240 pts (Psy Sociol)
Swansea – 240–300 pts (Psy joint courses)
Teesside – 240 pts (Psy; Foren Psy; Hlth Psy; Spo Exer Psy; Psy Crim)
Thames Valley – 240 pts (Psychology)
Winchester – 240–220 pts (Psy courses)

220 pts **Anglia Ruskin** – 220–260 pts (Psy courses)
Bath Spa – 220–260 pts (Psychology)
Central Lancashire – 220–240 pts (Psy courses except undere **260** pts)
Glamorgan – 220–260 pts (Psychology)
Hertfordshire – 220–260 pts (Psy courses except under **280 pts**)
Kingston – 220–280 pts (Psy joint courses)
Liverpool John Moores – 220 pts (Psy Biol; Psy Foren Sci)
Nottingham Trent – 220 pts (Eqn Spo Sci (Eqstrn Psy))
Plymouth – 220–280 pts (3AL) 220 pts (2AL) (Psy courses)
Queen Margaret – CCD 220 pts (Psy Media; Psy Sociol; PR Psy)
Sunderland – 220 pts (Psychology)
Winchester – 220 pts (Psy Comb courses)
Wolverhampton – 220–240 pts (Psy; Cnslg Psy; Ling Psy)

200 pts **Anglia Ruskin** – 200 pts (Psysoc St)
Birmingham City – 200 pts (Bus Psy courses)
Buckingham – 200 pts (Psy courses except under **240 pts**)
Cardiff (UWIC) – 200 pts (Consum Nutr Psy)
Chichester – 200–260 pts (Spo Exer Psy)
Cumbria – 200 pts (App Psy)
Dundee – BB (BSc Psy)
Gloucestershire – 200–280 pts (Psychology)
Greenwich – 200–180 pts (Psychology)
Huddersfield – 200 pts (Bhv Sci)
Middlesex – 200–220 pts (Psychology)
Napier – 200 pts (Psy; Psy Sociol; Spo Psy)
Newport – 200 pts (Psy courses)
Southampton Solent – 200 pts (Psychology)
Staffordshire – 200–280 pts (Psy; Psy Sociol; Spo Exer Psy)
York St John – 200 pts (Cnslg St Psy)

190 pts **London Met** – 190–240 pts (Bus Psy)
180 pts **Bedfordshire** – 180–240 pts (Psy; App Psy; Hlth Psy; Psy Crim Bhv; Psy St)
Bournemouth – 180–240 pts (Psy Comp)
De Montfort – 180 pts (Psy joint courses)
East London – 180 pts (Psy; Psy Crim; Psy Hlth St)

Northampton – 180–200 pts (Psy joint courses)
York St John – 180 pts (Psychology)
160 pts Abertay Dundee – 160–180 pts (Psy; Bhv Sci; Foren Psychobiol)
Canterbury Christ Church – CC (Psy courses)
Derby – 160–240 pts (Psy courses)
East London – 160 pts (Psysoc St)
Leeds Trinity and All Saints (Coll) – 160–240 pts (Psy courses)
London South Bank – CC **or** Ccc (Psy courses)
Middlesex – 160–200 pts (Psy joint courses)
Newman (UC) – CC 160 pts (Psy courses; Soc App Psy courses)
Norwich City (Coll) – 160–240 pts (Psy courses)
Roehampton – 160–180 pts (Psy Cnslg; Psy; Psy Hlth)
St Mary's (UC) – 160–200 pts (Psy courses)
Worcester – 160–120 pts (Psy courses)
140 pts Suffolk (Univ Campus) – 140–200 pts (Psy Sociol)
West Scotland – CD–DD (Psychology)
120 pts Bradford (Coll) – 120 pts (Cnslg Psy Commun Set)
Bucks New – 120–240 pts (Psy courses)
Cardiff (UWIC) – 120 pts (Psy Hum Biol)
Grimsby (IFHE) – 120–240 pts (Sociol Psy; Bus Psy)
North East Wales (IHE) – 120 pts (Psychology)
100 pts Swansea (Inst) – 100–160 pts (Psy courses)
80 pts East Lancashire (IHE) – 80–120 pts (App Psy)
London (Birk) – 80 pts for under 21s (over 21s varies) (p/t Psychology)
West Anglia (Coll) – 80–180 pts (Psysoc St)

Leeds Met – contact University
Open University – contact University

Alternative offers
See **Chapter 8** for grade/point equivalences and related information for the following examinations: Scottish qualifications, the Welsh Baccalaureate, the IB diploma (approximate points shown also in italics in the table of offers), the Irish Leaving Certificate, the European Baccalaureate and the French Baccalaureate.

EXAMPLES OF FOUNDATION DEGREES IN THE SUBJECT FIELD
Bedford (Coll); Bournemouth and Poole (Coll); Leicester; Milton Keynes (Coll); North Devon (Coll).

CHOOSING YOUR COURSE (SEE ALSO CH.1)
Course variations – Widen your options
Animal Behaviour and Psychology (Anglia Ruskin)
Sport Psychology and Coaching Science (Bournemouth)
Applied Criminal Justice Studies (Bradford)
Artificial Intelligence and Psychology (Bristol UWE)
Applied Psychology (Cardiff)
Consumer and Nutritional Psychology (Cardiff (UWIC))
Neuroscience (Edinburgh)
Health, Community, Social Care and Psychology (Gloucestershire)
Criminology and Psychology (Kingston)
Psychology and Ergonomics (Loughborough)
Psychology and Marketing (Middlesex)
Human Communication Studies (Sheffield)
Human Resource Management and Psychology (Stirling)
Health Psychology (Teesside)
Counselling Studies and Psychology (York St John)
CHECK PROSPECTUSES AND WEBSITES FOR OTHER UNIVERSITIES AND COLLEGES OFFERING THESE COURSES.

Universities and colleges teaching quality See www.qaa.ac.uk; www.unistats.com.

Top universities and colleges (Research) Aston; Bangor*; Birmingham*; Bristol*; Cambridge*; Cardiff*; Durham; Edinburgh; Essex; Exeter; Glasgow*; Lancaster; Leeds; London (Birk), (RH), (UCL)*; Manchester; Newcastle*; Nottingham; Oxford*; Plymouth; Reading*; St Andrews*; Sheffield; Southampton; Stirling; Surrey; Sussex; Warwick; York*.

Sandwich degree courses Aston; Bath; Birmingham City; Bournemouth; Bristol UWE; Brunel; Cardiff; Hertfordshire; Huddersfield; Kent; Lancaster; London Met; Loughborough; Manchester; Manchester Met; Middlesex; Oxford Brookes; Portsmouth; Queen Margaret; Surrey; Ulster; West Scotland; Wolverhampton.

ADMISSIONS INFORMATION

Number of applicants per place (approx) Abertay Dundee 5; Aston 6; Bangor 5; Bath 4; Birmingham 9; Bolton 5; Bournemouth 4; Bradford 14; Bradford (Coll) 2; Bristol 17; Bristol UWE 12; Brunel 20; Buckingham 1; Cardiff 10; Cardiff (UWIC) 5; Central Lancashire 13; Chester 20; City 6; Coventry 7; De Montfort 10; Derby 6; Dundee 6; Durham 20; East Anglia (Psysoc St) 6; Exeter 14; Glamorgan 6; Glasgow Caledonian 15; Gloucestershire 50; Greenwich 8; Hertfordshire 22; Huddersfield 3; Hull 14; Kent 15; Lancaster 20; Leeds 12; Leeds Trinity and All Saints (Coll) 13; Leicester 22; Liverpool 21; Liverpool John Moores 8; London (RH) 10, (UCL) 18; London South Bank 7; Loughborough 8; Manchester Met 27; Manchester Met/Manchester (CAT) (Psy p/t) 2; Middlesex 10; Napier 6; Newcastle 20; Newman (UC) 3; Northampton 4; Northumbria 2; Nottingham 27; Nottingham Trent 3; Oxford (success rate 23%); Oxford Brookes 29; Plymouth 5; Portsmouth 10; Roehampton 7; Salford 4; Sheffield 12; Sheffield Hallam 10; Southampton 10; Staffordshire 6; Stirling 9; Surrey 10; Sussex 5; Swansea 7; Teesside 10; Warwick 13; Westminster 6; Worcester 9; York 9; York St John 3.

Number of applicants (a UK b EU (non-UK) c non-EU d mature) Aston a800 b100 c70 d90; Bradford ab200 c20; Bristol ab1421 c91 d156; Derby a407 b152 c5; Leeds a1758 b36 c37 d165; London (UCL) abc 1500; Manchester Met/Manchester (CAT) abc14 d14; Swansea ab800 c50.

Advice to applicants and planning the UCAS personal statement Psychology is heavily oversubscribed so prepare well in advance by choosing suitable AS- and A-level subjects. Contact the Education and Social Services departments in your local authority office to arrange meetings with psychologists to gain a knowledge of the work. Make notes during those meetings and of any work experience gained and describe these fully on the UCAS application. English language courses available for non-EU students. **Bangor** Evidence of interest in caring-type work including voluntary or paid experience. **Birmingham** A science subject is desirable but not required. **East Anglia** (Psysoc St) For students wishing to study psychology as a research-based discipline, but not wishing to become psychologists. **Keele** Reference to introductory reading in psychology (many students have a distorted image of it). **Liverpool John Moores** Applicants studying AS psychology are more likely to receive an offer but must achieve grade C. **London (UCL)** Special provision is made for candidates over 21 who make up about 10% of the intake. **Manchester Met** Use UCAS application section 10 well. (Psy Sp Path) Observations with speech therapists working with children and adults. **St Andrews** Evidence of interest. Reasons for choosing the course. **Sheffield Hallam** Interest in psychology, preferably demonstrated through voluntary or other work experience. See also **Appendix 2**.

Misconceptions about this course Some believe a Psychology course will train them as therapists or counsellors – it will not. **Bath** They think that they are going to learn about themselves. **Birmingham** Some applicants underestimate the scientific nature of the course. **Exeter** It's scientific! **Lincoln** Applicants should be aware that this is a science-based course. Academic psychology is an empirical science requiring research methodologies and statistical analysis. **Reading** Not all applicants are aware that it is a science-based course and are surprised at the high science and statistics content. **Sussex** Applicants should note that the BSc course is not harder than the BA course. Many students mistakenly believe that psychology consists of counselling and that there is no maths. Psychology is a science. **York** Some students think psychology means Freud which it hasn't done for 50 years or more. They do not realise that psychology is a science in the same vein as biology, chemistry or physics. Only 20 per cent of Psychology graduates become professional psychologists. This involves taking a postgraduate degree in a specialist area of psychology.

Selection interviews **Yes** Blackpool and Fylde (Coll), Bolton, Brunel, Buckingham, Cambridge, Durham, Glamorgan, Glasgow Caledonian, Leeds Trinity and All Saints (Coll), London (UCL) 300 out of 1500 applicants, London Met, London South Bank, Middlesex, Newcastle, Northampton, Norwich City (Coll), Oxford, Oxford Brookes, Plymouth, Swansea; **Some** Aston, Bangor, Bristol, Cardiff, Derby (non-standard applications), Dundee, East Anglia, Exeter (mature students), Huddersfield (mature students), Keele, Leeds (mature students), Liverpool John Moores, Nottingham Trent (for non-standard applications), Roehampton, Salford, Sunderland.

Interview advice and questions Although some applicants will have studied the subject at A-level and will have a broad understanding of its coverage, it is still essential to have gained some work experience or to have discussed the career with a professional psychologist. Questions will be asked relevant to this experience and in previous years these have included: What have you read about psychology? What do you expect to gain by studying psychology? What are your parents' and teachers' views on your choice of subject? Are you interested in any particular branch of the subject? Is psychology an art or a science? Do you think you are well suited to this course? Why? Do you think it is possible that if we learn enough about the functioning of the brain we can create a computer that is functionally the same? What is counselling? Is it necessary? Know the differences between the various branches of psychology and discuss any specific interests, for example, in clinical, occupational, educational, criminal psychology and cognitive, neuro-, social or physiological psychology. What influences young children's food choices? What stereotypes do we have of people with mental illness? **Bangor** Each application is treated individually and considered on its own merits. **Oxford** Ability to evaluate evidence and to have the capacity for logical and creative thinking. See **Chapter 7**.

Reasons for rejection (non-academic) Lack of background reading and lack of awareness of psychology; poor communication skills; misunderstanding of what is involved in a degree course. Poor personal statement. Poor grades, especially in GCSE maths. **Exeter** Competition for places – we can select those with exceptional grades. **Sheffield** Poor predicted grades. **Surrey** Inarticulate. **Warwick** (BSc) Lack of science background.

AFTER-RESULTS ADVICE

Offers to applicants repeating A-levels **Higher** Birmingham, City, Loughborough, Newcastle, Portsmouth, Southampton, Swansea, Warwick, York; **Possibly higher** Aston, Northampton; **Same** Aston (Comb Hons), Bangor, Blackpool and Fylde (Coll), Bolton, Brunel, Cardiff, Cardiff (UWIC), Chester, Derby, Dundee, Durham, East Anglia, Huddersfield, Hull, Lincoln, Liverpool Hope, Liverpool John Moores, London (RH), London South Bank, Manchester Met, Newman (UC), Nottingham, Nottingham Trent, Oxford Brookes, Roehampton, St Mary's (UC), Salford, Sheffield Hallam, Staffordshire, Stirling, Suffolk (Univ Campus), Sunderland, Surrey, Thames Valley, Ulster, Wolverhampton, York St John; **No offers made** Cambridge.

GRADUATE DESTINATIONS AND EMPLOYMENT (2005/6 HESA)

Graduates surveyed 7840 **Employed** 3940 **In further study** 1260 **Assumed unemployed** 445.

Career note Clinical, educational and occupational psychology are the three main specialist careers for graduate psychologists, all involving further study. Ergonomics, human computer interaction, marketing, public relations, human resource management, advertising, the social services, the prison and rehabilitation services also provide alternative career routes.

OTHER DEGREE SUBJECTS FOR CONSIDERATION

Anthropology; Behavioural Science; Cognitive Sciences; Education; Health Studies; Neuroscience; Sociology

For information on how to read the Subject Tables, see **Chapter 8**.

QUANTITY SURVEYING

Quantity Surveying is a specialised field of surveying which focuses on the costing of the built environment. Students are introduced to construction studies, measurement cost studies, economics and law. The work is similar, in some aspects, to the work of an accountant and requires the same attention to detail. See also **Architecture**, **Building** and **Surveying** courses.

Useful website www.rics.org/careers.

NB The points totals shown to the left of the institutions are for ease of reference only. It must not be assumed that tariff points are always used by institutions or that they can be substituted for an offer in grades. The level of an offer is not necessarily indicative of the quality of a course.

COURSE OFFERS INFORMATION

Subject requirements/preferences **GCSE** English and mathematics grade A–C. **AL** No subjects specified; mathematics useful. **NB** A* grades are likely to form part of university offers in the higher ranges for students applying for places in 2008 for entry in 2009: check websites.

Your target offers

320 pts **Ulster** – 320 pts (Quant Surv)

300 pts **Loughborough** – 300 pts (Commer Mgt Quant Surv) *(IB 30 pts)*

280 pts **Kingston** – 280 pts (Quant Surv) *(IB 28 pts)*
Northumbria – 280 pts (Quant Surv) *(IB 26 pts)*

270 pts **Glasgow Caledonian** – 270 pts (Quant Surv)
Portsmouth – 270 pts (Prop Dev Quant Surv)
Sheffield Hallam – 270 pts (Quant Surv)

260 pts **Anglia Ruskin** – 260 pts (Quant Surv; Constr Econ Mgt)
Birmingham City – 260 pts (Quant Surv)
Heriot-Watt – 260 pts (Quant Surv courses) *(IB 29 pts)*
Reading – 260–280 pts (Quant Surv)

240 pts **Central Lancashire** – 240 pts (Commer Mgt Quant Surv)
Napier – 240 pts (Quant Surv)
Robert Gordon – CCC (Surv (Quant Surv))
Salford – 240 pts (Quant Surv)
Westminster – CCC (Quant Surv)

230 pts **Bristol UWE** – 230–290 pts (Quant Surv Commer Mgt) *(IB 24–28 pts)*
Liverpool John Moores – 230 pts (Quant Surv)
Reading – 230 pts (d/l Quant Surv)

220 pts **Bolton** – 220 pts (Quant Surv Commer Mgt)
Nottingham Trent – 220–280 pts (Quant Surv courses) *(IB 31 pts)*

180 pts **Birmingham City** – 180 pts (Constr Quant Surv)
Glamorgan – 180 pts (Quant Surv)
Greenwich – 180 pts min (Quant Surv)

160 pts **London South Bank** – CC (Commer Mgt (Quant Surv))
Wolverhampton – 160–220 pts (Quant Surv)

Leeds Met – contact University

Alternative offers

See **Chapter 8** for grade/point equivalences and related information for the following examinations: Scottish qualifications, the Welsh Baccalaureate, the IB diploma (approximate points shown also in italics in the table of offers), the Irish Leaving Certificate, the European Baccalaureate and the French Baccalaureate.

EXAMPLES OF FOUNDATION DEGREES IN THE SUBJECT FIELD

Adam Smith (Coll); Anglia Ruskin; Bolton; Manchester (CAT); Northumbria; Swansea (Inst).

CHOOSING YOUR COURSE (SEE ALSO CH.1)

Course variations – Widen your options
Construction Economics and Management (Anglia Ruskin)
Commercial Management and Quantity Surveying (Loughborough)
Quantity Surveying and Construction Commercial Management (Nottingham Trent)
Property Development and Quantity Surveying (Portsmouth)
CHECK PROSPECTUSES AND WEBSITES FOR OTHER UNIVERSITIES AND COLLEGES OFFERING THESE COURSES.

Universities and colleges teaching quality See www.qaa.ac.uk; www.unistats.com.

Top universities and colleges (Research) Salford.

Sandwich degree courses Birmingham City; Glasgow Caledonian; Greenwich; Kingston; Leeds Met; Napier; Nottingham Trent; Robert Gordon; Salford; Sheffield Hallam; Ulster; Wolverhampton.

ADMISSIONS INFORMATION

Number of applicants per place (approx) Anglia Ruskin 2; Birmingham City 14; Glamorgan 4; Glasgow Caledonian 3; Greenwich 11; Kingston 13; Liverpool John Moores 10; Loughborough 9; Napier 2; Northumbria 11; Nottingham Trent 10; Robert Gordon 5; Salford 16; Sheffield Hallam 7; Wolverhampton 6.

Advice to applicants and planning the UCAS personal statement Surveyors work with architects and builders as well as in their own consultancies and these organisations should be approached to discuss quantity surveying or to obtain work experience. Explain your interests fully. Read *The Chartered Quantity Surveyor* magazine. See also **Appendix 2**.

Selection interviews Yes Birmingham City, Glamorgan, Glasgow Caledonian, Heriot-Watt, Kingston, Liverpool John Moores, Nottingham Trent, Robert Gordon, Ulster.

Interview advice and questions Past questions have included: What is quantity surveying? What is the scope of the work? How do you qualify to do this work? Have you spoken to a quantity surveyor or spent any time in a quantity surveyor's office? See **Chapter 7**.

AFTER-RESULTS ADVICE

Offers to applicants repeating A-levels Higher Bolton, Nottingham Trent; **Possibly higher** Glamorgan, Liverpool John Moores; **Same** Salford.

GRADUATE DESTINATIONS AND EMPLOYMENT (2005/6 HESA)

No data available.

Career note See **Building** and **Property Management**.

OTHER DEGREE SUBJECTS FOR CONSIDERATION

Architectural Technology; Architecture; Building; Civil Engineering; Construction Management; Surveying.

RADIOGRAPHY

(including **Medical Imaging** and **Radiotherapy;** see also **Health Sciences/Studies**)

Many institutions offer both Diagnostic and Therapeutic Radiography but applicants should check this, and course entry requirements, before applying. Information on courses is also available from the Society of Radiographers (see **Appendix 2**). **Diagnostic Radiography** The demonstration on film (or other imaging materials) of the position and structure of the body's organs using radiation or other imaging media. **Therapeutic Radiography** The planning and administration of treatment for patients suffering from malignant and non-malignant disease using different forms of radiation. Courses lead to state registration.

Useful websites www.sor.org; www.radiographycareers.co.uk; www.nhscareers.nhs.uk.

NB The points totals shown to the left of the institutions are for ease of reference only. It must not be assumed that tariff points are always used by institutions or that they can be substituted for an offer in grades. The level of an offer is not necessarily indicative of the quality of a course.

COURSE OFFERS INFORMATION

Subject requirements/preferences GCSE Five subjects including English, mathematics and a science subject (usually at one sitting). **AL** One or two sciences required; mathematics may be acceptable. (Radiotherapy) One science subject required for some courses. **NB** A* grades are likely to form part of university offers in the higher ranges for students applying for places in 2008 for entry in 2009: check websites. **Other requirements** Applicants required to have an occupational health check and a Criminal Records Bureau (CRB) clearance.

Your target offers

300 pts	**Cumbria** – 300 pts (Diag Radiog)
	Portsmouth – 300 pts (Radiog (Diag) (Ther))
	Ulster – BBB 300 pts (Radiography) *(IB 25 pts)* (See **Ch.7**)
280 pts	**Bradford** – 280 pts (Diag Radiog)
	Salford – 280 pts (Diag Radiog) *(IB 30 pts)*
260 pts	**Cardiff** – BCC (Radiog (Diag Imag); Radiothera Onc) *(IB 24 pts)*
	Exeter – BCC 240 pts (Med Imag (Diag Radiog)) *(IB 25 pts)*
	Glasgow Caledonian – BCC (Rdtn Onc Sci; Diag Imag Sci)
240 pts	**Leeds** – CCC (Radiog (Diag))
	Liverpool – 240 pts (Diag Radiog; Radiothera) *(IB 26 pts)*
	Robert Gordon – 240 pts (Diag Radiog)
	Teesside – 240–320 pts (Diag Radiog)
220 pts	**Bangor** – CCD 240–260 pts (Diag Radiog Imag) *(IB 28 pts)*
	Birmingham City – 220 pts (Radiothera; Diag Radiog)
	Hertfordshire – 220 pts (Diag Radiog Imag; Radiothera Onc)
	London (St George's) – 220–240 pts (Diag Radiog; Ther Radiog)
200 pts	**Derby** – 200 pts (Diag Radiog)
180 pts	**Queen Margaret** – 180 pts (Diag Radiog; Ther Radiog)
160 pts	**Anglia Ruskin** – 160 pts (Radiog (Diag Imag))
	Bristol UWE – 160–200 pts (Diag Imag; Radiothera) *(IB 24 pts)*
	Canterbury Christ Church – CC (Diag Radiog)
	City – CC (Radiog (Diag) (Ther))
	London South Bank – CC–Ccc (Diag Imag (Radiog))
	Sheffield Hallam – 160 pts (Diag Radiog; Radiothera Onc)
	Suffolk (Univ Campus) – 160–180 pts (Diag Radiog; Onc Radiothera Tech)

Alternative offers

See **Chapter 8** for grade/point equivalences and related information for the following examinations: Scottish qualifications, the Welsh Baccalaureate, the IB diploma (approximate points shown also in italics in the table of offers), the Irish Leaving Certificate, the European Baccalaureate and the French Baccalaureate.

EXAMPLES OF FOUNDATION DEGREES IN THE SUBJECT FIELD

Anglia Ruskin; Leicester; Liverpool John Moores; Portsmouth; Salford.

CHOOSING YOUR COURSE (SEE ALSO CH.1)

Course variations – Widen your options

Diagnostic Imaging (Bristol UWE; London South Bank)
Radiotherapy (Birmingham City; Bristol UWE; Liverpool)
Oncology and Radiotherapy Technology (Suffolk (Univ Campus))
See also **Health Sciences/Studies**
CHECK PROSPECTUSES AND WEBSITES FOR OTHER UNIVERSITIES AND COLLEGES OFFERING THESE COURSES.

For a quick reference offers calculator, fold out the inside back cover.

Universities and colleges teaching quality See www.qaa.ac.uk; www.unistats.com.

ADMISSIONS INFORMATION

Number of applicants per place (approx) Bangor 7; Birmingham City (Radiothera) 8; Bradford 8; Cardiff 3; Derby 6; Glasgow Caledonian 7; Hertfordshire (Diag Radiog Imag) 8; Leeds 10; Liverpool 13; London (St George's) 7; London South Bank 9; Portsmouth 10; Robert Gordon 5; Salford 10; Sheffield Hallam 8, (Radiothera Onc) 3; Southampton 5; Suffolk (Univ Campus) 3; Teesside 10.

Advice to applicants and planning the UCAS personal statement Contacts with radiographers and visits to the radiography departments of hospitals should be discussed in full on the UCAS application. **Birmingham City** Evidence needed of a visit to at least one imaging department or oncology (radiotherapy) department before completing UCAS application. Evidence of good research into career. **Liverpool** Decision to choose between therapeutic and diagnostic pathways should be made before applying. **Salford** Communication skills, teamwork, work experience in public areas. See also **Appendix 2**.

Misconceptions about this course There is often confusion between radiotherapy and diagnostic imaging and between diagnostic and therapeutic radiography.

Selection interviews Yes Birmingham City, Cardiff, City, Derby, Hertfordshire, London South Bank, Queen Margaret, Salford, Sheffield Hallam; **Some** Bangor, London (St George's).

Interview advice and questions All applicants should have discussed this career with a radiographer and visited a hospital radiography department. Questions follow from these contacts. Where does radiography fit into the overall health care system? See **Chapter 7**.

Reasons for rejection (non-academic) Lack of interest in people. Poor communication skills. Occasionally students may be unsuitable for the clinical environment, for example, they express a fear of blood and needles; poor grasp of radiography as a career. Unable to meet criteria for

employment in the Health Service, for example, health factors, criminal convictions, severe disabilities.

AFTER-RESULTS ADVICE
Offers to applicants repeating A-levels **Higher** London (St George's); **Same** Derby, Salford.

GRADUATE DESTINATIONS AND EMPLOYMENT (2005/6 HESA)
No data available.

Career note Most radiographers work in the NHS in hospital radiography departments undertaking diagnostic or therapeutic treatment. Others work in private healthcare.

OTHER DEGREE SUBJECTS FOR CONSIDERATION
Audiology; Health Studies; Medical Physics; Nursing; Occupational Therapy; Physics; Podiatry; Speech Sciences.

RELIGIOUS STUDIES
(including **Biblical Studies, Divinity, Jewish Studies** and **Theology**)

Religious Studies courses cover four degree course subjects: Religious Studies, Divinity, Theology and Biblical Studies. The subject content of these courses varies and students should check prospectuses carefully. They are not intended as training courses for church ministry; an adherence to a particular religious denomination is not a necessary qualification for entry. (NB Religious studies is an acceptable second or third A-level for any non-scientific degree course.)

Useful websites www.guardian.co.uk/religion; www.cwmission.org.uk; www.miraclestudies.net; www.academicinfo.net/religindex.html; www.theologywebsite.com; www.jewishstudies.org; www.jewishstudies.virtualave.net; www.jewfaq.org; www.virtualreligion.net; www.jis.oxfordjournals.org.

NB The points totals shown to the left of the institutions are for ease of reference only. It must not be assumed that tariff points are always used by institutions or that they can be substituted for an offer in grades. The level of an offer is not necessarily indicative of the quality of a course.

COURSE OFFERS INFORMATION
Subject requirements/preferences **GCSE** English and mathematics. For teacher training, English and mathematics and science. **AL** Religious studies or theology may be required or preferred for some courses. **NB** A* grades are likely to form part of university offers in the higher ranges for students applying for places in 2008 for entry in 2009: check websites.

Your target offers
360 pts **and above**
  Bristol – AAA–AAB (Phil Theol)
  Cambridge – AAA (Theol Relig St)
  Cambridge (Hom) – AAA (BA Relig St Educ)
  Oxford – Offers vary eg AAA–AAB (Theology) *(IB 38–40 pts)*
  St Andrews – AAA (Bib St Int Rel)
340 pts **Cardiff** – AAB–BBC 340–260 pts (Cult Crit Relig St; Engl Lit Relig St; Hist Relig St; Maths Relig St) *(IB 32 pts)*
  Durham – AAB (Theol Comb Arts; Theol)
  Manchester – AAB–ABB (Compar Relig Soc Anth; St Relig Theol; St Relig Theol (Jew St) (Bib St) (Relig Soty) (S As St)) *(IB 32 pts)*
  St Andrews – AAB–ABB (Theol St courses; Bib St courses except under **360 pts**) *(IB 30 pts)*
320 pts **Birmingham** – ABB (Engl Theol; Hist Theol; Hist Art Theol; Mus Theol; Phil Theol)
  Durham – ABB (Phil Theol) *(IB 34 pts)*

Glasgow – ABB (Theol Relig St) *(IB 30 pts)*
Leeds – ABB (Engl Theol Relig St; Theol Relig St Hist)
London (King's) – ABB–BBB (Relig St; Theol; Relig Phil Eth) *(IB 34 pts)*
Nottingham – ABB (Engl St Theol)
Sheffield – ABB–BBB (Bib St Engl; Bib St Phil; Bib St Ling)

300 pts **Birmingham** – BBB–BBC (Theol courses except under **320 pts**) *(IB 30–32 pts)*
Bristol – BBB–CCC; BBC for joint courses (Theol Relig St; Theol Sociol) *(IB 32 pts H655)*
Cardiff – BBB (Relig St joint courses except under **340 pts**)
Durham – ABC (Theol (Euro St)) *(IB 30 pts)*
Edinburgh – BBB (Relig St; Div) *(IB 26–28 pts)*
Exeter – BBB–BBC 300–280 pts (Theol St; Class St Theol; Phil Theol) *(IB 26–28 pts)*
Lancaster – BBB/ABC (Engl Lit Relig St; Hist Relig St)
Leeds – BBB (Theol Relig St; Relig joint courses except under **320 pts**)
London (UCL) – BBB–BBC (Heb Jew St; Jew Hist) *(IB 30 pts)*
Nottingham – ABC (Theol; Phil Theol) *(IB 30 pts)*
Queen's Belfast – BBB–BBCb (Theol; Div) *(IB 29 pts)*
St Andrews – ABC (MTheol Theol)

280 pts **Bolton** – 280 pts (Phil Relig Eth)
Cardiff – BBC (Relig Theol St) *(IB 32 pts)*
Hull – 280–300 pts (Theol; Theol Crea Writ; Theol Film St; Theol Sociol; Theol Hist Art)
Kent – 280 pts (Relig St courses) *(IB 31 pts)*
Lancaster – BBB–BBC (Relig St; Relig St Sociol; Anth Relig; Eth Phil Relig; Phil Relig St) *(IB 28–29 pts)*
Oxford Brookes – BBC (Relig Cult Eth courses)
Sheffield – BBC–BCC **or** BBbb/BBcc/BCcc (Bib St; Bib St Ger; Bib St Mus) *(IB 30 pts)*
Stirling – BBC–CCC (Relig St courses)

260 pts **Birmingham** – BCC (Islam St)
Leo Baeck (Coll) – BCC (Heb Jew St)
London (Hey) – BCC (Theol; Phil Theol; Phil Relig Eth; Ab Religs Islam Chr Jud) *(IB 28–32 pts)*
London (SOAS) – 260–280 pts (St Relig)
Stranmillis (UC) – BCC (Relig St Educ)

240 pts **Aberdeen** – CCC (Div; Relig St; Theol)
Bangor – 240–280 pts (Relig St; Theol)
Chester – 240–260 pts (Theol Relig St courses)
Glasgow – CCC 1st yr entry (Theol Relig St; Relig Phil Educ)
Liverpool Hope – 240 pts (Theol Relig St)
UHI Millennium Inst (HTC) – AA–DD (Theol St)

For information on how to read the Subject Tables, see **Chapter 8.**

220 pts **Bath Spa** – 220–240 pts (St Relig)
Winchester – 220–240 pts (Theol Relig St)
200 pts **Central Lancashire** – 200 pts (Islam St Comb Hons)
Cumbria – 200 pts (Relig St)
Gloucestershire – 200–280 pts (Relig Phil Eth)
Roehampton – 200–280 pts (Theol Relig St)
180 pts **Bishop Grosseteste (UC)** – 180 pts (Educ St Theol)
Chichester – 180–220 pts (Theology)
Edge Hill – 180 pts (Relig Educ)
Lampeter – 180–240 pts (Theol; Relig St; Relig St Islam St; Relig St Hist; Div)
York St John – 180 pts (Theol Relig St)
160 pts **Canterbury Christ Church** – CC (Theol courses; Relig St courses)
Greenwich – 160 pts (Theol Relig courses)
Huddersfield – 160 pts (Relig Educ)
Leeds Trinity and All Saints (Coll) – CC–CCC 160–240 pts (Relig St; Theol)
Middlesex – 160–200 pts (Relig Cntxt courses)
Newman (UC) – 160–240 pts (Theol Educ St)
Newport – 160 pts (Relig St Phil)
St Mary's (UC) – 160–200 pts (Theol Relig St; Theol)
Wolverhampton – 160–220 pts (Relig St courses)
140 pts **Islam Advnc St (Coll)** – 140–220 pts (Islam St)
Trinity Carmarthen (Coll) – 140 pts (Relig St courses; Relig Educ; Chr Commun St)
120 pts **Cliff (Coll)** – 120–240 pts (Theology)

Brighton – contact University (BA Relig Educ St)

Alternative offers
See **Chapter 8** for grade/point equivalences and related information for the following examinations: Scottish qualifications, the Welsh Baccalaureate, the IB diploma (approximate points shown also in italics in the table of offers), the Irish Leaving Certificate, the European Baccalaureate and the French Baccalaureate.

EXAMPLES OF FOUNDATION DEGREES IN THE SUBJECT FIELD
York St John.

CHOOSING YOUR COURSE (SEE ALSO CH.1)
Course variations – Widen your options
Archaeology, Ancient History and Theology (Birmingham)
Religious Studies, Social Philosophy and Ethics (Cardiff)
Animal Behaviour and Theology (Chester)
Theology and Islamic Studies (Exeter)
Religious Studies and Classical and Archaeological Studies (Kent)
Religious Philosophy and Ethics (London (King's))
Study of Religions and Hebrew (London (SOAS))
Ethics and Spirituality and Theology and Religious Studies (Winchester)
Counselling Studies and Theology and Religious Studies (York St John)
CHECK PROSPECTUSES AND WEBSITES FOR OTHER UNIVERSITIES AND COLLEGES OFFERING THESE COURSES.

Universities and colleges teaching quality See www.qaa.ac.uk; www.unistats.com.

Top universities and colleges (Research) (including Theology and Divinity) Aberdeen; Birmingham; Bristol; Cambridge; Cardiff*; Durham; Edinburgh; Exeter; Glasgow; Lampeter; Lancaster; London (King's), (SOAS); Manchester*; Nottingham*; Oxford*; St Andrews; Sheffield; Stirling.

ADMISSIONS INFORMATION
Number of applicants per place (approx) Bangor 5; Birmingham 4; Bristol 7; Cambridge 2; Cambridge (Hom) 4; Chichester 6; Cumbria 12; Durham 6; Edinburgh 3; Exeter 7; Glasgow 4;

Greenwich 10; Hull (Theol) 10; Kent 13; Lampeter 7; Lancaster 6; Leeds 4; Leeds Trinity and All Saints (Coll) 4; Liverpool Hope 6; London (Hey) 4, (King's) 6, (SOAS) 1; Middlesex 4; Newman (UC) 2; Nottingham 10; Oxford (success rate 60%); Sheffield 7; Roehampton 2; Winchester 6; York St John 2.

Advice to applicants and planning the UCAS personal statement An awareness of the differences between the main religions is important as is any special research undertaken. Interests in the religious art and architecture of various periods and styles should be noted. Applicants should have an open-minded approach to studying a diverse range of religious traditions. **Bristol** Early application recommended. **St Andrews** Give evidence of interest and reasons for choosing the course.

Misconceptions about this course Some students think that you must be religious to study Theology – in fact, people of all faiths and none study the subject. A study of religions is not Christian theology. **Leeds** Some applicants are not aware of the breadth of the subject. We offer modules covering New Testament, Christian theology, Islamic studies, Hinduism, Buddhism, Sikhism, Christian ethics, sociology of religion.

Selection interviews Yes Aberystwyth, Cambridge, Chester, Durham, Edinburgh, Glasgow, Hull, Lampeter, Lancaster, Leeds, Leeds Trinity and All Saints (Coll), London (Hey), (SOAS), Nottingham, Oxford, Oxford Brookes, Roehampton, Sheffield, Winchester; **Some** Bristol, Cardiff, Southampton.

Interview advice and questions Past questions have included: Why do you want to study Theology/Biblical Studies/Religious Studies? What do you hope to do after obtaining your degree? Questions relating to the A-level syllabus. Questions on current theological topics. Do you have any strong religious convictions? Do you think that your religious beliefs will be changed at the end of the course? Why did you choose Religious Studies rather than Biblical Studies? How would you explain the miracles to a 10-year-old? (BEd course). Do you agree with the National Lottery? How do you think you can apply theology to your career? **Cambridge** There is a Christian priest who regularly visits India and converted to a Hindu priest. When he is in England he still practises as a Christian priest. What problems might this pose? Do you believe we should eradicate Christmas on the basis that it offends other religious groups? **Oxford** Ability to defend one's opinions and willingness to engage in a lively dialogue. See **Chapter 7**.

Reasons for rejection (non-academic) Students not attending Open days may be rejected. Too religiously conservative. Failure to interact. Lack of motivation to study a subject which goes beyond A-level. **Cardiff** Insufficiently open to an academic study of religion. **Leo Baeck (Coll)** Inability to fit into life of the College, bearing in mind that its main aim is to train rabbis for the Jewish community.

AFTER-RESULTS ADVICE

Offers to applicants repeating A-levels Higher Hull, Manchester, St Andrews; **Possibly higher** Cambridge (Hom); **Same** Bangor, Birmingham, Cardiff, Chester, Durham, Glasgow, Greenwich, Lampeter, Lancaster, Leeds, Liverpool Hope, London (SOAS), Nottingham, Roehampton, St Mary's (UC), Sheffield, Stirling, Winchester, Wolverhampton, York St John; **No offers made** Cambridge.

GRADUATE DESTINATIONS AND EMPLOYMENT (2005/6 HESA)

Graduates surveyed 890 **Employed** 355 **In further study** 265 **Assumed unemployed** 45.

Career note Although a small number of graduates may regard these courses as a preparation for entry to religious orders, the great majority enter other careers with teaching particularly popular.

OTHER DEGREE SUBJECTS FOR CONSIDERATION

Community Studies; Education; History; Philosophy; Psychology; Social Policy and Administration; Social Work.

RETAIL MANAGEMENT

This subject attracts a large number of applicants each year and at the outset, it is necessary to have work experience before applying. The work itself varies depending on the type of retail outlet. After completing their courses graduates in a large departmental store will be involved in different aspects of the business, for example supervising shop assistants, warehouse and packing staff. They could also receive special training in the sales of particular goods, for example food and drink, clothing, furniture. Subsequently there may be opportunities to become buyers. In more specialised shops, for example shoes, fashion and food, graduates are likely to work only with these products, with opportunities to reach senior management.

Useful websites www.brc.org.uk; www.retail-week.com; www.theretailbulletin.com; www.retailcareers.co.uk; www.retailchoice.com; www.nrf.com.

NB The points totals shown to the left of the institutions are for ease of reference only. It must not be assumed that tariff points are always used by institutions or that they can be substituted for an offer in grades. The level of an offer is not necessarily indicative of the quality of a course.

COURSE OFFERS INFORMATION

Subject requirements/preferences **GCSE** English and mathematics at grade C or above. **AL** No subjects specified. **NB** A* grades are likely to form part of university offers in the higher ranges for students applying for places in 2008 for entry in 2009: check websites.

Your target offers

320 pts **Loughborough** – ABB (Rtl Mgt) *(IB 36 pts)*

300 pts **Manchester** – BBB (Fash Tex Rtl; Des Mgt Fash Rtl)

Stirling – BBB 2nd yr entry (Rtl Mark)

Surrey – 300 pts (Rtl Mgt) *(IB 30 pts)*

260 pts **Stirling** – BCC 1st yr entry (Rtl Mark)

240 pts **Birmingham City** – 240 pts (Fash Rtl Mgt; Tex Des Rtl Mgt)

Bournemouth – 240 pts (Rtl Mgt)

Brighton – 240 pts (Rtl Mgt; Rtl Mark) *(IB 28 pts)*

De Montfort – 240 pts (Rtl Buy (Tex))

Huddersfield – 240 pts (Rtl Mgt)

Manchester Met – 240 pts (Rtl Mark Mgt; Fash Buy)

Oxford Brookes – CCC–CD (Rtl Mgt)

Robert Gordon – CCC (Rtl Mgt)

Westminster – 240 pts (Fash Mrchnds Mgt)

220 pts **Central Lancashire** – 220–260 pts (Rtl Mgt Buy; Rtl Mgt Fash; Rtl Mgt Mark; Rtl Mgt) *(IB 28 pts)*

Sunderland – 220 pts (Bus Rtl Mgt)

200 pts **London Met** – 200–240 pts (Bus Rtl Mgt)

180 pts **Birmingham (UC)** – 180 pts (Rtl Mgt; Fd Rtl Mgt)

Cardiff (UWIC) – 180 pts (Rtl Mgt)

Greenwich – 180 pts (Bus Admin Rtl Mgt)

Queen Margaret – 180 pts (Consum St Rtl; Rtl Bus)

Roehampton – 180–160 pts (Bus Mgt (Rtl Mgt Mark))

Southampton Solent – 180 pts (Mark Rtl Mgt)

160 pts **Arts London** – 160 pts (Rtl Mgt)

Canterbury Christ Church – 160 pts (Rtl Mgt)

Glasgow Caledonian – 160 pts (Retailing)

Northampton – 160 pts (Rtl Mark)

Teesside – 160–220 pts (Retailing) *(IB 24 pts)*

Wolverhampton – 160–220 pts (Rtl Mark)

140 pts **Harper Adams (UC)** – 140–240 pts (Fd Rtl Mgt)

Leeds Met – contact University

Alternative offers
See **Chapter 8** for grade/point equivalences and related information for the following examinations: Scottish qualifications, the Welsh Baccalaureate, the IB diploma (approximate points shown also in italics in the table of offers), the Irish Leaving Certificate, the European Baccalaureate and the French Baccalaureate.

EXAMPLES OF FOUNDATION DEGREES IN THE SUBJECT FIELD
Arts London (CComm); Birmingham (UC); Bournemouth and Poole (Coll); Canterbury Christ Church; Kent; London Met; Middlesex; Nottingham New (Coll); Plymouth; Preston (Coll); Southampton Solent; Wolverhampton.

CHOOSING YOUR COURSE (SEE ALSO CH.1)
Course variations – Widen your options
Fashion Retail Management (Birmingham City)
Food and Retail Management (Birmingham (UC))
Retail Marketing (Bournemouth)
Retail Management (Central Lancashire)
Retail Buying (Textiles) (De Montfort)
Exhibition and Retail Design (Huddersfield)
Advertising, Marketing Communications and Retail Management (London Met)
Retailing/Wastes Management (Northampton)
Marketing and Public Relations (Teesside)
CHECK PROSPECTUSES AND WEBSITES FOR OTHER UNIVERSITIES AND COLLEGES OFFERING THESE COURSES.

Universities and colleges teaching quality See www.qaa.ac.uk; www.unistats.com.

Top universities and colleges (Research) See **Business Courses**.

ADMISSIONS INFORMATION
Number of applicants per place (approx) Bournemouth 8; Manchester Met 10; Oxford Brookes 11; See also **Business Courses**.

Advice to applicants and planning the UCAS personal statement Manchester Met (Rtl Mark Mgt) Evidence of working with people or voluntary work experience (department unable to assist with sponsorships); see also **Business Courses**.

Misconceptions about this course See **Business Courses**.

Selection interviews See **Business Courses**.

Interview advice and questions See **Business Courses**.

Reasons for rejection (non-academic) See **Business Courses**.

AFTER-RESULTS ADVICE
Offers to applicants repeating A-levels See **Business Courses**.

GRADUATE DESTINATIONS AND EMPLOYMENT (2005/6 HESA)
See **Business Courses**.

Career note The majority of graduates work in business involved in marketing and retail work. Employment options include brand design, product management, advertising, PR sales and account management.

OTHER DEGREE SUBJECTS FOR CONSIDERATION
Business Studies; Consumer Sciences/Studies; E-Commerce; Human Resource Management; Psychology; Supply Chain Management.

RUSSIAN and EAST EUROPEAN STUDIES

(including **Bulgarian, Croatian, Czech, Finnish, Georgian, Hungarian, Polish, Romanian, Russian** and **Serbian;** see also **European Studies** and **Languages**)

East European Studies cover a wide range of the less popular language courses and should be considered by anyone with a love of and gift for languages. Many natural linguists often devote themselves to one of the popular European languages studied up to A-level, when their language skills could be extended to the more unusual languages, thereby increasing their future career opportunities.

Useful websites www.basees.org.uk; www.iol.org.uk; www.bbc.co.uk/languages; www.languageadvantage.com; www.languagematters.co.uk; www.reed.co.uk/multilingual; www.cilt.org.uk.

NB The points totals shown to the left of the institutions are for ease of reference only. It must not be assumed that tariff points are always used by institutions or that they can be substituted for an offer in grades. The level of an offer is not necessarily indicative of the quality of a course.

COURSE OFFERS INFORMATION

Subject requirements/preferences GCSE A foreign language. **AL** One or two modern languages may be stipulated. **NB** A* grades are likely to form part of university offers in the higher ranges for students applying for places in 2008 for entry in 2009: check websites.

Your target offers

360 pts   and above

   Cambridge – AAA (Russ; Modn Mediev Lang (Russ)) *(IB 38–42 pts)*

   Oxford – Offers vary eg AAA–AAB (Modn Langs (Russ+2nd Lang) (Cz Slov+2nd Lang); Engl Modn Langs (Russ)) *(IB 38–42 pts)*

340 pts   Bristol – AAB–BBB (Cz Fr/Ger/Ital/Port/Russ/Span; Russ courses) *(IB 29–32 pts H555–665)*

   Durham – AAB (Modn Langs (Russ+1–2 Langs)) *(IB 34 pts)*

   Manchester – AAB (Russ Chin/Fr/Ger/Ital/Jap/Span)

   St Andrews – AAB–ABB (Russ courses) *(IB 32 pts)*

320 pts   Bath – ABB–BBC (Modn Lang Euro St courses; Russ Pol) *(IB 32 pts)*

   Birmingham – ABB–BBB 300 pts (Russ St; Russ St joint courses)

   Durham – ABB (Russ Comb Hons)

   Exeter – ABB–BBB (Russ courses)

   Glasgow – ABB–BBB (Cnt E Euro St; Cz; Russ; Polh; Slav St)

   Nottingham – ABB–BCC (Russ St courses; Serb Cro St) *(IB 29 pts)*

300 pts   Edinburgh – BBB (Russ St Bus St; Russ St Ling; Russ St Euro Hist; Russ St Phil; Russ St Pol; Russ St Hist Art)

   London (LSE) – check with admissions tutor (Lang St (Russ))

   London (UCL) – BBB+AS (E Euro St; E Euro St Bulg/Cz/Finn/Hung/Slov/Polh/Romn/Serb Cro/Ukr; Russ St; Russ St (Pol Econ Cult Soty); Russ Hist) *(IB 32 pts)*

   Manchester – BBB (Russ courses except under **340 pts**)

   Sheffield – BBB–BBC (Russ courses) *(IB 30 pts)*

   Surrey – 300–260 pts (Modn Langs)

280 pts   Leeds – BBC–BCC (Russ St A and B courses; Russ joint Hons; Russ Civ courses; Russ St; Pol Russ)

   London (QM) – 280–320 pts (Russ Geog; Russ Econ; Russ Bus Mgt)

   London (SOAS) – BBC (Georgian)

260 pts   London (QM) – 260 pts (Russ courses except under **280 pts**) *(IB 32 pts)*

200 pts   European Bus Sch London – CDD 200 pts approx (Int Bus (Russ))

Alternative offers

See **Chapter 8** for grade/point equivalences and related information for the following examinations: Scottish qualifications, the Welsh Baccalaureate, the IB diploma (approximate points shown also in

italics in the table of offers), the Irish Leaving Certificate, the European Baccalaureate and the French Baccalaureate.

CHOOSING YOUR COURSE (SEE ALSO CH.1)

Course variations – Widen your options
International Business and Russian (Birmingham)
Arts Combined (Durham)
Czech/Russian (Glasgow)
Russian and Economics (London (QM))
Russian with an East European Language (London (UCL))
Russian and East European Civilisations (Nottingham)
See also **Languages**
CHECK PROSPECTUSES AND WEBSITES FOR OTHER UNIVERSITIES AND COLLEGES OFFERING THESE COURSES.

Universities and colleges teaching quality See www.qaa.ac.uk; www.unistats.com.

Top universities and colleges (Research) Birmingham; Bristol; Cambridge; Exeter; London (QM); Nottingham; Oxford*; Sheffield*; Surrey.

ADMISSIONS INFORMATION

Number of applicants per place (approx) Birmingham 3; Bristol 3; Durham 7; Leeds 3; London (UCL) (E Euro St Bulg) 1; Nottingham 5; Surrey 3.

Advice to applicants and planning the UCAS personal statement Visits to Eastern Europe should be mentioned, supported by your special reasons for wishing to study the language. A knowledge of the cultural, economic and political scene could be important. **Leeds** Fluent English important for non-EU students. See also **Languages**. **St Andrews** Evidence of interest, reasons for choosing the course. **Surrey** Evidence of wide reading, travel and residence abroad. Fluent English important. See also **Appendix 2** under **Languages**.

Selection interviews Yes Cambridge, Durham, Exeter, London (UCL), Oxford, Surrey; **Some** Nottingham.

Interview advice and questions Since many applicants will not have taken Russian at A-level, questions often focus on their reasons for choosing a Russian degree, and their knowledge of, and interest in, Russia. Those taking A-level Russian are likely to be questioned on the course and on any reading done outside A-level work. East European Studies applicants will need to show some knowledge of their chosen country/countries and any specific reasons why they wish to follow the course. **Leeds** See **Languages**. See **Chapter 7**.

Reasons for rejection (non-academic) Lack of perceived commitment for a demanding *ab initio* subject.

AFTER-RESULTS ADVICE

Offers to applicants repeating A-levels Higher Bristol, Glasgow, Leeds, St Andrews, Surrey (if candidate is re-sitting 2 A-levels); **Same** Durham; **No offers made** Cambridge.

GRADUATE DESTINATIONS AND EMPLOYMENT (2005/6 HESA)

Graduates surveyed 115 **Employed** 60 **In further study** 20 **Assumed unemployed** 5.

Career note See **Languages**.

OTHER DEGREE SUBJECTS FOR CONSIDERATION

Economics; European Studies; International Relations; Linguistics; Politics; other languages.

SCANDINAVIAN STUDIES

Scandinavian Studies provides students who enjoy languages with the opportunity to extend their language expertise to learn a modern Scandinavian language – Danish, Norwegian or Swedish – from beginner's level to Honours level in four years, including a year in Scandinavia. The three languages are very similar to each other and a knowledge of one makes it possible to access easily the literature and cultures of the other two. Viking Studies includes Old Norse, runology and archaeology.

Useful websites www.cilt.org.uk; www.iol.org.uk; www.bbc.co.uk/languages; www.languageadvantage.com; www.languagematters.co.uk; www.reed.co.uk/multilingual; www.scandinaviahouse.org; www.scandinavianstudy.org; www.nordicstudies.com.

NB The points totals shown to the left of the institutions are for ease of reference only. It must not be assumed that tariff points are always used by institutions or that they can be substituted for an offer in grades. The level of an offer is not necessarily indicative of the quality of a course.

COURSE OFFERS INFORMATION

Subject requirements/preferences **GCSE** Foreign language preferred for all courses. **AL** A modern language may be required. **NB** A* grades are likely to form part of university offers in the higher ranges for students applying for places in 2008 for entry in 2009: check websites.

Your target offers
360 pts   and above
        Cambridge – AAA varies between colleges (A-Sxn Nrs Celt) *(IB 38–42 pts)*
300 pts   Edinburgh – BBB (Scand St (Dan Norw Swed); Scand St Class; Scand St Euro Hist; Scand St Hist Art; Scand St Ling; Scand St Phil; Scand St Pol; Scand St Soc Pol; Scand St Scot Ethnol; Scand St Bus St; Scand St Celt) *(IB 34 pts H555)*
280 pts   London (UCL) – BBC+AS (Scand St (Dan) (Norw) (Swed); Scand St Hist; Ice; Vkg St) *(IB 32 pts)*
        Nottingham – BBC (Vkg St) *(IB 30 pts)*

Alternative offers
See **Chapter 8** for grade/point equivalences and related information for the following examinations: Scottish qualifications, the Welsh Baccalaureate, the IB diploma (approximate points shown also in italics in the table of offers), the Irish Leaving Certificate, the European Baccalaureate and the French Baccalaureate.

CHOOSING YOUR COURSE (SEE ALSO CH.1)

Course variations – Widen your options
Scandinavian Studies and Celtic (Edinburgh)
Icelandic (London (UCL))
See also **Languages**.
CHECK PROSPECTUSES AND WEBSITES FOR OTHER UNIVERSITIES AND COLLEGES OFFERING THESE COURSES.

Universities and colleges teaching quality See www.qaa.ac.uk; www.unistats.com.

Top universities and colleges (Research) Cambridge; Edinburgh; London (UCL).

ADMISSIONS INFORMATION

Number of applicants per place (approx) London (UCL) 3.

Advice to applicants and planning the UCAS personal statement Visits to Scandinavian countries could be the source of an interest in studying these languages. You should also be aware of cultural, political, geographical and economic aspects of Scandinavian countries. Knowledge of these should be shown in your statement.

Selection interviews **Yes** Cambridge.

Interview advice and questions Applicants in the past have been questioned on why they have chosen this subject area, on their visits to Scandinavia and on their knowledge of the country/ countries and their people. Future career plans are likely to be discussed. See **Chapter 7**.

Reasons for rejection (non-academic) One applicant didn't know the difference between a noun and a verb.

AFTER-RESULTS ADVICE
Offers to applicants repeating A-levels No offers made Cambridge.

GRADUATE DESTINATIONS AND EMPLOYMENT (2005/6 HESA)
Graduates surveyed 218 **Employed** 15 **In further study** none **Assumed unemployed** none.

Career note See **Languages**.

OTHER DEGREE SUBJECTS FOR CONSIDERATION
Archaeology; History; European History/Studies; other modern languages, including, for example, Russian and East European languages.

SCIENCE

(including **Combined and General Science;** see also **Biological Sciences** and **Natural Sciences**)

This table includes a range of specialised and general science degree subjects. General science degrees are interdisciplinary programmes, often giving a variety of subject combinations and a range of scientific skills.

Useful websites www.planet-science.com; www.scicentral.com; www.noisemakers.org.uk; www.intute.ac.uk; see also **Biology**, **Chemistry** and **Physics**.

NB The points totals shown to the left of the institutions are for ease of reference only. It must not be assumed that tariff points are always used by institutions or that they can be substituted for an offer in grades. The level of an offer is not necessarily indicative of the quality of a course.

COURSE OFFERS INFORMATION
Subject requirements/preferences GCSE Science/mathematics subjects. **Teacher Training courses** English, mathematics. **AL** One or two sciences may be required but courses in the History and Philosophy of Science may not necessarily require a science subject at A-level. **NB** A* grades are likely to form part of university offers in the higher ranges for students applying for places in 2008 for entry in 2009: check websites.

Your target offers
360 pts **and above**
   Cambridge – AAA (Nat Sci) *(IB 38–42 pts)*
350 pts **Queen's Belfast** – BBBb–BBCb (Hist Sci courses)
340 pts **Durham** – AAB (Nat Sci)
   London (UCL) – AAB+AS (Hist Phil Sci; Hist Phil Soc St Sci; Sci Comm Pol) *(IB 32–36 pts)*
   Manchester – AAB–BBB (Biol Sci Soty)
   St Andrews – AAB (Lgc Phil Sci (Comp Sci) (Maths) (Phys) (Stats); Intnet Comp Sci Lgc Phil Sci) *(IB 36 pts)*
320 pts **Leeds** – ABB (Hist Phil Sci)
   Liverpool – ABB–BBC (Sci Comb hons) *(IB 30–32 pts)*
300 pts **Stranmillis (UC)** – BBB (Sci Educ)
280 pts **Lancaster** – BBC (Nat Sci)
   Liverpool John Moores – 280–300 pts (Sci Ftbl)
   Nottingham Trent – 280 pts (Nat Sci)
260 pts **Leicester** – 260 pts (BSc Interd Sci)
   St Andrews – BCC (Sci Gen Deg)

240 pts **West Scotland** – CCC–EE (Gen Sci)
220 pts **Bradford** – 220 pts (BSc Comb St)
 Winchester – 220 pts (Sci P Educ)
200 pts **Glamorgan** – 200 pts (Sci Rgby; Out Learn Sci Advntr; Sci Fict Cult)
 Teesside – 200–260 pts (App Sci Foren Invstg; Crime Sc Sci)
180 pts **Heriot-Watt** – DDD 180 pts (BSc Comb St)
160 pts **Bishop Grosseteste (UC)** – 160 pts (Sci Educ St)
 Canterbury Christ Church – CC (Integ Sci; Sci QTS)
 Glamorgan – 160 pts (Comb Sci)
 London South Bank – CC (App Sci)
 Plymouth – 160–240 pts (Bed P Sci)
140 pts **Bath Spa** – CD (Comb awards)
120 pts **Huddersfield** – 120 pts (App Sci)
100 pts **Sheffield Hallam** – 100 pts (Fdn Sci Maths)
 80 pts **Farnborough (CT)** – 80–120 pts (Sci Mgt Exer Hlth)
 UHI Millennium Inst – 80 pts (Nat Env Sci)

 Open University – contact University

Alternative offers
See **Chapter 8** for grade/point equivalences and related information for the following examinations: Scottish qualifications, the Welsh Baccalaureate, the IB diploma (approximate points shown also in italics in the table of offers), the Irish Leaving Certificate, the European Baccalaureate and the French Baccalaureate.

EXAMPLES OF FOUNDATION DEGREES IN THE SUBJECT FIELD
Central Lancashire.

CHOOSING YOUR COURSE (SEE ALSO CH.1)
Course variations – Widen your options
Agricultural Science (Aberdeen)
Equine Science (Aberystwyth)
Coaching Science (Anglia Ruskin)
Biomedical Materials Science (Birmingham)
Nautical Science (Blackpool and Fylde (Coll))
Equine Dental Science (Bristol UWE)
Pharmaceutical Science (Huddersfield)
Actuarial Science (Kent)
Cognitive Science (Leeds)
Computer Science (London (Gold))
Forensic Science (London South Bank)
Sport Science (Loughborough)
Animal Production Science (Newcastle)
Biomedical Science (Portsmouth)
Aquatic Sciences (Salford)
Computer Games Science (Teesside)
Health and Exercise Science (Thames Valley)
CHECK PROSPECTUSES AND WEBSITES FOR OTHER UNIVERSITIES AND COLLEGES OFFERING THESE COURSES.

ADMISSIONS INFORMATION
Number of applicants per place (approx) Glamorgan 9; Heriot-Watt 2; Lancaster 7; Liverpool John Moores (Sci Ftbl) 10; West Scotland 4.

Advice to applicants and planning the UCAS personal statement **Liverpool John Moores** (Sci Ftbl) This is a lab-based course examining physical stress. See **Biology**, **Biological Sciences**, **Chemistry**, **Physics**. See also **Appendix 2**.

Misconceptions about this course Liverpool John Moores (Sci Ftbl) Some applicants believe that scientific ability is not needed for the course: this is not true. Both scientific and practical ability are essential.

Selection interviews Yes Cambridge, London (UCL).

Interview advice and questions Past applicants have been questioned on their A-level work and aspects they particularly enjoyed. See **Chapter 7**.

Reasons for rejection (non-academic) (Mainly academic) Lack of an active interest in scientific issues.

AFTER-RESULTS ADVICE
Offers to applicants repeating A-levels No offers made Cambridge.

GRADUATE DESTINATIONS AND EMPLOYMENT (2005/6 HESA)
See separate science tables.

Career note See also separate science tables.

OTHER DEGREE SUBJECTS FOR CONSIDERATION
Biochemistry; Biological Sciences; Biology; Health Sciences; Life Sciences; Natural Sciences; Physics; Sports Sciences.

SOCIAL and PUBLIC POLICY and ADMINISTRATION
(see also **Community Studies** and **Social Work**)

Social Policy is a multi-disciplinary degree that combines elements from sociology, political science, social and economic history, economics, cultural studies and philosophy. It is a study of the needs of society and how best to provide such services as education, housing, health and welfare services.

Useful websites www.lga.gov.uk; www.ippr.org.uk; www.swap.ac.uk; www.socialpolicy.net.

NB The points totals shown to the left of the institutions are for ease of reference only. It must not be assumed that tariff points are always used by institutions or that they can be substituted for an offer in grades. The level of an offer is not necessarily indicative of the quality of a course.

COURSE OFFERS INFORMATION
Subject requirements/preferences GCSE English and mathematics normally required. **AL** No subjects specified. **NB** A* grades are likely to form part of university offers in the higher ranges for students applying for places in 2008 for entry in 2009: check websites.

Your target offers
340 pts **Bristol** – AAB–BBC (Soc Pol Sociol; Soc Pol Pol) *(IB 29–32 pts H555/665)*
Warwick – BBBc–BBCc (Sociol Soc Pol)
320 pts **Glasgow** – ABB (Pblc Pol courses)
London (LSE) – ABB–BBB (Soc Pol; Soc Pol Crim; Soc Pol Gov; Soc Pol Sociol; Soc Pol Econ)
(IB 36 pts)
Southampton – ABB (Soc Pol Admin)
York – ABB (Pol Soc Pol)
300 pts **Aston** – BBB 300 pts (Pblc Pol Mgt Sociol)
Bath – BBB (Soc Pol Admin; Sociol Soc Pol) *(IB 32 pts)*
Cardiff – BBB–BCC (Soc Pol Crim; Sociol Soc Pol)
Edinburgh – BBB (Soc Pol Soc Econ Hist; Soc Pol Sociol; Soc Pol Law; Soc Pol Pol)
Leeds – BBB (Soc Pol Sociol; Soc Pol Theol Relig St; Soc Pol Span)

Nottingham – ABC–BBB (Soc Pol Admin; Soc Cult St)
Queen's Belfast – BBB–BBCb (Soc Pol courses)
Sheffield – BBB–BBC (Soc Pol Crim) *(IB 30–35 pts)*
Stirling – BBB 2nd yr entry (Sociol Soc Pol) *(IB 30 pts)*
York – BBB–BBC (Soc Pol; Sociol Soc Pol) *(IB 30–34 pts)*

280 pts **Bangor** – BBC 280–260 pts (Soc Pol Psy)
Birmingham – BBC–BCC 260–280 pts (Soc Pol; Pblc Soc Pol Mgt; Soc Pol Pol Sci; Soc Pol Sociol; Plan Pblc Pol Gov Mgt) *(IB 32 pts)*
Brighton – 280 pts (Soc Pol; Crim Soc Pol; Sociol Soc Pol) *(IB 28 pts)*
Leeds – BBC (Soc Pol)
Liverpool – BBC (Sociol Soc Pol)
Loughborough – 280–300 pts (Crim Soc Pol)

260 pts **Bangor** – 260–300 pts (Law Soc Pol)
Bristol – BCC (Soc Pol)
Stirling – BCC (Pblc Mgt Admin)
Stirling – BCC 1st yr entry (Soc Pol Sociol)

240 pts **Birmingham City** – 240 pts (Sociol Pol St)
De Montfort – 240 pts (Pblc Pol joint courses)
Kent – 240 pts (Soc Pol Pblc Sctr Mgt) *(IB 27 pts)*
Swansea – 240–280 pts (Soc Pol courses) *(IB 30 pts)*
Ulster – 240 pts (Soc Pol; Soc Pol Gov)

220 pts **Anglia Ruskin** – 220–260 pts (Soc Pol Crim; Soc Pol Law)
Bangor – 220–260 pts (Soc Pol courses)
Hull – 220–280 pts (Soc Pol Gndr St; Soc Pol Pblc Sctr Mgt)

200 pts **Anglia Ruskin** – 200 pts (Soc Pol Sociol; Bus Soc Pol)
Central Lancashire – 200–220 pts (Soc Pol Comb courses)
Lincoln – CDD 200 pts (Soc Pol)
London Met – 200 pts (Pblc Admin; Soc Pol; Soc Pol Sociol)
Middlesex – 200–240 pts (Soc Pol Pol Dev)

180 pts **Bradford** – 180–220 pts (Soc Pol Sociol)
Derby – 180 pts (Pblc Serv Mgt courses)
Salford – 180–200 pts (Soc Pol; Cnslg Soc Pol; Hlth Sci Soc Pol) *(IB 24 pts)*

160 pts **London South Bank** – CC (Soc Pol courses; Euro Pol St courses; Int Soc Pol)
Wolverhampton – 160–220 pts (Soc Pol courses)

140 pts **Anglia Ruskin** – 140 pts (Soc Pol)
Suffolk (Univ Campus) – 140 pts (Gov Pblc Pol)
West Scotland – CD (Soc Sci (Soc Pol))

120 pts **Llandrillo Cymru (Coll)** – 120–180 pts (Pblc Soc Pol)
Manchester Met – 120 pts (Pblc Serv)
Swansea (Inst) – 120–80 pts (Pblc Admin)
Worcester – 120 pts (Soc Welf courses)

Leeds Met – contact University

Alternative offers

See **Chapter 8** for grade/point equivalences and related information for the following examinations: Scottish qualifications, the Welsh Baccalaureate, the IB diploma (approximate points shown also in italics in the table of offers), the Irish Leaving Certificate, the European Baccalaureate and the French Baccalaureate.

EXAMPLES OF FOUNDATION DEGREES IN THE SUBJECT FIELD

Anglia Ruskin; Barnfield (Coll); Bath; Bournemouth and Poole (Coll); Bradford; Bristol City (Coll); City; City and Islington (Coll); Cornwall (Coll); De Montfort; Derby; Durham New (Coll); Exeter (Coll); Hull (Coll); Leeds Park Lane (Coll); Newman (UC); Plymouth; St Helens (Coll); Suffolk (Univ Campus); Sussex Downs (Coll); Truro (Coll); Walsall (Coll); West Anglia (Coll); Westminster Kingsway (Coll); Weymouth (Coll); Worcester; York St John.

For a quick reference offers calculator, fold out the inside back cover.

CHOOSING YOUR COURSE (SEE ALSO CH.1)

Course variations – Widen your options
Public Policy, Management and Sociology (Aston)
Psychology and Social Policy (Bangor)
Public Policy, Government and Management (Birmingham)
Local Policy (Gloucestershire)
Economics, Politics and Public Policy (London (Gold))
Social Policy and Government (London (LSE))
European Policy Studies (London South Bank)
International Social Policy (London South Bank)
Criminology and Social Policy (Loughborough)
Public Services (Manchester Met)
Health Sciences and Social Policy (Salford).
CHECK PROSPECTUSES AND WEBSITES FOR OTHER UNIVERSITIES AND COLLEGES OFFERING THESE COURSES.

Universities and colleges teaching quality See www.qaa.ac.uk; www.unistats.com.

Top universities and colleges (Research) Bath; Bristol; Kent*; Leeds; London (LSE)*; Sheffield; York.

Sandwich degree courses Aston; Bath; De Montfort; Loughborough; Middlesex.

ADMISSIONS INFORMATION

Number of applicants per place (approx) Aston 8; Bangor 6; Bath 6; Birmingham 3; Bristol 4; Cardiff 4; Central Lancashire 6; De Montfort 5; Hull 9; Kent 5; Leeds 10; London (LSE) (Soc Pol) 6, (Soc Pol Sociol) 8, (Soc Pol Econ) 7, (Soc Pol Gov) 14; Loughborough 5; Manchester Met 4; Middlesex 12; Nottingham 3; Southampton 6; Stirling 11; Swansea 6; York 3.

Advice to applicants and planning the UCAS personal statement Careers in public and social administration are covered by this subject; consequently a good knowledge of these occupations and contacts with the social services should be discussed fully on your UCAS application. Gain work experience if possible. **Aston** The course is specially tailored for students aiming for careers in NHS management, the civil service and local government. **Bangor** Ability to communicate and work in a group. **York** Work experience, including voluntary work relevant to social policy. (See **Appendix 2** for contact details of some relevant organisations.)

Misconceptions about this course York Some applicants imagine that the course is vocational and leads directly to social work – it does not. Graduates in this field are well placed for a wide range of careers.

Selection interviews Yes Birmingham, London (LSE), Swansea; **Some** Anglia Ruskin, Bangor, Bath (mature applicants), Cardiff, Kent, Leeds (mature students), Loughborough, Salford, Southampton, York.

Interview advice and questions Past questions have included: What relevance has history to social administration? What do you understand by 'public policy'? What advantage do you think studying social science gives when working in policy fields? How could the image of public management of services be improved? Applicants should be fully aware of the content and the differences between all the courses on offer, why they want to study Social Policy and their career objectives. See **Chapter 7**.

Reasons for rejection (non-academic) Some universities require attendance when they invite applicants to Open days (check). Lack of awareness of current social issues. **Bath** Applicant really wanted Business Studies: evidence that teacher, careers adviser or parents are pushing the applicant into the subject or higher education. See also **Social Work**.

AFTER-RESULTS ADVICE

Offers to applicants repeating A-levels Higher Glasgow, Leeds, Newcastle; **Same** Anglia Ruskin, Bangor, Bath, Birmingham, Brighton, Cardiff, Loughborough, Salford, Southampton, York.

For information on how to read the Subject Tables, see **Chapter 8**.

GRADUATE DESTINATIONS AND EMPLOYMENT (2005/6 HESA)

Graduates surveyed 885 **Employed** 430 **In further study** 130 **Assumed unemployed** 65.

Career note See **Social Studies/Science**.

OTHER DEGREE SUBJECTS FOR CONSIDERATION

Behavioural Science; Community Studies; Criminology; Economic and Social History; Economics; Education; Government; Health Studies; Human Resource Management; Law; Politics; Psychology; Social Work; Sociology; Women's Studies.

SOCIAL STUDIES/SCIENCE

(including **Criminology, Criminal Justice** and **Human Rights;** see also under specific subject tables in the Social Sciences field (eg **Anthropology, Politics, Psychology, Social and Public Policy and Administration** and **Sociology), Community Studies** and **Health Sciences/Studies**)

Most Social Studies/Science courses take a broad view of aspects of society, for example, economics, politics, history, social psychology and urban studies. Applied Social Studies usually focuses on practical and theoretical preparation for a career in social work. These courses are particularly popular with mature students and some universities and colleges offer shortened degree courses for those with relevant work experience.

Useful websites www.csv.org.uk; www.intute.ac.uk.

NB The points totals shown to the left of the institutions are for ease of reference only. It must not be assumed that tariff points are always used by institutions or that they can be substituted for an offer in grades. The level of an offer is not necessarily indicative of the quality of a course.

COURSE OFFERS INFORMATION

Subject requirements/preferences **GCSE** Usually English and mathematics; a science may be required. **AL** No subjects specified. **NB** A* grades are likely to form part of university offers in the higher ranges for students applying for places in 2008 for entry in 2009: check websites. **Other requirements** A Criminal Records Bureau (CRB) check may be required for some courses.

Your target offers

360 pts **and above**
   Cambridge – AAA (Soc Pol Sci) *(IB 38–42 pts)*
   Cardiff – AAA (Psy Crim)
340 pts **Birmingham** – AAB 340 pts (Hist Soc Sci)
   Durham – AAB (Comb Soc Sci)
   Lancaster – AAB (Law Crim)
320 pts **Aberystwyth** – 320 pts (Criminology) *(IB 32 pts)*
   Bath – ABB (Soc Sci)
   Cardiff – ABB–BBB 320 pts (Criminology)
   Kent – 320 pts (Law Crim)
   Manchester – ABB–BBC (Soc Sci Phil; Soc Sci Sci Psy; Soc Sci Class Civ Art Hist; Soc Sci Jew St; Soc Sci Blt Nat Env; Crim; Crim Soc Pol)
300 pts **Aston** – BBB 300 pts (Soty Gov)
   Brighton – BBB–BBC (Crim Soc Pol; Crim Sociol; Crim App Psy) *(IB 28 pts)*
   Cardiff – 300–260 pts (Soc Sci)
   Dundee – 300 pts 2nd yr entry (Arts Soc Sci)
   East Anglia – BBB–BBC (Soty Cult Media; Psysoc Sci)
   Edinburgh – BBB (MA Soc Sci)
   Essex – 300–280 pts (Sociol Crim; Law Hum Rts; Phil Hum Rts; Sociol Hum Rts; Crim Am St)
   Keele – 300–320 pts (Criminology) *(IB 32 pts)*
   Lancaster – BBB–BBC (Crim; Crim Sociol) *(IB 32–35 pts)*

Leeds – BBB 300 pts (Crim Just Crim; Soc Sci)
London (LSE) – BBB (Soc Pol Crim)
Nottingham – ABC–BBB (Soc Cult St)
Queen's Belfast – BBB–BBCb (Gndr St)
Southampton – BBB–BBC 300 pts (App Soc Sci (Crim))
Staffordshire – 300 pts (Criminology)
York – BBB–BBC (App Soc Sci (Child Yng Ppl) (Hlth) (Crm)) *(IB 30–32 pts)*
280 pts **Glasgow** – BBC–BCC (Scot St)
Leicester – BBC (Criminology)
Loughborough – 280–300 pts (Crim Soc Pol) *(IB 32 pts)*
Northumbria – 280–260 pts (Crim; Crim Sociol)
Ulster – 280 pts (Crim Crim Just)
260 pts **Brighton** – 260 pts (App Soc Sci)
Central Lancashire – 260 pts (Plc Crim Invstg)
Coventry – 260 pts (Crim Law; Crim Psy; Sociol Crim)
Cumbria – 260 pts (Sociol Crim; Soc Sci)
Glasgow Caledonian – BBD (Criminology)
Kent – 260 pts (Crim Soc Pol; Crim Sociol) *(IB 30–33 pts)*
Liverpool – BCC–ABB (Comb Hons Soc Sci)
Richmond (Am Int Univ) – 260 pts (Soc Sci)
Sheffield Hallam – 260 pts (Crim; Crim Psy; Crim Sociol; Pol Crim)
Stirling – BCC (Criminology)
Strathclyde – BCC (Arts Soc Sci)
Swansea – BCC–CCC 260–240 pts (Crm Soc Pol; Crim Psy)
240 pts **Bangor** – 240 pts (Crim Crim Just)
Birmingham City – 240 pts (Crim Just)
Bristol – CCC (Df St)
Bristol UWE – 240–300 pts (Crim joint courses)
Glamorgan – 240–280 pts (Plc Sci)
Kent – 240 pts (Env Soc Sci) *(IB 27 pts)*
Lincoln – 240 pts (Criminology)
Liverpool Hope – 240 pts (Criminology)
Liverpool John Moores – 240 pts (Crim Just Law; Crim)
Nottingham Trent – 240 pts (Criminology)
Plymouth – 240 pts (Crim Crim Just St)
Portsmouth – 240–300 pts (Crim Crim Just; Sociol Crim)
Salford – 240 pts (Crim Pol; Crim Sociol; Crim Cult St)
Sheffield Hallam – 240 pts (Soc Sci)
Westminster – CCC/BC (Soc Sci; Crim Just)
220 pts **Anglia Ruskin** – 220–260 pts (Crim courses)
Central Lancashire – 220 pts (Crim Crim Just)
Dundee – 220 pts 1st yr entry (Arts Soc Sci)
Edge Hill – 220 pts (Crim courses)
Glamorgan – 220–260 pts (Crim Crim Just)
Glasgow Caledonian – CCD (Soc Sci)
Hull – 220–300 pts (Crim courses)
Kingston – 220–280 pts (Crim courses; Hum Rts Crim)
Manchester Met – 220 pts (Criminology)
Sheffield Hallam – 220–200 pts (Soc Cult St Spo)
200 pts **Central Lancashire** – 200 pts (Df St; Rce Ethnic St courses; Crim Phil; Crim Soc Pol; Crim Sociol)
Coventry – 200pts (Soc Welf Commun St)
Derby – 200 pts (App Soc Cult St)
East Lancashire (IHE) – 200–220 pts (Soc Sci)
Huddersfield – 200–240 pts (Criminology)

Kent – 200 pts (Soc Sci)
Lincoln – 200 pts (Soc Sci)
London Met – 200 pts (Crim Law)
Napier – 200 pts (Soc Sci)
Newport – 200 pts (Crim Commun courses)
North East Wales (IHE) – 200 pts (Crim Just)
Nottingham Trent – 200 pts (Yth St)

180 pts **Bedfordshire** – 180–220 pts (Crim Sociol)
Bradford – 180–220 pts (App Crim Just St)
Chichester – 180–220 pts (Child Yth Soty)
De Montfort – 180–220 pts (App Crim; App Crim Foren Sci; App Crim Psy)
Havering (Coll) – 180 pts (Soc Sci)
East London – 180 pts (Crim courses)
Liverpool John Moores – 180 pts (App Commun Soc St)
Manchester Met – 180 pts (Crim Contemp Cult; Crim Sociol)
Northampton – 180 pts (Criminology)

160 pts **Abertay Dundee** – CC (Crimin St)
Canterbury Christ Church – CC (App Crim)
Derby – 160–240 pts (Crim Comb St)
Doncaster (Coll) – CC 160 pts (Law Crim; App Soc Sci)
East London – 160 pts (Psysoc St)
Glamorgan – 160–200 pts (Soc Sci)
Greenwich – 160 pts (Yth Commun St)
Lampeter – 160 pts (Vol Sctr St)
London South Bank – CC 160 pts (Crim; Crim Comb courses; Citzn St courses)
Manchester Met – CC 160 pts (Soc Commun St; Yth Commun Wk)
Middlesex – 160–200 pts (Criminology)
Newport – 160 pts (Cnslg St Soty; Soc Welf; Crim Commun Just; Yth Commun St)
Peterborough Reg (Coll) – 160 pts (Comb St)
Robert Gordon – CC (App Soc Sci)
Roehampton – 160–120 pts (Hum Rts Soc Anth; Crim)
South East Essex (Coll) – 160–180 pts (BSc Soc St)
Sunderland – 160 pts (Criminology)
Teesside – 160–200 pts (Crim; Crim Sociol; Yth St Crim)
Thames Valley – 160–180 pts (Crim Sociol; Crim Psy)
Winchester – 160 pts (Soc Cr St)
Wolverhampton – 160–220 pts (Crim Just; Soc Cr Crim Just; Interp (Br Sign Lang))

140 pts **West Scotland** – CD (Soc Sci)
120 pts **Bucks New** – 120 pts (Plc St Ctzn; Plc St; Crim Psy)
Marjon (UC) – 120–180 pts (Yth Commun Wk)
Roehampton – 120–160 pts (Child Soty Sociol)
South Devon (Coll) – 120–180 pts (Soc Sci)
Suffolk (Univ Campus) – 120–180 pts (Yth St)
Teesside – 120–200 pts (Yth St)
Trinity Carmarthen (Coll) – 120 pts (Yth Commun Wk)

100 pts **UHI Millennium Inst (IC)** – 100 pts (Soc Sci)
80 pts **Cornwall (Coll)** – 80–120 pts (Comb Soc Sci)
London (Gold) – EE contact admissions tutor (App Soc Sci Commun Dev Yth Wk; Sociol Cult St)
North East Wales (IHE) – 80–120 pts (Soc Sci; Sbstnc Use St)

Leeds Met – contact University
Open University – contact University

Alternative offers
See **Chapter 8** for grade/point equivalences and related information for the following examinations:

Scottish qualifications, the Welsh Baccalaureate, the IB diploma (approximate points shown also in italics in the table of offers), the Irish Leaving Certificate, the European Baccalaureate and the French Baccalaureate.

EXAMPLES OF FOUNDATION DEGREES IN THE SUBJECT FIELD

(see also Social and Public Policy and Administration) Barnfield (Coll); Bath; Bedford (Coll); Bedfordshire; Blackpool and Fylde (Coll); Bicton (Coll); Boston (Coll); Bournemouth; Bradford; Bradford (Coll); Brighton; Bristol City (Coll); Canterbury Christ Church; Carshalton (Coll); Central Lancashire; Croydon (Coll); Cumbria; De Montfort; Derby; Dunstable (Coll); East Lancashire (IHE); Grantham (Coll); Grimsby (IFHE); Hartlepool (CFE); Hertford Reg (Coll); Huddersfield; Hull (Coll); Huntingdonshire Reg (Coll); Leeds Park Lane (Coll); Leicester; Leicester (Coll); Liverpool Hope; London Met; Merthyr Tydfil (Coll); Newcastle (Coll); Newman (UC); Newport; Northbrook (Coll); Nottingham Castle (Coll); Nottingham Trent; Oaklands (Coll); Open University; Oxford and Cherwell Valley (Coll); Oxford Brookes; Peterborough Reg (Coll); Plymouth; Plymouth City (Coll); Portsmouth; Runshaw (Coll); Ruskin (Coll); St Helens (Coll); Sir Gar (Col); Staffordshire Reg Fed; Stratford-upon-Avon (Coll); Sunderland City (Coll); Sussex Downs (Coll); Teesside; Truro (Coll); Warrington (Coll); West Anglia (Coll); Worcester; Worcestershire New (Coll); Winchester; York St John; Yorkshire Coast (Coll)

CHOOSING YOUR COURSE (SEE ALSO CH.1)

Course variations – Widen your options
Society and Government (Aston)
Health and Social Care (Bangor)
Social Work and Applied Social Studies (Bath)
Sociology and Policy Studies (Birmingham City)
Social Welfare and Community Studies (Coventry)
Health Improvement and Social Change (Cumbria)
Social Sciences Combined (Durham)
Criminology and Social Psychology (Essex)
Social Policy and Public Sector Management (Hull)
Applied Community and Social Studies (Liverpool John Moores)
Social Policy and Government (London (LSE))
History, Philosophy and Social Studies (London (UCL))
Social and Cultural Studies in Sport (Sheffield Hallam)
Social Housing (Southampton Solent)
Social Work – Residential Child Care (Strathclyde)
Social Work – Learning Disabilities Nursing (Teesside)
CHECK PROSPECTUSES AND WEBSITES FOR OTHER UNIVERSITIES AND COLLEGES OFFERING THESE COURSES.

Universities and colleges teaching quality See www.qaa.ac.uk; www.unistats.com.

Top universities and colleges (Research) Bradford.

Sandwich degree courses Bath; Gloucestershire.

ADMISSIONS INFORMATION

Number of applicants per place (approx) Abertay Dundee 1; Aston 5; Bangor 2; Bath 6; Bath Spa 4; Bradford 15; Cambridge 7; Cornwall (Coll) 2; Coventry 7; Cumbria 4; De Montfort 1; Durham 3; East Anglia (Psysoc Sci) 4; East London 10; Edge Hill 5; Glasgow Caledonian 9; Hull 5; Kingston 5; Liverpool 13; London (King's) 5, (LSE) (all progs) 14; London South Bank 3; Manchester Met 10; Middlesex 26; Northampton 5; Nottingham 16; Nottingham Trent 2; Portsmouth 3; Roehampton 6; Salford 12; Sheffield Hallam 7; Southampton 2; Staffordshire 2; Strathclyde 9; Sunderland 11; Swansea 8; West Scotland 5; Westminster 14; Winchester 3.

Advice to applicants and planning the UCAS personal statement The Social Studies/Science subject area covers several topics. Focus on these (or some of these) and state your main areas of interest, outlining your work experience, personal goals and motivation to follow the course. See separate subject headings, for example, **Social and Public Policy and Administration**, **Sociology**,

Geography, **Economics**, **Politics** for further information. **Bristol** Evidence of a bright, lively mind. **East Anglia** (Psysoc Sci) This course is designed for those keen to study psychology as a research-based discipline but not wishing to become psychologists. **London (LSE)** Most students take a quarter of their studies outside their main subject area. We have a preference for 'traditional' academic subjects. **Nottingham Trent** GCSE grade C maths may be waived for mature applicants or those taking Access courses who can demonstrate equivalent competence in these areas. **Sheffield Hallam** Interest in current affairs. Details of work experience, paid or unpaid.

Misconceptions about this course **Cornwall (Coll)** That students transfer to Plymouth at the end of year 1: this is a three-year course in Cornwall.

Selection interviews **Yes** Anglia Ruskin, Bangor, Birmingham, Brunel, Cambridge, Coventry, Cumbria, Doncaster (Coll), Durham, East London, Edge Hill, Essex, Glasgow Caledonian, Hull, Kingston, Lampeter, London South Bank, Newcastle, Newport, Nottingham Trent, Oxford, Roehampton, Salford, Sunderland, Thames Valley, Westminster; **Some** Bath (mature students), Bristol, Cornwall (Coll), East Anglia, Robert Gordon, Staffordshire, Winchester, York.

Interview advice and questions Past questions have included: Define democracy. What is the role of the Church in nationalistic aspirations? Does today's government listen to its people? Questions on current affairs. How would you change the running of your school? What are the faults of the Labour Party/Conservative Party? Do you agree with the National Lottery? Is money from the National Lottery well spent? Give examples of how the social services have failed. What is your awareness of the social origins of problems? **Cambridge** Should obese people have free NHS treatment? What is Christmas? (Robinson) 'The main interview is to assess potential. Achievement is measured far more by school reports and the details on the Preliminary Application Form. The interview consists of three main elements. Firstly, the applicant is asked to think about issues which raise questions relating to the four topics in Part I of the course. He or she has to think about and discuss a current political issue, an anthropological question about ritual or how psychology experiments are carried out, for example. The applicant's views are not assessed, merely their ability to discuss their views in a serious and academic way. Next, the applicant is asked to discuss an unfamiliar and difficult text – handed out prior to interview – in order that interpretation and comprehension skills may be assessed. Lastly, we ask the applicant to bring with them an appropriate school essay.' See also **Chapter 7**.

Reasons for rejection (non-academic) Stated preference for other institutions. Incompetence in answering questions.

AFTER-RESULTS ADVICE
Offers to applicants repeating A-levels **Higher** Aston, Essex, Glasgow, Salford (possibly), Swansea; **Same** Anglia Ruskin, Bangor, Bath Spa, Bradford, Chester, Cornwall (Coll), Coventry, Cumbria, Durham, East Anglia, Gloucestershire, Leeds, Liverpool, London Met, London South Bank, Manchester Met, Newport, Nottingham Trent, Roehampton, Sheffield Hallam, Staffordshire, Stirling, Winchester, Wolverhampton; **No offers made** Cambridge.

GRADUATE DESTINATIONS AND EMPLOYMENT (2005/6 HESA)
See **Social and Public Policy and Administration**, **Social Work** and **Sociology**.

Career note Graduates find careers in all aspects of social provision, for example health services, welfare agencies such as housing departments, the probation service, police forces, the prison service, personnel work and residential care and other careers not necessarily linked with their degree subjects.

OTHER DEGREE SUBJECTS FOR CONSIDERATION
Business Studies; Community Studies; Economics; Education; Geography; Government; Health Studies; Law; Politics; Psychology; Public Administration; Social Policy; Social Work; Sociology; Urban Studies.

SOCIAL WORK

(see also **Community Studies** and **Social and Public Policy and Administration**)

Social Work courses (which lead to careers in social work) have similarities to those in Applied Social Studies, Social Policy and Administration and Community Studies and Health Studies. If you are offered a place on a Social Work course which leads to registration as a social worker, you must undergo the Criminal Records Bureau (CRB) disclosure check. You will also have to provide health information and certification. Check for full details of training and careers in social work with the General Social Care Council (see **Appendix 2**).

Useful websites www.gscc.org.uk; www.swap.ac.uk; www.ace.org.uk; www.samaritans.org; www.ccwales.org.uk; www.sssc.uk.com; www.niscc.info; www.socialworkandcare.co.uk.

NB The points totals shown to the left of the institutions are for ease of reference only. It must not be assumed that tariff points are always used by institutions or that they can be substituted for an offer in grades. The level of an offer is not necessarily indicative of the quality of a course.

COURSE OFFERS INFORMATION

Subject requirements/preferences GCSE English and mathematics usually required. **AL** No subjects specified. **NB** A* grades are likely to form part of university offers in the higher ranges for students applying for places in 2008 for entry in 2009: check websites.

Your target offers

320 pts **Glasgow** – ABB (Soc Wk)
Queen's Belfast – ABB (Soc Wk)

300 pts **Brighton** – 300 pts (contact admissions tutor) (Soc Wk)
Edinburgh – BBB (Soc Wk) *(IB 34 pts)*
Sussex – BBB+AS **or** 340 pts (3AL) (Soc Wk) *(IB 32 pts)*
Ulster – BBB 300 pts (Soc Wk)

280 pts **Bath** – BBC (Soc Wk App Soc St) *(IB 32 pts)*
East Anglia – 280–320 pts (Soc Wk)
Lancaster – BBC (Soc Wk) *(IB 30–32 pts)*
Leeds – BBC (Soc Wk)
London (Gold) – BBC (Soc Wk) *(IB 30 pts)*
Sheffield – BBC (Soc Wk) *(IB 30 pts)*
Strathclyde – BBC (Soc Wk)
York – BBC (Soc Wk) *(IB 30 pts)*

260 pts **Birmingham** – BCC (entry reqs vary according to age and education) (Soc Wk)
Bradford – 260 pts (Soc Wk)
Brunel – 260 pts (Soc Wk) *(IB 28 pts)*
Keele – BCC–BBC 260–280 pts (Soc Wk) *(IB 26–28 pts)*
London (RH) – 260 pts (Soc Wk)
Manchester – BCC (Soc Wk) *(IB 28 pts)*
Reading – 260 pts (3AL) 280 pts (4AL) (Soc Wk)
Stirling – BCC (min age 18) (Soc Wk)
Southampton – BCC 240 pts (Soc Wk) *(IB 28 pts H 13 pts)*
Wiltshire (Coll) – 260 pts (Soc Wk)

240 pts **Chester (Warrington)** – 240 pts (Soc Wk)
Coventry – 240–220 pts (Soc Wk)
Northumbria – 240 pts (Soc Wk)
Nottingham Trent – 240 pts (Soc Wk)
Swansea – 240 pts (Soc Wk)
Thames Valley – 240 pts (Soc Wk)

220 pts **Bangor** – 220–260 pts (Soc Wk)
De Montfort – 220 pts (Soc Wk)

Huddersfield – 220 pts (min age 19 on 1 July) (Soc Wk)
Lincoln – 220 pts (Soc Wk)
Winchester – 220 pts (Soc Cr St Comb courses)

200 pts **Anglia Ruskin** – 200 pts (Soc Wk)
Bournemouth – 200 pts (Soc Wk)
Coventry – 200 pts (Soc Welf Commun St)
Cumbria – 200 pts (Soc Wk)
Hull – 200 pts (Soc Wk)
Kent – 200 pts (Soc Wk) *(IB 27 pts)*
Kingston – 200–220 pts (Soc Wk)
Liverpool Hope – 200 pts (Soc Wk)
Middlesex – 200–280 pts (check with Univ) (Soc Wk)
Staffordshire – BB 200 pts (Soc Wk)

180 pts **Chichester** – 180–220 pts (Soc Wk) *(IB 28 pts)*
Edge Hill – 180–220 pts (Soc Wk St)
Glamorgan – 180–240 pts (Soc Wk)
Liverpool (CmC) – 180 pts (Soc Wk)
Liverpool John Moores – 180 pts (Soc Wk)

160 pts **Bedfordshire** – 160–240 pts (Soc Wk)
Birmingham City – CC 160 pts (Soc Wk)
Bristol UWE – 160–180 pts (Soc Wk)
Canterbury Christ Church – 160 pts (Soc Wk)
Cardiff (UWIC) – 160 pts (Soc Wk)
Central Lancashire – 160 pts (Soc Wk)
Derby – 160–120 pts (App Soc Wk)
Dundee – CC (Soc Wk)
Durham New (Coll) – 160 pts (Soc Wk)
East London – 160 pts (Soc Wk)
Essex (South East Essex (Coll)) – 160 pts (Soc Wk)
Glasgow Caledonian – CC (Soc Wk)
Greenwich – 160 pts (Soc Wk)
Hertfordshire – 160 pts (Soc Wk; Nurs (LD) Soc Wk)
London Met – 160 pts (min age 21) (Soc Wk)
London South Bank – CC–EE (Soc Wk)
Newport – 160 pts (Soc Wk)
Northampton – 160–180 pts (Soc Cr courses; Soc Wk)
Oxford Brookes – CC (Soc Wk)
Plymouth – 160 pts (Soc Wk)
Portsmouth – 160 pts (Soc Wk)
Robert Gordon – CC (Soc Wk)
Sheffield Hallam – 160 pts (Soc Wk St)
Suffolk (Univ Campus) – 160–120 pts (Soc Wk)
Sunderland – 160 pts (Soc Wk)
Winchester – 160 pts (Soc Cr St)
Wolverhampton – 160–220 pts (Soc Wk; Soc Cr)

140 pts **Manchester Met** – 140–180 pts (Soc Wk) *(IB 24 pts)*
Southampton Solent – 140 pts (Soc Wk)
West Scotland – CD (Soc Wk)

120 pts **Bucks New** – 120 pts (Soc Wk)
Cardiff (UWIC) – 120 pts (Hlth Soc Cr)
Gloucestershire – 120 pts (Soc Wk)
Manchester Met – 120 pts (Soc Wk)
North East Wales (IHE) – 120 pts (Soc Wk)
Salford – 120–180 pts (Soc Wk St)

Teesside – 120–240 pts (Soc Wk; Soc Wk Nurs LD/MH)
Worcester – 120 pts (Soc Welf courses)
100 pts **Bradford (Coll)** – 100 pts (Soc Wk)
 80 pts **Havering (Coll)** – 80 pts (check with admissions tutor) (Soc Wk)
Norwich City (Coll) – EE (Soc Wk)
Stockport (CFHE) – 80 pts (check with admissions tutor) (Soc Wk)

Leeds Met – contact University

Alternative offers
See **Chapter 8** for grade/point equivalences and related information for the following examinations: Scottish qualifications, the Welsh Baccalaureate, the IB diploma (approximate points shown also in italics in the table of offers), the Irish Leaving Certificate, the European Baccalaureate and the French Baccalaureate.

EXAMPLES OF FOUNDATION DEGREES IN THE SUBJECT FIELD
Chichester. See also **Social and Public Policy and Administration**.

CHOOSING YOUR COURSE (SEE ALSO CH.1)
Course variations – Widen your options
Social Work and Applied Social Studies (Bath)
Social Welfare and Community Studies (Coventry)
Social Work and Nursing (Learning Disabilities) (Mental Health) (Teesside)
See also **Social Studies/Science**
CHECK PROSPECTUSES AND WEBSITES FOR OTHER UNIVERSITIES AND COLLEGES OFFERING THESE COURSES.

Universities and colleges teaching quality See www.qaa.ac.uk; www.unistats.com.

Top universities and colleges (Research) East Anglia; Huddersfield; Kent*; Lancaster; Stirling; Swansea; York.

Sandwich degree courses Bath.

ADMISSIONS INFORMATION
Number of applicants per place (approx) Bangor 2; Bath 11; Bradford 10; Coventry 22; Dundee 6; London Met 27; Northampton 7; Nottingham Trent 6; Sheffield Hallam 4; Staffordshire 3.

Advice to applicants and planning the UCAS personal statement The statement should show motivation for social work, relevant work experience, awareness of the demands of social work and give relevant personal information, for example disabilities. Previous relevant experience in social work preferred in most cases. **Lincoln** Applicants must have had some voluntary or work experience working with people. **Salford** Applicants must be over 19 years on application. **Staffordshire** Awareness of the origins of personal and family difficulties, commitment to anti-discriminatory practice. See also **Social and Public Policy and Administration**. See also **Appendix 2**.

Selection interviews Yes Most courses; Bangor, Bradford, Chichester, Coventry, Liverpool Hope, Nottingham Trent, Salford, Sheffield Hallam, Staffordshire, Thames Valley, Wolverhampton, York; **Some** Dundee.

Interview advice and questions What qualities are needed to be a social worker? What use do you think you will be to society as a social worker? Why should money be spent on prison offenders? Your younger brother is playing truant and mixing with bad company. Your parents don't know. What would you do? See also **Social and Public Policy and Administration** and **Chapter 7**.

Reasons for rejection (non-academic) Criminal convictions.

AFTER-RESULTS ADVICE
Offers to applicants repeating A-levels Same Bangor, Lincoln, Liverpool Hope, Salford, Staffordshire; Suffolk (Univ Campus), Wolverhampton.

GRADUATE DESTINATIONS AND EMPLOYMENT (2005/6 HESA)
Graduates surveyed 2225 **Employed** 1465 **In further study** 110 **Assumed unemployed** 145.

Career note See **Social Studies/Science**.

OTHER DEGREE SUBJECTS FOR CONSIDERATION
Community Studies; Conductive Education; Criminology; Economics; Education; Health Studies; Law; Psychology; Public Sector Management and Administration; Social Policy; Sociology; Youth Studies.

SOCIOLOGY
(see also **Social and Public Policy and Administration** and **Social Studies/Science**)

Sociology is the study of social organisation, social structures, systems, institutions and practices. Courses are likely to include the meaning and structure of, for example, race, ethnicity and gender, industrial behaviour, crime and deviance, health and illness. NB Sociology is not a training course for social workers, although some graduates take additional qualifications to qualify in social work.

Useful websites www.britsoc.co.uk; www.asanet.org; www.sociology.org.uk; www.sociology.org.

NB The points totals shown to the left of the institutions are for ease of reference only. It must not be assumed that tariff points are always used by institutions or that they can be substituted for an offer in grades. The level of an offer is not necessarily indicative of the quality of a course.

COURSE OFFERS INFORMATION
Subject requirements/preferences **GCSE** English and mathematics usually required. **AL** No subjects specified. **NB** A* grades are likely to form part of university offers in the higher ranges for students applying for places in 2008 for entry in 2009: check websites.

Your target offers
360 pts **and above**
　　Cambridge – AAA (Soc Pol Sci) *(IB 38–42 pts)*
340 pts **Cardiff** – AAB–BCC 340–260 pts (Sociol joint courses; offers vary with 2nd subj)
320 pts **Bristol** – ABB–BBB (Sociol; Sociol Phil; Pol Sociol; Soc Pol Sociol; Theol Sociol)
　　Durham – ABB (Sociol Law; Pol Sociol)
　　East Anglia – ABB–BBB (Pol Sociol Contemp Cult; Soty Cult Media)
　　Exeter – ABB–BBC (Sociol; Sociol Arbc St; Sociol Fr/Ger/Ital/Russ/Span)
　　Glasgow – ABB (Sociology)
　　Lancaster – ABB (Org St Sociol)
　　Leeds – ABB–BBB (Sociol Span; Sociol Theol Relig St)
　　Loughborough – 320–330 pts (Econ Sociol)
　　Manchester – ABB–BBB (Sociol; Sociol Crim; Dev St Sociol; Bus St Sociol; Econ Sociol) *(IB 32 pts)*
　　Warwick – BBCc–BBBc (Sociol; Sociol (Soc Pol) (Gndr St) (Cult St) (Rsch Meth); Hist Sociol; Law Sociol; Fr Sociol) *(IB 32–33 pts)*
300 pts **Aston** – BBB 300 pts (Sociol courses)
　　Bath – BBB (Sociol; Sociol Soc Pol; Sociol HR Mgt)
　　Birmingham – BBB–BBC (Sociology) *(IB 32 pts)*
　　Cardiff – BBB–BCC (Sociol single Hons)
　　Durham – BBB (Sociology)
　　Edinburgh – BBB (Sociol; Sociol Pol; Sociol Soc Econ Hist; Sociol Anth; Sociol S As St)
　　Essex – 300–280 pts (Sociol; Sociol Crim; Sociol Media St) *(IB 30–32 pts)*
　　Lancaster – BBB (Sociol courses except under **280/320 pts**) *(IB 30–32 pts)*
　　London (LSE) – BBB (Sociol; Soc Pol Sociol) *(IB 36 pts)*
　　Newcastle – BBB (Sociol; Pol Sociol) *(IB 32 pts)*

Nottingham – ABC–BBB (Sociol; Sociol Soc Pol) *(IB 30–32 pts)*
Queen's Belfast – BBB–BBCb (Sociol courses)
Sheffield – BBB (Sociology)
Southampton – BBB (Sociol courses)
Surrey – BBB–BBC 300–280 pts (Sociol; Sociol Soc Rsch; Sociol Cult Media) *(IB 30–32 pts)*
Sussex – BBB **or** 340 pts 3AL+AS (Sociol courses)
York – BBB (Sociol Soc Pol; Sociol; Sociol Educ)

280 pts **Brighton** – 280 pts (Sociol Soc Pol) *(IB 28 pts)*
Durham – BBC (Anth Sociol)
Kent – 280 pts (Sociol; Sociol Yr Abrd; Sociol Ital) *(IB 27 pts)*
Lancaster – BBC (Relig St Sociol)
Leeds – BBC (Sociol; Soc Pol Sociol)
Liverpool – BBC (Sociol; Sociol Soc Pol; Crim Sociol) *(IB 30 pts)*
London (Gold) – BBC (Sociol Cult St) *(IB 28 pts)*
Oxford Brookes – BBC–BCC (Sociol courses)
Salford – 280 pts (Jrnl Sociol)

260 pts **Brighton** – 260 pts (Sociol Spo Leis)
Brunel – 260 pts (Sociol; Psy Sociol; Soc Anth Sociol; Sociol Media St) *(IB 28 pts)*
Chester – 260 pts (Sociology)
Coventry – 260 pts (Sociol; Sociol Psy; Sociol Crim)
Keele – 260–320 pts (Sociol courses) *(IB 30 pts)*
Leicester – 260–320 pts (Sociol; Psy Sociol; Sociol Comb courses) *(IB 28–30 pts)*
London (Gold) – BCC (Sociol; Sociol Pol) *(IB 28 pts)*
Loughborough – 260–300 pts (Sociology)
Northumbria – 260 pts (Sociol courses)
Oxford Brookes – BCC **or** BCcc (Pol Sociol)
Richmond (Am Int Univ) – 260 pts (Soc Sci (Sociol))
Stirling – BCC (Sociol courses)
Strathclyde – BCC/BB (Sociology)

240 pts **Aberdeen** – CCC (Sociol courses)
Cardiff (UWIC) – 240 pts (Sociol Pop Cult)
City – CCC–BCC (Sociol; Sociol Econ; Sociol Media St; Sociol Psy; Int Pol Sociol) *(IB 26 pts)*
Gloucestershire – 240 pts (Sociol courses)
Nottingham Trent – 240–280 pts (Sociol courses)
Portsmouth – 240–300 pts (Sociol; Sociol Crim; Sociol Media St; Sociol Psy)
Salford – 240 pts (Sociol Crim)
Sheffield Hallam – 240 pts (Sociology)
Ulster – 240–220 pts (Sociol; Sociol Ir Hist; Sociol Soc Pol)
Westminster – CCC/BC (Sociology)

220 pts **Bangor** – 220–260 pts (Sociology)
Birmingham City – 220 pts (Sociol; Sociol Crim; Sociol Psy; Sociol Cult St)
Hull – 220–280 pts (Sociol; Sociol Anth Gndr St; Sociol Soc Anth Span)
Kingston – 220–280 pts (Sociol courses)
Liverpool Hope – 220 pts (Sociol courses)
Manchester Met – 220–280 pts (Sociol joint courses) *(IB 24–28 pts)*
Queen Margaret – CCD 220 pts (Sociol Cult)
Salford – 220 pts (Sociol; Sociol Cult St)

200 pts **Anglia Ruskin** – 200 pts (Sociology)
Bath Spa – 200–240 pts (Sociol; Sociol Comb courses)
Bristol UWE – 200–260 pts (Sociology) *(IB 28 pts)*
Glamorgan – 200 pts (Sociology)
Huddersfield – 200 pts (Sociol; Sociol Crim)
Napier – 200 pts (Psy Sociol)
Plymouth – 200 pts (Sociol courses)
Staffordshire – 200 pts (Sociology)

For information on how to read the Subject Tables, see **Chapter 8**.

180 pts **Bangor** – 180–220 pts (Sociol Soc Pol (Welsh medium only))
Bradford – 180–220 pts (Sociol Psy; Interd Hum St)
Derby – 180 pts (Sociol Comb Hons)
Edge Hill – 180–220 pts (Sociol; Sociol Soc Wk St)
Greenwich – 180 pts min (Sociology)
Manchester Met – 180 pts (Sociol; Cult St Sociol)
Northampton – 180–200 pts (Sociology)
160 pts **Abertay Dundee** – CC (Sociology)
Canterbury Christ Church – 160 pts (Sociology)
Central Lancashire – 160 pts (Sociol courses)
East London – 160 pts (Sociol courses)
Glasgow Caledonian – CC–DD 160 pts (Hum Biol Sociol Psy)
Liverpool John Moores – 160–240 pts (Sociol courses)
London Met – 160 pts **or** Access course (Sociology)
London South Bank – CC (Sociology)
Middlesex – 160–200 pts (Sociology)
Norwich City (Coll) – 160 pts (Engl Cult St)
St Mary's (UC) – 160–200 pts (Sociol courses)
Sunderland – 160 pts (Sociology)
Teesside – 160 pts (Sociology)
Thames Valley – 160 pts (Sociol Hlth St; Sociol Psy; Sociol Lang)
Wolverhampton – 160–220 pts (Sociology)
Worcester – 160 pts (Sociology)
140 pts **Marjon (UC)** – 140–200 pts (Sociol courses)
West Scotland – CD (Soc Sci (Sociol))
120 pts **Bucks New** – 120–240 pts 2AL (Sociol courses)
Grimsby (IFHE) – 120 pts (Sociol Psy; Sociol St)
North East Wales (IHE) – 120 pts (Sociol courses)
Roehampton – 120 pts (Sociol courses)
Suffolk (Univ Campus) – 120–140 pts (Sociol courses)
100 pts **Swansea (Inst)** – 100 pts (Engl St Sociol)
West Anglia (Coll) – 100 pts (Sociol courses)

Leeds Met – contact University

Alternative offers

See **Chapter 8** for grade/point equivalences and related information for the following examinations: Scottish qualifications, the Welsh Baccalaureate, the IB diploma (approximate points shown also in italics in the table of offers), the Irish Leaving Certificate, the European Baccalaureate and the French Baccalaureate.

EXAMPLES OF FOUNDATION DEGREES IN THE SUBJECT FIELD
Bradford; Cornwall (Coll); East Lancashire (IHE); London Met; Winchester.

CHOOSING YOUR COURSE (SEE ALSO CH.1)
Course variations – Widen your options
Interdisciplinary Human Studies (Bradford)
Sociology of Sport and Leisure (Brighton)
Sociology with Study Abroad (Bristol)
Health Sciences and Sociology (Chester)
International Politics and Sociology (City)
Health Service Management with Sociology (East London)
Law and Society (Exeter)
Sociology and Criminology (Huddersfield)
Organisation Studies and Sociology (Lancaster)
Combined Honours (Liverpool)

For a quick reference offers calculator, fold out the inside back cover.

Childhood and Youth Studies and Sociology (London South Bank)
Applied Social Studies (Manchester Met)
Psychology and Sociology (Salford)
Crime, Deviance and Society (Staffordshire)
CHECK PROSPECTUSES AND WEBSITES FOR OTHER UNIVERSITIES AND COLLEGES OFFERING THESE COURSES.

Universities and colleges teaching quality See www.qaa.ac.uk; www.unistats.com.

Top universities and colleges (Research) Aberdeen; Bristol; Brunel; Cambridge; Cardiff; Edinburgh; Essex*; Exeter; Lancaster*; London (Gold)*, (LSE); Loughborough*; Manchester*; Queen's Belfast; Surrey*; Warwick; York.

Sandwich degree courses Aston; Bath.

ADMISSIONS INFORMATION
Number of applicants per place (approx) Aston 8; Bangor 1; Bath 6; Birmingham 8; Birmingham City 12; Bristol 8; Brunel 24; Cardiff 5; Cardiff (UWIC) 4; City 11; Durham 13; East Anglia 15; East London 8; Exeter 5; Gloucestershire 8; Greenwich 5; Hull 11; Kent 10; Kingston 9; Lancaster 12; Leeds 14; Leicester 6; Liverpool 9; Liverpool John Moores 10; London (Gold) 5, (LSE) 6; London Met 3; Loughborough 10; Northampton 3; Northumbria 18; Nottingham 7; Plymouth 9; Portsmouth 12; Roehampton 4; Sheffield Hallam 7; Southampton 8; Staffordshire 10; Sunderland 5; Surrey 6; Swansea 8; Warwick 20; Worcester 5; York 5.

Advice to applicants and planning the UCAS personal statement Show your ability to communicate and work as part of a group and your curiosity about issues such as social conflict and social change between social groups. **Birmingham** Discuss your interests in sociology on the personal statement. **Cardiff (UWIC)** (Non-EU students) Good command of written and spoken English required. **Liverpool John Moores** We look for intellectual curiosity about sociology and social problems. **London Met** Realistic awareness of the needs of living and studying in university conditions. **Northumbria** (Non-EU students) Fluency in English is required. See **Social Studies/Science**.

Misconceptions about this course Some applicants believe that all sociologists want to become social workers. **Birmingham** Students with an interest in crime and deviance may be disappointed that we do not offer modules in this area. **London Met** That it is the stamping ground of student activists and has no relevance to the real world.

Selection interviews Yes Aston, Birmingham City, Brunel, Cambridge, City, Derby, Durham, East London, Exeter, Hull, Lancaster, Leeds, Leicester, Liverpool, Liverpool Hope, London (Gold), Loughborough, Newcastle, Nottingham, Portsmouth, St Mary's (UC), Surrey, Swansea, Warwick; **Some** Bath (mature applicants), Bath Spa, Birmingham (mature applicants), Bristol, Cardiff, Kent, Liverpool John Moores, London Met, Nottingham Trent, Salford, Sheffield Hallam, Southampton, Staffordshire.

Interview advice and questions Past questions have included: Why do you want to study Sociology? What books have you read on the subject? How do you see the role of women changing in the next 20 years? **London Met** Questions will focus on existing level of interest in the subject and the applicant's expectations about studying. See also **Chapter 7**.

Reasons for rejection (non-academic) Evidence of difficulty with written work. Non-attendance at Open days (find out from your universities if your attendance will affect their offers). In the middle of an interview for Sociology a student asked us if we could interview him for Sports Studies instead! **Durham** No evidence of awareness of what the course involves. **London Met** References which indicated that the individual would not be able to work effectively within a diverse student group; concern that the applicant had not put any serious thought into the choice of subject for study. See also **Social and Public Policy and Administration**.

AFTER-RESULTS ADVICE
Offers to applicants repeating A-levels Higher Brunel, East London, Essex, Glasgow, Hull, Newcastle, Nottingham Trent, Swansea, Warwick, York; **Possibly higher** Leeds, Liverpool, Portsmouth; **Same** Aston, Bangor, Bath, Birmingham, Birmingham City, Bristol, Cardiff, Coventry, Derby, Durham,

Gloucestershire, Kingston, Lancaster, Liverpool Hope, Liverpool John Moores, London Met, Loughborough, Northumbria, Roehampton, St Mary's (UC), Salford, Sheffield Hallam, Southampton, Staffordshire; **No offers made** Cambridge.

GRADUATE DESTINATIONS AND EMPLOYMENT (2005/6 HESA)
Graduates surveyed 4200 **Employed** 2215 **In further study** 590 **Assumed unemployed** 270.

Career note See **Social Studies/Science**.

OTHER DEGREE SUBJECTS FOR CONSIDERATION
Anthropology; Economic and Social History; Economics; Education; Geography; Government; Health Studies; History; Law; Politics; Psychology; Social Policy; Social Work.

SPANISH

(including **Hispanic Studies** and **Portuguese; see also Languages** and **Latin American Studies**)

Spanish can be studied by focusing on the language and literature of Spain, although broader courses in Hispanic Studies are available which also include Portuguese and Latin American studies. See also **Appendix 2** under **Languages**.

Useful websites www.donquijote.co.uk; www.europa.eu; www.cilt.org.uk; www.iol.org.uk; www.bbc.co.uk/languages; www.languageadvantage.com; www.languagematters.co.uk; www.reed.co.uk/multilingual; www.studyspanish.com; www.spanishlanguageguide.com; see also **Latin American Studies**.

NB The points totals shown to the left of the institutions are for ease of reference only. It must not be assumed that tariff points are always used by institutions or that they can be substituted for an offer in grades. The level of an offer is not necessarily indicative of the quality of a course.

COURSE OFFERS INFORMATION
Subject requirements/preferences **GCSE** English, mathematics or science and a foreign language. **AL** Spanish required for most courses. **NB** A* grades are likely to form part of university offers in the higher ranges for students applying for places in 2008 for entry in 2009: check websites.

Your target offers
360 pts and above
        Cambridge – AAA (Modn Mediev Langs (Span)) *(IB 38–42 pts)*
        London (King's) – AAAb (Hist Port Braz St)
        London (QM) – AAA-BCC (Hisp St)
        London (UCL) – AAA-AAB (Mgt St Span; Lat Span; Hist Art Span) *(IB 34–36 pts)*
        Oxford – Offers vary eg AAA-AAB (Modn Lang (Port) (Span)) *(IB 38–42 pts)*
        Warwick – AABc-ABBc (Hist Cult (Span))
340 pts **Bristol** – AAB-BBC (Span; Span Port; Span Russ; Hisp St) *(IB 30–33 pts)*
        Bristol – AAB-BBB (Port courses)
        Cardiff – AAB (Cult Crit Span; Engl Lit Span) *(IB 30 pts)*
        Exeter – AAB-ABB (Engl Span)
        Lancaster – AAB (Euro Mgt Span)
        St Andrews – AAB-BBB (Span courses) *(IB 32 pts)*
320 pts **Aston** – ABB 320 pts (Int Bus Span) *(IB 30–31 pts)*
        Bath – ABB-BBB (Span Ital/Russ; Fr Span)
        Birmingham – ABB-BBB (Port courses; Hisp St courses) *(IB 32 pts)*
        Exeter – ABB-BBB (Span courses except under **340 pts**)
        Glasgow – ABB-BBB (Hisp St)
        Lancaster – ABB-BBB (Span courses except under **340 pts**)
        London (King's) – ABB (Fr Hisp St)

London (RH) – ABB–BBB (Span courses) *(IB 32 pts)*
Manchester – ABB–BBB (Span Port Lat Am St; Span Chin)
Newcastle – ABB (Ling Span; Span Bus St; Span Pol; Span Port Lat Am St)
Southampton – ABB 320 pts (Span courses; Port courses) *(IB 32 pts)*
300 pts **Aston** – 300 pts (Span courses)
Cardiff – BBB–BBC (Span courses except under **340 pts**)
East Anglia – BBB–BBC (Transl Media Span; Span courses)
Edinburgh – BBB (Span courses)
Essex – 300 pts (Econ Span)
Leeds – BBB–BBC (Port joint courses) *(IB 32 pts)*
Leeds – BBB (Span; Hisp Lat Am St) *(IB 32 pts)*
Liverpool – BBB 300 pts (Hisp St courses)
London (King's) – BBB+AS **or** BBbbb (Port Braz St courses)
London (LSE) – optional subj check with admissions tutor (Fr/Ger/Russ/Span)
London (UCL) – BBB+AS–BBC+AS (Hisp St; Modn Iber Lat Am Reg St)
Queen's Belfast – BBB–BBCb (Span courses)
Sheffield – BBB–BBC (Hisp St courses) *(IB 30–32 pts)*
Stirling – BBB 2nd yr entry (Span courses)
Surrey – BBB–BCC 300–260 pts (Law Span Law)
280 pts **Heriot-Watt** – BBC (App Langs Transl (Fr Span) (Ger Span))
Kent – 280–260 pts (Span courses; Pol Int Rel Span) *(IB 32 pts)*
Leicester – BBC–BCC (Span Ger/Fr/Ital) *(IB 28–30 pts)*
London (King's) – BBC+AS **or** BBbcc (Hisp St Modn Gk; Hisp St Engl; Hisp St Ling; Hisp St Port) *(IB 32 pts)*
Loughborough – 280–300 pts (Econ Span)
Nottingham – ABB–BBC (Hisp St courses) *(IB 32 pts)*
Westminster – 280 pts (Span courses)
260 pts **Aberystwyth** – 260 pts (Span courses)
Essex – 260 pts (Span St Modn Langs)
Kent – 260 pts (Hisp St)
London (Gold) – BCC (Euro St (Span))
Strathclyde – BCC/BB (Spanish)
240 pts **Aberdeen** – CCC (Hisp St courses; Span courses)
Bristol UWE – 240–300 pts (Span courses)
Chester – 240 pts (Span courses)
Coventry – 240 pts (Span courses)
Salford – 240–300 pts (Modn Langs Span)
Stirling – CCC 1st yr entry (Span courses)
Swansea – 240–300 pts (Span courses)
Ulster – CCC–CCD 240–220 pts (Span courses)
220 pts **Bangor** – 220–260 pts (Span Fr/Ger/Ital; Acc Span; Mgt Span; Span Tour)
Dundee – CCD–BCC 220–300 pts (Span courses)
Hull – 220–280 pts (Span courses)
Nottingham Trent – 220 pts (Span courses)
200 pts **Hertfordshire** – 200–240 pts (Span courses)
Napier – 200 pts (Tour Mgt Span)
Northumbria – 200–280 pts (Span courses)
Plymouth – 200–280 pts (Span courses)
Portsmouth – 200–280 pts (Span Lat Am St; Span St)
Sheffield Hallam – 200 pts (Int Bus Span; Span Mark; Span Tour)
180 pts **Anglia Ruskin** – 180–200 pts (Span courses)
Buckingham – 180–240 pts (Span courses)
European Bus Sch London – DDD (Int Bus Span)
Heriot-Watt – DDD (Chem Span)
Liverpool John Moores – 180–220 pts (Span courses)

160 pts	**Bucks New** – 160–180 pts (Span courses)
	Central Lancashire – 160–180 pts (Span Bus Span)
	Greenwich – DDE–BCC 160–260 pts (Span courses)
	Manchester Met – 160–180 pts (Span courses)
	Middlesex – 160–200 pts (Span courses)
	London Met – 160 pts (Span Lat Am St)
	Roehampton – 160 pts (Span courses; Transl Span)
	Wolverhampton – 160–220 pts (Span courses)
80 pts	**Kingston** – 80 pts (Span minor subj – lang req)
	London (Birk) – 80 pts (p/t Span Lat Am St; Span Port)

Leeds Met – contact University

Alternative offers

See **Chapter 8** for grade/point equivalences and related information for the following examinations: Scottish qualifications, the Welsh Baccalaureate, the IB diploma (approximate points shown also in italics in the table of offers), the Irish Leaving Certificate, the European Baccalaureate and the French Baccalaureate.

CHOOSING YOUR COURSE (SEE ALSO CH.1)

Course variations – Widen your options
European Studies French and Spanish (Aston)
Spanish and *ab initio* Russian/Italian/German (Bath)
Spanish and Portuguese (Bristol)
Arts Combined (Durham)
Interpreting and Translating with Double Honours Languages (East Anglia)
Latin American Studies (Essex)
Hispanic Studies and Business Administration (Kent)
TESOL and Spanish (Plymouth)
Law with Spanish Law (Surrey)
History and Culture – Spanish (Warwick)
CHECK PROSPECTUSES AND WEBSITES FOR OTHER UNIVERSITIES AND COLLEGES OFFERING THESE COURSES.

Universities and colleges teaching quality See www.qaa.ac.uk; www.unistats.com.

Top universities and colleges (Research) (Iberian and Latin American Languages) Birmingham; Cambridge*; Edinburgh; London (King's)*, (QM)*; Manchester*; Newcastle; Nottingham*; Oxford; St Andrews; Sheffield; Swansea.

ADMISSIONS INFORMATION

Number of applicants per place (approx) Birmingham 9; Bristol 3; Cardiff 3; Exeter 5; Hull 14; Leeds 10; Liverpool 3; London (Gold) 6, (King's) 6, (QM) 5, (UCL) 6; Middlesex 2; Newcastle 12; Nottingham 16; Portsmouth 4; Salford 5.

Advice to applicants and planning the UCAS personal statement Visits to Spanish-speaking countries should be discussed. Study the geography, culture, literature and politics of Spain (or Portugal) and discuss your interests in full. Further information could be obtained from embassies in London. **St Andrews** Give evidence of interest and your reasons for choosing the course. See also **Appendix 2** under **Languages**.

Selection interviews Yes Cambridge, Hull, London (Gold), (RH), (UCL), Nottingham, Oxford; **Some** Cardiff, Leeds, Roehampton, Swansea.

Applicants' impressions (A=Open day; B=Interview day) Exeter (A) The Open day consisted of a presentation about the University and the department and then an interview with the course tutor followed by a tour of the campus and halls. **London (UCL)** (Hisp St; B) The interview was followed by a brief talk and a Spanish TV programme.

Interview advice and questions Candidates offering A-level Spanish are likely to be questioned on their A-level work, their reasons for wanting to take the subject and on their knowledge of Spain and its people. Interest in Spain important for all applicants. Mostly questions about the literature I had read and I was given a poem and asked questions on it. Questions were asked in the target language. There were two interviewers for the Spanish interview; they did their best to trip me up and to make me think under pressure by asking aggressive questions. See **Chapter 7**.

AFTER-RESULTS ADVICE
Offers to applicants repeating A-levels **Higher** Glasgow, Leeds; **Same** Cardiff, Chester, Hull, Liverpool, London (RH), Newcastle, Nottingham, Roehampton, Swansea; **No offers made** Cambridge.

GRADUATE DESTINATIONS AND EMPLOYMENT (2005/6 HESA)
Graduates in Spanish surveyed 710 **Employed** 395 **In further study** 115 **Assumed unemployed** 40.

Graduates in Portuguese surveyed 55 **Employed** 25 **In further study** 10 **Assumed unemployed** 5.

Career note See **Languages**.

OTHER DEGREE SUBJECTS FOR CONSIDERATION
International Business Studies; Latin American Studies; Linguistics; see other **Language** tables.

SPEECH PATHOLOGY/SCIENCES/THERAPY

Speech Pathology/Sciences/Therapy is the study of speech defects caused by accident, disease or psychological trauma. Courses lead to qualification as a speech therapist. This is one of many medical courses. See also **Medicine** and **Appendix 2**.

Useful websites www.rcslt.org; www.speechteach.co.uk; www.asha.org.

NB The points totals shown to the left of the institutions are for ease of reference only. It must not be assumed that tariff points are always used by institutions or that they can be substituted for an offer in grades. The level of an offer is not necessarily indicative of the quality of a course.

COURSE OFFERS INFORMATION
Subject requirements/preferences **GCSE** English language, modern foreign language and biology/dual award science at grade B or above. **AL** At least one science subject; biology may be stipulated, psychology and English language may be preferred. **NB** A* grades are likely to form part of university offers in the higher ranges for students applying for places in 2008 for entry in 2009: check websites. **Other requirements** Criminal Records Bureau (CRB) and occupational health checks essential for speech sciences/speech therapy applicants.

Your target offers
340 pts **London (UCL)** – ABBe–BBBe (Sp Sci) *(IB 32–34 pts)*
320 pts **Manchester** – ABB (Sp Lang Thera)
 Newcastle – ABB (Sp Lang Sci) *(IB 35 pts H555 ST biol 6)*
 Queen Margaret – ABB (Sp Lang Thera) *(IB 32 pts)*
 Reading – 320 pts (Sp Lang Thera)
 Sheffield – ABB **or** ABab (Sp Sci) *(IB 33 pts)*
300 pts **Cardiff (UWIC)** – BBB (Sp Lang Thera) *(IB 28 pts)*
 City – BBB (Sp Lang Thera) *(IB 30 pts)*
 East Anglia – BBB (Sp Lang Thera) *(IB 32 pts H555)*
 Leeds – BBB (Ling Phn) *(IB 32 pts)*
 Manchester Met – BBB (Sp Path Thera; Psy Sp Path)
 Sheffield – BBB (Hum Comm Sci) *(IB 32 pts)*
 Strathclyde – BBB (Sp Lang Path) *(IB 30 pts)*
 Ulster – BBB (Sp Lang Thera) *(IB 25 pts)* (See **Ch.7**)

280 pts **De Montfort** – BBC (Hum Comm (Sp Lang Thera))
Marjon (UC) – BBC 280 pts (Sp Lang Thera))
260 pts **Birmingham City** – BCC 260 pts (Sp Lang Thera)
180 pts **Central Lancashire** – 180 pts (Df St) *(IB 28 pts)*

Leeds Met – contact University

Alternative offers
See **Chapter 8** for grade/point equivalences and related information for the following examinations: Scottish qualifications, the Welsh Baccalaureate, the IB diploma (approximate points shown also in italics in the table of offers), the Irish Leaving Certificate, the European Baccalaureate and the French Baccalaureate.

CHOOSING YOUR COURSE (SEE ALSO CH.1)

Course variations – Widen your options
Deaf Studies (Central Lancashire)
Linguistics and Phonetics (Leeds)
Psychology and Speech Pathology (Manchester)
Speech Science (Sheffield)
See also **Health Sciences/Studies**
CHECK PROSPECTUSES AND WEBSITES FOR OTHER UNIVERSITIES AND COLLEGES OFFERING THESE COURSES.

Universities and colleges teaching quality See www.qaa.ac.uk; www.unistats.com.

Top universities and colleges (Research) London (UCL); Manchester.

ADMISSIONS INFORMATION

Number of applicants per place (approx) Birmingham City 28; Cardiff (UWIC) 10; City 16; De Montfort 5; London (UCL) 9; Manchester Met 21; Newcastle 23; Queen Margaret 12.

Advice to applicants and planning the UCAS personal statement Contact with speech therapists and visits to their clinics are an essential part of the preparation for this career. Discuss these contacts in full, giving details of any work experience or work shadowing you have done and your interest in helping people to communicate, showing evidence of good 'people skills'. **Cardiff (UWIC)** Observation of speech and language therapists. Relevant work experience. **Manchester Met** Observation of speech therapists working with children and adults. (Non-EU students) Good English required because of placement periods. See also **Appendix 2** and **Chapter 7**.

Misconceptions about this course Some students fail to differentiate between speech therapy, occupational therapy and physiotherapy. They do not realise that to study speech and language therapy there are academic demands, including the study of linguistics, psychology, medical sciences and clinical dynamics, so the course is intensive. **Cardiff (UWIC)** Some are under the impression that good grades are not necessary, that it is an easy option and one has to speak with a standard pronunciation.

Selection interviews **Yes** De Montfort, London (UCL), Manchester Met, Marjon (UC), Queen Margaret, Sheffield.

Interview advice and questions Have you visited a speech therapy clinic? What made you want to become a speech therapist? What type of speech problems are there? What type of person would make a good speech therapist? Interviews often include an ear test (test of listening ability). What did you see when you visited a speech and language therapy clinic? **Cardiff (UWIC)** Interviewees must demonstrate an insight into communication problems and explain how one speech sound is produced. See also **Chapter 7**.

Reasons for rejection (non-academic) Insufficient knowledge of speech and language therapy. Lack of maturity. Poor communication skills. Written language problems.

AFTER-RESULTS ADVICE

Offers to applicants repeating A-levels **Higher** Birmingham City, Cardiff (UWIC); **Possibly higher** Manchester Met; **Same** City, De Montfort, Newcastle, Ulster.

GRADUATE DESTINATIONS AND EMPLOYMENT (2005/6 HESA)

No data available.

Career note Speech therapists work mainly in NHS clinics, some work in hospitals and others in special schools or units for the mentally or physically handicapped. The demand for speech therapists is high.

OTHER DEGREE SUBJECTS FOR CONSIDERATION

Audiology; Communication Studies; Deaf Studies; Education; Health Studies; Linguistics; Psychology.

SPORTS SCIENCES/STUDIES

(see also **Physical Education**)

In addition to the theory and practice of many different sporting activities, Sports Sciences/Studies courses also cover the psychological aspects of sports and business administration. The geography, economics and sociology of recreation may also be included. **Centres of Cricketing Excellence** The England and Wales Cricket Board has introduced the Universities Centres of Cricketing Excellence scheme (UCCE). The scheme is open to male cricketers with potential to play first class cricket and to female cricketers of senior county standard irrespective of their choice of degree subject. Details can be obtained from the following centres of excellence: Bradford (Univ) tel 01274 234867; Bradford (Coll) tel 01274 753291; Leeds (Univ) tel 0113 233 5096; Leeds Met (Univ) tel 0113 282 3113; Cambridge (Univ) tel 01223 336580; Anglia Ruskin (Univ) tel 01223 363271; Cardiff (Univ) tel 029 2087 4045; Cardiff (UWIC) tel 029 2041 6590; Glamorgan (Univ) tel 01443 482577; Durham (Univ) 0191 374 3463; Loughborough (Univ) tel 01509 223283; Oxford (Univ) tel 01865 245869; Oxford Brookes (Univ) tel 01865 483166. See also **Appendix 2**.

Useful websites www.isrm.co.uk; www.uksport.gov.uk; www.laureus.com; www.wsf.org.uk; www.sta.co.uk; www.olympic.org; www.sportscotland.org.uk; www.baha.org.uk; www.planet-science.com; www.london2012.org.

NB The points totals shown to the left of the institutions are for ease of reference only. It must not be assumed that tariff points are always used by institutions or that they can be substituted for an offer in grades. The level of an offer is not necessarily indicative of the quality of a course.

COURSE OFFERS INFORMATION

Subject requirements/preferences **GCSE** English, mathematics and, often, a science subject; check prospectuses. **AL** Science required for Sport Science courses. PE required for some Sport Studies courses. **NB** A* grades are likely to form part of university offers in the higher ranges for students applying for places in 2008 for entry in 2009: check websites. **Other requirements** A Criminal Records Bureau (CRB) check required for many courses.

Your target offers

360 pts **or above**
    Bath – AAA (Spo Exer Sci)
    Exeter – AAA (Psy Spo Exer Sci) *(IB 32–34 pts)*
    Loughborough – AAA–AAB (Spo Exer Sci) *(IB 32–34 pts)*
340 pts **Bath** – AAB (Spo Eng)
    Loughborough – 340–320 pts (Spo Sci Mgt)
    Sheffield – 340 pts (Spo Eng)

320 pts **Bath** – ABB (Coach Educ Spo Dev courses) *(IB 35–36 pts)*
Birmingham – ABB–BBB 320–300 pts (Spo Sci Mat Tech; Spo Exer Sci; App Glf Mgt St; Spo PE Commun St) *(IB 32–34 pts)*
Durham – ABB–BBB (Sport) *(IB 32–30 pts)*
Essex – 320–280 pts (Spo Exer Sci; Spo Sci Biol)
Exeter – ABB 320 pts (Exer Spo Sci)
Loughborough – 320–340 pts (Maths Spo Sci; Spo Tech)
Ulster – ABB (Spo courses)

300 pts **Aberdeen** – 300 pts 2nd yr entry (BSc Spo Exer Sci; Spo St (Spo Soty))
Cardiff (UWIC) – 300 pts (Spo Thera; Spo Exer Sci)
Central Lancashire – BBB (Spo Jrnl)
Dundee – 300 pts 2nd yr entry (Spo Biomed)
Glasgow – BBB (Spo Med)
Hertfordshire – 300 pts (Spo Thera)
Kent – 300 pts (Spo Thera Hlth Fit) *(IB 33 pts)*
Leeds – BBB (Spo Sci Physiol; Spo Sci (Out Actvts); Spo Exer Sci; Spo Mat Tech)
Salford – 300 pts (Spo Rehab)
Sheffield – BBB–BBC (Spo Eng)
Southampton – BBB (Spo Mgt Ldrshp; Spo St)
Teesside – 300 pts (Spo Thera)

280 pts **Brighton** – BBC (Spo Jrnl) *(IB 30 pts)*
Bristol UWE – 280–340 pts (Spo Thera Rehab)
Brunel – 280 pts (Spo Sci; Bus St Spo Sci; Spo Sci (Admin Dev) (Coach) (Exer Fit) (PE)) *(IB 28 pts)*
Cardiff (UWIC) – 280 pts (Spo Coach; Spo Dev)
Chichester – 280–320 pts (Spo Thera)
Gloucestershire – 280 pts (Spo Educ)
Heriot-Watt – BBC 2nd yr entry (Spo Exer Sci; Spo Exer Sci Psy)
Liverpool John Moores – 280–300 pts (Sci Ftbl; Spo Sci; Physl Actvt Exer Hlth; App Psy Spo Sci)
Loughborough – 280 pts (Spo Sci Phys)
Manchester Met – 280 pts (Spo Exer Sci) *(IB 28 pts)*
Northumbria – 280 pts (App Spo Exer Sci; Spo Mgt; Spo Dev Coach; Psy Spo Sci)
Nottingham Trent – 280 pts (Spo Exer Sci)
Sheffield Hallam – 280 pts (Spo Exer Sci)
Swansea – BBC 280 pts (Spo Sci)

260 pts **Bangor** – 260 pts (Spo Hlth PE; Spo Sci; Spo Sci Psy; Spo Sci (Out Actvt))
Bournemouth – 260 pts (Spo Dev Coach Sci; Spo Psy Coach Sci)
Cardiff (UWIC) – 260 pts (Spo Mgt)
Central Lancashire – 260 pts (Spo Psy; Spo Tech; Spo Tech (Glf); Spo Thera; Spo Sci)
Chester – 260 pts (Spo Thera)
Chichester – 260 pts (Spo Thera)
Coventry – 260 pts (Spo Thera)
Edinburgh – BCC (App Spo Sci; Spo Recr Mgt)
Huddersfield – 260 pts (Spo Prom Mark)
London (QM) – 260–340 pts (Spo Eng; Spo Mat)
Middlesex – 260 pts (Spo Rehab Injry Prvntn)
Northumbria – 260 pts (Geog Spo St)
Oxford Brookes – BCC (Exer Nutr Hlth courses; Spo Coach St)
Portsmouth – 260 pts (Wtr Spo Sci; Spo Sci)
Sheffield Hallam – 260 pts (Spo Dev Coach)
Stirling – BCC (Spo St courses; Spo Exer Sci)

240 pts **Aberdeen** – 240 pts 1st yr entry (BSc Spo Exer Sci; Spo St Spo Soty)
Aberystwyth – 240 pts (Spo Exer Sci) *(IB 26 pts)*
Bolton – 240 pts (Spo Rehab; Spo Exer Psy)

For information on how to read the Subject Tables, see **Chapter 8**.

Bournemouth – 240–260 pts (Spo Mgt (Glf))
Brighton – CCC–BCD 240–280 pts (Spo Exer Sci; Spo Leis Mgt; Sociol Spo Leis) *(IB 30 pts)*
Chester – 240 pts (Spo Dev)
Coventry – 240 pts (Spo Mgt; Spo Exer Hlth Sci; Spo Mgt; Spo Mark)
Dundee – 240 pts 1st yr entry (Spo Biomed)
Essex – 240 pts (Spo Exer Sci; Spo Sci Biol)
Gloucestershire – 240 pts (Spo courses except under **280 pts**)
Greenwich – 240 pts (Spo Sci (Prof Ftbl Coach); Spo Sci Fit)
Heriot-Watt – CCC 1st yr entry (Spo Exer Sci; Spo Exer Sci Psy)
Hertfordshire – 240 pts (Spo St courses)
Huddersfield – 240 pts (Spo Thera; Spo Exer St)
Hull – 240–280 pts (Spo Coach Perf; Spo Exer Sci; Spo Rehab; Spo Sci Geog)
Kent – 240 pts (Spo Exer Mgt; Spo Exer Fit Sci) *(IB 28 pts)*
Lincoln – 240 pts (Spo Exer Sci; Spo Dev Coach (Glf St))
Liverpool Hope – 240 pts (Spo courses)
Manchester Met – 240 pts (Coach Spo Dev)
Newport – 240 pts (Spo St)
Nottingham Trent – 240 pts (Spo Sci Mgt; Coach Spo Sci)
Portsmouth – 240 pts (Spo Dev)
Robert Gordon – CCC (Spo Exer Sci)
Salford – CCC 240 pts (App Spo Sci)
Staffordshire – 240 pts (Spo courses)
Strathclyde – CCC (Spo Eng; Spo Exer Sci)
Teesside – 240–260 pts (Spo Exer courses)

220 pts **Central Lancashire** – 220–240 pts (Spo Coach Spo Dev; Spo Mgt Spo St; Mtr Spo; Out Ldrshp)
Edge Hill – 220 pts (Spo Exer Sci; Spo Dev; Spo Thera; Coach Perf Dev; Spo St)
Glamorgan – 220–260 pts (Spo Dev; Spo Mgt)
Kingston – 220–260 pts (Spo Sci courses)
Liverpool John Moores – 220–260 pts (Spo Dev PE)
Napier – 220 pts (Spo Exer Sci; Spo Tech)
Nottingham Trent – 220 pts (Eqn Spo Sci courses; Spo Sci Maths; Spo Sci IT; Spo Mgt Bus)
Winchester – 220 pts (Spo St; Spo Dev courses; Spo Sci)
York St John – 220–160 pts (Spo St; Bus Mgt Spo St; Spo St Psy)

210 pts **Anglia Ruskin** – 210 pts (Spo Hlth Exer; Spo Sci; Coach Sci)

200 pts **Birmingham (UC)** – 200 pts (Spo Thera)
Bolton – 200 pts (Spo Leis Mgt; Spo Dev; Coach Sci)
Bradford – 200 pts (BSc Med Tech Spo)
Bristol UWE – 200–240 pts (Psy Spo Biol; Spo Bus Mgt) *(IB 30 pts)*
Central Lancashire – 200 pts (Spo Comb Hons)
Chichester – 200–260 pts (Spo Coach Sci; Spo Exer Psy; Spo Exer Sci)
Cumbria – 200 pts (Spo St; Spo St Spo Dev; Spo St Spo Hist)
Glamorgan – 200–260 pts (Sci Rgby; Spo Exer Sci; Spo Psy; Out Learn Sci Advntr)
Huddersfield – 200 pts (Spo Biol)
Liverpool John Moores – 200 pts (Spo Tech)
London Met – 200–240 pts (Spo Thera)
Manchester Met – 200 pts (Psy Spo Exer; Out St courses; Spo Comb Hons)
Middlesex – 200–240 pts (Spo Exer Sci)
Newport – 200 pts (Spo St; Spo Coach Dev)
Plymouth – 200 pts (App Mar Spo Sci; Srf Sci Tech)
Salford – 200 pts+fdn art (Spo Equip Des)
Salford – 200 pts (Exer Hlth Sci)
Southampton Solent – 200 pts (Spo St Bus; Spo Dev Mark; Ftbl St Bus; Spo; App Spo Sci; Wtrspo St Mgt)
Strathclyde – BB–AC (Spo Physl Actvt)

Sunderland – 200–220 pts (Spo courses)
Thames Valley – 200 pts (Hlth Exer Sci)
Worcester – 200–240 pts (Spo courses)
180 pts **Abertay Dundee** – DDD (Spo Coach Dev)
Birmingham (UC) – 180 pts (Spo Mgt)
Bristol UWE – 180–220 pts (Spo Biol)
Chichester – 180–220 pts (Spo St (Spo Dev))
Derby – 180 pts (Out Actvts Mgt)
Glamorgan – 180–220 pts (Spo St)
Greenwich – 180 pts (Spo Sci courses)
Lincoln – 180 pts (Eqn Spo Sci)
Marjon (UC) – 180–240 pts (Spo Dev courses)
Northampton – 180–220 pts (Spo courses)
St Mary's (UC) – BC 180–200 pts (Spo Rehab; Spo Sci; Spo Coach Sci; Strg Condit Sci)
Warwickshire (Coll) – 180 pts (Spo Sci (Eqn Hum))
160 pts **Bedfordshire** – 160–240 pts (Spo Exer Sci; Spo Thera; Spo Mgt)
Canterbury Christ Church – CC (Spo Exer Sci; Spo Exer Sci Psy)
East London – 160 pts (Spo Coach; Spo Exer Sci; Spo Dev)
Glasgow Caledonian – CC (Spo Mgt)
Hertfordshire – 160–240 pts (Spo St Comb St)
Leeds Trinity and All Saints (Coll) – 160–240 pts (Spo Hlth Exer Nutr; Spo Dev Mark; Spo Exer Psy; Spo Dev PE; Spo Hlth Leis Media)
London Met – 160 pts (Spo Mgt Spo Sci; Spo Sci Coach)
London South Bank – CC (Spo Exer Sci)
Loughborough – 160–200 pts (Fdn Spo Tech)
Manchester Met – 160–200 pts (Bus Spo)
Marjon (UC) – 160–120 pts (App Spo Sci Coach)
Newman (UC) – CC 160–240 pts (Spo St courses)
South East Essex (Coll) – 160 pts (Spo St)
Trinity Carmarthen (Coll) – 160 pts (Out Educ Spo St)
Wolverhampton – 160–220 pts (Spo Coach; Spo St; Spo Exer Sci courses)
140 pts **Suffolk (Univ Campus)** – 140–200 pts (Spo Sci courses)
Writtle (Coll) – 140 pts (Spo Exer Perf)
120 pts **Bucks New** – 120–180 pts (Spo Leis Mgt; Spo Mgt (Glf St) (Rgby St) (Ftbl); Spo Coach Mgt; Spo Psy)
London Met – 120 pts (Spo Psy Perf)
North East Wales (IHE) – 120 pts (Spo Sci; Spo Exer Mgt; Spo St)
Roehampton – 120–280 pts (Spo courses)
Swansea (Inst) – 120 pts (Spo Recr Mgt)
100 pts **UHI Millennium Inst (NHC)** – 100 pts approx (Glf Mgt)

Leeds Met – contact University

Alternative offers
See **Chapter 8** for grade/point equivalences and related information for the following examinations: Scottish qualifications, the Welsh Baccalaureate, the IB diploma (approximate points shown also in italics in the table of offers), the Irish Leaving Certificate, the European Baccalaureate and the French Baccalaureate.

EXAMPLES OF FOUNDATION DEGREES IN THE SUBJECT FIELD
Arts London (CComm); Askham Bryan (Coll); Barnfield (Coll); Bath; Bath City (Coll); Bedfordshire; Birmingham (UC); Bishop Burton (Coll); Blackpool and Fylde (Coll); Bradford (Coll); Bridgwater (Coll); Bucks New; Burnley (Coll); Central Lancashire; Cornwall (Coll); Derby; Dunstable (Coll); Durham New (Coll); East Durham (CmC); East Lancashire (IHE); Edge Hill; Exeter (Coll); Farnborough (CT); Gateshead (Coll); Glamorgan; Hartpury (Coll); Hastings (Coll); Herefordshire (CAD); Hertfordshire; Huddersfield; Kingston (Coll); Lancaster and Morecambe (Coll); Lincoln (Coll); London South Bank; Loughborough

(Coll); Manchester (CAT); Mid Cheshire (Coll); Middlesex; Milton Keynes (Coll); Myerscough (Coll); Nescot; Newcastle (Coll); Newport; North Devon (Coll); North Herefordshire (Coll); North Hertfordshire (Coll); Nottingham Trent; Oaklands (Coll); Park Lane Leeds (Coll); Pembrokeshire (Coll); Penwith (Coll); Peterborough Reg (Coll); Plymouth (CFE); Preston (Coll); Reaseheath (Coll); Richmond upon Thames (Coll); St Helens (Coll); St Mary's (UC); Sheffield (Coll); Somerset (CAT); South Cheshire (Coll); South Devon (Coll); Southampton Solent; Southport (Coll); Suffolk (Univ Campus); Sunderland; Sunderland City (Coll); Sussex Downs (Coll); Sutton Coldfield (Coll); Swindon New (Coll); Thames Valley; Truro (Coll); Tyne Met (Coll); Wakefield (Coll); Warwickshire (Coll); West Herts (Coll); West Nottinghamshire (Coll); West Suffolk (Coll); Wolverhampton; Worcester (CT); Writtle (Coll); Yeovil (Coll).

CHOOSING YOUR COURSE (SEE ALSO CH.1)

Course variations – Widen your options

Equine and Human Sport Science (Aberystwyth)
Sport, Health, Physical Education and Psychology (Bangor)
Coach Education and Sport Development (Bath)
Sports Engineering (Bath)
Adventure Recreation (Bedfordshire)
Applied Golf Management Studies (Birmingham)
Sport Journalism (Brighton)
Sport Therapy and Rehabilitation (Bristol UWE)
Sport Biomedicine and Nutrition (Cardiff (UWIC))
Motor Sport (Central Lancashire)
Adventure Leisure Management and Sports Development (Gloucestershire)
Sport Science with Professional Football Coaching (Greenwich)
Science and Football (Liverpool John Moores)
Sports Materials (London (QM))
Sport and Exercise Science (Sport Injuries) (Napier)

Applied Marine Sport Science (Plymouth)
Surf Science (Plymouth)
CHECK PROSPECTUSES AND WEBSITES FOR OTHER UNIVERSITIES AND COLLEGES OFFERING THESE COURSES.

Top universities and colleges (Research) Bangor; Birmingham*; Exeter; Glasgow*; Liverpool John Moores*; Manchester Met*.

Sandwich degree courses Bath; Bournemouth; Brighton; Bristol UWE; Brunel; Bucks New; Coventry; Glamorgan; Gloucestershire; Greenwich; Hertfordshire; Huddersfield; Kingston; London Met; Loughborough; Northumbria; Oxford Brookes; Sheffield Hallam; Sunderland; Swansea (Inst); Teesside; Ulster; Warwickshire (Coll); West Scotland; Wolverhampton; Writtle (Coll).

ADMISSIONS INFORMATION

Number of applicants per place (approx) Aberystwyth 5; Bangor 15; Bath (Coach Educ Spo Dev) 3; Birmingham 7; Brunel 6; Canterbury Christ Church 30; Cardiff (UWIC) 10; Chichester 4; Cumbria 14, (Spo St) 6; Durham 6; Edinburgh 11; Exeter 23; Gloucestershire 8; Kingston 13; Leeds 25; Leeds Trinity and All Saints (Coll) 35; Liverpool John Moores 4; Loughborough 20; Manchester Met 16; Northampton 4; Northumbria 30; Nottingham Trent 8; Portsmouth 12; Roehampton 8; St Mary's (UC) 4; Salford 30; Sheffield Hallam 7; South East Essex (Coll) 1; Staffordshire 12; Stirling 10; Strathclyde 28; Sunderland 2; Swansea 6; Teesside 15; Winchester 5; Wolverhampton 4; Worcester 10; York St John 4.

Advice to applicants and planning the UCAS personal statement **Cardiff (UWIC)** A strong personal statement required which clearly identifies current performance profile and indicates a balanced lifestyle. **Salford** Previous experience in a sporting environment will be noted. Previous study in biology/human biology, physics, chemistry, physical education/sports studies. Psychology is preferred. **Other comments** (Coach Sci) For these courses applicants must have proven coaching skills to gain a place. (Spo Sci) These are lab-based courses examining the physical stress of sport on the human body. A sound scientific aptitude is required. Although professional sporting qualifications and high level practical experience cannot take the place of scientific entry qualifications, they will be considered in any borderline applicants holding a conditional offer. Comment on any coaching or competitive experience. See also **Physical Education**. See also **Appendix 2**.

Misconceptions about this course **Bath** (Spo Exer Sci) This is not a sports course with a high component of practical sport: it is a science programme with minimal practical sport. (Coach Educ Spo Dev) This is not necessarily a course for élite athletes. **Birmingham** (App Glf Mgt St) Applicants do not appreciate the academic depth required across key areas (it is, in a sense, a multiple Honours course – business management, sports science, coaching theory, materials science). **Sheffield Hallam** (Spo Tech) Some applicants expect an engineering course! **Swansea** (Spo Sci) Applicants underestimate the quantity of maths on the course. Many applicants are uncertain about the differences between Sports Studies and Sports Science.

Selection interviews **Yes** Bath, Birmingham, Bristol UWE, Cumbria, Durham, Edinburgh, Leeds, Leeds Trinity and All Saints (Coll), Nottingham Trent, Swansea; **Some** Cardiff (UWIC), Chichester, Derby, Liverpool John Moores, Roehampton, St Mary's (UC), Salford, Sheffield Hallam, Staffordshire, Wolverhampton.

Applicants' impressions (A=Open day; B=Interview day) **Essex** (Spo Exer Sci; B) There were two interviewers, the interview lasted 10–15 minutes. It was well organised and very friendly. A tour of the campus followed but there was no chance to talk to students. I would recommend the university, but you need to talk to students to get a good idea of the course. **Leeds Met** (A) It was a worthwhile Open day. It cost a lot to get there but good to see the accommodation available.

Interview advice and questions Applicants' interests in sport and their sporting activities are likely to be discussed at length. Past questions include: How do you strike a balance between sport and academic work? How many, and which, sports do you coach? For how long? Have you devised your own coaching programme? What age-range do you coach? Do you coach unsupervised? **Loughborough** A high level of sporting achievement is expected. See **Chapter 7**.

For information on how to read the Subject Tables, see **Chapter 8**.

Reasons for rejection (non-academic) Not genuinely interested in outdoor activities. Poor sporting background or knowledge. Personal appearance. Inability to apply their science to their specialist sport. Illiteracy. Using the course as a second option to physiotherapy. Arrogance. Expectation that they will be playing sport all day. When the course is explained to them some applicants realise that a more arts-based course would be more appropriate.

AFTER-RESULTS ADVICE

Offers to applicants repeating A-levels **Higher** Swansea; **Same** Cardiff (UWIC), Chichester, Derby, Dundee, Lincoln, Liverpool John Moores, Loughborough, Plymouth, Roehampton, St Mary's (UC), Salford, Sheffield Hallam, Staffordshire, Stirling, Suffolk (Univ Campus), Sunderland, Winchester, Wolverhampton, York St John.

GRADUATE DESTINATIONS AND EMPLOYMENT (2005/6 HESA)

Graduates surveyed 4655 **Employed** 2385 **In further study** 775 **Assumed unemployed** 235.

Career note Career options include sport development, coaching, teaching, outdoor centres, sports equipment development, sales, recreation management and professional sport.

OTHER DEGREE SUBJECTS FOR CONSIDERATION

Anatomy; Biology; Human Movement Studies; Leisure and Recreation Management; Nutrition; Physical Education; Physiology; Physiotherapy.

STATISTICS

(see also **Business Courses** and **Mathematics**)

Statistics has mathematical underpinnings but is primarily concerned with the collection, interpretation and analysis of data. Statistics are used to analyse and solve problems in a wide range of areas, particularly in the scientific, business, government and public services.

Useful websites www.rss.org.uk; www.statistics.gov.uk.

NB The points totals shown to the left of the institutions are for ease of reference only. It must not be assumed that tariff points are always used by institutions or that they can be substituted for an offer in grades. The level of an offer is not necessarily indicative of the quality of a course.

COURSE OFFERS INFORMATION

Subject requirements/preferences **GCSE** English and mathematics. **AL** Mathematics required for all courses. **NB** A* grades are likely to form part of university offers in the higher ranges for students applying for places in 2008 for entry in 2009: check websites.

Your target offers
360 pts and above
> **Bath** – AAA (Stats; Maths Stats) *(IB 36 pts)*
> **Bristol** – AAA–AAB (Maths Stats) *(IB 36 pts H665)*
> **Durham** – AAA (Nat Sci (Stats)) *(IB 38–42 pts H maths 6/7)*
> **Imperial London** – AAA (Maths Stats) *(IB 38 pts H maths phys 6)*
> **London (LSE)** – AAA–AABB (Bus Maths Stats) *(IB 38 pts H766)*
> **London (UCL)** – AAAe–AABe (Econ Stats; Stats courses) *(IB 36–38 pts)*
> **Oxford** – AAA (Maths Stats) *(IB 38–40 pts)*
> **Southampton** – AAA–AAB (Maths Stats) *(IB 33 pts H 16 pts)*
> **Warwick** – AAA–AABa/b (Maths OR Stats Econ; Maths Stats)

340 pts Durham – AAB (Statistics) *(IB 34–36 pts H maths 6)*
> **Lancaster** – AAB (Stats N Am/Aus)
> **Leeds** – AAB (Stats courses)

Manchester – AAB–ABB (Maths Stats)
Newcastle – AAB (Stats courses)
St Andrews – AAB (Stats courses) *(IB 34 pts)*
320 pts Birmingham – ABB (Mathem Econ Stats) *(IB 34 pts)*
Cardiff – ABB–ABC (Maths OR Stats) *(IB 32 pts H maths 6)*
East Anglia – ABB–ABC (Maths Stats) *(IB 32 pts H maths 6)*
Edinburgh – ABB (Maths Stats) *(IB 30 pts)*
Glasgow – ABB–BBB (Statistics)
Lancaster – ABB (Stats; Maths Stats) *(IB 30 pts H maths 6)*
Liverpool – ABB (Maths Stats) *(IB 32 pts H maths 6)*
London (RH) – 320 pts (Maths Stats) *(IB 33 pts H maths 6)*
Surrey – 320 pts (Maths Stats)
York – ABB (Maths Stats)
300 pts Aberystwyth – 300 pts (Stats joint courses) *(IB 27 pts)*
Sheffield – BBB–BBbb (Econ Stats) *(IB 32 pts H maths 5)*
280 pts London (QM) – 280 pts (Statistics) *(IB 32 pts H maths 6)*
Oxford Brookes – BBC–CD (Bus Stats courses)
Reading – 280–300 pts (Maths App Stats; Maths Stats; Bus Stats; App Stats; Stats)
Strathclyde – BBC (Maths Stats Acc)
260 pts Brunel – 260 pts (Maths Stats Mgt) *(IB 28 pts)*
City – BCC 260 pts (Mathem Sci Stats) *(IB 28 pts)*
Kent – BCC (Maths Stats) *(IB 28 pts)*
Kingston – 260 pts (Stats Bus Mgt; Med Stats; Stats joint courses; Act Maths Stats)
240 pts Bristol UWE – 240–260 pts (Stats courses)
Heriot-Watt – BCD (Statistics)
Portsmouth – 240 pts (Maths Stats)
200 pts Coventry – 200 pts (Maths Stats)
Liverpool John Moores – 200 pts (Maths Stats Comp)
Plymouth – 200 pts (App Stats courses)
Sheffield Hallam – 200 pts (Maths Stats)
180 pts Greenwich – 180 pts (Stats Comb courses)
160 pts Middlesex – 160–200 pts (Stats courses)
Wolverhampton – 160–200 pts (Stats Sci courses)
120 pts London Met – 120 pts (Stats joint courses)
80 pts London (Birk) – 80 pts for under 21s (over 21s varies) (p/t Stats Econ; Stats Mgt)

Alternative offers
See **Chapter 8** for grade/point equivalences and related information for the following examinations: Scottish qualifications, the Welsh Baccalaureate, the IB diploma (approximate points shown also in italics in the table of offers), the Irish Leaving Certificate, the European Baccalaureate and the French Baccalaureate.

CHOOSING YOUR COURSE (SEE ALSO CH.1)
Course variations – Widen your options
Mathematical Economics and Statistics (Birmingham)
Mathematics, Statistics and Management (Brunel)
Mathematics, Operational Research and Statistics (Cardiff)
Mathematical, Statistical and Actuarial Sciences (Heriot-Watt)
Mathematics with Statistics for Finance (Imperial London)
Business Mathematics and Statistics (London (LSE))
Applied Statistics (Plymouth)
Logic and Philosophy of Science – Statistics (St Andrews)
CHECK PROSPECTUSES AND WEBSITES FOR OTHER UNIVERSITIES AND COLLEGES OFFERING THESE COURSES.

Universities and colleges teaching quality See www.qaa.ac.uk; www.unistats.com.

Top universities and colleges (Research) (including Operational Research) Bath; Bristol*; Glasgow; Heriot-Watt; Kent*; Imperial London; Lancaster*; Leeds; London (QM), (UCL); Newcastle; Oxford*; Sheffield; Southampton; Surrey; Warwick*.

Sandwich degree courses Bath; Coventry; Kingston; Liverpool John Moores; Portsmouth; Reading; Sheffield Hallam; Surrey; Wolverhampton.

ADMISSIONS INFORMATION

Number of applicants per place (approx) Bath 10; Bristol UWE 2; Cardiff 3; Coventry 3; East London 3; Heriot-Watt 6; Lancaster 11; Liverpool John Moores 6; London (UCL) 9; Newcastle 5; Sheffield Hallam 2; York 5.

Advice to applicants and planning the UCAS personal statement Love mathematics, don't expect an easy life. See **Mathematics**. See also **Appendix 2**.

Selection interviews **Yes** Bath, Birmingham, Liverpool, Liverpool John Moores, London (UCL), Newcastle, Sheffield, Sheffield Hallam; **Some** Greenwich.

Interview advice and questions Questions could be asked on your A-level syllabus (particularly in mathematics). Applicants' knowledge of statistics and their interest in the subject are likely to be tested, together with their awareness of the application of statistics in commerce and industry. See **Chapter 7**.

AFTER-RESULTS ADVICE

Offers to applicants repeating A-levels **Higher** Kent, Leeds, Liverpool, Liverpool John Moores, Newcastle, Swansea; **Same** Birmingham.

GRADUATE DESTINATIONS AND EMPLOYMENT (2005/6 HESA)

Graduates surveyed 220 **Employed** 105 **In further study** 45 **Assumed unemployed** 10.

Career note See **Mathematics**.

OTHER DEGREE SUBJECTS FOR CONSIDERATION

Accountancy; Actuarial Sciences; Business Information Technology; Business Studies; Computer Science; Economics; Financial Services; Mathematics.

TECHNOLOGY

(see also separate technologies, eg **Architecture, Broadcast, Business Information, Communications, Design, Fashion, Food, Information, Internet, Materials, Media, Music, Sound** and **Sport** under relevant subject tables)

Technology covers a wide range of activities and is commonly associated with the engineering industries although there are also scientific and artistic applications. See individual subject tables.

Useful websites www.techreview.com; www.intute.ac.uk.

NB The points totals shown to the left of the institutions are for ease of reference only. It must not be assumed that tariff points are always used by institutions or that they can be substituted for an offer in grades. The level of an offer is not necessarily indicative of the quality of a course.

COURSE OFFERS INFORMATION

Subject requirements/preferences **GCSE** English and mathematics required. **AL** Mathematics and/or a science may be required. **NB** A* grades are likely to form part of university offers in the higher ranges for students applying for places in 2008 for entry in 2009: check websites.

Your target offers
340 pts Warwick – AAB–ABB (MEng Comb Tech)

320 pts **Brunel** – 320 pts (Broad Media (Des Tech))
         Exeter – ABB–BBB (Phys Qntm Lsr Tech)
300 pts **Birmingham** – BBB 300 pts (Spo Sci Mat Tech)
         Oxford Brookes – BBB–DD (Mtrspo Tech)
         Surrey – BBB (BEng Phys Sat Tech)
         Warwick – BBB–BBC+AS (BEng Comb Tech)
280 pts **Bradford** – 280–260 pts (Media Tech Prod)
         Coventry – 280 pts (Mus Tech)
         Lancaster – 280 pts (Comb Tech)
         Staffordshire – 280 pts (Spo Tech Mgt; Ftbl Tech; Med Tech; Film Prod Tech; Des Tech; Mbl Dvc Tech)
         Surrey – BBC 280 pts (IT Bus Entre Tech)
260 pts **Aston** – BCC–CCC (Tech Ent Mgt; BEng Chem Tech Des) *(IB 30–34 pts)*
         Chester – 260–240 pts (Multim Tech courses)
240 pts **De Montfort** – 240 pts (Tech joint courses; Fash Tech; Electron Gms Tech; Mus Tech Innov; Des Tech)
         Glamorgan – 240–300 pts (Ltg Des Tech; Bus IT)
         Portsmouth – 240 pts (Mus Snd Tech; Comp Gms Tech)
         Strathclyde – CCC (Tech Bus St)
220 pts **Birmingham City** – 220–240 pts (Film Tech Prod)
         De Montfort – 220 pts (Aud Rec Tech)
         Glamorgan – 220–300 pts (Crea Tech)
         Manchester Met – 220–280 pts (Comp Gms Tech)
         Ulster – 220 pts (Tech Des)
200 pts **Bradford** – 200 pts (Tech Mgt; Clin Tech; E–Commer Tech; IT Mgt; Auto Des Tech)
         Glasgow – BB (Tech Mgt)
         Portsmouth – 200 pts (Mar Spo Tech; Intnet Tech)
         Sheffield Hallam – 200 pts (Spo Tech)
         Staffordshire – 200 pts (Des Tech)
180 pts **Derby** – 180 pts (Snd Lt Lv Evnt Tech; Des Tech)
         Huddersfield – 180 pts (Tech Bus Mgt)
         Manchester Met – 180–220 pts (Media Tech)
160 pts **Glasgow** – CC (Technol Educ)
140 pts **Glamorgan** – 140–180 pts (Eng Tech Mgt)
120 pts **West Scotland** – DD (Phys Med Tech)
100 pts **Oxford Brookes** – DE (Tech Fdn)

         Open University – contact University

Alternative offers
See **Chapter 8** for grade/point equivalences and related information for the following examinations: Scottish qualifications, the Welsh Baccalaureate, the IB diploma (approximate points shown also in italics in the table of offers), the Irish Leaving Certificate, the European Baccalaureate and the French Baccalaureate.

EXAMPLES OF FOUNDATION DEGREES IN THE SUBJECT FIELD
Accrington and Rossendale (Coll); Leeds Met; Manchester Met.

CHOOSING YOUR COURSE (SEE ALSO CH.1)
Course variations – Widen your options
Audio Technology (Anglia Ruskin)
Technology and Enterprise Management (Aston)
Fashion Design and Garment Technology (Birmingham City)
Music Technology (Bournemouth)

Dental Technology (Cardiff (UWIC))
Avionics Technology (Coventry)
Live Event Technology (Glamorgan)
Health and Information Technology (Greenwich)
Games Technology (Kingston)
Nanotechnology (Leeds)
Broadcast Technology (Liverpool John Moores)
Business Information Technology (London South Bank)
Textile Technology (Manchester)
Livestock Technology (Myerscough (Coll))
Small Craft Technology (Newcastle)
Architectural Technology (Northumbria)
Ship Technology and Naval Architecture (Plymouth)
Security Technology (Portsmouth)
CHECK PROSPECTUSES AND WEBSITES FOR OTHER UNIVERSITIES AND COLLEGES OFFERING THESE COURSES.

Sandwich degree courses Aston; Bradford; Coventry; De Montfort; Huddersfield; Oxford Brookes; Portsmouth.

ADMISSIONS INFORMATION

Number of applicants per place (approx) Aston 6.

Advice to applicants and planning the UCAS personal statement See **Engineering** courses and **Physics**.

Selection interviews **Yes** Aston, Glasgow, Staffordshire.

Interview advice and questions See **Engineering/Engineering Sciences** and **Chapter 7**.

AFTER-RESULTS ADVICE

Offers to applicants repeating A-levels **Same** Aston, Bradford, Staffordshire.

GRADUATE DESTINATIONS AND EMPLOYMENT (2005/6 HESA)

See **Engineering/Engineering Sciences**.

Career note See **Engineering/Engineering Sciences**.

OTHER DEGREE SUBJECTS FOR CONSIDERATION

Biotechnology; Design Technology; Engineering Sciences; Materials Science and Technology; Mechanical Engineering.

TOURISM and TRAVEL

(see also **Business Courses, Hospitality and Hotel Management** and **Leisure and Recreation Management/Studies**)

Tourism and Travel courses are popular; some are combined with Hospitality Management which provides students with specialisms in two areas. Courses involve business studies and a detailed study of tourism and travel. Industrial placements are frequently involved and language options are often included. See also **Appendix 2**.

Useful websites www.wttc.org; www.abta.com; www.baha.org.uk.

NB The points totals shown to the left of the institutions are for ease of reference only. It must not be assumed that tariff points are always used by institutions or that they can be substituted for an offer in grades. The level of an offer is not necessarily indicative of the quality of a course.

COURSE OFFERS INFORMATION

Subject requirements/preferences **GCSE** English and mathematics required. **AL** No subjects specified. **NB** A* grades are likely to form part of university offers in the higher ranges for students applying for places in 2008 for entry in 2009: check websites.

Your target offers

340 pts **Exeter** – AAB–BBB (Mgt Tour)

300 pts **Strathclyde** – BBB–BBC/AB (Tourism)

280 pts **Aberystwyth** – 280 pts (Tour Mgt) *(IB 26 pts)*
Northumbria – BBC (Trav Tour Mgt) *(IB 28 pts)*
Surrey – 280 pts (Tour Mgt)

260 pts **Oxford Brookes** – BCC (Tour Mgt courses)

240 pts **Bangor** – 240–280 pts (Langs Tour)
Brighton – 240 pts (Int Tour Mgt; Entre Trav Tour; Trav Tour Mark) *(IB 28 pts)*
Bristol UWE – 240–280 pts (Tour Mgt; Tour Env Mgt)
Chester – 240 pts (Tour courses) *(IB 24–28 pts)*
Coventry – 240–220 pts (Tour Mgt; Tour Mark; Tour Fr/Span; Spo Tour)
Kent – 240 pts (Tour Mgt; Tour Mgt Ind)
Manchester Met – 240 pts (Tour Mgt)
Northumbria – 240 pts (Bus Tour)
Staffordshire – 240 pts (Trav Tour Mgt)
Ulster – CCC 240 pts (Int Htl Tour Mgt; Int Htl Tour St)

220 pts **Bournemouth** – 220 pts (Tour Mgt)
Glamorgan – 220–260 pts (Tour Mgt; Tour Mark)
Liverpool Hope – 220 pts (Tour courses)
Stirling – CCD (Tour Mgt; Int Tour Mgt)
Westminster – 220 pts (Tour Bus; Tour Plan)
Winchester – 220–160 pts (Tour Herit Mgt; Tour Mgt Bus Mgt; Tour Mgt)

200 pts **Anglia Ruskin** – 200 pts (Tour St; Tour Mgt)
Bath Spa – 200–240 pts (Tour Mgt)
Bolton – 200 pts (Tour Mgt; Int Tour Mgt)
Cardiff (UWIC) – 200 pts (Tour Mgt courses; Tour St Fr/Ger/Span)
Gloucestershire – 200–280 pts (Tour Mgt courses; Spo Tour Mgt)
Hertfordshire – 200 pts (Tour courses)
Lincoln – 200 pts (Euro Tour; Int Tour; Tour)
Napier – 200 pts (Tour Mgt; Ecotour)
Plymouth – 200 pts (Tour Hspty Mgt; Bus Tour; Int Tour Mgt; Tour Mgt)
Salford – 200 pts (Tour Mgt)
Sheffield Hallam – 200 pts (Tour Mgt; Fr/Ger/Ital/Span Tour; Tour Hspty Bus Mgt)

190 pts **Aberystwyth** – 190–220 pts (Cntry Recr Tour)

180 pts **Birmingham (UC)** – 180 pts (Tour Bus Mgt; Mark Tour Mgt; Hspty Tour Mgt; Advntr Tour Mgt)
Central Lancashire – 180–200 pts (Int Tour Mgt; Tour Mgt)
Chichester – 180–220 pts (Tour Mgt courses)
Derby – 180–200 pts (Trav Tour Mgt)
Edge Hill – 180 pts (Geotourism)
Greenwich – 180 pts (Tour Mgt; Tour Mgt Fr/Ger/Span)
Hull – 180–200 pts (Tour Mgt courses)
Liverpool John Moores – 180 pts (Tour Leis courses)
Northampton – 180–220 pts (Tour courses)

160 pts **Bedfordshire** – 160–240 pts (Trav Tour; Spo Tour; Int Tour Mgt)
Canterbury Christ Church – CC (Tour courses)
East London – 160 pts (Int Tour Mgt)
Glasgow Caledonian – CC (Tour Mgt; Int Trav Mgt Tour)

For information on how to read the Subject Tables, see **Chapter 8**.

      Greenwich – 160 pts (Tour Mgt courses; Trav Tour Mgt)

      Huddersfield – 160 pts (Tour Leis Mgt)

      Liverpool John Moores – 160–180 pts (Out Educ Advntr Tour)

      London Met – 160 pts (Int Tour Mgt; Mark Trav Mgt; Tour Env)

      London South Bank – CC 160 pts (Tour Hspty; Tour courses)

      Middlesex – 160–200 pts (Int Tour Mgt)

      Queen Margaret – CC (Hspty Tour Mgt; Tour Mgt)

      Robert Gordon – CC (Int Tour Mgt)

      SAC (Scottish CAg) – CC 160 pts (Rur Recr Tour Mgt; Advntr Tour Out Prsts)

      St Mary's (UC) – CC 160 pts (Tour courses)

      Sunderland – 160 pts (Tour Dev; Tour Mgt; Tour Ent)

      Teesside – 160 pts (Tour Mgt; Leis Tour Mgt)

      Thames Valley – 160 pts (Trav Tour Mgt; Airln Airpt Mgt)

      West Scotland – CC (Tourism)

      Wolverhampton – 160–220 pts (Tour Mgt courses)

140 pts **Blackpool and Fylde (Coll)** – 140 pts (Int Tour Rsrt Mgt)

      Harper Adams (UC) – 140–200 pts (Tour Bus Mgt)

      Trinity Carmarthen (Coll) – 140 pts (Advntr Tour; Cult Tour)

      Writtle (Coll) – 140 pts (Advntr Tour)

120 pts **Bucks New** – 120–180 pts (Air Trav Mgt; Int Trav Tour Mgt)

      Southampton Solent – 120 pts (Tour Mgt; Tour Mgt Out Advntr)

100 pts **Arts London** – 100 pts check with admissions tutor (Int Trav Tour)

      Northbrook (Coll) – 100 pts (Bus Admin Trav Tour)

 80 pts **Greenwich (Sch Mgt)** – 80–120 pts (Bus Mgt Trav Tour – 2 yrs)

      Llandrillo Cymru (Coll) – 80 pts min (Mgt Trav Tour)

      Suffolk (Univ Campus) – 80–120 pts (Bus Mgt Tour Mgt)

      Swansea (Inst) – 80–340 pts (Int Trav Tour Mgt; Tour Mgt)

      Leeds Met – contact University

Alternative offers

See **Chapter 8** for grade/point equivalences and related information for the following examinations: Scottish qualifications, the Welsh Baccalaureate, the IB diploma (approximate points shown also in italics in the table of offers), the Irish Leaving Certificate, the European Baccalaureate and the French Baccalaureate.

EXAMPLES OF FOUNDATION DEGREES IN THE SUBJECT FIELD

Arts London (CComm); Bath Spa; Bedfordshire; Birmingham (UC); Bournemouth and Poole (Coll); Bradford (Coll); Bridgwater (Coll); Brighton; Brighton and Hove City (Coll); Bucks New; Canterbury Christ Church; Central Lancashire; Cornwall (Coll); Croydon (Coll); De Montfort; Derby; Durham New (Coll); Ealing, Hammersmith and West London (Coll); Edge Hill; Grimsby (IFHE); Harper Adams (UC); Herefordshire (CAD); Hertfordshire; Hugh Baird (Coll); Hull (Coll); Liverpool (CmC); Llandrillo (Coll); London Met; Loughborough (Coll); Mid-Kent (Coll); Myerscough (Coll); Newcastle (Coll); North Hertfordshire (Coll); Northampton; Northampton (Coll); Northbrook (Coll); Norwich City (Coll); Nottingham Castle (Coll); Oaklands (Coll); Park Lane Leeds (Coll); Pembrokeshire (Coll); Pershore (Coll); Plymouth; Plymouth (CFE); Preston (Coll); Riverside Halton (Coll); Runshaw (Coll); Somerset (CAT); South Devon (Coll); Southport (Coll); Sunderland; Sunderland City (Coll); Trinity Carmarthen (Coll); Tyne Met (Coll); Westminster Kingsway (Coll); Weston (Coll); Writtle (Coll).

CHOOSING YOUR COURSE (SEE ALSO CH.1)

Course variations – Widen your options

Sport Tourism (Bedfordshire)

Tourism Destination Management (Birmingham (UC))

International Tourism and Resort Management (Blackpool and Fylde (Coll))

Tourism and Spa Management (Bournemouth)
Tourism Management (Language/Licensed Premises) (Cardiff (UWIC))
Culture and Heritage Tourism (Derby)
Sport Development and Tourism (Liverpool Hope)
Ecotourism (Napier)
CHECK PROSPECTUSES AND WEBSITES FOR OTHER UNIVERSITIES AND COLLEGES OFFERING THESE COURSES.

Sandwich degree courses Aberystwyth; Bedfordshire; Birmingham (UC); Bournemouth; Brighton; Bristol UWE; Central Lancashire; Glamorgan; Gloucestershire; Harper Adams (UC); Hertfordshire; Huddersfield; Hull; Leeds Met; London Met; London South Bank; Manchester Met; Northumbria; Oxford Brookes; Plymouth; Sheffield Hallam; Staffordshire; Sunderland; Surrey; Swansea (IHE); Ulster; West Scotland; Writtle (Coll).

ADMISSIONS INFORMATION

Number of applicants per place (approx) Aberystwyth 3; Bath Spa 5; Birmingham (UC) 10; Bournemouth 16; Derby 4; Glamorgan 8; Glasgow Caledonian 30; Liverpool John Moores 10; Northumbria 6; Sheffield Hallam 12; Sunderland 2; Winchester 3.

Advice to applicants and planning the UCAS personal statement Work experience in the travel and tourism industry is important – in agencies, in the airline industry or hotels. This work could be described in detail. Any experience with people in sales work, dealing with the public – their problems and complaints – should also be included. Travel should be outlined, detailing places visited. Genuine interest in travel, diverse cultures and people. Good communication skills required. See also **Appendix 2**.

Misconceptions about this course Bath Spa The course is not purely vocational and operational: it also involves management issues. **Wolverhampton** Some applicants are uncertain whether or not to take a Business Management course instead of Tourism Management. They should be aware that the latter will equip them with a tourism-specific knowledge of business.

Selection interviews Yes Brighton, Derby, Glasgow Caledonian, Sunderland; **Some** Lincoln, Liverpool John Moores, Salford.

Interview advice and questions Past questions have included: What problems have you experienced when travelling? Questions on places visited. Experiences of air, rail and sea travel. What is marketing? What special qualities do you have that will be of use in the travel industry? See **Chapter 7**.

Applicants' impressions (A=Open day; B=Interview day) Bournemouth (A) A good tour of the University. The course was well explained. **Winchester** It was a very well organised Open day. There were talks about the University and the course, followed by an informal talk with the tutor.

Reasons for rejection (non-academic) Wolverhampton English language competence.

AFTER-RESULTS ADVICE

Offers to applicants repeating A-levels Same Birmingham (UC), Chester, Derby, Lincoln, Liverpool John Moores, Manchester Met, Northumbria, St Mary's (UC), Salford, Winchester, Wolverhampton.

GRADUATE DESTINATIONS AND EMPLOYMENT (2005/6 HESA)

Graduates surveyed 1195 **Employed** 815 **In further study** 55 **Assumed unemployed** 80.

Career note See **Business Courses**.

OTHER DEGREE SUBJECTS FOR CONSIDERATION

Business Studies; Events Management; Heritage Management; Hospitality Management; Leisure and Recreation Management; Travel Management.

TOWN and COUNTRY PLANNING

(including **Environmental Planning** and **Urban Studies;** see also **Development Studies, Environmental Science/Studies, Housing** and **Transport Management and Planning**)

Town and Country Planning courses are very similar and some lead to qualification or part of a qualification as a member of the Royal Town Planning Institute (RTPI). Further information from the RTPI (see **Appendix 2**).

Useful websites www.rtpi.org.uk; www.townplanningreview.org.

NB The points totals shown to the left of the institutions are for ease of reference only. It must not be assumed that tariff points are always used by institutions or that they can be substituted for an offer in grades. The level of an offer is not necessarily indicative of the quality of a course.

COURSE OFFERS INFORMATION

Subject requirements/preferences GCSE English and mathematics required. **AL** Geography may be specified. **NB** A* grades are likely to form part of university offers in the higher ranges for students applying for places in 2008 for entry in 2009: check websites.

Your target offers

300 pts **Birmingham** – BBB–BBC 300–280 pts (Urb Reg Plan courses) *(IB 32 pts)*
Cardiff – 300 pts (Geog (Hum) Plan) *(IB 32 pts)*
Dundee – BBB 300 pts 2nd yr entry (Twn Reg Plan; Geog Plan) *(IB 29 pts)*
Newcastle – BBB–BBC (Twn Plan; Geog Plan) *(IB 28 pts)*
Sheffield – BBB (Urb St Plan) *(IB 30–33 pts)*

280 pts **Cardiff** – 280 pts (City Reg Plan) *(IB 28 pts)*
Liverpool – 280–260 pts (Twn Reg Plan; Env Plan; Urb Regn Plan)
London (QM) – 280–320 pts (Cts Econ Soc Chng)
London (UCL) – BBC+AS (Urb St; Urb Plan Des Mgt)
Queen's Belfast – BBC–BBB (Env Plan)

260 pts **Heriot-Watt** – 260 pts (Urb Reg Plan)
Leeds – BCC (Env Trans Plan)
Manchester – BCC (Cty Reg Dev; Twn Cntry Plan) *(IB 28 pts)*
Northumbria – 260 pts (Plan Dev Surv)

240 pts **Aberdeen** – CCC (Spat Plan)
Anglia Ruskin – 240 pts (Env Plan)
Bangor – 240–280 pts (Env Plan Mgt)
Bristol UWE – 240–280 pts (Prop Dev Plan; Plan Hous Renew; Plan Trans; Twn Cntry Plan)
  (IB 26–30 pts)
Dundee – 240 pts CC+AL/2AS 1st yr entry (Twn Reg Plan; Geog Plan)

For a quick reference offers calculator, fold out the inside back cover.

Kent – 240 pts (Urb St (Soc Pol))
Oxford Brookes – CCC/BC **or** CCcc (Cty Reg Plan; Cits Env Des Dev)
230 pts **Sheffield Hallam** – 230 pts (Plan St; Plan Trans)
180 pts **Birmingham City** – 180 pts (Plan Dev)
Liverpool John Moores – 180 pts (Urb Plan)
160 pts **London South Bank** – CC (Urb Env Plan)

Leeds Met – contact University

Alternative offers
See **Chapter 8** for grade/point equivalences and related information for the following examinations: Scottish qualifications, the Welsh Baccalaureate, the IB diploma (approximate points shown also in italics in the table of offers), the Irish Leaving Certificate, the European Baccalaureate and the French Baccalaureate.

EXAMPLES OF FOUNDATION DEGREES IN THE SUBJECT FIELD
Lambeth (Coll); London (Birk); North East Wales (IHE).

CHOOSING YOUR COURSE (SEE ALSO CH.1)
Course variations – Widen your options
Planning and Public Policy (Birmingham)
Architecture and Planning (Bristol UWE)
Planning with Transport (Bristol UWE)
Geography (Human) and Planning (Cardiff)
Urban Studies (Kent)
Property, Planning and Development (Kingston)
Combined Honours (Liverpool)
Housing Studies (Middlesex)
Real Estate and Urban Planning (Reading)
Urban Land Economics (Sheffield Hallam)
CHECK PROSPECTUSES AND WEBSITES FOR OTHER UNIVERSITIES AND COLLEGES OFFERING THESE COURSES

Universities and colleges teaching quality See www.qaa.ac.uk; www.unistats.com.

Top universities and colleges (Research) Cardiff*; Leeds*; Newcastle; Sheffield.

ADMISSIONS INFORMATION
Number of applicants per place (approx) Birmingham 2; Birmingham City 6; Bristol UWE 6; Cardiff 6; Dundee 5; London (UCL) 6; London South Bank 3; Newcastle 9; Sheffield Hallam 6.

Advice to applicants and planning the UCAS personal statement Visit your local planning office and discuss the career with planners. Know plans and proposed developments in your area and any objections to them. Study the history of town planning worldwide and the development of new towns in the United Kingdom during the 20th century, for example Bournville, Milton Keynes, Port Sunlight, Welwyn Garden City, Cumbernauld, and the advantages and disadvantages which became apparent. See also **Appendix 2**.

Selection interviews Yes Bristol UWE, London (UCL), London South Bank, Newcastle; **Some** Birmingham City, Cardiff, Dundee.

Interview advice and questions Since Town and Country Planning courses are vocational, work experience in a planning office is relevant and questions are likely to be asked on the type of work done and the problems faced by planners. Questions in recent years have included: If you were re-planning your home county for the future, what points would you consider? How are statistics used in urban planning? How do you think the problem of inner cities can be solved? Have you visited your local planning office? See **Chapter 7**.

Reasons for rejection (non-academic) Lack of commitment to study for a professional qualification in Town Planning.

AFTER-RESULTS ADVICE

Offers to applicants repeating A-levels **Higher** Bristol UWE, Newcastle; **Same** Birmingham City, Cardiff, Dundee, London South Bank, Oxford Brookes.

GRADUATE DESTINATIONS AND EMPLOYMENT (2005/6 HESA)

Graduates surveyed 640 **Employed** 335 **In further study** 130 **Assumed unemployed** 30.

Career note Town planning graduates have a choice of career options within local authority planning offices. In addition to working on individual projects on urban development, they will also be involved in advising, co-ordinating and adjudicating in disputes and appeals. Planners also work closely with economists, surveyors and sociologists and their skills open up a wide range of other careers.

OTHER DEGREE SUBJECTS FOR CONSIDERATION

Architecture; Countryside Management; Environmental Studies; Geography; Heritage Management; Housing; Public Administration; Sociology; Surveying; Transport Management.

TRANSPORT MANAGEMENT and PLANNING

(including **Supply Chain Management;** see also **Business Courses, Engineering/Engineering Sciences** and **Town and Country Planning**)

Transport Management and Planning is a specialised branch of business studies with many applications on land, sea and air. It is not as popular as the less specialised Business Studies courses but is just as relevant and will provide the student with an excellent introduction to management and its problems.

Useful websites www.cilt-international.com; www.transportweb.com; www.nats.co.uk; www.ciltuk.org.uk.

NB The points totals shown to the left of the institutions are for ease of reference only. It must not be assumed that tariff points are always used by institutions or that they can be substituted for an offer in grades. The level of an offer is not necessarily indicative of the quality of a course.

COURSE OFFERS INFORMATION

Subject requirements/preferences **GCSE** English and mathematics required. **Birmingham** Mathematics grade B. **AL** No subjects specified. **NB** A* grades are likely to form part of university offers in the higher ranges for students applying for places in 2008 for entry in 2009: check websites.

Your target offers

340 pts **Leeds** – AAB (Mgt Trans St; Econ Trans St)
320 pts **Cardiff** – 320 pts (Bus Mgt (Log Ops))
          Leeds – ABB (Geog Trans Plan)
280 pts **City** – BBC (Air Trans Ops) *(IB 28 pts)*
          Northumbria – 280 pts+portfolio (Trans Des)
260 pts **Aston** – BCC–CCC (Trans Mgt; Log; Trans Plan) *(IB 29 pts)*
          Loughborough – 260–280 pts (Trans Bus Mgt; Air Trans Mgt) *(IB 30 pts)*
240 pts **Bristol UWE** – 240–280 pts (Plan Trans)
          City – 240 pts (Air Trans Eng) *(IB 28 pts)*
          Napier – 240 pts (Civ Trans Eng)
          Northumbria – 240 pts (Bus Log Sply Chn Mgt)
230 pts **Sheffield Hallam** – 230 pts inc 2AL (Plan Trans)
220 pts **Ulster** – CCD 220 pts (Transportation)
200 pts **Coventry** – 200–240 pts (Trans Des; Trans Des Fut)
          Liverpool John Moores – 200 pts (Mgt Trans Log)
          London Met – 200 pts (Avn Mgt; Trans courses)

For a quick reference offers calculator, fold out the inside back cover.

180 pts **Greenwich** – 180 pts (Bus Log Trans Mgt)
Huddersfield – 180–240 pts (Trans Log Mgt; Air Trans Log Mgt; Log Sply Chn Mgt; Log; Euro Log Mgt)
140 pts **Bolton** – 140 pts (Log Sply Chn Mgt; Mtr Veh Trans St)
Staffordshire – 140–160 pts (Trans Des)
Suffolk (Univ Campus) – 140 pts (Log Trans)
120 pts **Bucks New** – 120–180 pts check with admissions tutor (Air Trans Plt Trg; Air Trav Mgt)
Swansea (Inst) – 120–180 pts (Trans Mgt; Log Sply Chn Mgt)

Plymouth – Check with University (Crse Mgt)

Alternative offers
See **Chapter 8** for grade/point equivalences and related information for the following examinations: Scottish qualifications, the Welsh Baccalaureate, the IB diploma (approximate points shown also in italics in the table of offers), the Irish Leaving Certificate, the European Baccalaureate and the French Baccalaureate.

EXAMPLES OF FOUNDATION DEGREES IN THE SUBJECT FIELD
Anglia Ruskin; Bolton; Bucks New; London Met; Milton Keynes (Coll); Myerscough (Coll); Newcastle (Coll); Thurrock (Coll).

CHOOSING YOUR COURSE (SEE ALSO CH.1)
Course variations – Widen your options
Motor Vehicle and Transport Studies (Bolton)
Air Transport with Pilot Training (Bucks New)
Industrial Design (Coventry)
Business Logistics and Transport Management (Greenwich)
Transportation Design (Northumbria)
Airline and Airport Management (Thames Valley)
CHECK PROSPECTUSES AND WEBSITES FOR OTHER UNIVERSITIES AND COLLEGES OFFERING THESE COURSES.

Sandwich degree courses Aston; Huddersfield; Loughborough.

ADMISSIONS INFORMATION
Number of applicants per place (approx) Aston 5; Coventry 5; Huddersfield 5; Loughborough 11.

Advice to applicants and planning the UCAS personal statement Air, sea, road and rail transport are the main specialist areas. Contacts with those involved and work experience or work shadowing should be described in full. See also **Appendix 2**.

Selection interviews Yes Huddersfield, Loughborough; **Some** Aston.

Interview advice and questions Some knowledge of the transport industry (land, sea and air) is likely to be important at interview. Reading around the subject is also important, as are any contacts with management staff in the industries. Past questions have included: What developments are taking place to reduce the number of cars on the roads? What transport problems are there in your own locality? How did you travel to your interview? What problems did you encounter? How could they have been overcome? See **Chapter 7**.

AFTER-RESULTS ADVICE
Offers to applicants repeating A-levels Same Aston.

GRADUATE DESTINATIONS AND EMPLOYMENT (2005/6 HESA)
See **Tourism and Travel**.

Career note Many graduates will aim for openings linked with specialisms in their degree courses. These could cover air, rail, sea, bus or freight transport in which they will be involved in the management and control of operations as well as marketing and financial operations.

OTHER DEGREE SUBJECTS FOR CONSIDERATION

Environmental Studies; Marine Transport; Town and Country Planning; Urban Studies.

VETERINARY SCIENCE/MEDICINE

(including **Veterinary Nursing**)

Veterinary Medicine/Science degrees enable students to acquire the professional skills and experience to qualify as veterinary surgeons. Courses follow the same pattern and combine a rigorous scientific training with practical experience. The demand for these courses is considerable (see below) and work experience is essential prior to application. See also **Appendix 2**. Veterinary Nursing honours degree courses combine both the academic learning and the nursing training required by the Royal College of Veterinary Surgeons, and can also include practice management. Veterinary Nursing Foundation degrees are more widely available.

Useful websites www.vetweb.co.uk; www.rcvs.ac.uk; www.bmat.org.uk; www.bvna.org.uk; www.spvs.org.uk.

NB The points totals shown to the left of the institutions are for ease of reference only. It must not be assumed that tariff points are always used by institutions or that they can be substituted for an offer in grades. The level of an offer is not necessarily indicative of the quality of a course.

NB For places in Veterinary Science/Medicine, applicants may select only four universities. Applicants to the University of Bristol Veterinary School, the University of Cambridge Veterinary School and the Royal Veterinary College, University of London are required to sit the BioMedical Admissions Test (BMAT) (see **Chapter 7**).

COURSE OFFERS INFORMATION

Subject requirements/preferences GCSE (Vet Sci/Med) Grade B English, mathematics, physics, dual science if not at A-level. **Bristol, Glasgow** Grade A or B in physics. **Bristol** Grade A in five or six subjects. **Liverpool** English, mathematics, physics, dual science grade B if not at A-level. (Vet Nurs) Five subjects including English and two science. **AL** (Vet Sci/Med) See offers below. A science subject may be required for Nursing courses. **Cambridge** (Emmanuel) AEA in one science subject may be required when only two are taken (see **Chapter 7**). (Vet Nurs) Biology and another science may be required. **NB** A* grades are likely to form part of university offers in the higher ranges for students applying for places in 2008 for entry in 2009: check websites.

Your target offers

360 pts   and above
       Bristol – AAA +BMAT (Vet Sci) *(IB 38 pts H766)*
       Cambridge – AAA +BMAT (inc AL chem+1 from phys/biol/maths) (Vet Med) *(IB 38–42 pts)*

For a quick reference offers calculator, fold out the inside back cover.

Liverpool – AABb (Vet Sci) *(IB 38 pts H766)*

London (RVC) – AAA–AAB +BMAT (inc AL chem+1 from biol/phys/maths) (Vet Med)

340 pts **Edinburgh** – AAB (inc A chem+2AL from biol/maths/phys) (Vet Med) *(IB 36 pts)*

Glasgow – AAB (inc A chem+biol+phys/maths AB/BA) (Vet Med) *(IB 36 pts)*

Nottingham – AAB (Vet Med Srgy) *(IB 38 pts H76)*

300 pts **Bristol** – BBB (inc AL chem+1 sci inc 4AS inc 1 non-sci) (Vet Pathogen) *(IB 32 pts)*

Liverpool – BBB 300 pts (inc biol+sci) (Biovet Sci)

London (RVC) – BBB (BSc Biovet Sci 3yrs – **not** a qualification to practise as a veterinary surgeon)

Nottingham – BBB (inc biol/chem/maths/phys) (Pre-Vet Sci (Univ Cert) 5 places. Direct entry to St George's Grenada, West Indies)

280 pts **Lincoln** – 280 pts (Biovet Sci)

240 pts **London (RVC)** – CCC (1 yr Vet Gateway prog)

220 pts **Central Lancashire** – 220 pts (Vet Nurs)

Myerscough (Coll) – 220 pts (Vet Nurs)

200 pts **Anglia Ruskin** – 200 pts (Vet Nurs Sci)

Middlesex – 200–220 pts (Vet Nurs)

Napier – 200 pts (Vet Nurs)

180 pts **Bristol UWE (Hartpury)** – 180–240 pts (inc biol) (Biovet Sci; Vet Nurs Sci; Vet Prac Mgt; Eqn Dntl Sci)

160 pts **Bristol** – CC (inc AL sci, biol pref inc 2AS sci inc biol) (Vet Nurs)

Harper Adams (UC) – 160–240 pts (Biovet Sci; Vet Nurs Prac Mgt)

London (RVC) – CC–AA (Vet Nurs)

Alternative offers

See **Chapter 8** for grade/point equivalences and related information for the following examinations: Scottish qualifications, the Welsh Baccalaureate, the IB diploma (approximate points shown also in

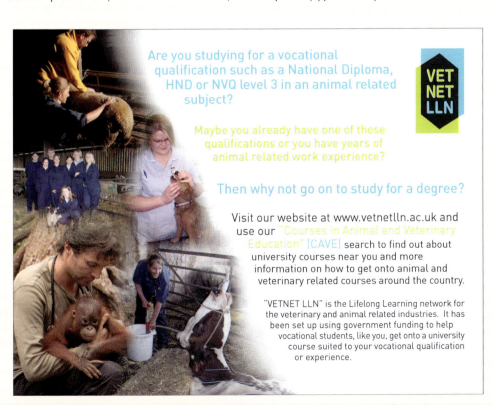

italics in the table of offers), the Irish Leaving Certificate, the European Baccalaureate and the French Baccalaureate.

EXAMPLES OF FOUNDATION DEGREES IN THE SUBJECT FIELD
Askham Bryan (Coll); Cornwall (Coll); Harper Adams (UC); Hartpury (Coll); Kingston Maurward (Coll); London (RVC); Myerscough (Coll); Nottingham Trent; Rodbaston (Coll); Sparsholt (Coll); Warwickshire (Coll).

CHOOSING YOUR COURSE (SEE ALSO CH.1)
Author's note Veterinary Science/Medicine is the most intensely competitive subject and, as in the case of Medicine, one or two offers and three rejections are not uncommon. As a result, the Royal College of Veterinary Surgeons has raised a number of points which are relevant to applicants and advisers:

(a) Every candidate for a Veterinary Medicine/Sciences degree course should be advised to spend a suitable period with a veterinarian in practice.
(b) A period spent in veterinary work may reveal a hitherto unsuspected allergy or sensitivity following contact with various animals.
(c) Potential applicants should be under no illusions about the difficulty of the task they have set themselves . . . five applicants for every available place . . . with no likelihood of places being increased at the present time.
(d) There are so many candidates who can produce the necessary level of scholastic attainment that other considerations have to be taken into account in making the choice. In most cases, the number of GCSE grade As will be crucial. This is current practice. Headteachers' reports and details of applicants' interests, activities and background are very relevant and are taken fully into consideration . . . applicants are reminded to include details of periods of time spent with veterinary surgeons.
(e) Any applicant who has not received an offer but who achieves the grades required for admission ought to write as soon as the results are known to the schools and enquire about the prospects of entry at the Clearing stage. All courses cover the same subject topics.

Course variations – Widen your options
Animal Management and Science (Askham Bryan (Coll))
Animal Behaviour and Welfare (Bristol)
Zoology (Animal Sciences) (Leeds)
Bioveterinary Science (London (RVC))
Equine Science and Management (Myerscough (Coll))
Applied Animal Studies (Northampton)
Animal Management (Wolverhampton)
CHECK PROSPECTUSES AND WEBSITES FOR OTHER UNIVERSITIES AND COLLEGES OFFERING THESE COURSES.

Universities and colleges teaching quality See www.qaa.ac.uk; www.unistats.com.

Top universities and colleges (Research) Bristol; Cambridge; Edinburgh; Glasgow; Liverpool; London (RVC).

ADMISSIONS INFORMATION
Number of applicants per place (approx) Bristol (Vet Sci) 16, (Vet Nurs) 4, (Vet Pathogen) 4; Cambridge 5; Edinburgh 17; Glasgow 20; Liverpool 12; London (RVC) 5.

Numbers of applicants (a UK b EU (non-UK) c non-EU d mature) London (RVC) a759 b71 c156 d172.

Advice to applicants and planning the UCAS personal statement Applicants for Veterinary Science must limit their choices to four universities and submit their applications by 15 October. They may add up to two alternative courses. However, if they receive and accept offers, and then perform better than expected, they will not be able to request vet schools to reconsider their applications. Work experience is essential for all applicants so discuss experiences in full, giving information about the size and type of practice and the type of work in which you were involved. **Bristol** Evidence of wide veterinary animal experience; evidence of initiative. The Veterinary Nursing course is a possible route to the BVSc degree. **Liverpool** The selection process involves three areas: academic ability to cope with the course; knowledge of vocational aspects of veterinary science acquired through work experience in veterinary practice and working with animals; personal attributes that demonstrate responsibility and self-motivation. **London (RVC)** Six weeks' hands-on experience needed: two weeks in a veterinary practice; two weeks with large domestic animals; two weeks with other animals, for example riding school, zoo, kennels. See also **Appendix 2**.

Misconceptions about this course Bristol UWE (Hartpury) (Vet Nurs Sci) Students think that the degree qualifies them as veterinary nurses but RCVS assessment/training is additional. **Liverpool** (Biovet Sci) Some applicants think that the course allows students to transfer to Veterinary Science: it does not.

Selection interviews All institutions.

Interview advice and questions Past questions have included: Why do you want to be a vet? Have you visited a veterinary practice? What did you see? Do you think there should be a Vet National Health Service? What are your views on vivisection? What are your views on intensive factory farming? How can you justify thousands of pounds of taxpayers' money being spent on training you to be a vet when it could be used to train a civil engineer? When would you feel it your responsibility to tell battery hen farmers that they were being cruel to their livestock? What are your views on vegetarians? How does aspirin stop pain? Why does it only work for a certain length of time? Do you eat beef? Outline the BSE problem and European attitudes. Questions on A-level science syllabus. **Glasgow** Applicants complete a questionnaire prior to interview. Questions cover experience with animals, reasons for choice of career, animal welfare, teamwork, work experience, stressful situations. See **Chapter 7**.

Applicants' impressions (A=Open day; B=Interview day) Bristol UWE (Hartpury) (Vet Nurs Sci; B) I had a 15-minute interview. The department was very well equipped.

Reasons for rejection (non-academic) Failure to demonstrate motivation. Lack of basic knowledge or understanding of ethical and animal issues.

AFTER-RESULTS ADVICE
Offers to applicants repeating A-levels Higher London (RVC); **Same** Bristol UWE (Hartpury) (Vet Nurs Sci), Harper Adams (UC) (Vet Nurs), Liverpool (candidates achieving the necessary grades are welcome to reapply); **Not acceptable** Edinburgh, Glasgow; **No offers made** Cambridge.

GRADUATE DESTINATIONS AND EMPLOYMENT (2005/6 HESA)
Graduates surveyed 335 **Employed** 295 **In further study** 10 **Assumed unemployed** 10.

Career note Over 80% of veterinary surgeons work in private practice with the remainder involved in research in universities, government-financed research departments and in firms linked with farming, foodstuff manufacturers and pharmaceutical companies. In 2006 only 2% of newly qualified veterinary surgeons were unemployed.

OTHER DEGREE SUBJECTS FOR CONSIDERATION
Agricultural Science; Agriculture; Animal Sciences; Biological Sciences; Biology; Dentistry; Equine Dental Science; Equine Management; Equine Studies; Medicine; Zoology.

WELSH (CYMRAEG) and CELTIC
(including **Gaelic** and **Irish Studies**)

Irish, Scottish, Gaelic, Welsh, Breton, Manx, Cornish, Gaulish and Celtiberian are all included in this subject area. Courses may also include the history and civilisation of the Celtic peoples.

Useful websites www.bwrdd-yr-iaith.org.uk; www.wales.gov.uk; www.bbc.co.uk/wales;

www.daltai.com; www.eisteddfod.org.uk; www.digitalmedievalist.com; www.gaelic-scotland.co.uk.

NB The points totals shown to the left of the institutions are for ease of reference only. It must not be assumed that tariff points are always used by institutions or that they can be substituted for an offer in grades. The level of an offer is not necessarily indicative of the quality of a course.

COURSE OFFERS INFORMATION

Subject requirements/preferences GCSE A foreign language or Welsh may be required. **AL** Welsh may be required for some courses. **NB** A* grades are likely to form part of university offers in the higher ranges for students applying for places in 2008 for entry in 2009: check websites.

Your target offers

360 pts and above

    Cambridge – AAA varies between colleges (A-Sxn Nrs Celt) *(IB 38–42 pts)*

320 pts Glasgow – ABB (Gael courses) *(IB 30 pts)*

300 pts Edinburgh – BBB (Celt; Celt Arch; Celt Ger; Celt Ling; Celt Scand St; Celt Scot Hist St; Scot Lit; Celt Engl Lang; Celtic Engl Lit) *(IB 34 pts H555)*

    Glasgow – BBB (Celt St; Celt Civ)

    Queen's Belfast – BBB–BBCb (Irish Celt courses)

260 pts Aberystwyth – 260–300 pts (Celt St; Ir Lang Lit; Welsh courses; Welsh Hist) *(IB 29 pts)*

    Cardiff – 260 pts (Welsh courses)

    Liverpool – BCC (Irish St Engl Lang Lit; Ir St Hist)

240 pts Aberdeen – CCC (Celt Civ courses; Celt St; Gael St)

    Bangor – 240–260 pts (Welsh courses (taught in Welsh medium))

    Liverpool – CCC 240 pts (Irish St) *(IB 32 pts)*

    Swansea – 240–300 pts (Welsh courses)

    Ulster – CCC–CCD 240–220 pts (Ir Lang Lit Ir St; Ir; Ir Lang)

220 pts Bangor – 220–200 pts (Cymraeg)

    Cardiff (UWIC) – 220 pts (Welsh courses)

180 pts Lampeter – 180–240 pts (Welsh St; Cymraeg; Welsh Transl Subtit; Welsh Subtit)

    UHI Millennium Inst – DDD 180 pts (Gael; Gael Lang Cult; Gael N Atlan St; Gael Trad Mus; Gael Media St)

160 pts St Mary's (UC) – 160–200 pts (Ir St)

140 pts Glamorgan – 140–160 pts (Prof Welsh courses)

    Trinity Carmarthen (Coll) – 140 pts (Welsh biling prac)

Alternative offers

See **Chapter 8** for grade/point equivalences and related information for the following examinations: Scottish qualifications, the Welsh Baccalaureate, the IB diploma (approximate points shown also in italics in the table of offers), the Irish Leaving Certificate, the European Baccalaureate and the French Baccalaureate.

CHOOSING YOUR COURSE (SEE ALSO CH.1)

Course variations – Widen your options
Law with Options in Gaelic Language (Aberdeen)
Celtic Civilisation and Gaelic Studies (Aberdeen)
Museum and Gallery Studies and Welsh History (Aberystwyth)
Irish Language Literature and Drama (Aberystwyth)
Law with Welsh (Bangor)
Archaeology and Welsh (Cardiff)
Combined Honours (Cornish Studies) (Exeter)
Media Studies and Welsh Studies (Lampeter)
Combined Honours (Liverpool)
Dance with Irish (Ulster)
CHECK PROSPECTUSES AND WEBSITES FOR OTHER UNIVERSITIES AND COLLEGES OFFERING THESE COURSES.

Universities and colleges teaching quality See www.qaa.ac.uk; www.unistats.com.

Top universities and colleges (Research) Aberystwyth*; Bangor*; Cambridge*; Cardiff; Edinburgh; Queen's Belfast; Swansea.

ADMISSIONS INFORMATION

Number of applicants per place (approx) Aberystwyth 6; Bangor 8; Cambridge 2; Cardiff 2; Lampeter 3; St Mary's (UC) 3; Swansea 7.

Advice to applicants and planning the UCAS personal statement Interests in this field largely develop through literature, museum visits or archaeology which should be fully described in the UCAS application.

Selection interviews Yes Aberystwyth, Lampeter; **No** St Mary's (UC).

Interview advice and questions Past questions have included: Why do you want to study this subject? What specific areas of Celtic culture interest you? What do you expect to gain by studying unusual subjects? See **Chapter 7**.

AFTER-RESULTS ADVICE

Offers to applicants repeating A-levels Same Aberystwyth, Bangor, Cardiff, Lampeter, Swansea.

GRADUATE DESTINATIONS AND EMPLOYMENT (2005/6 HESA)

Graduates surveyed 135 **Employed** 50 **In further study** 50 **Assumed unemployed** 5.

Career note See **Arts (General/Combined/Humanities/Modular)** and **Languages**.

OTHER DEGREE SUBJECTS FOR CONSIDERATION

Anthropology; Archaeology; History.

ZOOLOGY

(see also **Agricultural Sciences/Agriculture, Animal Sciences** and **Biology**)

Zoology courses have a biological science foundation and could cover animal ecology, marine and fisheries biology, animal population, development and behaviour and, on some courses, wildlife management and fisheries.

Useful websites www.scienceyear.com; www.zoo.cam.ac.uk/ioz; www.zsl.org; www.academicinfo.net/zoo.html.

NB The points totals shown to the left of the institutions are for ease of reference only. It must not be assumed that tariff points are always used by institutions or that they can be substituted for an offer in grades. The level of an offer is not necessarily indicative of the quality of a course.

COURSE OFFERS INFORMATION

Subject requirements/preferences GCSE English and science/mathematics required or preferred. **AL** One or two sciences will be required. **NB** A* grades are likely to form part of university offers in the higher ranges for students applying for places in 2008 for entry in 2009: check websites.

Your target offers

360 pts **and above**
        Cambridge – AAA (Nat Sci (Zool)) *(IB 38–42 pts)*
        London (UCL) – AABe–BBBe (Zoology) *(IB 32–36 pts)*
340 pts **Imperial London** – AAB–ABB (Zoology) *(IB 36 pts H66)*
        Manchester – AAB–BBB (Zool; Zool Ind; Zool Modn Lang)
        Sheffield – AAB (MBiol Sci Zool) *(IB 32 pts)*
320 pts **Birmingham** – ABB–BBB (Biol Sci (Zool))
        Bristol – ABB–BBB (Zoology) *(IB 33 pts H665)*
        Cardiff – ABB–BBB (Zoology) *(IB 32 pts H biol chem 5)*

Durham – ABB (Zool; Zool Ind) *(IB 34 pts H55)*
Liverpool – ABB–BBB (Zool; Zool Evol Psy) *(IB 28–30 pts)*
London (RH) – ABB–BBB (Zool; Zool Physiol)
Newcastle – ABB (Zoology) *(IB 32–35 pts)*
Nottingham – ABB–AAB (Zoology) *(IB 32 pts)*
300 pts **Aberdeen** – 300 pts 2nd yr entry (Zoology) *(IB 28 pts)*
Dundee – 300 pts 2nd yr entry (Zoology)
Edinburgh – BBB (Zoology) *(IB 30 pts)*
Leeds – BBB 300 pts (Zoology) *(IB 32 pts H 15 pts)*
Leicester – BBB (Biol Sci (Zool)) *(IB 32 pts)*
Reading – 300 pts (Zoology)
St Andrews – ABC–BBB (Zoology) *(IB 31 pts)*
Sheffield – ABB–BBB (BSc Zool; Anim Bhv) *(IB 32–33 pts)*
Southampton – BBB 300 pts (Zoology) *(IB 32 pts H 15 pts)*
280 pts **Glasgow** – BBC–CCC (Zoology) *(IB 28 pts)*
London (QM) – 280 pts (Zoology) *(IB 30 pts)*
Queen's Belfast – BBC–BCCb (Zoology) *(IB 28 pts H555)*
Swansea – 280–300 pts (3AL) 220–200 pts (2AL) (Zoology)
260 pts **Bangor** – 260–320 pts (Mar Biol Zool)
Hull – 260–300 pts (Aqua Zool; Zool)
240 pts **Aberdeen** – 240 pts 1st yr entry (Zoology)
Aberystwyth – 240–280 pts (Zool; Zool Microbiol)
Bangor – 240–280 pts (Zool; Zool Cons; Zool Mar Biol; Mar Biol Zool; Mar Vrtbrt Zool)
Dundee – 240 pts 1st yr entry (Zoology)
220 pts **Cumbria** – 220 pts (Wldlf Media)
Liverpool John Moores – 220 pts (Zoology)
Stirling – CCD (Anim Biol)
200 pts **Anglia Ruskin** – 200 pts (Zool; Wldlf Biol; Nat Hist courses)
Bolton – 200 pts (Biol Anim Biol)
Derby – 200 pts (Zoology)
Napier – 200 pts (Anim Biol)
Staffordshire – 200–260 pts (Anim Biol Cons)
180 pts **Salford** – 180 pts (Zool; Wldlf Cons Zoo Biol)
160 pts **Blackpool and Fylde (Coll)** – 160 pts (Sci Nat Hist Illus)
120 pts **Roehampton** – 120–200 pts (Zoology)
West Scotland – DD (Biol Zool; Multim Zool)
 80 pts **and below**
Eastleigh (Coll) – (Fdn Sci)

Alternative offers

See **Chapter 8** for grade/point equivalences and related information for the following examinations: Scottish qualifications, the Welsh Baccalaureate, the IB diploma (approximate points shown also in italics in the table of offers), the Irish Leaving Certificate, the European Baccalaureate and the French Baccalaureate.

EXAMPLES OF FOUNDATION DEGREES IN THE SUBJECT FIELD
(See also **Animal Sciences**) Cornwall (Coll); Sparsholt (Coll).

CHOOSING YOUR COURSE (SEE ALSO CH.1)
Course variations – Widen your options
Wildlife Biology (Anglia Ruskin)
Marine and Vertebrate Zoology (Bangor)
Zoology with Industrial Placement (Durham)
Aquatic Zoology (Hull)
Animal Science (Leeds)

For a quick reference offers calculator, fold out the inside back cover.

Animal Conservation Biology (Northampton)
Wildlife Conservation with Zoo Biology (Salford)
CHECK PROSPECTUSES AND WEBSITES FOR OTHER UNIVERSITIES AND COLLEGES OFFERING THESE COURSES.

Universities and colleges teaching quality See www.qaa.ac.uk; www.unistats.com.

Top universities and colleges (Research) Cambridge*.

Sandwich degree courses Cardiff; Durham; Manchester; West Scotland.

ADMISSIONS INFORMATION
Number of applicants per place (approx) Aberystwyth 8; Bangor 3; Bristol 13; Cardiff 8; Durham 11; Leeds 7; Liverpool John Moores 6; London (RH) 6, (UCL) 8; Newcastle 15; Nottingham 9; Swansea 6.

Advice to applicants and planning the UCAS personal statement Interests in animals should be described, together with any first-hand experience gained. Visits to zoos, farms, fish farms etc and field courses attended should be described, together with any special points of interest that you noted.

Selection interviews Yes Cambridge, Durham, Hull, Liverpool, London (RH), Newcastle; **Some** Cardiff, Derby, Dundee, Roehampton, Swansea.

Interview questions Past questions have included: Why do you want to study Zoology? What career do you hope to follow on graduation? Specimens may be given to identify. Questions usually asked on the A-level subjects. See **Chapter 7**.

AFTER-RESULTS ADVICE
Offers to applicants repeating A-levels Higher Bristol, Hull, Leeds, Swansea; **Same** Aberystwyth, Bangor, Cardiff, Derby, Dundee, Durham, Liverpool, Liverpool John Moores, London (RH), Roehampton, Swansea; **No offers made** Cambridge.

GRADUATE DESTINATIONS AND EMPLOYMENT (2005/6 HESA)
Graduates surveyed 650 **Employed** 300 **In further study** 135 **Assumed unemployed** 55.

Career note See **Biology**.

OTHER DEGREE SUBJECTS FOR CONSIDERATION
Animal Sciences; Aquaculture; Biological Sciences; Biology; Ecology; Fisheries Management; Marine Biology; Parasitology; Veterinary Science.

The choice of a subject to study (from over 50,000 degree courses) and of a university or college (from more than 300 institutions) is a major task for students living in the United Kingdom (UK). For overseas and European Union (EU) applicants it is even greater, and the decisions that have to be made need much careful planning, preferably beginning two years before the start of the course.

SELECTION POLICIES

The first reason for making early contact with your preferred institution is to check their requirements for your chosen subject and their selection policies for overseas applicants. For example, for all Art and some Architecture courses you will have to present a portfolio of work or slides. For Music courses your application often will have to be accompanied by a recording you have made of your playing or singing and, in many cases, a personal audition will be necessary. Attendance at an interview in this country is compulsory for some universities and for some courses. At other institutions the interview may take place either in the UK or with a university or college representative in your own country.

The ability to speak and write good English is essential and many institutions require evidence of competence, for example scores from the International English Language Testing System (IELTS) or from the Test of English as a Foreign Language (TOEFL) (see www.ielts.org and www.ets.org/toefl). For some institutions you may have to send examples of your written work. Each institution provides information about its English language entry requirements and a summary of this is given for each university listed below. International students should note that the recommended threshold for minimum English language requirements is IELTS 6.5–7.0. Recent research indicates that students with a lower score may have difficulty in dealing with their course.

In **Chapter 2** of this book you will find a directory of universities and colleges in the UK, together with their contact details. Most universities and colleges in the UK have an overseas student adviser who can advise you on these and other points you need to consider, such as passports, visas, entry certificates, evidence of financial support, medical certificates, medical insurance, and the numbers of overseas students in the university from your own country. All these details are very important and need to be considered at the same time as choosing your course and institution.

The subject tables in **Chapter 9** provide a comprehensive picture of courses on offer and of comparative entry levels. However, before making an application, other factors should be considered such as English language entry requirements (see above), the availability of English language teaching, living costs, tuition fees and any scholarships or other awards which might be offered. Detailed information about these can be obtained from the international offices in each university or college, from British higher education fairs throughout the world and from the British Council offices abroad and from websites: see www.britishcouncil.org; www.education.org.

Below is a brief summary of the arrangements made by each university in the UK for students aiming to take a full-time degree programme. The information is presented as follows:

* Institution.
* International student numbers.
* English language entry requirements for degree programmes shown in either IELTS or TOEFL scores. These vary between universities and courses. For the IELTS, scores can range from 5.5 to

7.5, and for the TOEFL computer-based test, scores can range from a minimum of 213; for the written TOEFL the usual minimum entry level is 5.0. For full details contact the university or college.

* Arrangements for English tuition.
* International Foundation courses.
* Annual tuition fees for degree courses (**approximate**). Tuition fees also usually include fees for examinations and graduation. These figures are approximate and are subject to change each year. EU students pay 'home student' fees, except for those from the Channel Islands and the Isle of Man; also, from 2007/8 students from the British Overseas Territories are treated as home students for fee purposes at universities and other institutions of higher education.
* Annual living costs. These are also approximate and represent the costs for a single student over the year. The living costs shown cover university accommodation (usually guaranteed for the first year only), food, books, clothing and travel in the UK, but not travel to or from the UK. (Costs are likely to rise year by year in line with the rate of inflation in the UK, currently around 3% per year.) Overseas students are normally permitted to take part-time work for a period of up to 20 hours per week.
* Scholarships and awards for non-EU students (most universities offer awards for EU students).

UNIVERSITY INFORMATION AND FEES FOR INTERNATIONAL STUDENTS

Aberdeen International students 14%, 115 nationalities; *English language entry requirement (or equivalent):* IELTS 6.0; for Medicine 7.0. Four-week English course available in August before the start of the academic year. *Fees:* Arts subjects £9200, Science subjects £11,700, Medicine £21,500. *Living costs:* £6200. Some scholarships and grants.

Abertay Dundee International students 10%; *English language entry requirement (or equivalent):* IELTS 5.5. Pre-sessional English course available, also full-time English course September to May and free English tuition throughout degree course. *Fees:* all courses £8200. *Living costs:* £5200. Several scholarships available, including special awards for students from India and from some countries in the Far East and the USA.

Aberystwyth A large number of international students. *English language entry requirement (or equivalent):* IELTS 6.5. Full-time tuition in English available. *Fees:* Arts subjects £7700, Science subjects £10,000, joint courses £9200. *Living costs:* £6200. Awards for students from the Far East.

American InterContinental There are 91 overseas students currently following courses at the University. *Living costs:* £10,200 (minimum).

Anglia Ruskin International students 21%. *English language entry requirement (or equivalent):* IELTS 5.5. A one-year International Foundation programme available. *Fees:* Arts subjects £7900, Science subjects £8900, Optometry £10,000, Nursing £13,200. *Living costs:* £7000.

Arts London A large number of international students. *English language entry requirement (or equivalent):* IELTS 6.5. Courses in Fashion Promotion, Acting, Directing require IELTS 7.5. Language Centre courses in academic English for 12, 24, 34 or 36 weeks. *Fees:* degree courses £10,700. *Living costs:* £12,000.

Aston Over 1000 students from over 80 countries, with 15% of the total student population from overseas. International Orientation programme at the beginning of the academic year. *English language entry requirement (or equivalent):* IELTS 6.0–6.5. International Foundation programme offered as a bridge to the degree courses. Pre-sessional English classes also available of five and ten weeks duration. *Fees:* non-Science programmes £8700, Engineering and Science courses £10,700. *Living costs:* £7200. Scholarships offered, including bursaries for Engineering and Science subjects.

Bangor Ten per cent of the student population is made up of international students from 70 countries. Lower cost of living than many other UK cities. *English language entry requirement (or equivalent):* IELTS 6.0. Pre-study English course starting September, January or April depending on level of English proficiency, leads to International Foundation course. One-month or two-month courses before starting degree course also offered. *Fees:* £8700. *Living costs:* £5700. Scholarships available.

Bath Over 1500 international students from around 100 countries. *English language entry requirement (or equivalent):* IELTS 6.0. Pre-degree language courses offered, ranging from one month to one year. *Fees:* Arts and Social Science subjects £9400, Science and Engineering courses £12,000. *Living costs:* £7700. Scholarships and awards available, including residential awards for applicants from the Far East and Kenya.

Bath Spa Students from 40 countries. *English language entry requirement (or equivalent):* IELTS 5.5 for subjects supported by the Undergraduate Course for International Students (UCIS). Foundation courses available for students below this score. Subjects not supported by UCIS, entry level IELTS 6.0. *Fees:* £8500–£10,000 (plus studio fees £200–£300 for Art and Design courses). *Living costs:* £6500.

Bedfordshire A new university (2006). 3000 EU and international students. *English language entry requirement (or equivalent):* IELTS 6.0. General English programmes are offered, including a summer school. *Fees:* One-year International Foundation course and English language course £6500, one-semester course £3600; Arts degree courses £7700, Science degree courses £8600. *Living costs:* £6000.

Birmingham Over 4000 international students from 152 countries. *English language entry requirement (or equivalent):* IELTS 6.0. Six, ten and 20-week English language programmes available, depending on language proficiency, ranging from IELTS 4.5 to 5.5. *Fees:* non-laboratory subjects £9000, laboratory subjects £11,500, clinical programmes £20,500. *Living costs:* £7600–£9700. International Foundation programme available. Awards are offered by some subject departments including Bioscience, Computer Science, Earth Sciences, Law, Psychology; there are also Engineering scholarships for students from Malaysia.

Birmingham City (Recently the University of Central England in Birmingham) Large number of international students. *English language entry requirement (or equivalent):* IELTS 6.0. Pre-sessional language courses and in-session language support. Orientation programme for all students. *Fees:* £8000–£9700. *Living costs:* £7000. Music bursaries.

Bolton 70 countries represented. *English language entry requirement (or equivalent):* IELTS 6.0. Courses start in September, some in February. Pre-sessional and in-session English tuition. *Fees:* £8300. *Living costs:* £6000.

Bournemouth A large number of international students. *English language entry requirement (or equivalent):* IELTS 6.0. Preparatory English programme offered, starting in January, April or July depending on applicant's level of English (entry IELTS 4.5/5.0/5.5). Several language schools in the town (see www.englishuk.com.uk or www.baselt.org.uk). Pre-sessional study skills programme also offered. *Fees:* £7400–£8400. *Living costs:* £8000. Some subject awards available.

Bradford Over 100 countries represented. *English language entry requirement (or equivalent):* IELTS 6.0. Some students may be admitted to Year 2, depending on qualifications. *Fees:* Science and Engineering courses £10,300, other courses £8000 (lower fees for students taking a sandwich year – see **Chapter 1**). *Living costs:* £7500. Ten scholarships to cover the duration of the course.

Brighton Some 2000 international students from over 100 countries. *English language entry requirement (or equivalent):* IELTS 6.0 (or 5.5 for less linguistically demanding subjects). New four-year degree programme (UK4) includes preparatory year. *Fees:* £8000. Fixed fees possible. *Living costs:* £8000. Links with other nationals at Brighton. Merit scholarships for students from some countries in the Far East, Africa and Norway.

Bristol Students from over 100 countries. *English language entry requirement (or equivalent):* IELTS 6.5 (possibly lower for some Science and Engineering subjects). *Fees:* Arts subjects £10,800, Science subjects £14,000, Clinical subjects £25,100. *Living costs:* £6000–£8500. Some bursaries and scholarships for one year from some subject departments including Law, Medicine, Dentistry and Veterinary Science.

Bristol UWE More than 1750 international students. *English language entry requirement (or equivalent):* IELTS 6.0. English language preparatory and pre-sessional courses offered. English modules can also be taken throughout your degree. *Fees:* classroom-based subjects £8000, laboratory subjects £8900. *Living costs:* £7000–£9000. Some partial fee scholarships available in Computing, Mathematics and Engineering, and Law scholarships for students from the Far East, South Africa, the West Indies and North America.

Brunel More than 2000 international students from over 110 countries. *English language entry requirement (or equivalent):* IELTS 6.0 for science/technology subjects, 7.0 for Law, 6.5 for other subjects. English language tuition offered during and before the course but only to improve existing skills. *Fees:* non-laboratory subjects £8400, laboratory subjects £10,900. *Living costs:* £8000. Twenty bursaries offered.

Buckingham Eighty nationalities represented at this small university. *English language entry requirement (or equivalent):* IELTS 6.0. *Fees:* £34,000 (total for two-year courses – check with university). *Living costs:* £7500. Tuition fee discount for students from the Bahamas, Bulgaria and India. Some scholarships for students from the Far East, Russia and Eastern Europe.

Bucks New (Buckinghamshire New) A new university (2007). 7.5% of students from overseas. *English language entry requirement (or equivalent):* IELTS 5.5/6.0. *Fees:* BA courses £7150, BSc courses £7750. *Living costs:* £7000.

Cambridge Over 1000 international undergraduate students. *English language entry requirement (or equivalent):* IELTS 7.0 overall, with minimum of 6.0 in each element. TOEFL (written) 600 (minimum) and at least 5.0 in TOEFL test of written English. *Fees:* classroom-based subjects £9700, laboratory-based subjects £11,800, clinical subjects £22,000; College fees (average) £3800. *Living costs:* £7000. Awards available, also scholarships for students from Hong Kong.

Canterbury Christ Church A new university (2005). *English language entry requirement (or equivalent):* IELTS 6.0. *Fees:* £7400–£8000. *Living costs:* £7000.

Cardiff 3500 international students from 100 countries. *English language entry requirement (or equivalent):* IELTS 6.5. Comprehensive selection of pre-sessional language courses from three weeks to nine months. Induction course for all students. International Foundation courses for Business, Law, Engineering, Computer Science and Health and Life Sciences. *Fees:* Arts courses £8800, science courses 11,300. *Living costs:* £7700. Law scholarships offered on the basis of academic merit.

Central Lancashire Large international student population from many countries. *English language entry requirement (or equivalent):* IELTS 6.0. Competence in written and spoken English required on application. *Fees:* £7400. *Living costs:* £6500.

Chester *English language entry requirement (or equivalent):* IELTS 6.0. International Foundation year available for Business Studies students. *Fees:* £7700. *Living costs:* £7500.

Chichester International students from several countries. *English language entry requirement (or equivalent):* IELTS 6.0. *Fees:* £7500–£9000. *Living costs:* £8000.

City A large international community. *English language entry requirement (or equivalent):* IELTS 6.0 (6.5 for Business, Law and Journalism). August and September pre-sessional English language courses, and in-session English workshops. International Foundation programmes in Law, Business, Engineering and Management. *Fees:* Arts-based programmes £8000, Journalism £9000, Music £10,300, Business programmes £9700, Engineering programmes £8700–£9600, Health Sciences £8100–£14,000, Law £7750–£12,275, Informatics £9900–£11,600. *Living costs:* £9500. Scholarships available for applicants for Actuarial Science, Engineering (Cypriot applicants only) and Law.

Coventry About 2500 international students. *English language entry requirement (or equivalent):* IELTS 6.0. *Fees:* £7700. *Living costs:* £7200. Scholarships available.

Cumbria A new university (2007). *English language entry requirement (or equivalent):* IELTS 6.0. *Fees:* Undergraduate £7500. English language programmes: 1 month £825, 2 months £1650, 3 months £2475. *Living costs:* £6500.

De Montfort Over 1000 international students from over 100 countries. *English language entry requirement (or equivalent):* IELTS 6.5 (lower for some faculties). In-session English tuition in some degree courses. One-year International Foundation Certificate courses in Business and Law. Orientation programme in September for all students. *Fees:* classroom subjects £9000, laboratory subjects £10,000. *Living costs:* £8000. Some scholarships for overseas students.

Derby Students from 70 countries. *English language entry requirement (or equivalent):* IELTS 6.0. Courses offered to those needing tuition in English language. Foundation courses (£5200) and pre-sessional intensive English tuition (£2000), and also language support whilst studying for degree. *Fees:* £7900. *Living costs:* £6800. International scholarships available for applicants from some countries in the Far East.

Dundee Students from 83 countries. *English language entry requirement (or equivalent):* IELTS 6.0. Foundation courses in English and for Business and Art and Design courses. *Fees:* classroom-based courses £8500, laboratory-based courses £10,800, clinical courses £21,500. *Living costs:* £7000. Some awards for overseas students in Arts and Social Sciences, Law, Accountancy, Science and Engineering and Art and Design.

Durham Some 1600 international students from over 120 countries. *English language entry requirement (or equivalent):* IELTS 6.5. Three-day induction programme before the start of the academic year. Intensive English language course if required if standard of English does not meet the required level. *Fees:* Clinical Medicine £20,000, Science, Engineering and Technology courses £11,100, all other courses £8800. *Living costs:* £5500, plus college fees (Durham); £2800 (Stockton). Scholarships for nationals from some Far Eastern countries.

East Anglia Over 2000 international students from 120 countries. *English language entry requirement (or equivalent):* IELTS 6.0 (higher for some courses). Four, eight and twelve-week pre-sessional courses in English and tuition during degree courses. *Fees:* classroom-based subjects £8700, laboratory-based subjects £11,100. *Living costs:* £570 per month. Scholarships available including awards, based on academic merit, cover part of the cost of tuition fees.

East London About 3300 international students from 120 countries. *English language entry requirement (or equivalent):* IELTS 6.0. One-year full-time preparatory English course available. *Fees:* £7500–£9500. *Living costs:* £12,000.

Edge Hill This university near Liverpool has a small number of international students. *English language entry requirement (or equivalent):* IELTS 6.5. *Fees:* £6800. *Living costs:* £5500.

Edinburgh Some 4000 international students from 120 countries. *English language entry requirement (or equivalent):* IELTS 6.0–6.5. English language support. *Fees:* £9800–£12,500, Clinical Medicine £23,500. *Living costs:* £8000. Awards include two India scholarships.

Essex International students from over 125 countries. *English language entry requirement (or equivalent):* IELTS 6.0–6.5. English language courses available before entry to degree course.

Fees: non-Science courses £8700, laboratory courses £11,175. *Living costs:* £8300. Some funding available for students in need.

Exeter Over 1500 international students from 120 countries. *English language entry requirement (or equivalent):* IELTS 6.5. Full-time Foundation programme in English, with opportunity to specialise in Physical Sciences, Computer Science, Business, Politics, History, Sociology or Law. Also pre-sessional courses in English starting in July, August or September as well as in-session support. *Fees:* non-Science programmes £9150, Science and Engineering programmes £11,000. *Living costs:* £8000. Awards available, including some subject and South East Asian scholarships.

Glamorgan Some 1500 international students from 60 different countries. *English language entry requirement (or equivalent):* IELTS from 5.0. Pre-sessional course offered in English, and also a 10–14-week English language skills programme. An International Foundation programme is also offered. *Fees:* £8800. *Living costs:* £9000.

Glasgow Over 2000 international students. *English language entry requirement (or equivalent):* IELTS 6.0 (higher for some courses). The English as a Foreign Language Unit offers intensive five-week presessional language courses in Foundation programme covering English language and study skills. *Fees:* classroom-based subjects £8900, Engineering, Sciences, Nursing £10,900, Clinical Medicine and Dentistry £19,300, Veterinary Medicine £15,900. *Living costs:* £8000. Fee-waiver scholarships and automatic Fourth Year scholarships available (not for Dentistry, Medicine or Veterinary Science).

Glasgow Caledonian Students from 70 countries. *English language entry requirement (or equivalent):* IELTS 6.0. English language programmes available. *Fees:* £7700–£8500. *Living costs:* £8000.

Gloucestershire *English language entry requirement (or equivalent):* IELTS 5.5. English language support and mentor scheme with other international students. *Fees:* £8500–£9200. *Living costs:* £6700.

Greenwich Over 4500 international students (including those from European countries). *English language entry requirement (or equivalent):* IELTS 6.0. Pre-sessional English courses, Access and International Foundation programmes. *Fees:* classroom-based subjects £8500, laboratory-based subjects £10,000. *Living costs:* from £10,000. Scholarships open to applicants from 25 countries.

Heriot-Watt Twenty-three per cent of the student population comes from over 90 countries. *English language entry requirement (or equivalent):* IELTS 6.5, and 6.8 for language courses. Several English language courses are offered; these range in length depending on students' requirements. *Fees:* £7900–£10,900. *Living costs:* £6300. Some international scholarships are available worth £1500–£2000 for one year.

Hertfordshire Students from over 90 countries are at present studying at the University. *English language entry requirement (or equivalent):* IELTS 6.0. English language tuition is offered in the one-year International Foundation course, in a course for the Foundation Certificate in English for Academic Purposes, and in a pre-sessional intensive English course held during the summer months. *Fees:* £9200–£10,000. *Living costs:* £8000.

Huddersfield International students from over 80 countries. *English language entry requirement (or equivalent):* IELTS 6.0. English language courses available and a one-year International Foundation course in English language with options in Business, Computing, Engineering, Mathematics and Music. Students guaranteed entry to Huddersfield courses on completion. *Fees:* classroom-based subjects £7900, laboratory-based subjects £8800, Foundation programme £6700. *Living costs:* £5700.

Hull Ten per cent of students from outside the EU. *English language entry requirement (or equivalent):* IELTS 6.0. English summer study programme through the three months before the start of the academic year. In-session study in English also available. Foundation programmes for Business and Management degrees. *Fees:* non-Science-based courses £8800, Science-based programmes £10,900, for the year in industry courses and for year-abroad courses £4500–£5500. *Living costs:* £6500. Hull has one of the best overseas scholarship provision of any British university, including full-tuition and 30 partial-tuition awards (50% of fees).

Imperial London Some 2200 international students from over 110 countries. *English language entry requirement (or equivalent):* IELTS 6.0–7.0. *Fees:* Mathematics and Computer Science £10,700, Chemistry £15,000, Computing £15,500, Pre-clinical Medicine £21,350, Clinical Medicine £31,900, other courses £14,300. *Living costs:* £12,000 (minimum). Scholarships available.

Keele Large number of overseas students. *English language entry requirement (or equivalent):* IELTS 6.0–6.5. English language summer school before the start of degree course. International Foundation year degree programmes (entry IELTS 4.5). *Fees:* classroom-based subjects £8700, Foundation year £8000, Science-based subjects £9900 (one science) £11,100 (two sciences), Science Foundation year £10,300. *Living costs:* £9000. Some bursaries valued at £1300 per annum.

Kent Comprehensive English language support service. *English language entry requirement (or equivalent):* IELTS 5.5. Foundation programmes (entry IELTS 5.0) to prepare students for Arts, Business, Science, Engineering and Law courses. Non-degree courses also offered for one year or less. *Fees:* laboratory courses £11,800, non-laboratory courses £9200. *Living costs:* £9000. Certificate of chest X-ray required. Limited number of scholarships available and some general scholarships for students from Hong Kong and Singapore.

Kingston More than 2000 international students from over 70 countries. *English language entry requirement (or equivalent):* IELTS 6.5. Foundation level Science and Technology courses. Pre-sessional English language courses and free English support during degree studies. *Fees:* classroom-based subjects £8700, studio-based subjects (including Design and some Computing and Science subjects) £9400, and most laboratory-based subjects £10,500. *Living costs:* £11,000.

Lampeter International students represented at this small distinctive university. *English language entry requirement (or equivalent):* IELTS 6.0. International Foundation programme. Accommodation possible for each year at university. *Fees:* £7500. *Living costs:* £5500.

Lancaster Twenty per cent of student population from over 100 countries. *English language entry requirement (or equivalent):* IELTS 5.5–6.0. Pre-sessional and in-session English language courses cover reading, writing, listening and speaking skills. On-campus accommodation throughout your degree course. *Fees:* £9000–£11,000. *Living costs:* £6500.

Leeds Approximately 4000 students from outside the UK. *English language entry requirement (or equivalent):* IELTS 6.0. *Fees:* Arts and Social Sciences £9000, for Engineering and Science subjects £11,800 and for Clinical Medicine and Dentistry £21,900. *Living costs:* £9000. Partial scholarships offered.

Leeds Metropolitan Over 2500 international students from 110 countries. *English language entry requirement (or equivalent):* IELTS 6.0 (IELTS 4.0 or 5.0 for the International Foundation programme, starting September or February). Also general English courses. *Fees:* £8100–£9500. *Living costs:* £9000. Small number of scholarships.

Leicester Fourteen per cent of full-time students are from outside the UK. *English language entry requirement (or equivalent):* IELTS 6.0 (IELTS 6.5 for Law, Medicine, Arts and Social Science programmes, 5.5 for the Foundation year). English language preparatory programmes and on-going support Foundation programme. *Fees:* £8900–£9900, Medicine £20,400. *Living costs:* £7500. Scholarships and bursaries awarded in a range of subjects, with special awards for students from India and Singapore.

Lincoln Over 2000 students from over 40 countries. *English language entry requirement (or equivalent):* IELTS 6.0. *Fees:* classroom-based subjects £8200, laboratory-based subjects £8700. *Living costs:* £7500.

Liverpool Approximately 2600 international students from over 100 countries. *English language entry requirement (or equivalent):* IELTS 6.0–6.5. International Foundation course (IELTS 5.0–5.5). *Fees:* Arts subjects £9100, Engineering and Science £11,650, Dentistry and Medicine £18,000, Veterinary Science £15,700. *Living costs:* £8800. Scholarships available, including special awards for students from Hong Kong and Singapore.

Liverpool Hope 700 international students. *English language entry requirement (or equivalent):* IELTS 6.0. Language courses available. *Fees:* £8800. *Living costs:* £8800.

Liverpool John Moores A large number of overseas students. *English language entry requirement (or equivalent):* IELTS 6.0. Pre-sessional and in-session English tuition available. *Fees:* classroom-based subjects £8200, laboratory-based subjects £8700. *Living costs:* £9000. Some awards available.

London (Central School of Speech and Drama) International students from over 40 countries are currently following courses. *Fees:* from £10,000. *Living costs:* £12,000.

London (Goldsmiths) Large number of overseas students. *English language entry requirement (or equivalent):* IELTS 6.5; IELTS 5.5 for Extension degrees and IELTS 5.0 for entry to the one-year Foundation course. Certificate course in Language and Contemporary Culture or pre-sessional programmes available. *Fees:* classroom-based subjects £8600, Art and Design, Computer Science, Drama, European Studies, Media and Communications and Social Work £11,400. *Living costs:* £12,000.

London (Heythrop College) A small college; students can take part in activities in any of the colleges belonging to London University. *English language entry requirement (or equivalent):* IELTS 6.0. *Fees:* £8900. *Living costs:* £12,000.

London (King's College) A large number of international students. *English language entry requirement (or equivalent):* IELTS 6.5 for Engineering, Nursing, Science courses, 7.0 for Dentistry, Law, Medicine, Physiotherapy and 7.5 for Humanities, Social Sciences. Pre-sessional summer courses and a one-year Foundation course available. *Fees:* classroom-based subjects £11,500, laboratory-based subjects £14,490, clinically based subjects £26,800. *Living costs:* £12,000. Awards available, including Hong Kong scholarships.

London (Queen Mary) Large number of international students. *English language entry requirement (or equivalent):* IELTS 6.5. International Foundation course covering English language tuition and specialist courses in Business, Management, Economics, Mathematics, Spanish, Geography and European Studies. The course guarantees progression to linked degree courses including Law. *Fees:* Arts, Social Studies, Law £8850, Engineering and Science £11,500, Medicine Years 1 and 2 £13,900, Years 3–5 £22,780, Dentistry Years 1 and 2 £12,000, Years 3–5 £22,000. *Living costs:* £12,000. Several departments operate scholarship schemes for overseas students.

London (Royal Holloway) Twenty per cent of students from over 120 countries. *English language entry requirement (or equivalent):* IELTS 4.0–5.5 for English language programmes. Ten-month Foundation course with studies in English language and introduction to specialist studies in a range of degree subjects. *Fees:* Foundation course £8500, classroom-based subjects £11,500, laboratory-based subjects £13,000, Computer Science and Media Arts £13,900. *Living costs:* £12,000. International student scholarships offered.

London (Royal Veterinary College) *Fees:* £16,900. *Living costs:* £12,000. Contact for further information tel 020 7468 5000; Fax 020 7388 2342.

London (St George's) *Fees:* BSc programmes £12,000, MBBS £10,000 for five years. *Living costs:* £10,000.

London (School of Economics) International students represent 150 countries. *English language entry requirement (or equivalent):* TOEFL 627 (paper test). Language Centre courses available. *Fees:* £12,000. *Living costs:* £12,000.

London (School of Oriental and African Studies) Large number of international students. *English language entry requirement (or equivalent):* IELTS 7.0. A one-year Foundation programme and English language courses available with an entry requirement of IELTS 4.0. Three-day International Students' Orientation programme. *Fees:* £11,000. *Living costs:* £12,000.

London (School of Pharmacy) *English language entry requirement (or equivalent):* IELTS 6.5. *Fees:* £11,400. *Living costs:* £12,000. For further information tel 020 7753 5831; Fax 020 7753 5829.

London (University College) Some 6460 students (34% of the total student body) are from countries outside the UK. *English language entry requirement (or equivalent):* Science and Engineering IELTS 6.5, Arts courses 7.0, Speech Science and Law 7.5. *Fees:* Arts and Social Sciences £10,900, Science, Engineering, Archaeology, Fine Art, Built Environment, Architecture £14,000, Law £11,000, Medicine £21,500. *Living costs:* £12,000. Scholarships available, including awards for students from Hong Kong and China.

London Metropolitan Over 4000 students from 147 countries. *English language entry requirement (or equivalent):* IELTS 5.5. One-year International Foundation programme (IELTS entry requirement 4.5). Full range of English courses. *Fees:* £7700, Foundation programme £5500. *Living costs:* £12,000.

London South Bank Approximately 2500 international students, including 1300 from the EU. *English language entry requirement (or equivalent):* IELTS 6.0. Pre-study English course and a University Foundation course for overseas students. *Fees:* £7500–£8000. *Living costs:* £12,000.

Loughborough Some 800 students from outside the UK. *English language entry requirement (or equivalent):* IELTS 6.5. Special courses offered by the English Language Study Unit. One-week residential course for international students before the start of the academic year. *Fees:* Arts courses £9500, Science and Engineering courses £12,500. *Living costs:* £6500. Eight merit-based scholarships offered.

Manchester A high proportion of international students. *English language entry requirement (or equivalent):* IELTS 6.0–7.5, depending on the high linguistic demands of courses eg Law, Management and Medicine. Foundation Year programme in Informatics, Engineering, Science and Biological Sciences. English language courses are also offered. *Fees:* Arts courses £9200, Science or studio-based courses £12,000, clinical courses in Medicine and Dentistry £22,000. *Living costs:* £8500. Some scholarships and bursaries are available.

Manchester Metropolitan A large number of international students. *English language entry requirement (or equivalent):* IELTS 6.0. English language courses in January, April and July. *Fees:* £8000–£8500, Architecture £11,000. *Living costs:* £8500.

Middlesex International students from 30 countries around the world. *English language entry requirement (or equivalent):* IELTS 6.0. Foundation course (IELTS entry requirement 4.5). Extended English language course from September to July. International summer school. *Fees:* International Foundation course £6300, degree courses £8900–£9400. *Living costs:* £12,000.

Napier Large intake of international students. *English language entry requirement (or equivalent):* IELTS 5.5. English language programmes in September and January; English language support through Foundation programmes. *Fees:* £7900–£9000. *Living costs:* £7000.

Newcastle Over 2500 students from outside the UK. *English language entry requirement (or equivalent):* IELTS 6.5 (7.0 for English, Law and Medicine). English language support and Foundation programmes in Arts and Social Sciences, Business and Finance, Computing, Science and Engineering. *Fees:* Tuition fees vary between courses: classroom-based subjects £9915–£12,000, laboratory, studio and pre-clinical Medicine £13,000, Clinical Medicine and Dentistry courses £20,500. *Living costs:* £7600. Some awards available.

Newport International students from 50 countries. *English language entry requirement (or equivalent):* IELTS 6.0. *Fees:* £7500–8500. *Living costs:* £5,500.

Northampton Over 700 students from over 100 countries are enrolled on courses at this new (2005) university. *English language entry requirement (or equivalent):* IELTS 6.0. English language courses available. *Fees:* £7500. *Living costs:* £6500.

Northumbria Approximately 2500 international students from over 80 countries. *English language entry requirement (or equivalent):* IELTS 5.5–6.5. English language and Foundation courses. *Fees:* classroom-based courses £7800, laboratory-based courses £9000. *Living costs:* £7600. Country scholarships for students from over 15 countries; some merit-based course scholarships.

Nottingham Students from over 130 countries. *English language entry requirement (or equivalent):* IELTS 6.0–6.5 (7.5 for Medicine). *Fees:* Arts, Law and Social Sciences £10,200, Science and Engineering £13,300, Medicine Years 1/2 £14,260, Years 3–5 £24500. *Living costs:* £7000. Scholarships for siblings and science applicants.

Nottingham Trent Large number of overseas students. *English language entry requirement (or equivalent):* IELTS 6.5. English language courses (19, 10 and 5 weeks duration) available. *Fees:* classroom-based subjects £8500, laboratory-based subjects £10,000. *Living costs:* £7000. Discounted overseas fees for some applicants for Art and Design courses.

Open University Courses are open to students throughout the world with study on-line or by way of educational partners. Tutorial support is by telephone, fax, computer conferencing or email. Non-EU students' fees vary depending on courses.

Oxford Large proportion of international students. *English language entry requirement (or equivalent):* IELTS 7.5 (minimum), TOEFL 650 (275 in the computer-based TOEFL). *Fees:* Arts subjects, Mathematics and Social Sciences £8800–£10,360, Science subjects, Music and Fine Art £11,840, Clinical Medicine £22,000. *Living costs:* £9250. University and college scholarships and awards.

Oxford Brookes Large number of international students. *English language entry requirement (or equivalent):* IELTS scores for Engineering and Construction 5.5; for Business, Social Sciences, Computing and Humanities 6.0; for Law and Psychology 6.5. Large number of English language support courses from two weeks to two years offered by the Centre for English Language Studies. *Fees:* £8700. *Living costs:* £9000. Engineering scholarships and family awards.

Plymouth *English language entry requirement (or equivalent):* IELTS 6.5. 'English for University' courses available with IELTS entry requirement of 4.5. *Fees:* £7900–£8500, depending on subject. *Living costs:* £7500. Scholarships for applicants from Malaysia.

Portsmouth Students from over 100 countries. *English language entry requirement (or equivalent):* IELTS 6.0 (5.5 for Foundation-level study). Induction, academic skills and language courses available. *Fees:* £8500–£9500. *Living costs:* £7500. Scholarships for first-year students.

Queen Margaret Four hundred international students from 50 countries. *English language entry requirement (or equivalent):* IELTS 5.5. *Fees:* English language classes (weekly) £172, classroom subjects £8000, laboratory subjects £8800. Some partial scholarships for self-funding students. *Living costs:* £7500.

Queen's Belfast Over 60 countries represented by 2400 international students. *English language entry requirement (or equivalent):* IELTS 6.0–6.5. Special English language summer schools and pre-university language courses are provided, also weekly language courses. Three-day orientation programme held before the start of the academic year. *Fees:* classroom subjects £8000, laboratory/workshop subjects £9800, Medicine/Dentistry pre-clinical £11,200, clinical £20,000. *Living costs:* £7500. Awards available.

Reading Over 3000 students from 135 countries. *English language entry requirement (or equivalent):* IELTS 6.5–7.0. International Foundation programme offering English language tuition and specialist studies in a choice of 14 subjects. Other pre-sessional English courses offered. *Fees:* £8600 for International Foundation programme, £8400–£9400 non-laboratory courses, £10,500 for courses with a significant laboratory content. *Living costs:* £6000. Some scholarships offered.

Richmond, The American International University in London Contact the Admissions Officer for details of entry requirements for all countries. Qualifications gained under education systems outside the American high school grading system will be assessed for equivalence. Students holding advanced qualifications (for example French Baccalaureate, GCE A-levels, the German Abitur) may be awarded course credit towards the Bachelor's degree. *Living costs:* £7500–£8500.

Robert Gordon Approximately 500 international students from over 50 countries. *English language entry requirement (or equivalent):* IELTS 6.0. Pre-entry English programme requirement IELTS 5.0 or above. *Fees:* £8500–£10,300. *Living costs:* £4500. Partial scholarship scheme.

Roehampton *English language entry requirement (or equivalent):* IELTS 5.5–6.0. *Fees:* £7900. *Living costs:* £7500.

St Andrews Twenty-six per cent of students from overseas. *English language entry requirement (or equivalent):* IELTS 6.5. Pre-entry English and study skills programmes and Foundation courses specialising in Arts, Science or Social Science subjects. *Fees:* Arts, Divinity and Sciences £11,300, Medicine £14,500. *Living costs:* £7500. Scholarships available.

Salford Some 1500 international students. *English language entry requirement (or equivalent):* IELTS 6.0. English study programmes and a very comprehensive International Foundation year. *Fees:* International Foundation courses £7300–£7900, classroom-based courses £8000, laboratory-based degree courses £10,200. *Living costs:* £8500.

Sheffield Over 3700 international students. *English language entry requirement (or equivalent):* IELTS 6.0. Preparatory English courses (one–nine months) and an international summer school with English classes. *Fees:* Arts and Social Sciences £10,100, Architecture £10,300, Law £9900, Science £10,300, Engineering £12,000, Medicine £21,000. *Living costs:* £7000. Scholarships available for applicants from Africa and the Far East, for siblings and alumni.

Sheffield Hallam Over 80 countries represented by 3000 international students. *English language entry requirement (or equivalent):* IELTS 6.0. English language tuition available on four, eight and twelve week courses (£810, £1700 and £2200 respectively and IELTS entry requirement 4.5). *Fees:* Arts subjects £7800, Science subjects £9000, Engineering £11,000. *Living costs:* £7000.

Southampton Over 2000 international students. *English language entry requirement (or equivalent):* IELTS 6.0–6.5. English courses offered and also an International Foundation course covering Arts, Humanities, Social Sciences and Law. *Fees:* Arts-based subjects £8800, Science-based subjects and Pre-clinical Medicine £11,000–£14,000, Clinical Medicine £21,500. *Living costs:* £7500. Awards available in Computer Science, Electronics, Law, Mathematics and Science.

Southampton Solent Students from over 50 countries. *English language entry requirement (or equivalent):* IELTS 6.0. Induction programme and language tuition available. *Fees:* £7500. *Living costs:* £7500.

Staffordshire Students from over 70 countries. *English language entry requirement (or equivalent):* IELTS 5.5–6.0. English tuition available. *Fees:* £8000. *Living costs:* £7500.

Stirling Thirteen per cent overseas students from 70 nationalities. *English language entry requirement (or equivalent):* IELTS 6.0. English language tuition available. *Fees:* classroom-based subjects £8400, laboratory-based subjects £11,000. *Living costs:* £6000. Some scholarships for students from South East Asia.

Strathclyde Students from 90 countries. *English language entry requirement (or equivalent):* IELTS 6.5. Pre-entry and pre-sessional English tuition available. *Fees:* Science and Engineering courses £10,700, Law, Arts and Social Sciences £8600, Education and Business £8700. *Living costs:* £6000.

Sunderland A large number of international students. *English language entry requirement (or equivalent):* IELTS 5.5–6.0. English language tuition available. *Fees:* Arts subjects £8400, Science subjects £8600. *Living costs:* £5500.

Surrey A large international community with 43% from the Far East. *English language entry requirement (or equivalent):* IELTS 6.0. English language courses and summer courses offered. *Fees:* Arts courses £8700–£9900, Science, Engineering and Management courses £11,500. *Living costs:* £6500. Scholarships and bursaries offered, including awards for students on Civil Engineering courses.

Sussex More than 2500 international students. *English language entry requirement (or equivalent):* IELTS 6.5. English language and study skills courses available. International Foundation courses offered, covering English language tuition and a choice from Humanities, Law, Media Studies, Social Sciences and Cultural Studies and Science and Technology. *Fees:* International Foundation courses £7500–£8800, classroom-based subjects £9400, laboratory-based subjects £12,800. *Living costs:* £7000. Forty international scholarships.

Swansea Students from over 100 countries. *English language entry requirement (or equivalent):* IELTS 6.0. Pre-sessional English language courses available and on-going support during degree courses. *Fees:* Arts-based courses £8400, Science-based courses £11,200. *Living costs:* £5500. Some overseas scholarships and prizes.

Swansea Metropolitan A new university (2008). *English language entry requirement (or equivalent):* IELTS 6.5. *Fees:* No information – contact the University. *Living costs:* £5500.

Teesside Students from over 75 countries. *English language entry requirement (or equivalent):* IELTS 6.5 for Law, English and Humanities, 5.5 for Engineering, Science, Technology and Computing courses and 6.0 for all other courses. Free English courses available throughout the year while following degree programmes. International summer school available. *Fees:* classroom-based courses £7400, laboratory-based courses £9000. *Living costs:* £5500.

Thames Valley A large number of international students. *English language entry requirement (or equivalent):* IELTS 5.0 for the International Foundation programme and 5.5 for undergraduate courses. English language support available and also pre-sessional courses. *Fees:* Arts-based courses £4500–£6000, Science-based courses £7800. *Living costs:* £12,000.

Ulster Students from over 40 countries. *Fees:* £7800 for degree and diploma courses, Foundation course £5400. *Living costs:* £5500.

Warwick Over 3500 international students. *English language entry requirement (or equivalent):* IELTS 6.0 for Science courses, 6.5 for Arts courses, 6.5 for MORSE courses, and 7.0 for Social Studies and Business courses. English support available. *Fees:* Arts courses £8800, Science courses £11,100, Medical School Year 1 £11,500, Years 2–4 £21,000. *Living costs:* £6500. Over 20 awards available for overseas students.

West Scotland (A new university formed in 2007 from the merger of the University of Paisley and Bell College) Over 1100 international students. *English language entry requirement (or equivalent):* IELTS 6.0. English language Foundation course available. *Fees:* classroom-based courses £7900, laboratory-based courses £8700. *Living costs:* £7000. Some first-year scholarships.

Westminster Students from 148 countries (51% Asian). *English language entry requirement (or equivalent):* IELTS 6.0. International Foundation certificate courses available focusing on the Built Environment, Mathematics and Computing or Social Sciences and Literature. *Fees:* classroom-based subjects £8500, laboratory-based subjects £9000. *Living costs:* £12,000.

Winchester A new university (2005). 150 international students from 30 countries. *English language entry requirement (or equivalent):* IELTS 6.0. Language courses available. *Fees:* £7000–£9000. *Living costs:* £7500.

Worcester *English language entry requirement (or equivalent):* IELTS 6.0. *Fees:* £7000–£8000. *Living costs:* £6000.

Wolverhampton A large number of international students. *English language entry requirement (or equivalent):* IELTS 6.0. English courses available over one or two months or longer. International student programme. *Fees:* undergraduate courses £7900, £6800 for the international student programme. *Living costs:* £6000. Twenty Scholarships for Excellence offered.

York Fifteen per cent of students from outside the UK. *English language entry requirement (or equivalent):* IELTS 6.0. Six-month and pre-sessional English language courses. Intensive vacation courses. *Fees:* sciences £11,500, other courses £8900. *Living costs:* £6500. Several scholarships for overseas students.

York St John *English language entry requirement (or equivalent):* IELTS 6.0 (3 year degree course or 4 year course including Foundation year). *Fees:* £7900, 10-week English language course £1900, Pre-sessional 4-week course £760. *Living costs:* £6500.

BRITISH OVERSEAS TERRITORIES STUDENTS

Students from British Overseas Territories are now treated as home students for fee purposes at universities and other institutions of higher education in the UK. The territories to which this policy applies are:

British Overseas Territories Anguilla, Bermuda, British Antarctic Territory, British Indian Ocean Territory, British Virgin Islands, Cayman Islands, Falkland Islands, Montserrat, Pitcairn Islands, South Georgia and the South Sandwich Islands, St Helena and its Dependencies, Turks and Caicos Islands.

Overseas Territories of other EU member states Greenland, Faroe Islands (Denmark), Netherlands Antilles (Bonaire, Curacao, Saba, St Eustatius, St Marten), Aruba (Netherlands), New Caledonia, French Polynesia, Wallis and Futura, Mayotte, St Pierre et Miquelon (France).

APPENDIX 1
INTERNATIONAL QUALIFICATIONS

Universities in the UK accept a range of international qualifications and those which normally satisfy the minimum general entrance requirements are listed below. However, the specific levels of achievement or grades required for entry to degree courses with international qualifications will vary, depending on the popularity of the university or college and the chosen degree programme. (The subject tables in **Chapter 9** provide a guide to the levels of entry to courses.) Students not holding the required qualifications should consider taking an International Foundation course.

International students whose mother tongue is not English and/or who have not studied for their secondary education in English will be required to pass an English test such as IELTS (International English Language Testing System) or TOEFL (the Test of English as a Foreign Language). Entry requirements vary between universities and courses. For the IELTS, scores can range from 5.5 to 7.5, for the TOEFL computer-based test scores can range from a minimum of 213, and for the TOEFL written test the minimum entry score is 5.0 (see www.ielts.org and www.ets.org/toefl).

Algeria Baccalaureate de l'Enseignement Secondaire
Argentina Completion of Year One of Licenciado/Professional Title
Australia Completion of Year 12 certificates
Austria Reifazeugnis/Maturazeugnis
Bahrain Two-year diploma or associate degree
Bangladesh Bachelor of Arts, Science and Commerce
Belgium Certificat d'Enseignement Secondaire Superieur
Bermuda Diploma of Arts and Science
Bosnia-Herzegovina Secondary School Leaving Diploma
Brazil Completion of Ensino Medio and a good pass in the Vestibular
Brunei Brunei GCE A-level
Bulgaria Diploma za Zavarshino Sredno Obrazovanie (Diploma of Completed Secondary Education)
Canada Completion of Grade 12 secondary/high school certificate or equivalent
Chile Completion of secondary education and a good pass in the Prueba de Conocimientos Especificos
China Completion of one year of a Bachelor degree from a recognised university with good grades
Croatia Matura (Secondary school leaving diploma)
Cyprus Apolytirion/Lise Bitirme Diploma with good grades
Czech Republic Vysvedceni o Maturitni Zkousce/Maturita
Denmark Studentereksamen (HF), (HHX), (HTX)
Egypt Completion of year one of a Bachelor degree or two-year Diploma
Finland Ylioppilastutkinoto/Studentexamen (Matriculation certificate)
France French Baccalaureate
Gambia West African Examinations Council Advanced Level
Georgia Successful completion of Year One of a Bachelor degree
Germany Abitur
Ghana West African High School Certificate/A-levels
Greece Apolytirion of Eniaio Lykeio (previously Apolytirion of Lykeio)
Hong Kong A-levels
Hungary Erettsegi/Matura

Iceland Studentsprof
India High grades from Standard XII School Leaving examinations from certain examination boards
Ireland Irish Leaving Certificate Higher Level
Israel Bagrut
Italy Diploma Conseguito con l'Esame di Stato (formerly the Diploma di Matura) with good grades
Japan Junior College Diploma
Kenya Cambridge Overseas Higher School Certificate
Lebanon Successful completion of year one of Licence
Malaysia Sijil Tinggi Persekolahan Malaysia (STPM, Malaysia Higher School Certificate)
Mauritius Cambridge Overseas Higher School Certificate or A-levels
Mexico Successful completion of year one of Licenciado
Netherlands Voorbereidend Wetenschappelijk Onderwijs (VWO)
Nigeria Successful completion of year one of a Bachelor degree
Norway Diploma of a completed 3-year course of upper secondary education
Pakistan Bachelor degree
Poland Matura/Swiadectwo Dojrzalosci
Portugal Certificado di Fim de Estudos Secundarios with good grades
Russian Federation Diploma of completed Specialised Secondary Education or successful completion of first year of Bakalav
Saudi Arabia Successful completion of first year of a Bachelor degree
Serbia and **Montenegro** Secondary School Leaving Diploma
Singapore Polytechnic Diploma or A-levels
South Korea Junior College Diploma
Spain Curso de Orientacion Universitaria (COU) with good grades
Sri Lanka A-levels
Sweden Fullstandigt Slutbetyg fran Gymnasieskolan
Taiwan Junior College Diploma
Thailand Successful completion of year one of a Bachelor degree
Turkey Devlet Lise Diplomasi (State High School Diploma) with good grades
Uganda East African Advanced Certificate of Education
Ukraine Successful completion of year one of Bakakavre
USA Good grades from the High School Graduation Diploma with SAT and/or APT

APPENDIX 2
PROFESSIONAL ASSOCIATIONS

Professional associations vary in size and function and many offer examinations to provide members with vocational qualifications. However, many of the larger bodies do not conduct examinations but accept evidence provided by the satisfactory completion of appropriate degree and diploma courses. When applying for courses in vocational subjects, therefore, it is important to check whether your chosen course is accredited by a professional association, since membership of such bodies is usually necessary for progression in your chosen career after graduation.

Information about careers, which you can use as background information for your UCAS application, can be obtained from the organisations below listed under the subject table headings used in **Chapter 9**. Full details of professional associations, their examinations and the degree courses accredited to them are published in *British Qualifications* (see **Appendix 3**).

Some additional organisations that can provide useful careers-related information are listed below under the subject table headings and other sources of relevant information are indicated in the subject tables of **Chapter 9** and in **Appendix 3**.

Accountancy/Accounting
Association of Accounting Technicians www.aat.org.uk
Association of Chartered Certified Accountants www.accaglobal.com
Association of International Accountants www.aia.org.uk
Chartered Institute of Management Accountants www.cimaglobal.com
Chartered Institute of Public Finance and Accountancy www.cipfa.org.uk
Chartered Institute of Taxation www.tax.org.uk
Institute of Accounting Technicians in Ireland www.iati.ie
Institute of Chartered Accountants in England and Wales www.icaew.co.uk
Institute of Chartered Accountants in Ireland www.icai.ie
Institute of Chartered Accountants of Scotland www.icas.org.uk
Institute of Financial Accountants www.ifa.org.uk
Institute of Internal Auditors www.iia.org.uk

Actuarial Science/Studies
Faculty of Actuaries www.actuaries.org.uk
Institute of Actuaries www.actuaries.org.uk

Agricultural Sciences/Agriculture
Royal Agricultural Society of England www.rase.org.uk

Animal Sciences
British Horse Society www.bhs.org.uk
British Society of Animal Science www.bsas.org.uk

Anthropology
Association of Social Anthropologists of the UK and Commonwealth www.theasa.org
Royal Anthropological Institute www.therai.org.uk

Archaeology

Council for British Archaeology www.britarch.ac.uk
Institute of Field Archaeologists www.archaeologists.net

Architecture

Chartered Institute of Architectural Technologists www.ciat.org.uk
Royal Incorporation of Architects in Scotland www.rias.org.uk
Royal Institute of British Architects www.riba.org

Art and Design

Arts Council England www.arts.org.uk
Association of Illustrators www.theaoi.com
Association of Photographers www.the-aop.org
British Association of Art Therapists www.baat.org
British Association of Paintings Conservator-Restorers www.bapcr.org.uk
British Institute of Professional Photography www.bipp.com
Chartered Society of Designers www.csd.org.uk
Crafts Council www.craftscouncil.org.uk
Design Council www.designcouncil.org.uk
Institute of Professional Goldsmiths www.ipgold.org.uk
National Society for Education in Art and Design www.nsead.org
Professional Accreditation of Conservator-Restorers www.pacr.org.uk
Royal British Society of Sculptors www.rbs.org.uk
Scottish Arts Council www.scottisharts.org.uk
Textile Institute www.texi.org

Astronomy/Astrophysics

Royal Astronomical Society www.ras.org.uk

Biochemistry (see also Chemistry)

Association of Clinical Biochemistry www.acb.org.uk
Biochemical Society www.biochemistry.org
British Society for Immunology www.immunology.org

Biological Sciences/Biology

British Society for Human Genetics www.bshg.org.uk
Genetics Society www.genetics.org.uk
Institute of Biology www.iob.org
Institute of Biomedical Science www.ibms.org

Building

Chartered Institute of Building www.ciob.org.uk
Chartered Institution of Building Services Engineers www.cibse.org
Construction Industry Training Board (CITB) www.citb.org.uk

Business Courses

Chartered Institute of Personnel and Development www.cipd.co.uk
Chartered Institute of Public Relations www.ipr.org.uk
Chartered Management Institute www.managers.org.uk
Communication, Advertising and Marketing Education Foundation (CAM Foundation)
     www.camfoundation.com
Council for Administration www.cfa.uk.com
Institute of Administrative Management www.instam.org

Institute of Chartered Secretaries and Administrators www.icsa.org.uk
Institute of Export www.export.org.uk
Institute of Management Consultancy www.imc.co.uk
Institute of Practitioners in Advertising www.ipa.co.uk
Institute of Qualified Professional Secretaries www.iqps.org
Institute of Sales and Marketing Management www.ismm.co.uk

Chemistry
Institute of Nanotechnology www.nano.org.uk
Royal Society of Chemistry www.rsc.org

Computer Courses
British Computer Society www.bcs.org
Institute for the Management of Information Systems www.imis.org.uk
Institute of Information Technology Training www.iitt.org.uk
Institution of Analysts and Programmers www.iap.org.uk

Consumer Studies/Sciences
Institute of Consumer Sciences (incorporating Home Economics) www.institute-consumer-sciences.co.uk

Dance
Council for Dance Education and Training www.cdet.org.uk

Dentistry
British Association of Dental Nurses www.badn.org.uk
British Association of Dental Therapists www.badt.org.uk
British Dental Association www.bda.org
British Dental Hygienists' Association www.bdha.org.uk
Dental Laboratories Association www.dla.org.uk
Dental Technicians Association www.dta-uk.org
General Dental Council www.gdc-uk.org

Dietetics
British Dietetic Association www.bda.uk.com

Drama
Equity www.equity.org.uk
National Council for Drama Training www.ncdt.co.uk
Society of British Theatre Designers www.theatredesign.org.uk

Economics
Royal Economic Society www.res.org.uk

Education and Teacher Training
Department for Children, Schools and Families www.dcsf.gov.uk
Department for Innovation, Universities and Skills www.dius.gov.uk
General Teaching Council for Scotland www.gtcs.org.uk
Training and Development Agency for Schools www.tda.gov.uk

Engineering/Engineering Sciences
Energy Institute www.energyinst.org.uk
Engineering Council UK www.engc.org.uk
Institute for Manufacturing www.ifm.eng.cam.ac.uk
Institute of Acoustics www.ioa.org.uk
Institute of Marine Engineering, Science and Technology www.imarest.org

Institution of Agricultural Engineers www.iagre.org
Institution of Civil Engineers www.ice.org.uk
Institution of Engineering and Technology www.theiet.org
Institution of Mechanical Engineers www.imeche.org.uk
Institution of Nuclear Engineers www.inuce.org.uk
Royal Aeronautical Society www.raes.org.uk

Environmental Science/Studies

Chartered Institute of Environmental Health www.cieh.org
Chartered Institution of Wastes Management www.ciwm.co.uk
Chartered Institution of Water and Environmental Management www.ciwem.org
Environment Agency www.environment-agency.gov.uk
Institute of Ecology and Environmental Management www.ieem.org.uk
Institution of Environmental Sciences www.ies-uk.org.uk
Institution of Occupational Safety and Health www.iosh.co.uk
Royal Environmental Health Institute of Scotland www.rehis.org
Society for the Environment www.socenv.org.uk

Film, Radio, Video and TV Studies

British Film Institute www.bfi.org.uk
Skillset (National training organisation for broadcast, film, video and multimedia) www.skillset.org

Finance (including Banking and Insurance)

Chartered Institute of Bankers in Scotland www.ciobs.org.uk
Chartered Institute of Loss Adjusters www.cila.co.uk
Chartered Insurance Institute www.cii.co.uk
Financial Services Skills Council www.fssc.org.uk
Institute of Financial Services www.ifslearning.com
Personal Finance Society www.thepfs.org
Securities and Investment Institute www.securities-institute.org.uk

Food Science/Studies and Technology

Institute of Food Science and Technology www.ifst.org
Society of Food Hygiene and Technology www.sofht.co.uk

Forensic Science

Forensic Science Society www.forensic-science-society.org

Forestry

Institute of Chartered Foresters www.charteredforesters.org
Institute of Wood Science www.iwsc.org.uk
Royal Forestry Society www.rfs.org.uk.

Geography

British Cartographic Society www.cartography.org.uk
Royal Geographical Society www.rgs.org
Royal Meteorological Society www.rmets.org

Geology/Geological Sciences

Geological Society www.geolsoc.org.uk

Health Sciences/Studies

British Academy of Audiology www.baaudiology.org
British and Irish Orthoptic Society www.orthoptics.org.uk

British Association of Prosthetists and Orthotists www.bapo.com
British Chiropractic Association www.chiropractic-uk.co.uk
British Occupational Hygiene Society www.bohs.org
British Osteopathic Association and General Osteopathic Council www.osteopathy.org.uk
Institute for Complementary Medicine www.i-c-m.org.uk
Institution of Occupational Safety and Health www.iosh.co.uk
Society of Homeopaths www.homeopathy-soh.org

History
Royal Historical Society www.rhs.ac.uk

Horticulture
Institute of Horticulture www.horticulture.org.uk

Hospitality and Hotel Management
Institute of Hospitality www.instituteofhospitality.org.uk
People 1st www.people1st.co.uk

Housing
Chartered Institute of Housing www.cih.org

Human Resource Management
Chartered Institute of Personnel and Development www.cipd.co.uk

Information Management
Association for Information Management www.aslib.co.uk
Chartered Institute of Library and Information Professionals www.cilip.org.uk

Landscape Architecture
Landscape Institute www.l-i.org.uk

Languages
Chartered Institute of Linguists www.iol.org.uk
Institute of Translation and Interpreting www.iti.org.uk

Law
Bar Council www.barcouncil.org.uk
Faculty of Advocates www.advocates.org.uk
Institute of Legal Executives www.ilex.org.uk
Law Society www.lawsociety.org.uk
Law Society of Northern Ireland www.lawsoc-ni.org
Law Society of Scotland www.lawscot.org.uk

Leisure and Recreation Management/Studies
Institute of Leisure and Amenity Management www.ilam.co.uk

Linguistics
British Association for Applied Linguistics www.baal.org.uk
Royal College of Speech and Language Therapists www.rcslt.org

Marine/Maritime Studies
Nautical Institute www.nautinst.org

Marketing
Chartered Institute of Marketing www.cim.co.uk
Institute of Sales and Marketing Management www.ismm.co.uk

Materials Science/Metallurgy
Institute of Materials, Minerals and Mining www.iom3.org

Mathematics
Council for Mathematical Sciences www.cms.ac.uk
Institute of Mathematics and its Applications www.ima.org.uk
London Mathematical Society www.lms.ac.uk
Mathematical Association www.m-a.org.uk

Media Studies
British Broadcasting Corporation www.bbc.co.uk/jobs
National Council for the Training of Journalists www.nctj.com
Skillset (National training organisation for broadcast, film, video and multimedia) www.skillset.org
Society for Editors and Proofreaders www.sfep.org.uk
Society of Authors www.societyofauthors.net

Medicine
British Medical Association www.bma.org.uk
General Medical Council www.gmc-uk.org
Institute for Complementary Medicine www.i-c-m.org.uk

Microbiology (see also Biological Sciences)
Society for General Microbiology www.sgm.ac.uk

Music
Incorporated Society of Musicians www.ism.org
Institute of Musical Instrument Technology www.imit.org.uk

Naval Architecture
Royal Institution of Naval Architects www.rina.org.uk

Nursing and Midwifery
Community Practitioners' and Health Visitors' Association www.amicustheunion.org/-cphva
Northern Ireland Practice and Educational Council for Nursing and Midwifery www.n-i.nhs.uk
Nursing and Midwifery Council www.nmc-uk.org
Royal College of Midwives www.rcm.org.uk
Royal College of Nursing www.rcn.org.uk

Nutrition (see Dietetics)

Occupational Therapy
British Association/College of Occupational Therapists www.cot.co.uk

Optometry
Association of British Dispensing Opticians www.abdo.org.uk
British and Irish Orthoptic Society www.orthoptics.org.uk
College of Optometrists www.college-optometrists.org
General Optical Council www.optical.org

Pharmacology
British Toxicology Society www.thebts.org
Royal Pharmaceutical Society of Great Britain www.rpsgb.org.uk

Pharmacy
Royal Pharmaceutical Society of Great Britain www.rpsgb.org.uk

Photography
Association of Photographers www.the-aop.org
British Institute of Professional Photography www.bipp.com
Royal Photographic Society www.rps.org

Physical Education (see Education and Sports Studies/Sciences)

Physics
Institute of Physics www.iop.org
Institute of Physics and Engineering in Medicine www.ipem.org.uk

Physiotherapy
Association of Chartered Physiotherapists in Animal Therapy www.acpat.org.uk
Chartered Society of Physiotherapy www.csp.org.uk

Plant Sciences (see Biological Sciences)

Podiatry
Society of Chiropodists and Podiatrists www.feetforlife.org

Property Management/Development
Chartered Institute of Building www.ciob.org.uk
Chartered Surveyors Training Trust www.cstt.org.uk
National Association of Estate Agents www.naea.co.uk
Royal Institution of Chartered Surveyors www.rics.org

Psychology
British Psychological Society www.bps.org.uk

Public Relations
Chartered Institute of Public Relations www.cipr.co.uk

Quantity Surveying
Chartered Institute of Building www.ciob.org.uk
Royal Institution of Chartered Surveyors www.rics.org

Radiography
Society and College of Radiographers www.sor.org

Social Work
Care Council for Wales www.ccwales.org.uk
General Social Care Council www.gscc.org.uk
Northern Ireland Social Care Council www.niscc.info
Scottish Social Services Council www.sssc.uk.com

Sociology
British Sociological Association www.britsoc.co.uk

Speech Pathology/Therapy
Royal College of Speech and Language Therapists www.rcslt.org

Sports Sciences/Studies
British Association of Sport and Exercise Sciences www.bases.org.uk
English Institute of Sport www.eis2win.co.uk
Institute of Sport and Recreation Management www.isrm.co.uk
Scottish Institute of Sport www.sisport.com
Society of Sports Therapists www.society-of-sports-therapists.org

Sport England www.sportengland.org
Sport Scotland www.sportscotland.org.uk
Sports Council for Wales www.sports-council-wales.co.uk
Sports Institute Northern Ireland www.sini.co.uk
UK Sport www.uksport.gov.uk

Statistics
Royal Statistical Society www.rss.org.uk

Tourism and Travel
Institute of Leisure and Amenity Management www.ilam.co.uk
Institute of Travel and Tourism www.itt.co.uk
TTC Training www.ttctraining.co.uk

Town and Country Planning
Royal Town Planning Institute www.rtpi.org.uk

Transport Management and Planning
Chartered Institute of Logistics and Transport www.cilt-international.com

Veterinary Science/Medicine/Nursing
Association of Chartered Physiotherapists in Animal Therapy www.acpat.org.uk
British Veterinary Nursing Association www.bvna.org.uk
Royal College of Veterinary Surgeons www.rcvs.ac.uk
Royal Veterinary College www.rvc.ac.uk

Zoology
Royal Entomological Society www.royensoc.co.uk
Zoological Society of London www.zsl.org

Unless otherwise stated, the publications in this list are all available from Trotman Publishing (www.trotman.co.uk / 0870 900 2665).

STANDARD REFERENCE BOOKS

British Qualifications, 38th edition, Kogan Page Ltd
British Vocational Qualifications, 9th edition, Kogan Page Ltd
The Big Guide 2009 Entry – the official universities and colleges entrance guide for 2009 entry, UCAS

OTHER BOOKS AND RESOURCES

Choosing Your Degree Course and University, 11th edition, Brian Heap, Trotman Publishing
Critical Choices: Applying to University, Trotman Publishing
Destinations of Leavers from Higher Education 2005/6, Higher Education Statistics Agency Services (available from HESA)
The Educational Grants Directory 2007/8, 8th edition, Directory of Social Change
Getting into the UK's Best Universities & Courses (Daily Telegraph Guide), Trotman Publishing
How to Complete Your UCAS Application for 2009 Entry, Trotman Publishing
Insiders' Guide to Applying to University (Daily Telegraph Guide), Trotman Publishing
Into Higher Education 2008: The Higher Education Guide for People with Disabilities, Skill
Making the Most of University, Kate van Haeften, Trotman Publishing
The Mature Students' Directory, 4th edition, Trotman Publishing
MPW Getting Into course guides: US and Canadian Universities, Art and Design Courses, Business and Management Courses, Dental School, Law, Medical School, Oxford and Cambridge, Physiotherapy Courses, Psychology Courses, Veterinary School, Trotman Publishing
The Push Guide to Which University 2007-8, Johnny Rich, Hodder Arnold
Student Book 2008, 29th edition, Klaus Boehm and Jenny Lees-Spalding, Trotman Publishing
Students' Money Matters 2008/09, 14th edition, Trotman Publishing
Study in Europe – UK Socrates-Erasmus Student Guide UK Socrates-Erasmus Council
The Times Good University Guide 2009, John O'Leary, Times Books
Trotman's Green Guides 2007, Trotman Publishing
University Scholarships, Awards and Bursaries, 7th edition, Brian Heap, Trotman Publishing
The Virgin 2008 Alternative Guide to British Universities, Piers Dudgeon, Virgin
Which Degree? 2008, Trotman Publishing
Your Gap Year, 5th edition, Susan Griffith, Vacation Works

USEFUL WEBSITES

Education, course and applications information
www.aimhigher.ac.uk
www.coursediscover.co.uk
www.direct.gov.uk/studentfinance
www.erasmus.ac.uk
www.hero.ac.uk
www.hesa.ac.uk

www.opendays.com (information on university and college open days)
www.skills.org.uk
www.unistats.com (official information from UK universities and colleges for comparing courses)
www.ucas.com

Careers information
www.armyjobs.mod.uk
www.careers.co.uk
www.careerseurope.co.uk
www.connexions.gov.uk
www.enginuity.org.uk
www.insidecareers.co.uk
www.isco.org.uk
www.milkround.com
www.nhscareers.nhs.uk
www.prospects.ac.uk
www.socialworkandcare.co.uk
www.tda.gov.uk
www.trotman.co.uk
www.ucreative.ac.uk

Gap years
www.gapyear.com
www.gap-year.com
www.yini.org.uk (Year in Industry)

Study overseas
www.acu.ac.uk
www.fulbright.co.uk
www.allaboutcollege.com

APPENDIX 4 CAMBRIDGE PRE-U DIPLOMA: A NEW QUALIFICATION

Readers may wish to be alerted to details of this new non-modular examination which is at present under development and consultation with schools and universities. The examination is equivalent to A-levels and the IB and will be offered by some schools from September 2008.

Cambridge Pre-U is a new post-16 qualification being developed by the University of Cambridge International Examinations (CIE). It aims to prepare students from across the world with the skills and knowledge required to make a success of their subsequent studies at university. Representatives from higher education have been involved in writing the syllabi and universities have shown great interest in the qualification.

Students can take **individual Cambridge Pre-U subjects** and build them up into a portfolio that suits their interests and ambitions. The structure of each Cambridge Pre-U syllabus is **linear**, and this differentiates it from AS and A-levels. All the assessment takes place at the end of the two-year course. Students can take a Cambridge Pre-U subject at Subsidiary level (in other words after one year) although the result would not count towards the full (Principal) qualification.

Twenty-four syllabi will be available from 2008: Mathematics, Further Maths, Economics, Chemistry, Physics, Biology, English, History, Geography, Business Studies, German, French, Spanish, Classical Heritage, Mandarin Chinese, Art History, Sport Science, Greek, Latin, Art and Design, Comparative Government and Politics, Psychology, Music, and Philosophy and Ethics.

Results will be reported for individual subjects on a scale of 1 to 10, with a separate grade for the full Diploma.

For the full **Cambridge Pre-U Diploma** students will offer at least three Principal subjects (some will want to offer more). The distinguishing feature is that students will have **complete freedom of choice** in their subjects, in other words they can specialise in, say, the natural sciences. To qualify for the full Diploma, students offer a programme that includes a core course in **Global Perspectives** – giving students the opportunity to engage with issues that will face every young person, wherever in the world they live and work.

Cambridge Pre-U will be taught from September 2008, with the first examinations in 2010. You can find out more about Cambridge Pre-U at www.cie.org.uk/cambridgepreu.

COURSE INDEX

INDEX OF ADVERTISERS

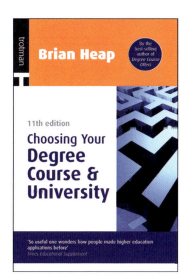